MW00759553

THE ANNENBERG FOUNDATION TRUST
AT SUNNYLANDS

The Annenberg Foundation Trust at Sunnylands'
Adolescent Mental Health Initiative

COMMISSIONS	COMMISSION CHAIRS
Anxiety Disorders	Edna B. Foa, Ph.D.
Depression and Bipolar Disorder	Dwight L. Evans, M.D.
Eating Disorders	B. Timothy Walsh, M.D.
Positive Youth Development	Martin E.P. Seligman, Ph.D.
Schizophrenia	Raquel E. Gur, M.D., Ph.D.
Substance and Alcohol Abuse	Charles P. O'Brien, M.D., Ph.D.
Suicide Prevention	Herbert Hendin, M.D.

Treating and Preventing Adolescent Mental Health Disorders

EDITED BY

The Commission Chairs
of The Annenberg Foundation Trust at Sunnylands'
Adolescent Mental Health Initiative

Dwight L. Evans, M.D.
Edna B. Foa, Ph.D.
Raquel E. Gur, M.D., Ph.D.
Herbert Hendin, M.D.
Charles P. O'Brien, M.D., Ph.D.
Martin E.P. Seligman, Ph.D.
B. Timothy Walsh, M.D.

Treating and Preventing Adolescent Mental Health Disorders

What We Know and What We Don't Know

A RESEARCH AGENDA FOR IMPROVING
THE MENTAL HEALTH OF OUR YOUTH

The Annenberg Foundation Trust at Sunnylands'
Adolescent Mental Health Initiative

OXFORD
UNIVERSITY PRESS

2005

OXFORD
UNIVERSITY PRESS

Oxford University Press, Inc., publishes works that further
Oxford University's objective of excellence
in research, scholarship, and education.

The Annenberg Foundation Trust at Sunnylands
The Annenberg Public Policy Center of the University of Pennsylvania
Oxford University Press

Oxford   New York
Auckland   Cape Town   Dar es Salaam   Hong Kong   Karachi
Kuala Lumpur   Madrid   Melbourne   Mexico City   Nairobi
New Delhi   Shanghai   Taipei   Toronto

With offices in
Argentina   Austria   Brazil   Chile   Czech Republic   France   Greece
Guatemala   Hungary   Italy   Japan   Poland   Portugal   Singapore
South Korea   Switzerland   Thailand   Turkey   Ukraine   Vietnam

Published by Oxford University Press, Inc.,
198 Madison Avenue, New York, New York 10016

www.oup.com

Oxford is a registered trademark of Oxford University Press

Library of Congress Cataloging-in-Publication Data
Treating and preventing adolescent mental health disorders : what we
know and what we don't know : a research agenda for improving the
mental health of our youth / edited by the commission chairs of the
Annenberg Foundation Trust at Sunnylands' Adolescent Mental Health
Initiative, Dwight L. Evans, . . . [et al.]
p. cm.   Includes bibliographical references and index.
ISBN-13 978-0-19-517364-2
ISBN 0-19-517364-3
1. Adolescent psychopathology.   2. Teenagers—Mental health.   3.
Mental illness—Treatment.   4. Behavioral assessment of teenagers.   I.
Evans, Dwight L.   II. Annenberg Foundation at Sunnylands.
RJ503.T75 2005
616.89'00835—dc22   2004019185

2 4 6 8 9 7 5 3 2 1

Printed in the United States of America
on acid-free paper

Contents

Adolescent Mental Health Initiative

Project Director   Kathleen Hall Jamieson, Ph.D.
Professor, Annenberg School for Communication, University of Pennsylvania
Director, Annenberg Public Policy Center, University of Pennsylvania

Commission on Adolescent Depression and Bipolar Disorder

Commission Chair   Dwight L. Evans, M.D.
Professor, Psychiatry, Medicine, and Neuroscience, University of Pennsylvania
Department Chair, Psychiatry, University of Pennsylvania
Chief of Psychiatry, Hospital of the University of Pennsylvania, Presbyterian
    Medical Center, Pennsylvania Hospital

Commission Members   William Beardslee, M.D.
Psychiatrist-in-Chief and Chairman, Psychiatry, Children's Hospital Boston
Professor, Child Psychiatry, Harvard Medical School

Joseph Biederman, M.D.
Professor, Psychiatry, Harvard University
Chief, Clinical and Research in Pediatric Psychopharmacology, Massachusetts
    General Hospital
Chief, Adult ADHD Program, Massachusetts General Hospital

David Brent, M.D.
Academic Chief, Child & Adolescent Psychiatry, Western Psychiatric Institute
    and Clinic
Professor, Child Psychiatry, Pediatrics & Epidemiology, University of
    Pittsburgh School of Medicine

Dennis Charney, M.D.
Chief, Mood and Anxiety Disorder Research Program and the Experimental
    Therapeutics and Pathophysiology Branch, National Institute of Mental
    Health

Joseph Coyle, M.D.
Professor, Psychiatry and Neuroscience, Harvard Medical School

W. Edward Craighead, Ph.D.
Professor, Psychology, University of Colorado, Boulder
Director, Clinical Psychology Program, University of Colorado, Boulder

Paul Crits-Christoph, Ph.D.
Professor, Psychology in Psychiatry, University of Pennsylvania
Director, Center for Psychotherapy Research, University of Pennsylvania

Robert Findling, M.D.
Director, Division of Child and Adolescent Psychiatry, Case Western Reserve
    University and University Hospitals of Cleveland
Associate Professor, Psychiatry and Pediatrics, Case Western Reserve University

Judy Garber, Ph.D.
Professor, Psychology and Human Development, Vanderbilt University
Senior Fellow, Institute for Public Policy Studies, Vanderbilt University

Investigator and Fellow, Kennedy Center for Research on Human
  Development, Vanderbilt University

Robert Johnson, M.D.
Professor and Chair, Pediatrics, University of Medicine and Dentistry of New
  Jersey
Professor, Psychiatry, University of Medicine and Dentistry of New Jersey
Director, Division of Adolescent and Young Adult Medicine, University of
  Medicine and Dentistry of New Jersey

Martin Keller, M.D.
Professor, and Chairman, Psychiatry and Human Behavior, Brown University
  School of Medicine

Charles Nemeroff, M.D., Ph.D.
Professor and Chairman, Psychiatry and Behavioral Sciences, Emory
  University School of Medicine

Moira A. Rynn, M.D.
Assistant Professor, Psychiatry, University of Pennsylvania School of Medicine
Medical Director, Mood and Anxiety Disorders Section, Department of
  Psychiatry, University of Pennsylvania School of Medicine

Karen Wagner, M.D., Ph.D.
Professor and Vice Chair, Psychiatry and Behavioral Sciences, University of
  Texas Medical Branch, Galveston
Director, Division of Child and Adolescent Psychiatry, University of Texas
  Medical Branch, Galveston

Myrna Weissman, Ph.D.
Professor, Psychiatry and Epidemiology, Columbia University College of
  Physicians
Chief, Division of Clinical and Genetic Epidemiology, New York State
  Psychiatric Institute

Elizabeth Weller, M.D.
Professor, Psychiatry and Pediatrics, University of Pennsylvania
Vice Chair, Department of Psychiatry, University of Pennsylvania

Commission on Adolescent Schizophrenia

Commission Chair Raquel E. Gur, M.D., Ph.D.
Professor, Psychiatry, Neurology, and Radiology, University of Pennsylvania
Director, Neuropsychiatry Section in Psychiatry, University of Pennsylvania

Commission Members Nancy Andreasen, M.D., Ph.D.
Chair, Psychiatry, University of Iowa
Director, Mental Health Clinical Research Center, University of Iowa

Robert Asarnow, Ph.D.
Professor, Psychiatry and Biobehavioral Sciences, Psychology, University of
  California at Los Angeles

Ruben Gur, Ph.D.
Professor, Psychiatry, Neurology, and Radiology, University of Pennsylvania
Director, Neuropsychology and the Brain Behavior Laboratory, University of
  Pennsylvania

Peter Jones, M.D.
Professor and Chair, Psychiatry, University of Cambridge

Kenneth Kendler, M.D.
Distinguished Professor, Psychiatry, and Professor, Human Genetics, Medical
    College of Virginia of Virginia Commonwealth University
Co-director, Virginia Institute for Psychiatric and Behavioral Genetics

Matcheri Keshavan, M.D.
Professor, Psychiatry, University of Pittsburgh School of Medicine
Director, Schizophrenia Inpatient Services, Western Psychiatric Institute and
    Clinic
Clinical Services Core, Center for the Neuroscience of Mental Disorders,
    Western Psychiatric Institute and Clinic

Jeffrey Lieberman, M.D.
Distinguished Professor, Psychiatry, Pharmacology, and Radiology, University
    of North Carolina School of Medicine
Director, Mental Health and Neuroscience Clinical Research Center,
    University of North Carolina School of Medicine

Robert McCarley, M.D.
Professor, Psychiatry, Harvard Medical School
Chair, Harvard Department of Psychiatry at the Brockton/West Roxbury VA
    Medical Center

Robin Murray, M.D.
Professor and Chair, Psychiatry, Institute of Psychiatry, King's College
    London

Judith Rapoport, M.D.
Chief, Child Psychiatry Branch, National Institute of Mental Health

Carol Tamminga, M.D.
Professor, Psychiatry and Pharmacology and Experimental Therapeutics,
    University of Maryland at Baltimore
Deputy Director, Maryland Psychiatric Research Center

Ming Tsuang, M.D., Ph.D.
Professor, Psychiatry, Harvard Medical School
Superintendent and Head, Harvard Department of Psychiatry at the
    Massachusetts Mental Health Center

Elaine Walker, Ph.D.
Professor, Psychology and Neuroscience, Emory University

Daniel Weinberger, M.D.
Chief, Clinical Brain Disorders Branch of the Intramural Research Program,
    National Institute of Mental Health

With contributions from Kristin Lancefield, MBBS MRCPsych
Honorary Specialist Registrar, Institute of Psychiatry, London

Commission Coordinator Stacy L. Moore III, B.A.
Academic Coordinator, Department of Neuropsychiatry, University of
    Pennsylvania

Commission on Adolescent Anxiety Disorders

Commission Chair

Edna B. Foa, Ph.D.
Professor, Clinical Psychology in Psychiatry, University of Pennsylvania
Director, Center for the Treatment and Study of Anxiety, University of
Pennsylvania

Commission Members

E. Jane Costello, Ph.D.
Associate Professor, Psychiatry and Behavioral Sciences, Duke University
Medical Center
Director, Center for Developmental Epidemiology, Duke University

Martin Franklin, Ph.D.
Assistant Professor, Clinical Psychology in Psychiatry, University of
Pennsylvania
Clinical Director, Center for the Treatment and Study of Anxiety, University
of Pennsylvania School of Medicine

Jerome Kagan, Ph.D.
Professor, Psychology, Harvard University

Philip Kendall, Ph.D.
Professor, Psychology, Temple University
Director, Child and Adolescent Anxiety Disorder Clinic, Temple University

Rachel Klein, Ph.D.
Professor, Psychiatry, New York University School of Medicine
Director, Anxiety and Mood Disorders Institute at the Child Study Center,
New York University School of Medicine

Henrietta Leonard, M.D.
Professor, Psychiatry and Human Behavior, Brown University
Director of Training, Child and Adolescent Psychiatry, Brown University

Michael Liebowitz, M.D.
Professor, Clinical Psychiatry, Columbia University
Director, Anxiety Disorders Clinic, New York State Psychiatric Institute

John March, M.D., M.P.H.
Professor, Psychiatry, Duke University
Director, Child and Adolescent Anxiety Disorders and Psychopharmacology,
Duke University Medical Center

Richard McNally, Ph.D.
Professor, Psychology, Harvard University

Thomas Ollendick, Ph.D.
Professor, Clinical Psychology, Virginia Polytechnic Institute and State
University
Director, Child Study Center, Virginia Polytechnic Institute and State
University

Daniel Pine, M.D.
Chief, Section on Development and Affective Neuroscience, National Institute
of Mental Health
Chief, Child and Adolescent Research Mood and Anxiety Disorders Program,
National Institute of Mental Health

Robert Pynoos, M.D.
Professor, Psychiatry and Biobehavioral Sciences, University of California at
    Los Angeles
Co-director, UCLA–Duke National Center for Child Traumatic Stress
Director, Trauma Psychiatry Program, University of California at
    Los Angeles

Wendy Silverman, Ph.D.
Professor, Psychology, Case Western University
Director, Child and Family Psychosocial Research Center, Florida International
    University

Linda Spear, Ph.D.
Distinguished Professor and Chair, Psychology Department, Binghamton
    University

Commission on Adolescent Eating Disorders

Commission Chair   B. Timothy Walsh, M.D.
Chair, Psychiatry, College of Physicians and Surgeons, Columbia University
Interim Executive Director, New York State Psychiatric Institute
Director, Eating Disorder Research Unit, New York State Psychiatric Institute

Commission Members   Cynthia M. Bulik, Ph.D.
Professor, Eating Disorders, Department of Psychiatry, University of North
    Carolina at Chapel Hill
Director, Eating Disorders Program, University of North Carolina at Chapel
    Hill

Christopher G. Fairburn, D.M., F.R.C.Psych., F.Med.Sci.
Professor, Psychiatry, Oxford University
Wellcome Principal Research Fellow, Department of Psychiatry, Oxford
    University

Neville H. Golden, M.D.
Professor, Clinical Pediatrics, Albert Einstein College of Medicine
Co-director, Eating Disorders Center, Schneider Children's Hospital

Katherine A. Halmi, M.D.
Professor, Psychiatry, Weill Medical College of Cornell University
Director, Eating Disorders Program, Cornell University

David B. Herzog, M.D.
Professor, Psychiatry and Pediatrics, Harvard Medical School
President and Founder, Harvard Medical School Eating Disorders Center
Director, Eating Disorders Unit, Massachusetts General Hospital

Allan S. Kaplan, M.D., F.R.C.P.(C)
Professor, Psychiatry, University of Toronto
Head, Program for Eating Disorders, Toronto General Hospital
Chair, Eating Disorders, Toronto General Hospital

Richard E. Kreipe, M.D.
Professor, Pediatrics, University of Rochester
Chief, Division of Adolescent Medicine, Children's Hospital at Strong,
    University of Rochester

James E. Mitchell, M.D.
Professor and Chair, Neurosciences, University of North Dakota School of
Medicine
President and Scientific Director, Neuropsychiatric Research Institute

Kathleen M. Pike, Ph.D.
Assistant Professor, Clinical Psychology in Psychiatry, Columbia Presbyterian
Medical Center
Chief Psychologist, Columbia Presbyterian Medical Center's Eating Disorders
Clinical Research Service

Eric Stice, Ph.D.
Associate Professor, Psychology, University of Texas at Austin

Ruth H. Striegel-Moore, Ph.D.
Professor, Psychology, Wesleyan University

C. Barr Taylor, M.D.
Director, Laboratory for the Study of Behavioral Medicine, Stanford University
School of Medicine
Director, Adult Residency Training Program, Stanford University School of
Medicine
Co-director, Stanford Cardiac Rehabilitation Program, Stanford University
School of Medicine

Thomas A. Wadden, Ph.D.
Professor, Psychology, University of Pennsylvania
Director, Weight and Eating Disorders Program, University of Pennsylvania

G. Terence Wilson, Ph.D.
Professor, Psychology, Rutgers University

With contributions   Meghan L. Butryn, M.S.
from   Graduate Student, Drexel University

Eric B. Chesley, D.O.
Fellow, Pediatric and Adolescent Medicine, University of Rochester

Michael P. Levine, Ph.D.
Professor, Psychology, Kenyon College

Marion P. Russell, M.D.
Clinical Fellow, Psychiatry, Brigham and Women's Hospital

Commission   Robyn Sysko, M.S.
Coordinator   Graduate Student, Rutgers University

Commission on Adolescent Substance and Alcohol Abuse

Commission Chair   Charles P. O'Brien, M.D., Ph.D.
Vice-Chairman, Psychiatry, University of Pennsylvania
Chief, Psychiatry, Philadelphia VA Medical Center
Director, Center for Studies of Addiction, University of Pennsylvania

Commission Members   James C. Anthony, Ph.D.
Professor and Chair, Epidemiology, College of Human Medicine, Michigan
State University

Kathleen Carroll, Ph.D.
Professor, Psychology in Psychiatry, Yale University School of Medicine

Director, Psychosocial Research, Division of Substance Abuse, Yale University
   School of Medicine

Anna Rose Childress, Ph.D.
Associate Professor, Psychology, University of Pennsylvania
Division Director, Penn Addiction Treatment Research Center

Charles Dackis, M.D.
Chief, Psychiatry, University of Pennsylvania Medical Center–Presbyterian
Medical Director, Adult Community Psychiatry, Department of Psychiatry,
   University of Pennsylvania

Guy Diamond, Ph.D.
Assistant Professor, Psychology in Psychiatry, Children's Hospital of
   Philadelphia
Director, Center for Family Intervention Science, Children's Hospital of
   Philadelphia

Robert Hornik, Ph.D.
Professor, Communication and Health Policy, Annenberg School for
   Communication of the University of Pennsylvania
Member, Health Communication Group, Annenberg Public Policy Center

Lloyd D. Johnston, Ph.D.
Distinguished Senior Research Scientist, Institute for Social Research,
   University of Michigan

Reese Jones, M.D.
Professor, Psychiatry, University of California, San Francisco
Director, Drug Dependence Research Center, University of California, San
   Francisco

George F. Koob, Ph.D.
Director, Division of Neuropsychopharmacology, The Scripps Research
   Institute
Director, Alcohol Research Center, The Scripps Research Institute

Thomas Kosten, M.D.
Professor, Psychiatry, Yale University

Caryn Lerman, Ph.D.
Professor, Psychiatry, University of Pennsylvania
Associate Director, Cancer Control and Population Science, University of
   Pennsylvania Cancer Center
Director, Tobacco Research Program, Leonard and Madlyn Abramson Family
   Cancer Research Institute

A. Thomas McLellan, Ph.D.
Professor, Psychology in Psychiatry, University of Pennsylvania
Director, Treatment Research Institute

Howard Moss, M.D.
Associate Director for Education and Career Development
National Institute on Alcohol Abuse and Alcoholism

Helen Pettinati, Ph.D.
Professor, Psychology in Psychiatry, University of Pennsylvania

Richard Spoth, Ph.D.
F. Wendell Miller Senior Prevention Scientist, and Director, Partnerships in
   Prevention Science Institute at Iowa State University

Commission on Adolescent Suicide Prevention

Commission Chair   **Herbert Hendin, M.D.**
Medical Director, American Foundation for Suicide Prevention
Professor, Psychiatry, New York Medical College

Commission Members   **David A. Brent, M.D.**
Academic Chief, Child and Adolescent Psychiatry, Western Psychiatric
  Institute and Clinic
Professor, Child Psychiatry, Pediatrics and Epidemiology, University of
  Pittsburgh School of Medicine

Jack R. Cornelius, M.D., M.P.H.
Professor, Psychiatry, University of Pittsburgh School of Medicine

Tamera Coyne-Beasley, M.D., M.P.H.,
Assistant Professor, Pediatrics and Internal Medicine
Co-Director, Adolescent Medicine Education
Principal Investigator, Firearm Injury Prevention Project, University of North
  Carolina at Chapel Hill

Ted Greenberg, M.P.H.
Research Associate, Child and Adolescent Psychiatry, Columbia University

Madelyn Gould, Ph.D., M.P.H.
Professor, Psychiatry and Public Health (Epidemiology), College of Physicians
  and Surgeons, Columbia University
Research Scientist, New York State Psychiatric Institute

Ann Pollinger Haas, Ph.D.
Research Director, American Foundation for Suicide Prevention
Professor, Health Services, Lehman College of The City University of New York

Jill Harkavy-Friedman, Ph.D.
Assistant Professor, Clinical Psychology in Psychiatry, Columbia University
Research Scientist, New York State Psychiatric Institute

Richard Harrington, M.D., F.R.C. Psych.
Professor, Child and Adolescent Psychiatry, University of Manchester
  (deceased)

Gregg Henriques, Ph.D.
Assistant Professor, Department of Psychology, James Madison University

Douglas G. Jacobs, M.D.
Associate Clinical Professor, Psychiatry, Harvard Medical School

John Kalafat, Ph.D.
Associate Professor, Graduate School of Applied and Professional Psychology,
  Rutgers University

Mary Margaret Kerr, Ed.D.
Associate Professor, Child Psychiatry and Education, University of Pittsburgh

Cheryl A. King, Ph.D.
Associate Professor, Psychiatry and Psychology, University of Michigan

Richard Ramsay, M.S.W.
Social Work, University of Calgary, and President, Living Works Education

David Shaffer, F.R.C.P., F.R.C. Psych.
Irving Philips Professor of Psychiatry, College of Physicians and Surgeons,
  Columbia University
Director, Child and Adolescent Psychiatry, College of Physicians and
  Surgeons, Columbia University

Anthony Spirito, Ph.D.
Professor, Psychiatry and Human Behavior, and Director, Clinical Psychology
  Training Consortium, Brown Medical School

Howard Sudak, M.D.
Clinical Professor, Psychiatry, University of Pennsylvania School of Medicine

Elaine Adams Thompson, Ph.D., R.N.
Professor, Psychosocial and Community Health, School of Nursing, University
  of Washington

Commission   Ann Pollinger Haas, Ph.D.
Coordinator

Commission on Positive Youth Development

Commission Chair   Martin E.P. Seligman, Ph.D.
Professor, Psychology, University of Pennsylvania
Director, Positive Psychology Network
Scientific Director, Values-in-Action Classification of Strengths and Virtues
  Project, Mayerson Foundation

Commission Members   Marvin W. Berkowitz, Ph.D.
Professor, Character Education, University of Missouri, St. Louis

Richard F. Catalano, Ph.D.
Professor, School of Social Work, University of Washington
Associate Director, Social Development Research Group, University of
  Washington

William Damon, Ph.D.
Professor, Education, Stanford University
Director, Center on Adolescence, Stanford University

Jacquelynne S. Eccles, Ph.D.
Professor, Psychology, University of Michigan

Jane E. Gillham, Ph.D.
Visiting Assistant Professor, Psychology, Swarthmore College
Co-director, The Penn Resiliency Project, University of Pennsylvania

Kristin A. Moore, Ph.D.
President and Senior Scholar, Child Trends

Heather Johnston Nicholson, Ph.D.
Director of Research, Girls Incorporated®

Nansook Park, Ph.D.
Assistant Professor, Psychology, University of Rhode Island

David L. Penn, Ph.D.
Assistant Professor, Psychology, University of North Carolina at Chapel Hill
Adjunct Assistant Professor, Psychiatry, University of North Carolina at
  Chapel Hill

Christopher Peterson, Ph.D.
Professor, Psychology, University of Michigan
Director of Clinical Training, University of Michigan

Margaret Shih, Ph.D.
Assistant Professor, Psychology, University of Michigan

Tracy A. Steen, Ph.D.
Postdoctoral Fellow, University of Pennsylvania

Robert J. Sternberg, Ph.D.
Professor, Psychology and Education, Yale University
Director, Center for the Psychology of Abilities, Competencies, and Expertise, Yale University

Joseph P. Tierney, M.A.
Director, Civic Initiatives for the Fox Leadership Program and the Center for Research on Religion and Urban Civil Society, University of Pennsylvania

Roger P. Weissberg, Ph.D.
Professor, Psychology and Education, University of Illinois at Chicago
Executive Director, the Collaborative for Academic, Social, and Emotional Learning

Jonathan F. Zaff, Ph.D.
Co-Founder and Executive Director, 18–35

Commission Coordinator   Tracy Steen, Ph.D.

Summary of Conclusions, Recommendations, Priorities

Joyce Garczynski, M.A.
Senior Research Assistant, Annenberg Public Policy Center, University of Pennsylvania

Michael Hennessy, Ph.D.
Senior Statistician, Annenberg Public Policy Center, University of Pennsylvania

Kimberly Hoagwood, Ph.D.
Professor, Clinical Psychology in Psychiatry, Columbia University
Director, Child and Adolescent Services Research, New York State Office of Mental Health

Kathleen Hall Jamieson, Ph.D.
Professor, Annenberg School for Communication, University of Pennsylvania
Director, Annenberg Public Policy Center, University of Pennsylvania

Patrick Jamieson, Ph.D.
Associate Director, Adolescent Risk Communication Institute, Annenberg Public Policy Center, University of Pennsylvania

Abigail Judge, B.A.
Graduate Student, Clinical Psychology, University of North Carolina at Chapel Hill

Mary McIntosh, Ph.D.
Principal and President, Princeton Survey Research Associates International

A. Thomas McLellan, Ph.D.
Professor, Psychology in Psychiatry, University of Pennsylvania
Director, Treatment Research Institute

Kathleen Meyers, Ph.D.
Senior Research Scientist, System Measures, Inc.
Adjunct Assistant Professor, Psychology in Psychiatry, University of
    Pennsylvania School of Medicine

David Penn, Ph.D.
Assistant Professor, Psychology, University of North Carolina at Chapel Hill
Adjunct Assistant Professor, Psychiatry, University of North Carolina at
    Chapel Hill

Daniel Romer, Ph.D.
Director, Adolescent Risk Communication Institute, Annenberg Public Policy
    Center, University of Pennsylvania

Foreword

Because the first sign that a person has a mental disorder often appears in adolescence, one would expect library shelves full of books for doctors, guidance counselors, and parents on the subject. Since early diagnosis and treatment increase the affected adolescent's chances for a productive adult life, one would expect that understanding how to prevent and treat depression, bipolar disorder, anxiety disorders, eating disorders, schizophrenia, and alcohol and drug abuse would be a national priority. One would expect as well a concerted national effort to prevent adolescent suicide and to find ways to promote mental health among the young. Although researchers have made sometimes stunning progress in treating adolescent mental disorders and in understanding ways to promote adolescent mental health, there have been surprisingly few attempts to digest what is known and what needs to be known.

To address this need, The Annenberg Foundation Trust at Sunnylands, founded in 2001 by Ambassadors Walter and Leonore Annenberg, convened seven scholarly commissions in 2003. Made up of leading psychiatrists and psychologists, and chaired by Edna B. Foa, Dwight L. Evans, B. Timothy Walsh, Martin E.P. Seligman, Raquel E. Gur, Charles P. O'Brien, and Herbert Hendin, the commissions were tasked with assessing the state of scientific research on the prevalent mental disorders whose onset occurs predominantly between the ages of 10 and 22. The collective findings of these commissions are presented in this book for the first time. As important, our commissions each identified the research agenda that would best advance our ability to prevent and treat the disorder on which they focused.

This book is significant not simply because it synthesizes a body of research on an important topic and charts future directions for research but also because it combines the disciplinary perspectives of those on the front lines of research and treatment. The work of psychologists and psychiatrists as well as scholars of social work is represented here. Noteworthy too is the fact that this book was produced without support from the pharmaceutical industry.

The publication of *Treating and Preventing Adolescent Mental Health Disorders* is the beginning of the Sunnylands Trust's multistaged effort to increase the likelihood that adolescents with mental disorders will be diagnosed and successfully treated. In partnership with the Annenberg Public Policy Center of the University of Pennsylvania, the Trust plans to widely disseminate this volume to scholars and practitioners. Companion volumes are now being prepared for school counselors and parents. A Web site, CopeCareDeal, will speak directly to teens.

The result, we hope, will not only help teens secure the care they deserve but also encourage those who shape the health policy of the nation to tackle the research and create and fund the delivery system needed to ensure the mental health of the nation's young.

Kathleen Hall Jamieson, Ph.D.
Director, Annenberg Foundation Trust at
Sunnylands
Director, Annenberg Public Policy Center
University of Pennsylvania
Philadelphia, PA

Introduction

Dwight L. Evans
and Martin E.P. Seligman

At least one in five youth suffers from a current developmental, emotional, or behavioral problem (Burns et al., 1995; Institute of Medicine, 1989; Irwin, Burg, & Cart, 2002; U.S. Department of Health and Human Services, 1999; Zill & Schoenborn, 1990). The prevention and treatment of such difficulties in adolescence is one of the major public health problems facing the United States. To help adolescents achieve their full potential both as youths and as adults, it is important that we focus resources on this issue now. Helping adolescents reach their potential involves the identification, treatment, and prevention of mental disorders that interfere with the adolescent's development into a successful adult. However, getting rid of the disorder is not enough. We need also to instill positive values and behaviors that enable formerly troubled young people to flourish, contribute to society, and be happy and healthy.

Our goal with this book is to provide a comprehensive evaluation of what we know, and what we don't know, about adolescent mental health to create a road map for further scientific study and point the way toward needed changes in social policy. Our hope is that the current volume can advance the field through a state-of-the-art summary of empirical research on adolescent mental health, positive youth development, and the treatment and prevention of mental disorders in this age group.

In this introductory chapter, we set the context for our evaluation of adolescent mental health. We first address the question, "why focus on adolescence?" Following this, we provide an introduction to the specific mental disorders that are the main focus of this book and define some of the terms used throughout the book. We next give an overview of some of these special characteristics of the adolescent period so as to give the reader an understanding of the importance of this period of life to mental health. This includes a brief introduction to brain development during adolescence and an overview of genetic and environmental processes that are important at this stage of life. We then orient the reader to the history and structure of this volume and provide the rationale for the set of concluding chapters.

WHY FOCUS ON ADOLESCENCE?

Adolescence, which we define here broadly as ages 10 to 22, is a unique and distinct period in the development of human beings. The unique aspects of this developmental period have enormous implications not only for mental health and disorder among young people but for adults as well. Adolescence is a critical period of development characterized by significant changes in brain development, endocrinology, emotions, cognition, behavior, and interpersonal relationships. This period of life is a transitional period of development that is foundational but also noticeably malleable and plastic from a neurobiological, behavioral, and psychosocial perspective.

From a mental health perspective, adolescence is important because most of the major mental disorders begin not in childhood but during adolescence. After onset in adolescence, many chronic mental disorders carry over into adulthood, leading to ongoing significant mental health impairment during the adult years. This later influence of adolescence applies to not only the major mental disorders but also a range of health habits that influence adult behavior and may influence medical diseases in adulthood. Specifically, adolescent development and behaviors set the stage for adult behavior in terms of use of substances (both legal and illegal) and dietary habits and can have an impact on the development and outcome of medical illnesses, such as cardiovascular disease, diabetes, obesity, osteoporosis, and HIV/AIDS.

The past two decades of research have revealed that many mental disorders are relatively common in adolescence. Details of epidemiological studies of mental disorders in adolescents are presented in each of the disorder-focused chapters in this volume. Some of the more striking examples are the following:

- The lifetime prevalence rate of major depressive disorder in adolescence is estimated to be about 15%, but 20% to 30% of adolescents report clinically significant levels of depressive symptoms (Chapter 1).
- Over half of young people have used an illicit drug by the time they graduate from high school (Chapter 17).
- The 12-month prevalence estimates for anxiety disorders in adolescents range from 9% to 21% (Chapter 9).
- Suicide is the third leading cause of death among youth (Chapter 21).

What is especially alarming is that the prevalence of some of these disorders has been on the rise over each successive generation. Certain changes over time in the nature of adolescence, and the environments that adolescents find themselves in, may be responsible for these observed increases in the prevalence of psychopathology in adolescence. A major factor is that adolescence itself is now more extended. Puberty has been occurring progressively earlier, particularly in developed countries such as the United States (Parent et al., 2003). At the other end, full-time work and marriage now occur later in life. Thus, if adolescence is defined in terms of the onset of puberty, the total time spent in adolescence is now longer than in the past, and if its upper end is defined as the end of formal schooling, the total time is now much longer. Access to and availability of potentially harmful environments and substances have increased. For example, many types of abusable drugs can now be ordered through the mail via the Internet (For-

man, 2003; National Drug Intelligence Center, 2002). Compounding the potentially negative consequences of harmful environments is the increasing behavioral independence of adolescents in association with less parental or even adult influence.

There are many unanswered questions about the ways in which the interplay between biology and environment lead to the alarming numbers of adolescents we now see afflicted with mental illness and why this seems to have worsened in recent years. However, what is clear is the need to make adolescent mental health a major public health priority. A decade ago, early childhood moved into the spotlight and became a major health priority, but from the point of view of mental health, adolescence may be the more critical transitional period given its neurobiological and behavioral plasticity. It is, moreover, likely the optimal time for prevention and treatment of psychopathology, and for the promotion of mental health and positive emotional and behavioral functioning. By increasing our knowledge of the causes, treatment, and prevention of mental disorders that begin in adolescence, we will help reduce the suffering and impairments associated with these disorders and reduce overall health care utilization. Furthermore, progress in adolescent mental health could prevent mental disorders in adulthood that have onset in adolescence and modify the prevalence or course of medical illnesses in adulthood that are related in part to adolescent behaviors or mental disorders.

WHY THESE DISORDERS?

For the current volume, we have chosen to concentrate on mood disorders, anxiety disorders, eating disorders, suicide, substance use disorders, and schizophrenia. These disorders represent the major mental disorders or public health issues among adolescents, with the exception that conduct disorder and attention-deficit hyperactivity disorder, two important disorders of adolescence, are not represented in the current volume. This decision was made because these disorders have clearer roots in childhood and they were extensively covered in the parallel book, *A Guide to Treatments That Work* (Nathan & Gorman, 2002), which focused primarily on adults.

Mood Disorders

Although for many years depression was considered a problem that afflicted only adults, in the last 30 years there has been increasing recognition that this disorder can and does occur in children, particularly in adolescents. Fifty years ago, its mean age of onset was near 30, but now it is closer to 15. As mentioned previously and reviewed in the chapters on mood disorders, major depressive disorder is now seen as not uncommon in adolescents. When it occurs, it often has a severe impact on school performance and interpersonal relationships of afflicted youth. Since depression is a recurring disorder, its onset in puberty predicts an increase in the incidence of major depressive disorder. This constellation of facts about depression suggests that the adolescent years are key to understanding the etiology and course of depressive disorders.

Although bipolar disorder occurs at a markedly lower prevalence than that of major depressive disorder, it often has an onset during adolescence and can progress into an extremely disabling condition during adulthood. Moreover, bipolar disorder is associated with high rates of suicide in adolescence. Identification and treatment of major depression and bipolar disorder in adolescence may be the key to preventing the insidious progression of these illnesses and thereby reducing the burden of the illness on the individual and society.

Anxiety Disorders

Each of the specific anxiety disorders (generalized anxiety disorder; panic disorder; agoraphobia; obsessive-compulsive disorder; posttraumatic stress disorder; simple phobia; social anxiety disorder; separation anxiety disorder) seen in youth occurs with relatively low prevalence, but combined together these disorders are relatively common. As described in chapters on anxiety disorders, some disorders (separation anxiety and phobic disorders) are more common in early childhood and then become less common by adolescence, whereas other disorders (panic disorder and agoraphobia) show the opposite developmental profile, increasing in adolescence. These changes suggest that something especially relevant to the nature and course of anxiety disorders is happening during the adolescent years and may provide clues to the etiology and prevention of these disorders.

Eating Disorders

The two major eating disorders, anorexia nervosa and bulimia nervosa, typically have their onset around the beginning of puberty. Aspects of adolescence provide a fertile context for the development of eating disorders during these years. As discussed in the chapters on eating disorders, there is a marked increase in energy requirements required to support normal growth and development, with caloric requirements for girls increasing by almost 50% and for boys, by 80%. Moreover, dieting related to self-perceived weight status is now extremely common among adolescents, with two of every three female high school students trying actively to lose weight. Both of these eating disorders are of concern from a public health point of view. The mortality rate among individuals with anorexia nervosa is particularly a concern. For bulimia nervosa, only about half of those with the disorder can be expected to recover, with the rest displaying an ongoing significant impact on physical and psychosocial functioning.

Suicide

Suicide among young people has become an increasing concern over the past several decades. Although there has been a decrease in suicides among youth recently, the suicide rate among youth is now over double what it was 50 years ago. Possible reasons for this increase, as discussed in the chapters on youth suicide, include higher rates of depression and substance use, lower family cohesion, and higher availability of firearms (which are used in about 60% of suicides). It may also be that increased awareness of suicide and documentation of suicides has contributed to an increase in recorded suicides over time. Although actual suicides are rare—about 8 per 100,000 among 15- to 19-year-olds—an alarming number of adolescents attempt suicide. Among U.S. high school students, almost 9% will have attempted a suicide in the past year. Despite the widely acknowledged importance of increased attention to the problem of youth suicide, the scientific evaluation of suicide prevention programs and risk factors associated with suicide is in its infancy. This area remains a high priority for the health of our nation.

Substance Use Disorders

Substance use is a ubiquitous problem among adolescents. Heroin, marijuana, cocaine, ecstasy, methamphetamine, inhalants, as well as new so-called club drugs such as gamma-hydroxybutyrate, flunitrazepam, and ketamine, are all used and abused by youths. As detailed in the chapters on substance use disorders, educational and preventive programs have had some success, with use of substances among adolescents decreasing slightly in recent years. Unfortunately, there is historical evidence to suggest that as soon as one birth cohort of adolescents shows reduced drug use after learning about the dangers and consequences of a particular drug through either education or personal experience, the next cohort of children enters adolescence without such knowledge and is prone to experience the dangers of a particular drug on their own. Moreover, new drugs continue to appear, such as the newer club drugs, for which there are few scientific studies of the short- or long-term effects and little accumulated street knowledge of the consequences of use. The advent of these new drugs further contributes to the ongoing high levels of substance use among adolescents.

The largest substance use problem among adolescents is not illicit drugs but alcohol. Surveys have documented that 0.4% to 9.6% of adolescents meet diagnostic criteria for alcohol abuse, and another 0.6% to 4.3% meet criteria for de-

pendence (Chapter 17). The behavioral and psychosocial effects of alcohol and drug abuse and dependence are alarming, with school performance and social functioning deteriorating significantly. Addiction to illicit drugs such as heroin and cocaine can lead to a variety of illegal activities, including dealing, prostitution, and robbery as ways to pay for a drug habit. Excessive drinking among adolescents has been linked to high-risk sexual behaviors, date rape, assaults, homicides, and suicides.

Of equal or greater concern are the long-term effects of substance use on the developing brain of adolescents. While the general public largely still views addiction as a moral or character problem, the scientific community increasingly has moved toward a disease model of addiction, with particular focus on the brain. Evidence for genetic vulnerability to addiction and the neuronal basis for many of the clinical features of substance dependence, including craving, tolerance, and withdrawal, have raised questions about the lasting effects of chronic drug use. In addition, as reviewed in the next section in this chapter, the adolescent brain is developing. There is a key neural vulnerability during the adolescent period: although the brain's reward system is fully developed in adolescents, other areas of the brain involved in decision making and judgment are not yet fully developed (see Chapter 17). Thus, the adolescent brain is ripe for experiencing the rewarding effects of drugs but without the decision-making capacity and judgment that would allow weighing the consequences of drug use.

Schizophrenia

Finally, although schizophrenia is often viewed as an adult disorder, it was included in this volume because its onset is often in adolescence. The outcome of schizophrenia is often devastating, with long-term chronic impairment lasting from adolescence or early adulthood throughout life. Basic research with neuroimaging and other techniques have begun to map out the relationship between brain development and the occurrence of schizophrenia in both children and adolescents. Thus, a focus on schizophrenia in adolescence can provide hope for a better understanding of the disorder, and early interventions at this stage of life can potentially lessen, if not prevent, some of the devastating effects of the disorder as it continues into adulthood.

WHAT IS ADOLESCENCE?

Adolescence is a distinct developmental period characterized by significant changes in hormones, brain and physical development, emotions, cognition, behavior, and interpersonal relationships. It has been defined as beginning with the onset of sexual maturation (puberty) and ending with the achievement of adult roles and responsibilities (Dahl, 2004). As mentioned previously, in terms of chronological age, the range for adolescence is broadly inclusive, roughly 10 to 22 years of age. For a number of reasons, this range is only a guide. First, there are wide individual differences in development. The onset of puberty, along with its associated hormonal and physical changes, occurs significantly earlier for some youth than for others. A second reason is that different facets of adolescent development are on a different time course. While hormonal changes occur at the beginning of adolescence, certain executive functions of the brain are not completely developed until the early 20s. Moreover, different developmental trajectories have been found for different cognitive and emotional processes (Rosso, Young, Femia & Yurgelun-Todd, 2004). A third reason for the difficulty in specifying an exact age range is evidence showing that, particularly in developed countries such as the United States, the onset of puberty is at an earlier average age than seen previously (Parent et al., 2003). At the other end, cultural changes, such as expanding enrollment in postgraduate education, have kept young people from assuming adult roles until well into their late 20s. Thus the typical age range of adolescence has been redefined over time, and there are differences in age range between cultures and countries. Regardless of the specific age range of adolescence, the nature of changes in the adolescent brain over time are crucial for understanding why this period of development is particularly important for mental health.

The Developing Brain

The brain undergoes changes throughout life, with intervals of modest change punctuated by periods of more rapid transformation (Spear, 2000). Periods of more dramatic change include not only prenatal and early postnatal eras but also adolescence (Spear, 2000). There are a number of specific changes in the brain during the adolescent years. These include synaptic changes, myelination (extensive maturation of myelin), changes in the relative volume and level of activity in different brain regions, and hormonal interactions with brain structures. Technological advances, particularly the development of functional magnetic brain imaging techniques, have contributed substantially to the recent increase in knowledge about these brain changes.

The primary synaptic change seen during adolescence is, counterintuitively, a major reduction in the number of synapses. Rakic, Bourgeois, and Goldman-Rakic (1994) estimate that up to 30,000 cortical synapses are lost every second during portions of the pubertal period in nonhuman primates, resulting in a decline of nearly 50% in the average number of synaptic contacts per neuron, compared with the number prior to puberty. There is a similar loss of synapses in the human brain between 7 and 16 years of age (Huttenlocher, 1979), but the scarcity of human postmortem tissue makes it difficult to provide a more detailed description of this phenomenon. Although the implications of the massive pruning remain speculative, it is likely that it reflects active restructuring of connections and the sculpting of more mature patterns, with a corresponding pruning of connections with very little activity. And we know, for example, that some forms of mental retardation are associated with unusually high density of synapses (Goldman-Rakic, Isseroff, Schwartz, & Bugbee, 1983).

The elimination of large amounts of synapses,

which are presumed to be excitatory, accompanied by a reduction in brain energy utilization, transforms the adolescent brain into one that is more efficient and less energy consuming (Chugani, 1996; Rakic et al., 1994). These changes may permit more selective reactions to stimuli that in younger children activate broader cortical regions (Casey, Giedd, & Thomas, 2000).

Myelination is another brain process that occurs during adolescence. The speed of neural transmission is greatly increased during myelination as a result of the glial cell membranes wrapping around axons. Although certain areas of the brain, such as the visual cortex, show maturation of myelin during childhood, myelination continues for the long-distance neural connections in the frontal, parietal, and temporal areas throughout adolescence (Luna & Sweeney, 2004). It is hypothesized that the myelination seen during adolescence further contributes to the development of executive functions of the brain, including faster information processing, by facilitating the integration of distributed brain areas and enhancing local connections (Luna & Sweeney, 2004).

Adolescence is also marked by changes in the relative volume and level of activity in different brain regions. For example, there is an increase in cortical white matter density (due to myelination) and a corresponding decrease in gray matter, especially in frontal and prefrontal regions (Giedd et al., 1999; Sowell et al., 1999a, 1999b). The overall result of these varied changes is a net decrease in volume of the prefrontal cortex (Sowell et al., 1999b; van Eden, Kros, & Uylings, 1990). In the hippocampus and the amygdala, however, gray-matter volumes continue to increase during late childhood and adolescence (Giedd, Castellanos, Rajapakse, Vaituzis, & Rapoport, 1997; Yurgelun-Todd, Killgore, & Cintron, 2003). While frontal white-matter volume peaks at about 11 years of age in girls and 12 years of age in boys, temporal gray matter volume peaks at about 16.7 years in girls and 16.2 years in boys (Giedd, 2004). In contrast, the dorsal lateral prefrontal cortex, which controls impulses, doesn't reach adult size until the early 20's (Giedd, 2004). Consistent with these changes in brain structure is the finding that by the end of adolescence there is improvement in prefrontal executive functions, including response inhibition and organizational and planning skills (Fuster, 1989).

There are also developmental shifts in patterns of innervation, including the circuits involved in the recognition and expression of fear, anxiety, and other emotions (Charney & Deutsch, 1996). The responsiveness of the cortical GABA–benzodiazepine receptor complex to challenge increases as animals approach puberty (Kellogg, 1998), and there are maturational changes in the hippocampus in humans and in animals (Benes, 1989; Wolfer & Lipp, 1995), especially increases in GABA transmission (Nurse & Lacaille, 1999). Further, pubescent animals show lower utilization rates of serotonin in the nucleus accumbens than do younger or older animals (Teicher & Andersen, 1999).

Developmental increases in amygdala–prefrontal cortex connectivity are seen during adolescence, in work conducted in laboratory animals (Cunningham, Bhattacharyya, & Benes, 2002). There are also alterations in amygdala activation (Terasawa & Timiras, 1968) and in the processing of emotional and stressful stimuli. Lesions of the amygdala have opposite effects on fearfulness to social stimuli according to whether those lesions are in infant or adult monkeys (Prather et al., 2001). Although levels of negative affect and anxiety have been correlated with amygdala activity in adults (Davidson, Abercrombie, Nitschke, & Putnam, 1999), recent studies using functional magnetic resonance imaging (fMRI) to examine amygdala activation in response to emotionally expressive faces in younger individuals have yielded a varying mosaic of evidence (Killgore, Oki, & Yurgelun-Todd, 2001; Pine et al., 2001).

Maturational changes in the cerebellum and in the circuitry connecting the cerebellum to the prefrontal cortex continue throughout adolescence. Lesions of the adult cerebellum disrupt the regulation of emotion and interfere with performance of tasks requiring executive functions (Schmahmann & Sherman, 1998), although this is less apparent in those younger than 16 years of age (Levisohn, Cronin-Golomb, & Schmahmann, 2000).

These brain changes related to the circuitry that involves emotions interact with hormonal changes during this period, leading to parallel emotional and behavioral changes during adolescence. Early adolescence is characterized by a lack of emotional regulation, but by the end of adolescence there is substantially greater emotional stability and control over behavior, particularly impulsive behavior.

There are several other changes in the human brain that, while not unique to adolescence, occur from birth through adulthood. One of these is postnatal neurogenesis (development of new neurons). This ongoing development of new neural cells is now known to occur in several brain areas, including the hippocampus, the olfactory bulb, the cingulate gyrus, and regions of the parietal cortex (Nelson, 2004). Neurotransmitter systems in the brain, which are key to current biological perspectives on many mental disorders, also do not reach full maturity until adulthood (White & Nelson, 2004).

Hormonal Changes in Adolescence

Puberty results from increased activation of the hypothalamic–pituitary–gonadal (HPG) axis, which in turn results in a rise in secretion of sex hormones (steroids) by the gonads in response to gonadotropin secretion from the anterior pituitary. Rising sex steroid concentrations are associated with other changes, including increased growth hormone secretion.

There is also more activity in the hypothalamic–pituitary–adrenal (HPA) axis during adolescence. This neural system governs the release of several hormones and is activated in response to stress. Cortisol is among the hormones secreted by the HPA axis, and researchers can measure it in body fluids to index the biological response to stress. Beginning around age 12, there is an age-related increase in baseline cortisol levels in normal children (Walker, Walder, & Reynolds, 2001).

The significance of postpubertal hormonal changes has been brought into clearer focus as researchers have elucidated the role of steroid hormones in neuronal activity and morphology (Dorn & Chrousos, 1997; Rupprecht & Holsboer, 1999). Neurons contain receptors for adrenal and gonadal hormones. When activated, these receptors modify cellular function and influence neurotransmitter function. Short-term effects of steroid hormones on cellular function are believed to be mediated by membrane receptors. Longer-term effects (genomic effects) can result from the activation of intraneuronal or nuclear receptors. These receptors can influence gene expression. Brain changes that occur during normal adolescence may be regulated by hormonal effects on the expression of genes that govern brain maturation.

Gonadal and adrenal hormone levels are linked with behavior in adolescents. In general, both elevated and very low levels are associated with greater adjustment problems. For example, higher levels of adrenal hormones (androstenedione) are associated with adjustment problems in both boys and girls (Nottelmann et al., 1987). Children with an earlier onset of puberty have significantly higher concentrations of adrenal androgens, estradiol, thyrotropin, and cortisol. They also manifest more psychological disorders (primarily anxiety disorders), self-reported depression, and parent-reported behavior problems (Dorn, Hitt, & Rotenstein, 1999). The more pronounced relationship between testosterone and aggressive behavior in adolescents who have more conflicts with their parents demonstrates the complex interactions between hormonal and environmental factors (Booth, Johnson, Granger, Crouter, & McHale, 2003).

It is conceivable that hormones partially exert their effects on behavior by triggering the expression of genes linked with vulnerability for behavioral disorders. Consistent with this assumption, the heritability estimates for antisocial behavior (Jacobson, Prescott, & Kendler, 2002) and depression (Silberg et al., 1999) increase during adolescence. Further, the relationship between cortisol and behavior may be more pronounced in youth with genetic vulnerabilities. For example, increased cortisol is more strongly associated with behavior problems in boys and girls with a mutation on the long arm of the X chromosome (fragile X syndrome) than in their unaffected siblings (Hessl et al., 2002).

Genetics

Genetics plays a significant role in our understanding of adolescent mental health. Historically, diathesis–stress models of mental illness suggested that a constitutional vulnerability interacting with environmental stress led to the development of mental disorders. Research in recent years, however, has shown that more complex models are needed to understand many disorders. Genes are turned on and turned off throughout one's lifetime, and multiple genes are likely involved in many mental disorders.

Many of the mental disorders prevalent in adolescents are the subject of promising, ongoing genetic research. Schizophrenia is one example. Several candidate genes have been identified that influence the development of the brain, including processes that have been linked to schizophrenia such as the excitability of glutamate neurons, hippocampal function, and regulation of dopamine neurons by the cortex. The authors of Chapter 5 on schizophrenia speculates that disruptions in these processes during adolescence may be particularly problematic because of the dramatic changes in cortical development that occur during this period.

Another example of the role of genetics is recent research on the relationship between a genetic variable, polymorphism of the serotonin transporter gene, and the development of depression after exposure to child abuse (Caspi et al., 2003). Individuals with a certain polymorphism of the serotonin transporter gene were found to be immune to the depressogenic affects of child abuse, whereas those with a different form of the polymorphism were highly likely to develop depression after child abuse (Caspi et al., 2003).

The Environmental Context of Adolescence

In the developing adolescent, the environmental context provides an influence that interacts (positively or negatively) with that child's biology to produce behavior. Families, schools, peers, youth sports and after-school activities, and community and religious organizations are the main social contexts in which adolescents

spend time and model interactions with adults and peers, and these contexts provide the general framework for adolescents to develop their own outlook on life. As youth move from childhood to adolescence, there is an increase in time spent with peers and a corresponding decrease in time spent with their family. Typically, there is also a natural tendency for conflicts with authority figures, including parents, to increase. These conflicts allow adolescents to find their own path in life and to begin to acquire the skills needed to succeed as an independent adult. As mentioned previously, the successful acquisition and application of skills to live independently mark the definition of the transition from adolescence to adulthood. There are also cultural differences in the nature and timing of the acquisition of these adult living skills during adolescence. Thus, environmental and cultural factors are inherently interwoven into the fabric of adolescence.

Each of the major external environmental contexts to which adolescents are exposed can have positive or negative influences on their mental health. Parents, friends, coaches, and teachers provide social support to adolescents that can bolster them during difficult times and help them develop in positive ways by serving as role models. But if these people are abusive, rejecting, or overly controlling toward a youth who is emotionally attached to them, the youth can suffer detrimental effects. Abuse, which is all too often physical and/or sexual abuse from adults, and trauma are also clearly risk factors for the development of mental disorders, such as posttraumatic stress disorder and major depression. Unfortunately, trauma and abuse are not uncommon in some settings. For example, a study of African-American male youth living in low-income housing in Alabama found that over three-fourths of the youth had been victims of violence. An even larger proportion (87%) reported witnessing at least one violent act (Fitzpatrick, 1997). Finally, a measurable impact of parental mental health, particularly parental depression, on child and adolescent mental health is beginning to be uncovered (see Chapter 1).

Although parental behavior or mental health has an impact on that of the child or adolescent, a case can be made that, beyond the extreme situation of abuse or neglect, parents are not the major influence on adolescents; instead, socialization that occurs in peer groups outside the home may be the more potent influence. Harris (1995) describes a number of influential processes that occur in peer groups. Adolescents who are part of a peer group are subject to "in-group" favoritism and "out-group" hostility. Peer groups also elicit within-group jockeying for status. Moreover, peer groups encourage adolescents to form close dyadic relationships, including the development of love relationships. Disruptions in these processes are part of the emotional turmoil of adolescence.

Peer groups, along with the media, also expose adolescents to popular culture, which can impact adolescent beliefs, values, and sexual behavior. One important example of this is described in Chapter 17: particularly during the 1960s to 1980s, popular culture affected the degree and nature of adolescent substance abuse.

Within each of the parts on mental disorders in adolescents, the role of environmental contexts as contributing factors or triggers in the development of such disorders is discussed. The positive influence of such environmental contexts is highlighted in Chapter 26 on positive youth development. These environmental contexts are important to understand, not only because of their etiologic or protective factors in regard to mental health, but also because they are the settings and vehicles for interventions among youth, as we discuss below.

Intervention in Adolescence

With all of the changes occurring during adolescence and the associated neurobehavioral vulnerabilities and resiliences, it is clear that this phase of life is an ideal time to target with interventions aimed at improving young people's lives. This is true for both the treatment of adolescent disorders and the prevention of both adolescent-onset and adult-onset disorders.

For many mental disorders, it is increasingly clear that the earlier the intervention, the better. For example, disorders such as schizophrenia and bipolar disorder have a progressive course, with onset in adolescence or early adulthood,

followed by the potential for further deterioration with the occurrence of each subsequent episode of illness. Therefore, rather than waiting for an individual to meet all diagnostic criteria from the *Diagnostic and Statistical Manual for Mental Disorders* (DSM) for a psychiatric disorder, it may be far better to identify and treat individuals who have risk factors or display some of the early signs of the illness. In the case of schizophrenia, such early-intervention programs have shown promise in reducing the annual incidence of first-episode psychosis (see Chapter 6; Falloon, Kydd, Coverdale & Laidlaw, 1996).

These early-intervention efforts and the targeting of high-risk and other nondisordered populations speak to the importance of interventions that have a preventive perspective. Although treatment of actual disorders in adolescence will remain an essential aspect of adolescent mental health research and practice, prevention may be the key to diminishing the burden of adolescent and adult disorders on society. Accordingly, the current volume has a major focus on prevention. There are many forms of prevention, therefore, a brief history of the concept and definitions of relevant terms are presented here.

Early Public Health Prevention Classification System

Different types of disease prevention efforts were first defined from a public health point of view in 1957 by the Commission on Chronic Illness (Commission on Chronic Illness, 1957). Three types of preventive interventions were identified: primary, secondary, and tertiary.

Primary prevention was defined as the reduction of the incidence of a disease or disorder through the prevention of the occurrence of *new cases* of a disease or disorder before they occur (Commission on Chronic Illness, 1957). This definition was expanded to include interventions designed to promote general optimum health by the specific protection of persons against disease agents or the establishment of barriers against agents in the environment (Leavell & Clark, 1965). Widespread vaccination is an example of primary prevention.

Secondary prevention was defined as the reduction in the prevalence in the general population of *recurrences* or exacerbations of a disease or disorder that already has been diagnosed (Commission on Chronic Illness, 1957). This includes early detection and intervention to reverse, halt, or at least retard the progress of a condition (Rieger, 1990). An example of secondary prevention is the use of antihypertensive medications among those with high blood pressure to reduce the risk of cardiovascular complications such as stroke.

In contrast to primary and secondary prevention, tertiary prevention efforts do not seek to reduce the prevalence of a disease or disorder. *Tertiary prevention* is only concerned with the reduction of the disability associated with an existing disease or disorder (Commission on Chronic Illness, 1957). For those with allergies, removal from exposure to the allergen would be a tertiary prevention approach.

Although these prevention terms were widely used in various public health domains, there are clear problems in attempting to apply this classification system for prevention efforts to the mental health field. The system requires an appreciation of the linkage between a disease or a disorder and the cause of that disorder at different stages of development (Haggerty & Mrazek, 1994). For example, the primary prevention of adolescent depression requires knowledge of the causal factors related to depression and their operational relationships. Secondary and tertiary prevention require a similar knowledge base. In practice, however, prevention interventions are often applied without this level of knowledge. As a practical matter, many preventive interventions have been based on indirect associations or statistical relationships with an outcome that is desirable to prevent. The strength or lack of strength of these associations has often diminished the effectiveness of these efforts. As more has been learned about etiology, it has become clear that physical and mental health events and outcomes cannot be explained by simple causal relationships. Rather, they are the result of the complex interplay of biological, social, environmental, and intrapersonal risk and protective factors. Thus, the original definitions of prevention break down when applied to adolescent mental health.

Gordon's Definitions of Prevention

An alternative to the Commission on Chronic Illness (1957) definitions of prevention was proposed by Robert Gordon. This new system was based on the "empirical relationships found in practically oriented disease prevention and health promotion programs" (Gordon, 1983). These included programs designed for universal, selective, and indicated prevention.

The definition of *universal prevention* included all interventions targeted to the general public or to an entire population group not selected on the basis of risk (Gordon, 1987). This would include interventions such as use of seat belts and immunization programs that are desirable for everyone in the eligible population. *Selective prevention* is defined by Gordon as interventions that target individuals, or a specific subgroup of the population, whose risk of developing a disorder is higher than average (Gordon, 1987). For example, condom use programs among sexually active adolescents is a selective prevention effort. Once an individual in a high-risk group exhibits the early signs or symptoms of a disorder, *indicated prevention* efforts would apply (Gordon, 1987).

Institute of Medicine Definitions

To reduce confusion emanating from the use of both the Commission on Chronic Illness (1957) and Gordon (1983) systems, and to suggest definitions more appropriate to the mental health field, the 1994 Institute of Medicine report, *Reducing Risk for Mental Disorders: Frontiers for Prevention Intervention Research*, offered new definitions. The term *prevention* was used in this report to refer only to interventions that occur before the initial onset of a disorder. Prevention included all three elements of Gordon's system. Efforts to identify cases and provide care for known disorders were called *treatment*, and efforts to provide rehabilitation and reduce relapse and reoccurrence of a disorder were called *maintenance*. Further distinctions were made within the prevention category using Gordon's (1983) terms. These are the definitions that we have used for the current volume. The specific distinctions within the prevention category are given below.

Universal mental health prevention interventions are defined as efforts that are beneficial to a whole population or group. They are targeted to the general public or a whole population group that has not been designated or identified as being at risk for the disorder being prevented. The goal at this level is the reduction of the occurrence of new cases of the disorder.

Selective mental health prevention interventions are defined as those efforts that target individuals or a subgroup of the population whose risk of developing the mental health disorder is significantly higher than average. The risk may be immediate or lifelong. Biological, psychological, or social risk factors associated with or related to the specific mental health disorder are used to identify the individual or group level risk.

Indicated prevention interventions are defined as those efforts that target high-risk individuals who are identified as having minimal but detectable signs or symptoms that predict the mental disorder or biological markers indicating predisposition to the disorder. For example, individuals who have some symptoms of major depressive disorder but do not yet meet criteria for the disorder would fall into this group. Although this definition includes early intervention, it excludes individuals whose signs and symptoms meet diagnostic criteria for the disorder. In the Institute of Medicine (1994) definitions, interventions with individuals who meet diagnostic criteria would be considered treatment.

Definition of Additional Prevention Terms

A further clarification of potentially confusing terms used within the prevention field was presented in the 1999 Surgeon General report on mental health (U.S. Department of Health and Human Services, 1999). In this report, *first (initial) onset* was defined as the initial point in time when an individual's mental health problems meet the full criteria for a diagnosis of a mental disorder. *Risk factors* were defined as those variables that, if present, make it more likely that a given individual, compared to someone selected at random from the general population, will develop a disorder. Although risk factors precede

the first onset of a disorder, they may change in response to development or environmental stressors. *Protective factors* include factors that improve an individual's response to an environmental hazard and result in an adaptive outcome. These protective factors can be found within the individual or within the family or community. They do not necessarily lead to normal development in the absence of risk factors, but they may make an appreciable difference in the influence exerted by risk factors. We have adopted these clarifications offered in the Surgeon General's (1999) report here.

It is also important to distinguish between the *risk of onset* and *the risk of relapse* of a disorder. This is important because the risks for onset, or protection from onset, of a disorder are likely to be somewhat different from the risks involved in relapse, or protection from relapse, of a previously diagnosed condition. In this book, the prevention of relapse is included in chapters on treatment, whereas the prevention of onset of a disorder is discussed in chapters on prevention.

Pharmacological Intervention in Adolescence

Psychopharmacological interventions in children and adolescents are now common. In part because of the availability of selective serotonin reuptake inhibitors (SSRIs) as well as increased recognition of depression and treatment seeking, there has been a substantial increase in antidepressant prescriptions for children and adolescents (Ofson, Marcus, Weissman, & Jensen, 2002; Zito et al., 2003). The U.S. Food and Drug Administration (FDA) has now granted approval for the SSRIs fluvoxamine, sertraline, and fluoxetine for the treatment of obsessive-compulsive disorder in children and adolescents, and for fluoxetine for the treatment of major depressive disorder in patients 8 years of age or older. In 2002, approximately 10.8 million total prescriptions were dispensed for the newer antidepressants among those 17 years and younger (Holden, 2004). About half of children and adolescents treated for depression in the United States receive medication (Olfson et al., 2003). Similarly, stimulant prescriptions for attention-deficit hyperactive disorder have also been on the rise, with one study finding that 9.5% of children 6 to 14 years of age were receiving such medication (Rushton & Whitmire, 2001).

The use of psychotropic medication in youth has recently come under scrutiny because of a possible link between use of antidepressants and increased suicidality. On the basis of an inspection of safety data, in late 2003 the U.K. drug regulatory agency recommended against the use of all SSRIs, except fluoxetine, in treating depression among youth under age 18 (Goode, 2003). After examining reports by pharmaceutical companies of their drug trials and listening to testimony at a public hearing on the issue, the FDA issued a public health advisory on antidepressants in March 2004 (FDA Public Health Advisory, 2004; Harris, 2004). In their statement, the FDA asked manufacturers of 10 specific SSRIs to place detailed information about the drugs' side effects prominently on their labels, and to specifically recommend close observation of adult and pediatric patients for the worsening of depression and the development and/or worsening of suicidality.

In September 2004, an FDA advisory committee met to further review the issue of suicide and SSRIs. The committee concluded that there was evidence for an increased risk of suicidality in pediatric patients, and that this risk applied to all drugs examined (Prozac, Zoloft, Remeron, Paxil, Effexor, Celexa, Wellbutrin, Luvox, and Serzone). On the basis of this risk, the advisory committee recommended that any warning related to an increased risk of suicidality in pediatric patients should be applied to all antidepressant drugs, including older antidepressants and medications that have not been tested in pediatric populations. However, the committee also recommended that these medications not be removed from the market in the United States because access to these therapies was important for those who could benefit from them. The FDA subsequently announced that it generally supported these recommendations and was working on new warning labels for all antidepressants. The chapters on mood disorders and suicide in this volume carefully consider the risks vs. benefits of antidepressant use in youth.

Positive Youth Development

In addition to our focus on the treatment and prevention of mental disorders in adolescence, this book adds another important perspective on adolescent mental health: positive youth development. Rather than focusing on symptomatology, disorders, or problems, positive youth development deals with each youth's unique talents, strengths, interests, and future potential.

There are two major reasons why positive youth development is an essential aspect of adolescent mental health and is therefore included prominently in this book. The first is our emphasis on prevention. Preventive programs that target nondisordered populations (e.g., universal mental health prevention) often are oriented toward building strengths, such as social competencies, rather than directly addressing negative behaviors, emotions, or symptoms. A full understanding of the range of positive virtues and strengths and their relation to competencies, well-being, and the development of disorders, problems, and symptoms is therefore necessary to successfully design preventive efforts and evaluate their effectiveness.

The second reason that positive youth development features prominently in this book is our view that adolescent mental health is much more than symptoms and disorders. As parents, teachers, and mental health professionals, our goals are to prepare young people for the demands of life. Having no symptoms or disorder is not likely to be sufficient to insure that adolescents thrive and form positive connections to the larger world as they transition into adulthood. Successful achievement of positive mental health, satisfaction with life, and adjustment to society may have more to do with certain positive characteristics such as curiosity, persistence, gratitude, hope, and humor than with the absence of symptoms. Indeed, research has shown that positive external (i.e., family support and adult mentors) and internal (commitment to learning, positive values, and sense of purpose) factors in youth are associated with academic success, the helping of others, leadership, and decreased problems (Benson, Leffert, Scales, & Blyth, 1998; Leffert et al., 1998; Scales, Benson,

Leffert, & Blyth, 2000; see Chapter 26 for more details).

The emphasis on positive youth development is complementary to the treatment and prevention of disorders. Adolescents will obviously continue to experience problems and disorders that need attention and treatment. Disorders themselves may be preventable or reducible through development of strengths and virtues. But by also addressing positive values and strengths, in disordered and nondisordered youth, we believe we can maximize the chances that successful lives will ensue.

The Settings for Interventions in Adolescence

The Mental Health and Substance Abuse Treatment System

Each of the chapters on disorders in this book identifies treatments and prevention programs that have been found to work. What has become increasingly clear is that the development of such efficacious treatment is only a first step toward improving public health. It is also essential to take into account the settings in which the interventions occur. Currently in the United States, there are significant challenges to providing quality care for youth and their families within the mental health and substance abuse treatment systems that serve these populations. The severity of these challenges are highlighted in two chapters on service delivery systems for adolescents, one by Myers and McLellan regarding the substance abuse service delivery system in the United States, and one by Hoagwood on the mental health service delivery system. Both of these chapters document systemic barriers to implementing evidence-based treatments in our existing service delivery system. One of the primary barriers, reviewed in greater detail in Chapters 28 and 29, is service fragmentation—that is, the fact that treatment of children and adolescents is performed by at least six separate systems: specialty mental health, primary health care, child welfare, education, juvenile justice, and substance abuse. Other barriers include poor access and use of services among minorities, lack of sustained family involvement, and fiscal dis-

incentives under managed care. Thus, a research agenda for the future would not be complete without an understanding of and improvement in the relevant service delivery systems.

School Settings

Schools have long been recognized as an important context for adolescent mental health development and service delivery. In fact, schools have been described as the de facto mental health service delivery system for children and adolescents, with between 70% and 80% of those that receive any form of mental health service obtaining such services from within the school setting (Burns et al., 1995). Higher prevalence rates of mental disorders and higher rates of comorbidity have been found among children and adolescents receiving services within the special education services of school than in specialty mental health clinics or in substance abuse clinics (Garland et al., 2001).

More than any other setting, schools provide access to adolescents for assessment and intervention. Student functioning, at least in terms of cognitive functioning needed for successful academic achievement, is tracked regularly, and behavior is assessed by multiple observers (teachers). At the first sign of problems, interventions could be initiated, rather than waiting until serious disorders develop and the adolescent is brought to a psychiatrist. Preventive interventions designed to target large populations of adolescents are particularly well suited for the school setting.

Unfortunately, as described in Chapter 31 on adolescent mental health and schools, the current state of mental health services in school is poor. There is wide variability across states and between urban and rural locations in the availability of mental health services in schools, with only about half of high schools having on-site mental health services (Brener, Martindale, & Weist, 2001; Slade, 2003). Increasing the availability and quality of school-based services for the assessment, treatment, and prevention of adolescent mental health problems is therefore a central component of any plan for improving the lives of adolescents.

Primary Care Settings

A particular component of the service delivery system, primary care medical practice, merits special attention in regard to adolescent mental health. In a typical year, over 70% of young people visit a primary care physician (Wells, Kataoka, & Asarnow, 2001). Primary care physicians typically serve as the gateway to obtaining specialist care, including mental health services. However, primary care physicians are typically poorly trained in psychiatry and psychology. Results of a national survey of primary care residency programs revealed that the average program devotes about 100 hours over the course of 3 years of residency to psychiatry training, with little or none of this specifically in child and adolescent psychiatry (Chin, Guillermo, Prakken, & Eisendrath, 2000). Compounding the problem is the fact that primary care physicians have enormous time constraints, especially since the advent of managed care and health maintenance organizations. These time constraints make it difficult for primary care physicians to adequately diagnose mental health problems. A recent study of over 20,000 youths visiting a primary care physician revealed that such physicians identified mood or anxiety syndromes at a rate substantially lower than that found in epidemiological studies (Wren, Scholle, Heo, & Comer, 2003). Inaccurate or missed diagnoses will lead to inadequate treatment.

Chapter 30 addresses in more detail the issues of identification and treatment of adolescent mental health problems in primary care settings. A unique aspect of this chapter is the presentation of a new study, commissioned by the Annenberg Adolescent Mental Health Initiative, which evaluates the practices of primary care physicians who treat large numbers of adolescents in the United States. This study found that physicians are concerned about the mental health of their adolescent patients and regard mental health as an important responsibility. In addition, the vast majority of primary care providers believe in the efficacy of treatment for mental disorders. However, primary care providers report low confidence in their ability to diagnose mental health problems, and only half employ any screening technique at all to detect mental health problems in their adolescent patients. These results suggest that enhancement of the recognition of mental disorders and referral practices in primary care represents a significant opportunity to increase appropriate treatment of adolescent mental health disorders.

THE PURPOSE AND STRUCTURE OF THIS BOOK

We have four main objectives with this book. The first is to review and summarize the adolescent literature for the six disorders and for positive youth development. To understand similarities and differences between adults and adolescents with these disorders, an additional objective is to review and briefly summarize the adult literature for the six disorders. On the basis of these literature reviews, each chapter provides recommendations for future research directions that we hope will serve as a template for guiding scientific developments in adolescent mental health. By fostering a specific scientific agenda, our larger objective is to help promote good mental health and positive youth development among adolescents.

This book was designed to be similar to a parallel volume addressing adult mental disorders (*A Guide to Treatments That Work*, Nathan & Gorman, 2002). Despite many similarities, unique aspects of adolescent mental health necessitated some differences from the Nathan and Gorman (2002) volume. The primary differences are the overriding focus on prevention and the theme of positive youth development. In addition, we have included several chapters that address the settings in which adolescent mental health and positive youth development efforts occur, and one discussing an important barrier (i.e., stigma) to enhancing adolescent mental health.

A substantial amount of effort went into the planning and creation of this book. The work began with the creation of seven commissions designed to discuss the issues and challenges in adolescent mental health regarding schizophrenia, anxiety disorders, mood disorders, eating disorders, substance abuse, suicide, and positive youth development. Researchers and clinicians from around the world with expertise in these areas were recruited for participation. Each commission initiated their work with a meeting during which initial ideas were presented and critiqued. Following this, initial drafts of chapters were prepared. A meeting of participants from all commissions, approaching 100 individuals, was then held in January 2004 to review and critique summaries of the literature and future recommendations. Final chapters were then prepared.

Throughout the preparation of the book, there was wide agreement among participants that the six disorders represented a somewhat artificial way to delineate the problems of adolescence. There was recognition that more work was needed on the current DSM system in regard to criteria for diagnosing adolescent disorders. More importantly, however, was the awareness, documented in a number of research studies, that comorbidity was extremely common among adolescent mental disorders, and therefore that the disorders as presently conceived may not "cut nature at the joints." Furthermore, it may be that what is most relevant to treatment and especially prevention is not the DSM disorders themselves but common pathways to these disorders. However, the six disorders were judged the best way to start the process of understanding adolescent mental health because the empirical literature is oriented around these disorders. The concept of common pathways is addressed within the recommendations of individual chapters, and again in the summary chapter.

Each of the disorder-focused chapters follows a common structure. The chapters begin by defining the disorder, including discussion of differences between childhood, adolescent, and adult manifestations of the disorder. Next, a review of epidemiological studies is presented to convey the public health significance of these disorders. This is followed by a review of theory and empirical studies pertaining to etiology and risk factors for the disorder. A broad perspective on etiology and risk factors is taken, so that empirical literature on personality and temperament, cognitive vulnerability, stress, interpersonal relationships, biological factors, genetics, gender, and early life traumas is summarized for each disorder, if relevant. All chapters then discuss comorbidity.

After thorough presentation of scientific knowledge concerning the nature of the disorder, each part then addresses intervention. This begins with treatment. A brief review of psychosocial studies in adults, including acute treatment as well as relapse prevention studies, is first given, followed by a more extensive review of adolescent acute-phase and relapse prevention studies. Pharmacological treatment studies in adults and adolescents are then reviewed. The concluding chapter of each part presents the commission's recommendations based on their literature reviews. These recommendations are outlined in terms of a research agenda for the future, summarized in regard to three questions asked separately about the nature of the disorder, treatment of the disorder, and prevention of the disorder: *(1)* What do we know? *(2)* What do we not know? *(3)* What do we urgently need to know? Chapter 26 on positive youth development necessarily deviates from the above structure but retains several of the elements, including parallel recommendations.

As mentioned previously, to improve adolescent mental health, some additional issues beyond research on treatment, prevention, or fostering of positive youth development also need to be considered. Four chapters on service delivery systems (mental health, substance abuse, primary care, and schools) provide the larger context needed for understanding how to foster improvements in adolescent mental health and positive youth development.

Chapter 27 addresses another significant barrier to improved mental health care: stigma. Penn et al. point out that often adolescents hold stigmatizing attitudes about those with mental disorders. By conveying these attitudes, the likelihood is reduced that those with disorders will seek and continue treatment. This chapter identifies factors that elicit or reinforce stigmatizing attitudes in both adults and youth, including negative labels, lack of contact with those with disorders, and negative portrayals in the mass media. The reduction of stigma is another way to increase the likelihood that adolescents will engage in treatment and prevention programs.

The concluding chapter of the book summarizes what has been learned about adolescent disorders, their treatment and prevention, service delivery systems, and barriers to care. In this chapter, a review of the key recommendations made by the seven commissions culminates in a call to the nation to make a sustained effort to enhance adolescent mental health through science and policy changes.

Adolescent mental health in the United States is, simply put, much poorer than it ought to be. We hope this book provides the reader with a new and comprehensive focus on adolescent mental health and positive youth development. To the extent that we have achieved that aim, we believe the recommendations contained here, if acted on, have the potential to *(1)* promote improved adolescent mental health and related physical health; *(2)* prevent adolescent and adult mental illness and related physical illness; *(3)* promote positive youth development and help adolescents reach their potential; *(4)* advance the treatment and rehabilitation of mental illness and related physical illness; and *(5)* raise the level of adolescent mental health to a standard that this nation can look on with pride.

Depression and Bipolar Disorder

COMMISSION ON ADOLESCENT DEPRESSION AND BIPOLAR DISORDER

Dwight L. Evans, *Chair*

William Beardslee

Joseph Biederman

David Brent

Dennis Charney

Joseph Coyle

W. Edward Craighead

Paul Crits-Christoph

Robert Findling

Judy Garber

Robert Johnson

Martin Keller

Charles Nemeroff

Moira A. Rynn

Karen Wagner

Myrna Weissman

Elizabeth Weller

part

Defining Depression and Bipolar Disorder

chapter **1**

The development of adolescent mood disorders involves a complex, multifactorial model (e.g., Akiskal & McKinney, 1975; Cicchetti, Rogosch, & Toth, 1998; Kendler, Gardner, & Prescott, 2002). No single risk factor accounts for all or even most of the variance. The most likely causal model will include individual biological and psychological diatheses that interact with various environmental stressors. There is little question that early onset is highly related to recurrence in adulthood, whether the data derive from clinical samples (Kovacs, Akiskal, Gatsonis, & Parrone, 1994), long-term population studies (Kessler and Walters, 1998), studies of high school students (Lewinsohn, Rohde, & Seeley, 1998), or studies of depressed patients (Rao et al., 1995). Over 50% of depressed adolescents had a recurrence within 5 years (Birmaher et al., 1996; Lewinsohn, Rohde, Seeley, Klein, & Gotlib, 2000), although only a small portion continues to have significant psychopathology in any one year. The few studies of depressed adolescents followed into adulthood show strong continuity between adolescent and adult depression (Trombonne, Wostear, Cooper, Harrington, & Rutter, 2001; Harrington, Fudge, Rutter, Pickles, & Hill, 1990; Weissman, Wolk, Goldstein et al., 1999; Weissman, Wolk, Wickramaratne, et al., 1999) and an increased risk of suicide attempts as well as psychiatric and medical hospitalization. Studies of prepubertal depression also show continuity into adolescence (Kovacs & Gatsonis, 1994). The most serious outcome is suicide, which is the third leading cause of death among adolescents. Other outcomes include lack of social development and skills, withdrawal from peers, poor school performance, less than optimal career and marriage choices, and substance abuse (Frost, Reinherz, Pakiz-Camra, Fiaconia, & Lekowitz, 1999; Rao et al., 1995; Weissman, Wolk, Goldstein, et al., 1999).

This chapter reviews the epidemiology and definitions of mood disorders in children and adolescence. The psychological, social, and biological factors that have been shown to increase the risk of mood disorders in children and adolescents are also discussed.

MAJOR DEPRESSION

For many years, children and adolescents were thought incapable of experiencing depression, according to the psychoanalytic concept of the underdeveloped superego. Thus depression was considered "an adult disease." However, case reports from as early as the 17th century described adolescents exhibiting symptoms resembling those observed in adults with depressive disorders. In 1975, the National Institute of Mental Health (NIMH) convened a meeting of thought leaders to discuss the incidence and diagnosis of depression among children. This meeting, followed by the publication of a book by Shulterbrant and Ruskin (1977), finally made clearer the diagnosis and the existence of depression acceptable in this population.

The last two decades have witnessed a burgeoning database on the age of onset of mood disorders. Major depressive disorder (MDD) is no longer seen primarily as a disorder of the middle-aged and elderly. Epidemiologic and clinical research from the United States and elsewhere has clearly documented that the age of first onset of major depression is commonly in adolescence and young adulthood and that prepubertal onsets, while less common, do occur. It is now clear that adolescent depression is a chronic, recurrent, and serious illness. The offspring of depressed parents, compared with children of nondepressed parents, have an over 2- to 4-fold increased risk of depression. Depressions occurring in adolescents share similar features with those of depression at other ages. Across ages, symptom patterns are similar; rates among females are higher (2-fold risk); there is high comorbidity with anxiety disorders, substance abuse, and suicidal behaviors; and high social, occupational, and educational disability can accompany depression (Angold, Costell, & Erkanli, 1999; Costello et al., 2002). In contrast, childhood MDD tends to be male predominant, mood reactive, and commonly associated with high levels of irritability and dysphoria and tends to have very heavy comorbidity with the disruptive behavior disorders (Biederman, Faraone, Mick, & Lelon, 1995; Leibenluft, Charney, Towbin, Bhangoo, & Pine, 2003).

The epidemiologic data on childhood and adolescent bipolar disorder are considerably sparser than those for MDD, in part because of the earlier erroneous belief that bipolar disorder begins in adulthood. It is also often quite difficult to assess boundaries between normal mood and mood irritability in youth, especially in community studies, and the first signs of bipolar disorder are frequently uncertain (Nottelman & Jensen, 1998). Most evidence on juvenile bipolar disorder comes from clinical samples in which efforts have been made, especially recently, to characterize early clinical presentations of bipolar disorder.

Unfortunately, until recently, persons under age 18 were excluded from epidemiological studies. Thus empirically based information on prevalence, risk factors, course, and treatment is scanty, especially for bipolar disorder. This situation is finally changing, but not rapidly enough; the consequences of mood disorders on future development in school, work, and marriage and on the next generation are often profound. This chapter will highlight the empirical basis for understanding the epidemiology, phenomenology, course, and comorbidity of MDD and bipolar disorder in youth. Because a sharp distinction between childhood and adolescent onset cannot be readily made, information on childhood (prepubertal-onset) disorder will be included when relevant.

Diagnosis

The same criteria defined in the *Diagnostic and Statistical Manual of Mental Disorders* (4th ed., with text revisions) (DSM-IV-TR) (American Psychiatric Association, 1994) to diagnose MDD in adults are used to diagnose MDD in adolescents (Table 1.1). Five or more of the following symptoms must be present nearly every day during the same 2-week period to diagnose an adolescent with a major depressive episode:

- Depressed or irritable mood most of the day
- Markedly diminished interest or pleasure in almost all activities, most of the day
- Significant weight loss or gain, or change in appetite; failure to gain expected weight
- Sleep disturbance

Table 1.1 Symptoms of Depressive Disorders

Categories	Symptoms
Affective	Anxiety, anhedonia, melancholia, depressed or sad mood, irritable or cranky mood
Motivational	Loss of interest in daily activities, feelings of hopelessness and helplessness, suicidal thoughts, suicidal acts or attempts
Cognitive	Difficulty concentrating, feelings of worthlessness, sense of guilt, low self-esteem, negative self-image, delusions or psychosis
Behavioral	Preference for time alone, easily angered or agitated, oppositional or defiant
Vegetative	Sleep disturbance, appetite change, lost or gained weight, energy loss, psychomotor agitation and retardation, lack of energy, decreased libido
Somatic	Physical or bodily complaints, frequent stomachaches and headaches

- Psychomotor agitation or retardation
- Fatigue or loss of energy
- Feelings of inappropriate guilt or hopelessness
- Indecisiveness or diminished ability to concentrate
- Recurrent thoughts of death or suicidal ideation, suicide attempt

At least one of the following two symptoms must be present: depressed or irritable mood, or markedly diminished interest or pleasure in almost all activities. These symptoms must cause clinically significant impairment in social, occupational, or other important areas of functioning. They cannot be due to the direct physiological effect of substance abuse or a general medical condition. Also, the symptoms should not be better accounted for by bereavement or schizoaffective disorder. A major depressive episode cannot be superimposed on schizophrenia, schizophreniform disorder, delusional disorder, or a psychotic disorder not otherwise specified.

More precisely, MDD can be rated as mild, moderate or severe; with or without psychotic symptoms; in full or partial remission. Depression should be diagnosed as chronic when the episode lasts more than 2 consecutive years. Furthermore, if loss of pleasure in almost all activities or lack of reactivity to usually pleasurable stimuli exists, the depression may be stated to have melancholic features. In addition, at least three of the following are required for melancholia:

- Depressed mood, which must be distinctly different from one felt from death of a loved one
- Morning depression being worse than that during the day or night
- Waking up several hours earlier than normal
- Evident psychomotor retardation or agitation
- Significant weight loss or anorexia
- Inappropriate or excessive guilt

Two of the following must be present to classify a depressive episode as having catatonic features:

- Motor immobility, catalepsy, or stupor
- Motor overactivity that is purposeless and not in response to external stimuli
- Extreme negativism or mutism
- Voluntary movement peculiarities such as posturing, grimacing, stereotypy, and mannerisms
- Echolalia or echopraxia

It is sometimes difficult but also important to establish the seasonality of the mood disorder because a major depressive episode can present initially as seasonal affective disorder in children and adolescents. To establish the presence of a true seasonal mood disorder, there must be a regular temporal relationship between the mood disorder (depression or mania) and a particular time of the year. A full remission or switching from depression to mania must occur within that particular time of the year. The adolescent also needs to experience two episodes of mood disturbance during the last 2 years and the seasonal episodes should greatly outnumber non-seasonal episodes. Seasonal mood disorder is often missed in adolescents because it is often

attributed to the stress of starting of a new school year in the fall. Postpartum depression in female adolescents is considered when the onset of depression is within 4 weeks of childbirth.

Another often undetected diagnosis in adolescents is *dysthymia*, which is defined in adolescents as depressed or irritable mood that must be present for a year or longer and the youth must never be symptom-free for more than 2 months. In addition, two or more of the following symptoms must be present:

- Change in appetite
- Change in sleep
- Decrease in energy
- Low self-esteem
- Difficulty making decisions or poor concentration
- Feelings of hopelessness

Similar to depression, dysthymia should not be diagnosed if it is a direct result of substance abuse or a general medical condition, or if it occurs during the course of a psychotic disorder such as schizophrenia. Moreover, if a major depressive episode is the first psychiatric disorder in an adolescent or the person has a history of manic, hypomanic, or mixed episodes, dysthymia should not be diagnosed.

Because dysthymia often starts in childhood, adolescence, or early adult life, it is often referred to as a "depressive personality disorder." Dysthymic disorder is considered chronic and if the age of onset is prior to 21, it is classified as early onset. Attention-deficit hyperactivity disorder (ADHD), conduct disorder (CD) specific developmental disorder, and a chaotic home environment are some of the more frequent predisposing factors for dysthymia in children and adolescents. Kovacs and associates (1984) have reported that dysthymic children are at risk for developing depression and mania on follow-up.

Adolescents who have dysthymic disorder and subsequently develop a major depressive episode are considered to have a "double-depression." When dysthymia coexists with disorders such as anorexia nervosa, anxiety disorder, rheumatoid arthritis, somatization disorder, or psychoactive substance dependence, it is referred to as "secondary dysthymia." In addition, adolescents can also exhibit atypical depressive features. Atypical features include mood reactivity with two or more of the following for a period of at least 2 weeks:

- Significant weight gain or increase in appetite
- Increased sleep
- Feelings of heaviness in arms or legs
- A pattern of long-standing rejection sensitivity that extends far beyond the mood disturbance episodes and results in significant social or occupational impairment. Atypical features are quite common among depressed adolescents.

Clinically it can be challenging to discern the difference between MDD and dysthymia in children and adolescents. However, with careful history taking with the child and the primary caregiver, this can be accomplished (Table 1.2).

Differentiating Prepubertal and Adolescent-Onset Major Depression

There are compelling reasons to differentiate between prepubertal- and adolescent-onset MDD (see Angold, Costello, & Worthman, 1998; Kaufman, Martin, King, & Charney, 2001). Although the frequency of MDD before puberty is not well established, it is hardly uncommon. Some estimates suggest that it may afflict as many as 2% of children at any one current period. Childhood-onset MDD tends to be male predominant, is commonly associated with irritability, and frequently is comorbid with disruptive behavior disorders (Biederman et al., 1995; Costello et al., 1996; Kessler, Foster, Webster, &

House, 1992; Rutter, 1996). Some studies of prepubertally depressed children have not found continuity into adulthood (Harrington et al., 1990; Weissman, Wolk, Goldstein, et al., 1999), whereas others have documented such continuity into adolescence (Kovacs et al., 1994). Prepubertally depressed children often develop a variety of psychiatric disorders in adulthood, especially increased rates of bipolar, anxiety and substance use disorders (Kovacs, 1998, 1990, 1996; Kovacs et al., 1984; Kovacs 1998).

There is good evidence to suggest that the onset of puberty as measured by Tanner stage and hormonal levels, rather than by chronological age per se, predicts the increase in onset of MDD in girls. Angold et al. (1998) studied 4,500 boys and girls, ages 9, 11, and 13, over 3 years who were sampled from the Great Smoky Mountains region of North Carolina. At each interview, assessments of major depression and pubertal status with Tanner staging (Tanner, 1962) were undertaken. Pubertal status, not chronological age at onset, was a better predictor of the emergent preponderance of major depression in girls. Consistent with the epidemiologic data, boys had a higher rate of MDD at prepubertal Tanner Stage I, with girls increasing and surpassing boys after Tanner Stage III.

Epidemiology

Rates

Epidemiologic data from large community surveys in the United States on the incidence of MDD among children and adolescents are sparse. This is in part due to the long-held view that MDD was rare before adulthood or was a self-limiting and normal part of growing up. In

Table 1.2 Comparison of Major Depressive Disorder and Dysthymic Disorder

Major Depressive Disorder	Dysthymic Disorder
Dysphoric mood	Dysphoric mood
Symptoms severe	Symptoms mild to moderate
Impaired functioning, common	Impaired functioning, less common
Psychosis may be present	No psychosis
Symptoms present every day	Symptoms usually fluctuating
Symptoms present every day for 2 weeks	Symptoms on and off for 1 year

addition, there has been controversy over the means of assessing young people and over who is the best informant, the child or the parent. A few surveys of adolescents have used self-report depression symptom scales assessing 1 week to 6 months prevalence. Rates based on established adult cutoff scores for clinically significant current depression range between 20% and 30% (Offord et al., 1987; Reinherz, Giaconia, Hauf, Wasserman, & Silverman, 1999; Wickstrom, 1999). However, self-reported symptom scales do not differentiate between mild and severe mood disorders, type of mood disorder, or other psychiatric disorders. Prevalence rates with self-report scales are generally considerably higher than those found in studies using diagnostic assessments.

Published epidemiologic studies of adolescents have been limited to school districts and high schools in one community (Lewinsohn, Hops, Roberts, Seeley, & Andrews, 1993; Whittaker et al., 1990) or limited geographic areas (Cohen et al., 1993; Costello et al., 1996), or have been conducted outside the United States in Canada (Flemming, Offord, & Boyle, 1989) or New Zealand (Fergusson & Woodward, 2002). With few exceptions (Flemming et al., 1989; Lewinsohn, Hops, et al., 1993); the samples of adolescents have usually been too small, under 1,000 and usually under 500, to be reliable estimates. The diagnostic methods and age groups of the adolescents vary widely among studies. The current lifetime prevalence rates of MDD from these studies have been estimated to be about 5%. The similarity between lifetime rates in adolescents and adults suggests that a large

percentage of those with major depression have onset while young.

The most comprehensive epidemiologic data in adults come from the National Comorbidity Survey (NCS; Kessler & Walters 1998), a nationally representative sample of over 8,000 persons from U.S. households ages 15 to 54 (Kessler & Walters, 1998). Although only 600 persons under age 18 were included in this sample, the rates from this U.S. population are consistent with published rates on adolescents. The lifetime prevalence for 15- to 18-year-olds was about 14% and an additional 11% were estimated to have a lifetime history of minor depression, with higher rates among females than among males. While the NCS did not sample persons under age 15, the sample was young enough so that reasonably good information from retrospective reports of age of first onset of MDD in childhood or adolescence could be obtained. Kaplan-Meier age-at-onset curves for major and minor depression in the NCS are presented in Figures 1.1 (major depression) and 1.2 (minor depression). Both curves show that meaningful risk begins in the early teens and continues to rise in a roughly linear fashion within groups of cohorts through the mid-20s (Kessler, Avenevoli, & Merikangas, 2001). The general shape of these curves is very similar to that of the onset curves reported in other epidemiologic studies of adolescent depression (e.g., Lewinsohn et al., 1998). The peak rise in rates in the late teens and early 20s is also consistent with the mean age of onset reported in the cross-national studies of adults (Weissman et al., 1996). Both curves show evidence of substantial prevalence increases in cohorts born af-

Figure 1.1 Kaplan-Meier cumulative lifetime prevalence curves for major depression in the total National Comorbidity Survey sample by cohort.

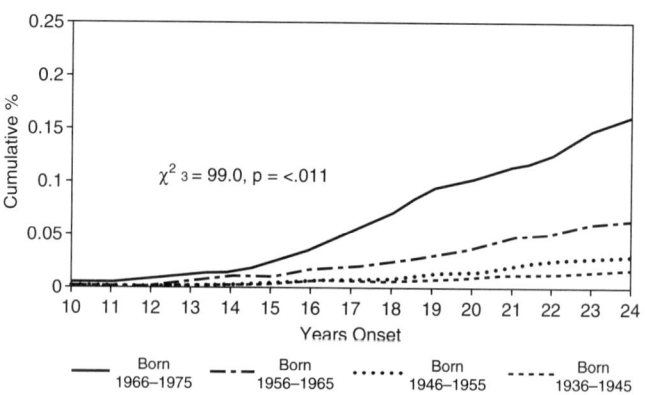

$\chi^2 3 = 99.0, p = <.011$

Cumulative %

Years Onset

| ——— Born 1966–1975 | — — Born 1956–1965 | ⋯⋯ Born 1946–1955 | - - - - Born 1936–1945 |

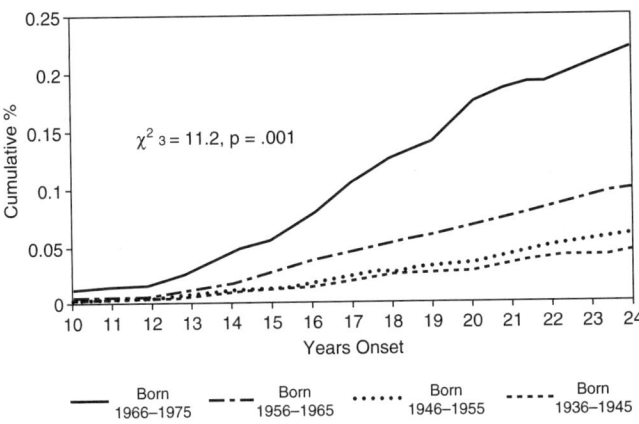

Figure 1.2 Kaplan-Meier cumulative lifetime prevalence curves for minor depression in the total National Comorbidity Survey sample by cohort.

ter the mid-1960s. A cohort effect (that is, secular changes in rates) has also been shown in cross-national epidemiologic studies of adults, spanning a considerable older age range (Cross-National Collaborative Group, 1992; Klerman & Weissman, 1989). These statistics need to be reconciled with data derived from clinical samples documenting that more than 30% of children referred to clinical centers suffer from major depression and that in many of these cases, the disorder starts in the preschool years. Moreover, recent reports from student health services on college campuses note a marked increase in requests for counseling for depression over the last decade and list suicide as the second leading cause of death among students (Voelker, 2003). In summary, there is good evidence that the first onset of MDD is frequently in adolescence and not uncommonly in childhood, and that the rates of MDD, especially in the young, have been increasing.

Comorbidity

Comorbidity with other psychiatric disorders in youth, as in adults, is the rule rather than the exception (see Angold et al., 1999 for a comprehensive review). Anxiety disorders are the most common, with over 60% of depressed adolescents having a history or a concomitant anxiety disorder. A frequent pattern of onset includes anxiety disorder, particularly phobias before puberty, with an emergence of major depression in adolescents (Pine, Cohen, Gurley, Brook, & Ma,

1998). Disruptive behavior disorders are frequent and emerge before puberty. Substance abuse in late adolescence with MDD is also common. Comorbidity with medical conditions in adolescents has been less well studied. However, a few studies have found an association between adolescent depression and obesity (Pine, Goldstein, Wolk, & Weissman, 2001); headaches (Pine, Cohen, & Brook, 1996) and asthma (Mrazek, Schuman, & Klinnert, 1998), as well as an increased risk of medical hospitalizations and accidents (Kramer et al., 1998).

Risk Factors

Information on risk factors for adolescent MDD comes both from epidemiologic and clinical studies. The two most consistent risk factors for MDD in both studies of adolescents and adults are female gender (2- to 3-fold increased risk) and a family history of MDD. The offspring of depressed parents are at 2- to 4-fold increased risk of MDD, an earlier age of onset, and recurrent episodes (Hammen, Burge, Burney, & Adrian, 1990; Weissman, Warner, Wickramaratne, Moreau, & Olfson, 1997; Weissman et al., 2004). The risk is transmitted across generations to grandchildren (Warner, Weissman, Mufson, & Wickramaratne, 1999).

Other risk factors that contribute to both the onset and recurrence of adolescent MDD are adverse family environments characterized by absence of supportive interactions; poor parental bonding; poor primary attachments; and harsh discipline (Fendrich, Warner, & Weissman, 1990; Garber & Little, 1999; Sheeber, Hops, & Davis, 2001). Separating out the effects of parental MDD from the risk factor studied is problematic, because parental MDD is frequently associated with the risk factors (e.g., divorce, poor parental bonding). One study of offspring at high and low risk of depression found that parental depression was the strongest risk factor for offspring depression, over and above other family risks, such as divorce or poor parental bonding. The rates of MDD were considerably lower in the offspring of nondepressed parents (low risk), but when MDD was present in the low-risk offspring, it was associated with poor parental bonding, parent–child conflict, and parental divorce (Fendrich et al., 1990; Nomura, Wickramaratne, Warner, Mufson, & Weissman, 2002).

Personality and Temperament

Several theorists have hypothesized a heritable trait vulnerability factor common to most, if not all, emotional disorders. This trait has been defined slightly differently and given various labels by different theorists, including harm avoidance (Cloninger, 1987), neuroticism (Eysenck, 1947), trait anxiety (Gray, 1982), behavioral inhibition (Kagan, Reznick, & Snidman, 1987), and negative affectivity (Watson & Tellegen, 1985), although the conceptual and empirical overlap among these constructs far outweighs the differences. Each implies a trait disposition to experience negative affect. The term *neuroticism* is often used to refer to this trait, and is consistent with the emergence of the Big Five model of personality as the dominant model of personality structure in children (e.g., Digman & Inouye, 1986; Digman & Shmelyov, 1996), adolescents (e.g., Digman, 1989; Graziano & Ward, 1992), and adults (e.g., Goldberg, 1992; McCrae & Costa, 1987).

Longitudinal studies have shown that neuroticism predicts later negative affect and symptoms of emotional distress (Costa & McCrae, 1980; Larson, 1992; Levenson, Aldwin, Bosse, & Spiro, 1988), even after controlling for initial symptom levels (Gershuny & Sher, 1998; Jorm, Christensen, Henderson, & Jacomb, 2000). Clark, Watson, and Mineka (1994) reviewed sev-

eral longitudinal studies showing that neuroticism predicts both subsequent diagnoses and chronicity of major depression. Since this review, studies reported by Hayward, Killen, Kraemer, and Taylor (2000), Kendler and colleagues (Kendler, Kessler, Neale, Heath, & Eaves, 1993; Kendler et al., 2002; Roberts & Kendler, 1999), and Krueger et al. (1996) have each obtained results consistent with the conclusions of Clark et al. (1994). For example, in a large adult female twin sample, Kendler et al. (1993) found that neuroticism predicted the onset of MDD over a 1-year period, and recently, Kendler et al. (2002; Kendler, Kuhn, & Prescott, 2004) tested a multifactorial model and showed that, after stressful life events, neuroticism was the strongest predictor of the onset of major depression.

The relation between neuroticism and depression may vary somewhat by age. Hirschfeld et al. (1989) found that whereas among 31- to 41-year-old individuals neurotic-like characteristics of decreased emotional strength, increased interpersonal dependency, and increased thoughtfulness predicted the first onset of depression, this was not the case for younger 17- to 30-year-old individuals. Similarly, Rohde, Lewinsohn, and Seeley (1990) found that adult participants who experienced a first episode of MDD had exhibited elevated levels of dependent traits 2 to 3 years earlier. Rohde, Lewinsohn, and Seeley (1994), however, found no differences with regard to prior levels of dependency between adolescents who later developed a first MDD and adolescents who were depression-free during a 1-year follow-up period.

In contrast, studies using other measures of neurotic-like traits in children have found evidence of a link with vulnerability for depression. Elevated levels of behavioral inhibition have been observed in laboratory tasks with young offspring of depressed parents (Kochanska & Kuczynski, 1991; Rosenbaum et al., 2000). Caspi, Moffit, Newman, and Silva (1996) reported that children who had been rated as inhibited, socially reticent, and easily upset at age 3 had elevated rates of depressive disorders at age 21. Similarly, van Os, Jones, Lewis, Wadsworth, and Murray (1997) found that physicians' ratings of behavioral apathy at ages 6, 7, and 11 predicted both adolescent mood disorders and chronic depression in middle adulthood. Finally, Gjerde (1995) reported that gender may moderate the relation between temperament and mood disorders. Whereas females with higher levels of chronic depression during young adulthood had been described as shy and withdrawn at 3 to 4 years of age, males with chronic depression exhibited higher levels of undercontrolled behaviors as young children. Thus, there is some evidence of an association between neurotic-like traits during childhood and subsequent depression, though it may depend on gender as well as how these traits are measured.

Neuroticism also has been found to be a risk factor for other forms of psychopathology, however, and thus it is not specific to mood disorders. For example, neuroticism has been shown to be a risk factor in the development of post-traumatic stress disorder (PTSD) following trauma (Breslau & Davis, 1992; Breslau, Davis, & Andreski, 1995; Helzer, Robins, & McEvoy, 1987). Behaviorally inhibited children are at greater risk for the development of multiple phobias and various anxiety disorders in later childhood (Biederman et al., 1990; Hirshfeld et al., 1992) and social phobias in adolescence. Hayward et al. (2000) also found that neuroticism predicted the development of panic attacks in a 4-year prospective study in adolescents. Thus, neuroticism appears to be a significant predictor of depression, though it might not be a specific vulnerability marker. Moreover, it is still difficult to distinguish among common cause, precursor, and predisposition models of the relation between neuroticism and depression (Klein, Durbin, Shankman, & Santiago, 2002).

Cognitive Vulnerability

According to cognitive theories of depression (Abramson, Metalsky, & Alloy, 1989; Abramson, Seligman, & Teasdale, 1978; Beck, 1967), depressed individuals have more negative beliefs about themselves, the world, and their future, and tend to make global, stable, and internal attributions for negative events. These negative cognitions are expected to be both concurrently associated with depression and to contribute to the onset and exacerbation of depressive symptoms. Cognitive theories of depression are in-

herently concordant with diathesis-stress theories. When confronted with stressful life events, individuals who have such negative cognitive tendencies will appraise the stressors and their consequences negatively, and hence are more likely to become depressed than are individuals who do not have such cognitive styles.

Several types of cognitions have been proposed to be related to depression, including low self-esteem, negative automatic thoughts, dysfunctional attitudes, and cognitive distortions (Beck, 1967); self-control (Rehm, 1977); control-related beliefs and self-efficacy (Bandura, 1977); depressive attributional style (Abramson et al., 1978); hopelessness (Abramson et al., 1989); and a ruminative response style (Nolen-Hoeksema, 2000). Cross-sectional studies with clinic and community samples of children have consistently shown a significant relation between negative cognitions, particularly low self-esteem and a pessimistic attributional style, and depression (Garber & Hilsman, 1992). Meta-analyses of studies reporting on attributional style and depression have demonstrated moderate to large effect sizes in cross-sectional studies suggesting a strong concurrent association between negative attributional style and higher levels of depressive symptoms in children and adolescents (Gladstone & Kaslow, 1995; Joiner & Wagner, 1995).

Longitudinal investigations of the role of cognitions in the prediction of childhood depression have yielded varying results. Global self-worth (Allgood-Merton, Lewinsohn, & Hops, 1990; Garber, Martin, & Keiley, 2002; Vitaro, Pelletier, Gagnon, & Baron, 1995) and perceived self-competence in specific domains (Hoffman, Cole, Martin, Tram, & Seroczynski, 2001; Vitaro et al., 1995) have predicted child and adolescent depressive symptoms (e.g., Allgood-Merton et al., 1990; Vitaro et al., 1995) and diagnoses (Garber, Martin, & Keiley, 2002), controlling for prior levels of depression. However, these same cognitive constructs also failed to predict depressive symptoms (Dubois, Felner, Brand, & George, 1999) and onset of new episodes. However, in one of these null studies, participants were selected from a drug and alcohol treatment clinic. The mean depression score in this sample was lower at the second assessment. Treatment procedures may have reduced depression levels during the assessment interval, making it difficult to predict maintenance or exacerbation of depression.

Attributional style generally has been investigated in the context of stress, though several studies have tested main-effects models or reported main effects in the absence of interactions. Significant prospective relations have been observed between attributional style and later depressive symptoms in children and young adolescents (Nolen-Hoeksema, Girgus, & Seligman, 1986; 1992; Panak & Garber, 1992), though a few studies have failed to find this relationship. In a longitudinal study of the developmental trajectories of negative attributions and depressive symptoms, Garber, Keiley, and Martin (2002) showed that attributional styles that were increasingly negative across time were associated with significantly higher initial levels and increasing growth of depressive symptoms during adolescence.

Prospective studies in children and adolescents have also found support for the cognitive diathesis–stress model of depression (Dixon & Ahrens, 1992; Hilsman & Garber, 1995; Lewinsohn, Joiner, & Rohde, 2001; Nolen-Hoeksema et al., 1992; Panak & Garber, 1992). Using different stressors (grades, peer rejection, and school transition) and different time periods, Garber and colleagues showed in three (Dixon & Ahrens, 1992; Panak & Garber, 1992; Robinson, Garber, & Hilsman, 1995) different short-term longitudinal studies that cognitions (attributions, self-worth) measured before the stressors occurred moderated the effect of the stressors on depressive symptoms in children. Among children who experienced high levels of stress, the relation between negative cognitions about the self or causes of events and depressive symptoms was stronger than in those without such negative cognitions. Lewinsohn et al. (2001) found that among adolescents who had experienced negative life events, intermediate levels of dysfunctional attitudes predicted the onset of depressive disorders a year later.

Developmental theorists (Nolen-Hoeksema et al., 1992; Weisz, Southam-Gero, & McCarty, 2001) have suggested that negative cognitions emerge over time and that their relation with depression becomes stronger with development.

For example, in a longitudinal study of children in grades 3 through 8, Nolen-Hoeksema et al. (1992) showed that attributional style alone and in conjunction with stress significantly predicted depressive symptoms in the older but not in the younger children. Similarly, in a cross-sectional comparison of children in grades 4, 6, and 8, Turner and Cole (1994) found that negative cognitions contributed to the prediction of depressive symptoms for the oldest children, but not for the two younger groups. Thus, the relation between the cognition–stress interaction and depressive symptoms appears to be increasing from middle childhood to early adolescence.

If negative cognitions contribute to the development of mood disorders, then "high-risk" offspring of depressed parents should be more likely to exhibit a cognitive vulnerability than children whose parents have not experienced mood disorders. Indeed, children of depressed mothers report significantly lower perceived self-worth and a more depressive attributional style than do children of well mothers (Garber & Robinson, 1997). Thus, children who are at risk for depression, but who have not yet experienced depression themselves, have been found to report a more negative cognitive style that likely represents a vulnerability to later depression.

In summary, correlational, predictive, and offspring studies have provided evidence that there is a cognitive style that represents a vulnerability to depression in children. This cognitive style involves beliefs about the self and explanations about the causes of negative events. Future studies need to examine the development of this cognitive vulnerability over time, and whether it needs to be primed in children (Ingram, Miranda, & Segal, 1998).

Stress

Common to all definitions of stress is a focus on environmental conditions that threaten to harm the biological or psychological well-being of the individual (Grant et al., 2003). Stress may occur either as an acute event or as chronic adversity, and as a major life event or as minor events with accumulated effects (either additive or multiplicative) (Grant et al, 2003). Stressful events may be normative (e.g., school transition) or pathological (e.g., abuse) and may be independent of, or directly related to and thus dependent on, an individual's actions. Objective environmental consequences of a stressor (i.e., can be reliably rated by objective observers) are hypothesized to have a direct effect on the development of depression. The subjective threat of a stressor involves individuals' appraisals of an event as stressful, which then may impact their psychological well-being (Lazarus, Delongis, Folkman, & Gruen, 1985). Finally, there may be specificity in the relation between stress and psychopathology such that certain subdomains of stressors may be more highly related to depression than others (Beck, 1967; Grant et al., 2003).

Stress plays a prominent role in most theories of depression, and a clear empirical link exists between stressful life events and depression in children and adolescents (Compas, Grant, & Ey, 1994). In infants, depressive symptoms have been associated with stressful life circumstances and often are responsive to changes in the environment (Moreau, 1996). One stressor particularly linked with depression in infants is separation. Spitz and Wolf (1946) noted that a common feature in depressed infants ages 6 to 8 months is separation from the mother. Separation in young children has been found to be associated with grief responses characterized by negative changes in sleep patterns, activity, heart rate, temperature, monoamine systems, immune function, and endocrine function (Kalin & Carnes, 1984). Spitz noted the phenomenon of hospitalism, referring to evidence that infants subjected to long hospital stays experienced a number of psychological difficulties. Longer and more frequent hospital stays and earlier age of entering the hospital were associated with more depressive symptoms in infants (Moreau, 1996).

In school-aged children, cross-sectional studies using either life events checklists or interview methods consistently have shown that depressive symptoms and disorders are significantly associated with both minor and major undesirable life events in children, particularly cumulative or chronic stressors, and negative life events are more prevalent among depressed than nondepressed children (Goodyer, Wright, & Altham, 1988). Cross-sectional studies, however, are not informative about the direction of the relation between stress and depression. Given the association between dependent stressors and depression (Garber, Martin, & Keiley, 2002), it is possible that depression contributes to the occurrence of stressors. Depressed individuals have been found to generate many of the stressors they encounter, and these stressors then serve to exacerbate and maintain the depressive symptoms (Bennett, Pendley, & Bates, 1995).

Laboratory animal studies have shown that antenatal stress impacts the developing physiology of the fetus and later physiological and behavioral outcomes in the offspring of stressed rat and primate mothers. These studies are reviewed in part in this section and in further detail later in this chapter. Henry, Kabbaj, Simon, Le Moal, and Maccari (1994) showed that prenatally stressed rat pups had an elevated corticosterone response to novel environments and reduced hippocampal corticosteroid receptor density, suggesting that prenatal stress may affect the neurobiological development of systems associated with depression. Behaviorally, rat pups stressed in utero had greater distress and defensive behavior (Takahashi, Baker, & Kalin, 1990) and reduced environmental exploration when exposed to aversive or stressful conditions (Poltyrev, Keshet, Kay, & Weinstock, 1996).

Prepartum exposure to stress also may result in hyperresponsiveness to later stressors. Clarke and associates (Clarke & Schneider, 1993; Clarke, Wittwer, Abbott, & Schneider, 1994) randomly assigned pregnant rhesus monkeys to stress and control conditions. The prenatally stressed offspring were less likely than control offspring to play and explore the environment and were more likely to engage in clinging, which is associated with distress in primates. Clarke and Schneider suggested that hypothalamic–pituitary–adrenal (HPA) axis activity was implicated in the hyperresponsiveness to later environmental stressors of prenatally stressed rhesus monkeys.

Thus, these data from animal models and additional data (see below) indicate that stress that occurs as early as at conception likely contributes to an increased vulnerability to depression. In human infants, stress during pregnancy is associated with negative outcomes for offspring (Lou et al., 1994). Although the mechanisms by which stress impacts the developing fetus are still unknown, it is hypothesized that fetal neurophysiological development may be sensitive to the intrauterine hormonal environment, and neurophysiological vulnerability (e.g., HPA axis dysregulation) may make these offspring more sensitive to stress and thereby predispose them to depression as they mature. Recently, Stowe and colleagues (unpublished observations) noted that infants of women depressed during pregnancy or postpartum had significantly greater salivary cortisol responses to a standardized stressor than offspring of normal control women or women with a past history of depression who were not depressed during the index pregnancy/postpartum period.

Longitudinal studies in which stressors are assessed prior to the onset of symptoms can be informative about the temporal relation between stress and depression. Prospective studies have found that stress predicts depressive symptoms, controlling for prior symptom levels in children (Goodyer, Herbert, & Altham, 1998) and adolescents (Allgood-Merten et al., 1990). The relationship is stronger when children's self-reports are used than when parents' reports of children's depressive symptoms are used (Stanger, McConaughy, & Achenbach, 1992).

Fewer studies have examined the contribution of negative life events to the onset of depressive disorders in children. Stress has predicted the onset of depressive symptoms in previously asymptomatic children (Aseltine, Gore, & Colten, 1994) and the onset of clinically significant depressive episodes, controlling for prior symptom levels in samples comprised of both children and adolescents (Hammen, 1991) and adolescents alone (Garber, Keiley, et al., 2002). Only three of these studies (Aseltine et al., 1994; Garber & Kaminski, 2000; Monroe, Rohde, Seeley & Lewinsohn, 1999) controlled for lifetime history of MDD to rule out the possibility that earlier depressive disorder contributed to onset.

Reports of stressful life events have been shown to increase for both boys and girls from childhood through adolescence, with increases being greater for girls (Ge, Longer, Lorenz, & Simons, 1994), paralleling increases in rates of depression for boys and girls (Hankin et al., 1998). However, few studies have found that gender moderates the relationship between stress and depression. Cohen (1987) reported that negative events predicted depressive symptoms in girls who had experienced minimal positive events in the same time interval, and Ge et al. (1994) showed that growth of stressful life events over time predicted growth in depressive symptoms for girls but not boys.

Although no one specific type of stressful event invariably leads to depression in children and adolescents, certain stressors consistently have been found to be associated with depression. Childhood abuse or maltreatment is an especially robust predictor of depression (Andrews, 1995; Bifulco, Brown, & Adler, 1991; Trad, 1994), and this is particularly true for women (Weiss, Longhurst, & Mazure, 1999). Sexual assault during childhood or adulthood has been found to increase the risk of depression by 2.4 in women (Burnam, Stein, Golding, Siegel, Sorenson, Forsythe, et al., 1988). Poverty also has been shown to contribute to vulnerability to depression (Bruce, Takeuchi, & Leaf, 1991; Grant et al., 2003; McLoyd, 1998). For example, the rates of depression among low-income mothers are about twice as high as in the general population (Bassuk, Buckner, Perloff, & Bassuk, 1998). Recently, Caspi et al. (2003) elegantly demonstrated the relationship between a genetic variable, polymorphism of the serotonin transporter (SERT), and the development of depression after exposure to child abuse. Individuals with the l/l form of the SERT were immune to the depressogenic affects of child abuse, whereas those with s/s allele were highly likely to develop depression after child abuse.

Events such as disappointments, loss, separation, and interpersonal conflict or rejection are also linked with depression (Aseltine et al., 1994; Goodyer, Herbert, Tamplin, & Altham, 2000; Panak & Garber, 1992). This is especially probable for individuals who tend to be more socially dependent or sociotropic. According to the specific vulnerability hypothesis (Beck, 1983, Blatt, Quinlan, Chevron, McDonald, & Zuroff, 1982), individuals whose self-esteem is derived from interpersonal relationships (sociotropy) are at increased risk for depression when they experience stressors within the social domain; in contrast, those who derive their self-worth from achievement-related goals are at greater risk for depression when they encounter occupational failure. Studies investigating this specific vulnerability hypothesis in children have been supportive (Garber & Kaminski, 2000).

In summary, a clear link exists between stress and depression. But by what mechanisms does stress increase an individual's vulnerability to depression? Although stressors often precede mood disorders, not all individuals exposed to stressors become depressed. Thus, there is not a perfect correspondence between exposure to negative life events and the onset of depressive symptoms. How individuals interpret and respond to events and how resilient they are also differentiates who does and does not become depressed. Some of the individual variability is due to differences in appraisals of the meaning of the events with regard to the self and future.

Interpersonal Relationships

Interpersonal perspectives on depression emphasize the importance of the social environment and the development of secure attachments. Vulnerability to depression presumably arises in early family environments in which the children's needs for security, comfort, and acceptance are not met. Bowlby (1980) argued that children with caretakers who are consistently accessible and supportive will develop cognitive representations, or "working models," of the self and others as positive and trustworthy. In contrast, caretakers who are unresponsive or inconsistent will produce insecure attachments leading to working models that include abandonment, self-criticism, and excessive dependency. Such working models may contribute to the development of negative cognitions about self and others, and presumably increase individuals' vulnerability to depression, particularly when exposed to new interpersonal stressors.

Reviews of the literature on the relation between the family environment and depression (Beardslee, Versage, & Gladstone, 1998; Rapee, 1997) indicate that families of depressed individuals are characterized by problems with attachment, communication, conflict, cohesion, and social support, as well as poor childrearing practices. Security in attachments helps infants cope

with the environment and a lack of such attachments may lead infants to seek protection by withdrawing from the environment altogether (Bowlby, 1980; Trad, 1994). Two-year-old children with secure attachments have been found to be more cooperative, persistent, and enthusiastic, show more positive affect, and function better overall than those with insecure attachments (Matas, Arend, & Sroufe, 1978). In adolescents, depression has been linked with less secure attachments to parents (Kenny, Moilanen, Lomax, & Brabeck, 1993). Moreover, adolescents undergoing stressful life events are more likely to become depressed if they had insecure attachments to their parents than adolescents with more secure attachments (e.g., Kobak, Cole, Ferenz-Gillies, Fleming, & Gamble, 1993).

Beyond attachment, other kinds of dysfunctional family patterns have been found to be associated with depression in children (Rapee, 1997). Serious abuse and neglect interfere with normal expressions of infants' emotions and lead to avoidant or resistant attachments, especially if the mother is the perpetrator of the abuse. Maltreatment also leads to withdrawal behaviors in infants and self-esteem deficits later in childhood (Trad, 1987). The parent–infant relationship is inevitably worsened from such abuse, which in turn puts the infant in higher danger of being abused again (Trad, 1987).

Two main parenting dimensions particularly associated with depression in children are acceptance/rejection and psychological control/autonomy (Barber, 1996). In retrospective studies, currently depressed adults recalled their parents as having been critical, rejecting, controlling, and intrusive (Parker, 1993). Currently depressed children have described their parents as authoritarian, controlling, rejecting, and unavailable (Stein et al., 2000), and they tend to perceive their families to be less cohesive and more conflictual than do nondepressed youth (Walker, Garber, & Greene, 1993; although see Asarnow, Carlson, & Guthrie, 1987, for contrary findings). Mothers of depressed children similarly describe themselves as more rejecting, less communicative, and less affectionate than mothers of both normal and psychiatric controls (Puig-Antich et al., 1985a). In observational studies, mothers of depressed children have been described as being less rewarding (Cole & Rehm, 1986) and more dominant and controlling than mothers of nondepressed children.

Several longitudinal studies have found a significant relation between the family environment and subsequent depressive symptoms (e.g., Barber, 1996; Sheeber, Hops, Alpert, Davis, & Andrews, 1997), whereas others have reported null findings (Burge et al., 1997). Barber (1996) showed that children's ratings of parents' psychologically controlling behavior predicted their depressive symptoms, controlling for prior levels of depression, although children's prior depressive symptoms also predicted their ratings of their parents' behavior. Burt, Cohen, and Bjorck (1988) found for girls' ratings of family expressiveness predicted depression after controlling for prior depressive symptoms. Other studies have shown that adolescents' reports of family adaptability and cohesion (Garrison, Jackson, Marsteller, McKeown, & Addy, 1990) and perceptions of family support (McFarlane, Bellissimo, & Norman, 1995) contribute to adolescent depressive symptoms, controlling for prior symptom levels. In addition, maternal hostile child-rearing attitudes have been found to significantly predict increases in children's depressive symptoms (Katainen, Raikkonen, Keskivaara, & Keltikangas-Jarvinen, 1999). Using observational data of parental warmth, hostility, and disciplinary skills, Ge et al. (1994) reported that increases in adolescent internalizing symptoms were predicted by lower levels of parental warmth and higher levels of maternal hostility. In this same sample, Rueter, Scaramella, Wallace, and Conger (1999) found that escalating parent–adolescent conflict predicted increases in adolescent internalizing symptoms, which in turn increased the risk of the onset of internalizing disorders.

Depressed children also have significant peer difficulties and social skills deficits (Altmann & Gotlib, 1988). Self-reported depression significantly correlates with teachers' reports of peer rejection in children (Rudolph, Hammen, & Burge, 1994). In laboratory studies, children with depressive symptoms were rated by their peers more negatively than were children without symptoms (Peterson, Mullins, & Ridley-Johnson, 1985). French, Conrad, and Turner

(1995) noted that rejection by peers predicted higher levels of self-reported depressive symptoms among antisocial, but not among non-antisocial youth. Panak and Garber (1992) found a significant relation between peer-rated rejection and self-reported depression, and this relation was mediated by perceived rejection. Kistner, Balthazor, Risi, and Burton (1999) similarly found that perceived rejection predicted increases in depressive symptoms during middle childhood. Finally, in a longitudinal study of children in sixth grade, Nolan, Flynn, and Garber (2003) found that a composite measure of rejection by peers, family, and teachers significantly predicted depressive symptoms across 3 years. Thus, depression in children is associated with high levels of interpersonal conflict and rejection from various members in their social domain.

Finally, relationships between depressed parents and their children have also consistently been found to be disrupted. Depressed parents report more conflict and less coherence in their families (Billings & Moos, 1983), are less involved and affectionate with their children, and experience poorer communication in parent–child relationships than nondepressed parents (Weissman, Paykel, Siegel, & Klerman, 1971). Moreover, depressed mothers tend to feel more hostile toward their children and less positive and competent about their parenting than do well mothers (Webster-Stratton & Hammond, 1988).

Observations of depressed mothers interacting with their children reveal that these mothers are more negative (Lovejoy, 1991), more controlling (Kochanska, Kuczynski, Radke-Yarrow, & Welsh, 1987), and less responsive and affectively involved (Cohn & Tronick, 1989) and use less productive communications (Gordon et al., 1989). Depressed mothers spend less time talking to and touching their infants and show more negative affect in their interactions with their infants who themselves show less positive affect, less activity, and more frequent protests (Field, 1995). Parental depression can also lead to disturbed attachment behavior and an inability by the infant to regulate emotions, thereby putting the infant at greater risk for developing depression (Gaensbauer, Harmon, Cytryn, & McKnew, 1984). Offspring of depressed parents have more insecure attachments than do offspring of well mothers (DeMulder & Radke-Yarrow, 1991; Teti, Gelfand, Messinger, & Isabella, 1995). Moreover, insecurely attached offspring of depressed mothers tend to have difficulties in their relationships with peers (Rubin, Booth, Zahn-Waxler, Cummings, & Wilkinson, 1991). Finally, negative reciprocal interaction patterns have been observed between depressed mothers and their children (Radke-Yarrow, Nottelman, Martinez, Fox, & Belmont, 1992).

In summary, two important findings emerge regarding the link between interpersonal vulnerability and depression. First, families with a depressed member tend to be characterized by less support and more conflict, and such family dysfunction increases children's risk of developing depression. Second, depressed individuals are themselves more interpersonally difficult, which results in greater problems in their social network. Thus, the link between interpersonal vulnerability and depression likely is bidirectional (Gotlib & Hammen, 1992). Longitudinal studies examining the contribution of family dysfunction, parent–child conflict, peer difficulties, and interpersonal rejection to increases in and maintenance of depressive symptoms in children have shown both that social problems temporally precede depression, and that depression contributes to interpersonal difficulties. Moreover, interpersonal difficulties appear to persist after depressive symptoms have remitted (Puig-Antich et al. 1985b). In addition, social adversities such as persistent poor friendships, low involvement of fathers, negative attitudes by family members, and stressful family environments can contribute to the maintenance or relapse of depressive disorders in youth (e.g., Asarnow, Goldstein, Tompson, & Guthrie, 1993).

The interpersonal environment clearly is an important and sometimes stressful context in which children develop schema about themselves and others, which can then serve as a vulnerability to depression. In addition, children's own reactions to these environments can exacerbate and perpetuate negative social exchanges, which furthers the interpersonal vicious cycle, thereby resulting in more rejection and depression. Thus, a transactional model of mutual influence probably best characterizes the association between depressed individuals and their social environment.

BIPOLAR DISORDER

The view that mania in younger people is extremely rare or nonexistent has been increasingly challenged by many case reports and by large-scale community surveys of adults; for example, Akiskal et al. (1985), in a case series of adolescent relatives of "classic" adult bipolar patients, found that despite frank symptoms of depression and mania and frequent mental health contacts, none of these youth had been diagnosed with an affective disorder. Weller, Weller, Tucker, and Fristad (1986) reviewed over 200 articles published between the years of 1809 and 1982 and identified 157 cases that would likely be considered manic by modern standards. However, approximately half of those subjects retrospectively diagnosed as manic according to DSM-III criteria were not considered so at the time of referral. More recently, Wozniak et al. (1999) reported that 16% of psychiatrically referred prepubertal children satisfied diagnostic criteria for bipolar disorder. Biederman et al. (1996) reported that a sizeable minority of children with ADHD has bipolar disorder. These reports suggested that mania in children/adolescents (pediatric mania) may not be rare, but difficult to diagnose. Despite continued debate and controversy over the validity of the diagnosis of mania in children (Biederman, 1998; Klein, Pine, & Klein, 1998), there is a growing consensus that many seriously disturbed children are afflicted with severe affective dysregulation and high levels of agitation, aggression, and dyscontrol that may be early bipolar disorder. These issues have received increased scientific attention, as evidenced by the scheduling of two NIMH workshops on bipolar disorder in children and adolescents and in exhaustive reviews that have supported the validity of the disorder in youth (Faedda et al., 1995; Geller and Luby, 1997; Weller, Weller, & Fristad, 1995). The NIMH Strategic Research Plan for Mood Disorder Research recommended the establishment of a multisite network program on pediatric onset bipolar disorder (Costello et al., 2002).

Agreement on what constitutes the first presentation of bipolar illness is critical for epidemiologic studies to obtain the true age of onset and estimate of prevalence and risk. The following questions need to be addressed: Does pediatric bipolar disorder differ from the adult form? What are the early signs and symptoms? What is the relationship of ADHD and other disruptive disorders to juvenile onset bipolar disorder? Answers to these questions are complicated by the uncertainty about the duration of a manic episode; that stems from the fact that youth more frequently report manic symptoms that persist only a few hours or days (Carlson and Kelly, 1998; Geller et al., 1995), and therefore do not fulfill adult criteria.

Differentiating Prepubertal and Adolescent Onset

In April 2000, the NIMH convened a meeting of experts to discuss diagnostic issues impeding research on children/adolescents bipolar disorder. There was general agreement that a diagnosis of bipolar disorder, using DSM criteria, is possible in prepubertal children. Children fall into two categories: *(1)* those who clearly have a bipolar disorder (because they meet DSM-IV criteria for bipolar I [the classic form of the illness characterized by recurring episodes of mania and depression] or bipolar II (A form of the illness characterized by milder episodes of hypomania that alternate with depression) and *(2)* those who may be bipolar but do not completely fit the adult phenotype defined in DSM-IV but suffer from severe mood disturbances and symptoms of bipolar disorder and are highly impaired.

Currently, severely ill children with an impaired mood disturbance, but not meeting full DSM-IV criteria for bipolar I or II, are not included in research studies of bipolar disorder because of the perceived uncertainty of their diagnosis. It was recommended that "bipolar-NOS" (not otherwise specified) could be used as a "working diagnosis" for advancing research on this broader phenotype, as long as the children are well described (with particular attention to symptoms of ADHD). Because available diagnostic instruments may not generate a reliable and

replicable diagnosis of bipolar-NOS, it was recommended that careful assessment include all of the behaviors that are impairing (Leibenluft et al., 2003).

Diagnosis

Pediatric mania tends to be chronic and continuous rather than episodic and acute (Carlson, 1983; Carlson, 1984; Feinstein and Wolpert, 1973; McGlashan, 1988). In a recent review of the past 10 years of research on pediatric mania, Geller and Luby (1997) concluded that childhood-onset mania is a nonepisodic, chronic, rapid-cycling, mixed manic state. Wozniak, Biederman, Kiely, et al. (1995) also found that the overwhelming majority of 43 children from an outpatient psychopharmacology clinic who met diagnostic criteria for mania on structured diagnostic interview had a chronic and mixed presentation. Carlson, Bromet, and Sievers (2000) reported that early-onset manics were more likely to have comorbid behavior disorders in childhood and, compared to adult-onset cases of mania, to have fewer episodes of remission over a 2-year period. A review by McElroy et al. (1997) described "mixed mania," which affects 20%–30% of adults with mania. Subjects with mixed mania tend to have a chronic course, absence of discrete episodes, onset of the disorder in childhood and adolescence, a high rate of suicide, poor response to treatment, and an early history of neuropsychological deficits highly suggestive of ADHD. Determination of the adult course of pediatric mania awaits data from longitudinal studies with larger samples. Presently, the same criteria defined in the DSM-IV-TR to diagnose bipolar disorder in adults are used for adolescents, as follows:

A. A distinct period of abnormally and persistently elevated, expansive, or irritable mood, lasting at least 1 week (or any duration if hospitalization is necessary)
B. During the period of mood disturbance, three (or more) of the following symptoms have persisted (four if the mood is only irritable) and have been present to a significant degree:

- Inflated self-esteem or grandiosity
- Decreased need for sleep
- More talkative than usual or pressure to keep talking
- Flight of ideas or subjective experience that thoughts are racing
- Distractibility
- Increase in goal-directed activity
- Excessive involvement in pleasurable activities that have a high potential for painful consequences

In addition, the symptoms do not meet the criteria of a mixed mood episode, in which both criteria for a manic episode and for MDD (except for duration) are met with symptoms nearly every day during at least a 1-week period. For hypomania, the elevated or irritable mood lasts for 4 days. The mood disturbance causes significant impairment and is not better accounted for by other psychiatric disorders or medical conditions. The DSM IV-TR notes that adolescents are more likely to exhibit psychotic features and may be associated with school difficulties, substance abuse, and antisocial behavior. It also notes that a significant minority of adolescents have a long-standing pattern of behavior problems that may represent an extended prodomal phase to bipolar disorder or, in fact, may represent a distinct disorder.

Epidemiology

Rates

Epidemiological data on juvenile bipolar disorder must be seen within the context of these diagnostic uncertainties. The 1980s Epidemiologic Catchment Area study (ECA), based on over 18,000 adults ages 18 and over for five U.S. communities, provided the first community-based data using modern diagnostic criteria and the first epidemiologic clue about the youth onset of bipolar disorder (Robins & Price, 1991) (Table 1.3). The lifetime prevalence of bipolar disorder was about 1/100, with few gender differences in rates and an overall median age of onset of 18 years.

The 1990 National Comorbidity Survey (NCS) included a representative national sample in the United States of over 8,000 subjects ages 15 to 54 (Kessler et al., 1994) and provided the best currently available epidemiologic information. The younger age included in the NCS was based on the ECA findings that many psychiatric disorders have a young age of onset. The overall lifetime prevalence of bipolar I disorder in the full sample was 1.7% (median age of onset, 21 years); in the sample ages 15 to 17 it was 1.3% with equal gender rates. Both the ECA and the NCS suggested that onset of bipolar disorder in adolescence and childhood is common.

In the 1990s, the Cross-National Collaborative Group was formed to directly compare rates and risk of psychiatric disorders by standardizing analysis to overcome the problem of disparate data among studies. Seven countries (U.S., Canada, Puerto Rico, Germany, Taiwan, Korea, and New Zealand) provided data on bipolar disorder (Table 1.4). The lifetime prevalence rates for bipolar I ranged from 0.3% in Taiwan to 1.5% in New Zealand (Weissman et al., 1996), with equal gender ratios across sites (with the exception of Korea) and median ages of onset of 18 to 25 years.

Efforts have been made to study children and adolescents directly in epidemiologic studies. Table 1.5 presents the prevalence rates from these efforts. There is considerable variability across these studies in the age ranges, diagnostic methods, and diagnostic criteria. All of these differences affect prevalence rates and may account for discordant findings.

The Methodological Epidemiologic Catchment Area study (MECA) was conducted in a population-based sample of children and adolescents (Shaffer, unpublished observations). Probability household samples of 1,285 youth aged 9 to 17 years were selected at four sites (Atlanta, Georgia; New Haven, Connecticut; Westchester County, New York; and Puerto Rico; see Lahey et al., 1996 for methods). Data were collected for both children and their parents. The current (6-month) prevalence for mania was 1.2% and for hypomania was 0.6% (unpublished); 4.5% of youth with suicide ideation and 7.1% with suicide attempts had mania, compared to 0.9% of those who had neither suicide ideation nor attempts (Gould et al., 1998). Significant associations between bipolar disorder

Table 1.3 Lifetime and Annual Prevalence/100 (SE) and Incidence Rate per 100 of Bipolar I Disorder in Five U.S. Sites

Factor	New Haven, CT	Baltimore, MD	St. Louis, MO	Durham, NC	Los Angeles, CA	Total
Number in sample	5,034	3,481	3,004	3,921	3,131	18,571
Response rate (%)	77	78	79	79	68	76
Female (%)	59	62	60	60	53	59
Lifetime Rate/100						
Total	1.2 (.21)	0.6 (.20)	1.0 (.20)	0.3 (.14)	0.6 (.16)	0.8 (.09)
Males	1.0 (.27)	0.7 (.22)	1.1 (.30)	0.1 (.11)	0.6 (.23)	0.7 (.12)
Females	1.3 (.30)	0.5 (.24)	1.0 (.27)	0.6 (.25)	0.5 (.21)	0.9 (.12)
M/F	0.8	1.4	1.1	0.2	1.2	0.8
Annual Rate/100						
Total	1.0 (.16)	0.5 (.14)	1.0 (.20)	0.2 (.08)	0.4 (.13)	0.6 (.07)
Males	0.9 (.22)	0.5 (.21)	1.0 (.30)	0.0	0.3 (.15)	0.5 (.09)
Females	1.1 (.23)	0.5 (.18)	1.0 (.27)	0.4 (.16)	0.5 (.20)	0.7 (.09)
M/F	0.8	1.0	1.0	0.0	0.1	0.7
Annual Incidence/100						
Total	0.6 (.12)	0.2 (.09)	0.1 (.07)	0.3 (.10)	0.5 (.15)	0.4 (.05)
Males	0.4 (.15)	0.0	0.0	0.1 (.09)	0.5 (.21)	0.2 (.06)
Females	0.7 (.19)	0.4 (1.6)	0.2 (.13)	0.5 (.18)	0.5 (.20)	0.5 (.08)
M/F	0.8	0.0	0.0	0.2	1.0	0.4
Age of Onset (years)						
Mean	21.3 (1.6)	22.3 (3.1)	14.6 (1.6)	20.7 (3.6)	16.1 (1.0)	18.6 (0.9)
Median	22.0	18.0	17.0	22.0	17.0	18.0

Data from Epidemiologic Catchment Area study; age = 18+ years.

Table 1.4 Lifetime Prevalence/100 (SE) Bipolar I Disorder in Cross-National Sample Lifetime Prevalence/100 (SE)

Country	Overall	Males	Females	M/F Ratio	Age of Onset (Years)	Median Age of Onset (Years)
United States		0.8 (.14)	1.0 (.15)	0.7	18.1 (.68)	18
ECA, 1980	0.9 (.10)					
NCS, 1990[a]	1.7 (.21)	1.6 (.29)	1.8 (.30)	0.9	24.0 (.92)	21
Edmonton, Canada	0.6 (.16)	0.7 (.25)	0.5 (.21)	1.4	17.1 (1.12)	22
Puerto Rico	0.6 (.23)	0.8 (.38)	0.5 (.27)	1.6	27.2 (3.40)	18
West Germany[b]	0.5 (.37)	—	1.0 (.71)	—	29.0	25
Taiwan	0.3 (.06)	0.3 (.09)	0.3 (.07)	1.0	22.5 (1.90)	22
Korea	0.4 (.09)	0.6 (.16)	0.2 (.09)	3.0	23.0 (2.54)	18
Christchurch, New Zealand	1.5 (.36)	1.7 (.56)	1.2 (.45)	1.4	18.2 (5.90)	18

ECA, Epidemiologic Catchment Study.

[a]Age 18–54 years in National Comorbidity Survey (NCS).

[b]Only one case of bipolar disorder was reported from West Germany.

Table 1.5 Prevalence Rates/100 of Bipolar Disorder from Studies in Children and Adolescents

Reference	Country (Year)	Sample Size	Age Range (Years)	Diagnostic Method	Diagnosis	Time Period	Rate/ 100
Shaffer, unpublished	USA (1992)	1,285	9–17	DISC	Mania	6 months	1.2
Lewinsohn, et al., 1995	Western Oregon (1987)	1,709	14–18	KSADS	BPD	Lifetime	1.0
Wittchen, et al., 1988	Bavaria, Germany (1988)	3,021	14–24	CIDI	BPI BPII	Lifetime	1.4 0.4
Aalto-Setälä et al., 2001	Helsinki, Finland (2000)	647	20–24	SCAN	BPI BPI, II, NOS	1 month 1 month	0.2 0.9

BPD, bipolar disorder; BPI, bipolar I; BPII, bipolar II; CIDI, Composite International Diagnostic Interview; DiSC, Diagnostic Interview Schedule for Children; KSADS, Kiddie Schizophrenia and Affective Disorders Schedule; NOS, not otherwise specified; SCAN, Schedules for Clinical Assessment in Neuropsychiatry.

and risk for suicide in youth has been previously reported by Brent et al. (1988), highlighting the long-held notion that bipolar disorder in youth is associated with not only high levels of morbidity but also mortality.

Lewinsohn, Klein, and Seeley (1995) studied 1,709 adolescents (14 to 18 years) randomly selected from nine senior high schools, representative of urban and rural districts in western Oregon. The lifetime prevalence of bipolar disorder (primarily bipolar disorder II and cyclothymia) was approximately 1.0%. An additional 5.7% of the sample reported experiencing a distinct period of abnormally elevated mood, expansive or irritable, although they never met the criteria for bipolar disorder per se. Both groups exhibited significant functional impairment and high rates of comorbidity (anxiety and disruptive behavior), suicide attempts, and mental health service utilization. The prevalence, age of onset, phenomenology, and course of bipolar disorder did not differ by gender. In a follow-up study, they found that less than 1.0% of adolescents with depression switched to bipolar disorder by age 24 (Lewinsohn, Rohde, Seeley, Klein, & Gotlib, 2000). The bipolar disorder and subsyndromal bipolar disorder subgroups both had elevated rates of antisocial and other personality symptoms. Both groups showed significant impairment in psychosocial functioning and had higher mental health treatment utilization. In general, adolescents with bipolar disorder showed significant continuity across developmental periods and adverse outcomes during young adulthood. Adolescent subsyndromal bi-

polar disorder was also associated with adverse outcomes in adulthood, but not with increased incidence of bipolar disorder, which questions the relationship of subsyndromal bipolar disorder in children and adolescents to true adulthood bipolar disorder.

A study from Bavaria, Germany, on a sample of 3,021 adolescents and young adults age 14 to 24 found a lifetime prevalence of 1.4% for bipolar I disorder and 0.4% for bipolar II disorder (Wittchen, Nelson, & Lachner, 1998). Ninety-four percent of the youth with either bipolar disorder considered themselves socially and economically impaired.

A 5-year follow-up of over 500 students of ages 20–24 years in Helsinki, Finland, found a 1-month prevalence rate of bipolar I of 0.2%. However, when bipolar II and bipolar-NOS were added, the prevalence rates were 0.9/100. In summary, the epidemiologic studies of adolescents and adults show an early age of onset of bipolar disorder and prevalence in adolescents close to what is found in studies of adults.

Comorbidity

With Attention Deficit Hyperactivity Disorder (ADHD)

The symptomatic overlap of childhood mania with ADHD is one major source of diagnostic controversy. Rates of ADHD range from 60% to 90% in pediatric patients with mania (Borchardt & Bernstein, 1995; Geller et al., 1995; West, McElroy, Strakowski, Keck, & McConville, 1995;

Wozniak, Biederman, Kiely, et al., 1995). Although the rates of ADHD in samples of youth with mania are universally high, the age at onset modifies the risk for comorbid ADHD. For example, while Wozniak, Biederman, Kiely, et al. (1995) found that 90% of children with mania also had ADHD, West et al. (1995) reported that only 57% of adolescents with mania had comorbid ADHD. Examining further developmental aspects of pediatric mania, Faraone, Biederman, Wozniak, et al., (1997) found that adolescents with childhood-onset mania had the same rates of comorbid ADHD as manic children (90%), and that both these groups had higher rates of ADHD than adolescents with adolescent-onset mania (60%). Most recently, Sachs, Baldassano, Truman, & Guille (2000) reported that among adults with bipolar disorder, a history of comorbid ADHD was only evident in those subjects with onset of bipolar disorder before 19 years of age. The mean onset of bipolar disorder in those with a history of childhood ADHD was 12.1 years (Sachs et al., 2000). Similarly, Chang, Steiner, and Ketter (2000) studied the offspring of patients with bipolar disorder and found that 88% of manic children had comorbid ADHD and that the onset of mania in adults with bipolar disorder and a history of ADHD was 11.3 years of age. These findings suggest that age of onset of mania, rather than chronological age at presentation, may be the critical developmental variable that identifies a highly virulent form of the disorder that is heavily comorbid with ADHD.

Although ADHD has a much earlier onset than pediatric mania, the symptomatic and syndromatic overlap between pediatric mania and ADHD raises a fundamental question—namely, do children presenting with symptoms suggestive of mania and ADHD have ADHD, mania, or both? One method to address these uncertainties has been to examine the transmission of comorbid disorders in families (Faraone & Tsuang 1995; Faraone, Tsuang, & Tsuang, 1999). If ADHD and mania are associated because of shared familial etiologic factors, then family studies should find mania in families of ADHD patients and ADHD in families of manic patients. Studies that examined rates of ADHD among the offspring of adults with bipolar disorder all found higher rates of ADHD among these children than in controls (Faraone, Biederman, Mennin, & Russell, 1998).

Wozniak, Biederman, Mundy, et al. (1995) used familial risk analysis to examine the association between ADHD and mania within families of manic children. They found that relatives of children with mania were at high risk for ADHD that was indistinguishable from the risk in relatives of children with ADHD and no mania. However, mania and the comorbid condition of mania plus ADHD selectively aggregated among relatives of manic youth compared with those with ADHD and comparison children (Wozniak, Biederman, Mundy, et al., 1995). Almost identical findings were obtained in two independently defined family studies of ADHD probands with and without comorbid mania (Faraone, et al., 1998; Faraone, Biederman & Monuteaux, 2001). Taken together, this pattern of transmission in families suggests that mania in children might be a familiarly distinct subtype of either bipolar disorder or ADHD.

With Conduct Disorder (CD)

Like ADHD, CD is also strongly associated with pediatric mania. This has been observed separately in studies of children with CD, ADHD, and mania. Kovacs and Pollak (1995) reported a 69% rate of CD in a referred sample of manic youth and found that the presence of comorbid CD heralded a more complicated course of mania. Kutcher et al. (1989) found that 42% of hospitalized youths with mania had comorbid CD. The Zurich longitudinal study found that hypomanic cases had more disciplinary difficulties at school and more thefts during their juvenile years than did other children (Wicki & Angst, 1991). These reports are consistent with the well-documented comorbidity between CD and major depression (Angold and Costello 1993), because pediatric depression often presages mania (Geller, Fox, & Clark, 1994; Strober and Carlson, 1982). It is not surprising that mania and CD are also frequently comorbid.

Biederman et al. (1999) (Biederman, Faraone, Hatch, et al., 1997) investigated the overlap between mania and CD in a consecutive sample of youth referred for treatment. They found a striking similarity in the features and age of onset of mania, regardless of comorbid CD. Whether or not CD was present, mania presented with a predominantly irritable mood, a chronic course, and was mixed with symptoms of major depression. Only two manic symptoms differed between those with versus without CD: "physical restlessness" and "poor judgment" were more common in the mania-with-CD group than in the mania-only group. Similarly, there were few differences in the frequency of CD symptoms between CD youth with and without comorbid mania. Nevertheless, it is important to assess for both diagnoses because delinquency and mania require different treatment strategies.

With Anxiety Disorders

Although anxiety is frequently overlooked in studies of mania, pediatric studies of youth with panic disorder and youth with mania document a bidirectional overlap. Biederman, Faraone, Marrs, et al. (1997) found that subjects with panic disorder and agoraphobia had very high rates of mania (52% and 31%), which were greater than those observed among psychiatric controls (15%). Wozniak, Biederman, Kiely, et al. (1995) and Bowen, South, & Hawkes (1994) reported significantly more panic and other anxiety disorders in children with mania. These findings indicate that mania at any age is frequently comorbid with severe anxiety that requires additional clinical and scientific scrutiny.

With Substance Use Disorders (SUD)

There is an extensive and bidirectional overlap between mania and substance use disorders (SUD) in youth (Biederman, Wilens, et al., 1997; West et al., 1996; Wilens, Bierderman, Abrantes, Spencer, & Thomas, 1997b) as well as in adults. Juvenile-onset mania may be a risk factor for SUD. For example, a prospective study of children and adolescents with and without ADHD found that early-onset mania was a risk factor for SUD independently of ADHD (Biederman, Wilens, et al., 1997). Similarly, controlled studies in

adults show that mania is often an antecedent and is strongly associated with SUD (Wilens et al., 1997b). Mania has also been shown to be overrepresented among youth with SUD (West et al., 1996; Wilens, Biederman, Abrantes, Spencer, & Thomas, 1997a).

Wilens et al. (1999) found that mania significantly increased the risk for SUD independently of conduct disorder. Furthermore, they reported that the risk for SUD was carried by those subjects with an adolescent-onset form of mania. While this may be consistent with the notion that, like adults, adolescents self-medicate manic symptoms with substances of abuse (Khantzian, 1997), it is also consistent with the hypothesis that child and adolescent onset mania are etiologically distinct forms of the disorder with different risk profiles and natural courses.

Risk Factors

Given the paucity of epidemiologic studies of bipolar disorder in youth and the fact that the relatively low lifetime prevalence (about 1%–2%) would require very large samples, risk factors have not been clearly identified from community-based studies. The most consistent risk factor for bipolar disorder is family history. While studies vary considerably in methods, sample size, and controls, they consistently show offspring of adult bipolar patients as having an increased risk, over 3-fold, of bipolar disorder as well as mood disorders, compared to offspring of controls (Carlson and Weintraub, 1993; Decina et al., 1983; Gershon et al., 1985; Hammen et al., 1990; Klein, Depue, & Slater, 1985; Nurnberger et al., 1988; Todd et al., 1996). Because most of the offspring have not lived through or even entered the age of risk, an accurate estimate of prevalence rates is not possible. However, it is important to note that although the risk to offspring of bipolar patients is increased, the majority of high-risk offspring will have neither a diagnosable bipolar illness nor any other mood disorder.

BIOLOGY OF CHILD AND ADOLESCENT MOOD DISORDERS

Although there has been an exponential increase in our understanding of the pathophysiology of major depression in adults, we are largely dependent on extrapolations from these findings to inform us on the biology of childhood and adolescent depression (Coyle et al., 2003). In the last two decades, considerably more research on the biology of depression in children has been forthcoming. Moreover, the neurobiology of bipolar disorder even in adults remains poorly understood (Berns & Nemeroff, 2003; Wang & Nemeroff, 2003), though it represents an active avenue of investigation. Not surprisingly, our understanding of the biology of childhood bipolar disorder is virtually nonexistent.

Genetics

As noted above, the age of onset of serious mood disorders is now known to occur in children and adolescents and to persist into adulthood. Thus, much of the information that has accrued concerning the pathophysiology of mood disorders in adulthood would appear to be applicable to the childhood onset mood disorders. One important difference, however, is the apparent lack of efficacy of tricyclic antidepressants in youth as compared to that of the selective serotonin reuptake inhibitors (SSRIs), though controversy surrounds the latter contention; clearly both classes are effective in adults (Wagner & Ambrosini, 2001).

Although heritable factors appear to be the most consistent predictors of risk for major depression in children, environmental factors also play an important role (Rice, Harold, & Thapar, 2002). Especially with regard to bipolar disorder, twin, family and adoption studies have shown that heritable factors are substantial predictors of risk (Smoller and Finn, 2003). In the case of bipolar disorder in the parents, the risk extends to major depressive disorder and early onset of mood symptoms in their children (Mortensen, Pedersen, Melbye, Mors, & Ewald, 2003). No specific genes have yet been identified that are un-

equivocally associated with mood disorders, regardless of age of onset. However, linkage studies, especially in bipolar disorder, have identified a number of regions on the human genome associated with high heritable risk for affective disorders (Schulze and McMahon, 2003; Tsuang, Taylor, & Faraone, 2004; Table 1.6). Given the evidence for interactions between risk genes and environment, and the important role of early trauma (Heim, Newport, Bonsall, Miller, & Nemeroff, 2001; Nemeroff, 2004), the risk for early-onset depression may be magnified by the impact of a parent with depression (e.g., postpartum disorder) on a genetically vulnerable child (Weinfeld, Stroufe, & Egeland, 2000).

Early Life Stress

In unipolar major depression, environmental influences are clearly substantial. Consistent with predications from early psychoanalytic models, losses early in life, maternal deprivation, and physical and sexual abuse appear to be major risk factors when controlled for heritable risks. Recent research has highlighted the seminal importance of early psychological insults contributing to the neurobiological processes thought to underlie the pathophysiology of major depressive disorder. The pronounced effects of early life stress (ELS) throughout the lifespan are believed to be mediated by the substantial plasticity of the developing central nervous system (CNS) as a function of experience. It has been proposed that stress and emotional trauma during development permanently shape the brain regions that mediate stress and emotion, leading to altered emotional processing and heightened stress responsiveness, which in the genetically vulnerable individual may then evolve into psychiatric disorders, such as depression.

Hypothalamic–pituitary–adrenal axis (HPA)

The system that has been most closely scrutinized in mood disorders is the HPA axis, with evidence of its hyperactivity in adult patients

Table 1.6 Genomic Regions Associated with High Heritable Risk for Affective Disorders

Genomic Location	Principle Report	Independent Confirmations	Comments
18p11.2	Berrettini et al., 1994 and 1997	Stine et al., 1995; Nothen et al., 1999; Turecki et al., 1999	Paternal parent-of-origin effect; see Schwab et al., 1998
21q22	Straub et al., 1994	Detera-Wadleigh et al., 1996; Smyth et al., 1996; Kwok et al., 1999; Morissette et al., 1999	
22q11–13	Kelsoe et al., 2001	Detera-Wadleigh et al., 1997 and 1999	Velocardiofacial syndrome region; possible overlap with a schizophrenia locus
18q22	Stine et al., 1995	McInnes et al., 1996; McMahon et al., 1997; De Bruyn et al., 1996	See Freimer et al., 1996
12q24	Morissette et al., 1999	Ewald et al., 1998; Detera-Wadleigh et al., 1999	Principal report in a Canadian isolate
4p15	Blackwood et al., 1996	Ewald et al., 1998; Nothen et al., 1997; Detera-Wadleigh et al., 1999	See Ginns et al., 1998

with unipolar depression and bipolar patients in the mixed state (Evans & Nemeroff, 1983; Swann et al., 1992). Upon stress exposure, neurons in the hypothalamic paraventricular nucleus (PVN) secrete corticotropin-releasing factor (CRF) into the hypothalamic-hypophyseal portal circulation, which stimulates the production and release of adrenocorticotropin (ACTH) from the anterior pituitary. Adrenocorticotropin in turn stimulates release of glucocorticoids from the adrenal cortex. Glucocorticoids have marked effects on metabolism, immune function, and the brain, adjusting physiological functions and behavior in response to the stressor. Glucocorticoids exert negative feedback control on the HPA axis by regulating hippocampal and PVN neurons. Persistent glucocorticoid exposure exerts adverse effects on hippocampal neurons, including reduction in dendritic branching, loss of dendritic spines, and impairment of neurogenesis. Such damage might progressively reduce inhibitory control of the HPA axis. Corticotropin-releasing factor neurons integrate information relevant to stress not only at the hypothalamic PVN but also in a widespread circuitry throughout the limbic system and brain stem. Direct CNS administration of CRF to laboratory animals produces endocrine, autonomic,

and behavioral responses that parallel signs of stress, depression, and anxiety, including loss of appetite, sleep disruption, decreased sexual behavior, despair, increased motor activity, neophobia, and enhanced startle reactivity.

Laboratory animal studies have provided direct evidence that ELS indeed leads to heightened stress reactivity and alterations in the aforementioned neural circuits that persist into adulthood. For example, adult rats separated from their dams for 180 minutes/day on postnatal days 2–14 exhibit up to 3-fold increases in ACTH and corticosterone responses to a variety of psychological stressors compared with control rats (Ladd et al., 2000; Plotsky and Meaney, 1993). Maternally separated rats also develop marked behavioral changes, including increased anxiety-like behavior, anhedonia, alcohol preference, sleep disruption, decreased appetite, and cognitive impairment. Subsequent studies revealed multiple CNS changes that likely underlie physiologic and behavioral sensitization to stress after maternal separation or lack of maternal care. These findings include increased activity (increased CRF mRNA expression) and sensitization of CRF neurons in hypothalamic and limbic regions, decreased glucocorticoid receptor density in the hippocampus and prefrontal cortex, increased mineralocorticoid receptor in the hippocampus, decreased mossy fiber development and neurogenesis in the hippocampus, as well as alterations in norepinephrine, GABA, and other systems (Heim, Plotsky, & Nemeroff, 2004; Ladd, Huot, Thrivikraman, Nemeroff, & Plotsky, 2004). Behavioral sensitization to fear stimuli have been observed in nonhuman primates reared by mothers exposed to unpredictable conditions with respect to food access over 3 months (Coplan et al., 1996, 2001). Taken together, ELS induces manifold changes in multiple neurocircuits involved in neuroendocrine, autonomic, and behavioral responses to stress. If similar changes also occur in humans exposed to ELS, these changes might indeed confer an enhanced risk for depression.

As noted earlier, several clinical studies have evaluated the long-term consequences of ELS in adult humans. In astonishing parallel to findings in rodents and nonhuman primates, women abused as children, including those with and those without current depression, exhibit greater plasma ACTH responses in a standardized stress paradigm than controls. The increase was more pronounced in abused women with current depression, and these women also showed greater cortisol and heart rate responses than controls (Heim et al., 2000). Several studies have reported similar neuroendocrine and neurochemical changes in abused children, which are reviewed in detail elsewhere (Heim & Nemeroff, 2001).

Magnetic Resonance Imaging

Among depressed patients, magnetic resonance imaging (MRI) analysis has revealed decreased hippocampal volumes only in adult women with ELS (Vythilingam et al., 2002). Because hippocampal volume loss is not observed in abused children or young adults (Teicher, 2002) (although corpus callosum, amygdala, and cortical development seems to be impaired), some have suggested that repeated bursts of cortisol secretion over the course of time may eventually result in smaller hippocampi. Enhanced CRF secretion during development may also contribute to progressive hippocampal volume loss (Brunson, Eghbal-Ahmadi, Bender, Chen, & Baram,

2001). The fact that adult patients with major depression exhibit HPA axis hyperactivity and profound CRF hypersecretion as evidenced in studies of cerebrospinal fluid (CSF) and postmortem tissue (Flores, Alvarado, Wong, Licinio, & Flockhart, 2004; Merali et al., 2004) and that these findings are also observed after ELS raises the question as to whether the HPA axis in general and the CRF system in particular play a role in the pathogenesis of childhood mood disorders.

Steingard and colleagues (2002) found significant reductions in frontal lobe volume and increased ventricular volume in a large cohort of children and adolescents with depressive disorders. In resolving white and gray matter, they found significant reductions in frontal white matter in adolescents with major depression. Furthermore, orbitofrontal choline levels are elevated in depressed adolescents (Steingard et al., 2000), consistent with findings in adults. A single photon emission computed tomography (SPECT) study found a significant elevation of the density of serotonin transporters in the hypothalamus and midbrain, but no change in the dopamine transporter in children and adolescents with major depression. Chang and colleagues (2004) used functional magnetic resonance imaging (fMRI) to compare 12 children and adolescents with bipolar disorder who had at least one parent with bipolar disorder and 10 age- and IQ-matched healthy male controls. Significant differences in brain activation patterns in prefrontal areas were noted in the bipolar subjects, compared to patterns in the controls, when performing both cognitive and affective tasks. Brain areas affected included the anterior cingulate cortical and dorsolateral prefrontal cortex. This same group (Chang et al., 2003) had previously reported a reduction in dorsolateral and prefrontal cortical N-acetyl-aspartate concentrations, a marker of neuronal integrity, in children with bipolar disorder, as measured by magnetic resonance spectroscopy (MRS). Children during a manic episode were also reported to exhibit increased anterior cingulate concentrations of myo-inositol (Davanzo et al., 2001).

Gender

Gender is well known to be an important but poorly understood factor influencing the risk of MDD. The prevalence of MDD, while equal between boys and girls prior to puberty, doubles in young women after puberty. This increase in females has been hypothesized to be secondary to hormonal changes occurring during puberty. These endocrine changes surely influence brain function, but the attendant social and psychological factors of puberty cannot be ignored. Nevertheless, twin studies suggest that the impact of genetic risk factors become more prominent as girls pass through puberty and enter adolescence (Silberg et al., 1999).

An early and logical focus of biological studies of child and adolescent mood disorders was neuroendocrinologic, motivated by the findings described above of significant HPA dysregulation in a sizeable proportion of adults with MDD. However, the results of a number of studies have found rare and only modest abnormalities in 24-hour cortisol secretion, the dexamethasone suppression test, and the CRF stimulation test. Recently, Feder and colleagues (2004) reported that of 86 children (depressed, anxious, or normal) tested, those children who exhibited an abnormally elevated cortisol concentration during the evening and an abnormal delay in the rise of cortisol during the night, whether depressed or not as children, exhibited depression as adults.

Puig-Antich and colleagues (1985a,b) observed a blunted growth hormone (GH) response in adolescents with MDD when challenged with insulin or growth hormone releasing hormone (GHRH), a finding previously reported in adults with major depression. However, the link between this abnormality and the underlying pathophysiology of depression remains obscure.

Conclusions

Accurate epidemiologic data are useful for determining the magnitude of the problem, identifying risk factors, monitoring changes of rates (epidemics), and identifying the underserved. Accurate estimates rest on accurate diagnosis. The explosive developments in neurosciences, genetics, and neuroimaging will undoubtedly help advance our pathophysiological understanding of these complex mood disorders afflicting the young. Such advances can help shed light on etiology, identify dysfunctional brain circuits and, most importantly, define subtypes of the disorder. This will undoubtedly lead to improved treatment of afflicted youth and their families. Longitudinal studies focusing on the biology and treatment response of childhood and adolescent mood disorders are sorely needed.

Treatment of Depression and Bipolar Disorder

chapter 2

Although it is clear that adolescent mood disorders exist and lead to significant immediate and lifelong impairment for the child, as shown in Chapter 1, there exists limited treatment research in this special population. This has led clinicians to consult with the adult literature to provide guidance in their treatment approaches. In fact, the adult research studies have provided the template for the present interventions being explored in adolescent treatment studies. To appreciate how the adult literature informs the field of adolescent mood disorder treatments, the current status of the adult literature for both psychosocial and psychopharmacologic treatments will be reviewed. This will be followed by an appraisal of the same treatment areas for adolescents.

PSYCHOSOCIAL TREATMENTS FOR MAJOR DEPRESSIVE DISORDER

Major depressive disorder (MDD) is one of the most common adult psychiatric disorders seen in the community and in outpatient psychiatric settings (Kessler et al., 2003). There is now substantial evidence that MDD can be treated successfully with certain targeted psychotherapies. This literature is briefly reviewed below.

Psychosocial Treatment of Major Depresssion in Adults

The strongest empirical evidence exists for three manual-based psychotherapies for the treatment of MDD—behavior therapy, cognitive therapy, and interpersonal therapy—with less evidence existing for two other forms of psychotherapy—brief dynamic therapy and problem-solving therapy.

Cognitive Therapy

The most widely studied psychotherapy for MDD is cognitive therapy (Beck, Rush, Shaw, & Emery, 1979). This treatment is based on the model that the cognitions (conscious or readily accessible to consciousness) of depressed individuals are negatively biased. This negative bias is evident in negative beliefs about the self, the

world, and the future. Such negative cognitions are one factor that plays a role in the initiation and maintenance of depressive symptoms. Cognitive therapy, typically consisting of 16 to 20 sessions over a period of 12 to 16 weeks, involves the application of both behavioral and cognitive techniques. The behavioral techniques serve to help patients engage in activities that give them pleasure, while cognitive techniques are used to help patients recognize negative cognitions and to evaluate the veracity of their beliefs.

Three meta-analyses of studies of cognitive therapy for MDD concluded that it is at least equal and often superior to other forms of treatment, including antidepressant medications (Dobson, 1989; Gaffan, Tsaousis, & Kemp-Wheeler, 1995; Agency for Health Care Policy Research, 1993). However, the comparison of cognitive therapy to medication continues to be controversial. While several studies have supported the finding that cognitive therapy and medication yield similar outcomes (Hollon et al., 1992; Murphy, Simons, Wetzel, & Lustman, 1984), another study (Elkin et al., 1989) failed to demonstrate that cognitive therapy is superior to pill placebo and yielded some evidence that, for more severely depressed patients, medication (imipramine) is superior to cognitive therapy (Elkin et al., 1995). Practice guidelines have recommended medication rather than psychotherapy for more severe depressions (American Psychiatric Association, 2000; Depression Guideline Panel, 1993). However, a direct examination of the comparative effects of cognitive therapy and medication across four studies revealed no evidence of a difference among those with moderate to severe depression (DeRubeis, Gelfand, Tang, & Simons, 1999).

Some further evidence on this issue has emerged from a two-site study by Hollon and DeRubeis (DeRubeis et al., in press) comparing standard cognitive therapy ($N = 60$), antidepressant medication (Paxil with augmentation by other agents if clinically indicated) $N = 120$; more patients were randomized to medication because of a subsequent continuation phase in which acute-phase medication responders were randomized to continuation medication or placebo), and placebo ($N = 60$) as acute treatments for moderate to severe MDD. At week 8, only

25% of placebo patients met criteria for clinical response, compared with 45% for cognitive therapy and 50% for medication (placebo treatment was ended at week 8 for ethical reasons). At week 16 (end of acute treatment), response rates for medication and cognitive therapy were identical (57%) and comparable to response rates from previous studies of cognitive therapy and medication in MDD.

Despite the lack of evidence that cognitive therapy is uniquely efficacious in the treatment of MDD, and some controversy over the comparative effects of medication and cognitive therapy in more severely depressed patients, the overall weight of the evidence is that cognitive therapy is an efficacious acute-phase treatment for MDD.

Behavior Therapy

The predominant behavioral model of MDD treatment is Lewinsohn and MacPhillamy's (1974) approach. In this model, the primary goal is to increase the frequency of pleasant activities in the patient's life. Using a group format for therapy, Shaw (1977) found that behavior therapy was superior to a wait-list control at the end of treatment. The largest study of behavior therapy for MDD found it to be significantly better than psychotherapy (an unstandardized, insight-oriented approach), relaxation therapy, and medication (amitriptyline) (McLean & Hakstian, 1979). In another study of MDD, Jacobson et al. (1996) compared three treatments: behavior therapy (behavioral activation), cognitive therapy with behavioral activation techniques plus techniques designed to address automatic negative thoughts, and cognitive therapy with behavioral activation techniques and automatic thought modification plus the addition of techniques designed to address enduring maladaptive beliefs. At the end of acute-phase treatment, remission rates (Beck Depression Inventory [BDI] score <8, no major depressive disorder) ranged from 56% for the full cognitive therapy package to 46% for behavior therapy, but no significant differences were evident on any measure.

One version of behavior therapy has been developed specifically for couples in which at least one member has MDD. The outcome of behav-ioral marital therapy for MDD was found to be not different from cognitive therapy when the couple was distressed, but inferior to cognitive therapy when the couple was not distressed (Jacobson, Dobson, Fruzzetti, Schmaling, & Salusky, 1991). Another study that included only distressed couples also found behavioral marital therapy to be equally effective to cognitive therapy, with both therapies being better than wait-list in the treatment of depression in the wife. The behavioral marital therapy, however, improved marital satisfaction more than cognitive therapy did.

As with cognitive therapy, there appears to be evidence that behavior therapy is an efficacious, but not uniquely effective, acute treatment for MDD.

Interpersonal Therapy for Depression

Klerman & Weissman (1989) interpersonal psychotherapy (IPT) for depression assumes that although depression is *caused* by a number of factors (genetic, biological, social) interacting in complex ways, it is usually *triggered* by problems in four interpersonal domains: role transition, grief, interpersonal deficits, and interpersonal disputes. In IPT, the interpersonal problem that triggered the current depressive episode is addressed and the person is helped to build communication and interaction skills to resolve it. The acute phase of IPT typically lasts for 16–20 sessions.

Several studies have supported the efficacy of IPT for acute treatment of MDD in adults seeking treatment in psychiatric and primary care settings. In one study, the efficacy of IPT was similar to that of amitriptyline, and both were superior to a minimal contact control in outpatients (DiMascio et al., 1979). In the National Institute of Mental Health (NIMH) Treatment of Depression Collaborative Research Program, results with IPT were not different from those with either imipramine or cognitive therapy. However, among more severely depressed patients (with a Hamilton Depression Rating scale [HAM-D] >20), imipramine and IPT were superior to placebo whereas CBT was not (Elkin et al., 1989). In a primary care setting, IPT was found to be better than usual care, and results from IPT were not different from those with nortriptyline at an 8-month assessment of depressed medical outpatients (Schulberg et al., 1996). Interpersonal therapy has also been tested with depressed HIV+ patients and was compared with imipramine, cognitive behavior therapy (CBT), and supportive psychotherapy. The IPT and imipramine showed similar efficacy and were both superior to CBT and to a lesser extent to supportive psychotherapy (Markowitz, Svartberg, & Swartz, 1998).

In the area of geriatric depression, IPT showed efficacy comparable to that of nortriptyline, but both failed to show significant difference from placebo in a 6-week trial (Schneider, Cooper, Staples, & Sloane, 1987). Interpersonal therapy has also been used to treat antepartum and postpartum depression. Treatment with IPT was superior to a parenting education program for women with antepartum depression in all measures of mood at termination (Spinelli & Endicott, 2003). Also, for symptomatic relief and social adjustment, IPT was superior to a wait-list control for women suffering from postpartum depression (O'Hara, Stuart, Gorman, & Wenzel, 2000). In a different study, IPT for postpartum depression was found to be as effective as a mother–infant therapy group and superior to a wait list control (Clark, Vittengl, Kraft, & Jarrett, 2003). Finally, in the only randomized, clinical trial of a Western psychotherapy adapted for Africa, group IPT was better than treatment as usual for depressed people in rural Uganda for depressive symptomatology and social functioning (Bolton et al., 2003).

Brief Dynamic Therapy

Psychodynamic psychotherapy comes in many forms. Brief versions of this treatment typically have a clear interpersonal or intrapsychic focus and use therapist interpretations as the key intervention designed to increase self-understanding about interpersonal or intrapsychic issues that might be contributing to or maintaining depressive symptoms. Manual-based, brief psychodynamic psychotherapy has been evaluated in the treatment of MDD in several studies. In two studies, an interpersonally oriented psychodynamic therapy (somewhat

similar to IPT) was found to yield comparable outcomes to those with CBT (Barkham, Hardy, & Startup, 1994; Shapiro et al., 1994). Similarly, in an elderly sample, brief psychodynamic therapy produced equal outcomes to those with behavioral and cognitive therapies (Thompson, Gallagher, & Breckenridge, 1987), although an earlier study using inexperienced therapists showed an advantage of CBT over psychodynamic therapy for depressed elders (Gallagher & Thompson, 1982). A study of clinically depressed elderly caregivers of frail, elderly relatives also found comparable efficacy for individual brief dynamic therapy and CBT (Gallagher-Thompson & Steffen, 1994). However, the duration of caregiving was an important factor, with brief dynamic therapy showing relatively better efficacy among the depressed elders who had been caregivers for a relatively briefer time period (≤ 3.5 years), whereas the CBT was relatively more efficacious with those that had been caregivers for longer than 3.5 years.

Although brief dynamic therapy appears to be a promising possibility for the acute treatment of MDD, more data on comparisons to credible control groups are needed.

Problem-Solving Therapy

Problem-solving therapy for MDD (Nezu, 1986) has been examined in several controlled studies. Nezu (1986) and Nezu and Perri (1989) found problem-solving treatment to be superior to a wait-list control group, using samples that were primarily female community volunteers. In each of these studies, the full version of problem-solving therapy was found to be better than a version that had some but not all of the key elements of the treatment. Problem-solving therapy has also been found to be as efficacious as routine medication treatment by general practitioners in one study (Catalan et al., 1991) and equal to amitriptyline but better than placebo in another (Mynors-Wallis, Gath, Lloyd-Thomas, & Tomlinson, 1995). In an elderly sample, Arean and colleagues (1993) found problem-solving therapy to yield roughly equivalent results to those with reminiscence therapy, but better results than those with wait-list.

Problem-solving therapy also appears to be

promising for the acute treatment of MDD. Additional larger studies are needed, as are comparisons to other standard psychotherapies for MDD, with samples recruited in psychiatric settings.

Prevention of Relapse and Recurrence

Studies that use naturalistic follow-up assessments of patients who have received a short-term course of treatment have suggested that cognitive therapy reduces relapse relative to discontinued medication (Blackburn, Eunson, & Bishop, 1986; Evans et al., 1992; Kovacs, Rush, Beck, & Hollon, 1981; Simons, Murphy, Levine, & Wetzel, 1986). In addition, for patients with residual depressive symptoms following pharmacotherapy, cognitive therapy has been found to reduce recurrence rates relative to maintenance medication only (Paykel et al., 1999) and treatment as usual (Teasdale et al., 2000). Several studies have examined continuation or maintenance psychotherapy for MDD patients who have achieved a clinical response or remission of symptoms following acute-phase treatment. In patients with recurrent MDD, continuation cognitive therapy has been found to reduce relapse relative to short-term cognitive therapy without continuation treatment (Jarrett et al., 2001). An earlier study found that both continuation-phase cognitive therapy alone or combined medication and continuation-phase cognitive therapy produced lower relapse rates than those with medication only (Blackburn et al., 1986). However, a subsequent study found that maintenance medication and maintenance cognitive therapy yielded similar prophylactic effects (Blackburn & Moore, 1997). Similarly, in patients treated to remission with fluoxetine (20 mg), Perlis et al. (2002) found that continuation treatment (28 weeks) with cognitive therapy plus fluoxetine (40 mg) yielded similar relapse rates to those with continuation treatment with fluoxetine (40 mg) alone.

Because residual symptoms of depression after successful treatment predicts the relapse or recurrence of MDD, research has examined the role of cognitive therapy in the treatment of such residual symptoms. Fava, Grandi, Zielezny, Rafanelli, and Canestrari, (1996) compared cog-

nitive therapy targeting residual symptoms with clinical management among patients who were successfully treated with antidepressant medications (in both treatments medications were gradually tapered and discontinued). Cognitive therapy resulted in substantially lower relapse rates than those after clinical management (Fava et al., 1996) over the course of a 4-year follow-up, and there were fewer depressive episodes at a 6-year follow-up assessment (Fava, Rafanelli, Grandi, Conti, & Belluardo, 1998).

In one large study of recurrent MDD maintenance, IPT (alone) was found to be inferior to medication and to medication plus IPT, but better than placebo (Frank et al., 1990). In a geriatric sample, MDD patients treated to remission with IPT plus nortrityline fared relatively poorer in maintenance IPT plus placebo treatment compared to IPT plus nortrityline (Reynolds et al., 1999). Maintenance IPT plus placebo, however, was superior to placebo in preventing recurrences of depressive episodes (Reynolds et al., 1999). Thus, overall, the evidence is stronger for cognitive therapy than for IPT as stand-alone continuation or maintenance treatment to prevent relapse or recurrences.

Conclusion

A relatively large and growing body of literature has substantiated the efficacy of targeted psychotherapies in the treatment of MDD in adults. Research evidence from controlled clinical trials in particular supports the efficacy of cognitive therapy, IPT, and behavioral therapy for MDD. Problem-solving therapy and certain forms of brief dynamic therapy appear promising, but further research is needed. Acute-phase cognitive therapy reduces the risk of relapse or recurrence of MDD, and continuation treatment reduces such risks further. Cognitive therapy and IPT generally have been found to be equally efficacious to medications, even with more severely depressed patients. However, a recent study suggests that chronic depression might best be treated with the combination of medication and psychotherapy.

Although many of the psychotherapeutic interventions studied in adults have been adapted to the treatment of adolescents, including IPT, cognitive therapy, and behavioral therapy, the adult literature is characterized by a much broader set of studies than in the child and adolescent MDD treatment literature. Even with this relatively large number of MDD studies conducted to date, numerous questions remain about psychotherapy for MDD in adults. Despite the success of certain psychotherapies in the treatment of adult MDD, it may be risky to assume such treatments are likely to be the best psychosocial treatments for childhood and adolescent MDD. The biological, developmental, cognitive, and experiential differences between children and adolescents and adults raise the question of whether wholly different intervention strategies may be most effective with children and adolescents (Mueller & Orvaschel, 1997). For example, psychodynamic psychotherapy, especially variants that rely heavily on symbolic interpretations, may not be appropriate for younger individuals who lack the cognitive maturity to understand such interventions. Treatments that have been little studied in adults, such as family therapy, may have much greater relevance among children and adolescents. New treatments that incorporate developmental issues may be needed. Although it may be hazardous to export treatment modalities developed for adults to children and adolescents, research on children and adolescents can benefit greatly from the methodological developments in the treatment of MDD in adults, particularly the study of prevention of relapse or recurrence. Ongoing dialogue and interchange among investigators in the adult and child areas is likely to facilitate the more rapid development of literature on treatment of children with MDD.

Psychosocial Treatment of Adolescent Major Depression

In this overview of psychosocial treatments for early-onset depression, we review the randomized clinical trials in children and adolescents with depressive disorders and symptomatology. The vast majority of the intervention trials have used CBT techniques. In addition, we review the handful of studies that have used interpersonal therapy and family therapy. Finally, given the frequent interrelationship between depression and suicidal behavior, we review the published clinical trials for the treatment of adolescent suicide attempters.

Cognitive Behavior Therapy of Youth Depression

In this section, we review controlled clinical trials of treating child and adolescent depressive disorders with CBT. The cognitive-behavioral approaches for youth depression focus on identifying and modifying negative thought patterns and improving disturbed behavioral self- and social-regulation skills thought to underlie the etiology of depression. In youth depression treatment, these foci have been addressed through the application of cognitive and behavioral techniques such as (1) mood monitoring; (2) cognitive restructuring; (3) behavioral activation, pleasant activity scheduling, and goal-setting strategies; (4) relaxation and stress management; (5) social skills and conflict resolution training; and (6) training in general problem-solving skills (Kaslow & Thompson, 1998; Kazdin & Weisz, 1998). Although the total number of youth depression treatment studies is relatively small, and different investigators have used varying combinations of these CBT techniques, preliminary evidence suggests that overall, CBT packages have beneficial effects on depression symptoms in youth. In two more recent meta-analyses of treatment of adolescent depression, mean effect sizes for comparisons of CBT to controls of CBT were estimated to be quite large, 1.02 and 1.27 post-treatment, respectively (Lewinsohn & Clarke, 1999; Reinecke, Ryan & DuBois, 1998).

To date, there have been 13 randomized studies of CBT with depressed youth—three in clinically referred samples, three in diagnosed community samples, and seven in symptomatic but not diagnosed community samples. Four studies were conducted in depressed children, and the remainder in adolescents. Most studies relied on samples of depressed youth recruited from school or community settings who may have mild to moderate symptoms of depression, as assessed by dimensional screening instruments; these studies are discussed only briefly here. Within the past 5 years, however, several investigative teams have published controlled trials in youth who meet diagnostic criteria for depression and are often clinically referred. We will begin our discussion with these more recent and well-developed treatment programs, and then briefly review historical work with subclinical samples of community youth. A summary of studies on clinic samples is shown in Table 2.1.

Wood, Harrington, and Moore (1996) compared the impact of a five- to eight-session CBT intervention with a comparable dose of relaxation training in the treatment of early- to middle-adolescent outpatients with depressive disorders, with 54% of the CBT group and 26% of the relaxation group remitting by the end of treatment. Similar results were obtained on self-report measures of depressive symptoms, self-esteem, and general psychosocial adjustment. Upon 6-month follow-up, the groups had converged, because of continued improvement in the relaxation group and symptomatic relapse in the CBT group. Younger age of diagnosis and higher level of functioning at intake were associated with better outcome (Jayson, Wood, Kroll, Fraser, Harrington, 1998). The addition of a median of six monthly booster CBT sessions after acute treatment resulted in a much lower relapse rate than acute treatment alone (20% vs. 50%; Kroll, Harrington, Jayson, Fraser, & Gowers, 1996).

Using a similar CBT treatment package to that of Wood et al. (1996), Vostanis, Feehan, Grattau, & Bickerton (1996) randomized depressed outpatients to either individual CBT or an attention-placebo condition termed nonfocused intervention (NFI). CBT and NFI were equivalent with regard to the proportion not meeting depressive criteria at the end of treatment (87% vs. 75%)

and at 9-month follow-up (71% vs. 75%) (Vostanis et al., 1996a). However, 46% of patients across conditions reported experiencing a "depressive episode" at some point during the follow-up period (Vostanis et al., 1996). On average, patients in both the CBT and NFI conditions attended six sessions with a therapist, but the range of sessions was from two to nine, occurring over a 1- to 5-month period.

Brent and colleagues (1997) tested CBT, derived from Beck et al. (1979), against systemic behavior family therapy (SBFT) and a nondirective supportive therapy (NST), using a primarily clinically referred sample (⅔ vs. ⅓ from newspaper advertisements) of depressed adolescents. In comparison to the treatment used by Wood et al. (1996) and Vostanis et al. (1996), these treatments were much longer and more regular (12 to 16 weekly sessions).

At posttreatment assessment, significantly fewer of those subjects receiving CBT (17%) than NST (42%) continued to have diagnosable MDD. Remission, as defined by the absence of MDD and at least three consecutive BDI scores < 9, was more common in the CBT cell (60%) than in either SBFT (38%) or NST (39%). Reductions in suicidality and improvements in general psychosocial adjustment were not different across groups. Cognitive behavior therapy resulted in greater change in cognitive distortions than did either SBFT or NST, although changes in depressive symptoms were not mediated by changes in cognitive style (Kolko, Brent, Baugher, Bridge, & Birmaher, 2000). Across treatment cells, poorer response was predicted by greater cognitive distortion, more severe depression at intake, and referral to an advertisement rather than by clinical

Table 2.1 Results of Cognitive Behavior Therapy Conducted in Clinical Samples (% Improved)

Study	N	CBT/IPT	Family	Supportive	Rate of Relapse
Wood et al., 1996[a]	53	54%	—	—	50%
Vostanis et al., 1996[a]	63	87%	—	75%	46%
Brent et al., 1997[a]	107	60%	38%	39%	30%
Mufsont et al., 1994[b]	48	75%	—	46%	—

CBT, cognitive-behavioral therapy; IPT, interpersonal therapy.
[a]There was no major depression and a significant reduction in symptoms; CBT was an active comparator.
[b]Interpersonal therapy was used.

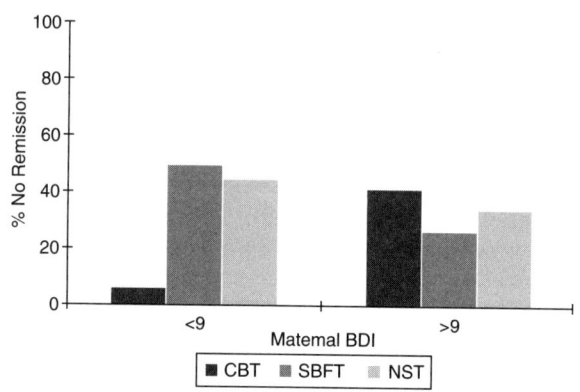

Figure 2.1 Failure to achieve remission as a function of self-reported maternal depression according to Beck Depression Inventory [data from D.A. Brent, D. Kolko, B. Birnaher, M. Bauger, J. Bridge, C. Roth, et al. (1988). Predictors of treatment efficacy in a clinical trial of three psychosocial treatments for adolescent depression. *Journal of the American Academy of Child and Adolescent Psychiatry, 37,* 906–914, used with permission].

referral. Removal from the study and dropout were predicted by double depression (depression comorbid with dysthymia) and greater hopelessness, respectively (Brent et al., 1998).

In the Brent et al. trial (1998), comorbid anxiety was associated with more robust response to CBT, and maternal depressive symptoms were associated with a poorer response to CBT (Fig. 2.1). At posttreatment, CBT was superior to NST and SBFT, even in the presence of multiple adverse predictors. This suggests that CBT, in addition to being efficacious under controlled conditions, may also be efficacious for use in real-world service settings with clinically complex cases (Fig. 2.2). Lifetime suicidality was associated with a poorer response to supportive treatment, where CBT appeared robust (Barbe, Bridge, Birmaher, Kolko, & Brent, 2004b). A history of sexual abuse, however, was associated with a poorer response to CBT (Barbe, Bridge, Birmaher, Kolko,

& Brent, 2004a). Subjects who entered the study via an advertisement fared much better than clinically referred subjects despite having nearly identifiable demographic, clinical, and family characteristics, and were 12 times less likely to have a recurrence of their depression on follow-up (Birmaher et al., 2000; Brent et al., 1998). The differential outcome of those who entered via an advertisement was in part mediated by hopelessness (Brent et al., 1998). At 2-year follow-up, differences between treatment groups on the presence of current MDD were not significant, although the descriptive data again favor CBT (6%) over SBFT (23%) and NST (26%). Recurrence of depression over the 2-year follow-up period was predicted by greater severity of depression symptoms at intake, higher levels of parent–child conflict, and a lifetime history of sexual abuse (Birmaher et al., 2000).

Table 2.2 shows a summary of the studies per-

Figure 2.2 Depression at the end of treatment as a function of the number of adverse conditions, including comorbid anxiety, clinical source of referral, high cognitive distortion, and hopelessness [data from D.A. Brent, D. Kolko, B. Birnaher, M. Bauger, J. Bridge, C. Roth, et al. (1988). Predictors of treatment efficacy in a clinical trial of three psychosocial treatments for adolescent depression. *Journal of the American Academy of Child and Adolescent Psychiatry, 37,* 906–914, used with permission].

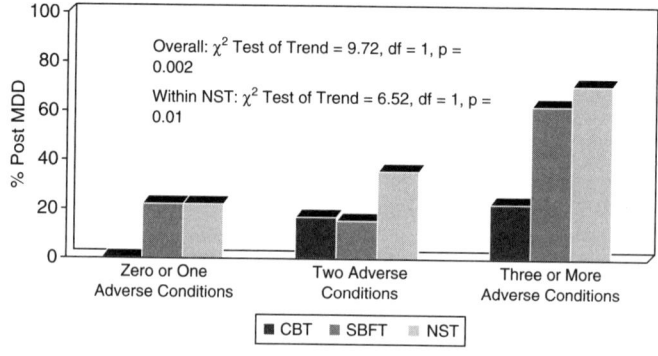

Table 2.2 Results of Cognitive Behavior Therapy Conducted in Diagnosed Samples (% Improved within Samples)

Study	N	CBT	IPT	WLC
Lewinsohn et al., 1990[a]	59	43%	—	5%
Clarke et al., 1999[a]	123	65%	—	48%
Rossello & Bernal, 1999[b]	71	59%	82%	—

CBT, cognitive-behavioral therapy; IPT, interpersonal therapy; WLC, wait-list control.

[a]There was no major depression.

[b]A "significant reduction in symptoms" was reported.

formed with community samples. The following set of studies used community samples of youth with diagnostic depression recruited either from schools or via advertisements.

Lewinsohn, Clarke, Hops, and Andrews (1990) randomized 59 participants to either Coping with Depression–Adolescent version (CWD-A) alone, CWD-A plus the parent group (consisting of 7 weekly sessions), or a wait-list control. The CWD-A consisted of 14 two-hour psychoeducationally oriented group sessions delivered over 7 weeks. The focus of CWD-A is on increasing social skills, pleasant events and activities, and problem-solving and conflict resolution skills, while reducing anxious and depressive cognitions. At the conclusion of treatment, 43% of the adolescent-only group and 48% of the adolescent-plus-parent group no longer met diagnostic criteria, compared to only 5% of the wait-list control subjects. Significantly decreased scores on self-report depression measures were also obtained for both treatment groups relative to the wait-list control group. Treatment gains persisted at 1-, 6-, 12-, and 24-month follow-up. The adolescent-plus-parent group did not result in better outcomes than the adolescent-only condition. Poor outcome was associated with greater depressive symptomatology, comorbid anxiety symptoms, and greater cognitive distortions at intake (Clarke, Hops, Lewinsohn, Andrew, & Williams, 1992).

Clarke, Lewinsohn, Rohde, Hops, and Seeley (1999) replicated these results, with 65%, 69%, and 48% of subjects in the adolescent-only,

adolescent-plus-parent, and wait-list control conditions, respectively, no longer meeting diagnostic criteria for MDD or dysthymia posttreatment. In this trial, there was a re-randomization to a one- to two-session booster condition that did not reduce the rate of depression recurrence for those who had remitted by the end of treatment. However, for patients who had not yet recovered from depression at the end of the acute treatment phase, booster sessions did accelerate their rate of recovery. Across both studies assessing the effects of CWD-A with diagnosed samples, a positive treatment response was predicted by a less severe initial depression, higher initial engagement in and enjoyment of pleasant activities, and fewer irrational thoughts (Clarke et al., 1992; Rohde, Clarke, Lewinsohn, Seeley, & Kaufman, 2001).

Clarke et al. (2002) examined the efficacy of group CBT for depressed adolescents whose parents were depressed. The sample was obtained through sampling the offspring of depressed parents. Subjects were assigned to either a 16-session group CBT program plus treatment as usual ($N = 41$) or treatment as usual alone ($N = 47$). Assessments were conducted at intake, after treatment, and at 12- and 24-month follow-up. According to intent-to-treat analyses, there was no advantage of group CBT over treatment as usual on rate of depressive disorders, depressive symptoms, nondepressive symptoms, or functional outcomes at the end of treatment or over the follow-up period. These findings are consistent with those of Brent et al. (1998), who also found that CBT, delivered individually, was no more effective than either family or supportive therapy in the face of significant maternal depressive symptoms.

Rohde et al. (2001) examined the impact of comorbidity on treatment outcome in an aggregated sample of depressed adolescents treated in the Lewinsohn et al. (1990) and Clarke et al. (1999) samples. Of 151 subjects enrolled in these trials, 40% had one or more comorbid diagnoses. Those with comorbid anxiety disorders showed a greater decrease in depression scores at posttreatment, similar to Brent et al. (1998). Lifetime substance abuse was associated with a slower time to recovery. Subjects with attention-deficit hyperactivity disorder (ADHD) and disruptive behavior disorders were more likely to experience a depressive recurrence. In general, the authors concluded that the effects of CBT were robust to the impact of comorbidity.

Symptomatic Community Samples

There are several community-based studies of symptomatic children and adolescents in which CBT is compared with other active treatments (e.g., relaxation treatment, self-control, modeling) as well as a wait-list control (Butler, Meizitis, & Friedman, 1980; Kahn, Kehle, Jenson, & Clark, 1990; Liddle & Spence, 1990; Reynolds & Coats, 1986; Stark, Reynolds, & Kaslow, 1987; Weisz, Thurber, Sweeney, Proffitt, & LeGagnoux, 1997). In general, all active interventions are superior to wait-list control conditions and the impact is sustained on follow-up, but with few exceptions, CBT showed no differential impact compared to the other active interventions. These studies are important because they are some of the only CBT studies of depressive symptoms in children, are usually delivered in a group format, and, therefore, may guide future efforts to prevent early-onset depression.

Prevention

Clarke and colleagues (1995) tested the efficacy of an adaptation of CWD-A, termed "coping with stress" (CWS), in preventing diagnosable depression in adolescents with subsyndromal depressive symptoms, but without a diagnosable depressive disorder. One hundred fifty high school students who scored high on the Center for Epidemiological Studies–Depression scale (CES-D) but failed to meet diagnostic criteria for a current depressive disorder were randomly assigned to the 15-session CWS or "usual care." At 12 months postintervention, fewer cases of depressive disorder (15%) had developed in the experimental group than in the control group (26%). Clarke et al. (2001) conducted a randomized clinical trial comparing the efficacy of group CBT plus treatment as usual versus treatment as usual alone for the adolescent offspring of depressed parents deemed to be at risk for the development of a depressive disorder (e.g., presence of subsyndromal symptoms of depression and/or a history of past mood disorder). Subjects

could not meet criteria for a current mood disorder. Ninety-four adolescent subjects were randomized to the experimental treatment ($N = 45$) and to usual care ($N = 49$). At 12-month follow-up, the cumulative rate of incident major depression was much lower in the experimental condition than that with treatment as usual (9.3% vs. 28.8%). The odds of new-onset depression was nearly six times higher in the control than in the experimental group, after adjusting for gender, age, past history of depression, and intake self-reported symptoms of depression (adjusted odds ratio [OR] = 5.6, 95% confidence interval [CI] = 1.6-20.4). Significant treatment by time interactions favoring the experimental treatment were found for self-reported depression and global functioning. On average, those exposed to the experimental group experienced 33 fewer depressed days than those in the treatment-as-usual condition.

One study examined the effect of CBT "bibliotherapy," or therapy involving pertinent reading materials, on adolescents with mild to moderate depression who were symptomatic volunteers (Ackerson, Scogin, McKendree-Smith, & Lyman, 1998). Twenty-two subjects were assigned to either reading the *Feeling Good* book by Burns (1980) or to a 4-week delayed-treatment condition, after which they received the bibliotherapy condition. Significant treatment by time interactions, favoring the experimental condition, were found for interview-, parent- and self-rated depression, and dysfunctional attitudes. Gains for the experimental condition were maintained at 1-month follow-up, and there was even evidence of continued improvement. Approximately 60% (59 to 64%) of subjects experienced a clinically significant improvement in their symptomatology, with evidence of sustained and even continued improvement on follow-up. Partial support was found for mediation of changes in depressive symptomatology by changes in dysfunctional thinking.

Interpersonal Psychotherapy for Adolescent Depression

Although CBT interventions have received the most attention from researchers of youth depression, there are a number of clinical trials that focus on changing the interpersonal aspects of depression. Interpersonal psychotherapy for depressed adolescents, family therapy, and social skills training have all been investigated in at least one controlled trial (Mufson et al., 1994; Diamond et al., 2002; Fine, Forth, & Gilbert, 1991). All three treatments target behavioral and environmental processes, although the social domain targeted by the interventions differs, as do the techniques used to affect change.

Interpersonal psychotherapy for adolescents (IPT-A), an adaption of IPT, is a time-limited, focused psychotherapy that addresses common adolescent developmental issues that are closely related to depression: separation from parents, authority and autonomy issues in the parent–teen relationship, development of dyadic interpersonal relationships, peer pressure, loss, and issues related to single-parent families. Interpersonal therapy has been adapted and tested for depressed adolescents (Mufson et al., 1994; Mufson, Weissman, Moreau, & Garfinkel, 1999). In a controlled, 12-week, clinical trial of IPT-A, 48 adolescents (12–18 years old) with MDD were randomly assigned to either weekly IPT-A or biweekly to monthly 30-minute sessions of clinical monitoring. The sample was largely Hispanic and female. Thirty-two of the 48 patients completed the protocol (21 IPT-A-assigned patients and 11 patients in the control group). At termination, a much lower proportion of those in IPT-A still met criteria for major depression (12.5% vs. 41.6%). As measured by the Clinical Global Improvement scale, 95.5% of those treated with IPT-A were rated as significantly better than at intake, compared to 61.5% of those treated with clinical management. Moreover, only 4.5% of those treated with IPT-A were rated as significantly worse, compared to 23.1% of those assigned to clinical monitoring. Patients who received IPT-A reported a significant decrease in depressive symptoms and greater improvement in overall social functioning, functioning with friends, and problem-solving skills. In the intent-to-treat sample, 18 (75%) of 24 patients who received IPT-A compared with 11 patients (46%) in the control condition met recovery criterion (HAM-D ≤6) at Week 12. These preliminary findings support the feasibil-

ity, acceptability, and efficacy of 12 weeks of IPT-A in acutely depressed adolescents in reducing depressive symptoms and improving social functioning and interpersonal problem-solving skills.

Mufson and colleagues assessed the effectiveness of IPT-A in school-based mental health clinics in New York City: they randomized 63 depressed adolescents referred for a mental health intake visit to IPT-A or treatment as usual, both performed by the clinic staff. The adolescents had either MDD, dysthymia, depressive disorder not otherwise specified (NOS), or adjustment disorder with a depressed mood. At termination, the adolescents in the IPT-A treatment experienced significantly higher symptomatic relief than the treatment-as-usual group (Mufson et al., 2004)

Rossello and Bernal (1999) compared the efficacy of a 12-week, individually administered CBT program to a similar dose of IPT and wait-list control in adolescents with diagnosed MDD and/or dysthymia referred by school personnel. Both active interventions were adapted to be culturally appropriate for use with Puerto Rican youth. Attendance problems occurred in both treatments, as only 68% of IPT cases and 52% of CBT cases completed over seven treatment sessions. To assess outcome, a clinical cutoff was selected on the Children's Depression Inventory (CDI) that was approximately 3 points lower than the mean intake CDI score for the sample. As measured by these criteria for clinically significant change (Jacobson and Truax, 1991), 59% of adolescents in the CBT condition and 82% of IPT cases achieved clinically significant improvement in depression symptoms by posttreatment; data were not provided for the wait-list control condition. Using an unspecified normative cutoff point for the CDI, the authors indicated that 56% of the IPT cases, 48% of the CBT cases, and 61% of wait-list cases were "severely depressed" at intake. At posttreatment, these percentages were 11%, 24%, and 34%, respectively, and 17% and 18% at 3-month follow-up (for IPT and CBT, respectively). Although this investigation has several methodological difficulties (e.g., substantial attrition and no intent-to-treat analyses conducted), these results provide some of the first information on the efficacy of CBT for depressed Latino youth and the only extant comparison of CBT and IPT for adolescent depression.

Attachment-Based Family Therapy

Diamond, Reis, Diamond, Siqueland, and Isaacs (2002) conducted a randomized clinical trial comparing Attachment-based family therapy (ABFT) with a wait-list control in 32 clinical referred adolescents meeting DSM-III-R criteria for major depression in a largely (69%) African-American, poor, inner-city sample. On average, subjects received eight sessions of ABFT, which focuses on strengthening family bonds, reducing conflict, improving trust, improving cross-generational empathy, and, subsequently, improving affect regulation, communication, and promotion of competence. Those in the wait-list condition received 15 minutes of weekly telephone monitoring of their clinical condition as well as a face-to-face assessment at Week 6, at which point those still meeting criteria for major depression were offered ABFT. The treatment data from these latter cases were not included in the primary outcome analyses. At posttreatment, 81% of those treated with ABFT no longer met criteria for depression, compared to 47% in the wait-list control group. A significantly greater number of those assigned to ABFT reported a BDI <9 (62% vs. 19%). A significant treatment-by-time interaction favoring ABFT was found for interview-rated depression, self-reported anxiety, and child-reported parent–child conflict, with nonsignificant trends favoring ABFT for attachment to mother, suicidal ideation, and hopelessness.

One limitation of the study was that ABFT was 12 weeks in duration whereas the control treatment lasted 6 weeks, so that it is hard to differentiate time versus treatment effects. Therefore, analyses were conducted focusing on the first 6 weeks. While most of these analyses were not statistically significant, a significantly greater proportion of those treated with ABFT showed a BDI <9 by 6 weeks (56% vs. 19%). Fifteen of those treated with ABFT were followed up for 6 months after the end of treatment and only 13% had a depressive relapse. These results suggest that ABFT may be a promising treatment for ad-

olescent major depression, and that it is efficacious in a poor, African-American population. It is important to note, however, that in the one clinical trial comparing CBT with family therapy for depressed adolescents (Brent et al., 1997), family therapy produced significantly worse outcomes than CBT. The model of family therapy in the Brent et al. (1997) study focused on problem solving and communication, but it did not address attachment issues as in the study of Diamond et al. (2002).

Social Skills Training

Fine, Forth, Gilbert, and Haley (1991) compared two forms of short-term group therapy, either social skills training or therapeutic support, for depressed adolescents in a randomized clinical trial. Subjects in the therapeutic support group showed significantly greater reductions in clinical depression and significant increases in self-concept, although there were no group differences by 9-month follow-up. Subjects in the support group maintained their gains, and those who attended the social skills group caught up.

Suicide Attempters

A high proportion of adolescent suicide attempters have mood disorders, and suicide attempts are a serious complication of mood disorder (Lewinsohn, Rohde, & Seeley, 1996). Therefore, we examine the three randomized clinical trials of adolescent suicide attempters that have been conducted thus far.

Rotheram-Borus et al. (1996) compared the efficacy of a cognitive behavior family therapy plus an emergency room intervention with that of family CBT alone. The family CBT plus emergency room intervention resulted in greater compliance with treatment. No baseline characteristics were reported, but end point analyses on maternal depression and general psychopathology, patient ideation, and parent-reported family interaction favored the combined intervention.

Harrington et al. (1998) compared a four-session, home-based family problem-solving intervention with treatment as usual for 162 adolescents who had taken an overdose. Subjects were assessed at intake and at 2 and 6 months after intake. There were no differences between the two groups with respect to suicidal ideation, hopelessness, or family variables. A post-hoc subgroup analysis showed that nondepressed subjects who received the family intervention (vs. treatment as usual) reported lower suicidal ideation. However, the authors note that the depressed subgroup had much more severe ideation, so that the intervention was not effective in the more severely suicidal group.

Wood, Trainor, Rothwell, Moore, and Harrington (2001) randomized 63 adolescents who, prior to randomization, had made at least two suicide attempts within a year to either a six-session group intervention or to treatment as usual. The group treatment consisted of a combination of interpersonal skills training, anger management, problem solving, addressing of depression and hopelessness, and conflict resolution. In intent-to-treat analyses, those who received the experimental treatment were 6.3 times less likely to have made two or more attempts over an average of 29 weeks of follow-up (6% vs. 31%). Subjects in the experimental treatment were 60% less likely to make at least one attempt, although this effect was not statistically significant. They were also less likely to use routine care, had better school attendance, and had a lower rate of disruptive disorders than those who received treatment as usual. However, the two treatments did not differ in their effects on depression or global outcome.

Conclusion

Cognitive behavior therapy for youth depression appears to be more efficacious than no treatment, wait-list control, or attention placebo controls. There is also evidence in clinically referred samples that CBT can produce better results than alternate active treatments (Brent et al., 1997; Wood et al., 1996). Cognitive behavior therapy may also be "robust" in the face of many of the adverse clinical predictors of poor outcome (e.g., comorbidity) (Brent et al., 1998; Rohde et al., 2001). A recently completed benchmarking study has also suggested that much of the advantage of CBT found in clinical trials can be sustained in outpatient clinic settings (Weersing,

Iyengar, & Birmaher, submitted). Efficacy also appears to be robust to format (group vs. individual), emphasis (behavioral vs. cognitive), and dose (5 to 16 sessions).

While these results are promising, many patients continue to have clinically significant levels of depression following CBT, and near majorities of patients experience at least one recurrence of depression within 2 years of treatment termination. It is perhaps not surprising that many patients (estimates range from 29% to 48%) seek additional services following acute CBT (Brent, Kolko, Birmaher, Baugher, & Bridge, 1999).

These studies provide some clues about the improvement of depression when CBT is used. Treatment with CBT fared more poorly in the face of maternal depressive symptoms, greater severity, and double depression; family discord also retarded recovery and predicted recurrence. Therefore, additional interventions that target maternal depression and family discord may well augment outcome. Moreover, particularly refractory and chronic conditions, such as double depression, may respond better to combinations of medication and CBT than to either as monotherapy alone, as suggested by comparable data in adults with chronic depression (Keller et al., 2000). Further work on improving outcome in patients with these poor prognostic risk factors needs to be conducted. There is little in the extant literature about the transportability of CBT to community settings. We do have evidence from benchmarking studies that CBT appears to be superior to community treatment and that it can yield similar results in clinical trials and in open treatment, under less controlled conditions (Weersing et al., 2003; Weisz & Weersing, 2002). We currently have very little information on the treatment of serious depression in preadolescents, and it is unclear how CBT may need to be adapted to take into account the more concrete cognitive style and greater dependence on parents seen in most preadolescent (as compared to adolescent) patients (Weisz & Weersing, 1999).

Much less is known about the efficacy of other forms of psychotherapy, such as interpersonal or family therapy. Interpersonal therapy for adolescents appears to be a promising treatment for adolescent depression and has been well accepted and efficacious in Latino populations. The one direct comparison of CBT and IPT is difficult to interpret, but IPT appeared at least as efficacious as CBT and with respect to some measures, more so (Rossello & Bernal, 1999). With additional studies of IPT it will be important to understand which factors predict good and poor response.

Despite numerous studies implicating family factors in adolescent depression, there have only been two studies that examine the efficacy of family therapy in child or adolescent depression. A skills-based family treatment did not appear to be as efficacious as CBT, whereas ABFT that focused on repairing and strengthening emotional bonds achieved results that were as good as those either with CBT or IPT-A (Brent et al., 1997; Diamond et al., 2002). This treatment mode clearly requires further study.

Relatively few studies have examined the impact of psychosocial intervention on the prevention of recurrent suicidal behavior, in part because those teens at higher risk for recurrence of suicide attempt are usually excluded from treatment trials for adolescent depression. The few studies that have been conducted are not definitive but suggest some utility for family cognitive behavior approaches and skills training. This vulnerable population deserves further scrutiny and study.

PSYCHOPHARMACOLOGICAL TREATMENT OF MAJOR DEPRESSION

In adults, effective antidepressants for the treatment of adult major depression include monoamine oxidase inhibitors (MAOIs) and tricyclic antidepressants (TCAs), selective serotonin reuptake inhibitors (SSRIs) and dual-action agents. Through these treatments at least partial symptomatic response is achieved, but often complete remission is difficult to obtain. The existence of residual symptoms may be the best predictor for a relapse or reoccurrence, which may have very significant implications if the first episode occurs in adolescence (Keller, 2003). Therefore, determination of the psychopharmacological approaches, both monotherapies or combinations,

that have the best outcome in adults may be significant for the treatment of adolescent depression.

Pharmacological Treatment of Adult Major Depression

Monotherapy

At this time the first line medication treatment for adult MDD is the SSRIs, which include fluoxetine (Prozac), sertraline (Zoloft), paroxetine (Paxil), fluvoxamine (Luvox), citalopram (Celexa), and escitalopram (Lexapro). They have a greater affinity for the serotonin transporter than for the noradrenergic transporter, and each compound selectively inhibits 5-hydroxytryptamine (5-HT) reuptake and has unique secondary binding properties. This class of drug is rarely associated with fatalities and given its safety profile provides an easy treatment option for the clinician (Farvolden, Kennedy, & Lam, 2003).

The latest generation of antidepressants is the selective serotonin and noradrenaline reuptake inhibitors (SNRIs), such as venlafaxine (Effexor), duloxetine (Cymbalta), and milnacipran. It appears that venlafaxine possesses a selective high affinity for the noradrenergic and sertonergic reuptake sites; however, it is only at higher doses (150 to 225 mg) that its noradrenergic reuptake becomes activated. This dual reuptake inhibition may contribute to the high rates of remission of depressive symptoms compared to those with SSRIs (Thase, Entsuah, & Rudolph, 2001). Although venlafaxine's side effect profile is similar to that of SSRIs, at higher doses >200 mg there is a 5.5% clinically significant elevation of blood pressure and at higher doses >300 mg the incidence of hypertension reaches 13%. Duloxetine is a newer SNRI with reportedly dual reuptake inhibition that is equal at clinical doses. Reboxetine is a selective norepinephrine reuptake inhibitor not approved in the United States for the treatment of major depression. Mirtazapine, which belongs to the piperazine-azepine group of compounds, has not been investigated in the treatment of pediatric depression.

Another novel compound used for the treatment of adult depression is bupropion, which has it effects by blocking noradrenergic and dopamine reuptake (Dong & Blier, 2001). It has the side effects of insomnia, nausea, increased anxiety, and restlessness. Another potential side effect is an increased incidence of seizures, which occur at a rate of 0.4% with daily doses below 450 mg and 2.4% with daily doses between 450 and 600 mg (Johnston et al., 1991). However, one important advantage of this compound in treating adults is that it has been found to cause no weight gain or sexual dysfunction.

Nefazodone and trazodone inhibit the 5-HT2A receptors. This class of compounds is effective for the symptom of insomnia; however, sedation is a common problematic side effect along with orthostatic hypotension. A common clinical practice is to use low doses of trazodone for insomnia while simultaneously starting an SSRI. Trazodone is associated with a rare side effect of priaprism. In addition, hepatic toxicity and liver failure have been found to be associated with these compounds.

Older classes of antidepressants efficacious in treating adult MDD, such as the tricyclic and heterocyclic antidepressants (amitriptyline, amoxapine, clomipramine, desipramine, doxepin, imipramine, maprotiline, nortriptyline, and protriptyline) inhibit different combinations of serotonin, noradrenergic, and dopamine receptors. Their antagonism at other receptor types causes difficult side effects such as dry mouth, confusion, orthostatic hypotension, tachycardia, weight gain, urinary retention, and constipation. In addition, doses outside of the therapeutic range may be lethal because of conduction abnormalities. The MAOIs (phenelzine and tranylcypromine) irreversibly inhibit the monoamine oxidase isozymes A and B. It is thought that the blockade of the isozyme A lends these compounds their clinical efficacy (Mann et al., 1989). One major issue with this class of antidepressants is the required tyramine-restricted diet, which if not adhered to can prove to be fatal with dangerous elevation of the patient's blood pressure. Also, drugs that increase synaptic monoamines must be avoided, such as over-the-counter cold medications, TCAs, SSRIs, stimulants, and cocaine. There is also a risk of lethal, rare hyperthermic reactions that occur with meperidine and other opiates. Given these issues of tolerability and potential serious adverse events,

TCAs and MAOIs have been more often reserved as second- and third-line agents for patients who have failed treatment with one of the newer antidepressant classes.

Pharmacological Combination and Augmentation Therapy

The definition of treatment-resistant depression is the failure to clinically respond to one or two antidepressant trials with an adequate amount of time and dosage. There are several strategies for treating adults with this clinical problem: maximize the dose and duration of treatment; switch to another antidepressant within a class or another class; use a combination of antidepressants; and augment with other compounds. Response rates when switching to another type of antidepressant have ranged from 40% to 60% (Thase, Trivedi, & Rush, 1995). There is evidence that supports the use of lithium and triodothyronine as augmentation treatment for patients who are TCA nonresponders (Aronson, Offman, Joffee, & Naylor, 1996; Freemantle, Anderson, & Young, 2000). There are limited data available on the efficacy of lithium and triodothryonine augmentation with SSRIs (one study with citalpram and one with fluoxetine) and newer antidepressant nonresponders (Baumann, 1996; Katona et al., 1993). Open studies of combinations of antidepressants from different classes suggest possible usefulness for the strategy, but more controlled research is required (Seth, Jennings, Bindman, Phillips, & Bergman, 1992). In addition, there is some evidence for the usefulness of novel antipsychotic agents in combination with antidepressants for treatment-refractory depression, such as the combination of fluoxetine and olanzapine (Shelton et al., 2001).

Pharmacologial Treatment of Adolescent Major Depression

The FDA has issued an advisory to physicians that the use of antidepressants may lead to suicidal thinking or attempts in depressed youths (see Part VI: Youth Suicide, Chapter 4). The FDA has requested that a warning be added to the product label of these antidepressants, with information highlighting the need for close observation for worsening of depression and the emergence of suicidality in adults and children treated with these medications. This advisory is based on the available evidence from pediatric major depression trials that seem to suggest modest efficacy of antidepressants for this illness and a small increased risk for suicidal thinking in some of these studies. This is a complex issue, and the available pediatric data do not clearly support or refute these treatment concerns for pediatric depression. However, these issues highlight the need for continued research to examine the efficacy and safety of both acute and long-term use of these medications in the pediatric population.

To date, the only medications that have demonstrated safety and efficacy in double-blind, placebo-controlled trials for children and adolescents with major depression are the SSRIs. Fluoxetine was the first SSRI shown to be efficacious in the treatment of children and adolescents with major depression. In a single-site 8-week trial, fluoxetine 20 mg was significantly superior to placebo. Fifty percent of the fluoxetine group compared to 33% of the placebo group were much or very much clinically improved (Emslie et al., 1997). In a subsequent multicenter study of 219 outpatient youths with major depression, significantly greater improvement in depression as assessed by the Children's Depression Rating Scale–Revised (CDRS-R) scores was found for the fluoxetine group compared to the placebo group. Fifty-two percent of the fluoxetine group was much or very much clinically improved compared to 37% of the placebo group (Emslie et al., 2002). On the basis of the positive findings of this study, fluoxetine received FDA approval for the treatment of major depression in children and adolescents.

The efficacy of paroxetine has been assessed in two pediatric studies, one with adolescents only and one with children and adolescents. In a multicenter study of 275 adolescent outpatients with major depression, patients were randomized to paroxetine (up to 40 mg), imipramine (up to 300 mg), or placebo for an 8-week trial. Sixty-six percent of the paroxetine group was much or very much clinically improved, compared to 52% of the imipramine group and 48% of the placebo group. However, on the pri-

mary efficacy measure of the HAM-D total score, there was no statistically significant difference among the groups (Keller et al., 2001). Adverse events most commonly reported for paroxetine were headache, nausea, dizziness, dry mouth, and somnolence, which occurred at rates similar to those in the placebo group except for somnolence. The most common adverse events in the imipramine group were dizziness, dry mouth, headache, nausea, and tachycardia. In a multicenter double-blind, placebo-controlled trial of paroxetine treatment of children and adolescents with major depression, there was no statistically significant difference in the response rates between the paroxetine and placebo groups (GlaxoSmith Kline, data on file).

Citalopram treatment for major depression in children and adolescents was assessed in 174 youths, ages 7 to 17 years. In this double-blind, placebo-controlled, 8-week trial, patients were randomized to citalopram (mean 23 mg/day) or placebo. Significantly greater improvement in depression, based on change in CDRS-R scores from baseline to end point, was found for the citalopram group compared to the placebo group. Remission rates, defined as a CDRS-R score $\leq$ 28, were 36% in the citalopram group and 24% in the placebo group. Headache, nausea, rhinitis, abdominal pain, and influenza-like symptoms were the most frequent side effects in the citalopram group (Wagner et al., 2001).

The efficacy and safety of sertraline were assessed in two identical multicenter studies of 376 children and adolescents ages 6 to 17 years with major depression. Patients were randomized to sertraline (mean 131 mg/day) or placebo during this 10-week, double-blind, placebo-controlled trial. On the basis of change in CDRS-R scores from baseline to end point, the sertraline group showed significantly greater improvement in depression than the placebo group. Response rates, defined as a decrease of >40% in the CDRS-R score, were 69% in the sertraline group and 59% in the placebo group. Headache, nausea, insomnia, upper respiratory tract infection, abdominal pain, and diarrhea were the most common side effects in the sertraline-treated group (Wagner et al., 2003).

With regard to other antidepressant classes, nefazadone was evaluated in a double-blind, placebo-controlled trial of 195 adolescents with major depression. Adolescents were randomized to nefazadone in targeted daily doses of 300–400 mg/week or placebo over 8 weeks. Although greater improvement was found with nefazadone than with placebo, this was not statistically significant. In a second multicenter trial for children and adolescents ages 7–17 years, nefazadone did not differentiate from placebo (Rynn et al. 2002).

Double-blind, placebo-controlled trials of TCAs in the treatment of depressed youths have not demonstrated superiority of TCAs over placebo. Approximately 500 children and adolescents have been included in aggregate in these studies (Ryan, 2003) (Table 2.3).

The efficacy of venlafaxine, mirtazapine, and bupropion have not been established in children and adolescents with depression. Dietary restrictions markedly limit the utility of MAOIs for pediatric patients.

Therefore, for medication treatment of major depression in children and adolescents, only the SSRIs have demonstrated efficacy and tolerability in acute, short-term treatment studies. The SSRIs are currently first-line pharmacological treatment for children and adolescents who are suffering from depression, although care must be taken to monitor the possible emergence of suicidal ideation.

Conclusion

Controlled, large-scale studies demonstrating the efficacy of antidepressants in the treatment

Table 2.3 Selected Monotherapy Studies in Treatment of Adolescent Depression

Study	Agent(s) Used	Study Design	Study Length (weeks)	Sample Size	Comments
Esmlie et al., 1997	Fluoxetine	Double-blind, placebo-controlled	8	64	Fluoxetine 20 mg superior to placebo
Esmlie et al., 2002	Fluoxetine	Double-blind, placebo-controlled	8	219	Fluoxetine effective 52% vs. 37% placebo; FDA approval in pediatric MDD on the basis of this study
Keller et al., 2001	Paroxetine, imipramine	Double-blind, placebo-controlled	8	275	Overall response rates were as follows: Paroxetine = 66% Imipramine = 52% Placebo = 48%
GlaxoSmithKline (data on file)	Paroxetine	Double-blind, placebo-controlled	10		Not statistically significant between paroxetine and placebo
Wagner et al., 2001	Citalopram	Double-blind, placebo-controlled	8	174	On the basis of CDRS-R scores, citalopram showed significant improvement over placebo
Wagner et al., 2003	Sertraline	Double-blind, placebo-controlled	10	376	Sertraline showed significant improvement over placebo
Rynn et al., 2002	Nefazadone	Double-blind, placebo-controlled	8	195	Nefazadone not superior to placebo on primary outcome (CDRS-R), but significant on secondary outcome (HAM-D)
Ryan, 2003	Tricyclic antidepressants	Aggregate studies		500	Tricyclics not superior to placebo

CDRS-R, Children's Depression Rating Scale–Revised; FDA, Food and Drug Association; HAM-D, Hamilton Depression Rating Scale; MDD, major depressive disorder.

of youths with major depression are limited to acute SSRI trials. Moreover, it remains to be determined whether children and adolescents respond similarly, since these trials were not adequately powered to determine the relative efficacy of treatment between these age groups.

There are a number of limitations to these acute SSRI treatment trials that limit their generalizability to the pediatric population. Commonly occurring comorbid disorders were often exclusion criteria in these studies. For example, in the study of citalopram treatment for major depression, ADHD was an exclusion criterion. Comorbidity has been shown to affect response rates of SSRI treatment. In a subset analysis of the study by Keller and colleagues (2001), the presence of comorbid ADHD significantly reduced response rates in all of the treatment groups. On the basis of Clinical Global Improvement ratings of very much improved or much improved, the response rates among patients without ADHD were as follows: paroxetine, 71%; imipramine, 64%; and placebo, 59%. For patients with ADHD, response rates were as follows: paroxetine, 25%; imipramine, 31%; and placebo, 13% (Birmaher, McCafferty, Bellew, & Beebe, 2001). Substance abuse was an exclusion criterion in all of the SSRI treatment trials. There was minimal ethnic diversity in the patients included in these trials—i.e., the majority of patients were Caucasian.

Other than the SSRIs, there are no data available to support the efficacy of other classes of antidepressants in treating children and adolescents with major depression. Because children have been shown to have high placebo response rates in depression studies, open studies with other antidepressants provide little information about the efficacy of these agents in youths.

Very little information is known about the optimal treatment duration for a child with major depression. The only controlled data available for children and adolescents are from a study by Emslie et al. (2001), which showed that extending treatment 19 weeks after the end of acute treatment with fluoxetine decreased the relapse rate to 34%, compared to 60% in the placebo group.

There is a paucity of data about augmentation strategies for youths who have an inadequate response to an antidepressant. Lithium augmentation (Ryan, Myer, et al., 1988; Strober, Freeman, Rigali, Schmidt, & Diamond, 1992) and MAOI augmentation (Ryan, Puig-Antich, et al., 1988) to TCAs for depressed adolescents have been reported. However, since TCAs are now rarely used to treat depression in youths, these earlier augmentation studies are less clinically relevant.

There is little known about the long-term safety of antidepressant use in children. The longest duration of safety data available is from a 52-week open-extension study of sertraline following an acute 10-week trial for the treatment of obsessive-compulsive disorder in children and adolescents (Cook et al., 2001).

There is a pressing need to identify effective medication alternatives to the SSRIs for treating depression in youth. It is important that future studies be powered sufficiently to determine efficacy and safety of antidepressants in both child and adolescent populations. Ethnic diversity should be an aim of subject inclusion. Long-term studies of antidepressants are required to evaluate their safety profile in children. This information will enable a risk-benefit analysis of extended antidepressant use.

Maintenance studies are needed to guide optimal medication treatment duration. Strategies for relapse prevention need to be developed. Studies of antidepressants should focus on remission of symptoms rather than treatment response. The role of antidepressant medications in improving cognitive functioning, peer relationships, family harmony, and overall quality of life needs to be assessed.

Predictors of treatment response and remission should be evaluated in pediatric pharmacological studies. Some factors that may influence outcome are age of onset of illness, severity and duration of illness, comorbid disorders, family history of major depression, and current episode of parental major depression.

Medication augmentation strategies and the role of psychotherapy to enhance treatment response require further investigation. The order of treatment selection—i.e., medication, psychotherapy, or combined medication and psychotherapy—should be established, particularly as it relates to depression severity.

Information is needed as to whether early treatment interventions affect the course of the illness or prevents its later occurrence in adulthood. A new area of investigation is treatment for youths at risk for the development of major depression. Clark et al. (2003) found that adolescent offspring of depressed parents who had subsyndromal depressive symptoms benefited more from a group cognitive therapy prevention program than from the usual health maintenance organization care. At 12 months follow-up, cumulative major depression incidence was 9% in the cognitive treatment group and 29% in the usual-care group. It remains to be determined whether pharmacological treatment of youths at risk for depression will reduce the likelihood or prevent the occurrence of major depression.

In summary, a medication treatment algorithm based on empirically derived information in pediatric populations is necessary to provide optimal care to children and adolescents suffering from major depression.

COMBINED PSYCHOTHERAPY AND MEDICATION

Adult Depression

Reviews of controlled studies have historically concluded that the combination of medication and psychotherapy does not yield appreciable benefits above the effects of either medication or psychotherapy alone (Conte, Plutchik, Wild, & Karasu, 1986; Depression Guideline Panel, 1993; Robinson, Powers, Cleveland, & Thyer, 1990). However, the combination of medication and psychotherapy may be especially beneficial for certain subtypes of MDD. Along these lines, Thase et al. (1997) combined the data from six trials involving cognitive therapy, IPT, and/or combined medication and cognitive therapy or IPT for acute-phase treatment of MDD. The results revealed that combined treatment and psychotherapy alone were equally effective for non-severe, nonrecurrent MDD, but combined treatment was more effective than psychotherapy alone for recurrent or severe MDD.

Particularly striking results for the value of combined treatment were evident in a recent trial

examining nefazodone, cognitive-behavioral analysis system of psychotherapy (CBASP), and the combination, as treatments for chronic forms of MDD (Keller et al., 2000). The CBASP is a new psychotherapy, developed specifically for chronic forms of depression, that draws elements from cognitive, behavioral, and interpersonal therapies. Using a problem-solving approach, the treatment teaches patients to examine the consequences of their interpersonal behavior as a means of resolving interpersonal conflicts. In the Keller et al. (2000) study, combined nefazodone and CBASP resulted in significantly greater acute depression–phase treatment response rates (73%) than those with nefazodone alone (48%) and CBASP alone (48%). Although these results for combined CBASP and nefazodone deserve attention, the lack of a placebo control or alternate form of psychotherapy prevents any inferences about whether CBASP is uniquely effective in combination with nefazodone, or whether any other form of psychotherapy would have achieved similar results.

Adolescent Major Depression

The comparative efficacy of medication, psychotherapy, and the combination of medication and psychotherapy remains to be determined. A NIMH-funded multicenter, randomized trial has just been completed to determine the efficacy of fluoxetine vs. CBT vs. fluoxetine plus CBT vs. placebo in the treatment of adolescents with major depression (Treatment for Adolescents with Depression Study Team, 2003). The preliminary results from the first 12 weeks ($N = 378$) showed that 71% responded well to combination treatment, compared to 61% who received fluoxetine alone, 43% who received CBT alone, and 35% of those treated with placebo (March et al., 2004). The study also reported that patients became significantly less suicidal regardless of the treatment that they received. For suicide attempts, 4 occurred in the combination treatment group, 2 in the fluoxetine alone, and 1 in CBT alone. There were no completed suicides. It is hoped that with subsequent analyses of this study there will be a better understanding of the treatments that work best for particular adolescents.

There are no data available about treatment strategies for depressed youth who fail to respond to usual treatment with an SSRI. An NIMH-funded multicenter trial is under way to assess the efficacy of treatments for SSRI-resistant depression in adolescents. In this study, adolescents are randomized to an alternative SSRI, alternative SSRI plus CBT, venlafaxine, or venlafaxine plus CBT.

BIPOLAR DISORDER

Mood disorders by definition disrupt functioning in several areas of an individual's life, including school, family, and peer relationships. Practice guidelines for the treatment of bipolar disorder in adults recognize both pharmacotherapy and psychotherapy as essential components of optimal treatment (American Psychiatric Association, 1994). From a developmental standpoint, research supports the notion that early psychosocial impairment tends to promote later impairment, as the individual arrives at each progressive stage of development with inadequate resources available to meet the challenges unique to the ensuing developmental period (Cicchetti, Rogosch, & Toth, 1998). Thus, it is crucial that treatment be provided promptly and effectively to maintain a normal developmental trajectory as much as possible, and minimize the effects that symptoms have on functioning.

Given the more recent recognition of bipolar disorder in childhood, it is not surprising that little is known about treatment strategies, both pharmacologic and psychotherapeutic, for this population. To date, no randomized, controlled trials of psychosocial intervention with a pediatric bipolar disorder population have been completed; however, several are currently under way. Potentially promising treatment approaches for pediatric bipolar disorder rely on the literature for treatment of adult bipolar disorder. In the next section we review the literature on the psychosocial treatment of adult bipolar disorder. This is followed by suggestions for adaptation of adult psychosocial treatments for use with children and adolescents.

Psychosocial Treatment of Adult Bipolar Disorder

Several different manualized psychosocial treatments have been applied to the treatment of bipolar disorder in adults; although they are based on different theoretical orientations, they share the goal of diminishing relapse to ultimately improve quality of life. Common areas of treatment focus include increasing treatment compliance, enhancing protective factors (e.g., support, self-care routines), and decreasing risk factors associated with relapse (e.g., stress, substance use).

Cognitive Behavior Therapy

Cognitive behavior therapy conceptualizes mood swings as a function of negative thought and behavioral patterns. These maladaptive patterns are then targeted in the therapy. Three randomized, controlled clinical trials with bipolar adults (for a review see Craighead, Miklowitz, Frank, & Vajk, 2002) suggest that adjunctive CBT leads to increased medication compliance, fewer hospitalizations, and improved social and occupational functioning.

Interpersonal Therapy and Social Rhythm Therapy

Interpersonal therapy, as discussed earlier, is a short-term, present-oriented, problem-focused individual therapy developed and supported for the alleviation of symptoms of major depression (Klerman et al., 1987). In IPT, the onset of the depressive episode is placed in the context of interpersonal relationships, and current interpersonal difficulties are addressed. With the knowledge that circadian rhythm disturbances are linked to bipolar disorder (Ehlers, Frank, & Kupfer, 1988), Frank and colleagues supplemented IPT with social rhythm therapy (SRT) to create IPSRT for bipolar disorder. The focus of IPSRT is on the regularization of both social and circadian rhythms to control mood cycling. Results of a controlled trial with bipolar adults indicate that IPSRT is most effective in controlling the depressive symptoms of bipolar disorder, and also affects greater stabilization of sleep–wake cycles than case management treatment (Frank et al., 1997).

Family-Based Therapies

Several randomized, controlled trials of family-based treatments have been documented in the literature. Inpatient family intervention (IFI; Clarkin et al., 1990), a nine-session intervention focused on psychoeducation, aims to modify negative family patterns and increase coping skills. Results indicate that female patients had better global and symptomatic functioning than those receiving standard hospital treatment (Clarkin et al., 1990).

Miklowitz and Goldstein (1990) developed family-focused therapy (FFT), a 9-month treatment incorporating psychoeducation, communication skills training, and problem-solving skills training. In a randomized trial, patients receiving FFT experienced fewer depressive symptoms, increased compliance with medication regimens, had fewer hospitalizations, and experienced a longer period to mood relapse than patients in a case management condition (Miklowitz et al., 2000).

At present, a multisite, randomized, controlled trial of family-focused therapy for adolescents (FFT-A; Miklowitz & George, 2000), a modified version of Miklowitz and Goldstein's (1990) FFT, is under way. We know that familial climate is related to relapse in bipolar adults (Miklowitz, Goldstein, Neuchterlein, Snyder, & Mintz, 1988). Therefore, family-based interventions among the families of bipolar children and adolescents may shed light on the role of family involvement in intervention with a pediatric bipolar population.

Group Psychotherapy

Among adults with bipolar disorder, several different group approaches have been successful. For example, Colom and colleagues (2003) demonstrated increased time to relapse of mood symptoms, as well as lower rates of rehospitalization among remitted bipolar adults attending a psychoeducational group, compared with those receiving standard treatment (medications alone). Another structured group approach, The

Life Goals Program (Bauer, McBride, Chase, Sachs, & Shea, 1998), consists of psychoeducation, behavioral skills, and individually tailored goals; at present, no data are available on outcome.

Psychosocial Treatment of Adolescent Bipolar Disorder

In adapting existing psychosocial treatments used with bipolar adults for children and adolescents, several considerations should be made. For example, modifications should take into account the developmental level of the patient. Thus, information provided within an age-appropriate context may be more understandable and more widely accepted by the patient and family members; this may include the use of age-appropriate language rather than medical terminology. Psychoeducation conducted against the backdrop of a normal developmental trajectory may help distinguish normal childhood tantrums and adolescent moodiness from bipolar disorder. Given the high rate of comorbidity in pediatric bipolar disorder (Papolos & Papolos, 2002), information about comorbidly existing conditions may be included as part of psychoeducation. Comparative risks and benefits of psychotropic medications used with this population should be included, given that medications commonly used for the treatment of pediatric bipolar disorder have been understudied in randomized, controlled trials and are often used off-label (Ryan, 2002). Psychoeducation may focus on the manner in which early-onset bipolar disorder differs from adult bipolar disorder—childhood bipolar disorder often manifests in less discrete episodes and more frequent mood swings (Papolos & Papolos, 1999). Additionally, the manner in which symptoms manifest themselves may need to be considered within a developmental framework, as children exhibit several affective symptoms differently than adults (Geller et al., 2002). Similarly, the literature has indicated that there may be symptoms of bipolar disorder that are unique to this population (e.g., gory dreams; Papolos & Papolos, 1999). Furthermore, age-specific issues may be targeted, including substance use, suicide prevention, family conflict, teasing, and academic concerns, that may not be relevant in an adult population. Finally, because bipolar disorder is highly familial, it is likely that at least one of the parents of a child with pediatric bipolar disorder has either unipolar or bipolar mood disorder (Geller, Fox, & Clark, 1994). The course of a parent's mood disorder is likely to be intimately related to the child's presentation, compliance, and management. Given that parental depression may interfere with a mood-disordered child's response to treatment (Brent et al., 1998), it is particularly important that the parent's own affective illness be addressed when treating a bipolar child or adolescent.

Conclusion

The empirical literature on psychosocial treatment of adult bipolar disorder suggests that several forms of therapy, including CBT, IPT supplemented with SRT, family-based treatments, and group therapy, are useful adjunctive treatments. These treatments have been found to produce better medication compliance, fewer hospitalizations, and improved social and occupational functioning.

PHARMACOTHERAPY FOR BIPOLAR DISORDERS

Pharmacological Treatment for Adult Bipolar Disorder

Mood Stabilizers

Lithium has been shown through placebo-controlled trials to significantly reduce episodes of new manic and/or depressive episodes in adults. However, approximately 42% to 64% of patients do not respond to lithium (Solomon et al., 1995). To obtain maximum benefit and prevention of relapses, it appears that the blood level of lithium needs to be titrated to and maintained at a blood level range of 0.8 to 1.2 mmol/L (Gelenberg et al., 1989). At this higher blood level the patient may experience an increase in side effects, such as tremor, diarrhea, weight gain, increased urinary frequency, and gastrointestinal distress. Long-term treatment with lithium may lead to hypothyroidism, renal compromise, and cardiovascular side effects. Patients who are diagnosed with mixed states, rapid cycling, and mania due to medical disorders may be less responsive to lithium treatment (Bowden et al., 1997).

Divalproex and carbamazepine are anticonvulsants used to treat acute symptoms of bipolar disorder as well as for long-term maintenance treatment. Bowden and colleagues (1994) published a double-blind, randomized, parallel-group trial in which patients hospitalized with acute mania ($N = 179$) were randomly assigned to 3 weeks of treatment with lithium, divalproex, or placebo. Both lithium and divalproex significantly reduced patients' symptoms of mania compared to placebo. Bowden and colleagues (2000) completed a double-blind, randomized maintenance treatment trial of lithium vs. divalproex vs. placebo for patients diagnosed with bipolar I. The study's primary end point was the time to develop any mood episode and there was no difference found between the three groups. However, divalproex was shown to significantly reduce the number of patients who dropped from the study because of relapse and it also showed a significantly improved outcome of secondary mood measurements.

Lamotrigine has been shown to be an effective treatment for bipolar I depression (Hirschfeld et al., 2002) and for long-term treatment of in patients with bipolar II disorder and rapid cycling (Bowden et al., 1999). Treatment with lamotrigine is associated with a 5% incidence of a skin rash. Most of these rashes appear in the first 8 weeks of treatment and resolve with cessation of drug treatment. However, these skin rashes can evolve to a more serious form of a skin reaction such as Stevens-Johnson syndrome (Wong, Kennedy, & Lee, 1999). At this time, there are limited data to support the use of gabapentin or topiramate as mood stabilizers.

Atypical Antipsychotics

Olanzapine is presently the most studied atypical antipsychotic medication for the treatment of bipolar disorder and was approved by the FDA for treatment of acute mania (Tohen et al., 1999). The most concerning side effect with this medication is weight gain. Segal, Berk, and Brook (1998) showed in a randomized study that risperidone, compared to lithium and haloperidol, produces similar improvement in manic symptoms. It has also been shown in combination as an add-on therapy with a mood stabilizer to have superior efficacy to that of monotherapy, as found in a study using quetiapine (Sachs, Grossman, Ghaemi, Okamoto, & Bowden, 2002).

Antidepressants

There are conflicting views on the use of antidepressants for the treatment of bipolar depression. However, there is agreement that antidepressants should only be used in combination with a mood stabilizer for the treatment of bipolar depression (Thase, Bhargave, & Sachs, 2003). For patients who are suffering from a severe depressive episode it is recommended that lithium or lamotrigine be used as first-line therapy. If the patient is nonresponsive, then a combination is recommended, such as the addition of lamotrigine, bupropion, or paroxetine. Another option would be to add an SSRI, venlafaxine, or an MAOI. It appears that SSRIs have a lower risk of inducing mania than that with TCAs (Moller & Nasarallah, 2003). For bipolar depression, there are limited data available that compare the treatment outcome of treating only with a mood stabilizer versus the combination of a mood stabilizer with an antidepressant.

Pharmacological Treatment of Adolescent Bipolar Disorder

Compared with what is known about the pharmacotherapy of bipolar disorder in adults, relatively little is known about the medication management of bipolar disorder in young people. This is unfortunate, as there has been an increased appreciation over the past few years that bipolar disorder is a chronic, debilitating condition when it occurs in children and adolescents. Most prospective pharmacotherapy studies in pediatric bipolar disorder are uncontrolled, focused on the manic phase of the illness, and of brief duration. Therefore, definitive conclusions about the best way of treating mania or depressive symptomatology both acutely and over the long term cannot be made.

Fortunately, there has been a substantial increase in the number of medication studies within this patient population over the past few years. These data can provide practicing clinicians practical information on rational treatment approaches to the pharmacotherapy of this illness.

Monotherapy

Several agents have been examined within the context of acute prospective monotherapy treatment trials (Table 2.4). More research has been done to examine the use of lithium for the treatment of mania than any other compound. Although several open-label studies have been conducted, at present there has only been one published, methodologically rigorous study that has examined the acute efficacy of lithium in the treatment of mania in young people (Kowatch & DelBello, 2003). In that study, 25 adolescents with bipolar-spectrum disorders with secondary substance abuse dependence were randomized to receive either lithium monotherapy or placebo for 6 weeks. The average age of the subjects was 16 years. The authors found that subjects treated with lithium had superior global functioning and fewer positive urine drug assays than those who were treated with placebo (Geller et al., 1998).

A review of the available treatment studies suggest that lithium carbonate may often be useful in ameliorating symptoms of bipolar disorder in young people and is generally well tolerated. The available data also suggest that approximately half of patients treated with this agent will respond to acute treatment with lithium (Chang & Ketter, 2001; Kowatch et al., 2000). The implication of this observation is that a substantial number of patients will not experience a meaningful response to lithium treatment alone. Moreover, many patients treated with lithium monotherapy who benefit from substantial symptom reduction will not experience syn-

Table 2.4 Selected Monotherapy Studies in Treatment of Pediatric Bipolarity

Study	Agent(s) Used	Study Design	Study Length (weeks)	Sample Size	Comments
Geller et al., 1998	Lithium	Double-blind, placebo-controlled	6	25	Lithium superior to placebo
Wagner et al., 2002	Divalproex sodium	Open-label, prospective	8	40	Divalproex effective with 61% response rate
Kowatch et al., 2000	Lithium, carbamazepine, divalproex sodium	Prospective, open-label, random assignment to one of the 3 agents	6	41 (13 to CBZ, 13 to Li, 15 to DVPX)	Overall response rates were as follows: CBZ = 34%, Li = 42%, DVPX = 46%
Frazier et al., 2001	Olanzapine	Open-label, prospective	8	23	Treatment was noted to be effective in 61%. Mean weight gain = 5.0 kg

CBZ, carbamazepine; DVPX, divalproex sodium; Li, lithium.

dromal remission when treated with lithium alone.

At present, there are no published placebo-controlled studies that have examined the efficacy of divalproex sodium (Depakote) in the treatment of pediatric mania. There are several open trials that have examined the acute effectiveness of divalproex sodium (Depakote) in young patients with mania or mixed states. In the largest of these trials, 40 youths between the ages of 7 and 19 who were suffering from either a manic, hypomanic, or mixed episode were treated with open-label divalproex sodium for up to 8 weeks (Wagner, 2002; Wagner et al., 2002). Overall, the authors reported that divalproex sodium was an effective and reasonably well-tolerated intervention in the study subjects. Approximately 60% of the subjects were considered to be treatment responders.

On the basis of results of this trial and other published reports, the available data suggest that, similar to lithium, divalproex sodium may be an effective treatment for young patients with mania and related mood states (Wagner, 2002; Wagner et al., 2002). Like lithium, it appears that a substantial number of youths will not respond to monotherapy and only a small number of patients will experience syndromal remission with divalproex sodium monotherapy.

Carbamazepine has historically been given as a treatment to young people with a variety of

neuropsychiatric conditions. Most reports describing the use of this drug in young people with neuropsychiatric conditions lack methodological rigor. At present, there is only one prospective study that has examined this agent's utility in young people with bipolar disorder. In that trial, Kowatch and colleagues treated 42 youths with an average age of 11 years, 20 of whom met diagnostic symptom criteria for bipolar 1 disorder and 22 of whom met diagnostic symptom criteria for bipolar II disorder (Kowatch et al., 2000). In order to be enrolled in this trial, the subjects had to have moderate symptoms of mania. Upon enrollment, subjects were randomized to open treatment with carbamazepine, divalproex sodium, or lithium. Of the 41 youths who completed at least 1 week of medication therapy, 13 were treated with carbamazepine. Treatment with carbamazepine was associated with an effect size of 1.00 with an overall response rate of 34 percent. Although these numbers were more modest than those seen with lithium or divalproex sodium, no statistically significant differences in effectiveness were noted between the three different study drugs.

At present there is one prospective open-label trial that has examined the use of olanzapine in youths suffering from a manic, mixed, or hypomanic episode (Frazier et al., 2001). In that trial, the 23 patients (mean age, 10.3 years) were treated with olanzapine in doses that could range between 2.5 and 20 mg/day. The authors noted that treatment was associated with reductions in symptoms of mania and that the agent was generally well tolerated, with the most common reported adverse events being increased appetite and sedation. The average weight gain over the course of the study was 5 kg.

There are several other agents that have been noted to have possible roles in the treatment of bipolar disorder in adults. These include lamotrigine, gabapentin, omega-3 fatty acids, verapamil, and topiramate. At present, none of these agents have been examined in a methodologically sound prospective treatment study in pediatric patients with bipolar disorder. Therefore, definitive statements about these agents' possible utility cannot be made.

Psychopharmacological Combinations

Since a substantial number of patients do not appear to derive optimal clinical response from acute treatment with a single drug, investigators have begun to explore whether treatment with more than one agent may be useful in the acute therapy of young people who present with symptoms of mania. The majority of these studies have explored treatment with an atypical antipsychotic combined with a traditional mood stabilizer.

In a retrospective chart review, Kowatch and colleagues (1995) described five youths with bipolar disorder and mixed presentations between the ages of 8 and 15 years who were treated with clozapine. In four of these five cases, clozapine was an adjunct to other psychotropic agents (most commonly lithium). At clozapine doses ranging from 75 to 150 mg/day, the authors noted that all five patients had a "marked" response to clozapine. The authors also observed that clozapine therapy was generally well tolerated. The authors concluded that clozapine might be an effective treatment for treatment-refractory patients.

The response of 35 adolescent inpatients treated predominantly with lithium plus haloperidol or lithium plus risperidone for up to 4 consecutive weeks has been described (Kafantaris, Coletti, Dicker, Padula, & Kane, 2001).

These youths, who were between the ages of 12 and 18, had prominent symptoms of psychosis as well as moderate symptoms of mania at the time of treatment initiation. At the end of the trial, almost all of the subjects had their psychotic symptoms fully resolved, with most subjects experiencing significant amelioration of mood symptoms. The authors then took some of the subjects who responded to combination treatment and discontinued their antipsychotic. The authors found that most patients experienced clinical deterioration during lithium monotherapy. This response suggests that they would have benefited from continued combination treatment.

In a chart review study, Frazier and colleagues (1999) examined the use of risperidone in a group of 28 young people with bipolar-spectrum disorders. All but one patient was being treated with one or more concomitant medications during risperidone administration. These concomitant agents most commonly included mood stabilizers and ADHD medications (stimulants and α_2-agonists). At an average total daily dose of 1.7 mg, the authors noted that risperidone appeared to be effective in symptom reduction and that the risperidone appeared to be generally well tolerated.

There is one published study that has rigorously examined quetiapine treatment as an adjunct in young people ages 12 to 18 suffering from bipolar I disorder (DelBello, Schwiers, Rosenberg, & Strakowski, 2002). In that 6-week trial, 30 hospitalized adolescents with mania or mixed presentations were treated with divalproex sodium at an initial dose of 20 mg/kg/day. Half of the subjects were randomized to receive adjunctive quetiapine and half were randomized to receive adjunctive placebo. The quetiapine was titrated to a total daily dose of 450 mg. Results from this trial noted greater reductions in manic symptomatology in the cohort of youths randomized to receive combination therapy. However, sedation was also more common in these youths.

The largest prospective trial that has examined combination pharmacotherapy in pediatric bipolar disorder described the response of 90 outpatients with a mean age of about 11 years who were treated with combination lithium and divalproex sodium therapy for up to 20 weeks (Findling et al., 2003). In that trial, the authors observed that the response rates were larger than those seen in other prospective trials in this patient population. The authors also found that response rates were higher than those described in adults using a similar combination treatment paradigm. In addition, it was noted that combination treatment was well tolerated. Of particular interest was the observation that residual depressive symptomatology was not manifest after combination lithium plus divalproex treatment in this patient population. This is in direct contrast to adults, in whom depression was often seen as a problematic residual mood state.

Conclusion

On the basis of available evidence, it appears that combination pharmacotherapy with more than one mood stabilizing agent may be a rational approach for some youth who have manic, hypomanic, or mixed states. Whether treatment should begin with drug monotherapy or combination pharmacotherapy should be a topic of further study.

Maintenance Trials

At present, there are no published prospective trials that have examined the maintenance pharmacotherapy of pediatric bipolar disorder. The first data to suggest that lithium maintenance therapy might be useful in the treatment of adolescents with bipolar disorder were published in 1990. That report described the results of a naturalistic, prospective, 18-month follow-up study of 37 youth with bipolar I disorder who had responded to lithium treatment (Strober, Morrell, Lampert, & Burroughs, 1990). In that trial, the authors found that in the 13 youth who discontinued lithium maintenance therapy, the relapse rate was 2.5 times greater than that in those who continued lithium treatment. Despite methodological limitations inherent in this study design, these data suggest that maintenance lithium treatment in young people who respond to administration of this compound may be beneficial.

There is one unpublished prospective trial of maintenance pharmacotherapy in pediatric bipolarity. In that trial, 60 youths who had responded to acute treatment with combination therapy using both lithium and divalproex sodium were randomized to receive monotherapy treatment with either lithium or divalproex for up to 76 weeks in a double-blind fashion (Findling, Gracious, McNamara, & Calabrese, 2000). The authors found that the overall median survival time in the study was approximately 100 days. It was also noted that lithium and divalproex sodium had similar effectiveness as monotherapy.

Conclusions

There are only limited data from methodologically rigorous trials in pediatric bipolarity. Evidence, predominantly from open-label trials, suggests that monotherapy with lithium, carbamazepine, divalproex sodium, and olanzapine may be useful in the treatment of young patients with mania and related mood states. A consistent theme from the extant literature is that a substantial number of patients do not respond to monotherapy with these agents. For this reason, investigators have begun to explore combination pharmacotherapy. It seems that simultaneous treatment with more than one agent may be a rational form of intervention for some patients. What has yet to be identified are those circumstances in which combination drug therapy might be most rationally employed. Because pediatric bipolarity is a chronic condition, it appears that young people suffering from this illness will need long-term treatment. Although maintenance pharmacotherapy data are lacking, patients who respond to a given acute pharmacotherapy regimen may continue to benefit from ongoing treatment with the drug(s) that led to successful symptom amelioration.

In summary, pediatric bipolarity is a chronic condition associated with substantial dysfunction and human suffering. There is a paucity of methodologically sound pharmacological treatment studies, thus more research on this topic is sorely needed.

Prevention of Depression and Bipolar Disorder

The prevention of an individual's first episode of depression is worthy of greater study among investigators concerned with mood disorders. Not only is the first episode devastating for individuals and those around them but it is a major burden within our health system and society (Murray & Lopez, 1997). Once the first episode of major depressive disorder (MDD) occurs, the sequelae are substantial. Following an episode of MDD, the probability of subsequent episodes is significantly increased, even to the point that many now consider MDD to be a chronic disease. As noted in Chapter 1, the sequelae to MDD are numerous and include poorer social relationships, increased substance abuse, increased use of medical services, interference with long-term cognitive functioning, significant comorbidity with major health problems, and younger ages of death (even when deaths by suicide are taken into account). Most investigators of mood disorders believe that the first episode lays down neural pathways that are difficult to overcome and, without modification via medications or psychosocial interventions or their combination, are likely to be lasting pathways that impact individuals' lives.

Even though prevention of MDD is an important topic, empirical work in this area is difficult and has been slow to progress. Some recent work has been conducted on the prevention of second and subsequent episodes (Craighead, Hart, Craighead, & Ilardi, 2002), but the work designed to prevent the first episode of MDD has been meager. Before addressing the empirical work on prevention of MDD, it is important to note again the conceptual and historical context in which general prevention research has been defined.

HISTORICAL CONTEXT AND DEFINITIONS

A Brief History of Prevention in Mental Health

During the last decade, three reports have established a historical context and defined the mental health prevention classification system:

1. *Reducing Risk for Mental Disorders: Frontiers for Prevention Intervention Research*, Institute of Medicine (1994)

2. *Priorities for Prevention Research at NIMH: A Report by the National Advisory Mental Health Council Workgroup on Mental Disorders Prevention Research*, National Institutes of Health, National Institute of Mental Health (1998)

3. *Mental Health: A Report of the Surgeon General*, U.S. Department of Health and Human Services (US-DHHS), Substance Abuse and Mental Health Services Administration, Center for Mental Health Services, National Institutes of Health, National Institute of Mental Health (1999)

In 1998, the National Institute of Mental Health (NIMH) established an ad hoc committee to review the progress of mental health prevention research. The committee's report, *Priorities For Prevention Research at NIMH: A Report by the National Advisory Mental Health Council Workgroup on Mental Disorders Prevention Research*, traced the history of prevention in mental health and proposed the following generational taxonomy:

The first generation of efforts to prevent mental disorder began in the 1930s when, as an outgrowth of the turn-of-the-century mental hygiene movement, the focus gradually expanded beyond ameliorating the plight of those in asylums to include the prevention of many forms of social and emotional maladjustment. The new goal was to assure the well-being and "positive mental health" of the general population through primary-prevention interventions aimed at creating health-promoting environments for all. These efforts were based on humanitarian concern, but had few, if any, research underpinnings.

The second generation of interventions to prevent mental disorder, which began in the late 1960s, reflected the impact of a growing health and mental health research knowledge base. Some scientists retained their broad-based emphasis on primary prevention, while others began to target specific "at-risk" groups for study and intervention. During the 1960s there had been a burgeoning of research on the causes, mechanisms, and effects of stress on bodily and mental functioning. "At-risk" persons were defined as those who would predictably experience periods of substantial life stress, such as domestic violence, divorce, bereavement, or unemployment as precursors of mental distress or disorder. Changing behavior for health also became an active area of study and prevention during the same period. Those studies placed a strong emphasis on preventing lung cancer and heart disease through programs to prevent or reduce smoking, obesity, high cholesterol intake, and sedentary life styles.

NIMH, 1998

This NIMH committee observed that over the next decade mental health prevention interventions continued to proliferate. After reviewing progress in this field, however, the 1978 President's Commission on Mental Health determined that previous investigation had been "unfocused and uncoordinated." As a remedy the commission recommended the establishment of a Center for Prevention at NIMH to coordinate and enhance research in mental health primary prevention research. The NIMH report determined that "during the last 20 years The NIMH Center for Prevention Research and its programmatic successors have stimulated considerable progress in building the scientific foundation of an interdisciplinary field of prevention research in areas of epidemiology, human development, and intervention research methodology" (NIMH, 1998). The committee concluded that sufficient progress had been made in establishing the scientific basis for mental health prevention science to declare that we were then in a third generation of prevention activity. Thus, prevention research could build on prior accomplishments of prior preventive interventions and integrate these with advances in the biomedical, behavioral, and cognitive sciences.

Despite the described significance and need for prevention research and this sanguine view of the 1998 NIMH committee, the amount of work studying the prevention of an initial episode of depression has remained meager. In contrast, considerable progress has been made in the development of a nomenclature for prevention research. In order for the field to progress, it was

necessary to develop a clear terminology for investigators to follow.

Early Classification Systems

The Commission on Chronic Illness (1957) developed the original public health classification system of disease prevention. Three types of preventive interventions were identified: primary, secondary, and tertiary. During the last 40 years the definitions of these types of prevention have expanded to include an array of nuanced but related meanings.

Gordon's Definitions

In 1983 and in 1987, Robert Gordon proposed an alternative classification of prevention that was based on the empirical relationships found in practically oriented disease prevention and health promotion programs. These included programs which he labeled universal, selective, and indicated prevention.

Although Gordon's classification system was to be distinct from that of the Commission on Chronic Health, the use of these two classification systems slowly deteriorated into a confusing, merging and mixing of definitions, e.g., "universal primary prevention." This confusion was particularly problematic when this terminology was applied to the classification of the prevention of psychiatric disorders, because the classical public health prevention classification system and Gordon's reclassification were both designed for use in the description of the prevention of biological disorders, not of interventions to prevent psychiatric and psychological disorders. The 1994 Institute of Medicine (IOM) report, *Reducing Risk for Mental Disorders: Frontiers for Prevention Intervention Research*, presented a cogent discussion of the inherent pitfalls in applying general prevention classifications to problems in mental health:

> One of the main problems has been the notion of "caseness" that is used in public health. It is often more difficult to document that a "case" of mental disorder exists than it is to document a physical health problem. Agreement regarding the occurrence of a

case of mental disorder varies with time and with the instruments and diagnostic systems employed and with the theoretical perspective of the evaluators. Also symptoms and dysfunctions may exist even though criteria for a DSM-III-R diagnosis are not present. Finally, the outcomes in very young children (birth to age 5) are often not diagnosable as "psychiatric caseness" but rather as impairments in cognition and psychosocial development.

IOM, 1994

Recent Attempts to Define Prevention

The IOM report chose to resolve the confusion in terminology by using the term *prevention* to refer only to interventions that occur before the initial onset of a disorder. In this system, prevention included all three elements of Gordon's system (1983, 1987). Efforts to identify cases and provide care for known disorders were called *treatment*, and efforts to provide rehabilitation and reduce relapse and reoccurrence of a disorder were called *maintenance/interventions*. Further distinctions were made within the prevention category. We have employed these definitions throughout this chapter. The definitions are described in the following paragraphs.

Universal mental health prevention interventions are defined as efforts that are beneficial to a whole population or group. They are targeted to the general public or a whole population group that has not been designated or identified as being at risk for the disorder being prevented. The goal at this level of prevention is the reduction of the occurrence of new cases of the disorder.

Selective mental health prevention interventions are defined as those efforts that target individuals or a subgroup of the population whose risk for developing the mental health disorder is significantly higher than average. The risk may be immediate or lifelong. Biological, psychological, or social risk factors associated with or related to the specific mental health disorder are used to identify the individual or group level of risk. Those with the identified risk factors are referred to as those "at risk."

Indicated prevention interventions are defined as

those efforts that target high-risk individuals who are identified as having minimal but detectable signs or symptoms that predict the mental disorder or biological markers indicating predisposition to the disorder. For example, individuals who have some symptoms of MDD but do not yet meet criteria for the disorder would fall into this group. Indicated prevention excludes individuals whose signs and symptoms meet diagnostic criteria for the disorder.

The IOM identified three aims or desired outcomes for mental health prevention: *(1)* reduction in the number of new cases of the disorder; *(2)* delay in the onset of illness; and *(3)* reduction in the length of time the early symptoms continue as well as halting the progression of severity so that individuals ultimately do not meet diagnostic criteria. The 1999 *Mental Health: A Report of the Surgeon General* agreed with the IOM and defined prevention as the "prevention of the initial onset of a mental disorder or emotional or behavioral problem, including prevention of comorbidity" (US-DHHS, 1999). In addition, the report defined other terms that were often imprecisely used in discussions of prevention. They are listed below:

- *First (initial) onset*: the initial point in time when an individual's mental health problems meet the full criteria for a diagnosis of a mental disorder
- *Risk factors*: "characteristics, variables, or hazards that, if present for a given individual, make it more likely that this individual, compared to someone selected at random from the general population, will develop a disorder" (US-DHHS, 1999). Although risk factors precede the first onset of a disorder, they may change in response to the disorder, development, or stressors.
- *Protective factors*: Factors that "improve a person's response to some environmental hazard resulting in an 'adaptive outcome.' These factors can be found within the individual or within the family or community. They do not necessarily cause normal development in the absence of risk factors, but they may make an appreciable difference in the influence exerted by risk factors" (US-DHHS, 1999).

- *Risk of onset vs. risk of relapse*: The terminologies that refer to the risk of the development of a disorder are often used without specification of the risk of onset vs. the risk of relapse. This is a key distinction because "the risks for onset of a disorder are likely to be somewhat different from the risks involved in relapse of a previously diagnosed condition" (US-DHHS, 1999). Undoubtedly, this same distinction is true for factors that protect against onset or relapse. As will be noted later, not all "prevention" projects have made this distinction between initial and second or subsequent episodes of MDD.

Goals of Prevention Programs

In addition to the IOM's goals of reducing the number of new cases and delaying the onset of MDD and the insidious nature of the onset and course of MDD, there are other ancillary and associated goals of prevention programs. For example, prevention of initial MDD is likely to have an impact on school and work performance, social skills, and quality of life, reduce the need of medical services, and reduce MDD-related substance abuse disorders. In the long run, prevention programs may actually extend the lives of individuals who were at risk but did not develop the disorder, by reducing both the risk of suicide completion and the behavioral and biological sequalae of the disorder.

Another goal of prevention programs is to teach resiliency to the program participants. Individuals at risk for MDD are likely to experience negative and traumatic events, as are other individuals in our society. Prevention programs have a goal of teaching at-risk individuals to become more resilient—to develop skills and abilities to spring back from or adapt to adversity.

A further goal of prevention programs is to enhance and enrich the positive aspects of living. By changing cognitive patterns, enhancing social skills, and increasing resiliency, individuals who otherwise might live a marginally happy life may have the opportunity to develop greater self-esteem and self-efficacy and live a more successful and adaptive life. This positive adaption in life may lead to the development of more adaptive neurological pathways. Emotional intelligence (Goleman, 1995) may also be enhanced by successful preventive programs.

The societal goals of depression prevention programs are also numerous. For example, even a modest reduction in new cases of MDD would reduce the economic burden of the disorder. The disorder itself would not have to be treated so frequently, nor would the associated (sometimes self-treatment) problems of alcohol, tobacco, and other forms of substance abuse. Each prevented case of MDD would increase the limited resources available to other health initiatives. Productivity would be increased in the workplace. Thus, the call for effective programs to prevent the first episode of MDD is a forceful and significant one—significant for individuals, families, and society as a whole.

RISK FACTORS FOR MAJOR DEPRESSION

To develop programs for individuals "at risk" for MDD, it is necessary to develop knowledge and understanding of factors and their interactions that render one likely to develop MDD. Chapter 1 provided evidence for many of the risk factors for MDD, so the details will not be reiterated here. These risk factors include dysfunctional parenting and family interactions; gender; personality and temperament; cognitive vulnerabilities; internal and external stress, including negative life events; and poor interpersonal relationships.

In addition to the preceding risk factors, the following risk factors that have implications for prevention of MDD are important and worthy of further detailed review. These include subsyndromal depression, poverty, violence, and cultural factors.

Subsyndromal Depression

Among adults, subsyndromal depression (two or more symptoms for 2 weeks or longer) appears to cause as much health impairment and economic burden as MDD, and these individuals are at increased risk for developing subsequent MDD (Fava, 1999; Johnson, Weissman, & Klerman,

1992; Judd, Akiskal, & Paulus, 1997). In a longitudinal study, subsyndromal depression among adolescents predicted poorer functioning as these individuals became adults (Devine, Kempton, & Forehand, 1994). Subsyndromal depressive symptoms among adolescents predicted MDD later on in adolescence and young adulthood (Pine, Cohen, & Brook, 1999; Rao et al., 1995; Weissman, Warner, Wickramaratne, Moreau, & Olfson, 1997). Lewinsohn, Solomon, Seeley, and Zeiss (2000) found that increasing levels of depressive symptoms among a large sample of nondepressed adolescents (average age of 16½) predicted increased levels of social dysfunction and incidence of MDD, as well as increased substance abuse at age 24. These data indicate that subsyndromal depression renders adolescents at risk for a first episode of MDD, and they are prime candidates for depression prevention programs.

Poverty

Poverty has been linked with an early onset of depression. It is not clear whether this represents an independent risk factor or can be grouped among the more general examples of diversity that are associated with depression. Results from epidemiological studies have linked lower socioeconomic status with depression and a multitude of other mental health problems (Robins, Locke, & Reiger, 1991). This vulnerability is particularly strong for families living at poverty levels (Bruce, Takeuchi, & Leaf, 1991). This relationship may be explained in part by a phenomenon of selection, whereby those with mental health problems are more inclined to drift toward economic disadvantage and remain there (Dohrenwend et al., 1992). Longitudinal data have also demonstrated that socioeconomic disadvantage is largely a cause of higher vulnerability to psychiatric disorder, particularly for depression (Dohrenwend et al., 1992; Gilman, Kawachi, Fitzmaurice, & Buka, 2002; Johnson, Cohen, Dohrenwend, Link, & Brook, 1999). In a study of over 4,000 Australian families, poverty caused a small but significant increase in risk when other sociological variables were controlled (Spence, Najman, Bar, O'Callaghan, & Williams,

2002); this effect was more pronounced in girls than in boys.

If we consider poverty as a generator for a variety of stressors, the possible mechanisms driving poverty-induced vulnerability appear boundless. A number of mediators between socioeconomic disadvantage and depression have been studied empirically. These include external mediators such as access to health care, quality of social networks and resources, quality of parenting and parent availability, and, of course, level of exposure to violence. Children of families who are of lower socioeconomic status are most likely to witness violence and to be the victims of abuse (Buka, Stichik, Birdthistle, & Earls, 2001; Sedlak & Broadhurst, 1996).

Internal individual mediators include self-esteem, health-risk behaviors, cognitive deficits, interpersonal skills, and academic achievement. Several comprehensive reviews on the consequences of poverty and mediating factors demonstrate the vast amount of knowledge we have accumulated on the relation between poverty and depression (Aber, Bennett, Conley, & Li, 1997; Leventhal & Brooks-Gunn, 2000; Turner & Lloyd, 1999). This literature highlights the importance of two larger factors: (*a*) the need for universal health care with parity for mental illness and physical illness and parity for services for adults and children; and (*b*) the need to address large-scale public health risk factors that have a strong effect on the occurrence of adolescent depression (i.e., exposure to violence).

Violence

Exposure to violence during childhood is a potent risk factor for future psychological and psychiatric disorders (Kilpatrick et al., 2003; MacMillan et al., 2001) as well as physical health-risk behaviors (Felitti et al., 1998), in both the short and long term. The violence to which children are exposed has many forms. This includes being a victim of sexual or physical abuse as well as witnessing violence in the home (Kilpatrick et al., 2003). A large number of children also frequently witness violence in the community (Buka et al., 2001). Children who are exposed to violence are most often exposed to more than one type, and evidence suggests that the amount of violence-related adversities a child encounters has a substantial impact on the severity of the outcome (Felitti et al., 1998). The most disturbing illustration of this accumulation phenomenon is the gradation effect of violence-related adversities on risk for suicide attempt. Results from the Adverse Childhood Experiences Study demonstrated that for every additional adversity experienced as a child, the risk of suicide attempts increased from 2- to 5-fold, such that children or adolescents who encounter seven or more adversities are 50 times as likely to attempt suicide as those without violence exposure (Dube et al., 2001).

Although the mental health consequences of violence exposure are diverse, the most prevalent and commonly studied are posttraumatic stress disorder (PTSD) and major depression. This makes sense, particularly if violence exposure is viewed as a form of trauma. The consequences of our country's recent dealings with terrorism have provided an especially graphic picture of how violence-related trauma is linked to PTSD and depression (North et al., 1999; Schlenger et al., 2002). Survivors of the Oklahoma City bombing, for instance, were studied by North and colleagues (1999) about 6 months after the disaster. Of these individuals, 45% had some form of post-disaster psychiatric disorder (34.3% had PTSD, and 22.5% had MDD). Psychiatric comorbidity predicted functional impairment and treatment. Fifty-six percent of depressed subjects had never been depressed before the incident.

Violence-related trauma experienced during childhood can have particularly devastating effects, because the trauma is inflicted during a critical period of development. Neurobiological and neuroendocrine studies of depressed women, which look at the volume of certain brain regions and at hormonal stress-response mechanisms, provide evidence that violence-related trauma experienced during childhood can have profound and lasting effects on brain structure and function (Heim, Newport, Bonsall, Miller, & Nemeroff, 2001; Vythilingam et al., 2002). These alterations, in turn, increase vulnerability to stress-related disorders like depression.

Depression that is comorbid with PTSD or other disorders, as well as depression that has an established neurobiological etiology like that experienced by childhood victims of trauma, are forms of the disorder that are particularly resistant to treatment and are associated with increased levels of impairment (Mervaala et al., 2000; Petersen et al., 2001). Thus, it is essential that prevention strategies attend to violence exposure.

Cultural Factors

The role of ethnocultural factors has been understudied. Some ethnic groups appear to have higher rates of adolescent depression than others. For example, Mexican Americans and African-American adolescents appear to have higher risk for depression whereas American adolescents of Chinese descent may be at lesser risk (Barrera & Craighead, 2004; Roberts, Roberts, & Chen, 1997). It appears that some groups (such as African-American or Hispanic adolescents) may not show the gender disparity following puberty that is seen among Caucasian adolescents (Hayward, Gotlib, & Schraedley, 1999).

PREVENTION PROGRAMS FOR ADOLESCENTS

During the past decade, a number of promising strategies for the prevention of childhood depression have emerged. The overarching principles of these programs are similar, and the specifics of preventive interventions for children and adolescents have taken into account the development level of the participants. The evaluated preventive strategies are based primarily on cognitive behavioral and family-educational approaches that seek to reduce risk factors and enhance protective and resiliency factors associated with depression in youth.

In general, progress in the field of prevention science has been made through the introduction of rigorous standards for the development and evaluation of manualized preventive strategies that are based on well-established theoretical frameworks and proceed through a series of orderly stages. This is best described in the 1994

IOM's *Report on the Prevention of Mental Disorder.* The IOM suggested that prevention development and evaluation proceed through five stages. The first and second stages are identifying risk factors and describing the relative contributions of different factors to the disorder. The third stage is applying strategies developed in pilot studies and completing efficacy trials to evaluate the overall effectiveness of these approaches. The fourth stage, carrying out effectiveness trials, involves the examination of such strategies in multiple sites in large-scale investigations under nonideal, real-world conditions. The final stage consists of implementing such strategies in large-scale public health campaigns. Following this sequence and the articulation of a set of rigorous empirical standards by which to test preventive intervention approaches, a number of important strategies for prevention of depression have emerged. These have begun to be tested in randomized trial designs according to the recommended guidelines.

Consideration of the prevention of depression also must take place in the context of the remarkable progress in developmental neuroscience, the sequencing of a human genome, and in psychiatric epidemiology. As these important scientific advances unfold, they will offer important opportunities for future prevention programs. These findings will need to be integrated with adolescents' developmental, social, cultural, and family contexts in the development of preventive interventions.

To date, there have been two major conceptual frameworks that have guided most of the development of the prevention studies. First, cognitive behavioral programs have been used and show considerable promise—e.g., those of Seligman and Clarke in the United States, programs of Shochet and Spence in Australia, and the program of Arnarson and Craighead in Iceland. In addition, Beardslee and colleagues have developed and evaluated a program designed to prevent depression in the family context. All of these programs have in common a strong theoretical orientation—an orientation toward building of strengths and resiliency; they have all been written into manuals for dissemination; and they have been or are being tested with randomized trials designs.

Penn Prevention Program

In the Penn Prevention Program, Seligman and colleagues (Gillham & Reivich, 1999; Gillham, Reivich, Jaycox, & Seligman, 1995; Jaycox, Reivich, Gillham, & Seligman, 1994) developed and evaluated a school-based "indicated" prevention program targeting 10- to 13-year-old children in school districts in the Philadelphia suburbs. The youth were defined as at risk for depression on the basis of elevated self-reported depressive symptomatology, self-reported parental conflict, or both. This prevention program was based on a model of explanatory style introduced by Seligman and colleagues (Nolen-Hoeksema, Girgus, & Seligman, 1992) and on research identifying core cognitive deficits associated with youth depression, including negative self-evaluation, dysfunctional attitudes, poor interpersonal problem solving, and low expectations for self-performance (Garber, Weis, & Shanley, 1993; Kaslow, Rehm, & Siegel, 1984; Quiggle, Garber, Panak, & Dodge, 1992). Participants recruited for the treatment group were assigned to one of three treatment programs: a cognitive training program, a social problem-solving program, or a combined program. Eighty-eight students, whose scores were matched to prevention participants, were recruited from nearby schools and comprised the no-participation control group. Assessments included child self-report, teacher-report, and parent-report questionnaires.

Results indicated that relative to control participants, children who participated in any of the treatment groups reported significantly fewer depressive symptoms immediately following the program and at the 6-month and 2-year follow-ups, but not at the 12-month and 3-year follow-ups. Moreover, teacher reports at follow-up revealed better classroom behavior in treatment participants than in control participants. Finally, overall treatment effects were more significant for children who, at the screening phase of the study, reported more significant depressive symptomatology and more significant parental conflict at home. The major limitations of the study are the lack of randomization to intervention conditions, the use of only self-report measures, attrition of approximately 30% of participants during follow-up, and the failure to include diagnoses for clinical depression.

More recently, Seligman and his group at Penn have focused on "positive psychology" programs, which are likely to have an indirect effect of preventing episodes of MDD. These programs are included in Part VII of this book.

Clarke and Colleagues

Clarke and colleagues (Clarke et al., 1995) in Oregon were among the first to study prevention of MDD among adolescents. In an excellent study, 150 adolescent students from 9th and 10th grades were assigned randomly to either a "prevention" or "usual-care" group. The prevention program, entitled "Adolescent Coping with Stress Course" was delivered in groups and was a prevention-focused version of this group's "Adolescent Coping with Depression Course" (Clarke, Lewinsohn, & Hops, 1990). The 5-week intervention was conducted within the adolescents' school setting and comprised fifteen 45-minute group sessions (3 after-school meetings per week). The usual-care youngsters were free to continue with preexisting treatment or seek new treatment. This program employed both behavioral and cognitive coping techniques designed to reduce vulnerability to future depressive episodes.

Participants were followed for 1 year, and the results were positive. Namely, significantly ($p <$ .05) fewer prevention group (14.5%; 8 of 55) subjects were diagnosed with MDD or dysthymia than control group subjects (25.7%; 18 of 70). The major strengths of this program include random assignment of subjects, adequate sample sizes, diagnoses of clinical mood disorders, and encouraging outcomes. It is important to note, however, that approximately 36% of their participants had suffered a prior episode of MDD. Because 30% to 50% of adolescents who have had a prior episode can be expected to have a relapse or recurrence of the disorder during the time (18 months) of this study (Hart, Craighead, & Craighead, 2001; Lewinsohn, Rohde, Seeley, & Fischer, 1993; Rao et al., 1995), it very well may be that Clarke and colleagues actually had their

biggest impact on preventing relapse or recurrence rather than on preventing a first episode of MDD. In addition, it should be noted that there was differential dropout between conditions in this study (Clarke et al., 1995), but as the authors suggested, this probably operated against their favorable outcomes.

In an expansion of this program, Clarke and associates (2001) applied this approach to a health maintenance organization (HMO) population of adolescents of parents with diagnosed depression and youngsters already manifesting symptoms. They screened all those at risk and divided them into three groups: low or no depressive symptomatology, medium symptomatology, and those already in episode. Those already meeting criteria for MDD were referred for treatment, and those with no depressive symptomatology were excluded. In this trial, those adolescents (ages 13–18) with moderate symptomatology were randomized into a usual-care condition ($N = 49$) or their cognitive behavioral intervention group ($N = 45$). As in their previous study, prevention group subjects participated in 15 group sessions.

This intervention yielded substantial preventive effects, with significant treatment-by-time effects in the expected direction on the Center for Epidemiological Studies–Depression (CES-D) and the Global Assessment of Functioning scales—i.e., adolescents in the prevention condition did much better than those in the usual-care condition. Survival analysis indicated that over a 15-month follow-up period, there was a cumulative rate of major depression of only 9% in the experimental group in contrast to 28% in the usual-care condition (Clarke et al., 2001). Even though this is the most sophisticated prevention study to date, its specific implications for prevention are limited by the choice to include adolescents who had previously suffered from an episode of depression; these subjects comprised 67% of the adolescents in this study. Thus, as with the prior study, it is impossible to determine if the study prevented first episodes or relapse and recurrence of prior episodes of MDD. Currently, Clarke, Garber, Beardslee, and Brent are conducting a four-site effectiveness study of this preventive intervention.

Programs in Australia

Two prevention programs in Australia have recently been described and evaluated: one by Shochet and colleagues, and the other by Spence and associates. Shochet and colleagues (2001) evaluated a "universal" prevention program applied in a school setting in Australia. This was a skills-based program of 11 sessions offered by a psychologist and based on a downward extension of principles of cognitive behavior therapy (CBT) and interpersonal therapy (IPT). The student sessions could be supplemented with three parental sessions, but not many parents took advantage of this offer. There were 240, 12- to 15-year-old subjects, who were assigned to assessment-only control, prevention without parental sessions, or prevention with parental sessions.

Students who completed either prevention program (no differences were obtained between the two prevention groups) showed fewer depressive symptoms on one measure of depression (but not another) than controls. The prevention program subjects also reported less hopelessness at the end of the project. All of these effects were maintained at a 10-month follow-up. The limitations of this program include the lack of random assignment of subjects (controls participated in one academic year, and intervention subjects in the next academic year), a small sample size, and assessments conducted at different times of the year in different conditions. The findings, though limited, were encouraging for such a short program and short follow-up period.

A very sophisticated study evaluated the long-term impact of a universal, teacher-implemented, and school-based prevention program that was developed by Spence, Sheffield, and Donovan (2003) in Australia. The program, Problem Solving for LIFE (PSFL), is a combination of cognitive restructuring and problem-solving approaches, and it is designed to prevent a first episode of depression. Subjects were 1,500 eighth-grade (ages 12–14; mean = 12.9) students attending 16 participating high schools in the Brisbane region of Queensland, Australia. The eight 1-hour classroom-session program was implemented by 28 teachers in eight randomly as-

signed schools ($N = 751$), while the control subjects ($N = 749$) attended the other eight schools. There were approximately equal numbers of girls and boys.

Appropriate data analyses indicated that the program significantly decreased depressive symptoms between the beginning and end of the program. This finding, however, was only true for those adolescents who had elevated ("high risk," defined as 13 or higher on the Beck Depression Inventory) depression scores at the beginning of the study. Unfortunately, this difference was not maintained at a 12-month follow-up.

These two well-conducted studies are not particularly encouraging for the effectiveness of "universal" prevention programs for MDD. There are some hints, however, that similar studies conducted with at risk samples (i.e., selected or indicated prevention programs) might be more effective. For example, in the Spence study (replicating the Penn Study) it appears that students with greater depressive symptomatology (but not MDD) may respond better to prevention programs.

Arnarson and Craighead (Iceland)

Because of the stable population of Iceland and because most of the citizens live in one city, Reykjavik, Arnarson and Craighead have spent the past several years translating and standardizing the assessment instruments and developing a manualized, developmentally based, behavioral and cognitive program designed to prevent depression. It has been labeled the "Thoughts and Health" program, and it includes a student workbook as well as a program manual. The program consists of 15 group sessions (6–8 students per group) that are delivered in the school setting by the local school psychologists.

In their most recent report of this work (Arnarson & Craighead, 2004), they had studied 72 students at risk for MDD. *At risk* was defined as scoring above 13 on the Children's Depression Inventory *or* at the 75th percentile or higher on the negative composite of the Children's Attributional Style (CAS) Questionnaire (see Alloy et al., 2000). Thirty-two of the subjects from five schools were randomly assigned (within their respective schools) to the prevention program, and 40 subjects were randomly assigned (within their respective schools) to an assessment-only control condition. All at risk subjects were interviewed with the Children's Assessment Scale, and any subjects who were currently depressed or had suffered a previous depressive episode were excluded (currently depressed subjects were referred for treatment), as were subjects with attention deficit hyperactivity disorder or conduct disorder.

At the end of the intervention, there were no differences between the two groups on depressive symptoms or attributional style. However, at the 6-month follow-up interview (CAS interview), 18% of the assessment-only control subjects had developed MDD or dysthymia, whereas only one (3%) of the prevention program subjects had developed either disorder. Arnarson and Craighead are currently evaluating their prevention program with 96 at-risk (as previously defined) students in six schools in Iceland. They are also developing a similar program for use with 16- to 18-year-old students in a commercial or trade school setting.

Beardslee and Associates

Beardslee and associates, following the IOM stages, first studied risk and resilience, then developed pilot interventions and conducted a large efficacy trial, and are now exploring the effectiveness phase. Their prevention programs were designed to be public health interventions and useful to all families in which a parent is depressed. The programs are to be used by a range of health practitioners, including internists, pediatricians, school counselors, and nurses, as well as by mental health practitioners such as child psychiatrists, child psychologists, and family therapists. Moreover, this approach includes a strong emphasis on treatment, given that so much depression is undiagnosed and untreated.

A variety of studies from different theoretical points of view have in common the finding that children of depressed parents are at risk for depression and other conditions. Rates of depression are two to four times higher in children of depressed parents than those for children of parents with no illness (Beardslee, Versage, & Gladstone, 1998). To understand the transmission of depression, it is important to recognize that in many instances, depression in parents serves as an identifier of a constellation of risk factors that, taken together, cause poor outcomes. In Rutter's classic epidemiologic studies, six factors were identified, including maternal psychiatric disorder. When only one was present, there was no increased risk to the child, but when two or more risk factors were present, the risk went up dramatically. In a random HMO sample over a 4-year period, Beardslee and associates (1996) demonstrated that the same principles were evident in predicting who became depressed. They devised an adversity index consisting of parental major depression, parental nonaffective illness, and a prior history of disorder in the child. When no risk factors were present, less than 10% of the children became ill. When all three were present, 50% of the children became ill, with a gradation in between.

In studying resilience, Beardslee and associates identified three characteristics that described resilient children of depressed parents. The three characteristics, which were incorporated into the preventive intervention, were *(1)* support for activities and accomplishment of developmental tasks outside of the home; *(2)* a deep involvement in human relationships; and *(3)* the capacity for self-reflection and self-understanding, in particular, in relationship to the parent's disorder. Resilient youth repeatedly said that understanding that their parent was ill, that the disorder had a name, and that they were not to blame for it contributed substantially to their doing well. This, then, became a central part of the preventive intervention.

Initial studies of these intervention programs revealed that they were safe and feasible, and that families believed them to be helpful. In an initial random assignment study of the first 20 families enrolled, promising effects were observed 6 months after intervention, and a further follow-up study of parents' reports showed sustained effects over 3 years. In addition, pilot studies revealed that greater benefits were associated with the clinician-facilitated intervention than with the lecture condition. More recent reports on a portion of the sample at the third assessment point have indicated that both conditions resulted in family improvements, and that parents in the clinician-facilitated condition reported significantly greater levels of assessor-rated and self-reported change in family understanding and problem-solving strategies than did participants in the lecture condition.

Most recently, Beardslee, Gladstone, Wright and Cooper (2003) presented findings from follow-up interviews conducted with their entire sample of families at the fourth data point, nearly 2.5 years after intervention. They chose this interval because it was long enough to begin to see substantial, sustained changes in several main domains hypothesized to be affected by participation in the prevention programs. They focused on effecting change in a mediating variable that they described as parental child-related behavior and attitude change.

Results revealed several important findings about the primary prevention of depression and other forms of psychopathology in children at risk for dysfunction due to parental mood disorder. They found that these programs did have long-standing effects in how families problem solve about parental depression (i.e., behavior and attitude change). There was evidence that the clinician-facilitated program was initially more beneficial than the lecture program, and that the amount of change in parent's child-related behaviors and attitudes increased over time. They also found that children reported an increased understanding because of the intervention. They found a significant relation between the amount of child-related behavior and attitude change manifested by parents and the amount of change in understanding manifested by children, even though change was rated entirely separately by assessors blind to the knowledge of the other subjects' reports. Finally, they found that children who participated in the intervention programs reported decreased internalizing symptomatology over time.

After the success of the randomized trial, Beardslee and associates examined the mechanisms by which change took place. Briefly, they found that when families did make changes, they talked repeatedly about depression. Often,

breaking the silence about depression led the families to talk and strategize successfully about many other things. This process was named the "emergence of the healer within." Similarly, they found that what works for a child at 12 does not work for the same child at 16. In this sense, *understandings of depression* change both as the course of parental illness changes and as children grow and mature. Finally, many parents, despite the negativism and self-doubt of depression, end up functioning effectively as parents. In essence, they made peace with their disorder and moved on.

FUTURE DIRECTIONS AND RECOMMENDATIONS

1. The number of empirical studies of effectiveness of preventive interventions needs to be dramatically increased.
2. We need to continue to expand the study of cognitive behavioral and educational approaches based on public health principles. The promising interventions described here need much further study, but the core principles are likely to be highly applicable.
3. A number of methodological issues need to be clarified: *(1)* how to increase retention of participants in prevention studies; and *(2)* how to identify who drops out of prevention studies (dropouts may be those at highest risk—e.g., high family conflict, more negative life events, and greater depressive symptoms).
4. The optimal timing of prevention interventions needs to be established. Current data suggest that ages 13–14 may be the best time, because this is the age just before a sharp upturn (ages 15–18) in initial episodes of MDD and bipolar disorder.
5. The low rate of "caseness" of mood disorders must be taken into account in calculating the sample sizes necessary for prevention studies. At-risk samples are likely to result in 40%–50% of individuals (ages 13–14) with MDD during a 3-year follow-up, whereas, universal programs are more likely to see a control group caseness in a much lower range.

6. We need continually to expand the science base of depression, particularly regarding the question of its heterogeneity. It is important to identify robust subtypes of depression because specific programs for some of these subtypes are likely to be more effective than general prevention programs for a heterogenous overall MDD. Robust subtypes of MDD are also likely to yield important genetic information. It is likely that certain vulnerabilities to depression are conveyed by multiple genes acting in concert and expressed in stressful situations. Promising leads include the work of Garber (Garber & Martin, 2002) on the stress diathesis hypothesis, work by Goodman and associates (Goodman & Gotlib, 1999) on ways in which genes and the stressors in families with parental depression interact, and Reiss and colleagues' (Reiss, Neiderhiser, Hetherington, & Plomkin, 2000) work on behavioral genetics. Recent work points to other subtypes and suggests that depression may represent an underlying dysregulation of emotion (Dahl, 2001), or that it may be part of a general phenomenon of inhibition (Kagan & Snidman, 1991). The more we understand risk factors and risk mechanisms (i.e., how risks come together), the better we will be able to mount preventive interventions.

7. It is also very important to remember that better treatments make a huge difference in the lives of families—e.g., quicker recoveries, less misunderstanding. And, as better interventions are found, they will contribute to the prevention of depression among other family members.

8. We need more study of prevention programs in different contexts with an awareness of cultural, racial, and ethnic differences.

9. The occurrence of depression in either a parent or a child requires educational support from the other family members. Important opportunities exist for prevention in these situations. Some groups have found that adult family members with MDD do not want their children to know of the disorder; this attitude needs to be overcome by reducing stigma associated with mood disorders.

10. Prevention of depression is closely related to other preventive efforts—in particular, the prevention of suicide and the consideration of victimization by violence. The work by Marikangas and colleagues suggests the possibility that MDD may be prevented by preventing the development of anxiety, which is a risk factor for subsequent development of MDD (Marikangas, Avwneoli, Dierker, & Grillon, 1999).

11. Community/political intervention. Although the prevention of adolescent depression is a common goal in adolescent health, it is rarely approached in a comprehensive and systematic manner that includes continuous attention to all aspects of prevention. Most often, adolescent depression rises to the attention of the local or national health agenda after a series of well-publicized adolescent suicides. National and local advocacy groups have been effective in raising the public visibility of issues such as teenage pregnancy and drug abuse. A similar approach is needed for the prevention of adolescent depression. Three specific approaches are needed:

   a. Campaigns to educate local and national governmental agencies and institutions and assist them in developing policies and programs that ensure utilization of effective and comprehensive models that prevent adolescent depression at all stages.

   b. Advisory groups that work with national professional organizations to assist them to develop protocols and professional standards that place a higher priority on the prevention of adolescent depression. These efforts should include all professions that interact with youth—health care, education, social service, and juvenile justice.

   c. Self-help groups that work on the local level with families, communities, and youth development agencies to assist them in the development of effective prevention interventions.

Research Agenda for Depression and Bipolar Disorder

chapter 4

MAJOR DEPRESSIVE DISORDER

The Disorder

What We Know

Basic knowledge about major depressive disorder (MDD) in adolescence has begun to accumulate over the past two decades. Most importantly, MDD is now no longer seen primarily as a disorder of the middle-aged and elderly. It is clear that MDD often begins in adolescence and has a serious impact on the adolescent's development into adulthood. In contrast, prepubertal onset is less common, with a higher proportion of males who experience mood reactivity, irritability, dysphoria, and comorbidity with disruptive disorder. Adolescent MDD is chronic and recurrent, sharing diagnostic features with those of adult MDD, including high comorbidity with anxiety and substance abuse disorders, and risk for suicide. Adolescent MDD is associated with a lack of social development and skills, withdrawal from peers, and poor school performance.

Information on risk factors for the development of adolescent MDD has also begun to emerge. The most consistent risk factors for MDD in both adolescents and adults are female gender (2- to 3-fold increased risk) and a family history of MDD. Offspring of depressed parents are at increased risk (2- to 4-fold) for depression. A previous episode is a major risk factor for the occurrence of additional episodes; over 50% of adolescents with MDD have a recurrence within 5 years, and MDD episodes often continue into adulthood. This confers an increased risk of suicide attempts and psychiatric and medical hospitalizations. Adverse family environments, especially the absence of supportive interactions, poor parental bonding, poor primary attachments, and harsh discipline, are also risk factors that contribute to both the onset and recurrence of adolescent MDD. Negative cognitions about the self appear to mediate the relation between stressful life events and the occurrence of depressive symptoms.

Biologically, there are abnormalities in hypothalamic–pituitary–adrenal (HPA) axis activity in adolescence similar to those found in adults, as well as thyroid dysfunction.

What We Do Not Know

We have only begun to characterize the possible adverse effects of depression on brain structure and function. We have limited data on brain plasticity and neurogenesis. In addition, the way in which treatment interventions (psychosocial and/or psychopharmacological) impact brain plasticity and neurogenesis is unknown. No specific genes have yet been identified that are unequivocally associated with MDD, regardless of age of onset.

Although there appears to be a clear link between life events and depression, we do not know the mechanisms by which stress increases an individual's vulnerability to depression or the genetic and environmental factors that influence vulnerability or resilience. Furthermore, it is known that various forms of stressors often precede mood disorders, but it is not known why only some individuals exposed to these stressors become depressed. There is some evidence that a patient's response to an external stressor may be moderated by the individual's genetic constitution, by possessing a functional polymorphism in the promoter region of the serotonin transporter gene. Some evidence has pointed to negative cognitive appraisals of the self and life events as mediators of the relation between stress and depression, but these factors do not appear to tell the whole story. Thus, other mediators are likely. Moreover, we know little about the ways in which such negative cognitions develop in adolescence, and whether they can be prevented.

The biological mechanisms that mediate the relation between life events and risk of MDD in adolescents are also not known. We do not know whether the presence of adolescent depression is a risk factor for the development of other medical diseases and how its presence may affect the course of the medical illness. In addition, we do not know if treatment and/or prevention of depression decreases the potential impact and severity of the expressed medical illness.

Research Priorities: What We Need to Know

Research on adolescent MDD needs to proceed on many fronts. To facilitate research across broad aspects of the disorder, we propose that highest priority be given to the following areas:

- Studies of the prodromal phase of child and adolescent mood disorders. Such research would allow for better identification of the illness and how it evolves over time to its full clinical course.
- Integrative studies of the range of possible psychological, sociological, familial, and biological variables that contribute to the development of adolescent depression. By identifying which variables are most important and contribute the most to the development of adolescent MDD, we can target treatment and prevention efforts to such risk factors and yield the best outcomes.
- Examination of the mediational links between environmental stressors, cognitive and personality variables, genetics, biological systems, and depressive symptoms. Uncovering these links will provide information on the causal chain of events that leads to the clinical disorder, and suggest avenues for the further development of new treatments and preventive programs.

Treatment

What We Know

As found in the adult depression treatment literature, cognitive behavioral treatment (CBT) and interpersonal therapy for youth depression appears to be more efficacious than no treatment, wait-list control, or attention placebo controls. In addition, there is preliminary evidence suggesting that attachment-based family therapy may be useful for the treatment of adolescent depression. To date, the only medications that have demonstrated safety and efficacy in double-blind, placebo-controlled trials for children and adolescents with major depression are the selective serotonin reuptake inhibitors (SSRIs). Fluoxetine was the first SSRI and the only one with federal Food and Drug Administration (FDA) approval for the treatment of pediatric depression. Recently, the National Institute of Mental Health (NIMH) funded study entitled "Treatment of Adolescents with Depression

Study" (TADS) showed that 71% of patients responded well to combination treatment of CBT with fluoxetine compared with 61% who received fluoxetine alone, 43% who received CBT alone, and 35% of those treated with placebo. The study also reported that patients became significantly less suicidal regardless of the treatment they received. In addition, after reviewing 24 double-blind, placebo-controlled pediatric trials using antidepressants, an FDA panel has determined that SSRIs may carry an increased risk of suicidal ideation or behaviors for a small proportion of users (perhaps 2% or 3%). The FDA has labeled all antidepressants with a warning about the potential risk of increased suicidal thinking and behavior and the need for close medical monitoring, particularly in the first month of treatment and when the medication dose is adjusted. The FDA expects physicians to educate patients and families about the risks and benefits of these medications and to watch for behavioral changes in the child, such as irritability, aggression, and impulsivity. In spite of these concerns, antidepressants can be very effective in treating mood and anxiety disorders in this group.

What We Do Not Know

Although initial treatment studies have been promising, many patients continue to have clinically significant levels of depression after psychotherapy and medication treatment, and most patients experience at least one recurrence of depression within 5 years of treatment termination. Thus, we know little about achieving remission and favorable long-term outcomes in adolescent MDD populations. Presently, the TADS program is continuing to follow children over a one-year period after completing the acute phase of the study. This will provide much needed information about long-term treatment outcomes for adolescents with depression. Moreover, we do not know which specific psychosocial or pharmacologic treatments are most efficacious and for which patients. In addition, there is little known about the efficacy of sequencing or combining various treatments. There is no information regarding the management of partial and nonresponse in the treatment of adolescent depression. We have limited information about the optimal length of time for any of these treatments and how to maintain the treatment response once achieved by using such options as booster sessions and/or varying the length of medication treatment. There is also little information on how our present treatments that target adolescent depression impact comorbid psychiatric disorders such as substance abuse, disruptive disorders, and anxiety disorders.

Research Priorities: What We Need to Know

We have identified a number of high-priority topics for treatment research on MDD in adolescence:

- There is a need for more research into the safety and efficacy of SSRIs. The benefits vs. risks of using SSRIs with adolescents should be carefully assessed in such studies.
- Future studies need to have adequate statistical power to determine the efficacy and safety of antidepressants in both child and adolescent populations.
- There is a particular need to research the use of antidepressant treatment in suicidal adolescents. Independent, federally funded centers should be established to evaluate treatment to prevent suicide.
- Long-term studies of antidepressants are required to evaluate their safety profile in children. This information will enable a risk/benefit analysis of extended antidepressant use. In addition, maintenance studies are needed to guide optimal medication treatment duration.
- There is a need for antidepressants studies focussing on remission of symptoms and full functional recovery, rather than just treatment response.
- The development and testing of interventions that focus on maternal depression and family discord might be an effective way of preventing adolescent depression.
- Additional treatment research such as the TADS program is needed to explore further the acute efficacy of combination treatment, with a particular focus on determining

which subpopulation of patients will do best with monotherapy vs. combined treatment.

- Treatment research is needed on refractory and chronic conditions, such as "double depression" in adolescence. These chronic disorders may respond better to combinations of medication and CBT than to either monotherapy alone, as suggested by comparable data on adults with chronic depression.
- Interventions designed to improve outcome in patients with poor prognostic risk factors need to be examined.
- There is little in the literature about the transportability of manualized treatments to the community settings; this important issue needs to be addressed.

Prevention

What We Know

A number of promising strategies for the prevention of childhood and adolescent depression have emerged over the past decade. Of special significance is the fact that these emerging prevention strategies make a point of taking the developmental level of participants into account. The evaluated preventive strategies are based primarily on cognitive-behavioral and family-educational approaches, with the focus of reducing risk factors and enhancing protective and resiliency factors associated with depression in youth. Rigorous standards for the development and evaluation of manual-based preventive approaches have been introduced, and these innovations have greatly facilitated research in this area.

To date, we have initial evidence that these prevention programs are more effective than both no treatment and usual care (staying in existing treatment or patients seeking treatment on their own) in reducing future episodes of MDD. These effects are particularly evident for those at highest risk of MDD and for those with the greatest severity of depressive symptoms.

What We Do Not Know

Despite the promising studies on prevention of depression, much remains to be learned. There are not enough data about the timing of preventive interventions or about the appropriate setting for such interventions to be assured that the expected outcomes occur for the targeted population. Most studies have used samples that include adolescents who have had previous episodes of MDD (high-risk samples). Thus, we know little about the prevention of first episodes of MDD. Long-term follow-up data are scarce but crucial to understanding whether preventive interventions have an impact on the occurrence of MDD episodes into adulthood.

Research Priorities: What We Need to Know

Prevention research is in its infancy; therefore, a number of basic studies are sorely needed. These include the following:

- More prevention programs based on the full range of risk factors for MDD need to be developed and tested.
- Comparisons among existing preventive programs need to be conducted.
- Further research on the active ingredients of preventive programs and the mediators of change should be performed.
- We need to examine prevention programs in different contexts with an awareness of cultural, racial, and ethnic differences.
- We need to learn how to disseminate prevention programs so that they reach the families most at need and at risk. This is especially a challenge because of the lack of sophisticated delivery systems of prevention programs.
- The impact of prevention programs for individuals with different types of risk factors for MDD needs to be evaluated.

BIPOLAR DISORDER

The Disorder

What We Know

We now know that variants, or precursors, of bipolar disorder may be more common in adolescence than previously thought. There is a growing consensus that youth who are afflicted with severe affective dysregulation, high levels of agitation, aggression, and dyscontrol may be suffering from an early form of bipolar disorder. This issue has received increased scientific attention, as is evident in the scheduling of two NIMH workshops on bipolar disorder in children and adolescents and in exhaustive reviews that have supported the validity of the disorder in youth.

Bipolar disorder is highly heritable. There are several loci of the human genome that have been associated with the disorder.

What We Do Not Know

We know little about how to accurately identify the early signs and symptoms of bipolar disorder in youth. This challenge of early disorder identification has limited epidemiologic information on this illness. There is still controversy over the definition of early-onset mania; this is complicated by the fact that this disorder is highly comorbid with other psychiatric disorders. In particular, we know little about the overlap of attention deficit hyperactivity disorder (ADHD) and conduct disorder with bipolar disorder in youth.

We also do not know whether pediatric bipolar disorder differs from the adult form of the disorder. Related to this, there is little information on the adult course of pediatric-onset mania. Other than a likely genetic contribution, little is known about the risk factors for the development of bipolar disorder in youth.

Research Priorities: What We Need to Know

Several priorities for research can be suggested:

- Most importantly, additional epidemiologic studies are needed to determine the prevalence of pediatric and adolescent bipolar disorder.
- Long-term longitudinal studies are needed to clarify the relation of adolescent onset of symptoms to the course of bipolar disorder in adulthood. These data would assist with informing us about the clinical course and acute and long-term treatment outcome.
- The relationship of comorbid disorders such

as ADHD and conduct disorder to juvenile-onset bipolar disorder needs to be further evaluated.

Treatment

What We Know

As learned from treatment of adults diagnosed with bipolar disorder, the complexity of this illness in adolescents requires a combination of medication and psychosocial interventions to effectively reduce the burden of the illness. We also know that patients who respond to a given acute pharmacotherapy regimen continue to benefit from ongoing treatment with the medication that led to successful symptom amelioration.

What We Do Not Know

There are very few controlled studies of specific psychosocial or pharmacologic interventions for pediatric bipolar disorder. Psychosocial interventions specifically targeting adolescent bipolar disorder are just now starting to evolve. There are few studies of maintenance treatment, which is essential for this disorder. For both psychosocial and pharmacologic treatments, there is minimal empirical evidence to clearly inform the clinician as to what types of treatment combinations are most effective for the adolescent suffering from bipolar disorder. It may be that combination pharmacotherapy with more than one mood-stabilizing agent may be a rational approach for some youth who have manic, hypomanic, depressed, or mixed states.

There are also limited data on the impact of long-term exposure to psychotropic compounds on the developing brain. We also do not have studies of the side effects that arise from medication treatment over a long period of time.

Research Priorities: What We Need to Know

Treatment studies of highest priority would include the following:

- More, and larger, efficacy studies of medications and psychosocial treatments are urgently needed.

- Whether treatment should begin with drug monotherapy or a combination of medications, or medication plus psychotherapy, should be a topic of further study.
- Treatment of nonresponders to standard bipolar treatment should be evaluated.
- Studies of maintenance pharmacotherapy and psychotherapy are sorely needed.
- Given the chronicity of this disorder and the high risk for these patients to die from suicide, there needs to be research on the development of prevention programs that would target patients at risk for this disorder that have an impact on prevention of suicide, the most serious consequence of the illness.

Prevention

What We Know and Do Not Know

Unfortunately, we know almost nothing about the prevention of bipolar disorder in youth. One factor hindering prevention research is the challenge of making an accurate diagnosis. Not until we can accurately identify high-risk cases and the emergence of the actual disorder in adolescence can studies on prevention begin. At this point in time, even if we could properly identify a target population and clinical end point, we do not yet know how best to design and evaluate preventive strategies for this disorder.

Research Priorities: What We Need to Know

As mentioned above, scientific advancement in accurately characterizing the early signs and full emergence of bipolar disorder in youth is a crucial first step. The next step is further research on risk factors for the development of bipolar disorder in youth. Once these goals have been accomplished, we need to design and evaluate preventive programs that target such risk factors. Although such preventive studies are in the future, they represent one of the more important directions for alleviating the burden of this serious and potentially debilitating disorder in adulthood.

Schizophrenia

COMMISSION ON ADOLESCENT SCHIZOPHRENIA

Raquel E. Gur, *Commission Chair*

Nancy Andreasen

Robert Asarnow

Ruben Gur

Peter Jones

Kenneth Kendler

Matcheri Keshavan

Jeffrey Lieberman

Robert McCarley

Robin Murray

Judith Rapoport

Carol Tamminga

Ming Tsuang

Elaine Walker

Daniel Weinberger

With contributions from
Kristin Lancefield

part II

Defining Schizophrenia

chapter **5**

Schizophrenia is a chronic and severe mental disorder with a typical onset in adolescence and early adulthood and a lifetime prevalence of about 1%. On average, males have their illness onset 3 to 4 years earlier than females. Onset of schizophrenia is very rare before age 11, and prior to age 18 the illness has been called "early-onset schizophrenia" (EOS), while onset before age 13 has been termed "very early-onset schizophrenia" (VEOS; Werry, 1981).

Prior to examining topics in schizophrenia, we must address a basic question as to the definition of *adolescents* and *adults*. The way these groups will be defined is partly related to the question being asked. That is, research studies that emphasize the study of neural development or finding links between endocrine changes and onset of schizophrenia are likely to place more emphasis on defining adolescence in terms of body or brain maturation. For example, *adolescence* could be defined as the period between the onset and offset of puberty. Alternatively, it could be defined on the basis of our current knowledge of brain development, which suggests that maturational processes accelerate around the time of puberty but that they continue on into what is often considered young adulthood. Most recent studies of normal brain development suggest that brain maturation continues to the early 20s. If this rather extended definition of adolescence is used, then the appropriate adult contrast groups are likely to be somewhat older—people in their late 20s, 30s, or even 40s.

Under the general rubric of phenomenology, four major topics need to be considered as we explore the relevance of research on adults to the understanding of adolescents. These four topics are diagnostic criteria, phenomenology, the relationship of phenomenology to neural mechanisms, and the use of phenomenology to assist in identifying the phenotype for genetic studies.

OVERVIEW

Diagnostic Criteria

Two different sets of diagnostic criteria are currently used in the world literature. For most stud-

ies that emphasize biological markers, and for almost all of those conducted in the United States, the standard diagnostic criteria are from the *Diagnostic and Statistical Manual of Mental Disorders, Fourth Edition* (DSM-IV, American Psychiatric Association, 1994). However, international epidemiologic studies are likely to use the World Health Organization's *International Classification of Diseases, Tenth Revision* (WHO's ICD-10, World Health Organization, 1992). Differences in the choice of diagnostic criteria may affect the results of studies.

There are many similarities between the ICD and DSM, largely as a consequence of efforts by the ICD and DSM work groups to achieve as much concordance as possible. Both require 1 month of active symptoms and the presence of psychotic symptoms such as delusions or hallucinations. There are, however, important differences between the ICD and DSM. In most respects, the DSM provides a slightly narrower conceptualization of schizophrenia than does the ICD. For example, the ICD only requires 1 month of overall duration of symptoms, whereas the DSM requires 6 months. In addition, the ICD includes schizotypal disorder and simple schizophrenia within its nomenclature under the general heading of the diagnosis of schizophrenia. In the DSM, simple schizophrenia is excluded, and schizotypal disorder is placed among the personality disorders. Other less significant differences include a greater emphasis on first-rank symptoms in the ICD, as well as a much more specific and complex system list.

How important is the choice of diagnostic criteria for research on adolescents? It could be very important. Setting criteria boundaries more broadly or more narrowly will have a significant impact on the groups of adolescents chosen for study. Furthermore, although the developers of these criteria paid close attention to examining the reliability and, when possible, their validity, it was assumed almost without question that the criteria could and should be the same for children, adolescents, and adults. This decision was not based on any published empirical data but rather, primarily on "clinical impressions."

A frequently expressed clinical impression among those who study schizophrenia or psychosis in children and adolescents, however, is that making a diagnosis in these younger age ranges is much more difficult than diagnosing individuals in their 20s. Multiple issues arise for a diagnosis in the adolescence age range. One important issue is comorbidity. Teenagers frequently may meet criteria for multiple diagnoses, such as conduct disorder or attention-deficit hyperactivity disorder (ADHD). Although the DSM tends to encourage the use of multiple diagnoses, this policy also has no empirical basis. An alternative approach that might be considered from research on adolescents is to try to identify a single "best" diagnosis that would summarize the child parsimoniously.

Many adolescents also abuse substances of many different kinds. This factor is important to consider in the diagnosis of adults who may have schizophrenia, but it poses even greater problems among adolescents. Abuse of substances such as amphetamines may potentially induce a psychotic picture that is very similar to schizophrenia. We do not know whether young people who continue to meet criteria for schizophrenia after discontinuing amphetamine use should be considered "typical schizophrenics" or whether they should in fact be given another diagnosis such as substance-induced psychotic disorder. However, because amphetamines have a significant effect on the dopamine system—a key neurotransmitter implicated in the neurochemical mechanisms of schizophrenia—it is at least plausible that amphetamines (and perhaps other substances as well) be considered triggers or inducers of schizophrenia. According to this view, substance abuse could be one of the many factors that rank among the nongenetic causes of schizophrenia. However, there is still no strong consensus on this issue.

In summary, there are many unanswered research questions under the heading of diagnosis. More studies are needed to explore how well existing diagnostic criteria actually work in children and adolescents. Specifically, studies of both the reliability and validity of these criteria are needed, as well as studies examining issues of comorbidity and longitudinal studies examining changes in both diagnosis and phenomenology in cohorts of adolescents and of adults.

Phenomenology

The concept of phenomenology can be relatively broad, describing clinical symptoms, psychosocial functioning, cognitive functioning, and "neurological" measures such as soft signs. Here we will focus primarily on clinical symptoms and psychosocial functioning.

For the assessment of clinical symptoms in schizophrenia, choosing the appropriate informant is a key issue. Whatever the age, patients suffering from schizophrenia frequently have difficulty in reporting their symptoms and past history accurately. Optimally, one gets the best information from several informants, usually a parent plus the patient. In the case of adolescents, a friend may be a good additional informant. Another critical issue in phenomenology when assessing adolescents is to determine the distinction between "normal" adolescent behavior and psychopathology. Again, this can be difficult in assessing adults, but it is even more difficult in adolescents. It can be hard to draw the line between "teenage scruffiness" and disorganization, or a withdrawal to seek privacy versus avolition. As discussed above, drug use or abuse can also confound the picture. For example, when an adolescent known to be using marijuana regularly exhibits chronic apathy and avolition, is this due to marijuana use or is it a true negative symptom? At the moment, no data are available to help us address any of these issues pertaining to the assessment of clinical symptoms in adolescents versus those in adults. This is clearly an area in which more information is needed.

Another issue is the identification of appropriate developmental milestones and needs that are appropriate to the adolescent age range for the assessment of psychosocial functioning. For example, when we assess peer relationships in young or older adults with schizophrenia, we are evaluating the extent to which they have a circle of friends with whom they get together socially. In the case of adolescents, peer relationships are far more important and are more intensely driven by a need to establish independence from the family setting and to bond with others from the same age range. Likewise, the assessment of family relationships among adolescents is guided by quite different conditions than those for mature adults. Finally, the "work" of an adolescent is quite generally to do well in school, whereas the "work" of an adult is normally to find a paying job. Again, assessment tools have simply not been defined for assessing these aspects of psychosocial functioning in adolescents.

Expression of Early Symptoms and Illness Course

A wide range of symptoms has been described (Table 5.1) and the initial clinical features vary from one patient to another. The identification of these as prodromal symptoms is essentially retrospective, being diagnosed only after the first psychotic episode heralds. Using detailed assessment of such symptoms by a structured interview, studies have shown that the prodromal symptoms may begin 2 to 6 years before psychosis onset (Hafner et al., 1992). Negative symptoms of the prodrome may begin earlier than the positive symptoms (Häfner, Maurer, Löffler, & Riecher-Rossler, 1993). Over the past decade, attempts have been made to characterize the prodromal phase prospectively, with operational criteria (Yung & McGorry, 1996). However, several such patients may not develop schizophrenia, leading to the problem of false positives; it is therefore critical that we identify more specific predictors of conversion to psychosis among prospectively identified prodromal patients.

The onset of the first episode of psychosis (the beginning of clearly evident psychotic symptoms) is to be distinguished from the illness onset, which often begins with symptoms and signs of nonspecific psychological disorder (Häfner et al., 1993). The *prodromal phase* refers to the period characterized by symptoms marking a change from the premorbid state to the time frank psychosis begins (Fig. 5.1). The onset of both the prodrome and the psychotic episode are difficult to define precisely.

Although the clinical features of adolescent-onset and adult-onset schizophrenia are overall quite similar, early onset of schizophrenia may have an impact on its initial clinical presentation. In general, early-onset schizophrenia patients have more severe negative symptoms and cognitive impairments and are less responsive to treatment. Children and adolescents with schizophrenia often tend to fail in achieving expected levels of academic and interpersonal achievement. Very early-onset cases tend to have an insidious onset, whereas adolescent-onset cases tend to have a more acute onset. Patients with EOS or VEOS are also more often diagnosed as an undifferentiated subtype, because well-formed delusions and hallucinations are less frequent (Nicolson & Rapoport, 1999; Werry, McClellan, & Chard, 1991).

In summary, a challenge in the study of schizophrenia is the variability, or heterogeneity, in the clinical manifestations, and associated biological changes and course. This heterogeneity may have lead to inconsistencies in research findings (Keshavan & Schooler, 1992). Identifying early symptoms and signs and functional impairment can help our efforts in improving early diagnosis and in understanding the biological and genetic heterogeneity. Knowledge of the illness onset in adolescence may also help elucidate the brain developmental and possibly neurodegenerative processes in this illness, as proposed by recent pathophysiological models. Furthermore, an understanding of the course of clinical and neurobiological characteristics in the early phase of schizophrenia, such as the duration of untreated illness, can help in predicting outcome and presents important opportunities for secondary prevention.

Some of the key research questions in the area of the phenomenology of adolescent schizophrenia are as follows:

Table 5.1 Prodromal Features in First-Episode Psychosis Frequently Described in Adolescent Patients

Reduced concentration, attention

Decreased motivation, drive, and energy

Mood changes: depression, anxiety

Sleep difficulties

Social withdrawal

Suspiciousness

Irritability

Decline in role functioning, e.g., giving less to academic performance, quitting established interests, neglecting appearance

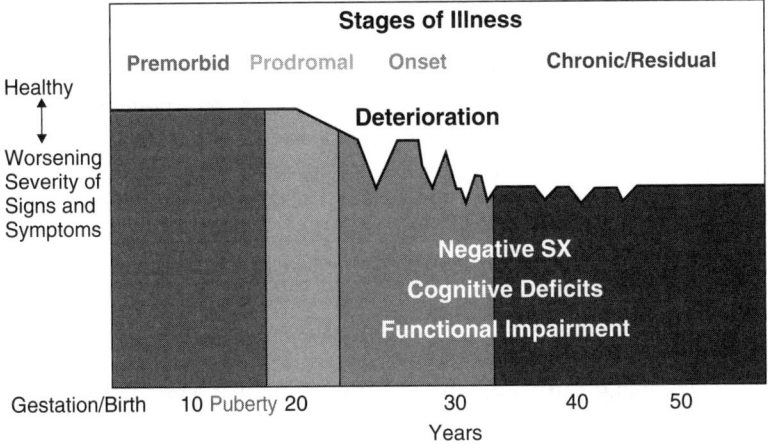

Figure 5.1 Natural history of schizophrenia.

- Should the same criteria be used for adolescents and adults?
- Are there differences in phenomenology between the two?
- What is the validity of current assessment tools in the "real" research world? The reliability?
- What is (are) the best source(s) of information?
- What impact do differences in "life developmental stages" have on phenomenology?
- What is the best way to assess comorbidity and boundary issues in relationship to other disorders such as schizotypal disorder?

The consensus on these questions is at best modest. Almost no empirical data are available to answer them. In the area of phenomenology in adolescents suffering from schizophrenia, more well-designed, empirical studies are needed to improve assessment tools and to compare adults and adolescents.

Linking Phenomenology to Its Neural Basis

Through the use of neuroimaging, neuropathology, and neurogenetics, substantial progress in understanding the neural underpinnings of schizophrenia is being made. Excellent work has been done recently that examines the relationship between brain development and the occurrence of schizophrenia in children and adoles-

cents, as described in other chapters (DeLisi, 1997; Giedd et al., 1999; Gur, Maany, et al., 1998; 1999; Ho et al., 2003; Jacobsen et al., 1998; Kumra et al., 2000; Lieberman, Chakos, et al., 2001; Rapoport et al., 1997; Thompson, Vidal, et al., 2001). As this work continues to mature, however, more work needs to be done to examine precisely how the specific symptoms of schizophrenia arise in the human brain, and whether imaging and other tools can be used to assist in diagnosis, treatment planning, and ultimately prevention.

This work must also address several questions in the realm of phenomenology. Specifically, how should we proceed as we attempt to link phenomenology to neural mechanisms? As discussed above, the phenomenology has multiple levels and aspects—symptoms, outcome, cognitive function, and psychosocial function. Which of these should be linked to imaging and other "biological" measures?

Most work to date has taken several different approaches. At the simplest level, investigators have conducted studies linking specific symptoms to neural measures. For example, studies have used positron emission tomography (PET) to identify brain regions active during auditory hallucinations (e.g., Silbersweig et al., 1995). Other investigators have examined symptoms such as thought disorder in relation to brain measures (e.g., Shenton et al., 1992). One of the critical conceptual issues, however, is the fact that the phenomenology of schizophrenia is complex. That is, the illness cannot be characterized on the basis of a single symptom. Although auditory hallucinations are common in schizophrenia, they are not omnipresent. Therefore, other investigators have proceeded by examining groups of symptoms that are correlated with one another, or "dimensions." Many factor analytic studies have examined the factor structure of the symptoms of schizophrenia; nearly all find that the symptoms group naturally into three dimensions: psychoticism, disorganization, and negative symptoms (Andreasen, 1986; Andreasen, O'Leary, et al., 1995; Andreasen, Olsen, & Dennert, 1982; Arndt, Alliger, & Andreasen, 1991; Arndt, Andreasen, Flaum, Miller, & Nopoulos, 1995; Bilder, Mukherjee, Rieder, & Pandurangi, 1985; Gur et al., 1991; Kulhara, Kota, & Joseph, 1986; Lenzenweger, Dworkin, & Wethington, 1989; Liddle, 1987). Some studies have used the dimensional approach to examine brain–behavior relationships. Several studies also suggest that these three dimensions may have different functional neural substrates as seen with PET, or different structural brain correlates as evaluated with magnetic resonance imaging (MRI), and may also have different and independent longitudinal courses (Andreasen, Arndt, Alliger, Miller, & Flaum, 1995; Andreasen et al., 1996, 1997; Arndt et al., 1995; Flaum et al., 1995, 1997; Gur et al., 1991; Miller, Arndt, & Andreasen, 1993; O'Leary et al., 2000).

In concert with this work examining the symptoms of schizophrenia, other investigators have pursued the study of relationships between cognition and brain measures. Some have argued that some form of cognitive dysfunction may ultimately provide the best definition of the phenotype of schizophrenia, and that ultimately cognitive measures may replace symptom measures in defining the phenomenology of schizophrenia (Andreasen, 1999). Again, however, a consensus has not been achieved.

Defining the Phenotype for Genetic Studies

Contemporary geneticists applying the tools of modern genetics have become very much aware of how important it is to have good definitions of complex disorders such as schizophrenia. In fact, reflecting this awareness, they are beginning to speak about a new (but actually old) field, referred to as "phenomics," the genetic underpinnings of phenomenology. The emergence of this term reflects the fact that the definition of the phenotype of illnesses like schizophrenia may be the single most important component of modern genetic studies.

Here the issues are very similar to those discussed above, involving the relationship between clinical presentation and neural mechanisms. At what level should the phenotype be defined? The symptom level? Dimension level? Diagnosis level? Cognitive level? Or should we abandon these more superficial clinical measurements and attempt to find more basic definitions, often referred to as "endophenotypes," or "measurable components unseen by the unaided eye along the pathway between disease and distal genotype" (Gottesman & Gould, 2003)?

In this instance, there may be some consensus. Many investigators believe that endophenotypic definitions may provide a better index of the presence of this disorder than classic symptom-based definitions, such as those created by the DSM or ICD. There is as of yet, however, no strong consensus on what the "best" endophenotypes may be. Some candidates that have been proposed include problems with working memory, eye tracking, or prepulse inhibition. To date, most of this work has been conducted with adults. The application of this approach to defining and identifying the schizophrenia endophenotype in children and adolescents is another important future direction, as is the search for additional new candidate endophenotypes.

ETIOLOGY

Two complementary approaches have emerged as providing much needed insight into the causes and underlying substrates of schizophrenia: neurobiology and genetics. Current efforts in neurobiology are to integrate data from behavioral measurements with the increasingly informative data from work with neuroimaging and electrophysiology. Neurobiological studies were stimulated by the well-documented neuro-behavioral deficits that are present in schizo-phrenia. Some of the impairments are evident at the premorbid phase of illness and progress during adolescence, with onset of symptoms. These have become targets for therapeutic interventions. The application of structural and functional neuroimaging has enabled researchers to obtain in vivo measures and highlight the brain circuitry affected in schizophrenia. Progress in genetics has moved the field from earlier efforts relying on family studies of the phenotype to molecular studies that probe the underlying biology. In this section, we will review neuro-behavioral measures, proceed to describe studies of brain structure and function, review the impact of hormones critical during adolescence, describe the implicated brain circuitry, and conclude by presenting the genetics of schizophrenia.

Neurobehavioral Deficits

Cognitive deficits have been recognized since early descriptions of schizophrenia, when it was called "dementia praecox." More recent evidence confirms that cognitive deficits are evident in vulnerable individuals, are present at the onset of illness, and predict outcome. Furthermore, as summarized in Chapters 6 and 7, early detection and efforts at intervention may hold a key for ameliorating the ravages of schizophrenia later in life. Here we will describe evidence for deficits in neuromotor and neurocognitive functioning, with special emphasis on early presentation.

Neuromotor Functions

Prior to the advent of antipsychotic medications, there were reports in the scientific literature on the occurrence of movement abnormalities in patients with schizophrenia (Huston & Shakow, 1946; Walker, 1994; Yarden & Discipio, 1971). After treatment of patients with antipsychotics became widespread, attention shifted to drug-induced abnormalities in motor behavior. Because motor side effects were of such great concern, they temporarily eclipsed research on

naturally occurring motor dysfunction in schizo-phrenia. But in recent decades, the findings from prospective and retrospective studies have rekindled interest in the signs of motor dysfunction that often accompany schizophrenia in the absence of treatment.

Because the association between motor deficits and brain dysfunction is so well established, motor behaviors are particularly interesting to researchers in the field of schizophrenia (Walker, 1994). In clinical practice, neurologists are often able to identify the locus of brain lesions based on the nature of motor impairments. To date, the motor signs observed in schizophrenia have generally been too subtle and nonspecific to suggest a lesion in a particular brain structure. Nonetheless, there is extensive evidence that motor dysfunction is common in schizophrenia, and it may offer clues about the nature of the brain dysfunction subserving the disorder.

Research has shown that motor deficits predate the onset of schizophrenia, and for some patients are present early in life. Infants who later develop schizophrenia show delays and abnormalities in motor development (Fish, Marcus, Hans, & Auerbach, 1993; Walker, Savoie, & Davis, 1994). They are slower to acquire coordinated patterns of crawling, walking, and bimanual manipulation. They also manifest asymmetries and abnormalities in their movements. These include abnormal postures and involuntary movements of the hands and arms. It is important to note, however, that these early motor signs are not specific to schizophrenia. Delays and anomalies in motor development are present in children who later manifest a variety of disorders, as well as some who show no subsequent disorder. Thus, we cannot use motor signs as a basis for early diagnosis or prediction. But the presence of motor deficits in infants who subsequently manifest schizophrenia suggests that the vulnerability to the disorder involves the central nervous system and is present at birth.

Deficits in motor function extend beyond infancy and have been detected throughout the premorbid period in schizophrenia, including adolescence. Studies of the school and medical records of individuals diagnosed with schizophrenia in late adolescence or early adulthood reveal an elevated rate of motor problems. Both school-aged children and adolescents at risk are more likely to have problems with motor coordination (Cannon, Jones, Huttunen, Tanskanen, & Murray, 1999). Similarly, prospective research has shown that children and adolescents who later develop schizophrenia score below normal controls on standardized tests of motor proficiency (Marcus, Hans, Auerbach, & Auerbach, 1993; Niemi, Suvisaari, Tuulio-Henriksson, & Loennqvist, 2003; Schreiber, Stolz-Born, Heinrich, & Kornhuber, 1992). Again, the presence of these deficits before the onset of clinical schizophrenia suggests that they are indicators of biological vulnerability.

As mentioned, there is an extensive body of research on motor functions in adult patients diagnosed with schizophrenia, both medicated and nonmedicated (Manschreck, Maher, Rucklos, & Vereen, 1982; Walker, 1994; Wolff & O'Driscoll, 1999). The research has revealed deficits in a wide range of measures, from simple finger tapping to the execution of complex manual tasks. In addition, when compared to healthy comparison subjects, schizophrenia patients manifest more involuntary movements and postural abnormalities.

It is noteworthy that motor abnormalities have also been detected in adolescents with schizotypal personality disorder. Compared to healthy adolescents, these children show more involuntary movements and coordination problems (Nagy & Szatmari, 1986; Walker, Lewis, Loewy, & Palyo, 1999). Further research is needed to determine whether schizotypal adolescents with motor abnormalities are more likely to succumb to schizophrenia.

The nature of the motor deficits observed in schizophrenia suggests abnormalities in subcortical brain areas, in particular a group of brain regions referred to as the basal ganglia (Walker, 1994). These brain regions are a part of the neural circuitry that connects subcortical with higher cortical areas of the brain. It is now known that the basal ganglia play a role in cognitive and emotional processes, as well as motor functions. As our understanding of brain function and motor circuitry expands, we will have greater opportunities for identifying the origins of motor dysfunction in schizophrenia. In addi-

tion, research on motor abnormalities in schizophrenia has the potential to shed light on the neural substrates that confer risk for schizophrenia. Some of the important questions that remain to be answered are: What is the nature and prevalence of motor dysfunction in adolescents at risk for schizophrenia? Is the presence of motor dysfunction in schizophrenia linked with a particular pattern of neurochemical or brain abnormalities? Can the presence of motor dysfunction aid in predicting which individuals with prodromal syndromes, such as schizotypal personality disorder (SPD), will develop schizophrenia? Would neuromotor assessment aid in the prediction of treatment response?

Neurocognition

Early studies examining cognitive function in schizophrenia focused on single domains, such as attention or memory, and preceded developments in neuroimaging and cognitive neuroscience that afford better linkage between cognitive aberrations and brain circuitry. Neuropsychological batteries, which have been initially developed and applied in neurological populations, attempt to link behavioral deficits to brain function. When applied in schizophrenia, such batteries have consistently indicated diffuse dysfunction, with relatively greater impairment in executive functions and in learning and memory (Bilder et al., 2000; Censits, Ragland, Gur, & Gur, 1997; Elvevag & Goldberg, 2000; Green, 1996; Gur et al., 2001; Saykin et al., 1994).

It is noteworthy that the pattern of deficits is already observed at first presentation and is not significantly changed by treatment of the clinical symptoms. Therefore, study of adolescents at risk or at onset of illness avoids confounding by effects of treatment, hospitalization, and social isolation that may contribute to compromised function. Although the literature evaluating the specificity of cognitive deficits in schizophrenia is limited, there is enough evidence to show that the profile and severity are different from bipolar disorder. Thus, early evaluation during adolescence may have diagnostic and treatment implications. Given the evidence on cognitive deficits at the premorbid stage, it would be important to evaluate whether a pattern of deficits in adolescents at risk can predict the onset and course of illness. The executive functions impaired in adults with schizophrenia are the very abilities that are essential for an adolescent to make the transition to young adulthood, when navigation through an increasing complexity of alternatives becomes the issue.

In addition to the cognitive impairment, emotion-processing deficits in identification, discrimination, and recognition of facial expressions have been observed in schizophrenia (Kohler et al., 2003; Kring, Barrett, & Gard, 2003). Such deficits may contribute to the poor social adjustment already salient before disease onset. Emotional impairment in schizophrenia is clinically well established, manifesting in flat, blunted, inappropriate affect and in depression. These affect-related symptoms are notable in adolescents during the prodromal phase of illness preceding the positive symptoms. While these may represent a component of the generalized cognitive impairment, they relate to symptoms and neurobiological measures that deserve further research.

Several brain systems are implicated by these deficits. The attention-processing circuitry includes brainstem-thalamo-striato-accumbens-temporal-hippocampal-prefrontal-parietal regions. Deficits in working memory implicate the dorsolateral prefrontal cortex, and the ventromedial temporal lobe is implicated by deficits in episodic memory. A dorsolateral-medial-orbital prefrontal cortical circuit mediates executive functions. Animal and human investigations have implicated the limbic system, primarily the amygdala, hypothalamus, mesocorticolimbic dopaminergic systems, and cortical regions including orbitofrontal, dorsolateral prefrontal, temporal, and parts of parietal cortex. These are obviously complex systems and impairment in one may interact with dysfunction in others. Studies with large samples are needed to test models of underlying pathophysiology.

The link between neurobehavioral deficits and brain dysfunction can be examined both by correlating individual differences in performance with measures of brain anatomy and through the application of neurobehavioral probes in functional imaging studies. With these paradigms, we can investigate the topography of

brain activity in response to engagement in tasks in which deficits have been noted in patients. Thus, there is "online" correlation between brain activity and performance in a way that permits direct examination of brain–behavior relations (Gur et al., 1997).

Neuroanatomic Studies

The availability of methods for quantitative structural neuroimaging has enabled examination of neuroanatomic abnormalities in schizophrenia. Because the onset of schizophrenia takes place during a phase of neurodevelopment characterized by dynamic and extensive changes in brain anatomy, establishment of the growth chart is necessary to interpret findings. Two complementary lines of investigation have proved helpful. By examining the neuroanatomical differences between healthy people and individuals with childhood-onset and first-episode schizophrenia, as well as individuals at risk, regional abnormalities early in the course of illness may be identified. Complementary efforts are needed to examine changes associated with illness progression. An understanding of the neuroanatomic changes in the context of the dynamic transitions of the developing brain during adolescence, however, requires careful longitudinal studies during this critical period. A brief introduction to the methodology of quantitative MRI and its application to examine neurodevelopment is needed to appreciate findings in schizophrenia.

Several approaches have been developed in the early 1990s, and these have now become standard and have been shown to produce reliable results (e.g., Filipek, Richelme, Kennedy, & Caviness, 1994; Kohn et al., 1991). These methods have provided data on the intracranial composition of the three main brain compartments related to cytoarchitecture and connectivity: gray matter (GM), the somatodendritic tissue of neurons (cortical and deep); white matter (WM), the axonal compartment of myelinated connecting fibers; and cerebrospinal fluid (CSF).

In one of the first studies examining segmented MRI in children and adults, Jernigan and Tallal (1990) documented the "pruning" process proposed by Huttenlocher's (1984) work. They found that children had higher GM volumes than adults, a finding indicating loss of GM during adolescence. This group has more recently replicated these results by use of advanced methods for image analysis (Sowell, Thompson, Holmes, Jernigan, & Toga, 1999). Their new study also demonstrated that the pruning is most "aggressive" in prefrontal and temporoparietal cortical brain regions. As a result of this work, we now recognize that both myelination and pruning are important aspects of brain development.

In a landmark paper published in 1996, a National Institutes of Health (NIH) group reported results of a brain volumetric MRI study on 104 healthy children ranging in age from 4 to 18 (Giedd et al., 1996). Although this group did not segment the MRI data into compartments, they did observe developmental changes that clearly indicated prolonged maturation beyond age 17. In a later report on this sample, in which segmentation algorithms were applied, the investigators were able to pinpoint the greatest delay in myelination, defined as WM volume, for frontotemporal pathways (Paus et al., 1999). This finding is very consistent with the Yakovlev and Lecours (1967) projections. The NIH group went on to exploit the ability of MRI to obtain repeated measures on the same individuals. Using these longitudinal data, they were able to better pinpoint the timing of preadolescent increase in GM that precipitates the pruning process of adolescence. Of importance to the question of maturation as defined by myelogenesis are results indicating that the volume of WM continued to show increases up to age 22 years (Giedd et al., 1999).

A Harvard group developed a sophisticated procedure for MRI analysis (Filipek et al., 1994) which they applied to a sample of children with the age range of 7 to 11 years and used to compare results with those of adults (Caviness, Kennedy, Richelme, Rademacher, & Filipek, 1996). They found sex differences suggesting earlier maturation of females, and generally supported the role of WM as an index of maturation. Their results also indicated that WM shows a delay in reaching its peak volume until early adulthood.

Another landmark study, published by a Stanford group, examined segmented MRI on a "retrospective" sample of 88 participants ranging in age from 3 months to 30 years and a "prospective" sample of 73 healthy men aged 21 to 70 years (Pfefferbaum et al., 1994). Scans for the retrospective sample were available from the clinical caseload, although images were carefully selected to include only those with a negative clinical reading; the prospective sample was recruited specifically for research and was medically screened to be healthy. The results demonstrated a clear neurodevelopmental course for GM and WM, the former showing a steady decline during adolescence whereas the latter showed increased volume until about age 20 to 22 years.

A Johns Hopkins group used a similar approach in a sample of 85 healthy children and adolescents ranging in age from 5 to 17 years (Reiss, Abrams, Singer, Ross, & Denckla, 1996). Consistent with postmortem and the other volumetric MRI studies, these investigators reported a steady increase in WM volume with age that did not seem to peak by age 17. Unfortunately, they did not have data on older individuals. Their results are consistent with those of Blatter et al. (1995) from Utah, although the extensive Utah database combines ages 16 to 25 and therefore does not permit evaluation of changes during late adolescence and early adulthood.

In the only study to date that has examined segmented MRI volumes from a prospective sample of 28 healthy children aged 1 month to 10 years and a small adult sample, Matsuzawa et al. (2001) applied the segmentation procedures developed by the Penn group. Matsuzawa et al. demonstrated increased volume of both GM and WM in the first postnatal months, but whereas GM volume peaked at about 2 years of age, the volume of WM, which indicates brain maturation, continued to increase into adulthood (Figure 5.2). Furthermore, consistent with the postmortem and other MRI studies that have examined this issue, the frontal lobe showed the greatest maturational lag, and its myelination is unlikely completed before young adulthood.

Magnetic resonance imaging studies in first-episode patients have indicated smaller brain

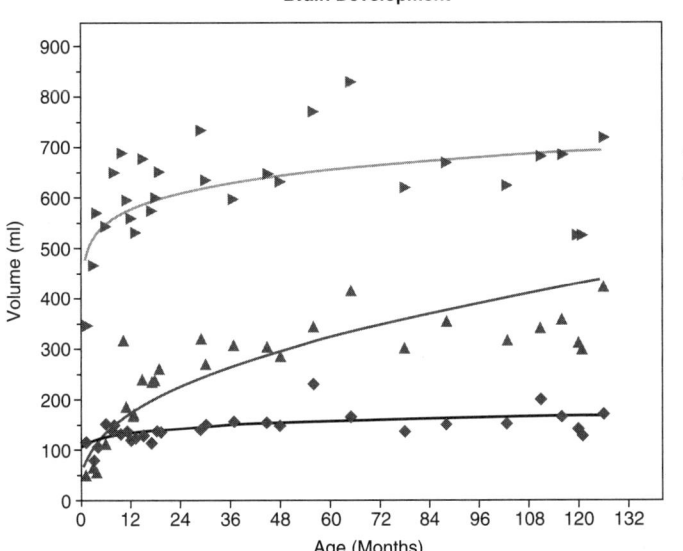

Brain Development

Figure 5.2 Compartmental volumes of gray matter (GM), white matter (WM), and cerebrospinal fluid (CSF) from birth [from Matsuzawa. J., Matsui, M., Konishi, T., Noguci, K., Gur, R.C., Bilker, W., & Miyawaki, T. (2001). Age-related volumetric changes of brain gray and white matter in healthy infants and children. *Cerebral Coretex, 11*, 335–342, used with permission].

volume and an increase in CSF relative to that in healthy people (e.g., Gur et al. 1998a; Ho et al., 2003). The increase is more pronounced in ventricular than in sulcal CSF. Brain and CSF volumes have been related to phenomenological and other clinical variables such as premorbid functioning, symptom severity, and outcome. Abnormalities in these measures are likely to be more pronounced in patients with poorer premorbid functioning, more severe symptoms, and worse outcome. The concept of brain reserve or resilience may apply to schizophrenia as well, with normal brain and CSF volumes as preliminary indicators of protective capacity. As our understanding of how brain systems regulate behavior in health and disease improves, we can take advantage of neuroimaging to examine specific brain regions implicated in the pathophysiology of schizophrenia.

Gray and white matter tissue segmentation can help determine whether tissue loss and disorganization in schizophrenia are primarily the result of a GM deficit or whether abnormalities in WM are also involved. Several studies using segmentation methods have indicated that GM volume reduction characterizes individuals with schizophrenia, whereas the volume of WM is

normal. The reduction in GM is apparent in first-episode, never-treated patients and supports the growing body of work that schizophrenia is a neurodevelopmental disorder (e.g., Gur et al., 1999).

In evaluating specific regions, the most consistent findings are of reduced volumes of prefrontal cortex and temporal lobe structures. Other brain regions also noted to have reduced volumes include the parietal lobe, thalamus, basal ganglia, cerebellar vermis, and olfactory bulbs. Relatively few studies have related sublobar volumes to clinical or neurocognitive measures. Available studies, however, support the hypothesis that increased volume is associated with lower severity of negative symptoms and better cognitive performance (e.g., Gur et al., 2000a,b; Ho et al., 2003).

The question of progression of tissue loss has been addressed in relatively few studies and in small samples, reflecting the difficulty of recruiting for study patients in the early stages of illness. Longitudinal studies applying MRI have examined first-episode patients. One group of investigators found no ventricular changes in a follow-up study, conducted 1 to 2 years after the initial study, of 13 patients and 8 controls (Degreef et al., 1992). Another study evaluated 16 patients and 5 controls, studied 2 years after a first psychotic episode (DeLisi et al., 1991). Patients showed no consistent change in ventricular size with time, although there were individual increases or decreases. With a slightly larger group of 24 patients and 6 controls, no significant changes were observed in ventricular or temporal lobe volume at follow-up (DeLisi et al., 1992). Subsequently, 20 of these patients and 5 controls were rescanned over 4 years, and greater decreases in whole-brain volume and enlargement in left ventricular volume were observed in patients. The authors concluded that subtle cortical changes may occur after the onset of illness, suggesting progression in some cases (DeLisi et al., 1995).

In a longitudinal study with a larger sample, 40 patients (20 first-episode, 20 previously treated) and 17 healthy participants were rescanned an average of 2.5 years later. Volumes of whole brain, CSF, and frontal and temporal lobes were measured (Gur, Cowell, et al., 1998). First-episode and previously treated patients had smaller whole-brain, frontal, and temporal lobe volumes than controls at intake. Longitudinally, a reduction in frontal lobe volume was found only in patients, and was most pronounced at the early stages of illness, whereas temporal lobe reduction was seen also in controls. In both first-episode and previously treated patients, volume reduction was associated with decline in some neurobehavioral functions.

The question of specificity of neuroanatomic findings to schizophrenia was addressed in a recent study that evaluated 13 patients with first-episode schizophrenia, 15 patients with first-episode affective psychosis (mainly manic), and 14 healthy comparison subjects longitudinally, with scans separated by 1.5 years (Kasai et. al., 2003a). The investigators reported that patients with schizophrenia had progressive decreases in GM volume over time in the left superior temporal gyrus, compared with that in both of the other groups. The existence of neuroanatomical abnormalities in first-episode patients indicates that brain dysfunction occurs before clinical presentation. However, the longitudinal studies suggest evidence of progression, in which anatomic changes may impact some clinical and neurobehavioral features of the illness in some patients. There is also evidence that progression is significantly greater in early-onset patients during adolescence than it is for adult subjects (Gogate, Giedd, Janson, & Rapoport, 2001).

Findings from MRI have been most consistent for GM volume reduction, but more recently, WM changes have also been reported. In the coming years the availability of diffusion tensor imaging will enhance the efforts to examine compartmental abnormalities. The growing understanding of brain development and MRI data obtained from children suggest that the neuroanatomic neuroimaging literature in schizophrenia is consistent with diffuse disruption of normal maturation. Thus, there is clear evidence for structural abnormalities in schizophrenia that are associated with reduced cognitive capacity and less clearly with symptoms. Future work, perhaps with more advanced computerized parcellation methods, is needed to better chart the brain pathways most severely affected.

Electrophysiology

The *electroencephalogram* (EEG) measures the electrical activity of the brain; it originates from the summated electrical potentials generated by inhibitory and excitatory inputs onto neurons. The main source of the scalp-recorded EEG is in the cortex of the brain, which contains the large and parallel dendritic trees of pyramidal neurons whose regular ordering facilitates summation. One of the important advances in EEG-based research was the development of a technique to isolate the brain activity related to specific events from the background EEG; this activity related to specific events is termed *event-related potentials,* or ERPs. Using averaging techniques, it is possible to visualize events related to one of the many different brain operations reflected in the EEG. Typically, these ERPs are related to the specific processing of certain sensory stimuli.

In recent years, many new means of measuring brain structure and function have been developed, each with its advantages in study of the brain. Electroencephalographic and ERP measures are unsurpassed in providing real-time, millisecond resolution of normal and pathological brain processing, literally at the speed of thought, whereas functional magnetic resonance imaging (fMRI) and PET have temporal resolutions some thousand-fold less. Moreover, fMRI and PET only indirectly track neural activity through its effects on blood flow or metabolism. However, the ability of EEG and ERP techniques to localize sources of activity is much less than that of fMRI and PET, and these methods, together with structural MRI, are needed to supplement EEG and ERP information.

Current Event-Related Potential Research in Schizophrenia

Space limitations preclude discussion of all ERPs. We provide here a sample of current work designed to illuminate a fundamental question in schizophrenia research—namely, how the brains of patients suffering from this disorder differ from those of healthy subjects. Event-related potentials provide a functional window on many aspects of brain processing. These include the most elementary ones, likely involving cellular circuitry (gamma band activity), early, simple signal detection and gating (P50), and automatic detection of changes in the environment (mismatch negativity activity), and more complex activity such as conscious updating of expectations in view of unusual events (P300).

In this section we will first briefly review studies of ERP processes in adults with schizophrenia that illustrate the potential of these measures to provide clues about the cellular circuitry that may be impaired in schizophrenia. The auditory modality plays a special role because it is severely affected in schizophrenia, as evinced in the primacy of auditory hallucinations and speech and language pathology. The data presented here support the hypothesis that schizophrenia involves abnormalities in brain processing from the most simple to the most complex level, and that the anatomical substrates of auditory processing in the neocortical temporal lobe, most carefully investigated in the superior temporal gyrus, themselves evince reduction in GM volume. Next, we briefly summarize a series of studies of adolescents with schizophrenia in which ERPS are recorded while the youngsters perform

poorly on cognitive tasks that make extensive demands on processing resources. These studies use ERPs in an attempt to identify the earliest stage of cognitive processing at which deficits emerge in adolescents with schizophrenia.

Gamma-band activity and neural circuit abnormalities at the cellular level. The first ERP we will consider is the steady-state gamma-band response. *Gamma band* refers to a brain oscillation at and near the frequency of 40 Hertz (Hz) or 40 times per second; *steady-state* refers to its being elicited by a stimulus of the same frequency. At the cellular level, gamma-band activity is an endogenous brain oscillation thought to reflect the synchronizing of activity in several columns of cortical neurons, or between cortex and thalamus, with this synchronization facilitating communication. At the cognitive level, work in humans suggests that gamma activity reflects the convergence of multiple processing streams in cortex, giving rise to a unified percept. A simple example is a "fire truck"; a particular combination of form perception, motion perception, and auditory perception are melded to form this percept. Gamma activity at its simplest, however, involves basic neural circuitry composed of projection neurons, usually using excitatory amino acid (EAA) neurotransmission, linked with inhibitory gamma-aminobutyric acid (GABA)ergic interneurons. Studies of gamma activity in schizophrenia aim to determine if there is a basic circuit abnormality present, such as might arise from a deficiency in recurrent inhibition, postulated by a number of workers (see review in McCarley, Hsiao, Freedman, Pfefferbaum, & Donchin, 1996). Gamma-band studies themselves, however, cannot reveal any specific details of neural circuitry abnormality.

Kwon and colleagues (1999) began the study of gamma in schizophrenia using an exogenous input of 40-Hz auditory clicks, leading to a steady-state gamma response. The magnitude of the brain response was measured by power, the amount of EEG energy at a specific frequency, with the degree of capability of gamma driving being reflected in the power at and near 40 Hz. Compared with healthy controls, schizophrenia patients had a markedly reduced power at 40-Hz input, although they showed normal driving at slower frequencies, which indicated that this was not a general reduction in power but one specific to the gamma band.

Spencer and colleagues (2003) took the next logical step and evaluated the gamma-band response to visual stimuli in schizophrenia, to determine whether high-frequency neural synchronization associated with the perception of visual gestalts is abnormal in schizophrenia patients. Previous studies of healthy individuals had reported enhancements of gamma-band power (Tallon-Baudry & Bertrand, 1999) and phase locking (Rodriguez et al., 1999) when gestalt objects are perceived. In the study by Spencer et al., individuals with schizophrenia and matched healthy people discriminated between square gestalt stimuli and non-square stimuli (square/no-square conditions). In schizophrenia patients, the early visual system gamma-band response to gestalt square stimuli was lacking. There were also abnormalities in gamma-band synchrony between brain regions, with schizophrenia patients showing decreasing rather than increasing gamma-band coherence between posterior visual regions and other brain regions after perceiving the visual gestalt stimuli. These findings support the hypothesis that schizophrenia is associated with a fundamental abnormality in cellular neural circuitry evinced as a failure of gamma-band synchronization, especially in the 40-Hz range.

Sensory gating and the P50—early sensory gating. Several ERPs have been related to the search for an electrophysiologic concomitant of an early sensory gating deficit in schizophrenia. These include, for example, the startle response, for which the size of a blink to an acoustic probe is measured. Schizophrenia patients appear to be unable to modify their large startle response when forewarned that a probe is coming, in contrast with controls (e.g., Braff et al., 1978).

Another ERP thought to be sensitive to an early sensory gating abnormality in schizophrenia is the P50. In the sensory gating paradigm, an auditory click is presented to a subject, eliciting a positive deflection about 50 msec after stimulus onset, the P50 component. After a brief interval (about 500 msec), a second click elicits a much smaller-amplitude P50 in normal adult subjects, who are said to show normal gating: the first stimulus inhibits, or closes the gate to, neu-

rophysiological processing of the second stimulus. Patients with schizophrenia, by contrast, show less reduction in P50 amplitude to the second click, which is referred to as a failure in gating (Freedman, Adler, Waldo, Oachtman, & Franks, 1983). This gating deficit occurs in about half the first-degree relatives of a schizophrenic patient, a finding suggesting that it may index a genetic factor in schizophrenia in the absence of overt psychotic symptoms (Waldo et al., 1991). Patients with affective disorder may show a gating deficit, but the deficit does not persist after successful treatment; in patients with schizophrenia, the deficit occurs in both medicated and unmedicated patients and persists after symptom remission (Adler et al., 1991; Freedman et al., 1983).

The gating effect is thought to take place in temporal lobe structures, possibly the medial temporal lobe (Adler, Waldo, & Freedman, 1985). P50 gating is enhanced by nicotinic cholinergic mechanisms, and it is possible that smoking in patients with schizophrenia is a form of self-medication. Freedman et al. (1994) have shown that blockade of the α_7-nicotinic receptor, localized to hippocampal neurons, causes loss of the inhibitory gating response to auditory stimuli in an animal model. The failure of inhibitory mechanisms to gate sensory input to higher-order processing might result in "sensory flooding," which Freedman suggests may underlie many of the symptoms of schizophrenia.

Mismatch negativity and postonset progression of abnormalities. Mismatch negativity (MMN) is a negative ERP that occurs about 0.2 sec after infrequent sounds (deviants) are presented in the sequence of repetitive sounds (standards). Deviant sounds may differ from the standards in a simple physical characteristic such as pitch, duration, intensity, or spatial location. Mismatch negativity is primarily evoked automatically, that is, without conscious attention. Its main source is thought to be in or near primary auditory cortex (Heschl gyrus) and to reflect the operations of sensory memory, a memory of past stimuli used by the auditory cortex in analysis of temporal patterns.

There is a consistent finding of a reduction in amplitude of MMN in chronically ill schizophrenia patients that appears to be traitlike and not ameliorated by either typical (haloperidol) or atypical (clozapine) medication (Umbricht et al., 1998). A point of particular interest has been the finding that the MMN elicited by tones of different frequency (the pitch MMN) is normal in patients at the time of first hospitalization (Salisbury, Bonner-Jackson, Griggs, Shenton, & McCarley, 2001; confirmed by Umbricht, Javitt, Bates, Kane, & Lieberman, 2002), whereas the MMN elicited by the same stimuli is abnormal in chronic schizophrenia. This finding suggests that pitch MMN might index a postonset progression of brain abnormalities. Indeed, the prospective longitudinal study of Salisbury, McCarley, and colleagues (unpublished data) now has preliminary data showing that schizophrenia subjects without a MMN abnormality at first hospitalization develop an abnormality over the next 1.5 years.

In the same group of patients, the Heschl gyrus, the likely source of the MMN, demonstrates a progressive reduction in GM volume over the same time period (Kasai et al., 2003b). In participants with both MRI and MMN procedures, the degree of GM volume reduction was found to parallel the degree of MMN reduction, although the number of subjects examined is currently relatively small and this conclusion is tentative. Although the presence of postonset progression of abnormalities is controversial in the field, it is of obvious importance to our understanding of the disorder and of particular importance to the study of adolescents with onset of schizophrenia, because it would prompt a search for possible medication and/or psychosocial treatment that might ameliorate progression.

Recent multimodal imaging (Wible et al., 2001) has demonstrated the presence of a deficiency of fMRI activation (BOLD) in schizophrenia to the mismatch stimulus within Heschl's gyrus and nearby posterior superior temporal gyrus.

Because MMN may reflect, in part, N-methyl-D-aspartate (NMDA)-mediated activity, a speculation about the reason for progression is that NMDA-mediated excitotoxity might cause both a reduction in the neuropil (dendritic regression) and a concomitant reduction in the MMN in the months following first hospitalization. Only further work will determine whether this specula-tion is valid. It is noteworthy that the MMN abnormalities present in schizophrenic psychosis are not present in manic psychosis.

P300 and the failure to process unusual events. The P300 is an ERP that occurs when a low-probability event is detected and consciously processed. Typically, subjects are asked to count a low-probability tone that is interspersed with a more frequently occurring stimulus. The P300 differs from the typical MMN paradigm in that the stimuli are presented at a slower rate (typically around one per second) and the subject is actively and consciously attending and processing the stimuli, whereas the MMN stimuli are not consciously processed. P300 is larger when the stimulus is rare. Whereas MMN is thought to reflect sensory memory, by definition preconscious, P300 is thought to reflect an updating of the conscious information-processing stream and of expectancy.

Reduction of the P300 amplitude at midline sites is the most frequently replicated abnormality in schizophrenia, although P300 reduction is also found in some other disorders. This widespread P300 reduction also appears to be traitlike and an enduring feature of the disease. For example, Ford and colleagues (1994) demonstrated that although P300 showed moderate amplitude increases with symptom resolution, it did not approach normal values during these periods of remission. Umbricht et al. (1998) have reported that atypical antipsychotic treatment led to a significant increase of P300 amplitudes in patients with schizophrenia.

In addition to the midline P300 reduction, both chronically ill and first-episode schizophrenic subjects display an asymmetry in P300 with smaller voltage over the left temporal lobe than over the right. The more pronounced this left temporal P300 amplitude abnormality, the more pronounced is the extent of psychopathology, as reflected in thought disorder and paranoid delusions (e.g., McCarley et al., 1993, 2002). It is possible the increased delusions reflect a failure of veridical updating of cognitive schemata. This left temporal deficit is not found in affective (manic) psychosis.

There are likely several bilateral brain generators responsible for the P300, with a generator in the superior temporal gyrus (STG) likely underlying the left temporal deficit, since, in schizophrenia, the greater the reduction in GM volume in posterior STG, the greater the reduction in P300 amplitude at left temporal sites in both chronic and first-episode schizophrenia patients. It is of note that the posterior STG, on the left in right-handed individuals, is an area intimately related to language processing and thinking (it includes part of Wernicke's area), and an area where volume reductions are associated with increased thought disorder and severity of auditory hallucinations.

Event-related Potential Measures in Children and Adolescents with Schizophrenia

Event-related indices of information processing deficits. Brain activity reflected in ERPs recorded during performance of information-processing tasks can be used to help isolate the component or stage of information-processing that is impaired in schizophrenia. A series of ERP studies of children and adolescents with schizophrenia, conducted by the UCLA Childhood Onset Schizophrenia program, are summarized below (see Strandburg et al., 1994a and Asarnow, Brown, & Strandburg, 1995 for reviews). These studies examined ERP components while children and adolescents with schizophrenia performed tasks like the span of apprehension (Span; Strandburg, Marsh, Brown, Asarnow, & Guthrie, 1984) and a continuous performance test (CPT; Strandburg et al., 1990). Several decades of studying mental chronometry with ERPs has produced a lexicon of ERP components with well-established neurocognitive correlates (Hillyard & Kutas, 1983). These ERP components can be used to help identify the stages of information processing that are impaired in schizophrenia.

The UCLA ERP studies have focused primarily on four components: contingent negative variation (CNV), hemispheric asymmetry in the amplitude of the P1/N1 component complex, processing negativity (Np), and a late positive component (P300). The CNV measures orienting, preparation, and readiness to respond to an expected stimulus. There are at least two separate generators of the CNV: an early frontal component believed to be an orienting response to

warning stimuli, and a later central component associated with preparedness for stimuli-processing and response (Rohrbaugh et al., 1986).

Healthy individuals typically have larger visual P1/N1 components over the right cerebral hemisphere. Many of the UCLA studies compared hemispheric laterality between healthy and schizophrenia individuals. Differences in lateralization during visual information-processing tasks could reflect either differences in the strategic use of processing capacity of the hemispheres or a lateralized neural deficit.

The Np is a family of negative components that occur within the first 400 msec after the onset of a stimulus, indicating the degree to which attentional and perceptual resources have been allocated to stimulus processing. Because the Np waves occur contemporaneously with other components (P1, N1, and P2), they are best seen in difference potentials resulting from the subtraction of non-attend ERPs from attend ERPs (Hillyard & Hansen, 1986; Naatanan, 1982). Finally, as described above, the P300 is a frequently studied index of the recognition of stimulus significance in relation to task demands.

Event-related potential results in child and adolescent schizophrenia. Table 5.2 summarizes by component the ERP results from six UCLA studies of children or adults with schizophrenia. In all the studies summarized in this table there were large and robust performance differences between groups in both the accuracy and reaction times of signal detection responses. Thus, the behavioral paradigms were successful in eliciting information-processing deficits in these patients.

The CNV differences between normals and schizophrenics were not consistently found across studies. In the span task (which includes a warning interval) all possible results were obtained (normals > schizophrenics; normals = schizophrenics; and normals < schizophrenics). For the CNV-like negative wave occurring in the CPT task, no group differences were found in either experiment. Because the warning interval was short and the wave was largest frontally, the CNVs in both tasks were most likely the early wave related to orienting. Thus, differences in prestimulus orienting do not seem to reliably ac-

Table 5.2 Information-Processing Tasks in Child and Adolescent and Adult-Onset Schizophrenia: Summary of Evoked Potential Studies.

Reference	Task	P300	Group Tested	CNV	P1/N1 Asymmetry	Np
Strandburg et al., 1984	Span	Norm > schiz	Schizophrenic children	Norm > schiz	Norm > schiz	Norm > schiz[a]
Strandburg et al., 1990	CPT	Norm > schiz	Schizophrenic children	Norm = schiz	Norm > schiz	—
Strandburg et al., 1991	Span	—	Schizophrenic children	Norm = schiz	Norm > schiz	Norm > schiz
Strandburg et al., 1994a	Span	Norm > schiz	Schizophrenic adults	Schiz > norm	Norm > schiz	Norm > schiz
Strandburg et al., 1994b	CPT	Norm > schiz[b]	Schizophrenic children	Norm = schiz	Norm > schiz	Norm > schiz
Strandburg et al., 1997	Idiom recognition	Norm > schiz	Schizophrenic adults	Norm > schiz	—	—

[a] Larger task-difficulty increased more in N1 amplitude in normals than in schizophrenics.

[b] Normals had larger P300 than schizophrenics for targets in the single-target CPT task.

CNV, contingent negative variation; CPT, continuous performance task; Np, processing negativity; P300, late positive component.

count for the poor performance of schizophrenics on these tasks. There are mixed results in CNV experiments on adults with schizophrenia, although most studies found smaller CNVs in schizophrenics (Pritchard, 1986). A longer warning interval than that used in the UCLA experiments (500 msec in the span and 1250 msec ISI in the CNV) may be required to detect preparatory abnormalities in schizophrenia.

In every study summarized in Table 5.2 in which processing negativities were measured, Nps were found to be smaller in schizophrenics. This deficit was seen in both children and adults, with both the span and CPT (Strandburg et al., 1994c) tasks. In contrast, a group of children with ADHD studied while they performed a CPT task showed no evidence of a smaller Np. Diminished Np amplitude is the earliest consistent ERP index of schizophrenia-related information-processing deficit in the UCLA studies. These results suggest impaired allocation of attentional and perceptual resources.

Most studies of processing negativities during channel selective attention tasks (Nd) find that adults with schizophrenia produce less attentional-related endogenous negative activity than do normal controls (see reviews by Cohen, 1990, and Pritchard, 1986). The UCLA results compliment this finding in adults by using a discriminative processing task and extend these findings to childhood- and adolescent-onset schizophrenia. Reductions in the amplitude of Np in schizophrenia result from impairments in executive functions responsible for the maintenance of an attentional trace (Baribeau-Braun, Picton, & Gosselin, 1983; Michie, Fox, Ward, Catts, & McConaghy, 1990). Baribeau-Braun et al. (1983) observed normal Nd activity with rapid stimulus presentation rates, but reduced amplitudes with slower rates, findings suggesting that the neural substrates of Nd are intact but improperly regulated in schizophrenia. Individuals with frontal lobe lesions resemble individuals with schizophrenia in this regard, in that both groups do not show increased Np to attended stimuli in auditory selection tasks (Knight, Hillyard, Woods, & Neville 1981).

As noted earlier, reduced amplitude P300 in schizophrenic adults has been consistently found using a wide variety of experimental paradigms (Pritchard et al., 1986). As can be seen in Table 5.2, the UCLA studies also consistently observed smaller P300 amplitude in studies of both schizophrenic children and adults, in the span, CPT, and idiom recognition tasks. P300 latency was also measured in two of these studies. Although prolonged P300 latency was found in one study (Strandburg et al., 1994c), no differences were found in another (Strandburg et al., 1994b). The majority of ERP studies have reported normal P300 latency in schizophrenics (Pritchard, 1986).

Absence of right-lateralized P1/N1 amplitude in visual ERPs has been a consistent finding in all five of the UCLA studies that used the CPT and span tasks. Abnormally lateralized electrophysiological responses, related either to lateralized dysfunction in schizophrenia or a pathology-related difference in information-processing strategy, is a consistent aspect of both adult- and childhood-onset schizophrenia. These results are consistent with abnormal patterns of hemispheric laterality in schizophrenics (e.g., Tucker & Williamson, 1984).

In summary, ERP studies of schizophrenic adults and children performing discriminative processing tasks suggest that the earliest reliable electrophysiological correlate of impaired discriminative processing in schizophrenia is the Np component. It appears that children and adolescents with schizophrenia are deficient in the allocation of attentional resources necessary for efficient and accurate discriminative processing. Although diminished amplitude processing negativities have been observed in ADHD in auditory paradigms (Loiselle, Stamm, Maitinsky, & Whipple, 1980; Satterfield, Schell, Nicholar, Satterfield, & Freese, 1990), Np was found to be normal in ADHD children during the UCLA CPT task (Strandburg et al., 1994a). Diminished Np visual processing may be specific to schizophrenic pathology. Later ERP abnormalities in schizophrenia (e.g., diminished amplitude P300) may be a "downstream" product of the uncertainty in stimulus recognition created by previous discriminative difficulties, or they may be one of additional neurocognitive deficits. Abnormalities in later ERP components are not specific to schizophrenia, having been reported in studies of ADHD children (reviewed by Klorman, 1991).

The absence of P1/N1 asymmetry in the visual ERPs of schizophrenics is contemporaneous with diminished Np. However, the fact that Np amplitude varies with the processing demands of the task, whereas P1/N1 asymmetry does not, suggests that the Np deficit plays a greater role in the information-processing deficits manifested by children and adolescents with schizophrenia.

Magnetoencephalography—A Complement to Electroencephalography

Magnetoencephalography (MEG) is the measure of magnetic fields generated by the brain. A key difference between the physical source of the MEG and that of the EEG is that the MEG is sensitive to cells that lie tangential to the brain surface and consequently have magnetic fields oriented tangentially. Cells with a radial orientation (perpendicular to the brain surface) do not generate signals detectable with MEG. The EEG and MEG are complementary in that the EEG is most sensitive to radially oriented neurons and fields. This distinction arises, of course, because magnetic fields are generated at right angles to electrical fields. One major advantage that magnetic fields have over electrical potentials is that, once generated, they are relatively invulnerable to intervening variations in the media they traverse (i.e., the skull, gray and white matter, and CSF), unlike electrical fields, which are "smeared" by different electrical conductivities. This has made MEG a favorite technology for use in source localization, in which attention has been especially focused on early potentials.

Perhaps because of the expense and nonmobility of the recording equipment needed for MEG, there has been relatively little work using MEG in schizophrenia to replicate and extend the findings of ERPs. A search of Medline in 2000 revealed only 23 published studies using MEG measures of brain activity in schizophrenia. The extant studies have shown interesting results. Reite and colleagues demonstrated that M100 component (the magnetic analogue to the N100) showed less interhemispheric asymmetry in

male schizophrenics and had different source orientations in the left hemisphere. The recent review by Reite, Teale, and Rojas (1999) should be consulted for more details of the work on MEG in schizophrenia.

In summary, electrophysiology has the advantage of providing real-time information on brain processing, with a resolution in the millisecond range. In schizophrenia, it shows abnormalities of processing from the very earliest stages (Np, mismatch negativity, P50, gamma activity) to later stages of attentive discrepancy processing (P300) and semantic processing (N400). This suggests a model of disturbance that encompasses a wide variety of processing and is most compatible with a brain model of circuit abnormalities underlying processing at each stage, particularly in the auditory modality. This is also compatible with MRI studies of abnormal GM regions associated with abnormal ERPs.

One of the more intriguing potential applications to schizophrenia in adolescence is using ERPs to track progression of brain abnormalities. The mismatch negativity ERP is normal at onset (first hospitalization) of schizophrenia but becomes abnormal in the course of the disorder (this developing abnormality is associated with a loss of GM in auditory cortex). The mismatch negativity is thus potentially of use in tracking the ability of therapeutic interventions to minimize brain changes. It is not yet known if gamma abnormalities become evident early or late in the course of schizophrenia.

Neuroendocrinology

In recent years, the postpubescent period received increasing attention from researchers in the field of schizophrenia (Stevens, 2002). This interest stems largely from the fact that adolescence is associated with a significant rise in the risk for psychotic symptoms, particularly prodromal signs of schizophrenia (van Oel, Sitskoorn, Cremer, & Kahn, 2002; Walker, 2002). Further, rates of other psychiatric syndromes, including mood and anxiety disorders, escalate during adolescence. It has been suggested that hormonal changes may play an important role in this developmental phenomena, making adolescence a critical period for the emergence of mental illness (Walker, 2002).

Puberty results from increased activation of the hypothalamic-pituitary-gonadal (HPG) axis, which results in a rise in secretion of sex hormones (steroids) by the gonads in response to gonadotropin secretion from the anterior pituitary. Rising sex steroid concentrations are associated with other changes, including increased growth hormone secretion.

There is also an augmentation of activity in the hypothalamic-pituitary-adrenal (HPA) axis during adolescence. This neural system governs the release of several hormones and is activated in response to stress. Cortisol is among the hormones secreted by the HPA axis, and researchers can measure it in body fluids to index the biological response to stress. Beginning around age 12, there is an age-related increase in baseline cortisol levels in normal children. The change from pre- to postpubertal status is linked with a marked rise in cortisol (Walker, Walder, & Reynolds, 2001) and a significant rise in cortisol clearance and in the volume of cortisol distribution.

The significance of postpubertal hormonal changes has been brought into clearer focus as researchers have elucidated the role of steroid hormones in neuronal activity and morphology (Dorn & Chrousos, 1997; Rupprecht & Holsboer, 1999). Neurons contain receptors for adrenal and gonadal hormones. When activated, these receptors modify cellular function and impact neurotransmitter function. Short-term effects (nongenomic effects) of steroid hormones on cellular function are believed to be mediated by membrane receptors. Longer-term effects (genomic effects) can result from the activation of intraneuronal or nuclear receptors. These receptors can influence gene expression. Brain changes that occur during normal adolescence may be regulated by hormonal effects on the expression of genes that govern brain maturation.

Gonadal and adrenal hormone levels are linked with behavior in adolescents. In general, both elevated and very low levels are associated with greater adjustment problems. For example, higher levels of the adrenal hormones (androstenedione) are associated with adjustment problems in both boys and girls (Nottelmann et

al., 1987). Children with an earlier onset of puberty have significantly higher concentrations of adrenal androgens, estradiol, thyrotropin, and cortisol. They also manifest more psychological disorders (primarily anxiety disorders), self-reported depression, and parent-reported behavior problems (Dorn, Hitt, & Rotenstein, 1999). The relationship between testosterone and aggressive behavior is more pronounced in adolescents with more conflictual parent-child relationships, and this demonstrates the complex interactions between hormonal and environmental factors (Booth, Johnson, Granger, Crouter, & McHale 2003).

It is conceivable that hormones are partially exerting their effects on behavior by triggering the expression of genes that are linked with vulnerability for behavioral disorders. Consistent with this assumption, the heritability estimates for antisocial behavior (Jacobson, Prescott, & Kendler, 2002) and depression (Silberg et al., 1999) increase during adolescence. Further, the relationship between cortisol and behavior may be more pronounced in youth with genetic vulnerabilities. For example, increased cortisol is more strongly associated with behavior problems in boys and girls with fragile X than in their unaffected siblings (Hessl et al., 2002).

To date, there has been relatively little research on the HPG axis and schizophrenia, and there is no database on gonadal hormones in adolescent schizophrenia patients. The available reports on adult schizophrenia patients suggest that estrogen may serve to modulate the severity of psychotic symptoms and enhance prognosis (Huber et al., 2001; Seeman, 1997). Specifically, there is evidence that estrogen may have an ameliorative effect by reducing dopaminergic activity.

The role of the HPA axis in schizophrenia has received greater attention. A large body of research literature suggests a link between exposure to psychosocial stress and symptom relapse and exacerbation in schizophrenia (Walker & Diforio, 1997). It has been suggested that activation of the HPA axis mediates this effect (Walker & Diforio, 1997). Dysregulation of the HPA axis, including elevated baseline cortisol and cortisol response to pharmacological challenge, is often found in unmedicated schizophrenia patients (e.g., Lammers et al., 1995; Lee, Woo, & Meltzer, 2001; Muck-Seler, Pivac, Jakovljevic, & Brzovic, 1999). Patients with higher cortisol levels have more severe symptoms (Walder, Walker, & Lewine, 2000) and are more likely to commit suicide (Plocka-Lewandowska, Araszkiewicz, & Rybakowski, 2001).

Basic research has demonstrated that cortisol affects the activity of several neurotransmitter systems. This includes dopamine, a neurotransmitter that has been implicated in the etiology of schizophrenia (Walker & Diforio, 1997). The assumption is that increased dopamine activity plays a role in psychotic symptoms. Cortisol secretion augments dopamine activity. Thus it may be that when patients are exposed to stress and elevations in cortisol ensue, dopamine activity increases and symptoms are triggered or exacerbated.

Although there are no published reports on cortisol secretion in adolescents with schizophrenia, HPA axis function has been studied in adolescents with schizotypal personality disorder (Weinstein, Diforio, Schiffman, Walker, & Bonsall, 1999). Schizotypal personality disorder (SPD) involves subclinical manifestations of the symptoms of schizophrenia, including social withdrawal and unusual perceptions and ideas. This disorder is both genetically and developmentally linked with schizophrenia. The genetic link is indicated by the higher rate of SPD in the family members of patients diagnosed with schizophrenia. From a developmental perspective, there is extensive evidence that the defining symptoms of SPD often predate the diagnosis of schizophrenia, usually arising during adolescence.

When compared to healthy adolescents, adolescents with SPD show elevated baseline levels of cortisol (Weinstein et al., 1999) and a more pronounced developmental increase in cortisol when measured over a 2-year period (Walker et al., 2001). Further, SPD adolescents who show a greater developmental rise in cortisol are more likely to have an increase in symptom severity over time. This suggests that increased activation of the HPA axis may contribute to the worsening of symptoms as the child progresses through adolescence.

Research on the role of neurohormones in schizophrenia, especially the gonadal and adrenal hormones, should be given high priority in the future. In particular, it will be important to study hormonal processes in youth at risk for schizophrenia. There are several key questions to be addressed in clinical research. Are hormonal changes linked with the emergence of the prodromal phases of schizophrenia? Do rising levels of adrenal or gonadal hormones precede the onset of symptoms? Is there a relationship between hormonal factors and the brain changes that have been observed in the prodromal phase of schizophrenia? At the same time, basic science research is expected to yield new information about the impact of hormones on gene expression. This may lead to clinical research to explore the role of adolescent hormone changes on the gene expression in humans.

BRAIN CIRCUITRY IN SCHIZOPHRENIA

Information processing in the brain is a complex task, and even simple sensory information, such as recognizing a sight or a sound, engages circuits of cells in multiple regions of the brain. Scientists early in the 20th century imagined that brain function occurred in discrete steps along a linear stream of information flow. However, the recent emergence of brain imaging as an important tool for understanding the neuroscience of cognition and emotion has demonstrated that the brain operates more like a parallel processing computer with feed-forward and feedback circuitry that manages information in distributed and overlapping processing modules working in parallel. Thus, abnormal function in one brain region will have functional ripple effects in other regions, and abnormal sharing of information between regions, perhaps because of problems in the connectional wiring, can result in abnormal behavior even if individual modules are functionally intact.

In light of the elaborate and complex symptoms of schizophrenia, it is not surprising that researchers have increasingly focused on evidence of malfunction within distributed brain circuits rather than within a particular single brain region or module. Most of this work has been based on in vivo physiologic techniques, such as imaging and electrophysiology. At the same time, basic research in animals and to a lesser extent in humans has shown that the elaboration of brain circuitry is a lifelong process, especially the connection between cells in circuits within and between different regions of the cortex. This process of development and modification of connections between neurons is particularly dynamic during adolescence and early adult life. In this section, we will review some of the recent evidence that local and distributed abnormalities of brain circuitry are associated with schizophrenia and their implications for adolescent psychosis.

Frontal-Temporal Circuits

Two of the most often cited areas of the brain said to be abnormal in schizophrenia are the cortices of the frontal and temporal lobes. Indeed, damage to these regions caused by trauma, stroke, or neurological disease is more likely to be associated with psychosis than is damage to other brain regions. Recent studies using neuroimaging techniques have suggested that malfunction at the systems level—that is, at the relationship of processing in the temporal and frontal lobes combined—best characterizes the problem in patients with schizophrenia. For example, in a study of identical twins discordant for schizophrenia, differences within each twin pair in volume of the hippocampus predicted very strongly the difference in the function of the prefrontal cortex assayed physiologically during a cognitive task dependent on the function of the prefrontal cortex (Weinberger, Berman, Suddah, & Torrey, 1992).

A peculiar disturbance in the use of language, so-called thought disorder, is one of the cardinal signs of schizophrenia. Language is highly dependent on frontotemporal circuitry, which is disturbed in schizophrenia. When patients are asked to generate a list of words beginning with a specific consonant, instead of activating the frontal lobes and deactivating the temporal lobes, as seen in healthy subjects, they do the opposite. More detailed analyses have examined declarative memory encoding, storage, and retrieval as related to language. Encoding is ma-

nipulated by instructing subjects to process material more deeply, as, for example, to make semantic judgments about to-be-remembered words, such as whether the words represent living or nonliving, or abstract or concrete words. This deeper, more elaborate encoding is compared with a shallower, more superficial level of encoding, such as having subjects judge the font (upper case versus lower case) of each word presented. Compared with healthy controls, patients with schizophrenia show different patterns of fMRI activation for semantically encoded words, with significantly reduced left inferior frontal cortex activation but significantly increased left superior temporal cortex activation (Kubicki et al., 2003). During tests of word retrieval, patients with schizophrenia tend to show underengagement of the hippocampus, but at the same time their prefrontal cortex is overactive (Heckers et al., 1998). During performance of effortful tasks, by contrast, people with schizophrenia show increased activity in hippocampus and an alteration in the connection between hippocampus and anterior cingulate cortex (Holcomb et al., 2000; Medoff, Holcomb, Lahti, & Tamminga, 2001). These studies suggest that the information-processing strategy for encoding and retrieving learned information, which depends on an orchestrated duet between frontotemporal brain regions, is disturbed in patients with schizophrenia.

Similar results have been found in studies focused on prefrontal mediated memory, so-called working memory, in which the normal relationships between prefrontal activation and hippocampal deactivation are disrupted in schizophrenia (Callicott et al., 2000). Finally, recent statistical approaches to interpreting functional imaging results based on patterns of intercorrelated activity across the whole brain have demonstrated that abnormalities in schizophrenia are distributed across cortical regions. In particular, the pattern based on the normal relationships between prefrontal and temporal cortical activity is especially abnormal (Meyer-Lindenberg et al., 2001). This apparent functional abnormality in intracortical connectedness has been supported by anatomical evidence from diffusion tensor imaging, which has pointed to an abnormality in the WM links between frontal and temporal lobes (e.g., Kubicki et al., 2002).

The evidence for abnormal function across distributed cortical circuitry is quite compelling in schizophrenia, and other regions representing other circuits are also implicated (Tamminga et al., 2002; Weinberger et al., 2001). Indeed, it is not clear that any particular area of cortex is normal under all conditions. This may reflect simply the interconnectedness of the brain or it may suggest that schizophrenia is especially characterized by a "dysconnectivity." It is impossible at the current level of our understanding of the disease to differentiate between these possibilities.

Schizophrenia disrupts not only circuitry linking brain regions but also the microcircuitry within brain regions, as shown by abnormal electrophysiologic activity during simple, early-stage "automatic processing" of stimuli, processing relatively independent of directed, conscious control. For example, healthy subjects automatically generate a robust EEG response in and near primary auditory cortex to tones differing slightly in pitch from others in a series ("mismatch" response), whereas the processing response in schizophrenia to the mismatch is much less pronounced (Wible et al., 2001).

Prefrontal-Striatal Circuitry

Neurophysiological studies have focused largely on function of the cerebral cortex, but the pharmacological treatment of schizophrenia targets principally the dopamine system, which has long implicated the striatum and related subcortical sites. In fact, cortical function and activity of the subcortical dopamine system are intimately related, consistent with circuitry models of brain function. Animal studies have demonstrated conclusively that perturbations in cortical function, especially prefrontal function, disrupt a normal tonic brake on dopamine neurons in the brainstem, leading to a loss of the normal regulation of these neurons and to their excessive activation (Weinberger et al., 2001). It is thought that the prefrontal cortex helps guide the dopamine reward system toward the reinforcing of contextually appropriate stimuli. In the absence of such normal regulation, reward

and motivation may be less appropriately targeted.

Neuroimaging studies of the dopamine system in patients with schizophrenia, particularly those who are actively psychotic, have found evidence of overactivity in the striatum (Laruelle, 2000). Recently, two studies reported that this apparent overactivation of the subcortical dopamine system is strongly predicted by measures of abnormal prefrontal cortical function (Bertolino et al., 2000; Meyer-Lindenberg et al., 2002). Moreover, reducing dopaminergic transmission with dopamine antagonists in subcortical dopamine-rich regions is associated with substantial alterations in frontal cortex function (Holcomb et al., 1996), presumably mediated through circuits connecting the striatum to the frontal cortex (Alexander & Crutcher, 1990). These data illustrate that what happens in the prefrontal cortex is very important to how other brain systems function and that the behavioral disturbances of schizophrenia involve dysfunction of diverse and interconnected brain systems.

Brain Circuitry and Implications for Adolescence

Contrary to long-held ideas that the brain was mostly grown-up after childhood, it is now clear that adolescence is a time of explosive growth and development of the brain. While the number of nerve cells does not change after birth, the richness and complexity of the connections between cells do, and the capacity for these networks to process increasingly complex information changes accordingly. Cortical regions that handle abstract information and that are critical for learning and memory of abstract concepts—rules, laws, codes of social conduct—seem to become much more likely to share information in a parallel processing fashion as adulthood approaches. This pattern of increased cortical information sharing is reflected in the patterns of connections between neurons in different regions of the cortex. Thus, the dendritic trees of neurons in the prefrontal cortex become much more complex during adolescence, which indicates that the information flow between neurons has become more complex (Lambe, Krimer, & Goldman-Rakic, 2000). The possibility that schizophrenia involves molecular and functional abnormalities of information flow in these circuits suggests that such abnormalities may converge on the dynamic process of brain maturation during adolescence and increase the risk of a psychotic episode in predisposed individuals.

Pathophysiology of Schizophrenia in Adolescence

Despite over a century of research, we have only a limited understanding of what causes schizophrenia and related psychotic disorders. Early studies of the biological basis of schizophrenia relied mostly on either postmortem studies of brains of people with this illness or brain imaging studies typically of older patients with chronic schizophrenia, many of whom were treated with medications. It was therefore difficult to know to what extent the observed changes were the results of aging, illness chronicity, or medication effects. One can avoid such difficulties by conducting studies of individuals in the early phases of schizophrenia (Keshavan & Schooler, 1992). First, these studies allow us to clarify which of the biological processes may be unique to the illness and which ones might be a result of medications or of persistent illness. Second, first-episode studies allow us to longitudinally evaluate the course of the brain changes, and how such changes can help us predict outcome with treatment. Follow-up studies suggest that less than half of early psychosis patients go on to develop a chronic form of schizophrenia with poor level of functioning and intellectual deficits (Harrison et al., 2001). An understanding of which patients may have such an outcome will greatly help treatment decisions early in the illness. Finally, not all who have features of the prodromal phases of the illness go on to develop the psychotic illness (Yung et al., 2003). Studies of the prodromal and early course of psychotic disorders provide an opportunity to elucidate the neurobiological processes responsible for the transition from the prodromal to psychotic phase of the illness.

Several conceptual models of the biology and causation of schizophrenia have been recently suggested, and serve to guide research into the early phase of this illness. One view, which dates back to the late 1980s, is the so-called early neurodevelopmental model (Murray & Lewis, 1987; Weinberger, 1987). This model posits abnormalities early during brain development (perhaps at or before birth) as mediating the failure of brain functions in adolescence and early adulthood. Several lines of evidence, such as an increased rate of birth complications, minor physical and neurological abnormalities, and subtle behavioral difficulties in children who later developed schizophrenia, support this view. However, many nonaffected persons in the population also have these problems; their presence cannot inform us with confidence whether or not schizophrenia will develop later in life. The fact that the symptoms typically begin in adolescence or early adulthood suggests that the illness may be related to some biological changes related to adolescence occurring around or prior to the onset of psychosis. Childhood is characterized by proliferation of synapses and dendrites, and normal adolescence is characterized by elimination or pruning of unnecessary synapses in the brain, a process that serves to make nerve cell transmission more efficient (Huttenlocher et al., 1982). This process could go wrong, and an excessive pruning before or around the onset phase of illness (Feinberg, 1982b; Keshavan, Anderson, & Pettegrew, 1994) has been thought to mediate the emergence of psychosis in adolescence or early adulthood. Our understanding of the underlying neurobiology of this phase of illness remains poor, however. Another view is that active biological changes could occur after the onset of illness, during the commonly lengthy period of untreated psychosis. This model proposes progressive neurodegenerative changes (Lieberman, Perkins, et al., 2001). It is possible that all three processes are involved in schizophrenia (Keshavan & Hogarty, 1999); additionally, environmental factors such as drug misuse (Addington & Addington, 1998) and psychosocial stress (Erickson, Beiser, Iacono, Fleming, & Lin, 1989) may trigger the onset and influence the course of schizophrenia. Careful studies of the early phase of schizophrenia can shed light on these apparently contrasting models. The three proposed pathophysiological models might reflect different critical periods for prevention and therapeutic intervention.

THE GENETICS OF SCHIZOPHRENIA

Remarkable progress has been made in understanding genetic factors related to schizophrenia. We will summarize this work in the following section. Since almost no work has been done specifically on the genetics of adolescent-onset schizophrenia, we focus on studies of typical samples of adult-onset cases.

Is Schizophrenia Familial?

The most basic question in the genetics of schizophrenia is whether the disorder aggregates (or "runs") in families. Technically, familial aggregation means that a close relative of an individual with a disorder is at increased risk for that disorder, compared to a matched individual chosen at random from the general population. Twenty-six early family studies, conducted prior to 1980 and lacking modern diagnostic procedures and appropriate controls, consistently showed that first-degree relatives of schizophrenia patients had a risk for schizophrenia that was roughly 10 times greater than would be expected in the general population (Kendler, 2000). Since 1980, 11 major family studies of schizophrenia have been reported that used blind diagnoses, control groups, personal interviews, and operationalized diagnostic criteria. The level of agreement in results is impressive. Every study showed that the risk of schizophrenia was higher in first-degree relatives of schizophrenic patients than in matched controls. The mean risk for schizophrenia in these 11 studies was 0.5% in relatives of controls and 5.9% in the relatives of schizophrenics. Modern studies suggest that, on average, parents, siblings, and offspring of individuals with schizophrenia have a risk of illness about 12 times greater than that of the general population, a figure close to that found in the earlier studies.

Recently, results of the first methodologically

rigorous family study of child-onset schizophrenia have been reported. Compared to parents of matched normal controls and children with ADHD, parents of childhood-onset schizophrenia had an over 10-fold increased risk for schizophrenia. This finding supports the hypothesis of etiologic continuity between childhood- and adult-onset schizophrenia (Asarnow, Tompson, & Goldstein, 2001).

To What Extent Is the Familial Aggregation of Schizophrenia Due to Genetic Versus Environmental Factors?

Resemblance among relatives can be due to either shared or family environment (nurture), to genes (nature), or to both. A major goal in psychiatric genetics is to determine the degree to which familial aggregation for a disorder such as schizophrenia results from environmental or genetic mechanisms. Although sophisticated analysis of family data can begin to make this discrimination, nearly all of our knowledge about this problem in schizophrenia comes from twin and adoption studies.

Twin studies are based on the assumption that "identical," or monozygotic (MZ), and "fraternal," or dizygotic (DZ), twins share a common environment to approximately the same degree. However, MZ twins are genetically identical, whereas DZ twins (like full siblings) share on average only half of their genes. Results are available from 13 major twin studies of schizophrenia published from 1928 to 1998 (Kendler, 2000). Although modest differences are seen across studies, overall, the agreement is impressive. Across all studies, the average concordance rate for schizophrenia in MZ twins is 55.8% and in DZ twins, 13.5%. When statistical models are applied to these data to estimate heritability (the proportion of variance in liability in the population that is due to genetic factors), the average across all 13 studies is 72%. This figure, which is higher than that found for most common biomedical disorders, means that, on average, genetic factors are considerably more important than environmental factors in affecting the risk for schizophrenia.

Adoption studies can clarify the role of genetic

and environmental factors in the transmission of schizophrenia by studying two kinds of rare but informative relationships: *(1)* individuals who are genetically related but do not share their rearing environment, and *(2)* individuals who share their rearing environment but are not genetically related. Three studies conducted in Oregon, Denmark, and Finland all found significantly greater risk for schizophrenia or schizophrenia-spectrum disorders in the adopted-away offspring of schizophrenic parents than that for the adopted-away offspring of matched control mothers. The second major adoption strategy used for studying schizophrenia begins with ill adoptees rather than with ill parents and compares rates of schizophrenia between groups of biologic parents and groups of adoptive parents. In two studies from Denmark using this strategy, the only group with elevated rates of schizophrenia and schizophrenia-spectrum disorders were the biological relatives of the schizophrenic adoptees (Kety et al., 1994).

Twin and adoption studies provide strong and consistent evidence that genetic factors play a major role in the familial aggregation of schizophrenia. Although not reviewed here, evidence for a role for nongenetic familial factors is much less clear. Some studies suggest they may contribute modestly to risk for schizophrenia, but most studies find no evidence for significant nongenetic familial factors for schizophrenia.

What Psychiatric Disorders Are Transmitted Within Families of Individuals With Schizophrenia?

Since the earliest genetic studies of schizophrenia, a major focus of such work has been to clarify more precisely the nature of the psychiatric syndromes that occur in excess in relatives of schizophrenic patients. To summarize a large body of evidence, relatives of schizophrenia patients are at increased risk for not only schizophrenia but also schizophrenia-like personality disorders (best captured by the DSM-IV categories of schizotypal and paranoid personality disorder) and other psychotic disorders (Kendler, 2000). However, there is good evidence that relatives of schizophrenia patients are not at in-

creased risk for other disorders, such as anxiety disorders and alcoholism. The most active debate in this area is the relationship between schizophrenia and mood disorders. Most evidence suggests little if any genetic relationship between these two major groups of disorders, but some research does suggest a relationship particularly between schizophrenia and major depression.

The evidence that other disorders in addition to schizophrenia occur at greater frequency in the close relatives of individuals with schizophrenia has led to the concept of the schizophrenia-spectrum—a group of disorders that all bear a genetic relationship with classic or core schizophrenia.

What Is the Current Status for Identifying Specific Genes That Predispose to Schizophrenia?

Given the evidence that genetic factors play an important role in the etiology of schizophrenia, a major focus of recent work has been to apply the increasingly powerful tools of human molecular genetics to localize and identify the specific genes that predispose to schizophrenia. Two strategies have been employed in this effort: linkage and association. The goal of linkage studies is to identify areas of the human genome that are shared more frequently than would be expected by relatives who are affected. If such areas can be reliably identified, then these regions may contain one or more specific genes that influence the liability to schizophrenia. The method of linkage analysis has been extremely successful in identifying the location of genes for simple, usually rare medical genetic disorders (termed "Mendelian" disorders) in which there is a one-to-one relationship between having the defective gene and having the disorder. This method, however, has had more mixed results when applied to disorders such as schizophrenia that are genetically "complex." Such complex disorders are likely to be the result of multiple genes, none of which have a very large impact on risk, interacting with a range of environmental risk factors.

Eighteen genome scans for schizophrenia

have been published between 1994 and 2002. None of these scans has revealed evidence for a single gene with a large impact on risk for schizophrenia. Indeed, these results suggest that the existence of a single susceptibility locus that accounts for a large majority of the genetic variance for schizophrenia can now be effectively ruled out.

The most pressing scientific issue in the interpretation of linkage studies of schizophrenia has been whether there is agreement at above-chance levels across studies on which individual regions of the genome contain susceptibility genes for schizophrenia. Until recently, the across-study agreement had not been very impressive.

Two recent findings have increased our confidence that linkage studies of schizophrenia may be producing reliable results. First, in a large-scale study of families containing two or more cases of schizophrenia, conducted in Ireland, the sample was divided, prior to analysis, into three random subsets (Straub, MacLean, et al., 2002). When a genome scan was performed on these three subsets, three of the four regions that most prominently displayed evidence for linkage (on chromosomes 5q, 6p, and 8p) were replicated across all three subsets. Interestingly, one region, on chromosome 10p, was not replicated even within the same study. Probably more important, Levinson and collaborators were able to obtain raw data from nearly all major published genome scans of schizophrenia to perform a meta-analysis—a statistical method for rigorously combining data across multiple samples (Lewis et al., 2003). Ten regions produced nominally significant results including 2q, 5q, 6p, 22q, and 8p. The authors concluded: "There is greater consistency of linkage results across studies than had been previously recognized. The results suggest that some or all of these regions contain loci that increase susceptibility to schizophrenia in diverse populations."

On the Cusp of Gene Discovery in Schizophrenia

The evidence for replicated linkages in schizophrenia represents an important step toward the ultimate goal of identifying susceptibility genes and characterizing their biologic effects. Because the human genome contains within its 23 pairs of chromosomes over three billion nucleotides (i.e., "letters" in the genetic alphabet) and 30,000 genes (i.e., protein-encoding units), it is a large territory to explore. *Linkage* is a strategy to narrow the search and to provide a map of where the treasure (i.e., the genes) may lie. The linkage results in schizophrenia so far have highlighted several regions of the genome for a more thorough search. Association (also called linkage disequilibrium) is the next critical step in this search for the treasure. *Linkage* represents a relationship between regions of the genome shared by family members who also share the phenotype of interest—here, schizophrenia. It provides a low-resolution map because family members share relatively large regions of any chromosome. *Association*, however, represents a relationship between specific alleles (i.e., specific variation in a gene or in a genetic marker) and illness in unrelated individuals. It provides a high-resolution map because unrelated people share relatively little genetic information. For a given allele to be found more frequently in unrelated individuals with a similar disease than it is in the general population, the probability that this specific allele is a causative factor in the disease is enhanced. If the frequency of a specific allele (i.e., a specific genetic variation) is greater in a sample of unrelated individuals who have the diagnosis of schizophrenia than it is in a control population, the allele is said to be associated with schizophrenia. This association represents one of three possibilities: the allele is a causative mutation related to the etiology of the disease; the allele is a genetic variation that is physically close to the true causative mutation (i.e., in "linkage disequilibrium" with the true mutation); or the association is a spurious relationship reflecting population characteristics not related to the phenotype of interest. This latter possibility is often referred to as a *population stratification artifact*, meaning that differences in allele frequencies between the cases and control samples are not because of disease but because of systematic genetic differences between the comparison populations.

Association has become the strategy of choice

for fine mapping of susceptibility loci and for preliminary testing of whether specific genes are susceptibility genes for schizophrenia. The strategy involves identifying variations ("polymorphisms") in a gene of interest and then performing a laboratory analysis of the DNA samples to "type" each variation in each individual and determine its frequency in the study populations. Genetic sequence variations are common in the human genome and public databases have been established to catalog them. The most abundant sequence variations are single nucleotide polymorphisms (SNPs), which represent a substitution in one DNA base. Common SNPs occur at a frequency of approximately one in every 1,000 DNA bases in the genome and over two million SNPs have been identified. While SNPs are relatively common, most SNPs within genes either do not change the amino acid code or are in noncoding regions of genes ("introns") and are thus not likely to have an impact on gene function.

Early association studies in schizophrenia focused on genes based on their known function and the possibility that variations in their function might relate to the pathogenesis of the disease. These so-called functional candidate gene studies had no a priori probability of genetic association. A number of studies compared frequencies of variations in genes related to popular neurochemical hypotheses about schizophrenia, such as the dopamine and glutamate hypotheses, in individuals with schizophrenia with those in control samples. In almost every instance the results were mixed, with some positive but mostly negative reports. Many of the positive studies were compromised by potential population stratification artifacts. However, because the effect on risk of any given variation in any candidate gene (e.g., a dopamine or glutamate receptor gene) is likely to be small (less than a twofold increase in risk), most studies have been underpowered to establish association or to rule it out.

Recent association studies have been much more promising, primarily because of the linkage results. Using the linkage map regions as a priori entry points into the human genetic sequence databases, genes have been identified in each of the major linkage regions that appear to represent at least some of the basis for the linkage results. Moreover, confirmation of association in independent samples have appeared, which combined with the linkage results comprise convergent evidence for the validity of these genetic associations. In the August and October 2002 issues of the *American Journal of Human Genetics*, the first two articles appeared that claimed to identify susceptibility genes for schizophrenia, starting with traditional linkage followed by fine association mapping. Both of these were in chromosomal regions previously identified by multiple linkage groups: dysbindin (*DTNBP1*) on chromosome 6p22.3 (Straub, Jiang, et al., 2002) and neuregulin 1 (*NRG1*) on chromosome 8p-p21 (Stefansson et al., 2002). Both groups identified the genes in these regions from public databases and then found variations (SNPs) within the genes that could be tested via an association analysis. In both studies, the statistical signals were strong and unlikely to occur by chance. In the January 2003 issue of the same journal, two further articles were published, replicating, in independent population data sets also from Europe, association to variations in the same genes (Schwab et al., 2003; Stefansson et al., 2003). In the December 2002 issue of the same journal, authors of a study on a large population sample from Israel reported very strong statistical association to SNPs in the gene for catechol-*O*-methyltransferase (*COMT*), which was mapped to the region of 22q that had been identified as a susceptibility locus in several linkage studies (Shifman et al., 2002). Positive association to variation in *COMT* had also been reported in earlier studies in samples from China, Japan, France, and the United States (Egan et al., 2001). Starting with the linkage region on chromosome 13q34, a group from France discovered a novel gene, called *G72*, and reported in two population samples association between variations in this gene and schizophrenia (Chumakov et al., 2002). The SNP variations in *G72* have recently been reported to be associated with bipolar disorder as well.

In addition to these reports based on relatively strong linkage regions, several other promising associations have emerged from genes found in weaker linkage regions. For example, a weak linkage signal was found in several genome scans in 15q, a region containing the gene for the α_{-7}-nicotine receptor (*CHRNA7*; Raux et al., 2002). This gene has been associated with an intermediate phenotype related to schizophrenia, the abnormal P50 EEG evoked response. Preliminary evidence has been reported that variants in *CHRNA7* are associated with schizophrenia as well. *DISC-1* is a gene in 1q43, which was a positive linkage peak in a genome linkage scan from Finland. A chromosomal translocation originating in this gene has been found to be very strongly associated with psychosis in Scottish families having this translocation (Millar et al., 2000). Finally, in a study of gene expression profiling from schizophrenic brain tissue, a gene called *RGS4* was found to have much lower expression in schizophrenic brains than in normal brains. This gene is found in another 1q region that was positive in a linkage scan from Canada, and SNPs identified in *RGS4* have now been shown to be associated with schizophrenia in at least three population samples (Chowdari et al., 2002). This convergent evidence from linkage and association studies implicates at least seven specific genes as potentially contributing risk for schizophrenia.

From Genetic Association to Biological Mechanisms of Risk

Genetic association identifies genes but it does not identify disease mechanisms. Most of the genes implicated thus far are based on associations with variations that are not clearly functional, in the sense that they do not appear to change the integrity of the gene. Most are SNPs in intronic regions of genes, which do not have an impact on traditional aspects of gene function, such as the amino acid sequence or regulation of transcription. So, the associations put a flag on the gene but they do not indicate how inheritance of a variation in the gene affects the function of the gene or the function of the brain. More work is needed in searching for variations that may have obvious functional implications and in basic cell biology to understand how gene function affects cell function.

In two of the genes implicated to date, there is evidence of a potential mechanism of increased risk. Preliminary evidence suggests that SNPs in the promotor region of the *CHRNA7* gene that are associated with schizophrenia affect factors that turn on transcription of the *CHRNA7* gene, presumably accounting for lower abundance of *CHRNA7* receptors, which has been reported in schizophrenic brain tissue (Leonard et al., 2002). This receptor is important in many aspects of hippocampal function and in regulation of the response of dopamine neurons to environmental rewards. Both hippocampal function and dopaminergic responsivity have been prominently implicated in the biology of schizophrenia. The COMT valine allele, which has been associated with schizophrenia in the *COMT* studies, translates into a more active enzyme, which appears to diminish dopamine in the prefrontal cortex. This leads to various aspects of poorer prefrontal function, in terms of cognition and physiology, which are prominent clinical aspects of schizophrenia, and to intermediate phenotypes associated with risk for schizophrenia (Weinberger et al., 2001). The COMT valine allele also is associated with abnormal control of dopamine activity in the parts of the brain where it appears to be overactive in schizophrenia (Akil et al., 2003). Thus, inheritance of the COMT valine allele appears to increase risk for schizophrenia because it biases toward biological effects implicated in both the negative and positive symptoms of the illness.

Schizophrenia-Susceptibility Genes and Adolescence

It is not obvious how the genes described would specifically relate to adolescence and the emergence of schizophrenia during this time of life. The evidence so far suggests that each of the candidate susceptibility genes has an impact on fundamental aspects of how a brain grows and how it adapts to experience. Each gene may affect the excitability of glutamate neurons—directly or through GABA neuron intermediates, and indirectly through the regulation of dopamine neurons by the cortex. These are fundamental processes related to the biology of schizophrenia. These are also processes that may be especially crucial to adolescence because cortical development and plasticity are changing dramatically during this period. Thus, it is conceivable that the variations in the functions of these genes associated with schizophrenia lead to compromises and bottlenecks in these processes.

The Potential Gene-Finding Utility of Intermediate or Endophenotypes

Despite encouraging results from recent linkage and association studies, the literature also contains prominent failures and inconsistencies. Failures to replicate linkage and association signals for schizophrenia suggest that genomic strategies may benefit from a redirection based on our current understanding of the pathophysiology of schizophrenia. For example, the power of genetic studies may increase by examining linkage with quantitative traits that relate to schizophrenia rather than with a formal diagnosis itself. The concept of using intermediate phenotypes, or *endophenotypes*, is not new (Gottesman & Gould, 2003), but has only recently started to enjoy widespread popularity among those seeking genes for schizophrenia. Gottesman and Shields suggested over 30 years ago that features such as subclinical personality traits, measures of attention and information processing, or the number of dopamine receptors in specific brain regions might lie "intermediate to the phenotype and genotype of schizophrenia" (Gottesman & Shields, 1973). Today, other traits, such as eye-movement dysfunctions, altered brain-wave patterns, and neuropsychological and neuroimaging abnormalities, are under consideration as potentially useful endophenotypes of schizophrenia, because all of these are more common or more severe in schizophrenic patients and their family members than in the general population or among control subjects (Faraone et al., 1995). These deficits may relate more directly than the diagnosis of schizophrenia to the aberrant genes. At the biological level, this is a logical assumption, as genes do not encode for hallucinations or delusions; they encode primarily for proteins that have an impact on molecular processes within and between cells. Thus, endophenotypes may serve as proxies for schizophrenia that are closer to the biology of the underlying risk genes.

Early Findings from Molecular Genetic Studies of Endophenotypes

While much recent work has been dedicated toward establishing the heritability of endophenotypes, only a handful of molecular genetic studies of endophenotypes have emerged. Results observed to date have been encouraging, in that some chromosomal loci that have been found to harbor genes for schizophrenia have also shown evidence for linkage with an endophenotype. For example, linkage with an auditory-evoked brain wave pattern (the P50 endophenotype) has been observed independently in two samples of schizophrenia pedigrees on chromosome 15 at the locus of the α_{-7}-nicotinic receptor gene, where some evidence for linkage had previously been observed using traditional diagnostic classifications (Leonard et al., 1996; Raux et al., 2002). However, the greater potential of endophenotype studies is that genes might be identified that would not be implicated from regions of the genome highlighted in linkage regions. This is because minor genes for schizophrenia may turn out to be major genes for some index of central nervous system dysfunction. The proof of this has been supported by evidence that *COMT*, which is a weak susceptibility gene for schizophrenia, is a relatively strong factor in normal human frontal lobe function (Weinberger et al., 2001).

Whether classical criteria or quantitative phenotypes are used to further study schizophrenia, refining the definition of an "affected" individual is a top priority for genetic studies. Because not all individuals with schizophrenia-susceptibility genes develop the actual disorder, understanding the measurable effects of these aberrant genes is a critical step in tracking their passage through affected pedigrees and in identifying their clinical biology. In the near future, the amount and types of expressed protein products of these disease genes may be used as the ultimate endophenotype for schizophrenia. To the extent that we can reduce measurement error and create measures that are more closely tied to individual schizophrenia genes, we will greatly improve our understanding of the genetics of schizophrenia.

Genetic Counseling Issues and Schizophrenia

With increasing attention in the media to issues relating to genetics and particularly the role of genetic factors in mental illness, an increasing number of individuals will likely be seeking genetic counseling for issues related to schizophrenia. In our experience, by far the most common situation is a married couple who are contemplating having children and the husband or wife has a family history of schizophrenia. They typically ask any combination of three questions: First, is there a genetic test that can be performed on us to determine whether we have the gene for schizophrenia and whether we might pass it on to our children? Second, is there an in utero test that can be given that would determine the risk of the fetus to develop schizophrenia later in life? Third, what is the risk for schizophrenia to our children?

Unfortunately, given the current state of our knowledge, answers to the first two questions are no, we are not yet in the position of having a genetic test that can usefully predict risk for schizophrenia. We would also often add a statement to the effect that this is a very active area of research and there is hope that in the next few years, some breakthrough might occur that would allow us to develop such a test. But, right now we really do not know when or even if that will be possible.

By contrast, useful information can be provided for the third question. Most typically, the husband or wife has a parent or sibling with schizophrenia and they themselves have been mentally healthy. Therefore, the empirical question is what is known about the risk of schizophrenia to the grandchild or niece or nephew of an individual with schizophrenia. Interestingly, this is a subject that has not been systematically

studied since the early days of psychiatric genetics in the first decades of the 20th century. The results of these early studies have been summarized in several places, most notably by Gottesman (Gottesman & Shields, 1982), with aggregate risk estimates for schizophrenia of 3.7% and 3.0%, respectively, in grandchildren or nieces and nephews of an individual with schizophrenia. However, this is a considerable overestimate if the parent with the positive family history remains unaffected. That is, the risk to a grandchild or niece or nephew of an individual with schizophrenia when the intervening parent never develops the illness is probably under 2%. Most individuals find this information helpful and broadly reassuring.

FUTURE WORK

By the time this chapter is read, a great deal more information is likely to have accumulated about the scientific status of these findings. At this early stage, several trends are noteworthy. First, including unpublished reports known to the authors, at least some of these potential gene discoveries have now been replicated enough times that it is increasingly unlikely that they are false-positive findings (due, for example, to the performance of many statistical tests). Second, we can expect that the biochemical pathways represented by these genes will be explored at the level of basic cell biology and new leads about pathogenesis and potential new targets for prevention and treatment will be found. Third, we can expect a number of studies to emerge that will try to understand whether expression of these genes are changed in the brains of schizophrenia patients. Fourth, efforts are already under way to try to understand how these genes influence psychological functions such as attention, sensory gating, and memory that are disturbed in schizophrenia. Fifth, intense efforts will be made to try to determine whether these different genes are acting through a common pathway as, for example, has been postulated for the four known genes for Alzheimer's disease.

Treatment of Schizophrenia

Interest in psychological treatments for schizophrenia has increased in recent years, particularly in Europe and Australia, driven by understandable patient dissatisfaction with purely pharmacological approaches. The recognition that 40% of patients do not achieve symptom resolution with drug treatment (Kane, 1996) has added impetus to the search for alternatives and adjuncts. Unfortunately, the paucity of data concerning the application of such approaches to adolescents suffering from schizophrenia means that, at least for the time being, inferences have to be drawn mainly from studies of adult populations.

Nevertheless, the similar lack of data regarding efficacy and safety of antipsychotic drug treatment in adolescents and the observation that adolescents may be especially sensitive to the adverse effects of typical antipsychotics (e.g., extrapyramidal side effects; Lewis, 1998) and clozapine (e.g., neutropenia and seizures; Kumra et al., 1996) mean that there is a real need for alternative or supplementary interventions. Indeed, one could hypothesize that psychological treatments might be more effective in adolescents than in adults. This is a group with a greater degree of neural plasticity and a still evolving personality, and who are especially likely to have an ongoing system of support in the form of family and educational input. Furthermore, the latter presents opportunities for early detection. Alongside early treatment with antipsychotics, there is potential for psychotherapeutic interventions to lessen the impact of positive symptoms, improve coping strategies, and potentially to reduce the cognitive deficits, which so impair psychosocial function.

EARLY AND EDUCATIONAL INTERVENTIONS

Like those who go on to develop other serious mental disorders, individuals who develop schizophrenia in later life often, but not invariably, demonstrate interpersonal and emotional difficulties during childhood and adolescence. Cannon et al. (2002) reported that schizophrenia was specifically predicted by the presence of deficits in receptive language, neuromotor function, and cognitive development between 3 and 11 years of age.

Schools

Because such abilities are already observed and assessed, to an extent, as part of a child's schooling, there is potential for the development of predictors and the identification of targets for psychological intervention. Studies examining the ability of teachers and other educational professionals, in day-to-day contact with adolescents, to predict future sufferers of schizophrenia do show some statistical power, but this is at the cost of many false positives and even more false negatives (Isohanni, et al., 2004) unless restricted to high-risk populations (Kravariti, Dazzan, Fearon, & Murray, 2003). One possible exception was the study by Davidson et al. (1999) linking the Israeli Draft Board Registry with the National Psychiatric Hospitalization Case Registry. Adolescent boys, aged 16 to 17 years, underwent preinduction assessments to determine suitability for military service. Those admitted to a psychiatric hospital with schizophrenia 4 to 10 years later were matched with control individuals from their school class at the time of original assessment. Identified predictors for schizophrenia in the male adolescents included deficits in social and intellectual functioning and organizational activity. The predictive model derived by the authors had 75% sensitivity, 100% specificity, and a positive predictive value of 72%. However, as highlighted in a commentary by Jones and van Os (2000), the predictive power of this model was achieved by excluding from the sample those school classes without individuals who later became schizophrenic.

So far the best prediction has come not from teachers but from a psychiatric interview. In the Dunedin study (Poulton et al., 2000), 11-year-old children were asked about experiences of quasi-psychotic symptoms. The questions were as follows:

1. Do you believe in mind reading or being psychic? Have other people ever read your mind?

2. Have you ever had messages sent just to you through the television or radio?
3. Have you ever thought that people are following you or spying on you?
4. Have you heard voices other people can't hear?
5. Has something ever gotten inside your body or has your body changed in some way?

Those who answered positively to one of the five questions or possibly positively to two were 16 times more likely to develop a schizophrenia-like psychosis by age 26 years. Teachers or school nursing staff could be advised of the value of such questions. However, little work aiming at primary prevention (i.e., preventing progression from premorbid abnormalities to prodrome) is in progress.

Early Treatment Projects

Falloon initiated an early intervention for "prodromal" symptoms in adolescents and adults, in the form of the Buckingham project, a "shared care model" between primary and secondary care (using low doses of medication, interventions designed to reduce stress, psychoeducation, and follow-up for 2 years after the symptoms had occurred). He claimed that this reduced the annual incidence of first-episode psychosis from 7.4 per 100,000/year, as measured by the same group in 1989, to 0.75 per 100,000/year during the 4-year study period (Falloon, Kydd, Coverdale, & Laidlaw, 1996).

Unfortunately, adolescents developing schizophrenia suffer the same delays as their older counterparts, often not receiving diagnosis or treatment for a prolonged period. Consequently, a number of projects have been developed to reduce this unnecessary period of untreated psychosis.

Projects such as the Personal Assessment and Crisis Evaluation (PACE) clinic in Melbourne, Australia, and the early Treatment and Intervention in Psychosis (TIPs) project in Norway aim at secondary prevention (i.e., preventing progression from prodrome into syndrome) in adolescents and adults. Such programs are motivated by the belief that the chronicity of schizophrenia

may develop in the early stages of the illness and that long-term outcomes may be linked to the duration of untreated psychosis, or DUP that is, the time period between onset of symptoms and initiation of treatment. However, the latter hypothesis remains theoretical. Norman and Malla (2001) reviewed the concept of DUP and while they confirmed that there was evidence to suggest a relationship between DUP and the ease with which first remission of symptoms is achieved, they could not find evidence to support a link with disease progression. Although the concept of DUP focuses on initiation of pharmacological treatment, de Haan, Linszen, Lenoir, de Win, and Gorsira (2003) suggest that delay in initiating intensive psychosocial treatment may have similar implications for outcome, particularly in relation to negative symptoms at follow-up.

The TIPS project is a prospective clinical trial that started in Norway in 1997, comparing an experimental sector with two other control sectors (age range 15 to 65 years). The experimental sector developed a system for early detection and also established a comprehensive information, service, and education program aimed at both the general public and professionals involved in health care and education (Johannessen et al., 2001). In the 2 years after the initiation of the TIPs project, mean DUP decreased from 1.5 years to 0.5 years.

The PACE was established in Melbourne, Australia, in 1994; the aim was to evaluate the prodromal phase, develop interventions that prevent further deterioration and maximize function, and set up a clinical service to identify and engage young people experiencing potential early psychosis. Preliminary results, which are further discussed in Cognitive Behavior Therapy, below, show that early intervention in the prodrome can at least delay onset of first-episode psychosis.

It seems likely that the wider-ranging public and educative measures occurring in the TIPS project and PACE clinic are vital to any health service initiatives or collaboration, especially in view of adolescents' poor primary care attendance. It is important to note, however, that while a number of the early-intervention services cover the adolescent age range, their goal is actually to intervene in an early stage of the disorder rather than to specifically target those who develop schizophrenia in adolescence.

PSYCHOLOGICAL TREATMENTS

Cognitive Behavior Therapy

Cognitive behavior therapy (CBT) addresses problems in the here-and-now by targeting dysfunctional thoughts and behaviors within a collaborative therapeutic relationship. Efficacy of CBT and acceptability by those with disorders such as depression and anxiety have been demonstrated (Beck, Sokol, Clark, Berchick, & Wright, 1992; Kovacs, Rush, Beck, & Hollon, 1981). In support of the growing (but relatively underevaluated) practice of CBT in adults with schizophrenia, Rector and Beck (2002) suggest that since the inferential errors and faulty logic in hallucinations and delusions are similar to those seen in other disorders, CBT should also work in schizophrenia. They describe CBT for psychosis as an active, structured therapy, usually of 6 to 9 months duration, given individually.

Adolescent Studies

Unfortunately, we could not find any reports of the use of definitive CBT in specifically adolescent individuals. However, data are beginning to accumulate from the early-intervention programs, reporting on the use of CBT in early-onset psychosis. McGorry et al. (2002) conducted a randomized controlled trial (RCT) with 14- to 30-year-olds at the Early Psychosis Prevention and Intervention Centre, Melbourne, which is associated with the PACE clinic discussed earlier. This study compared interventions designed to reduce the risk of progression to first-episode psychosis, in a clinical sample aged 14 to 30 years, termed ultra-high risk (first-degree family history of schizophrenia and subthreshold symptoms). The interventions comprised a needs-based intervention and a specific preventive intervention (low-dose risperidone and CBT) for 6 months with assessments at baseline and 6 and 12 months, using a defined threshold

outcome rather than a formal diagnosis of schizophrenia. Ten of 28 in the needs-based intervention versus 3 of the 31 in the specific intervention had reached the defined outcome by the end of treatment; however, there was no significant difference at 6-month follow-up. When the data were assessed, taking into account drug adherence, a significant difference was found between the fully adherent specific intervention group and the needs-based group. It seemed that the specific intervention delayed onset.

Adult Studies

Dickerson (2000) reviewed all studies investigating CBT for schizophrenia in adult populations (although age data are not supplied) between 1990 and 1999. She examined the available data for seven different CBT approaches, some focusing on acute psychosis, others on persisting positive symptoms. Her conclusion was that there were some CBT strategies that reduced positive symptomatology, especially in individuals with clearly defined symptoms that they themselves viewed as problematic. The most beneficial outcome appeared to be in reducing conviction in and distress about delusions; there was little evidence to suggest that CBT was efficacious in negative symptoms or social functioning. The overall superiority of CBT was reduced when the control condition was matched for therapist input.

Even more disappointing, a Cochrane meta-analysis of CBT in schizophrenia (Cormac, Jones, & Campbell, 2002) found no evidence that CBT, in addition to standard care, reduces the relapse and readmission rate in the short or longer term (1 year) any more than standard care alone. Moreover, there was no overall difference between CBT and supportive psychotherapy, with respect to relapse rate or improvements in mental state.

Pilling et al. (2002) conducted a systematic review of RCTs of CBT (and family interventions, social skills training, and cognitive remediation). The trials reviewed compared CBT with supportive therapies and standard care in predominantly chronic psychosis. There was no evidence for increased effectiveness of CBT during treatment, although CBT showed a clear advantage over the comparison treatment at follow-up when measured continuously in terms of "important improvement." This superiority persisted for up to 18 months after treatment. Furthermore, CBT groups had lower dropout rates. It was not possible to identify any particular responder characteristics or the optimum frequency or length of treatment.

Although the Study of Cognitive Reality Alignment Therapy in Early Schizophrenia (SoCRATES; Lewis et al., 2002) was conducted among individuals with an average age of 27, it is one of the more relevant adult studies to this discussion because the patients recruited were in the early phases of their illness. The RCT compared CBT with routine care, supportive counseling and routine care, and routine care alone, all for 5 weeks duration only, in individuals suffering their first or second episode of schizophrenia. Use of CBT showed only transient advantages over the other two intervention conditions in speeding remission from acute symptoms in this group of individuals.

In summary, the adult literature suggests that, although CBT might have some beneficial effects, questions such as defining the length of treatment required, which patients would benefit, and at which stages in their illness it should be implemented still remain unanswered. Until these questions are answered in adult populations, it would be foolish to commence large trials in adolescent individuals, especially without adequately defined aims. This caution should not prevent CBT techniques from being borrowed in part in the development of specific interventions targeted at the special needs of adolescents with schizophrenia.

Cognitive Remediation Therapy

Deficits in cognitive function such as working memory, attention, and executive functioning are core features of schizophrenia. *Cognitive remediation therapy* (CRT) aims to teach people thinking skills. More specifically, it uses material that is not personal to the individual and targets the specific domains affected in schizophrenia. Cognitive remediation therapy can be character-

ized into three generic approaches (Bellack & Brown, 2001):

1. Practice and brief training on neurocognitive tests or computer tasks to improve a single domain of functioning
2. Repetitive practice on a battery of computer tasks aimed at multiple domains
3. Strategies to improve cognitive functioning in general by increasing self-confidence, interest, and initiative

The assessment of efficacy of CRT has again been hampered by methodological constraints, in particular, the heterogeneity of intervention packages used and then inappropriately compared. Wykes et al. (2001) have made attempts to reduce this phenomenon by describing a typology for classification of methods.

Adolescent Populations

Techniques specifically targeted at cognitive differentiation, attention, memory, and social perception are being evaluated in adolescent populations by Rund and colleagues in Oslo. Ueland and Rund (2004) carried out an RCT comparing the effects of psychoeducation and cognitive training with those of psychoeducation in a small group of adolescents with early-onset psychosis. They did not detect any significant between-group differences in any of their treatment scores, although there were some specific significant improvements in visual long-term memory and early visual information processing and Brief Psychiatric Rating Scale (BPRS) scores, limited to the remediation group. This group has also focused on the remediation of more specific cognitive deficits. Ueland et al. (2004) assessed the effect of enhanced instructions and contingent monetary reinforcement on attentional skills. A group of adolescents with early-onset psychosis received the span of apprehension performance (SPAN) at baseline, three times as an intervention, and then after testing and at 10-day follow-up. Improvements in performance were evident at the end of the intervention, diminishing slightly after testing but recovering at 10-day follow-up.

Adult Populations

Research into CRT in adults, based on the third category listed above, has recently shown an effect on memory durable to 6 months of follow-up, which, if large enough, gives rise to associated improvement in social performance (Wykes et al., 2001). We await with interest the ongoing study this group is conducting of patients between 16 and 21 years of age. Furthermore, a study involving "cognitive enhancement therapy" in early-course patients, some of whom will be within the adolescent age range, is being undertaken by G. Hogarty's team in Pittsburgh (personal communication).

Interpersonal Psychotherapy

Very little evaluative work has been published in the area of interpersonal therapy (IPT) since the 3-year trial conducted by Hogarty et al. (1997). Although this study was aimed at reducing the "late relapse" observed to occur in the second year after psychotherapeutic intervention, and was conducted in a mixed adult and adolescent cohort (16 to 55 years old), it warrants discussion because its conclusions seem particularly pertinent to the adolescent population. This study examined relapse and noncompliance in outpatients with schizophrenia and schizoaffective disorder in two concurrent trials. One trial concerned individuals who resided with their families who were randomly assigned to personal therapy, family therapy, personal therapy and family therapy, or supportive therapy; the other trial studied those individuals who lived alone who were randomly assigned to either personal or supportive therapy.

Personal therapy occurred in three stages, and although it focused on internal, personal responses to stress, and not the regulation of external triggers, it did not use symbolic interpretation or analysis of unconscious factors. It aimed more specifically to identify and manage the "affect dysregulation" that might mediate relapse or inappropriate behavior. All patients were on the minimum effective dose of medication. The overall rate of relapse over the 3-year period was 29% over all groups, which was lower than expected. For individuals residing with their family, the group receiving personal therapy relapsed less than the other groups, although this was only significant for family intervention. For individuals living alone, personal therapy significantly increased relapse rates, compared to those for supportive treatment, even though the latter was particularly rich in its provisions. The authors suggested that the group living away from their family may not have reached a stable independence; they may have been too distracted to prioritize the therapy or the intervention itself may have overloaded them. Perhaps this conclusion should serve as a more global caution: full assessment of levels of independence and subjective perceptions of stability may be required before initiating any form of psychotherapy.

Social Skills

Social skills training is a structured educative program that involves modeling, role-play, and reinforcement (Bellack & Mueser, 1993). It is based on the hope that the improved social skills generalize to real-life situations and might even improve symptomatology and reduce relapse. These interventions are targeted at the profound impairments in social functioning that characterize schizophrenia and affect life in the workplace, family, and wider community. There are three forms of social skills training as detailed by Bellack and Mueser (1993): the basic model, the social problem-solving model, and the cognitive remediation model (considered in the previous section).

The basic model involves breaking down complex social interactions into smaller elements. The patients are therefore taught the steps and then the combined elements by means of role-play and areas such as self-care, medication management, and conversation are targeted. Bustillo, Lauriello, Horan, and Keith (2001) reviewed reports from 1996 to 2001 and found that the basic model was repeatedly efficacious in improving social skills and that this effect continued for up to 12 months. However, there was not much to suggest that this treatment affected overall social performance. Evidence from studies of the problem-solving approach suggests modest benefits on very discrete areas of social functioning that appear to have some durability.

Although such research seems old-fashioned and potentially out of sync with the dilemmas and challenges facing an adolescent suffering from schizophrenia, the approach may have merits. For a child, the transition into adolescence and then adulthood is a difficult process requiring support and structure. Development of schizophrenia during this process can disrupt personal development in an infinite number of ways. Therefore, there is a real need for research among groups of adolescents with schizophrenia into developing ways to teach them social skills that generalize to real life.

Family Therapies

Successful family therapies have psychoeducation at their heart, taking the form of a collaborative respectful relationship with the family, provision of information, and teaching of family members less stressful ways of communicating and solving problems. It seems intuitive that family interventions, in a nonspecific sense, would be particularly beneficial for adolescents with schizophrenia, especially those who remain still dependent on their parents.

The need for intervention is supported by reports that children with schizotypal personality disorder or schizophrenia and the parents of such children tend to show increased rates of thought disorder during direct family interactions (Tompson, Asarnow, Hamilton, Newell, & Goldstein, 1997). Some reports claim that the parents also show increased communication deviance (an index of difficulties associated with a failure to establish and maintain a shared focus of attention; Asarnow, 1994). It is not possible to know at this stage whether this represents a shared genetic vulnerability to psychosis or a parental response to their child's illness.

Additional support comes from the work on expressed emotion (EE). Although this was originally investigated in adult populations, most data assessing family interventions in adolescents are based on EE. The concept of EE, which encompasses critical comments, hostility, and

overinvolvement, arose out of a body of research focused on the effect of the family environment on the maintenance of schizophrenia and other severe mental disorders (Brown, Monck, Carstairs, & Wing, 1962). Family interventions evolved, again targeted at adults, that aimed to reduce high EE and thus reduce relapse rates (Leff, Kuipers, Berkowitz, Eberlein-Vries, & Sturgeon, 1982).

Adolescents

The applicability of therapies directed at high EE in adolescent schizophrenia is hampered by three problems. First, adolescent families have less EE or different EE. Asarnow, Tompson, Hamilton, Goldstein, and Guthrie (1994) found relatively low parental EE (compared to families of adults with schizophrenia) when measuring criticism and overinvolvement on the Five-minute Speech Sample Expressed Emotion (FMSS-EE) scale. Twenty-three percent of families of adolescents with schizophrenia or schizotypal personality disorder were rated as having high EE, compared to 44% of families of adults with schizophrenia in a similar study by Miklowitz et al. (1989).

The second problem in using EE-related therapies for adolescents is the lack of stability over time and lack of response to treatment. Lenior, Dingemans, Schene, Hart, and Linszen (2002) conducted a longitudinal study to analyze the stability of parental EE in individuals with recent-onset schizophrenia, aged 15 to 26 years, in the 8 years following discharge from two interventions from inpatient care: community care alone and community care with additional family intervention according to the model of Falloon, Boyd, and McGill (1984). The families were stratified according to high and low EE before allocation and EE was measured over the follow-up period using the FMSS. According to these measurements, EE did change over time, although the study failed to detect any overall treatment effect on EE levels. In addition, this group found no intervention effect on the number of months of psychosis during 5-year follow-up.

Nugter, Dingemans, van der Does, Linszen, and Gersons et al. (1997) studied individuals, aged 16 to 25, with recent-onset schizophrenia and related disorders who were randomly allocated to individual treatment with or without a family intervention (modeled on Falloon et al., 1984). At the end of treatment (1 year), there were no significant between-group differences in EE (as assessed by the FMSS). There were no detectable relationships between EE and relapse, except that in the individual group, changeable EE (in whichever direction) was correlated with relapse rate.

The third difficulty with using EE in treatment for adolescents is its lack of specificity to schizophrenia. A meta-analysis of EE-outcome relationships in mental disorders (Butzlaff & Hooley, 1998), though confirming EE as a significant predictor of relapse in schizophrenia, found significantly larger effect sizes for EE in mood and eating disorders. This study did not specify age ranges covered by the reviewed studies. Thus, attempts to evolve therapies targeted at underlying problems, particularly in younger populations, have been complicated.

Linszen et al. (1996) found that adding a behavioral family intervention (after Falloon et al., 1984) to an individual psychosocial intervention in patients aged 15 to 26 years made no difference to rates of psychotic relapse in the 15 months following first-episode psychosis. In fact, Linszen's group found a near-significant increase in relapse rate in low-EE families subjected to the intervention, possibly because of the families' perception of the therapy as artificial, critical, or interfering in their reactions to their offspring's illness. However, during that 15-month intervention period, the relapse rate was 15%, which suggests that early intervention improved outcome. The cohort was then referred for care by other agencies and at 5-year follow-up, the low relapse rate had not been maintained. The authors suggest that sustained intervention above and beyond regular services might be required to improve outcome in the longer term. This result, taken in conjunction with the increase in relapse of low-EE families, calls into question the value and possibly the ethics of using this intervention in early psychosis.

Asarnow et al. (2001) concluded that although available data support the use of family interven-

tions in the treatment of adolescents with schizophrenia, it is not yet possible to determine which model is most effective. There is, however, an encouraging shift from reducing putative risk factors to empowering and channeling this resource. We concur with this viewpoint but would welcome more work into alternative means of monitoring response to family therapy.

Adult Studies

The preliminary results from the multicentered National Institute of Mental Health (NIMH) Treatment Strategies Study (Schooler et al., 1997), which compared variable medication strategies in conjunction with a "supportive family management" (psychoeducational workshop for relatives with a monthly support group for 2 years) and "applied family management" (which included the former and an intensive at-home family intervention based on the Falloon et al. behavioral program), suggest that the latter, more intensive program does not yield better results and does not permit the use of lower or intermittent medication regimes.

McFarlane et al. (1995) conducted a pilot study in which psychoeducation administered in single-family groups was compared with that in multiple-family groups for individuals aged 18 to 45 years. There were lower relapse rates (12.5% at 12 months and 25% at 24 months) in the multiple-family groups (compared to 23.5% and 47.1%, respectively). Both of these programs resulted in lower relapse rates than those achieved in a multiple-family program without a psychoeducational model.

In Pilling et al.'s (2002) systematic review, family intervention data were also analyzed. The mean age of studied individuals was 31 years, and the mean number of admissions per individual was 2.7. All family interventions (single and multiple) were more effective than the control condition at reducing relapse in the first 12 months of treatment, especially when it consisted of standard care. Only single-family interventions reduced readmission during this time. At 1 to 2 years only, single-family interventions were still reducing relapse, although all treatments were effective at reducing readmission. Interestingly, all family interventions studied had higher rates of treatment compliance to both the family intervention and concurrently prescribed medication. It is important to note, however, that not all the studies included in this review used a supportive individual program as the control condition. Some control conditions actually comprised a family intervention itself, as noted in a response to the review (Bentsen, 2003).

The Family to Family Education Program developed by the National Alliance for the Mentally Ill, detailed on their Web site (http://www.nami.org), involves a highly structured program conducted by trained family members for 2- to 3-hour sessions over 12 weeks. Participants report decreases in family members' "worry and displeasure" and "subjective burden," with increased empowerment and knowledge and improved coping strategies. This program is cheap, popular with family members, and can be widely disseminated, thus aiding implementation.

Compliance Therapy

Compliance therapy is a brief, pragmatic intervention in which cognitive behavioral techniques, very closely linked with motivational interviewing, are used to focus on improving treatment adherence. This therapy evolved out of initial work in programs using psychoeducational and behavioral techniques (e.g., Eckman et al., 1992), and its further development was encouraged by the UK National Health Service, which declared noncompliance a research priority. It was tested in a pilot study, modified, and then used by Kemp, Hayward, Applewhaite, Everitt, and David (1996) in an RCT of inpatients with psychotic illnesses with follow-up to six months. Eighteen-month follow-up was reported (Kemp, Kirov, Everitt, Hayward, & David, 1998) using an expanded sample. The therapy itself takes place over four to six sessions of 20 to 60 minutes each, approximately biweekly and involves the following:

1. Review of the individual's treatment history and his or her views and understanding of the illness and treatment

2. Exploration of symptoms and side effects and thus evaluation of pros and cons of treatment
3. Discussion of stigma

Despite the fact that the therapy was biased to encourage only positive attitudes to treatment, the therapy also aimed to reframe the use of medication as a decision, freely chosen to enhance quality of life, referred to as an "insurance policy" or "protective layer." Immediately after the intervention, the compliance therapy had significantly improved insight and compliance, compared to a supportive counseling matched for therapist time, with the same therapists. This effect was maintained at 6-month follow-up with a 23% difference between groups, with those with higher IQ achieving better results. It was not possible to determine whether these gains resulted in increased function or diminished relapse rate. The 18-month follow-up confirmed that compared to the control condition, compliance therapy improved compliance and insight in the intervention group by 19% and improved global functioning, especially as time progressed. It had no overall effect on improving symptomatology or reducing time spent in the hospital over the follow-up period. The positive effects on compliance were not replicated by O'Donnell et al. (2003) in an RCT of adult inpatients with schizophrenia. Compliance therapy, administered according to Kemp et al. (1996, 1998), conferred no advantage in compliance, symptomatology, or overall function outcomes at 1 year post-therapy, compared to a control condition of equivalent duration with nonspecific counseling. Furthermore, one struggles to see how such a therapy could exert such a persuasive effect in a teenager in the throes of puberty and a battle for independence. Yet again, there is a real need for adaptation of such techniques to adolescent populations, followed by RCTs evaluating their effect.

Illicit Drugs

Although many illicit substances are used by individuals with psychosis, our discussion of such substances will be limited to cannabis because it is by far the most common illicit substance used by adolescents.

Treatment

There is much evidence to suggest that cannabis consumption among those already schizophrenic has a detrimental effect. The strength of this effect is not yet certain, however (Johns, 2001). Unfortunately, there is even less evidence concerning what can be done about it.

Prevention

Zammit, Allebeck, Andreasson, Lunberg, & Lewis (2002) conducted a further analysis of the Swedish conscript data for 1969–1970 (>97% of the country's male population aged 18 to 20). They separated the cohort into those with psychosis onset < 5 years and those with onset > 5 years after data collection to rule out the possibility of prodrome at the time of conscription. They found a significant dose-related relationship between cannabis and increased risk of developing schizophrenia, strongest in those who had onset of psychosis within 5 years of conscription and present in both those who used cannabis alone and cannabis with other drugs. Similar results were obtained when only those with onset >5 years were analyzed.

This study could not determine, however, whether cannabis use in adolescence was a result of preexisting psychotic symptomatology or a cause in itself for psychosis. This issue was addressed by the Dunedin study (Arsenault, Cannon, Witton, & Murray, 2003), a longitudinal, prospective study that assessed preexisting psychotic symptoms at age 11, drug use at 15 and 18 years of age, and psychiatric outcome measures at 26 years. This study showed that adolescents who used cannabis at 15 and 18 years of age had significantly more symptoms of schizophrenia than controls at 26 years of age. Furthermore, these results remained significant when quasi-psychotic symptoms at 11 years were controlled for. Use of cannabis at 15 years increased adult risk of schizophreniform disorder by a factor of 4, although these results did not remain significant when psychotic symptoms at age 11 were controlled for. Thus cannabis use, especially earlier in life, increases the risk of schizophrenia symptoms. This effect is not explained by use secondary to psychosis and this effect appears to be specific to cannabis use. Although cannabis is not thought to be necessary or sufficient to cause the onset of psychosis, it is estimated that 8% of schizophrenia cases in New Zealand could be prevented by the cessation of cannabis use in the general population (Arsenault et al., 2003).

Therefore, in addition to discouraging the legalization and supply of cannabis, mental health initiatives should educate adolescents on the previously unrecognized risks of cannabis misuse. Such initiatives could occur concurrently with the campaigns already implemented by early-intervention services.

Summary

Studies attempting to assess efficacy of psychological treatments have been hampered by a multitude of methodological problems. Often very different versions of a treatment model are described as one and the same. They are often applied to heterogenous populations (e.g., different ages or illness stages) and compared with a control condition unmatched for therapist time and attention.

Debate also continues about the best way to assess the outcome of such interventions. Bellack and Brown (2001) feel that judging psychosocial treatments on the same outcome measures as pharmacological intervention might not be appropriate. Rather than evaluating therapies on whether they reduce symptoms, induce remission, or prevent relapse, they recommend focusing on their effect in reducing impairments in social role functioning and improving overall quality of life and treatment adherence. So they recommend rehabilitation rather than treatment, taking into account the confounding effect of cognitive deficits and the need for newly learned skills to generalize to real life in the community. They liken psychosocial therapies to the use of Braille in visually impaired individuals.

Outcome studies in schizophrenia tend to focus on categorical measures, such as hospital admission, and on professional observations of relapse, symptomatology, or cognitive impairment. Very few assess psychosocial outcome or quality of life, especially as rated by users of services and their caregivers. Such measures of outcome are particularly important for adolescent populations. Lay, Blanz, Hartmann, and Schmidt (2000) conducted a 12-year follow-up study of 96 consecutively admitted individuals with schizophrenia (aged 11 to 17). Of the 68% reassessed at 12 years, 66% had serious social disability, which was predicted by severity of positive symptoms in the early stages and by admissions numbering more than two; 75% were financially dependent. Jarbin, Yngve, & Von Knorring (2003) conducted a 10-year follow-up of adolescents (age <19 years) who were diagnosed with first-episode early-onset psychosis in the 1980s and early 1990s; 79% of those with early-onset schizophrenia spectrum disorders suffered a chronic course with poor outcome.

The collaborative and empowering nature of many of the psychotherapeutic options, though incompletely evaluated and not always available, switches our focus from such sobering outcomes and inflicted choices to a more patient-driven framework. It is encouraging to see that the quest for alternatives and adjuncts to pharmacological treatments has been stepped up and that attempts are being made to improve the methodological quality of their evaluation.

However, a clinician faced with an adolescent newly diagnosed as having schizophrenia would find it extremely difficult to tease out which interventions might be helpful and of these, which might be a cost-effective use of available resources. Adolescents continue, as before, to fall between child and adult services in terms of service provision (National Institute of Clinical Excellence [NICE], 2002). Perhaps mental health initiatives, building on the continuing outcomes of early-intervention programs, can shape devoted services to be targeted at problems that beset adolescents with schizophrenia by virtue of their developmental stage. Such initiatives need to be designed specifically for young minds and hearts.

PHARMACOLOGICAL MANAGEMENT OF PRODROMAL AND FIRST-EPISODE SCHIZOPHRENIA AND RELATED NONAFFECTIVE PSYCHOSES

As noted in Chapter 5, schizophrenia is a severe mental illness characterized by abnormalities of thought and perception that affects about 1% of the population worldwide over the course of a lifetime (Bourdon, Rae, Locke, Narrow, & Regier, 1992; Eaton, 1985; Hare, 1987; Helgason, 1964; Jablensky, 1986; Kramer, 1969; Robins et al., 1984). The optimal time to treat this illness with the currently available therapeutic agents is as early in the course and as close to the onset as possible. Often the onset of the illness precedes the manifestation of symptoms diagnosable at the syndromal level by a considerable period of time. As also summarized in Chapter 5, the onset of the formal symptoms of schizophrenia is generally preceded by a prodromal phase. So-called prodromal symptoms and behaviors (i.e., those that herald the approaching onset of the illness) include attenuated positive symptoms (e.g., illusions, ideas of reference, magical thinking, superstitiousness), mood symptoms (e.g., anxiety, dysphoria, irritability), cognitive symptoms (e.g., distractibility, concentration difficulties), social withdrawal, or obsessive behaviors, to name a few (McGlashan, 1996; Yung & McGorry, 1996). Because many of these prodromal phenomena extensively overlap with the range of mental experiences and behaviors of persons in the ages of risk who do not subsequently develop schizophrenia, prodromal symptoms cannot be considered diagnostic. It is precisely their nonspecificity and lack of high predictive validity that limits their utility for the purposes of early intervention (Gottesman & Erlenmeyer-Kimling, 2001; Schaffner & McGorry, 2001).

The development of frank psychotic symptoms marks the formal onset of first-episode schizophrenia, although this is usually not diagnosed for some time, until the patient seeks or is brought to medical attention. Indeed, the duration of psychotic symptoms prior to diagnosis and treatment averages about 1 year, and if time since prodromal symptoms first appeared is considered, the average duration is about 3 years

(McGlashan, 1996). Despite this, most individuals recover symptomatically from the first episode. However, most patients proceed to have one or more subsequent episodes in the form of psychotic relapses from which some proportion fail to recover, at least to the same degree as they had during their first or prior episode (Lieberman et al., 1993, 1996; Robinson et al., 1999a). This process of psychotic relapses, treatment failure, and incomplete recovery leads many patients to a chronic course of illness. Finally, persistent disturbances and deficits in perceptions, thought processes, and cognition affect development (Lieberman, 1999; McGlashan, 1988). In this way, patients accumulate morbidity in the form of residual or persistent symptoms and decrements in function from their premorbid status. The process of accruing morbidity in the context of exacerbations and (relative) remissions has been attributed to progression of the illness (Kraepelin, 1919) and described as "clinical deterioration" (Bleuler, 1980). Interestingly, the deterioration process occurs predominantly in the early phases of the illness, in the prepsychotic prodromal period and during the first 5 to 10 years after the initial episode (see Figure 5.1). For these reasons, early intervention is highly indicated. In this context, treatment serves two purposes: first, it is remedial for active symptoms of whatever level of severity or syndromal criteria; second, it may be preventive of the deterioration, which can occur and is the most devastating consequence of the illness. However, there are several challenges for treating patients optimally in the earliest stages of schizophrenia. First, patients usually do not seek (or are not brought in for) treatment until they have had the symptoms for often lengthy periods of time. Second, the symptoms by which persons in the prodromal stage and at imminent risk for psychosis are identified are not highly specific or sufficiently validated to use in clinical practice. Third, the optimal treatment agents and strategies for prodromal patients have not been determined. Fourth, patients in the prodromal stages and experiencing first episodes of schizophrenia are reluctant to take medications for sustained periods of time, as they have limited insight into the nature of their illness and are sensitive to and often object to side effects.

Acute Treatment

There have been relatively few studies on first-episode schizophrenia and very few on patients in the prodromal phase. There are currently two published studies of controlled or standardized acute treatment of patients with prodromal symptoms of schizophrenia and eight published studies of controlled or standardized acute treatment of patients with first-episode schizophrenia (summarized in Tables 6.1 and 6.2; Emsley, 1999; Kopala et al., 1996; Lieberman et al., 1993; May, Tuma, Yale, Potepan, & Dixon, 1976; Sanger et al., 1999; Scottish Schizophrenia Research Group, 1987; Szymanski et al., 1994). From these data and those from some uncontrolled studies and secondary analyses, several principles can be suggested to provide guidance for the treatment of patients experiencing a first episode of schizophrenia and for future research on improving the standard of care for this critical stage of psychotic disorders. With such limited data available on the management of prodromal and first-episode schizophrenia, practice will be guided by a hybrid of clinical trials evidence, real-life studies, and clinical experience.

Dosing and Selection of Pharmacologic Agents for Early Stages of Schizophrenia

The pharmacology of treating the prodromal stages of schizophrenia and related psychotic disorders has not been sufficiently well developed. Many agents have been suggested (by theories of pathogenesis) as preventive agents for schizophrenia to be used in the prodromal stage. These include a wide variety of treatments (antioxidants, benzodiazepines, phospholipids, lithium and mood-stabilizers, antidepressants, glutamatergic and nicotinic agents, selective DRD 1, 3, 4 dopamine receptor antagonists, and antipsychotic drugs). For both prodromal and first-episode patients, if an antipsychotic drug is to be used, the general consensus is that this be one of the second-generation antipsychotic drugs (Addington, 2002; Bhana, Foster, Olney, & Plosker, 2001; Bustillo, Lauriello, & Keith, 1999; Green & Schildkraut, 1995; Lieberman, 1996; NICE, 2002; Sartorius et al., 2002). Currently,

Table 6.1 Studies of Acute Treatment in Prodromal Stages of Schizophrenia

Reference	Population	Inclusion/Exclusion	Design/Protocol	Response Criteria	Response Rates
McGorry et al., 2002	59 patients at incipient risk of progression to first-episode psychosis ("high risk")	Ages 14–30, living in Melbourne metropolitan area; met criteria for 1 or more of 3 operationally defined "high-risk" categories	Single-blind, random-ized, controlled trial with blinded interviews. Subjects were random-ized to need-based inter-vention (according to presenting or existing problems) and specific preventive intervention, which included 1–2 mg risperidone and a modi-fied CBT.	Progression to psychosis at 6 months (postinter-vention) and 12 months (follow-up) after study entry, defined by a pre-determined threshold of positive symptoms sus-tained for 1 week or more (based on BPRS and comprehensive as-sessment of symptoms and history)	Needs-based interven-tion: 36% postinterven-tion, 36% at 12 months Specific prevention in-tervention: 10% postin-tervention, 19% at 12 months
Woods et al., 2002	60 patients from 4 North American centers diag-nosed by means of the Structured Interview for Prodromal Symptoms	Not available in pub-lished abstract	Randomized to 5–15 mg olanzapine daily or pla-cebo	SOPS at 8 weeks; weight gain	Olanzapine: least-squares SOPS mean = -14.0 ± 3.3 versus -2.1 ± 3.4. Olanzapine patients gained significantly more weight ($p = .001$).

BPRS, Brief Psychiatric Rating Scale; CBT, cognitive behavior therapy; SOPS, Scale of Prodromal Symptoms.

Table 6.2 Studies of Acute Treatment in First-Episode Schizophrenia

Reference	Population	Inclusion/Exclusion	Design/Protocol	Response Criteria	Response Rates
May et al., 1976	228 patients selected from consecutive admissions to a state psychiatric hospital between 1959 and 1962	Inclusions: first-admission patients with diagnosis of schizophrenia and "no significant prior treatment" Exclusions: those judged unlikely to be discharged and those who remitted fairly quickly (within 18 days)	Randomization to either individual psychotherapy, trifluoperazine, psychotherapy in combination with trifluoperazine, electroconvulsive therapy, or milieu therapy only	Release from hospital after a "fair trial" (6–12 months) of the assigned treatment	Individual psychotherapy (65%), trifluoperazine (96%), psychotherapy in combination with trifluoperazine (95%), ECT (79%), and milieu therapy only (58%)
Scottish Schizophrenia Research Group, 1987	46 patients with first-episode schizophrenia admitted to hospital	Inclusion: diagnosis of first-episode criteria on clinician's ICD-9	5-week, double-blind, randomized trial of flupenthixol versus pimozide Adjunctive medications allowed	"Responders": able to enter maintenance treatment on their assigned drug therapy "Non-responders": those who received further treatment, either ECT or another antipsychotic "Non-completers": those who did not proceed to maintenance therapy but were clearly not "non-responders"	63% were "responders" overall Positive symptoms improved significantly ($p < .01$) for both drugs during the study period, but negative symptoms did not change
Lieberman et al., 1993; Robinson et al., 1999b	70 RDC-diagnosed patients with schizophrenia ($N = 54$) and schizoaffective disorder ($N = 16$)	1. No prior psychotic episodes 2. Age 16–40 years 3. No history of neurological or general medical illness that could influence diagnosis or biological variables being studied	Open, prospective study using a standardized antipsychotic protocol of sequential trials until response criteria were met with fluphenazine, haloperidol, molindone, and clozapine	Operationally defined as a CGI rating of "much" or "very much" improved and a rating of mild or less on specified SADS-C+PDI items with response sustained for at least 8 weeks	83% of patients remitted by 1 year with mean and median times to remission of 35.7 and 11 weeks, respectively

Study	Sample	Diagnostic criteria	Design/treatment	Response definition	Results
Szymanski et al., 1994	10 patients in the Lieberman et al. (1993) study	Patients in the above study who had failed treatment with a standardized protocol of 3 typical antipsychotics	After a 2-week washout period, patients were treated for 12 weeks on clozapine	20% reduction in BPRS score and a CGI severity of illness score of ≤3	30% (3 of 10)
Kopala et al., 1996	22 neuroleptic naive patients consecutively admitted for the first time; mean age of 25 years	DSM-IV diagnosis of a first episode of schizophrenia	Open trial of risperidone monotherapy for a mean duration of treatment was 7.1 weeks (SD = 3.2, range 1.8–14.1). Benzotropine for EPS and lorazepam or clonazepam for insomnia were the only adjunctives allowed.	20% reduction in total PANSS score	59% Negative symptoms improved less than positive symptoms.
Sanger et al., 1999	83 first-episode patients out of 1,996 patients enrolled in a multicenter trial of olanzapine versus haloperidol in psychotic disorders	1. First episode of psychosis with a DSM-II-R diagnosis of schizophrenia, schizophreniform, or schizoaffective disorder 2. Duration of episode of <5 years 3. No more than 45 years old at episode onset 4. Minimum BPRS score of 18 or intolerant to current antipsychotic therapy	6-week, double-blind, randomized trial of olanzapine (N = 59) or haloperidol (N = 24) at mean modal doses of 11.6 (SD = 5.9) and 10.8 (SD = 4.8) mg/day, respectively	Defined a priori as a ≥40% reduction in total BPRS from baseline, also calculated for a 20% reduction	40% BPRS reduction in total BPRS: olanzapine 67.2% response rate, haloperidol 29.2% (Fisher's exact p = .003) 20% BPRS reduction: olanzapine 82.8% response rate, haloperidol 58.3% (Fisher's exact p = .03)
Emsley, 1999	183 patients recruited in multiple international sites	1. Ages 15–40 years 2. Diagnosis of provisional schizophreniform disorder or schizophrenia according to DSM-III-R 3. No prior treatment beyond 3 days of emergency antipsychotics 4. No clinically relevant medical abnormalities	6-week, double-blind study of risperidone versus haloperidol 2–16 mg/day Antiparkinsonian drugs or benzodiazepines administered only if essential	50% improvement in total PANSS scores was defined a priori as clinical response	Risperidone: 63% response rate Haloperidol: 56% response rate

(continued)

Table 6.2 (Continued)

Reference	Population	Inclusion/Exclusion	Design/Protocol	Response Criteria	Response Rates
Yap et al., 2001	24 patients recruited from Woodbridge Hospital and Geylang Psychiatric Outpatient Clinic	Previously untreated male and female patients aged 18–65 with DSM-IV schizophreniform disorder or DSM-IV schizophrenia for no longer than 12 months	Open-label, 8-week study of risperidone	20% reduction in total PANSS score, response for 50% reduction in total PANSS score was also calculated	Responder rate (≥20% reduction in total PANSS score) was 87.5% 13 patients (54.2%) exhibited ≥50% reduction in total PANSS score
Lieberman, Gu, et al., 2003	160 Chinese patients in first-episode schizophrenia	1. Ages 16–45 years 2. Diagnosis of provisional schizophreniform disorder or schizophrenia according to DSM-IV 3. No prior antipsychotic treatment 4. No clinically relevant medical abnormalities	52-week, double-blind RCT of clozapine and chlorpromazine and trihexyphenidyl		
Lieberman, Tollefson, et al., 2003	263 patients recruited from 14 sites in N. America and W. Europe	1. Ages 16–40 years 2. Diagnosis of provisional schizophreniform disorder, schizophrenia, or schizoaffective disorder according to DSM-IV 3. Prior lifetime treatment <16 weeks 4. No clinically relevant medical abnormalities	12-week, acute treatment results of 2-year double-blind RCT of olanzapine (5–15 mg/day) and haloperidol (2–20 mg/day). Antiparkinsonian drugs or benzodiazepines administered only if essential	Total PANSS response defined as 30% reduction of PANSS and CGI severity <4 (moderately ill)	Significantly greater reduction in total PANSS and PANSS Negative Scale with olanzapine on mixed models but not LOCF analysis 55% of olanzapine and 46% of haloperidol met response criteria by week 12

BPRS, Brief Psychiatric Rating Scale; CGI, Clinical Global Impression; ECT, electroconvulsive therapy; LOCF, last-observation-carried-forward; PANSS, Positive and Negative Syndrome Scale for schizophrenia; RCT, randomized control trial; RDC, Research Diagnostic Criteria; SADS-C+PDI, Schedule for Affective Disorders and Schizophrenia Change Version with Psychosis and Disorganization Items rating scale; SD, standard deviation.

there are no specific guidelines or sufficient evidence to determine which second-generation antipsychotic to use. Side effects are the primary distinguishing features among the various drugs.

Young patients without prior exposure to antipsychotic drugs may be more sensitive to the antipsychotic side effects than patients in other stages of the illness. In a sample of 70 treatment-naive patients who received fluphenazine at 20 to 40 mg/day for the first 10 weeks of treatment, 34% developed parkinsonism, 18% developed akathisia, and 36% developed dystonia (Chakos, Mayerhoff, Loebel, Alvir, & Lieberman, 1992). Lower doses of antipsychotics may be adequate to achieve positive symptom remission, but less likely to cause side effects (Cullberg, 1999; Zhang-Wong, Zipursky, Beiser, & Bean, 1999). For example, in a post hoc analysis, low-dose risperidone (maximum of ≤6 mg/day) was more effective and better tolerated than high-dose risperidone (maximum of ≥6 mg/day; Emsley, 1999). Another recent study of 49 acutely psychotic, neuroleptic-naive patients with schizophrenia, schizophreniform disorder, or schizoaffective disorder treated with either 2 mg or 4 mg daily of risperidone showed the two doses to be comparable in efficacy with an advantage for the lower dose in fine motor functioning (Merlo et al., 2002). The greater sensitivity to side effects of first-episode patients than that of chronic patients was dramatically demonstrated by McEvoy, Hogarty, and Steingard (1991) in comparing their neuroleptic thresholds for extrapyramidal symptoms. In the context of a gradual dose titration paradigm, first-episode patients exhibited lower thresholds to develop signs of extrapyramidal symptoms than previously treated more chronic patients. Younger patients are also more susceptible to other side effects, such as weight gain (Kumra et al., 1998; Lieberman, Gu, et al., 2003). Consistent with these studies, the Schizophrenia Patient Outcomes Research Team recommended that patients in a first psychotic episode be treated with relatively lower doses (300 to 500 mg chlorpromazine equivalents per day) of antipsychotics than for patients with schizophrenia in general (300 to 1,000 mg chlorpromazine equivalents per day; Lehman & Steinwachs, 1998). Clinical experience and available research findings suggest that lower doses of antipsychotics are as effective as higher doses in patients experiencing a first episode of schizophrenia, with superior tolerability.

Since the first episode is a time when patients form their attitudes about treatment, efforts to minimize unpleasant side effects may influence patients' willingness to take medications over the long term. In a study of first-episode patients, the only variable that predicted whether patients would attend a follow-up assessment was antipsychotic dosage, with those on higher doses less likely to comply (Jackson et al., 2001).

Treatment of Positive Symptoms

Available data indicate that in prodromal and first-episode patients, positive symptoms, including hallucinations and delusions, will usually remit with antipsychotic treatment. Thus, clinicians should expect remission of positive symptoms in prodromal and first-episode patients. A series of adequate trials of available agents should be employed with this goal in mind. If residual symptoms persist, a trial of clozapine or the addition of adjunctive treatments should be considered.

Treatment of Negative and Cognitive Symptoms

While positive symptoms in first-episode patients tend to respond well to antipsychotic drug treatment, negative and cognitive symptoms of schizophrenia generally take longer to respond or are less responsive to antipsychotic medications (Kopala et al., 1996; Sanger et al., 1999; Scottish Schizophrenia Research Group, 1987). This indicates that negative and cognitive symptoms may have a different time course for response than positive symptoms or that the relative refractoriness of negative and cognitive symptoms may contribute to the less than optimal functional recovery that is often observed in first-episode patients. Improving treatments for negative and cognitive symptoms in the first episode of schizophrenia is an area of major importance in future research and drug development efforts, especially since these symptoms likely affect these patients' functional abilities.

Adjunctive Treatments of Residual Symptoms and Comorbid Syndromes

Often antipsychotic medications are insufficient by themselves to achieve full symptom remission and functional recovery in early-stage schizophrenia patients. For these reasons, a variety of adjunctive treatments both pharmacologic and nonpharmacologic can be used to enhance and optimize treatment response. Adjunctive treatments have different roles in the management of first-episode schizophrenia, targeting residual symptoms and treating comorbid syndromes. A clinical approach to treatment-refractory, first-episode schizophrenia, as described in a recent manual on first-episode schizophrenia, should include the strategies that promote medication adherence, attention to substance abuse, sequential trials of antipsychotic agents, or dose adjustment if clinical improvement is not seen by 6 to 12 weeks of treatment, and consideration of clozapine even early in the course of treatment (Edwards & McGorry, 2002).

While not yet systematically studied in prodromal or first-episode patients, data from studies in chronic patients suggest that cognitive therapy also may benefit residual symptoms (Cormac et al., 2002). Even given the lack of specific trials in first-episode patients, it is likely that CBT may have a role in the treatment of prodromal and first-episode schizophrenia, especially in helping patients to comply with treatment and the transition to outpatient care.

Adjunctive treatments that have been studied in the treatment of schizophrenia include benzodiazepines, anticonvulsants, and antidepressants. Benzodiazepines are often used as adjuncts to antipsychotics in acute schizophrenia. There have been no controlled studies of benzodiazepines in groups of first-episode patients with schizophrenia. Literature on mixed populations of patients with schizophrenia suggest overall that benzodiazepines have a role in treating agitation, anxiety, and aggression in patients with acute psychosis (Barbee, Mancuso, Freed, & Todorov, 1992; Battaglia et al., 1997; Kellner, Wilson, Muldawer, & Pathak, 1975; Salzman et al., 1991) and in preventing an impending psychotic relapse (Carpenter, Buchanan, Kirkpatrick, & Breier, 1999).

Mood stabilizers, including anticonvulsants and lithium, are widely used in patients with schizophrenia (Citrome, Levine, & Allingham, 2000), and there is some evidence that they may also have a role in reducing aggression and agitation (Christison, Kirch, & Wyatt, 1991; Ko, Korpi, Freed, Zalcman, & Bigelow, 1985; Leucht, McGrath, White, & Kissling, 2002; Linnoila & Viukari, 1979; Wassef et al., 2000). Although there is no evidence as to their efficacy in early stage patients, mood stabilizers should be considered for patients who have mood symptoms of excitement and mood lability during residual to the prodromal and first episodes of schizophrenia.

Depressive syndromes are common in prodromal and first-episode patients. Patients who ultimately manifest symptoms of schizophrenia often report a previous depressive episode (Hafner, Loffler, Maurer, Hambrecht, & an der Heiden, 1999) or suicide attempt in their prodromal period (Cohen, Lavelle, Rich, & Bromet, 1994). On presentation with an acute psychotic episode, first-episode patients often have mood symptoms (Addington, Addington, & Patten, 1998). Depressive symptoms will often resolve as psychotic symptoms remit (Koreen et al., 1993), however, in some cases they may persist or occur in the episode's aftermath ("postpsychotic depression"). Antidepressants should be used cautiously in prodromal and first-episode schizophrenia as they could possibly provoke or exacerbate psychotic symptoms. In addition, residual negative symptoms that persist after the stabilization of the acute episode may respond to antidepressant treatment (Berk, Ichim, & Brook, 2001; Hogarty et al., 1995; Silver, Barash, Aharon, Kaplan, & Poyurovsky, 2000; Silver & Nassar, 1992).

Suicidal behavior can occur in prodromal and first-episode schizophrenia patients (Steinert, Wiebe, & Gebhardt, 1999). While depression in the presenting psychotic episode or in the postpsychotic period is an important risk factor for suicide (Axelsson & Lagerkvist-Briggs, 1992), prodromal and first-episode patients with schizophrenia may attempt suicide in the absence of prominent depressive symptoms as a result of hallucinations, paranoia, disorganization, or other symptoms considered more primary to psychosis or other factors. Mounting literature supports the use of clozapine (Meltzer et al., 2003; Meltzer & Okayli, 1995; Reid, Mason, & Hogan, 1998; Sernyak, Desai, Stolar, & Rosenheck, 2001) in patients with psychotic disorder and suicidal behaviors. Although use of clozapine in first-episode schizophrenia has been studied recently (Lieberman, Gu, et al., 2003), it is not considered at this time a first-line drug for first-episode schizophrenia. It should be considered early in the course of treatment only in patients who are unresponsive to other second-generation antipsychotic drugs.

Another important comorbid syndrome in the treatment of first-episode schizophrenia is substance abuse with its possible role in lowering initial vulnerability to the onset or recurrence of psychosis (Chouljian et al., 1995; DeQuardo, Carpenter, & Tandon, 1994; Gupta, Hendricks, Kenkel, Bhatia, & Haffke, 1996; Hambrecht & Hafner, 2000; Linszen, Dingemans, & Lenior, 1994; Rabinowitz et al., 1998). Thorough evaluations of substance abuse habits of prodromal and first-episode schizophrenia patients are critical to directing appropriate clinical attention to this issue throughout care of the patient.

Treatment After Remission of Symptoms in Prodromal and First-Episode Schizophrenia

Continuation and Maintenance Treatment

As the symptomatic response to treatment of young early stage patients is generally very good, clinicians should expect and aim for achieving maximal remission of symptoms, recognizing that psychosis may resolve first and then negative and cognitive symptoms. Residual symptoms should be targeted with adjunctive therapies as needed. After achieving optimal treatment response, the next goal of treatment is to maximize the functional recovery of patients. To an extent, this is dependent on the resolution of symptoms but may not necessarily occur fully concurrently with symptom remission. Maximization of functional recovery involves

the use of adjunctive pharmacologic treatments for any residual symptoms but then various non-pharmacologic treatments to enhance functional recovery. These may include psychoeducation about the nature of the illness, supportive psychotherapy, supported employment, social and vocational rehabilitation, and case management. We think of many of these psychosocial interventions as being associated with the care of chronic patients; however, they can and should also be adapted to young early-stage patients. It is also important to keep in mind that it is necessary to be patient and not rush patients prematurely into the activities with which they may have been previously engaged.

The need for interventions aimed at achieving functional recovery is reflected by the results of outcome studies in first-episode patients. Although patients typically recover from a first episode of schizophrenia, the long-term course for most patients is still characterized by chronic illness, disability, and relapse. Studies report that a minority of patients, about 15% to 20%, will maintain good symptomatic and functional recovery from a first episode. For example, in a study of 349 patients followed up to 15 years after their first onset of schizophrenia, 17% had no disability at follow-up, whereas 24% still suffered from severe disability, and the remaining 69% had varying degrees of disability (Wiersma et al., 2000; Wiersma, Nienhuis, Sloof, & Giel, 1998). The long-term prognosis of patients in the pre-antipsychotic era is similar, with about 20% of patients having good symptomatic and functional recovery (Bleuler, 1978). In a study of first-episode patients with operationally defined criteria for recovery (a period of 2 years of remission of positive and negative symptoms, fulfillment of age-appropriate role expectations, performance of daily living tasks without supervision, and engagement in social interactions), 16.8% of the 118 patients achieved full functional recovery (Robinson et al., 1999b). However, a recent study of 1,633 patients with psychotic disorders from diverse cultures found more optimistic rates of favorable outcome, with nearly half of the patients with schizophrenia considered to be recovered (Harrison et al., 2001).

The next question in the clinical management

of prodromal and first-episode patients is, after achieving maximal therapeutic response, how long should treatment (particularly pharmacologic treatment) be continued? There are not sufficient data to answer that question in prodromal patients. Thus, treatment of prodromal symptoms should be considered time limited and aimed at alleviating current symptoms and stabilizing the patient. There is a growing body of evidence on first-episode patients, however, that suggests the value of continuing medication for a sustained and possibly indefinite period. Ideally, this decision would be informed by data from prospective, controlled studies answering the following questions: *(1)* How likely is relapse with and without antipsychotic medication? *(2)* Is it possible to predict who will relapse after remission of a first episode? *(3)* Will antipsychotic therapy improve the course and long-term outcome of the illness or merely suppress symptoms in the short to medium term? Table 6.3 summarizes the six controlled studies of maintenance antipsychotic treatment of remitted first-episode schizophrenia (Crow, MacMillan, Johnson, & Johnstone, 1986; Gitlin et al., 2001; Kane, Rifkin, Quitkin, Nayak, & Ramos-Lorenzi, 1982; McCreadie et al., 1989; Nuechterlein et al., 1994).

The risk of eventual relapse after recovery from a first psychotic episode is very high and is greatly diminished by maintenance antipsychotic treatment. However, even with strong evidence of the risk of relapse without antipsychotic medication, there is still no clear consensus on the recommended duration of treatment for patients who have recovered from a first episode of schizophrenia. Clinicians may have a difficult time convincing patients who have recovered from one episode of schizophrenia that indefinite and possibly lifelong antipsychotic treatment is indicated because of the diagnostic uncertainty and instability associated with a first psychotic episode (Amin et al., 1999), limited patient understanding and awareness of the illness (Thompson, McGorry, & Harrigan, 2001), and risks of long-term antipsychotic therapy. Most practice guidelines for the treatment of patients with schizophrenia recommend that patients who have had only one episode of positive symptoms and have been symptom-free

during the subsequent year of maintenance therapy can be considered for a trial period without medication, provided that dose reductions are made gradually over several months with frequent visits (Rose, 1997). Similarly, the Schizophrenia Patient Outcomes Research Team (Lehman & Steinwachs, 1998) recommended in their report that patients continue treatment for at least 1 year after remission of acute symptoms, with continual reassessment of the maintenance dose for possible reduction. The draft consensus statement of 26 international consultants (Addington, 2002) recommends taking into consideration the severity of the first episode when deciding how long to continue maintenance treatment. They suggest that patients who achieve full remission be offered gradual withdrawal of medication after 12 months of maintenance treatment, but that patients experiencing more severe episodes and are slow to respond be maintained for 24 months. This panel further suggests that patients who respond incompletely to medication, but clearly benefit from treatment, be maintained for 2 to 5 years on medication.

Conclusion

Patients in the prodromal phase or first episode of schizophrenia respond very favorably to antipsychotic treatment in terms of their positive symptoms. However, cognitive and negative symptoms are often slower to respond or are refractory to treatment, leaving many of these individuals with significant social disability. Sequential trials of adequate dose and duration of antipsychotics and adjunctive treatments should be employed to help patients achieve their optimal response. Psychosocial therapies such as CBT and education groups may be helpful in addressing residual symptoms and helping patients to adhere to their medication regimens.

In addition to lessening the morbidity of the presenting episode, early intervention in prodromal and first-episode schizophrenia may improve the long-term course of the disorder, as evidenced by studies showing an inverse correlation between the duration of untreated psychosis and outcome. The outcome of schizo-

Table 6.3 Studies of Maintenance Treatment in First-Episode Schizophrenia

Reference	Population	Inclusion/Exclusion	Design/Protocol	Relapse Criteria	Relapse Rates
Kane et al. 1982	28 patients referred for aftercare with a diagnosis of a single episode of schizophrenia; 19 of 28 patients met RDC criteria for schizophrenia	1. At least 4 weeks of remission 2. 1 year or less since hospitalization 3. No treatment prior to 3 months before hospitalization 4. No evidence of drug abuse, alcoholism, or important medical illness	Double-blind, 1-year duration Random assignment to fluphenazine hydrochloride (5–20 mg/day), fluphenazine decanoate (12.5–50 mg/2 weeks) or placebo. Only patients thought to have possible compliance problems were randomized to decanoate. Procyclidine hydrochloride for all patients, with substitution of placebo in second month for placebo patients	Substantial clinical deterioration with a potential for marked social impairment Patients were considered dropouts only if they showed no clinical deterioration at the time they left the study	For all patients: 0% (0 out of 11) on fluphenazine and 41% (7 out of 17) on placebo relapsed Of those with RDC schizophrenia: 0% (0 out of 6) on fluphenazine and 46% (6 out of 13) on placebo relapsed Follow-up with 26 patients (mean interval of 3.5 years): 69% had a second relapse; 54% had a third relapse
Crow et al., 1986	120 patients diagnosed with first-episode schizophrenia, recruited from both psychiatric and district general practices in Harrow, England	1. Age 15–70 years 2. Suffering from a first psychotic episode that was "not unequivocally affective" 3. Admission to an inpatient psychiatric unit for at least 1 week 4. Clinical diagnosis of schizophrenia 5. Absence of organic disease of probable etiological significance	Drugs [fluphenthixol (40 mg/month IM), chlorpromazine (200 mg/day orally), haloperidol (3 mg/day orally), pimozide (4 mg/day), or trifluoperazine (5 mg/day)] chosen by clinicians, then patients randomized to either drug or placebo 1 month after remission of initial episode Adjunctive medications allowed	Psychiatric readmission for any reason; readmission deemed necessary by treating clinician, but not possible; or active antipsychotic medication considered to be essential because of features of imminent relapse Relapse determinations made by treating clinicians	Actuarial relapse rates: 6 months: placebo 43%, drug 21%; 12 months: placebo 63%, drug 38%; 18 months: placebo 67%, drug 46%; 24 months: placebo 70%, drug 58%

(continued)

Table 6.3 Continued

Reference	Population	Inclusion/Exclusion	Design/Protocol	Relapse Criteria	Relapse Rates
Scottish Schizophrenia Research Group, 1987	15 patients who had suffered a first episode of schizophrenia	Patients had to respond to acute treatment and then be relapse-free for an additional year of treatment on either once-weekly pimozide or IM fluphenthixol decanoate	Double-blind trial of active medication (either once-weekly pimozide or IM fluphenthixol decanoate) or placebo for 1 year	Deterioration in schizophrenia symptoms or behavior sufficient to warrant patient's withdrawal from study	0% (0 out of 8) of the patients who received active drug, but 57% (4 out of 7) who received placebo were readmitted in second year of study treatment
Nuechterlein et al., 1994	106 patients from four public hospitals and an outpatient clinic of an academic medical center 66% had never taken antipsychotic medication and the remainder had a mean duration of treatment of 2.7 months (SD = 3.1)	Inclusion: recent-onset psychotic symptoms lasting at least 2 weeks and not more than 2 years, age 18–45 years, and RDC diagnosis of schizophrenia or schizoaffective disorder (mainly schizophrenia) Exclusions: known neurological disorder, recent significant substance abuse, or African-American descent[a]	Phase I: stabilized patients were treated with 12.5 mg fluphenazine decanoate every 2 weeks for 12 months Phase II: those who remitted in Phase I were recruited into Phase II. They were treated for 12 weeks with either placebo or fluphenazine, followed by crossover to the opposite treatment	Operationally defined as a 2-point worsening on any three BPRS psychotic items, excluding changes where the scores remained at nonpsychotic levels; a score of 6 or 7 was obtained on any three items; or clinical deterioration warranting a change in treatment as judged by treating psychiatrist	Phase I: 11 patients needed to have dose lowered because of side effects and 6 were prescribed antidepressants Phase II: 6% (3 of 53 subjects) had a relapse while on active medication and 13% (7 out of 53) relapsed on placebo
Robinson et al., 1999b	104 patients who responded to treatment of their index episode of schizophrenia and were at risk for relapse	1. RDC-defined diagnosis of schizophrenia or schizoaffective disorder 2. Total lifetime exposure to antipsychotic medications of ≤12 weeks 3. Rating of ≥4 (moderate) on at least one psychotic symptom item on SADS-C+PD 4. No medical contraindications to treatment with antipsychotic medications 5. No neurologic or endocrine disorder or neuromedical illness that could affect diagnosis or biological variables in study	Patients were treated openly according to a standard algorithm, progressing from one phase of the algorithm to the next until they met response criteria. The sequence was initial treatment with fluphenazine, then haloperidol, then lithium augmentation, then molindone hydrochloride or loxapine, then clozapine	At least "moderately ill" on the CGI Severity of Illness Scale, "much worse" or "very much worse" on the CGI Improvement Scale, and at least "moderate" on one or more of the SADS-C+PD psychosis items listed above; these criteria had to be sustained for a minimum of 1 week	5-year overall relapse rate: 81.9%; the second relapse rate. By 4 years after recovery from a second relapse, the cumulative third relapse rate was 86.2%. Discontinuing antipsychotic drug therapy increased the risk of relapse by almost 5 times

| Gitlin et al., 2001 | 53 patients with RDC schizophrenia or schizoaffective disorder who had been stabilized for 1 year on fluphenzine decanoate | Patient who completed Phase II of the Nuechterlein et al. study (above) and did not relapse | Open-label discontinuation of drugs | Two-point worsening on any three BPRS psychotic items, excluding changes where the scores remained at nonpsychotic levels, a score of 6 or 7 was obtained on any three items, or the treating psychiatrist deemed that there was clinical deterioration warranting change in treatment | 78% relapsed by 1 year and 96% by 2 years with low threshold for relapse. Only 13% required hospitalization |

[a] Excluded because of differences in electrodermal conductivity from other groups because this was a biological variable being studied.

BRPS, Brief Psychiatric Rating Scale; CGI, Clinical Global Impression; IM, intramuscular; RCT, randomized control trial; RDC, Research Diagnostic Criteria; SADS-C+PDI, Schedule for Affective Disorders and Schizophrenia Change Version with Psychosis and Disorganization Items rating scale; SD, standard deviation.

phrenia is variable, and despite a large literature, we know relatively little about the predictors of outcome. Duration of untreated illness in various studies also varies widely, ranging between 22 and 166.4 weeks (Norman & Malla, 2001). Several studies have suggested that prolonged duration of untreated illness (DUI) may predict poor outcome as evidenced by longer time to and level of remission. Based on such findings, it has been suggested that decreasing DUI, perhaps by early identification and intervention, might lead to a more favorable outcome. It has also been argued that prolonged untreated illness might be causally related to poor outcomes, perhaps as a result of a neurotoxic process. However, controversy has shrouded this literature, as some studies have not found an association between DUI and outcome.

Prevention of schizophrenia through presymptomatic treatment is an exciting possibility, but future research is needed to develop the methodology by which to reliably identify those at risk before this strategy can become part of routine clinical practice. Once remission from the first episode is reached, maintenance with antipsychotic treatment is indicated for at least 1 year. The overwhelming majority of individuals who do not remain on antipsychotic therapy eventually experience a relapse. This raises the question of the optimal length of continuation and maintenance treatment for patients who have recovered from a first episode of schizophrenia or related psychoses. Clinically useful predictors of the small minority who maintain remission without pharmacotherapy have not yet been identified.

Atypical antipsychotics represent an advance in the treatment of first-episode schizophrenia, with strong evidence for greater tolerability with equal or better therapeutic efficacy. While future research will help to characterize their efficacy relative to one another and define the effect of their use on the long-term outcomes of schizophrenia, available evidence and consensus expert opinion support their use as first-line treatment in first-episode schizophrenia.

Prevention of Schizophrenia

There are currently recognized precursors of schizophrenia that are apparent during adolescence. A wide variety of early-intervention techniques have been developed that draw on the knowledge of these precursors to identify individuals at risk for the illness and to prevent the predisposition toward schizophrenia from developing into the full disorder. Unfortunately, most of the research that has enabled the identification of these precursors and the development of these intervention techniques has been performed retrospectively in adults with schizophrenia, with little specific research attention directed toward forms of schizophrenia that manifest during adolescence. In addition, prevention efforts have necessarily lagged behind studies of the risk factors, detection, and early intervention of the disease. Yet, a great deal has already been learned about risk-profiling and early intervention in schizophrenia generally, and those aspects that may be useful in understanding the adolescent forms of the illness are discussed below.

What Guides the Development of Early Intervention and Prevention Efforts?

Traditionally, prevention efforts have been classified at three levels: *(1)* primary prevention, which is practiced prior to the onset of the disease; *(2)* secondary prevention, which is practiced after the disease is recognized, but before it has caused suffering and disability; and *(3)* tertiary prevention, which is practiced after suffering or disability has been experienced, to prevent further deterioration. The primary/secondary/tertiary classification scheme is attractive and simple, but it does not serve to distinguish between preventive interventions that have different epidemiological justifications and require different strategies for optimal utilization. For example, this classification into primary, secondary, and tertiary prevention focuses on intended outcomes rather than on target populations or prevention strategies.

More recently, the terms *universal, selective,* and *indicated* have been adopted as a valuable way to distinguish preventive interventions. All three of these preventive intervention strategies

refer to the target population. Universal preventive interventions are applied to whole populations, and aim at reducing risk and promoting protective factors. Because obstetric complications have been linked to the subsequent onset of schizophrenia in several studies (Zorenberg, Buka, & Tsuang, 2000), one potentially effective universal prevention strategy would be to focus on lowering the incidence of such complications through improved pre-, peri-, and postnatal care.

In contrast to universal prevention strategies, selective and indicated interventions target specific subgroups for intervention. Selective interventions target those who are at elevated risk based on group-level characteristics that are not directly related to etiology. Because schizophrenia is a familial and heritable disorder (Gottesman, 1991), a selective prevention program for schizophrenia might focus on asymptomatic children with first-degree affected relatives or, more specifically, on those with particular combinations of schizophrenia-risk–specific gene variants, as they become known.

Finally, an indicated intervention involves targeting individuals who either have signs of the disorder but are currently asymptomatic, or are in an early stage of a progressive disorder. Because there are no universal signs of schizophrenia, indicated interventions for this disorder have a somewhat broad definition. Two lines of research that may lead to indicated interventions for schizophrenia include the study of individuals with prodromal signs of schizophrenia (Eaton, Badawi, & Melton, 1995) and the characterization of individuals with schizotaxia, which can be defined as the underlying predisposition to schizophrenia that may or may not be expressed as prodromal symptoms (Tsuang, Stone, Tarbox, & Faraone, 2002).

In order to develop and refine selective and indicated prevention efforts for schizophrenia, the disorder itself (as well as its precursors) must be thoroughly understood. Some of the risk factors for schizophrenia, such as birth complications and a family history of the disorder, are widely recognized. Others are just becoming known or are still being validated. When a wide variety of schizophrenia-specific precursors are available, these features can be used to maximize the efficiency and effectiveness of preventive efforts by narrowly specifying the characteristics of at-risk individuals, allowing only those who would benefit from intervention to be selected to receive it.

PREMORBID ASPECTS OF SCHIZOPHRENIA

The etiology of schizophrenia is complex, most likely involving a range of genetic and gene-environment interactions that are well summarized as the "epigenetic puzzle" (Gottesman & Shields, 1982; Plomin, Reiss, Hetherington, & Howe, 1994), as discussed in Chapter 5. The schizophrenia syndrome—the delusions, hallucinations, thought disorder, negative features, and cognitive dysfunction—is manifest at some stage during the lives of around 1 in 100 people. Figure 7.1 shows that the occurrence begins to take off in the early teenage and adolescent years, being rare before puberty and becoming less common in the second half of life. However, important events may occur in the period leading up to illness and in the early years of development, the so-called prodromal and premorbid periods.

Prodromal and Premorbid Phases of Schizophrenia

In most cases, schizophrenia does not come totally out of the blue; there are important changes that occur before the psychotic syndrome. Fragmentary psychotic symptoms, depression, changes in behavior, attenuated general functioning, and other nonspecific features commonly occur in the weeks, months, and sometimes years before the first psychotic break. This period before the schizophrenia syndrome is established is known as the *prodrome*, and is a change that can frequently be identified by either the affected individual or by their family.

The prodrome is a period of considerable interest from a clinical and theoretical point of view because it may be possible to intervene early during this time and thus prevent the onset of psychosis or improve its outcome. This exciting prospect of early intervention, considered elsewhere in this volume (Chapter 6), is technically complex because of the nonspecific nature of some of the symptoms in the prodrome. Schizophrenia or other psychoses are by no means inevitable in a group of adolescents who show apparently prodromal features. Looking back to adolescents who have developed schizophrenia, the psychological difficulties are, of course, much more difficult. Much research is aiming to understand the biology underlying this period just before and around the onset of schizophrenia when important neuropsychological and structural changes may be occurring (Pantelis et al., 2003; Wood et al., 2003). There is general agreement, however, that earlier-onset cases such as these occurring in childhood or ad-

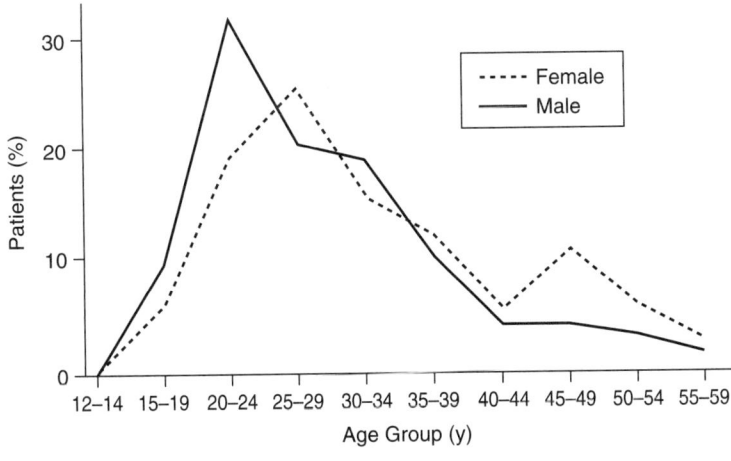

Figure 7.1 Age at onset distribution of schizophrenia [from Hafner, H., Maurer, K., Loffler, W., & Riecher-Rossler, A. (1993). The influence of age and sex on the onset and early course of schizophrenia. *British Journal of Psychiatry, 162,* 80–86, used with permission].

olescence are likely to have more severe premorbid abnormalities (Nicolson & Rapoport, 1999; Nicolson et al., 2000).

There are other differences and abnormalities that occur well before the period of risk shown in Figure 7.1 begins. They are not just in a psychological domain and show no obvious continuity with the schizophrenia syndrome. Rather than being changes from the preexisting state that herald the illness during a prodrome, these differences are more a long-term part of the person, his or her personality, and early development.

These differences are known as *premorbid* features. The distinction from the prodrome is not always clear, particularly in younger people, but may have theoretical importance because they seem to point toward early vulnerability or predisposing factors, rather than to events that occur as an illness is triggered or precipitated. The existence of premorbid abnormalities and differences in those who will develop schizophrenia years later suggests that parts of the epigenetic puzzle are put in place in very early life. In childhood-onset cases, the distinction may be almost impossible because of the severity and insidious onset of schizophrenia before age 13 (Alaghband-Rad et al., 1995). Why look in early life for premorbid differences and causes of schizophrenia?

From its first descriptions, schizophrenia has had a longitudinal dimension. Thomas Clouston (Clouston, 1892; Murray, 1994; Murray & Jones, 1995) recognized a syndrome that he called "developmental insanity" in which developmental physical abnormalities were associated with early-onset psychotic phenomena, particularly in adolescent boys. When defining the schizophrenia syndrome more clearly, both Kraepelin (1896/1987) and Bleuler (1908/1987, 1911/1950) noted that many of the people who developed the psychotic syndrome had been different from their peers long before the psychosis began. Here is a description from one of Bleuler's (1911/1950) early accounts of what has become known as schizophrenia:

It is certain that many a schizophrenia can be traced back into the early years of the patient's life, and many manifest illnesses are

simply intensifications of an already existing character. . . . All ten of my own school comrades who later became schizophrenics were quite different from the other boys.

If some of the seeds of schizophrenia are sown in early life, then there ought to be other evidence. The excess of minor physical abnormalities (Green, Satz, Gaier, Ganzell, & Kharabi, 1989; Gualtieri, Adams, Shen, & Loiselle, 1982; Guy, Majorski, Wallace, & Guy, 1983; Lane et al., 1997; Lohr & Flynn, 1993; Sharma & Lal, 1986), and the dermatoglyphic or fingerprint abnormalities in people with schizophrenia (Bracha, Torrey, Gottesman, Bigelow, & Cunniff, 1992; McGrath et al., 1996) are seen as "fossilized" reminders of insults very early in life, during the first or second trimester of pregnancy, such as infections and nutritional problems (reviewed in Tarrant & Jones, 1999). These factors and some of the neuropathological data are probably best explained in terms of developmental processes having gone awry (Weinberger, 1995).

However, these processes are difficult to observe directly. Genetic high-risk studies in which the offspring of people with schizophrenia are followed up have shown subtle differences in the neurological development of these children at special risk, and in those not known to be so (Erlenmeyer-Kimling et al., 1982; Fish, 1977; Fish, Marcus, Hans, Auerbach, & Perdue, 1992; Walker & Lewine, 1990). Genetic studies such as these are discussed in Chapter 5.

What Are the Premorbid Differences Seen in Schizophrenia?

Bleuler wasn't very precise when he mentioned that many of the people he'd known who developed schizophrenia as adults were different from other boys as children. It's certainly interesting that he mentions boys specifically, because tightly defined schizophrenia does seem to be more common in men than in women, and the early developmental differences are often more obvious in boys than in girls. This may be partly an artifact of some research designs, as well as an effect of differences in the wiring of male and female brains.

Many aspects of development can be seen to be slightly different in children who will later develop schizophrenia. Often these differences are subtle and would not be noticed at the time by parents or professionals. Usually, differences can be noted in characteristics that are developing rapidly according to the age of the child, things that are on the cusp of the developmental wave, and the child appears to catch up later on. Following are some examples.

Early Milestones and Motor Development

Direct evidence of neurodevelopmental differences is available (Weinberger, 1995). One source is a remarkable piece of opportunistic research by Walker and colleagues (Walker, Grimes, Davis, & Smith, 1993; Walker & Lewine, 1993) who studied home movies of families in which one child later developed schizophrenia. Facial expression of emotion and general motor functions were rated blind to that child's identity among siblings. The preschizophrenic children were distinguished on both accounts, some with fairly gross but transitory motor differences. These may point to the basal ganglia of the brain as being involved in the underlying mechanism, reminding us that subtle motor disturbances are apparent at the beginning of schizophrenia, before any treatment (Gervin et al., 1998).

Such developmental differences have now been demonstrated in large, population-based or epidemiological samples. In the British 1946 birth cohort, a group of several thousand people born in 1 week in March 1946 have been studied regularly throughout their lives. Their mothers were asked about development when the children were age 2 years, before anyone knew what would happen later on. All the milestones of sitting, standing, walking, and talking were slightly though clearly delayed in those who developed schizophrenia as adults, but there was nothing that would have alarmed parents at the time. There were other indications that language acquisition was different before onset of schizophrenia. Nurses were more likely to notice a lack of speech by 2 years in the children who developed schizophrenia as adults, and school doctors noted speech delays and problems in them throughout childhood.

Developmental differences have been replicated in similar cohort studies in other domains, such as bladder control, fine motor skill, and co-ordination during late childhood and adolescence (Cannon et al., 1999; Crow, Done, & Sacker, 1995). The motor and language delays were replicated and extended in a birth cohort study from Dunedin, New Zealand (Cannon et al., 2002), where over a thousand children have been followed during childhood. Those who indicated in their mid-20s that they had experienced symptoms suggestive of schizophrenia, mania, and other disorders were compared with those who said that they had never had such phenomena.

Figure 7.2 shows how a summary motor performance score was lower throughout most of childhood for those who experienced a schizophreniform disorder than that of the other groups. Figure 7.3 indicates that there was also a receptive language problem in those who later had hallucination, delusion, and thought disorder.

Developmental differences before onset of schizophrenia were observed during the first year of life in the North Finland 1966 birth cohort. This comprises about 12,000 babies due to be born in this geographical area during 1966 (Rantakallio, 1969). Their early development was charted in the first year of life and later linked to information about who had developed schizophrenia through adolescence and into the early 30s (Isohanni et al., 2001). Figure 7.4 shows the incidence of schizophrenia in male subjects according to how quickly the little boys learned to stand without support or "toddle" during the first year. The figure for girls was similar.

It is clear that not only was there an effect whereby the later a boy learned to toddle, the greater his chance of developing schizophrenia in later life, but also that this effect seemed to hold true throughout the range of variation in reaching this milestone, all of which might be considered normal. If one were looking only for very late developers, then one might be more likely to find them within the preschizophrenia group than in those who did not develop the illness. However, this approach would completely obscure the widespread nature of this association, the meaning of which is considered later on in this chapter.

Figure 7.2 Mean standardized scores for motor performance at four ages during childhood for adults who indicated symptoms of schizophreniform disorder (36), mania (20), or anxiety/depression (278), compared with controls (642) [from Cannon, M., Caspi, A., Moffitt, T.E., Harrington, H., Taylor A., & Murray, R.M. (2002). Evidence for early-childhood, pan-developmental impairment specific to schizophreniform disorder: results from a longitudinal birth cohort. *Archives of General Psychiatry, 59*, 449–456. Copyright © 2002, American Medical Association. All rights reserved, used with permission].

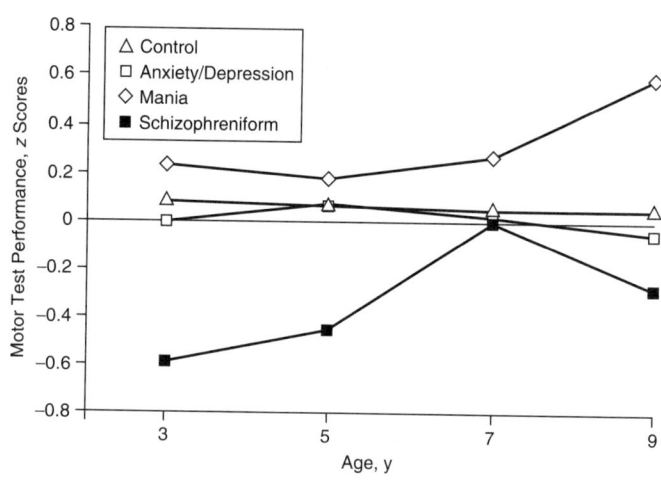

Figure 7.3 Mean standardized scores for expressive and receptive language performance at four ages during childhood for adults who indicated symptoms of schizophreniform disorder (36), mania (20), or anxiety/depression (278), compared with controls (642) [from Cannon, M., Caspi, A., Moffitt, T.E., Harrington, H., Taylor A., & Murray, R.M. (2002). Evidence for early-childhood, pan-developmental impairment specific to schizophreniform disorder: results from a longitudinal birth cohort. *Archives of General Psychiatry, 59*, 449–456. Copyright © 2002, American Medical Association. All rights reserved, used with permission].

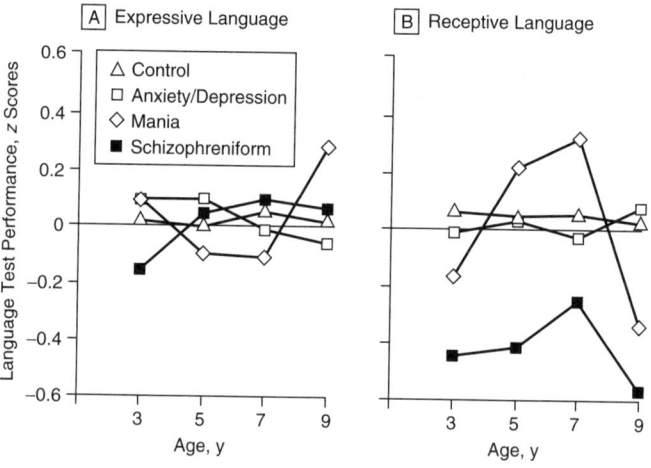

There is another finding apparent from Figure 7.4. For the boys who passed the milestone early, in the 9-month and 10-month categories, the relatively few individuals who developed schizophrenia all did so in their mid-teens to mid-20s; their period of risk seems fairly short. For those who were later developers, the period of risk is longer; these groups are still accruing cases of schizophrenia into their early 30s and beyond. It may be that the overall risk period for schizophrenia is shorter when neurodevelopment is more efficient, and longer when it is less efficient.

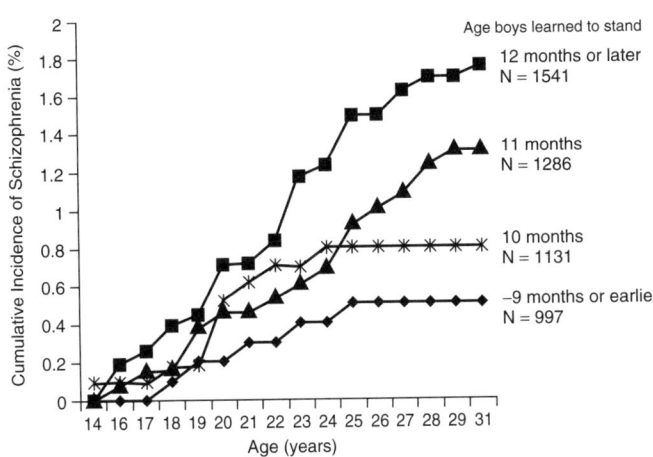

Figure 7.4 Relationship between age at standing without support, or toddling, and later schizophrenia in boys from the 1966 North Finland birth cohort (Isohanni et al., 2001). The later boys could stand during the first year of life, the greater the risk of schizophrenia, even when the milestone was passed within normal limits [from Isohanni, M., Jones, P.B., Moilanen, K., Rantakallio, P., Veijola, J., Oja, H., Koiranen M., Jokelainen, J., Croudace, T.J., & Järvelin, M-R. (2001). Early development milestones in adult schizophrenia and other psychoses. A 31-year follow-up of the north Finland 1966 birth cohort. *Schizophrenia Research*, 52, 1–19, used with permission from Elsevier].

Behavioral Development

Bleuler's description of schizophrenia most obviously implies differences in behavior and temperament. Studies in this area have also moved on through retrospective research methodologies to cohort designs. Sophisticated rating scales for the retrospective assessment of behavior and personality demonstrate differences prior to psychosis, with the most common being characteristics of a shy, "schizoid" habit (Ambelas, 1992; Cannon-Spoor, Potkin, & Wyatt, 1982; Foerster, Lewis, Owen, & Murray, 1991; Gittleman-Klein & Klein, 1969).

Robins (1966) undertook a pioneering, historical cohort study in which she followed a group of boys who had been referred to a child guidance clinic in St. Louis, Missouri. Here antisocial behavior was associated with later schizophrenia. Watt and Lubensky (1976; Watt, 1978) traced the school records of people with schizophrenia who came from a geographically defined neighborhood in Massachusetts. Girls who were to develop schizophrenia were introverted throughout kindergarten into adolescence. Boys who were to become ill were more likely to be rated as "disagreeable," but only in

the later school grades (7 to 12). This pattern has been identified (Done, Crow, Johnson, & Sacker, 1994) in a British cohort using a similar set of behavioral ratings and in the Dunedin cohort mentioned above (Cannon et al., 2002). The 1946 British birth cohort contained children's own ratings of their behavior at age 13 years and teachers' ratings 2 years later. These data showed no evidence of antisocial traits in the preschizophrenia group, but a strong association with shy, "schizoid" behaviors at both ages. The two views gave a very similar picture; the shyer someone seemed as a child, the greater the risk. Other studies, however, remind us of the varied childhood psychiatric conditions that predate schizophrenia (Kim et al., in press).

The behavioral differences seem to persist toward the prodrome, though are independent from it. Malmberg, Lewis, David, and Auerbach (1998) studied a sample of some 50,000 men conscripted into the Swedish army at age 18 to 20 years when they underwent a range of tests and assessments. Four behavioral variables at age 18 were particularly associated with later schizophrenia: having only one or no friends, preferring to socialize in small groups, feeling more sensitive than others, and not having a steady girlfriend. Cannon et al. (1997) also noted the same relationship.

Another twist to the story about premorbid behavioral differences comes from the recent recognition that some of the individual parts of the schizophrenia syndrome, such as hallucinations or delusions, can exist in otherwise well-functioning individuals in the population. However, they are indeed associated with greater risk of occurrence of subsequent schizophrenia whether they occur in early adolescence (Poulton et al., 2000) or adulthood (Myin-Germeys, Krabbendam, Delespaul, & Van Os, 2003).

Thus, there seems to be a consistency over childhood and adolescence and across several types of study regarding the presence of premorbid behavioral differences. People who will develop schizophrenia as adolescents and adults are different from their peers in terms of behavior in childhood, just as Bleuler noted a century ago; the effects may be even more widespread than he thought.

Cognitive Function and IQ

This aspect of psychological function also shows differences in the premorbid period. Aylward,

Walker, and Bettes (1984) have provided a comprehensive review of intelligence in schizophrenia. They concluded that intellectual function is lower in prepsychotic individuals than in age-matched controls. Linking the prepsychotic deficit to outcome, they raised the question as to whether IQ may be an independent factor that can protect otherwise vulnerable individuals, or whether the deficits are part of that vulnerability.

Once again, the birth cohort studies shed light on the question. Cannon et al. (2002) showed that mean IQ test scores were consistently lower during childhood in those children who developed schizophreniform disorder (Fig. 7.5). This mean shift in premorbid IQ was also seen in two British cohorts (Jones & Done, 1997). When the childhood IQ data from the 1946 cohort (Pidgeon, 1964, 1968) is studied in greater detail, it is clear that the lower mean premorbid IQ is not due to a subset of people with very low scores; rather, the whole distribution of those who develop schizophrenia when they reach adolescence or adulthood is shifted down—most children seem not to be doing as well as they might have been expected to perform (Jones, Rodgers, Murray, & Marmot, 1994). This is a similar situation to the motor findings in the Finnish cohort (Cannon et al., 1999). It is not that there is a

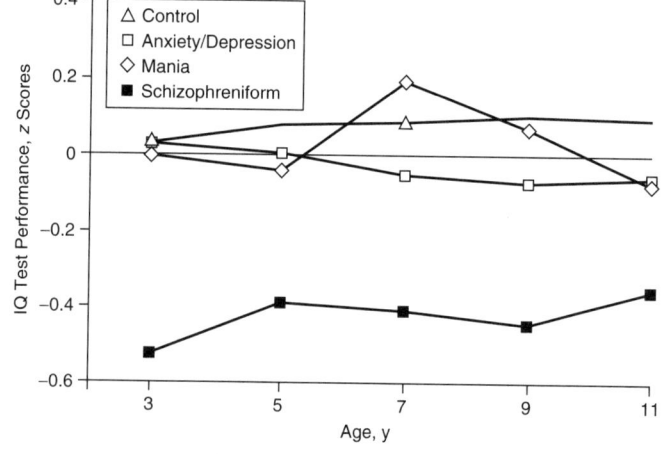

Figure 7.5 Mean standardized scores for IQ performance at four ages during childhood for adults who indicated symptoms of schizophreniform disorder (36), mania (20), or anxiety/depression (278), compared with controls (642) [from Cannon, M., Caspi, A., Moffitt, T.E., Harrington, H., Taylor A., & Murray, R.M. (2002). Evidence for early-childhood, pan-developmental impairment specific to schizophreniform disorder: results from a longitudinal birth cohort. *Archives of General Psychiatry, 59,* 449–456. Copyright © 2002, American Medical Association. All rights reserved, used with permission].

group of very abnormal individuals driving the findings; the effects are seen across the normal range.

David, Malmberg, Brandt, Allebeck, and Lewis (1997; see above) replicated this result in the Swedish conscript study, although the measures were later in life at age 18. There was no evidence of a threshold effect below or above which this relationship did not hold. Very bright individuals can develop schizophrenia, but they are less likely to than those who are less able. Put another way, any individual is more likely to develop schizophrenia than someone who is more able in terms of IQ, although the effect is small. Recent interest in the cognitive aspects of schizophrenia (David & Cutting, 1994; Green, 1998) suggests a parsimonious conclusion that prepsychotic IQ deficits (and perhaps social characteristics) may be manifestations of the same abnormal cognitive processes that later result in psychosis.

What Do Premorbid Abnormalities Mean?

The range of differences in the developmental histories of people who develop schizophrenia when they are older suggests that something to do with the causes of this syndrome is active long before the characteristic features begin (Marenco & Weinberger, 2000). There is evidence for many such early factors, including genetic effects (Jones & Murray, 1991; Fish et al., 1992), obstetric complications (Cannon et al., 2002), psychosocial stresses, famine, infections, and other toxic events during brain development (see Jones, 1999, for review).

It seems that many events that may lead to early brain development being suboptimal may increase the risk of later schizophrenia. There may be specific causes or combinations of causes, such as gene–environment interactions, that make people vulnerable to developing the schizophrenia syndrome, perhaps after later, necessary events that act as triggers. These may include normal (Weinberger, 1987, 1995) or abnormal brain development (Feinberg, 1982a, 1997; Pogue-Geile, 1997), as well as traditional precipitants such as psychosocial stressors or drugs (see Chapter 6).

The behavioral, motor, language, and cognitive differences shown in the premorbid period may be manifestations of vulnerability or predisposition to schizophrenia; they may not be risk modifiers in themselves. These indicators seem remarkably homogeneous—in retrospect, like a final common pathway. The idea of only a subgroup of individuals having this manifest vulnerability, as suggested in the seminal views of developmental aspects of schizophrenia (Murray & Lewis, 1987), is not supported by recent research. Most people or even every person who develops the syndrome may have had a degree of developmental vulnerability, although this will not have been obvious at the time.

The early motor findings in the Finnish birth cohort (Fig. 7.4) are consistent with the vulnerability being due to developmental processes being generally less efficient, the formation or enhancement of functional neural networks, for instance. The greater the inefficiency, the greater the risk of schizophrenia when that same inefficiency is played out in the formation of complex and integrative systems later in adolescence and adult life (Chapter 5).

There are several candidates to explain this unifying vulnerability. These include hormonal events (Walker & Bollini, 2002) that are able to tie together motor and other system abnormalities in early life and links with psychosocial stress in models of predisposition and precipitation (Walker, Lewis, Loewy, & Palyo, 1999). Molecular biology and the investigation of not only the presence but also the functional activity of genes and the proteins that code them may yield other dimensions of vulnerability. For instance, Tkachev et al. (2003) showed that expression of genes associated with glial cells facilitate the nutritional support of nerve cells (oligodendrocytes) and with myelin, the insulating sheaths provided for these neurons, were down-regulated in the frontal cortex of brains of deceased people who had suffered from schizophrenia. Expression seems a very good candidate for the homogeneous vulnerability factor posited in this account of premorbid abnormalities before schizophrenia, and may be an endophenotype or hidden manifestation of the disorder. The deficient gene expression remains to be demonstrated before onset of schizophrenia and will itself have its own prior causes.

As mentioned at the beginning of this section, premorbid features of schizophrenia are not yet of use in terms of prediction and early intervention. They occur in multiple domains, but many of the effects we can measure are subtle and leave individuals remaining well within the wide range of normality. Premorbid features tell us a great deal about what we should be looking for in terms of underlying mechanisms and causes of schizophrenia and when these may operate; these features are signposts toward these mechanisms. As we learn about the processes that underpin the behavioral, cognitive, and motor differences that we can measure in the premorbid phase of schizophrenia, we may become able to identify those individuals who are vulnerable with enough precision to be able to do something useful for them.

Developmental Precursors of Adolescent-Onset Schizophrenia

There are precursors of schizophrenia prior to the first onset of psychosis in many but not all adolescents who develop schizophrenia. As will be seen below, the precursors of schizophrenia can be subtle changes in basic brain functions such as motor functions, attention and memory, certain behavior problems, or attenuated schizophrenic symptoms. Identifying the developmental precursors of adolescent-onset schizophrenia has important implications for both enhancing our understanding of the underlying neurobiology of schizophrenia and developing of preventive interventions for schizophrenia.

Neurobiological factors present in individuals at high risk for developing a schizophrenic disorder, prior to the onset of frank psychotic symptoms, may represent potential etiological factors for schizophrenia. A number of brain systems known to be disturbed in schizophrenia, including prefrontal and medial temporal lobes (Selemon & Goldman-Rakic, 1999; Weinberger, 1986), may underlie certain neurocognitive impairments in children at risk for schizophrenia (Asarnow, 1983; Cannon et al., 1993). Determining how these neurobiological factors evolve

when a schizophrenic disorder develops could provide important clues about how the diathesis for schizophrenia is potentiated into the overt disorder. A combination of disease-related progressions and maturational changes are hypothesized to exacerbate these dysfunctions when individuals at risk for the disorder convert to having the disorder.

Research Methods Used to Identify Developmental Precursors

Two broad classes of methods have been used to identify developmental precursors of schizophrenia. The first class of methods is *prospective* studies of children. A common feature of prospective methods is identifying, then characterizing, a group of children and following them up to determine which children subsequently develop a schizophrenic disorder. One important prospective method is to study children who are at increased statistical risk of developing a schizophrenic disorder. The lifetime risk for schizophrenia in the general population is less than 1%. Very large samples are required to prospectively identify the precursors of schizophrenia by following up children drawn from the general population. Given the population base rate of schizophrenia (<1%), one would need to start off with at least 2,500 children (without accounting for subjects being lost to follow-up) to identify the developmental precursors of schizophrenia in 25 individuals. High-risk studies ascertain individuals with an increased lifetime risk for schizophrenia for inclusion in prospective, longitudinal studies. This is typically accomplished by studying the children of parents with schizophrenia. The lifetime risk for schizophrenia for children of one parent with schizophrenia is approximately 10% to 12%, an approximately 10-fold increase in risk for the disorder. High-risk studies frequently measure putative etiological factors for schizophrenia prior to the onset of the disorder. In this way, studies of children at risk for schizophrenia provide a vehicle for testing hypotheses about etiological factors in schizophrenia.

Most (85% to 90%) patients with schizophrenia do not have parents with a schizophrenic disorder. This has raised the concern that findings from "genetic high-risk" samples may not accurately describe the developmental precursors of schizophrenia in the much larger number of individuals who develop schizophrenia but do not have a schizophrenic parent. Recognition of this problem has led to an interest in complementary strategies for identifying developmental precursors of schizophrenia. *Birth cohort studies* are prospective studies that can provide information on precursors of schizophrenia but do not have some of the ascertainment biases inherent in high-risk studies. In contrast to studies of children at risk for schizophrenia, birth cohort studies follow up large, representative samples of entire birth cohorts. Birth cohort studies are designed to provide information about a wide range of medical, psychiatric, and social conditions, so they use very large samples, literally thousands of subjects. For example, the 1946 British birth cohort study that provided important data on developmental precursors of schizophrenia studied almost 5,400 children born during the week of March 9, 1946, then systematically followed them up to determine that 30 children developed schizophrenia as well as a broad range of other psychiatric and medical outcomes. A great strength of birth cohort studies is the large, representative sample size. However, a limitation of birth cohort studies is that because they are not typically designed to test hypotheses about any particular disorder, they use a rather broad range of measures, which are not specifically tailored to measure potential precursors of schizophrenia.

By studying children prior to the onset of the disorder it becomes possible to identify the precursors or antecedents of the disorder, not the consequences of the disorder—for example, the initiation of antipsychotic drug treatment. We will review some of the key findings that have emerged from three decades of studies of children at risk for schizophrenia and from birth cohort studies.

A second class of methods involves the collection of information on the premorbid development of individuals, usually adults, who have been diagnosed with schizophrenia. Some of the earliest studies of this type relied on *retrospective* reports from informants who knew the patient as a child. This approach has obvious limita-

tions, among them being that recollections of the past may be subject to bias. The *follow-back* method features the ascertainment of individuals with schizophrenia and then, using different types of archival material, characterization of them prior to the onset of psychosis. Since the focus of this section is on adolescent-onset schizophrenia, we will emphasize the few studies that ascertained adolescent-onset schizophrenics.

Follow-back studies vary in the type of archival material used to describe the premorbid characteristics of individuals who develop schizophrenia. There is wide agreement (see Watt, Grubb, & Erlenmeyer-Kimling, 1982) about the advantages of using contemporaneous childhood records over retrospective interviews to reconstruct the premorbid histories of individuals who develop schizophrenia. The major limitation of follow-back studies is that the childhood evaluations were not guided by specific hypotheses about the age-specific manifestations of schizophrenia, and as a consequence, the most informative measures may not have been collected. These studies also have ascertainment biases, the nature of which varies depending on how the sample of schizophrenia patients was identified.

Birth cohort and follow-back studies can show associations between childhood characteristics and the development of schizophrenia because in both types of studies, individuals with schizophrenia have been identified. These associations are prospective in birth cohort studies, and retrospective in follow-back studies. Because the data used to describe childhood risk factors in birth cohort and follow-back studies were not collected with the intent of testing hypotheses about schizophrenia, the measures may not be sensitive to some of the more subtle manifestations of liability to schizophrenia. In contrast, the measures included in more recent studies of children at risk for schizophrenia were specifically designed to tap vulnerability to schizophrenia. Most studies of children at risk for schizophrenia, while intended to be longitudinal, were not able to follow up subjects through the age of risk to determine which high-risk subjects developed a schizophrenic disorder. Consequently, although there are extensive cross-sectional comparisons of children at risk for schizophrenia to controls, there are far fewer data on the long-term predictive validity of childhood risk factors identified in high-risk studies.

If the results of follow-back studies of adolescent-onset schizophrenia patients yield converging results to those of children at risk for schizophrenia and birth cohort studies, then the generalizability and validity of the results will hold more value for future research and treatment.

A Developmental Perspective on Risk Factors

There are relatively age-specific manifestations of liability to schizophrenia (see J. Asarnow, 1988; R. Asarnow, 1983; Erlenmeyer-Kimling et al., 2000; Walker, 1991 for reviews), and the manifestations to liability to schizophrenia are somewhat different at different ages. For example, one of the interesting findings that emerges from a review of developmental precursors of schizophrenia is that some deficits observed during infancy that are frequently found in high-risk, birth cohort, and follow-back studies are not found in later stages of development. Another important reason to attend to the developmental progression of risk factors is that, from the point of view of targeting individuals for prevention, risk factors more proximal to the period of time when schizophrenia develops may have better diagnostic accuracy than, for example, infancy predictors.

Table 7.1 summarizes some of the major findings concerning precursors of schizophrenia at three different developmental periods: infancy, early childhood, and middle childhood and early adolescence. Table 7.1 is not an exhaustive summary of the results of high-risk, birth cohort, and follow-back studies. Rather, Table 7.1 presents the characteristics that best differentiate high-risk children from controls or predict later development of schizophrenia that have thus far been identified in the literature. Cited below are comprehensive reviews of the results of high-risk, birth cohort, and follow-back studies.

The format of Table 7.1 was modeled after a review by J. Asarnow (1988), and the entries for

studies on high-risk children come from reviews by J. Asarnow (1988), Erlenmeyer-Kimling (2000, 2001), R. Asarnow (1983), and Cornblatt and Obuchowski (1997). The entries for birth cohort studies are based on reviews by Jones, Rogers, Murray, and Marmot (1994) and by Jones and Tarrant (1999). The data for entries of follow-back studies of adolescent-onset schizophrenia come from Watkins, Asarnow, and Tanguay (1988) and Walker, Savoie, and Davis (1994). Watt and Saiz (1991) provided a broad review of follow-back studies of adult-onset schizophrenia.

Two types of risk characteristics are differentiated into separate columns in Table 7.1: endophenotypes versus clinical and behavioral features. *Endophenotypes* are putative reflections of the underlying schizophrenic genetic diathesis. Most of the putative endophenotypes employed in high-risk studies are neuromotor or neurocognitive functions (e.g., language, attention, and memory) believed to tap central nervous system disturbances that reflect liability to schizophrenia. In contrast, clinical and behavioral features are either nonschizophrenic psychiatric symptoms or behavior problems which, while they may reflect the underlying genetic diathesis, are much more proximal to the overt symptoms of schizophrenia. The reason for making this distinction is that these two different classes of risk characteristics have somewhat different implications as targets for prevention.

High-Risk Studies

The results of high-risk studies have to be considered in the context of a major limitation: there are limited data on how well the cross-sectional differences between children at risk for schizophrenia and matched controls predict the later onset of schizophrenia. Only six studies of children at risk for schizophrenia have obtained diagnostic evaluations in adulthood or late adolescence: *(1)* the New York High-Risk study (Fish, 1984); *(2)* the Copenhagen High-Risk project (Cannon et al., 1993; Mednick & Schulsinger, 1968); *(3)* the Israeli High-Risk study (Ingraham, Kugelmass, Frankel, Nathan, & Mirsky, 1995); *(4)* the New York High-Risk project (Erlenmeyer-

Table 7.1 Developmental Precursors of Schizophrenia Identified by Means of Three Different Research Strategies

Life Stage	Children At Risk for Schizophrenia Retrospective Studies		Birth Cohort Studies		Follow-Back Studies	
	CNS Functioning	Symptoms and Behaviors	CNS Functioning	Symptoms and Behaviors	CNS Functioning	Symptoms and Behaviors
Infancy (0–2 years)	Impaired motor and sensory functioning; High or variable sensitivity to sensory stimulation; Abnormal growth patterns; Short attention span; Low IQ	Difficult temperament; Passive, low energy, quiet, inhibited; Absence of fear of strangers; Low communicative competence in mother–child interaction, less social contact with mothers	Delays in motor milestones; Speech problems or delays; Delayed potty training		Abnormal motor functioning; Impaired language	
Early childhood (2–4 years)	Low reactivity; Poor gross and fine motor coordination; Inconsistent, variable performance on cognitive tests	Depression and anxiety; Angry and hostile disposition; Schizoid behavior (i.e., emotionally flat, withdrawn, distractible, passive, irritable, negativistic); Low reactivity; More likely to receive a diagnosis of developmental disorder	Speech problems; Motor problems	Solitary play	Impaired language; Neuromotor impairments	Solitary play
Middle childhood/ early adolescence years (4–14 years)	Neurological; Passive motor impairment (poor fine motor coordination, Socially balance, sensory perceptual isolated signs, delayed motor development); Poor social adjustment; Attentional impairment under ADD overload conditions; Anxious/Variance-scatter on depressed intellectual tests	Poor affective control (emotional instability, aggressive, disruptive, hyperactive, impulsive); Poor interpersonal relationships, withdrawn; Cognitive slippage disturbance; Mixed internalizing–externalizing symptoms, fearful; ADD-like syndrome	Twitches, grimaces; Poor academic achievement; Poor balance, clumsiness	Solitary play; Less socially confident; "Schizoid" social development	Reduced general intelligence; Poor academic achievement; Poor attention; Neuromotor impairments	Passive; Specially isolated; Poor social adjustment; ADD

ADD, attention-deficit disorder; CNS, central nervous system.

Kimling et al., 2000); *(5)* the Swedish High-Risk study (McNeil, Harty, Blennow, & Cantor-Graae, 1993); and *(6)* the Jerusalem Infant Development study (Hans et al., 1999). The New York High-Risk project studied the largest number of subjects for the longest period of time and therefore provides the most extensive data on the diagnostic accuracy of childhood and adolescent predictors of schizophrenia-related psychoses. None of these studies focused on the prediction of adolescent-onset schizophrenia. Indeed, there are very few cases of adolescent-onset schizophrenia in the entire high-risk literature. As a consequence, we are making the assumption that the factors that predict adult-onset schizophrenia are germane to the prediction of adolescent-onset schizophrenia.

Infancy. In most but not all studies (see Walker & Emory, 1985, for review), during infancy neurological signs or neuromotor dysfunctions are found more frequently in children at risk for schizophrenia than in controls. In these studies neuromotor anomalies were assessed by observation during a pediatric neurological examination or by performance on standardized tests of infant development (e.g., the Bayley). Neurological signs and neuromotor dysfunctions are not specific to infants at risk for schizophrenia and are not rare events in the general pediatric population. Neurological abnormalities in neonates typically tend to improve. In contrast, it appears that these abnormalities in children at risk for schizophrenia persist, and may worsen over time. Infants with neurological or neuromotor abnormalities are the high-risk infants most likely to develop schizophrenic disorders in adolescence and early adulthood (Fish, 1987; Marcus et al., 1987; Parnas, 1982). Neurologic dysregulation in infancy predicts the development of schizophrenia spectrum disorders (Fish, 1984). Impaired performance on tasks with extensive motor demands during middle childhood also predicts the presence of schizophrenia spectrum disorders during adolescence (Hans et al., 1999).

Disturbances in early social development are found more frequently in children at risk for schizophrenia than in controls. Depending on the study, these disturbances are manifested in difficult temperaments, apathy or withdrawal, being inhibited, less spontaneous, and imitative, reduced social contact with mothers, and absence of fear of strangers. The absence of fear of strangers during infancy could be an indication that the child does not differentiate between familiar adults to whom the child is attached (for example, the parents) and others. This absence of the fear of strangers may reflect inadequately developed attachment. These disturbances are not specific to children at risk for schizophrenia. They are also associated with broad risk factors such as socioeconomic status, general maternal distress, early trauma or neglect, and poor quality of parenting. Although there are scant data on how well these disturbances in infant social development predict the development of schizophrenia, many of these findings are related to the development of social competencies (Watt & Saiz, 1991).

Early childhood. During early childhood (2 to 4 years of age), children at risk for schizophrenia are more likely than controls to show poor fine and gross motor coordination and low reactivity. Although poor fine and gross motor coordination was found in a sample of children that was different from the samples of infants at risk for schizophrenia who showed a variety of neurological signs and neuromotor dysfunction, these data suggest that the dysfunctions observed in infancy are persistent.

In early childhood there is an increased occurrence of internalizing symptoms (depression and anxiety), angry and hostile dispositions, and schizoid behavior (emotionally flat, socially withdrawn, passive and distractible) in children at risk for schizophrenia. Again, these characteristics are not specific to children at risk for schizophrenia and there is no evidence that these characteristics are strongly predictive of the later development of schizophrenia.

Middle childhood and early adolescence. Neuromotor impairments, including gross motor skills (Marcus et al., 1993), are found more frequently in children at risk for schizophrenia than in controls during middle childhood and early adolescence (4 to 14 years of age). One of the most robust cross-sectional findings during middle childhood and early adolescence is the presence of neurocognitive impairments, especially on measures with high attention demands.

A subgroup of children at risk for schizophrenia showed impairments on some of the same tasks for which patients with schizophrenia show impairments (Asarnow, 1988). The neurocognitive tasks for which children at risk for schizophrenia show impairments include measures of sustained attention (various continuous performance tests) and secondary memory (e.g., memory for stories). For example, children at risk for schizophrenia, as well as acutely disturbed and partially remitted schizophrenia patients, performed poorly on a partial-report-span-of-apprehension task (Asarnow, 1983) in the high attention/processing demand condition. The span of apprehension measures the rate of early visual information processing (Fig. 7.6).

There are some data on the predictive validity of the neurocognitive impairments identified during middle childhood and early adolescence. In the New York High-Risk project, the presence of impairments on a number of attentional tasks (an Attentional Deviance Index) given in middle childhood predicted 58% of the subjects who developed schizophrenia-related psychoses by mid-adulthood (Erlenmeyer-Kimling et al., 2000). Attentional impairments in middle childhood were also associated with anhedonia (Freedman, Rock, Roberts, Cornblatt, &

Erlenmeyer-Kimling, 1998) in adolescents prior to the onset of schizophrenia and social deficits during early adulthood (Cornblatt, Lenzenweger, Dworkin, & Erlenmeyer-Kimling, 1992; Freedman et al., 1998). Neuromotor dysfunction during childhood (assessed by the Lincoln-Oseretsky Motor Development Scale) identified 75% of the high-risk children who developed schizophrenia-related psychoses during adulthood (Erlenmeyer-Kimling et al., 2000). A verbal short-term memory factor that included a childhood digit span task and a complex attention task predicted 83% of the New York high-risk children who developed schizophrenia-related psychoses during adulthood and showed high specificity to those psychoses (Erlenmeyer-Kimling et al., 2000). If replicated, these findings would suggest that the combination of genetic risk (being the child of a parent who has schizophrenia) and neurocognitive impairments during middle childhood might identify individuals with a greatly increased risk for developing schizophrenia. The sensitivity (correctly predicting the onset of schizophrenia-related psychoses) was higher for the verbal memory (83%) and motor skills (75%) factors than for the attentional factor (58%). Conversely, the false-positive rate (incorrectly predicting that a child

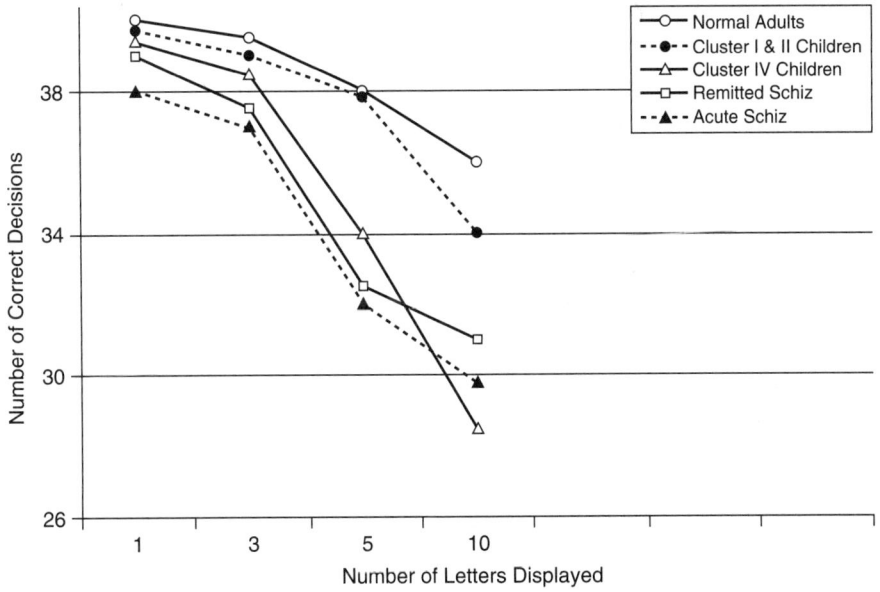

Figure 7.6 Span of apprehension data [from Asarnow, Steffy, MacCrimmon, & Cleghorn, 1978].

would develop schizophrenia) was lower for the Attentional Deviance Index (18%) than for the memory factor (28%) and motor factor (27%).

The short-term follow-up in the Jerusalem High-Risk study provides an important link between the attentional impairments frequently observed in children at risk for schizophrenia during adolescence and the motor impairments found during infancy and early childhood. The children who showed impaired neuromotor performance during childhood were the subjects most likely to show impairments on a variety of measures of attention and information processing during early adolescence (Hans et al., 1999).

During middle childhood, children at risk for schizophrenia receive an increased frequency of a variety of psychiatric diagnoses, including an attention deficit disorder (ADD)-like syndrome. Poor affective control, including emotional instability and impulsivity, as well as aggression and disruptive behaviors are found more frequently in children at risk for schizophrenia than in controls. Early precursors of thought disorder may be reflected in the presence of cognitive slippage. Poor peer relations are one of the more frequently found behavioral characteristics during middle childhood and early adolescence. None of these symptoms is specific to children at risk for schizophrenia. For example, poor affective control is found in children who subsequently develop an affective disorder.

Birth Cohort Studies

A British birth cohort study of almost 5,400 people born the week of March 9, 1946, complements the studies of individuals at risk for schizophrenia by virtue of being representative of the general population. Thirty cases of schizophrenia were identified among individuals between the ages of 16 and 43 in this cohort, which reflects the population base rate of the disorder. A 1956 birth cohort study in Northern Finland (Isohanni et al., 2001) yielded 100 cases of DSM-III schizophrenia.

Across the major birth cohort studies, including the British birth cohorts of 1946 (Jones, Rodgers, Murray, & Marmot, 1994) and 1958 (Done, Crow, Johnson, & Sacker, 1994; Jones & Done, 1997) and the Northern Finland 1956

birth cohort (Isohanni et al., 2001), a number of developmental precursors of schizophrenia have been identified. Neurologic signs, reflected in various forms of motoric dysfunction ranging from tics and twitches, poor balance and coordination and clumsiness, to poor hand skill, are consistently identified as developmental precursors of individuals who later go on to develop schizophrenia (Done et al., 1994; Jones et al., 1994). There was an increased frequency of speech problems up to age 15 in patients who subsequently developed schizophrenia. Low educational test scores at ages 8 and 11 were also risk factors (Jones et al., 1994).

During early and late middle childhood, individuals who subsequently developed a schizophrenic disorder could be differentiated from their peers by their preference for solitary play, poor social confidence, and a "schizoid" social development.

In general, birth cohort studies suggest that there appears to be "consistent dose-response relationships between the presence of developmental deviance and subsequent risk" (Jones & Tarrant, 1999). The more deviant an individual is toward the "abnormal" end of a population distribution, the greater the risk of the disorder.

There is considerable overlap between the developmental precursors of affective disorders and schizophrenia (Van Os, Jones, Lewis, Wadsworth, & Murray, 1997). For example, lower educational achievement is associated with affective disorders in general, whereas delayed motor and language milestones are associated with childhood onset of an affective disorder. As in schizophrenia, there is evidence of persistence of motor difficulties, with an excess of twitches and grimaces noted in adolescents.

Follow-back Studies

With regard to endophenotypic characteristics, during infancy, children who subsequently develop schizophrenia as adolescents are characterized by the presence of abnormal motor functioning and impaired language. Neuromotor and language impairments and decreases in positive facial emotion are also present in early childhood (Walker et al., 1993). During middle childhood the language impairments fade; however, the neuromotor impairments persist. In addition, during middle childhood, children who subsequently develop a schizophrenic disorder are characterized by poor academic achievement, poor attention, and reduced general intelligence.

During middle childhood, children who subsequently develop a schizophrenic disorder are characterized as being passive and socially isolated, with poor social adjustment. They frequently present with symptoms of attention-deficit hyperactivity disorder (ADHD) and/or anxiety and depression.

A novel approach to using archival data to characterize the premorbid histories of individuals who develop schizophrenia is the use of home movies to identify infant and childhood neuromotor dysfunctions (Walker et al., 1994). In such studies, ratings were made of neuromotor functioning in children who subsequently developed schizophrenia, in their healthy siblings, in preaffective disorder participants, and in their healthy siblings. The preschizophrenia subjects showed poorer motor skills, particularly during infancy, than those of their healthy siblings and preaffective disorder participants and their siblings. The abnormalities included choreoathetoid movements and posturing of the upper limbs, primarily on the left side of the body.

Consistency of Findings Across Methods

Endophenotypes. Table 7.1 shows a consistency across studies of children at risk for schizophrenia, birth cohort studies, and retrospective studies in the presence of motor and language problems during infancy. This consistency is particularly impressive given the considerable variation across studies in the ways in which motor functioning and language were assessed.

During early childhood (2 to 4 years of age), neuromotor problems are observed in all three types of studies. In birth cohort studies and retrospective studies, impaired language is noted. In high-risk studies children at risk for schizophrenia are noted as being depressed, anxious, angry, and schizoid, whereas in birth cohort studies they are noted as preferring solitary play.

During middle childhood (4 to 14 years of age) there is a persistence of neurologic impairments

reflected in poor motor functioning in high-risk, birth cohort, and follow-back studies. High-risk studies, unlike birth cohort studies and retrospective studies, included laboratory measures of attention information processing. On these tasks, children at risk for schizophrenia showed attentional impairment under conditions of high processing demands. This may be related to the poor academic achievement observed in birth cohort studies and retrospective studies during middle childhood as well as the frequent diagnosis of ADHD. In contrast to the persistence of neuromotor problems, language problems tend to diminish over time, so by middle childhood they are rarely noted across the three classes of studies. In adolescents who develop a schizophrenic disorder, language functions are relatively preserved compared to visual-spatial and motor functioning (Asarnow, Tanguay, Bott, & Freeman, 1987).

The results of this brief review suggest a developmental pathway from precursors first identified in infancy to the development of schizophrenia-related psychoses in late adolescence and early adulthood. Neurologic signs or neuromotor dysfunctions are present in infancy and persist through early and middle childhood and early adolescence. Neuromotor dysfunction in early childhood predicts the presence of attentional impairments under high processing demands during early adolescence. Neuromotor dysfunctions and attentional impairments during adolescence predict the development of schizophrenia-related psychoses. Because the characterization of key points in this developmental sequence is based on only one or two studies, clearly this model needs to be tested in future research.

The developmental pathway sketched here has potentially interesting implications for our understanding of the neurobiology of schizophrenia. What brain systems are involved in the control of simple motor functions and attention? The developmental link between early neuromotor dysfunction and later attentional impairments may implicate cortical-striatal pathways that support both motor functions and attentional control mechanisms. Striatal dysfunction results in impaired sequential motor performance and chunking of action sequences.

Impairments in a variety of attentional functions, including set shifting and self-monitoring, are also associated with striatal dysfunction (Saint-Cyr, 2003).

Clinical and behavioral characteristics. In high-risk studies, the precursors of later difficulties in developing social relations can first be detected in infancy. In some studies, children at risk for schizophrenia have less social contact with their mothers and less fear of strangers, as well as having a difficult temperament.

Poor peer relations are one of the most frequently found behavioral characteristics during middle childhood and early adolescence. A preference for solitary play, poor social confidence, and a generally "schizoid" social development are frequent precursors of schizophrenia. Studies of children at risk for schizophrenia, birth cohort studies, and retrospective studies all find an increased frequency of nonpsychotic symptoms, particularly internalizing symptoms and poor affective control (including emotional instability and impulsivity) during middle childhood and early adolescence. However, none of these symptoms are specific to children at risk for schizophrenia. Many of these symptoms and behavioral characteristics are found in children who subsequently develop an affective disorder.

Limitations: What We Don't Know

Neuromotor and attentional dysfunctions appear to be putative developmental precursors to schizophrenia. They consistently appear with increased frequency in high-risk, birth cohort, and follow-back studies. In a number of high-risk studies, infancy and childhood neuromotor impairments predicted the later onset of schizophrenia-related psychosis. Attentional impairments during middle childhood and early adolescence in the New York High-Risk project predicted the development of schizophrenia-related psychosis.

The endophenotypic indices that appear to have the greatest predictive validity are neuromotor dysfunction and impaired performance on measures that tap processing under high attention demands, or measures of secondary memory. It remains unclear whether these mea-

sures tap schizophrenic-related processes specifically. A number of the measures (including continuous performance tests, partial-report-span-of-apprehension tasks, and secondary verbal memory tests) that are sensitive to subtle neurocognitive impairments in children at risk for schizophrenia in middle childhood and adolescence also detect neurocognitive impairments in children with ADHD and learning disabilities. It is unlikely that these impairments have cross-sectional diagnostic specificity.

Although the ability of childhood and adolescent measures of attention to predict schizophrenia-related psychosis in the New York High-Risk project is promising, those results need to be replicated in an independent sample. Future studies will need to determine the extent to which childhood and adolescent neurocognitive measures predict schizophrenia-related psychosis conditioned on the presence of a second risk factor—having a parent who is schizophrenic. In effect, the analyses reported by the New York High-Risk project contained two risk factors that predicted schizophrenia-related psychosis: being the child of a schizophrenic parent and having attentional, verbal short-term memory or neuromotor impairments. These factors did not predict the onset of schizophrenia in the children of parents with an affective disorder nearly as well as they did in the children of parents with schizophrenia. As noted above, children with other, more common psychiatric diagnoses show deficits on these types of tasks. More research is needed on the diagnostic accuracy of these measures when they are used in the general pediatric population before they can be used to screen children for precursors for schizophrenia. At present, all that we know is that these measures have some promise in predicting which children who have a parent with schizophrenia are likely to develop a schizophrenic disorder themselves.

What is needed in the next generation of studies is not merely the demonstration of group mean differences between high-risk and control groups. If endophenotypic measures are to be used as candidates for preventive intervention programs, then diagnostic accuracy analyses that specify the sensitivity and specificity of tasks by means of various cutting scores need to be developed. Cutting scores can be created, depending on the purpose, that optimize sensitivity (detecting true positives) or specificity (false negatives). For example, if the intervention can produce significant adverse events, it might be desirable to set a cutting score to minimize false positives.

Poor peer relations, a preference for solitary play, a "schizoid" social development, various nonpsychotic symptoms (particularly internalizing symptoms), and poor affective control occur frequently during middle childhood and early adolescence in high-risk, birth cohort, and follow-back studies. While these behavior problems and symptoms are precursors of schizophrenia, they are not diagnostically specific. Many of these symptoms are associated with other psychiatric disorders. For example, poor affective control is both a symptom of and precursor to affective disorders. Poor peer relationships are associated with the presence of both externalizing and internalizing disorders. There are relatively few data on the diagnostic accuracy (i.e., specificity and sensitivity) of symptoms and behavior problems detected in middle childhood and early adolescence as predictors of schizophrenia-related psychoses.

The behavior problems and symptoms that are putative precursors of schizophrenia are associated with psychiatric disorders (e.g., depression and ADHD) that are much more common than schizophrenia in the general population. Thus high false-positive rates may result if these symptoms are used in the general pediatric population in an attempt to identify individuals likely to develop schizophrenia.

Implications for Preventive Intervention

There is great interest in developing preventive interventions for schizophrenia, in part because of the belief that once the disorder emerges, a neurodegenerative process is initiated that can only be partially forestalled by currently available treatments. The neurocognitive impairments, nonschizophrenic symptoms, and behavior problems that are putative developmental precursors of schizophrenia may have important implications for the development of preventive interventions for this disorder. These precursors could be used to identify children who might benefit from preventive intervention and serve as targets of interventions.

The neurocognitive impairments that are putative developmental precursors of schizophrenia have potential utility in identifying candidates for preventive interventions. Depending on the risk profile of the intervention, cutting scores on neurocognitive indices could be constructed to either maximize sensitivity or minimize false positives. However, as noted above, before the cutting scores for putative neurocognitive precursors of schizophrenia can be applied to the general pediatric population, additional research is required to evaluate the diagnostic efficiency of these measures in populations without a genetic risk. The neurocognitive precursors of schizophrenia seem to be unlikely targets for preventive interventions. There is no evidence that mitigating attentional, memory, and neuromotor impairments forestalls the development of schizophrenia-related psychoses. Identifying neurocognitive precursors of schizophrenia does advance attempts to develop new somatic treatments for schizophrenia by helping to elucidate the dysfunctional neural networks that underlie this complex disorder.

The diagnostic accuracy of the behavior problems and symptoms that are putative precursors of schizophrenia thus far identified in high-risk, birth cohort, and follow-back studies have not been carefully examined. Given the nonspecificity of these behavior problems and symptoms, it seems likely that they would yield high rates of false positives if used to identify candidates for preventive interventions for schizophrenia. It may be that clinical features more proximal to the onset of schizophrenia-related psychoses, such as prodromal signs and symptoms, have greater diagnostic accuracy in predicting which children will develop schizophrenia. A number of research groups are currently addressing this question.

The behavior problems and symptoms that are putative precursors of schizophrenia are potentially interesting targets for interventions. To the extent that poor peer relations, the presence of internalizing symptoms, and poor affective control pose difficulties for the child and parent, they become worthy targets of therapeutic interventions. Behavioral (e.g., social skills training) and pharmacological (mood stabilizing drugs) interventions for these problems are based on symptomatic presentations. The nonspecificity of these problems is not particularly problematic in this case. While there is no reason to believe that successfully enhancing social skills and controlling affective symptoms will forestall the development of schizophrenia, there is good reason to believe that enhancing social skills and controlling affective symptoms will enhance the current quality of life and may also improve the postpsychotic episode adaptation. The best predictor of postpsychotic psychosocial functioning is the level of premorbid social competencies.

What Are the Precursors of Schizophrenia?

One of the best ways to develop early-intervention efforts for schizophrenia is to start by identifying key features of those individuals who are or will become schizophrenic and determine how these features differ from those seen in normal individuals who are not ill and are not likely to ever become afflicted with the illness. Several research designs can accomplish this goal. For example, cross-sectional studies of patients and control subjects can be used to characterize each group on as many potentially meaningful variables as possible, including behavior, personality, social activity, neuropsychological abilities, brain structure and function, and genetics. One problem with this method, however, is that any differences observed between the two groups cannot necessarily be attributed a causal role in the development of disease. For example, if total brain volume were lower among a group of schizophrenic patients than it was among a group of well-matched controls, this might indicate that low brain volume is a precursor or predictor of the development of schizophrenia. However, from such a cross-sectional design, it is unclear if the brain volume deficit in the patient group actually preceded the onset of schizophrenic illness. In fact, it is possible that it did, but it is also possible that the onset of schizophrenia caused a decline in brain volume due to some degenerative process. Alter-

natively, other factors, such as treatment with antipsychotic medication, may have precipitated the decline in brain volume. It is further possible that the brain volumetric decline in the patient group was concurrent with the onset of illness but causally unrelated to it.

Numerous cross-sectional studies have unearthed a wealth of information regarding the ways in which schizophrenic patients are different from patients with other psychiatric illnesses and from normal control subjects. However, because of the limitations on causal inference that exist in these types of studies, their results can only guide further research; they are not powerful enough to dictate a specific pattern of behavioral, neuropsychological, or biological characteristics that would be useful for identifying individuals for targeted prevention efforts. As already mentioned, studies of individuals with prodromal signs of schizophrenia and individuals with schizotaxia provide more insight into those traits that precede the disorder than do cross-sectional studies. Thus, great efforts have been made to enable identification of individuals in the earliest stages of the illness or even in the premorbid period so that they may be targeted for intervention.

By characterizing the prodromal phase of schizophrenia, subtle changes in behavior have been noted in those who are beginning to deteriorate into the early stages of the disease, and these changes are now being used to identify other clinically at-risk individuals for inclusion in early intervention programs. Some of the more pronounced changes observed during the prodrome occur in domains of thought, mood, behavior, and social functioning (Phillips, Yung, Yuen, Pantelis, & McGorry, 2002). Specifically, difficulties in concentration and memory may emerge, as well as preoccupations with odd ideas and increased levels of suspiciousness. Mood changes may include a lack of emotionality, rapid mood changes, and inappropriate moods. Beyond simply odd or unusual behavior, the prodrome may also be characterized by changes in sleep patterns and energy levels. Social changes can be quite marked, with withdrawal and isolation being the most predominant features. These characteristics may be particularly informative of the disease process in schizophrenia, because they are by definition not related to the effects of medication or the degenerative effects of being ill for a prolonged period.

Perhaps the most powerful window into the premorbid changes in preschizophrenic individuals comes from the longitudinal study of children and adolescents who are genetically at high risk for the illness. By studying the biological children of schizophrenic parents, the clinical, behavioral, and biological features of schizotaxia can be revealed. Longitudinal studies of individuals such as these, who harbor the latent genetic liability toward schizophrenia, can be extremely informative for early intervention and prevention efforts because they can track the emergence of schizophrenia precursors before any signs of illness are apparent. Thus, any differences observed between children of schizophrenic patients and children of control subjects can be definitively attributed to factors other than the effects of antipsychotic medication, the degenerative effects of the illness, or any other factors that are subsequent to disease onset. The observed differences can be viewed as antecedents to the illness, which is as close to a causal relationship as can be ascribed in human research studies in which group membership cannot be experimentally assigned.

Studies of children of patients with schizophrenia have yielded a variety of findings of altered behavioral, neuropsychological, and biological processes. The richness and diversity of measures taken on these subjects can make profiling the premorbid genetic susceptibility to schizophrenia difficult. Such studies have also produced some surprisingly uniform findings, which simplify our understanding of what may be the most central or universal deficits among those who are at the highest risk for schizophrenia.

Certain personality characteristics seem to reliably differentiate children of schizophrenic parents from children of control subjects (Miller et al., 2002). For example, schizotypal personality features, including social withdrawal, psychotic symptoms, socioemotional dysfunction, and odd behavior, have been shown to precede the onset of psychosis among genetically high-risk children. Deficits of social functioning are also commonly observed in this group (Dworkin

et al., 1993). Specifically, children of schizophrenic patients are more likely than children of controls to have more restricted interests, significantly poorer social competence (especially in peer relationships and hobbies and interests), and greater affective flattening. Some neuropsychological deficits have also been reliably observed in these high-risk individuals (Asarnow & Goldstein, 1986; Cosway et al., 2000; Erlenmeyer-Kimling & Cornblatt, 1992; Schreiber et al., 1992). For example, several studies have replicated a pattern of impaired discrimination, sustained attention, and information processing on the visual continuous performance test among children of schizophrenic patients. These high-risk individuals also exhibit marked impairments on memory for verbal stimuli and in executive functioning, as well as neuromotor deficits such as soft neurological signs, gross and fine motor impairments, and perceptual-motor delays.

Perhaps underlying these personality, social, and neuropsychological deficits, children of schizophrenic patients have also been shown to have altered brain structure and function compared to that of children of control subjects (Berman, Torrey, Daniel, & Weinberger, 1992; Cannon et al., 1993; Liddle, Spence, & Sharma, 1995; Mednick, Parnas, & Schulsinger, 1987; Reveley, Reveley, & Clifford, 1982; Seidman et al., 1997; Weinberger, DeLisi, Neophytides, & Wyatt, 1981). The most commonly observed structural brain abnormality among children of schizophrenic patients is a reduced volume of the hippocampus and amygdala region. Loss of volume in the thalamus has also been observed in these children, and there has been some support for enlarged third ventricular volume and smaller overall brain volume in this group. Children of schizophrenic patients also have been found to exhibit linear increases in cortical and ventricular cerebrospinal fluid to brain ratios with increasing genetic load—that is, children with the greatest number of affected biological relatives showed the highest ratios.

Ultimately, these clinical, behavioral, social, and biological profiles of risk for emergent schizophrenia will be augmented by information on specific genes that increase susceptibility. Recently, genes coding for neuregulin 1

(*NRG1*; Stefansson et al., 2002), nitric oxide synthase (*NOS1*; Shinkai, Ohmori, Hori, & Nakamura, 2002), and dystrobrevin-binding protein 1 (*DTNBP1*; Straub, Jiang, et al., 2002) have been reported to have an association with schizophrenia, but these findings will require verification. Many other polymorphisms have shown a positive association with the disorder, but attempts to replicate these findings have often failed. For several of these widely studied polymorphisms, meta-analysis has been used to clarify the presence or absence of a true allelic association with the disorder in the presence of ambiguity. In fact, using this approach, some candidate genes, including those that code for the serotonin 2A receptor (*HTR2A*) and the dopamine D2 (*DRD2*) and D3 (*DRD3*) receptors, have already been shown to have a small, but reliable, association with the disorder (Dubertret et al., 1998; Glatt, Faraone, & Tsuang, 2003; Williams, McGuffin, Nothen, & Owen, 1997). Eventually, other gene variants, including perhaps *NRG1, NOS1,* and *DTNBP1*, will be found to be reliably associated with schizophrenia. This may make it possible to create a genetic risk profile that will be predictive of future onsets of schizophrenia, especially in combination with other known risk indicators.

Together, the various abnormal features of children of schizophrenic patients provide a "composite sketch" of the underlying premorbid susceptibility toward schizophrenia. Because the probability of developing schizophrenia among children of one or two affected individuals (12% and 46%, respectively) is far greater than that probability among children of control subjects (1%), these abnormalities signal the subsequent development of schizophrenia with a relatively high degree of sensitivity and reliability. However, it is also clear that these trends are not absolute, and many children of schizophrenic patients will not exhibit these signs, nor will they ever develop schizophrenia.

Do Early Intervention and Prevention Efforts Work?

It has been recognized for some time that the duration of untreated illness in schizophrenia is correlated with the prognosis for the disease, such that those with the longest period of untreated psychosis experience the least favorable outcomes (Browne et al., 2000). Recently, it has also been discovered that outcome correlates with the duration of illness as measured from the onset of the prodrome rather than only from the onset of frank psychosis. From this line of evidence, the rationale for early-intervention efforts was born. It was reasoned that, if early treatment of the illness led to a more favorable outcome, early intervention even before the onset of the illness might further inhibit the progression of the illness, either delaying its onset, decreasing its severity, or both.

A fundamental question in designing early intervention protocols is, what will be the target of the intervention? There is no single best answer to this question, which may be why various targets are being used in current early intervention efforts. The earliest interventions might realize the greatest opportunities to divert high-risk individuals from the subsequent development of schizophrenia, but the ability to predict schizophrenia accurately might be greatest in the period closest to disease onset. For example, targeting attention problems in young children of schizophrenic parents might allow the identification of the children who are at highest risk of transitioning to psychosis and afford ample time to intervene in that process; yet because of the restricted sensitivity and specificity of this deficit, targeting attention problems may also cause some high-risk children to be excluded from the protocol while, inevitably, some of the children who were included in the protocol would not go on to develop the illness. Targeting the changes of the prodrome, by contrast, such as the emergence of odd behaviors or increased suspiciousness, might lower false-positive and false-negative classification errors, but the ability of the intervention protocol to influence the course of the illness might be relatively restricted compared to earlier interventions. Thus, a balance must be maintained between the potential effectiveness of the intervention and the specificity of the intervention to the target population.

Another key question in developing early intervention protocols is, at what level should the intervention be administered? Again, this is a question without a simple answer. Universal and selected interventions will have the greatest likelihood of reaching those individuals most in need of intervention—that is they will have the greatest sensitivity. However, these may also be too expensive to implement successfully. Indicated interventions will be more feasible, simply because of their more restricted nature, but this will prevent such protocols from reaching some individuals who may benefit from them. In fact, interventions administered at multiple levels may work better than protocols designed to intervene only at a single level.

Perhaps the least consensus in the design of early intervention trials is on the form of the intervention. The effectiveness of various early-intervention programs is currently an active area of research and, quite fortunately, multiple types of interventions have shown promise for keeping at least some high-risk individuals from developing schizophrenia. In fact, educational programs, as well as psychosocial and psychotherapeutic interventions, have all shown some degree of promise in either reducing the duration of untreated psychosis or postponing the onset of schizophrenia, which suggests that these methods may also be useful in decreasing the likelihood of schizophrenic illness altogether. In Norway, for example, the establishment of a comprehensive, multilevel, multitarget psychosis education and early detection network reduced the average duration of untreated psychosis in the catchment area by approximately 75% over a 5-year period (Johannessen et al., 2001).

The preventive effects of various psychotherapeutic techniques, such as individual cognitive behavior therapy or family-based cognitive remediation, have yet to be evaluated with great rigor, but pharmacologic intervention has received a fair amount of empirical support for efficacy in preventing or delaying the transition from prodrome to psychosis. A variety of psychopharmacological compounds may have efficacy in suppressing schizophrenia, including second-generation antipsychotic drugs such as risperidone, antidepressants such as the selective-serotonin reuptake inhibitors, mood stabilizers such as lithium and valproate, and antianxiolytics such as benzodiazepines, but few of

these have been tested for such a role. Of these, the novel antipsychotic risperidone has shown tremendous promise in preventing descent into schizophrenia among prodromal individuals when compared with needs-based therapy alone, even up to 6 months after discontinuation of treatment (McGorry & Killackey, 2002). Risperidone has also been shown to improve neuropsychological functioning among the nonpsychotic, nonprodromal schizotaxic relatives of schizophrenic patients (Tsuang et al., 2002).

In light of these successes, it is not so troubling that consensus is difficult to reach on which form of intervention is the most appropriate; it seems that the method of intervention is not quite as important as the fact that any intervention is better than none. There are, however, a number of problems with current early-intervention efforts. For example, because our screening criteria cannot definitively identify individuals who are at risk for developing psychosis, early-intervention efforts are sometimes administered to individuals who do not need them or cannot benefit from them. Alternatively, because the warning signs of psychotic decompensation sometimes go unrecognized, some individuals who should have received intervention do not. Furthermore, little is known about the potential harm that may be caused by informing individuals that they are at risk for schizophrenia, but presumably there may be some negative consequences of receiving this knowledge. In addition, the benefits of some of our most promising early-intervention and prevention protocols (pharmacotherapies) may be offset by the potential side effects of individual compounds.

A careful analysis of the benefits and the risks of early intervention has led to the general consensus that intervention in the prodrome of schizophrenia is warranted. There is less agreement about the feasibility of selective and indicated intervention in the premorbid phase of schizotaxic individuals, who may or may not ultimately develop a schizophrenia-spectrum illness. Studies have shown that pharmacological intervention can improve the subclinical deficits experienced by some nonschizophrenic genetically at-risk individuals; however, at such an early stage of research and with a limited understanding of schizotaxia, it is not yet clear if these benefits outweigh their associated risks when the selection of proper candidates for intervention may still be suboptimal. As the phenomenology and time course of schizotaxia becomes better understood, criteria for inclusion in preventive and early-intervention efforts will improve, along with the efficiency of such protocols in treating only those individuals who will receive maximal benefit while sustaining little harm.

Research Agenda for Schizophrenia

We have learned a great deal about the early course of schizophrenia during the past two decades, leading to therapeutic optimism. However, several key areas of research continue to be a priority. First, we need to identify specific clinical characteristics in the premorbid and prodromal phases that can help us predict the individuals at a high risk for developing psychosis. Second, we do not know how to prospectively identify the early beginnings of the psychotic illness with an adequate degree of reliability to be able to intervene early. We also need to better understand the pathways to care for these patients. Educating the public and health care providers in early signs and symptoms can reduce the delay in care. Third, we need to further clarify the clinical features in the first psychotic episode that can help us predict subsequent illness course. Finally, we need to better understand the neurodevelopmental and neurodeteriorative processes that may underlie both the emergence and the subsequent course of the first psychotic episode.

It is readily apparent that the single greatest research need regarding adolescent-onset schizophrenia is simply more studies of this form of the illness apart from its more traditional manifestations. While schizophrenia is among the most widely studied psychiatric disorder, adolescent schizophrenia is rarely examined as a clinical entity onto itself. Yet it is necessary to conduct such studies, as early-onset forms may not just reflect an enrichment of risk factors for schizophrenia or greater severity of the illness, they may in fact have their own distinct etiologies and separate ranges of severity. To determine the degree of continuity and etiological similarity between adolescent- and adult-onset schizophrenia, twin, adoption, and longitudinal studies of the early-onset form of the disease should be considered a high priority.

The study of schizophrenia can serve as a model for how adolescent schizophrenia should itself be studied. More specifically, the precursors of adolescent schizophrenia must be delineated through the examination of individuals in the premorbid stages of the illness. The most effective way to accomplish this goal may be through the use of the genetic high-risk paradigm. The ascertainment of individuals who are at the highest genetic risk for illness (e.g., children of parents with schizophrenia) would allow the collection of a sample of individuals who also have the highest likelihood of developing a severe form of illness. If adolescent schizophrenia is etiologically related to other forms of the illness and represents a more severe or genetically driven form of the disease, then such a sample would also be enriched with individuals who will develop schizophrenia during adolescence. Longitudinal studies of these individuals, beginning before adolescence and continuing throughout the period of disease risk, would allow investigtors to identify changes that signal the impending expression of latent schizophrenia susceptibility. Once detected, such features could then be compared to similar profiles of premorbid change in adult preschizophrenia to determine if any of these emergent abnormalities are specific for adolescent versus adult onset of the illness. If adolescent-onset specific changes were elucidated, these would then form the screening criteria for subsequent early intervention and, ultimately, prevention efforts for schizophrenia in adolescents.

The developments in genetics and neurobiology provide investigators with powerful new tools to extend our undertanding of the evolution of schizophrenia. Such an understanding will go beyond the current emphasis on symptomatic characterizations and will include measures of behavioral and neurobiological endophenotypic vulnerability markers. Adolescence is pivotal for brain maturation and longitudinal data are necessary to establish bridges between the phenotypic manifestations of schizophrenia and the neurobiologic substrate. It is likely that multimodal intervention methods will be shaped by such knowledge in a way that will eventually delay, ameliorate, and perhaps even thwart the devastating impact of schizophrenia.

Anxiety Disorders

COMMISSION ON ADOLESCENT ANXIETY DISORDERS

Edna B. Foa, *Commission Chair*

E. Jane Costello

Martin Franklin

Jerome Kagan

Philip Kendall

Rachel Klein

Henrietta Leonard

Michael Liebowitz

John March

Richard McNally

Thomas Ollendick

Daniel Pine

Robert Pynoos

Wendy Silverman

Linda Spear

part

Defining Anxiety Disorders

chapter

9

Before discussing the anxiety disorders, it is important to consider the concept of anxiety and its heterogeneity. *Anxiety* refers to multiple mental and physiological phenomena, including a person's conscious state of worry over a future unwanted event, or fear of an actual situation. Anxiety and fear are closely related. Some scholars view anxiety as a uniquely human emotion and fear as common to nonhuman species. Another distinction often made between fear and anxiety is that fear is an adaptive response to realistic threat, whereas anxiety is a diffuse emotion, sometimes an unreasonable or excessive reaction to current or future perceived threat.

DISTINGUISHING *ANXIETY* FROM *ANXIETY DISORDERS*

Defining the boundaries between extremes of normal behavior and psychopathology is a dilemma that pervades all psychiatry. For some very extreme conditions, such as Downs syndrome, diagnostic decisions are straightforward. Milder forms, by contrast, present problems when one attempts to define the point at which "caseness" begins. A few symptoms escape this definitional conundrum by virtue of their being deviant, regardless of their severity. This applies to symptoms such as delusional beliefs or hallucinations. In the case of anxiety, however, it is especially problematic to establish the limits between normal behavior and pathology because when mild, anxiety plays an adaptive role in human development, signaling that self-protective action is required to ensure safety. Because anxiety can be rated on a continuum, some investigators suggest that extreme anxiety represents only a severe expression of the trait, rather than a distinct or pathological state. Distributions may consist of distinct entities, however. For example, some cases of mental retardation, as caused by neurological injury, represent a quantal departure from factors influencing normal variations in intelligence. By analogy, the fact that anxiety falls on a continuum of severity does not preclude the presence of qualitatively distinct disorders at any point in the distribution (Klein & Pine, 2001).

Anxiety may become symptomatic at any age when it prevents or limits developmentally appropriate adaptive behavior (Klein & Pine, 2001). However, anxiety about particular circumstances may develop at one or another developmental stage, based on the typical age-related experiences that occur during this stage. For example, anxiety about separation represents a normal aspect of development that is experienced by many young children. Similarly, in adolescence, particular questions arise concerning anxiety about social situations, given changes in the social milieu that are experienced as stressful by many adolescents. A useful rule of thumb for determining the diagnostic threshold is the person's ability to recover from anxiety and to remain anxiety-free when the provoking situation is absent. For example, it is not necessarily deviant for adolescents to respond with acute discomfort or anxiety when meeting a peer that they find attractive. Such reactions reach clinical levels, however, when adolescents are unable to recover from the anxiety (as manifested by recurrent doubts or ruminations about how they behave), or when adolescents avoid such encounters on a consistent basis. Similarly, clinical anxiety in this situation might be characterized by the development of concerns about future meetings with unfamiliar peers or even avoidance of activities that might require peer interactions. Therefore, an adolescent's lack of flexibility in affective adaptation is an important pathological indicator. In addition, the degree of distress and dysfunction influences diagnostic decisions; these vary with developmental stage, as well as with cultural and familial standards. When anxiety symptoms are developmentally inappropriate, subjective distress is relatively more informative. For example, separation anxiety is developmentally more congruent with early childhood than with adolescence. In brief, three clinical features impinge on the definition of pathological anxiety. Two of these, distress and dysfunction, vary in importance as a function of developmental stage. The third, symptomatic inflexibility, is diagnostically relevant regardless of age.

The ability to draw firm conclusions on the ideal criteria for disorders will remain limited so long as signs and symptoms are the exclusive basis for establishing the presence of psychiatric disorders. Longitudinal research can provide some answers by identifying specific symptom patterns and thresholds that have long-term significance. In practice, however, such evidence has proved to be informative but rarely conclusive.

The past two decades have witnessed a great expansion in the study of anxiety disorders. An earlier emphasis on rating scales or interviews assessing multitudes of unrelated fears and worries has been replaced by an emphasis on the study of diagnostic groups that reflect explicit clinical criteria. Scale ratings can be grouped to generate overall scores of anxiety, or what has come to be called "internalizing" symptoms, such as in the widely used Child Behavior Checklist (CBCL; Achenbach, 1991), but as the evidence shows, scale ratings correspond poorly to clinical entities.

Difficulties in separating "normal" from "pathological" anxiety are clearly reflected in results from epidemiological studies, in which the prevalence of anxiety disorders changes markedly with relatively minor changes in the definition of impairment (reviewed Klein & Pine, 2001). However, adolescents with anxiety disorders who seek treatment typically suffer from markedly impairing anxiety, and there is little ambiguity about determining whether they have "normal" or abnormal levels of anxiety.

This challenge poses both practical and conceptual problems. The practical problem concerns the timing of treatment. Two mistakes are possible. An adolescent who needs treatment may fail to receive it if the threshold for diagnosing the disorder is set too high ("a false negative"). An adolescent whose anxiety reflects a reasonable response to adverse circumstances may receive unnecessary treatment ("a false positive"). The decision to treat versus not treat is linked to costs and benefits that inform decisions about each adolescent.

The conceptual problem concerns the need to provide a principled basis for distinguishing disorder from nondisorder beyond the current imperfect clinically based principles. In an ideal circumstance, these principles would be based on understandings of pathophysiology. Consistent with this perspective, some philosophers of medicine have attempted to provide objective, biological criteria for demarcating disorder (e.g., major depression) from distressing states that fall within the bounds of normal unhappiness (e.g., grief). Others have claimed that all ascriptions of disorder reflect nothing more than societally determined value judgments about undesirable states and behavior.

Merging these polarized views, Wakefield (1992) proposed a harmful dysfunction account of disorder, holding the position that *disorder* is a hybrid concept comprising a factual component and an evaluative component. The factual component specifies what is dysfunctional—a derangement in a psychobiological function—and the value component specifies the resultant harm—usually emotional suffering, social maladjustment, or both. Therefore, ascription of *disorder* requires that two interrelated criteria be met: a psychobiological mechanism is malfunctioning, and this underlying dysfunction results in suffering, maladaptation, or both.

Wakefield's criteria imply that a person may be characterized by internal dysfunction but not qualify as having a disorder because no resultant harm occurs. For example, some youngsters characterized by extreme shyness or behavioral inhibition may find niches for themselves that enable them to adapt without marked distress. Even though the dysfunction requirement is met, these children would not be considered disordered because their dysfunction does not result in suffering or maladaptation. Conversely, some youngsters, bullied by larger children for example, may experience chronic anxiety at school. But because their suffering does not arise from dysfunction in the psychobiological mechanisms for estimating threat, Wakefield's criteria would suggest that they not be diagnosed as disordered. Mechanisms for detecting threat work precisely as they are "designed" to work: the bullied youngsters experience chronic anxiety because they are continually exposed to threat, not because they have a mental disorder. It is important to note that this is only one definition of a "mental disorder."

Wakefield's (1992) framework is not without its limitations. Attempts to elucidate a value-free perspective on *function*—especially when cast within an evolutionary framework (McNally, 2001a)—raises yet another set of thorny problems. Nevertheless, the harmful dysfunction provides a useful model for posing questions regarding the distinction between normal psychological distress and its pathological variants.

DESCRIPTIONS OF THE ANXIETY DISORDERS

In the following sections we will describe each of the anxiety disorders listed in the *Diagnostic and Statistical Manual of Mental Disorders*, 4th ed., (DSM-IV; American Psychiatric Association, 1994). For an accompanying list of signs and symptoms see Table 9.1.

Specific Phobia

A *specific phobia* is an extreme or unreasonable feeling of fear or anxiety linked to a specific animal, object, activity, or situation. Individuals usually experience anxiety when they encounter or think about the feared target. The diagnosis of phobic disorder requires that the person experience extreme distress and impairment in normal functioning. Although phobic disorders can begin at an early age, they often occur in childhood. Although there are many possible phobic targets, most children fear the same limited range of objects or events. Although most phobias do not have a distinct biological profile, blood phobia is an exception for it is accompanied by a sudden drop of blood pressure and heart rate and often fainting. This profile is not characteristic of phobic reactions to most other feared targets.

Separation Anxiety Disorder

Onset of separation anxiety disorder, defined by unrealistic worry accompanying separation from home or caretaker that interferes with appropriate behavior, usually occurs in late childhood but before adolescence. Indeed, this is the only disorder in which onset must occur before the person is 18 years old. Because separation anxiety disorder is accompanied by a reluctance to engage in activities that require separation from a caretaker, it can take the form of fear of school attendance. Although some adolescents develop separation anxiety disorder, refusal of school attendance among adolescents can occur because of social anxiety, rather than anxiety over separation.

Social Anxiety Disorder

The central clinical feature in social anxiety disorder, also called *social phobia*, is extreme worry over ridicule, humiliation, or embarrassment in a social situation that is not the result of a serious cognitive or physical impairment in the ability to interact with others. Havelock Ellis, writing a century ago, called such patients "modest" and regarded their fear as instinctual and possessing a sexual component (Ellis, 1899). Although these children avoid social situations, some are unable to articulate these concerns and simply feel uncomfortable in unfamiliar social settings. The diagnosis of social anxiety disorder requires that the child or adolescent experience distress with peers. There are two categories of social anxiety disorder. One type involves a restricted range of fears, limited to performance situations. A second category, called the generalized subtype, is applied when the anxiety is evoked in a majority of social settings. This definition typically encompasses situations feared by individuals with performance-limited social anxiety. This generalized form usually has an earlier onset, lasts for a longer time, and is often comorbid with other symptoms.

There is variability in the application of nosological definitions of social anxiety disorder in clinical settings. Some clinicians apply it to individuals who are anxious in one or two situations. Others apply the same diagnosis to patients who experience performance or test anxiety (worry over public speaking or examinations), or who feel anxiety when eating with strangers but not when interacting with others.

Obsessive-Compulsive Disorder

The diagnosis of obsessive-compulsive disorder (OCD) is made when the individual has recur-

Table 9.1 Signs and Symptoms of Adolescent Anxiety Disorders

Disorder	Key Diagnostic Feature	Other Criteria for the Disorder	Other Relevant Clinical Signs and Symptoms
Panic disorder	The occurrence of spontaneous panic attacks. These are paroxysms of fear or anxiety associated with somatic symptoms, such as palpitations or shortness of breath.	Panic attacks must be recurrent and must be associated with either concern about additional attacks, worry about the implication of the attacks, or changes in behavior. Panic disorder is frequently associated with agoraphobia, or anxiety about being in places where escape might be difficult.	Spontaneous panic attacks are very rare before puberty. Typical developmental course for progressive forms of the disorder involves initial development of isolated spontaneous panic attacks around puberty, followed by recurrent panic attacks, and then agoraphobia in adulthood. This process can take years to unfold across maturation from adolescence to adulthood.
Social anxiety disorder	The occurrence of extreme fear in social situations in which an individual is exposed to unfamiliar people	Exposure to social situations provokes anxiety that is associated with severe distress or impairment. The individual must show the capacity for age-appropriate social relationships.	This condition typically develops in late childhood or early adolescence. The disorder is associated with shyness or other subclinical behavioral features, such as certain temperamental types.
Separation anxiety disorder	Extreme anxiety about being separated from home or from an individual to whom a child is attached	The anxiety is associated with either distress upon separation, worry about harm to an attachment figure, avoidance of situations requiring separation, or physical complaints when separation is anticipated.	This condition is among the most prevalent mental disorders in children. The condition typically develops in early childhood, showing high rates of remission between childhood and adolescence. Some data suggest a familial or longitudinal association with panic disorder in adults.
Obsessive compulsive disorder (OCD)	Recurrent, persistent, intrusive, anxiety-provoking thoughts (obsessions) or repetitive acts (compulsions) that a person feels driven to perform	This pattern of intrusive thoughts or acts is recognized as unreasonable and consumes an hour of each day. These symptoms produce significant interference or distress.	This condition typically presents with stereotyped thoughts or acts. These might include concerns that the individual is in some way dirty or that the person has sinned. The disorder is frequently associated with tics and attention deficit disorder during childhood.
Posttraumatic stress disorder (PTSD)	Following exposure to trauma, in the form of a frightening event, an individual develops recurrent reexperiencing of the event, attempts to avoid stimuli associated with the event, and develops signs of increased arousal.	Reexperiencing can involve flashbacks, nightmares, or images. Avoidance can involve changes in behavior, changes in cognition, or new-onset feelings of detachment. Increased arousal can involve insomnia, exaggerated startle, or irritability.	PTSD is associated with many comorbid disorders, including major depression, other anxiety disorders, and behavior disorders. Different types of traumas may involve different symptomatic manifestations. For example, symptoms may differ in acute vs. chronic trauma.

(continued)

Table 9.1 Continued

Disorder	Key Diagnostic Feature	Other Criteria for the Disorder	Other Relevant Clinical Signs and Symptoms
Generalized anxiety disorder (GAD)	A pattern of excessive worry on most days for a period of 6 months. This worry is difficult to control.	Worry is characterized as apprehension when anticipating an upcoming feared event. Worry is associated with restlessness, fatigue, reduced concentration, or difficulty falling asleep.	GAD shows very high rates of comorbidity with a range of conditions, particularly anxiety disorders. In clinical settings, GAD virtually never presents as an isolated condition but is complicated by another comorbid disorder. Beyond the relationship with other anxiety disorders, GAD shows an unusually strong association with major depression.
Specific phobia	Marked and excessive fear of a specific object, such that exposure to the object precipitates extreme anxiety	The fear either causes avoidance that interferes with functioning or produces marked distress in the individual.	Specific phobia generally produces lower levels of impairment than other anxiety disorders. Phobias can be divided according to the nature of the feared object into various types, including animal type, natural-environment type, blood-injury type, or situational type.

rent obsessive thoughts or repetitive behaviors called *compulsions* that the individual feels he or she must perform. Young children are more often characterized by compulsions than by obsessions. Some children spend considerable time involved in elaborate rituals surrounding cleaning or checking routines, providing vague justifications for these behaviors. Adolescents are both more willing and better able to describe the obsessive thoughts that accompany their compulsions. Patients with OCD sometimes exhibit tics and attention deficit hyperactivity disorder (ADHD). Although OCD had been considered a rare condition, recent research suggests that as many as 1% of children exhibit this disorder.

Generalized Anxiety Disorder

A diagnosis of generalized anxiety disorder (GAD) is given to adolescents who worry about a variety of events or life circumstances—usually schoolwork, appearance, money, or their future. Age of onset of GAD is usually later than for most other disorders, although many patients report

having been anxious for many years. Further, GAD is likely to be comorbid with other symptoms, but the primary symptom is a chronic state of worry, rather than chronically avoidant behavior.

Panic Disorder

The essential feature of panic disorder is the repeated experience of intense fear of impending doom or danger following the unprovoked experience of bodily symptoms, especially rapid heart rate, shortness of breath, choking sensations, and sweating, or a feeling of depersonalization. The onset of this disorder is usually in late adolescence or early adulthood. Some patients with panic attacks will develop a fear of leaving home to avoid a panic attack; these patients are called *agoraphobic*. Panic disorder usually begins with sporadic isolated episodes of anxiety that accompany a panic attack and becomes a full-blown panic disorder between adolescence and adulthood (Pine, Cohen, Gurlet, Brook, & Ma, 1998).

Although young children can have an occasional panic reaction, it is unclear whether these attacks are accompanied by thoughts of impending danger. Moreover, it is extremely rare for children to experience panic reactions spontaneously in the absence of a trigger. Spontaneous panic attacks are the essential element of the diagnosis. Hence, there is some controversy over the degree to which panic disorder occurs in preadolescents. If this disorder does occur in children, it is relatively infrequent. Some investigators believe that the essential missing component in early childhood is the unprovoked change in bodily sensations, rather than the ability to impose a catastrophic interpretation.

Posttraumatic Stress Disorder

Unlike the other anxiety disorders, a diagnosis of posttraumatic stress disorder (PTSD) rests on a clearer causal sequence in which a person is first exposed to a traumatic event, feels frightened because of the threat to personal integrity, and then develops the disorder. Patients with PTSD present three kinds of symptoms. First, the patient must suffer from episodes of reexperiencing the traumatic event, which can include recollections of the event manifested in flashbacks or recurring dreams. Second, patients must attempt to avoid any event or place associated with the trauma, and the avoidance is accompanied by feelings of numbness or reduced responsivity. Finally, PTSD patients must experience signs of increased physiological arousal, especially difficulty falling asleep, increased irritability, or exaggerated startle. As with panic disorder, there is some debate over whether children exposed to trauma manifest all three symptoms. Children are likely to display separation anxiety disorder following a traumatic event. Nonetheless, the diagnostic criteria for PTSD in the DSM-IV are the same for children and adults.

PREVALENCE OF THE ANXIETY DISORDERS

Accurate estimates of the prevalence of DSM anxiety disorders are only available for children older than 8 years of age because studies of younger children have failed to have population-based samples and clear diagnostic criteria (these studies often use symptom scales rather than diagnostic indices) or have failed both requirements. The best estimates of the prevalence of anxiety disorders in preschool children, based on a primary care clinic sample (Lavigne et al., 1996, 1998, 2001), were very low. The following sections summarize prevalence data based on samples from the general population and studies published over the past decade (Costello, Egger, & Angold, 2004). The prevalence of any anxiety disorder increases with the duration of time over which the symptom's presence is counted. Thus 3-month estimates range from 2.2% to 8.6%, 6-month estimates from 5.5% to 17.7%, 12-month estimates from 8.6% to 20.9%, and lifetime estimates from 8.3% to 27%.

Specific Anxiety Disorders

The most prevalent diagnoses are DSM-III-R overanxious disorder (OAD) (0.5% to 7.1% with a median of 3.6%), DSM-IV specific phobias (0.1% to 12.2% with a median of 3.5%), and social phobia (0.3% to 15.1% with a median of 3.5%). Panic disorder (0.1% to 3.1%, median of 1.1%) and OCD (0.1% to 7.1%, median of 0.6%) are far less common. The use of adult diagnostic instruments such as the Disorders Interview Schedule (DIS) produce higher rates of specific and social phobias, agoraphobia, and OCD. By contrast, instruments designed specifically for children yield lower prevalence rates. Thus caution should be exercised when adult diagnostic instruments are used with children.

Anxiety and Disability

The relation between the diagnosis and everyday functioning remains a focus of controversy. Health maintenance organizations, insurance companies, and governmental agencies are concerned with whether children diagnosed with anxiety disorder require treatment (Costello, Burns, Angold, & Leaf, 1993). One perspective requires that a child show significant impairment or disability to receive a diagnosis, in which *disability* can refer to a particular symptom or the entire syndrome. Clinicians could rate a child's psychological functioning but fail to make a clinical diagnosis (Hodges, Doucette-Gates, & Liao, 1999; Shaffer et al., 1983).

The prevalence of anxiety disorders varies according to whether disability is or is not part of the definition. If a child must meet the criteria for a diagnostically relevant symptom as well as impairment in everyday functioning, the prevalence of a diagnosis is reduced by two-thirds. Further, requiring both specific impairment as well as severe scores on the Children's Global Assessment Scale (CGAS; Shaffer, Fisher, Dulcan, & Davies, 1996) reduced the prevalence of disorder by almost 90%. The prevalence of simple phobia was affected most severely; the prevalence fell from 21.6% if no impairment was required to an estimate of only 0.7% when impairment in daily functioning was required. Thus, all estimates of the frequency of the anxiety disorders depend in a serious way on the source of evidence and the criteria adopted. There is no "correct" prevalence in the sense that there is a correct height, in meters, for the Empire State Building.

Gender and Age Differences in Prevalence

Most investigators report that girls are more likely than boys to have an anxiety disorder. For example, more girls than boys between ages 9 and 16 years participating in the Great Smoky Mountains Study had an anxiety disorder (12.1% vs. 7.7%; Costello et al., 2004). Three studies revealed more phobias in girls, two reported more panic disorder and agoraphobia in girls, and only one study found more separation anxiety disorder and OAD in girls than in boys. In one of the few studies that examined the potential confounding factors linked to gender, the excess of anxiety disorder in girls was not eliminated after controlling for 15 possible confounding factors (Lewinsohn, Gotlib, Lewinsohn, Seeley, & Allen, 1998). One confound was the fact that the child's age is often correlated with the time frame used to estimate symptoms. Investigators who used 3-month prevalence rates reported the

lowest prevalence but studied the youngest subjects. By contrast, investigators using 12-month estimates had the highest prevalence but worked with the oldest children. In the Great Smoky Mountains Study the prevalence of separation anxiety decreased with age, whereas social phobia, agoraphobia, and panic disorder increased with age. It is difficult to draw conclusions about gender differences in the fears, worries, and anxieties of clinic-referred samples (either clinically anxious samples or other types of clinical samples) given the limited amount of research that has been conducted. Further research in this area is of critical importance (see Silverman & Carter, in press).

Summary

On any one day, between 3% and 5% of children and adolescents suffer from an anxiety disorder. Rates of GAD and specific phobias remain constant across childhood and adolescence. Although girls are more likely than boys to have an anxiety disorder, the gender difference is not as marked in the general population as it is in clinical samples, perhaps because boys are less likely to be referred for treatment. Numerous studies have demonstrated that girls who mature earlier than their peers exhibit higher rates of anxiety symptoms and disorders (e.g., Caspi & Moffitt, 1991); such findings have not been obtained with boys.

Comorbidity

Comorbidity among the anxiety disorders has been a problem for nosology, epidemiology, diagnosis, and treatment. The high level of comorbidity in clinical samples is mirrored in community samples (Brady & Kendall, 1992; Kendall & Clarkin, 1992; Kendall, Kortlander, Chansky, & Brady, 1992; Table 9.2). A review by Costello et al. (2004) yielded equivocal results because not all diagnoses were present in every study, there was a lack of consensus regarding controls for comorbidity, and concurrent comorbidity and sequential comorbidity were not always distinguished.

Table 9.2 Summary of Comorbidity from Pediatric Samples

Anxiety Disorder	Community Samples	Clinical Samples
Social anxiety disorder, selective mutism	Specific phobias, separation anxiety disorder	Other anxiety disorders, major depression, substance abuse
Generalized anxiety disorder (formerly overanxious disorder)	Depression, possibly alcohol and other substance abuse	Separation anxiety disorder, specific phobia, social anxiety disorder
Separation anxiety disorder	OAD/GAD, specific phobia, social anxiety disorder, possibly *subsequent* panic disorder	OAD/GAD, specific phobia, social anxiety disorder
Specific phobias	Separation anxiety disorder, social anxiety disorder	Separation anxiety disorder, social anxiety disorder
Panic disorder	Possibly social anxiety disorder, specific phobia	GAD
Obsessive compulsive disorder		Depression, other anxiety disorders, tic disorders
Posttraumatic stress disorder	Depression, other anxiety disorders, externalizing disorders	Depression, panic disorder, social anxiety disorder, GAD, externalizing disorders

GAD, generalized anxiety disorder; OAD, overanxious disorder.

Generalized Anxiety Disorder with Overanxious Disorder

The new formulations in DSM-IV for GAD indicate that children who formerly received a diagnosis of OAD should be placed in a new category called *generalized anxiety disorder*, or GAD. The criteria for GAD are permissive, hence a child could receive this diagnosis if he or she displayed only one of the six critical symptoms (restlessness, fatigue, difficulty concentrating, irritability, muscle tension, or sleep disturbance). The GAD symptoms are different from those that define OAD (worry about the past or future, concern about one's competence, need for reassurance, somatic symptoms, excessive self-consciousness, and muscle tension). Further, the new criteria for GAD resemble those used to diagnose major depressive episodes; examination of the overlap between OAD and GAD should take into account the possibility of a correlation with depression.

The Great Smoky Mountains Study, involving 1,420 children, which examined comorbidity among OAD, GAD, and depression (Costello, Mustillo, Erklani, Keeler, & Angold, 2003), found that among children who were comorbid (5.4% of the entire sample or 47% of those with any of

the three diagnoses), more than half had all three disorders, and only 12 children (16% of those with GAD or OAD) had both disorders but no signs of depression.

Comorbidity Among the Phobias

Most published studies confirm comorbidities among the three phobias: specific, social, and agoraphobia. However, none had any association with PTSD after investigators controlled for other anxious comorbidities. This finding suggests that PTSD is a distinct disorder (Pine & Grun, 1999).

Comorbidity Between Panic Disorder and Separation Anxiety Disorder

There is no significant concurrent comorbidity between panic disorder and separation anxiety, but this tendency does not rule out the possibility of sequential comorbidity. Early appearance of separation anxiety appears to predict panic disorder (Black, 1994; Klein, 1995; Silove, Manicavasagar, Curtis, & Blaszczynski, 1996), but no community studies have tested this hypothesis adequately. There is little association between separation anxiety and either phobias or OAD.

Comorbidity With Other Disorders

Comorbidity between any one anxiety disorder on the one hand, and ADHD, conduct disorder, depression, or substance abuse disorder on the other, reveals the highest level of comorbidity with depression, with a median odds ratio of 8.2 (95% confidence interval (CI) 5.8–12; Costello, Egger, et al., 2004).

There is also a sequential link between early anxiety and later depression (Costello et al., 2003); Orvaschel, Lewinsohn, & Seeley, 1995). It is not clear, however, whether depression or anxiety increases the subsequent risk for the complementary disorder or whether the natural sequence is from an initial anxiety disorder to the later development of depression.

The odds ratio for the comorbidity of anxiety with risk for conduct disorder/oppositional disorder is 3.1 (95% CI 2.2–4.6), and with ADHD it is 3.0 (95% CI 2.1–4.3). These confidence intervals imply a significant degree of comorbidity. Although the bivariate odds ratios that involve substance use or abuse were significant in some studies, an association between anxiety and substance abuse disappeared when comorbidity between anxiety and other psychiatric disorders was controlled (Costello et al., 2004).

Although there is little concurrent comorbidity for anxiety and substance abuse (Weissman et al., 1999), childhood onset of an anxiety disorder might predict either lower or higher rates of substance abuse in adolescence. Kaplow, Curran, Angold, and Costello (2001) reported that children with separation anxiety were less likely than others to begin drinking alcohol, and if they did, they did so at a later age than that of most youth. But children with GAD were more likely to begin drinking and abuse alcohol earlier in adolescence.

Onset and Course

The evidence does not permit a confident reply to the question of whether anxiety disorders in preschool children are precursors of similar disorders in adolescents. Retrospective data, which are always fallible, indicate that adolescents with anxiety disorders recalled their first onset of anx-

iety being at around 7 years of age (Costello, Erkanli, Federman, & Angold, 1999; Orvaschel et al., 1995). The Great Smoky Mountains Study revealed that specific phobias, GAD, separation anxiety, and social phobia all appeared around the time the child began school, while agoraphobia, OAD, and OCD appeared several years later, usually at 9 to 11 years of age (Costello et al., 2003).

Although early anxiety disorder appears to be a precursor of later depression (Alloy, Kelly, Mineka, & Clements, 1990; Breslau, Schultz, & Peterson, 1995; Kendler, Neale, Kessler, Heath, & Eaves, 1992; Lewinsohn, Zinbarg, Seeley, Lewinsohn, & Sack, 1997; Silberg, Rutter, & Eaves, 2001a, 2001b; Silberg, Rutter, Neale, & Eaves, 2001), we do not know the influence of anxiety on the timing or occurrence of other psychiatric disorders, with the sole exception that early separation anxiety and GAD have different predictive consequences for the later abuse of alcohol (Kaplow, Curran, Angold, & Costello, 2001).

Summary of Prevalence

Separation anxiety and phobic disorders are seen in early childhood but become rare by adolescence. However, panic disorder and agoraphobia have the opposite developmental profile; they are rare in childhood and increase in adolescence. We do not yet know whether some adolescent disorders are later manifestations of an underlying syndrome that was displayed earlier or whether they represent new forms of psychiatric illness. An answer to this question requires longitudinal research.

THEORIES OF ETIOLOGY AND MAINTENANCE

Learning Theories

Early behavioral models for the treatment of anxiety have been based on two primary suppositions. First, fears and phobias are acquired through classical conditioning, i.e., through the formation of association between a neutral stimulus and an aversive stimulus such that the former acquires the aversive properties of the latter. The neutral stimulus is then designated as a *conditioned stimulus* (CS) and the original aversive stimulus is called an *unconditioned stimulus* (US). Second, the acquired fears can be unlearned through extinction, i.e., through presentation of the CS in the absence of the US. This conceptualization gave rise to exposure therapy, in which patients are taught to systematically confront their feared situations, objects, responses (e.g., tachycardia), or memories, under safe circumstances with the goal of extinguishing their phobic fear. While there have been debates about the mechanisms through which exposure therapy reduces anxiety symptoms, the benefit of this therapy has been demonstrated by a large body of research (cf., Barlow, 2001; Ollendick & March, 2004).

Discontent with nonmediational (automatic) accounts for acquisition and extinction of pathological anxiety led to the development of theories that posited a pivotal role for cognitive factors in anxiety (e.g., Beck, Emory, & Greenberg, 1985). The assumption here is that it is not the events themselves but rather their threat "meaning" that is responsible for the evocation of anxiety. Meaning in these theories is often assumed to be represented in language. Accordingly, in cognitive therapy for anxiety disorders, verbal discourse is used to challenge the patient's threat interpretations of events and to help replace them with more realistic ones, especially so with adolescents. With young children, however, cognitive therapy frequently takes the simpler form of thought replacement such that fearful thoughts are replaced with brave ones (e.g., "I am a brave boy. I can handle this."). The child is provided new thoughts to replace the old ones (see Ollendick & Cerny, 1981).

The focus on the meaning of events as accounting for pathological anxiety paralleled the reconceptualization of conditioning in learning theories. For example, Rescorla noted that "conditioning depends not on the contiguity between the CS and US but rather in the information that the CS provides about the US" (Rescorla, 1988, p. 153) and that the "organism is better seen as an information seeker using logical and perceptual relations among events along with its own pre-conception to form a sophisti-

cated representation of its world" (Rescorla, 1988, p. 154). In the same vein, when discussing the phenomenon of extinction, Bouton (1994, 2000) stated that "in the Pavlovian conditioning situation, the signal winds up with two available 'meanings' " (Bouton, 2000, p. 58). Obviously, for rats the meaning of events cannot be represented in verbal language; rather, it is represented as associations among stimuli, responses, and outcomes.

Advances in information processing theories of conditioning and of pathological anxiety (e.g., Lang, 1977) influenced conceptualizations of treatment for the anxiety disorders. One such conceptualization, emotional processing theory, was proposed by Foa and Kozak (1986). In this theory, fear is viewed as a cognitive structure in memory that serves as a blueprint for escaping or avoiding danger that contains information about the feared stimuli, fear responses, and the meaning of these stimuli and responses. When a person is faced with a realistically threatening situation (e.g., a car accelerating at you, a fierce-looking dog approaching you) the fear structure supports adaptive behavior (e.g., swerving away, running away). A fear structure becomes pathological when the associations among stimulus, response, and meaning representations do not accurately reflect reality; in this instance, harmless stimuli or responses assume threat meaning. In emotional processing theory, meaning is thought to be embedded in associations among stimuli, responses, and consequences (as in Rescorla, 1988), as well as in language, especially in the form of thoughts, beliefs, and evaluations (as in Beck, 1976).

Within emotional processing theory the anxiety disorders are thought to reflect the operation of specific pathological fear structures (cf. Foa & Kozak, 1985). For example, the fear structure of individuals with panic disorder is characterized by erroneous interpretations of physiological responses associated with their panic symptoms (e.g., tachycardia, difficulty breathing) as dangerous (e.g., leading to heart attack). As a result of this misinterpretation, individuals with panic disorder avoid locations where they anticipate experiencing panic attacks or similar bodily sensations, such as physical exertion. In contrast, the fear structure of individuals with OCD most often involves the erroneous interpretation of safe stimuli (e.g., brown spots) as dangerous (e.g., AIDS-contaminated blood). Accordingly, the core pathology in panic disorder lies in the erroneous meaning of physiological responses, whereas the core pathology of OCD lies in the erroneous meaning of external events. The supposition that inaccurate negative cognitions underlie the anxiety disorders has also been at the heart of theories posed by cognitive therapists (e.g., Clark, 1986; Rapee & Heimberg, 1997; Salkovskis, 1985).

If fear and avoidance reflect the activation of an underlying cognitive fear structure, then changes in the fear structure should result in corresponding changes in emotions and behavior. Indeed, Foa and Kozak (1986) proposed that psychological interventions known to reduce fear, such as exposure therapy, achieve their effects through modifying the fear structure. According to emotional processing theory two conditions are necessary for therapeutic fear-reduction to occur: first, the fear structure must be activated; second, information that is *incompatible* with the pathological aspects of the fear structure must be available and incorporated into the existing structure. Thus, within this framework, exposure therapy is thought to correct the erroneous cognitions that underlie the specific disorder (e.g., tachycardia equals heart attack). This is also the explicit mechanism by which cognitive therapy is thought to reduce fear. In this way the mechanisms that are thought to operate during exposure greatly overlap with those of cognitive therapy. Moreover, some cognitive therapists explicitly posit that fear activation is necessary to refute the patient's false interpretations, and cognitive therapy programs routinely include an exposure component in the form of "behavioral experiments." It must be noted that the evidence for change in cognitions as the central mechanism in fear reduction is somewhat incomplete at this time; accordingly, additional work on the mediators or mechanisms of change in both the cognitive and behavior therapies is drastically needed. Such research is especially needed with children and adolescents, in whom the exact role of cognitions has been less frequently examined (Prins & Ollendick, 2003).

Cognitive Correlates of Anxiety Disorders

The cognitive approach to anxiety disorders comprises two research traditions (McNally, 2001b). In one tradition, researchers assume that introspective self-reports of anxious individuals can reveal aberrant cognition underlying symptom expression. These scholars administer questionnaires and conduct interviews to ascertain, for example, the intensity, frequency, and content of the worries and fears of children and adolescents. One such study revealed that school-age children worry most about school, health, and personal harm, especially the latter (Silverman, La Greca, & Wasserstein, 1995). Another indicated that children and adolescents suffering from anxiety disorders report the same kinds of worries as those of their healthy counterparts, but that the intensity (not the number) of worries distinguished youngsters with anxiety disorders from those without anxiety disorders (Weems, Silverman, & La Greca, 2000). Researchers in this tradition have also studied the *fear* of anxiety symptoms (i.e., anxiety sensitivity; Reiss & McNally, 1985). Silverman and colleagues have developed the Childhood Anxiety Sensitivity Index (CASI; Silverman, Fleisig, Rabian, & Peterson, 1991; Silverman & Weems, 1999) to investigate this phenomenon.

In the second tradition, researchers eschew self-report as insufficiently sensitive to measure abnormalities in cognitive mechanisms that often operate rapidly, and outside of awareness. These scientists apply the methods of experimental cognitive psychology to elucidate biases favoring processing of threat-related information in anxiety-disordered patients (McNally, 1996; Williams, Watts, MacLeod, & Mathews, 1997). In this section, we review experiments on information-processing biases in anxious children and adolescents (see also Vasey, Dalgleish, & Silverman, 2003; Vasey & MacLeod, 2001).

Attentional Bias for Threat

Because attentional capacity is limited, people can attend only to certain stimuli at a given time, and any bias for selectively attending to threat-related stimuli should increase a person's likelihood of experiencing anxiety. Two experimental tasks have confirmed that adults with anxiety disorders are characterized by an attentional bias for processing information about threat. In the emotional Stroop task (Williams, Mathews, & MacLeod, 1996), subjects are shown words of varying emotional significance and are asked to name the colors in which the words appear while ignoring the meanings of the words. Delays in color-naming ("Stroop Interference") occur when the meaning of the word automatically captures the subject's attention despite the subject's effort to attend to the color in which the word is printed. Most studies have shown that patients with anxiety disorders take longer to name the colors of words related to their threat-related concerns than to name the colors of other emotional or neutral words, and take longer to name the colors of threat words than do healthy subjects.

Although the emotional Stroop task has been traditionally interpreted as tapping an *attentional* bias for threat, debate continues about the mechanisms underlying the effect (Williams et al., 1996). For example, the emotional Stroop may reflect an inhibitory problem rather than an attentional one. That is, delayed color-naming of trauma-related words may reflect difficulty suppressing the meaning of trauma-related concepts once they are activated rather than selective attention per se (McNally, 2003, pp. 301–302).

Studies on the emotional Stroop in children have revealed mixed results. Relative to control subjects, spider-fearful children take longer to name the colors of spider words (Martin, Horder, & Jones, 1992) and colors of line drawings of spiders (Martin & Jones, 1995). Adolescents who developed PTSD after having survived a shipwreck exhibited Stroop interference for trauma-related words (Thrasher, Dalgleish, & Yule, 1994). Children who developed PTSD after being either physically or sexually abused exhibited similar patterns of trauma-related Stroop interference (Dubner & Motta, 1999). Relative to control subjects, children and adolescents (aged 9–17 years) with PTSD arising from either road traffic accidents or exposure to violence exhibited greater interference for trauma words than for neutral words (Moradi, Taghavi, Neshat-Doost, Yule, & Dalgleish, 1999). The magnitude of this trauma-

related interference effect was unrelated to the age of the patients.

However, not all Stroop studies have confirmed an anxiety-linked attentional bias for threat cues in youngsters. For example, nonanxious as well as anxious children have exhibited delayed color-naming of threat words (Kindt, Bierman, & Brosschot, 1997; Kindt, Brosschot, & Everaerd, 1997). A pictorial version of the spider Stroop (naming colors of background against which spider pictures appeared) did not reveal a fear-related effect in children (ages 8–11; Kindt, van den Hout, de Jong, & Hoekzema, 2000).

A second paradigm provides a much less controversial measure of attentional bias. In the Dot Probe Attention Allocation Task (MacLeod, Mathews, & Tata, 1986), subjects view two words on a computer screen, one appearing above the other. On some trials, one word is threat related, whereas the other is not. After the words disappear, a small dot replaces one of the words. Subjects press a button as soon as they detect the dot. Relative to healthy control subjects, patients with anxiety disorders are faster to respond when the dot replaces a threat word than when it replaces a neutral word. Because threat cues capture attention in anxious patients, these individuals are especially quick to respond to a neutral cue that follows a threat cue.

Using this task, Vasey, Daleiden, Williams, and Brown (1995) found that children (ages 9–14 years) with anxiety disorders exhibited an attentional bias for threat, whereas control children did not. The attentional bias increased with age and with reading ability. Relative to their nonanxious counterparts, test-anxious school children (ages 11–14 years) exhibited an attentional bias for threat words (both socially and physically threatening; Vasey, El-Hag, & Daleiden, 1996). Patients with GAD (ages 9–18 years) exhibited an attentional bias for threat words, whereas patients with mixed anxiety and depression or healthy control subjects did not (Taghavi, Neshat-Doost, Moradi, Yule, & Dalgleish, 1999). The GAD patients did not show an attentional bias for depression-related words, and the attentional bias for threat words was unrelated to the age of the subject. Finally, patients with PTSD (ages 9–17 years) arising from either non-domestic violence or road traffic accidents exhibited an attentional bias for social threat words (but not physical threat words), whereas control subjects did not (Dalgleish, Moradi, Taghavi, Neshat-Doost, & Yule, 2001).

Interpretive Bias for Threat

Anxious children tend to interpret ambiguous information in a threatening fashion. In one study, children (ages 7–9 years) heard homophones (e.g., *whipping*) that could be interpreted in either a threatening or a nonthreatening fashion (Hadwin, Frost, French, & Richards, 1997). The higher a child's self-reported trait anxiety, the more likely the child selected threatening pictures (e.g., rope) over nonthreatening pictures (e.g., cream) that made the homophones (e.g., *whipping*) unambiguous. In another study, GAD patients (ages 8–17 years) and healthy control children were shown homographs (e.g., *hang*), each possessing a threatening and a nonthreatening meaning (Taghavi, Moradi, Neshat-Doost, Yule, & Dalgleish, 2000). They were asked to construct a sentence including the homograph. Relative to the sentences constructed by control children, the anxious children more often constructed sentences incorporating the threatening interpretation of the homograph, implying that they had interpreted the ambiguous word in terms of its threatening meaning. This interpretive bias was unrelated to the age of the subjects.

Researchers asked anxious and nonanxious children to provide interpretations of ambiguous scenarios. Anxious fourth and fifth graders were more likely than their nonanxious peers to interpret nonhostile scenarios in a threatening fashion, whereas both groups interpreted ambiguous scenarios in a hostile fashion (Bell-Dolan, 1995). Patients with anxiety disorders (ages 9–13 years) exhibited a bias for interpreting ambiguous scenarios in a threatening manner, and this effect was strongly predicted by level of trait anxiety (Chorpita, Albano, & Barlow, 1996). Relative to healthy control children, patients ranging in age from 7 to 14 years who had anxiety disorders (overanxious, separation anxiety, social phobia, simple phobia), exhibited a bias for interpreting ambiguous scenarios in a threatening fashion (Barrett, Rapee, Dadds, & Ryan, 1996). This bias,

however, was even more pronounced in patients with oppositional-defiant disorder.

Conclusions

Anxious children and adolescents exhibit threat-related attentional and interpretive biases that resemble those exhibited by anxious adults. Moreover, within most studies, the extent of bias did not vary as a function of the child's age. Still, questions remain. In one study, the responses of anxious children to two measures of attentional bias (dot probe and emotional Stroop) were uncorrelated, indicating that these tasks tap distinct constructs (Dalgleish et al., 2003). Further, researchers have yet to test whether these biases disappear following successful psychological or pharmacological treatment. A more detailed critique of information processing in adolescent psychopathology is available elsewhere (Vasey et al., 2003).

Biological Features of Adolescents and Anxiety States

Although the exact timing of puberty is not easy to specify, scientists agree that the psychological and biological features of the era called adolescence are influenced by cultural setting. Some cultures, like our own, delay the assumption of adult roles; others require a clear transition, with or without a rite-of-passage ceremony (Schlegel & Barry, 1991). Nonetheless, there is an identifiable period between 12 and 18 years, ubiquitous across societies, characterized by changes in hormones, brain structure, and behavior. These properties may have been conserved over evolution to promote autonomy and to foster dispersal of some individuals from the natal territory to another in order to avoid inbreeding (Schlegel & Barry, 1991; Spear, 2000).

Adolescence is marked by a reactivation of the hypothalamic–pituitary–gonadal axis, development of secondary sexual characteristics, and the onset of reproductive capacity, even though the increased circulation of sex hormones does not account for much of the variance in the behavior of adolescents (Brooks-Gunn, Graber, & Paikoff, 1994). The timing of pubertal signs is influenced by gender and environment; onset of puberty may be influenced more strongly by environmental stressors in girls than in boys (Moffitt, Caspi, Belsky, & Silva, 1992).

Brain Changes

The brain undergoes changes throughout life (Eriksson et al., 1998), with intervals of modest change punctuated by periods of more rapid transformation (Spear, 2000). Periods of more dramatic change include not only pre- and early postnatal eras but also adolescence (Spear, 2000). Rakic, Bourgeios, and Goldman-Rakic (1994) estimate that up to 30,000 cortical synapses are lost every second during portions of the pubertal period in nonhuman primates, resulting in a decline of nearly 50% in the average number of synaptic contacts per neuron, compared with the number prior to puberty. There is a similar loss of synapses in the human brain between 7 and 16 years of age (Huttenlocher, 1979), but the scarcity of human postmortem tissue makes it difficult to provide a more detailed description of this phenomenon. Although the implications of the massive pruning remain speculative, it is likely that it reflects active restructuring of connections and the promotion of more mature patterns. Some forms of mental retardation are associated with unusually high density of synapses (Goldman-Rakic, Isseroff, Schwartz, & Bugbee, 1983).

The elimination of synapses that are presumed to be excitatory, accompanied by a reduction in brain energy utilization, transform the adolescent brain into one that is more efficient and less energy consuming (Chugani, 1996; Rakic et al., 1994). These changes could permit more selective reactions to stimuli that in younger children activate broader cortical regions (Casey, Geidd, & Thomas, 2000).

Adolescence is also marked by changes in the relative volume and level of activity in different brain regions. For example, there is an increase in cortical white matter density (reflected in myelinated fiber tracts) and a corresponding decrease in gray matter, especially in frontal and prefrontal regions (Giedd et al., 1999; Sowell et al., 1999a, 1999b). The overall result of these varied changes is net decrease in the volume of the prefrontal cortex (Sowell et al., 1999b, van Eden, Kros, & Uylings, 1990). In the hippocampus and the amygdala however, gray matter volumes continue to increase during late childhood and adolescence (Giedd et al., 1997; Yurgelun-Todd, Killgrove, & Cintron, 2003).

There are also developmental shifts in patterns of innervation, including the circuits involved in the recognition and expression of fear, anxiety, and other emotions (Charney & Deutsch, 1996). The responsiveness of the cortical gamma-aminobutyric acid (GABA)–benzodiazepine receptor complex to challenge increases as animals approach puberty (Kellogg, 1998), and there are maturational changes in the hippocampus in humans as well as in animals (Benes, 1989; Wolfer & Lipp, 1995), especially increases in GABA transmission (Nurse & Lacaille, 1999). Further, pubescent animals show lower utilization rates of serotonin in the nucleus accumbens than younger or older animals (Teicher & Andersen, 1999).

Developmental increases in amygdala–prefrontal cortex (PFC) connectivity are seen during adolescence in work conducted in laboratory animals (Cunningham, Bhattacharyya, & Benes, 2002), along with alterations in amygdala activation (Terasawa & Timiras, 1968) and the processing of emotional and stressful stimuli. Lesions of the amygdala have opposite effects on fearfulness to social stimuli when those lesions are in infant versus adult monkeys (Prather et al., 2001). Although levels of negative affect and anxiety have been correlated with amygdalar activity in adults (Davidson, Abercrombie, Nitschke, & Putnam, 1999), recent studies using functional magnetic resonance imaging (fMRI) to examine amygdalar activation in response to emotionally expressive faces in younger individuals have yielded a varying mosaic of evidence (Killgore, Oki, & Yurgelun-Todd, 2001; Pine, Grun, et al., 2001).

Maturational changes in the cerebellum, and the circuitry connecting the cerebellum to the prefrontal cortex, continue through adolescence. Lesions of the adult cerebellum disrupt the regulation of emotion and interfere with performance on tasks requiring executive functions (Schmahmann & Sherman, 1998), although this is less apparent in those younger than 16 years

(Levisohn, Cronin-Golomb, & Schmahmann, 2000).

One consequence of·this restructuring of the brain during adolescence is that early developmental compromises might be exposed. That is, brain regions vulnerable to dysfunction, due either to genetics or to adverse early experience, might be unmasked by the combination of brain restructuring and stressful life experiences (Goldman-Rakic et al., 1983; Hughes & Sparber, 1978).

BIOLOGY AND ANXIETY DISORDERS

There is great interest in detecting the biological variables that might distinguish anxious from nonanxious patients. Many, but not all, of these biological measures are influenced directly or indirectly by activity of the amygdala, bed nucleus, and their projections to the brain stem, autonomic nervous system, endocrine targets, cortex, and central gray matter (Pine, 1999, 2001, 2002; Pine, Cohen, & Brook, 2001; Pine, Fyer, et al., 2001; Pine, Grun, et al., 2001). It is relevant that connectivity between the amygdala and prefrontal cortex, along with level of amygdalar activation, increases during adolescence (Cunningham, Bhattacharyya, & Benes, 2002; Terasawa & Timiras, 1968).

Does the Amygdala Respond to Threat or Novelty?

There is debate over whether the amygdala is activated primarily by events that are potentially harmful or events that are unexpected or discrepant. Support for the former, more popular, position comes from the elegant research of LeDoux (1996, 1998, 2000) and Davis (1992, 1998) who have shown that acquisition of conditioned body immobility or bodily startle in rats, via Pavlovian conditioning with electric shock as the unconditioned stimulus, requires the integrity of the amygdala. But the amygdala also responds to discrepant and unexpected events that are harmless. Select neurons in the amygdala, as well as in the bed nucleus, hippocampus, and brainstem sites, reliably respond to

unexpected or discrepant events, regardless of whether they are threatening or harmful (Wilson & Rolls, 1993). And the reactivity of amygdalar neurons to unexpected or discrepant events habituates, often rapidly, as the event becomes expected and loses its surprise value (La Bar, Gatenby, Gore, Le Doux, & Phelps, 1998).

Nonetheless, Ohman and Mineka (2001) argue that the amygdala reacts primarily to signs of danger rather than to novelty. They suggest that all animals inherit a fear module, located in the amygdala, that reacts without conscious awareness and free of cognitive control to events that pose a threat to the integrity of the body (confrontation with snakes and spiders are classic examples of fear-evoking events). There are serious problems with this theoretical position.

First, the behavioral reactions of monkeys, chimpanzees, and human infants to a snake are no different from their reactions to discrepant events that are harmless (for example, a tortoise or seaweed). The British psychiatrist Isaac Marks (1987) described the terror his 2½-year-old son displayed when he first saw thousands of dried skeins of seaweed. However, the boy lost his fear following repeated exposures to these stimuli.

Only 30% of monkeys born and reared in the laboratory showed more prolonged withdrawal to a live snake than to blue masking tape (Nelson, Shelton, & Kalin, 2003). If snakes were a biologically potent incentive for fear, a majority of monkeys should have shown an immediate withdrawal reaction.

It is relevant that discrepant events that pose no danger can produce the same level of amygdalar activation as dangerous ones. Adults in an fMRI scanner looking at faces with neutral expressions showed amygdalar activation to new, compared with familiar faces, even though no face had a fearful, disgusting, or threatening expression (Schwartz et al., 2003).

These data suggest that the amygdala is biologically prepared to react to unexpected or discrepant events, a hypothesis supported by Cahill and McGaugh (1990), who believe that a primary function of the amygdala is to initiate a cascade of physiological reactions to novel or unexpected events. The degree of activation of the amygdala is correlated with the degree of arousal produced by the unexpected event, and not with its potential for danger or level of aversiveness. Although some might argue that every unexpected event also elicits a fear state this assumption seems a bit difficult to defend when the discrepant event is a neutral face, unexpected food for a rat, or the sudden appearance of a smiling parent from behind a screen of closed hands saying "peek a boo."

The phenomena of conditioned freezing or bodily startle in an animal, proposed as a model for human anxiety disorders, have so deeply penetrated contemporary thought that many clinicians and researchers have forgotten that humans do not become fearful or anxious to events qua events, but to the symbolic interpretations imposed on them. An anthropologist who studied the Ojibwa Indians of Northern Canada over 60 years ago (Hallowell, 1955) observed that adults report a state of fear when they fall chronically ill because prolonged illness means that a sorcerer has cast a spell on them. The symbolic meaning of the illness, not the somatic distress of being sick, is the origin of the adult fear.

Americans who report a fear of snakes are aware of the discrepant features of this species. Snakes have unusual skin covering, a typical ratio of head to body, and locomote in an unusual way. Seventeen of 22 adults with an animal phobia reported that it was the discrepant form of the animal's locomotion or appearance that upset them. No phobic patient had experienced any harm as a result of encountering the feared animal (McNally & Steketee, 1985).

An American woman with a phobia of birds supports this argument. The woman dates the origin of her fear to an afternoon when, as a seven year old, she was watching Hitchcock's film, "The Birds," which showed large flocks of birds attacking humans. The woman remembers feeling very surprised by the fact that birds, which she had regarded as benevolent and beautiful, could be aggressive to humans. The sharp disconfirmation of her childhood belief could have activated the amygdala. Because the film displayed birds attacking humans, the idea of harm became associated with amygdalar activation and the accompanying somatic consequences produced by the feeling of surprise. If the girl had not been surprised by the birds' behavior, it is likely that the phobia for birds would not have developed.

However, because some unexpected events are potential threats—the attack of a large dog or a scorpion on the bedspread—it is likely that some anxiety disorders, but probably not most, are the result of Pavlovian conditioning mechanisms.

Biological Correlates of Adolescent Anxiety Disorders

Advances in genetics, imaging, and cognitive neuroscience provide the opportunity to combine discoveries in neuroscience with insights from clinical psychobiology. Current views of adolescent anxiety disorders are influenced by two limiting facts. The first is that the research on adolescents has been modeled on investigations of adults; the second is that all current anxiety disorders are heterogeneous in their origin. This second fact means that investigators would profit from using biological variables to distinguish between patients with transient symptoms and those with more persistent disorders (Merikangas, Avenevoli, Dierker, & Grillon, 1999; Pine, Wasserman, & Workman, 1999).

Autonomic Nervous System

Many, but not all, adults with anxiety disorders show abnormalities of autonomic regulation, especially lability of the cardiovascular system. This feature is most common among adults with panic disorder, social anxiety, and GAD (Gorman & Sloan, 2000). These abnormalities occur in both the sympathetic and parasympathetic systems and probably contribute to the association between anxiety disorder and cardiovascular mortality (Gorman & Sloan, 2000). Although children at risk for one or more anxiety disorders, because of a temperamental bias, show high sympathetic tone in the cardiovascular system (Kagan, Snidman, McManis, & Woodward, 2001), this relation is not robust and children with different disorders often display similar autonomic profiles (Pine et al., 1998). One mechanism that ties autonomic regulation to psychology is the result of peripheral feedback from the cardiovascular system to the brain. If this somatic activity pierces consciousness, the person might conclude that a threat is imminent (Moss & Damasio, 2001). Perturbations in respiratory function are characteristic of panic disorder (Pine, 1999) and lead panic patients to experience a heightened feeling of anxiety (Coryell, Fyer, Pine, Martinez, & Arndt, 2001; Pine et al., 2000).

Hypothalamic–Pituitary–Adrenal Axis

Patients with an anxiety disorder often show perturbations in the HPA axis. Further, both rodents and nonhuman primates show changes in the hypothalamic–pituitary–adrenal (HPA) axis during acute stress, as well as after a stress experienced early in life (Essex, Klein, Cho, & Kalin, 2002; Kaufman, Plotsky, Nemeroff, & Charney, 2000; Meaney, 2001; Monk, Pine, & Charney, 2002). The strongest association between activation in the HPA axis and anxiety disorder is seen in PTSD (Bremner, 1999; Bremner et al., 1999; Yehuda, 2002). Although enhanced feedback sensitivity in the HPA axis is often associated with an anxiety disorder, unfortunately, some children with an anxiety disorder exhibit the opposite pattern of reduced feedback sensitivity (Coplan et al., 2002; De Bellis, 2001; Heim & Nemeroff, 2002).

Neurochemistry

Brain chemistry can affect the excitability of a particular brain region in diverse ways. Neurochemical regulation in adult anxiety disorders is studied most often with pharmacological challenges, positron emission tomography, or measurement of peripheral neurochemical metabolites. Because the first two techniques are invasive, data on adolescents are restricted primarily to peripheral measures.

Adults with anxiety often show enhanced activity in the neurons of the locus ceruleus (Coplan et al., 1997; Sullivan, Coplan, & Gorman, 1998; Sullivan, Coplan, Kent, & Gorman, 1999). For example, adults with panic disorder and children with separation anxiety disorder show an abnormal response to the administration of yohimbine (Sallee, Sethuraman, Sine, & Liu, 2000). However, children and adults with a diagnosis of

OCD show an abnormal, neurohormonal response to clonidine (Sallee et al., 1998). There is also an association between environmental stress and a prolactin response to serotonergic probes (Heim & Nemeroff, 2002), and adults with anxiety disorders show abnormalities in serotonergic regulation.

Immunology

A dramatic indication of a relation between immunology and anxiety disorder comes from studies of children with OCD. Earlier work had found a specific association between OCD and neurological conditions affecting the basal ganglia, including pediatric Snydenham's chorea. This discovery led to the recognition of a specific form of OCD, called *Pediatric Autoimmune Neuropsychiatric Disorder Associated with Streptococcus* (PANDAS; Swedo, 2002), marked by anxiety, OCD, and motor tics that emerge following infection with group A ß-hemolytic streptococcus. This syndrome reflects an immunological reaction within underlying fronto-striatal-thalamo-cortical-circuitry. It may be relevant that the offspring of adults with panic disorder show selected allergic disorders reflecting anomalies in the immune system (Kagan et al., 2001; Slattery et al., 2002).

Brain Imaging

A variety of techniques have been used to study anxiety disorder. These include MRI, fMRI, magnetic resonance spectroscopy (MRS), and electrophysiology.

Morphometric MRI evidence, which provides information on brain structure, reveals that OCD adults have abnormalities in the circuit involving the prefrontal cortex, basal ganglia, and thalamus (Rauch, Savage, Alpert, Fischman, & Jenicke, 1997). Some of these abnormalities have been observed in children and adolescents with OCD (Rosenberg & Hanna, 2000; Rosenberg, MacMillan, & Moore, 2001). Adults with PTSD have reduced volume in the hippocampus; but children with PTSD do not show these specific reductions, even though they have a smaller brain volume (De Bellis et al., 1999). Children with GAD show increased volume of the amygdala and superior temporal gyrus of the right hemisphere (De Bellis et al., 2002).

Functional magnetic resonance imaging quantifies brain activity. Despite these advantages it relies on measures of blood flow and therefore is an indirect index of neuronal events. Moreover, fMRI does not measure absolute amount of blood flow, but differences in changes in blood flow during an experimental task compared with a control task.

Despite these caveats, adults with PTSD show enhanced amygdalar activation (Rauch et al., 2000), and children with anxiety disorders show activation to faces with fearful expressions (Thomas et al., 2001a, 2001b). However, this latter response could be due to the surprise of seeing fearful faces, because healthy children show enhanced amygdalar activation to neutral faces (Thomas et al., 2001a, 2001b).

Magnetic resonance spectroscopy (MRS) is a noninvasive technique that can reveal aspects of brain neurochemistry. One study with MRS found a reduction in levels of N-acetylaspartate in the cingulate gyrus of children who had PTSD (De Bellis, Keshavan, Spencer, & Hall, 2000).

Electroencephalogram Activity

The electroencephalogram (EEG) represents the synchronized activity of large numbers of cortical pyramidal neurons which, at any moment, have a dominant frequency of oscillation at particular sites. A state of mental and physical relaxation is usually but not always associated with more power in the alpha frequency band (8–13 Hz) in frontal areas. A state of psychological arousal is associated with greater power in the higher-frequency beta band (14–30 Hz). The change to higher frequencies could be the result of more intense volleys from the amygdala to the cortex.

In addition, there are usually small hemispheric differences in the amount of alpha power on the right, compared with the left, side at frontal and parietal sites. Because alpha frequencies are associated with a relaxed psychological state, the less alpha power at a particular site, the more likely that site is neuronally active. The technical term for loss of alpha power is *desynchronized*, and investigators assume that desyn-

chronization of alpha frequencies is a sign that the individual has moved to a more aroused state.

Subjects reporting higher anxiety tend to have greater activation in the right frontal area than the left, whereas normal controls show more activation in the left frontal area. A preference for display of right versus left frontal activation could reflect either a stable trait or a transient state. It appears that a stable preference for right or left frontal activation can be influenced by an individual's temperament and, therefore, could reflect a stable property (Fox, Henderson, Rabin, Caikins, & Schmidt, 2001). McManis, Kagan, Snidman, and Woodward (2002) have found that 11-year-old children who had been highly reactive infants and fearful toddlers were likely to show right frontal activation under resting conditions. However, an asymmetry of activation can also reflect a transient state. Infants watching the approach of a stranger showed greater right frontal activation during that brief period of time (Fox & Bell, 1990). Hagemann and colleagues, who gathered EEG data on four separate occasions on a sample of 59 adults, concluded that 60% of the variance in asymmetry of activation reflected a stable trait while 40% was attributable to the specific occasion of testing (Hagemann, Naumann, Thayer, & Bartussek, 2002).

The event-related potential is a time-locked, post-synaptic potential generated by large numbers of cortical pyramidal neurons to a specific stimulus. The first waveform that represents the detection of a discrepancy is called N2 because it usually peaks at about 200 msec to an unexpected event. The two most frequently studied waveforms, P3 and N4, appear a bit later with peak voltages at about 400 msec, and are prominent at frontal sites when the subject is passive and has no task to perform. Kagan and colleagues have unpublished data indicating that 11-year-old children who had been highly reactive infants and fearful toddlers showed a larger negative waveform at 400 msec to nonthreatening discrepant scenes. Although this research is preliminary, it suggests that future investigators should examine EEG profiles and event-related potentials in their study of anxiety and anxiety disorders.

Genetics

Years of work have affirmed that genetic factors influence the risk for anxiety disorders. One study of adults found modest heritability for GAD for both men (15%) and women (20%) and no effect of shared environment (Hettema, Prescott, & Kendler, 2001; see Table 9.3). Other research affirms the heritability of panic disorder (Crowe, 1985; Gorwood, Feingold, & Ades, 1999; Marks, 1986; Skre, Onstad, Torgersen, Lygren, & Kringlen, 1993). Merikangas and Risch (2003) suggest heritability estimates of 50% to 60% for adult panic disorder, with risk ratios ranging from 3 to 8 for first-degree relatives of adult probands with panic disorder. A meta-analysis by Hettema, Neale, and Kendler (2001) uncovered a modest genetic contribution to four anxiety categories and little or no effect of shared environment. One of the most extensive explorations of the contribution of genes to anxiety disorders is the Virginia Twin Study of Adolescent Behavioral Development (VTSABD; Eaves et al., 1997). This corpus, which relies primarily on self-report data, discovered strong additive genetic effects for OAD in both boys and girls (37%), with little effect of shared environment (Topolski et al., 1997). Silberg and colleagues (Silberg, Rutter, Neale, & Eaves, 2001) reported that 12% to 14% of the variance in OAD in girls was attributable to genes, and most of the remaining variance to nonshared environment.

The Virginia Twin Study corpus indicated a smaller genetic contribution to separation anxiety (only 4%), but large nonshared environmental effects (40% and 56%). The data for girls revealed minimal genetic effects on separation anxiety and a greater contribution of shared environment (11% for children 8 to 12 years old, 23% for children 14 to 17 years old; Silberg, Rutter, Neale et al., 2001). However, parent-report checklists from an Australian national twin registry found a higher genetic loading for separation anxiety symptoms in girls (50%) and a much lower one for boys (14%) (Feigon, Waldman, Irwin, Levy, & Hay, 2001).

The Virginia Study indicated that about 9% to 10% of the variance in phobic symptoms was genetic in girls; the remainder was attributable to nonshared environment (Topolski et al., 1997). However, a Swedish study found that shared environmental factors explained considerably more of the variance for fears of animals, unfamiliar situations, and mutilations than nonshared environment (Lichtenstein & Annas, 2000). Thus, it is important to appreciate that conclusions based on twin studies can vary markedly as a function of the site of the laboratory, as well as the informant supplying the relevant information. When mothers reported on separation anxiety disorder in a population-based sample of female twins living in Missouri, heritability estimates were high (62%) and there was only a modest effect of shared environment.

Weissman (1988) argued almost 20 years ago that high rates of separation anxiety in children of parents who were comorbid for panic and depression disorder implied an association between separation anxiety disorder in childhood and the later development of panic disorder. There was a fairly specific association between separation anxiety in children who had been

Table 9.3 Genetics of Anxiety Disorders: Result of Meta-Analysis of Studies of Adults

Disorder	Odds Ratio[a]	Heritability	Shared Environment	Nonshared Environment
Panic disorder	5	.37–.43		.57–.63
Generalized anxiety disorder	6	.22–.37	0–.25	.51–.78
Phobias	4	0–.39	0–.32	.61–.80
Obsessive-compulsive disorder	4			

[a] Ratio of prevalence in relatives of probands to that of relatives of comparison subjects
Source: From Hettema, Neale, and Kendler (2001).

brought to clinics and separation anxiety in the parents when they were children years earlier (Manicavasagar, Silove, Rapee, Waters, & Momartin, 2001).

In addition, there is evidence for genetic contributions to personality traits such as neuroticism and introversion (Eaves, Eysenck, & Martin, 1989), shyness (Daniels & Plomin, 1985), and behavioral inhibition (DiLalla, Kagan, & Reznick, 1994; Kagan, 1994). A group of very shy 7-year-old Israeli children were more likely than others to inherit the long form of the allele for the serotonin transporter promoter region polymorphism (Arbelle et al., 2003); however, not all studies have found this association.

Despite these findings, many studies fail to meet the highest research standards, which include the following: *(1)* clearly operationalized diagnostic criteria; *(2)* systematic ascertainment of probands and relatives; *(3)* direct interviews with a majority of subjects; *(4)* diagnostic assessment of relatives by investigators blind to the proband's status; and *(5)* family studies with inclusion of comparison groups (Hettema, Neale, & Kendler, 2001). These standards are occasionally met in studies with adults, but rarely in studies with children and adolescents.

Genes are only expressed within a certain envelope of environments and individuals both shape and select their environments (Rutter, Silberg, O'Connor, & Siminoff, 1999a, 1999b). Finally, it should be appreciated that the attribution of a genetic risk to an individual should not invite fatalism (Rutter et al., 1990). Some heritable conditions can be treated and a few can be controlled. The classic example is phenylketonuria, for which the cognitive impairment is caused by an inherited metabolic defect that can be controlled by restricting the child's diet.

By developing personalized treatment plans, the revolution in molecular genetics promises to transform the identification and treatment of anxiety disorders across the lifespan. Two complementary approaches are described. Pharmacogenomic studies use genomic technologies to identify chromosomal areas of interest and, hence, potential drug targets (see, for example, Arbelle et al. 2003; Smoller et al., 2003); pharmacogenetic studies identify candidate genes that moderate drug response (see, for example,

Basile, Masellis, Potkin, & Kennedy, 2002), or adverse event profile (see, for example, Murphy, Kremer, Rodrigues, & Schatzberg, 2003). Identified difference may interact with age, gender, race and ethnicity (Lin, 2001).

In the adult literature on genetic factors, the most robust findings involve polymorphisms in the serotonin transporter (Weizman and Weizman, 2000). In comparison to progress in ADHD (Rohde, Roman, & Hutz, 2003), however, little is known about pharmacogenetic or pharmacogenomic approaches to anxiety disorders in the pediatric population. Shyness (Arbelle et al., 2003) and behavioral inhibition (Smoller et al., 2003) but not internalizing symptoms (Young, Smolen, Stallings, Corley, & Hewitt, 2003) all have been linked to candidate gene variation, illustrating how lack of consistency in phenotypic identification among other factors limits progress despite clear evidence from statistical genetic methods regarding the importance of genetic factors (Stein, Chavira, & Jang, 2001).

Future progress will depend on an improved understanding of the nature and identification of disease states and their natural course, which in turn will allow the development of more specific treatments, better risk prediction, and the implementation of preventive strategies based in pharmacogenomic and pharmacogenetic approaches (Gottesman and Gould, 2003; Pickar, 2003).

SUMMARY

The research of the past few decades has expanded our understanding of the phenomena linked to the concepts of anxiety and anxiety disorder. A comparison of contemporary reports with those of the last half century provides reason for optimism, for we have learned several important facts.

First, the state we call anxiety in humans is not unitary in origin or consequence and can be the result of living with realistic threat, past history, conditioning, or a temperamental bias for unexpected somatic sensations that are interpreted as meaning one is anxious. Second, epidemiological and genetic data imply distinct biological profiles for the varied anxiety disorders, many of which implicate neurochemical processes. Finally, clinicians and investigators now have an initial set of cognitive and biological procedures that promise to aid differential diagnosis of individuals who report anxiety. Major advances will occur when investigators and clinicians add these procedures to their interview data. The results of this work will permit the parsing of individuals who have a particular diagnosis into subgroups with more homogeneous biological and psychological features. This knowledge should lead to a more fruitful set of psychiatric classifications.

Treatment of Anxiety Disorders

chapter

10

Concurrent with the emergence of a growing psychopathology literature, child and adolescent clinical psychology and psychiatry have moved away from nonspecific interventions toward problem-focused treatments keyed to specific diagnoses in the *Diagnostic and Statistical Manual of Mental Disorders,* 4th ed. (American Psychiatric Association, 1994; DSM-IV) and, within diagnoses, targets (Kazdin, 1997). The past 40 years have seen the emergence of diverse, sophisticated, empirically supported, cognitive-behavioral and pharmacological therapies that cover the range of childhood-onset anxiety disorders (Ollendick & March, 2004). Before reviewing what is known about the treatment of anxiety disorders in adolescence, we first provide a brief overview of the history and rationale for cognitive-behavioral therapy (CBT), for pharmacotherapy, and for the combination of the two in the treatment of youth with anxiety disorders. Because of increasing emphasis in the field on evidence-based approaches, those interventions that have not been subjected to treatment outcome study by means of accepted research methodology, such as psychodynamic approaches, "play therapy," and other approaches, are not reviewed in this chapter.

COGNITIVE-BEHAVIORAL THERAPY

Current cognitive-behavioral theories regarding the etiology and maintenance of anxiety disorders posit that internal mental phenomena play an important role in mediating pathological anxiety. Foa and Kozak (1985, 1986) proposed that specific "fear structures" which contain erroneous information about the fear stimuli, fear responses, and their meaning underlie the anxiety disorders. Kendall (2000b) also referred to "cognitive structures" as being important in anxiety disorders in childhood. Accordingly, the goal of cognitive-behavioral treatment is to provide information that is incompatible with the erroneous elements of the fear structure.

Most mental health clinicians are familiar with treatments that assume psychological distress stems from historical relationship problems that must be uncovered in therapy. In contrast to this approach, the CBT clinician addresses the anxiety symptoms directly by confrontation with the feared stimuli in a therapeutic environment and by teaching the patient a set of adaptive coping skills for specific symptoms associated with distress and impairment (Kendall, 2000b). Thus, unlike some other psychotherapeutic approaches, CBT fits into a problem management framework in which the symptoms of the disorder and associated functional impairments are specifically targeted for treatment.

The cognitive-behavioral approach is not a single, monolithic approach. Quite the contrary is true. The generic approach labeled "cognitive-behavioral" involves working with parents, enhancing emotional processing, changing social and peer influences, and using behavioral contingencies and cognitive processing. Similarly, CBT is not one treatment. Rather, treatments of childhood anxiety disorders, though held together by common components and guiding theory, have emerged from different clinics, in different countries, and with variations in the length and specifics of treatment. Nevertheless, there are numerous common themes, strategies, and guiding principles.

One CBT program has received research attention, and though not exactly prototypic, serves as an illustrative example of this approach. (For futher discussion of CBT programs, the reader is referred to the several programs that are described in detail within each of the sections on the several disorders.) This program is manual based and time limited (Kendall, 2000b). This program integrates elements of cognitive information processing associated with anxiety with behavioral techniques (e.g., relaxation, imaginal and in vivo exposure, role-playing) that are known to be useful in the reduction of anxiety. In this program, children with anxiety typically participate in a structured 16- to 20-week treatment program divided into two phases: education and practice.

The first phase includes training, education, and skill-building, during which the therapist works with the child to recognize signs of anxiety, acquire relaxation skills, and identify anxious cognitive processing. Through self-monitoring homework assignments and in-session role-playing, the child learns about anxiety and, more importantly, the cognitive, somatic, emotional, and behavioral aspects of his or her own personal anxious experience. These sessions also allow the child to begin to think about various ways to overcome his or her anxiety.

Education and Skill-Building

During initial sessions, the anxious child learns to distinguish between various bodily reactions to emotions as well as the somatic reactions that are specific to his or her anxiety. Coupled with this awareness, the child is taught relaxation exercises designed to help the child develop further awareness of and control over physiological and muscular reactions to anxiety (see King, Hamilton, & Ollendick, 1994). This segment may be especially beneficial for children whose worry is accompanied by more severe somatic symptoms (see also Eisen & Silverman, 1998). In this way, anxious children may develop an awareness of their physiological responses to anxiety and use this as an "early warning signal" to initiate relaxation procedures.

Next, children are taught how to identify and modify anxious cognition (their internal dialogue). Therapist and child then discuss such thoughts and the child is encouraged to ask himself or herself the various possibilities that may occur in a given situation. It is believed that helping children to challenge their distorted or unrealistic cognition will promote more constructive ways of thinking and less dysfunctional emotional and behavioral responses. For example, the "perfectionistic" nature of many anxious children can be challenged as these children become better able to examine, test out, and reduce their negative self-talk, modify unrealistic expectations, generate more realistic and less negative self-statements, and create a plan to cope with their concerns. Importantly, the idea here is not necessarily to fill the child with positive self-talk. Rather, the ameliorative power rests in the reduction of negative self-talk, or the "power of non-negative thinking" (Kendall, 1984). This phenomenon is supported by recent evidence indicating that changing children's anxiety-ridden and negative self-talk—but not positive self-talk—mediates the changes in anxiety that

are associated with treatment-produced gains (Treadwell & Kendall, 1996). Children learn problem-solving skills that help them to devise a behavioral plan to cope with their anxiety. This includes learning to recognize the problem, brainstorming and generating alternatives to managing their anxiety, weighing the consequences of each possible alternative, and then choosing and following through with their plan (see D'Zurilla & Goldfried, 1971). The therapist serves as a model during each phase of problem solving by, for example, reminding the child that problems and challenges are part of life or by brainstorming ideas without judgment. With the acquisition of problem-solving skills, children develop confidence in their ability to handle anxiety-provoking situations as well as everyday challenges that arise. They learn to judge the effectiveness of their efforts and reward themselves for these efforts. They also learn to identify those things they liked about how they handled a situation and those things that they may want to do differently. Here, children are encouraged to reward both complete and partial successes. Children with anxiety may have exceedingly high standards for achievement and be unforgiving and critical of themselves if they fail to meet these standards. Therefore, it is important for the therapist to emphasize and encourage self-reward for effort and partial success.

Exposure Exercises

The second phase of treatment focuses on exposure exercises in which children practice the newly acquired skills. In these sessions, participant youth are prepared for and exposed to various situations that induce anxiety. They are first exposed to imaginary and low-anxiety situations and gradually are exposed to moderate- and then high-anxiety situations. Through imaginal and in vivo exposures, the therapist assists the child in preparing for the exposure by, for example, discussing aspects of the situation that are likely to be troubling, working through the steps of the plan, and rehearsing. The in vivo exposures are extremely important, as these situations provide the child real opportunities to practice. Thus, they should be tailored to address the specific worries (sources of anxious distress) of the child.

The therapist also facilitates children's postexperience processing of the exposures, helping them to evaluate their performances and think of a reward. In so doing, the therapist helps to frame the current exposure experience in terms of a pattern for future coping. When designing the graduated hierarchy of exposures, it is beneficial for the therapist and child to collaborate to create in vivo exposures that are meaningful and memorable for the child. Homework assignments are an important feature of this program. Throughout the treatment, children complete tasks in a personal notebook, which allow them to practice their steps and to use their skills outside of session. Rewards are provided upon completion of the assignments.

As the end of the time-limited treatment approaches (starting with 3 weeks left), the therapist and child begin to discuss how the child will create and produce a "commercial" about his or her experiences in the program to be presented and videotaped during the last session of the treatment. Children are encouraged to use their imagination and create a videotape, audiotape, or booklet describing their experiences to help in telling other children about strategies for coping with anxiety. This effort is designed to not only help children organize their experiences but also afford them the opportunity to "go public" with their newly acquired skills and recognize their accomplishments. The commercial also serves as a tangible reward that children can take home with them once the treatment is completed and, although it may not be described as such, it is an in vivo exposure task with emotional, social, creative, and organizational features.

Developmental Considerations

The treatment manuals that have been written and evaluated in research (e.g., Kendall, Chu, Pimentel, & Choudhury, 2000) were designed for children between the ages of 8 and 13 years. Also designed for this age range, *The Coping Cat Workbook* (Kendall, 2000a) contains exercises that parallel treatment sessions in an effort to facilitate the child's involvement in the program and the acquisition of skills. Although some manual-based treatments have acquired the reputation of being somewhat rigid, the therapist working with this program is allowed flexibility, as life can be "breathed" into the manual to better fit the needs and functioning of the child (Kendall, Chu, Gifford, Hayes, & Nauta, 1998). Although adaptations can be made when working with older children, younger children may not have yet developed the cognitive skills necessary to participate fully in or benefit maximally from this intervention and children with an IQ below 80 may not have the prerequisite skills. Additionally, with developmental considerations, it is important to be cognizant of possible age-related increases in physiological functioning, emotional vulnerability, social and peer pressures, and comorbid conditions, as well as any other changes that these children may be experiencing. Accordingly, a CBT therapist manual and a related workbook for teenagers (Kendall, 2000a) are also available.

PHARMACOTHERAPY

Progress in the neurobiology of anxiety has focused on *(1)* identifying the central nervous system (CNS) substrates of anxiety and *(2)* the effects of rearing and environment in the progression of anxiety states with reference to their somatic substrates (Pine & Grun, 1999) in an evolutionary context (Leckman & Mayes, 1998). Convergent evidence from both child studies of stress and trauma as well as primate rearing and deprivation studies suggests that the effects of stress in the genesis of anxiety disorder can be profound. Important substrates for this "stress-response system" include brainstem arousal centers, particularly the locus ceruleus, which provides noradrenergic input to brainstem and more rostral arousal mechanisms (McCracken, Walkup, & Koplewicz, 2002); the amygdala located in the anterior temporal lobe, which processes threat cues and safety signals, with particular emphasis on social threat (Bremner, Krystal, Charney, & Southwick, 1996); the septal–hippocampal system that mediates glucocorticoid sensitive context-conditioning within the framework of learned experience; striatal and neoriatal structures, such as the caudate nucleus, which with their cortical targets comprise the circuitry that mediates habitual automatic behaviors, such as those seen in obsessive-compulsive disorder (OCD; Rosenberg & Hanna, 2000); the orbital-frontal cortex, which assigns complex negative affective valence to cognitive attributions (Graybiel & Rauch, 2000); paralimbic structures, such as the anterior cingulate gyrus, which play an important role in directed and selective attention to threatening stimuli (Davidson, Abercrombie, Nitschke, & Putnam, 1999); and the dorsolateral and ventromedial prefrontal cortex, which respond to and modulate subcortical input and output, generating adaptive responses or, in the case of disease states, maladaptive anxiety-maintaining behaviors (Davidson et al., 1999). From an integrationist point of view, extensive afferent and efferent connections between these brain regions process a wide variety of internal and external threat cues and safety signals, integrate current experience with previous experience, and generate affective and cognitively mediated approach and avoidance behaviors that are either appropriate or inappropriate to the individual's current context.

The understanding of the neurobiology of anxiety has been propelled by new pharmacologic agents that impact CNS receptors within the stress–response system (Heim, Owens, Plotsky, & Nemeroff, 1997). For example, the serotonin system is involved in generating and maintaining normal and pathological fear (Stein, Westenberg, & Liebowitz, 2002). Modulation of this system with a serotonin reuptake inhibitor provides an effective treatment for OCD (March, Biederman, et al., 1998) and may be useful for separation anxiety, panic, and social phobia (Research Units of Pediatric Psychopharmacology (RUPP) Anxiety Group, 2001). Other major neurotransmitter systems that appear to be involved in pathological anxiety include the GABAergic/glutamergic, noradrenergic, and dopaminergic systems, with recent evidence also suggesting important roles for the neuropeptides cholecystokinin, neuropeptide Y, and corticotropin-releasing hormone (CRH) (Sallee & March, 2001). These neurotransmitter systems

appear to work in concert to provide homeostasis with respect to the phasic management of threat, and dysregulation in the information processes linked to these substrates may be linked to anxiety states in children and adolescents. They also appear to interface with Kagan's notion of "behavioral inhibition," which as a stable temperamental characteristic appears to be an index of biological vulnerability that under certain circumstances (e.g., separation-stress exposure) can contribute to the generation of an anxiety disorder (Biederman, Rosenbaum, Chaloff, & Kagan, 1995).

Brain mechanisms of response to threat that are highly conserved in evolutionary terms and are exquisitely sensitive to learned experience provide the CNS substrate for the information processes that, when dysregulated, produce pathological anxiety, as well as for normal fears and worry. Pharmacotherapy presumably biases these processes directly by influencing the neurotransmitter milieu within which these hierarchically distributed neural networks operate.

COMBINED TREATMENT

In a biopsychosocial approach, combined treatment may be the rule rather than the exception (e.g., the treatment of juvenile rheumatoid arthritis with ibuprofen and physical therapy). In a perfectly evidence-based world, selecting an appropriate treatment for the anxious child or adolescent from among the many possible options would be reasonably straightforward. In the complex world of research and clinical practice, choices are rarely clear-cut. In this regard, the treatment of the anxious child can be thought of as being partially analogous to the treatment of juvenile-onset diabetes, with the caveat that the target organ, the brain in the case of mental disorders, requires psychosocial interventions of much greater complexity. The treatment of diabetes and anxiety disorder can both involve medication—insulin in diabetes and in anxiety, typically a serotonin reuptake inhibitor. Each also involves an evidence-based psychosocial intervention. In diabetes, the psychosocial treatment of choice is diet and exercise, and in anxiety, exposure-based CBT. Depending on the presence of risk and protective factors, not every participant has the same outcome. Bright youngsters from well-adjusted, two-parent families typically may do better with either diabetes or anxiety than those beset with tremendous psychosocial adversity and family hardship. Also, not everybody recovers completely even with the best of available treatment, so some interventions need to target coping with residual symptoms, such as diabetic foot care in diabetes and helping patients and their families cope skillfully with residual symptoms in anxiety disorders.

Psychosocial treatments may be combined with a medication for one of several reasons. First, in the acute treatment of the severely anxious child, two treatments may provide a greater "dose" and thus, may promise a better and perhaps speedier outcome. For example, patients with OCD may opt for a combined treatment even though CBT alone may offer equal benefit (March & Leonard, 1998). Second, comorbidity may require two treatments, since different targets may require varied treatments. For example, treating an 8-year-old who has attention-deficit hyperactivity disorder (ADHD) and separation anxiety disorder (SAD) with a psychostimulant and CBT is a reasonable treatment strategy. Third, in the face of partial response, an augmenting treatment can be added to the initial treatment to improve the outcome. A selective serotonic reuptake inhibitor (SSRI) can be added to CBT or CBT can be added to an SSRI. In an adjunctive treatment strategy, a second treatment can be added to a first one to positively impact one or more additional outcome domains. For example, an SSRI can be added to CBT to address comorbid depression.

As our understanding of both mental disorders in youth and adolescent development increases, treatment innovations inevitably will accrue, including knowledge about when and how to combine treatments (see Table 10.1). The good news is that the National Institute of Mental Health (NIMH)-funded comparative treatment trials that include a combination cell as well as CBT and medication monotherapy conditions are currently under way. Unfortunately, adolescent cases play too small a role and appear in too small a number in these ongoing trials to allow for specific examination of the effects of CBT, medication, and their combination on adolescents with anxiety disorders. The clear mandate is for similar programmatic research with adolescent cases. Before such work is undertaken, however, we offer a review of what is known to date. Because the state of knowledge varies by disorder, our review will consider each of the anxiety disorders separately (i.e., social phobia, generalized anxiety disorder, separation anxiety disorder, specific phobia, panic disorder, obsessive-compulsive disorder, and posttraumatic stress disorder). The information will be provided within the categories of *(a)* acute treatment, *(b)* maintenance treatment, and *(c)* management of partial response and nonresponse. In each category we very briefly summarize what is known about the treatment of adults and then provide more detailed coverage of treatments for youth. As noted above, there are very few studies of combined treatments of any kind in child or adolescent samples. Moreover, with few exceptions (e.g., Barlow, Gorman, Shear, & Woods, 2000), most of the combined-treatment studies in adults have not included a CBT plus pill placebo condition, which leaves an important mechanism question essentially unanswered by the extant literature.

ACUTE TREATMENT

Social Anxiety Disorder

Treatment of Social Anxiety Disorder in Adults

With respect to psychosocial interventions, behavioral, cognitive, and combined cognitive-behavioral interventions have each been found to be efficacious in the acute treatment of social phobia in adults, delivered either in groups or individually. Direct comparisons of behavioral and cognitive-behavioral treatments have been mixed, and it is unclear as yet whether there is a strong advantage for one over the other. As with pharmacotherapy, residual impairment remains an issue (for a comprehensive review see Hambrick, Turk, Heimberg, Schneier, & Liebowitz, 2003).

A variety of medications have been found use-

Table 10.1 Summary of Literature on Pediatric Treatment Outcome by Anxiety Disorder

Anxiety Disorder	Standards of Evidence	Summary of Key Type 1 Studies
Social anxiety disorder	*Psychosocial Treatment* Three Type 1 studies, several Type 3 studies A few dismantling studies (e.g., Spence et al., 2000; CBT + family therapy failed to separate from CBT delivered individually) Multiple Type 1 CBT studies that included SAD patients but did not analyze separately (e.g., Flannery-Schroeder & Kendall, 2000) *Pharmacotherapy* Multiple Type 3 studies Type 1 study: RUPP study of fluoxetine vs. placebo, SAD patients included	Beidel, Turner, & Morris (2000): Social effectiveness therapy > nonspecific treatment (Testbusters) Hayward et al. (2000): Group CBT > assessment only Spence et al. (2000): CBT, CBT + family therapy > WL RUPP (2001, 2003): Fluvoxamine > placebo overall, but SAD diagnosis identified as a moderator of treatment outcome in that those with social anxiety disorder did not fare as well as those with GAD or separation anxiety
Selective mutism	*Psychosocial Treatment* Type 6 case studies provide preliminary support for various behavioral techniques (e.g., contingency management, exposure, self-modeling) No Type 1 or Type 2 studies for any behavioral or cognitive-behavioral therapy *Pharmacotherapy* Only one Type 1 study: fluoxetine vs. placebo	Black & Uhde (1994): Fluoxetine > placebo in a small randomized, double blind trial that also included a single-blind placebo lead-in
Generalized anxiety disorder (GAD)	*Psychosocial Treatment* Five Type 1 studies support the efficacy of CBT packages for anxious youth; many, but not all, of subjects were diagnosed with GAD *Pharmacotherapy* Several Type 3 studies provide preliminary support for use of several classes of medication, including benzodiazepines Some negative findings in Type 3 studies of benzodiazepines, plus concerns about dependency and withdrawal (e.g., Rickels et al., 1990) Some Type 1 studies of TCAs for youth with "school refusal," some of whom may have had GAD Concerns about cardiac risks with TCAs Some preliminary evidence for the SSRIs, plus two Type 1 studies (1 for sertraline, 1 for fluvoxamine)	Kendall (1994): CBT package ("Coping Cat") > WL Kendall et al. (1997): Coping Cat > WL Barrett (1998): Group CBT, group family-based CBT > WL; family-based treatment afforded advantages over CBT alone on some measures Rynn et al. (2001): Sertraline > placebo RUPP (2001, 2003): Fluvoxamine > placebo; unlike SAD, GAD not found to be a predictor of non-response
Separation anxiety disorder (SAD; including school refusal behavior)	*Psychosocial Treatment* Several Type 1 studies of school refusal, which included many individuals with separation anxiety (e.g., Bernstein et al., 2000) Several Type 1 studies of anxious children and adolescents that included separation-anxious participants (e.g., Kendall et al., 1999, Silverman et al., 1999a)	King et al. (1998): CBT > WL for school refusal behavior Last et al. (1998): CBT = educational support for school refusal behavior, with children and parents' ratings of improvement generally higher than that found by study investigators

(continued)

Table 10.1 Continued

Anxiety Disorder	*Standards of Evidence*	*Summary of Key Type 1 Studies*
	Family and teacher involvement in CBT was found initially superior to CBT alone for school refusal behavior, which presumably included separation anxious participants (Heyne et al., 2002)	Gittleman-Klein & Klein (1971): Imipramine > placebo
		Klein, Kopelwicz, et al. (1992): Failed to replicate earlier positive findings for imipramine
	Pharmacotherapy	
	Several Type 1 studies, with mixed results: imipramine was first efficacious but then a later study found no difference (Gittleman-Klein & Klein, 1971; Klein, Koplewicz, et al., 1992); benzodiazepines did not separate from placebo (Graae et al., 1994)	Graae et al., 1994: Benzodiazepine did not separate from placebo
		RUPP (2001, 2003): Fluvoxamine > placebo; unlike SAD, separation anxiety not found to be a predictor of nonresponse
	SSRIs have had efficacy (RUPP, 2001, 2003) and are generally considered first-line option	
Specific phobia	***Psychosocial Treatment***	Silverman et al. (1999b): Contingency management, self-control > educational support in terms of clinically significant improvement, but all three groups improved functioning
	Participant modeling and reinforced practice are well established; other behavioral methods are "probably efficacious" in children (Ollendick & King, 1998, 2000)	
	Two completed Type 1 studies, one large study still in progress	Öst et al. (2001): One-session CBT > WL
	Type 3 study suggested that one-session CBT is comparable if not superior to longer treatments (Muris et al., 1998)	Ollendick & Öst (in progress): One-session CBT compared with educational support and WL
	Pharmacotherapy	
	No Type 1 studies of any medication have been conducted; Type 3 study of fluoxetine suggested efficacy	
Panic disorder	***Psychosocial Treatment***	Mattis et al. (2001): Panic control treatment for adolescents (PCT-A) compared with self-monitoring; preliminary evidence from this trial is encouraging: PCT-A > self-monitoring in reducing panic attack severity and other symptoms of panic disorder
	Preliminary evidence for CBT packages based on Barlow's panic control treatment was found in Type 3 studies (Barlow & Seidner, 1983; Ollendick, 1995)	
	Pharmacotherapy	
	Type 3 evidence for SSRIs (e.g., Renaud et al., 1999)	
	No Type 1 studies of any class of medication	
Obsessive compulsive disorder (OCD)	***Psychosocial Treatment***	De Haan et al. (1998): EX/RP > clomipramine, both yielded significant reductions
	Multiple Type 3 studies provide preliminary evidence for efficacy of CBT involving EX/RP for children and adolescents (e.g., Piacentini et al., 2002)	Pediatric OCD Collaborative Study Group: Compared combined treatment with CBT and sertraline, and all with placebo
	Preliminary evidence from Type 3 studies shows that EX/RP augments SRI pharmacotherapy (e.g., March et al., 1994; Wever & Rey, 1997)	Piacentini (1999): Describes a soon-to-be-completed study comparing EX/RP + family therapy with relaxation control
	Preliminary evidence from Type 3 study shows that intensive EX/RP and weekly EX/RP are comparable (Franklin et al., 1998)	
	One completed Type 1 study directly comparing EX/RP with pharmacotherapy suggested an advantage for EX/RP (DeHaan et al., 1998)	DeVeaugh-Geiss et al. (1992): Clomipramine > placebo

Table 10.1 Continued

Anxiety Disorder	Standards of Evidence	Summary of Key Type 1 Studies
	Two large-scale Type 1 studies of EX/RP are underway, one of which examines EX/RP + SSRI (sertraline)	March, Biederman, et al. (1998): Sertraline > placebo
	Pharmacotherapy	Riddle et al. (2001): Fluvoxamine > placebo
	Several Type 1 studies of clomipramine (e.g., Leonard et al., 1989), including a multicenter study (DeVeaugh-Geiss et al., 1992)	Geller et al. (2001): Fluoxetine > placebo
	Multiple large-scale, multicenter Type 1 studies of SSRIs (e.g., March, Biederman, et al., 1998)	Garvey et al. (1999): Oral penicillin = placebo in children diagnosed with PANDAS, but penicillin administration may have been ineffective in preventing reinfection with GABHS
	Type 3 studies examining augmentation of SSRIs with atypical neuroleptics	
	Investigational Treatments	
	Two Type 1 studies examining treatments for children and adolescents diagnosed with PANDAS	Perlmutter et al. (1999): Plasma exchange = IV immunoglobulin > IV placebo for PANDAS
Posttraumatic stress disorder	**Psychosocial Treatment**	Deblinger et al. (1996, 1999): CBT > community treatment as usual
	Several Type 3 studies provide preliminary evidence for individual + group CBT (Goenjian et al., 1997) or group CBT (e.g., Layne, Pynoos, Saltzman, et al., 2001; March, Amaya-Jackson, et al., 1998); one study for a form of EMDR (Chemtob et al., 2002)	King et al. (2000): CBT = CBT + family involvement
	Four Type 1 studies of CBT for PTSD associated with child sexual abuse	Cohen & Mannarino (1996a, 1996b): CBT > supportive therapy
	No other Type 1 studies of CBT for other forms of trauma	Cohen & Mannarino (1998): CBT > supportive therapy
	Pharmacotherapy	
	Limited to Type 3 studies	

CBT, cognitive-behavioral therapy; EMDR, eye movement desensitization and reprocessing; EX/RP, exposure and response prevention; GABHS, group A β-hemolytic streptococcal infection; IV, intravenous; PANDAS, pediatric autoimmune neuropsychiatric disorders associated with streptococcal infection; SRI, serotonin reuptake inhibitor; RUPP, Research Units on Pediatric Psychopharmacology; SSRI, selective serotonin reuptake inhibitor; TCA, tricyclic antidepressant; WL, wait list.

ful for social anxiety disorder. There are no controlled trials of patients with nongeneralized social anxiety disorder, and studies containing both generalized and nongeneralized patients include too few of the latter to be definitive. Placebo-controlled trials of patients with the generalized subtype suggest efficacy for phenelzine, clonazepam, paroxetine, sertraline, fluvoxamine, venlafaxine, gabapentin, and pregabelin. The average responder rate in these trials is 40%–55%, defining response as a 1 or 2 on the Clinical Global Impression (CGI) Improvement scale. A majority of the patients classified as responders in these trials still have clinically significant symptoms. Patients with comorbid major depressive disorder (MDD) or significant substance abuse have usually been excluded. Drugs such as phenelzine or sertraline have shown greater acute efficacy than CBT in trials comparing the two modalities. Phenelzine plus CBT, and sertraline plus CBT, showed modestly greater efficacy than the respective drug monotherapies alone in controlled trials. Remission has not been assessed in any trials, and there is also no agreement on the criteria to define remission in social anxiety disorder. Negative findings from controlled trials exist for buspirone, atenolol, moclobemide, and fluoxetine in generalized social anxiety disorder (for a review see Roy-Byrne & Cowley, 2002).

Social Anxiety Disorder in Children and Adolescents

Increased self-consciousness and preoccupation with social matters are extremely common during late childhood and early adolescence, a developmental stage in which the importance of peers is typically heightened. Accordingly, adult epidemiological studies have also consistently indicated that onset of social phobia is common during late childhood, with onset typically occurring between ages 11 and 12 (Albano, 2003). Differentiating normative adolescent social concerns from the clinical social anxiety disorder poses difficulties for clinicians, parents, teachers, and adolescents alike, and perhaps the best way to parse the two is to examine functional impairment and concomitant symptoms: compared to non-anxious counterparts, youth with social anxiety disorder more often report depressed mood, high trait anxiety, and perceived social incompetence (Albano, Chorpita, & Barlow, 2003), higher levels of loneliness and fewer friends (Beidel, Turner, & Morris, 1999), a wide range of social avoidance (Albano, Detweiler, Logsdon-Conradsen, Walker, & Ollendick, 1999), and, in at least some cases, social anxiety is associated with school refusal (Kearney & Drake, 2002). Given the potentially serious consequences of social anxiety disorder and its sequalae for the life trajectory of adolescents, detection and treatment are especially important.

Psychosocial Treatment for Social Anxiety Disorder in Children and Adolescents

There is an increasing body of evidence demonstrating the efficacy of CBT approaches for children and adolescents with anxiety disorders, which has included those with social phobia (or with the previous diagnostic term, avoidant disorder). A number of controlled trials targeting anxious children have included those diagnosed with social phobia (Barrett, Dadds, & Rapee, 1996; Barrett, 1998; Cobham, Dadds, & Spence, 1998; Dadds et al., 1999; Dadds, Spence, Hol-

land, Barrett, & Laurens, 1997; Flannery-Schroeder & Kendall, 2000; Ginsburg & Schlossberg, 2002; Kendall, 1994; Kendall et al., 1997; Last, Hansen, & Franco, 1998; Lumpkin, Silverman, Weems, Markham, & Kurtines, 2002; Silverman et al., 1999a, 1999b).

Three Type 1 randomized, controlled cognitive-behavioral treatment studies specifically for children and adolescents with social phobia have reported positive clinical response. Hayward et al. (2000) randomly assigned 35 female adolescents with social phobia to cognitive-behavioral group therapy (CBGT) ($N = 12$) or no treatment ($N = 23$). Eleven of the 12 cases completed the active treatment. After 16 weeks of treatment, significantly fewer treated patients met criteria for social phobia. At 1-year follow-up, however, there was no difference between the two groups, suggesting that the CBGT may result in a moderate short-term effect. Spence, Donovan, and Brechman-Toussaint (2000) randomly assigned 50 children with social phobia, ages 7–14 years, to either child-focused CBT, CBT plus parent involvement, or a wait-list control. The integrated CBT program involved intensive social skills training with graded exposure and cognitive challenging. After treatment, children in both CBT groups had a greater decrease in social and general anxiety and a greater increase in parental ratings of child social skills than did those in the wait-list control group. At 12-month follow-up, both CBT groups had retained their improvement. Beidel, Turner, and Morris (2000) demonstrated the efficacy of social effectiveness therapy for children (SET-C) in comparison to an active but nonspecific intervention (Testbusters): children ages 8–12 treated with SET-C had enhanced social skill, reduced social anxiety, decreased associated psychopathology, and increased social interaction both at posttreatment and at 6-month follow-up.

Researchers have also examined whether the treatment should be delivered individually, with family, or with peers. In the Spence et al. (2000) study described above, superior results seemed to have emerged when parents were involved in CBT treatment, but this effect was not statistically significant. In a Type 3 study, Masia, Klein, Storch, and Corda (2001) piloted a school-based behavioral treatment for adolescents and concluded that the school setting is a logical place to deliver the treatment because it is where the individuals with social anxiety endure the most distress.

Current research is attempting to identify the necessary or sufficient components in the psychosocial treatment of social phobia, as well as the optimal context. Based on meta-analyses of adult studies, exposure in some form may be a key ingredient (Beidel et al., 2000). Treatment of the adolescent with social phobia may require different treatment interventions from those used in the younger ages (Beidel et al., 2000; Spence et al., 2000).

Pharmacotherapy of Social Anxiety Disorder in Children and Adolescents

As recently as 1999, no definitive data existed on the efficacy of psychopharmacology in the treatment of anxiety disorders in youth (excluding OCD) (Labellarte, Ginsburg, Walkup, & Riddle, 1999). In 2001, fluvoxamine, an SSRI, was studied in children and adolescents 6 to 17 years of age with either social phobia, SAD, or generalized anxiety disorder (GAD; Walkup et al., 2001). Youth ($N = 153$) were evaluated and enrolled in a 3-week open treatment trial with supportive psychoeducational therapy. Only five children improved with brief psychoeducation and did not go on to medication therapy. One hundred and twenty-eight children were assigned to either fluvoxamine or placebo for 8 weeks. The fluvoxamine dose was increased every week by 50 mg to a maximum of 300 mg/day for adolescents and 250 mg/day for children less than 12 years of age. The average dose of fluvoxamine was 2.9 + 1.3 mg/kg, and the average last dose was 4.0 + 2.2 mg/kg. The medication was generally well tolerated; five children in the fluvoxamine group and one in the placebo group discontinued because of adverse effects. Adverse effects were more common in the medication group; abdominal discomfort was significantly greater in the fluvoxamine group than in the placebo group, and there was a trend toward a greater frequency of increased motor activity in the fluvoxamine group. The youth in the fluvoxamine group had significantly greater reductions in symptoms of anxiety and higher rates of clinical response

than did the children in the placebo group. On the CGI scale, 48 of 63 (76%) of children had a response to treatment, in comparison to only 19 of 65 children (29%; $p < .001$). The study led to the conclusion that fluvoxamine is an effective treatment for children and adolescents with social phobia, SAD, or generalized anxiety.

In follow-up analyses, Walkup and colleagues (RUPP, 2003) examined the data for moderators and mediators of pharmacologic response in these 128 youths. Interestingly, no significant moderators of efficacy were identified, except for lower baseline depression scores, based on "parent" (but not "child") report, which were associated with greater improvement. Patients with social phobia and greater severity of illness, irrespective of medical assignment, were less likely to improve. Further study will be needed to determine why the diagnosis of social phobia predicted a less favorable outcome in this specific study.

Although there have been few studies examining the effects of treatments that combine CBT and medication in adults, no systematic studies of combined treatment for children and adolescents with social phobia exist. Given the lack of information about adolescents with anxiety disorders, efficacy studies on both CBT and pharmacotherapy and on the relative efficacy of each treatment alone and in combination are very much needed.

Selective Mutism: Is It a Form of Social Phobia?

Over the last 10 years, the literature has focused on the relationship between selective mutism and social phobia across developmental phases, in particular as to whether selective mutism is a childhood form of later social phobia. Selective mutism is currently classified under "disorders usually first diagnosed in infancy, childhood or adolescence," in DSM-IV (American Psychiatric Association, 1994). There is an emerging consensus that it is most consistent with an anxiety disorder. Although still somewhat debated, selective mutism may represent a childhood form of social phobia (Black & Uhde, 1992, 1995; Dummit et al., 1997; Steinhausen & Juzi, 1996). Some have argued that selective mutism should not continue to be a separate diagnostic category but rather be considered a symptom, or subtype, of social phobia (Anstendig, 1999; Black & Uhde, 1995; Dummit et al., 1997).

Psychosocial (Behavioral) Treatment for Selective Mutism

Behavioral treatment of selective mutism has generally been the initial and the primary intervention in clinical practice, but there are no randomized controlled trials (RCTs) evaluating behavioral treatment. On the basis of Type 6 case reports and single case designs, contingency management, exposure-based techniques, and self-modeling are the most frequently used behavioral interventions (Anstendig, 1998; Cunningham, Cataldo, Mallion, & Keyes, 1984; Holmbeck & Lavigne, 1992; Kehle, Owens, & Cressy, 1990).

Pharmacological Treatment of Selective Mutism

Despite the paucity of controlled trials on the efficacy of medications for the treatment of selective mutism, pharmacotherapy is often used in clinical practice. In one Type 1 report, Black and Uhde (1994) treated 16 children with selective mutism with single-blind placebo for 2 weeks. The 15 placebo nonresponders were then randomly assigned to double-blind treatment with fluoxetine ($N = 6$) or placebo ($N = 9$) for 12 weeks. The mean maximum dose of fluoxetine was 21.4 mg/day (range 12–27 mg/day, 0.60 to 0.62 mg/kg/day). Side effects were minimal, and all double-blind patients completed the 12 weeks. Patients on fluoxetine ($N = 6$) were significantly better than those on placebo ($N = 9$) on parent's rating of mutism change and global change. However, clinician and teacher ratings did not show any significant differences between those receiving medication and those on placebo. The authors suggested that this could in part be due to the small number of patients or the more severe baseline symptoms of the medication group. Nevertheless, the authors cautioned that despite improvement for some,

patients in both groups remained very symptomatic at the end of the study.

Generalized Anxiety Disorder

Treatment of Generalized Anxiety Disorder in Adults

Several CBT programs have been developed and empitacally evaluated for GAD. As might be expected given the nature of GAD, some of these protocols place less emphasis on exposure to specific fear cues and instead focus primarily on the development of effective coping strategies, of which exposure-based procedures (e.g., worry time) are among several techniques used. The outcome data for CBT are generally encouraging, with several meta-analytic reports indicating very large within-subjects effects and moderate to large effects in comparison to psychosocial control treatments and to low-dose diazepam treatment (Borkovec & Ruscio, 2001; Gould, Buckminster, Pollack, Otto, & Yap, 1997). Although the efficacy of several CBT programs has been established, outcome studies also suggest that there is significant room for improvement, especially with respect to the percentage of patients who achieve high end-state functioning (Orsillo, Roehmer, & Barlow, 2003). This observation has prompted recent innovations in GAD treatment, including the addition of interpersonal elements into the existing CBT programs (Borkovec, Newman, & Castonguay, 2003).

Several medications have been found effective for acute treatment of GAD. Benzodiazepines, such as alprazolam, have demonstrated short-term efficacy for reducing GAD symptoms, with response rates (usually defined as a 40%–50% improvement in symptoms on the Hamilton Anxiety Scale or a CGI improvement rating of "moderately" or "much" improved) as high as 75%. Benzodiazepines have the advantage of being faster acting than alternative medications. Despite concerns about side effects (e.g., sedation, memory loss, physiologic dependence, withdrawal syndromes), benzodiazepines are still among the most widely used medications for treatment of GAD. Buspirone has also been found effective in controlled trials and its side-effect profile (e.g., not sedating) may be better tolerated by some patients than that of benzodiazepines.

Antidepressant medications have shown efficacy for GAD in controlled trials. Because of very high rates of comorbidity of GAD with depressive disorders and symptoms, antidepressant medications may provide additional benefits for GAD patients. However, most antidepressants are slower acting than benzodiazepines, often taking 3–4 weeks for benefits to become obvious. Tricyclic antidepressants (TCAs) such as imipramine demonstrated benefit over placebo in early controlled trials, yet recent controlled trials have shown benefits for newer antidepressants such as the SSRI paroxetine and the dual serotonin–norepinephrine reuptake inhibitor (SNRI) venlafaxine-XR. The latter is the first antidepressant to receive a U.S. Food and Drug Administration (FDA) indication for treatment of GAD. These antidepressants are well tolerated and lend to long-term treatment, and not surprisingly have quickly become commonplace for treatment of GAD. For a detailed review of pharmacotherapy for adult GAD see the report by Roy-Byrne and Cowley (2002).

In examining the relative and combined efficacy of CBT and medication, Power et al. (1990) randomly assigned 113 patients to one of five treatment conditions: CBT + diazepam (DZ), CBT + placebo (PBO), CBT alone, DZ alone, and PBO. Percent responders, defined as reduction of >2 standard deviations from pretreatment, at posttreatment were 90.5% for CBT + DZ, 83% for CBT + PBO, 86% for CBT, 68% for DZ, and 37% for PBO. All active treatments were superior to PBO, but did not differ from one another. Percent responders at 6-month follow-up were 71% for CBT + DZ, 67% for CBT + PBO, 71% for CBT, and 41% for DZ; chi-squared analysis revealed the superiority of treatments that included CBT treatments over medication (DZ) alone.

Generalized Anxiety Disorder in Children and Adolescents

Generalized Anxiety Disorder is primarily excessive worry in one or more areas of one's life. Youth with GAD are often viewed by others as "little adults" because their worries may focus on keeping schedules, family finances, the environment, health issues, relationships, and perfectionism—themes that are more typically concerns for adults. Youth with GAD may not be disruptive or acting-out in their behavior, so their difficulties may go unnoticed by parents, family, and teachers. Nevertheless, their internal distress interferes with their overall functioning.

Preliminary data evidences developmental differences in symptom report between older and younger children with GAD (formerly overanxious disorder [OAD]), and it seems that with age, children's manifestation of GAD changes in both content and in symptom number (Kendall & Pimentel, 2003; Strauss, Lease, Last, & Francis, 1988). There also appear to be differences across GAD symptoms with respect to their efficiency in yielding a DSM-IV diagnosis (Pina, Silverman, Alfano, & Saavedra, 2002). In addition, older children, over the age of 12, present with a higher number of overall symptoms, as well as more anxiety about past events. This increase in symptom report may be somewhat GAD-specific, rather than a mere function of increased age, as findings with youth with SAD often reveal that younger children report more symptoms than do older children (Francis, Last, & Strauss, 1987).

Psychosocial Treatment of Generalized Anxiety Disorder in Children and Adolescents

Historically, a wide range of treatments has been used to treat youth with GAD, including various psychological approaches (e.g., behavioral, cognitive-behavioral, psychodynamic, family, play) as well as medications. Only a very small number of treatments have met the criteria for and have been assigned the label of "empirically supported." With regard to GAD, much of this research has been with children, not with adolescents. Our descriptions here of the treatment of GAD in youth will place an emphasis on the treatments that have received empirical support.

The results of several Type 1 randomized clinical trials using CBT, conducted by different research groups, support the application of this approach (Barrett, Rapee, Dadds, & Ryan, 1996; Flannery-Schroeder & Kendall, 2000; Kendall, 1994; Kendall et al., 1997; Mendlowitz et al., 1999). Evidence to date suggests that CBT for children and adolescents is effective compared to no-treatment control conditions (e.g., Barrett, Dadds, & Rapee, 1996; Kendall, 1994; Kendall et al., 1997) and that CBT for youth with anxiety is a "probably efficacious" treatment (Chambless & Hollon, 1998).

An initial Type 1 randomized clinical trial evaluated a CBT protocol with 8- to 13-year-old children (Kendall, 1994). The manual-based CBT intervention (called the "Coping Cat") targets one or more of the following disorders; SAD, social phobia, and GAD. A large percentage of the cases in the report were highly comorbid and many had GAD as the primary disorder. Cognitive-behavioral therapy addresses the cognitive biases associated with anxiety through psychoeducation, cognitive restructuring to change self-talk, relaxation training, guided imagery, problem solving, and numerous graded exposure tasks. In this RCT, 47 children ages 8 to 13 years were randomized to either CBT or a wait-list condition. Children in the CBT condition demonstrated significant improvement from pre- to posttreatment on self-reported distress, parent-reported distress of child, and, importantly, diagnostic status. Specifically, 66% of treated children no longer met criteria for their principal anxiety diagnosis following treatment.

In a second Type 1 randomized clinical trial (Kendall et al., 1997), 94 children aged 9 to 13 years were randomized to the CBT protocol or a wait-list condition. Over 50% of treated youth were free of their principal diagnosis at posttreatment, with significant reductions in disorder severity even for the youth remaining symptomatic. Other controlled trials (e.g., Barrett, 1998) support the efficacy of CBT in childhood anxiety (for review see Kazdin & Weisz, 1998; Ollendick & King, 2000) and CBT protocols have also been adapted to the group format (Flannery-Schroeder & Kendall, 2000; Manassis et al., 2002; Silverman et al., 1999a).

When considering the treatment of adolescents with GAD, one must take into account that the literature on the treatment of "child and adolescent" anxiety is based primarily on studies that have evaluated treatments for youth ages 7 to 14, with a mean age around 10.6 (e.g., Barrett, Dadds et al., 1996; Kendall, 1994; Kendall et al., 1997). Moreover, in one of these studies (Barrett, Dadds, et al., 1996), the treatment effects were not the same across age ranges, showing that a combined CBT and family intervention was significantly more effective than CBT alone for 7- to 10-year-old children, but not for 11- to 14-year-old children. This finding suggests that older children might respond differently than younger children to the same treatment. More research on this important topic is sorely needed.

Most of the CBT treatments that have been empirically supported for children have substantial room for improvement when applied to adolescents. First, we cannot assume that previous findings from children ages 7 to 14 automatically apply to all adolescents. Second, adolescence is a transitional period, characterized by more biological, physical, psychological, and social role changes than any other stage except infancy (Kendall & Williams, 1986). However, these developmental differences among children and adolescents have been largely ignored in treatment outcome studies of anxious youth. Holmbeck and colleagues (2000) note, "although many authors advocate for adaptations of treatment manuals in ways that take development into account, few provide methods for doing so" (Holmbeck et al., 2000, p. 339). Similarly, Weisz and Hawley (2002) assert that one of the long-term goals for the field of treatment outcome research should be to "develop an array of developmentally tailored treatments that are effective with clinically referred teens" (p. 21). Because treatments have not fully addressed the developmental changes of adolescence, one could argue that the impact of the treatment on the adolescent's anxiety disorder has not yet been examined empirically.

To date, no controlled studies have investigated CBT for adolescent GAD. It is important for such studies to be conducted because GAD is prevalent in adolescents (see Merikangas & Avenevoli, 2002).

Pharmacotherapy of Generalized Anxiety Disorder in Children and Adolescents

There are limited data on pharmacotherapy of GAD, and anxiety disorders in youth in general, with the exception of OCD (March, Biederman, et al., 1998). This situation exists despite the fact that there has been an increase in the use of psychotropic medications in child and adolescent samples (Pincus et al., 1998; Zito et al., 2000). There are few adequately designed studies available that establish the safety and efficacy of any class of medication for childhood GAD (Allen, Leonard, & Swedo, 1995; Bernstein, Borchardt, & Perwein, 1996). Medication options for the treatment of GAD in children and adolescents would appear to include the benzodiazepines, the nonbenzodiazepine anxiolytic buspirone, the SSRIs, and the TCAs. These medications have efficacy in adult GAD (Rickels, Downing, Schweizer, & Hassman, 1993) and venlafaxine has also been shown to be effective for adult GAD (Derivan, Entsuah, Haskins, Rudolph, & Aguiar, 1997; Rickels, Pollack, Sheehan, & Haskins, 2000). However, at this juncture there are not adequate data with regard to the use of medications with adolescents.

Although there exists a literature on the effectiveness of benzodiazepines in adult anxiety disorders (Rickels et al., 1983; Rickels, Schweizer, Case, & Greenblatt, 1990), there have been only a few studies, with small sample sizes, to examine the use of benzodiazepines in childhood anxiety disorders (Biederman, 1987; Graae, Milner, Rizzotto, & Klein, 1994; Simeon et al., 1992). Most of the studies involve children and adolescents with additional comorbidities such as major depression, panic disorder, and school refusal (Bernstein, Garfinkel, & Borchardt, 1990; Kutcher & Mackenzie, 1988). The results of these studies are mixed, with some finding positive results and others finding limited efficacy for benzodiazepines. Because of the inconsistency in results, reports of potentially serious side effects (Rickels et al., 1990, 1993), and risk of dependency and withdrawal, the benzodiazepines cannot be considered a front-line treatment.

Although buspirone has been shown to have both anxiolytic and antidepressants affects in adults (Rickels et al., 1990, 1991), it does not appear to be a highly effective or broad-spectrum anxiolytic in youth (Pohl, Balon, Yergani, & Gershon, 1989; Sheehan, Raj, Sheehan, & Soto, 1990).

Most of the clinical trials in which TCAs were used did not have children and adolescents with GAD only, but rather the much more complicated comorbid group of "school-refusing" children. The several Type 1 placebo-controlled studies of TCAs for children with anxiety-based school refusal provide conflicting results (Berney et al., 1991; Bernstein et al., 1990; Gittelman-Klein & Klein, 1973; Klein, Manuzza, Chapman, & Fyer, 1992). None of these studies were designed to examine children with the primary diagnosis of GAD, so no conclusions can be drawn as to the efficacy of TCAs for this anxiety disorder. Another issue of concern with TCA use in children is associated with a growing recognition of cardiac risk (Popper & Ziminitzky, 1995; Riddle, Geller, & Ryan, 1993; Riddle, Nelson, et al., 1991; Varley & McClellan, 1997). Given the uncertain clinical efficacy of TCAs for anxiety-disordered children (including GAD) plus the significant side effects, this class of medication is not a first choice.

The SSRI antidepressants are potential candidates for the treatment of childhood GAD. The safety of the SSRIs recommends them, as does their effectiveness in treating depression, which may be comorbid with childhood GAD. The SSRIs have shown preliminary efficacy in the treatment of adult GAD (Pohl, Wolkow, & Clary, 1998) and there is some evidence to suggest the use of SSRIs to treat childhood GAD. Unfortunately, the majority of studies include patients with GAD, SAD, social phobia, selective mutism, and anxiety disorder not otherwise specified. In Type 3 open trials, fluoxetine has shown some preliminary benefit for overanxious disorder, SAD, and social phobia (Birmaher et al., 1994; Fairbanks et al., 1997; Manassis & Bradley, 1994). In a Type 1 study, Rynn, Siqueland, and Rickels (2001) randomized ($n = 22$) children meeting the diagnosis of GAD to receive either placebo or 50 mg (maximum dose) of sertraline for 9 weeks, with positive results. The main side effects of the sertraline-treated children, as compared to the placebo-treated children, were dry mouth, drowsiness, leg spasms, and restlessness. The RUPP study (2001), mentioned earlier, also provides supportive evidence.

There have been previous reports of activation or agitation with the SSRIs, and it appears to be dose related (Apter et al., 1994; Riddle, Harin, & King, 1990; Riddle, King, et al., 1991). With these recent positive studies, it appears that SSRIs are emerging as the first line medication treatment for childhood anxiety disorders. Because of withdrawal symptoms being reported with the discontinuation of SSRIs, including nausea, headache, dizziness, and agitation (Labellarte, Walkup, & Riddle, 1998), these medications should not be abruptly discontinued.

The combination of medications and CBT for the treatment of GAD has several potential merits and a few potential enigmas. First, the GAD youth who is nonresponsive to one of the approaches may be responsive to the other or to their combination. Second, on the optimistic side, it may be that the combined treatment effect is additive—medications reduce initial distress and prepare the client for a more active and involved participation in CBT treatment. A less optimistic view of the combined treatment is that a medication may detract from the efficacy of CBT. That is, if exposure to the situation and the facing of the unwanted emotional distress in that situation contribute to the efficacy of CBT, then it is possible that the medication-produced nonanxious condition will prevent the CBT participant from experiencing the anxiety during exposure to in vivo tasks. The effectiveness of the medications could undermine one of the thought-to-be-active aspects of CBT (habituation to anxiety in the situation). Clearly, research on this question is very much needed.

Separation Anxiety Disorder

Distress upon separation from home or caretakers is a normal developmental feature. However, it can become so intense as to cause marked interference with ordinary function. In the extreme, children or adolescents are limited in their independent activities, unable to venture out alone, and may resist going to school. In young children fear of going to school (school phobia) is almost invariably due to separation anxiety, whereas in adolescence, social anxiety or depression may be involved. Likewise, childhood school refusal behavior is often associated with SAD, whereas school refusal behavior in adolescents may be more strongly linked to social anxiety disorder.

Psychosocial Treatment of Separation Anxiety Disorder in Children and Adolescents

Indirect information on psychosocial treatment comes from a Type 1 controlled study of behavior therapy combined with either imipramine or a placebo in 45 6- to 14-year-olds with school refusal specifically due to separation anxiety (Gittelman-Klein & Klein, 1971, 1973). To enter the drug study, children had to fail 4 weeks of vigorous behavioral therapy (Gittelman-Klein, 1975)—half (50%) of the children responded. With another 6 weeks of behavior therapy, now combined with a placebo, another 20% improved; thus 70% of severely separation-anxious children derived marked benefit from 10 weeks of behavior therapy. The comprehensive behavioral treatment in the Gittelman-Klein report had beneficial impact, but its precise efficacy is unknown because there were no comparison conditions. A Type 3 naturalistic study of school refusers reported superior efficacy of behavior therapy compared to inpatient care and to home schooling (Blagg & Yule, 1984). The lack of randomization weakens the conclusions.

Type 1 studies of CBT for children with school refusal behavior have also been conducted (King, Leonard, & March, 1998; Last, Hansen, & Franco, 1998). King et al. (1998) found that 4 weeks of CBT was superior to a wait-list control. School attendance was higher in the treated children than in the untreated children (89% vs. 60%), and ratings of anxiety also showed meaningful differences. In contrast, Last et al. (1998) found no significant difference in the improvement rate between CBT and standardized educational support treatment: mean percentages of school attendance were 67% and 60%, respectively. The more stringent criterion of 95% school attendance was met by 22% of the CBT group and 21% of those receiving educational support. In both treatments, a high rate of children judged themselves to be improved, as did parents and clinicians (90% to 100%), but considerably less were considered well by independent raters.

Other studies of CBT have not focused solely on SAD but have included youth with this disorder in addition to other anxiety disorders. These studies have reported efficacy in treating SAD (e.g., Kendall, 1994; Kendall et al., 1997). Another Type 1 study (Silverman et al., 1999a) focused mostly on specific fears, the majority (67%) consisting of anxiety at bedtime requiring the presence of a parent, a cardinal symptom of separation anxiety. Following 10 weeks, children showed similar patterns of improvement with CBT, behavior therapy focusing on training parents in contingency management, or educational support.

Some investigators have examined whether parental involvement in treatment contributes to childrens' improvement. Of all the childhood anxiety disorders, SAD can be said to have the most direct impact on the family. Consequently, there is a strong rationale for parental involvement in treatment. A study of anxious school refusers reported significant superiority for the condition involving parents and teachers in the children's treatment, compared to treatment without this component (Heyne et al., 2002), but the advantage was not sustained over a 5-month follow-up. In a recent Type 1 study, group CBT was compared to a group family anxiety management program and to a wait-list control for youth with mixed anxiety disorders, 43% of whom had separation anxiety (Barrett, 1998). The treatments were superior to the wait-list condition, but did not differ from each other on most outcome measures.

Pharmacotherapy of Separation Anxiety Disorder in Children and Adolescents

The first use of a pharmacological agent, imipramine, in SAD derived from a postulated re-

lationship between this childhood condition and adult panic disorder (Klein, 1964; Klein & Fink, 1962). Marked clinical benefit for imipramine (mean 125 mg/day) versus a placebo was reported in a Type 1 study of 45 children with school phobia and separation anxiety (Gittelman-Klein & Klein, 1971). A smaller study (N = 20) failed to replicate earlier positive findings (Klein, Koplewicz, & Kanner, 1992). These two treatment studies targeted SAD specifically. Another study failed to observe a significant advantage in school-phobic children treated with relatively low doses of clomipramine (75 mg/day) (Berney et al., 1981). More recently, a Type 1 controlled trial in adolescent school refusers reported efficacy for imipramine (Bernstein et al., 2000), but interpretation is complicated by the comorbidity of major depression. The well-documented cardiotoxic effects of high doses of TCAs have limited their usefulness, especially since SSRIs do not present such a risk.

Clinical reports have claimed benefit from high-potency benzodiazepines (i.e., clonazepam) in mixed anxiety, but the only Type 1 controlled trial did not confirm these clinical observations (Graae et al., 1994). The design of this trial was less than rigorous, however. Benzodiazepines can induce behavioral disinhibition in children, which limits their application.

As noted earlier, a Type 1 multisite, placebo-controlled study (N = 128) of fluvoxamine (up to 300 mg/day) in children with separation anxiety, social anxiety, and generalized anxiety disorders reported a marked advantage for the medication (RUPP, 2001) with an overall improvement rate of 78% for fluvoxamine vs. 29% for placebo. There were no interactions for diagnosis and treatment outcome, except for the lesser response rate among patients with social phobia than that among those with other diagnoses (RUPP, 2003). Therefore, it may be surmised that SAD responded to fluvoxamine.

At this time, SSRIs may be the first-line pharmacological treatment for childhood SAD, but we are in need of information specifically regarding adolescents. On the whole, the SSRIs are well tolerated and have a favorable side effect profile, and some have demonstrated efficacy.

Specific Phobia

Treatment of Specific Phobia in Adults

Although it is relatively uncommon for adults with only a specific phobia to seek treatment, it is also one of the most effectively treated disorders. The primary treatment for specific phobias is CBT. Several controlled studies have found that up to 90% of participants experienced significant symptom reduction within 2 to 3 hr of therapy (Öst, 1989; Öst, Ferbee, & Furmark, 1997; Öst, Salkovskis, & Hellstroem, 1991). The effectiveness of CBT is likely the result of exposing the patient to feared stimuli in a supportive environment. This is commonly done systematically, with the therapist using a hierarchy to address the patient's fears. Research has also shown that although exposures tend to be more effective when therapists model the treatment tasks for the patient, direct observation in and of itself is generally not sufficient (e.g., Öst et al., 1997). With the exception of dental phobias (e.g., Jerremalm, Jaansson, & Öst, 1986), cognitive therapy alone has not been examined in the treatment of specific phobias.

Researchers have examined the effectiveness of benzodiazepines, beta-blockers, and SSRIs in treating specific phobias. Some controlled studies have found benzodiazepines to be helpful for patients who are averse to initial exposures to feared stimuli, or who simply need acute symptom relief (e.g., Schmidt, Koselka, & Woolaway-Bickel, 2001). However, both controlled and uncontrolled studies have found long-term use of benzodiazepines to be associated with unsatisfactory outcome and a myriad of other complications (Sanderson & Wetzler, 1993; Westra & Stewart, 1998). These unwanted effects include depression, a higher rate of symptom relapse once drugs are discontinued, and a risk of drug tolerance, dependence, and abuse (Spiegel & Bruce, 1997).

The use of benzodiazepines in conjunction with exposure therapy was found to interfere with the treatment efficacy of exposure (e.g., Marks et al., 1993; Wilhelm & Roth, 1997). Studies have shown benzodiazepines to interfere with both the acquisition and retention of new information (Barbee, Black, & Tordorov, 1992) and to affect the way new information is stored in memory (Gray, 1987). This interference can cause state-dependent learning, whereby information encoded in the presence of the drug may not be properly retrieved in a drug-free state. In addition, uncontrolled studies have reported that the use of benzodiazepines can interfere with the development of tolerance to anxiogenic stimuli on a neurochemical level (Gray, 1987). It has been speculated that these medications interfere with the central nervous system's ability to adapt to persistently elevated levels of neurotransmitters involved in the stress response (Anisman & Zacharko, 1992). More research is needed to further examine these potentially important findings.

Specific Phobia in Children and Adolescents

Fear is a normal response to active or imagined threat that is characterized by affective, behavioral, and cognitive components. As discussed elsewhere (King et al., 1988; Ollendick, King, & Muris, 2002), nearly all children and adolescents experience some degree of fear. For the most part, these fears are adaptive—they appear to emanate from day-to-day experiences of children and they reflect their emerging cognitive and representational capabilities. Moreover, most of these fears do not involve intense or persistent reactions, and they are short-lived. This is not so with specific phobias.

Psychosocial Treatment of Specific Phobia in Children and Adolescents

Using criteria established for empirically supported treatments (see Chambless & Hollon, 1998; Chambless & Ollendick, 2000), Ollendick and King (1998, 2000) have indicated that two psychosocial treatments have attained "well-established" status (participant modeling, reinforced practice) and five treatments have achieved "probably efficacious" status (imaginal desensitization, in vivo desensitization, live modeling, filmed modeling, and verbal self-instruction) in the treatment of phobic disorders in children. The well-established treatments have been shown to be more effective than credible placebo controls in at least two RCTs, whereas probably efficacious treatments have been shown to be more effective than wait-list control conditions in at least two RCTs or to be more effective than a credible placebo control in at least one RCT. Support for these interventions has come solely from intervention studies with children 12 or 13 years of age and younger. None of the studies treated specific phobia in adolescents. More research is needed with adolescents to determine the efficacy of behavioral treatments for them. Two recent studies conducted have examined cognitive-behavioral interventions in samples that included adolescents.

In the first Type 1 study examining the treatment of both children and adolescents, Silverman et al. (1999b) examined the relative benefits of an operant-based contingency management treatment and a cognitive-based self-control treatment, in comparison to an education-support control group. Graduated in vivo exposure was used in both the self-control and the contingency management conditions but not in the education-support condition. Phobic children ($N = 81$) between 6 and 16 years of age along with their parents were evaluated using child, parent, and clinician measures. The children were assigned randomly to one of the three 10-week manualized treatment conditions (i.e., self-control, contingency management, or education support). Although all three conditions were found to impart improvement in the child's functioning as measured by the reports of children, parents, and clinicians, clinically significant improvements were noted only in the two cognitive-behavioral treatment conditions. Specifically, on a measure of clinical distress at posttreatment, 80% of the participants in the self-control and 80% of the participants in the contingency management conditions reported very little or no distress, compared to only 25% in the education-support condition. Notably, 88% of the participants in the self-control condition no longer met diagnostic criteria at posttreatment compared to 55% in the contingency management and 56% in the education-support condition.

In the second Type 1 study, Öst, Svensson, Hellström, and Lindwall (2001) evaluated the effects of a cognitive-behavioral procedure referred to as "one-session treatment" on phobic children and adolescents 7 to 17 years old. The hall-mark of this one-session treatment is a graduated, systematic, prolonged exposure to the phobic stimulus combined with the active dissuading and repair of faulty cognition. As such, it involves a combination of strategies including cognitive restructuring, in vivo graduated exposure, participant modeling, and social reinforcement. Notably, this treatment has been designed to be maximally effective in one session, and therefore lasts 3 or more hours in length. Results indicated that the treatment was superior to wait-list and produced significant gains both immediately posttreatment and at 1-year follow-up (Öst et al., 2001). Also, in a Type 3 study, one-session treatment has been found to be comparable to other, longer treatments with more sessions (see Muris, Merckelbach, Holdrinet, & Sijsenaar, 1998). Presently, Ollendick and Öst are completing a larger Type 1 study examining the effectiveness of one-session treatment in comparison to educational support and wait-list conditions. Approximately 200 youth with specific phobias are participating in this trial, which is being conducted in the United States and Sweden.

Pharmacotherapy of Specific Phobia in Children and Adolescents

At present, no randomized pharmacological treatment studies of specific phobia in children and adolescents have been completed (Ginsburg & Walkup, 2004). The lack of such studies appears to be related to the common misconception that specific fears are a part of normal experience and not a condition associated with impairment. On the basis of the findings obtained with adults, however, SSRIs may be effective among children and adolescents with specific phobia (in contrast to the benzodiazepines and TCAs). A recent Type 3 open trial suggests their utility. Fairbanks et al. (1997) completed a 9-week trial of fluoxetine in children ages 9 to 18 years with mixed anxiety disorders ($N = 16$). After not responding to brief psychotherapy, patients were started on low-dose fluoxetine (5 mg/day), which was then increased weekly until side effects or improvement occurred to a maximum of 40 mg/day (children) and 80 mg/day (adolescents). Of the 16 patients enrolled, 6 had specific phobia and 4 of the 6 responded to fluoxetine. The medication was also generally well tolerated.

To date, no randomized clinical trials have examined the joint efficacy of psychosocial and pharmacologic treatments with children or adolescents. Given the promise of several treatments, however, there is reason to believe that beneficial effects of combined treatment may occur. Research into their combinatorial effects is needed before any conclusions can be drawn.

Panic Disorder

Treatment of Panic Disorder in Adults

The efficacy of cognitive, behavioral, and cognitive-behavioral treatment programs has been examined and is now well established for panic disorder. Under a broad theoretical umbrella, the emphasis in treatment has been on disconfirming mistaken beliefs about the meaning of physical sensations (Clark, 1986, 1996) and on exposing the patient to the feared physical sensations (Barlow, 1988). Cognitive-behavioral therapy has proven efficacious even when cognitive therapy is condensed (Clark et al., 1999). A commonly used protocol, panic control treatment, has been found to be efficacious in several studies (e.g., Zarate, Craske, & Barlow, 1990), and in the largest combined treatment study published to date, it was superior to pill placebo at the end of acute treatment but not superior to imipramine alone (Barlow et al., 2000). Notably, although panic control treatment typically includes breathing retraining, a procedure designed to minimize panic sensations, a recent controlled study indicated that the inclusion of breathing retraining did not provide incremental benefit above and beyond CBT alone, and on some outcome measures actually yielded less favorable outcome (Schmidt et al., 2000).

A wide range of medications have demonstrable efficacy for panic in the initial phase of treatment, including TCAs, low- and high-potency benzodiazepines, monoamine oxidase inhibitors (MAOIs), and SSRIs. Because of the comparable efficacy to that of older medications, yet a vastly superior side-effect profile, SSRIs are now considered first-line medications for treating panic. Pa-

roxetine was the first SSRI approved by the FDA for panic disorder and its antipanic effects have been demonstrated in placebo-controlled studies. A 12-week double-blind, placebo-controlled study of 367 panic patients found that both paroxetine and clomipramine were superior to placebo (Lecrubier, Bakker, Dunbar, & Judge, 1997). Compared to clomipramine, paroxetine acted more quickly to block spontaneous panic attacks, overall was associated with less adverse effects, and for 9 months after the 12-week acute phase demonstrated improvement. In a double-blind, placebo-controlled study, Ballenger, Davidson, Wheadon, and colleagues (1998) compared different doses of paroxetine and concluded that 40 mg daily was the most effective dosage. Sertraline (now also FDA approved), fluvoxamine, and fluoxetine have all shown significant ability to block panic compared to placebo. The general pattern of treatment response is as follows. First, spontaneous panic attacks are blocked, usually within the first 6 to 8 weeks. This is followed by a gradual reduction in anticipatory anxiety and agoraphobic avoidance behavior. A critical issue that has emerged from virtually all studies of SSRI treatment for panic is the vulnerability of these patients to jitteriness, restlessness, and increased anxiety during initial dosing. Starting with low doses is thus recommended (e.g., paroxetine 10 mg/day, sertraline 25 mg/day, fluvoxamine 50 mg/day, fluoxetine 10 mg/day) with gradual increases to the optimal target dose.

High-potency benzodiazepines are also effective for panic disorder. Alprazolam and clonazepam have been the most widely studied. In Phase 1 of the Cross-National Collaborative Panic study of 481 panic patients, alprazolam at a mean dose of 5.7 mg/day was more effective than placebo with a 55% response rate (compared to 32% placebo rate) at the 8-week end point (Ballenger, Davidson, Lecrbier, et al., 1998). Rosenbaum, Moroz, and Bowden (1997) conducted a multicenter, parallel group, placebo-controlled, fixed-dose study of clonazepam in 413 patients. Patients were randomly assigned to one of five fixed doses. The results indicated significant improvement at all doses but a differentiation of the four higher doses from the 0.5-mg dose and placebo. The minimum effective dose was 1 mg; beyond this dose all doses were equally efficacious. Reticence to prescribe benzodiazepines for panic has been based on the (unwarranted) assumption that patients will gradually escalate the dose to achieve therapeutic effect in a pattern similar to that seen in substance abusers. However, controlled studies have shown that panic disorder patients are not likely to increase dosages and actually found such increases to be uncomfortable and associated with unwanted effects (Salzman, 1993).

With respect to TCAs, imipramine has been the most studied antipanic agent, with several studies demonstrating superiority over placebo. The serotonergic-acting clomipramine also has strong antipanic effects and in one placebo-controlled trial was actually superior to imipramine and placebo (Modigh, Westberg, & Eriksson, 1992). However, the majority of studies point to equivalent efficacy for TCAs and SSRIs yet a superior side-effect profile with SSRIs (Bakker, Spinhoven, van der Does, van Balkom, & van Dyck, 2002). Although venlafaxine, nefazodone, and mirtazapine have not been studied in a controlled fashion, they have all been shown to exhibit antipanic action, particularly in patients with comorbid depression. For a detailed review of the literature on panic disorder treatment outcome see Roy-Byrne and Cowley (2002).

Panic Disorder in Children and Adolescents

Panic disorder can be a disabling condition accompanied by psychosocial, family, peer, and academic difficulties (Birmaher & Ollendick, 2004; Moreau & Weissman, 1992; Ollendick, Mattis, & King, 1994). In addition, panic disorder is associated with increased risk for other anxiety disorders, major depressive disorder (MDD), and substance abuse (Birmaher & Ollendick, 2004; Moreau & Weissman, 1992). Moreover, such adverse outcomes are more prevalent in adults whose panic disorder starts early in life (before 17 years of age; see Weissman et al., 1997). Despite this, it takes on average 12.7 years from the onset of reported symptoms for adults to initiate and seek treatment (Moreau & Follet, 1993). Unfortunately, it appears that very few youngsters

with panic disorder seek help at all (Essau, Condradt, & Petermann, 1999).

Psychosocial Treatment of Panic Disorder in Children and Adolescents

Psychosocial treatments for panic disorder have been based largely on cognitive and cognitive-behavioral theories (Chambless & Ollendick, 2000), and the few studies of cognitive-behavioral treatment of panic disorder in children and adolescents have used a protocol based largely on panic control treatment (Barlow, 1988). This treatment consists of three primary strategies: relaxation training and breathing retraining to address neurobiological sensitivities to stress, interoceptive exposure to address heightened somatic symptoms, and cognitive restructuring to address faulty misinterpretations associated with the somatic symptoms. Adolescent treatment studies based on Barlow's model have been sparse; however, two Type 3 case series studies lend initial support to its use and one randomized, large-scale, Type 1 treatment outcome study appears promising. In the first of the Type 3 studies, Barlow and Seidner (1983) treated three adolescents who had panic disorder with agoraphobia using an early version of panic control treatment. The patients were treated in a 10-session group-therapy format and were accompanied by their mothers, who were enlisted to facilitate behavior change. Following treatment, two of the three adolescents showed considerable improvement in their symptoms; the third did not show significant change. In the second of the Type 3 studies, Ollendick (1995) used a multiple baseline design to illustrate the effects of an adapted version of panic control treatment with four adolescents who had panic disorder with agoraphobia. The adolescents ranged in age from 13 to 17 years; however, their panic attacks began when they were between 9 and 13 years of age, nearly 4 years on average prior to the beginning of treatment. The patients were treated individually but, as in Barlow and Seidner's (1983) study, their mothers were enlisted to facilitate behavior change. Treatment varied in duration but lasted between 10 and 12 sessions for the four adolescents. Treatment was effective for all the patients eliminating panic attacks, reducing agoraphobic avoidance, decreasing accompanying negative mood states, and increasing self-efficacy for coping with previously avoided situations and panic attacks should they occur in the future.

Presently, Mattis and colleagues are in the final stages of a Type 1 RCT of a developmental adaptation of panic control treatment for adolescents (PCT-A) and a self-monitoring control condition in the treatment of panic disorder. Three aspects of panic disorder are addressed in this 11-session, manualized intervention: *(1)* the cognitive aspect of panic disorder or the tendency to misinterpret physical sensations as catastrophic; *(2)* the tendency to hyperventilate or overbreathe, thus creating and/or intensifying physical sensations of panic; and *(3)* conditioned fear reactions to the physical sensations. Although the trial is still under way, initial findings suggest a reduction in severity of panic attacks and panic disorder in patients receiving PCT-A relative to those in the monitoring control group (Mattis et al., 2001).

Pharmacotherapy of Panic Disorder in Children and Adolescents

No RCTs for the pharmacological treatment of panic disorder in children and adolescents have yet been completed (Birmaher & Ollendick, 2004). In children and adolescents, anecdotal case reports suggest that benzodiazepines and the SSRIs (Birmaher & Ollendick, 2004) may be efficacious for panic disorder. For example, in a prospective Type 3 open trial, Renaud, Birmaher, Wassick, and Bridge (1999) treated 12 children and adolescents with panic disorder with SSRIs for a period of 6 to 8 weeks. Nearly 75% of the youth showed much to very much improvement with SSRIs without experiencing significant side effects. At the end of the trial, eight (67%) no longer fulfilled criteria for panic disorder whereas four (33%) continued to have significant and lasting effects.

Panic disorder is accompanied frequently by a variety of other mental health disorders (Biederman, Faraone, et al., 2001; Mattis & Ollendick, 2002). Treatment of these comorbid conditions may be needed to improve the youngster's overall functioning. Fortunately, two of the common comorbid disorders, depression and other anxiety disorders, also respond to CBT and/or SSRIs (Birmaher et al., 1994; Brent et al., 1997; Emslie et al. 1997; Kendall et al., 1997; Ollendick & King, 1998; RUPP, 2001).

To date, no randomly controlled clinical trials have examined the joint efficacy of psychosocial and pharmacologic treatments with children or adolescents with panic disorder. Given the independent promise of both treatments, however, there is reason to believe that synergistic effects could occur. Nevertheless, research into their separate and combined effects, such as that pursued in adult populations (e.g., Barlow et al., 2000), is needed.

Obsessive-Compulsive Disorder

Treatment of Obsessive-Compulsive Disorder in Adults

Among the psychosocial treatments for OCD, exposure and response (or ritual) prevention (EX/RP) is the most well-established treatment for adults, having been found superior to a variety of active and control treatments (for a review see Franklin & Foa, 2002). In this treatment patients gradually confront situations that evoke their obsessional fears (e.g., sitting on the floor, where they feel contaminated by germs) and at the same time are refrained from reducing their discomfort by performing ritualistic behaviors (e.g., excessive washing and cleaning).

The only medications studied in randomized clinical trials and reported to be efficacious for OCD are serotonin reuptake inhibitors (e.g., clomipramine) and the SSRIs (e.g., fluoxetine, fluvoxamine, sertraline, paroxetine, citalopram). The data suggest a 20% to 40% reduction in symptoms, but many patients classified as responders in these trials still have clinically significant symptoms. Moreover, patients with severe comorbid MDD or significant substance abuse have usually been excluded (for a review see Dougherty, Rauch, & Jenike, 2002).

Several RCTs examining the efficacy of combined treatment have been conducted in OCD (Cottreaux et al., 1990; Foa, Rothbaum, & Furr, 2003; Hohagen et al., 1998; Marks et al., 1988; van Balkom et al., 1998), and their collective results suggest that combined treatment, at least as applied simultaneously, has not proven to be a panacea (Foa, Franklin, & Moser, 2002; Franklin & Foa, 2002). In trials directly comparing serotonin reuptake inhibitors (SRIs) and CBT (including EX/RP), outcome has been influenced by the design of the study, the SRI dosage, and the quality and the quantity of the EX/RP delivered. When intensive EX/RP (e.g., 15 sessions delivered five times per week for 3 weeks) was compared to adequately dosed clomipramine over 12 weeks, arguably the two most efficacious OCD treatments, the two treatments were both superior to placebo and EX/RP was superior in most analyses (Foa et al., 2005). Further, when results from this study using an intensive CBT approach are compared with a study employing weekly CBT with and without concomitant medication (Cottraux et al., 1990), intensive CBT alone appears to fare better than weekly CBT alone, with no differences evident in the combined treatment groups (Foa, Franklin, & Moser, 2002). It is important to note that response prevention in the study by Foa et al. (2005) appears to have been more strictly applied than that in the Cottraux et al. study (1990), and thus the effects of the visit schedule cannot be isolated in this comparison. Nevertheless, perhaps the addition of medication may enhance outcome when EX/RP is not implemented intensively or when variations are made to the EX/RP protocol.

Obsessive-Compulsive Disorder in Children and Adolescents

Children and adolescents with OCD typically present with both obsessions and compulsions, although the youngest sufferers may have difficulty articulating their obsessions. As is the case with adults, the cardinal feature of OCD in youth is neutralizing: when the patient describes anxiety-inducing thoughts or images and attempts to relieve this anxiety or reduce the chances that feared consequences would occur by performing some overt or covert neutralizing behavior, the OCD diagnosis should be considered. Functional impairment is required for diagnosis as well, as subclinical obsessions and compulsions are probably ubiquitous. Insight

into the senselessness of obsessional concerns is not required for diagnosis in children and adolescents, and, as with adults, probably exists along a continuum from complete awareness of their senselessness to no insight (Foa, Hearst-Ikeda, & Perry, 1995). In general pediatric OCD is formally similar to OCD in adults, yet the content of obsessions and compulsions is likely to be influenced by developmental factors. For example, younger children are generally more "magical" in their thinking and thus may have more superstitious OCD symptoms (e.g., "If I don't retrace my steps then something really bad will happen to my little sister"). As with adults, some pediatric OCD patients are able to identify feared consequences of not ritualizing (e.g., books will be stolen if the locker is not checked), whereas others experience anxiety and distress in the absence of articulated consequences. Further, although the logic of some patients' feared consequences is shared by many in their culture (e.g., contracting disease via direct contact with a public toilet seat), other patients' fears are extremely unusual (e.g., losing their essence by discarding trash that has touched them). It is important to recognize that bizarre content does not necessarily preclude a diagnosis of OCD and that patients with such unusual fears may also be responsive to CBT (Franklin, Tolin, March, & Foa, 2001).

A subgroup of children with pediatric onset of either OCD or a tic disorder has been described by the term *PANDAS* (Pediatric Autoimmune Neuropsychiatric Disorders Associated with Streptococcal infection). These children have an abrupt onset of symptoms after a group A β-hemolytic streptococcal infection (GABHS), and their course of illness is characterized by dramatic acute worsening of symptoms with periods of remission (Swedo 1994, Swedo et al., 1998). The PANDAS subgroup is defined by five clinical characteristics: *(1)* presence of OCD and/or a tic disorder; *(2)* prepubertal symptom onset; *(3)* dramatic onset and acute exacerbations with an episodic course of symptom severity; *(4)* temporal association between symptom exacerbations and GABHS infections; and *(5)* associated neurological abnormalities (e.g., choreiform movements) (Swedo et al., 1998). Identification of this subtype is important because the symptoms may require a different assessment and treatment. In a child who has an acute onset of OCD and/or tics or has had a dramatic deterioration, medical illnesses (including seemingly benign upper respiratory infections) in the prior months should be carefully considered. A throat culture, antistreptolysin O (ASO) titer, and anti-DNaseB streptococcal titer may help to diagnose such an infection, even in the absence of clinical symptoms of pharyngitis (Murphy & Pichichero, 2002; Swedo et al., 1998).

Psychosocial Treatments of Obsessive-Compulsive Disorder in Children and Adolescents

Expert Consensus Guidelines (March, Francis, Kahn, & Carpenter, 1997) and the American Academy of Child and Adolescent Psychiatry (AACAP) Practice Parameters for OCD (King et al., 1998) consider CBT, specifically the features of EX/RP, an important intervention, and recommend starting with CBT or CBT plus an SSRI, depending on severity and comorbidity. Exposure and response prevention involves therapist-assisted in vivo exposure to feared situations, imaginal exposure to feared "disasters," and instructions to refrain from rituals and avoidance behaviors. In the treatment of OCD, cognitive therapy procedures are sometimes used to identify faulty cognition, engage in cognitive restructuring and, with behavioral experiments, have the patient be exposed to situations that are designed to "disconfirm" the faulty cognition. Notably, exposure exercises provide the patient with the information that is needed to "correct" their distorted thinking without formal cognitive therapy.

Although CBT (specifically EX/RP) is recommended for children by Expert Concensus Guidelines and AACAP Practice Parameters (King et al., 1998; March, Frances, et al., 1997), there are no published large RCTs of CBT with children or adolescents. Uncontrolled CBT treatment trials reported to date suggest that most of the patients were responders, with a mean symptom decrease from 50% to 67%. March, Mulle, and Herbel (1994) reported on the outcome of a Type 3 study of a manualized and structured CBT protocol with 15 youth ages 8 to 18 years. There

were significant differences between pre- and posttreatment, with a mean reduction in symptom severity of about 50%. Sixty-seven percent of the patients had better than 50% symptom improvement (which was maintained at follow-up). Only 20% were nonresponders. At the end of treatment, 40% were rated as asymptomatic, and at follow-up 60% were rated as such. Forty percent of the sample was able to discontinue medication with booster sessions. This work has led to a manual for children and adolescents with OCD (8 to 17 years) (March & Mulle, 1998), and an RCT comparing the relative efficacy of this CBT manual, sertraline, combined treatment, and placebo has just been completed (Franklin, Foa, & March, 2003); a second RCT comparing EX/RP plus family therapy to relaxation is also nearing completion (J. Piacentini, personal communication).

Franklin and colleagues (1998) conducted a Type 3 study and reported that 14 youth (ages 10 to 17 years) had a 67% improvement at posttreatment, and found no difference in response between those who received CBT alone and those with CBT in combination with an SRI. Others have also reported generally positive results for CBT in Type 3 open studies (Piacentini et al., 1994; Wever & Rey, 1997). Most of the studies used a weekly therapy regimen, generally over 3 months. Wever and Rey (1997) used a more intensive CBT protocol of 10 daily sessions over 2 weeks and found generally similar results. Franklin and colleagues (1998) reported that there was no difference in results, regardless of whether the treatment was delivered in 14 weekly sessions over 14 weeks or in 18 sessions over 4 weeks, although there was no random assignment.

In the only published direct Type 1 comparison of CBT and pharmacotherapy for pediatric OCD, de Haan, Hoogduin, Buitelaar, and Keijsers (1998) reported that whereas CBT and clomipramine both appeared to reduce OCD symptoms, CBT was superior to clomipramine. Until the systematic comparisons of single and combined treatments are completed, the relative efficacy cannot be directly compared, although the existing data suggest that CBT may provide more durability than medication.

The family context may play an important

role in treating OCD. Freeman, Garcia, and Leonard (2003) proposed that the family is a vehicle for treatment of OCD in youth and in the treatment of childhood anxiety disorders more broadly (Barrett, Dadds, et al., 1996; Howard & Kendall, 1996; Sanders, 1996; Siqueland & Diamond, 1998). Cognitive-behavioral therapy with family intervention can and often does involve parents and significant others as "behavior change agents." Because the affective and cognitive aspects of the parent–child relationship, as well as the anxiety targets of intervention, are dealt with, the approach has been called cognitive-behavioral family therapy. Freeman and colleagues (2003) have manualized a treatment for children and their families with OCD, and initial pilot results are promising.

Pharmacotherapy of Obsessive-Compulsive Disorder in Children and Adolescents

The systematic efficacy studies of the SRIs for the treatment of pediatric OCD form the largest body of work in the pharmacotherapy of the childhood psychiatric disorders, other than that of ADHD. An increasing literature supports the acute efficacy of clomipramine and the SSRIs in the treatment of children and adolescents with OCD.

The TCA clomipramine (an SRI) was the first medication systematically studied in children and adolescents with OCD. Three studies supported the efficacy of clomipramine for pediatric OCD (DeVeaugh-Geiss et al., 1992; Flament et al., 1985; Leonard et al., 1989). Flament and colleagues (1985) reported in a Type 1 study that in 23 youth in a 10-week double-blind, placebo-controlled, crossover study, clomipramine (in doses of 3 mg/kg) was significantly more effective than placebo in decreasing OCD symptomatology at week 5. For some patients, a reduction in symptoms was seen by 3 weeks. Of the 19 children who completed the trial, 75% had a moderate to marked improvement, and only 16% of the patients were unchanged. Extending this finding in an 8-week multicenter double-blind, parallel Type 1 study, DeVeaugh-Geiss and colleagues (1992) reported that clomipramine was superior to placebo for the treatment of OCD in youth. The 31 patients on clomipramine

had a mean reduction in OCD severity scores of 37%, compared to 8% in the 29 patients on placebo. This study led to FDA approval for an SRI in pediatric OCD (children 10 years and older). The studies reported that clomipramine was generally well tolerated and had an anticholinergic adverse-effects profile. Periodic electrocardiograms (EKGs) are obtained during ongoing clinical care because of concerns about tachycardia and prolongation of the QTc interval.

To address whether the serotonergic specificity of clomipramine was critical, a double-blind crossover Type 1 study of clomipramine and desipramine (a selective noradrenergic reuptake inhibitor without serotonergic activity) was completed in 48 children and adolescents with OCD (Leonard et al., 1989). In this 12-week double-blind design, a patient received two weeks of placebo, then 5 weeks of clomipramine and 5 weeks of desipramine in a crossover. Clomipramine (targeting 3 mg/kg/day and not exceeding 5 mg/kg/day) was significantly better than desipramine in decreasing the OCD symptoms at week 5. Desipramine was no more effective in reducing OCD symptoms than placebo was in the Flament et al. (1985) study. The study noted that some of the patients who had received clomipramine in the first phase and desipramine in the second phase had a return of their symptoms when transferred to desipramine in the last phase, which suggests that the serotonergic reuptake inhibition may be critical.

With the development of the SSRIs, there is considerable discussion as to whether clomipramine is more effective than the SSRIs and at what point it should be chosen over the SSRIs. Initial meta-analysis (Griest, Jefferson, Kobak, & Katzelnick, 1995) indicated that clomipramine might be somewhat more effective than an SSRI for OCD in adults, but small head-to-head comparisons of clomipramine and fluvoxamine (Freeman, Trimble, Deakin, Stokes, & Ashford, 1994) and of fluvoxamine, paroxetine, and citalopram (Mundo, Bareggi, Pirola, & Bellodi, 1997) suggest that they have equivalent efficacy. The Expert Consensus Guidelines (March, Frances, et al., 1997) suggest that clomipramine be used when a patient has failed two or three adequate trials of an SSRI in combination with CBT.

The SSRIs have now emerged as the first-line

pharmacotherapeutic agent for OCD. They have the advantage over clomipramine of having a generally more tolerable side-effect profile with few anticholinergic effects, safer profile in over-doses, and no required EKG monitoring. Large multicenter Type 1 efficacy studies have shown that fluoxetine, fluvoxamine, and sertraline were each superior to placebo for children and ado-lescents with OCD (Geller et al., 2001; March, Biederman, et al., 1998; Riddle et al., 2001). Type 3 open studies support the use of citalopram and paroxetine (Rosenberg, Stewart, Fitzgerald, Taw-ile, & Carroll, 1999; Thomsen, 1997). The FDA has approved sertraline for the treatment of OCD in children ages 6 years and older, fluvox-amine for children ages 8 years and older, and fluoxetine for 8 years and older.

March, Biederman, and colleagues (1998) re-ported on 187 children and adolescents (ages 6 to 17 years of age) with OCD in a randomized double-blind, placebo-controlled, 8-week trial of sertraline (forced titration to 200 mg/day) versus placebo. Patients on sertraline, in comparison to those on placebo, showed significantly greater improvement on the several scales. Significant differences (with intent-to-treat analyses) be-tween the two groups were seen as early as week 3 and continued for the entire study.

Riddle and colleagues (2001) reported the safety and efficacy of fluvoxamine for 120 youth (ages 8 to 17 years) with OCD in an RCT in which youth received either fluvoxamine (50–200 mg/day) or placebo for 10 weeks. Patients in the flu-voxamine group had a significant improvement (as measured on the Children's Yale-Brown Ob-sessive-Compulsive Scale, CY-BOCS) in compar-ison to the placebo group, and a difference could be measured as early as the first week. In the flu-voxamine group, 42% were responders (defined as a 25% decrease in measure of OCD symptom severity, CY-BOCS) in comparison to 26% in the placebo group, which was significantly different.

Geller and colleagues (2001) randomized 103 youth with OCD to either fluoxetine (starting at 10 mg/day) or placebo (in a 2:1 ratio) for 8 weeks. Intent-to-treat analyses reported that those in the fluoxetine group had significantly better im-provement on CY-BOCs than did the placebo group. The authors concluded that fluoxetine at 20 to 60 mg daily was effective and well tolerated

in the pediatric group. In contrast, Liebowitz and colleagues (2002) randomized 43 patients to ei-ther fluoxetine or placebo for 8 weeks. Respond-ers then went into an 8-week maintenance phase. Fluoxetine dosage was fixed at 60 mg/day for 6 weeks and then could be increased to 80 mg/day. At week 8, fluoxetine was not signifi-cantly better than placebo on the CY-BOCs or CGI-Improvement scale; authors attributed this to either low power or short duration of treat-ment. The fluoxetine group continued to im-prove during the maintenance phase such that at week 16, 57% of the fluoxetine patients, as compared to 27% of the placebo patients (using data at week 8), were much or very much im-proved. The authors concluded that fluoxetine's effect took more than 8 weeks to develop.

Review of adverse effects of the SSRIs suggests that dropouts from blinded active medication as-signment are usually less than 13%, and in many studies there are no significant differences be-tween the dropouts receiving medication or pla-cebo (March, 1999). Generally, the most com-mon side effects seen with the SSRIs include sedation, nausea, diarrhea, insomnia, anorexia, tremor, sexual dysfunction, and hyperstimula-tion (March, Biederman, et al., 1998; Riddle et al., 2001). Children and adolescents may be more vulnerable to agitation or activation while on SSRIs than are adults, but this is not well stud-ied. Rare adverse reactions include apathy syn-drome, serotonin syndrome, and extrapyramidal symptoms. Pharmacokinetic studies of sertraline (Alderman, Wolkow, Chung, & Johnston, 1998) and of paroxetine (Findling et al., 1999) reported wide intra- and between-individual pharmaco-kinetic variability but generally similar results to those reported in adults.

How large is the treatment response on an SSRI? The pediatric treatment response is similar to that reported in adults. In general, a 30%–40% reduction in OCD symptoms, which corre-sponds to an average 6- to 8-point decrease on the CY-BOCS (Scahill et al., 1997), is reported in the medication treatment group in the SSRI con-trolled studies (March, 1999). Unlike some of the other disorders, there is little or no placebo effect reported. Clinical benefits may begin as early as 3 weeks and typically plateau at about 10 weeks (March, 1999).

The Expert Consensus Guidelines (March, Frances, et al., 1997) and the AACAP Practice Parameters for OCD (King et al., 1998) both recommend starting treatment in children with CBT or CBT plus an SSRI, depending on severity and comorbidity. Both guidelines recommend that patients started on SSRI alone who are partial responders should have a trial of CBT. The study of the relative efficacy of medication, of CBT, and their combination has just been completed using a Type 1 randomized controlled trial (Franklin et al., 2003; Pediatric OCD Collaborative Study Group, 2004; Foa & March, personal observations).

Investigational Treatments

Hypotheses concerning whether Sydenham's chorea and PANDAS might share similarities in their pathophysiology have led to the question of whether penicillin prophylaxis would reduce neuropsychiatric symptom exacerbation in children with PANDAS by preventing streptococcal infection. An 8-month, Type 1 double-blind, placebo-controlled, crossover trial of oral penicillin V (250 mg twice daily) and placebo was conducted in 37 children (Garvey et al., 1999). There was no significant difference between phases in either the OCD or tic symptom severity; however, penicillin administration failed to provide adequate prophylaxis against GABHS (as evidenced by the fact that 14 of 35 GABHS infections occurred during the penicillin phase). A number of children received antibiotic treatment multiple times during the placebo phase. The authors concluded that because of the failure to achieve an acceptable level of streptococcal prophylaxis, no conclusions could be drawn regarding the efficacy of penicillin prophylaxis in preventing tic or OCD symptom exacerbation. Further studies are needed that use a more effective prophylactic agent and include a larger sample size. Clinical experience would recommend workup for GABHS infection in children with abrupt and sudden onset of OCD or tics and dramatic exacerbations (Murphy & Pichichero, 2002; Swedo et al., 1998).

If post-streptococcal autoimmunity is the cause of the exacerbations in this subgroup, then children with PANDAS might benefit from immunomodulatory therapies that have been shown in preliminary findings to treat symptoms of Sydenham's chorea. In a Type 1 study, children with severe, infection triggered exacerbations of OCD or tic disorders were randomly assigned to plasma exchange (five single-volume exchanges over 2 weeks), intravenous immunoglobulin (IVIG;1 g/kg daily on 2 consecutive days), or placebo (saline solution given in the same manner as IVIG). Plasma exchange and IVIG were both effective in lessening of symptom severity for this group of children. Ratings were completed at 1 month and symptom gains were maintained at 1 year (Perlmutter et al., 1999). It should be noted that these children were more much significantly impaired than the average child with OCD or tics, and thus these invasive interventions were considered. These interventions are investigational and should only be considered in the context of research approved by a human investigations committee and not in the context of routine clinical care (Leonard & Swedo, 2001).

Posttraumatic Stress Disorder

Treatment of Posttraumatic Stress Disorder in Adults

With respect to psychotherapy for addressing posttraumatic stress disorder (PTSD), treatments derived from behavioral and cognitive theoretical models have been most carefully examined. In RCTs, the efficacy of several CBT treatments has been evaluated, including prolonged exposure (PE), anxiety management, eye movement desensitization and reprocessing (EMDR), cognitive therapy, and treatment packages that combine approaches.

Summaries of the studies of PE with veterans (e.g., Cooper & Clum, 1989; Glynn et al., 1999; Keane, Fairbank, Caddell, & Zimmering, 1989a) have consistently indicated that although exposure therapy is superior to various control conditions, the magnitude of the improvement has been somewhat limited. Because of the extent and chronicity of their problems and the presence of incentives for the veterans to minimize acknowledging treatment gains (e.g., losing service-connected disability compensation), evaluating the efficacy of a treatment within a veteran population is a very strict and difficult test. Indeed, in contrast to the exposure therapy findings with veterans, RCTs examining the efficacy of PE and other CBT interventions in civilian populations have generally yielded very positive results. Among the comparative outcome studies conducted using civilian samples, exposure therapy has been found to be as or more effective than relaxation, self-instructional training (SIT), and cognitive therapy (e.g., Devilly & Spence, 1999; Echeburua, Corral, Zubizarreta, & Sarasua, 1997; Foa et al., 1999; Marks, Lovell, Noshirvani, Livanou, & Thrasher, 1998; Resick, Nishith, & Griffin, 2003). Moreover, the addition of CBT procedures to exposure therapy alone does not augment its efficacy (Foa et al., 2003).

Multiple medications and classes of medications have been found to be effective in treating PTSD (Albucher & Liberzon, 2002). But there are relatively few placebo-controlled trials of medications outside the class of SSRIs (Albucher & Liberzon, 2002). Sertraline (Davidson, Rothbaum, van der Kolk, Sikes, & Farfel, 2001), paroxetine (Marshall, Beebe, Oldhau, & Zaninelli, 2001; Tucker et al., 2001), and fluoxetine (Martenyi et al., 2002a, 2002b) were found to be significantly more efficacious than placebo for symptom reduction and have few side effects (Albucher & Liberzon, 2002). Both have received FDA indication for PTSD. The SSRIs are considered the first-line pharmacotherapy for PTSD related to both interpersonal and wartime trauma as well as acute and chronic PTSD (Marshall et al., 2001; Smajkic et al., 2001; Tucker et al., 2001). A clinician-administered PTSD scale evidenced a 25%–30% reduction, but most of the patients classified as responders still have clinically significant symptoms despite significant reductions in number and severity of symptoms after an average of 12 weeks of medication (Marshall et al., 2001).

Other classes of medications shown to be effective for symptom reduction in double-blind, placebo-controlled trials include reversible and irreversible MAOIs, TCAs, and the anticonvulsant lamotrigine (Hageman, Andersen, & Jorgensen, 2001). However, these medications all have higher rates of side effects than the SSRIs (Albucher & Liberzon, 2002; for a review see Hembree & Foa, 2003).

Posttraumatic Stress Disorder in Children and Adolescents

Adolescence represents a developmental transition in the maturation of self-efficacy in the face of danger. There is increasing reliance on the peer group for appraisal of danger and estimation of needed protective actions along with greater engagement of the peer group in dangerous and protective behavior. Developmental epidemiology suggests that adolescence carries a high risk of exposure to a spectrum of traumatic situations, subsequent PTSD, comorbid psychopathology, and age-related impairments. Included among the salient types of exposure are adolescent physical and sexual abuse (Kaplan et al., 1998; Pelcovitz, Kaplan, DeRosa, Mandel, & Salzinger, 2000); interpersonal and community violence (Berman, Kurtines, Silverman, & Serafini, 1996; Kilpatrick, Acierno, Resnick, Saunders, & Best, 1997; Wolfe, Scott, Wekerlee, & Pittman, 2001); serious accidental injury, especially traffic accidents; traumatic losses, including those by homicide, suicide, and fatal automobile accidents; and life-threatening medical illness accompanied by life-endangering medical procedures (e.g., kidney and liver transplant) (Shemesh et al., 2001). For example, juveniles are two times more likely than adults to be victims of serious violent crime and three times more likely to be victims of simple assault. There are differential rates of exposure, with boys more likely to experience criminal assault and girls, dating violence and rape. A national survey of adolescents found that 23% reported having been both a victim of assault and a witness to violence, and that over 20% met lifetime criteria for PTSD (Kilpatrick, Saunders, Resnick, & Smith, 1995). In addition to general rates of exposure to war and disasters, international studies indicate that adolescents in these situations are often engaged in resistance and rescue efforts (Nader et al., 1989) that expose them to many stressful experiences. Studies among adolescents suggest that there may be multiple forms of exposure, with co-morbid admixtures of PTSD, depression, and SAD (Pelcovitz, Kaplan, DeRosa, et al., 2000; Warner & Weist, 1996). Finally, adolescent exposures may be superimposed on prior trauma histories and untreated chronic posttraumatic stress symptoms.

Considerable evidence indicates that traumatized adolescents are at increased risk for a spectrum of adverse psychosocial difficulties and functional impairments. These include reduced academic achievement; aggressive, delinquent, or high-risk sexual behavior; substance abuse and dependence (Cavaiola & Schiff, 1988; Collins & Bailey, 1990; Farrell & Bruce, 1997; Kilpatrick et al., 2000; Saigh, Mroueh, & Bremner, 1997; Saltzman, Pynoos, Layne, Steinberg, & Aisenberg, 2001); and nonadherence to prescribed posttransplant medical treatment (Shemesh et al., 2001). Further, trauma in adolescence has been linked with long-term developmental disturbances, including disrupted moral development, missed developmental opportunities, delayed preparation for professional and family life, and disruptions in close relationships (Goenjian et al., 1999; Layne, Pynoos, & Cardenas, 2001; Malinkosky-Rummell & Hansen, 1993; Pynoos, Steinberg, & Piacentini, 1999). Ongoing reactive behavior to trauma reminders in adolescence carries the bimodal risk of reckless behavior or extreme avoidant behavior that can derail the adolescent's life.

Psychosocial Treatment of Posttraumatic Stress Disorder in Children and Adolescents

Given the high rates of trauma and serious adverse consequences, the treatment of PTSD in adolescence is emerging as an important area for the identification of evidence-based interventions. Advances are being made and the field of child and adolescent PTSD is at the cusp of placing the treatment of PTSD on an evidence-based foundation.

Beginning in the early 1980s, school-age children and adolescents were found to be able to describe their posttraumatic stress symptoms and to engage in the work needed to address their acute traumatic experiences. Pilot studies suggested clinical improvement in posttraumatic stress symptoms after (1) exploration of the complexity of the experience; (2) identification of the most traumatic moments; (3) repeated attention to the subjective and objective features of these moments, especially experiences of helplessness, fear, and ineffectualness; (4) clarification of distortions, misattributions, and confusions; and (5) identification of current trauma reminders and an increase in cognitive, emotional, physiological and behavioral management. At the same time, features of traumatic bereavement were distinguished from primary PTSD (Cohen et al., 2002; Pynoos, 1992). Similar to the treatment of adults, school-age children and adolescents were found to be capable of being helped to contend with their anticipatory anxieties about addressing their traumatic experience and were capable of mustering the needed courage to participate in treatment.

In the past decade, there have been continuous advances in treating PTSD in youth. The approaches have included individual, group, and family therapy modalities and psychopharmacology. Studies among school-age children, adolescents and young adults have provided preliminary evidence about the effectiveness of different interventions for adolescent PTSD. Key Type 1 randomized studies among school-age children have primarily examined CBT approaches for sexually abused children, using both symptoms and sexually inappropriate behavior as outcome measures. In a study of 100 sexually abused children Deblinger and colleagues (Deblinger & Heflin, 1996; Deblinger, Steer, & Lippman, 1999) provided evidence for the effectiveness of a 12-week CBT treatment that emphasizes gradual confrontation of traumatic thoughts, feelings, and memories, using response to even subtle trauma reminders to more fully explore their traumatogenic origins and ongoing cognitive, emotional, and physiological reactions. The CBT treatment included exposure components and cognitive therapy. Children treated alone or with their parents were significantly improved in PTSD symptoms, depression, and externalizing behavior, compared with treatment for the mothers only and with treatment as usual in community-based clinics.

Studies of child sexual abuse treatment will benefit from follow-up into adolescence to measure treatment effects on later psychosexual developmental challenges and new sets of reminders. Pertinent to adolescent treatment strategies, when the age range of subjects extended from school age through late adolescence, a randomized clinical trial on treatment of child sexual abuse found no effect of parent involvement in treatment (King, Gaines, Lambert, Summerfelt, & Bickman, 2000). Cohen and Mannarino (1996a, 1996b, 1998) provided evidence for CBT effectiveness in comparison to supportive therapy for preschool and early adolescent subjects. Their CBT emphasizes developmental skills in emotional labeling and regulation. The effect size among adolescents was considerably greater than that for younger children. Each of these three treatment protocols includes a section devoted to promoting safety behaviors both currently and in the future.

Using a staggered start comparison group, March, Amaya-Jackson, Murry, and Schulte (1998) reported a robust beneficial effect of an 18-week CBT for school-age children and adolescents who experienced a single-incident traumatic experience. In this small size study (14 of 17 completers), there was significant improvement in PTSD, symptoms, depression, anxiety, and anger. The treatment was modeled on prolonged exposure (Foa & Rothbaum, 1998). Treatment began with anxiety management techniques and included a preparatory individual break-out session to establish a trauma hierarchy and initial trauma narrative before group exposure work. The treatment then moved toward a focus on "worst moments," augmented by homework that addressed avoidant behavior, then promoted anger management skills, restructured future expectations, and finished with attention to relapse prevention. The study confirmed that adolescents can engage in this extended, demanding treatment with acceptance, safety, and effectiveness.

Two comparison studies reported the effectiveness of delayed, intermediate school-based trauma-focused interventions for school-age children and adolescents after large-scale disasters. One and one-half years after the catastrophic 1988 earthquake in Armenia, Goenjian et al. (1997) employed a five-foci approach (trauma reminders, traumatic experience[s], traumatic bereavement, secondary adversities, developmental progression) over six 90-min combined classroom and individual sessions for adolescents with severe chronic PTSD. When treated and untreated adolescents were compared 3 years after the earthquake, treatment was associated with significant improvement in PTSD and stable depressive symptoms, whereas untreated adolescents suffered a worsening of PTSD and exacerbation of depressive symptoms that reached clinical diagnostic levels. In this extremely traumatized population with persistent and pervasive postearthquake adversities, treatment gains were maintained for 1 and ½ years posttreatment and, even without specific strategies to ameliorate depression, this intervention appeared to have protected against adolescent depression.

Three and one-half years after Hurricane Iniki, Chemtob, Nakashima, and Carlson (2002) used a lagged group design to treat a group of school-aged children who continued to experience moderate levels of PTSD after being unresponsive to an earlier psychoeducational intervention. With a form of EMDR, this intermediate intervention sequentially addressed in four sessions positive cognition, worst memories, worst reminders, and fears about future hurricanes. Both treatment groups demonstrated pre- to posttreatment reductions in PTSD symptoms and moderate reductions in anxiety and depression. These gains were maintained at 6-month follow-up. These studies demonstrated the potential usefulness of school-based interventions across disasters of different magnitudes and ranges of PTSD outcomes, even if delayed by postdisaster circumstances.

More recently, manualized school-based, trauma-focused, adolescent group therapy has been studied among adolescents exposed to multiple traumatic experiences during war or urban community violence. The same five foci of treatment used by Goenjian et al. (1997) were employed, and specific adolescent measures were used to evaluate the targeted outcome improvement for each module. Layne, Pynoos, Saltzman, and colleagues (2001) reported on the treatment of 55 war-traumatized students from schools in Bosnia-Hercegovina 3 years after the Dayton Accords ended the war. The treatment resulted in significant reduction in PTSD, depression, and traumatic grief reactions. Saltzman, Pynoos, Layne, Steinberg, and Aisenberg (2001) reported on the treatment of chronic PTSD and academic impairment among urban adolescents living in a high-crime area. Similar results were achieved as in the Layne et al. study, with additional evidence for significant improvement in grade point average (GPA), especially reflected in reduced number of failed classes. As the study authors point out, the improvement in GPA to a "C" range carries significant developmental importance, as these adolescents were able to participate once again in many school interpersonal and enrichment activities that promote adolescent developmental progression. The group intervention was preceded by an individual session in which the adolescent formed a hierarchy of prior traumatic experiences, identified salient features and developmental impact, and selected one to focus on in treatment. As a prelude to core trauma-specific group and homework exposure exercises, the use of beginning strategies to inventory and enhance management of current trauma and loss reminders served as a useful introduction for adolescents to make the work immediately relevant, understandable, and acceptable. Since many adolescent exposures entail traumatic deaths, a specific module directed at traumatic bereavement was included. Beyond a focus on PTSD-related avoidant behavior, the last module focused on resumption of adolescent activities in response to missed developmental opportunities, restoration of investment in the social contract, and engagement in prosocial activities. These programs indicate the advantage of school-based interventions, with each study reporting nearly 100% completion rates. They also suggest that group formats may be powerful among adolescents, providing the opportunity to engage the peer group in reexamination of appraisal of danger and protective action. School-based group interventions also provide a potentially cost-efficient method of delivering mental health services to the under-

served population of youth with unaddressed PTSD.

Pharmacotherapy of Posttraumatic Stress Disorder in Children and Adolescents

Pharmacotherapy of PTSD for children and adolescents is limited, with open trial reports and only one RCT (Cohen, 2001). The strategies include targeting specific symptoms, for example, sleep disturbance, that carry significant functional consequence, as well as overall symptom remission. The earliest report documented overall clinical improvement in a small sample of sexually and/or physically abused young children treated with propanolol (Famularo, Spivak, Bunshaft, & Berkson, 1988). Isolated clinical reports also suggest effective treatment of significant sleep disturbance in young children with clonidine or guanfacine (e.g., Harmon, Morse, & Morse, 1996). A clinical report on the use of carbamazepine in treatment of PTSD among a series of 28 children and adolescents suggested remission of PTSD, although children with comorbid conditions (half of the sample) required additional medications. With evidence for the efficacy of SSRIs in the treatment of adult PTSD discussed above, there is interest in conducting RCTs with children and adolescents.

Table 10.2 provides some tentative recommendations of acute treatment strategies for use with adolescents suffering from anxiety disorders. It is important to emphasize that the outcome literature remains underdeveloped and thus our suggestions should be viewed as just that, rather than as specific recommendations that have been rigorously tested with large samples.

MAINTENANCE OF GAINS AFTER ACUTE TREATMENT

There is a paucity of knowledge about what happens after the acute phase of treatment with adults, children, and adolescents. Studies of CBT have commonly reported uncontrolled follow-up data, but did not control the treatments that patients received during the naturalistic follow-

Table 10.2 Recommendations for Acute Treatment Strategies

Anxiety Disorder	Psychosocial Treatment	Pharmacotherapy
Social anxiety disorder, selective mutism	CBT involving some form of exposure; needs to be adjusted to address specific fears in selective mutism (e.g., hearing own voice)	SRIs
Generalized anxiety disorder	CBT; development of problem-focused coping strategies to handle frequently changing themes	SRIs; possibly also TCAs, benzodiazepines, buspirone
Separation anxiety disorder	CBT; graded exposure rather than flooding	SRIs
Specific phobias	Exposure for most fears, possibly 3-hr sessions	If CBT is not available and problem is severe, possibly SRIs
Panic disorder	CBT, exposure to interoceptive cues	SRIs, possibly imipramine or benzodiazepines
Obsessive-compulsive disorder	CBT involving both exposure and response prevention	SRIs
Posttraumatic stress disorder	CBT involving exposure to traumatic memories and to objectively safe yet fear-evoking trauma-related situations	SRIs

CBT, cognitive-behavioral therapy; SRI, serotonin reuptake inhibitor; TCA, tricyclic antidepressant.

up period. These data suggest that on the average, a meaningful degree of maintenance of the gains that accrues from CBT, with few studies reporting only mild overall relapse. Although more data are needed, one study reported favorable maintenance of gains at a 7.4-year follow-up of cases treated with CBT (Kendall, Safford, Flannery-Schroeder, & Webb, 2004). Traditionally, the vast majority of psychopharmacological trials have focused entirely on efficacy during acute, short-term treatment. More recently, studies have examined the effects of treatment during a longer, maintenance phase and after medication discontinuation. Even less is known about these effects in children and adolescents. Below we discuss what we know about maintenance of treatment gains and discontinuation of treatment in each disorder, for adults, children, and adolescents.

Social Anxiety Disorder

Maintenance trials with phenelzine, paroxetine, and sertraline in adults suggest that responders maintain their gains with continued medication

(Liebowitz et al., 1992; Stein et al., 1996; Walker et al., 2000). However, discontinuation trials with phenelzine (after 9 months treatment), sertraline (after 20 weeks treatment), and paroxetine (after 13 weeks treatment) suggest that relapse rates are high when medication is discontinued. Use of CBT showed good continuation of gains during maintenance and after discontinuation in a comparative trial with phenelzine, and in another study in comparison with a psychoeducational condition. Knowledge about optimal lengths of treatment to minimize relapse and about predictors of who can discontinue when without relapsing are lacking, as are studies of maintenance of gains and treatment discontinuation in treated children and adolescents.

Separation Anxiety Disorder and Selective Mutism

No adult studies have examined these conditions that almost invariably occur exclusively during childhood and adolescence. Studies of CBT that have included separation-anxious children in the samples have generally shown maintenance of gains following treatment discontinuation (e.g., Barrett, Rapee, et al., 1996; Kendall et al., 1997) and SAD diagnosis has not been a predictor of poor outcome in these studies. Thus it can be surmised that CBT provides lasting benefits for these children. As mentioned above, SAD may be more common in young children, and its treatment and maintenance of gains have not been studied in adolescent samples. The treatment of selective mutism has also received little attention in the acute treatment literature, thus even less is known about maintenance of gains, especially in adolescents. In general, the available data indicate partial response to acute treatment, which suggests continued impairment. What is unknown is whether the posttreatment gains are maintained over time.

Generalized Anxiety Disorder

Relapse rates following discontinuation of acute benzodiazepine treatment in adults are as high as 80%, indicating the absence of maintenance of medication-produced gains (Rickels, Case, & Diamond, 1980; Rickels, Case, Downing, & Fridman, 1986). A few studies demonstrate lasting benefit for GAD patients treated for 6 months or more with benzodiazepines and buspirone. However, concern over physiologic dependence and potential for abuse make long-term treatment with benzodiazepines controversial. A recent placebo-controlled trial of venlafaxine XR showed that benefits from this medication continued following 6 months of treatment and that it was well tolerated over the long term. Several CBT studies involving GAD in youth have indicated maintenance of gains up to 12 months after CBT discontinuation. In addition, there are supportive data for 3.5-year (Kendall & Southam-Gerow, 1996), 6-year (Barrett, 1998), and 7.4-year (Kendall et al., 2004) follow-ups. Although not all of these treated cases had GAD as the principal diagnosis and not all evidenced complete initial benefit from CBT, those individuals who do benefit seem to be able to maintain their gains for several years, even without continued treatment.

Specific Phobia

The adult literature on maintenance of gains following treatment of specific phobias generally suggests that benefits associated with CBT are lasting even when the treatment is delivered in a single 3-hour long session (Öst, 1989; Öst et al., 1991, 1997). Studies of children and adolescents have indicated that CBT produces significant gains immediately after treatment up to and at 1-year follow-up (Öst et al., 2001; Silverman et al., 1999a). The pharmacotherapy literature on this topic is underdeveloped and thus no conclusions can be drawn about maintenance of gain over time using this approach.

Panic Disorder

Mavissakalian and Perel (1992) compared patients who responded to 6 months of acute treatment with adult patients who had a similar response to a 6-month acute treatment period and then additionally received 1 year of half-dose maintenance imipramine treatment. Both groups entered a double-blind discontinuation study for 3 months, followed by a 3-month drug-free period. The group who had acute and maintenance treatment did significantly better during this 6-month period than the group that had only acute treatment. Maintenance treatment with antidepressants may have a significant prophylactic effect and reduce the rate of relapse after treatment discontinuation (Mavissakalian & Perel, 1992). A follow-up study found prophylactic efficacy for maintenance treatment continued beyond 1 year of maintenance and into a second year. However, the persistence of difficult side effects, particularly weight gain, was noted with imipramine over long-term treatment (Mavissakalian & Perel, 2001). A recent naturalistic study (Simon et al., 2002) involving 78 patients who achieved remission in an 8-week acute phase (with benzodiazepine alone, antidepressant alone, or both) and then received maintenance pharmacotherapy for 2 years found that 46% of these patients relapsed over the maintenance phase and that combination therapy did not confer any added advantage.

As briefly noted earlier, a multicenter trial studied the efficacy of medication therapy and CBT and explored whether combined therapy (medication plus CBT) is more effective than either therapy alone in a randomized, double-blind placebo study (Barlow et al., 2000). In terms of acute response, combined treatment did not differ from medication or CBT alone, but was better than placebo. The 6-month maintenance response rate of the combination therapy was high (approximately 57% for the Panic Disorder Severity Scale [PDSS] and 60% for the CGI) and significantly different from medication alone or CBT alone but not significantly different from CBT plus placebo. After the 6-month maintenance phase, patients had treatment discontinued and were followed for 6 months. Improvement in CGI was highest for CBT plus placebo (41%), 32% for CBT alone, 20% for imipramine alone, and 26% for combined treatment. This study and another large-scale RCT using alprazolam (Marks et al., 1993) indicate that combined treatment for panic disorder may be advantageous at posttreatment and during maintenance but may attenuate the benefits of CBT following medication discontinuation (for a review see Foa, Franklin, & Moser, 2002). Ollendick's (1995) small multiple-baseline study included follow-up over a 6-month interval, and these results affirmed the lasting effects of a similar treatment for a pediatric sample. Much more research employing controlled designs needs to be done using pediatric samples.

Obsessive-Compulsive Disorder

Little is known about how long SRI medication should be continued in OCD. In practice, many adult patients continue taking their medication for at least one year; some seem to require indefinite treatment. There are only three published double-blind SRI discontinuation studies (Koran, Hackett, Rubin, Wokow & Robinson, 2002; Pato, Zohar-Kadouch, Zohar, & Murphy, 1988; Romano, Goodman, Tamura, Gonzales, & the Collaborative Research Group, 2001) in adults with OCD. Each uses a different SRI (clomipramine, fluoxetine, sertraline) and comes to a different conclusion regarding the effects of dis-

continuing the SRI (substantial [89%] recurrence over 12 weeks for clomipramine, moderate relapse [32%] after one year and not different from staying on SRI [21%] for fluoxetine, low rate of recurrence [24%] after 28 weeks but significantly more than staying on SRI [9%] for sertraline). Given the paucity of blind studies and the methodological differences between them (e.g., relapse definition, length of follow-up, procedure for placebo substitution), the posttreatment effects of SRIs in OCD remain unclear.

A recent comparative trial of clomipramine and EX/RP in adults suggested that the relapse rate with clomipramine may not be as high (i.e., 45%) as previously thought. However, even with this lower relapse rate, EX/RP showed superior maintenance of gains 12 weeks after treatment discontinuation (Simpson et al., 2004). Optimal lengths of SRI treatment to minimize relapse, and predictors of who can discontinue without relapsing are lacking. Moreover, there is no agreement on the criteria to define relapse. The few open studies of CBT in pediatric OCD that have included follow-up data suggest good maintenance of gains following treatment discontinuation (Franklin et al., 1998; March et al., 1994; Wever & Rey, 1997), and the one study of pharmacotherapy discontinuation in pediatric OCD suggests that relapse is common (e.g., Leonard et al., 1991). A systematic follow-up study (done when clomipramine was available only investigationally and access to CBT was limited) of 54 children and adolescents with OCD treated acutely with clomipramine was completed (Leonard et al., 1993). Of the 54 subjects, 38 (70%) were taking psychoactive medication at follow-up; 23 of 54 (43%) patients still met diagnostic criteria for OCD, and 43 (80%) were improved from baseline. Of the six patients (11%) who were totally asymptomatic, three were taking medication at the time of reevaluation; thus, only three could be considered to be in true remission. This finding suggested that patients were improved at follow-up, but most were on medication maintenance, and only 3 of 54 were asymptomatic and not on medication. Although not every patient had attempted discontinuation of medication, this study for patients treated with an SRI indicates that they may require long-term maintenance therapy.

Posttraumatic Stress Disorder

Deblinger and colleagues' (Deblinger and Heflin, 1996; Deblinger et al., 1999) work with sexually abused children provided evidence for the long-term effectiveness of a 12-week CBT treatment. March, Amaya-Jackson, et al. (1998) reported a robust beneficial effect and maintenance of gains up to 6 months in a small study of CBT for school-age children and adolescents who experienced a single incident traumatic experience. Pharmacological studies in adolescents need to take into account the two adult randomized studies of SSRIs in the treatment of PTSD that indicate relapse with discontinuation of medication (Martenyi, et al., 2002a). These adult studies raise the same issue as that in the treatment of other anxiety disorders—whether a combination of medication and trauma-focused CBT would provide greater resistance to relapse.

A Comment on Relapse Prevention in Children and Adolescents

It is important to note that there has been no research specifically addressing maintenance treatment and relapse prevention for anxiety disorders in youth and adolescents. In general, the ultimate goal of most psychosocial treatment programs for anxiety disorders is to equip children with skills that will help them manage anxious distress after treatment discontinues; a "cure" for anxiety is not the goal (see Kendall, 1989). Because some degree of anxious arousal is likely to persist after treatment, modifying dysfunctional expectations and distorted processing styles can help to enable more adaptive functioning. The use of in vivo exposure tasks in treatment provides performance-based experiences of coping that bolster a child's confidence for future situations. Therapeutic intervention may be only a first step, but it is a step that helps to alter the maladaptive developmental trajectories of these children so that they are better able to address the inevitable challenges emerging in their lives. Upon completion of a treatment program, the guiding principle (and hope) is for the child to continue to practice the skills learned.

There are several clinical strategies to help guide youth toward consolidation of treatment-produced gains. First, the therapist should shape and encourage "effort" attributions regarding the management of anxiety. Youth should be encouraged to reward their hard work and coping efforts, even if the successes are only partial. A second principle for continued posttreatment functioning includes introducing children to the concept of "lapses in efforts," rather than "relapses" (see also Brownell, Marlatt, Lichtenstein, & Wilson, 1986; Marlatt & Gordon, 1985). Mistakes and partial successes are not viewed as incompetence or inability; rather, they can be constructively framed as vital and inextricably linked to the learning process. Within this framework, children can label and accept inevitable setbacks as temporary and then proceed to work on forward-looking problem solving. Mistakes are viewed as an acceptable part of the learning process and not as excuses for giving up or confirming anxious cognition.

Maintenance treatment may require combinations of CBT and medications, booster sessions, or a return and reexperience of the initial therapy. Alternate approaches, or even as-yet undeveloped treatments may be needed, especially for cases that are refractory to the otherwise reasonably successful program. To date, the field is lacking information about how best to maintain treatments, prevent relapses, and integrate psychological and pharmacological approaches to maximize long-term gains.

MANAGEMENT OF PARTIAL RESPONSE AND NONRESPONSE

Social Anxiety Disorder

There are no controlled studies in any age group on how to address partial responders and nonresponders with social anxiety disorder. Cognitive-behavioral therapy is a logical candidate to augment partial drug response, and Liebowitz and colleagues have recently found CBT to be helpful in augmenting partial SSRI responders in an open trial (unpublished data). Gabapentin and clonazepam are also considered possible augmenting agents for partial SSRI responders. Complicating this research is the fact that there is no accepted definition of partial response.

Generalized Anxiety Disorder

Most adult GAD patients who improve with acute treatment do not reach full remission of symptoms. In early trials, full remission occurred in as few as one-third of GAD patients. Unfortunately, there are no systematic studies of treatment options for patients with partial medication response in GAD. Partial response and a nonresponder rate also characterize CBT outcomes for GAD. Unfortunately, there are no systematic trials assessing nonresponders to initial treatment.

Specific Phobia

There are no controlled data on how to address or augment partial responders and there are no controlled data on how to treat nonresponders to an initial drug or CBT trial.

Panic Disorder

A recent double-blind, placebo-controlled trial with adults found that pindolol had a beneficial augmentation effect on fluoxetine-treated panic patients (Hirschmann et al., 2000). Patients with panic disorder ($N = 25$) who had not responded to 8 weeks of fluoxetine (and prior to that, two other trials of antidepressants) were randomly assigned to pindolol or placebo for 4 weeks. The pindolol group achieved significant improvement on ratings compared to the placebo group. However, since the augmentation period studied was so brief, it is difficult to determine if these effects would be sustained and whether they would actually lead to remission. Three studies have examined the effects of benzodiazepine treatment combined with antidepressant treatment. Imipramine plus alprazolam was compared to imipramine plus placebo. The combi-

nation group responded with therapeutic effect more quickly. Clonazepam augmentation of paroxetine was shown to be superior to paroxetine alone (Mathew, Coplan, & Gorman, 2001). Goddard et al. (2001) studied 50 panic patients and randomized them to either .5 mg of clonazepam three times per day plus sertraline or placebo clonazepam plus sertraline for the first 4 weeks. At week 1, 41% of the combination group evidenced improvement compared to 4% of the placebo group. At 3 weeks, there was a significantly higher (63%) response rate in the combination group than that in the placebo group (32%), but this difference did not emerge at any other point in the trial. This study suggests that benzodiazepine augmentation of SSRIs at the beginning of treatment can lead to earlier improvement. Recently, Kampman, Keijsers, Hoogduin, and Hendriks (2002) found that paroxetine augmentation of 43 nonresponders to an acute phase of CBT significantly reduced overall anxiety and agoraphobic behaviors. Nonresponders pose a special challenge, yet there is a paucity of systematic investigation in this area.

Obsessive-Compulsive Disorder

In considering medication augmentation, a benzodiazepine, such as clonazepam, is occasionally added, but disinhibition, dependence, and tolerance to the medication have limited the enthusiasm for this choice in the long run (Leonard et al., 1994). Adult studies support a trial of neuroleptic augmentation in SRI non- or partial responders (McDougle et al., 1995). In a Type 1 controlled risperidone versus placebo SRI augmentation study, risperidone addition was superior in reducing OCD symptoms (McDougle et al., 2000). Neuroleptic augmentation has not been systematically studied in children; a case series of children who were refractory to SRI therapy improved significantly after risperidone was added (Fitzgerald, 1999). T. Owley, S. Owley, Leventhal, and Cook (2002) reported four cases of 8- to 25-year-olds who were partial responders to an SSRI and subsequently responded after mixed salts of dextroamphetamine (Adderall) was added. The authors speculated that the "delicate" balance of serotonergic and dopaminergic systems may be affected by both neuroleptic or Adderall augmentation, resulting in increased serotonergic transmission.

There is no accepted definition of a nonresponder. Sometimes *nonresponders* have meant patients who have had a suboptimal response to one therapy, but such a definition would include both partial responders and nonresponders. If a *nonresponder* is defined as someone who has had absolutely no improvement from an initial treatment, there are no published controlled data on how to treat such patients.

Posttraumatic Stress Disorder

There is only one placebo-controlled study on augmentation for partial responders: combat veterans with PTSD who were minimally responsive on an SSRI (sertraline) were given augmentation with the atypical antipsychotic medication olanzepine (Stein, Westenberg, & Liebowitz, 2002). Olanzapine augmentation was associated with statistically significantly greater reduction than that with placebo in specific measures of posttraumatic stress, depressive, and sleep disorder symptoms (Petty et al., 2001). One recently completed study found an augmentation effect for PE compared to sertraline continuation in patients who evidenced at least a 20% symptom reduction following 10 weeks of open label sertraline (Foa, Franklin, & Moser, 2002). In a subgroup analysis of these data, patients who experienced only a marginal response to 10 weeks of open label sertraline benefited substantially when PE was added, compared to those who continued on sertraline for an additional 5 weeks.

There are no controlled data on how to treat nonresponders to pharmacologic or CBT treatment for PTSD in adults. Given the high rates of comorbidity with PTSD, it is recommended that patients be given evidence-based treatments for their comorbid conditions and that thereafter the patient's PTSD symptoms be reassessed.

A Comment on Management of Partial Response and Nonresponse in Children and Adolescents

There is little to no research on the management of partial response and nonresponse in the treatment of adolescent anxiety disorders. This area is one that sorely needs to be addressed in future research. Although the literature has yet to provide the data needed to guide evidence-based treatments for partial responders and nonresponders, several issues still warrant our consideration.

The evidence accrued to date informs us about the choice of an initial treatment to be undertaken for anxious children and, at least to some extent, anxious adolescents. There is a noted absence of studies specifically about adolescents and what to do for them at the various other stages of treatment. Studies reviewed above have evaluated the efficacy of various treatments for children identified with anxiety disorders and these data guide our treatment choices. However, it is likely that some of the cases treated in these studies had prior experience with one or another treatment, and may or may not have been partially refractory to those earlier treatments. More detailed analyses of initial treatment response may reveal useful information about the moderating role of prior treatment experiences in the efficacy of the treatment being evaluated. The field has nevertheless made meaningful progress in identifying at least a few initial treatments that are quite promising for anxious youth.

We know little about what to do when the youthful patient's response to treatment is not favorable. Even when approximately two-thirds of patients respond favorably to CBT, for example, there are still one-third of the patients who did not respond well and may need something additional. One might speculate that within the CBT approach, a combination of more practice, increased exposure tasks, and help with the use of new skills in new, challenging situations would be worthwhile. One might also speculate that a combination of approaches may be valuable. Treatment of a nonresponsive client can be complicated by the fact that a nonresponder to one treatment approach (psychosocial, medication) may then seek another approach as a way to rectify the less-than-preferred previous outcomes. Again, more information is needed about prior treatment history and its effect on the evaluation of a current intervention, and there is a real need for studies of the preferred treatment for patients whose response to treatments are less than satisfactory.

Insufficient research on adults and almost none on youth regarding the continuation and maintenance treatment phases for specific phobia have been carried out. In adults with anxiety disorders, it may be recommended that medications be continued for at least 12–18 months and, thereafter, if the person is judged to be stable, that the medications be reduced very slowly to avoid withdrawal side effects. It is conceivable that at least some children and adolescents will require treatment for years, consistent with findings from the adult literature. As in other psychiatric and medical illnesses, after achieving a therapeutic response it is important to continue the same treatment (CBT and/or medications) to prevent relapses. During these phases, depending on the youngster's clinical status, she or he may need to be seen less frequently.

It is important that an adequate trial be conducted (dose and duration of an SSRI; expertise and number of sessions of CBT) prior to concluding that a patient is a partial responder. For example, the Expert Consensus Guidelines for OCD recommend clomipramine after two or three failed SSRI trials (March, Frances, et al., 1997). Cognitive-behavioral therapy would be a first choice for an augmentation strategy after a partial response or nonresponse to adequate pharmacotherapy with an agent of known efficacy, although availability of trained therapists is sometimes limited, and some children are not motivated to participate. Systematic study of CBT dissemination strategies is sorely needed, as is the development of CBT techniques designed specifically to enhance motivation to engage fully in treatment. Such study is well under way in adult anxiety disorders, and clearly needs to be addressed next in children and adolescents. Much more needs to be done to establish the efficacy and safety of such augmentation for adolescents with anxiety disorders. Clinically we know that many are treated with this strategy, but the literature supporting this approach has yet to be developed.

Prevention of Anxiety Disorders

chapter 11

THEORETICAL AND CONCEPTUAL MODELS OF PREVENTION AND CHANGE

The case for efforts in preventing anxiety disorder in youth has been made elsewhere (e.g., Weissberg, Kumpfer, & Seligman, 2003), but warrants brief reiteration here: *(1)* anxiety disorders are common (Kessler, 1994); *(2)* pediatric onset is also common (March, 1995); *(3)* anxiety disorders are associated with significant morbidity and comorbidity that often extends into adulthood (Costello & Angold, 1995); *(4)* the economic burden of anxiety disorders in the United States is enormous ($42.3 billion in 1990; Greenberg et al., 1999); and *(5)* most pediatric sufferers do not receive adequate care (Kendall & Southam-Gerow, 1995). Prevention efforts should target both risk and protective factors associated with the etiology and maintenance of the disorders. Some risk and protective factors may be less modifiable than others (e.g., gender, familial factors), and thus the interventions need to target mediating variables. The issue of timing is also important to consider because certain risk and protective factors may be more likely to exert their influence during certain developmental periods relative to other periods. For example, it may be when an adolescent needs to make the transition from middle to high school that being behaviorally inhibited (described in Chapter 9 and briefly below) heightens the adolescent's risk for developing an anxiety disorder. Consequently, the development of effective prevention of anxiety disorders will require *(1)* comprehensive knowledge of the risk and protective factors as well as their complex interrelationships during different periods in development; *(2)* advances in methods to detect the presence and/or absence of these factors; and *(3)* interventions that increase protective factors and/or reduce risk factors, or both. The goal of such programs is to reduce the enormous individual and societal burdens imposed by anxiety disorders.

In reviewing the studies on prevention of anxiety disorder conducted to date with children and adolescents, we used the system advocated by the Institute of Medicine's Committee on Prevention of Mental Disorders (Mrazek & Haggerty, 1994; Munoz, Mrazek, & Haggerty, 1996) and adopted by several prevention experts (e.g., Craske & Zucker, 2001; Donovan & Spence, 2000; Winett, 1998a). According to this system, prevention programs are classified as *(1)* indicated prevention programs, which target at-risk individuals who already have symptoms and/or a biological marker but do not fully meet diagnostic criteria for the disorder; *(2)* selective prevention programs, which target individuals presumed to be at high risk for the development of a disorder (e.g., witnesses of violence); and *(3)* universal prevention programs, in which entire populations are targeted regardless of risk factors (e.g., third graders).

Before considering the intervention studies, it is important to briefly consider what is known about risk and protective factors at the individual, familial, and societal level, because it is knowledge of these factors and their interrelations that should inform the development of specific intervention strategies. Unfortunately, knowledge of such factors is limited, and perhaps the paucity of prevention studies in anxiety disorders is a direct result of this limited knowledge.

Of particular concern is the absence of evidence about protective factors that are *specific* to anxiety disorders. That is, although the youth resilience literature has generally underscored the importance of factors such as high IQ, self-esteem, social support, and positive coping in serving to protect young people from the development of psychopathology in general, there is a paucity of literature regarding whether any protective factor(s) may serve to protect against anxiety disorders in particular. Certainly, development of effective prevention programs will continue to be hampered until evidence-based knowledge has accumulated in this area. The summary below is thus reflective of this in proportion to the literature; that is, considerable more coverage is paid to risk factors than to protective factors.

INDIVIDUAL RISK AND PROTECTIVE FACTORS

Individual Psychological Characteristics

Elevated but Subsyndromal Anxiety Symptoms

Many children exhibit symptoms of anxiety at some time before adulthood, and two questions are of particular interest here: *(1)* Do children with elevated but subsyndromal levels of anxiety show greater than normal levels of impaired functioning in their roles at home, at school, or with peers? *(2)* Does subsyndromal anxiety predict later psychiatric disorder, whether an anxiety disorder or some other diagnosis? To answer both questions it is necessary to control for comorbidity with other symptoms and disorders; that is, impaired functioning or future anxiety disorder must be linked directly to the anxiety symptoms, not to other symptoms or disorders that may co-occur.

To address the question of whether adolescents with elevated but subsyndromal levels of anxiety show greater than normal levels of impaired functioning in their roles at home, at school, or with peers, it is helpful to draw upon data from the Great Smoky Mountains Study of youth aged 9 to 16 (Costello, Mustillo, Erkanli, Keeler, & Angold, 2004). In this study, in which 1,420 children and adolescents and their parents were interviewed annually, children and adolescents with an anxiety disorder but no other psychiatric diagnoses were twice as likely to show functional impairment as those with no disorder. Even among youths with no diagnoses, those with symptoms of anxiety were twice as likely to have impaired functioning compared to those with no symptoms. This was true of both pre- and postpubertal youths. Thus, in this population-based sample, subsyndromal anxiety symptoms were associated with youths' impaired ability to function well at home, at school, and with peers.

Regarding whether subsyndromal anxiety predict later psychiatric disorder, data from the same study were used to compare children and adolescents who had an anxiety disorder at least once in the 8-year period of observation with those who had *never* had an anxiety disorder. Youths who had an anxiety disorder at least once during that period had an average of two symptoms during the years when they did not have a diagnosis; the average for those who never had an anxiety disorder was 0.4 symptoms. This finding suggests that youths with a vulnerability to anxiety disorders show clinical symptoms even at times when they would not meet formal diagnostic criteria.

Among children and adolescents without a history of anxiety disorders, those who developed one disorder in any given year of the study had three times as many subsyndromal anxiety symptoms in the year before they developed a disorder compared to those who did not develop an anxiety disorder (2.0 vs. 0.7 symptoms). Almost half of the youths who developed a new anxiety disorder the following year had at least two clinically significant symptoms the previous year, compared with one in five youths who would not develop a disorder. This finding suggests that it should be possible to identify high-risk children and adolescents for prevention programs with a high degree of accuracy.

It is important to remember, however, that anxiety disorders are not all that common among children and adolescents. In the Great Smoky Mountains Study, although subsyndromal symptoms quadrupled the likelihood that a youth without a previous history of anxiety disorders would develop one, the likelihood was increased from 1% to 4% only. It follows that 96% of the children and adolescents with two or more anxiety symptoms did not develop a disorder within the next year. Overall, children and adolescents with the highest likelihood of an anxiety disorder were those with a past history of anxiety disorders (13%).

Autonomic Reactivity

Although research findings are consistent in showing that children and adolescents who display anxiety display alterations in autonomic reactivity, Sweeny and Pine (2004) have noted limits in studies that have relied on cardiovascular measures as indices of autonomic activity. These limits include the fact that cardiovascular measures are regulated by a wide variety of neural structures and thus provide relatively indirect information about the state of brain systems that might be implicated in anxiety disorders. In addition, abnormalities in cardiovascular control appear to occur in other conditions, and so they do not appear to be specific to anxiety disorders. The context in which cardiovascular measures are obtained can also influence any reactivity that might be observed on these measures, thereby raising a concern about whether such findings are actually epiphenomena (Sweeny & Pine, 2004).

Respiratory indexes, in contrast, are relatively free of the limits noted above with cardiovascular measures (Sweeny & Pine, 2004). Respiratory indexes that have been used in this area of research include minute ventilation (the amount of air breathed every minute), tidal volume (size of each breath), and respiratory rate. Guided by Klein's (1993) theory that panic attacks are a suffocation alarm triggered by cues of suffocation, most of the research using respiratory indexes has focused on using samples of patients with panic disorder or an anxiety disorder other than panic disorder as well as "normal" controls and have had the participants breathe air that has an increased concentration of carbon dioxide.

Although research findings generally show that patients with panic disorder experience high degrees of anxiety, panic attacks, and changes in respiratory parameters in response to carbon dioxide exposure whereas other patient groups and normal controls do not (e.g., Papp et al., 1993; Papp, Martinez, Klein, Coplan, & Gorman, 1995), these findings have not emerged in all studies (e.g., Rapee, Brown, Antony, & Barlow, 1992; Woods & Charney, 1998). Only one study (Pine, Cohen, Gurley, Brook, & Ma, 1998) has extended this work to young people (ages 7 to 17; mixed sample of anxiety disorders), but separate analyses were not conducted for the preadolescent versus adolescent subsamples. Pine et al.'s findings with this sample of youth paralleled the positive findings obtained with adults. In light of the paucity of research conducted with adolescent samples, considerable more research is needed before firm conclusions can be drawn about the influence of adolescents' autonomic reactivity as a risk factor for anxiety disorders.

Behavioral Inhibition

The detailed review of the temperamental vulnerability to behavioral inhibition was also presented earlier. It is currently known from two independent labs that children who were highly reactive to novel stimuli as infants were more likely than others to display extreme shyness, timidity, and restraint to unfamiliar people, situations, and objects when they were 2, 4, 7, and 11 years of age (Fox, Henderson, Rabin, Caikins, & Schmidt, 2001; Kagan, 2002), and were more likely to show biological differences that may implicate the amygdala. Although these children are at 3- to 4-fold increased risk for development of an anxiety disorder compared to other children, most do not go on to develop one. Thus, behavioral inhibition is not a strong predictor of later anxiety disorder. This finding points to the importance of identifying protective factors that limit the rate of later anxiety disorders in vulnerable individuals.

Cognitive Factors

There are several characteristics of the individual that have been linked with anxiety and its disorders in children and adolescents. In Chapter 9, mention was made of information-processing biases and anxiety sensitivity. In this section, two additional cognitive characteristics are indicated: coping skills and perceived control. Individuals' coping skills strategies, which refer to a variety of methods individuals employ in an attempt to cope with negative or aversive situations, may be categorized as *(1)* problem-focused, *(2)* avoidant, or *(3)* emotion-focused. *Problem-focused coping* refers to strategies that either directly address or minimize the effect of the problem. *Avoidant coping* focuses on either avoiding or escaping the problem. Emotion-*focused coping* is directed toward the subjective level of distress associated with the problem. There is research evidence that problem-focused methods such as actively seeking out information, positive self-talk, diversion of attention, relaxation, and thought-stopping are associated with reduced levels of anxiety and emotional distress in 8- to 18-year-olds (Brown, O'Keefe, Sanders, &

Baker, 1986). Generally, children's and adolescents' use of problem-focused coping strategies has been found to be more associated with positive psychological adjustment than their use of emotion-focused coping strategies. Interestingly, adolescent use of avoidant coping has been found to be associated with high levels of depression in adolescence (Ebata & Moos, 1991). There has been little systematic research on the association between specific types of coping strategies and the development and maintenance of anxiety disorders in adolescence. There also has been little systematic research on which specific coping skills should be taught to adolescents across diverse anxiety-provoking situations. Research in this area is clearly of importance given that coping-skills training represents a major feature of cognitive-behavioral treatments (see Chapter 10). Another characteristic of the individual that relates to cognitions is individuals' perceived control. Specifically, Barlow (2001) has suggested that children who experience uncontrollable events early in life may develop a propensity to perceive or process events as not being under their control, which for some youngsters may serve as a risk for the development of anxiety and its disorders. Chorpita, Brown, and Barlow (1998) have presented some interesting data showing that perceived control may serve as a mediator of family environment among youths with anxiety disorders. Clearly, further research on the role of perceived control as a protective and risk factor in anxiety disorders is needed, particularly on its specificity (or lack thereof) to anxiety.

Genetics

As discussed in greater detail in Chapter 9, genetic factors clearly influence the risk for anxiety disorders and, taken together, the epidemiological and genetic data imply distinct biological profiles for the varied anxiety disorders, many of which implicate neurochemical processes. A recent meta-analysis found only a modest genetic contribution to four anxiety categories, and no evidence for a significant effect of shared environment (Hettema, Neale, & Kendler, 2001). When the individual studies themselves are reviewed, however, inconsistencies emerge with respect to the degree to which genetics were implicated in transmission of anxiety disorders; rates appear to vary as a function of the site of the laboratory, as well as the informant supplying the relevant information. There is evidence for genetic contributions to personality traits such as neuroticism, introversion (Eaves, Eysenck, & Martin, 1989), shyness (Daniels & Plomin, 1985), and behavioral inhibition (DiLalla, Kagan, & Reznick, 1994; Kagan, 1994), each of which may increase risk for the subsequent development of anxiety disorder. In general, many studies of the genetics of anxiety disorders involving children and adolescents have substantive methodological limitations, thus there remains a great deal to discover in this area. Also, it is important to note that the presence of a genetic influence for anxiety disorders does not imply that the course of illness is immutable. From the perspective of prevention, it may be that studying other risk factors in youth at genetic risk for anxiety disorders may prove especially fruitful, and may suggest roads to interventions that reduce the genetic risk.

ENVIRONMENTAL FACTORS

Familial Factors

Parent–Child Interaction and Attachment

All four of the attachment styles in children according to the classification by Ainsworth, Blehar, Waters, and Wall (1978) and by Main and Solomon (1990)—secure, insecure-avoidant, insecure-ambivalent, and insecure-disorganized—have been found to be represented in children with anxiety disorders. The highest risks for developing an anxiety disorder are associated with disorganized attachment, which is associated with unresolved trauma or loss, and ambivalent attachment (Cassidy, 1995; Manassis, Bradley, Goldberg, Hood, & Swinson, 1994; Warren, Huston, Egeland, & Sroufe, 1997). The specificity of an association between disorganized attachment in terms of its link with a specific type of anxiety disorder, such as separation anxiety disorder, has not been established.

Retrospective studies. Lutz and Hock (1995) examined whether adult mental representations of attachment relationships and memories of childhood experiences with parents contributed to a mother's anxiety about separation from her own infant. Mothers with insecure attachment representations, when asked to remember details of their own childhood, reported more negative recollections of early parental caregiving, particularly rejection and discouragement of independence. Cassidy (1995) found that adolescents and adults with generalized anxiety disorder reported more caregiver unresponsiveness, role-reversal and enmeshment, and feelings of anger and vulnerability toward their mothers than controls. Systematic and formal assessments of the adolescents' and adult attachment styles were not conducted in this sample, however.

Prospective studies. Manassis et al. (1994) examined adult attachment and mother–child attachment in 20 mother–child dyads (children ages 18 to 59 months) in which the mothers suffered from anxiety disorders. The mothers all had insecure adult attachments, and 80% also had insecure attachments with their children. Among the insecurely attached children, 3 of 16 met diagnostic criteria for anxiety disorders; none of the secure children did. Two had separation anxiety disorder (one with disorganized attachment, one with avoidant attachment) and one had avoidant disorder (with disorganized attachment). Insecure children also had higher internalizing scores on the Child Behavior Checklist than those of secure children. When the dyads who had been classified as disorganized and mothers who had been classified as unresolved were assigned their "best" alternate category, and combined with the remaining three attachment categories, a higher than expected rate of ambivalent/resistant attachment and a lower than expected rate of secure attachment were found.

Warren et al. (1997) studied 172 adolescents aged 17.5 years who had participated in assessments of mother–child attachment at 12 months of age. Of these 172 adolescents, 26 (15%) met diagnostic criteria for anxiety disorders. More of the disordered adolescents were classified as anxious/resistant in infancy than the adolescent without anxiety disorders. More adolescents di-

agnosed with other disorders (not anxiety) were, as infants, classified as avoidant. Furthermore, being classified as anxious/resistant attachment doubled the risk of subsequently developing an anxiety disorder and better predicted adolescent anxiety disorders than either maternal anxiety or child temperament. The interaction between anxious/resistant attachment and one aspect of temperament (slow habituation to stimuli) further increased the risk of a subsequent anxiety disorder. However, secure, insecure-avoidant, and insecure-resistant attachment were *all* represented among the adolescents with anxiety disorders (data on the insecure-disorganized classification were unavailable).

Linkages have also been found between attachment and subclinical levels of anxiety. Female undergraduates who were insecurely attached were perceived by their friends as being more anxious than their counterparts who were securely attached (Barnas, Pollina, & Cummings 1991). Crowell, O'Connor, Wollmers, and Sprafkin (1991) found that children with behavioral disturbances whose mothers were classified as secure on the Adult Attachment Interview rated themselves as less anxious and depressed than children with behavioral disturbances whose mothers were insecure-dismissing. Cassidy and Berlin (1994) reported increased fearfulness across several studies of insecure-ambivalent/resistant children.

Belsky and Rovine (1987) have suggested a potential linkage between attachment and anxiety when attachment is placed on a spectrum from the style associated with the most overt distress (ambivalent/resistant) to that associated with the least overt distress (avoidant). Secure individuals are in the middle of the spectrum, with some exhibiting relatively high distress and some exhibiting relatively low distress (Belsky & Rovine, 1987). Consistent with Belsky and Rovine (1987), 2.5-year-old children who were either insecure-ambivalent/resistant or secure with relatively high distress showed higher indices of fear and separation distress than children in the other attachment classifications (Stevenson-Hinde & Shouldice, 1990).

In summary, insecure attachment has been linked with both clinical and subclinical anxiety in children of different age ranges. The link may be stronger when the child also has temperamental vulnerability to anxiety, although the evidence for this is not as clear. Limitations of this research include paucity of prospective studies, the varying definitions of anxiety (e.g., anxiety symptoms, anxiety disorders) used across studies, and small sample sizes.

Parenting

The research conducted on parenting has focused primarily on parental rearing styles, with the latter conceptualized along two orthogonal dimensions: warmth versus hostility, and control versus autonomy (Boer, 1998; Cassidy, 1995; Dadds, Barrett, Rapee, & Ryan, 1996; Lutz & Hock, 1995; Manassis et al., 1994; Rapee 1997; Siqueland, Kendall, & Steinberg, 1996; Warren et al., 1997).

Retrospective reports. In a meta-analysis of five studies, with a total of 463 patients in the experimental groups, Gerlsma, Emmelkamp, and Arrindell (1990) found that adults with phobias reported a parental rearing style characterized by less affection and more control. Studies of adults meeting diagnostic criteria for panic disorder or social phobia/avoidant personality disorder have demonstrated a similar recollection of childrearing patterns, in that these adults view their parents, and their relationship with them, as low in affection and overcontrolling (Rapee, 1997).

Empirical research has documented an influence of parental rearing styles on the development of anxiety (see Rapee, 1997, for review). Interestingly, adults with insecure-preoccupied attachments frequently report parental rejection and control (Main & Goldwyn, 1991), which suggests that parenting style may be related to adult attachment status.

Prospective reports and behavioral observations. In an early study, Bush, Melamed, & Cockrell (1989), using a self-report measure of parental rearing patterns, found parental reported use of positive reinforcement, modeling, and persuasion was associated with lower levels of child anxiety during their child's undergoing of a fearful medical procedure; parental use of punishment, physical force, and reinforcement of dependency was associated with higher levels during the medical procedure. Siqueland et al.

(1996) found that parents of children with anxiety disorders were rated by observers as less granting of psychological autonomy than were the parents of "normal" controls. In addition, children with anxiety disorders rated their mothers and fathers as less accepting and less granting of psychological autonomy compared to control children's ratings of their parents.

Direct observations of parent–child interactions have provided further evidence of family processes that may be specific to families of children with anxiety disorders, and these processes may serve to either bring out and/or maintain these disorders in children (e.g., Chorpita, Albano, & Barlow, 1996; Dadds et al., 1996; Ginsburg, Silverman, & Kurtines, 1995). For example, Dadds et al. (1996) studied specific sequences of communication exchanged between parents and children (ages 7 to 14) in a discussion of ambiguous hypothetical situations. Parents of children with anxiety disorders ($n = 66$) were less likely to grant and reward autonomy of thought and action than controls ($n = 18$). Dadds et al. also found that these parents fostered cautiousness and avoidance of taking a social risk by modeling caution, providing information about risk, expressing doubt about the child's competency, and rewarding the child for avoidance by expressing agreement and nurturance when the child decided he or she would not join in with the other children. Dadds et al. referred to this finding as the FEAR effect (Family Enhancement of Avoidant and Aggressive Responses).

In a study with 16 children (mean age = 11 years) of agoraphobic mothers and 16 children of mothers with no history of psychopathology matched by age, gender, and socioeconomic status (Capps, Sigman, Sena, & Henker, 1996), agoraphobic mothers reported more maternal separation anxiety with regard to their child than the control group. Maternal separation anxiety correlated negatively with children's perceived control (Capps et al., 1996). The effect probably is best interpreted as the result of a reciprocal relation between caregiver and child: when a child is more anxious, there may be greater cause for the parent's anxiety about separation.

More recently, Hudson and Rapee (2002) studied 57 children and adolescents (37 children with anxiety disorders, 20 nonclinic-referred children; aged 7 to 16 years) and found that mothers and fathers were overly involved not only with their anxiety-disordered child but also with the child's sibling (without anxiety disorders). The authors concluded that because parental overinvolvement does not occur exclusively in youths with anxiety disorders, it probably is not simply a response to difficulties with anxiety and coping that they have observed with the diagnosed youth. It also suggests that parental overinvolvement does not in and of itself cause anxiety disorders.

Anxious parents could increase their offsprings' risk of anxiety disorders by *(1)* having difficulty modeling appropriate coping strategies; *(2)* reacting to their children's fears negatively because they represent an aspect of themselves that they would rather deny; or *(3)* becoming overly concerned about their children's anxiety, resulting in overprotection and thus reducing opportunities for desensitization. The latter two reactions are consistent with dismissive and preoccupied adult attachment types, respectively. Anxious parents who are securely attached, by contrast, may be able to empathize with their children's fears, which may then be perceived as supportive. Thus, the transmission of parental anxiety may depend on the interaction between attachment and parental psychopathology (Radke-Yarrow, DeMulder, & Belmont, 1995).

Peer, School, and Community

The ecology of adolescent development and culture includes an expanded network of peer, school, and community affiliations. The transition to middle and high school constitutes a period of high developmental risk, in which there is an increased incidence of school truancy, failure and dropout, engagement in high-risk sexual and self-injurious behaviors, smoking and drug use, initiation into gangs, and contact with the juvenile justice system. It is also a period of increased exposure to interpersonal violence. For example, in 1999, almost 10% of 9th to 12th graders reported being hit or physically hurt by a boyfriend or girlfriend. In the sections below, particular high-risk activities engaged in by adolescents and their associated risk with anxiety are discussed.

Smoking

Initiation into cigarette smoking in adolescents is recognized as a major public health problem. As summarized by Upadhyaya, Deas, Brady, and Kruesi (2002) from a number of national surveys, approximately 3,000 adolescents start smoking each day, resulting in about 21% of high school seniors smoking daily, and a total of 4 million adolescent smokers. Smoking prevention and early treatment are important components of universal and selective public health prevention strategies, especially given that the American Health Association estimates that addiction to tobacco during adolescence accounts for 80% of adult smokers. As Upadhyaya et al. (2002) discuss, there is continuing interest in the interaction between onset of adolescent psychiatric conditions and smoking behavior, including experimental smoking and cessation difficulty. Among the disorders studied, Johnson et al. (2000) report that heavy cigarette smoking (defined as over 20 cigarettes per day) is associated with higher rates of agoraphobia, anxiety, and panic disorders in adolescents. Other studies have reported an even stronger association of adolescent smoking with attention-deficit hyperactivity disorder (Johnson et. al., 2000) and major depressive disorder (Dierker et al., 2001). Most of these studies note the importance of the relationship between peer smoking influences and individual psychiatric vulnerabilities. The general conclusion is two-pronged: first, smoking prevention and cessation programs need to incorporate screening for adolescent psychiatric disorders, including anxiety disorders and, second, attention to adolescent anxiety and comorbid disorders need to include strategies to address risks of tobacco addiction.

Drug Use

Adolescence is a developmental period in which experimentation with alcohol and drugs is common. It also is a time of development risk for early onset of alcohol and substance abuse and dependence. Nelson and Wittchen (1998) found that among youth and young adults, the peak incidence of alcohol disorders occurred at 16–17 years of age. Alcohol and drug use problems in adolescents are a strong predictive factor of adult alcohol and drug dependence (Swadi, 1999). Studies of substance abuse and alcohol motivation in adolescents suggest a multifactorial explanatory framework. Among the many factors, Comeau, Stuart, and Loba (2001) found that high anxiety sensitivity predicts conformity motives for alcohol and marijuana use, whereas anxiety traits are associated with coping motives for alcohol and cigarette use. Zucker, Craske, Barrios, and Holguin (2002) reported that among young adults with panic disorder, up to one in five cases had an onset related to an adolescent experience with a psychoactive drug. In a review of studies of adolescent use of the recreational drug "ecstasy," Montoya, Sorrentino, Lukas, and Price (2002) found a strong association between repeated drug use and anxiety disturbances, with potential neurobiological consequences that are of concern within this critical developmental stage.

Initiation and use of alcohol and drugs among adolescents are also related to life stresses, including traumatic events (Wills, Vaccaro, & McNammar, 1992). In one study, substance-abusing adolescents were found to be five times more likely to have a history of trauma and concurrent posttraumatic stress disorder (PTSD) compared to a community sample (Deykin & Buka, 1997). In a large study of adolescents enrolled in four drug treatment programs, a high positive correlation was found between severity of posttraumatic stress symptoms and higher levels of substance use and HIV risk behavior (Stevens, Murphy, & McNight, 2003).

As with cigarette addiction, prevention strategies for adolescent substance abuse need to include early intervention for anxiety vulnerable and traumatized youth and at the same time recognize that prevention or early intervention for adolescent substance abuse may also constitute an anxiety disorder prevention strategy.

Gang Affiliation and Other Criminal Behavior

Gang affiliation is a serious cultural problem in adolescence. There are an estimated 24,000 gangs, with over 772,000 members active across the United States (U.S. Department of Justice, 2002). There is a complexity to youth involvement in gangs. Many studies have examined the confluence of risk factors that predict gang membership, including neighborhood, family, school, peer group, and individual variables (Hill, Levermore, Twaite, & Jones, 1996). There is an emerging literature about the extent of trauma and loss exposure associated with gang membership and delinquent behavior more generally (Wood, Foy, Layne, Pynoos, & James, 2002). Despite high rates of trauma exposure prior to gang membership, commonly youth report that their worst traumatic experiences are gang related and the source of current PTSD symptoms (Wood et al., 2002). Ages 11–13 are primary years for solicitation and inculcation into gang affiliation and activities, contributing to years of increased trauma and loss exposure during adolescence. Consequently, intervention programs to prevent youth from becoming involved in gangs should be considered an adjunct prevention strategy for adolescent PTSD.

Adolescence is also the time when involvement in the justice system accelerates. Approximately 1.8 million youth go through the juvenile justice system each year, with over 360,000 detained and 176,000 incarcerated (U.S. Department of Justice, 2002). Recently, attention has turned to the high prevalence of adolescent psychiatric disorder present among juvenile justice detainees. Of importance, the rate of anxiety disorders is as high as one in three and equal to or exceeds those of mood disorder. Of the anxiety disorders, studies vary in the prevalence of specific anxiety disorders. Studies that have assessed PTSD have found it to be among the highest (Wasserman, McReynolds, Lucal, Fisher, & Santos, 2002). Interestingly, separation anxiety disorder among adolescents (an age-range where it is less expected) is surprisingly high among African-American and Hispanic and Latino detained youth (Teplin, Abram, McClelland,

Dulcan, & Mericle, 2002). The juvenile justice contact provides a key opportunity for mental health intervention that can play a significant role in an overall public mental health approach to adolescent anxiety disorders and delinquency prevention programs.

Social Support

The adult literature is replete with studies that suggest the possible beneficial effects of social support following exposure to traumatic events, but less is known about its role in mitigating anxiety disorder symptoms outside the context of trauma, and even less about the influence of social support in adolescent anxiety disorders. Studies of veterans from the Vietnam, Gulf, and Lebanon wars have found that veterans' perceptions of poor social support are associated with worse PTSD symptoms; the relationship remains regardless of whether veterans report retrospectively about the support they received immediately after his or her return from duty (Barrett & Mizes, 1988; Fontana, Schwartz, & Rosenheck, 1997; Foy, Resnick, Sipprelle, & Carroll, 1987; Solomon, Mikulincer, & Avitzur, 1988; Stretch, 1985, 1989; Sutker, Davis, Uddo, & Ditta, 1995) and even when controlling for level of combat exposure, another robust predictor of PTSD symptoms among veterans (Boscarino, 1995; King, Leonard, & March, 1998). Among civilian victims of violence, poor social support also has been linked to PTSD symptoms in victims of violent nonsexual assault (Bisson & Shepherd, 1995), domestic violence (Astin, Lawrence, & Foy, 1993; Kemp, Green, Hovanitz, & Rawlings, 1995), and rape survivors (Resick, 1993; Steketee & Foa, 1987; Zoellner, Foa, & Brigidi, 1999). Moreover, Fontana and Rosenheck (1998) found that good postdischarge social support was strongly predictive of less PTSD in female veterans who were victims of sexual harassment, rape, or attempted rape. Social support is also associated with recovery among victims of "noninterpersonal" traumas, such as natural disasters (e.g., Madakasira & O'Brien, 1987), motor vehicle accidents (Buckley, Blanchard, & Hickling, 1996), and chronic, life-threatening illness, including patients treated for breast cancer (Andrykowski & Cordova, 1998), African-American women

with HIV/AIDS (Myers & Durvasula, 1999), and survivors of childhood leukemia and their mothers and fathers (Kazak et al., 1997).

There are a number of shortcomings to the extant adult literature on social support in the wake of trauma. First, although a large body of research supports the conclusion that social support is associated with decreased PTSD symptomology (e.g., Greene, Grace, & Gleser, 1985; Keane, Zimering, & Caddell, 1985; most of these studies have relied on retrospective reports (some as many as 30 years after the fact) of social support. Second, the studies typically have aggregated and equally weighted the influence of friends, co-workers, and neighbors with that of immediate family, which may obscure the more influential effects for the latter (Griffith, 1985). Third, and perhaps most importantly for the purpose of considering prevention efforts, no studies have attempted to delineate the mechanism responsible for the apparent positive impact of social support on posttrauma recovery. Pennebaker and Seagal (1999) suggest that painful events, which have not been structured in a narrative format, may contribute to the continued experience of negative feelings and are more likely to remain in consciousness as unwanted thoughts (Wegner, 1989). Foa and Riggs (1993) suggest that trauma disclosure within naturally occurring social support systems provides three potential benefits: First, disclosure enables the trauma survivor to confront frightening memories in a relatively safe environment, allowing habituation of fear reactions, much as is accomplished in flooding treatment of PTSD (Foa et al., 1999; Foa, Feske, Murdock, Kozak, & McCarthy, 1991; Keane, Fairbank, Caddell, & Zimmering, 1989b; Richards, Lovell, & Marks, 1994). Second, given the observation that traumatic memories are often disjointed and confused, disclosure, particularly repeated disclosure, provides the survivor with an opportunity to create a more coherent memory. Finally, disclosure is thought to provide an opportunity for survivors to evaluate potentially mistaken cognitions regarding the impact on themselves (e.g., I am incompetent or worthless) or the world (e.g., the world is unpredictably dangerous). Herman (1992) suggests that disclosure may also serve to "reconnect" the trauma survivor to others within the social arena. That is, the act of disclosing the trauma to another person may provide an opportunity for the survivor to redevelop a sense of trust and attachment to others. Thus, disclosing the trauma to a supportive person may function in multiple ways to facilitate recovery.

There is also evidence that social support may mitigate the impact of negative life events in children and adolescents whose parents are divorcing (Cowen, Wyman, Work, & Parker, 1990) and in those who have been exposed to community violence (Berman, Kurtines, Silverman, & Serafini, 1996; Hill, Levermore, Twaite, & Jones, 1996; White, Bruce, Farrell, & Kliewer, 1998) and hurricanes (e.g., La Greca, Silverman, Vernberg, & Prinstein, 1996; Vernberg, La Greca, Silverman, & Prinstein, 1996). For example, White and colleagues (1998) found a strong negative relation between anxiety level and family social support in a longitudinal study investigating the effects of family social support on anxiety in 11- to 14-year-olds exposed to community violence. Unfortunately, little else has been done to explore the specific role of this potentially important protective factor. Perhaps acceptance into a supportive social network attenuates the effects of the putative anxiety disorder risk factors described earlier. Thus, social support serves as one possible explanation for so many children and adolescents elevated on these risk factors (e.g., behavioral inhibition) not going on to develop full-blown disorders. The importance of the adolescent's peer group suggests that social support may be particularly relevant during this period (see Table 11.1 for a summary of putative risk factors).

Table 11.1 Who May Be at Risk?

Factor	Description
Individual Factors	
Elevated but subsyndromal anxiety symptoms	Increased risk of developing full-blown disorder in next 2 years if elevated symptoms are already present
Behavioral inhibition (temperament)	Tendency to avoid novel stimuli and experiences; excessive shyness in response to new people
Anxiety sensitivity	Tendency to interpret physiological sensations of anxiety as threatening in and of themselves
Cognitive factors	Avoidant coping style, low perceived control
Family Factors	
Parenting	Insecure attachment, possibly interacting with behaviorally inhibited temperament
Parent–child interactions	Parental tendency to suggest avoidant problem-solving strategies; overinvolvement and overprotection in response to child's fears; poor modeling of coping responses
Peer, School, and Community Factors	
Smoking	Association with panic disorder in particular
Alcohol and other drug use	Elevates other risk factors (e.g., MVAs), may also elevate risk in and of itself
Gang affiliation and criminal behavior	Exposure to traumatic events, commission of interpersonal violence
Trauma exposure	Criterion A trauma increases the risk for PTSD and other anxiety symptoms, perhaps especially in those who are already vulnerable or in response to certain traumas regardless (e.g., sexual assault)
Poor social support	Associated with more symptoms and poorer outcomes in adults, possibly a mediating factor

MVA, motor vehicle accident; PTSD, posttraumatic stress syndrome.

Early Detection and Screening

The success of prevention intervention programs for anxiety disorders in adolescents depends a great deal on having early detection and screening strategies in place at key access points where youths might be identified. The types of early detection and screening strategies are likely to vary with the type of preventive intervention program being implemented (universal, selective, indicated). In this section, key access points are identified and specific types of screens that might be administered, depending on the type of preventive intervention strategy, are summarized.

Before proceeding with this discussion, a general point is first worth noting. For the majority of access points or settings where early detection and screening strategies might be conducted, some type of rating scale is recommended for initial use. Because of their objective scoring procedure, rating scales minimize the role of clinical inference and interpretation. As a result, there is no need to use highly trained staff for administration and scoring. In addition, most rating scales contain questions that would be of clear concern to non-mental health professionals, such as school board institutional review board members, because the scales contain items that are face valid. Finally, a wide range of rating scales is available for administration to various informants, including children and adolescents, as well as parents, teachers, and clinicians. Consequently, information can be obtained from either a single source (e.g., adolescent only) or multiple sources (e.g., adolescent, parent) depending on one's available resources. If resources are limited, the consensus in the field is that information from youths themselves should be obtained for screening and assessing for internalizing problems, including anxiety (Loeber, Green, & Lahey, 1990).

Despite the advantages in using rating scales for the purpose of early detection and screening, several caveats are worth noting. One is that although the measures mentioned in this section all possess adequate psychometric properties in terms of reliability and validity, their actual utility for screening purposes awaits further empirical evaluation. For example, data on the measures' sensitivity (the percentage of individuals who receive the diagnosis who were positively identified by the rating scale; true positives) and specificity (the percentage of individuals who do not receive the diagnosis and who are not identified by the rating scale as anxious; true negatives) (Vecchio, 1966) are scarce when it comes to child and adolescent samples, particularly nonwhite samples. Second, currently available rating scales are likely to select more false positives than true positives (Costello & Angold, 1988). That is, youths identified as anxious at an initial screen are likely not to be anxious or depressed at the second stage of an investigation. Consequently, a useful and cost-efficient approach for early detection and screening for indicated intervention programs would employ a multistage sampling design (e.g., Ialongo, Edelsohn, Werthamer-Larsson, Crockett, & Kellam, 1993; Kendall, Cantwell, & Kazdin, 1989; Roberts, Lewinsohn, & Seeley, 1991). At the first stage, a rating scale would be administered to informants to identify youths who score 1 or 2 standard deviations from the sample mean or who deviate from normative data. These identified cases would then undergo more precise and comprehensive assessments (e.g., structured diagnostic interviews) at the second or third stage of the research.

Potential Access Points for Early Detection and Screening

School. The school setting is an obvious access point for early detection and screening of anxiety and its disorders because this is where the children and adolescents are. If a preventive interventionist is interested in developing and implementing an indicated prevention program, there are several rating scales that can be administered to target high-risk children and adolescents who may demonstrate minimal but detectable symptoms of anxiety and/or anxiety disorders. In general, most of the research studies that have used rating scales for screening anxiety symptoms and disorders have used largely preadolescent samples of children. There is a paucity of work in which the study's samples involved adolescents specifically.

For anxiety symptoms, the most widely used

child and adolescent self-rating scale measure is the Revised Children's Manifest Anxiety Scale (RCMAS; Reynolds & Richmond, 1978), which was used as an initial screen in the Queensland Early Intervention and Prevention of Anxiety Project (Dadds et al., 1999; Dadds, Spence, Holland, Barrett, & Laurens, 1997), described below. The RCMAS is a 37-item scale: 28 items are summed yielding a Total Anxiety score; the other nine items are summed to yield a Lie score. Youths respond either yes or no to all 37 items. Factor analytic studies have also provided support for the RCMAS's three-factor subscale structure (Physiological, Worry/Oversensitivity, and Concentration) as well as the Lie scale (e.g., Reynolds & Richmond, 1978). Positive scale convergence between the RCMAS and other widely used child self-rating scales of anxiety and related constructs (trait anxiety, fear, depression) in community samples have also been found (e.g., Muris, Merckelbach, Ollendick, King, & Bogie, 2002). In addition, there is considerable evidence supporting the reliability of the RCMAS and its subscales in community samples. For example, Pela and Reynolds (1982) reported test–retest reliability of $r = .98$ of the Total Anxiety scale using a 3-week interval. Internal consistency of the RCMAS is also excellent, with estimates ranging from .82 to .85.

For anxiety symptoms linked more directly to DSM-IV anxiety disorders, the Multidimensional Anxiety Scale for Children (MASC; March, Parker, Sullivan, & Stallings, 1997), the Screen for Child Anxiety Related Emotional Disorders (Birmaher et al., 1997), and the Spence Children's Anxiety Scale may be useful. The MASC, for example, is a 45-item scale that yields a Total Anxiety Disorder Index and four main factor scores: Social Anxiety (with performance anxiety and humiliation as subfactors), Physical Symptoms, (with tension-restlessness, somatic-autonomic arousal as subfactors), Harm/Avoidance (with perfectionism, anxious coping as subfactors), and Separation/Panic. In addition, six items yield an Inconsistency Index to identify careless or contradictory responses. Youths may be identified on the basis of either specific subscale scores on these measures or the total score.

For social anxiety, the Social Anxiety Scale for Children–Revised (La Greca & Stone, 1993) and

the adolescent version (La Greca & Lopez, 1998) as well as the Social Phobia and Anxiety Inventory for Children (Beidel, Turner, & Morris, 1995) have been found to be helpful in identifying highly social anxious children (Epkins, 2002; Morris & Masia, 1998), although variations in the two measures' classification correspondence indicated variation with sample, age, and gender. In light of this variation, coupled with the fact that both the Epkins (2002) and Morris and Masia (1998) studies did not sample adolescents (Epkins's sample was 8 to 12 years; Morris and Masia's was 9 to 12 years), additional research on the utility of these measures for screening among adolescents is needed. Moreover, research on all of these scales' utility in the context of prevention is lacking.

The Childhood Anxiety Sensitivity Index (CASI; Silverman, Fleisig, Rabian, & Peterson, 1991) has been used in a number of studies and appears useful as a screen for adolescents who may be at risk for displaying panic attacks and panic disorder (Hayward, Killen, Wilson, & Hammer, 1997; Weems, Hayward, Killen, & Taylor, 2002). In fact, it appears to be the only measure that has been used as a screen for adolescents specifically. Consequently, further description of the scale might be in order.

The CASI consists of 18 items that assess the extent to which children and adolescents believe the experience of anxiety will result in negative consequences. Sample items include: "It scares me when I feel like I am going to throw up" and "It scares me when my heart beats fast." Youths respond to each item using a 3-point scale: none (1), some (2), or a lot (3). The CASI yields a total score by summing the ratings across all items. The CASI scores can range from 18 to 54, with higher scores reflecting higher levels of anxiety sensitivity. Silverman et al. (1991) reported internal consistency estimates (coefficient alphas) of .87 for both a nonclinical and clinical sample, and test–retest reliability estimates (using a retest interval of 2 weeks) of .76 and .79 for the nonclinical and clinical samples, respectively.

Recent research provides strong support for a hierarchical model for anxiety sensitivity as represented in the CASI with a single second-order factor and four facets (first-order factors) labeled Disease Concerns, Unsteady Concerns, Mental

Incapacitation Concerns, and Social Concerns (Silverman, Goedhart, Barrett, & Turner, 2003). This type of research on the facets of anxiety sensitivity has the potential to further our understanding about the prevention of anxiety problems to the extent that the specific facets of anxiety sensitivity may be more related to a given pathological condition than the total anxiety sensitivity construct as recent research suggests (Joiner et al., 2002).

Silverman et al. (2003) also tested for factorial invariance (equal factor loadings) of the completed four-factor model across gender and age (two age groups: children, ages 7 to 11 years, and adolescents, ages 12 to 17 years). The hypothesis of equal factor loadings on the four factors across age and gender and across samples could not be rejected, thereby indicating factor stability. The only age difference to emerge in this study was that children displayed a higher level of Unsteady and Disease Concerns (and consequently a higher level of Total Concerns) than adolescents, a finding that is consistent with age differences in frequency and intensity of common fears (Gullone, 2000). Perhaps a higher level of fearfulness and less knowledge of physical processes in children than in adolescents constitutes a higher level of worrying among children about their physical condition. Whether the emergence in children of higher levels of Unsteady and Disease Concerns is something that would be worth assessing early on by means of the CASI, with possible intervenion as a preventative step, would be an interesting avenue to pursue.

In addition, evidence indicates that a large proportion of children and adolescents who display school refusal behavior are likely suffering from some type of anxiety disorder, particularly separation anxiety disorder in young children and social anxiety, panic, or generalized anxiety disorder in older children and adolescents (Kearney & Silverman, 1997). Thus it is critical that school counselors and psychologists be informed and educated about the nature of school refusal behavior so that they can help detect such cases and refer students for appropriate therapeutic, rather than disciplinary, action.

If a preventive interventionist is interested in developing and implementing a selective prevention program in a school setting, specific groups or individuals considered to be at risk for developing anxiety and its disorders need to be identified. At the preschool level, Rapee (2002) used a mother-completed rating scale of the child's temperament, followed by a laboratory observation of behavioral inhibition, as a screen for selecting youngsters in the Macquarie University Preschool Intervention Program (described below).

In light of the high rates of traumatic exposure among young people, particularly adolescents, youths who have been exposed to traumatic events are another group that should be considered for early detection and screening in the school setting, with focus particularly on posttraumatic stress and anxiety reactions. Successful efforts in such screening, using most frequently the Reaction Index (Frederick, Pynoos, & Nader, 1992), have appeared in the area of community violence (e.g., adolescent sample: Berman, Kurtines, Silverman, & Serafini, 1996), natural disasters (e.g., child sample; La Greca et al., 1996; Vernberg et al., 1996); and sniper shootings (e.g., child sample; Pynoos, Frederick, Nader, & Arroyo, 1987). March, Amaya-Jackson, Terry, and Costanzo (1997) and, more recently, Foa, Johnson, Feeny, and Treadwell (2001) have developed and conducted psychometric evaluation of the Child and Adolescent Trauma Survey (CATS) and the Child PTSD Symptom Scale (CPSS), respectively; both have been found to be psychometrically sound.

The CPSS, for example, assesses traumatic stress symptoms in children and adolescents, 8 to 18 years of age. The CPSS items assess all 17 DSM-IV symptom criteria for PTSD and yield a Total Severity Score (17 items) and three empirically derived factor scale scores representing DSM-IV clusters B (Re-experiencing), C (Avoidance), and D (Arousal). The CPSS also includes a seven-item impairment rating scale to assess functioning in such domains as family, peers, and school. Evidence has indicated moderate to excellent internal consistency, retest reliability, and concurrent validity as well as excellent sensitivity and specificity (Foa, Cashman, Jaycox, & Perry, 1997). All together, these PTSD scales have the potential for use in early detection and screening of youths at high risk for developing posttraumatic stress and anxiety reactions from their exposure to traumatic events. Further evaluative research regarding their utility for such purposes is needed, however. In addition, because many adolescent-onset problems such as cigarette smoking frequently co-occur with anxiety and its disorders, as noted earlier in this section, screening for anxiety with one of the anxiety symptoms scales (e.g., RCMAS, MASC) may be worthwhile to include, whenever beginning work with adolescents for any such problems.

Finally, Beidel and colleagues (Beidel & Turner, 1988; Beidel, Turner, & Trager, 1994) conducted a series of studies showing that the Test Anxiety Scale for Children (Saranson, Davidson, Lighthall, & Waite, 1958) could serve as a useful screen in identifying children who may show detectable symptoms of anxiety disorders, including social anxiety disorder, specific phobia, and generalized anxiety disorder. Clearly, as "high-stakes" testing (e.g., SATs, ACTs) becomes more of a stressor with adolescence, the potential utility of test anxiety as a marker, and the Test Anxiety Scale as a screen among adolescent samples, deserves scrutiny.

Health-care settings. There are multiple access points for early detection and screening in healthcare settings, particularly in pediatrics, obstetrics-gynecology (ob-gyn), and psychiatry. The pediatric setting, for example, is the natural site for early detection and screening of young children with pediatric onset of either obsessive-compulsive disorder (OCD) or a tic disorder following an abrupt onset of symptoms after a group A β-hemolytic streptococcal infection, which is referred to as PANDAS (see Chapter 10). The MASC Obsessive-Compulsive Screener (March, Parker, et al., 1997), together with the Conners-March Developmental Questionnaire, may identify such cases; the former could be used to identify OCD symptoms in both pediatricians' and dermatologists' offices. Indeed, for a large proportion of families, the pediatrician office is the "first gate" they enter when their child or adolescent begins to show disturbances associated with anxiety and its disorders, such as somatic complaints and panic attack symptoms. It would thus seem critical for primary care physicians to have understanding of and knowledge about anxiety disorders so that they could inquire about the presence or absence of key symptoms of the various disorders (described in Chapter 9), and refer, as necessary, to a mental health professional for further evaluation based on the results of these initial queries.

Given the preponderance of female cases of anxiety disorders relative to male cases particularly from adolescence and beyond, ob-gyn settings represent yet another potentially useful and critically important access point for early detection and screening. Studies have demonstrated that pubertal maturation in adolescent girls, particularly early onset, may constitute a risk factor for developing anxiety symptoms and disorders (e.g., Caspi & Moffit, 1991; Graber, Brooks-Gunn, Paikoff, & Warren, 1994), particularly panic attacks (Hayward, Killen, Kraemer, et al., 1997). Such findings suggest the potential utility of educating physicians in the ob-gyn area about the risks of anxiety problems in their young adolescent female patients. The manner in which such young patients may become overly sensitive to the physical changes that occur during the menstrual cycle (i.e., high anxiety sensitivity) might be carefully considered and even assessed using the CASI (Silverman et al., 1991). Relatedly, research findings, albeit sparse, suggest that hormonal fluctuations during the female reproductive cycle may serve to either exacerbate or reduce anxiety symptoms and disorders. For example, among some women, the postpartum period may be a risk for the onset and exacerbation of anxiety symptoms and disorders (March & Yonkers, 2001). Also among some women, pregnancy may be a period when past episodes of panic disorder improves (Shear & Oommen, 1995). In light of such findings, it seems critically important that ob-gyn physicians carefully consider their female patients' emotional states during regularly scheduled appointments. Adult anxiety rating scales, such as the Hamilton Scales, may be worth administering as a potential screen for the presence of anxiety symptoms in these patients.

Finally, psychiatry departments housed in medical settings, community mental health settings, or in private practice represent yet another important, though again, largely untapped access point by which to conduct early detection and screening. In light of the strong evidence for familial transmission of anxiety disorders, adult patients who present with anxiety disorders, depressive disorders, or both (Weissman, 1988) should be carefully queried about the functioning of their children and adolescents. For such purposes, parent rating scales such as the Child Behavior Checklist (CBCL; Achenbach, 1991) and the Connors Rating Scales (Conners, 1997) could be administered. Although parents with anxiety problems are likely to endorse high levels of internalizing problems in their offspring with the CBCL (e.g., Silverman, Cerny, Nelles, & Burke, 1988), some of which might be due to the parent's own pathology, as noted earlier, this initial step is a screen. Further follow-up would then be conducted with the children themselves by means of structured interview schedules, such as the Anxiety Disorders Interview Schedule for Children (ADIS-C): DSM-IV (Silverman & Albano, 1996). This interview schedule is the one most widely used in child and adolescent anxiety disorders and includes a child and a parent version. Previous research demonstrates good to excellent test-retest reliability for the diagnosis of anxiety disorders (e.g., κ = .63 to .83 for the ADIS-C child version, κ = .65 to .88 for the ADIS-C parent version, and κ = .80 to .92 for the composite diagnosis; Silverman, Saavedra, & Pina, 2001).

Web-based surveys. Finally, recent survey studies involving adults' reactions to the terrorist attacks of September 11, 2001 employed Web-based measures (e.g., Schuster et al., 2001), which allowed for efficient data collection from large numbers of subjects. The method is not without its shortcomings, however, the most prominent of which is the possibility of sampling bias: *(1)* those most interested in the topic and affected by the events might be most likely to participate, which will perhaps overestimate effects; and *(2)* despite the appearance of ubiquity in our culture, it is estimated that fewer than 50% of urban homes have personal computers, and thus Web-based surveys are likely to exclude large numbers of participants. It may be that use of Web-based surveys in the school context may be a useful way to proceed, however: it would avert a problem of having little unscheduled time during the school day to conduct research studies, and may improve participation among adolescents, who are increasingly computer-

savvy. The problem of excluding youngsters who do not have a computer in their home could be addressed by allowing the use of school and/or researcher-provided laptops for this purpose.

Model Programs

The outcome literature on the prevention of anxiety disorders is insufficiently developed to describe any existing program as a "model" and reflects the fact that the complex interplay among the many putative risk and protective factors for anxiety disorders is not well understood. Nevertheless, several studies have been undertaken and are described below. Most of these studies have been conducted using adult samples; however, a handful of studies have employed pediatric samples. Moreover, as is the case with anxiety disorder treatment studies, no adolescent-specific prevention intervention protocols have been developed as yet. Thus, although there are limitations inherent to extrapolating findings from studies comprised of adult samples to adolescent populations, the paucity of research on prevention of anxiety disorders in adolescents requires greater reliance on the adult literature. Efforts at anxiety disorders prevention are also hampered by insufficient and sometimes inconsistent information about the longitudinal course of disorders, the efficacy of procedures designed to reduce modifiable risk factors (e.g., anxiety sensitivity), the influence of protective factors, and the possible additive if not multiplicative effects of multiple risk factors. Further, as indicated earlier, immersion in adolescent culture represents a time of increased risk for a variety of negative life experiences and, as such, adolescents are at increased risk for the development of at least certain anxiety disorders. Thus, the research literature in this area remains underdeveloped, and addressing these critical gaps will be important in developing adolescent-specific prevention programs.

Interventions

We have organized the review of the extant literature using the categories recommended by the Institute of Medicine's Committee on Prevention of Mental Disorders: *(1)* indicated prevention programs, *(2)* selective prevention programs, and *(3)* universal prevention programs. Notably, some prevention intervention programs have been developed to target general psychopathology risk factors (e.g., children whose parents recently divorced; Pedro-Carroll & Cowen, 1985). However, because the link between these broader risk factors and the development of anxiety disorders is even more tenuous than the link between anxiety disorders and the specific anxiety disorder risk factors described above, we limit our discussion here to those studies that focused more specifically on prevention of anxiety symptoms and anxiety disorders. A comprehensive review of these studies is available elsewhere (Hudson, Flannery-Schroeder, & Kendall, 2004).

Indicated prevention programs. These programs are most similar to the treatments for fully syndromal individuals with which the field is most familiar, in that patients are already experiencing symptoms of a disorder and are at high risk for the development of the full-blown syndrome. Harvey and Bryant (1998) reported that 78% of adult motor vehicle accident survivors who met criteria for acute stress disorder (ASD) suffered from PTSD 6 months after the trauma, compared to only 4% of survivors who did not meet criteria for ASD. Thus, ASD is considered a major risk factor for PTSD. It is important to note, however, that there are many shared features between the two disorders and this overlap may be the main contributor to the predictive relationship between ASD and PTSD. Indeed, severity of PTSD symptoms shortly after the traumatic event is a very strong predictor of PTSD severity later on. Foa, Hearst-Ikeda, and Perry (1995) conducted the first PTSD prevention study. Women who were recent victims of sexual and nonsexual assault and who met symptom criteria for PTSD received either a brief cognitive-behavioral therapy (CBT) program consisting of four weekly 1.5-hr sessions or four weekly assessments of their PTSD related symptoms. At 2 months postintervention assessment, the CBT group had a recovery rate of 10% for PTSD vs. 70% in the assessment control group. Using five sessions of Foa et al.'s prevention program (adding one additional session), Bryant, Harvey,

Sackville, Dang, and Basten (1998) compared it to supportive counseling (SC) for male and female survivors of motor vehicle and industrial accidents who met diagnostic criteria for ASD. At posttreatment, only 8% of CBT participants met criteria for PTSD, compared to 83% of the SC patients. Although rates of PTSD increased over the course of a 6-month follow-up, CBT remained superior (17% PTSD incidence) to SC (67% PTSD incidence). In a subsequent study, Bryant, Sackville, Dangh, Moulds, and Guthrie (1999) modified the brief CBT by limiting it to psychoeducation and exposure, eliminating anxiety management (e.g., relaxation training) and cognitive restructuring, and compared this modified protocol to the full protocol and to SC. At posttreatment, 20% of participants in the full treatment program and 14% of participants in the brief CBT met criteria for PTSD, in comparison to 56% of participants in the SC condition. At 6 months, incidence of PTSD was 23%, 15%, and 67% for the full treatment program, exposure, and SC, respectively. In a more recent study, Foa, Zoellner, and Feeny (2004) again found that CBT accelerates recovery after sexual assault, compared to SC.

Another group presumably at risk for the development of an anxiety disorder is adults who present to emergency rooms with panic attack symptoms. Swinson, Soulios, Cox, and Kuch (1992) conducted an intervention study with such individuals, 40% of whom met full symptom criteria for panic disorder, thus rendering this study an indicated prevention/treatment hybrid. Nevertheless, at 6 months follow-up, participants randomized to a 1-hr exposure-based condition were improved on panic and anxiety measures, whereas those assigned to a 1-hr reassurance control intervention were no better. Subgroup analyses examining outcome for those with full syndromal panic disorder and those who were subthreshold were not reported, however. Gardenschwartz and Craske (2001) also targeted the prevention of panic disorder, but recruited college students who had experienced a panic attack within the last year, evidenced elevated anxiety sensitivity, and did not meet DSM criteria for panic disorder. Participants were randomly assigned to either a wait list or a day-long CBT workshop that included psychoeducation about agoraphobia and panic, behavioral and cognitive strategies, and interoceptive exposure. At 6 months follow-up, 14% of the wait-list group had gone on to develop fully syndromal panic disorder, compared with only 2% of the workshop participants; significant effects were also seen on other relevant indices (e.g., panic attack frequency × intensity index). As the authors note, a longer follow-up period may not have yielded similar outcome, as the workshop's effects may have been transient.

Only two randomized control trials (RCTs) involving indicated prevention programs have been conducted using pediatric samples. LaFreniere and Capuano (1997) examined the effects of a program directed at mothers of preschool children ($N = 43$) exhibiting anxious or withdrawn behavior, comparing it to no treatment. The intervention lasted for 6 months and consisted of four phases: *(1)* assessment; *(2)* education of the parents about their child's developmental needs; *(3)* determination of specific objectives for the family; and *(4)* implementation of the intervention during 11 home visits with child-directed interaction, modification of behavior problems, training in parenting skills, and enhancement of the effectiveness of social support systems. Given the age of the children, outcome variables included teacher ratings in social competence within the preschool setting and cooperation and enthusiasm during a problem-solving task rather than symptoms of a specific anxiety disorder. Results indicated that maternal stress was reduced and anxious–withdrawn behavior of the child was significantly lower at posttreatment in both conditions, although the social competence of children whose mothers received the intervention was greater prior to intervention than that of those whose mother received no treatment. The relatively brief follow-up period and the lack of information about anxiety disorder symptoms limit the utility of the findings. Nevertheless, the study offers preliminary and encouraging findings about the potential benefit of such programs for behaviorally inhibited young children.

The second pediatric study, known as the Queensland Early Intervention and Prevention of Anxiety Project, constitutes the most comprehensive effort made thus far in evaluating the efficacy of a prevention program for children and adolescents (Dadds et al., 1997, 1999). As in the Swinson et al. (1992) adult panic disorder prevention study described above, Dadds et al.'s study can be better characterized as a hybrid-indicated prevention and early-intervention study because 55% of the selected children met diagnostic criteria for at least one anxiety disorder. A total of 1,786 children (ages 7 to 14 years) were screened for anxiety problems by use of teacher nominations and children's self-ratings. After initial diagnostic interviews, 128 children were selected and randomly assigned to either a 10-week school-based psychosocial intervention based on Kendall's Coping Cat protocol (2000a), or to a monitoring group. The intervention was conducted over 10 weekly, 1- to 2-hr sessions at each intervention school. Group sizes ranged from 5 to 12 children. Parental sessions were conducted at the intervention schools in weeks 3, 6, and 9. Anxiety disorder diagnostic status was assessed at posttreatment and at 6-month, 12-month, and 24-month follow-up and yielded interesting results: the CBT and control groups differed significantly with respect to anxiety disorder diagnostic status at 6 months (27% vs. 57%) and at 24 months (20% vs. 39%), but did not differ at 12-month follow-up (37% vs. 42%). Notably, treatment benefits were most evident for those children who initially had moderate to severe clinician ratings of severity, with approximately 50% of these children retaining a clinical diagnosis at the 2-year follow-up, if they did not receive the intervention. For those children who initially showed symptoms of anxiety but who did not have a clinically significant anxiety disorder, there was minimal difference between the preventive intervention and the monitoring-only condition at 24 months follow-up, with 11% showing an anxiety disorder in the intervention group and 16% in the monitoring condition. In other words, children with subclinical anxiety problems did not appear to be at high risk of developing a more severe anxiety disorder if left untreated and benefited only minimally from the intervention.

Selective prevention programs. Selective prevention intervention programs are delivered to individuals or groups considered to be at high risk for anxiety disorders yet are not evidencing anxiety disorder symptoms. There is a paucity of studies on these programs. To date, most selective prevention intervention programs have targeted individuals or groups exposed to stressful life events such as parental divorce (e.g., Alpert-Gillis, Pedro-Carroll, & Cowen, 1989; Hightower & Braden, 1991; Hodges, 1991; Short, 1998; Zubernis, Cassidy, Gillham, Reivich, & Jaycox, 1999); transition between primary and secondary school, which can be associated with a number of psychological difficulties (e.g., peer relationships, school refusal behavior, substance use; Felner & Adan, 1988); medical and dental procedures (Peterson & Shigetomi, 1981); and having a chronically ill sibling (e.g., Bendor, 1990). Although the findings from these studies generally yield positive effects, their direct relevance to preventing anxiety disorders in adolescents is unclear.

The only selective prevention intervention program designed specifically for anxiety disorders is the Macquarie University Preschool Intervention Program (Rapee, 2002). Children (ages 3.5 to 4.5 years) were recruited mainly via questionnaires distributed to preschools. Inclusion in the study was based on mother-completed ratings on the Australian version of the Childhood Temperament Scale (Sansan, Pedlow, Cann, Prior, & Oberklaid, 1996), followed up by laboratory observation of behavioral inhibition. Behaviorally inhibited children were randomly assigned to either an intervention condition or a monitoring condition. The intervention was conducted with parents only and focused on education about the nature of withdrawal and anxiety, parental anxiety management strategies, information about the importance of modeling competence and promoting independence, development of exposure hierarchies for the children and practice of graded exposure, and discussion of future development. The intervention was conducted in groups of six families and lasted for six sessions. Results at 12 months revealed that mothers in the intervention condition had self-ratings that indicated significantly greater decreases in their child's inhibited temperament as well as in the number of child anxiety diagnoses compared to mothers in the control condition. However, laboratory observations indicated that children in the

both groups had reduced behavioral inhibition with no significant differences between the two groups.

Universal prevention programs. As an extension of the indicated prevention work conducted in Australia and reviewed above, encouraging preliminary data have emerged from a school-based FRIENDS program for children ages 10–12 years (Barrett & Turner, 2001) and a second sample of children ages 10–13 years (Lowry-Webster, Barrett, & Dadds, 2001). The FRIENDS acronym stands for *F*eeling worried; *R*elax and feel good; *I*nner thoughts; *E*xplore plans of action; *N*ice work, reward yourself; *D*on't forget to practice; and *S*tay cool. The program is cognitive-behavioral in orientation, can be delivered by teachers or psychologists, is conducted weekly for 10 weeks and followed by booster sessions, and has been compared to an untreated control group. Children who received the intervention had lower self-rated anxiety levels than those of controls at posttreatment; moreover, no statistical differences were found in outcome when FRIENDS was delivered by either teachers or psychologists (Barrett & Turner, 2001). These preliminary reports are encouraging, although the full sample has yet to be accrued, and the follow-up period (6 months) is insufficient to determine whether participation in the program affects anxiety symptoms and the development of anxiety disorders in the long run, especially for those anxiety disorders (e.g., panic disorder) that are more likely to develop in adolescence than in childhood.

Lowry-Webster et al. (2001) randomly assigned 594 children (10 to 13 years) within different schools to receive either the FRIENDS program or assessment only. The intervention was implemented by trained classroom teachers and three separate sessions for parents were also conducted. Pre- to postintervention changes were examined universally and for children who scored above the clinical cutoff for anxiety at pretest. Results revealed that children in the FRIENDS intervention condition reported less anxiety symptoms, regardless of their risk status, relative to the comparison condition. Notably, those who were already in the clinically anxious range on the Spence Children's Anxiety Scale fared better in the FRIENDS program than in the wait-list condition, which, as found by Dadds et al. (1997), suggests again that the FRIENDS program may be a useful intervention for children who are already experiencing significant problems with anxiety. Further research evaluating its efficacy with older adolescent samples is needed, however, before conclusions for its utility with this population can be drawn.

The FRIENDS program was also conducted and evaluated with culturally diverse migrant groups of non-English-speaking background (Yugoslavian, Chinese, and mixed-ethnic; $N = 121$ in Australia (Barrett, Sonderegger, & Sonderegger, 2001). The sample consisted of 106 primary and 98 high school students and were randomly assigned to either the FRIENDS program or a wait-list control condition (10 weeks wait). Participants in the FRIENDS program exhibited lower anxiety and a more positive future outlook than wait-list participants at posttest. Although the findings suggest the potential of the FRIENDS program in reducing anxiety associated with cultural change, the long-term effects of the program for this purpose have yet to be determined. Also unclear is the extent to which the youths involved in this program were actually suffering from clinically significant anxiety or were undergoing transitory duress due to their being of new immigration status.

As noted by Winett (1998a) and by Donovan and Spence (2000), an infrastructure capable of supporting such large-scale projects must be in place before a universal prevention program can be conducted, and the necessary resources can only be marshaled if anxiety disorders prevention is given a significant level of priority on a societal, school, and community level. It is notable that the only study of this kind specifically targeting reduction of anxiety symptoms was conducted with children rather than with adults, perhaps because schools contain the infrastructure that is needed for the implementation of universal prevention programs. Another reason to focus on children in prevention programs is the belief that early intervention will prevent the vulnerable individual from having experiences that will increase risk for developing an anxiety disorder (e.g., being bullied by peers). One advantage of universal prevention is that it does not label any individuals as being "at risk," a process that may serve to increase anxiety about anxiety and initiate avoidant coping.

Evaluating and Measuring Success

What Constitutes Success?

As noted above, the small number of intervention studies that have been conducted thus far have focused primarily on the reduction of anxious symptoms as measured by self-report (e.g., Lowry-Webster et al., 2001), although some studies examined whether patients met diagnostic status for an anxiety disorder at both post-intervention and, perhaps more importantly, at follow-up (e.g., Dadds et al., 1997). Both symptoms and diagnostic status are relevant, although the latter is less sensitive because participants can lose the diagnosis at a particular assessment point yet still remain elevated symptomatically and thus presumably also remain at risk for increased symptoms down the road. No studies have examined anxious symptoms and diagnostic status longitudinally through adolescence and into early adulthood. Such studies would yield data that truly test the success of prevention interventions. Yet another kind of successful outcome for universal intervention programs would be destigmatization of anxiety as a character flaw or weakness. Clearly, most youth who participate in universal prevention programs are at low risk for the development of anxiety disorders, yet informing this majority of the nature and impact of anxiety may help reduce problems that often face anxious youth in the social context, such as ostracism, teasing, and peer rejection.

What Are the Active Ingredients?

The few prevention intervention studies that have been conducted thus far have not shed light on the mechanisms involved because most of the designs used have compared active treatment packages to repeated assessment only. The superiority of the CBT packages examined thus far could therefore be attributable to a wide variety of nonspecific factors, such as treatment credibility and therapist contact. Dismantling studies typically follow the establishment of efficacy (e.g., Schmidt et al., 2000), and thus the field may be a long time from discovering the impact of specific treatment interventions and their underlying mechanisms.

What Outcomes Are Targeted?

As noted above, in the small number of studies conducted to date, the outcomes targeted have focused primarily on anxiety symptoms and disorders. It might be worthwhile for future research to move beyond symptoms and diagnosis and pay increased attention to whether functional impairment has improvement. For example, are there improvements in the adolescent's grades or in his or her peer relationships? These are the outcomes that would seem to matter most and should be seriously considered in the design and evaluation of future prevention studies.

In addition, the potential of "positive psychology" has yet to be seriously considered in the context of preventing anxiety disorders in adolescents and targeting outcomes. Positive psychology is devoted to creating a science of human strengths that act as buffers against mental illness, including anxiety (Seligman, 2002). Dick-Niederhauser and Silverman (2003) have adapted positive psychology principles and have suggested their utility in serving as outcome targets for anxiety prevention studies. Thus, potential outcome targets might include the instilling of hope and the active pursuit of goals in young people, which in turn have been linked to the development of courage. Courage in turn has been linked with increased optimistic cognitive processing, a sense of self-efficacy, and skillful coping. Although measures exist to assess some positive psychological concepts, further instrument development and evaluation is needed for positive psychology principles to be fully implemented and studied in the context of anxiety prevention research.

Conceptual, Methodological, and Practical Issues

Methodological and conceptual issues vary across types of prevention program. That is, the methodological concerns arising in universal prevention that target the broad population of adolescents are different from those in selected and indicated prevention intervention. The former requires more streamlined assessments that would increase participation and compliance (thus ensuring sample representativeness) and reduce cost (thus assuring feasibility). Accordingly, a major issue in universal prevention program research is finding the best ways to prompt adolescents to participate in a study that addresses a problem that they probably do not have. Universal prevention programs are especially likely to be conducted in conjunction with school administrators, thus capitalizing on the schools' past successes in encouraging student participation will be important. As noted earlier, a brief survey conducted via a Web site might capture the interest of teens in particular, thus computer technologies may prove essential in this kind of work. The costs of universal programs may ultimately require a political commitment on the level of state or federal government. For the selective and indicated programs, the primary methodological concern is how to encourage participation while at the same time protecting student confidentiality. This may be especially important if the intervention itself is conducted at school and during school hours, when absence might be conspicuous; negative social costs both real and imagined may impact participation. Moreover, if the intervention is conducted in groups, confidentiality among group members needs to be considered. Students who have been identified for intervention participation because of having experienced a trauma or for being excessively shy might be reluctant to share their experiences if they do not have assurance that what is discussed in session will not be discussed outside with nonmembers. The provision of sufficient time to foster group cohesion to alleviate this concern would therefore be important in any selective and indicated prevention effort that involves discussion of personal matters in a group setting.

Another issue that warrants consideration is when to intervene. As discussed above in relation to trauma exposure, immediate intervention provided to all individuals exposed to the trauma has not been found helpful with adults and thus should probably be avoided when conducting interventions with youth who have been exposed to a traumatic event, such as shootings at the school.

Yet another issue is the match between the type of intervention and the developmental stage of the individuals. Perhaps group interventions can be particularly successful in adolescence when the value of the peer group is quite powerful and, if properly harnessed, may enhance the efficacy of the intervention. Interventions with younger children, by contrast, need to be targeted at parents, particularly interventions that target the parental risk factors thought to be associated with increased risk for anxiety disorders.

The choice of place for conducting prevention interventions is another important consideration. Often the school would be the most practical place and would allow for the accrual of the kinds of large sample sizes required to detect effects for intervention programs. The pediatrician's office can also be a useful place to conduct certain indicated prevention program interventions, such as providing psychoeducation about anxiety and anxiety disorders to youngsters who present frequently for treatment of gastrointestinal problems. Many of these youngsters may have subclinical anxiety symptoms and thus they may constitute an appropriate population for psychopathology and intervention research. Swinson et al.'s (1992) hybrid treatment/indicated prevention study on the use of psychoeducation for adults who presented to emergency rooms with panic symptoms serves as a model for this sort of study. The provision of prevention intervention in the medical context raises questions of feasibility of delivery: managed care has minimized the amount of time available in a visit to discuss seemingly peripheral issues such as anxiety symptoms. Thus the development of brochures, self-help programs, or interventions that can be delivered by support staff should be considered.

Prevention research by its nature requires longitudinal follow-up. One major issue is how best to retain participation in the study and how to guard against attrition over time. Here again informed consent from the student and family and active collaboration with the school will be helpful, but it is important to keep in mind that the most valuable assessment points for prevention programs take place years after the intervention is delivered. Thus it is imperative that studies be funded in a manner that will ensure the collection of data well into the future; inadequate participation in follow-up for these kinds of studies imperils the entire enterprise, as detection of sampling bias (e.g., better follow-up with less impaired participants or vice versa) threatens to compromise conclusions that could be drawn about the efficacy of intervention. Treatment studies have had to address this problem and have requested that the family provide the names of family and friends who will know how to contact them in the future if they move, Social Security numbers, and other such information to facilitate participation in long-term follow-ups.

A final issue that affects all prevention programs involves the ongoing assessment of risk, and responsibility for risk. Those at risk for anxiety may also be at increased risk for other psychiatric comorbidity, thus procedures must be enacted within prevention intervention programs to manage clinical emergencies. Moreover, the role of the parent in these programs must be considered: if the child or adolescent is found to be at increased risk for anxiety disorders upon screening and is then eligible to participate in the program, how much or how little the parent should be involved or have access to the information discussed in assessment and/or treatment needs to be specified up front, as it will certainly affect both entry and active participation.

Problem of Sustainability (Boosters, Ongoing Programs, Training)

Little is known about the long-term effects of prevention intervention methods for anxiety disorders in youth, as the longest follow-up period reported on thus far is 2 years (Dadds et al., 1997). The studies that have included follow-up have generally suggested maintenance of the intervention effects, but here again these studies have focused on young or very young children and thus cannot inform the field about retention of benefits into and through adolescence and adulthood. A related question is whether booster sessions are needed to retain the gains from preventions programs, since the fairly predictable stressful life events that face young children growing into adolescence might compromise long-term maintenance. For example, studies discussed earlier suggest that young children with elevated but subclinical anxiety disorders may benefit most from prevention programs; transition from middle to high school may threaten these gains, and thus it may be reasonable to reinstitute the intervention during this transition. It is unknown whether this is the case, but the relation between loss of gains and stressful life events constitutes an especially important area for future study.

Problem of Contagion

There is no evidence of these undesirable effects from the studies of group treatment of youth that have been conducted thus far (e.g., Kendall et al., 1997), but the possibility for such effects remains. Although it is possible that discussion of anxiety themes may activate new fears in those who are already vulnerable, especially if the interventions involve group discussions, there is no evidence of these effects from group treatment studies (e.g., Kendall et al., 1997; Silverman et al., 1999a), including in groups in which the patients involved were very heterogeneous with respect to both age (i.e., child and adolescent patients) and primary anxiety diagnosis (e.g., OCD, specific phobia) and other clinical features (e.g., presence or absence of school refusal behavior; Lumpkin, Silverman, Weems, Markham, & Kurtines, 2002). However, the example of Critical Incident Stress Debriefing (CISD) suggests that the long-term recovery of certain adults who have experienced a trauma and have attended group meetings may be impeded by participating, and possibly the mechanism by which this effect is realized involves exposure to other participants' narratives of the traumatic event (e.g., Mayou, Bryant, & Ehlers, 2001). Provided that secondary gains (e.g., missing trigonometry class) for attending prevention intervention sessions are minimized, there is little reason for concern that students without anxious symptoms or risk factors would feign such problems.

Age-Appropriate Interventions (Developmental Approach)

The prevention intervention programs that have been evaluated thus far in research (e.g., Lowry-Webster et al., 2001) were designed for children rather than for adolescents. Adaptations to accommodate the developmental needs of adolescents should be made with specific attention to possible age-related increases in physiological functioning, emotional vulnerability, social and peer pressures, and comorbid conditions, as well as any other changes that these youngsters may be experiencing. In particular, prevention programs must consider the importance of the peer group within the intervention program itself, but also with an eye towards the social implications of participating in the program among nonparticipating students, especially if the program is either selective or indicated. Insufficient attention to these factors may reduce the number of teens willing to enter the program altogether, and can limit active participation within the program itself if a group format is implemented. One way to address this potentially important concern is to incorporate program graduates who may serve as role models for new participants, as a way to alleviate concerns that program participants may not be perceived as "cool" among the larger student population. Another way to make participation more palatable is to present information about adult role models who have struggled with anxiety and have openly discussed their difficulties, such as television host Mark Summers. However this is accomplished within a protocol, it is imperative that the culture of adolescence and the importance of the peer group be taken into consideration when developing appropriate interventions for teens.

Ethical Issues

A Note of Caution from Adult Early-Intervention Research

Longitudinal studies of trauma survivors (e.g., Riggs, Rothbaum, & Foa, 1995; Rothbaum et al., 1992) indicate that most individuals experience elevated levels of PTSD symptoms shortly after the traumatic event. In addition, elevated levels of depression and general anxiety often accompany PTSD symptoms. For most trauma survivors, however, these symptoms decline significantly over the ensuing 3 months without any professional intervention. That said, a significant minority of trauma survivors continues to experience high levels of posttrauma distress that, without professional treatment, may persist for months or years (Kessler, Sonnega, Bromet, Hughes, & Nelson, 1995).

As discussed above, it is now well established that various forms of CBT are effective in reducing PTSD symptom severity as well as associated anxiety and depression (e.g., Foa et al., 1999). While there are effective treatments for individuals suffering from chronic PTSD, many sufferers either do not seek treatment for their trauma-related symptoms or do not have access to treatment. As a consequence, individuals' suffering and their inability to function can be prolonged. They are also vulnerable to associated comorbidity such as substance abuse. Such considerations have prompted trauma therapists to develop brief interventions applied shortly after the traumatic event to facilitate recovery and thereby prevent the development of chronic PTSD. Two approaches to facilitating recovery following a traumatic event have been researched. Abbreviated CBT packages such as those developed by Foa et al. (1995) and adopted by Bryant and colleagues (1998, 1999) have been found to be efficacious in accelerating recovery and reducing the likelihood of chronic PTSD. The other approach involves psychological debriefing (PD). Such programs typically comprise one session and are applied shortly after a traumatic event (frequently within 48–72 hr). In this session (which can be conducted in groups or individually), participants are encouraged to describe the traumatic event, including their thoughts, impressions, and emotional reactions. The ses-

sion also includes normalization of the trauma survivors' reactions and planning for coping with the trauma and its sequelae. Results of RCTs for PD are somewhat mixed, but an important pattern is emerging. In general, participants in PD studies subjectively find the intervention to be helpful (i.e., high consumer satisfaction), yet objective measures of specific posttrauma symptoms typically yield no differences between those receiving PD and those who do not. Thus, the improvement typically observed following PD is better attributed to natural recovery, rather than to an active ingredient of the intervention (e.g., Bisson, 2003; Rose, Brewin, Andrews, & Kirk, 1999). Moreover, a few studies have found PD actually interfered with natural recovery (e.g., Mayou et al., 2000). The results of PD studies highlight the need for caution in using one-session interventions conducted shortly after traumatic events involving children and adolescents.

Stigmatization

As noted earlier, unlike universal prevention programs, selective and indicated prevention programs specifically select participants on the basis of elevations of anxious symptoms or putative anxiety disorder risk factors. In the school context, where most prevention interventions are likely to take place, the latter program types require identification of a subgroup of participants from among the broader population who will be either encouraged or required to participate. The potential negative implications of this strategy have already been considered in the academic context with respect to educational issues, and have led to the gradual reduction of labeling for academic tracking systems (e.g., honors, regents, and basic classes) and to increased mainstreaming of special education students. Similar problems may be encountered in identifying already anxious or anxiety-vulnerable students for special attention or services. As discussed above, adolescence is a stage in life when similarity with the relevant peer group is valued, and intervention efforts that do not deal sensitively with this issue may be poorly attended or, worse yet, yield unintended negative consequences. Little has been written about this issue in the context of anxiety prevention programs implemented thus far, but methods to prevent such unintended consequences should be carefully considered.

Postvention, Follow-up, Dissemination (Monitoring Dissemination)

The studies conducted thus far have involved acute treatment and, at least in some studies, follow-up assessment only. It is unknown how to encourage ongoing use of skills learned in the prevention programs, nor is it known how best to encourage participation in follow-up assessments. Because the primary dependent variable of interest in prevention programs must be measured years later than the intervention was conducted, it is imperative to develop methods that encourage cooperation with long-term follow-up. Because most prevention interventions will likely be conducted in the school context, active collaboration with school administration will be critical to promote collection of these data. Families may also be able to facilitate participation, thus direct contact with families may be advisable. However, this raises issues with respect to confidentiality and the need to discuss up front with the young participant what will and will not be shared with parents and/or guardians.

The preliminary success of the FRIENDS program in the hands of teachers bodes well for transportability of this program to treatment providers other than mental health professionals with expertise in CBT. Clearly the implementation of CBT-oriented prevention programs cannot realistically be limited to Ph.D.-level psychologists, and a multidisciplinary approach may be the best way to proceed. This raises interesting questions about the best way of disseminating CBT and the degree of expert supervision needed in the short and long run to optimize treatment delivery; these questions touch on cost-effectiveness of prevention programs. Research on the treatment of adult PTSD suggests that masters-level counselors can be trained to successfully deliver prolonged exposure for women who have been sexually assaulted; indeed, these counselors were as effective in delivering prolonged exposure as were CBT experts (Foa et al., 2002). However, the counselors received weekly supervision from CBT experts, which increased the cost of the program. The next research question being currently examined is whether reduction in the amount of expert supervision for the counselors will reduce their success. A similar line of research needs to be pursued in adolescent anxiety disorder prevention, since the broad application of such interventions appears to be dependent on successful training of school personnel to implement these programs in the school context.

Impediments to Prevention

The first set of impediments to developing successful prevention intervention is the lack of knowledge about the complex interrelations among the various risk and protective factors for the development of anxiety disorders. Much is known about some specific factors but little is known about how they interact, which leaves the field bereft of a strong theoretical foundation upon which to build prevention programs. This may be the reason why prevention research has languished relative to treatment research: the factors associated with etiology may not be the same as those associated with maintenance, and thus comprehensive knowledge about the latter will allow for the development of treatment interventions even in the relative absence of the former.

Practical considerations have stunted the development of prevention programs as well. Prevention efforts are likely to be costly, as they necessarily involve collection of data from large samples over a long period of time. Large samples are needed because of the relatively low base rates of anxiety disorder in the population of interest, and because there is insufficient information about who will actually go on to develop an anxiety disorder. Consequently, it is important to conduct broad screens to obtain sufficient numbers of vulnerable children and adolescents for inclusion in the studies. For example, most behaviorally inhibited infants do not develop an anxiety disorder later in life, and thus a large sample of inhibited children would be needed to detect the efficacy of a prevention program targeting behavioral inhibition. Further, because the relevant outcome is the future development of anxiety disorders and perhaps of subsequent comorbid conditions (e.g., depression, substance abuse), prevention studies require data collection for years after the intervention to determine its ultimate impact. The need to conduct longitudinal follow-ups of these large numbers for long periods of time renders the study of prevention programs impractical, especially when the primary funding sources for anxiety disorders research (e.g., National Institute of Mental Health) typically favor shorter studies with more tangible impact. Thus, new sources of funding must be identified to generate knowledge that will inform the development of anxiety disorder prevention programs. Given the potential for anxiety disorders to derail adolescent development and thereby result in substantial personal and economic impact, these programs should be a major priority for a society that promises to leave no child behind.

Research Agenda for
Anxiety Disorders

12

THE ANXIETY DISORDERS

What We Know

Empirical work and theory over the past 25 years have illuminated many issues related to the concept of anxiety. First, investigators recognize that there are distinct temperamental vulnerabilities to various forms of anxiety and sets of symptoms in individuals. We have also learned that the neurochemistry of the limbic system probably makes a contribution to some of these temperamental biases. Each bias renders certain individuals susceptible to distinct symptom profiles. For example, patients with social phobia can be distinguished from individuals with blood phobia because the former are vulnerable to a vasovagal reaction to the sight of blood and, as a result, often feel faint. By contrast, social phobics have a more labile sympathetic nervous system characterized by increases in heart rate and blood pressure rather than a sudden drop in blood pressure to their feared targets. Given the large number of possible neurochemical profiles it is likely that there are many different anxiety disorders, each characterized by a specific class of symptoms.

Scientists have also learned that the history of experience contributes to a development of an anxiety disorder. Children growing up in economically disadvantaged homes with less educated parents are more vulnerable to certain anxiety disorders than are advantaged children. Further, independent of social class background, the experience of abuse, neglect, or trauma increases the risk of developing an anxiety disorder. However, the cultural setting to which the child and adolescent must adapt is a relevant factor. Adolescents living in large urban centers in America and Europe are more vulnerable to social anxiety than those living in rural areas or small towns where there are few unfamiliar people and settings and greater social support.

Each period of development is marked by anxiety over different targets. The human infant is provoked to anxiety by encounters with strangers or separation from caretakers. Three-year-old children experience anxiety when they anticipate or actually implement actions that violate family prohibitions. Six- to eight-year-old children are made anxious by failing at tasks that are valued by their family or peers and adolescents are anxious over rejection or isolation from peers, and identification with a person or group categorized by the individual as undesirable or impotent and following detection of inconsistency among their beliefs. Thus, adolescents do not experience more intense anxiety than younger children. The important point is that their state of anxiety is linked to very different events and thoughts.

What We Do Not Know

Scientists have not yet learned in any detail the specific biology that characterizes the varied temperamental vulnerabilities. That is, it is likely that each of the anxiety disorders is characterized by a profile of measures that includes reactivity of the sympathetic and parasympathetic nervous systems, as well as the propensity to secrete corticotropin-releasing hormone, norepinephrine, dopamine, GABA, glutamate, or any one of the opioids after encountering a challenge or stress. The task is to determine the specific profile that characterizes each anxiety disorder.

We do not yet know the childhood and adolescent experiences that either exacerbate or mute the risk of developing an anxiety disorder. There is some research to show that infants who are at risk for developing social anxiety are helped if their parents do not overprotect them during the first year of life. We also need to know whether success in school tasks or on peer value activities reduces the risk of anxiety disorder in individuals who are temperamentally vulnerable.

We do not know whether there have been historical trends in the prevalence of each of the anxiety disorders over the past century or two. Nor do we know whether females are more vulnerable to anxiety than males because of a combination of biology and cultural values or personal experience and culture alone. The female in almost all mammalian species is more avoidant to unfamiliarity than the male, which suggests a biological basis for the sex ratio. However, most cultures are more accepting of avoidant symptoms and the experience of anxiety in girls and women than in boys and men.

Finally, we need to know more about the contribution of the amygdala to the development of any one of the anxiety disorders. The popular view at the present time is that the amygdala is the seminal structure mediating the acquisition of anxiety and fear because it is prepared to be responsive to threat. However, the amygdala is also responsive to unfamiliar or unexpected events. Therefore, we need to learn whether the amygdala is responsive to the threat of harm over and above its responsivity to unfamiliar events. This research should have profound implications for theory, for if the amygdala is not biologically prepared to react to dangerous events, the current animal model for human anxiety will be subject to critique.

Research Priorities

Research is needed in four broad areas. First, we must determine or discover the fundamental anxiety disorder categories. This will require gathering reliable data on each individual's temperament, current biology, and life history. Currently, the diagnostic categories are defined only by self-reported symptoms, and as a result, each category is heterogeneous with respect to its etiology. It will be necessary to add behavioral and biological variables to interview and questionnaire data to arrive at the more fundamental anxiety disorder categories.

Second, we should determine whether adolescents with distinct symptoms (for example, a panic reaction) have a special vulnerability that renders them vulnerable to develop anxiety over a specific class of target. As noted earlier, adolescents with a low threshold for a vasovagal reaction may be vulnerable to develop blood phobia, whereas those with a labile sympathetic system may be vulnerable to develop social phobia. This research, which is so critical for theoretical progress, must include a variety of biological variables, including power profiles and the asymmetry of activation in the electroencephalogram, event-related potential waveforms to threaten-

ing and unfamiliar events, functional magnetic resonance imaging and positron emission tomography scanning, measures of the cardiovascular system and hypothalamic–pituitary axis, and, in the future, the concentrations of varied neurochemicals in the central nervous system.

Finally, we need research to determine the experiential contributions to the various anxiety disorders by gathering a large number of psychological and sociological variables on every patient. These could include social class, ethnicity, educational attainment, academic performance, and family and peer relations. In addition, preliminary data point to the influence of month of conception and body build. For example, several reports indicate that children who are conceived in early fall when the light is decreasing are at slightly higher risk for becoming shy than those who are conceived in other seasons of the year. Individuals with an ectomorphic body build are at higher risk for social anxiety than children who are mesomorphic. If investigators gathered such a core set of variables on all subjects, we would gain a richer insight into the more fundamental categories of anxiety disorder and the contribution of experience to these phenomena.

TREATMENT OF ADOLESCENTS WITH ANXIETY DISORDERS

What We Know

We can be fairly confident that treatments that have been empirically supported with anxiety-disordered adults, when adjusted to be developmentally appropriate, also appear to be efficacious for youth with these disorders. Most of our knowledge, however, refers to the acute phase of treatment and less is known about long-term maintenance or relapse. Cognitive-behavioral therapies (CBT) that involve some form of exposure to feared situations, objects, or thoughts appear to be especially helpful. The medications that have been reported as effective for adults, most notably the SSRIs, are also being found superior to placebo in several anxiety disorders such as OCD and GAD. Thus, the studies conducted to date suggest that CBT, medication, and/or their combination are the treatment of choice for anxiety conditions in youth.

We also know that, as is the case with adults, some patients do not respond to CBT and pharmacotherapy and many remain somewhat symptomatic. Progress will come from further understanding of biological and psychological mechanisms underlying the disorders and the ways in which our treatment ameliorates anxiety symptoms. Anther avenue worthy of pursuit is the study of predictors for treatment response and failure.

What We Do Not Know

For most child and adolescent anxiety disorders we rely on only a few randomized control trials (RCTs) to guide our decisions about initial treatments, a situation that is in stark contrast to the adult literature, where dozens of studies have been conducted within almost every disorder. Also, with the exception of OCD, there are no completed RCTs that examine the relative and combined efficacy of psychosocial and pharmacological treatments for children and adolescents with anxiety disorders. The adult literature informs us that simultaneous administration of CBT and pharmacotherapy has generally not enhanced outcome of monotherapies. This may be because the effects of many medications are delayed in anxiety disorders, producing symptom reduction after about three months, when most CBT protocols are completed. To maximize the utility of combining treatments, it may be an option to initiate medication first, and begin CBT after medication has reduced anxiety sufficiently to enhance tolerability and to promote information processing from CBT exercises. A recently completed study with adult PTSD sufferers indicates that the addition of exposure therapy to sertraline enhanced medication effects, especially for partial responders (Cahill et al., 2004). No such investigations have been made in youth as yet. In contrast, an initial successful trial with medication may undermine the potency of the exposure task and preclude or reduce its effectiveness.

There is little to no research regarding the management of partial response and nonre-

sponse in the treatment of anxiety disorders in youth, and the effect of prior treatment with one modality on response to the other has also not been explored. Moreover, although it is unknown at this time, findings from the adult literature suggest that perhaps some children and adolescents will require medication treatment for years. The efficacy and safety of continued pharmacotherapy have not been studied sufficiently. Given recent concerns about growth suppression in youth taking SSRIs and possible increased risk for suicidal ideation in youth receiving paroxetine, the lack of studies of long-term effects of medication in youth constitute a critical gap in our knowledge. With CBT, most studies with adults and youth report long-term naturalistic follow-ups. However, no studies (in adults and youth) available examined the short and long differential responding to different doses of treatment (e.g., 10 vs. 20 sessions). Studies of the effectiveness of different lengths of CBT, both long and short term, are very much needed.

The treatment outcome literature with youth thus far consists of studies that have included wide age ranges, with the majority of participants being younger children. The samples of adolescents in most studies are too small to examine whether children respond differently than adolescents. Given the special developmental stage of adolescence, it is imperative that treatments effective for adults and younger children not be applied blindly to adolescents. Thus, there is a large and significant gap in our knowledge regarding how applicable the available treatments are to adolescents with an anxiety disorder.

Research Priorities

Given the available and impressive evidence with adults and the emerging evidence with young children that the various anxiety disorders can be treated effectively, and given the evidence that adolescence is a stage in the lifespan that is fundamentally different from both childhood and adulthood, it is essential that treatments specifically designed for adolescents be developed and that large-scale RCTs be conducted to evaluate their acute and long-term safety and efficacy. After a series of RCTs, assuming favorable outcomes from more than a single site and across dependent variables and evaluators, examination of the specific contribution of treatment components would then be needed. With psychopharmacology, issues of tolerance and dosage need to be studied; with regard to psychological treatments, issues related to the role of parents and the influence of peers should be emphasized. It is also extremely important to examine whether the effects of treatment provided during adolescence persist (maintenance of gain), preventing the negative sequelae of anxiety so often seen in adults with these disorders, such as major depression, substance abuse, and underemployment. Studies of samples that span adolescence may also be needed, however, if findings suggest that adolescence itself may moderate outcomes and comparisons across ages would be deemed necessary and appropriate.

Medications tested thus far with youth have generally been well tolerated in the acute treatment, but more information is needed to see whether any gains are maintained as the adolescent faces new challenges. One set of common SSRI side effects that may be especially relevant for adolescents are the sexual side effects, as it is often during this period of life that young people begin to explore their sexuality. Specifically, difficulties with anorgasmia and retarded ejaculation may lead to reduced medication compliance. Much more information is needed to examine this important clinical management issue, although this is but one example of an untoward medication effect that needs to be studied in youth. It is also crucial to explore the interaction between pharmacotherapy and experimentation with alcohol and other drugs, as here again adolescence is a time in life when such experimenting often begins.

Most studies of anxious youth combine patients with various anxiety disorders. Future research should use homogenous samples to evaluate the specificity and generality of the interventions. Such studies will tell us whether medications and/or psychosocial treatments (e.g., for OCD, PTSD, GAD) are differentially effective for adolescents with varying principal diagnoses, or are applicable to more than one diagnostic presentation. We also need to examine the possible complicating role of psychiatric comorbidity, as perhaps we may learn that combined treatments are most needed for patients with other significant and impairing problems beyond the primary diagnosis. To achieve this goal, studies will need to include patients with a wide range of comorbidity.

More information is also needed about prior treatment history and its effect on the evaluation of a current intervention, and there is need for studies of the preferred treatment for treatment-resistant patients. Studies examining the prediction of partial response are also needed, as perhaps a triage approach could be employed if we learned up front which patient and disorder characteristics predict partial response or relapse following delivery of acute treatments.

Fundamental issues facing the field regarding psychosocial treatments for anxiety disorders are as follows:

1. The optimal therapeutic time to be dedicated to exposure to feared situations
2. The relative benefits of massed versus spaced sessions
3. The extent to which interventions designed to target specific symptoms produce a more general reduction in symptoms and improvement in functioning
4. The degree to which treatment that results in symptom improvement should be augmented by interventions that enhance developmental progression, rehabilitation of developmental competencies, treatment of comorbid conditions, and relapse prevention
5. The optimal inclusion of parents, siblings, and other caretakers in a combined therapeutic approach

Recognition of the social, biological, cognitive, and emotional changes that emerge during adolescent development should be used to design treatments specific for adolescents with anxiety disorders. Treatment development and treatment evaluation should follow a logical course, with empirical data on the nature of adolescence used to provide a basis for the intervention. Initially, treatment development should be guided by empirical data on the nature of adolescence. That is, as treatments are developed, the biological changes and the cognitive and emotional processing features of adolescents should inform them. Given pubertal development and the emerging autonomy and independence of adolescents, researchers need to consider how best to provide treatments (e.g., role of parental involvement). Once developed, these empirically based treatments would then need to be evaluated in RCTs.

PREVENTION OF ANXIETY DISORDERS IN ADOLESCENTS

What We Know

We know that the ecology of adolescent development and culture involves an expanded network of peer, school, and community affiliations and that this expanded network increases adolescent risk for exposure to events and circumstances that have been empirically linked with the development of anxiety disorders. The events and circumstances associated with the development of anxiety disorders include possible high-risk sexual and self-injurious behaviors, smoking and drug use, and exposure to traumatic events (e.g., interpersonal and community violence). Some of these factors appear to put young people (i.e., children *and* adolescents) at risk for developing anxiety disorders as adults. Identifying which factors place young people at risk is a beginning step toward developing selective prevention intervention programs.

Specifically, we know that there are distinct temperamental vulnerabilities to anxiety disorders and anxiety symptoms in some individuals. Moreover, anxiety disorders tend to aggregate in families, and such familial aggregation is due to genetic contributions as well as family environment. A family environment that limits youth independence may particularly put young people at risk. Furthermore, the interactions of children and parents, in which either the child or parent has an anxiety disorder, maintain anxiety and its disorders in young people. Another individual characteristic, anxiety sensitivity, may also serve as a potential risk factor for anxiety

disorders, especially panic attacks and panic disorder. A third factor, the presence of anxiety symptoms, at a subthreshold level, may also place young people at risk for developing full-blown DSM-IV anxiety disorders.

We know that not all vulnerable children develop anxiety disorders—in fact, relatively few do. Thus, there are factors that protect young people (i.e., children and adolescents) from developing anxiety disorders. In addition to knowledge about risk factors, knowledge about protective factors constitutes the building block for developing selective preventive interventions programs that will foster protection from pathological anxiety.

Specifically, individual characteristics such as child perceived competence, child coping skills and behavior, level of intelligence, and general "resourcefulness" (e.g., knowing how to solve problems and whom to seek out to help solve problems) serve protective function. Certain environmental resources, such as adequate social support systems (and knowing how to reach out to these systems), and parents who are relatively free of psychopathology and serve as model of coping, also may serve a protective function.

What We Do Not Know

Although research has informed us about potential risk and protective factors, we do not know which factors are linked *specifically* to anxiety disorders, rather than being *general* risk and protective factors that play a role in the development of psychopathological conditions (either internalizing, externalizing, or both). Moreover, we do not know how the risk and protective factors differentially affect specific anxiety disorders. The research conducted to date has included diagnostically heterogeneous samples of youths with anxiety disorders (e.g., SAD, GAD, etc.), and participants often are comorbid with other disorders. This limitation is more pronounced in research of protective factors than of risk factors. Further, we know much less about protective and risk factors of anxiety disorders in ethnic and racial groups and in socially and economically disadvantaged groups.

Studies of risk and protective factors conducted thus far have primarily used "main-effects" models, rather than "interactive models." Consequently, we do not how risk and protective factors interact with one another or whether they serve to either mediate or moderate (or both) anxiety or other psychopathology. We also do not know when in the developmental trajectory of the child potential risk and protective factors have particular influence. Most of the research on risk factors has included either mixed samples of younger and older children (including adolescents) or younger children only. Studies using samples of adolescents only are rare. We should not presume that potential risk and protective factors operate in a similar fashion across developmental stages.

From a selective preventive intervention perspective, we do not know whether targeting any of identified risk factors, protective factors, or some combination (or "packages") of risk and protective factors in certain subsamples of adolescents would in fact lead to a prevention of anxiety disorders. Relatedly, we do not know whether targeting either particular risk factor(s) (i.e., reducing risk factors), protective factors (i.e., enhancing protective factors), or some combination thereof (i.e., reducing and enhancing risk and protective factors, respectively) would lead to "resilience-building" in adolescence. Indeed, no prevention or resilience building research in the context of anxiety and its disorders has been conducted among adolescents.

We also do not know whether prevention programs aimed at a universal level, which target particular facets of the ecology of adolescent development and culture, reduce anxiety disorders in adolescents. For example, do teen smoking cessation programs reduce or prevent anxiety disorders in teens? If they do, what might be the mediational processes that are operating and might they be moderated by certain adolescent characteristics? We are not even close to knowing the answers to such questions.

Research Priorities

It is critical that more research be conducted on obtaining basic knowledge about *specific* risk and protective factors of anxiety disorders in adolescents. This research must carefully consider the context of adolescent development and culture in trying to discern the particular factors and the manner in which these factors *interact*. Most risk studies to date combine patients with various disorders, anxiety and otherwise. Future research should use homogenous samples to evaluate the specificity of these factors to anxiety. In addition, research needs to be focused exclusively on specificity of protective factors of adolescents. This research needs to consider carefully not only the role of these factors in the "mainstream" population but also in diverse samples that represent the adolescent population of the United States.

A particularly high research priority is to develop and evaluate selective intervention programs (i.e., programs that target particular risk and protective factors) to learn about their efficacy in preventing anxiety disorders, building resilience, or both in adolescence. If preliminary data indicate that such prevention programs have some positive outcome, the field can move on to discerning more specific questions about enhancing program effectiveness, as well as why these program work and for whom.

As with the development of treatment interventions, recognition of the social, biological, cognitive, and emotional changes that emerge during adolescent development should be used to design prevention programs specific for adolescents; thus far this important work has not been done. Given pubertal development and the critical role of the social network for teenagers, programs developed for adolescents should carefully consider how best to provide such interventions in the school setting and at the same time take into account the possible issues that arise by implementing interventions in schools (e.g., problems with confidentiality).

Eating Disorders

COMMISSION ON ADOLESCENT EATING DISORDERS

B. Timothy Walsh, M.D., *Commission Chair*

Cynthia M. Bulik

Christopher G. Fairburn

Neville H. Golden

Katherine A. Halmi

David B. Herzog

Allan S. Kaplan

Richard E. Kreipe

James E. Mitchell

Kathleen M. Pike

Eric Stice

Ruth H. Striegel-Moore

C. Barr Taylor

Thomas A. Wadden

G. Terence Wilson

We acknowledge the assistance
of Robyn Sysko, M.S.,
Meghan L. Butryn, M.S.,
Eric B. Chesley, D.O.,
Michael P. Levine, Ph.D.,
and Marion P. Russell, M.D.

IV

part

Defining Eating Disorders

chapter

13

The wide range of human food preferences and of human practices surrounding food preparation and consumption makes the definition of an eating disorder challenging. This challenge is amplified by the fact that dramatic changes occur in energy requirements during adolescence for supporting normal growth and development. For example, between ages 9 and 19, the estimated caloric requirements for girls increases by almost 50% and those for boys, by 80% (Committee on Dietary Reference Intakes, 2002). In addition, dieting related to self-perceived weight status is now extremely common among adolescents (Strauss, 1999). These and other factors provide a fertile environment for the development of disordered eating, yet researchers have paid surprisingly little attention to the task of defining an eating disorder.

The most widely used definitions of eating disorders are those provided by the American Psychiatric Association's *Diagnostic and Statistical Manual of Mental Disorders,* fourth edition (DSM-IV, 2000). Only two distinct syndromes, anorexia nervosa and bulimia nervosa, are described in DSM-IV. A residual category, eating disorder not otherwise specified (EDNOS), is provided for all other disorders of eating. A prominent example within the EDNOS category is binge eating disorder, and tentative criteria for binge eating disorder are presented in an appendix in DSM-IV. As is described in more detail below, it appears that most adolescents and adults who present for treatment of an eating disorder do not meet full criteria for either of the two formally defined syndromes and are therefore classified as having an EDNOS. Precisely how to characterize and subdivide this large heterogeneous group is a significant problem for the field. It should also be noted that the state of being overweight or obese is not considered an eating disorder. The presence of excess body fat is viewed in the DSM-IV system as a general medical problem, not a mental disorder. The relationship between obesity and eating disorders, especially binge eating disorder, is a topic of considerable interest.

Although most eating disorders begin in adolescence, surprisingly little research has focused on this age range. The ability to make firm treatment recommendations for adolescent patients is thus severely limited. In the chapters that follow, our current knowledge of the definition, treatment, and prevention of eating disorders will be reviewed. Chapter 13 includes the etiology of eating disorders; the diagnostic criteria for anorexia nervosa and bulimia nervosa and assessment of how well these criteria apply to adolescents; the demographics and prevalence of eating disorders among adolescents; issues of comorbidity, outcome, and diagnostic migration for adolescents with eating disorders; and the medical complications of anorexia nervosa and bulimia nervosa. Chapter 14 describes psychological and pharmacological treatments for adolescents with eating disorders, and studies of relapse prevention in which psychological or pharmacological interventions are used. Chapter 15 addresses the risk factors for the development of anorexia nervosa and bulimia nervosa, the relationship between treatment of obesity and the development of eating disorders, and prevention. Chapter 16 suggests promising directions for future study in this field.

ETIOLOGY OF EATING DISORDERS

A variety of biological, environmental, and psychosocial factors are associated with the development of an eating disorder, thus such factors may play a causative role in their evolution. However, as is discussed in greater detail in Chapter 15, there is no conclusive evidence that any characteristic or event is specifically associated with the development of anorexia nervosa or bulimia nervosa.

Both of these disorders affect primarily women and usually begin around the time of or soon after puberty, thus developmental factors may play a crucial role in the onset of eating disorders. It is not clear, however, whether biological changes that accompany adolescence, psychological changes, or an interaction between the two types of phenomena account for the occurrence of eating disorders. Social factors may also influence the development of eating disorders among adolescents, as adolescents may model overconcern with body shape and weight, dieting, or binge eating behavior observed among peers. This behavior suggests that contagion may play a role in the development of eating disturbances, although this phenomenon has received little study.

Because these disorders are described primarily in developed countries, Western influence may play an important role, but precisely how cultural factors interact with other phenomena in the development of these disorders is not well understood. Evidence for the impact of Western culture, specifically the influence of mass media, was found in a naturalistic study of adolescents in Fiji, where increased rates of body image and eating disturbances were observed following the introduction of Western media (Becker, Burwell, Gilman, Herzog, & Hamburg, 2002). An experimental study found that exposure to images of the cultural thin-ideal, such as those in fashion magazines, were associated with an increase in negative affect among vulnerable adolescents who reported increased perceived pressure to be thin and body dissatisfaction (Stice, Spangler, & Agras, 2001).

There is little question that psychological distress is common within the families of adolescents with serious eating disorders, but it is not clear to what degree such disturbances precede rather than follow development of the eating disorder. There is growing evidence that genetic influences contribute to an individual's vulnerability to develop an eating disorder, but genes specifically linked to the development of anorexia nervosa or bulimia nervosa have not been identified, and it is uncertain how genetic influences may operate to influence the risk of a disorder. In short, despite extensive information about the clinical characteristics of eating disorders and much discussion of potential causes, solid knowledge of the etiology of eating disorders is elusive.

In addition, it is likely that different factors contribute to the onset and maintenance of eating disorders. If risk and maintenance factors are distinct, then prevention efforts and treatment interventions likely need to be aimed at somewhat different targets and, potentially, at different populations. However, there is currently insufficient evidence to differentiate with confidence those factors that increase the risk of developing an eating disorder from those that perpetuate the disorder once it has begun. The lack of knowledge about such issues clearly limits the development of more effective prevention and treatment interventions.

DIAGNOSTIC CRITERIA FOR EATING DISORDERS

Diagnostic Criteria for Anorexia Nervosa

The most widely used diagnostic criteria for anorexia nervosa are those of the American Psychiatric Association's *Diagnostic and Statistical Manual of Mental Disorders* (DSM-IV, 1994a). The DSM-IV diagnostic system is based on a practical foundation and aims to *(1)* facilitate meaningful communication among clinicians, *(2)* aid replication of research findings, *(3)* gauge treatment efficacy by means of carefully defined criteria, and (4) foster further elucidation of the disorder under investigation. The specific DSM-IV criteria for anorexia nervosa are listed in Table 13.1. None of the criteria in the DSM-IV diagnosis of anorexia nervosa is perfect, and further refinement of the criteria is needed. The World Health Organization's 10th Revision of the *International Classification of Diseases and Related Health Problems* (ICD-10, 1990) also provides diagnostic criteria similar to those of the DSM-IV for eating disorders. However, there are sufficient differences between the two criteria sets that the populations defined are not identical. In this section we will focus on the DSM-IV criteria, as they are widely employed in the research literature. The first criterion deals with weight loss and would seem to be noncontroversial; however, there is no consensus on how weight loss should be calculated, especially during adolescence. Some investigators emphasize the amount lost from an original baseline, and others emphasize weight loss below a normal weight for age and height. The term *refusal* in the first criterion is also problematic, because it implies a voluntary decision not to eat. In anorexia nervosa, dieting behavior often has an obsessive quality and is difficult for

Table 13.1 DSM-IV Diagnostic
Criteria for Anorexia Nervosa

A. Refusal to maintain body weight at or above a
   minimally normal weight for age and height
   (e.g., weight loss leading to maintenance of
   body weight less than 85% of that expected;
   or failure to make expected weight gain during period of growth, leading to body weight
   less than 85% of the expected)

B. Intense fear of gaining weight or becoming
   fat, even though underweight

C. Disturbance in the way in which one's body
   weight or shape is experienced, undue influence of body weight or shape on self-
   evaluation, or denial of the seriousness of the
   current low body weight

D. In postmenarcheal females, amenorrhea, i.e.,
   absence of at least three consecutive menstrual cycles (A woman is considered to have
   amenorrhea if her periods occur only following hormone, e.g., estrogen, administration.)

Specify Type

Restricting type During the current episode of anorexia nervosa, the person has not regularly
   engaged in binge-eating or purging behavior
   (i.e., self-induced vomiting or the misuse of
   laxatives, diuretics, or enemas).

Binge eating/purging type During the current
   episode of anorexia nervosa, the person has
   regularly engaged in binge-eating or purging
   behavior (i.e., self-induced vomiting or the
   misuse of laxatives, diuretics, or enemas).

Source: Reprinted with permission from the *Diagnostic
and Statistical Manual of Mental Disorders, Fourth Edition,
Text Revision*, Copyright 2000. American Psychiatric Association.

patients to control, thus *inability* might be more accurate than *refusal*.

Many individuals with anorexia nervosa acknowledge the core phenomenon described in Criterion B, an intense fear of gaining weight or becoming fat. However, younger individuals and individuals who are not motivated for treatment sometimes deny that they fear gaining weight, despite engaging in behaviors that strongly suggest an intense fear of fatness. It is possible that this criterion might be better worded to capture the characteristic behaviors rather than focusing on a psychological parameter. Criterion C is complex, as it describes three rather distinct phe-

nomena in an attempt to define the core psychological features of anorexia nervosa. The disturbance in the experience of body weight or shape is observable from statements of feeling fat or of perceiving specific parts of the body as being too large, even when the person is emaciated. Individuals with anorexia nervosa are remarkably successful at remaining underweight, thereby deriving a feeling of accomplishment by evaluating themselves in terms of their thinness. An admission of the seriousness of low body weight would imply an acknowledgment of the necessity of changing behavior and gaining weight, which are overwhelming and terrifying notions.

The final criterion for the diagnosis of anorexia nervosa, amenorrhea, remains controversial. The physiological implications of the amenorrhea are not entirely clear; some investigators have suggested that its presence might be indicative of a primary disturbance of hypothalamic function (Pirke, Fichter, Lund, & Doerr, 1979; Russell, 1969), whereas others maintain that amenorrhea is merely a reflection of dieting and weight loss (Katz, Boyar, Roffwang, Hellman, & Weiner, 1978). Several reports have suggested that the characteristics of individuals who meet all diagnostic criteria for anorexia nervosa except amenorrhea do not differ from those of individuals who meet all the criteria (Cachelin & Maher, 1998; Garfinkel et al., 1996). These observations, in addition to the occasional difficulty of obtaining an accurate history of menstrual patterns from patients, suggest that amenorrhea may be a less useful criterion for anorexia nervosa.

The DSM-IV suggests that individuals with anorexia nervosa be further described as belonging to one of two mutually exclusive subtypes, the restricting type (AN-R) and the binge eating/purging type (AN-B/P). These subtypes were included in the DSM-IV criteria for anorexia nervosa because of data indicating that in comparison with AN-R patients, AN-B/P patients have a higher frequency of impulsive behaviors such as suicide attempts, self-mutilation, stealing, and alcohol and substance abuse (Casper, Eckert, Halmi, Goldberg, & Davis, 1980; Garfinkel, Moldofsky, & Garner, 1980). In addition, the binge eating and purging behaviors of individuals with AN-B/P predispose these individuals to medical problems less frequently associated with AN-R (Halmi, 2002).

Comparison of Anorexia Nervosa in Adolescents and Adults

The DSM-IV system of classification does not suggest that a different set of criteria be employed for adolescents with anorexia nervosa. It is of interest to note that the third edition of the *Diagnostic and Statistical Manual of Mental Disorders* (DSM-III; American Psychiatric Association, 1980) placed the anorexia nervosa criteria in the section on child and adolescent disorders, which reflects the fact that most cases of anorexia nervosa have their onset during adolescent years. Several studies provide information on whether there are substantial differences in the clinical characteristics of adolescent and older individuals with anorexia nervosa.

Halmi, Caspar, Eckert, Goldberg, and Davis (1979) examined correlations between a variety of clinical characteristics and age of onset of anorexia nervosa. Younger patients were hospitalized somewhat sooner than older patients after the onset of their illness, and older age of onset was associated with a greater weight loss from normal. Most of the typical anorectic behaviors and attitudes occurred with a greater frequency in patients with a younger age of onset. In general, however, there were very few significant age-related correlations. Heebink, Sunday, and Halmi (1995) compared clinical characteristics of four age groups of female inpatients on an eating disorders unit: early adolescence (ages 12 through 13), middle adolescence (ages 14, 15, and 16), late adolescence (ages 17, 18, and 19), and adult (age 20 and older). Few psychological differences were observed between the adults and the adolescents. Onset of anorexia nervosa before age 14 and primary amenorrhea were associated with the greatest maturity fears. Among AN-R patients, adolescents aged 17 through 19 had the highest drive for thinness, and the lowest levels of depression and anxiety were seen in patients younger than age 14. These data suggest that eating disorder symptomatology is fairly consistent in presentation over the life cycle.

Fisher, Schneider, Burns, Symons, and Mandel (2001) compared patients between the ages of 9 and 19 years with patients aged 20 to 46. On most variables, there were no significant differences between the adolescents and adults. The adults were more likely to have a history of binge eating, laxative abuse, diuretic and ipecac use, and prior use of psychiatric medications. The adolescents were more likely than adults to have a diagnosis of EDNOS, and the adolescents had a lower global severity score, greater denial, and less desire for help. Although the study showed some age-related differences between adolescents and adults, changes to the DSM-IV diagnostic criteria for the adolescent population were not recommended.

Additionally, in a study comparing the general psychopathology of early-onset anorexia nervosa to that defined as classic adolescent-onset anorexia nervosa (Cooper, Watkins, Bryant-Waugh, & Lask, 2002), the specific eating disorder psychopathology and general psychopathology in the early onset anorexia nervosa group were very similar to those of the late-onset anorexia nervosa sample. Thus, there is little evidence to suggest that the core clinical characteristics of adolescents with anorexia nervosa differ substantially from those of adults, and it does not appear necessary to modify the diagnostic criteria for anorexia nervosa for use with adolescents.

Diagnostic Criteria for Bulimia Nervosa

The DSM-IV diagnostic criteria for bulimia nervosa are listed in Table 13.2. As with anorexia nervosa, the diagnostic criteria for bulimia nervosa are at times difficult to interpret. Criterion A, which provides a definition of a binge eating episode, addresses amount ("larger than most people would eat"), duration ("in a discrete period of time"), and psychological state ("a sense of a lack of control"). The relative importance of these elements and the definitions offered are open to interpretation. For example, many patients with bulimia nervosa state that they are binge eating when they eat amounts of food that are not larger than what most people eat and believe that the sense of loss of control is more important than the amount ingested.

Table 13.2 DSM-IV Diagnostic Criteria for Bulimia Nervosa

A. Recurrent episodes of binge eating. An episode of binge eating is characterized by both of the following:

   i. Eating, in a discrete period of time (e.g., within any 2-hour period), an amount of food that is definitely larger than most people would eat during a similar period of time and under similar circumstances

   ii. A sense of lack of control over eating during the episode (e.g., a feeling that one cannot stop eating or control what or how much one is eating)

B. Recurrent inappropriate compensatory behavior in order to prevent weight gain, such as self-induced vomiting; misuse of laxatives, diuretics, enemas, or other medications; fasting; or excessive exercise

C. Binge eating and inappropriate compensatory behaviors both occur on average at least twice a week for 3 months.

D. Self-evaluation is unduly influenced by body shape and weight.

E. The disturbance does not occur exclusively during episodes of anorexia nervosa.

Source: Reprinted with permission from the *Diagnostic and Statistical Manual of Mental Disorders, Fourth Edition, Text Revision*, Copyright 2000. American Psychiatric Association.

Criterion B, which describes recurrent and inappropriate behaviors, includes some behaviors that are easily characterized (self-induced vomiting) and others that are open to interpretation (for example, what is "misuse" of laxatives and diuretics?). Particularly problematic is the question of what constitutes excessive exercise.

Criterion C requires that the binge eating and inappropriate compensatory behaviors occur on average at least twice a week for 3 months, but studies suggest that individuals with somewhat lower reported frequencies of binge eating closely resemble individuals who meet Criterion C. Criterion D, that self-evaluation is unduly influenced by body shape and weight, is part of the anorexia nervosa criteria as well, and attempts to capture an important psychopathological variable. But the line between "undue influence" and normative overconcern with body shape and weight among female adolescents is uncertain.

Evaluation of DSM-IV Classification for Adolescents with Eating Disorders

One indicator of the utility of the diagnostic criteria for eating disorders is the degree to which they capture the signs and symptoms reported by patients who present for assessment because of distress about their symptoms or because of medical, psychological, or social impairment resulting from these problems. Most patients treated in clinical settings do not meet full criteria for either anorexia nervosa or bulimia nervosa but instead must be grouped into the ED-NOS category, which includes some specific examples of eating patterns that do not meet the full criteria for anorexia nervosa or bulimia nervosa but which remains for the most part poorly characterized.

For example, in data collected as part of an eating disorder database system involving five clinical centers (Neuropsychiatric Research Institute/University of North Dakota; University of South Florida; University of Toledo; Ohio State University; University of Chicago) and including a total of 704 patients, the percentage of subjects meeting full criteria for bulimia nervosa ranged from 12% to 20% and for subjects meeting full criteria for anorexia nervosa from 3% to 17%. The percentage of those diagnosed with EDNOS ranged from 49% to 71%. Of the adolescent patients in this database ($N = 163$), 86 (53%) received a diagnosis of EDNOS. This finding is reflected in other literature as well. Fisher and colleagues (2001) compared adolescents and young adults at presentation to an eating disorder program, and found that the likelihood of EDNOS was high in both populations but was highest among the adolescents. Others have discussed the high rate of EDNOS in adolescents and the inadequacy of the DSM criteria as well (Brewerton, 2002; Dancyger & Garfinkel, 1995; Eliot & Baker, 2001; Engelsen, 1999; Fisher et al., 1995; Muscari, 2002; Nicholls, Chater, & Lask, 2000).

Factors that appear to be risk factors for the later development of eating disorders, which are discussed in detail in Chapter 15, are common among adolescent girls, and some are so common as to be considered normative. A question relevant to both devising prevention efforts and considering the most appropriate diagnostic criteria is where to draw the line, to decide that a clinically significant eating problem has developed. Are cognitive concerns sufficient, are early behavioral symptoms necessary, or does a well-established pattern of such behaviors need to emerge? Prior research has shown that the altering of severity criteria would result in substantial changes in base rates of bulimia nervosa (Thaw, Williamson, & Martin, 2001).

Alternatives to DSM-IV Classification

As described above, the DSM-IV system fails to provide useful categories for a substantial number of individuals with significant eating disorder symptoms. A possible alternative to the DSM-IV categories for an adolescent population is provided by the Diagnostic and Statistical Manual for Primary Care (DSM-PC), Child and Adolescent Version (Wolraich, Felice, & Drotar, 1996), developed by the American Academy of Pediatrics. This manual provides a broader classification scheme and includes a hierarchy of clinical presentations that do not reach full DSM-IV diagnostic criteria but that nonetheless deserve clinical attention. "Variations" represent minor dysfunctional symptoms related to eating or body image and "problems" reflect more serious disturbances. The utility of this system has received little empirical examination. The clinical characteristics of individuals in these categories are unknown, as is the prevalence of these characteristics. In addition, it is not known how often or whether DSM-PC variations or problems advance to become DSM-IV full syndromes. Nonetheless, this system provides a potentially useful method for defining a wide range of important eating problems among adolescents.

In an attempt to describe the wide range of eating problems seen among children, the Great Ormond Street criteria were developed (Lask & Bryant-Waugh, 2000). These criteria include determined weight loss, abnormal cognitions about body weight and shape, and morbid preoccupation with body weight and shape for the diagnosis of anorexia nervosa. The bulimia nervosa criteria include recurrent binges and purges, a sense of lack of control, and morbid preoccupation with shape and weight. A unique feature of these criteria is the inclusion of specific criteria for additional disorders, such as food avoidance emotional disorder, selective eating, functional dysphagia, and pervasive refusal syndrome. The utility of the Great Ormond Street criteria is just beginning to be explored empirically.

Summary

The DSM-IV criteria for anorexia nervosa and bulimia nervosa are widely used and are useful in recognizing and describing both adolescents and adults with severe disturbances of eating behavior. However, it is not completely clear how several of the criteria for both anorexia nervosa and bulimia nervosa should be interpreted. The criterion requiring amenorrhea for the diagnosis of anorexia nervosa is particularly problematic and may need to be eliminated. The available literature strongly suggests that the criteria sets provided by DSM-IV fail to describe many adolescents and adults with clinically significant eating problems. Indeed, EDNOS is the most common diagnosis assigned in eating disorder programs. Thus, the DSM-IV criteria may need to be broadened, and other categories for less severely affected individuals may need to be added.

DEMOGRAPHICS AND PREVALENCE OF EATING DISORDERS

Despite exponential growth in eating disorders research the past few decades (Theander, 2002), epidemiological research has lagged behind research in other areas, such as studies of the clinical presentation of eating disorders and research on treatment interventions. Although the symptoms of eating disorders are known to originate primarily during adolescence, epidemiological studies have focused principally on adult populations. Consequently, data on the prevalence and distribution of anorexia nervosa and bulimia nervosa among adolescents are quite limited.

Even among adults, knowledge about the number of individuals having an eating disorder or about particular vulnerability to developing anorexia nervosa, bulimia nervosa, or their variants (for review, see Striegel-Moore & Cachelin, 2001) is limited. For example, only one study in the United States, conducted about 25 years ago, has provided prevalence data for eating disorders based on a nationally representative sample (Robins & Regier, 1991). Rates of bulimia nervosa were not documented, as this disorder had not yet been introduced into the psychiatric nomenclature.

Experts have concluded that eating disorders occur in approximately 1% (anorexia nervosa) to 3% (bulimia nervosa) of women, and prevalence rates among men are approximately one tenth of those observed in women (for review, see Hoek, 2002). Large samples are needed to describe even the most easily identified epidemiological parameters such as gender or ethnicity, and as the review by Hoek, van Hoeken, and Katzman (2003) illustrates, even in samples exceeding 1,000 girls, some studies have not identified a single girl with past or current anorexia nervosa (e.g., Johnson-Sabine, Wood, Patton, Mann, & Wakeling, 1988). Because of the rather preliminary stage of epidemiological research among adolescent samples, studies based on relatively small or select samples or only on self-report are not reviewed in this chapter.

Fifteen recent studies (summarized in Tables 13.3 and 13.4) have provided interview-based information about the prevalence of anorexia nervosa and bulimia nervosa as defined by DSM-III (1980) and DSM-IV criteria. In some instances, the prevalence of partial syndrome eating disorders in community-based samples was also determined. Some studies recruited not only adolescents but also younger children or adults; these studies are also reviewed (e.g., Newman et al., 1996).

Prevalence Studies of Anorexia Nervosa and Bulimia Nervosa: Methodological Considerations

Ideally, epidemiological studies recruit adequately large, representative population samples and provide detailed information about the sampling frame, recruitment procedures, and participation rates. Because eating disorders are fairly uncommon in adults (Hoek, 2002), sample sizes of several thousand (for studies focused on girls) to tens of thousands of participants (for studies focusing also on eating disorders in boys) are needed for stable estimates of eating disorders. Most studies reviewed in this chapter had fewer than 1,000 participants and only one study had over 10,000. Regrettably, the latter did not report detailed information about eating disorder cases, leaving unknown the specific disorders found (anorexia nervosa or bulimia nervosa) or the gender of those affected by an eating disorder (Emerson, 2003).

Most studies were conducted in European countries (ranging from Norway to Italy) and included populations representing Western industrialized nations. Five studies were conducted in the United States (Graber, Tyrka, & Brooks-Gunn, 2003; Johnson, Cohen, Kasen, & Brook, 2002; Lewinsohn, Hops, Roberts, Seeley, & Andrews, 1993; McKnight Investigators, 2003; Whitaker et al., 1990) and one was done in New Zealand (Newman et al., 1996). A considerable variety of sampling frames was used (ranging from the recruitment of girls at a single school, to the use of sophisticated stratification schemes, to the recruitment of an entire birth cohort in a particular county). Only two studies recruited national probability samples of children in a particular age range (Emerson, 2003: Great Britain; Verhulst, van der Ende, Ferdinand, & Kasius, 1997: the Netherlands). Unfortunately, although they included both girls and boys, neither study reported gender-specific eating disorder rates. None of the studies examined ethnic differences in the prevalence of eating disorders.

In nine studies (summarized in Table 13.3) a two-stage case-finding approach was used: a questionnaire was given to the entire sample and was followed by a diagnostic interview of those individuals whose responses to the initial screening suggested the presence of an eating disorder. In some studies, a random subset of those participants who screened negatively for an eating disorder were also interviewed. The two-stage screening approach permits a relatively cost-effective assessment of large samples through use of an inexpensive survey method first, reserving the expensive interview method for

Table 13.3 Two-stage Studies of Prevalence of Anorexia Nervosa and Bulimia Nervosa in Community Samples of Adolescents

Study	Country (city or state)	Sample[a]	Age (years)	Sample Size (response rate in %)	Screening[b] Interview (response rate in %)	Diagnostic Criteria[c]	AN Point	AN Lifetime	BN Point	BN Lifetime
Whitaker et al., 1990	United States (county in New Jersey)	1	13–18	F 2544 (91) / M 2564	EAT-40, Interview (75)	DSM-III	F / M	0.3 / 0	F / M	2.5 / 0.2
Rathner & Messner, 1993	Italy (Brixen)	2	11–20	F 517 (81) / M 0	EAT, ANIS, Interview (88)	DSM-III-R	F 0.58		F 0	
Wlodarczyk-Bisaga & Dolan, 1996	Poland (Warsaw)	2	14–16	F 747 (93) / M 0	EAT-26, Interview (92)	DSM-III-R	F 0		F 0	
Graber et al., 2003	United States, New York City	3	Mean: 16	F 155 / M 0	EAT, SCID	DSM-III-R	F	3.9	F	3.2
Szabo & Tury, 1991	Hungary (Debrecen)	2	14–18	F 416 (49) / M 119	EAT-40, BCDS, ANIS Interview	DSM-III-R	F— / M—		F 0 / M 0	
Steinhausen et al., 1997	Switzerland (Zurich Canton)	2	14–17	F 276 / M 307	EDE-S, DISC-P	DSM-III-R	F 0.7 / M 0		F 0.05 / M 0	
Verhulst et al., 1997	Netherlands	4	13–18	F/M 853 (82)	CBCL DISC-C/-P (91)	DSM-III-R	F/M 0.3		F/M 0.3	
Santonastaso et al., 1996	Italy (Padova)	2	16	F 359 (91) / M 0	EAT-40, BMI, Interview (93)	DSM-IV	F 0	0	F 0.5	1.0
Rosenvinge et al., 1999	Norway (Buskerud)	2	15	F 464 (78) / M 214	EDI, DSED	DSM-IV	F 0.4 / M 0		F 1.1 / M 0	

[a] 1 = entire enrollment of grades 9 through 12 in a single New Jersey county, including public, private and parochial schools; 2 = public school students; 3 = private school students; 4 = national probability sample.

[b] ANIS, Anorexia Nervosa Inventory Scale; BCDS, Bulimic Cognitive Distortions Scale; BMI, Body Mass Index; CBCL, Children's Behavior Check List; DISC, Diagnostic Interview Schedule for Children (DISC-P, parent version, DISC-C, child version); DSED, Diagnostic Survey for Eating Disorders; EAT, Eating Attitudes Test; EDE-S, Eating Disorder Examination, screening version; EDI, Eating Disorder Inventory; SCID, Structured Clinical Interview for DSM-IIIR.

[c] DSM, Diagnostic and Statistical Manual for Mental Disorders (DSM III, 3rd edition; DSM III-R, 3rd, revised edition; DSM IV, 4th edition).

[d] AN, anorexia nervosa; BN, bulimia nervosa; F, female; M, male; Point, point prevalence, based on 6 months (Verhulst et al., 1997), 12 months (Steinhausen et al., 1997), or "current" (i.e., at the time of the interview; Rathner & Messner, 1993; Rosenvinge et al., 1999; Santonastaso et al., 1996; Szabo & Tury, 1991; Wlodarczyk-Bisaga & Dolan 1996).

those participants whose self-report responses suggest the presence of an eating disorder. The quality of the two-stage method depends in part on the participation rates at each assessment. For example, some data suggest that screening efforts may miss eating disorder cases and thus underestimate the prevalence of eating disorders (Fairburn & Beglin, 1990). The sensitivity of the screening instrument is also important: in an uncommon disorder, the omission of even a few cases because of an insensitive screen produces underestimates of the true prevalence of the disorder.

In six studies (summarized in Table 13.4), there was no initial screening; rather, the entire sample participated in a diagnostic interview. In general, eating disorder status was assessed in the context of a comprehensive evaluation of psychiatric disorders, rather than in an interview focused specifically on eating disorders. This approach can be advantageous—because participants are not recruited specifically for a study of eating disorders, participation rates are likely unaffected by the participants' attitudes about eating disorders (e.g., wanting to avoid detection of one's eating disorder). There are also limitations to using a one-step assessment design. These studies generally have lower participation rates than those of two-stage studies, possibly because of a greater subject burden from the requirement that all participants complete the diagnostic interview. Also, in an effort to reduce assessment time and subject burden, interviewers usually employ a branched approach to diagnostic assessment: "gated" questions about the key symptom(s) are required for a diagnosis; if these are answered negatively, any further assessment of symptoms is terminated (Feehan, McGee, Raja, & Williams, 1994). Hence, unless the participant acknowledges the initial question (e.g., voluntary efforts to achieve low weight in the case of anorexia nervosa, and recurrent binge eating in the case of bulimia nervosa), no further information is gathered about eating disorder symptoms. It is unclear whether the clinical presentation of eating disorders in children is less prototypic than that in adults. If it is, then a higher number of cases among children would be missed using a one-step approach.

The *prevalence rate* is the actual number of cases in a population at a certain point in time. Some studies only report either point prevalence rates or "lifetime" rates, and a few studies report both point-prevalence and lifetime rates. *Point prevalence* is reported over various time frames, ranging from the present (or the time of interview) to within the last 12 months. *Lifetime prevalence* can be a problematic term, given that participants may have not yet reached the age of maximum risk for developing an eating disorder. In the studies reviewed in this chapter, *lifetime prevalence* connotes the number of individuals who ever met criteria for anorexia nervosa or bulimia nervosa. Retrospective reports of age of onset from adult samples suggest that full-syndrome status is not reached until mid- to late adolescence (16–18 years) or even young adulthood (18–21 years). In adult community samples, the mean age of onset of anorexia nervosa ranges from 16 to 19 years (Fairburn, Cooper, Doll, & Welch, 1999; Garfinkel et al., 1996; Walters & Kendler, 1995) and that of bulimia nervosa ranges from 18 to 20 years (Garfinkel et al., 1995; Kendler et al., 1991). Few eating disorders begin before age 10 or after age 25, and the rate of new cases climbs steadily in between those ages (Bushnell, Wells, Hornblow, Oakley-Browne, & Joyce, 1990; Lewinsohn, Striegel-Moore, & Seeley, 2000). Hence, "lifetime" prevalence, especially in young samples, should be adjusted to reflect these age-related patterns.

Prevalence Studies of Anorexia Nervosa and Bulimia Nervosa: Major Findings

Full-Syndrome Anorexia Nervosa

Full-syndrome current anorexia nervosa is not uncommon among adolescent girls, with rates ranging from 0% to 0.9%, depending on the study. Epidemiologically, it is undetectable among boys. It is difficult to discern a clear trend in prevalence rates for girls because of the considerable variations in methodology used across studies. Those studies in which no girls were identified with a diagnosis of current anorexia nervosa included relatively young samples (ages 11 to 16 years; McKnight Investigators, 2003; Santonastaso, Zanetti, Sala, & Favaretto, 1996; Wlodarczyk-Bisaga & Dolan, 1996). Rathner and

Table 13.4 Interview-based Studies of Prevalence of Anorexia Nervosa and Bulimia Nervosa in Community Samples of Adolescents

Study	Subjects Country (city or state)	Sample[b]	Age (years)	Sample Size (response rate in %)	Methods Interview[c]	Diagnostic Criteria[d]	Prevalence Rates (%)[e] AN Point	AN Lifetime	BN Point	BN Lifetime
Lewinsohn et al., 1993	United States (Oregon)	1	15–18	F 797 (61) M 711	K-SADS	DSM-III-R	F 0 M 0	0.74 0	F 0.49 M 0	1.6 0.14
Newman et al., 1996	New Zealand (Dunedin)	2	21	F 469 (84) M 492	DIS	DSM-III-R	F 0.9 M 0.0		F 1.5 M 0.4	
Wittchen et al., 1998	Germany (Munich)	3	14–24	F 1488 (71) M 1533	M-CIDI	DSM-IV	F 0.3 M 0	1.0 0.1	F 0.7 M 0	1.7 0
Johnson, Cohen, Kasen, et al., 2002[a]	United States (New York)	4	9–23	F 366 M 351	DISC-I	DSM-IV	F 0 M 0.28		F 4.0 M 0.28	
McKnight Investigators, 2003	United States (Arizona, California)	1	11–14	F 1103 M 0	MEDE	DSM-IV	F 0		F 0.37	
Emerson, 2003	Great Britain	5	5–15	F/M 10,438	DAWBA	DSM-IV	F/M 0.1–0.4 (current eating disorder)			

[a] Rates reported reflect the number of respondents who either at early adolescence (9 to 19 years) or mid-adolescence (11 to 23 years) assessment met criteria.

[b] 1 = school students; 2 = entire birth cohort 4/72–3/73; 3 = city residents; 4 = representative sample of two counties; 5 = national sample.

[c] DAWBA, Development and Well-Being Assessment; DIS, Diagnostic Interview Schedule; DISC-I, Diagnostic Interview Schedule for Children; K-SADS, Kiddie Schedule for Affective Disorders and Schizophrenia; M-CICI, Munich-Composite International Diagnostic Interview; MEDE, McKnight Eating Disorder Examination.

[d] DSM, *Diagnostic and Statistical Manual for Mental Disorders* (DSM III-R, 3rd, revised edition; DSM IV, 4th edition).

[e] AN, anorexia nervosa; BN, bulimia nervosa; F, female; M, male; point, point prevalence, based on 3 months (McKnight Investigators, 2003), 12 months (Johnson, Cohen, Kasen, et al., 2002a), or "current" (i.e., at the time of the interview; Emerson, 2003).
2002a; Lewinsohn et al., 1993; Newman et al., 1996; Wittchen et al., 1998).

Messner (1993) initially observed a 0.39% rate for anorexia nervosa, but found additional cases for a total rate of 0.58%, and reported that none of the current cases identified in their Italian sample were under age 15 years. In a randomly selected population sample of 15-year-old girls in Southern Norway, by contrast, about 4 in 100 current anorexia nervosa cases were found (Rosenvinge, Borgen, & Boerresen, 1999). An earlier study from the Mayo Clinic had a prevalence rate of 0.48% among 15- to 19-year-old girls, a rate higher than that for any other age group (Lucas, Beard, O'Fallon, & Kurland, 1991).

In a large study of 14- to 24-year-old Germans, Wittchen, Nelson, and Lanchner (1998) over-sampled 14- and 15-year-olds, which may explain why only 0.3% of current anorexia nervosa cases were identified among the female participants, despite the wider age range of the study sample. A relatively large number of girls with current anorexia nervosa (0.7%) was observed in a Zurich Canton sample of 14- to 17-year-olds. In this study, confirmatory interviews were conducted with a parent, rather than with the child, as in most other studies (Steinhausen, Winkler, & Meier, 1997). Denial is a hallmark of anorexia nervosa, and future studies are needed to determine whether parental reports result in better detection of anorexia nervosa than that from child self-report only. Finally, the highest point prevalence rate (past 12 months), 0.9%, was reported in a New Zealand study (Newman et al., 1996) and was based on diagnostic interviews when the girls were 21 years old. This well-controlled, longitudinal study of an entire birth cohort of children born between April 1972 and March 1973 had previously reported prevalence rates for major mental disorders, but not eating disorders, based on assessments at ages 11 years (Anderson, Williams, McGee, & Silva, 1987), 13 years (Frost, Moffitt, & McGee, 1989), 15 years (McGee et al., 1990), and 18 years (Feehan, McGee, & Williams, 1993; Feehan et al., 1994). It is unclear whether rates from earlier assessments would have been similar to those found in the other large-scale studies conducted in the United States (Johnson, Cohen, Kasen, & Brock, 2002; Lewinsohn et al., 1993) or the large Munich study (Wittchen et al., 1998) in which a majority of girls were younger than 21 years.

For girls, lifetime rates (ever having met criteria for anorexia nervosa) range considerably, with rates as low as 3 in 100 (Whitaker et al., 1990) in a study using DSM III criteria (which are more restrictive for anorexia nervosa than later editions of the DSM) and as high as 3.9 (Graber et al., 2003).

Partial-Syndrome Anorexia Nervosa

Only a few studies have provided data about partial anorexia nervosa, and when such data are reported, typically rates for partial anorexia nervosa have exceeded those for full-syndrome anorexia nervosa (McKnight Investigators, 2003; Rathner & Messner, 1993; Wittchen et al., 1998). Wittchen and colleagues (1998) found an additional 1.3% of females and 0.4% of males who fell "just short one DSM IV criterion" (p. 116) for having ever experienced anorexia nervosa, for a combined lifetime rate of partial anorexia nervosa or anorexia nervosa of 2.3% in females and 0.5% in males. In the young sample from the McKnight study, five girls (0.37%) met criteria for current partial anorexia nervosa, defined as meeting all but the amenorrhea criteria (McKnight Investigators, 2003, p. 249). Despite the use of quite liberal criteria for partial anorexia nervosa ("at least one DSM IV criterion not met," p. 385), Rosenvinge and colleagues (1999) found no cases of partial anorexia nervosa in their sample of 15-year-olds. Not surprisingly, rates of partial anorexia nervosa also seem to be correlated with age of the sample, with higher rates found in samples of older girls. For example, Rathner and Messner (1993) found no partial anorexia nervosa among the younger girls (ages 11 to 14 years), but found a rate of 1.3% among the older girls (15 to 20 years).

Full-Syndrome Bulimia Nervosa

Reported prevalence rates for current bulimia nervosa in girls vary considerably, and with the possible exception of age of the sample, these variations do not seem to reflect methodological differences across the studies. Only two studies found any current male cases and the reported rates were very low (Johnson, Cohen, Kasen, et al., 2002; Wittchen et al., 1998). Rates for females

(0.5% or less) were reported to be low in several European countries (e.g., Italy: Rathner & Messner, 1993; Switzerland: Steinhausen et al., 1997; Hungary: Szabo & Tury, 1991; the Netherlands: Verhulst et al., 1997; Poland: Wlodarczyk-Bisaga & Dolan, 1996) but not uniformly so (e.g., Norway: Rosenvinge et al., 1999; Germany: Wittchen et al., 1998).

Studies reporting relatively higher point prevalence rates have tended to include older participants. Specifically, 12-month prevalence rates were 0.7% in the female Munich sample (ages 14 to 24; Wittchen et al., 1998), 1.5% in the female Dunedin sample (age 21; Newman et al., 1996), and an astonishingly high 4% in the U.S. sample of students from New York state (Johnson, Cohen, Kasen, et al., 2002). In this study, any student who had met criteria during either early adolescence or mid-adolescence (spanning the ages 9 to 23 years) was counted. Johnson, Cohen, Kasen, and Brook have published several reports on eating disorders in their sample, and in one of these they indicated that in early adolescence (mean age 13.8, range 9–19 years), the 12-month prevalence for bulimia nervosa among girls was 1.4% (Johnson, Cohen, Kotler, Kasen, & Brook, 2002). It further bears noting that in general, rates were higher in the studies that employed a one-time assessment strategy rather than the more common two-stage approach. Consistently, the studies found that bulimia nervosa is very rare among adolescent boys (Lewinsohn et al., 1993; Wittchen et al., 1998; Woodside et al., 2001). In most studies, there were no cases of current or lifetime male bulimia nervosa, and when such cases were detected, they were far less common than female cases.

Partial-Syndrome Bulimia Nervosa

As has been observed for anorexia nervosa, partial-syndrome bulimia nervosa is more common than full-syndrome bulimia nervosa (Johnson, Cohen, Kasen, et al., 2002; McKnight Investigators, 2003; Newman et al., 1996; Rathner & Messner, 1993; Rosenvinge et al., 1999; Wittchen et al., 1998). Rathner and Messner (1993) found no full-syndrome bulimia nervosa cases and reported that the two girls with partial

bulimia nervosa (0.39%) were among the older girls (>15 years). In the study conducted by the McKnight Investigators (2003), 1.2% of girls met criteria for partial bulimia nervosa, for a combined rate of partial bulimia nervosa and bulimia nervosa of 1.6%. A fairly inclusive definition of partial bulimia nervosa was used: all cases in which either binge eating and purging were less frequent than that required by DSM-IV or subjective binges occurred in the presence of at least weekly purging were reported (McKnight Investigators, p. 249).

Using another broad definition, the presence of "all but one of the required symptoms," Wittchen and colleagues (1998) identified 1.5% female partial bulimia nervosa cases and 0.6% male partial bulimia nervosa cases. The combined rate of partial bulimia nervosa and bulimia nervosa was 3.2% in females and 0.6% in males. Finally, in what may be the most inclusive definition, "at least one DSM IV criterion not met," Rosenvinge at al. (1999) detected 1% of girls but no boys with partial bulimia nervosa. Although it is clear that a broader definition of bulimia nervosa results in increased rates, the lack of a systematic definition of partial bulimia nervosa makes it impossible to draw any conclusions about the prevalence of more broadly defined bulimia nervosa in adolescents.

Prevalence of Binge Eating Disorder

Only three studies have reported specifically on the prevalence of binge eating disorder (defined mutually exclusively from partial bulimia nervosa or eating disorder not otherwise specified). The McKnight Investigators (2003) reported that 0.59% of the 11- to 14-year-old girls in their study met 3-month point prevalence criteria for binge eating disorder. Using 12-month prevalence criteria, Johnson, Cohen, Kasen, et al. (2002) identified no male binge eating disorder cases and reported 0.55% of female binge eating disorder cases. The highest rates were found by Rosenvinge and colleagues (1999), who reported that 1.5% of the 15-year-old school girls and none of the boys studied met point prevalence (time frame not specified) for binge eating disorder. As described earlier, this particular study found relatively high rates for all eating disorders, considering the young age of the sample, yet there is no apparent explanation for these high rates (e.g., some obvious methodological peculiarity).

In clinical samples, onset of binge eating disorder (as determined by retrospective report) has been described to occur later than that of bulimia nervosa (Wilfley, Schwartz, Spurrell, & Fairburn, 2000). There are some indications from nonrepresentative community samples that in adults, binge eating disorder is more prevalent than bulimia nervosa (Spitzer et al., 1993; Spitzer, Williams, Kroenke, Hornyak, & McMurray, 2000). On the basis of the very limited evidence, this does not seem to be the case, but the evidence of binge eating disorder in adolescents is too preliminary to permit firm conclusions. Given the emerging data about recurrent binge eating as a risk factor for obesity (Fairburn, Cooper, Doll, Norman, & O'Connor, 2000), future studies need to include the requisite diagnostic questions to identify binge eating disorder in adolescents.

Conclusions from the Data on Prevalence

The prevalence of anorexia nervosa and bulimia nervosa in adolescent samples clearly is lower than rates reported for adult samples. The lack of studies with adequate sample sizes and the considerable variation in methodology make it difficult to answer confidently the question of

---

Red Flags Signaling the Potential Development of an Eating Disorder

- An abnormally low weight or significant fluctuations in weight not due to medical illness
- Purging behaviors intended to induce weight loss
- Persistent intense concerns with weight or shape
- Persistent attempts to diet or lose weight despite being at a normal or low weight
- Social withdrawal and isolation for activities involving food and/or eating
- Unexplained amenorrhea

---

how many adolescents experience an eating disorder. A major gap in studies from the United States is the lack of data adequately representing the ethnic diversity of its population.

Experts have expressed concern that the data on prevalence of eating disorders in adolescents are misleading because the strict diagnostic criteria do not permit diagnosis of anorexia nervosa or bulimia nervosa among adolescents who show evidence of the core features of these disorders yet have not yet developed the requisite severity or duration of symptoms (Golden et al., 2003). Examination of the prevalence of behavioral eating disorder symptoms, is therefore indicated. These symptoms may represent the first signs of development of a full-syndrome disorder, and data on their prevalence thus give an indication of the size of the "at-risk" group.

Symptoms of Eating Disorders in Adolescent Girls and Boys

In 1990, the Centers for Disease Control and Prevention developed the Youth Risk Behavior Surveillance System to monitor health risk behaviors that contribute markedly to the leading causes of death, disability, and social problems among youth and adults in the United States. The system includes national, state, and local school-based Youth Risk Behavior Surveys (YRBS; 2003) conducted every 2 years, of representative samples of 9th through 12th grade students. Students complete the anonymous surveys during a class period at school. In the 2001 YRBS (Grunbaum et al., 2002), the overall participation rate was 63% but varied considerably across states. The YRBS includes questions about current attempts to lose weight and questions about weight loss or weight maintenance efforts, such as vomiting, diet pills, and "other methods."

Consistently, the YRBS has found that about two of every three female students report trying to lose weight, compared to one in four male students. Trying to gain weight is quite common among boys (about 40%), whereas only a minority of girls (about 8%) engage in efforts to become heavier (Grunbaum et al., 2002; Lowry et al., 2002; Middleman, Vasquez, & Durant, 1998). The YRBS also includes questions about behaviors that are considered in the DSM to be "inappropriate compensatory behaviors." Data collected in 1999 and 2001 suggest that inappropriate efforts to lose weight or keep from gaining weight are disturbingly common, especially among girls. Specifically, in 1999, fasting, use of diet pills, and vomiting or laxative abuse were reported by 18.8%, 10.9%, and 7.5% of girls, respectively, compared to 6.4%, 4.4%, and 2.2% of boys (Lowry et al., 2002). Data for 2001 showed similar rates for these behaviors (Grunbaum et al., 2002).

The YRBS includes an ethnically diverse sample, permitting the examination of ethnic group differences in the prevalence of weight-related behaviors. In 2001, white and Hispanic girls were found to be significantly more likely than black girls to report inappropriate compensatory behaviors. Almost one in four (23.1%) female Hispanic students and one in five white students (19.7%), compared to 15% of black students, reported that she had gone without eating for 24 or more hours to control her weight. Vomiting or laxative use to control weight was reported by 10.8%, 8.2%, and 4.2% of Hispanic, white, and black girls, respectively (Grunbaum et al., 2002). These findings suggest that additional study of disordered eating among minority groups is needed. Whether girls in this sample would meet diagnostic criteria for an eating disorder is unclear, because the YRBS does not include questions covering the complete set of diagnostic criteria for anorexia nervosa and bulimia nervosa. Nevertheless, a considerable subset of female students practice potentially health-damaging behaviors, such as vomiting, which is cause for concern.

Although the YRBS does not assess binge eating, a recent study of boys and girls in public middle and high schools has provided information about binge eating in adolescents (Ackard, Neumark-Sztainer, Story, & Perry, 2003). Binge eating was considered present if the child answered "yes" to a question about overeating with loss of control, at least a few times a week, and feeling upset "some" or "a lot" by overeating. More girls (3.1%) than boys (0.9%) met criteria for binge eating, and the results suggested that binge eating was significantly correlated with body mass index (BMI) in girls and boys. Binge

eating was only slightly more common in white girls (2.6%) than in black (1.6%) or Hispanic (1.7%) girls, and was reported by a surprisingly large number of Asian American girls (5.9%). Therefore, binge eating may occur among ethnically diverse groups.

Summary

Epidemiological research on eating disorders in adolescence is limited in several important ways. Nationally representative samples, including ethnic minority children, are needed to determine the prevalence of eating disorders among American youth. Studies of ethnic minorities in European countries (e.g., Bhugra & Kamaldeep, 2003) and among adolescents in non-Western countries (e.g., Huon, Mingyi, Oliver, & Xiao, 2002; Nobakht & Dezhkam, 2000) have reported significant rates of eating disorders among minorities. These results indicate that eating disorder research should be more inclusive in its sampling frames.

While the diagnostic criteria for anorexia nervosa and bulimia nervosa are well articulated, definitions of eating pathology that fail to meet diagnostic criteria are quite varied. Since eating pathology that fails to reach diagnostic significance may represent the early stages of a full-syndrome eating disorder for some adolescents, a more uniform definition of partial syndrome is needed. Studies should also include criteria for binge eating disorder to permit estimates of the prevalence of this syndrome.

The lack of a uniform instrument for measuring eating disorder symptoms also limits current epidemiological research. One-step assessment studies that use standardized psychiatric interviews, in which individuals "skip out" of the eating disorder module if a gated question is answered negatively, may have produced an underestimation of eating pathology, especially in young samples, in whom the clinical presentation of anorexia nervosa or bulimia nervosa could be atypical (Kreipe et al., 1995). Finally, parent reports might improve the detection of anorexia nervosa, a disorder in which denial is a hallmark.

Eating disorders may be transient (albeit in

many cases recurrent) and point prevalence rates may therefore not reflect fully the extent of eating pathology in adolescents (Patton, Coffey, & Sawyer, 2003). Even if an adolescent's eating disorder is time limited and nonrecurring, it may represent a marker for psychopathology that conveys important clinical information. For example, Johnson, Harris, Spitzer, & Williams (2000) demonstrated that an adolescent's history of an eating disorder is associated with elevated risk for other Axis I disorders in adulthood. Adolescent eating disorders, even when fully remitted, are associated with a broad range of indicators of impaired psychosocial functioning (Striegel-Moore, Seeley, & Lewinsohn, 2003).

Information about the incidence of eating disorders requires longitudinal data. Although a few studies have included longitudinal follow-ups, these studies have not focused specifically on eating disorders and did not provide incidence data. There is one exception, however. Lewinsohn and colleagues (2000) classified an eating disorder sample into onset prior to or after age 19 and reported that first incidence for anorexia nervosa was significantly more likely to occur prior to age 19. An incidence rate for anorexia nervosa of 0.1% was found for the age group of 19–23 years. For bulimia nervosa, the incidence rates for before age 19 and after were comparable: 1.5% and 1.3%, respectively. Clearly, more detailed data are needed on the incidence of eating disorders.

In conclusion, epidemiological research of eating disorders is quite limited. In light of the considerable public health significance of anorexia nervosa and bulimia nervosa and their spectrum variants, such research is urgently needed.

COMORBIDITY, OUTCOME, AND DIAGNOSTIC MIGRATION

In addition to examining the diagnostic categories and prevalence of eating disorders, it is important to know what other emotional and psychological problems individuals with eating disorders are prone to develop and to describe what is likely to occur over time to individuals with eating disorders. Knowledge of comorbidity, outcome, and migration between diagnostic categories is important in helping to refine the definition of adolescent eating disorders and in assessing the effectiveness of treatment. A number of studies have addressed comorbidity, course, and outcome of adult patients with eating disorders, but studies of adolescents have only included patients with anorexia nervosa.

Comorbidity of Anorexia Nervosa

The lifetime rates of psychiatric comorbidity among patients with anorexia nervosa are approximately 80% (Halmi et al., 1991). Affective disorders, anxiety disorders, substance use disorders, and personality disorders are commonly associated with anorexia nervosa. The affective disorder that most commonly co-occurs with anorexia nervosa is major depressive disorder, with a lifetime comorbidity of 50%–68% (Herzog, Nussbaum, & Marmor, 1996). Lifetime rates of anxiety disorders are between 55% and 65% (Godart, Flament, Perdereau, & Jeammet, 2002; Halmi et al., 1991); the most common comorbid anxiety diagnoses are social phobia (55%) and obsessive-compulsive disorder (OCD) (25%–69%; Godart et al., 2002; Halmi et al., 1991). Lifetime prevalence of substance use disorders ranges between 12% and 21% (Herzog, Keller, Sacks, Yeh, & Lavori, 1992; Stock, Goldberg, Corbett, & Katzman, 2002), compared to 11% of women in the general population (Bulik, Sullivan, McKee, Weltzin, & Kaye, 1994). Patients with AN-B/P are more likely than those with AN-R to manifest substance use disorders (Herzog, Keller, Sacks, et al., 1992; Stock et al., 2002).

When patients with anorexia nervosa present for treatment, over 70% report an additional current psychiatric disorder. Approximately 66% have a co-occurring affective disorder, 49% are diagnosed with a personality disorder, 5% have a substance use disorder, and 56% report an anxiety disorder (Braun, Sunday, & Halmi, 1994; Herpertz-Dahlmann et al., 2001; Herzog, Keller, Sacks, et al., 1992; Wonderlich & Mitchell, 1997). Cluster C personality disorders, which include avoidant, dependent, obsessive-compulsive, and passive-aggressive personality disorder, are also common among patients with anorexia nervosa (Herzog, Keller, Lavori, Kenny, & Sachs, 1992).

The developmental sequence of anorexia nervosa in relation to other comorbid conditions can vary significantly. Affective disorders may begin before or after the onset of anorexia nervosa, or the disorders can begin concurrently (Braun et al., 1994). Anxiety disorders, in particular social phobia and OCD, frequently predate the onset of anorexia nervosa (Anderluh, Tchanturia, Rabe-Hesketh, & Treasure, 2003; Braun et al., 1994; Bulik, Sullivan, & Joyce, 1997), whereas substance use disorders often develop after anorexia nervosa (Braun et al., 1994).

Comorbidity of Bulimia Nervosa

Nearly 83% of patients with bulimia nervosa report a lifetime history of an additional psychiatric disorder (Fichter & Quadfleig, 1997); affective disorders, anxiety disorders, substance use disorders, and personality disorders are commonly associated with bulimia nervosa. While there is a significant amount of variability in the rates of comorbidity, more than 50% of patients with bulimia nervosa have a lifetime history of a mood disorder. Major depressive disorder has been shown to be the most common mood disorder diagnosis among patients with bulimia nervosa. In community samples, approximately one third are depressed, a rate that increases to 65% in inpatient and outpatient samples. In clinical samples, the lifetime rates of comorbidity with at least one anxiety disorder ranges from 13% to 65% (Herzog, Keller, Sacks, et al., 1992). Social phobia (17%) and OCD (8%–33%) are the most frequently diagnosed anxiety disorders in bulimia nervosa, and panic disorder is also commonly observed (Brewerton et al., 1995; von Ranson, Kaye, Weltzin, Rao, & Matsunaga, 1999). The lifetime prevalence of substance use disorders is approximately 25% (Bulik et al., 1994), and patients with bulimia nervosa most frequently abuse alcohol, cocaine, and marijuana. Patients with bulimia nervosa and substance use disorders commonly exhibit impulsivity in multiple domains, including suicide attempts, self-injurious acts, and stealing.

When patients with bulimia nervosa present for treatment, approximately 75% meet criteria for an additional psychiatric disorder (Fichter & Quadfleig, 1997). Approximately 50% have a co-occurring affective disorder, 34% have a substance use disorder, and 56% have an anxiety disorder (Halmi et al., 2002; Herzog, Keller, Sacks, et al., 1992; Mitchell, Specker, & de Zwaan, 1991; Wonderlich & Mitchell, 1997). Cluster B personality disorders, such as antisocial, borderline, histrionic, and narcissistic personality disorder, are also common in bulimia nervosa (Herzog, Keller, Lavori, et al., 1992).

As in anorexia nervosa, the sequence development of bulimia nervosa and comorbid conditions varies, as onset of the comorbid disorder can occur prior to, at the same time as, or following the development of bulimia nervosa (Braun et al., 1994). As with anorexia nervosa, anxiety disorders commonly predate the onset of bulimia nervosa, whereas substance use disorders more often develop after the onset of bulimia nervosa (Braun et al., 1994; Bulik et al., 1997).

Outcome of Anorexia Nervosa

The available data suggest that approximately 50%–70% of adolescents with anorexia nervosa recover, 20% are improved but continue to have residual symptoms, and 10%–20% have chronic anorexia nervosa (Herpertz-Dahlmann et al., 2001; Morgan, Purgold, & Welbourne, 1983; Steinhausen, 2002; Steinhausen et al., 1997). Adolescents with anorexia nervosa continue to recover over time; for example, Strober, Freeman, and Morrell (1997) reported a 1% probability of adolescents reaching full recovery at 3 years, which increased to 72% after 10 years. Those anorexia nervosa patients experiencing persistent symptoms typically display abnormalities in weight, eating behaviors, menstrual function, comorbid psychopathology, and difficulties with psychosocial functioning (Herpertz-Dahlmann et al., 2001; Steinhausen, 1997; Strober et al., 1997; Wentz, Gillberg, Gillberg, & Rastam, 2001). Relapse is common after weight gain in hospitalized patients, with up to one third of adolescent anorexia nervosa patients relapsing soon after discharge (Herzog et al., 1999; Strober et al., 1997).

Anorexia nervosa has one of the highest mortality rates among psychiatric disorders. Approximately 5.6% of patients diagnosed with anorexia nervosa die per decade of illness (Sullivan, 1995), and anorexia nervosa patients are 12 times more likely to die than women of a similar age in the general population (Keel et al., 2003). Although the combined mortality rate for anorexia nervosa among adolescents and adults is over 5% (Steinhausen, 2002), the mortality rate during adolescence is low. The most common causes of death among patients with anorexia nervosa are suicide and the effects of starvation. The suicide rate among women with anorexia nervosa is 57 times higher than that for women of a similar age in the general population (Keel et al., 2003). Some studies have found lower weight at presentation, longer duration of illness, and severe alcohol use to be associated with higher risk of mortality (Keel, Mitchell, Miller, Davis, & Crow, 1999; Patton, 1988).

Few variables are consistently associated with outcome in anorexia nervosa, but the most positive outcomes are seen in patients between the ages of 12 and 18 with a short duration of illness. Poor outcome is associated with extremely low weight at presentation and, in some studies, by vomiting. The relationship of binge eating to outcome of anorexia nervosa is not clear, as patients with AN-R and those with AN-B/P have a similar time to recovery (Herzog et al., 1999).

Outcome of Bulimia Nervosa

Most adolescents and adults with bulimia nervosa improve over time, with recovery rates ranging from 35% to 75% at 5 or more years of follow-up (Fairburn et al., 2000; Fichter & Quadfleig, 1997; Herzog et al., 1999). Bulimia nervosa is a chronic relapsing condition, and approximately one third of individuals with bulimia nervosa relapse (Keel & Mitchell, 1997), often within 1 to 2 years of recovery (Herzog et al., 1996). Although approximately 50% of patients with bulimia nervosa recover, the remaining individuals continue to be symptomatic, often with substantial impact on physical and psychosocial functioning. Mortality is a rare outcome in bulimia nervosa, with rates as low as 0.5%

(Keel et al., 1999). Few prognostic factors have been consistently reported across studies of bulimia nervosa, but low self-esteem, longer duration of illness prior to presentation, higher frequency or severity of binge eating, substance abuse history, and a history of obesity have been associated with poor outcome (Bulik, Sullivan, Joyce, Carter, & McIntosh, 1998; Fairburn, Stice, et al., 2003; Keel et al., 1999).

Diagnostic Migration

Few studies address diagnostic migration, or the movement from one eating disorder subtype, or eating disorder, to another, within the adolescent eating disorder population. While some patients migrate from bulimia nervosa to anorexia nervosa (Kassett, Gwirtsman, Kaye, Brandt, & Jimerson, 1988), the most frequent change among diagnostic categories is from the subtype AN-R to AN-B/P, reflecting the development of bulimic symptomatology. Some individuals gain weight in association with the binge eating, leading to a change in diagnostic status from the subtype AN-R or AN-B/P to bulimia nervosa. In one study, more than 50% of AN-R patients, both adolescents and adults, developed bulimic symptomatology (Eddy et al., 2002), and only a small fraction of patients with AN-R remained in that diagnostic subtype. The remaining patients with AN-R who did not develop binge eating or purging were partially or fully recovered. It is unknown what factors lead to the development of bulimic symptoms among patients with AN-R, and what the precise time course of this development is.

Summary

The occurrence of other psychiatric disorders is extremely common in association with both anorexia nervosa and bulimia nervosa, and this complicates treatment. Unfortunately, many treatment studies of eating disorders exclude patients with serious comorbid disorders, such as substance use disorders. Adolescents with anorexia nervosa have a better prognosis when they receive treatment early in the course of their illness. However, anorexia nervosa is a severe psychiatric disorder, and those who remain ill have high rates of psychiatric comorbidity and are at risk for premature death. Diagnostic migration appears to be common between AN-R to AN-B/P and AN-B/P to bulimia nervosa. Little is known about the course and outcome of bulimia nervosa among adolescents, but among adults, bulimia nervosa is a chronic relapsing condition with a 50% recovery rate and a low mortality rate.

MEDICAL COMPLICATIONS OF EATING DISORDERS

Eating disorders are associated with significant medical morbidity and mortality. Most complications of eating disorders result from physiologic adaptations to the effects of malnutrition or occur as a result of unhealthy weight-control behaviors. Many, but not all, of the complications are reversible with nutritional rehabilitation and symptomatic improvement. In an adolescent whose growth and development are not yet complete, however, the medical consequences of eating disorders can be long-lasting and potentially irreversible. Particularly worrisome complications for adolescents include growth retardation, pubertal delay or arrest, impaired acquisition of bone mass, and structural brain changes.

During normal pubertal development, body weight doubles and maturation of various organs occurs with increases in the size of the heart, brain, lungs, liver, and kidneys. Approximately 17%–18% of final adult height is achieved (Abbassi, 1998) and between 40% and 60% of peak bone mass is accrued (Golden & Shenker, 1992; Katzman, Bachrach, Carter, & Marcus, 1991).

The medical complications of anorexia nervosa and bulimia nervosa are listed in Table 13.5. Individuals with symptoms of both disorders (e.g., patients with AN-B/P) are at risk for complications of both. Adolescents who have symptoms of eating disorders but do not meet full criteria for anorexia nervosa or bulimia nervosa may also be at risk of complications. Most of the complications occur with equal frequency in

adults and adolescents. In contrast to adults, however, a young adolescent with incompletely formed stores of body fat and other substrates can suffer significant medical compromise after a relatively small degree of weight loss.

Medical Complications of Anorexia Nervosa

The most notable medical complications of anorexia nervosa result from malnutrition. Subcutaneous tissue is lost, muscle wastes, and patients display sunken cheeks and prominence of bony protuberances. Body temperature is usually low and patients often wear multiple layers of clothing to keep warm. The hands and feet may be cold and blue (acrocyanosis); the skin may be pale, dry, and yellow in color. Fine downy hair (lanugo) may be present over the arms, back, and abdomen. Scalp hair is dry, listless, and brittle and there may be evidence of hair loss. Resting pulse and blood pressure are both low, and dizziness and fainting may occur upon standing, as a result of changes in pulse and blood pressure. There may be generalized muscle weakness.

In anorexia nervosa, life-threatening complications include electrolyte disturbances and cardiac arrhythmias. Patients may present with dehydration and abnormal serum levels of sodium, potassium, chloride, carbon dioxide, and blood urea nitrogen. Electrolyte disturbances are more likely in those who are vomiting or abusing laxatives or diuretics. Hyponatremia (low sodium levels) can occur in those who drink excessive amounts of water to either satisfy hunger urges or falsely elevate body weight prior to a medical visit. Water intoxication with hyponatremia can cause seizures, coma, and death. Serum phosphorus levels may be normal on presentation but may drop upon refeeding, and hypophosphatemia may play a role in the development of cardiac arrhythmias and sudden unexpected death seen in the "refeeding syndrome" (Kohn, Golden, & Shenker, 1998).

Resting pulse rates among patients with anorexia nervosa may be as low as 30–40 beats per minute (Palla & Litt, 1988) and systolic and diastolic blood pressures are low. Within the first 4 days of hospitalization, 60%–85% of patients demonstrate orthostatic pulse changes on stand-

Table 13.5 Signs and Symptoms in Adolescence

Factor	Anorexia Nervosa[a]	Bulimia Nervosa
Weight	Markedly decreased	Usually normal
Menstruation	Absent	Usually normal
Skin/extremities	Growth of fine downy hair (lanugo) Cold blue hands and feet (acrocyanosis) Swelling of feet (edema)	Calluses on back of hand
Cardiovascular	Low heart rate (bradycardia) Hypotension	—
Gastrointestinal	Elevated liver enzymes Delayed gastric emptying Constipation	Salivary gland enlargement Dental erosion Esophagitis
Hematopoietic	Normochromic, normocyctic anemia Leukopenia Low erythrocyte sedimentation rate	—
Fluid/electrolytes	Increased blood urea nitrogen Increased creatinine Hyponatremia	Hypokalemia Hypochloremia Alkalosis
Endocrine	Hypoglycemia Low estrogen or testosterone Low luteinizing hormone Low follicle stimulating hormone Low to normal thyroxine Normal thyroid stimulating hormone Increased cortisol Delayed puberty Growth retardation	—
Skeletal	Osteopenia	—

[a] Individuals with anorexia nervosa who engage in binge eating with or without purging may also develop signs and symptoms of bulimia nervosa.

Partially adapted from Walsh, B. T. (2001). Eating disorders. In E. Braunwald, S. L. Hauser, A. S. Fauci, D. L. Longo, J. L. Jameson, & D. L. Kasper (Eds.), *Harrison's Principles of Internal Medicine* (15th ed., p. 488).

ing (Shamim, Golden, Arden, Filiberto, & Shenker, 2003). Electrocardiographic (EKG) abnormalities have been noted in up to 75% of hospitalized adolescent patients (Palla & Litt, 1988; Galetta et al., 2002). A prolonged QTc interval, one type of EKG abnormality, is of particular concern because it appears to precede ventricular arrhythmias and sudden death in patients hospitalized with anorexia nervosa (Isner, Roberts, Heymsfield, & Yager, 1985). A pericardial effusion (fluid around the heart) can develop in very malnourished patients (Silverman & Krongrad, 1983). Mitral valve prolapse has been reported in patients with anorexia nervosa (Johnson, Humphries, Shirley, Mazzoleni, & Noonan, 1986; Meyers, Starke, Pearson, & Wilken, 1986), but the apparent prolapse is reversible with weight restoration, whereas true

prolapse is a permanent degeneration of the mitral valve (Schocken, Holloway, & Powers, 1989). Congestive heart failure does not usually occur in the starvation phase and is more likely to occur during refeeding (Powers, 1982).

Bloating and constipation are frequent complaints of patients with anorexia nervosa and reflect delayed gastric emptying and decreased intestinal motility. Liver enzymes are elevated in 4%–38% of patients with anorexia nervosa (Mickley, Greenfeld, Quinlan, Roloff, & Zwas, 1996; Palla & Litt, 1988; Sherman, Leslie, Goldberg, Rybczynski, & St. Louis, 1994). Cholesterol levels may be high but most frequently are normal (Arden, Weiselberg, Nussbaum, Shenker, & Jacobson, 1990; Boland, Beguin, Zech, Desager, & Lambert, 2001; Mehler, Lezotte, & Eckel, 1998). Serum carotene levels may be elevated in

13%–62% of cases and may lead to a yellowish discoloration of the skin (Sherman et al., 1994; Boland et al., 2001). The cause of the high serum carotene levels is not clear but is thought to be a combination of increased dietary intake of pigmented vegetables such as carrots and derangements of hepatic conversion of beta-carotene to vitamin A. In contrast to other forms of malnutrition, serum albumin levels are usually normal in anorexia nervosa. Rapid weight loss is associated with gallstone formation. With malnutrition, the metabolic rate slows down as an adaptive response to starvation. In anorexia nervosa, measured resting energy expenditure may be 65%–70% of predicted values (Schebendach et al., 1995). Consequently, in the malnourished state, caloric requirements are lower. With nutritional rehabilitation, metabolic recovery occurs over a 4- to 6-week period and caloric requirements increase dramatically (Schebendach, Golden, Jacobson, Hertz, & Shenker, 1997).

Suppression of the bone marrow occurs frequently in anorexia nervosa, resulting in low white blood cell, red blood cell, and platelet counts. Leukopenia (low white blood cell count) has been reported in one to two thirds of patients with anorexia nervosa and is thought to be secondary to bone marrow suppression (Palla & Litt, 1988; Sharp & Freeman, 1993). Despite the low white blood cell count, there does not appear to be an increased risk of infection. Once a bacterial infection is present, however, low complement levels may prolong the course of the infection. All hematologic abnormalities are reversed with nutritional rehabilitation.

The major neurological complications of eating disorders are seizures and cerebral atrophy, found on computed tomography (CT) and magnetic resonance imaging (MRI) scans (Enzmann & Lane, 1977; Golden et al., 1996; Katzman et al., 1996; Nussbaum, Shenker, Marc, & Klein, 1980). Muscle weakness and a peripheral neuropathy can also occur. Neuropsychological testing has demonstrated impairment of attention, concentration, and memory, with deficits in visuospatial ability (Kingston, Szmukler, Andrewes, Tress, & Desmond, 1996). Although the ventricular enlargement and white matter changes revert to normal after weight restoration

(Golden et al., 1996; Katzman, Zipursky, Lambe, & Mikulis, 1997), the gray-matter volume deficits and regional blood flow disturbances may persist. It may be that these changes predate the illness (Golden et al., 1996; Gordon, Lask, Bryant-Waugh, Christie, & Timimi, 1997; Katzman et al., 1997). Similarly, some but not all of the cognitive deficits improve with weight restoration (Kingston et al., 1996).

Adolescents who develop anorexia nervosa prior to the completion of growth can exhibit growth retardation and short stature. Patients are shorter than expected (Nussbaum, Baird, Sonnenblick, Cowan, & Shenker, 1985) and growth stunting may even be the presenting feature (Modan-Moses et al., 2003; Root & Powers, 1983). Growth retardation is more likely to occur in adolescent boys because boys grow, on average, for 2 years longer than girls. In girls, growth is almost complete by menarche, which occurs at an average age of 12.4 years in the United States (Chumlea et al., 2003). Catch-up growth can occur with nutritional rehabilitation, but even with intervention, these adolescents may not reach their genetic height potential (Lantzouni, Frank, Golden, & Shenker, 2002).

Hypothalamic dysfunction is evidenced by amenorrhea (loss of menses) as well as disturbances in satiety, difficulties with temperature regulation, and decreased ability to concentrate urine (Mecklenberg, Loriaux, Thompson, Andersen, & Lipsett, 1976). There is activation of the hypothalamic–adrenal axis with high levels of serum cortisol. Clinically, patients with anorexia nervosa have symptoms that look very much like those seen in hypothyroidism (dry yellow skin, low heart rate, low metabolic rate, amenorrhea, and constipation). Disturbances in thyroid function tests resolve with improved nutrition and should not be treated with thyroid hormone replacement.

Pubertal delay is frequently found among patients who develop anorexia nervosa prior to the completion of puberty (Palla & Litt, 1988; Russell, 1985). Amenorrhea is a cardinal feature of anorexia nervosa, caused by a combination of malnutrition, increased exercise, emotional stress, low body weight, and decreased stores of body fat. Pituitary and ovarian hormones controlling menstruation are all low and the uterus and ovaries shrink in size (Golden & Shenker, 1992). In most instances, amenorrhea is associated with weight loss, but in approximately 20% of cases loss of menses may precede significant weight loss (Golden et al., 1997). Weight gain is usually accompanied by restoration of normal hypothalamic–pituitary–ovarian function and resumption of spontaneous menses, but in many cases amenorrhea may be prolonged.

Provided weight is restored and menses are regular, the ability to conceive should be normal. Persistence of low body weight and weight control behaviors, however, may be associated with infertility (Bates, Bates, & Whitworth, 1982). A recent study found that women who had a history of anorexia nervosa in the past had pregnancy rates similar to those of healthy controls and were no more likely to have received treatment for infertility (Bulik, Sullivan, Fear, Pickering, & Dawn, 1999). The women with a history of anorexia nervosa, however, were more likely to have a miscarriage, presumably because they continued with inappropriate weight-control behaviors during pregnancy.

The most serious complication of prolonged amenorrhea and a low estrogen state is osteopenia, a substantial reduction in bone mass. In anorexia nervosa, osteopenia may occur after a relatively short duration of illness (Bachrach, Guido, Katzman, Litt, & Marcus, 1990; Grinspoon et al., 2000). Osteopenia is related to a combination of poor nutrition, low body weight, estrogen deficiency, excessive exercise, and high levels of cortisol in the blood stream. The degree of osteopenia in anorexia nervosa is more severe than that seen in women with other conditions associated with amenorrhea and a low estrogen state. This finding suggests that in addition to estrogen deficiency, nutritional factors play an important role (Grinspoon et al., 1999).

Adolescence is a critical time for bone mass acquisition. Approximately 60% of peak bone mass is accrued during the adolescent years, and there is very little net gain in bone mass after 2 years following menarche (Bonjour, Theintz, Buchs, Slosman, & Rizzoli, 1991; Golden & Shenker, 1992; Katzman et al., 1991; Theintz et al., 1992). Whether a young woman will develop osteoporosis in later life depends not only on the rate of bone loss in adulthood but also on the

amount of bone present at skeletal maturity, often referred to as "peak bone mass." Multiple studies have shown that peak bone mass is achieved toward the end of the second decade of life (Bonjour et al., 1991; Faulkner et al., 1996; Katzman et al., 1991; Southard et al., 1991). A woman who develops anorexia nervosa during adolescence will not reach her peak bone mass, thus she will be at increased risk of developing fractures. Because of the lower peak bone mass, the increased fracture risk may persist for years after recovery from anorexia nervosa. Recent studies have demonstrated that more than 90% of adolescents and young adults with anorexia nervosa have reduced bone mass at one or more skeletal sites (Golden, 2003; Grinspoon et al., 2000). Osteopenia that occurs in adolescence may not be completely reversible (Rigotti, Neer, Skates, Herzog, & Nussbaum, 1991; Soyka et al., 2002). Weight gain is associated with some improvement in bone mineral density, but levels do not return to normal (Bachrach, Katzman, Litt, Guido, & Marcus, 1991). A recent study conducted on women who had been in recovery from anorexia nervosa for an average of 21 years found that bone mineral density of the hip remained lower than that of controls, and a relatively high percentage of patients reported a history of pathologic bone fractures (Hartman et al., 2000). Although there are no proven therapies and estrogen has been shown to be ineffective, recent studies have shown that insulin-like growth factor-1 (IGF-1), a nutritionally dependent hormone, may prevent bone loss (Grinspoon, Thomas, Miller, Herzog, & Kilbanski, 2002).

Medical Complications of Bulimia Nervosa

For patients with bulimia nervosa, fluctuations in body weight can be observed, and reflect cycles of dehydration, electrolyte disturbances, and water retention associated with vomiting and abuse of laxatives and diuretics. Massive swelling of the hands and feet can occur among those who abruptly discontinue the use of laxatives or diuretics. Examination of the hands may reveal calluses or scars over the knuckles or skin of the dominant hand (Russell's sign), which are caused by abrasions by the teeth during self-induced vomiting.

Hypokalemia, a reduced level of potassium in the blood, is the most frequently found significant electrolyte disturbance in patients who vomit or use laxatives or diuretics. Hypokalemia can be associated with life-threatening cardiac arrhythmias, and a low serum potassium level should be carefully corrected. Periods of caloric restriction result in episodes of bradycardia and vital sign instability, although not to the same degree as that seen in patients with anorexia nervosa.

Ipecac, a medication used to induce vomiting after accidental poisoning, is abused by some patients with bulimia nervosa. Ipecac contains the alkaloid emetine, which is toxic to both skeletal and cardiac muscle, and excessive intake may cause muscle weakness, congestive heart failure, and cardiac arrest. Ipecac use is cumulative and ipecac abuse can be a cause of sudden death among adolescents with bulimia nervosa (Schiff et al., 1986).

Enlargement of the parotid and salivary glands occurs in 10% to 30% of patients with bulimia nervosa and is thought to be secondary to binge eating and vomiting (Ogren, Huerter, Pearson, Antonson, & Moore, 1987). Erosion of the dental enamel is most evident on the lingual aspects of the anterior teeth and is caused by the gastric acid. Recurrent vomiting leads to gastroesophageal reflux, esophagitis, tears of the esophagus, and, less frequently, esophageal rupture. Small tears may be evidenced by blood-stained vomiting. Esophageal rupture is a catastrophic event and is usually fatal. Esophagitis is associated with epigastric or retrosternal chest pain and warrants treatment.

Treatment of Medical Complications

The goals of medical management of patients with eating disorders are acute medical stabilization, normalization of eating behaviors, and reversal of medical complications. For patients with anorexia nervosa, weight restoration is an important goal of treatment and is usually associated with improvements in mood and eating disorder symptoms.

Refeeding in Anorexia Nervosa

The greatest risk of cardiac decompensation and electrolyte disturbances occurs during the refeeding phase and, in particular, during the first 7–10 days of refeeding. It is during this time when the "refeeding syndrome," consisting of cardiac, neurologic, and hematologic complications, is most likely to occur. The syndrome can occur after intravenous, nasogastric, or oral refeeding. Hypophosphatemia occurs in over one quarter of adolescents hospitalized with anorexia nervosa (Ornstein, Golden, Jacobson, & Shenker, 2003). Hypophosphatemia is more likely to occur in those who are very malnourished (less than 70% of ideal body weight) and may predispose patients to ventricular arrhythmias and sudden death.

The refeeding syndrome can be prevented by monitoring of heart rate and serum electrolytes (especially phosphorus) during the first 7–10 days of treatment. Caloric requirements of children and adolescents with anorexia nervosa are usually higher than those for adults and may be 3,000–4,500 kcals/day. The rate of weight gain should be 2–3 lbs/week for inpatient programs, 1–2 lbs/week for partial hospitalization programs (when such programs are step-down programs from inpatient units), and 0.5–1 lb/week for outpatient management (American Psychiatric Association Work Group on Eating Disorders, 2000).

Treatment of Osteopenia in Anorexia Nervosa

Few controlled trials have evaluated the treatment of osteopenia in anorexia nervosa, and fewer still have specifically focused on adolescents; most studies enrolled only a modest number of subjects. Therefore, the preferred treatment of anorexia nervosa–related osteopenia is unknown. Calcium supplementation is known to improve bone mass in healthy adolescents (Cadogan, Eastell, Jones, & Barker, 1997; Johnston et al., 1992; Lloyd et al., 1993) and in postmenopausal women with osteoporosis (Reid, Ames, Evans, Gamble, & Sharpe, 1995), but there have been no published controlled trials with anorexia nervosa patients. The Institute of Medicine recommends a dietary intake of 1,300 mg/ day of calcium for healthy girls aged 9–18 years (Standing Committee on the Scientific Evaluation of Dietary Reference Intakes for Calcium, 1997) and the American Academy of Pediatrics recommends a calcium intake of 1,200–1,500 mg/day for adolescents (American Academy of Pediatrics Committee on Nutrition, 1999). Without scientific evidence demonstrating the efficacy of calcium supplementation in adolescents with anorexia nervosa, it may be most prudent to suggest calcium supplementation for patients whose dietary intake contains less than the recommended amount.

A number of studies have shown that body weight, and particularly lean body mass, is a significant determinant of bone mineral density in healthy subjects (Glastre et al., 1990; Henderson, Price, Cole, Gutteridge, & Bhagat, 1995; Southard et al., 1991) and in those with anorexia nervosa (Bachrach et al., 1990; Goebel, Schweiger, Kruger, & Fichter, 1999; Golden et al., 2002; Gordon, Goodman, et al., 2002; Grinspoon et al., 1999; Soyka et al., 2002). Although bone mineral density increases with weight gain, even with weight restoration, osteopenia is not entirely reversible (Bachrach et al., 1991; Golden et al., 2002; Hartman et al., 2000; Rigotti et al., 1991).

Both weight-bearing and resistance exercise programs increase bone mineral density of the spine in children and young women (McKay et al., 2000; Snow-Harter, Bouxsein, Lewis, Carter, & Marcus, 1992), but exercise programs for patients with anorexia nervosa have not been studied. Excessive exercise, commonly used by patients with anorexia nervosa to control weight, could interfere with weight gain and produce amenorrhea. Therefore, any exercise should be undertaken cautiously.

Hormone replacement therapy is frequently prescribed to treat osteopenia in adolescents with anorexia nervosa (Robinson, Bachrach, & Katzman, 2000), on the assumption that estrogen deficiency contributes to the bone loss. The only randomized controlled trial published to date (Klibanski, Biller, Schoenfeld, Herzog, & Saxe, 1993) found no significant increase in bone mineral density for adult subjects with anorexia nervosa randomly assigned to receive es-

trogen treatment, in comparison to those who did not receive hormone treatment. The only suggestion of benefit was for those who were very malnourished (<70% of ideal body weight); hormone treatment may have provided a protective effect. In that subgroup, spinal bone mass increased 4% in those who received estrogen, but decreased 20.1% in those who did not. Golden et al. (2002) found that estrogen-progestin treatment in adolescents did not significantly increase bone mineral density, compared with standard treatment at 1-year follow-up. In subjects followed for 2–3 years, osteopenia was persistent and in some cases progressive, despite weight gain, in both experimental treatment groups (estrogen-progestin treatment and standard care).

Thus, there is currently no evidence of efficacy of hormone replacement therapy for the treatment of osteopenia in anorexia nervosa. Furthermore, prescribing estrogen to a young adolescent may cause premature closure of the epiphyses, which might result in further growth arrest. Ongoing randomized controlled trials are evaluating the use of new modalities such as IGF-1 (Grinspoon et al., 1996, 2002), dehydroepiandrosterone (DHEA; Gordon et al., 1999; Gordon, Grace et al., 2002), and the bisphosphonates for the treatment of osteopenia in anorexia nervosa. Current treatment recommendations include weight restoration with resumption of menses, calcium (1,300–1,500 mg/day) and vitamin D (400 IU/day) supplementation, and carefully monitored weight-bearing exercise (Golden, 2003).

Treatments to Increase Weight in Adolescents

The goal weight should be set in treatment on an individual basis, taking into account pubertal stage, prior growth percentiles, and height and age. For adolescents, the goal weight is a "moving target," and normal growth and development necessitate a recalculation of this number every 6 months. Height and weight tables used for adults are inappropriate for adolescents. The National Center for Health Statistics (NCHS) tables provide a useful resource of normative height and weight data for children and adolescents in the United States (National Center for Health Statistics, 1973); however, the tables provide only normative weight data, not specific guidance for what is an "ideal body weight."

The goal, or "ideal," weight should be the weight at which normal physical and sexual development occurs; for girls this is the weight at which menstruation and ovulation are restored. In postmenarcheal girls, a weight approximately 90% of ideal body weight (the median weight for age and height according to the NCHS tables) is a reasonable goal weight, since 86% of patients who achieve that weight will resume menses within 3 to 6 months (Golden et al., 1997). For those who were previously overweight, treatment goal weight may need to be higher. In a premenarcheal girl or an adolescent boy whose growth and development are not yet complete, treatment goal weight should be 100% of ideal body weight to maximize growth potential.

Summary

Most of the medical consequences of eating disorders are secondary to malnutrition and are reversible with nutritional rehabilitation and interruption of binge–purge activity. Heart rate returns to normal after approximately 12 days, vital sign instability resolves after approximately 21 days, and resting energy expenditure increases slowly and normalizes after approximately 6 weeks (Schebendach et al., 1997; Shamim et al., 2003). The amount of time needed for weight gain varies, and resumption of menses usually occurs within 3–6 months after achieving treatment goal weight. Difficulties with body image distortion and preoccupation with weight and shape, however, may take longer to resolve. Although most of the medical complications are reversible, growth retardation, osteopenia, and, possibly, structural brain changes may not be entirely reversible.

Treatment of Eating Disorders

Ideally, treatment efficacy should be evaluated by means of randomized control trials (RCTs) (National Institute for Clinical Excellence, 2004; Wilson & Fairburn, 2002). Surprisingly, for adolescents with eating disorders, only a handful of relatively small RCTs have been completed. In the absence of the requisite empirical base, the evaluation and recommendations described in this chapter are derived from the following sources: extrapolation from evidence-based treatments for eating disorders in adults, generalizations from closely related psychological and pharmacological treatments of anxiety and mood disorders in adolescents, and consensus views of clinicians who are experienced in the treatment of eating disorders.

PSYCHOLOGICAL TREATMENTS FOR ADOLESCENTS WITH EATING DISORDERS

Psychological interventions are a mainstay of the treatment of eating disorders in adults. Despite the need for effective treatment of eating disorders in affected adolescents, there are remarkably few controlled studies of psychological interventions in this age group. There have been only five RCTs of outpatient-based psychological treatments for adolescents with anorexia nervosa (National Institute for Clinical Excellence, 2004) and no studies of adolescents with bulimia nervosa (Weisz & Hawley, 2002). The lack of research in the treatment of adolescents with eating disorders is not unique, as relatively less attention has been paid to treatment outcome studies of adolescent psychiatric disorders in general than to those of either adults (Weisz & Hawley, 2002) or younger children (Kazdin, Bass, Ayers, & Rodgers, 1990). Because symptoms of both anorexia nervosa and bulimia nervosa generally begin in adolescence (Mitchell, Hatsukami, Eckert, & Pyle, 1985; Schmidt, Hodes, & Treasure, 1992), it is difficult to explain the complete lack of research done with adolescent bulimia nervosa patients and the relatively low number of bulimia nervosa patients who present for treatment. It is possible that adolescents with anorexia nervosa are more easily identified by parents and professionals and are therefore encouraged to seek treatment, whereas adolescents

with bulimia nervosa can more easily hide their behaviors, thus their disorder escapes detection.

Psychological Treatments for Adolescents with Anorexia Nervosa

Randomized Controlled Trials of Treatment of Anorexia Nervosa

Russell and colleagues, from the Maudsley Hospital in London (Russell, Szmukler, Dare, & Eisler, 1987), published the first RCT of the treatment of adolescents with anorexia nervosa. The aim of this study was to evaluate two treatment approaches, family therapy and individual treatment for the management of patients who had initially been treated in a hospital. The average duration of the patients' hospital stay was 10 weeks, and the mean weight on discharge was $88.9 \pm 7.4\%$ average body weight. Although patients are typically still symptomatic at the end of hospitalization, the next stage of treatment, is sometimes described as "relapse prevention." This study was an evaluation of treatment at this stage.

The study did not consist of a single RCT; rather, there were four separate RCTs, each involving slightly different groups of patients. One of these groups (subgroup 1) was composed of 21 adolescents with anorexia nervosa who had a mean age of 16.6 ± 1.7 years and a mean duration of illness of 1.2 ± 0.7 years. These 21 patients were randomized to receive either 1 year of family therapy or 1 year of individual psychotherapy. The form of family therapy used has since come to be known as the "Maudsley method," described in a recently published manual (Lock, Le Grange, Agras, & Dare, 2001). The Maudsley method, a specific form of family therapy designed for adolescent patients with anorexia nervosa, is quite unlike more generic family-based treatments. As described by Lock and colleagues (2001), this treatment has three stages: refeeding the patient, negotiating for a new pattern of relationships, and addressing adolescent issues and treatment termination.

In the initial implementation of the Maudsley treatment (Russell et al., 1987), there are two main phases. The first phase occurs after the patient and family have been engaged in therapy and focuses largely on the patient's eating and weight. Here the parents are helped to take control over the way the patient eats. In the second phase, once the patient's weight is under control, responsibility for weight management is transferred to the patient and treatment focuses on more general family and individual concerns.

The comparison individual treatment used by Russell et al. (1987) was devised specifically for this study. In content, it was based on conventional posthospitalization follow-up appointments (as practiced at the Maudsley Hospital), but the sessions were more frequent and lasted longer than usual, to match the intensity of the family treatment. The individual treatment is probably best characterized as a form of supportive psychotherapy that encourages patients to eat healthily and maintain an appropriate weight.

The results of the Russell et al. (1987) study favored the family therapy approach. At the end of treatment (1 year after discharge from the hospital), 6 out of 10 patients who received family therapy were judged to have a good outcome, as assessed via the Morgan-Russell scales (Morgan & Russell, 1975), compared with 1 out of 11 patients who received the control treatment ($p <$ .02). Also, the family therapy patients had a better outcome in terms of weight regain (from their prehospitalization weight); the percentage weight regain in the two treatment conditions was 25.5% and 15.5%, respectively ($p <$ .01). Similarly, the family therapy patients were better at maintaining their new higher weight, with 5 out of 10 patients keeping their weight above 85% average body weight, compared with 1 out of 11 patients who received the control individual psychotherapy ($p <$ .05). There was also a lower dropout rate among the patients who received family therapy (1/10, vs. 7/11 in the control condition, $p =$ .024).

A major strength of this study was that the patients were followed up 5 years after the completion of treatment (Eisler et al., 1997). At this time point, both patient groups had done well; the mean percentage of average body weight was 103.4 ± 13.2% in the group treated with family therapy and 94.4 ± 16.8% in the control group ($p = ns$). In terms of overall outcome on the Morgan-Russell scales, the results continued to favor the family therapy group, with 9 out of 10 patients having a good outcome, vs. 4 out of 11 patients in the control group ($p =$ .024). This study is limited by its modest scale and the post-hospitalization design, but has had a major influence on the design of more recent investigations and on current treatment recommendations.

The later studies from the Maudsley group have focused on family therapy alone, the premise being that family therapy is "established as an effective treatment for anorexia nervosa in adolescence" (Dare & Eisler, 2002, p. 317). The next investigation (Le Grange, Eisler, Dare, & Russell, 1992) was a pilot study for a subsequent trial (Eisler et al., 2000). The goal was to compare two different ways of delivering the Maudsley method of family therapy: one involved all the family being seen together (subsequently termed "conjoint family therapy," the original method), the other consisted of separate treatment sessions for the patient and the parents (subsequently termed "separated family therapy"). In contrast with the Russell et al. (1987) study, family therapy was provided from the outset of treatment rather than after a period of hospitalization. This study is of greater relevance to the routine management of patients with anorexia nervosa, most of whom are not admitted to a hospital.

This pilot study involved just 18 patients (mean age 15.3 ± 1.8 years; mean duration of illness 13.7 ± 8.4 months; mean percentage of average body weight 77.9 ± 7.6%). Both groups responded well, despite receiving a modest number of treatment sessions (8.9 ± 4.1 sessions over 6 months), with substantial weight regain and improvement on various measures of psychopathology. Not surprisingly, given the small sample size, there were no statistically significant differences in outcome between the two groups.

The third study in the Maudsley series (Eisler et al., 2000) followed from the Le Grange et al. (1992) pilot study. It involved a comparison of the same two family-based treatments, but on a larger scale. Forty patients were randomized to the two treatments, their mean age being 15.5 ± 1.6 years and mean duration of disorder being 12.9 ± 9.4 months. Treatment took place over 1 year and involved on average 16 sessions. The conjoint sessions lasted 1 hour, whereas the separated sessions lasted 90 minutes.

Once again, both groups of patients improved markedly; their percentage average body weight increased from 74.3 ± 9.8% to 87.0 ± 13.0% (p = .001), and the equivalent figures for body mass index (BMI) increased from 15.4 ± 2.0 kg/m^2 to 18.5 ± 3.6 kg/m^2 ($p < .001$). There was a substantial decrease in eating disorder features—for example, the total score on the Eating Attitudes Test (Garner & Garfinkel, 1979) decreased from 47.7 ± 25.7 to 19.7 ± 16.1 ($p < .001$), and there was improvement on the Morgan-Russell scales. The analysis of differences in outcome between the two treatments revealed few statistically significant findings, although the pattern of the findings suggested that separated family therapy might be more potent at addressing the specific psychopathology of eating disorders, whereas conjoint family therapy might be more effective at addressing general psychopathology, such as depressive and obsessional features. With only 20 patients per treatment condition, however, the study did not have sufficient power for comparisons of this type. Nevertheless, the findings do suggest that family meetings of the type required for conjoint family therapy may not be needed for the Maudsley method to achieve its effects.

The fourth RCT was by Robin and colleagues (Robin, Siegel, Koepke, Moye, & Tice, 1994; Robin et al., 1999). They compared "behavioral family systems therapy," a treatment similar to the original Maudsley method, with "ego-oriented individual therapy," a psychodynamically oriented treatment in which patients are seen individually, with occasional supportive sessions for their parents. In the latter condition there was little or no direct emphasis on changing eating habits or increasing body weight.

Thirty-seven patients were randomized to the two treatments, the mean ages of the family therapy and individual therapy groups being 14.9 years and 13.4 years, respectively ($p < .05$), and their baseline BMI being 15.2 ± 1.8 kg/m^2 and 16.6 ± 2.1 kg/m^2, respectively ($p = .038$). All the patients had developed anorexia nervosa within the previous 12 months. The two treatments were more intensive and multifaceted than those provided by the Maudsley group, and

involved 12 to 18 months of treatment with weekly sessions for half of the treatment and sessions every other week thereafter. In addition, both groups of patients saw a dietician who prescribed a diet designed to restore body weight at a rate of 1 lb/week. Furthermore, those patients whose weight was below 75% of ideal or who had significant cardiac problems were hospitalized at the outset and received a structured refeeding program until they reached 80% of their target weight and were medically stable. This applied to 58% of the family therapy group and 28% of those receiving individual therapy ($p = .099$). While in the hospital, the patients also received their assigned form of psychotherapy.

The outcome of both groups was positive, both at the end of treatment and 1 year later. There was one statistically significant difference between the groups: patients in the family therapy group had a greater increase in BMI. The mean BMI posttreatment and at 1 year follow-up was 19.9 ± 1.9 kg/m^2 and 20.7 ± 2.7 kg/m^2 in the family therapy group, and 18.9 ± 1.9 kg/m^2 and 19.8 ± 3.1 kg/m^2 for those receiving individual therapy. On all other measures of outcome there were no statistically significant differences between the two groups. At the end of treatment, two thirds of the patients had reached their target weight. By the end of 1-year follow-up, 80% of those who had received family therapy had reached their target weight; there was no such increase for those who had received individual therapy. In considering these findings, it is important to note that it is not possible to attribute the changes observed specifically to the two psychotherapies received. All the patients also received extensive dietary advice, and many were hospitalized during the initial stages of treatment (especially those receiving family therapy).

The most recent of the five RCTs (Geist, Heinmaa, Stephens, Davis, & Katzman, 2000) compared two 16-week family-based interventions. The interventions occurred in the context of considerable additional treatment, including an initial period of inpatient treatment (lasting on average 6 weeks) that involved an assertive refeeding program, as well as milieu therapy, and individual and group psychotherapy. In addition, following discharge from the hospital patients had continuing medical and nursing contact that was designed to encourage further weight regain. A further complicating factor is that many patients and their families declined to take part in the study: 59% of the eligible patients refused, and only 29 patients entered the trial. The two treatment groups did not differ in their outcome.

Evaluation of Research on Psychological Treatments for Anorexia Nervosa

There has been little research on the treatment of adolescents with anorexia nervosa. The studies that have been conducted are small, with the largest study including just 20 patients per treatment condition. Thus the power of these studies to detect differences between treatments is minimal, and it is difficult to evaluate the findings of these studies. Three larger studies (I. Eisler, personal communication, 2003; S. G. Gowers, personal communication, 2002; J. Lock, personal communication, 2002) are currently under way, and may provide additional information about the efficacy of treatments for adolescents with anorexia nervosa.

Another limitation of this research is the quality of the assessment measures used. None of the studies has employed standardized and psychometrically sound instruments of the type routinely used in adult eating disorder treatment trials. As a result, it is difficult to gauge the true extent of the patients' improvement.

In addition, limited data are available on the longer-term effects of treatment. Such data are important, because not only is relapse into anorexia nervosa common but the eating disorder may evolve into bulimia nervosa or an eating disorder not otherwise specified (EDNOS) (Fairburn & Harrison, 2003). To assess the frequency of diagnostic migration and determine whether treatments differ in their ability to influence the long-term course of the disorder, repeated assessments are required and measures capable of characterizing any form of eating disorder must be used.

None of the studies in this area has included a delayed-treatment ("waiting list") control condition. It is conceivable that once adolescent patients and their parents request help, changes

have already begun to take place that will lead to symptomatic improvement. And even if this were not true of the majority of patients, it might be true for a significant minority. However, the serious psychological and medical morbidity of anorexia nervosa makes the employment of a waiting-list condition ethically problematic, and there has been very little discussion of what might constitute appropriate control conditions against which new interventions for anorexia nervosa should be compared.

Family Therapy

It is widely accepted that family therapy is the treatment of choice for adolescents with anorexia nervosa (e.g., National Institute for Clinical Excellence [NICE], 2004). This is surprising given the modest evidence to support it. Only two studies have compared family therapy to another form of treatment (Robin et al., 1999; Russell et al., 1987), and the findings of the second are difficult to interpret.

The superiority of family therapy over individual therapy has not been clearly established. In the family treatment used in the Russell et al. (1987) trial, great emphasis was placed on getting patients to eat well and maintain a healthy weight; the control treatment did not have the same focus on eating and weight. The same is true of the two treatments studied in the Robin et al. (1999) trial. Thus, in both studies any differences in outcome between the family-based treatment and individual therapy could have been a result of their relative emphasis on eating and weight rather than the modality of the treatment.

The Maudsley Method

As noted earlier, research on the treatment of adolescent anorexia nervosa has concentrated on a very particular form of family therapy. Two ways of delivering this treatment have been compared (Eisler et al., 2000; Le Grange et al., 1992), but no other type of family therapy has been adequately tested. It is important that clinicians be aware of this when deciding how to treat their adolescent patients. It is of note that the Maudsley group has progressively modified their

family-based treatment and now view their original method as "slightly out of date" (Dare & Eisler, 2002; p. 318). They favor treating groups of
families at one time (so-called "multi-family
group therapy"; Dare & Eisler, 2000), not least
because this form of treatment is well received
by patients and their families, and are in the process of evaluating this method.

Summary

There is a pressing need for more research on the
psychological treatment of adolescents with anorexia nervosa. Family therapy is widely used but
its effectiveness has not been definitively established, and individual therapy has been largely
ignored. Further well-designed psychological
treatment trials are needed and are feasible.

Psychological Treatments for Adolescents with Bulimia Nervosa

No RCTs of psychological treatments for adolescents with bulimia nervosa have been published.
Treatments such as the Maudsley family-therapy
approach are nonetheless being adapted for adolescents with bulimia nervosa (LeGrange, Lock,
& Dymek, 2003). Although it cannot be assumed
that effective treatments for adults with eating
disorders will be as effective for adolescents, a
case can be made for the feasibility of adapting
evidence-based treatments for adults to adolescents.

In adults, cognitive-behavioral therapy (CBT)
for bulimia nervosa has been intensively evaluated in a large number of RCTs (NICE, 2004).
Cognitive-behavioral therapy has been shown to
be consistently superior to assignment to a
waiting-list, as those receiving the latter have
typically shown no improvement across a range
of measures. On average, CBT has eliminated
binge eating and purging in roughly 30% to 50%
of patients in controlled outcome studies. The
percentage reduction in binge eating and purging across all patients treated with CBT has typically been 80% or more. Dysfunctional dieting
is decreased, and patients' attitudes about their
body shape and weight are improved. In addition, there is usually a reduction in the level of
general psychiatric symptoms and an improvement in self-esteem and social functioning.

Cognitive-behavioral therapy has been found
to be equal or superior to all the treatments with
which it has been compared. It has been shown
to be more effective than antidepressant medication, an intensively researched treatment for
bulimia nervosa that has been consistently
shown to be significantly more effective than pill
placebo (Hay & Bacaltchuk, 2000; NICE, 2004;
Whittal, Agras, & Gould, 1999; Wilson & Fairburn, 2002). Cognitive-behavioral therapy has
also proved to be more effective than several
other psychological treatments, including supportive psychotherapy, supportive-expressive
psychotherapy, stress management therapy, and
a form of behavior therapy that did not address
cognitive features of bulimia nervosa (Whittal et
al., 1999; Wilson & Fairburn, 2002).

Cognitive-behavioral therapy is based on a
model that emphasizes the critical role of both
cognitive and behavioral factors in the maintenance of the disorder. Of primary importance is
the value attached to an idealized body weight
and shape, which leads women to restrict their
food intake in rigid and unrealistic ways. As a
result, they may become physiologically and
psychologically susceptible to periodic loss of
control over eating, namely binge eating. Purging and other extreme forms of weight control
are then attempts to compensate for the effects
of binge eating. The purging helps maintain the
binge eating by reducing the patient's anxiety
about potential weight gain and disrupting
learned satiety that regulates food intake. In
turn, the binge eating and purging cause distress
and low self-esteem, thereby reciprocally fostering the conditions that lead to more dietary restraint and binge eating (Fairburn, 1997a; Fairburn, Cooper, & Shafran, 2003).

Cognitive-behavioral therapy consists of procedures for developing a regular pattern of eating
that includes previously avoided foods, and
more constructive skills to cope with high-risk
situations for binge eating and purging; for modifying abnormal attitudes to eating, shape, and
weight; and for preventing relapse at the conclusion of treatment (Fairburn, Marcus, & Wilson,

1993). Treatment is time limited, directive, and problem oriented.

Some research suggests that guided self-help programs based on the principles of CBT (Fairburn et al., 1995) can be effective with at least a subset of patients with bulimia nervosa (Thiels, Schmidt, Treasure, Garthe, & Troop, 1998). Accordingly, a stepped-care approach to the treatment of bulimia nervosa might begin with guided self-help (Wilson, Vitousek, & Loeb, 2000).

Interpersonal Psychotherapy

Interpersonal psychotherapy (IPT) was originally developed by Klerman, Weissman, Rounsaville, and Chevron (1984) as a short-term treatment for depression. The primary focus of IPT is to help patients identify and modify current interpersonal problems. As adapted for bulimia nervosa (Fairburn, 1997b), IPT focuses exclusively on interpersonal issues, with little or no attention directed to the modification of binge eating, purging, disturbed eating, or overconcern with body shape and weight. Specific eating problems are viewed as a means of understanding the interpersonal context that is assumed to be maintaining them.

Two major comparative outcome studies of adult bulimia nervosa patients demonstrated that at the end of treatment IPT was significantly less effective than CBT (Agras, Walsh, Fairburn, Wilson, & Kraemer, 2000; Fairburn et al., 1993). At 1-year follow-up, however, the difference between the two treatments was no longer statistically significant. In the absence of a control condition it is not possible to attribute the improvement associated with IPT to any specific treatment effect. However, in the study by Fairburn et al. (1995), both IPT and CBT fared significantly better than a suitable comparison treatment (a form of behavior therapy without the cognitive features of CBT) over the course of follow-up. Given that the behavior therapy treatment was equivalent in the amount of therapist contact and ratings of suitability and expectancy, this single study provides specific evidence of the efficacy of IPT for bulimia nervosa.

A variety of psychological treatments other than CBT or IPT are commonly used to treat bulimia nervosa (e.g., psychodynamic therapy, family therapy; Garner & Garfinkel, 1997), but none has been systematically evaluated in controlled research. None can be considered an evidence-based treatment (NICE, 2004).

Application of Cognitive-Behavioral Therapy to Adolescents with Bulimia Nervosa

It can be predicted that CBT will prove comparably effective for adolescents with bulimia nervosa, as conceptually and procedurally similar forms of CBT that were originally developed as treatments for adults with anxiety disorders and major depression have been readily adapted to adolescent populations. Cognitive-behavioral therapy has been shown to be reliably effective in the treatment of adult anxiety and mood disorders (Barlow, 2002; Hollon, Thase, & Markowitz, 2002; Nathan & Gorman, 2002). Manual-based CBT is as effective as antidepressant medication as an acute treatment of panic disorder and major depression, and has more sustained effects if medication is discontinued (Barlow, 2002). The CBT interventions that have been successfully used in treating adults have been adapted to adolescents.

Manual-based CBT for adolescents with major depression results in greater improvement and faster remission than being assigned to a waiting-list or alternative forms of psychotherapy, including family and supportive therapy, at the end of acute treatment (Curry, 2001). Cognitive-behavioral therapy has also been successfully used to prevent the onset of depression in at-risk adolescents with no prior history of depression (Clarke et al., 2001). There is also evidence of the efficacy of CBT in treating anxiety disorders (Donovan & Spence, 2001); a large RCT found CBT to be significantly more effective than a waiting-list control at post-treatment on a variety of outcome measures. Therapeutic improvement was maintained at 1-year follow-up (Kendall et al., 1997). Replications of this CBT treatment for anxiety disorders in children have shown maintenance of treatment effects for up to 6 years (Kazdin, 2003).

Although not studied as extensively as treatments for adult disorders, psychological therapies for depression and anxiety disorders in adolescence have proven effective. The theoretical models, treatment principles, and technical interventions that comprise these therapies are similar to those that would be applied to bulimia nervosa. It should also be noted that depression and anxiety disorders are commonly comorbid with bulimia nervosa (Bulik, 2002).

Interpersonal psychotherapy for treatment of depression in adolescents.   Two controlled studies have shown that IPT is effective with adolescents with major depression (Mufson, Weissman, Moreau, & Garfinkel, 1999; Rossello & Bernal, 1999). According to Curry (2001), IPT meets criteria "for possible efficacy in treating adolescent major depression" (p. 1092). In light of these data and the frequent co-occurrence of depression and bulimia nervosa, studies of the utility of IPT for adolescents with bulimia nervosa would be of interest.

Psychological Therapy for Adolescents with Eating Disorders: General Considerations

Developmental psychologists emphasize a connection between the psychological dimensions of development and the treatment of adolescents. Weisz and Hawley (2002) focused on the following issues: motivation, cognition, and social development.

Motivation.   The issue here is that many adolescents in treatment are not self-referred but pressured by family into seeking help. Weisz and Hawley (2002) state that interventions programs tacitly assume motivation for treatment. They recommend that therapists assess motivation prior to starting treatment and implement specific strategies for enhancing it.

Cognition.   Weisz and Hawley (2000) argue that the adolescent's developing cognitive abilities may impose limits on the utility of some therapeutic interventions. They emphasize the importance of three cognitive skills in adolescence "that are especially relevant to therapy: abstraction, consequential thinking, and hypothetical reasoning" (Holmbeck et al., 2000). They suggest that this might be especially relevant to CBT, with its explicit cognitive focus.

Social development.   Developmental change in social interactions is a distinguishing feature of adolescence. Peer group and family relationships loom large in adolescent adjustment. Weisz and Hawley (2002) underscore the relevance of addressing interpersonal skills and relationship issues in adolescent treatments. They also assert that an adolescent's psychological and social adjustment and school performance can be enhanced by "authoritative parenting," namely, "consistently enforced guidelines and limits with warmth and psychological autonomy granting" (p. 30). They suggest that the former is especially relevant to "externalizing" problem behaviors such as substance abuse, whereas the latter applies particularly to "internalizing" problems such as anxiety and depression. It can be argued that both sets of problems often characterize eating disorders, and that both limit setting and autonomy granting, a "complicated balancing act," are required. Treatment of adolescents inescapably raises the question of how to involve parents in the therapy. Somewhat surprisingly, fewer than half the studies of empirically supported treatments identified by Weisz and Hawley addressed family relationships in therapy. Among those that did, the evidence on outcome was mixed.

Psychological Therapy for Adolescents with Bulimia Nervosa: Specific Considerations

The conceptual model of the maintenance of bulimia nervosa and the therapeutic principles and procedures of CBT appear to mesh well with the psychology of adolescence and the developmental factors summarized above. Bulimia nervosa occurs predominantly in females, and much is known about the developmental challenges (psychosocial tasks) facing adolescent girls (Striegel-Moore, 1993). Girls, far more than boys, are socially oriented. Girls' sense of personal identity is said to be interpersonally constructed, with self-esteem being strongly influenced by the perceptions of others' approval. Social approval is closely linked to physical attractiveness, and girls are socialized to evaluate themselves in terms of appearance. Striegel-Moore (1993) has argued that girls with an insecure identity who are concerned about how others view them may focus disproportionately on physical appearance as a concrete way to construct a sense of self. Bulimia nervosa is often marked by problems with social adjustment and social-self difficulties. These findings about bulimia nervosa and the psychology of adolescence for girls indicate that treatment needs to address interpersonal relationships.

Although body shape and weight concerns have been documented in prepubertal girls, it is the key developmental milestone of reaching puberty that poses biological and psychological challenges for adolescent girls. Concerns about body image are commonplace, and severe dissatisfaction with body shape and weight and pressure to be thin can drive the rigid, unhealthy dieting and negative affect (because appearance is a key evaluative dimension for females) that are proximal triggers for bulimia nervosa (Fairburn, 1997a; Stice, 2001).

Psychological Treatments for Other Adolescent Eating Disorders

As discussed previously, most adolescent patients who present for treatment do not meet the DSM-IV diagnostic criteria for anorexia nervosa or bulimia nervosa. Their eating disorder is therefore categorized as eating disorder not otherwise specified (Brewerton, 2002; Dancyger & Garfinkel, 1995; Eliot & Baker, 2001; Engelsen, 1999; Fisher et al., 1995; Muscari, 2002; Nicholls et al., 2000). Thus, treatment for adolescents must be able to accommodate a wide range of eating disorder pathology.

A recently described manual-based form of CBT provides a transdiagnostic model of eating disorders (Fairburn, Cooper, & Shafran, 2003): specific therapeutic interventions are matched to particular clinical features of the eating disorder, rather than a heterogeneous diagnostic category. The flexibility of this enhanced CBT allows different clinical features to be targeted with theory-driven and evidence-based treatment modules within the overall framework of the core CBT approach. This approach could be useful in treating adolescent patients with an eating disorder not otherwise specified.

Summary

Cognitive-behavioral therapy is the leading evidence-based therapy for bulimia nervosa

among adults (NICE, 2004) and is likely to be adaptable to the treatment of adolescents. The flexibility of CBT and recent evidence for its utility in preventing relapse among adults with anorexia nervosa (see below) suggest that when suitably adapted, it may be useful for the wide spectrum of eating disturbances in adolescents. Examination of the efficacy of CBT for adolescents with bulimia nervosa is clearly warranted. Interpersonal psychotherapy has some utility in the treatment of adults with bulimia nervosa and has been successfully employed in the treatment of depression among adolescents. Thus IPT might be useful for adolescents with bulimia nervosa. Finally, the apparent success of family-based interventions for anorexia nervosa suggests that this approach may also have merit in the treatment of bulimia nervosa.

PHARMACOLOGICAL TREATMENTS FOR ADOLESCENTS WITH EATING DISORDERS

With rare exception (e.g., Biederman et al., 1985), there are no studies of the efficacy of pharmacological treatment for adolescents with eating disorders. Therefore, as is the case with psychological treatments for adolescents, information about pharmacological interventions must be adapted from the literature for adults. Recent evidence that some pharmacological treatments of clear efficacy for adults with disorders such as major depression can be successfully employed for adolescents (Varley, 2003) should encourage further research on the utility of pharmacological treatments for adolescents with eating disorders.

Pharmacological Treatments for Anorexia Nervosa

There are no empirically supported pharmacological treatments for the acute symptoms of anorexia nervosa in either adolescents or adults. As in the case of the existing psychotherapy research, however, data from pharmacological studies of adults with eating disorders may provide some guidance in developing promising therapeutic interventions.

Antidepressant Medications

Four placebo-controlled trials of antidepressants in the treatment of anorexia nervosa have been published (Attia, Haiman, Walsh, & Flater, 1998; Biederman et al., 1985; Halmi, Eckert, LaDu, & Cohen, 1986; Lacey & Crisp, 1980). None of the trials documented more than a slight therapeutic effect. Given the evidence of utility of antidepressant medication for conditions with substantial symptomatic overlap with anorexia nervosa, such as major depression and bulimia nervosa, the lack of any significant effect is surprising and raises the possibility that the malnutrition inherent in anorexia nervosa somehow interferes with the therapeutic action of antidepressant medication. Circumstantial evidence consistent with this hypothesis has emerged from studies of serotonin function. For example, in healthy women, dieting significantly lowers plasma levels of tryptophan, the precursor of serotonin (Andersen, Parry-Billings, Newsholme, Fairburn, & Cowen, 1990). Individuals with anorexia nervosa who are malnourished have reduced plasma tryptophan availability (Schweiger, Warnoff, Pahl, & Pirke, 1986) and reduced levels of cerebrospinal fluid 5-hydroxyindoleacetic acid (CSF 5-HIAA), the major metabolite of serotonin, which increases with weight gain (Kaye, Gwirtsman, George, Jimerson, & Ebert, 1988). Depletion of serotonin in anorexia nervosa might interfere with the effects of antidepressants in general and the selective serotonin reuptake inhibitors (SSRIs) in particular (Delgado et al., 1990).

Atypical Antipsychotic Medications

Almost 50 years ago, experience with chlorpromazine, the first antipsychotic medication in clinical use, led to substantial enthusiasm about its potential role in the treatment of anorexia nervosa. With greater experience, however, the enthusiasm waned, and two small, placebo-controlled trials of antipsychotic medication found little evidence of efficacy (Vandereycken, 1984; Vandereycken & Pierloot, 1982). The recent introduction of the atypical antipsychotic drugs, a number of which are associated with considerable weight gain, has prompted reconsideration of this class of medication as a treatment for acute anorexia nervosa. Several case reports and open studies have described improvement associated with olanzapine treatment of children, adolescents, and adults with anorexia nervosa (Boachie, Goldfield, & Spettigue, 2003; Hansen, 1999; Jensen & Mejlhede, 2000; La Via, Gray, & Kaye, 2000; Mehler et al., 2001; Powers, Santana, & Bannon, 2002). By contrast, one open study reported no appreciable weight gain with olanzapine among patients treated on a specialized inpatient unit (Gaskill, Treat, McCabe, Marcus, 2001). In the absence of randomized placebo-controlled trials, no conclusion about the role of atypical antipsychotic medications in the treatment of anorexia nervosa in either adults or adolescents is possible. This is nonetheless a potentially promising area for new research.

Other Medications

Zinc deficiency is associated with weight loss, a decrease in appetite, changes in taste perception, amenorrhea, and depression, all symptoms described by patients with anorexia nervosa. This observation, coupled with reports of zinc deficiency associated with anorexia nervosa, has prompted several controlled trials of zinc supplementation. While one controlled trial in adults found zinc to be associated with an increased rate of weight gain (Birmingham, Goldner, & Bakan, 1994), two other trials among adolescents found no effect (Katz et al., 1987; Lask, Fosson, Rolfe, & Thomas, 1993). The role of zinc supplementation as a treatment for anorexia nervosa is uncertain.

The benefits of lithium in the treatment of bipolar (manic-depressive) disorder among adults are very well established, and, like many antipsychotic medications, the use of lithium is associated with weight gain. These considerations prompted a single controlled trial of lithium among inpatients with anorexia nervosa, which provided little support for the utility of this agent (Gross, Ebert, Faden, Goldberg, Nee, & Kaye, 1981).

Issues to Consider in Treating Adolescents with Pharmacotherapy

The pharmacokinetics and pharmacodynamics of psychotropic drugs in children and adolescents are not well studied. Some biological factors inherent to adolescents may affect the metabolism and efficacy of psychiatric medications, such as immature neurotransmitter systems, rapid hepatic metabolism, and shifting hormonal levels in adolescents (Hazell, O'Connell, Heathcote, Robertson, & Henry, 1995). Dramatic shifts in weight, especially weight loss, can also occur much more rapidly in adolescents than in adults with eating disorders. As a result, there may be differences in the metabolism and/or the effects of medications in adolescents with eating disorders, which could necessitate adjustments in dosage and medication response.

The safety of psychotropic medications should be considered when prescribing medications for patients with an eating disorder, especially when patients are medically unstable. Tricyclic antidepressants (TCAs) and mood stabilizers, which tend to be less frequently used today than in the past, have potential for serious side effects. In particular, although a clear causal link has not been documented, TCAs have been associated with sudden death among adolescents without eating disorders (Geller, Reising, Leonard, Riddle, & Walsh, 1999), and the cardiac abnormalities associated with anorexia nervosa, in theory, should increase the risks of tricyclic use in this population. Careful medical and psychiatric monitoring is required when prescribing psychotropic drugs to adolescents with eating disorders. As with adults, adolescent patients with eating disorders are prone to develop other behavioral problems, such as substance abuse, which may increase the risk of side effects. In addition, in sexually active adolescents, ensuring adequate birth control is important to prevent the potential harmful effects of medications during pregnancy (Kotler & Walsh, 2000). Finally, concerns have recently been raised about the potential for some SSRIs to increase suicidal ideation among adolescents (Dalrymple, 2003; Harris, 2003; United Kingdom Department of Health, 2003; United States Food and Drug Administration, 2004). The potential for SSRIs to increase the risk of suicide among ad-

olescents is controversial, but suggests a need for close monitoring of suicidal ideation when such treatment is initiated.

Finally, as noted in the discussion of psychotherapeutic approaches, the motivation of adolescents for treatment is quite variable, and a lack of motivation may compromise patients' compliance with following treatment recommendations, including taking psychotropic drugs as prescribed. For adolescents, compliance may be increased by family psychoeducation and parental involvement with treatment.

Pharmacological Treatments for Bulimia Nervosa

Antidepressant Medications

Virtually every class of antidepressant medication has been studied in placebo-controlled, double-blind trials for adult patients with bulimia nervosa. Antidepressant medications, including both TCAs and SSRIs, appear to have approximately equal efficacy in the acute treatment of bulimia nervosa; however, SSRI antidepressants are generally better tolerated and have fewer side effects (Zhu & Walsh, 2002), thus they are the first pharmacological treatment of choice for adults with bulimia nervosa. Specifically, the SSRI fluoxetine is the only drug approved by the U.S. Food and Drug Administration for the treatment of bulimia nervosa. It is most effective at a dose of 60 mg/day, significantly higher than the standard dose used to treat major depression. A recent open trial suggests that fluoxetine at this dose is well tolerated and may be useful for adolescents with bulimia nervosa (Kotler, Devlin, Davies, & Walsh, 2003). Newer selective noradrenergic/serotonergic reuptake inhibitors such as venlafaxine have not been systematically studied in treatment of bulimia nervosa.

Although wide variability exists across studies, the rates of reduction in binge eating and vomiting with antidepressant treatment have ranged between 50% and 75% in controlled trials. A comprehensive review of the overall effectiveness of such studies (Agras, 1997) found a median reduction in binge eating and vomiting of about 70% and complete abstinence in about 30% of subjects. The mechanism of action of antidepressant medications in bulimia nervosa may be different from that in depression, as the response to antidepressant drugs in bulimia nervosa is independent of mood state; nondepressed bulimia nervosa patients respond equally as well as depressed bulimia nervosa patients to these drugs (Hughes, Wells, & Cunningham, 1986; Walsh, Hadigan, Devlin, Gladis, & Roose, 1991). Many patients with eating disorders are reluctant to use medication and a significant number of patients who initiate medication terminate treatment prematurely. In addition, despite convincing empirical evidence of efficacy in treating bulimia nervosa with antidepressant medications, residual symptoms persist in the majority of subjects treated with a single antidepressant medication (Nakash-Eisikovits, Dierberger, & Westen, 2002).

Several studies have examined the effectiveness of a combination of antidepressant pharmacotherapy with psychotherapy, usually CBT, for adults with bulimia nervosa. A meta-analysis of controlled trials using combined treatments for bulimia nervosa (Nakash-Eisikovits et al., 2002) demonstrated that combined treatments are superior to medication alone, but the advantage of combined treatments over psychotherapy alone is small.

Other Medications

Experience with several novel pharmacological agents may hold promise for the development of other medications for bulimia nervosa. Both the antiobesity agent sibutramine and the anticonvulsant topiramate may be beneficial for the treatment of binge eating in adults (Appolinario et al., 2002; McElroy et al., 2003). The serotonin antagonist ondansetron, which is used for the treatment of chemotherapy-induced nausea and vomiting, has been found to be of use in the treatment of adults with refractory bulimia nervosa (Faris et al., 2000). However, much work will be required to extend these preliminary findings to the treatment of adolescents.

Summary

Despite the widespread use of psychotropic medications for adolescents with eating disorders,

there is little empirical information about the utility and safety of such interventions. Reports that atypical antipsychotic medications may be useful for adolescents with anorexia nervosa are encouraging but need to be examined in controlled trials. Antidepressant medications have been shown to be useful in the treatment of adults with bulimia nervosa, but studies are needed to assess their utility and safety for adolescents with bulimia nervosa.

Combined Treatments for Anorexia Nervosa and Bulimia Nervosa

Virtually all of the studies of acute pharmacological treatment for anorexia nervosa have been conducted in settings such as hospitals where patients receive psychological treatment in addition to medication. There have been no controlled trials examining the combination of psychological and pharmacological treatment for anorexia nervosa. Given the dearth of evidence that medication is useful in the treatment of anorexia nervosa, it is not possible to draw any conclusions about the potential utility of combined treatments.

For adults with bulimia nervosa, studies suggest that the addition of antidepressant medication to psychotherapy leads to a small but detectable increase in improvement of bulimic symptoms (Walsh et al., 1997). There have been no controlled studies of combined treatments in adolescents with bulimia nervosa.

PREVENTION OF RELAPSE WITH PSYCHOLOGICAL TREATMENTS

Relapse prevention, as initially formulated by Marlatt and colleagues, was conceptualized as a maintenance therapy for individuals who had completed initial treatment and had achieved a certain measure of symptomatic recovery (Brownell, Marlatt, Lichtenstein, & Wilson, 1986; Marlatt & Gordon, 1985). The prevention of relapse among anorexia nervosa and bulimia nervosa patients is an essential goal and an integral step in the course of recovery. Standardized definitions of relapse, or uniform goals of relapse prevention interventions, have not been established, however. By definition, relapse occurs with a resurgence of symptoms or deterioration of condition subsequent to attaining a clinically significant degree of improvement. Because the operationalized definitions of initial treatment response have varied from study to study, empirical estimates of relapse are difficult to interpret. Moreover, follow-up studies often fail to differentiate reports of chronicity and relapse. Given these limitations and variations in terminology, current estimates of relapse are imprecise, and caution must be used when comparing across studies.

With anorexia nervosa, the definition of relapse usually involves weight loss coupled with a clinical deterioration following a successful response to treatment. In the past decade, attention to relapse and relapse prevention initiatives has increased, with a focus on the need for continuing care following initial improvements in weight and psychological and behavioral symptoms. However, without operationalized and consistent terminology for assessing treatment response and relapse in research studies, it is difficult to develop standardized clinical guidelines for preventing relapse. For bulimia nervosa, binge eating and purging are the core behavioral components that define treatment response and relapse; however, treatment response and recovery can include many other dimensions of functioning, including a range of attitudinal and psychological variables. As with anorexia nervosa, the field does not have accepted standards for defining response and relapse in bulimia nervosa, and reports of response and relapse vary considerably across studies. In addition, much of the available data have been obtained from studies of adults and may not strictly apply to adolescents.

Relapse Rates and Relapse Prevention for Anorexia Nervosa

Outpatient Treatment

Data from outpatient trials of psychological treatments for anorexia nervosa report that an overwhelming percentage of individuals, between 60% and 70%, fail to achieve full recovery or even a good response to treatment (Dare, Eisler, Russell, Treasure, & Dodge, 2001; McIntosh et al., 2002). In some cases, high rates of attrition among anorexia nervosa outpatients result in an inability to analyze treatment response (e.g., Serfaty, Turkington, Heap, Ledsham, & Jolley, 1999). Treatment of anorexia nervosa with the Maudsley family therapy has resulted in more success, with approximately 75% of adolescents achieving full recovery by the end of treatment (Lock et al., 2001). Follow-up data of outpatients treated solely with the Maudsley therapy have not been published, thus the rates of maintenance and relapse for individuals who participate in this type of therapy are unknown.

In most types of outpatient anorexia nervosa treatment, a large percentage of patients fail to achieve a good response to treatment. Thus it is extremely difficult to report relapse rates following outpatient treatment, and there are virtually no data on relapse prevention strategies for those individuals who do achieve a significant response to outpatient treatment. As a result, it is somewhat premature to discuss relapse prevention for individuals with anorexia nervosa treated on an outpatient basis, as the first-line intervention for reducing relapse for these patients is to improve initial response rates.

Inpatient Treatment

The data indicate that most hospitalized anorexia nervosa patients respond to treatment (Anderson, Bowers, & Evans, 1997; Attia et al., 1998; Baran, Weltzin, & Kaye, 1995), despite the greater severity of illness seen in hospitalized patients. However, follow-up studies indicate that the posthospitalization period is fraught with difficulty, with a significant resurgence of symptoms and relapse rates generally ranging from 30% to 50% (for review see Pike, 1998); some rates run as high as 70% (Lay, Jennen-Steinmetz, Reinhard, Schmidt, 2002). In addition to symptomatic relapse, it is not uncommon for individuals with AN-R subtype to develop binge eating following hospitalization. The reported median latency is 24 months for adolescents (Strober, Freeman, & Morrell, 1997).

Posthospitalization relapse rates are significant for both adolescent and adult patients. In a study of 95 patients between the ages of 12 to almost 18 years old, Strober and colleagues (1997) reported that nearly 30% of patients who successfully completed their inpatient program relapsed following discharge, with a mean time to relapse of 15 months and a median of 11 months. In an older sample (mean age = 20 ± 5.4 years), Eckert and colleagues reported that 42% of women who achieved weight normalization in the hospital relapsed within 1 year of discharge, but if weight normalization was maintained for 1 year, the risk of subsequent weight loss declined dramatically (Eckert, Halmi, Marchi, Grove & Crosby, 1995).

Psychological Treatments Aimed at Relapse Prevention following Hospitalization for Anorexia Nervosa

Family therapy. As discussed above, the Maudsley approach to family therapy for anorexia nervosa was originally designed as a post-hospitalization treatment, delivered over the course of 1 year following inpatient treatment. The findings from the initial study of this treatment (Russell et al., 1987) reported that family treatment was more effective than individual supportive therapy for individuals whose onset of anorexia nervosa was at 18 years or younger and whose illness had a duration of less than 3 years. Treatment gains in this group were largely maintained at a 5-year follow-up assessment (Eisler et al., 1997), suggesting that changes effected by family therapy serve to prevent relapse and enhance long-term efficacy for this group of patients with anorexia nervosa.

Cognitive-behavioral therapy. A version of CBT treatment has been designed to treat anorexia nervosa patients in the year following the successful completion of inpatient treatment. Consistent with the fundamental components of CBT for eating disorders (Fairburn et al., 1993; Garner, Vitousek, & Pike, 1997; Pike, Devlin, & Loeb, 2003), this intervention focuses on the cognitive and behavioral processes involved in the overvaluation of weight and shape, dysregulation of eating behavior, and deficits in self-esteem and self schemata that are thought to be at the core of maintaining the eating disorder.

Initially, treatment focuses on specific cognitive distortions and behavioral dysfunction pertaining to eating and weight that increase the risk of relapse. As treatment progresses, schema-based approaches are used to address a range of issues that extend beyond the specific domains of eating and weight but remain fundamental to the individual's self-schema, self-esteem, and eating disorder. On the basis of a sample of 33 patients, a survival analysis demonstrated a statistically significant advantage of CBT over the comparison treatment of nutritional counseling (log-rank statistic = 8.39, $p < .004$). According to Morgan-Russell outcome criteria, 44.4% of the CBT group met criteria for good outcome, compared to 6.7% of the nutritional counseling group ($c^2 = 5.89$; $p < .02$), and 16.7% of the CBT group met criteria for full recovery, compared to none in the nutritional counseling group ($c^2 = 2.75$, $p < .097$) (Pike, Walsh, Vitousek, Wilson, & Bauer, 2003). These data provide preliminary support for CBT in preventing relapse and promoting recovery following inpatient hospitalization for adult women with anorexia nervosa.

Relapse Rates and Relapse Prevention for Bulimia Nervosa

Naturalistic follow-up studies, which do not control for specific treatment effects, estimate a relapse rate of approximately 30% for patients with bulimia nervosa (Herzog et al., 1999; Keel & Mitchell, 1997). None of the published clinical trials evaluating psychological treatments for the acute symptoms of bulimia nervosa specifically focused on relapse prevention for this disorder; instead, relapse prevention was typically an integrated component of the initial intervention. Follow-up data on CBT and IPT, two evidence-based treatments for bulimia nervosa, indicate that the two psychotherapies do not differ in rates of relapse at 1-year follow-up. Some studies suggest that therapeutic changes are well maintained for most individuals who respond well to initial CBT or IPT treatment, with the most enduring recovery being reported by individuals who achieve complete remission of binge eating and purging by the end of treatment (Agras et al., 2000, Fairburn et al., 1995). However, another study has indicated that as many as 30% of individuals who are abstinent from binge eating and purging at the end of CBT treatment report some resurgence of symptoms during 1-year follow-up (Halmi et al., 2002). It is unclear whether these patients should be classified as "relapsed," on the basis of the severity of their symptoms. A similar rate of 30% relapse has been reported among individuals who had responded to an eating disorders day program (Olmsted, Kaplan, & Rockert, 1994).

A significant fraction of individuals who receive CBT or IPT fail to achieve full remission of binge eating and purging at the end of treatment. Data suggest that the risk of relapse is greater for this group than for those who achieve complete abstinence of binge eating and purging (Halmi et al., 2002). Therefore, treatment interventions for bulimia nervosa should be targeted not only at those individuals who fail to respond to initial treatment but also those who have a significant but incomplete response to treatment. Maintenance and relapse prevention treatments should promote further recovery and also mitigate against lapses and relapse for these individuals.

Summary

Anorexia Nervosa

The data on relapse rates for anorexia nervosa suggest that the risk of posthospitalization relapse is approximately 30%–50% for adolescents as well as for adults. Long-term outcome studies of anorexia nervosa indicate that early onset of anorexia nervosa and early intervention (i.e., short duration of illness at time of presentation for treatment) may be associated with a better long-term prognosis; it is likely, however, that the journey to recovery will include periods of relapse, as documented by Strober et al. (1997). Family therapy has been shown to be effective in preventing relapse among adolescent anorexia nervosa patients. It is important to note that the family therapy data are strongest for a very specific group of patients, i.e., those who develop anorexia nervosa before 18 years of age

and who have a very short duration of illness (less than 3 years). Cognitive-behavioral therapy has support for relapse prevention among adult patients, but there are no data on the efficacy of this treatment for adolescents.

Bulimia Nervosa

Clinical trials have not specifically targeted adolescents with bulimia nervosa and data for the adolescent patients in these trials have generally not been sufficient to analyze separately. Given that bulimia nervosa typically begins in adolescence, initiatives aimed at getting individuals into treatment earlier in the course of their disorder may result in improved outcome and reduced risk for relapse. Currently, LeGrange, Lock, and Dymek (2003) are adapting the Maudsley family therapy approach for anorexia nervosa to the treatment of adolescent bulimia nervosa. Although this treatment is not specifically a relapse prevention intervention, it aims to assist patients in achieving significant and lasting recovery. Empirical data on the clinical efficacy of treatments for adolescents with bulimia nervosa, both in the short term and in preventing relapse in the longer term, are needed to help inform evidence-based clinical practice.

RELAPSE PREVENTION WITH PHARMACOLOGICAL TREATMENTS

Anorexia Nervosa

As described above, trials evaluating antidepressant medications for underweight patients with anorexia nervosa have failed to show a difference between active medication and placebo for the treatment of eating disorders or mood symptoms. Antidepressant medications may lack efficacy in anorexia nervosa because of the neurochemical disturbances associated with low body weight (Attia et al., 1998). Despite their apparent lack of utility for underweight patients, antidepressant medications may be useful in the prevention of relapse after weight gain.

One placebo-controlled study has addressed this issue (Kaye et al., 2001). Following inpatient hospitalization, patients were randomized to receive either fluoxetine or placebo in a double-blind fashion. Some patients also received psychological treatment, which was not standardized. Fluoxetine-treated patients were more likely to complete the trial (63% completed) than were patients receiving placebo (16% completed, $p = .0001$). Patients who completed the trial tended to experience more weight gain and psychological improvement than patients who did not complete the trial. The average age of the patient sample was 22.5 years old, and it is not clear whether any adolescent patients were included.

Bulimia Nervosa

In the last 15 years, more than a dozen RCTs have demonstrated that antidepressant medications are effective in the treatment of adult bulimia nervosa patients (Zhu & Walsh, 2002). Although antidepressant medications have been shown to reduce bulimic symptoms in the short term, the role of continued pharmacological treatment in sustaining clinical improvement over time is unclear. Several controlled trials have examined the efficacy of antidepressant medications in preventing relapse among bulimia nervosa patients.

Some studies have evaluated continuing treatment with pharmacotherapy to prevent relapse after an initial positive response to medication (Pyle et al., 1990; Romano, Halmi, Sarkar, Koke, & Lee, 2002; Walsh et al., 1991), and an additional study randomized patients to receive either medication or placebo for relapse prevention after receiving a course of inpatient treatment (Fichter, Kruger, Rief, Holland, & Dohne, 1996). A consistent finding across studies has been the significant rate of symptomatic relapse despite continued pharmacological treatment. There is also an indication that TCAs, specifically imipramine and desipramine, and the SSRI fluoxetine may diminish the rate of relapse for patients maintained on antidepressant medications, compared to patients maintained on placebo. These studies suggest that, despite a significant rate of relapse on antidepressant medications, the rate of relapse is greater when medication is discontinued after a few months

(Romano et al., 2002). Although the studies evaluating pharmacotherapy as a means to prevent relapse have generated similar results, there have been a relatively limited number of studies in this area, with modest sample sizes and large dropout rates across trials.

All four controlled trials evaluating pharmacotherapy to prevent relapse enrolled only adult bulimia nervosa patients. Therefore, it is unclear whether the results of these studies are applicable to an adolescent population, or if there are special considerations for using antidepressant medications with younger patients for the prevention of relapse.

Summary

Pharmacological interventions may be useful in the prevention of relapse of anorexia nervosa following initial treatment. However, replication of the Kaye et al. (2001) results is necessary before firm conclusions can be drawn about the benefits of antidepressant medications for adults with anorexia nervosa. If such a benefit is established for adults, it will be important to extend studies to an adolescent population. Clearly, for some adult patients with bulimia nervosa who initially respond to medication, symptomatic relapse occurs despite continued pharmacotherapy. Therefore, continued treatment with medication after an initial positive response cannot guarantee against relapse. The data from placebo-controlled studies do suggest that when bulimia nervosa patients respond to a medication and are maintained on that medication, they experience lower rates of relapse than those of patients who are switched to placebo (Pyle et al., 1990; Romano et al., 2002; Walsh et al., 1991). Therefore, continuation of an effective pharmacological intervention may reduce the rate of relapse but does not ensure against the return of bulimic symptoms. The question remains as to the optimal length of time to maintain a patient on medication to prevent symptomatic relapse. Additionally, given the absence of data in adolescent samples, it is not known if the pattern of results from the controlled studies of pharmacotherapy for relapse prevention apply to a younger population.

EVALUATION OF THE EFFICACY AND EFFECTIVENESS OF TREATMENTS FOR EATING DISORDERS IN ADOLESCENTS

The previous discussion has focused on the specific efficacy of psychological and pharmacological treatments. There are a number of other questions that need to be addressed when evaluating the treatment of eating disorders in adolescents: When is the best time to begin treatment? What is the optimal treatment setting? Do adolescents with eating disorders need specialized services? Finally, who should provide the treatment?

When Should Treatment Begin?

Ideally, patients should be identified at the earliest possible point in the course of the disorder, and treatment should begin as soon as the adolescent, the parent(s), or other professional(s) recognizes a clinically significant eating problem. As implied in the previous section, treatment should frequently be initiated before symptoms have become sufficiently severe to meet full diagnostic criteria for anorexia nervosa or bulimia nervosa. Among the factors to be considered in initiating treatment are the intensity, severity, and duration of symptoms, and the motivation of the adolescent and the family for treatment.

Where Should Adolescents Be Treated?

A fundamental and noncontroversial tenet is that treatment should occur in the least restrictive setting in which effective treatment can be provided. A primary real-world consideration is the availability of treatment settings to which the adolescent has access. Larger cities are more likely to have university-based programs, with a full spectrum of treatment options such as outpatient clinics, intensive outpatient and partial hospitalization programs, and inpatient hospitalization. Although referral to more intensive treatment settings, such as residential facilities or inpatient units, may be resisted by adolescents or their parents because of the distance from home, the disruption of family life or schooling, or financial burden, this option may be necessary if other types of treatment are not effective. Treatment options in smaller towns or rural areas are often limited to therapists with varying degrees of interest and expertise in treating adolescents with eating disorders. The skills and interests of the adolescent's treatment providers help to determine where an adolescent will be treated, as some primary care physicians may not feel comfortable monitoring the physical health of adolescents with eating disorders, and some therapists may limit their practice to adults. In these situations, adolescents who might otherwise be treated in their home community may need to be referred to a specialty program. It is best if an appropriate treatment team or program is available locally, allowing an adolescent to live at home and engage in outpatient therapy while also remaining in school and continuing to develop important peer relationships. The challenge for the provider is to determine the balance between ideal treatment and available treatment.

Even when services are available, there are very limited data to guide the practitioner in determining the most appropriate type and duration of clinical services for anorexia nervosa. A recent study suggests that more expensive, intensive inpatient treatment early in the course of anorexia nervosa is associated with reduced relapse and long-term personal, social, and financial costs (Striegel-Moore, Leslie, Petrill, Garvin, & Rosenheck, 2000). For adults with bulimia nervosa, an initial brief and less intensive treatment, followed by more intensive and specialized care for nonresponders within a stepped-care framework, as noted above, might be effective (Garner & Needleman, 1997; Wilson et al., 2000).

Currently, there are no agreed-upon specific treatment protocols for adolescents with eating disorders to guide practitioners in matching the treatment setting and intensity to the patient's clinical status. Instead, adolescents tend to begin in outpatient treatment settings, with visits to medical and mental health services, then progress to more intensive treatment approaches if they do not have a positive response to treatment.

Are There Special Considerations in Treating Adolescents with Eating Disorders?

One aspect of treatment that is unique to adolescents is the involvement and authority of the family in the treatment process. The development of a therapeutic relationship between care providers and parents can be critical to success, but also challenging if parents deny the existence of a problem or blame the adolescent for the problem. Conversely, if the care providers attribute blame or fault to the parents, it will be difficult to foster a collaborative relationship with the parents.

Who Should Provide the Treatment?

Especially for anorexia nervosa, treatment often begins with a specialist in adolescent medicine because of the physical symptoms associated with weight loss (e.g., amenorrhea, fatigue, cold intolerance, weakness, fainting). Adolescents with anorexia nervosa tend to be more willing to be evaluated for these "medical problems" than for any associated psychological symptoms. In addition to addressing the presenting medical symptoms, primary care providers can suggest the need for additional mental health services. By focusing on the signs and symptoms that precipitated a medical evaluation and emphasizing healthy meal planning and completion, the primary care provider can shift the focus away from the presence of an eating disorder and toward the behaviors needed to improve health, thereby enhancing motivation for treatment. In the case of continuing medical instability or significant eating problems, adolescent patients can be referred for additional specialist services. Appropriately trained health-care professionals can usually treat bulimia nervosa on an outpatient basis, but some patients with bulimia nervosa need to be monitored for potential medical complications.

Government Guidelines

In the United Kingdom, the National Institute for Clinical Excellence has completed a compre-hensive and rigorous evaluation of the literature on eating disorders. A guideline that makes recommendations for the identification, treatment, and management of anorexia nervosa, bulimia nervosa, and atypical eating disorders (including binge eating disorder) was published in January 2004 (NICE, 2004). The guidelines contains specific recommendations regarding the treatment of adolescents with anorexia nervosa and bulimia nervosa (see http://www.nice.org.uk/).

Professional Guidelines

Although not based on empirical studies addressing the appropriate timing, location, and provider of treatment for adolescents with eating disorders, several professional organizations have developed guidelines for the treatment of anorexia nervosa and bulimia nervosa.

The American Psychiatric Association (APA) published its first practice guideline for the treatment of patients with eating disorders in 1993, with a revision in 2000. In this guideline, presentation of the disorder in the younger child and older adult were described, but the specific treatment needs of adolescents were not addressed. A strength of this guideline is the advice provided to practitioners on the medical management of anorexia nervosa. The choice of a treatment site and the potential collaborative arrangements among different health care professionals are similarly addressed. The APA practice guideline notes that bulimia nervosa patients rarely require hospitalization. Family therapy is said to be especially useful for adolescents, according to the Russell et al. (1987) study (see our analysis of this research above, under Psychological Treatments for Adolescents with Anorexia Nervosa).

In 2003, the Society for Adolescent Medicine (SAM) published guidelines that are similar to the 2000 APA recommendations (Golden et al., 2003) with five major positions on the treatment of adolescents with eating disorders:

1. Diagnosis should be considered in the context of normal adolescent growth and development, because adolescents, especially younger ones, may have significant health

risks associated with dysfunctional weight control practices, even though they do not meet full DSM-IV criteria.

2. Treatment should be initiated at lower symptom levels than for adults.
3. Nutritional management should reflect the patient's age, pubertal stage, and physical activity level.
4. Family-based treatment should be considered an important part of treatment for most adolescents, and mental health services should address the psychopathologic patterns of eating disorders, developmental tasks of adolescence, and possible comorbid psychiatric conditions.
5. The assessment and treatment of adolescents is best accomplished by a treatment team that is knowledgeable about normal adolescent physical and psychological growth and development. Hospitalization would be necessary in the presence of severe malnutrition, physiologic instability, severe mental health disturbance, or failure of outpatient treatment.

The American Academy of Pediatrics (AAP) also published a statement about the treatment of adolescents with eating disorders in 2003, noting the potential role for primary care providers in the identification and treatment of these disorders (Rome et al., 2003). The AAP emphasized the unique position of primary care pediatricians in detecting the onset of eating disorders and stopping their progression at the earliest stages of the illness as part of routine, preventive health care. Additionally, because of their existing relationship with a patient, primary care providers already have an established trusting relationship with the patient and the family, and usually have the necessary knowledge and skills to monitor health. The AAP policy statement also advocated rapid and aggressive treatment of eating disorders, and noted that hospitalization might be required in the case of emerging medical or psychiatric needs or failure to respond to intensive outpatient treatment.

Summary

There are no scientific studies to indicate the optimal treatment for adolescents, in terms of when treatment should begin, where that treatment should be delivered, or who should provide the treatment. The consensus view is that therapy should begin as soon as possible after a clinically significant eating problem has been identified, with the treatment provider, parents, and patient working to individualize treatment. The setting for the treatment is partially determined by availability, but the severity and duration of illness, especially with regard to medical complications, must also be considered. The optimal professional to treat an adolescent with an eating disorder is again determined in part by availability. Eating disorders can be effectively managed by a variety of different professionals, including physicians (psychiatrists, primary care providers, or adolescent medicine specialists), psychologists, social workers, and nutritionists who are familiar with efficacious treatment of eating disorders.

Prevention of Eating Disorders

For any disorder, understanding the risk factors, or variables that predict the development of the disorder, is vital to prevention efforts. In eating disorders, considerable progress has been made in identifying risk factors for the development of the syndrome of bulimia nervosa and for a number of the behavioral and psychological symptoms of eating disorders; however, much less is know about risk factors for anorexia nervosa. Through recent efforts we have begun to identify risk factors and to examine how they increase the probability that an eating disorder will develop. This information is being used to inform rational prevention efforts.

DEFINITIONS

A *risk factor* is an agent or exposure that increases the probability of an adverse outcome, in this case, eating disorders. In order to be demonstrated conclusively as a risk factor, the agent in question should be assessed prospectively (prior to development of the eating disorder), show temporal precedence to the onset of the eating disorder, and show some degree of specificity with the eating disorder (i.e., not be merely a general risk factor for psychopathology).

One of the first factors mentioned in most discussions of risk factors for eating disorders is *dieting* (Schmidt, 2002). The term *dieting* is complex, laden with many meanings, and used to refer to a variety of attitudes and behaviors. The National Task Force on the Prevention and Treatment of Obesity (2000) defines dieting as "the intentional and sustained restriction of caloric intake for the purposes of reducing body weight or changing body shape, resulting in a significant negative energy balance." This useful and relatively straightforward definition implies that dieting, because it results in negative energy balance, must be associated with weight loss. Therefore, attempts to restrict caloric intake that do not result in weight loss might properly be termed "unsuccessful dieting"; such attempts are frequently described by individuals with symptoms of eating disorders. The literature on eating disorders uses *dieting* to refer to both successful and unsuccessful attempts to restrict caloric intake, making it difficult to determine whether successful dieting and unsuccessful dieting play similar roles in the development of eating disorders.

The terms *restrained eating* and *dietary restraint* are theoretical constructs frequently employed in discussions of risk factors for the development and maintenance of eating disorders. *Dietary restraint* refers to a mental or cognitive set linked with the attempt to diet, and tends to be associated with unsuccessful dieting (Lowe, 1993). However, like the term *dieting, dietary restraint* and *restrained eating* are used to describe a range of attitudes and behaviors, including food avoidance.

Finally, the syndromes of anorexia nervosa and bulimia nervosa are characterized by what may be termed "unhealthy weight loss behaviors." These include a wide range of activities associated with some risk of physical harm, such as self-induced vomiting, laxative and diet pill abuse, complete food avoidance for extended periods of time (fasting), and excessive exercise to lose weight. These types of behavior are relevant in discussions of risk factors for eating disorders, as a considerable number of young people engage in unhealthy weight loss behaviors, and it is possible that such individuals are at high risk for the development of eating disorders meeting full DSM-IV criteria.

In this chapter, we will attempt to use the terms *dieting, unsuccessful dieting, dietary restraint,* and *unhealthy weight loss behaviors* in the narrow sense just described. However, the range of ways in which these terms have been used in the literature and the failure of many studies to define them add to the difficulties of interpreting the literature on risk factors for eating disorders.

BACKGROUND ON RISK FACTORS FOR ANOREXIA AND BULIMIA NERVOSA

In order to explore the literature on risk factors for anorexia nervosa and bulimia nervosa, slightly different approaches are necessary. In part, this divergence stems from necessity. Anorexia nervosa is more rare than bulimia nervosa, and fewer prospective studies of anorexia nervosa have been performed. Despite decades of study, no true risk factor for anorexia nervosa has been clearly demonstrated and confirmed. A greater number of prospective studies of bulimia nervosa exist. Nonetheless, the outcome is often varying degrees of bulimic pathology, rather than the occurrence of the syndrome of bulimia nervosa meeting full DSM-IV criteria. Unlike the study of risk factors for anorexia nervosa, there have been attempts to study bulimia nervosa risk factors experimentally, with some intriguing results. When prospective and experimental studies exist, they are highlighted, as these designs permit firmer inferences regarding the potential risk factors that promote psychiatric disturbances.

In the absence of prospective and experimental studies, the review of risk factors for anorexia nervosa necessitates a greater reliance on cross-sectional data. Although such data can be useful for generating hypotheses on potential risk factors for eating pathology, this type of design does not allow for differentiation of a precursor from a concomitant or consequence of a psychiatric condition. One exception is research on genetic factors, because one's genetic make-up is determined before birth, and therefore temporal precedence is ensured, although complicated by complex gene–environment interactions and gene–environment correlations. In addition, in this review, studies that used retrospective reports were de-emphasized or excluded, because temporal precedence could not be demonstrated and retrospective data are subject to a variety of biases.

RISK FACTORS FOR ANOREXIA NERVOSA

Several factors have contributed to our relative lack of understanding of risk factors for anorexia nervosa. First, there is the pervasive sense that anorexia nervosa is a disorder "chosen" by women in pursuit of an unrealistic sociocultural body size ideal. Such beliefs can hamper attempts at identifying true risk factors. From a basic epidemiological perspective, identification of risk factors for anorexia nervosa has been difficult. The prevalence of the disorder in the population is relatively low, no more than 1% or 2%

among females (see Chapter 13), and the prediction of a rare event is challenging, as evidenced by longitudinal studies in which no incident cases of anorexia nervosa emerged (McKnight Investigators, 2003; Stice, Presnell, & Bearman, 2001).

Unfortunately, few if any studies have satisfied the standards outlined above for identification of true risk factors. Although the available study designs have yielded suggestions about possible risk factors, confounds in their design have made it impossible to determine whether the traits examined are truly risk factors or phenomena associated with anorexia nervosa in some other way. Ultimately, novel designs will likely be required to identify factors that increase risk for anorexia nervosa.

In the absence of definitive studies, this discussion will include a range of potential risk factors that have been associated with anorexia nervosa via a variety of research designs. Three axes—temporal precedence, or, "Did the event occur prior to the onset of anorexia nervosa?"; time of reporting, or, "Was the temporal precedence determined prospectively or retrospectively?"; and the nature of the outcome event, or, whether the observed outcome is DSM-IV anorexia nervosa or a broadly defined anorexia nervosa syndrome or symptom—will be considered. Although longitudinal data suggest temporal stability of severe anorexia nervosa symptoms that emerge in childhood and persist throughout adolescence and adulthood (Kotler, Cohen, Davies, Pine, & Walsh, 2001), the relation between symptoms that do not meet criteria for DSM-IV anorexia nervosa and the subsequent development of DSM-IV anorexia nervosa is less certain. The correlation of anorexia nervosa symptoms ranges from 0.4 to 0.5 over time. Table 15.1 presents the putative risk factors and their ratings on each of the three axes.

The mechanisms of action by which these putative risk factors may operate to increase risk of anorexia nervosa have not begun to be explored. Similarly, there are no data on the timing of exposure and whether there are critical windows for exposure that lead to differential risk. Nor have factors that may protect against the development of anorexia nervosa been examined in any detail.

Table 15.1 Risk Factors for Anorexia Nervosa

Factor	Temporal Precedence	Prospectively Assessed	Persists after Recovery	Associated with Full Syndrome of AN	Associated with Subthreshold Symptoms
Gender	+	+	+	+	+
Puberty	+	+		+	+
Societal emphasis on thinness					+
Race					
SES					
Perinatal events	+	+		+	
Personality, temperament			+	+	
Early feeding problems	+				+
Obesity (self)					
Obesity (familial)					+
Dieting			+		+
Body dissatisfaction			+		+
Depression			+	+	+
Anxiety	+	+	+	+	+
Attachment					
Family environment					+
CSA				+	
Life events	+		+	+	
Social support					
High-risk activities					+
Family history, genetics	+		+	+	+

AN, anorexia nervosa; CSA, childhood sexual abuse; SES, socioeconomic status.

General Risk Factors

Gender

Being female is perhaps the most reliable risk factor for anorexia nervosa. The female-to-male ratio for anorexia nervosa has been consistently estimated to be approximately 10:1 in both clinical and epidemiological samples (Garfinkel et al., 1995; Hoek, 1991; Jones, Fox, Babigan, & Hutton, 1980; Lucas, Beard, O'Fallon, & Kurland, 1988; Lucas, Beard, O'Fallon, & Kurland, 1991; Rand & Kuldau, 1992; Rastam, Gillberg, & Garton, 1989; Soundy, Lucas, Suman, & Melton, 1995; Wells, Bushnell, Hornblow, Joyce, & Oakley-Browne, 1989). The uneven gender distribution cannot yet be explained, and although theories ranging from sociocultural to bi-

ological (Garner & Garfinkel, 1980) factors exist, no definitive answer has been found as to why a differential risk for gender is so consistently observed across cultures.

Puberty

The onset of anorexia nervosa typically occurs during the peripubertal or postpubertal period (Lucas et al., 1988, 1991). Prepubertal anorexia nervosa exists (Cooper, Watkins, Bryant-Waugh, & Lask, 2002), but is uncommon (Stein, Chalhoub, & Hodes, 1998). Disturbances in eating and weight-related behaviors are clearly present, however, in preadolescent girls (Graber, Brooks-Gunn, Paikoff, & Warren, 1994; Killen et al., 1994; Leon, Fulkerson, Perry, & Cudeck, 1993;

Sands, Tricker, Sherman, Armatas, & Maschette, 1997). The extent to which these disturbances overlap with anorexia nervosa is not entirely known (Kotler et al., 2001). Onset of anorexia nervosa can occur throughout the life span (Beck, Casper, & Andersen, 1996; Inagaki et al., 2002), but the highest risk period for onset is around puberty (Lucas et al., 1988, 1991). As is true with gender, there is no definitive answer as to why puberty increases risk, and theories range from sociocultural (during puberty girls become more vulnerable to social pressures to be thin, especially in the context of their changing bodies; Gowers & Shore, 2001) to biological (hormonal changes during puberty trigger other relevant biological processes; see Muñoz & Argente, 2002, for a review). In contrast to binge eating disorder (Reichborn-Kjennerud, Bulik, Tambs, Harris, & Sullivan, submitted) early menarche has not been associated with risk for anorexia nervosa (Fairburn, Cooper, Doll, & Welch, 1999; Stice et al., 2001).

Societal Emphasis on Thinness

Weight concerns and dieting are normative in developed countries (Rodin, Silberstein, & Striegel-Moore, 1985; Striegel-Moore, Silberstein, & Rodin, 1986), a cultural phenomenon thought to be a necessary but not sufficient precondition for the development of eating disorders (Brownell, 1991; Garner & Garfinkel, 1980). The incidence of anorexia nervosa on Curaçao suggests, however, that anorexia nervosa is not confined to areas embracing the Western ideal of slimness (Hoek, van Harten, van Hoeken, & Susser, 1998). The precise role of sociocultural factors in increasing risk for anorexia nervosa is unclear, as exposure to thin ideals and dieting are nearly universal in industrialized countries, but only a very small number of young women actually develop clinically significant eating disorders. Individuals may be susceptible to the cultural pressures toward dieting and body dissatisfaction in proportion to their degree of genetic predisposition (Bulik, 2003). Thus, although all individuals are exposed to these forces, those at greater genetic risk may be more adversely affected. Immigration and the rapid introduction of Western body ideals have been shown to af-

fect the incidence of eating disorder–related behaviors (Becker, Burwell, Gilman, Herzog, & Hamburg, 2002; Bulik, 1987; Fichter, Weyerer, Sourdi, & Sourdi, 1983; Katzman, Nasser, & Gordon, 2001). It is unclear whether exposure to Western ideals or major nonspecific life stress (i.e., immigration) is associated with the emergence of eating pathology.

Race and Socioeconomic Status

Traditionally, anorexia nervosa was considered to be a disorder confined to the white upper-middle class. This perception may result from the failure of many community-based studies to include non-white participants or from sampling highly homogeneous populations (Bushnell, Wells, Hornblow, Oakley-Browne, & Joyce, 1990; Götestam & Agras, 1995; Hoek et al., 1995; Kendler et al., 1991). Anorexia nervosa occurs across races and cultures (Hoek et al., 1998; Katzman et al., 2001). In terms of socioeconomic status, in a large population-based study of female twins, Walters and Kendler (1995) found that a greater number of years of parental education (a proxy variable for SES) was associated with anorexia nervosa. In addition, Striegel-Moore, Dohm, et al. (2003) found that 15 white (1.5%) and no black women in a geographically and economically diverse community sample of young women who had previously participated in the 10-year National Heart, Lung, and Blood Institute (NHLBI) Growth and Health Study met lifetime criteria for anorexia nervosa.

Perinatal Events

Cnattingius, Hultman, Dahl, and Sparen (1999), using the link between the Swedish birth registry and the Swedish psychiatric inpatient registry, found that girls born prematurely (especially if they were small for gestational age) and those born with cephalhematoma (a collection of blood under the scalp of a newborn) were at increased risk for developing anorexia nervosa. This study employed a design capable of identifying true prospective risk factors. The authors hypothesized that subtle brain damage at birth could result in early feeding difficulties and increase risk for anorexia nervosa. It is also possible that prematurity and small size for gestational age of infants were secondary effects of lingering eating disorders in the mother. Shoebridge and Gowers (2000) also noted higher rates of perinatal or infant loss in mothers of a clinical sample of individuals with anorexia nervosa, and greater maternal anxiety and concern during pregnancy. Emerging data in animals suggest that even moderate maternal undernutrition around the time of conception can produce a precocious fetal cortisol surge and preterm birth (Bloomfield et al., 2003), a phenomenon which could occur in women with anorexia nervosa symptoms around the time of conception. Additional data indicate that individuals with current or past anorexia nervosa have a higher risk of birth complications, cesarean deliveries, and postpartum depression (Bulik, Sullivan, Fear, Pickering, & Dawn, 1999; Franko & Walton, 1993; Franko et al., 2001). Perinatal adverse events may therefore increase the risk of developing anorexia nervosa, and a past history of anorexia nervosa may increase the risk of experiencing adverse perinatal events, thus perpetuating a cycle of risk.

Individual Risk Factors

Personality Characteristics

Psychometric studies have consistently linked anorexia nervosa to a cluster of personality and temperamental traits—specifically, negative self-evaluation, low self-esteem, extreme compliance, obsessionality, perfectionism, neuroticism, and harm avoidance (Anderluh, Tchanturia, Rabe-Hesketh, & Treasure, 2003; Brewerton, Dorn, & Bishop, 1992; Bulik, Sullivan, Weltzin, & Kaye, 1995; Bulik, Tozzi, et al., 2003; Fairburn, Cooper, et al., 1999; Gual et al., 2002; Karwautz et al., 2001; Kleifield, Sunday, Hurt, & Halmi, 1994; Srinivasagam et al., 1995; Strober, 1990; Tyrka, Waldron, Graber, & Brooks-Gunn, 2002; Vitousek & Manke, 1994; Waller et al., 1993; Walters & Kendler, 1995). These traits continue to characterize individuals with anorexia nervosa even after recovery (Bulik, Sullivan, Fear, & Pickering, 2000; Casper, 1990; Kaye, Weltzin, & Hsu, 1993; Srinivasagam et al., 1995). In the absence of premorbid personality data on large

samples of individuals who later develop anorexia nervosa, some studies have used a "recovery" design, in which traits that persist after recovery are assumed to represent enduring traits that preceded the onset of the disorder and are thought to represent vulnerability factors. The potential weakness of this design is that these traits may not have existed premorbidly and instead could represent personality or trait "scars" from having had anorexia nervosa.

Specific Eating and Weight-Related Risk Factors

Obesity and Body Mass Index

Parental obesity is less frequently associated with risk for anorexia nervosa than for bulimia nervosa, and familial obesity appears to be more common in family members of women with bulimia nervosa than women with anorexia nervosa (Garfinkel, Moldofsky, & Garner, 1980; Grace, Jacobson, & Fullager, 1985; Vieselman & Roig, 1985). Fairburn, Welch, Doll, Davies, and O'Connor (1997) also found a differential obesity risk between individuals with anorexia nervosa and bulimia nervosa, with anorexia nervosa women having lower familial risk of obesity. Only one study explored the opposite phenomenon, whether parents of individuals with anorexia nervosa tend to be thinner than parents of healthy controls (Halmi, Struss, & Goldberg, 1978), and there was no evidence to suggest that either mothers or fathers weighed less than parents of controls.

Dieting

The prevalence of dieting has been estimated to be between 14% and 77% and is highest in young women (French, Perry, Leon, & Fulkerson, 1994). In most of these studies dieting was simply defined as whether individuals had ever restricted their intake to lose weight, and therefore may have captured both successful and unsuccessful dieters. In a study of 36,320 public school students, dieting frequency was strongly related to poor body image, fears of being unable to control eating, and more prevalent history of binge eating. Dieting was also related in a "dose–response" fashion to a range of psychosocial and health behavior variables (French, Story, Downes, Resnick, & Blum, 1995). Walters and Kendler (1995) found dieting status to be associated with anorexia nervosa in a population-based sample of twins; however, dieting was not measured prior to the onset of anorexia nervosa. In contrast, in a series of studies of anorexia nervosa, bulimia nervosa, and binge eating disorder in which subjects were asked to report on the premorbid presence of potential risk factors, Fairburn, Cooper, et al. (1999) found that although dieting dimensions were relevant to the emergence of both bulimia nervosa and binge eating disorder, they were not associated with anorexia nervosa. Dieting was not elevated in a study of affected sisters of discordant sister pairs (Karwautz et al., 2001). Thus, the data from clinical and epidemiological studies do not resolve whether dieting should be considered a risk factor for anorexia nervosa.

Body Dissatisfaction and Slim Body Ideal

Dissatisfaction with the size or shape of one's body is often thought to be the psychological motivator for dieting behavior (Stice, 1994) and a key contributor to the gender differential in prevalence of eating disorders. In puberty, body satisfaction begins to decrease in young girls, and this dissatisfaction may be secondary to the increase in body fat percentage associated with female pubertal development (Marino & King, 1980). Dissatisfaction with body shape or size is thought to be the driving force for the onset of dieting behavior (Cash & Henry, 1995; Hawkins & Clement, 1984; Rodin et al., 1985; Tiggemann, 1994; Van Strien, 1989).

Comorbidity

As previously discussed in Chapter 13, other significant psychiatric disorders, especially major depression and anxiety disorders, commonly co-occur with anorexia nervosa (Braun, Sunday, & Halmi, 1994; Bulik, 2001; Bulik, Sullivan, Fear, & Joyce, 1997; Deep, Nagy, Weltzin, Rao, & Kaye, 1995; Halmi et al., 1991). Well over half of women with anorexia nervosa report a lifetime presence of an anxiety disorder—most

commonly, overanxious disorder, obsessive-compulsive disorder, or social phobia. In many cases, onset of the anxiety disorder precedes the onset of anorexia nervosa (Bulik et al., 1997; Deep et al., 1995). Retrospective accounts of premorbid symptoms among children who later develop anorexia nervosa often emphasize the presence of pervasive anxiety (Bruch, 1973; Lask & Bryant-Waugh, 2000). This pattern of onset may reflect the natural course of the two disorders (i.e., the average age of onset of many anxiety disorders is younger than the average age of onset of anorexia nervosa), but it may also indicate that childhood anxiety is a significant risk factor for the development of anorexia nervosa. In a population-based sample of over 2,000 female twins, odds ratios for generalized anxiety disorder, phobias, and panic disorder were significantly elevated among women with varying definitions of anorexia nervosa (Walters & Kendler, 1995).

In addition, several outcome studies suggest that depression and anxiety commonly persist after recovery from anorexia nervosa (Löwe et al., 2001; Sullivan, Bulik, Fear, & Pickering, 1998). Significantly elevated relative risks for mood disorders have been reported among relatives of probands with anorexia nervosa (Gershon et al., 1984; Hudson, Pope, Jonas, & Yurgelun-Todd, 1983; Logue, Crowe, & Bean, 1989; Rivinus et al., 1984), although these rates may be highest among relatives of individuals with anorexia nervosa who are themselves depressed (Strober, Lampert, Morrell, Burroughs, & Jacobs, 1990). Twin studies have shown that the genetic risk factors for anorexia nervosa and depression are correlated (Wade, Bulik, Neale, & Kendler, 2000), and there appears to be a unique genetic factor that influences the emergence of both early eating and early anxiety disorder symptoms (Silberg & Bulik, submitted).

Other "Environmental" Risk Factors

Attachment

Early family theories of the etiology of anorexia nervosa posited dysfunctional family patterns marked by enmeshment and rigidity (Minuchin, Rosman, & Baker, 1978). Studies have generally found that women with eating disorders display anxious attachment styles and separation distress (Armstrong & Roth, 1989), greater fears of abandonment, and lack of autonomy in relationships (Becker, Bell, & Billington, 1987; Kenny & Hart, 1992); the more insecure the attachment with parents, the greater the disordered eating pathology (Heesacker & Neimeyer, 1990). Shoebridge and Gowers (2000) noted higher rates of near exclusive maternal childcare, severe distress at first separation, high maternal trait anxiety, and later age for sleeping away from home in patients with anorexia nervosa in comparison to controls.

Family Environment

Research does not support the existence of a "typical" anorexia nervosa family; indeed, studies that have compared family environment across eating disorders tend to identify more family dysfunction in families with bulimia nervosa offspring than those with anorexia nervosa offspring. Schmidt, Tiller, and Treasure (1993) found that women with bulimia nervosa had experienced more family arrangements, parental indifference, excessive parental control, physical abuse, and violence among family members than members of other eating disorders subgroups. Murphy, Troop, and Treasure (2000) reported that sisters with anorexia nervosa had higher levels of maternal control and more antagonism toward and jealousy of their sisters than did their unaffected sisters. In a population-based sample of female twins, Walters and Kendler (1995) reported higher maternal overprotectiveness in individuals with anorexia nervosa.

Sexual Abuse

Childhood sexual abuse (CSA) has been reported in women with anorexia nervosa (Herzog, Staley, Carmody, Robbins, & van der Kolk, 1993; Horesh et al., 1995), and there is some evidence that CSA is more prevalent in women with anorexia nervosa who exhibit purging behavior (Waller, Halek, & Crisp, 1993). Given the relative rarity of anorexia nervosa, few population-based estimates of the prevalence of CSA in these women

exist. Romans, Martin, and Mullen (1994) studied 3,000 women in New Zealand and found that there was a higher frequency of anorexia nervosa and bulimia nervosa in women who reported CSA. However, CSA did not appear to act independently, as poor parenting and growing up away from both parents also contributed independently to risk of eating disorders. Kinzl, Traweger, Guenther, and Biebl (1994) highlighted the importance of the familial environment in which CSA occurs and the difficulty in teasing out the long-term effects of CSA without considering the family context that mediates the experience of abuse (Alexander, 1992). The current data suggest overall that CSA and abuse of other types, although more common in women with anorexia nervosa, may be more general risk factors for psychopathology.

Life Events

Horesch et al. (1995) found that adolescents with anorexia nervosa reported more adverse life events than healthy controls, and more adverse life events relating to family than psychiatric controls. Fairburn, Cooper, et al. (1999) found that a history of events including abuse and death of close relatives increased the risk of anorexia nervosa. Schmidt, Tiller, Blanchard, Andrews, and Treasure (1997) found that individuals with anorexia nervosa experienced significantly more adverse events and difficulties with the potential to evoke sexual shame or disgust, in the year prior to onset of anorexia nervosa. An increase in such events was also found by Karwautz et al. (2001) in a study of discordant sisters: sisters with anorexia nervosa reported more teasing about breast development. Whether individuals with eating disorders actually experience more adverse life events, whether they remember adverse life events better than patients without such events, or whether they are more susceptible to the impact of life events remains unknown.

Social Support and Interpersonal Relationships

Women with eating disorders report less successful social adjustment and problematic interpersonal relationships (Norman & Herzog, 1984; Pike & Rodin, 1991; Striegel-Moore, Silberstein, & Rodin, 1993). Problems with social adjustment often persist after recovery (Casper, 1990; Fava et al., 1990; Yager, Landsverk, & Edelstein, 1987; Yager, Landsverk, Edelstein, & Jarvik, 1988).

Participation in Sports and Activities, Professions with Focus on Body Shape and Weight

Activities that place substantial emphasis on weight and appearance (e.g., ballet, gymnastics) have been investigated as independent risk factors for the development of anorexia nervosa. Ballet participation has received substantial attention (Klump, Ringham, Marcus, & Kaye, 2001) because of the high levels of required exercise and pressures for thinness and athletic excellence (Garner & Garfinkel, 1980; Vaisman, Voet, Akivis, & Sive-Ner, 1996; Weeda-Mannak & Drop, 1985). An increased prevalence of both diagnosable eating disorders as well as disordered eating symptoms has been observed in ballet dancers, with a prevalence of DSM-IV anorexia nervosa that is 4 to 25 times higher in ballet dancers than that in the general population (4%–25%) (Garner & Garfinkel, 1980; Szmukler, Eisler, Gillies, & Hayward, 1985; Vaisman et al., 1996).

Unlike data from other athlete groups (Powers, Schocken, & Boyd, 1998), ballet dancers' scores on measures of eating pathology are similar to those of individuals with diagnosable eating disorders. In addition, disturbed eating attitudes and behaviors appear to persist after retirement in ballet dancers (Khan et al., 1996), which has not been observed in other athlete groups, including gymnasts (O'Connor, Lewis, Kirchner, & Cook, 1996). Moreover, athletic, artistic, and professional environments may attract individuals who are preoccupied with facets central to eating disorder pathology. This pairing can then contribute to the emergence of the syndromes.

Biological Risk Factors

Several lines of evidence suggest that women with anorexia nervosa have a disturbance of serotonin (5-hydroxytryptamine [5-HT]) neuronal transmission. Serotonin function in the brain is involved in the regulation of both mood and behavior, including eating behavior. Increased 5-HT activity may contribute to core emotional and attitudinal factors, such as anxiety, perfectionism, harm avoidance, and body image distortions, which, when coupled with psychosocial influences, may increase an individual's risk for developing anorexia nervosa (Kaye et al., submitted). Disturbances of 5-HT activity and anxious, obsessive symptoms persist after recovery from anorexia nervosa, and recovered women have increased levels of the major serotonin metabolite 5-hydroxyindoleacetic acid (5-HIAA) in cerebrospinal fluid (CSF) (Kaye, Gwirtsman, George, & Ebert, 1991). Moreover, the antidepressant medication fluoxetine, which affects the serotonergic system, may reduce the rate of relapse among anorexia nervosa patients (Kaye et al., 2001).

Genetic Risk Factors

A series of family studies have demonstrated a significantly greater lifetime prevalence of eating disorders among relatives of eating disordered individuals than among relatives of controls (Gershon et al., 1983; Hudson, Pope, Jonas, Yurgelun-Todd, & Frankenburg, 1987; Kassett et al., 1989; Lilenfeld et al., 1998; Strober et al., 1990; Strober, Freeman, Lampert, Diamond, & Kaye, 2000). Relatives of individuals with anorexia nervosa and bulimia nervosa also have significantly increased rates of eating disorders that do not meet full diagnostic criteria, compared to relatives of controls (Lilenfeld et al., 1998; Strober et al., 2000), which suggests a broad spectrum of eating-related pathology in families. Thus, anorexia nervosa appears to be familial (see Lilenfeld, Kaye, & Strober, 1997, for a review). In addition, twin studies (Klump, Miller, Keel, McGue, & Iacono, 2001; Kortegaard, Hoerder, Joergensen, Gillberg, & Kyvik, 2001; Wade et al., 2000) suggest that the observed familial links may be accounted for by genetic effects.

Linkage studies have begun to identify areas of the human genome that may harbor susceptibility genes for anorexia nervosa, with the most promising areas being identified on chromosome 1 (Devlin et al., 2002; Grice et al., 2002). Several groups have investigated the relation between a variety of candidate genes and eating disorders (for a review, see Tozzi, Bergen, & Bulik, 2002). These studies have chosen candidate genes based on systems and functions associated with food intake, body weight, regulation of feeding behavior, motor activity, energy expenditure, metabolic adaptation to fasting, and other related characteristics and symptoms of eating disorders. Although a number of positive findings have been documented, no single gene or set of genes has consistently emerged as being strongly associated with either anorexia nervosa or bulimia nervosa. As anorexia nervosa is a complex disorder whose etiology is influenced by multiple genes and multiple environmental factors, ultimate understanding of risk will have to include the elucidation of Gene × Environment, Gene × Gene, and Environment × Environment interactions.

Summary

Numerous studies have been conducted to identify risk factors that predict the onset of anorexia nervosa, but enhanced efforts are needed to identify true risk and protective factors for anorexia nervosa. Studies of recovered individuals, while valuable, are not sufficient to discriminate between risk factors for anorexia nervosa and residual effects of anorexia nervosa. The identification of protective factors is equally critical, as the identification of factors that are associated with both the emergence of anorexia nervosa and the failure to develop the disorder has implications for both detection and prevention of the disorder.

RISK FACTORS FOR BULIMIA NERVOSA

As mentioned previously, this review of risk factors for bulimia nervosa will emphasize prospective and experimental studies. Such studies, properly conducted, are powerful in being able to establish with some clarity whether the introduction of a putative risk factor leads to an increase in symptoms. Cross-sectional data, although essential for hypothesis generation in studies of anorexia nervosa, are less valuable, as it is difficult or impossible to establish whether a variable is causally linked to the development of the disorder or only associated with it in some way. It should be noted, however, that the prospective and experimental studies focus on risk factors for the development of broadly defined bulimic symptoms rather than the full syndrome of bulimia nervosa. Crucial unanswered questions are the nature of the relation between bulimic symptoms and bulimia nervosa, and the degree of overlap between risk factors for bulimic symptoms and risk factors for bulimia nervosa.

Societal Emphasis on Thinness

As with anorexia nervosa, the cultural emphasis on thinness has been implicated as a risk factor for the development of bulimia nervosa. Pressure to be thin has been shown to predict increases in body dissatisfaction, dieting, and negative affect (Cattarin & Thompson, 1994; Field et al., 2001; Stice, 2001; Stice & Bearman, 2001; Stice & Whitenton, 2002; Wertheim, Koerner, & Paxton, 2001) and to contribute to bulimic symptom onset (Field, Camargo, Taylor, Berkey, & Colditz, 1999; Stice & Agras, 1998; Stice, Presnell, & Spangler, 2002). Experiments have found that acute and long-term exposure to ultraslender media images and peers produces increased body dissatisfaction, negative affect, dieting, and bulimic symptoms, but that these effects are stronger for girls with preexisting body image disturbances and social support deficits (Cattarin, Thompson, Thomas, & Williams, 2000; Groesz, Levine, & Murnen, 2002; Irving, 1990). Thus, perceived pressure to be thin appears to be a risk factor for body dissatisfaction, dieting, negative affect, and bulimic symptoms, and these effects may be amplified for at-risk individuals.

Early Feeding Problems

Several studies have examined the extent to which early problems with feeding constitute risk factors for the later development of broadly defined eating disorder symptoms. In data obtained from a long-term prospective study, Marchi and Cohen (1990) found that symptoms of bulimia nervosa in later adolescence were related to both digestive problems and pica in early childhood and to efforts at weight loss in early adolescence. Stice, Agras, and Hammer (1999) found that a higher infant body mass index (BMI) predicted the emergence of overeating and that longer duration of infant sucking predicted overeating-induced vomiting in children; however, the relationship of these phenomena to the development of bulimia nervosa is unknown.

Early Menarche

Early menarche is thought to produce increased adipose tissue, which may result in a perceived deviation from the thin ideal and decreased body dissatisfaction and could, in turn, lead to dieting, negative affect, and bulimic symptoms. Early sexual development can also lead to increased sexual attention and unwanted comments and teasing. However, early menarche did not predict future increases in body dissatisfaction, dieting, negative affect, or bulimic symptoms (Cooley & Toray, 2001a; Hayward et al., 1997; Stice & Whitenton, 2002). Therefore, the currently available research does not support early pubertal development as a risk factor for these symptoms.

Perfectionism and Impulsivity

Perfectionism has been evaluated as a risk factor for eating pathology because this personality trait may promote a relentless pursuit of the thin ideal. Three studies have found that perfectionism did not predict future bulimic symptomatology (Killen et al., 1996; Vohs, Bardone, Joiner, Abramson, & Heatherton, 1999; Vohs et al., 2001), although neither study used DSM-IV criteria for bulimia nervosa as an outcome. Another personality characteristic, a deficit in impulse control, has also been considered a risk factor for bulimic pathology, as deficits in impulse control might increase the propensity for episodes of uncontrollable binge eating. Data from three pro-

spective studies indicate that impulsivity does not predict subsequent increases in bulimic symptoms (Wonderlich, Connolly, & Stice, in press). Thus, while there is currently no empirical evidence for a role of perfectionism or impulsivity as risk factors for bulimic pathology, additional studies are required to determine whether these traits influence risk for threshold bulimia nervosa.

Negative Affect

Negative affect has been shown to predict increases in bulimic symptoms and subthreshold/threshold bulimic pathology among adolescents (Cooley & Toray, 2001a; Killen et al., 1996; Stice, 2001; Stice & Agras, 1998), and experimentally induced negative affect produced increases in body dissatisfaction in one study (Taylor & Cooper, 1992). One prevention trial found that an intervention that reduced negative affect produced decreases in bulimic pathology (Burton, Stice, Bearman, & Rohde, submitted). These results are consistent in suggesting that negative affect is a risk factor for bulimic pathology.

Obesity and Body Mass Index

Elevated body mass, or being at a higher weight, has been shown to predict increases in perceived pressure to be thin, in body dissatisfaction, and in attempted dieting (Cattarin & Thompson, 1994; Field et al., 2001; Patton, Johnson-Sabine, Wood, Mann, & Wakeling, 1990; Stice & Whitenton, 2002; Vogeltanz-Holm et al., 2000), but not increases in depression (Lewinsohn et al., 1994; Stice & Bearman, 2001; Stice, Hayward Cameron, Killen, & Taylor, 2000). Therefore, individuals at a higher weight may experience pressure to be thin from family or peers, which could result in increased drive for thinness or body dissatisfaction, and increased risk for bulimic symptoms. Increased BMI predicted the onset of bulimic symptoms in several studies (Killen et al., 1994; Stice, Presnell, & Spangler, 2002; Vogeltanz-Holm et al., 2000), but other studies found no association (Cattarin & Thompson, 1994; Cooley & Toray, 2001b; Killen et al.,

1996; Stice & Agras, 1998). Thus, while increased weight is a risk factor for pressure to be thin, body dissatisfaction, and attempted dieting, it may play a more important role in promoting other risk factors for bulimia nervosa than in directly fostering bulimic symptoms.

Dieting

Self-report dietary restraint measures predicted increases in negative affect (Stice & Bearman, 2001; Stice et al., 2000) and onset of bulimic pathology (Field, Camargo, Taylor, Berkey, & Colditz, 1999; Killen et al., 1994, 1996; Stice, 2001; Stice & Agras, 1998). However, experiments manipulating dietary restriction have not supported dietary restriction as a risk factor for bulimic symptoms. Random assignment to a low-calorie diet (Goodrick, Poston, Kimball, Reeves & Foreyt, 1998; Presnell & Stice, 2003; Reeves et al., 2001) or a weight-maintenance diet (Klem, Wing, Simkin-Silverman, & Kuller, 1997; Stice, Presnell, Groesz, & Shaw, submitted), relative to a waiting-list condition, resulted in reduced negative affect and bulimic symptoms among obese and nonobese samples. Although these findings appear contradictory, it has been reported that self-report dietary restraint scales do not measure actual caloric restriction (Stice, Fisher, & Lowe, 2004), which indicates that these scales may not be valid measures of dietary restriction. Thus, although prospective studies suggest that dieting is a risk factor for negative affect and bulimic pathology, experimental studies suggest that prescribed dietary restriction is not a causal risk factor for bulimic pathology. It is important to note that caloric restriction as implemented in experimental situations may not mimic the types of dysfunctional dieting behavior that occur among individuals prone to eating disorders.

Body Dissatisfaction and Slim Body Ideal

Body dissatisfaction predicts increases in attempted dieting (Cooley & Toray, 2001a; Patton et al., 1990; Stice, 2001; Wertheim, Koerner, & Paxton 2001), negative affect (Rierdan, Koff, & Stubbs, 1989; Stice & Bearman, 2001; Stice et al., 2000), bulimic symptom onset (Field et al., 1999; Killen et al., 1994, 1996; Stice & Agras, 1998), and bulimic symptoms (Cooley & Toray, 2001a; Stice, 2001). An intervention that reduced body dissatisfaction produced decreases in negative affect and bulimic symptoms (Bearman, Stice, & Chase, 2003).

The societal ideal for thinness is very difficult to attain, and may promote dieting in the absence of body dissatisfaction. Body dissatisfaction and attempted dieting, in turn, are thought to increase the risk for negative affect and bulimic pathology. Thin-ideal internalization predicts increases in body dissatisfaction, attempted dieting, negative affect (Stice, 2001; Stice & Whitenton, 2002) and is associated with bulimic symptom onset (Field et al., 1999; Stice & Agras, 1998; Stice et al., 2002). The effects of thin-ideal internalization appear to be stronger for heavier girls (Stice et al., 2002; Stice & Whitenton, 2002). Interventions that reduce thin-ideal internalization result in decreased body dissatisfaction, dieting, negative affect, and bulimic symptoms (Stice & Shaw, 2004). Thus, the thin-ideal internalization may be a risk factor for body dissatisfaction, dieting, negative affect, and bulimic symptoms, and these effects are potentiated by elevated body weight.

Genetic Risk Factors

Twin studies have yielded heritability estimates ranging from 31% to 83% for bulimia nervosa (e.g., Bulik, Sullivan, & Kendler, 1998; Kendler et al., 1991; Wade et al., 1999). Significant linkage has been reported on chromosome 10p, which suggests that this is an area of the genome worthy of further investigation for containing genes that may influence risk for bulimia nervosa (Bulik, Devlin, et al., 2003). However, researchers have been unable to identify specific genes that may influence the risk of developing bulimia nervosa. It may be that bulimia nervosa is a complex syndrome with both genetic and environmental underpinnings.

Although it is likely that risk factors for bulimia are interactive and multiplicative, the prospective evidence examining this issue is minimal. In a recent review, Stice (2002) concluded that there was some evidence that negative affect, perfectionism, and early menarche are potentiating factors that amplify the effects of other risk factors. He also noted that although early menarche did not emerge as a significant risk factor for eating pathology in univariate models, it did appear to interact with life stressors to predict emergence of negative affect and eating disturbances (Stice, 2002). These promising leads should be followed in future studies.

How Are Risk Factors Acquired?

As noted above, prospective studies have suggested that the perceived pressure to be thin, internalization of a thin ideal, body dissatisfaction, and negative affect are risk factors for the development of bulimic symptoms, and other studies have begun to examine the development of such factors (Stice, 2002). Their acquisition is undoubtedly complex, involving the adolescent's innate susceptibility, developmental stage, and exposure to sociocultural factors such as teasing from family members and peers, social modeling (e.g., Furman & Thompson, 2002; Jackson, Grilo, & Masheb, 2000; Stice, Maxfield, & Wells, 2003; van den Berg, Wertheim, Thompson, & Paxton, 2002), and media pressure (e.g., Field, Camargo, Taylor, Berkey, & Colditz, 1999; Field et al., 2001; Taylor et al., 1998). Although few longitudinal studies have demonstrated the developmental sequence of exposure to risk factors, interventions designed to reduce the impact of risk factors may need to address a range of sociocultural factors.

Summary

A number of factors, including perceived pressure to be thin, thin-ideal internalization, body dissatisfaction, and negative affect, have been identified as risk factors for the development of bulimic symptoms. Some studies suggest that attempted dieting is a risk factor for the development of bulimic symptoms, whereas other data indicate that actual experimentally prescribed dietary restriction is not a risk factor. It is not clear whether dysfunctional dieting, especially severe caloric restriction, is a risk factor for full-syndrome bulimia nervosa. Low self-esteem, perfectionism, early menarche, and impulsivity do not appear to be risk factors for bulimic symptoms. The conclusions from the studies of risk factors for bulimia nervosa indicate that prevention programs that target thin-ideal internalization, pressure to be thin, modeling of eating disturbances, body dissatisfaction, and negative affect may prove useful in preventing the development of bulimic symptoms. Although currently unproven, it seems logical to assume that a reduction in bulimic symptoms in a population would lead to a reduction in the incidence of full-syndrome bulimia nervosa as well.

TREATMENT OF OBESITY AS A RISK FACTOR FOR EATING DISORDERS

As discussed previously, although the empirical evidence is mixed, dieting is frequently implicated in the pathogenesis of eating disorders (Schmidt, 2002). The presumed association between dieting and the development of symptoms of eating disorders has led school-based eating disorder prevention programs to warn students about the ill effects of dieting (e.g., Kater, Rohwer, & Levine, 2000). With obesity rapidly becoming a major public health problem for America's youth, it is important to understand whether treatments for obesity, specifically recommendations to restrict caloric intake, increase the risk for the development of eating disorders.

Recent data indicate that 15.5% of adolescents are overweight, a 3-fold increase since 1980 (National Center for Health Statistics, 2003; Troiano, Flegal, Kuczmarski, Campbell, & Johnson, 1995), and an additional 22% of adolescents are at risk of being overweight, compared to 15.7% in 1980 (Troiano et al., 1995). Approximately 80% of overweight teenagers will become obese adults and consequently will experience increased risks of cardiovascular disease, hyperlipidemia, hypertension, diabetes mellitus, gallbladder disease, several cancers, and psychosocial complications (Casey, Dwyer, Coleman, & Valadian, 1992; Garn, Sullivan, & Hawthorne, 1989). Adults suffer adverse health effects as a result of teenage obesity (DiPietro, Mossberg, &

Stunkard, 1994; Must, Jacques, Dallal, Bajema, & Dietz, 1992), but obese teens may not be spared from health complications until they reach adulthood. Twenty years ago, Type 2 diabetes was rare in children and adolescents. However, recent reports demonstrated that one third of adolescents diagnosed with diabetes had the Type 2, or adult-onset, form of this disease, which represents a 10-fold increase from rates in 1982 (Pinhas-Hamiel et al., 1996; Glaser 1997; Phillips & Young, 2000). Investigators fear that diabetes progresses more quickly in youth than in adults (Styne, 2001).

A combination of decreased caloric intake (i.e., dieting) and increased physical activity is the cornerstone of weight management in overweight adolescents, as in obese adults. Some clinicians and researchers fear, however, that dieting may increase the risk of eating disorders, particularly in adolescent females, and that weight loss interventions may do more harm than good (Garner & Wooley, 1991; Hirschmann & Munter, 1988; Polivy & Herman, 1985). By contrast, obesity experts generally believe that early intervention is desirable. Family support for change is likely to be available, eating and activity habits may be more amenable to modification, and adipose tissue cell proliferation may be curtailed (Goldfield & Epstein, 2002). Early treatment may also be cost-effective. Preventing overweight children and adolescents from becoming obese adults could reduce the health-care costs of treating obesity-related complications.

The question of whether dieting increases the risk of eating disorders in overweight adolescents and older children who seek weight loss is particularly important given the increasing rates of obesity. However, the vast majority of adolescent dieters do not develop eating disorders, as 44% of teenage girls report trying to lose weight, but the prevalence of eating disorders is between 1% (anorexia nervosa) and 3% (bulimia nervosa) of women, and prevalence rates among men are approximately one tenth of those observed in women (Hoek, 2002). As discussed above, other factors, including a genetic predisposition and negative affect, appear to contribute to the development of eating disorders in the presence of attempts to diet (Schmidt, 2002).

Other issues must also be examined when considering whether dieting is a risk factor for the development of eating disorders in overweight adolescents. First, studies of average weight or lean youth may have limited relevance to overweight adolescents. Although average-weight individuals experience adverse behavioral and psychological effects from severe caloric restriction (Keys, Brozek, Henschel, Mickelson, & Taylor, 1950), obese adults who have lost 10% of their initial weight have shown improvements in mood and premorbid binge eating frequency (National Task Force on the Prevention and Treatment of Obesity, 2000). A second consideration already discussed is that dieting can take many forms, from unhealthy weight control practices such as fasting or starvation, to moderate energy restriction, to a preoccupation with purportedly "good" and "bad" foods. Some interventions would appear more likely than others to be associated with adverse effects, therefore, it is important to understand the types of treatments used with overweight or obese children and adolescents.

Weight Loss Interventions for Children and Adolescents

Effective management of overweight in children and adolescents consists of diet, physical activity, and behavior change, and often requires parental participation (Goldfield, Raynor, & Epstein, 2002). Dietary change may include reduction of calorie or fat intake, or improved adherence to dietary guidelines, such as the Food Guide Pyramid (Epstein, Myers, Raynor, & Saelens, 1998). A popular approach to diet modification in youth is provided by the Traffic Light Diet, which classifies foods into red (*stop*), yellow (*caution*), or green (*go*) categories based on caloric value and nutrient density (Epstein & Squires, 1988). Typically, the initial goal is to limit intake to 1,000–1,300 calories per day, adjusted to promote a weight loss of 0.25 kg/week.

To increase physical activity, programs typically encourage structured aerobic exercise, such as swimming, jogging, or basketball, and lifestyle activity, which increases physical activity throughout the day (e.g., using the stairs rather than escalators). Preliminary studies demonstrated that lifestyle activity was more effective than structured exercise in facilitating the maintenance of weight loss (Goldfield et al., 2002). Reducing sedentary behaviors, including watching television and playing video games, has also been shown to contribute significantly to weight management (Epstein et al., 1995).

Parental participation in treatment is critical for children and also benefits adolescents (Goldfield et al., 2002). Parents may reward changes in their child's diet or physical activity, or modify their own eating or activity habits to model healthy behaviors. Similarly, parents can limit high-fat and high-sugar foods available in the home, while increasing consumption of fruits, vegetables, and other healthy choices. One study found that using parents as the exclusive agents for their child's behavior change resulted in greater decreases in overweight than treating the child alone (Golan, Weizman, Apterm, & Fainaru, 1998).

Family-based behavioral programs reduce children's percentage of overweight by as much as 25% and produce successful weight maintenance for as long as 10 years (Goldfield & Epstein, 2002). More typical reductions in percentage overweight have ranged from 5% to 15% (Goldfield et al., 2002). Decreases in weight (or fat) have been associated with significant reductions in systolic and diastolic blood pressure, fasting serum cholesterol, triglycerides, and hyperinsulinemia, and significant increases in high-density lipoprotein serum cholesterol (Epstein et al., 1998).

Effects of Dieting and Weight Loss on Eating Behavior

A family-based behavior modification program for severe pediatric overweight (Levine, Ringham, Kalarchian, Wisniewski, & Marcus, 2001) produced an average decrease in overweight of 11% during treatment, but this reduction was not maintained approximately 8 months later. Symptoms of eating disorders were measured by the Children's Eating Attitudes Test (ChEAT), which is designed to assess attitudes toward eating and dieting behavior, perceived

body image, obsessions and preoccupations with food, and dieting practices. At follow-up, preoccupation with dieting, unhealthy dieting behaviors, and concerns about being overweight decreased. Thus, neither significant weight loss nor weight regain caused an increase in eating disorder symptoms.

Epstein and colleagues evaluated an intervention in which all participants followed the standard Traffic Light Diet intervention (described above), and some also received problem-solving skills training (Epstein, Paluch, Saelens, Ernst, & Wilfley, 2001). Follow-up assessments, conducted 18 months after completion of treatment, indicated that percentage overweight decreased an average of 13% across conditions. Weight dissatisfaction, purging and restricting, and total symptoms of disordered eating, assessed by the Kids' Eating Disorder Survey (KEDS; Childress, Jarrell, & Brewerton, 1993), showed no significant changes over time.

A third study evaluated a cognitive-behavior modification (CBM) program that taught self-regulation and problem-solving skills and promoted lifestyle change (Braet & Van Winckel, 2000). Cognitive-behavior modification was delivered in a group, individual, or summer-camp format and was compared to a one-session advice condition. At the 4.6-year follow-up assessment, percentage overweight (which did not differ between groups) had decreased an average of 11% from baseline. None of the participants had anorexia nervosa at follow-up. Assessment with the Dutch Eating Behavior Questionnaire (DEBQ; Van Strien, Frijters, Bergers, & Defares, 1986) indicated that external eating decreased and restrained eating increased between baseline and follow-up, which indicated that the program helped children control external food stimuli and develop the restraint necessary for weight control. Emotional eating, also measured with the DEBQ, did not change. Five participants (9%) scored 1 standard deviation above the reference group mean for the bulimia subscale of the Eating Disorders Inventory, which indicates a greater risk for developing an eating disorder. However, the proportion of higher-risk participants did not appear elevated when compared with community samples of adolescents.

A 10-year follow-up study, the longest to date,

evaluated outcomes for participants enrolled in one of four weight control programs during childhood (Epstein, Myers, Raynor, & Saelens, 1998). All of the interventions were family based and used the Traffic Light Diet. At follow-up, percentage overweight decreased an average of 10%–20% for participants in most treatment groups, whereas participants in control groups increased their percentage overweight by as much as 12%. Four percent of participants reported that they had been treated for bulimia nervosa over the course of the 10-year follow-up, and none reported treatment for anorexia nervosa. These rates are consistent with rates from community samples.

These four studies suggest that professionally administered weight loss interventions pose minimal risks of precipitating eating disorders in overweight children and adolescents. Cross-sectional studies examining the relationship between dieting and binge eating in clinical populations support this view, as past participation in diet programs does not appear to increase the occurrence of binge eating (Berkowitz, Stunkard, & Stallings, 1993). Similarly, about half of adults with binge eating disorder report that dieting did not precede the onset of their disorder (Yanovski, 2002).

Effects of Dieting on Psychological Status

Dieting and weight loss have also been identified as precipitants to adverse emotional reactions, including depression, anxiety, and irritability (Stunkard, 1957; Stunkard & Rush, 1974). Myers, Raynor, and Epstein (1998) evaluated children's psychological status, as determined by mothers' reports on the Child Behavior Checklist (CBCL; Achenbach, 1991), while they participated in a family-based behavioral program. From baseline to 1-year follow-up, participants' percentage overweight decreased an average of 20%, and during this time, global child psychopathology decreased significantly, while global competence increased. The proportion of children who met clinical criteria for at least one behavior problem decreased from 29% at baseline to 13% at follow-up. Improvements in some aspects of psychological status, including somatic complaints and so-

cial competence, were positively associated with weight loss.

Levine and colleagues (2001) found significant reductions in symptoms of depression and anxiety at the end of treatment that were maintained at 8-month follow-up. Epstein and colleagues (2001) observed that total behavior problems and internalizing behavior problems (as measured by the CBCL) decreased significantly at 18-month follow-up. Twelve percent of participants reported seeking treatment for depression during the decade of the Epstein, Valoski, Wing, & McCurley (1994) follow-up, a rate that does not appear high for children who have sought professional weight reduction services (Goldsmith et al., 1992). These findings, as a whole, do not indicate that dieting has a negative effect on mood (e.g., Polivy & Herman, 1985).

Evidence from Research on Obese Adults

Professionally administered weight control programs for overweight youth do not appear to precipitate disordered eating, a finding supported by research on the effects of dieting on binge eating behaviors in obese adults (National Task Force on the Prevention and Treatment of Obesity, 2000; Wilson, 2002). Behavioral programs that prescribed moderate caloric restriction were associated with significant decreases in binge eating episodes in individuals with preexisting binge eating pathology. Studies that used very low–calorie diets (VLCDs) also generally reported improvements in binge eating, although one investigation reported an increase in this behavior (Telch & Agras, 1993). In reviewing the literature, the National Task Force on the Prevention and Treatment of Obesity (2000) concluded that dieting and weight loss, in overweight or obese adults, were not associated with the development of eating disorders, and that weight loss was associated with improvements in depression, anxiety, and related complications. The inclusion, in most programs, of behavior therapy to promote weight loss may have contributed to the observed improvements in mood (Wadden, Stunkard, & Liebschutz, 1988; Wadden, Stunkard, & Smoller, 1986). Long-term studies also found that weight regain, while upsetting to dieters, was not associated with significant increases in depression, anxiety, or binge eating (Foster, Wadden, Kendall, Stunkard and Vogt, 1996; National Task Force, 2000; Wilson, 2002).

Summary

Professionally administered weight loss programs for *overweight* children and adolescents generally do not increase symptoms of eating disorders and are associated with significant improvements in psychological status. Thus, concerns about the possible adverse effects of dieting should not deter our nation's growing number of overweight youth from pursuing sensible methods to lose weight or, at least, to prevent the progression of adiposity. A critical issue to address in future research is how to craft public health messages that are health promoting. Clearly approaches aimed at moderation (neither too much nor too little) could effectively target overweight children and youth who tend toward caloric restriction associated with eating disorders. Given the electricity and lack of clarity associated with the term *dieting*, other terminology should be sought that focuses on healthy portion sizes, moderation of intake, and healthy levels of physical activity.

PREVENTION OF EATING DISORDERS

The prevention of eating disorders remains an important but elusive goal. The literature on eating disorders prevention is relatively limited compared to the voluminous work on the prevention of other problems seen in adolescence. For instance, Durlak and Wells (1997) used meta-analysis to examine 177 primary prevention programs designed to prevent behavioral and social problems in young people under the age of 18. Tobler et al. (2000) found 207 universal prevention programs designed to reduce substance abuse. Nevertheless, the existing data can be useful in evaluating the current state of research on the prevention of eating disorders.

This section reviews empirical studies of prevention, with a focus on universal and targeted

prevention activities. In universal prevention, attempts are made to reduce the incidence of a disease by eliminating or reducing risk factors in a population. Increasing exercise levels and reducing intake of high levels of saturated fat to reduce the prevalence of obesity would be categorized as a universal prevention intervention. Ideally, the reduction of risk factors would decrease the incidence of eating disorders such that the benefits of the change outweigh any attendant risks for the population as a whole. Targeted preventive interventions focus on reducing risk factors in individuals who are at high risk of developing subthreshold or threshold eating disorder syndromes. A more in-depth definition of universal and targeted prevention programs is given in the Introduction to this book.

For both universal and targeted interventions, risk factors must be identified and subsequently tested to determine whether a reduction in the risk factor decreases the incidence of the disorder. No risk factor for eating disorders has yet passed this test. Although some investigators have argued that preventive activities should also focus on "protective" factors, such as building higher levels of self-esteem to reduce the risk of developing an eating disorder, no such protective factors have been identified in prospective risk factor studies. Targeted preventive interventions must identify high-risk individuals accurately, which could involve the use of highly sensitive and specific screening tools to partition a population into no-risk, high-risk, or case (diagnosed with the disorder) groups. High-risk individuals could receive targeted preventive interventions, or monitoring, whereas cases could be referred for treatment. But there is currently no instrument that can satisfactorily partition individuals into these groups.

Universal Prevention

Most studies evaluating universal prevention efforts target older students and use curricula designed to change the knowledge, beliefs, attitudes, intentions, and behaviors of individual students. Most programs promote healthy weight regulation, discourage calorie-restrictive dieting, and address ways in which body image and eating are influenced by developmental, so-cial, and cultural factors, or a healthy weight reg-ulation (HWR) model. Other studies focus on broader issues such as increasing self-esteem, empowerment, confidence, and general skills, or a self-esteem/social competence (SESC) model. Many studies focus on reducing the onset of eat-ing disorder symptoms, particularly bulimic pa-thology. Little is known about prevention of the onset of anorexia nervosa, but given the low prevalence of this disorder, it would be difficult for prevention studies to recruit sufficient sam-ple sizes to detect significant effects.

Elementary School

Studies of universal prevention efforts in ele-mentary school have produced some encourag-ing results in demonstrating increases in knowl-edge about eating disorders, but have been less successful in altering attitudes and behaviors. Smolak and Levine (2001) evaluated a 10-lesson HWR model curriculum for girls and boys ages 9 through 11 which also emphasized tolerance and appreciation for diversity in weight and shape. Students in the original sample were reas-sessed 2 years later. Compared to young adoles-cents from schools not included in the original study, participants were more knowledgeable, had higher body esteem, and used fewer un-healthy weight management techniques. Scores for the original control group were intermediate, suggesting "cross-contamination" or "spillover" between the original groups. Cross-talk among control and treatment groups at the same school creates a major confound for controlled school-based studies.

Middle School

At least 22 studies have evaluated universal pre-vention interventions with middle-school chil-dren. Killen et al. (1993) randomized 967 sixth- and seventh-grade girls to an 18-lesson program grounded in the HWR model or to standard cur-riculum control. The intervention produced only modest increases in knowledge and no short- or long-term changes in attitudes or be-haviors. The authors also examined changes in the students at "risk," on the basis of scores of a

measure designed to predict the onset of eating disorders (Weight Concerns). At 2-year follow-up, the effect sizes of Weight Concerns for at-risk students in the preventive intervention and control classes were moderate. Thus, the inter-vention may have been effective for high-risk students.

McVey and Davis (2002) implemented a cur-riculum of six 1-hour lessons combining features of the HWR and SESC models for 11- to 12-year-old girls beginning the transition into adoles-cence. There were no significant differences in body satisfaction and eating attitudes between schools that received the intervention and schools that did not. In a controlled evaluation of another HWR intervention, Stewart, Carter, Drinkwater, Hainsworth, and Fairburn (2001) found significant decreases between the pre- and postintervention assessments, including shape concerns, Eating Disorders Examination Ques-tionnaire (EDE-Q), and Eating Attitudes Test (EAT) scores, but scores on these variables re-verted to baseline at 6-month follow-up.

A controlled evaluation of an intensive school-based obesity prevention program for youth ages 11 through 13 (Austin, Field, & Gort-maker, 2002) found more positive effects from curricula following the HWR model. Among the 188 girls who were not dieting or eating disor-dered at baseline, only 1 (0.5%) program partic-ipant reported purging or using diet pills 2 years later, as compared to 9 (5.5%) in the control con-dition. Promising results have also been reported in a series of studies using elements of the SESC model. For example, Steiner-Adair et al. (2002) developed a curriculum designed to help girls be-come more assertive and supportive of one another as they learned to critically evaluate cul-tural messages and recognize prejudices pertain-ing to gender, beauty, weight, and eating. This curriculum, called *Full of Ourselves*, consists of 70 activities, organized into eight units delivered across 2–4 months. Students learn assertion skills and learn how to be more supportive of one an-other. The curriculum also discusses issues re-lated to prejudice about weight and teaches stu-dents to critically evaluate various cultural messages pertaining to gender, beauty, weight, and eating. Students are encouraged to take active leadership roles in social-justice issues concerning body image (Steiner-Adair, 1994). The girls are given the opportunity to work closely with trained adult mentors and to serve as mentors themselves for girls ages 9 to 11.

Among 500 seventh-grade girls in 24 schools, significant pre- to postintervention effects were found on measures of eating disorder knowledge and weight-related body esteem, which were maintained at 6-month follow-up. There were no apparent effects on weight management behavior.

High School

Universal prevention has been evaluated in at least 23 studies with high school students (ages 14 through 18.). Two studies (one in Israel and one in Italy) demonstrated sustained benefits for low-risk students receiving an HWR curriculum (Neumark-Sztainer, Butler, & Palti, 1995; Santonastaso et al., 1999). Four controlled studies of the HWR model with variations of the SESC model have produced positive pre- to postprogram changes, but the positive effects were limited to drive for thinness (Wiseman et al., 2002), attitudes about sociocultural factors (Kelton-Locke, 2001; Moriarty, Shore, & Maxim, 1990; Phelps, Sapia, Nathanson, & Nelson, 2000), or intentions to diet (Phelps et al., 2000). Two other well-designed studies of prevention programs with substantial elements of the HWR and SESC models (Buddeberg-Fischer, Klaghofer, Reed, & Buddeberg, 2000; Paxton, 1993) and a number of other small-scale or uncontrolled studies have found negative results.

Environmental Interventions

Eating-disordered attitudes and behaviors are difficult to alter because they are strongly reinforced by a variety of family, peer, medical, and other cultural factors. Consequently, some prevention researchers have argued for the need to change the environment of children and adolescents, specifically, the school environment (Neumark-Sztainer, 1996; Piran, 1999; see also Levine & Piran, 2001). Piran (1999), an advocate of this approach, has demonstrated that system-wide changes can reduce eating disorders in the high-risk setting of an elite ballet school. Neumark-Sztainer, Sherwood, Coller, and Hannan (2000) designed a community-based intervention to prevent disordered eating among preadolescent girls, and randomized 226 Girl Scout troop members into control and intervention groups. The intervention consisted of six 90-minute sessions focusing on media literacy and advocacy skills, with some training for troop leaders. At 3-month follow-up, the program demonstrated a positive influence on media-related attitudes and behaviors including internalization of sociocultural ideals, self-efficacy to impact weight-related social norms, and print media habits. Unfortunately, manipulation of system or setting variables to prevent the development of eating disorders has not been well tested in other settings or by other researchers.

Targeted Prevention

A number of studies, usually focused on older adolescents or college students, have shown that interventions targeted at high-risk students can be effective. Because most of these studies included self-selected and older samples, extrapolation of their success to adolescents should be made cautiously. Stice, Trost, and Chase (2003) randomly assigned high school and college students to a dissonance treatment, a healthy weight management condition, or a waiting-list control. With this approach, the participants were asked to help create a program to teach younger girls body acceptance and to avoid internalizing the thin-body ideal. The theory is that participating students will change their own attitudes and beliefs to better conform to the messages they are developing for the younger girls. At 6-month follow-up, the dissonance group had a sustained reduction in internalization of the thin ideal, but the effects for the other measures dissipated after the program (body dissatisfaction) or at 6-month follow-up (negative affect and bulimic behavior). If anything, the healthy weight intervention resulted in longer-term improvements in negative affect and bulimic symptoms.

Results from other studies reporting the effects of both brief and more intense psychoeducational programs have also been mixed. Mann et al. (1997) evaluated the effects of recovered classmates describing their experience with having an eating disorder and providing information about eating disorders to fellow students. At the posttest, intervention participants had slightly *more* symptoms of eating disorders than did controls. Franko (1998) found little benefit from a more intensive eight-session psychosocial support group, whereas Stice and Ragan (2002) and Springer, Winzelberg, Perkins, and Taylor (1999) found some positive effects of college courses on body image and disordered eating.

In a series of studies using a computer-assisted HWR program, Taylor and colleagues found improvements in body image and eating behaviors of self-selected high-risk college students (Taylor, Winzelberg, & Celio, 2001). Studies of students with borderline symptoms of clinical disorders have also been promising. For instance, Kaminski and McNamara (1996) randomized 315 at-risk female college students to a no-treatment control or a cognitive-behavioral group, and at 1-month follow-up the intervention group demonstrated significant improvements in weight management behavior, body satisfaction, and self-esteem, and less fear of negative evaluation. These and more clinically focused studies show that intensive, targeted interventions can reduce risk factors, at least in the short term.

Combining Targeted and Universal Prevention

Luce et al. (submitted) demonstrated that students in a population can be screened for eating disorder risk and participate in interventions appropriate to their needs and interests. On the basis of answers to an on-line risk-factor screen, and self-reported height and weight, students in this study were offered various on-line options, including a general nutrition and healthy weight regulation program, and an intensive psychoeducational program focused on body image enhancement and/or weight maintenance. Students completed one of the programs, provided 1 hour/week for 4 weeks, and participated in a monitored discussion group germane to their group. Of the 11 students who reported vomiting and/or laxative abuse preintervention, 10 reported a decrease at postintervention, and the 11th entered therapy.

High-Risk Populations and Settings

Aside from a few studies with ballet dancers (Piran, 1999, Yannakoulia, Sitara, & Matalas, 2002), preventive interventions for particular at-risk populations or high-risk settings have received little attention. Olmsted, Daneman, Rydall, Lawson, and Rodin (2002) randomly assigned adolescent girls with insulin-dependent diabetes to a psychoeducational program. At 6-month follow-up, significant reductions in body dissatisfaction, drive for thinness, dietary restraint, and eating concerns were observed. Students participating in certain types of athletic activities can also be considered high risk, but there are no studies of adolescents with these characteristics.

Summary

The prevention of disordered eating is an important issue in public health. Many young girls and women, as well as boys, suffer from severe and potentially chronic problems with body image, eating, and various forms of unhealthy weight management. In addition, efforts to combine prevention efforts for eating disorders and obesity are important, as some of the fundamental factors that influence disordered eating may also contribute to obesity. The data on the prevention of both eating disorders and cigarette smoking and other drug use (Tobler et al., 2000) also suggest that curricula in the schools alone are not sufficient to produce sustained preventive effects.

Universal prevention efforts with elementary school children have produced positive changes in the relevant knowledge and attitudes of students. Programs that focus on changing factors with broad application, such as increasing self-esteem, creating a stronger sense of connection to peers and mentors, and transforming critical awareness into cultural change, have proved promising with middle school students, but it is unclear whether interventions using the HWR model are of benefit to children in middle school. High school students are a very difficult target audience for universal prevention, as evidenced by nine studies in five different countries producing no significant effects on attitudes and behaviors. Thus it remains unclear whether universal prevention interventions are effective for preventing eating disorders.

A recent meta-analysis of universal prevention studies concluded that the evidence does not "allow any firm conclusions to be made about the impact of prevention programs for eating disorders in children and adolescents" (Pratt and Woolfenden, 2002), and with similar data, others have concluded that universal prevention is ineffective and should be abandoned. However, a dearth of universal prevention studies is different from a proven lack of effectiveness, particularly when well-designed studies of multidimensional interventions are rare. Many questions remain about universal prevention programs, such as how these programs can have stronger and more long-lasting effects on risk factors, what the ideal age is for such interventions, what the advantages and disadvantages are of combined interventions, how to include environmental and family factors, and whether programs should be provided to both boys and girls in the same setting.

The general lack of effectiveness of programs aimed at preventing eating disorders in adolescents also needs to be put in the context of substantial research done on prevention of substance abuse, high-risk sexual behavior, and juvenile delinquency and violence (Nation et al., 2003). In an extensive review, the authors concluded that effective prevention programs need to be comprehensive, include varied teaching methods, provide sufficient dosage, be theory driven, provide opportunities for positive relationships, be developmentally appropriate and socioculturally relevant, include outcome evaluation, and involve well-trained staff. Few of the eating disorder prevention studies meet all these characteristics.

A number of studies have demonstrated that interventions targeting high-risk students can be effective, but because many of these studies focused on self-selected and older samples, caution is needed in generalizing the findings to adolescents. Analyses of universal prevention studies suggest that the HWR model might work for high-risk students, but surprisingly little research has focused on students in high-risk settings. Although targeted interventions have proven effective, their effects are generally short-lived and specific to a few dimensions. The challenges in delivering targeted interventions, particularly to populations, are substantial. For example, in school settings, the identification and motivation for high-risk individuals to participate in interventions may be difficult.

Research Agenda for
Eating Disorders

Research on eating disorders has produced a substantial base of knowledge regarding the definitions of eating disorders, their treatment, and their prevention. There are major gaps, however, in our understanding of eating disorders, especially those occurring among adolescents. Most of the research literature on eating disorders has focused on adults, and the findings may not apply to younger individuals. Thus, the research agenda for eating disorders among adolescents is large.

DEFINING EATING DISORDERS

Diagnostic Criteria for Anorexia Nervosa and Bulimia Nervosa

The DSM-IV diagnostic criteria for eating disorders are useful but imperfect. Perhaps the most glaring problem is that the current criteria do not provide a category, beyond the nonspecific eating disorder not otherwise specified, for a substantial fraction of the individuals who present to clinicians for evaluation and treatment. Eating disturbances that do not meet the full DSM-IV criteria for anorexia nervosa or bulimia nervosa are inadequately described, and it is unclear how clinically significant eating problems are to be differentiated from other eating pathologies, and whether individuals classified as having eating disorder not otherwise specified will develop full-blown disorders. Several promising approaches to these problems have been developed in recent years, such as the Great Ormond Street criteria (Lask & Bryant-Waugh, 2000) and the categories of the Diagnostic and Statistical Manual for Primary Care (DSM-PC), and these deserve further examination. Longitudinal examinations of the course of eating disorder symptoms during adolescence and the course of associated psychological and physical problems (e.g., obesity) would also be very valuable in defining the evolution and characteristics of adolescent eating disorders.

Epidemiology

In adults, anorexia nervosa and bulimia nervosa affect approximately 1% and 3% of women, re-

spectively, with rates among men estimated at one tenth of those observed in women (Hoek, 2002). The small number of methodologically rigorous epidemiological studies leads to significant uncertainty about the prevalence and incidence of anorexia nervosa and bulimia nervosa among adolescents. The peak incidence (number of new cases per year) of anorexia nervosa appears to occur in late adolescence (Hoek & van Hoeken, 2003), but the combined prevalence (number of current cases) of anorexia nervosa and bulimia nervosa appears to be somewhat less among adolescents than among adults. Methodologically rigorous studies may find that the published rates do not adequately reflect the true prevalence of eating disorders in adolescents. Epidemiological research on eating disorders among adolescents is limited in several important ways. Nationally representative samples are needed to determine more precisely how common eating disorders are among American youth. The extant (and limited) evidence suggests that ethnic minority children need to be included to gain a more accurate understanding of risk for eating disorders in non-white youth.

The epidemiological literature has, for the most part, used clearly articulated diagnostic criteria for anorexia nervosa and bulimia nervosa, and the difficulties in defining the spectrum of other eating disturbances have presented a significant barrier to describing the prevalence of other potentially important but less well–defined conditions. For example, future studies should include criteria for binge eating disorder to permit estimates of the prevalence of this syndrome. A uniform instrument for measuring eating disorder symptoms that is efficient and accurate in detecting anorexia nervosa, bulimia nervosa, and binge eating disorder and is standardized across studies would be of great value. Psychiatric interviews that "skip out" of the eating disorder questions after a negative answer may underestimate eating pathology, especially in young samples with atypical clinical presentations of anorexia nervosa or bulimia nervosa (Kreipe et al., 1995). Finally, parent reports of eating behavior might improve the detection of anorexia nervosa, a disorder in which denial is a hallmark.

Future studies should assess both current and

past eating disorders. Several population-based studies have shown that eating disorders may be transient (albeit in many cases recurrent) and point prevalence rates may therefore not fully reflect the extent of eating pathology in adolescents (Patton, Coffey, & Sawyer, 2003). Even when the adolescent's eating disorder is time limited and nonrecurring, it may represent a marker for psychopathology that conveys important clinical information.

Comorbidity, Outcome, and Migration

Psychiatric comorbidities are common among both adolescents and adults with anorexia nervosa and bulimia nervosa, and include mood disorders, anxiety disorders, and substance use disorders. However, the relationship between anorexia nervosa, bulimia nervosa, and comorbid disorders is unclear. The outcome of adolescent patients with anorexia nervosa who receive early treatment appears better than that of patients who do not; however, those patients who remain ill have high rates of psychiatric comorbidity and are at risk for premature death. Most adolescent anorexia nervosa patients improve or get well, but a substantial percentage remains permanently symptomatic. The data on the course and outcome of adolescent bulimia nervosa are very limited. Diagnostic migration occurs frequently from anorexia nervosa-restricting subtype (AN-R) to anorexia nervosa-binge purge subtype (AN-B/P), and from AN-B/P to bulimia nervosa. It is currently not possible to identify those patients likely to migrate.

Future studies of adolescents with eating disorders should include individuals with comorbidities, such as substance use disorders, to aid in developing treatment strategies for these dual-diagnosis conditions. Studies of the course and outcome of adolescent bulimia nervosa are needed, and early identification and intervention strategies need to be developed.

Medical Complications

While most medical complications associated with eating disorders are reversible with nutri-

tional rehabilitation and cessation of the binge–purge cycle, there are indications that growth retardation, osteopenia, and, possibly, structural brain changes are not entirely reversible. Studies probing structural brain changes in anorexia nervosa and their relationship to neuropsychological changes are needed. In addition, there is a pressing need to develop efficacious treatments for osteopenia among adolescents with anorexia nervosa.

TREATMENTS FOR EATING DISORDERS

Arguably, the most compelling need for future research is to develop effective treatments for adolescents with eating disorders. A significant body of information is available on interventions for adults with bulimia nervosa, and there are promising developments in the treatment of adolescents with anorexia nervosa. It is imperative to build on these initial efforts.

Psychological Treatment of Anorexia Nervosa

There is only one evidence-based treatment for adolescents with anorexia nervosa, the Maudsley method of family therapy, whether delivered in a conjoint or separated format. The empirical evidence supporting the treatment is limited, however. Whereas a subgroup of anorexia nervosa patients may have an inherently good prognosis, it is clear that significant numbers of these patients do not do well. For example, Eisler et al. (2000) found in their study (in which all the patients received the Maudsley method of family therapy) that 15 of 40 patients were judged to have a "poor" outcome on the Morgan-Russell scales and 4 patients had to be admitted to the hospital because of continuing weight loss. At the end of the study by Robin et al. (1999), the authors note that "even with comprehensive, multidisciplinary interventions such as those evaluated in this study, not all adolescents with anorexia nervosa will improve. Twenty to 30 percent of the patients did not reach their target weights, and 40% to 50% did not reach the 50th percentile of BMI by 1-year follow-up. Clinicians and researchers will need to continue to develop innovative approaches to helping these more resistant patients" (p. 1489).

A potentially promising treatment for adolescent anorexia nervosa patients is cognitive-behavioral therapy (CBT). This therapy is the leading evidence-based treatment for bulimia nervosa (National Institute for Clinical Excellence, 2004; Wilson & Fairburn, 2002), a disorder that has much of the same psychopathology as that of anorexia nervosa (Fairburn & Harrison, 2003; Fairburn, Cooper, & Shafran, 2003). Additionally, CBT is already used with adults with anorexia nervosa (e.g., Garner, Vitousek, & Pike, 1997), and a recent cognitive-behavioral conceptualization of anorexia nervosa may pertain to adolescent patients, given its emphasis on the early stages in the evolution of the disorder (Fairburn, Shafran, & Cooper, 1999). Finally, CBT has been successfully used to treat other psychiatric disorders in adolescence (Kazdin, 2003; Kendall, 2000).

If CBT were to be developed as a treatment for these patients, it would need to be adapted in certain ways. It would need to be based on a model of the maintenance of anorexia nervosa, focusing on the processes involved in recent-onset cases (e.g., Fairburn, Shafran, et al., 1999). The therapy would need to take account of the developmental psychology of adolescence and the specific concerns of adolescents, and it would need to be adjusted to accommodate the developmental variability seen among adolescents (Holmbeck et al., 2000; Weisz & Hawley, 2002). It would also need to involve the patient's family and possibly the school.

A challenging issue in the study of new treatments for anorexia nervosa is the choice of the comparison, or "control," treatment. In theory, it might be useful to compare the effect of a new intervention with that of no treatment at all or a waiting-list condition. While such a comparison neatly controls for the effect of time alone, it is difficult to justify a delay of treatment for individuals with a disorder having such serious medical and psychiatric morbidity. Furthermore, documentation that a new treatment is superior to doing nothing does not provide strong evidence of specific clinical utility. A comparison between two interventions likely to be useful

(e.g., the Maudsley method and suitably adapted CBT) may be difficult to interpret without controls for the effect of time and for the nonspecific effects provided by any intervention. The notion of a "treatment-as-usual" comparison group has appeal, but the definition and implementation of such an intervention in the context of a research study are far from clear.

Psychological Treatment of Bulimia Nervosa

Controlled trials are needed to identify and evaluate the efficacy of psychological treatments for adolescents with bulimia nervosa. Both CBT and interpersonal psychotherapy (IPT) have been shown to be effective for adult bulimia nervosa patients. These treatments should be adapted and applied to adolescents, because CBT and IPT have been successfully adapted to treating adolescents with other problems. The case is particularly compelling for CBT, as it is the treatment of choice for bulimia nervosa in adults, its adaptation to depressed and anxious adolescents has received the most study and enjoys the most empirical support, and it meshes well with the generic and specific considerations governing psychological treatment of adolescents.

Alternative psychological therapies should also be explored. An adaptation of the family-based treatment developed by Lock, Le Grange, Agras, and Dare (2001) is an obvious candidate for study, given its apparent efficacy with adolescent anorexia nervosa. Research is also needed to assess the comparative efficacy of evidence-based psychological treatments, such as CBT, IPT, or family therapy, with antidepressant medication and their combination (sequencing).

Pharmacological Treatments for Eating Disorders

Few controlled studies have evaluated the utility and safety of pharmacological treatments for adolescents with eating disorders, although medications are frequently used in the clinical treatment of these patients. Antidepressant medications have demonstrated efficacy in reducing binge eating and vomiting behaviors for adults with bulimia nervosa, but additional study will be necessary before any conclusions can be reached about the use of these medications with younger patients. There is currently no evidence for the efficacy of pharmacological treatments in low-weight adults with anorexia nervosa. However, recent reports have suggested a utility of atypical antipsychotic medications, such as olanzapine, with adolescent anorexia nervosa patients, and future research should evaluate these medications in a controlled manner.

Relapse Prevention

For both adolescents and adults with anorexia nervosa, the risk of posthospitalization relapse is approximately 30%–50%. The Maudsley form of family therapy appears to have efficacy for preventing relapse among adolescent anorexia nervosa patients, but family therapy may be most effective for patients who develop anorexia nervosa before age 18 and who have less than 3 years duration of illness. Although there are no data on the efficacy of CBT for relapse prevention among adolescents, this treatment has support for relapse prevention in adult patients. A single controlled study in adults suggests that antidepressant medication may reduce the rate of relapse following weight restoration, but there are no data on the utility of this intervention to prevent relapse among adolescents.

Adolescents with bulimia nervosa have not been the focus of clinical treatment trials, and studies that include adolescent patients are not sufficient to draw conclusions about relapse prevention for these patients. Little is known about the efficacy of psychological or pharmacological treatments for adolescents with bulimia nervosa, both for the acute treatment of the disorder and the prevention of relapse.

Methodological and logistical challenges hamper progress in the development of effective relapse prevention interventions. Operationalized and consistent definitions of treatment response, relapse, remission, and recovery, and a standardized assessment battery would enhance the study of both initial interventions and re-lapse prevention. Clinical trials require tremendous resources, and the failure to develop consensus in the field on core terminology and assessment procedures will continue to hinder development of empirically supported treatments. Discussions of relapse and relapse prevention lead to dichotomous distinctions: either an individual has responded to treatment or not; either an individual has relapsed or not. In reality, change in clinical status is continuous, which complicates the establishment of thresholds and standardized classifications. Several authors have attempted to address this important issue (Orimoto & Vitousek, 1992; Pike, 1998).

Intensive but expensive initial treatments for anorexia nervosa, such as inpatient or partial hospitalization, are arguably the most successful in achieving weight restoration, especially among severely and chronically ill patients. Weight restoration is an essential goal in achieving recovery and is the first step in preventing relapse. However, economic pressures on reducing health-care expenditures, at least in the United States, are limiting patients' ability to receive sufficient care to achieve weight restoration. Studies of the short- and long-term costs and benefits of interventions of a range of intensity would be extremely valuable in helping to define which treatments are most cost-effective.

Treatments for Adolescents: Summary

The encouraging work on the utility of the Maudsley method for adolescents with anorexia nervosa should be pursued in studies comparing this intervention to other standard and novel approaches. Empirically supported psychological treatments for adults with eating disorders, including CBT and IPT, should be adapted to the treatment of adolescents. This process should include collaboration between treatment researchers and developmental psychologists who study adolescence. Treatments should be designed to address issues specific to adolescent patients, including motivation, cognitive processing, interpersonal functioning, body image, control, and family issues. The utility and safety of psychopharmacological interventions for adolescents with eating disorders are in need of critical examination, as such agents are commonly employed despite the current absence of evidence of efficacy.

Because eating disorders are uncommon, multisite studies will be necessary for the definitive examination of treatment efficacy and of relapse prevention. Multisite studies will further support initiatives to establish standards for terminology and assessment, as standardization is required for the execution of such trials. Another significant advantage of multisite studies is that the enhanced power will provide the opportunity to conduct more specific investigations of the relationship between eating disorder subtype, comorbidity, treatment response, and relapse.

In addition, novel approaches to study design and procedures in the treatment of adolescents with eating disorders should be considered not only for developmental considerations in treating younger patients but also because many eating disorder research centers serve as secondary and tertiary referral centers and therefore do not currently treat significant numbers of younger, new-onset cases. The particular ethical considerations and the reluctance of parents to have their children participate in clinical research are also critical issues that need to be addressed to increase clinical research initiatives focused on adolescents with eating disorders.

PREVENTION OF THE DISORDER

Risk Factors for Anorexia Nervosa

While there have been numerous studies to identify risk factors for the development of anorexia nervosa, few true risk or protective factors for the development of anorexia nervosa have been definitively established. Population-based longitudinal databases, which include prospectively collected data on large populations that include incident cases, may shed light on questions of etiological relevance to anorexia nervosa. Such projects must be viewed as a priority. Research on the risk factors for anorexia nervosa must be appropriately divided between biological–genetic and environmental factors. Because anorexia nervosa is influenced by both biological and environmental factors, a comprehensive exploration of gene and environment interactions may provide valuable information about the etiology of this disorder.

Risk Factors for Bulimia Nervosa

Factors such as perceived pressure to be thin, thin-ideal internalization, body dissatisfaction, and negative affect have been identified as risk factors for the development of bulimia nervosa. Future research should be directed at identifying new risk factors for bulimia nervosa, as most of the established risk factors have relatively modest effect sizes (Stice, 2002). Promising variables include hypersensitivity to negative interpersonal transactions, cognitive factors (e.g., affect regulation expectancies), feeding avidity, and individual differences in reinforcement from eating. In addition, the role of dieting in the development of bulimic pathology should be clarified.

Research should also begin to examine potential biological risk factors for bulimic pathology (e.g., serotonin abnormalities and structural differences in the orbitofrontal cortex); research has yet to identify a single biological risk factor for bulimic pathology. Furthermore, studies should continue to search for genetic factors that influence risk for this eating disorder.

Relatively little is known about the ways in which risk factors work together to promote the development of this disorder or about possibly distinct etiologic pathways in bulimia nervosa. Thus future research should test multivariate models to determine how the various risk factors work in concert to promote bulimic pathology. It will be particularly important to focus greater attention on identifying protective and potentiating factors and on the means by which psychosocial and biological factors work together to foster bulimic pathology.

Research should also investigate whether the risk factors for symptom onset differ from those for symptom escalation and maintenance. This is important because the former are germane to the design of universal and selected prevention programs, but the latter are necessary for the design of optimally effective indicated prevention programs and treatment interventions.

More generally, the use of prospective and experimental designs should be encouraged. These research methods are potentially powerful means of elucidating the etiologic processes that give rise to eating disorders.

Treatment of Obesity as a Risk Factor for Eating Disorders

Research on professionally administered weight loss programs for overweight children and adolescents indicates that these programs do not appear to increase symptoms of eating disorders. Conclusions about the relationship between the treatment of obesity and eating disorders are based on a very limited number of studies, and further research is needed before firm conclusions can be reached. In particular, studies are needed to reconcile findings of the apparently benign effects of dieting, as practiced in behavioral weight loss programs, to determine whether dieting precipitates eating disorders. Several issues must be considered.

First, healthy dieting, which encourages only modest caloric restriction, in combination with increased consumption of low-fat dairy products and fruits and vegetables, appears to present few risks to overweight youth. As previously mentioned, this type of dieting is likely to improve the nutritional value of foods consumed. By contrast, unhealthy weight loss behaviors, which include severe caloric restriction (e.g., crash diets) and the prohibition of certain foods (e.g., fad diets), could significantly increase the risk of eating disorders and emotional complications. This is possible in overweight youth, as well as in normal-weight girls who diet aggressively in pursuit of an ever-thinner ideal. Similarly, chronic restrained eating may pose risks that are not associated with healthy dieting.

Second, disturbances in eating behavior and mood must be clearly defined and measured. The pediatric obesity studies reviewed in this volume did not assess criteria for the diagnosis of bulimia nervosa, binge eating disorder, or eating disorder not otherwise specified. None, for example, measured objective or subjective binge episodes, as defined by Fairburn and Cooper (1993). Future studies could incorporate efforts to modify the

Eating Disorder Examination (Fairburn & Cooper, 1993) for use with children and adolescents (Bryant-Waugh, Cooper, Taylor, and Lask, 1996).

Third, some overweight youth may be at greater risk for adverse behavioral consequences of dieting and weight loss, even when they participate in a professionally administered program. Longitudinal studies, for example, have shown that severe body image dissatisfaction and weight and shape preoccupation are the most robust predictors of the development of eating disorders in adolescent girls. Thus, overweight teenagers with marked body image dissatisfaction, depression, or other psychiatric complications may be at greatest risk of experiencing binge eating episodes when subjected to even modest caloric restriction, and research in this area is needed.

Finally, weight regain is common in overweight adolescents, as in obese adults. Studies of adults have not found weight cycling (i.e., weight loss followed by regain) to be associated with clinically significant behavioral consequences; however, in overweight youth with a history of psychiatric complications, weight cycling might produce different effects. Whenever possible, follow-up assessment should be conducted through late adolescence when symptoms of bulimia nervosa or binge eating disorder might emerge.

Ultimately, large-scale randomized controlled trials will be needed to determine the behavioral risks posed by different weight loss interventions for overweight youth. Ethical constraints will limit investigators from using such trials to assess the effects of crash diets and other fundamentally unsound approaches. In addition, given the generally low occurrence of eating disorders, case–control studies may provide a better mechanism of identifying dietary practices most likely to be associated with adverse behavioral effects. Health professionals, teachers, and parents will continue to be concerned about misguided weight loss efforts in children and teenagers, but all should be increasingly concerned about the growing epidemic of pediatric obesity. Fifteen percent of America's adolescents are already overweight and as adults will experience serious medical and psychosocial consequences of this condition. Concerns about potential ill effects of dieting should not impede efforts to improve the treatment of pediatric obesity. More important, such concerns should not discourage urgently needed efforts to prevent the development of overweight in both children and adults.

Eating Disorder Prevention Research

Prevention research is an important issue in eating disorder research, even though the impact of eating disorder prevention programs for children and adolescents is not clear (Pratt & Woolfenden, 2002). Future research should include longitudinal studies of universal prevention with an integrated, multidimensional, and systemic approach to schools and other important parts of the community. These studies should demonstrate significant reductions in risk factors and a reduction in incidence of the disorders. In addition, studies of targeted interventions are needed to focus on valid and ethical ways to identify individuals and environments that are at-risk and provide interventions that reduce risk factors and incidence of the disorders. Research should demonstrate that significant and important changes in the putative risk factors or protective factors can be achieved and maintained.

Substance Use Disorders

V
part

Defining Substance
Use Disorders

chapter 17

An occasion of drug taking may be a passing indulgence of an adolescent, perhaps initiated in a moment of immature judgment. All too often, the drug taking can become repetitive and may lead to a syndrome of abuse or addiction, possibly in an interaction of inherited vulnerability traits with environmental conditions and processes. The development of addiction and the dependence syndrome in adolescents are emotion-laden, controversial, and often misunderstood topics. Public opinion leaders often do not appreciate the scientific evidence that tends to favor a disease concept of addiction or dependence on alcohol, tobacco, and other drugs such as cocaine or cannabis (McLellan, Lewis, O'Brien, & Kleber, 2000). This evidence includes a neuronal basis for many of the prominent clinical features of dependence (Dackis & O'Brien, 2003), genetic vulnerability (Vanyukov & Tarter, 2000), and a characteristic chronic, relapsing course that resembles that of many medical illnesses. Unfortunately, these biological bases of addiction are often forgotten or misunderstood by a nonetheless opinionated American public that can view adolescent drug problems as purely behavioral and morally objectionable. Consequently, many affected adolescents end up being managed by their parents, school authorities, or the judicial system rather than being treated in specialized adolescent treatment programs. Even those seeking treatment often discover that appropriate programs do not exist in their geographic region or are difficult to access because of low capacity or managed care policies. While there would be a public uproar if treatment were not available to adolescents with head injuries, diabetes, or cancer, obvious disparities in addiction treatment have been tolerated for decades and may well reflect public skepticism about the biological bases of drug dependence and addiction. Unfortunately, we have much to learn about the onset, nature, and treatment of these conditions in adolescents. It is our contention that gaps in our knowledge should be addressed with research and clinical experience, and not cited to justify an inadequate treatment infrastructure.

Syndromes of alcohol, tobacco, and other drug abuse and addiction have been defined and redefined over the past several decades and these definitions have now achieved international acceptance. The central clinical features generally include *(a)* disturbances of mental life in the form of obsession-like ruminations or even craving for drugs or drug-related experiences, *(b)* disturbances of behavior in the form of compulsion-like repetitive drug-taking or drug-related behaviors to the detriment of normal activities, and *(c)* manifestations of neuroadaptation to drug exposure, in the form of pharmacological tolerance and (sometimes) observable and characteristic withdrawal syndromes when there is an abrupt cessation of drug use. Many definitions of abuse and addiction reference a loss of control during cycles of euphoria and craving. Any definition must account for the continuum of severity that ranges from minimal use with limited consequences on one end to compulsive use with serious functional impairment on the other end. Some adolescents show progressive impairment and move along the continuum whereas others remain at a relatively stable level of severity. The American Psychiatric Association's (1994) *Diagnosis and Statistical Manual of Mental Disorders*, 4th ed. (DSM-IV) uses the label *substance abuse* to describe use with limited negative consequences, whereas the term *dependence* refers to a generally more serious loss of control of drug taking and a clinical syndrome with a running together of the clinical features mentioned above. The term *dependence* as used in the official DSM-IV manual often leads to semantic confusion with *dependence* in the pharmacological sense, which is a normal response to repeated use of many different types of medications, including drugs for the treatment of hypertension, depression, and pain. Thus many clinicians prefer the term *addiction* when referring to dependence as defined in DSM-IV. This definition applies the same diagnostic criteria to all pharmacological classes, acknowledging that similar disturbances of mental life and behavior, as well as manifestations of neuroadaptation, may develop regardless of whether the drug taking involves alcoholic beverages, tobacco (nicotine), or other drugs such as cocaine, heroin, or cannabis. Accordingly, alcohol is grouped with other dependence-producing drugs in the DSM-IV classification and will be categorized as such in this volume.

Seeking a fundamental understanding of the processes that lead toward drug addiction, clinical investigators have found evidence that drug-induced euphoria is linked to pharmacological activation of reward-related brain regions that normally mediate natural reward, including reward circuits influenced by food, sex, and drinking fluids (Dackis & O'Brien, 2003b). Reward-related circuits that have evolved over millions of years to ensure survival may actually be dysregulated by the chronic use of drugs. The clinical features of craving, loss of control, and impaired hedonic function also have linkages with the dysregulation of brain reward centers (Dackis & O'Brien, 2001, 2003b).

Tolerance is manifested in an escalation of drug dose to achieve a stated level of drug-induced effect. The process of developing tolerance can begin with the first exposure to the drug, with subsequent compensatory neuradaptational changes that often oppose the acute effect of the drugs. For example, the chronic administration of heroin and diazepam can produce so much tolerance that a 100-fold increase in dose is required to produce certain pharmacological effects that were apparent at the first low dose. Tolerance may also occur over brief periods, as evidenced by ever-decreasing euphoria with successive cocaine doses during a protracted binge. Tolerance develops more rapidly to some drug effects than to others, and drug-induced euphoria typically requires ever-increasing doses; in contrast, toxic effects may not initially require a greater dose (e.g., heroin-induced respiratory depression). Individual variability in rates of development of tolerance appear to be genetically determined and may help explain variations in the risk of drug overdose.

In contrast with pharmacological tolerance as ordinarily defined, a reverse tolerance or *sensitization* can occur, as manifest in an increased drug response after repeated administration. For instance, successive equal doses of cocaine can be followed by motor activity increases (i.e., the opposite of what is expected if tolerance has developed) in rats given the drug at daily intervals. Examples of reverse tolerance or sensitization in humans are difficult to demonstrate but may include cocaine-induced psychosis, seizures, and cue-induced craving (Dackis & O'Brien, 2001).

Tolerance and sensitization phenomena are influenced by genetic factors that affect receptor responses and the distribution of drugs in the body (pharmacokinetics) and the nervous system adaptations (pharmacodynamics) once drug exposure has occurred.

A withdrawal syndrome is seen most clearly when there is abrupt discontinuation of repetitive drug-taking. It is possible to conceive of the withdrawal features as manifestations of compensatory or homeostatic brain changes that have been established in response to chronic or repeated drug exposures. If the drug is abruptly discontinued, these changes are suddenly unopposed and there can be a rebound in the form of a characteristic cluster of withdrawal signs and symptoms. These clusters or drug withdrawal syndromes can vary markedly across classes of addictive drugs and typically include clinical features that are opposite those seen during intoxication. The onset, duration, and clinical course of withdrawal also can vary from one individual to another. It should be emphasized that withdrawal from alcohol or sedative or hypnotic agents (especially barbiturates) is potentially lethal and often requires intensive medical inpatient treatment. Treatment of drug withdrawal (detoxification) is often accomplished by administering descending doses of a medication with the same types of action as the dependence-producing drug. Therefore, opioids (such as methadone) are used to reverse heroin withdrawal, longer-acting benzodiazepines are used to counter withdrawal from shorter-acting benzodiazepine drugs, and longer-acting barbiturates are used to counter withdrawal due to shorter-acting barbiturates. In addition, benzodiazepines and barbiturates effectively reverse the alcohol withdrawal syndrome, based on their shared action on underlying neuronal (GABA) circuitry. Although detoxification is an important clinical intervention that allows the brain to equilibrate in the absence of the dependence-producing drug, detoxification is seldom sufficient to arrest the cycle of craving and euphoria. Consequently, detoxified patients require referral to continued drug rehabilitative treatment.

As we seek an understanding of vulnerability to drug dependence and addiction, we can turn to three major domains of influence. This triad includes *(1)* the drug used (the "agent"), *(2)* the constitutional characteristics of the user (the "host"), and *(3)* the physical and psychosocial setting (the "environment"). As we look across classes of drugs, the nature and potency of drug-induced euphoria vary considerably, and this euphoria may be an important reinforcer of repetitive drug-taking behavior. Among addiction specialists, there is a general consensus about a hierarchy of addictiveness or dependence liability among drugs, although it is arguable how central stimulants, opioids, alcohol, nicotine, sedative and hypnotics, marijuana, and hallucinogens should be specifically ranked. Animal models provide one means of gauging the reinforcing functions of each drug as an agent in the process of developing drug dependence. When properly equipped with intravenous delivery systems, laboratory animals will self-administer various drugs with varying enthusiasm. For instance, laboratory animals with unlimited access to cocaine or amphetamine generally will self-administer these agents until they die; in contrast, training animals to self-administer alcohol or cannabis can be difficult. Evidence for the biological basis of drug reward includes the phenomenon that animals will self-administer drugs like cocaine without special training, as well as the finding that nearly all drugs with dependence liability (cocaine, amphetamine, heroin, alcohol, nicotine, marijuana) share a common action of activating brain reward systems, as indicated by elevated dopamine levels in the nucleus accumbens (Dackis & O'Brien, 2003b). In fact, researchers routinely use this neurochemical signature of drug reward to screen the addictive potential of compounds synthesized in pharmaceutical research and development process. Natural rewards such as food, water, and sex also increase dopamine levels in the nucleus accumbens, consistent with the notion that these drugs produce euphoria by activating natural pleasure pathways. Although dopamine plays a central role in natural and drug-induced reward, there is also evidence that endogenous opioids, glutamate, γ-aminobutyric acid (GABA), and serotonin systems are mechanistically involved.

The ability of a drug to induce euphoria in humans is correlated with its dependence liability or addictiveness and can be greatly enhanced when the drug is taken by routes of administration that produce rapidly rising brain levels of the agent. The importance of the route-of-administration principle is illustrated in the history of cocaine use. People living in the Andes Mountains have chewed coca leaves since antiquity with few deleterious effects, largely because cocaine brain levels increase very slowly when the drug is absorbed through the buccal mucosa. However, once pure cocaine was chemically isolated from the coca leaf in the form of hydrochloride powder (HCl), it became possible to administer high doses by the more efficient intranasal and intravenous routes. Once cocaine HCl powder was administered intravenously or intranasally, its toxic effects became more obvious. During the 1980s the by-then illegal cocaine marketplace changed markedly when an underground pharmaceutical innovation appeared in the form of crack-cocaine, which is heated and vaporized so that the fumes can be inhaled ("smoked"). Whereas a typically intranasal route of administration might yield a cocaine "high" over the course of minutes after insufflation, the onset of the cocaine high is more rapid with smoked crack-cocaine. Indeed, within seconds after being smoked and then absorbed in the lungs, the vaporized cocaine reaches the brain and an almost instantaneous rush of euphoria may fuel a crack-associated rapid emergence of the cocaine dependence process, as indicated by recent epidemiological evidence (Chen & Anthony, 2004). A similar rapid onset of effects can be achieved by injecting cocaine, but smoking crack is more convenient and more socially acceptable than injecting cocaine, especially when adolescents already have a history of smoking cigarettes or marijuana.

In addition to characteristics of the drug agent and its route of administration, host factors can contribute significantly to the onset and course of the dependence process. Disenfranchised adolescents might use drugs to gain peer acceptance, and thrill-seeking adolescents may be attracted to drug euphoria. Adolescents with clinical features of depression, anxiety, or phobias may sometimes use drugs for relief of these symptoms. Unfortunately, chronic brain changes produced by drugs often exacerbate the very symptoms they initially alleviated, and these drugs may well produce far more psychiatric symptoms than they relieve.

Inherited traits correlated with a family history of drug dependence are also now appreciated as important host characteristics associated with the risk of becoming drug-dependent. Children of alcoholics are at increased risk of developing alcoholism, even after they have been adopted at birth and raised by nonalcoholic parents, and identical twins are more likely than fraternal twins to be concordant for alcoholism (Schuckit, 2000) and nicotine dependence (Sullivan & Kendler, 1999). Drug effects vary markedly from one individual to another and are influenced by genetic variations that affect drug absorption, metabolism, excretion, and receptor-mediated neuronal responses. Researchers are actively investigating profiles of candidate genes that encode the enzymes or other protein products related to these functions, as described in later sections about specific agents.

Individuals with extensive family history loadings for drug dependence do not necessarily become addicted, however, partly because environmental factors (supply, psychosocial norms, and peer pressure) also influence the onset and development of dependence processes. Drug supply is an essential and permissive factor that has been targeted by law enforcement initiatives. Without drug access, there can be no addiction. Aside from the physical availability of a drug, access can also be affected by its cost, with, for example, the increased use of cocaine and heroin in the past decade coinciding with the declining street price of these drugs. Psychosocial norms also affect the timing of first and subsequent uses of addictive drugs. In some communities, drug users and drug dealers are actually viewed as successful role models to be respected and emulated by young people. This unfortunate situation is often compounded by inadequate educational, vocational, and diversionary options that would otherwise offset the attractiveness of a drug-related lifestyle. Drug users often attempt to re-

gain control of their drug use, but relapse to compulsive use is almost inevitable. When the user returns to a neighborhood where he or she previously used drugs, the environmental cues may reflexively precipitate craving and resumption of drug taking. The role of environmental cues (people, places, and things) that can trigger craving are important research-based principles that influence both continued drug use and relapse after treatment (O'Brien, Childress, McLellan, & Ehrman, 1992). Since agent, host, and environmental factors are cumulatively involved in addictive illness, effective prevention and treatment interventions typically address all three realms.

THE EXTENT AND NATURE OF THE PROBLEMS

The field of epidemiology offers a description in statistical terms of the nature and extent of problems associated with adolescent use of alcohol, tobacco, and other psychoactive drugs. In this section, we describe trends and offer estimates for the prevalence of different forms of drug taking, as well as the occurrence of the clinically defined syndromes of abuse and addiction. As we seek to understand the nature and extent of associated problems we stress the plural. Indeed, a description of "the problem" would oversimplify the complex phenomenon of drug use and addiction described previously in this chapter.

Evolution of the Drug Epidemic Among Mainstream Youth in the United States: 1960s–1990

Against a background of quite prevalent alcohol and tobacco use in the United States, the prevalence of illegal drug use grew dramatically among American adolescents beginning in the 1960s. Since then, there have been dynamic changes. New drugs have emerged (e.g., crack-cocaine; MDMA, or ecstasy). Major historical events led to great social upheaval and alienation among many youth (e.g., the Vietnam War, the Watergate scandal). Concurrently, youth involvement in illegal drug use changed from being a set of experiences and behaviors concentrated mostly in fairly small, identifiable subgroups on the periphery of mainstream American society to becoming a widespread and more normative set of experiences and behavior. In terms of numerical increases of new users and previously observed and expected numbers, these illegal drug use experiences came to be characterized as an epidemic, and drug use became an important "generation gap" issue, with youths and adults often holding radically different views of the acceptability of drug use—particularly the use of certain drugs such as marijuana and hallucinogens (National Commission on Marijuana and Drug Abuse, 1972).

At the peak of this epidemic of illegal drug use, between 1975 and 1980, fully two thirds of American adolescents had tried an illegal drug by the time they finished high school (Johnston, O'Malley, & Bachman, 2002a; see also Substance Abuse and Mental Health Services Administration (SAMHSA), 2002a). This represented a dramatic increase over the prevalence proportions observed in the mid-1960s, when the epidemic began (Johnston, 1973; National Commission on Marijuana and Drug Abuse, 1972). During this interval, illegal drug use came to be associated with political beliefs—particularly, being against the Vietnam War—and with certain lifestyle orientations, as reflected in the counterculture (Johnston, 1973; Zinburg & Robertson, 1972). At the population level, there were also associations with other forms of rule-breaking behavior, deviance, or delinquency unrelated to using drugs. These associations remain, even though many drug-using youths are otherwise rule abiding and do not show other conduct problems, and some youths with conduct problems do not take illegal drugs (Jessor & Jessor, 1977; Johnston, 1973; Osgood, Johnston, O'Malley, & Bachman, 1988).

If the Vietnam War and other historical events of the 1960s and early 1970s accounted for the dramatic increase in the epidemic of illegal drug use, one might have expected a downward trend with passage of time since these events. That turned out not to be the case. The Vietnam War ended in 1973, but the rise in drug use continued into the late 1970s, albeit with some fading of the symbolic meanings of illegal drug use. During this interval, the illegal drug use epidemic developed its own forward momentum.

As gauged in relation to the number of new adolescent users year by year, it was not until the late 1970s that the epidemic trend turned downward. Even so, the proportion of young people continuing to use drugs did not decline across the board until after 1985. The decline in each year's prevalence proportion persisted into the early 1990s. During this interval of time, norms among young people against the use of many of the illegal drugs strengthened considerably. Our surveys showed an increased appreciation of harms associated with illegal drug use, in particular marijuana, cocaine, crack, and phenlcyclidine (PCP) (Bachman, Johnston, & O'Malley, 1990, 1998; Johnston, 2003).

This change in perceptions about drugs and a concomitant decline in prevalence of illegal drug use during the late 1980s, however, may have helped to sow the seeds of its own reversal and to create a context for emergence of a noteworthy "failure of success." By this we mean that important new historical events were emerging in the late 1980s and early 1990s to take the center stage of the popular imagination. Headlines and media attention shifted away from domestic matters such as illegal drug use and toward concerns about terrorism abroad, the Iraqi invasion of Kuwait, and the emerging Gulf War. With these declines in coverage of the drug issue by the media, Congressional attention and budgeting for drug prevention programs shrank considerably, and political attention to the issue declined generally. Young people were hearing and reading much less about illegal drug use, and perhaps more importantly, their perceptions reflected less familiarity with hazards that go along with illegal drug use (Johnston, 1991, 2003). In our retrospective analysis of the domains of influence that govern youths' appreciation of the hazards of illegal drug use, we build from a foundation of observations by historian David Musto and others, highlighting (a) media coverage, (b) drug prevention programming, (c) personal experiences, and (d) vicarious experiences (i.e., learning vicariously from peers, parents, or other relatives of the drugs' hazards experienced by others). To the extent that society achieves success in dampening the prevalence of illegal drug use (by whatever means), we may expect controllable declines in the first two domains: *(a)* media coverage falls, and *(b)* support for prevention programming wanes. Part and parcel with declines in the prevalence of illegal drug use are less personal experience with these drugs, fewer chances to try the drugs, and fewer young people experiencing the hurt that often goes along with drug taking. In addition, there is less vicarious experience with the associated hazards as can be gained by personal acquaintance with other young people or adults whose lives have been harmed by illegal drug use. Hence, on the downward side of an epidemic curve of illegal drug use, the same processes that fuel the continuing decline in the behavior of illegal drug use are fueling a decline in adolescents' personal and vicarious knowledge of the hazards of illegal drug use. In this sense, a "success" in the form of declining prevalence of illegal drug use sows the seeds for a "failure" and later rebound—to the extent that the knowledge of drug-associated hazards helps to promote resistance when the young person faces the first or subsequent chance to try an illegal drug.

These seeds for a resurgence of illegal drug use among American adolescents had been sown in the late 1980s and early 1990s, and for most illegal drugs, the epidemic curve turned upward in the early 1990s, with a generally persistent trend of increasing proportions of new users and continuing users into the late 1990s. Marijuana use exhibited the sharpest rise during this "relapse phase" in the epidemic, but use of most of the drugs in the ever-growing list of alternatives increased during this period as well (Johnston, O'Malley, & Bachman, 2003b; SAMHSA, 2002a,b).

By the late 1990s there were once again signs of improvement, with prevalence of inhalant use beginning to decline in 1996, and prevalence of marijuana use peaking or stabilizing by 1997. Other drugs began to decline at various points, including LSD (lysergic acid diethylamide), cocaine, and finally heroin. But one drug was growing sharply in popularity in the late 1990s— namely, ecstasy, or MDMA (3,4-methylenedioxymethamphetamine). With respect to prevalence of recent use, this newcomer to the list of popular drugs reached peak values in the 2000–2002 interval, and there now may be a persisting downward trend in prevalence of MDMA use, concomitant with increases in the proportion of young people perceiving adverse effects and hazards of MDMA use, as happened with a number of other drugs in prior years (Johnston et al., 2003b).

The ecstasy epidemic among youth and young adults illustrates one very important feature of the larger epidemic of illegal drug use over the past three decades: that there has been a continuing march of new drugs onto the scene, each presenting youths with new alternatives. While American youth may have learned about the dangers of most of the existing alternatives on the menu, we may expect continuing innovations and "designer drugs," perhaps with claims that the new drug compounds have no adverse consequences. As an elaboration of the "failure-of-success" concept, we now appreciate that when one birth cohort of adolescents comes to appreciate the dangers of a drug, by learning about its consequences through the media, prevention programming, and personal and vicarious experience, and enters the lower-risk developmental period of adulthood, the more recently born cohorts of children enter adolescence without the history of accumulated knowledge and belief about the hazards connected with the drug. These adolescents are thus prone to reexperience and relearn these dangers on their own.

The ecstasy/MDMA example illustrates another important point of particular relevance to prevention. A careful examination of the trends over time of the various classes of illegal drugs will show that to a considerable degree, they each have unique cross-time profiles (Johnston et al., 2003a; SAMHSA, 2002a). The use of one drug may be rising at the same time that the use of another is falling and perhaps a third is holding steady. This means that the different drugs are responding to influences that are specific to them—very likely, factors such as the perceived benefits of using that drug as well as the perceived dangers of doing so. Although there may be some larger social forces, such as the Vietnam War, that change the overall proportions of youth willing to engage in illegal drug use generally, there are also many important drug-specific influences that must be taken into account. This means that drug education, communication, and persuasion efforts may be most valuable when they address each class of drug separately. The attitudes and beliefs related to drugs are so varied that in addition to pursuing goals common to all drugs, such as strengthening resistance to peer influence in favor of any illegal drug, there should be educational efforts specific to individual drugs (Johnston et al., 2003a; SAMHSA, 2002a).

Major Data Sources Documenting Adolescent Drug Experiences in the United States

There are several ongoing survey series available for assessing the size and nature of the American adolescent drug experience, based on scientifically selected national samples. Two are based on in-school surveys using self-completed paper-and-pencil questionnaires administered to students in group settings: the Center for Disease Control and Prevention's (CDC's) Youth Risk Behavior Study (YRBS), and the University of Michigan's Monitoring the Future (MTF) study, sponsored by the National Institute on Drug Abuse. The MTF was launched in 1975 and the YRBS in 1991.

In the YRBS, a nationally representative sample of some 13,000 to 14,000 students in grades 9 through 12, enrolled in about 150 public and private high schools, are surveyed by means of self-administered, optically scanned questionnaires (Grunbaum et al., 2002; Kann, 2002). Data are gathered biennially. Measurement is spread across a range of risk behaviors for adolescents, so little information is gathered on attitudes, beliefs, or social surroundings specifically related to drug use. This is a repeated cross-section design.

In the MTF, some 45,000 students in grades 8, 10, and 12, enrolled in public and private schools in the coterminous United States, are surveyed annually. Self-administered, optically scanned questionnaires are used in this study as well. Extensive information is gathered on attitudes, beliefs, and various social influences from the family, school, work, and mass-media environments. In addition, representative panels of

high school seniors are selected for follow-up each year and are then surveyed by mail for some years after high school graduation in this cohort-sequential study design.[1]

The third source of population survey data derives from national household surveys that include and report separately on youth 12 to 17 years old—the National Household Survey on Drug Use and Health (NHSDUH), known until very recently as the National Household Survey on Drug Abuse (NHSDA).[2] Data were gathered from adolescents for many years by personal interview in combination with private answer sheets on drug use, but very recently the methodology has shifted to computer-assisted interviewing. This series began in 1971 with a survey for the National Commission on Marijuana and Drug Abuse (1972). Over the years there have been a number of changes in measurement content, measurement methods, and sample sizes, all of which have made accurate trend estimation more of a challenge. In general, however, trends have been reasonably parallel to those generated by MTF and YRBS. The NHSDUH uses a repeated cross-section design, with surveys conducted at various intervals in the past, but on an annual basis in recent years.[3]

The National Comorbidity Survey (NCS; Kessler, 1994) represents a somewhat different approach to generating prevalence data on drug use, in that it measures the prevalence and correlates of DSM III-R disorders, as well as the connection of drug dependence and related disorders to the various other psychiatric disorders (Anthony, Warner, & Kessler, 1994). One key finding is that there is a significant level of such comorbidity among individuals with a drug de-

---

1. A full listing of publications from MTF may be found at www.monitoringthefuture.org

2. In the past, estimates that emanate from the National Household Surveys have been lower than those that derive from the school surveys, possibly because of greater concealment in the household setting or other sampling or measurement differences (e.g., see Harrison, 2001). Since MTF covers a considerably longer time period, more classes of drugs, and more information on related attitudes, beliefs, and environmental factors than the YRBS, it will be used as the source for most of the estimates presented here. The YRBS, begun in 1991, generates prevalence estimates that tend to be slightly higher than those from MTF, but shows trends that tend to be quite similar.

3. A listing of publications on the NHSDUH may be found at http://www.samhsa.gov/oas/nhsda.htm

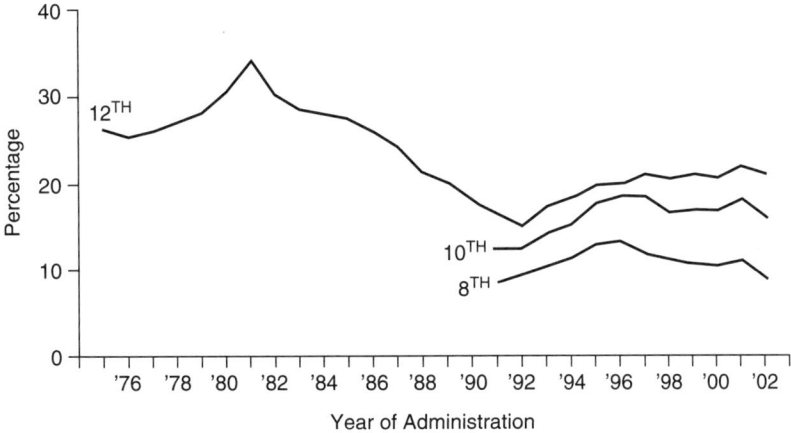

Figure 17.1 Trends in annual prevalence of any illicit drug other than marijuana in three populations.

pendence syndrome (see, for example, Kessler et al., 1996, 2001).[4] Unfortunately, the relatively small samples of adolescents in the first iteration in the NCS put limitations on the precision of estimates specific to adolescents. The NCS household sample included around 8,000 people from ages 15 to 54 in the noninstitutionalized population of the United States, and it was fielded between 1990 and 1992. Sequel surveys are now being carried out that will, among other things, provide trend estimates on many of the conditions measured in the first wave. In addition, and of particular relevance here, a supplementary sample of 10,000 adolescents is included in the current work to specifically examine the prevalence and correlates of drug dependence and other disorders among adolescents.

Still another, completely different, type of information is gathered nationwide from hospital emergency rooms and coroners' offices as part of the Drug Abuse Warning Network (DAWN; e.g., SAMHSA, 2002b), in which case counts are made of people treated for medical emergencies involving any of a range of drugs and of people who die with identifiable evidence of drug use present. Unlike the population surveys, which attempt to estimate prevalence and trends in drug use in major segments of the national pop-

4. A full list of publications from the National Comorbidity Study may be found at http://www.hcp.med.harvard.edu/ncs/publicationbyyear.htm

ulation, the DAWN system is intended to generate data on case counts of drug-related "casualties."

Prevalence and Trends in the Adolescent Use of Various Drugs

Prevalence rates of adolescent use of specific substances (heroin, cocaine, alcohol, and tobacco especially) are given in the discussion of those substances later in this chapter. Here we focus on the prevalence rates and trends of use across various substances.

The 2002 MTF survey shows that a quarter (25%) of today's young people have tried some illegal drug before finishing eighth grade—that is, by ages 13 or 14—and more than half (53%) have done so by the end of high school (Johnston et al., 2003b). If inhalants are included in the definition of illegal drugs, the numbers are even higher (32% and 55%, respectively). Prevalence rates for any illegal drug, marijuana, cigarettes, and binge drinking of alcohol observed among 8th-, 10th-, and 12th-grade students in these nationally representative surveys are given in Figures 17.1–17.4. (Grade 8 students are 13 or 14 years old for the most part, and grade 12 students are mostly 17 or 18 years old.) Trend data for the three grades illustrate a number of the points made above, including the dynamic na-

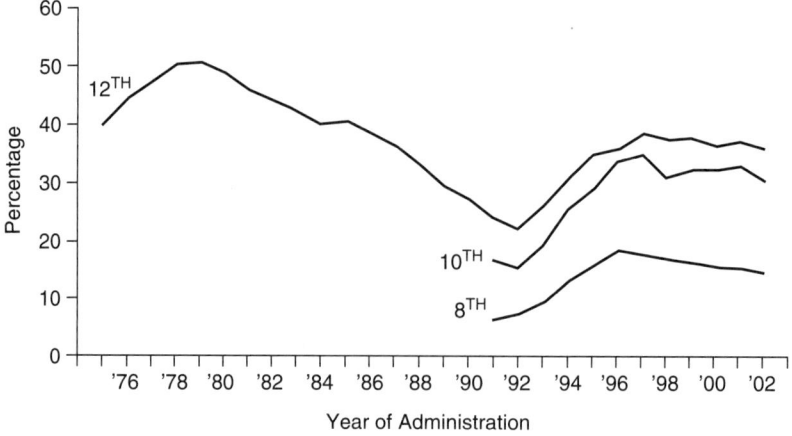

Figure 17.2 Trends in annual prevalence of marijuana in three populations.

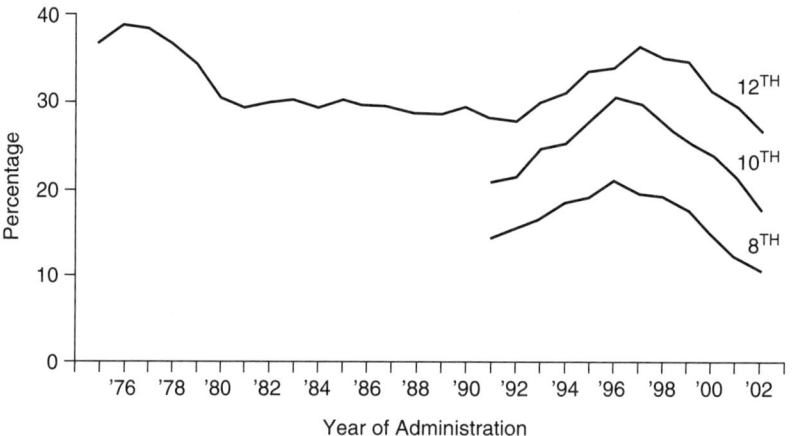

Figure 17.3 Trends in 30-day prevalence of cigarette smoking in three populations.

ture of this class of problem behaviors among youth, and that different drugs tend to vary independently of the others.[5]

By comparison, Tables 17.1 and 17.2 provide trends in the proportion of 8th-, 10th-, and 12th-grade students in MTF who reported receiving treatment for their use of alcohol and/or illegal drugs in recent years.[6] As would be expected, the values rise with age (and, therefore, with prevalence), but not as much as one might expect. Among 12th graders (the only ones asked about the distinction) the number receiving outpatient treatment or counseling exceeds the number receiving inpatient treatment by a ratio of 3:1 to 5:1 in recent years, but by larger ratios in earlier years. The lifetime prevalence of treatment also rose toward the end of the 1990s, no doubt reflecting the relapse in the epidemic of adolescent drug use from the early to mid-1990s.

Other important survey series that attempt to measure clinically defined cases of drug depen-

5. It should be noted that data based on school surveys, such as MTF or YRBS, of necessity omit the out-of-school segment of the youth population. How great an omission varies with age, of course. At 8th grade less dropping out has occurred; more has occurred before the end of 10th grade, although most states have compulsory attendance laws through the age of 16. By 12th grade, it is estimated from Census data that perhaps 15% of an age cohort has permanently dropped out. (See Johnston, et al., 2003b, Appendix A, for a more detailed discussion of this issue and for numerical estimates of the degree of underreporting likely to occur as a result of dropping out and absenteeism.)

6. Pairs of years have been combined to increase the reliability of the estimates.

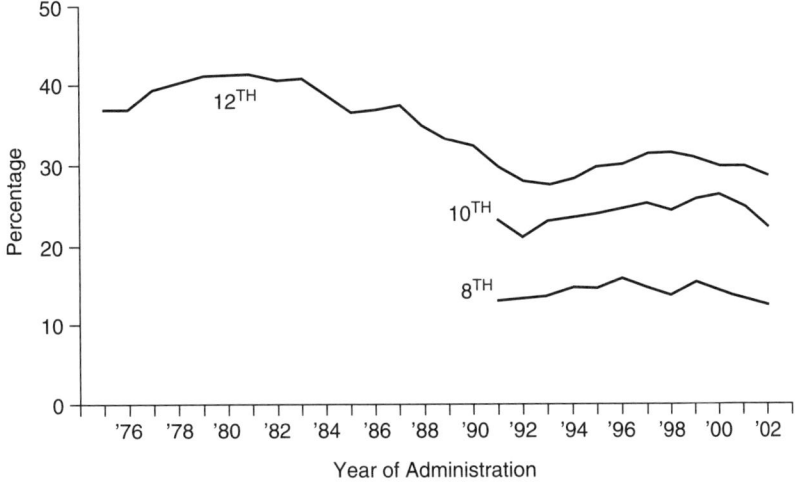

Figure 17.4 Trends in 2-week prevalence of binge drinking in three populations.

dence and related problems are the National Household Surveys mentioned above (e.g., SAMHSA, 2002a) and the National Comorbidity Study (Anthony, Warner, & Kessler, 1994; Kessler, 1994). However, as is explained above, it is still too soon to derive much from the NCS with specific regard to adolescents.

Subgroup Differences in Substance Use

Not all adolescent and young adult subgroups in society are at equal risk of being a recently active drug user (Johnston et al., 2002a; Wallace et al., 2003). During adolescence, at least, African-American youngsters have substantially lower prevalence of use of the full range of legal and illegal substances than their white, Hispanic, or Native American counterparts, although there seems to be some reversal of this difference in early and later adulthood (SAMHSA, 2002a). Native Americans tend to have the highest prevalence of use, and in early adolescence, Hispanic youth tend to have the next highest. Adolescent boys are somewhat more likely than girls to use most drugs, and quite a bit more likely to use them frequently. Van Etten, Anthony, and colleagues have pursued a line of research that traces the basic male–female difference in drug experience back to an earlier male excess in the experience of the first chance to try drugs; that

Table 17.1 How Many Have Ever Received Drug Treatment or Counseling?: Cumulative Proportion (%) Estimated for Each Year, 1988–2001

Grade	1988– 1989	1990– 1991	1992– 1993	1994– 1995	1996– 1997	1998– 1999	2000– 2001	Average
8			2.9	2.7	3.3	3.0	2.8	2.9
10			2.7	3.1	3.9	3.9	4.0	3.5
12 (total)	3.7	3.6	3.3	3.9	4.5	4.7	4.1	4.0
12 (residential)	1.2	1.1	1.1	1.5	1.4	1.2	1.1	1.2
12 (outpatient)	3.3	3.4	2.9	3.4	3.9	4.5	3.7	3.6

Source: Johnston, L. D., O'Malley, P. M., & Bachman, J. G. (2002a). *National survey results from the Monitoring the Future study, 1975–2001. Volume I: Secondary school students.* Bethesda, MD: National Institute on Drug Abuse.

Table 17.2 How Many Received Drug Treatment or Counseling Each Year?: Prevalence Proportion (%) Estimated for Each Year, 1988–2001

Grade	1988–1989	1990–1991	1992–1993	1994–1995	1996–1997	1998–1999	2000–2001	Average
8			1.4	1.2	1.5	1.4	1.4	1.4
10			1.3	1.5	1.9	2.0	1.9	1.7
12 (total)	1.6	1.6	1.6	1.9	2.3	2.2	1.9	1.9
12 (residential)	0.4	0.2	0.4	0.5	0.4	0.5	0.5	0.4
12 (outpatient)	1.6	1.5	1.4	1.8	2.1	2.1	1.7	1.7

Source: Johnston, L. D., O'Malley, P. M., & Bachman, J. G. (2002a). *National survey results from the Monitoring the Future study, 1975–2001. Volume I: Secondary school students.* Bethesda, MD: National Institute on Drug Abuse.

is, males have the chance to try illegal drugs earlier than girls and at any given age are more likely to have experienced a chance to try these drugs. However, once the first chance to try a drug is presented, girls are just as likely as boys to actually consume the drug (e.g., see Van Etten & Anthony, 2001; Van Etten, Neumarks, & Anthony, 1999). Contrary to popular opinion, rural areas now generally do not have lower prevalence of most types of drug use than more urban areas, and sometimes actually have higher rates, which speaks to how thoroughly the drug epidemic has diffused to all parts of American society. The finding that most forms of drug use do not vary much as a function of the educational level of the parents, a measure of socioeconomic status, also reflects this diffusion. The use of certain drugs does tend to concentrate in particular regions of the country—crystal methamphetamine use in the West, for example—but for the most part regional similarities are more noteworthy than the differences. Sometimes, when a new drug is coming onto the scene, such as crack in the 1980s and ecstasy in the late 1990s, there are larger geographic differences until the diffusion process takes place. Most of the demographic and family background subgroup differences mentioned above tend to enlarge during periods of greater use of a drug and to diminish during periods of contraction in use; but still they tend to remain consistent as to direction over long historical periods, with very few exceptions. Regional differences in cocaine use expanded dramatically in the early 1980s, at the height of the cocaine epidemic, with the West

and the Northeast United States attaining considerably higher prevalence of use than the South or the North Central. But during the contraction period that followed, beginning in 1997, the West and Northeast also showed the most dramatic declines (Johnston, et al., 2003b).

An International Comparison

The American drug epidemic of the 1960s and 1970s spread around the globe, as a mobile generation of young people traveled the world. Even so, illegal drug use generally did not penetrate so deeply into youth populations of other countries. A recent 30-country prevalence survey of illegal drug use among 15-year-olds (mostly in European countries) shows generally larger values for American adolescents than for any of the 30 other countries (Hibell et al., 2000). Despite the long-ago passing of forces giving special impetus to the American epidemic, and despite progress in prevention, we still are in the top rank.[7]

A caution is in order, however. When an epidemic has occurred, as happened with cocaine in the 1970s and early 1980s, it can give rise to a considerable population of continuing, dependent users. A result is that "casualty" counts of impaired users needing treatment can lag behind general trends in prevalence of use.

7. It should be noted that with regard to use of the legal drugs, alcohol and tobacco, the United States has enjoyed one of the lowest prevalence proportions of any of the countries compared, a fact of considerable consequence for the long-term health and longevity of this generation of youth.

CLINICAL ASPECTS OF SPECIFIC SUBSTANCE USE DISORDERS

Our understanding of adolescent addiction, in both pharmacological and behavioral realms, is somewhat limited, and research advances in this area have been thwarted by several considerations. First, the typical pharmacologic experiments involving controlled administration of drugs commonly done with adult research volunteers for the most part have not been possible with adolescents. Thus much of what is known about the pharmacology of drugs in adolescents must be inferred from experience with adults. The logistics, particularly ethical, regulatory, and related informed-consent issues, are such that much of the pharmacologic research on drugs that adolescents should not be using must necessarily take place with animal models or with adult volunteers. Of course, useful information can be learned from clinical experience and observations, but even our clinical experience has been limited by adolescent resistance to treatment, by social stigma, and by an inadequate addiction treatment infrastructure in the United States. Furthermore, anecdotal clinical information is much less reliable than that gleaned from controlled studies, as have been performed on adult substance abusers. Experience from clinical settings, such as emergency rooms and treatment clinics, provides information on the pharmacology of adverse drug consequences, but provides less information on the more typical pharmacologic effects of illicit drug use experienced by the majority of adolescent users who never appear for treatment of adverse consequences.

Another consideration when describing effects of drugs in adolescents is that it is traditional to present and discuss the pharmacology of each drug or drug class individually. However, adolescents who abuse drugs, particularly those of most concern who use drugs regularly, seldom take only one drug during an evening or day of drug use. All of the drugs reviewed here are typically used more in various combinations rather than individually. For example, when considering the pharmacology of cannabis, hardly anyone begins to use cannabis regularly before becoming experienced with alcohol and tobacco,

although recent data suggest this pattern may be changing. More often than not, after becoming a regular user, all of these three drugs (and often others) are used in close proximity or together. This is true to varying degrees for all the drugs attractive to some adolescents. The pharmacology and toxicity of drug combinations can be complex and different from the pharmacology of the drugs used individually.

Heroin and Other Opioid Dependence in Adolescence

Most adolescents view heroin to be extremely dangerous and few if any plan to become addicted to this agent. Yet heroin use has increased since 1992 among all age groups and the average age of first time use has declined (SAMHSA, 1997). Furthermore, heroin is now available to adolescents living in urban, suburban, and even rural settings, where alarming numbers of adolescents are seeking treatment for heroin addiction and presenting to emergency rooms with heroin-related problems. There has also been an uptrend among adolescents in the abuse of prescription pills with opioid agonist action (see Table 17.3) that are capable of producing the same clinical elements characteristic of heroin dependence. In past years heroin was primarily injected and the reluctance of adolescents to use needles probably provided a significant barrier to their first-time use. But the purity of heroin has increased significantly and the drug is now widely administered by the less efficient but more socially acceptable nasal route, making first-time use less onerous to adolescents who are

Table 17.3 Opioid Pain Relievers

Codeine (Phenergan, Robitussin)
Hydrocodone (Hycodan)
Hydromorphone (Dilaudid)
Meperidine (Demerol)
Methadone (Dolophine)
Morphine (Roxanol)
Oxycodone (Oxycontin, Percocet, Percodan)
Pentazocine (Talwin)
Propoxyphene (Darvocet, Darvon)

introduced to heroin by peers, acquaintances, and family members. In addition, a precipitous decline in the price of heroin has made the drug affordable to adolescents.

Data on adolescents from the National Household Surveys on Drug Use and Health (NHSDUH) reported that in the 12- to 17-years age range, there were 47,000 active heroin users in the United States (0.2% prevalence), of which 34,000 had recently begun using heroin (0.1% incidence) (SAMHSA, 2000). Chen and Anthony (under review) studied the clinical course of adolescent heroin users by analyzing NHSDUH data from calendar years 2000 and 2001 and found that approximately 22% of first-time users became addicted. In addition, clinical features reported by the adolescent heroin users (time spent seeking heroin and recovering from its effects, failed efforts to quit, dose escalation, continued use despite emotional and physical problems, reduction in nondrug activities) were generally much greater than corresponding estimates for stimulants, alcohol, marijuana, hallucinogens, sedative and hypnotics, and inhalants. There are approximately 1,262,000 adolescents using prescription pain relievers (5.4% prevalence), 722,000 recent-onset users (3.3% incidence), and a 9% likelihood of becoming addicted (SAMHSA, 2000).

The addictiveness of heroin stems largely from the intense euphoria associated with heroin intoxication. Heroin euphoria has been compared to sexual orgasm or described as "God's warmest blanket" by heroin users who often become obsessed with the drug. The rewarding effect of heroin and of all opioid agonists derives from their ability to activate endogenous opioid receptors that densely populate reward-related brain regions. Opioid receptors are normally activated by endogenous opioid peptides (i.e., β-endorphin, enkephalin, dynorphin) that play important roles in natural reward and satiety (Dackis & O'Brien, 2003b). An injection of heroin leads to a rush of euphoria that lasts several minutes and is followed by a persistent period of sedation and satiety, during which time the user typically nods and falls asleep. It is noteworthy that this tranquil response to heroin contrasts markedly with the stimulation, gregariousness, and intense craving that follows cocaine use.

Tolerance develops more rapidly to the rewarding effect of heroin than to its toxic effects, such as respiratory depression, which increases the risk of lethal overdose in users pursuing euphoria. In the presence of adequate supply, heroin users can progressively increase their daily dose by 100-fold. Street heroin varies widely in potency and unusually pure shipments are notorious for leaving a trail in the medical examiner's office. Although naloxone (an opioid receptor antagonist) rapidly reverses heroin overdose, timely medical treatment is often unavailable in adolescent overdose situations that can easily result in death. Heroin is often used in combination with other drugs of abuse: benzodiazepines, cocaine, alcohol, marijuana, and prescription opioids. It is common for intravenous users to inject heroin and cocaine simultaneously (termed "speedballing") to experience additive subjective effects of these agents.

Heroin addiction produces marked functional impairment in adolescents as they progressively lose control over the amount used and over behaviors directed toward heroin procurement. Reports indicate that the risk of developing specific clinical features of drug dependence is consistently greater for heroin than other drugs of abuse (SAMHSA, 2002a). School performance, family relations, and social functioning typically deteriorate significantly as heroin becomes the adolescent's first priority. Heroin-addicted adolescents often resort to illegal activities, including shoplifting, dealing, prostitution, and robbery, as a means of paying for their increasing heroin dose requirement. Consequently, they risk arrest, conviction, and incarceration, along with the stigma and disadvantages that are associated with a criminal record. Heroin users also risk physical trauma associated with the dangerous drug-seeking lifestyle. As their heroin addiction intensifies, adolescents are usually shielded from their impairment by denial, an essential feature of the addiction. Minimization, rationalization, intellectualization, and other aspects of denial must be addressed by treatment interventions that make adolescents aware of their loss of control.

Adolescents who experiment with heroin are often surprised by the rapid onset of heroin withdrawal. Heroin withdrawal symptoms usually emerge within days or weeks after the first use of heroin, typically emerging within 8 to 12 hr of abstinence and lasting for 3 to 5 days. Physiological, genetic, and psychological factors can significantly affect the duration and severity of heroin withdrawal. It is noteworthy that the signs and symptoms of heroin withdrawal are diametrically opposite those of heroin intoxication. This phenomenon results from the fact that compensatory brain responses to chronically administered heroin are unopposed during heroin abstinence, resulting in rebound withdrawal symptoms (O'Brien, 2001). Although the heroin withdrawal syndrome (see Table 17.4) is extremely unpleasant, it is not medically dangerous.

Heroin-addicted individuals experience panic and intense irritability during withdrawal, and their urgent drive for heroin often leads to risky drug-seeking behaviors. This tendency is compounded in adolescents who are characteristically impulsive. Generally, heroin users will actively avoid withdrawal symptoms by using heroin on a regular and daily basis. Consequently, the binge pattern of use that is charac-

teristic of cocaine dependence is seldom reported among heroin users. Heroin users routinely experience withdrawal symptoms when their supply of heroin or money is interrupted. Furthermore, severely addicted individuals must use heroin several times per day to avoid withdrawal, and are constantly oscillating between periods of heroin intoxication and withdrawal, creating a vicious cycle that positively (euphoria) and negatively (withdrawal/ craving) reinforces continued heroin use. When alcohol or other sedatives (benzodiazepines, barbiturates) are also abused, sedative withdrawal symptoms may complicate the symptoms of opioid withdrawal.

Cocaine and Other Stimulant Dependence in Adolescence

Cocaine is the most heavily abused nervous system stimulant in the United States and therefore the primary focus of this section. Other central stimulants (most notably methamphetamine, amphetamine, and dextroamphetamine) pro-

Table 17.4 Signs and Symptoms of Heroin Intoxication and Withdrawal

Heroin Intoxication	Heroin Withdrawal
Signs (Observed)	
Bradycardia	Tachycardia
Low blood pressure	Elevated blood pressure
Low body temperature	Fever, sweats
Sedation	Insomnia
Small (pinpoint) pupils	Enlarged pupils
Reduced movement	Pacing
Slurred speech	Piloerection ("gooseflesh")
Head nodding	Yawning, tearing, runny nose
Slow breathing	Increased breathing rate
Symptoms (Reported)	
Euphoria	Anxiety, depression
Reduced pain threshold	Bone and muscle pain
Calmness	Cramps, nausea, vomiting, diarrhea
Satiation	Craving for heroin
	Restlessness, irritability
	Reduced pain threshold

duce cocaine-like subjective effects that result from their similar neurotransmitter actions in reward-related brain circuits (Dackis & O'Brien, 2001). Methamphetamine is used predominantly in the western regions of the United States, and is particularly addicting when injected or smoked. Although many adolescents are able to experiment with stimulants without suffering long-term consequences, others are pulled into a tenacious cycle of addiction that all too often persists into adulthood. About 6% of the adolescents who try cocaine become addicted within 1 year, and most of the additional 10% who ultimately become addicted do so within 3 years (Wagner & Anthony, 2002a). The constitutional and environmental vulnerabilities that predispose individuals to cocaine addiction are not entirely understood, and it is very difficult to predict which adolescents will ultimately become afflicted. Considerable resources have been allocated to prevention, on the basis of the undeniable fact that cocaine addiction cannot occur if cocaine is never tried. Prevention initiatives include educational and advertising campaigns that convey the dangers of cocaine, school and community programs, and law enforcement efforts that target the key variable of cocaine supply. However, preventive measures (discussed in Chapter 19) are most likely to benefit cocaine-naive individuals and are of limited value to adolescents who are already in the grips of full-fledged cocaine addiction.

The historic use of cocaine has varied extensively, reaching epidemic levels when its addictiveness was unappreciated and receding when perceived risk was great. The chemical isolation of cocaine in 1860 produced a white powder that could be efficiently consumed by oral, intranasal, and intravenous routes. Cocaine became immensely popular in Europe and the United States in the 19th century, and was sold in wine or soda (a bottle of Coca-Cola originally contained 10 mg of cocaine) for its medicinal, antidepressant, and energy-enhancing qualities. Its availability and perceived harmlessness proved to be essential ingredients that quickly unleashed a cocaine epidemic in the late 19th century. Cocaine use declined precipitously after the risk of medical, psychiatric, and behavioral consequences became widely appreciated. Amphet-

amine was developed in the mid-20th century and widely abused until perceived risk became appreciated, partly in response to the "speed kills" prevention initiative. Its appearance illustrates both the latent human demand for stimulants and the potential danger posed by new compounds, including designer drugs that have similar actions on reward-related brain circuits. The reversibility of perceived risk was demonstrated by the reemergence of cocaine in the 1980s as a popular drug with a mythology of harmlessness.

In recent years, it is likely that the availability of inexpensive crack has actually increased cocaine access to adolescents. Crack can now be purchased for as little as $2 in many regions of the United States. Although there was a reduction in cocaine use among adolescents between 1985 and 1995, findings of the U.S. Substance Abuse and Mental Health Service Administration (SAMHSA) and the United Nations Office for Drug Control and Crime Prevention provide evidence that cocaine use in the United States and throughout the world actually increased during the late 1990s (Chen & Anthony, 2004). Data on American adolescents (ages 12–17) from the National Household Surveys on Drug Use and Health (SAMHSA, 2000) reported 397,000 active cocaine (including crack) users (1.7% prevalence) and 275,000 (1.2% incidence) recent-onset users. Stimulants other than cocaine were actively used by 561,000 (2.4% prevalence) adolescents, of which 322,000 (1.4% incidence) were recent-onset users. These data indicate that many adolescents continue to experiment with cocaine and other stimulants even though their risks are widely known.

Crack provides adolescents with a convenient and highly efficient means of administering cocaine that is particularly acceptable to adolescents who are already smoking tobacco or marijuana. Marketing inexpensive crack, whether by design or chance, has apparently provided the illegal drug industry with adolescent cocaine customers that number in the hundreds of thousands. In addition, smoking crack (a freebase form of cocaine that can be vaporized without loss of potency) has long been recognized to be more hazardous than snorting cocaine HCl (Hatsukami & Fischman, 1996). Crack is taken by the intrapulmonary route that delivers cocaine to the brain much more rapidly than snorting (6 to 8 sec vs. 3 to 5 min), resulting in more intense euphoria and a greater likelihood of addiction (Volkow, Fowler, & Wang, 1999). A recent epidemiological study concluded that smoking crack might double the likelihood of developing cocaine dependence (Chen & Anthony, 2004). To make matters worse, crack is often sold in dangerous urban areas where drug trafficking, crime, prostitution, and infectious diseases present convergent hazards for adolescents. The risk of suffering procurement-related medical hazards, including trauma, is especially high because adolescents who use drugs are more likely to engage in unprotected sex and illegal behavior (Jessor, 1991).

Although there are large numbers of adolescents who need effective treatment for cocaine dependence, specialized adolescent addiction treatment programs are scarce and difficult to access throughout the United States. This situation is incongruous with the clinical importance of arresting a progressive and reversible disorder at an early stage, thereby averting functional impairment, morbidity, and mortality. In fact, adolescence is the ideal age for recovery. Unfortunately, cocaine addiction often persists into adulthood with predictable medical, psychiatric, behavioral, and societal ramifications that probably exhaust more resources than would be expended by a serious attempt to establish an appropriate treatment infrastructure for our children.

The transition from cocaine use to addiction is influenced by the route of administration (Chen & Anthony, 2004), the environment (Dackis & O'Brien, 2001), and constitutional factors that affect the attractiveness and rewarding qualities of cocaine (Tsuang et al., 1999). Environmental and psychosocial factors strongly influence the likelihood of first-time use. In some communities, drug dealers are viewed as successful role models and are actually emulated by adolescents who have few educational or vocational alternatives. Disenfranchised adolescents might be particularly vulnerable to cocaine use as a means of gaining peer acceptance, and parents are well advised to be cognizant of peer group changes (DuRant, 1995). Family members, particularly older siblings, are often instrumental in providing adolescents with their first dose of cocaine or normalizing its use through example. Studies indicate that the vulnerability for cocaine dependence is enhanced when there is a family history of alcoholism or drug dependency. Epidemiological studies conclude that the vulnerability to develop cocaine dependence is partially inherited. Twin studies report significantly higher concordance rates for identical twins than for nonidentical twins (Cadoret, Troughton, O'Gorman, & Heywood, 1986; Tsuang et al., 1996; van den Bree, Johnson, Neale, & Pickens, 1998), although research into candidate genes that encode enzymes involved in cocaine metabolism and receptors that mediate cocaine effects has not identified reliable genetic vulnerability markers.

Clinical Aspects of Stimulant Dependence

The reinforcing effect of stimulants correlates directly with the rate by which these drugs enter the brain and block dopamine transporters (Volkow, Fowler, et al., 1999), which are membrane-based proteins that regulate the amount of dopamine available to stimulate postsynaptic receptors. Cocaine euphoria has also been associated to a lesser degree with glutamate, β-endorphin, GABA, norepinephrine, and serotonin neuronal systems (Dackis & O'Brien, 2003a). By activating brain pleasure centers, cocaine places adolescents at immediate risk of developing stimulant addiction (Dackis & O'Brien, 2001). In fact, the powerful biological basis of stimulant reward is illustrated by the fact that animals with unlimited access will consistently self-administer cocaine and amphetamine to the point of death.

Cocaine administration produces a rush of euphoria that lasts only a few minutes but far exceeds the normal range of human pleasure, explaining its remarkable ability to dominate thoughts, behaviors, and priorities of adolescents. Cocaine intoxication also produces racing thoughts, self-confidence, increased energy, heightened alertness, reduced appetite, and enhanced libido (see Table 17.5). The last effect may lead to promiscuity and unprotected sex, with the accompanying risk of pregnancy and

Table 17.5 Signs and Symptoms of Cocaine Intoxication and Withdrawal

Cocaine Intoxication	Cocaine Withdrawal
Signs (Observed)	
Elevated blood pressure and pulse	Slow pulse
Elevated body temperature, perspiration	Low body temperature
Alertness, vigilance	Somnolence
Pacing, sweats, enlarged pupils	Reduced movement
Symptoms (Reported)	
Euphoria, grandiosity	Depression, low self-esteem
Increased energy	Low energy
Reduced appetite	Increased appetite
Increased sex drive	Reduced sex drive, impotence
Racing thoughts	Poor concentration
Insomnia	Oversleeping

venereal disease. Interestingly, cocaine euphoria appears to last only as long as brain cocaine levels are rising, and declining levels (even when still very elevated) are associated with craving and cocaine-seeking behavior (O'Brien, 2001). Physical manifestations of cocaine intoxication, which may provide warning signs to parents or teachers, include dose-dependent tachycardia, dilated pupils, diaphoresis, excessive movement, pressured speech, elevated blood pressure, and increased body temperature. Cocaine-intoxicated adolescents are likely to be talkative and gregarious, although higher doses can precipitate irritability, aggressiveness, and psychosis (especially paranoia and hallucinations) with a host of behavioral risks.

Within minutes, cocaine euphoria gives way to depression, irritability, and cocaine-induced craving (Jaffe, Cascella, Kumor, & Sherer, 1989; O'Brien et al., 1992). Cocaine's ability to beget its own craving promotes a characteristic binge use pattern that typically exhausts the available supply of cocaine and cash. In fact, the unexplained disappearance of money may be the first indication that an adolescent is using cocaine. At the end of a cocaine binge, alcohol, sedatives, and even heroin might be used to reduce insomnia, paranoia, and irritability. The combination of alcohol and cocaine is particularly hazardous because of the formation of cocaethylene, a psychoactive substance with cocaine-like actions that has much more toxicity and lethality than

cocaine alone (McCance-Katz, Kosten, & Jatlow, 1998). Cocaine has a half-life of 50 min and the major route of metabolism involves the hydrolysis of both ester groups to form benzoylecgonine, which can be detected for 2 to 5 days after a cocaine binge.

At the end of a cocaine binge, cocaine withdrawal symptoms may develop. The cocaine withdrawal syndrome includes depression, overeating, low energy, somnolence, psychomotor retardation, bradycardia, and poor concentration (Weddington et al., 1990). Although most symptoms resolve within 1 to 3 days, cocaine withdrawal can affect the motivation and school performance of adolescents who binge frequently. Severe cocaine withdrawal is associated with poor clinical outcome and may result from cocaine-induced disruptions of brain reward centers that have been hypothesized to produce hedonic dysregulation (Dackis & O'Brien, 2002). Stimulant withdrawal can also be associated with profound depression and suicidality.

Cocaine craving can persist after weeks, months, and even years of abstinence, especially in response to environmental cues that have been associated with cocaine through conditioning. Cue-induced cocaine craving has been extensively studied in the laboratory and is associated with robust limbic activation in addicted individuals on the basis of positron emission tomography (PET) (Childress, Mozley, McElgin, Fitzgerald, Reivich, & O'Brien, 1999) and functional magnetic resonance index (fMRI) studies (Garavan et al., 2000). Since the same limbic regions can be activated by sexually explicit videos (Garavan et al., 2000), sexual arousal and cocaine craving appear to share common neuronal substrates. One might imagine how difficult it would be for adolescents, notoriously vulnerable to sexual drive, to resist a similar lure to use cocaine. In actively addicted individuals, cocaine craving alternates with cocaine euphoria to form a cycle of addiction that becomes increasingly tenacious and uncontrollable.

Whereas some individuals may use cocaine intermittently for years, others experience rapidly progressive impairment that involves family, educational, interpersonal, medical, psychiatric, and legal domains. These impairments, resulting from loss of control over drug intake, are typically minimized by denial. Denial may be particularly formidable in adolescents who notoriously view themselves as invincible. Poor school performance is common in adolescent cocaine users and may be an early warning sign of the problem. Legal and behavioral problems (especially theft) should also raise the question of cocaine use. Medical complications of cocaine include sudden death (usually as a result of cardiac arrest or hyperthermia), myocardial infarction, seizures, cardiac arrhythmias, aortic dissection, and hemorrhage. Many of the medical complications of cocaine result from its ability to constrict blood vessels and impede blood supply, potentially leading to stroke, renal failure, spontaneous abortion, and even bowel necrosis. Psychiatric problems include depression, especially during cocaine withdrawal, suicide, and panic anxiety. Paranoia is a classic complication of cocaine and amphetamine intoxication, and may be associated with hallucinations and violent behavior.

Central stimulants may produce tolerance or sensitization, depending on the response in question. During cocaine bingeing, tolerance often develops rapidly to the euphoric effect of cocaine. Cocaine also produces sensitization in animal models, as evidenced by an increase in cocaine-induced hyperactivity with repeated dosing. The relevance of sensitization in the clinical arena is unclear. It has been hypothesized that cocaine users become sensitized to cocaine-induced seizures and cocaine-induced psychosis. Sensitization may also be associated with cue-induced craving as both phenomena are persistent and involve similar perturbations in dopamine and glutamate neurotransmission (Dackis & O'Brien, 2002).

Marijuana Use and Abuse in Adolescence

Marijuana is the most commonly used illicit drug among adolescents in the United States (see Figs. 17.1 and 17.2 for comparison). It shares some attributes and possible health consequences with tobacco in that marijuana is a plant material, is most commonly smoked, and contains hundreds of compounds including at least 60 termed *cannabinoids* that are unique to the cannabis plant. The pharmacology of most of the cannabinoids is relatively unknown, but the most potent psychoactive agent, δ-9-tetrahydrocannabinol (THC), has been isolated, can be synthesized, and has been well researched in adults since the early 1970s. The noncannabinoid materials in the plant and its combustion products when smoked are similar to many of those from tobacco leaf smoking with, of course, the exception of nicotine.

In recent years the technology of growing and distributing illicit marijuana has become sophisticated and much improved. The THC content of plants from different sources and strains varies a great deal. Improved growing techniques, particularly plant breeding, have changed the THC content from a typical 10 mg in a marijuana cigarette in the 1960s to a 1 g marijuana cigarette that contains 150 to 200 mg. One consequence of the increased potency is that much of the human research done in the 1970s and 1980s with relatively low-potency smoked marijuana may be less relevant to the pharmacology of and consequences from marijuana now readily available to adolescents in most parts of the world. What is clear from past research is that the biological effects of THC are dependent on dose. The availability of potent marijuana has greatly increased so that far higher doses of THC are now available to adolescent marijuana users than was possible 10 or 20 years ago.

Although marijuana is typically smoked in the

form of cigarettes or from pipes, THC can also be easily extracted with ethanol and the THC extract or raw plant material can be added to baked goods or to sugar cubes or even an oral spray. Because THC and other cannabinoids are not water soluble, intravenous use leads to major toxic effects unless very special preparations and delivery systems are used.

The pharmacokinetics—that is, the manner in which cannabinoids are distributed and metabolized in the body—are more complex than that of most psychoactive drugs. As with the use of any smoked drug, the final absorbed dose is very much under the control of the individual and subject to learning processes similar to those involved in learning to smoke tobacco. Thus, beginning adolescent marijuana smokers may well underdose or overdose themselves until they learn how to smoke. That traditionally most marijuana smoking follows some prior experience with tobacco smoking probably facilitates the learning process. About half of the THC in a marijuana cigarette enters the lungs and most is absorbed rapidly, reaching the brain within seconds of a puff. After oral ingestion, absorption is much less, slower, and more variable. The onset of effects after an oral dose of THC can be delayed as long as an hour and absorption continues slowly. Thus either through chance or for other reasons, overdose with oral ingestion is more likely than after smoking.

THC and other cannabinoids move rapidly into fat and other body tissues during smoking but are only very slowly released from those tissue stores back into blood (and brain) over days, weeks, and months; they are gradually cleared from the body in urine and feces. Thus, the half-life of elimination of even a single, modest dose of THC from tissue stores is very slow, from 7 to 18 days with complete elimination of cannabinoids from one smoked dose taking up to 30 or more days. One consequence of this pattern of slow elimination from the body is that, with repeated doses, even doses taken only a few times weekly, cannabinoids gradually accumulate throughout the body, including the brain. Concentrations in brain areas vary but are highest in cortical, limbic, sensory, and motor areas of the brain. Cannabinoids are primarily metabolized in the liver into a host of metabolites, most of

which are not known to be biologically active. The metabolites are very slowly cleared from the body, thus making urine tests useful as an indicator of past marijuana use. Because of the very long presence of cannabinoids in the body, there is no relationship between plasma or urine concentrations of THC or metabolites and degree of intoxication once an hour or less has passed after smoking.

THC alters brain functions by binding to specific receptors widely distributed throughout the brain and elsewhere in the body. As the actions of naturally occurring ligands (hormones) that alter the state of these receptors have become better understood, it has become apparent that there is a complex system of multiple cannabinoid receptors interacting with a series of endogenous ligands. One of these ligands or hormones is called *anandamide*. The neuropharmacology of this cannabinoid receptor system is only beginning to be understood, but it appears to involve cannabinoids acting as neuromodulators of the large family of other neurotransmitters such as dopamine. Given the extensive distribution of cannabinoid receptors, it should not be surprising that virtually every system in the body is affected to some degree by marijuana. Marijuana appears to have sedative, analgesic, anxiolytic, hallucinogenic, appetite-suppressing, and appetite-enhancing properties and less well-characterized effects on the immune system. Firm conclusions about any medical treatment applications of marijuana are premature, but the discussions of marijuana use as a treatment makes it a more interesting drug to an adolescent.

Marijuana is used by adolescents to produce a mild, relatively short period of intoxication, often imprecisely characterized as euphoria. THC is an extremely potent psychoactive drug, so that less than a milligram smoked can produce relaxation, decreased anxiety, and feelings of less inhibition. The intoxication typically lasts a few hours. With higher doses, or with an inexperienced or sensitive individual, a single dose can produce severe anxiety, paranoid delusional thinking, and perceptual distortions that are not unlike those produced by hallucinogen drugs. Individuals with a genetic predisposition for developing schizophrenia, depression, or other mood disorder may be particularly vulnerable to such adverse effects resulting from marijuana doses well tolerated by others.

Cannabis-induced intoxication clearly impairs cognitive and psychomotor performance, with complex, demanding tasks being more affected and in a dose-dependent manner. The spectrum of behavioral effects is similar to those of other central nervous system (CNS) depressant drugs such as alcohol and are additive to effects produced by concurrently used depressant drugs. The magnitude of marijuana-produced perceptual and psychomotor alterations measurable in research settings is such that it is reasonable to assume that complex tasks such as driving or other tasks that have high demands on attention and information processing and reaction responses would be impaired. Of particular relevance when considering consequences of adolescent marijuana use is that in a laboratory setting, overlearned or well-practiced tasks are relatively less affected by marijuana. Thus, a beginning or relatively inexperienced driver may be more subject to marijuana-induced cognitive, motor, and perceptual impairments than an adult who has been driving for many years.

Although the evidence for cognitive impairment for some hours after a dose of marijuana is quite consistent and has been repeated in experiments in many laboratories over many years, there is less unanimity about the consequences of long-term chronic cannabis use. The consensus of recent studies is that individuals who have used cannabis over long periods of time have impaired performance on tests even when not acutely intoxicated. The cognitive functions that are impaired are attention, memory, and processing of complex information, and appear to last months, perhaps years, after cessation of use. Uncertainty remains as to whether some of the individuals had impaired performance before becoming involved with cannabis, but the data are quite consistent that the performance of heavy, frequent users is impaired when compared with shorter-term, less infrequent marijuana users.

Tolerance to many of cannabis's subjective and behavioral effects develops rapidly with relatively few exposures, not unlike the pattern of tolerance that develops to nicotine and cocaine effects when smoked. For many users, tolerance likely leads to more frequent or high-dose use to achieve the sought-after psychological effects. A cannabis withdrawal state has been clearly demonstrated in laboratory animals given marijuana or other cannabinoids over a relatively short period of time. Clinically significant cannabis withdrawal symptoms have been well described in both human laboratory studies and clinical settings. With abrupt discontinuation after only a few days of repeated administration of THC or marijuana in a laboratory setting, disturbed sleep, decreased appetite, restlessness, irritability, sweating, chills, nausea, and markedly disturbed sleep rapidly develop within hours of the last dose. Although most symptoms disappear in a day or two, irritability and sleep disturbance can persist for weeks. Frequent marijuana users in a clinical setting report similar symptoms when they stop marijuana smoking, along with a craving for marijuana, depressed mood, increased anger, wild dreams, and headaches. The pattern of withdrawal symptoms suggests to some investigators that it may contribute to continued use of marijuana in cannabis-dependent individuals. As with other addicting drugs, the precise links between withdrawal symptoms and continued or relapse to drug use is still a matter of some uncertainty.

As with nicotine dependence, it appears that early exposure to cannabinoids during adolescence may have more adverse consequences, including patterns of drug taking consistent with addiction. Individuals who began regular use of cannabis in adolescence appear to be at greater risk, relative to cannabis users who began regular use at an older age, in terms of greater use of other illicit drugs, depression, suicidal ideation and suicide attempts, and violent or property crimes. When adolescents were followed over time into adulthood, weekly cannabis use when an adolescent predicted an increased risk of dependence when a young adult.

The sometimes marked cardiovascular and autonomic system effects of cannabis appear to be well tolerated by adolescent users. However, when used heavily and over time, smoking marijuana is associated with pulmonary symptoms and problems. Pulmonary toxins are present in marijuana smoke as they are in tobacco smoke.

Recent estimates that in the future as many as 30,000 deaths a year may result in Britain from smoking cannabis reflect reasonable extrapolations from the toxic effects of marijuana to what is known about the adverse effects of tobacco smoking. Laboratory models of cannabinoid-induced alterations in immune system response are such that questions remain about the likelihood of clinically relevant immune system impairments from prolonged marijuana exposure.

Alcohol Use and Abuse in Adolescence

In this section we provide an overview of the phenomenology of alcohol drinking and alcohol use disorders (AUDs) in adolescents ages 11 to 19 years of age. Included in this overview is a current description of "drinking youths"; prevalence rates of adolescent drinking, binge drinking, AUDs, and drinking-related consequences; pertinent diagnostic issues; and potential etiological factors that may enhance our understanding of alcohol use and the development of problem drinking in adolescents.

Alcohol is a sedative and it is the only drug in this category to be discussed in this chapter. Other sedatives such as benzodiazepines, barbiturates, and other sleeping pills are used so uncommonly that they do not merit a full discussion. Notably, a discussion of alcohol leads to some overlap in content with discussions of other substance use disorders in adolescents, discussed elsewhere in this chapter. However, there are some important distinctions to bear in mind. Alcohol use by persons 21 years or older is legal in the United States, making it more readily available to adolescents and exposing them to seductive advertisements. In addition, low to moderate alcohol use is an integral part of our adult community life. It is available in many restaurants, sold in grocery stores in many states, and is available in liquor stores throughout the country. It is readily accepted in social settings, frequently accompanying a meal, and incorporated in many religious ceremonies. Over the past decade, the health benefits of one or two glasses of wine per day have been widely covered by the media. Finally, parents and other authorities frequently overlook adolescent drinking,

relegating it to experimentation or "rites of passage." In contrast, the illegality of many of the other abused substances (e.g., marijuana, cocaine, heroin) makes them taboo in most adult circles and causes much alarm and concern in adult communities when adolescent use of illegal substances is uncovered.

General Description of Adolescent Drinking

Drinking alcohol can be a highly pleasurable experience for many people, regardless of age. It is frequently described as relaxing, euphoric, anxiety reducing, and disinhibiting. Nonetheless, as alcohol is absorbed, metabolized, and eliminated from the body, it can also be associated with poor motor coordination, some confusion, irritability, depression, sleeplessness, nausea, and vomiting, among other ill effects. Ingesting excessive amounts of alcohol in a relatively brief period of time can cause extreme confusion, unconsciousness, and sometimes death.

Beer is the most commonly consumed alcoholic beverage among adolescents. The National Center on Addiction and Substance Abuse (CASA) at Columbia University estimated that nearly 20% of all alcoholic beverages purchased in 1999 was consumed by underage drinkers (CASA, 2003). For these underage drinkers (12 to 20 years of age), 76% of the expenditures was for beer, 19% for liquors (distilled spirits), and 4% for wine. These percentages are likely to change as alcohol manufacturers market new types of beverages that appeal to adolescents. The most recent arrivals are sweet-tasting, fruit-flavored, malt-based, colorful beverages, known as "alcopops" or "malternatives." These beverages are gaining in popularity, easily accessible, and preferred to beer and mixed drinks by adolescents (CASA, 2003). While adolescents will use elaborate means to obtain alcohol (e.g., having fake identification cards made; asking strangers to buy alcohol for them), they more commonly obtain alcohol from their own homes, their friends' homes, their parents, or from other adults (CASA, 2003; National Research Council and Institute of Medicine [NRCIM], 2003).

Adolescents report drinking for many of the same reasons that adults drink—that is, they expect positive effects from drinking. Younger adolescents report that drinking alcohol reduces tension and they like the mild impairment it causes to their cognitive and behavioral functioning. Older adolescents say they drink primarily because of the euphoria they experience and/or the altered social and emotional behaviors that occur when they drink. Oldest adolescents refer to the empowerment effects of alcohol. Adolescent males rate the pleasurable effects and sexual enhancement of alcohol more highly than females, who, in contrast, rate the tension-reduction effects more favorably (CASA, 2003; NRCIM, 2003).

Problem Drinking in Adolescents

The hallmarks of problem drinking are loss of control over drinking (i.e., drinking more than planned or in inappropriate settings) and the occurrence of negative consequences from drinking (driving under the influence [DUI], high-risk sexual behaviors, fights, medical problems). The development of addiction is associated with re-peated, heavy drinking over time, potentially as a continual attempt to recreate the pleasurable state associated with initiating drinking and intoxication. Repeated drinking can also lead to the development of physiological dependence, marked primarily by tolerance to alcohol, and withdrawal symptoms between drinking periods. *Tolerance* is defined as the need to drink progressively greater amounts of alcohol to yield the same pleasurable effects that can be experienced when drinking alcohol. Tolerance is one of the most commonly reported dependence symptoms in community samples and clinical samples of adolescents (Chung, Martin, Armstrong, & Labouvie, 2002; Martin & Winters, 1998).

Although less frequently reported among adolescents than among adults, heavy drinking can also lead to alcohol withdrawal symptoms between drinking periods (see Table 17.6). Severe withdrawal can be life threatening and may present as delirium tremens (DTs), which include symptoms of confusion, delirium, hallucinations, and psychosis (Dackis & O'Brien, 2003b).

Table 17.6 Signs and Symptoms of Alcohol Intoxication and Withdrawal

Alcohol Intoxication	Alcohol Withdrawal
Signs (Observed)	
Decreased heart rate	Increased heart rate
Lower blood pressure	Elevated blood pressure
Lower body temperature	Elevated body temperature
Sedation	Sweating
Decreased respiration	Tremors and muscle spasm
Loss of balance	Vomiting and diarrhea
Restlessness	Seizures
Slurred speech	Confusion
	Delirium
	Psychosis
Symptoms (Reported)	
Relaxation	Craving for alcohol
Sense of well-being	Anxiety
Euphoria	Irritability
Dizziness	Insomnia
Fatigue	Nausea
Nausea	Hallucinations
Blackouts	

Delirium tremens are more likely if patients are malnourished, dehydrated, or suffer from infection or electrolyte imbalance. A careful history is critical, because withdrawal can produce seizures, especially if they have occurred before.

The psychological, behavioral, and physical effects of alcohol are related to the blood alcohol level (BAL) of an individual, which is determined primarily by the quantity, frequency, and potency of alcohol consumed. The BAL (the ratio of milligrams of alcohol per 100 ml of blood) can be easily estimated by exhaling into instruments called breathalyzers, which are commonly available to treatment providers and law enforcement agencies. Impaired judgment and impaired coordination due to alcohol are legally determined by a BAL of 0.08% (i.e., as of May 2003, 39 states have this as their legal limit; for the latest statistics see http://www.nhtsa.dot.gov/people/Crash/crashstatistics/). Most European countries set the legal limit lower because discernable impairment from alcohol usually begins at about 0.05% or below. Adolescents may have higher BAL levels than adults because of their high-quantity, peer-influenced drinking patterns (Deas, Riggs, Langenbucher, Goldman, & Brown, 2000). Nonetheless, all states have zero-tolerance laws and allow no legal BAL for drivers under the age of 21.

Prevalence of Adolescent Use and Abuse of Alcohol

It is generally acknowledged that some use of alcohol is the norm among adolescents (Schulenberg & Maggs, 2002; Windle, 1999). According to national surveys, alcohol is the most widely used psychoactive substance in adolescents (excluding caffeine) (Grunbaum et al., 2002; Johnston et al., 2003b). The most recent Monitoring the Future (MTF) annual survey found that by senior year, nearly 80% of students reported some use of alcohol (Johnston et al., 2003b). In 1992, the CDC began conducting the Youth Risk Behavior Surveillance Survey (YRBSS) every 2 years, interviewing approximately 11,000 youths (ages 12 to 21) from a nationally representative sample. The results from their most recently available survey (2001) indicated that the percentage of high school students who had at

least one drink of alcohol ranged from 73.1% of 9th graders to 85.1% of 12th graders (Grunbaum et al., 2002). Data are also available from the National Survey of Parents and Youths, conducted by the Annenberg School for Communications at the University of Pennsylvania (Hornik, 2003). This survey included a nationally representative sample of 2,435 youths who were initially interviewed in 2000 and reinterviewed 18 months later. Use of any alcohol increased in a linear fashion from about 5% at age 11 to approximately 89% at age 18. Thus, the most recent national surveys indicate that by senior year, approximately 80% to 90% of high school students have had at least a drink of alcohol.

Binge drinking. One particular concern is the amount of binge drinking by adolescents. Wechsler and colleagues (Wechsler, Davenport, Dowdall, Moeykens, & Castillo, 1994) are generally credited with first using the term *binge drinking* in referring to excessive alcohol drinking by some adolescent and college-aged drinkers. Excessive or binge drinking has been defined in multiple ways (NRCIM, 2003), but the standard definition is drinking five or more drinks in a single episode (CASA, 2003; Wechsler, et al., 1994; Windle, 1999). This pattern of drinking in adolescents is associated with a broad range of problems, including date rape, vandalism, and academic failure (Baer, 1993). According to the YRBSS survey (Grunbaum et al., 2002), 25.5% of 9th graders, 28.2% of 10th graders, 32.2% of 11th graders, and 36.7% of 12th graders had had at least one binge-drinking episode in the past 30 days. The MTF survey (Johnston et al., 2003b) obtained information on binge drinking in the 2 weeks prior to the interview and found that 12.4% of 8th graders, 22.4% of 10th graders, and 28.6% of 12th graders had at least one binge-drinking episode. The MTF survey also asked respondents to report if they had been "drunk" in the past month, and found that 6.7% of 8th graders, 18.3% of 10th graders, and 30.3% of 12th graders responded affirmatively.

Perhaps some of the most innovative work to date has combined a developmental perspective in defining more homogeneous adolescent–young adult subgroups with respect to their amount of binge drinking. Schulenberg, O'Malley, Bachman, Wadsworth, and Johnston

(1996) identified six different patterns or trajectories of binge drinking on the basis of data from MTF. These trajectories accounted for 90% of the sample. The most common trajectories were "never" (36%) or "rarely" (17%) reported binge drinking; however, the other four trajectories were 12% decreased binge drinking over time, 10% increased binge drinking, 10% increased and then decreased, and 7% sustained chronic binge drinking over time.

Drinking-related consequences among adolescents. According to the National Institute on Alcohol Abuse and Alcoholism (NIAAA), "underage alcohol use is more likely to kill young people than all illegal drugs combined" (NIAAA, 2003). As in adult circles, excessive drinking and intoxication have serious consequences in the adolescent population. Most notable are automobile accidents. In 2001, 22.1% of high school seniors drove after drinking, and 32.8% rode with a driver who had been drinking (Grunbaum et al., 2002). Driving skills appear to be more readily impaired by alcohol in adolescent than adult drivers, and the alcohol-involved fatality rate is twice as high among adolescent than adult drivers (NIAAA, 2003).

Other harmful behaviors frequently related to excessive drinking among adolescents are high-risk sexual behaviors (unplanned with no protection); rapes, including date rape; assaults; homicides; and suicides (NIAAA, 2003; Windle, 1999). Having multiple sexual partners, failing to use condoms, and performing other high-risk sexual behaviors have been associated with alcohol use in adolescents (NIAAA, 2003). Furthermore, alcohol use by the offender, victim, or both has been linked to sexual assault, including date rape. Using the MTF data, Bachman and Peralta (2002) reported that heavy alcohol use increased the likelihood of violence for either gender, even after controlling for home environment, grades, and ethnicity. Alcohol generally is a disinhibiting intoxicant and it may also potentiate mood and stress states that lead to suicide attempts or other life-threatening behaviors. For example, heavy drinking has been correlated with suicide attempts in eighth-grade girls (Windle, Miller-Tutzauer, Domenico, 1992). Finally, alcohol is considered by some to be a "gateway" substance (along with nicotine) for illicit drugs

such as marijuana (Hornik, 2003; Wagner & Anthony, 2002b). That is, on the basis of a longitudinal study of a nationally representative sample (Hornik, 2003), researchers concluded "that marijuana is a behavior taken up after alcohol and tobacco use, and only if these behaviors are present as well" (p. 342). The gateway hypothesis is discussed further in Chapter 19 on prevention.

Alcohol use disorders in adolescents. The national surveys mentioned above are representative of the general population drinking patterns but do not specifically address the prevalence of AUDs in adolescents. Recently, Chung and colleagues (2002) reviewed the epidemiological literature on diagnosing AUDs in adolescents. Although this review summarized both community and clinical groups, the community groups are of specific relevance here. Five community samples were identified from studies in peer-reviewed journals whose sample sizes ranged from 220 to 4,023 adolescents, ages 12 to 19. Two of the studies were representative of the entire U.S. population and the other three were representative of individual states (North Carolina, Oregon, and Pennsylvania). In these surveys, the percentage of adolescents meeting criteria for alcohol abuse ranged from 0.4% to 9.6%, and for alcohol dependence, from 0.6% to 4.3%.

Issues in Determining Alcohol Use Disorders in Adolescence

Diagnostic criteria for alcohol abuse and dependence are detailed in the DSM-IV (American Psychiatric Association, 1994), and are identical to the criteria for all substance disorders in all populations. To meet a diagnosis of alcohol abuse, one of four abuse criteria must be met:

1. Recurrent use causing serious consequences
2. Being physically dangerous
3. Use causing legal problems
4. Use resulting in persistent social or interpersonal problems

To meet a diagnosis of alcohol dependence (alcoholism), three of seven dependence criteria must be met:

1. Withdrawal
2. Tolerance
3. Larger amounts consumed than intended
4. Unsuccessful attempts to stop
5. Excessive time spent drinking
6. Important activities given up
7. Continued use despite awareness of negative effects of drinking

While the number and type of symptoms needed to determine a diagnosis appear to be valid for adults (e.g., Schuckit et al., 2001), investigators have questioned the validity of the DSM-IV diagnostic criteria for identifying AUDs in adolescent populations (Winters, 2001). This skepticism is not surprising given that six of the seven research sites from the DSM-IV field trials did not contribute data on adolescents (Cottler et al., 1995). In addition, symptoms such as "risky sexual behaviors" are not explicitly assessed in the currently accepted list of symptoms used to determine a diagnosis of alcohol abuse or dependence.

Pollack and Martin (1999) studied 372 adolescent regular drinkers. More than 10% of this sample reported symptoms of alcohol dependence but not enough to have a diagnosis, and they also did not have symptoms of alcohol abuse (termed "diagnostic orphans"). However, these individuals had drinking-related problems similar to those of adolescents who did meet diagnostic criteria for an AUD, and they had significantly more drinking-related problems than did adolescents with no symptoms of alcohol abuse or dependence. In the review by Chung and colleagues (2002), "diagnostic orphans" represented from 1.9% to 16.7% of adolescent community samples and from 7.5% to 33.7% of adolescent clinical samples. Clearly additional conceptual and empirical research is needed to adequately diagnose AUDs in adolescents.

Finally, the two physiological symptoms (withdrawal and tolerance), that are part of the diagnostic DSM-IV criteria for determining if an individual has an AUD may have limited utility in diagnosing AUDs in adolescents (Martin, Kaczynski, Maisto, Bukstein, & Moss, 1995). Withdrawal symptoms are infrequently reported by adolescents (Chung et al., 2002), even in clinical samples, presumably because these symptoms

take years to develop. Tolerance, by contrast, seems to develop quickly in most adolescents, but does not readily distinguish problem from normative drinkers in the adolescent population.

Etiology: Risk and Protective Factors

The greater number of risk factors an adolescent has for developing an AUD, the more likely he or she is to abuse or to be dependent on alcohol (Jaffe & Simkin, 2002; Newcomb, 1997). However, sometimes there are protective factors that counteract risk factors. For example, a strong religious commitment, dedication to constructive activities such as sports, intense anti-alcohol beliefs, and high self-esteem all can serve to neutralize inherent risk factors for developing an AUD (Liepman, Calles, Kizilbash, Nazeer, & Sheikh, 2002).

The relevance of some of the risk factors varies with the age, gender, and ethnicity of the adolescent. In addition, other factors have been identified that influence the risk for AUDs as well as other substance use disorders. Newcomb (1997) classified these risk factors into four generic domains: cultural/societal, interpersonal, psychobehavioral, and biogenetic. The first three factors are summarized here. Discussion of genetic factors is given at the end of this chapter.

Cultural and societal factors.   While many factors contribute to the availability and acceptability of alcohol in a community (cultural, economic, legal, etc.), probably the single, most influential factor that relates to alcohol consumption in adolescents is the attitude of the adult community in the particular geographic location (see review by Newcomb, 1997). For example, the purchase of alcohol by underage drinkers is prohibited in all 50 states. However, in some places, the laws are not regularly enforced by police officers, and the liquor stores and bars do not consistently require identification from minors (Windle, 1999). Underage drinking at family gatherings or special celebrations may be acceptable to parents and relatives in some communities. An in-depth examination of the relationship between community attitudes and alcohol availability (economic and legal) is of paramount importance but beyond the scope of this book.

Interpersonal factors. Interpersonal factors that relate to AUD risk are parental (referring to other than heredity), sibling, and peer influences. Despite waning parental influence with the passage of time, parents' level of nurturing, monitoring, communication, and their own alcohol use affects the amounts and patterns of alcohol drinking in their adolescents (see reviews by Gilvarry, 2000; Liepman et al., 2002; Schulenberg & Maggs, 2002; Windle, 1999). That is, although adolescents may reject many of their parents' ideas and behaviors, the majority do not seem to reject their parents' drinking behaviors. Higher levels of maternal and paternal alcohol consumption are related to higher levels of alcohol use among adolescents (e.g., Kilpatrick et al., 2000; Webb & Baer, 1995). However, parents can have a positive influence on their adolescents. Higher levels of emotional support and warmth (nurturance), higher levels of appropriate monitoring and limit setting, more time spent together, and higher levels of parent–adolescent communication have been associated with lower levels of adolescent alcohol-related problems (Windle, 1999).

Siblings represent another familial influence. Older siblings typically serve as role models and there is a greater likelihood that younger siblings will drink alcohol before they are adults if their older siblings drink. This relationship is stronger if the older sibling is closer in age and the same gender (Windle, 1999).

The commonly held notion that peers exert considerable influence on the initiation and maintenance of alcohol use is sustained empirically (Schulenberg & Maggs, 2002). But there is little support for overt peer pressure causing the initiation of alcohol use. Rather, most studies support a more complex, developmental interactional process in which an adolescent selects and unselects peer groups. The individual is influenced by the course of behaviors and attitudes of these groups and in turn influences them (Schulenberg & Maggs, 2002). However, overt peer pressure can play a role in relapse (Brown, 1993).

Psychobehavioral influences. Newcomb (1997) cites age of onset and comorbid psychopathology as primary psychobehavioral influences in alcohol use. An earlier age of first use of alcohol is frequently associated with increased alcohol-related problems then and later in life. But it is not clear whether excessive drinking in early adolescence is a marker of serious preexisting or coexisting psychopathological factors (e.g., fractured gene pool, flawed personality, poor parental modeling, nurturing, monitoring, etc.), or, alternatively, whether excessive alcohol drinking in adolescence introduces a "toxin" that negatively impacts a person who is still experiencing a critical period of growth toward adulthood.

Recently, Ellickson, Tucker, and Klein (2003) published a 10-year prospective study in which students recruited from 30 Oregon and California schools were assessed at grades 7 and 12, and then later at age 23 ($N = 6,338$, $4,265$, and $3,369$, respectively). Young drinkers in both middle school and high school, compared to nondrinkers, were more likely to report academic problems, delinquent behaviors, and other substance use. At age 23, compared to nondrinkers, those who had been adolescent drinkers were more likely to report employment problems, continued "other" substance abuse, and criminal and violent behaviors.

These findings were supported by several retrospective reports as well. According to adults interviewed as part of the National Longitudinal Alcohol Epidemiological Survey, Grant and Dawson (1997) found that over 40% of adults who had reported using alcohol before age 14 had developed alcohol dependence later in their lives. This compared to a rate of less than 10% of alcohol-dependent adults who said they did not start drinking alcohol until after the age of 18. Also, DeWit, Adlaf, Offord, & Ogborne (2000) examined a larger health survey of adult reports. Of 5,856 drinkers, 501 had a DSM-IV diagnosis of lifetime alcohol abuse, and 473 had a DSM-IV diagnosis of lifetime alcohol dependence. Approximately 13.6% of the respondents who said they had their first drink between 11 and 14 years of age met diagnostic criteria for alcohol abuse 10 years later. This compares to only 2% of alcohol abusers who said they had had their first drink after the age of 18. These rates were parallel in adults diagnosable with alcohol dependence. That is, 15.9% of the respondents who said they had their first drink between 11 and 12 years of age reported alcohol dependence 10 years later. In comparison, those who said they had their first drink after age 18 represented only 1% of the respondents.

Comorbidity. Comorbid psychiatric disorders frequently co-occur with AUDs (Deas & Thomas, 2002; Gilvarry, 2000), but it is often difficult to distinguish etiological from consequential associations. For example, it is easy to imagine that a psychiatric disorder can result from continual, excessive alcohol consumption, especially in a physiological and psychological developmental period such as adolescence. In this example, the AUD would precede the comorbid disorder. Another scenario, however, is drinking alcohol to treat the symptoms of a psychiatric disorder; this is called "self-medication." For example, an individual with a social phobia may desire the relaxing and disinhibitory effects of a few drinks prior to attending a social gathering. In this case, if an AUD is identified, it is likely that the comorbid disorder preceded the AUD. Finally, both AUD and a psychiatric disorder may have the same etiology (e.g., genetic, neurochemical). Naturally, an understanding of the etiology of both concomitant disorders can guide treatment decisions.

Behavioral disorders, mood disorders, and anxiety disorders have been frequently associated with AUDs (Deas & Thomas, 2002; Gilvarry, 2000). Attention deficit-hyperactivity disorder (ADHD) has been associated with AUDs, but its independence from conduct disorder (CD) has not been well established (Gilvarry, 2000). In a 4-year longitudinal study of ADHD children and controls (6 to 15 years old), there was no difference in the prevalence of AUDs between youths with and without ADHD (Biederman et al., 1997). Conduct disorder proved to be a significant predictor of AUDs in the target and control groups. In another study, Moss and Lynch (2001) used structural modeling to illustrate an association between ADHD and AUD for adolescent males but not females, yet CD symptoms had the strongest association with AUD in adolescents.

As implied above, there is strong empirical evidence relating CD and similar disorders (e.g., oppositional defiant disorders [ODD]) with AUDs (Clark, Vanyukov, & Cornelius, 2002). Clark, Bukstein, and Cornelius (2002) provide convincing evidence that childhood antisocial behaviors precede and predict adolescent AUDs. They argue that the association between the behavior disorders and AUDs is best understood as manifestations of common underlying causes. These include poor behavioral regulation (possibly related to prefrontal cortex abnormalities), common genetic pathways (for instance, genetic variations influencing the dopamine system), and similar environmental factors (for instance, low levels of parental monitoring). Early identification and intervention efforts for these individuals with childhood antisocial behaviors may ameliorate later AUDs.

In adults, a person with alcohol dependence is nearly four times more likely to have major depression than a person without alcohol dependence (Petrakis, Gonzalez, Rosenheck, & Krystal, 2002). Gilvarry (2000) reported that up to one third of adolescents in addiction treatment facilities are diagnosed with mood disorders, especially major depression and dysthymia. Deas-Nesmith, Campbell, and Brady (1998) reported that 73% of inpatient adolescents who used substances met diagnostic criteria for depression. Furthermore, in 80% of those cases, the depressive symptoms predated the substance use, suggesting that the mood disorder for these adolescents was an important risk factor for developing a subsequent AUD. In the Biederman et al. (1997) study, bipolar disorder predicted substance use disorders, independent of ADHD. Although not all studies have found that mood disorders predate substance use disorders (e.g., Rohde, Lewinsohn, & Seeley, 1996), these observations suggest that mood disorders may be a risk factor for developing an AUD in some adolescents.

Anxiety disorders, especially social phobia and posttraumatic stress disorder (PTSD), may also be risk factors for AUDs. Rohde and colleagues (1996) reported that alcohol use among female high school students was associated with anxiety disorders that preceded the alcohol problems. Deas-Nesmith, Brady, and Campbell (1998) found that 60% of adolescents seeking treatment for addiction met diagnostic criteria for a social anxiety disorder. Furthermore, the anxiety symptoms generally predated substance dependence by about 2 years.

Posttraumatic stress disorder has also been implicated as a risk factor for AUDs. Kilpatrick and colleagues (2000) explored PTSD as a risk factor for substance use problems in adolescents. These investigators found that physical or sexual abuse, assault, or the witnessing of violence (e.g., murder, sexual assault) increased the risk of abuse of several illicit drugs, including alcohol. In another study, Clark et al. (1997) found that adolescents with an AUD were more likely to have a history of physical and sexual abuse compared to an adolescent control group. Furthermore, the association of PTSD and alcohol dependence was stronger in females than in males.

Special Case of College Drinking

Thus far, this chapter has focused on alcohol drinking and disorders observed in adolescent youth, with most of this population attending middle school and high school. However, there are significant numbers of adolescents in the age group who have just graduated from high school and may be attending college (average college age ranges from approximately 18 to 24 years). It should be noted that drinking on college campuses has its own culture, with easy access to alcohol. This clearly distinguishes it from our traditional view of adolescent drinking patterns, prevalence, and disorder development. In addition, access to alcohol on most college campuses, from both attitudinal and economic perspectives, is unparalleled in any other large, established adult community, and has been associated with a high frequency of serious and sometimes life-threatening drinking-related negative behaviors. While it is not within the scope of this chapter to detail the phenomenology of college campus drinking, we briefly mention the nature of the problem here and the need for further research.

Basically, the prevalence of drinking and heavy drinking among college students is higher than that of their peers who do not attend college (U.S. Department of Health and Human Services [DHHS], 2002). This difference is due to many factors, including specific ones such as the influence of sororities and fraternities, greater

amounts of unstructured time, easy access to those who can obtain alcohol legally, differential economic issues (parents or scholarships typically provide some financial support), and special advertising of alcoholic beverages targeted to the college population. College surveys reveal that approximately 40% of college students report heavy drinking in the 2 weeks prior to the survey. Consumption is heavier among males, highest among Caucasian students, and highest among the Northeast and North Central regions of the country (DHHS, 2002).

Hingson, Heeren, Zakocs, Kopstein, and Wechsler (2002) recently reported on the serious consequences of college drinking in the United States. On an annual basis, alcohol consumption is associated with 1,400 deaths, 500,000 unintentional injuries, 600,000 assaults, and 70,000 sexual assaults of college students. Approximately 2.1 million college students drive while intoxicated each year, 400,000 report having unprotected sex while drinking, and over 150,000 develop health-related problems due to their drinking (Hingson et al., 2002). In an effort to address the serious problems of college drinking, the NIAAA (2003) recently released a program announcement "to provide a rapid funding mechanism for timely research on interventions to prevent or reduce alcohol-related problems among college students" (see http://grants1.nih .gov/grants/guide/pa-files/PAR-03-133.html).

Tobacco Use in Adolescence

Adolescent tobacco use is widely recognized as a major public health problem (Windle & Windler, 1999). According to recent data, 64% of adolescents reported ever having smoked cigarettes, 28% reported having smoked on at least 1 day in the past month, and 14% reported having smoked on at least 20 of the last 30 days (CDC, 2002b). Among high school seniors who indicated that they currently smoked, 29% reported symptoms that met the DSM-III-R criteria for nicotine dependence (Stanton, 1995). Moreover, over one half of adolescents indicated that they experience withdrawal symptoms following a quit attempt and 70% regret ever having started smoking (CDC, 1998; Colby, Tiffany, Shiffman,

& Niaura, 2000a). Thus, early patterns of tobacco use among adolescents may develop into lifelong nicotine addiction.

Nicotine and Nicotine Dependence

Nicotine, a potent alkaloid in tobacco leaves, is what sustains tobacco smoking, which efficiently delivers nicotine to the brain (Benowitz, 1990). Nicotine, steam distilled from burning tobacco plant material in a cigarette, is inhaled into the lungs on small tar droplets and absorbed rapidly into arterial blood, reaching the brain within 20 sec after each puff. Nicotine has similarities to the neurotransmitter acetylcholine, binding to a complex family of nicotine cholinergic receptors distributed throughout the brain and elsewhere in the body. During cigarette smoking, with each puff, nicotine levels in brain tissues briefly rise and then decline rapidly, more because of the rapid distribution into tissues than of being broken down by metabolism. Each puff acts like an individual dose of drug.

Blood and brain nicotine levels peak immediately after each cigarette, but gradually nicotine accumulates during 6 to 10 hr of repeated smoking because of nicotine's 2-hr half-life. During sleep, nicotine levels fall, but upon awakening, when the first cigarette of the day is smoked, levels begin to rise. Thus, someone smoking 10 cigarettes a day exposes their brain to nicotine 24 hr a day but along with rewarding perturbations in brain levels of nicotine after each of the 100 puffs. Each cigarette in effect delivers about 10 separate doses of nicotine to the brain. With marijuana or cocaine smoking, a similar pattern of drug delivery is involved.

Adolescent smokers quickly learn to regulate, on a puff-by-puff basis, their smoked nicotine dose by maintaining a brain concentration of the drug that just avoids nicotine toxicity but satisfies the increasing need for nicotine as dependence develops. Tobacco smoking is initially aversive for almost everyone. It is unlikely that a young person would begin tobacco or other drug smoking without the support and teaching from peers, the observations of admired or envied adult smokers, and the reinforcement associated with the tobacco industry's multibillion-dollar advertising that promotes the rewards of cigarette smoking.

Nicotine delivered by cigarettes offers a beginning smoker individualized and personal control of psychoactive drug dose unobtainable by any other drug delivery system. Rapid onset of nicotine toxicity, particularly the early symptoms of nausea, weakness, and sweating, gives rapid feedback that the absorbed dose is higher than optimal, exceeding the acquired tolerance level. After repeated exposure to smoking, the difficulty in concentrating and other symptoms of nicotine withdrawal that develop when brain levels are falling offer another set of cues that it is time for a cigarette to be smoked.

If nicotine toxicity is avoided, adult tobacco smokers report enhanced concentration and improved mood. Attention to task performance improves, as does reaction time and problem solving. Adult smokers report enhanced pleasure and reduced anger, tension, depression, and stress after a cigarette. Whether performance and enhanced mood after smoking are due to relief of abstinence symptoms rather than intrinsic effects of nicotine remains unclear. However, enhanced performance of nonsmokers after nicotine suggests some direct nicotine enhancement. Reports from adolescent tobacco users parallel those of adults, which suggests that nicotine has these same pharmacologic effects in an adolescent smoker (Corrigall, Zack, Eissenberg, Belsito, & Scher, 2001).

Nicotine, by its effects on nicotinic cholinergic receptors in the brain, enhances or modulates release of many neurotransmitters—dopamine, norepinephrine, acetylcholine, serotonin, vasopressin, β-endorphin, glutamate, GABA, and others (Tobacco Advisory Group Royal College of Physicians, 2000). Thus changes in brain neurochemistry after nicotine exposure are profound. Neurotransmitter release is assumed to mediate nicotine's positive effects on arousal, relaxation, cognitive enhancement, relief of stress, and depression. The mesolimbic dopamine system is important in mediating the pleasurable and other rewards of nicotine, as with other drugs of abuse, and is important for understanding the withdrawal phenomena as well.

When brain nicotine levels decrease, diminished neurotransmitter release contributes to a relative deficiency state. The resulting symptoms of withdrawal—craving, lethargy, irritability, anger, restlessness, inability to concentrate, anxiety, depressed mood, and other symptoms that characterize a nicotine withdrawal syndrome—develop rapidly (DiFranza et al., 2002). Regular adolescent smokers report withdrawal symptoms similar to those reported by adults. Whether the withdrawal symptoms experienced by an adolescent nicotine addict are more or less intense after comparable levels of nicotine exposure is not established.

Young smokers who are still experimenting are likely to become regular smokers surprisingly rapidly. The precise numbers that go on to regular smoking and factors that influence progression from experimentation to regular smoking for any single individual remain uncertain. Measurable symptoms of nicotine dependence occur within weeks of the beginning of occasional nicotine use, probably well before daily smoking has been established. One third to one half of adolescents who experiment with more than a few cigarettes become regular smokers (Colby, Tiffany, Shiffman, & Niaura, 2000).

Nicotine dependence is associated with tolerance, cravings for tobacco, desire to use tobacco, withdrawal symptoms when nicotine dose is decreased or unavailable, and loss of control over frequency and duration of use. The criteria common to all drugs are used to diagnose dependence as defined in the DSM-IV (American Psychiatric Association, 1994).

Although traditionally it has been assumed that a period of sustained, daily use is required to produce dependence, in recent years clinical observations of adolescent smokers and data from animal laboratory experiments suggest that dependence develops rapidly in adolescent smokers and in adolescent laboratory animals (Abreu-Villaca et al., 2003; DiFranza et al., 2000; Slotkin, 2002). Some adolescent smokers demonstrate evidence of nicotine dependence well before becoming daily smokers and possibly after only a few days of intermittent tobacco smoking (DiFranza et al., 2000; O'Loughlin, Tarasuk, DiFranza, & Paradis, 2002).

This pattern is consistent with a variety of evidence from animal research showing that an adolescent brain is more susceptible to rapid development of nicotine dependence (Abreu-Villaca et al., 2003). Animal researchers have focused on possible brain mechanisms that account for the special susceptibility of adolescent brains (Slotkin, 2002). For example, nicotine exposure in adolescent rats results in greater and more persistent nicotine receptor up-regulation and cholinergic activity than in adult animals. The rapidity of change in the animal models is consistent with adolescent smokers who develop evidence of nicotine dependence after only a few days' experience with just a few cigarettes (DiFranza et al., 2000, 2002). Brief nicotine exposure results in alterations in cholinergic receptor activity lasting at least 1 month after exposure in rats, which suggests that brief exposure to nicotine changes cholinergic tone in a persistent manner. The level of exposure in the animal models was thought to be in the range experienced by adolescents occasionally smoking three to five cigarettes a day. The data suggest the possibility that brain mechanisms that account for nicotine dependence can be activated by nicotine exposure from only occasional smoking. Although nicotine has a variety of systemic effects in a smoker, particularly cardiovascular and neuroendocrine changes, some animal researchers believe they have found evidence of a primary neurotoxicity as well (Slotkin, 2002) with lasting cell injury, particularly cholinergic system cells. There is no evidence of cholinergic toxicity in human studies. In summary, animal experiments with nicotine suggest rapid and persistent changes in nicotinic receptor and cholinergic function in adolescent rat brains with doses perhaps as little as one tenth of those ingested by regular tobacco smokers.

Determinants of Smoking

Nicotine is essential to maintain tobacco smoking, but the beginning of tobacco addiction, as with other addictions, is influenced mostly by nonpharmacologic, learned, or conditioned factors. Peer influence, social setting, personality, and genetics determine who begins and who continues to smoke. In order to develop and implement more effective prevention and treatment programs for adolescent tobacco use, a greater understanding of the determinants of these behaviors is needed. The following summarizes a few of these determinants.

Socioenvironmental factors. Socioenvironmental factors can have an important influence on youth tobacco use. For example, smoking among peers is a powerful determinant of smoking initiation and progression (Choi, Pierce, Gilpin, Farkas, & Berry, 1997; Conrad, Flay, & Hill, 1992). Tobacco industry promotional activities can also have a significant impact on adolescent smoking behavior (Choi, Gilpin, Farkas, & Berry, Pierce, 1998). Of particular relevance to prevention strategies are socioenvironmental factors that protect against youth smoking. For example, adolescents who are involved in interscholastic sports and non-school-related physical activity are less likely to be established smokers (Escobedo, Marcus, Holtzman, & Giovino, 1993; Patton et al., 1998; Thorlindsson & Vihjalmsson, 1991). Religious affiliation appears to be protective against smoking (Heath, Madden et al., 1999), as are school and home smoking restrictions (Farkas, Gilpin, White, & Pierce, 2000; Wakefield et al., 2000).

Psychological factors. Relatively less attention has been devoted to the role of psychological factors in youth smoking. Available data suggest that tobacco use and nicotine dependence are more common among adolescents who experience depression symptoms (Escobedo, Kirch, & Anda, 1996; Wang et al., 1999), particularly those with more serious psychiatric conditions (Breslau, 1995). Adolescents with ADHD are at greater risk for tobacco use (Milberger, Biederman, Faraone, Chen, & Jones, 1997). And weight concerns appear to promote smoking initiation and current smoking in female adolescents (French, Perry, Leon, & Fulkerson, 1994).

While some socioenvironmental and psychological factors appear to play an important role in the early stages of smoking uptake, genetic factors may be more influential in the development of nicotine dependence. Differentiation of the precise set of factors that are important in each of these transitions is a critical step toward developing effective strategies to prevent progression to addicted smoking and facilitate quitting.

Individual variability. There are abundant data supporting the heritability of cigarette smoking (see discussion at the end of this chapter). This variability influences the subjective effects of nicotine. Nicotine has both positive reinforcing effects (e.g., enhances alertness, arousal, pleasure) and negative reinforcing effects (relieves adverse mood and withdrawal symptoms) (Pomerleau & Pomerleau, 1984). Individual differences in the rewarding effects of the initial dose of nicotine from a cigarette may account for the observation that some young adults become dependent smokers, whereas others can experiment and not progress to nicotine dependence (Eissenberg & Balster, 2000; Flay, d'Avernas, Best, Kersell, & Ryan, 1983). In support of this hypothesis, one cross-sectional analysis found that pleasant emotional and physiological effects of the initial smoking experience discriminated teens who continued to experiment with cigarettes and those who did not (Friedman, Lichtenstein, & Biglan, 1985). Among adults, retrospective reports of the rewarding effects of the initial smoking experience (e.g., pleasurable rush or buzz, relaxation) were associated with current levels of nicotine dependence (Pomerleau, Pomerleau, & Namenek, 1998). Studies of genetic influences in nicotine metabolism may lead to better forms of smoking prevention and treatment. For example, on the basis of this new knowledge, researchers are testing medications that may reduce nicotine metabolism rate, thereby increasing aversive effects of initial smoking experiences (Sellers, Tyndale, & Fernandes, 2003).

Personality traits. Novelty seeking as a personality trait has been linked to tobacco use during adolescence (Wills, Vaccaro, & McNamara, 1994; Wills, Windle, & Cleary, 1998) and early onset of smoking in adolescent boys (Masse & Tremblay, 1997). Genetic studies have related novelty seeking with genetic variants in the dopamine pathway (Noble et al., 1998; Sabol et al., 1999), suggesting that these genetic effects on smoking behavior may be mediated in part by novelty-seeking personality traits. For example, adolescents who are novelty seekers or risk takers may be exposed at a younger age to peer smoking influences. There is also evidence to suggest that hostility, impulsivity, or anxiety-related traits might mediate the influence of serotonergic gene variants on smoking behavior (Gilbert & Gilbert, 1995). While not yet tested in the tobacco arena, interventions that include messages and format targeted to adolescents with these predisposing personality traits may be more effective than broad-based appeals (Lerman, Patterson, & Shields, 2003).

Other Substances

MDMA (Ecstasy)

MDMA (3,4-methylenedioxymethamphetamine), also called ecstasy and other names, has similarities to other amphetamines with stimulant and hallucinogen-like properties (Green, Mechan, Elliott, O'Shea, & Colado, 2003). Usually taken orally, it can also be injected. MDMA produces feelings of energy along with a pleasurable, altered sense of time and enhanced perception and sensory experiences. MDMA effects last 3 to 6 hr. A typical oral dose is one or two tablets, each containing 60 to 120 mg of MDMA, although recently the average dose may be increasing. As is characteristic of all illicit drugs, the chemical content and potency of the MDMA tablets vary, thus dose estimates or even unverified assumptions about the actual drug ingested are only estimates (Cole, Bailey, Sumnall, Wagstaff, & King, 2002).

Perhaps MDMA has a special appeal to adolescents because its usual effects include, along with mental stimulation, feelings of relatedness and empathy toward other people and feelings of well-being (Cole & Sumnall, 2003). These mood effects along with the experience of enhanced sensory perception make MDMA an appealing drug, particularly as typically used in social gatherings, dances, and concerts. At higher doses or in susceptible individuals, undesirable effects include rapid onset of anxiety, agitation, and feelings of restlessness (Gowing, Henry-Edwards, Irvine, & Ali, 2002). During the period of marked intoxication, memory is impaired, sometimes for days or longer in regular users. Information processing and task performance are disrupted. Regular users and sometimes even occasional users report withdrawal phenomena when MDMA effects are wearing off. Withdrawal effects include feelings of depression, difficulty concentrating, unusual calmness, fluctuating mood, and feelings of pervasive sadness sometimes lasting a week or more after an evening of moderate MDMA use (Parrott et al., 2002).

MDMA can be associated with addictive drug-using patterns. Some users report continued use to relieve the feelings that follow MDMA use. Compared to nonusers, regular MDMA users report increased anxiety, greater impulsiveness, and feelings of aggression, sleep disturbance, loss of appetite, and reduced sexual interest (Parrott, 2001). Whether reports from users result from their MDMA use or are symptoms and behaviors that predate MDMA use is not established.

As with other amphetamine-like stimulant drugs, high doses of MDMA, particularly if used with other stimulants, can be associated with nausea, chills, sweating, muscle cramps, and blurred vision. Anxiety, paranoid thinking, and, later, depression are common. After higher doses, markedly increased blood pressure, loss of consciousness, and seizures may occur, and under certain conditions of dose, or drug combinations and heat, the body's thermoregulation mechanisms fail. The resultant marked increase in body temperature (hyperthermia) under some circumstances is rapidly followed by multiple organ failure and death (Schifano, 2003). MDMA is commonly used with alcohol, increasing MDMA toxicity.

The nature of MDMA metabolism in the body contributes to toxicity. After a dose of MDMA is rapidly absorbed, it slows its own breakdown, resulting in unexpectedly high MDMA concentrations with repeated doses (Farre et al., 2004; Green, Mechan, et al., 2003). After regular use, tolerance to the desired MDMA effects develops (Verheyden, Henry, & Curran, 2003). This tolerance leads regular MDMA users to take larger or more frequent doses, resulting in the accumulation of toxic blood levels because of the drug-induced slowdown in its own metabolism.

MDMA increases the activity of brain serotonin, dopamine, and norepinephrine (Gerra et al., 2002; Vollenweider, Liechti, Gamma, Greer, & Geyer, 2002). When compared with methamphetamine, MDMA produces greater serotonin and less dopamine release. In animals, moderate to high doses of MDMA are toxic to serotonergic nerve cells and are associated with persistent cellular changes. As MDMA behavioral effects wear off, serotonin levels decrease for days, perhaps longer. One controversy about the toxicity of MDMA involves the correct extrapolation of human doses to doses used in animal models in which signs of toxic effects can be directly observed (Green, Mechan, et al., 2003).

A relative serotonin deficit experienced by frequent MDMA users may account for the mood, sleep, and other behaviors and symptoms associated with frequent MDMA use (Parrott, 2002). As with all psychoactive drugs, the general considerations of gender, dose, frequency of exposure, and concurrent use of other drugs, along with genetic and environmental factors, are probably important determinants of the consequences of MDMA exposure for any specific individual (Daumann et al., 2003; De Win et al., 2004; Obrocki et al., 2002; Roiser & Sahakian, 2003). Certainly many people have used MDMA and appear to have avoided measurable harm, but some have died after taking MDMA. As with nicotine, animal experiments suggest that younger brains may be more susceptible to the neurotoxic effects of MDMA (Williams et al., 2003), although important experiments with adolescent animals have not yet been reported.

Inhalant Abuse

Thousands of chemicals produce vapors or can be delivered as aerosols and inhaled to produce psychoactive effects (Anderson & Loomis, 2003). Inhalants can be organized by their chemical classification (toluene or nitrous oxide, for example), by their legitimate use (as an anesthetic, solvent, adhesive, fuel, etc.), or by their means of delivery (as a gas, a vapor, or an aerosol) (Balster, 1987). What inhalants have in common is that they are rarely taken by other routes when abused, although some can be swallowed or injected.

Volatile solvents include common household and workplace products—cleaning fluids, felt-tip markers, glues, paint thinners, and gasoline (Anderson & Loomis, 2003). Volatile medical anesthetics, halothane or isofluane, and other ethers occasionally turn up among adolescent inhalant users. Another category of inhalants, aerosols, is available as the solvents in spray cans that deliver paint, deodorants, hairspray, insecticides, and other products. Inhalant gases include household and commercial gases—butane in cigarette lighters, and nitrous oxide in whipped cream delivery cans or from medical sources. Nitrites are a special class of inhalants occasionally encountered by adolescents. When inhaled, nitrites dilate blood vessels, relax smooth muscles, and, unlike other inhalants, are more stimulating than depressant and are used primarily to enhance sexual activities.

Inhalants have been used as intoxicants for hundreds of years. Inhalants, particularly solvents, are often one of the first psychoactive drugs used by children. An estimated 6% of children had tried inhalants on at least one occasion by the fourth grade. Inhalants stand out among abused drugs by being used more by younger than older children, though on occasion, inhalant abuse persists into adulthood (Balster, 1987). Although inhalant abusers generally use whatever is available, preferred agents exist, varying from region to region in an almost fad-like way.

National and state surveys indicate inhalant use peaks around the seventh to ninth grades, with 6% of eighth graders reporting use of inhalants within the previous 30 days. The prevalence of inhalant use in young adolescents exceeds marijuana use and is more frequent in boys and in adverse socioeconomic conditions. Poverty, childhood abuse, poor grades, and early school dropout are associated with greater inhalant abuse (Beauvais, Wayman, Jumper-Thurman, Plested, & Helm, 2002; Kurtzman, Otsuka, & Wahl, 2001).

Inhalants are easy to self-administer and readily available, which explains their appeal to children. The solvents can be inhaled from a bag, from a cloth held over the face, or by sniffing from the container. Aerosol propellants can be sprayed directly into the mouth, inhaled from a balloon, or sprayed into a bag and then inhaled.

As with smoked drugs, inhalant effects depend on the substance used, efficiency of the inhalant delivery system, and the amount inhaled. Length and frequency of use are important because tolerance to many effects develops.

When inhaled, the drugs move from the lungs to brain and an onset of effects occurs within seconds. Psychoactive effects dissipate within minutes when inhalation is stopped. The chemicals are distributed to other organs, potentially damaging the liver, kidneys, and peripheral nerves. The experience produced by most inhalants is similar to that of drinking alcohol: an initial feeling of relaxation, anxiety relief, and feelings of disinhibition. As the intoxication increases with repeated doses, speech becomes slurred, fine motor movements and ability to walk are impaired, and, with increasing and repeated doses, loss of consciousness and an anesthetic state or coma occur. The neural mechanisms by which inhalant intoxication occurs are not well understood (Balster, 1998). During the period of intoxication many neural systems become dysfunctional.

As intoxication wears off, a hangover state commonly ensues. The severity of the postintoxication effect depends on dose, duration of exposure, and the amount used, but typically includes headache or nausea. Inadvertent overdose is possible, particularly when the bag or other inhalant delivery system becomes positioned so that when consciousness or coordination is lost, delivery of the inhalant continues.

Long-term effects vary with inhalant and frequency of use, but can include central nervous symptoms such as fatigue, difficulty concentrating, and impaired memory (Lorenc, 2003). Some solvents or aerosols produce nosebleed, bloodshot eyes, cough, and sores on the lips, nose, or mouth. If used over long periods of time, permanent brain damage or other organ damage (kidney, liver, and peripheral nerves) can develop (Aydin et al., 2002). Tolerance to the depressant effects develops with repeated use. In frequent users, withdrawal phenomena have been described on cessation of inhalant use.

A common cause of death during inhalant use is rapid inhalation of large amounts of solvents, followed by strenuous activity. This results in impaired cardiac function and arrhythmias. Injury and death may result from accidents associated with impaired judgment, motor impairment, or falls. Suffocation from inadequate air during the inhalation of concentrated gases or solvents is possible, and because many inhalants are flammable, fires or explosions may lead to injury or death.

When asked, children typically report that they sniff inhalants because it's fun and they like the feeling of intoxication. Initial use is often in a group with considerable peer pressure. Some users report that the intoxicated state is a way to avoid experiencing or dealing with worries and problems. Although most child inhalant use is transient and initially stems from curiosity, with the wrong kind of group pressure, it becomes a repeated behavior.

GHB (Gammahydroxybutyrate; Liquid Ecstasy, Georgia Home Boy, and Other Names)

A potent CNS depressant, GHB is typically taken to produce euphoria and a relaxed and uninhibited state, similar to that produced by alcohol (Nicholson & Balster, 2001; Teter & Guthrie, 2001). GHB is a clear, odorless, slightly salty-tasting liquid. Because of its steep dose–effect curve inadvertent overdose is frequent. Nausea, vomiting, slowed heart rate, loss of consciousness, coma, respiratory depression, and seizures can require emergency treatment. Coma, along with vomiting and an obstructed airway, can lead to death. The purity and the strength of individual doses of GHB vary greatly and can contribute to overdoses, particularly by inexperienced users. When GHB is taken with other CNS depressants, lethality increases. Deaths from GHB typically occur after combined use with alcohol. GHB is so rapidly metabolized that postmortem toxicology statistics may underestimate its frequency.

Regular users of GHB report that they must increase the dose to attain euphoric and relaxing effects; thus tolerance seems likely. A withdrawal state with increased heart rate, restlessness, anxiety, agitation, delirium, and disrupted sleep follows sudden cessation of regular GHB use (Miotto et al., 2001). GHB has been perceived as a safe drug because it was available in health food stores as a dietary supplement. Its potential toxicity may be underestimated by adolescents (Mason & Kerns, 2002). Although now a controlled drug, GHB precursors are readily available through Internet distributors. Because it is odorless and relatively tasteless, GHB has reportedly been added to the drink of unsuspecting victims. It can sedate or anesthetize an unwary recipient, leading to its use as a date rape drug (Schwartz, Milteer, & LeBeau, 2000).

Rohypnol: Flunitrazepam (Roofies, Rophie, Forget Me)

Rohypnol is a potent benzodiazepine sedative drug with similarities to Valium or Xanax, except for its increased potency (Simmons & Cupp, 1998). Although a prescribed medication in some countries, Rohypnol is not approved for prescription use in the United States. Taken by mouth in tablet form or when dissolved in beverages, Rohypnol rapidly produces profound sedation or loss of consciousness and marked amnesia for events occuring during the period of intoxication. With no odor, and almost tasteless, it can easily be administered to someone without their knowledge. Like GHB it has been associated with date rape and other sexual assaults (Schwartz et al., 2000; Slaughter, 2000).

Hallucinogens

Hallucinogens are a pharmacologically diverse group of drugs. They have in common the ability to produce profound distortions in sensory perception but accompanied by a relatively clear level of consciousness (Hollister, 1968). The perceptual distortions are typically termed *hallucinations,* though in fact true hallucinations are relatively uncommon. The sought-after alterations in visual images, perception of sounds, and bodily sensations are sometimes accompanied by intense mood swings and feelings of being out of control that can be disturbing to the uninitiated (Strassman, 1984).

Some humans have valued hallucinogenic drugs for thousands of years. The older hallucinogenic plants, for example, mescaline, psilocybin, or ibogaine, contain chemicals structurally similar to brain neurotransmitters such as serotonin, dopamine, and norepinephrine. Historically, drug-induced hallucinogenic states were typically part of social and religious rituals rather

than entertainment. Plant-based hallucinogens are still available and are even sold over the Internet (for example, psilocybin mushrooms and peyote cacti), but since the 1960s the prototype hallucinogen has been LSD (lysergic acid diethylamide), an extremely potent, chemically synthesized drug, readily available through illicit sources and, compared to many drugs, relatively inexpensive (Hofmann, 1994). LSD's physiologic effects are relatively few and mild—dilated pupils, increased deep tendon reflexes, increased muscle tension, and mild motor incoordination. Heart rate increases as does blood pressure and respiration, but not greatly. Nausea, decreased appetite, and increased salivation are common.

In nontolerant users, about 25 μg of LSD is a threshold dose. The psychological and perceptual state produced by LSD is in general similar to that produced by mescaline, psilocybin, and hallucinogenic amphetamine analogs. The major difference is potency. LSD is hundreds to thousands of times more potent. Acquired tolerance to LSD can be profound. After 3 days of successive daily doses, a 4- or 5-day drug-free period is necessary to again experience the full sensory effects. This limits, to some extent, frequency of use.

In recent years, LSD has been distributed as "blotter acid"—that is, on sheets of paper perforated into postage stamp size squares with each square containing 30 to 75 μg of LSD, ingested as a chewed dose. The effects of a single dose last from 6 to 12 hr, diminishing gradually.

LSD alters the function of brain serotonin receptors (Aghajanian & Marek, 1999). At higher doses LSD can produce a distressing drug-induced psychosis with similarities to naturally occurring psychotic states, such as acute schizophrenia. The user has difficulty in recognizing reality, thinking rationally, and communicating easily with others (Blaho, Merigan, Winbery, Geraci, & Smartt, 1997; Strassman, 1984).

For reasons not well understood, an LSD-induced experience can be psychologically traumatic, particularly for poorly prepared novices. The symptoms persist long after the pharmacologic effects of LSD have worn off (Blaho et al., 1997). An LSD persistent psychosis with mood swings ranging from mania to depression, visual disturbances, and hallucinations is relatively uncommon. Individuals who are predisposed, for genetic or other unknown reasons, to developing schizophrenia may be more likely to experience this (Hollister, 1968).

A disorder known as flashbacks, or more formally in DSM-IV, hallucinogen-persisting perception disorder, has been described (Halpern & Pope, 2003). Recurrent, primarily visual disturbances follow even a single exposure to LSD or other hallucinogen and recur over days or months. Flashback symptoms typically last only a few seconds. Only an occasional disorder following hallucinogen use, a flashback can be a substantial problem when it occurs. Considering the multiple hallucinogen doses taken by millions of people since the late 1950s, relatively few cases of flashback phenomena have been reported in the scientific literature (Halpern & Pope, 1999).

Other hallucinogens such as mescaline, consumed in the form of peyote buttons from cacti, or tryptamine hallucinogens, for example, dimethyltryptamine (DMT), are less commonly used, probably because they are less available to adolescents. In recent years, however, trafficking over the Internet has enhanced availability (Halpern & Pope, 2001). Psilocybin is occasionally available to adolescents, usually ingested as psilocybin-containing mushrooms. Psilocybin sold illicitly as pills or capsules more likely contains phencyclidine or LSD rather than psilocybin.

Newly rediscovered hallucinogens appear regularly. An example is *Salvia divenorum*, recently popularized through Internet resources (Halpern & Pope, 2001). Salvia illustrates the rapid awareness, increased interest, and progression of use of an old substance that, without the Internet, would likely have remained a relatively unknown plant hallucinogen. Salvia is a mint plant long used as a medicine and sacred sacrament in rural Mexico (Sheffler & Roth, 2003). A relatively mild hallucinogen at usually ingested doses, it is easily cultivated and now extensively discussed, advertised, and sold inexpensively via the Internet. Its active and potent component, salvinorin-A, is absorbed when the plant is chewed or the leaves are smoked. Salvia's pharmacologic effects and metabolite fate have not been adequately researched.

Phencyclidine (PCP, "Angel Dust") and Ketamine (K, Special K, Vitamin K, Kat Valium)

Phencyclidine (PCP) and a shorter-acting analogue, ketamine, were developed as surgical anesthetics (Reich & Silvay, 1989). At lower doses both alter perception and produce feelings of detachment and of being disconnected or dissociated from the environment, leading to use of the term *dissociative anesthetics* to describe this class of drugs and distinguish them from hallucinogens. At anesthetic doses patients are quiet but with eyes open, fixed in a gaze, and in a seeming cataleptic state without experiencing pain during a surgical procedure. Both PCP and ketamine produce similar effects by altering the distribution of an important brain neurotransmitter, glutamate.

Phencyclidine anesthesia produced a sometimes distressing delirium as the anesthetic was wearing off, so ketamine, which is shorter acting and slightly less potent but associated with briefer and less troublesome delirium, replaced it. Most abusers do not overdose to full anesthetic levels (Freese, Miotto, & Reback, 2002). However, depending on drug dose and tolerance, PCP or ketamine intoxication can progress from feelings of detachment and perceptual changes through confusion, delirium, and psychosis to coma and coma with seizures (Dillon, Copeland, & Jansen, 2003; Jansen & Darracot-Cankovic, 2001). After overdose, the progression to recovery follows the reverse pattern. Treatment of symptoms is primarily supportive. Ketamine produces a shorter period of intoxication; in a surgical setting a single anesthetic dose produces coma for only 10 minutes as compared to a much longer coma after a single large dose of phencyclidine. When abused, these drugs can be taken by mouth or, for more rapid effects, smoked or sniffed. When used medically they are injected. With frequent use, tolerance and dependence develop (Pal, Berry, Kumar, & Ray, 2002).

Ketamine is odorless and tasteless and can be surreptitiously added to someone's drink to produce a period of impaired awareness and amnesia. Thus ketamine has been used during sexual assaults and date rape. Phencyclidine is inexpen-

sive to produce and distribute so it is often sub-
stituted for other illicit drugs—for example, it is
misrepresented as MDMA or THC.

Club Drugs

The term *club drugs* refers to a variety of drugs
that have in common only that they are typically used at all-night parties or "rave" dances,
clubs, and bars (Smith, Larive, & Romanelli,
2002; Weir, 2000). The drugs in this group are
varied. Their pharmacology and patterns of use
vary in different regions (Gross, Barrett, Shestowsky, & Pihl, 2002). Patterns of use, dose, and
popular drug mixes change over time. The most
common club drugs, particularly marijuana, cocaine, MDMA (ecstasy), and methamphetamine,
are discussed elsewhere in this chapter. Club
drugs that have come to the attention of adolescents include GHB, flunitrazepam (Rohypnol),
and ketamine. Thus the list includes stimulants,
depressants, and hallucinogens. MDMA, GHB,
and Rohypnol have received the most recent attention as club drugs. The special appeal of club
drugs to an adolescent includes their novelty and
fad-like qualities. Unfortunately, among users
there is a misperception about the relative safety
of club drugs (Koesters, Rogers, & Rajasingham,
2002). Their use, particularly by novices, can lead
to serious health problems (Tellier, 2002).

THE NEUROBIOLOGY OF ADDICTION

As discussed above, most adolescents who experiment with drugs do not progress to clinical
problems. Some of them progress to the level of
abuse and a smaller number progress to addiction (dependence). The latter has been the focus
of much biological research because the chronic
relapsing nature of addiction suggests that
changes in the brain underlie its persistent
course. Over the past several decades, neuroscientists have uncovered compelling evidence
supporting the notion that addiction is a disease,
primarily affecting specific brain regions that
mediate motivation and natural reward. With
the help of animal models and direct studies on
addicted human subjects, scientists are rapidly
unraveling neuronal mechanisms that underlie
many of the clinical features of addiction, in-

cluding drug euphoria, tolerance, withdrawal,
craving, and hedonic dysregulation. It is now apparent that brain reward circuitry is stimulated
by addictive agents during drug-induced euphoria and disrupted over the course of chronic exposure. The chronic dysregulation of these
reward-related regions explains many of the
clinical manifestations of addiction, and the restoration of normal hedonic function through
medical interventions should ultimately improve the prognosis of this refractory disorder.
Interestingly, addictive agents as diverse as heroin, alcohol, and cocaine (to name only a few)
produce many similar neurochemical effects,
supporting the established classification of different substance dependence disorders within
the single category of addiction.

The interaction between an addictive exogenous agent and endogenous reward-related circuitry produces two powerful forces, euphoria
and craving, that initiate and drive addiction.
Whether motivated by curiosity, boredom, peer
pressure, or thrill seeking, the initial use of a euphoric drug indelibly embeds the experience
into memory. Since we organisms are neurolog-
ically "wired" to repeat pleasurable experiences,
drug euphoria positively reinforces subsequent
use. When used excessively, addictive drugs produce unpleasant states (craving, withdrawal, impaired hedonic function) that negatively reinforce use and alternate with euphoria to produce
a vicious cycle of addiction that becomes increasingly entrenched and uncontrollable, regardless of negative consequences. Although
psychological, psychosocial, and environmental
factors play critical roles in the initiation and
perpetuation of addiction, brain involvement
explains many of its paradoxes and provides important clues for the development of more effective and durable treatments.

Biological Research Based on Animal Models

Since the discovery of "pleasure centers" by Olds
in the early 1950s, extensive research has been
conducted using animal models that address the
acute and chronic effects of addictive drugs on
reward-related brain regions. These studies have
contributed tremendously to our understanding

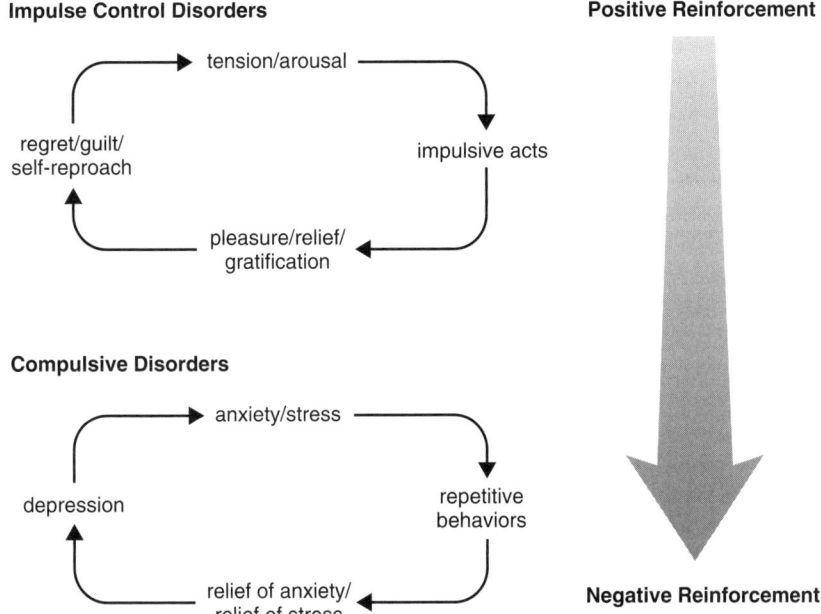

Figure 17.5 Impulse control disorders and compulsive disorders in drug addiction.

of addiction by delineating relevant neuronal mechanisms and proposing hypotheses to define the disorder. Drug addiction, also known as substance dependence (American Psychiatric Association, 1994), is a chronically relapsing disorder that is characterized by *(1)* compulsion to seek and take the drug, *(2)* loss of control in limiting intake, and *(3)* emergence of a negative emotional state (e.g., dysphoria, anxiety, irritability) when access to the drug is prevented (defined here as dependence; Koob and Le Moal, 1997). In experimental animals, the occasional but limited use of an addictive agent is very distinct from escalated drug use and the emergence of chronic drug dependence. Therefore, an important goal of current research is to understand the neuropharmacological and neuroadaptive mechanisms within reward-related neurocircuits that mediate the transition between occasional, controlled drug use and the loss of behavioral control over drug seeking and drug taking that defines chronic addiction (Koob and Le Moal, 1997).

Historically, addiction was originally defined as the presence of an acquired abnormal state where a drug is needed to keep a normal state (Himmelsbach, 1943). Eventually, the definition

of addiction became tied to the emergence of intense physical disturbances when drug taking ceased (Eddy, Halbach, Isbell, & Seevers, 1965). However, this definition did not capture many aspects of addiction that are unrelated to physical withdrawal, necessitating a second definition of "psychic" dependence in which a drug produces "a feeling of satisfaction and a psychic drive that require periodic or continuous administration of the drug to produce pleasure or to avoid discomfort" (Eddy et al., 1965). Producing pleasure and avoiding discomfort, encountered clinically as euphoria and craving, are now accepted as the primary forces that drive addiction.

From a modern perspective, drug addiction has aspects of both impulse control disorders and compulsive disorders (Fig. 17.5). Impulse control disorders are characterized by an increasing sense of tension or arousal before committing an impulsive act; pleasure, gratification, or relief is felt at the time of committing the act; and following the act there may or may not be regret, self-reproach, or guilt (American Psychiatric Association, 1994). In contrast, compulsive disorders are characterized by anxiety and stress before committing a compulsive repetitive be-

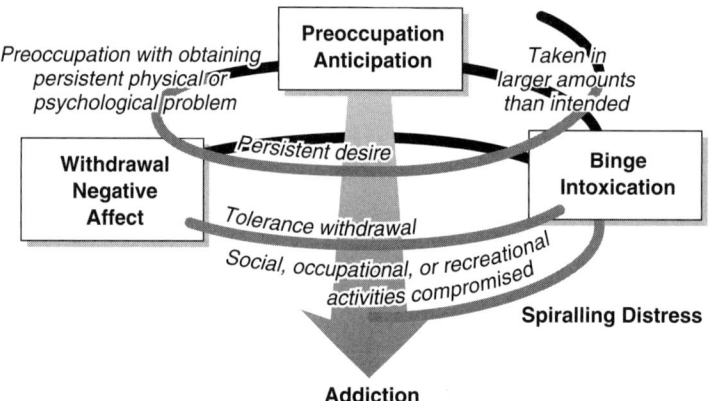

Figure 17.6 Criteria for substance dependence (DSM-IV).

havior, and relief from the stress by performing the compulsive behavior. As an individual moves from an impulsive disorder to a compulsive disorder there is a shift from positive reinforcement (euphoria) driving the motivated behavior to negative reinforcement (craving, or discomfort) driving the motivated behavior. Drug addiction can be viewed as a disorder that progresses from impulsivity to compulsivity in a collapsed cycle of addiction comprised of three stages: preoccupation and anticipation, binge intoxication, and withdrawal and negative affect (Fig. 17.6). These stages have biological, social, and psychological aspects that feed into each other, intensify, and ultimately lead to the pathological state known as addiction (Koob & Le Moal, 1997).

Given these considerations, the modern view of addiction has shifted from a focus of physical withdrawal symptoms to the motivational aspects of addiction. This shift in emphasis is supported by the clinical axiom that mere detoxification (the elimination of drug from the body with pharmacological suppression of physical withdrawal symptoms) is insufficient treatment for addiction. More central to the transition from drug use to addiction is the emergence of negative emotions, including craving, anxiety, and irritability, when access to the drug is prevented (Koob & Le Moal, 2001). Indeed, some have argued that the development of such a negative affective state should define addiction.

Animal Models of Drug Reward

Through extensive animal research, the neurotransmitters and brain circuits that mediate drug reward, have been largely delineated; the biological basis of drug reward is exemplified by the fact that laboratory animals will press levers to receive addictive substances. When provided unlimited access, animals will consistently self-administer cocaine and amphetamine to the point of death, and the power of drug reward should not be underestimated in the clinical setting. Diverse classes of addictive drugs affect different neurotransmitter systems and produce distinct activation patterns within reward circuits. Many addictive substances (including heroin, cocaine, amphetamine, alcohol, nicotine, and marijuana) acutely increase the neurotransmitter dopamine in elements of the ventral striatum, specifically the nucleus accumbens, but this increase is most robust for psychomotor stimulants and much more modest for sedative hypnotics. Other neurotransmitter systems are also involved, including opioid peptides, GABA, glutamate, and serotonin, and play more critical roles as one moves out of the domain of psychomotor stimulants. Dopamine levels in the nucleus accumbens are also elevated during activities that lead to natural rewards, providing compelling evidence that addictive drugs tap into natural motivational circuits.

Animal Models of Motivational Effects of Withdrawal

Although considerable focus in animal studies has been directed toward neuronal sites and mechanisms that produce drug reward, new animal models have been developed to examine negative emotional states produced by neuroadaptations caused by repeated drug administration. Although drug reward certainly reinforces repeated use, the transition to drug addiction appears to require an additional source of reinforcement, the reduction of negative emotional states that are associated with repeated drug administration. The ability of addictive drugs to produce reward and negative emotional states (which they temporarily alleviate) is a powerful combination that positively and negatively reinforces the compulsive cycle of addiction. Negative emotional states can be measured by using animal models that evaluate hedonic function through the use of electrical current delivered directly into brain reward regions, which is termed intracranial self-stimulation (ICSS). Animals will press levers to deliver this current, but after chronic exposure to drugs (including cocaine, morphine, alcohol, marijuana, and nicotine), more current is required to support ICSS (Koob, Sanna, & Bloom, 1998). These animal studies support the hypothesis that repeated drug use leads to hedonic dysregulation, which is thought to be manifested clinically by craving, anxiety, irritability, and other unpleasant feelings that arise during drug withdrawal.

A framework that models the transition from drug use to addiction involves prolonged access to intravenous cocaine self-administration. Typically, after learning to self-administer cocaine, rats allowed access to cocaine for 3 hr or less per day establish highly stable levels of intake and patterns of responding between daily sessions. When animals are allowed longer access to cocaine, they consistently self-administer almost twice as much at any dose tested. These findings further suggest that there is an upward shift in the set point for cocaine reward when intake is escalated (Ahmed and Koob, 1998). In addition, escalation in cocaine intake was highly correlated with reduced hedonic function, as measured by ICSS. The decreased function of the reward system failed to return to baseline levels before the onset of each subsequent self-administration session, thereby deviating more and more from control levels. These studies provide compelling evidence for brain reward dysfunction in compulsive cocaine self-administration.

Extended Amygdala: A Key Component of the Brain Reward System

Historically, the brain reward (pleasure) system was thought to be a series of brain cells and pathways that projected bidirectionally from the midbrain to forebrain, and forebrain to midbrain, and it was called the medial forebrain bundle. A part of the forebrain component of the reward system has been termed the extended amygdala (Heimer & Alheid, 1991) and may represent a common anatomical substrate for acute drug pleasure and the dysphoria associated with compulsive drug use. The extended amygdala is made up of three major structures: the bed nucleus of the stria terminalis (BNST), the central nucleus of the amygdala, and a transition zone in the medial subregion of the nucleus accumbens (shell of the nucleus accumbens; Heimer and Alheid, 1991). Each of these regions shares certain cell types and connections (Heimer and Alheid, 1991), receives information from limbic structures such as the basolateral amygdala and hippocampus, and sends information to the lateral hypothalamus, a brain structure long associated with processing basic drives and emotions.

A principal focus of research on the neurobiology of the pleasurable effects of drugs of abuse has been the origins and terminal areas of the midbrain dopamine system, and there now is compelling evidence for the importance of this system in drug reward (Le Moal & Simon, 1991). The major components of this circuit are the projection of brain cells containing dopamine from the ventral tegmental area (the site of dopaminergic cell bodies) to the basal forebrain, which includes the nucleus accumbens. Other chemical transmitters form the many neural inputs and outputs that interact with the ventral tegmental area and the extended amygdala and include opioid peptides, GABA, glutamate, and serotonin (Koob, 1992). While dopamine is critical for the reward associated with cocaine, methamphetamine and nicotine, it has a less critical role in the pleasure associated with opiates, PCP, and alcohol. Endogenous opioid peptides (such as β-endorphin and enkephalin) and their receptors have important roles in opiate and alcohol reward.

Role of the Extended Amygdala in the Dysphoria Associated With Addiction

Addictive drugs may produce dysphoric effects during their withdrawal by disrupting the same sites that they activate during drug reward. As such, negative emotional states associated with chronic drug exposure may reflect the dysregulation of the extended amygdala and midbrain dopamine systems that are implicated in drug reward. There is considerable evidence that dopamine activity is decreased during drug withdrawal (as opposed to being increased during drug reward), and alterations in the activity of other reward-related neurotransmitter systems, such as glutamate, endogenous opioids, GABA, and serotonin, have also been reported.

Stress-related chemical systems in the extended amygdala may also contribute to the dysphoria associated with dependence. Drugs of abuse not only activate the brain pleasure systems but also activate the "stress" systems within the brain. One major component of the brain stress system is the brain peptide corticotropin-releasing factor (CRF), which controls the master gland (pituitary) hormonal response to stress, the sympathetic system (fight or flight) response to stress, and behavioral (emotional) responses to stress (Koob & Heinrichs, 1999). Increases in brain and pituitary CRF are associated with the dysphoria of abstinence from many drugs, including alcohol, cocaine, opiates, and marijuana (Koob et al., 1998). Another component of the brain stress systems is the chemical norepinephrine, which also is associated with the dysphoria of drug withdrawal. Conversely, the acute withdrawal from some drugs such as alcohol is associated with decreases in the levels of the brain

"anti-stress" neuropeptide Y (NPY) in the extended amygdala (Roy & Pandey, 2002). It has been hypothesized that decreased NPY activity, combined with increased CRF activity, may contribute significantly to the dysphoric effects of drug withdrawal. This suggests that addictive drugs not only reduce the functional integrity of reward-related neurotransmitter systems but also produce stress by enhancing stress-related chemicals (CRF and norepinephrine) and reducing the NPY anti-stress system. Should even a small part of these changes persist beyond acute withdrawal, a powerful drive for resumption of drug taking would be established.

Animal Models for Conditioned Drug Effects

Through classical conditioning, environmental cues that have been repeatedly paired with drug administration can acquire drug-like (rewarding) and drug-opposite (dysphoria) properties that contribute significantly to drug craving and relapse in the clinical setting. Human studies have shown that the presentation of stimuli previously associated with drug delivery or drug withdrawal produce craving and increase the likelihood of relapse (Childress, McLellan, Ehrman, & O'Brien, 1988; O'Brien, Testa, O'Brien, Brady, & Wells 1977). A number of animal models are available to characterize the conditioning effects imparted on formerly neutral environmental stimuli that are subsequently paired with drug self-administration. For instance, stimuli that previously signaled drug availability will cause an animal to continue to press the lever even when drug is no longer available. In other situations, animals can be trained to work for a previously neutral stimulus that predicts drug availability. In an extinction procedure, responding with and without drug-related cues provides a measure of the rewarding effects of drugs by assessing the persistence of drug-seeking behavior. Drug-related cues can also reinstate responding by animals long after drug responding has been extinguished. These findings are important because the learning reinforced by drugs persists long after the drug has been eliminated from the body. In humans, these learned or conditioned effects can produce drug craving and possible relapse long after the patient is discharged from a drug-free rehabilitation program.

Brain studies support an important role for discrete glutamate-containing brain regions in conditioned cue-related phenomena associated with addictive drugs, providing insight into the mechanism of craving and relapse vulnerability. Destruction of parts of the glutamate-rich basolateral amygdala (called "lesioning") blocks the development of conditioned drug-like effects in a variety of situations, indicating that this region may be an important neural substrate for drug craving. Interestingly, these results are consistent with brain imaging studies in humans that have shown that cocaine cue-induced craving is associated with activation of the amygdala and anterior cingulate cortex. The neurochemical substrates underlying drug-like effects also involve the dopamine and opioid chemical systems located in the basal forebrain (for review, see Hyman & Malenka, 2001; Weiss et al., 2001). Evidence supports a role for opioid peptide systems in cue-induced reinstatement of drug administration, and previously neutral stimuli associated with opiate withdrawal have long been associated with dysphoric-like effects in animal models of conditioned withdrawal (Goldberg & Schuster, 1967). These animal studies are consistent with clinical findings that the opiate antagonist naltrexone attenuates craving associated with exposure to alcohol cues and reduces relapse rates in abstinent alcoholics (O'Brien, Childress, Ehrman, & Robbins, 1998). There are reciprocal interactions between dopamine and glutamate neurotransmission in the nucleus accumbens and hippocampus that are important in regulating the expression of long-term potentiation (LTP), a process considered essential for learning and memory. Thus addiction-related learning factors may involve limbic glutamate-dependent neuroadaptations.

The extended amygdala and its connections may also be critical substrates for drug-opposite effects. Basolateral amygdala lesions block the development of conditioned drug-opposite effects (Schulteis, Ahmed, Morse, Koob, & Everitt, 2000), and animal studies indicate that the aversive aspects of opiate withdrawal may involve both the central nucleus of the amygdala and the nucleus accumbens. The shell of the nucleus accumbens and central nucleus of the amygdala, key elements of the extended amygdala, showed the greatest opiate withdrawal-induced nerve cell activation that paralleled the development of conditioned place aversions (Schulteis & Koob, 1996).

In summary, brain substrates implicated in conditioned drug effects have been intensely researched, paired both with drug administration and drug withdrawal. The amygdala, and specifically the basolateral amygdala, is an important substrate in reward-related memory and conditioning. This structure has a critical role in the consolidation of emotional memories that have long been recognized as an essential component of the addictive process (Cahill & McGaugh, 1998). How such drug memories relate to memory circuitry in general and contribute to the dysregulation of already strained reward circuits is a subject for future studies.

Molecular Aspects of Addiction

The chronic administration of diverse addictive drugs produces similar molecular changes in second messengers (the immediate chemical actions that occur after a drug binds to a receptor), signal transduction pathways, and transcription factors (chemicals that change gene expression) within cells that populate reward centers (Koob et al., 1998). The prolonged expression of transcription factors produced by drugs of abuse, such as cocaine, may be relevant to the sustained dysregulation of reward centers (Self & Nestler, 1995). One such transcription factor, Δ FosB, is produced at increased levels in specific brain regions after the repeated administration of addictive drugs (Nestler, Kelz, Chen, & Fos, 1999). The chronic administration of alcohol also produces molecular changes, including reduced activity of cyclic adenosine monophosphate response element binding (CREB) protein in the central nucleus of the amygdala that is linked to alcohol withdrawal (Pandey, Zhang, & Roy, 2003). Decreased CREB activity has been linked to reduced expression of NPY in the central nucleus of the amygdala, which was previously described as an important anti-stress chemical affected by addictive drugs. Thus, changes in transcription factors may provide a model by which molecular events translate into neurochemical changes in the extended amygdala that affect motivation and contribute to the development of addiction.

Neuroadaptations and Allostasis

The counteradaptation hypothesis presented in this section essentially states that within reward-related circuits, the acute rewarding effect of a drug is counteracted by regulatory changes that exert aversive states (Siegel, 1975; Solomon & Corbit, 1974). While the pleasurable effects of drugs occur immediately in response to the pharmacological activation of reward centers, negative hedonic effects emerge later, persist, and intensify with repeated exposure. Hedonic dysregulation worsens over time because repeated use, while providing temporary relief, merely exacerbates the problem. The concept of "allostasis" has been proposed to explain how physiological brain changes contribute to relapse vulnerability. In contrast to homeostasis, in which a system returns to normal function, allostasis defines a brain reward system that does *not* return to normal but remains in a persistent dysphoric condition because of a shift in the reward set point (Koob and Le Moal, 2001). Fueled not only by the dysregulation of reward circuits but also by the activation of brain and hormonal stress systems, this process leads gradually to the loss of control over drug intake. Disruptions in reward-related neurotransmitter systems (dopamine, glutamate, opioids, serotonin, GABA) that contribute to emotional dysfunction in drug addiction and alcoholism persist long into abstinence, and are reasonable targets for pharmacological treatments. Restoring normal hedonic function in drug addiction and alcoholism could significantly reduce relapse in these treatment-refractory conditions.

Vulnerability of the Developing Nervous System: Focus on Adolescents

Despite great interest and relevance to the ultimate development of drug abuse and dependence, relatively little work has been done on the potentially unique vulnerability of the developing nervous system to drugs of abuse. Researchers have been slow to adapt animal models in the drug abuse field to studies of adolescent animals largely because many of the established models such as intravenous self-administration historically have required extensive time and technical expertise to establish, and the window of adolescence in rodent models is quite short (postnatal days 28–42; Varlinskaya, Spear, & Spear, 2001). However, recent studies with nicotine and alcohol have begun to characterize a pattern of results in adolescent rats that may provide critical insights into the importance of adolescent exposure for future vulnerability to addiction. When treated with nicotine, amphetamine, and alcohol, for instance, adolescent rodents show smaller responses to the acute effects of the drugs and less of a withdrawal response (Levin, Rezvani, Montoya, Rose, & Swartzwelder, 2003; Spear, 2002).

Human adolescents commonly experiment with drugs but relatively few go on to develop entrenched patterns of addiction. It is not known why some individuals are more vulnerable to addiction, although family studies support a contributing hereditary role. Neuroscientists have identified reward-related molecular machinery (circuits, receptors, and enzymes) that could be encoded by specific genetic polymorphisms that significantly affect the rewarding and aversive qualities of addictive drugs. Constitutional factors might thereby enhance addiction vulnerability, affect drug preference, or provide inherent protection. Many questions also exist regarding the effects of addictive drugs on the adolescent brain, which continues to develop and mature well into early adulthood. Does early experimentation, even in childhood, enhance the likelihood of addiction? Does the early abuse of one substance, particularly marijuana or nicotine, biologically predispose the individual to developing other substance dependence disorders? Does early drug experimentation produce persistent, clinically significant brain changes? Unfortunately, these questions remain unanswered. However, the current rate of knowledge expansion should shed light on these and other critical issues, enhancing our understanding of addiction and guiding the development of more effective interventions.

Adults afflicted with addiction often report that their substance use began in adolescence. However, as stated above, only a relatively small subgroup of those adolescents who try alcohol or cigarettes or use illicit drugs will progress to addiction. Adolescence is clearly a period of vulnerability for those who will continue to addiction, but what is the nature of the vulnerability? Recent brain imaging research with addicted adults suggests that the vulnerability to addiction may lie in the function (and dysfunction) of two critical brain systems: *(1)* the ancient brain motivational system, which underlies the powerful motivation for natural rewards such as food and sex (and is described above), and *(2)* the brain's inhibitory or executive function systems, responsible for inhibiting behavior and putting on the brakes, for deciding when pursuit of a desired reward would be a danger or a disadvantage, in the long term.

Deficits in Executive Inhibitory Circuitry

In adolescents, changes in the reward system are powerfully evident, with hormonal changes readying the system's response to rewards (e.g., sexual opportunity) that will reinforce the all-important (from an evolutionary standpoint) behaviors directed toward reproduction. In contrast, the brain's executive circuitry is not yet fully developed in adolescence: the frontal lobes, so critical for good decision making, are now known to continue to mature well into the 20s. This asymmetry, of a fully developed reward system and a vulnerable, not yet fully developed executive inhibitory system may help account for several familiar phenomena of normal adolescence, including the new pull of sexual rewards, increased risk taking, and decision making weighted more in the moment than in the future. The imbalance between these opposing brain systems in adolescence may represent a critical period of developmental vulnerability for exposure to powerfully rewarding drugs of abuse. The adolescent brain is able to respond to rewards, including powerful drug rewards, but the brain's systems for governing the pursuit of

these rewards and for weighing the potential negative consequences of this pursuit are often lagging behind.

Individual differences in the brain's reward circuitry and in the powerful motivational response to drug cues may be important contributors to adolescent addiction vulnerability. However, there are now growing indications that defects in the brain's executive inhibitory circuitry may be an equally critical and complementary source of addiction vulnerability. The brain's frontal regions usually exert a modulatory or "braking" function on the downstream reward regions. Intact frontal regions are critical for good decision making and especially allow the individual to weigh the promise of immediate reward against other competing rewards. This attribute is particularly relevant to addiction because negative consequences resulting from active addiction are typically delayed, whereas the reward of drug intoxication is immediate. In children, the brain's frontal functions are not yet developed, which explains why young children have difficulty inhibiting impulses toward a reward, delaying gratification, and making decisions that go beyond the moment. These abilities develop further in adolescence, but the brain's frontal lobes, and their associated functions, continue maturing into young adulthood.

There appear to be striking individual differences in the effectiveness of the brain's executive inhibitory circuitry; addicted adults show a variety of deficits. For instance, subjects with substance dependence often perform poorly on tests of long-term strategy and decision making (Monterosso et al., 2001; Petry, 2001) and show deficits in neuropsychological tests that assess their ability to inhibit overtrained or prepotent responses (Petry, 2001). Brain imaging data from chronic cocaine users show both functional and structural defects in frontal regions. Functionally there is evidence of lower frontal activity (both blood flow and glucose metabolism are reduced) in these critical frontal regions of cocaine patients than that in nonusers (Childress, Mozley, et al., 1999; Volkow et al., 1992, 1993). Structurally there is evidence for less concentrated gray matter (fewer nerve cells) in the frontal regions of cocaine patients (Franklin et al.,

2002), and chronic alcoholics show a similar finding (Lingford-Hughes et al., 1998). These differences in the brain's executive inhibitory circuitry might explain why substance abusers find it so difficult to inhibit or manage their cravings for drugs. Glutamate-enhancing drugs, such as modafinil, might ultimately play a role in bolstering prefrontal function (Dackis & O'Brien, 2003a).

As with some of the previously discussed findings, it is not possible to tell from a cross-sectional imaging study of addicted adults whether an observed brain difference predates the long history of drug use or whether it reflects the impact of long-term drug exposure. Studies with primates do show that chronic exposure to stimulants can undermine frontal inhibitory functions (Jentsch, Olaussen, De La Garza, & Taylor, 2002), which may help explain the poor frontal function in some human cocaine users. But the primate findings do not preclude the possibility that adolescents with poorer frontal function may be at early risk for making poor choices regarding drug experimentation or other risky behaviors. Such adolescents would be very poorly equipped for handling the motivational significance of drug and drug cues. Consistent with this latter notion, childhood psychiatric disorders such as ADHD and conduct disorder are risk factors for adolescent substance abuse (Biederman, Wilens, Mick, Spencer, & Faraone, 1999; Wilens, Faraone, Biederman, & Gunawardene, 2003), and both these disorders are associated with frontal deficiencies (Biederman et al., 1999). Even children who fail to meet the full clinical criteria for ADHD or conduct disorder may have some degree of frontal impairment that would increase their risk for managing the pull of rewarding drugs and their associated cues. The neurological basis of adolescent vulnerability is reviewed in more detail by Chambers, Taylor, and Potenza (2003).

Brain Imaging: The Addicted Brain

Although addiction has a very long human history, we have only recently acquired the technology to measure alterations in the living human brain that contribute to addiction vulnerability. Within the past two decades, human brain imaging techniques have revolutionized the field of psychiatric and neurological research, allowing us to visualize both the structure and the function of living human brains. Imaging research has also begun to identify differences in the reward and executive inhibitory brain systems of addicted individuals that may be critical in addiction vulnerability.

Most of the brain imaging research in addiction has been conducted with addicted adults, posing a difficulty in applying these findings to the adolescent brain. For instance, which of the brain differences observed in adults may have existed in childhood and adolescence, as a vulnerability that predated and perhaps even predisposed the person to drug addiction? Alternatively, which brain differences in the addicted adult brain *result* from years of exposure to the drug of abuse? Imaging studies at only one time point in adulthood have trouble answering this important "chicken-or-the-egg" question. Imaging studies in adolescents who are at risk for drug use but have not yet begun to use the drug will be critical in analyzing the findings in adult brains. The approach in this overview is to highlight several recent findings from brain imaging in addicted adults that may provide clues about the vulnerability to addiction in adolescence. Using the framework of reward and inhibition, this overview will also identify gaps in our current knowledge and potential implications of the brain findings for treatment and prevention.

Differences in Reward Systems of Addicted Individuals

The brain's reward circuitry is composed of an ancient network of interconnected structures whose evolutionary function is to ensure pursuit of the natural rewards necessary for daily survival (food) and for survival of the species (sex). For survival, it is not sufficient simply to appreciate the natural rewards whenever they happen to occur; it is critical to learn which cues in the environment signal the critical rewards, so that the rewards can be accessed again and again. The learned signals for reward, such as the sight of a desired food or reproductive partner, have a powerful "pull" or incentive value. As previously discussed, drugs of abuse activate the brain's circuitry for natural rewards. However, reward center activation by addictive drugs greatly exceeds that of natural rewards, which explains why drugs like cocaine can produce euphoria that is outside the range of normal human experience. The powerful subjective effects (which, in the case of cocaine and heroin, are likened to "orgasm, but much stronger") of drugs result in powerful reactions to drug cues.

Although many chemical messenger systems are involved in the brain circuitry for reward and reward signals, the neurotransmitter dopamine has been the focus of most research in human brain imaging (Volkow et al., 1990; Volkow, Wang, Fischman, et al., 1997; Volkow, Wang, et al., 1999). This focus is due in part to the large number of animal studies that implicate a role for dopamine in reward function (Di Chiara, 1999; Di Chiara, Acquas, Tanda, & Cadoni, 1993; Koob & Nestler, 1997; Roberts & Ranaldi, 1995; Schultz, 2002; Wise, 1996). The focus on dopamine is also due to a current research limitation: there are several dopamine-related tracers available for human imaging research, but very few are available for the other transmitter systems. As previously noted, most drugs of abuse acutely increase the level of dopamine in the nucleus accumbens and other reward-related brain regions. This allows more dopamine to bind specialized dopamine receptors, increasing transmission of the dopamine message. Increased dopamine neurotransmission may be associated with an increase in positive mood, energy, arousal, and motor activity, all of which are effects that have been linked to the dopamine system.

Low D2 Dopamine Receptors

In terms of addiction vulnerability, one might expect that individuals with more dopamine receptors would potentially experience a greater (positive) drug effect and might therefore be *more likely* to become addicted. However, brain imaging research suggests the opposite may be true. Cocaine-addicted adults with long histories of addiction had low numbers of dopamine (type D2) receptors in the striatum (a critical waystation in the reward circuitry), compared with controls who had no history of any substance abuse (Volkow et al., 1990, 1993).

For some years, the finding of low D2 dopamine receptors in cocaine patients was regarded as a possible consequence of the cocaine use. This interpretation was based on knowledge (from animal studies) that the increased flood of dopamine caused by cocaine or other drugs of abuse can often trigger adaptive and compensatory responses in the brain. In the case of excessive dopamine message, as occurs during drug intoxication, reductions in dopamine synthesis, release, or reduction in dopamine receptors could help reduce the transmission of the message and help bring the dopamine system back into homeostatic balance. Dramatic recent findings from imaging studies suggest that low D2 receptors may also predate drug use, and may constitute a vulnerability factor in their own right. In a study of normal controls without addiction, those individuals within the group who "liked" an infusion of the stimulant methylphenidate had D2 receptor levels that were as low as those in cocaine patients addicted for many years (Volkow, Wang, et al., 1999). In the same study, individuals with a higher level of D2 receptors rated stimulant administration as "too much" and downright unpleasant. The study suggests that a higher level of D2 dopamine receptors may actually be protective against stimulant addiction by reducing the pleasurable effects of the powerful stimulant.

The potential protective effect of higher dopamine D2 receptors and the interaction of environmental experience with this effect was dramatically demonstrated in recent imaging studies with nonhuman primates given the opportunity to administer cocaine (Morgan et al., 2002). Individually housed male monkeys were imaged and some were then group housed, allowing dominance hierarchies to be established. Alpha-male monkeys, who had achieved dominance in the group-housing situation, showed a significant increase in dopamine D2 receptors in the striatum, and did not find cocaine initially appealing. However, the subordinate monkeys who had low D2 dopamine receptors avidly self-administered cocaine (Morgan et al., 2002).

These imaging findings suggest that a genetically determined trait, the initial level of D2 dopamine receptors in the striatal portion of the reward system, may be one vulnerability factor for enjoyment of drugs, drug taking, and eventual addiction. The findings equally demonstrate the critical role of the environment in determining whether a genetic vulnerability is expressed or even is reshaping the trait itself. For example, the human control subjects with low D2 receptors (those who liked drugs in the methylphenidate study) had survived adolescence and early adulthood without developing addiction. The mastery experiences of the alpha-male monkeys apparently reshaped a biological risk factor for addiction into one of protection.

We have no imaging studies of D2 dopamine receptor function in adolescents. This represents an important gap in our knowledge. Consequently, we do not yet know whether adolescents with low D2 dopamine receptor levels will have more preference for stimulants and experience enhanced vulnerability of future addiction. The D2 dopamine receptor imaging technique is unlikely to be used in research with adolescents and children because it currently requires minute amounts of a radioactive tracer. However, other "surrogate" measures of dopamine receptor function may be obtained without radioactive imaging, e.g., by measuring the subjective response to a stimulant challenge and/or by testing the impact of a known dopaminergic agent within a nonradioactive imaging modality such as functional magnetic resonance imaging (fMRI). In addition, some cognitive tasks are sensitive to dopaminergic manipulations, and an adolescent's performance on these (within or outside an imaging setting) could be used to indirectly determine tonic dopamine function.

For those at risk, an implication of these findings for prevention and treatment might be to reset the D2 receptor numbers to a more protective level. The teaching of social and behavioral coping tools to increase mastery and control over stressors could help turn a vulnerable individual (with low D2 dopamine receptors) into one who is more like the alpha monkey—ready to take on challenges and challengers. Once these monkeys had established dominance, they were much less attracted to cocaine. Alternatively, a medication could be used to reset the reward system to a more protective level. Agents

that occupy the dopamine D2 receptors but block their action should, over time, lead to a compensatory increase in the D2 receptors. Unfortunately, the chronic administration of dopamine-blocking drugs (e.g., the typical antipsychotic neuroleptic medications such as chlorpromazine and haloperidol) often have prohibitive side effects, including sedation and a Parkinson-like neurological syndrome, that make these medications undesirable for long-term treatment. Medications that reduce the activity of the dopamine system but do not completely block it are better tolerated. For example, GABA agonists reduce dopamine neurotransmission without producing side effects associated with neuroleptics and might theoretically produce a gradual (compensatory) increase in D2 dopamine receptors. Consistent with this prediction, the GABA-B agonist baclofen has shown some early promise in the treatment of cocaine (Ling, Shoptaw, & Majewska, 1998), alcohol (Addolorato et al., 2000), and opiate (Akhondzadeh et al., 2000) dependence (trials in nicotine dependence are just beginning). Whether GABA-B agonists could also have a prophylactic effect in those *at risk* for addiction has not yet been tested, but this benefit might be predicted by the adult imaging findings with D2 dopamine receptors.

Brain Response to Drugs of Abuse and Drug-Related Cues

As previously described, drugs of abuse increase dopamine in critical parts of the reward circuitry, and this increase is most robust for psychomotor stimulants. Animal research also shows that the learned signals, or "cues," for these drugs (as well as for natural rewards) also increase dopamine release in these same brain regions. In humans, drug cues trigger strong craving and arousal and may precede relapse. The brain response to drugs, and to cues that signal the availability of drugs thus represent two additional sources of potential addiction vulnerability in the reward system.

Research in animals has shown that under certain circumstances, the brain response to drugs of abuse (as measured by either brain dopamine release or behavioral activation) can "sensitize" or increase with repeated exposures to the drug. This might lead to the prediction that chronic drug use in humans would similarly lead to an increased brain response, compared with those who have not previously used the drug. Contrary to this expectation, imaging studies in chronic cocaine users have shown that the brain dopamine response to administration of a stimulant in chronic users is actually *lower* than the response of non–drug users (Volkow, Wang, et al., 1997). Though this lower brain response can be interpreted as evidence for tolerance (a reduced response to drug with repeated administrations), we do not yet know whether the response is indeed an effect of cocaine exposure or (as with lower D2 receptors) possibly a preexisting neurochemical condition that predated chronic cocaine use. How could a lower brain response to rewards be a risk factor in adolescence? One possibility is that a lower brain dopamine response to natural rewards would mean that these rewards are insufficiently engaging, whereas the powerful, supranormal stimulation by drugs of abuse might be experienced as "just right." Some theories of sensation seeking and thrill seeking take this view. For sensation seekers, the arousal produced by natural rewards may be low, and thus high-intensity, high-arousal experiences are pursued and experienced as pleasurable (Zuckerman, 1986; Zuckerman & Kuhlman, 2000). In contrast, for those with a normal response to natural rewards, the high-intensity (often higher-risk) experiences (parachuting, bungee jumping, etc.) could be experienced as overwhelming and unpleasant.

We do not yet know whether adolescents at risk for substance abuse have a blunted brain response to natural rewards or to drugs of abuse. Although imaging studies that probe dopamine tone require small amounts of radioactive tracers and thus would not be permitted in adolescents, other nonradioactive imaging techniques could be used to measure response to the presentation of common rewards (money, food, etc.). Nonradioactive techniques such as fMRI use magnetic fields to map the regional change in brain blood flow, an index of increased brain activity. This technique is currently being used with adults to map the normal response of the brain to monetary (Elliott, Newman, Longe, & Deakin, 2003),

food (Small, Zatore, Dagher, Evans, & Jones-Gotman, 2001), or sexual stimuli (Karama et al., 2002). These studies demonstrate that research on the reward circuitry could be conducted in adolescents.

As previously described, animal research has shown activation of the brain reward circuitry by both drugs of abuse and the cues signaling these drugs. The drug and the cues for the drug lead to dopamine increases at important nodes in the reward circuitry. In humans, cues regularly associated with drug use (e.g., the sight of a drug-using friend, dealer, location, or drug paraphernalia) can come to trigger profound craving and motivation for their drug of choice, potentially leading to drug use and relapse in the clinical setting (Childress, Franklin, Listerud, Acton, & O'Brien, 2002). Brain imaging studies of this conditioned motivational state in addicted adults have shown activation of several way stations in the motivational/reward circuitry, including those linked to attention, affect, autonomic arousal, and the rapid assignment of emotional valence to incoming stimuli (Childress, Mozley et al., 1999; Childress et al., 2002). Studies also demonstrate significant similarity in the brain regions activated by the cues for cocaine (Bonson et al., 2002; Childress, Mozley, et al., Garavan et al., 2000, 1999; Grant et al., 1996; Kilts et al., 2001; Maas et al., 1996), heroin (Daglish et al., 2001; Sell et al., 1999), alcohol (Schneider et al., 2001), and cigarettes (Brody et al., 2002). Similar actions by diverse drugs on motivational circuitry provide biological evidence that supports the commonality of substance abuse disorders. This circuitry also normally manages the motivation for natural rewards, as demonstrated by human brain imaging studies using food (chocolate) (Small et al., 2001) or sexual (Karama et al., 2002) stimuli. Addicted adults often report their craving for drugs exceeds their desire for natural rewards. A very recent fMRI study in adolescents with alcohol use disorder indeed found that the brain response (which included regions in the reward circuitry) to visual cues of their preferred alcohol beverage was larger than the response to pictures of a nonalcohol beverage (Tapert et al., 2003).

Most substance-dependent individuals find that behavioral techniques are difficult to apply when they are already in the throes of a full-blown craving episode. Therefore, medications that help bring the powerful brain reward system into a more manageable range are much needed. The GABA-B agonist medications baclofen, described above as having the potential to reset dopamine receptors, has also shown promise in blunting the response to cocaine (Brebner, Childress, & Roberts, 2002; Roberts, Andrews, & Vickers, 1996) or heroin (Di Ciano & Everitt, 2003) cues in animals, and it also blunts the craving and brain activation by cocaine cues in humans (Brebner et al., 2002; Childress, McElgin, et al., 1999). Other candidate medications for reducing the brain response to drug cues are discussed in Chapter 18.

Conclusions on Neurobiology

A large body of neuroscience research, only partially reviewed in this section, supports the notion that addiction is a disease that disrupts brain pleasure centers, including the extended amygdala and its numerous connections with other reward-related systems. Neurobiological research has provided an understanding of brain mechanisms that can guide medication development and potentially improve outcome. While the anatomy and circuitry of reward neurocircuits have been largely delineated, we know little about molecular changes within these regions that mediate the transition into addiction, enhance relapse vulnerability, and produce hedonic dysregulation. Nevertheless, the disease concept of addiction is supported by its strong biological basis, which is conclusively demonstrated by several lines of animal and human research. Although addictive drugs produce pleasure by activating brain reward circuits, their long-term effect is to inhibit these regions, leading to hedonic dysregulation and unpleasant emotional states. The short-term fix of more drug use provides temporary relief but then merely worsens this vicious cycle. Animal models of addiction have identified specific neurochemical alterations in reward-related and stress-related systems that contribute to dysphoric motivational states associated with drug abstinence, and the pharmacological reversal of these

neuroadaptations is a promising strategy to improve outcome in clinical practice. Human studies likewise demonstrate functional and structural brain abnormalities associated with addiction, especially in the prefrontal cortex and amygdala, although the issue of causality has not been adequately addressed. Are these abnormalities produced by repeated drug administration, or do they predate and even contribute to addictive vulnerability? Can they be normalized with abstinence or through specific interventions? Will brain abnormalities identified through imaging techniques eventually serve to identify individuals who are most at risk of developing addiction? The issue of vulnerability is particularly important to identify adolescents who might benefit from specific interventions, be they preventive or therapeutic. Unfortunately, prodigious gaps exist in our knowledge of the neurobiology of addiction in adolescents, which represents an important area for future research.

THE ROLE OF GENETICS

Overview of Genetic Models

Research using both animal and human models is advancing our understanding of the role of genetic factors in substance use. Animal models of drug addiction can manipulate genetic factors through selective breeding or "knock-outs" (mice that are lacking a critical gene) to explore general and specific genetic effects on behavioral responses to drugs and propensity to self-administer drugs. As reviewed by Ponomarev and Crabbe (2002), this line of research has generated important knowledge about the role of genetic factors in initial sensitivity to drugs, neuroadaptive changes from chronic exposure, withdrawal syndromes, and reinforcing effects. Of particular relevance to adolescent substance use, animal research is elucidating how the adolescent brain may be especially vulnerable to the stimulating effects of both novel environment and drugs of abuse (Laviola, Adriani, Terranova, & Gerra, 1999). This work suggests that adolescence is a critical period during which exposure to drugs may interfere with more adaptive coping strategies and produce lifelong behavioral substance abuse patterns.

In humans, twin models have been used to explore the relative contribution of genetic and environmental factors to substance use and dependence. This is accomplished by comparing concordance rates for a particular trait in monozygotic twins who share all of their genes in common to those for dizygotic twins who share roughly 50% of their genes (Kendler, 2001). As described in greater detail below, this methodology has been used to study the role of heritable factors for smoking, alcohol use, and use of illegal drugs.

Once a particular behavioral trait (also referred to as a "phenotype") has been established as heritable, molecular genetic approaches are used to identify the specific genetic variants that may be responsible. One such approach identifies candidate genes based on neurobiological or biochemical pathways (e.g., dopamine or serotonin genes) and uses a case–control study design to compare the frequency of genetic variants (alleles) in these pathways among persons with and without the phenotype (e.g., nicotine-dependent persons vs. nondependent persons) (Sullivan, Jiang, Neale, Kendler, & Straub, 2001). Several studies employing the candidate gene approach to investigate substance abuse genes are described below. The role of specific genetic variants can be also investigated through family-based designs that examine allele sharing or allele transmission for candidate genes within families (Spielman et al., 1996). This latter approach controls for potential bias due to ethnic admixture, but has less statistical power and is more costly to implement.

In contrast to these hypothesis-driven approaches, genetic linkage analysis can be used to search for as yet unidentified genetic variants that may be linked with substance use phenotypes. In this approach families or relative pairs (e.g., sibling pairs) are used to look for linkage with anonymous markers across the genome. Because the effect sizes of any individual gene conferring susceptibility to a behavioral trait are expected to be small (Comings et al., 2001), this approach requires a large number of family members. As described below, the results of such studies are beginning to reveal regions of interest

in the genome; however, it is likely to take several years before specific loci are identified and validated as being important in substance use and dependence.

Below, we summarize the literature on the heritability and specific genetic effects for tobacco use, alcohol use, and use of illegal drugs. Although most of these studies used adult populations, we highlight investigations that included adolescent participants. The results of both adolescent and adult studies provide insights into the biobehavioral basis of substance use and its relevance to prevention in high-risk youth.

Genetic Contributions to Tobacco Use

Abundant data from twin studies provide evidence for the heritability of cigarette smoking. Using the Australian twin registry, Heath and Martin (1993) found that inherited factors accounted for 53% of the variance in smoking initiation. More recent data suggest that the heritability of a diagnosis of nicotine dependence is even higher (Kendler et al., 1999; True et al., 1999). Sullivan and Kendler (1999) summarized data from a large number of twin studies indicating that additive genetic effects account for 56% of the variance in smoking initiation and 67% of the variance in nicotine dependence. Significant genetic influences have also been documented for age at smoking onset (True et al., 1999) and for smoking persistence (Madden et al., 1999).

Genes in the dopamine pathway have been studied most extensively with respect to tobacco use and addiction. It is speculated that individuals with low-activity genetic variants may experience greater reinforcement from nicotine because of its dopamine-stimulating effects. In support of this hypothesis are three studies showing a higher prevalence of the more rare A1 or B1 allele of the dopamine 2 receptor (*DRD2*) gene among smokers than among nonsmokers (Comings et al., 1996; Noble et al., 1994; Spitz et al., 1998). However, a small, family-based analysis did not provide evidence for significant linkage of smoking to the *DRD2* locus (Bierut et al., 2000).

In a case–control study of smokers and non-smokers, Lerman and colleagues (1999) found that *DRD2* interacted with the dopamine transporter (*DAT*) gene in its effects on smoking behavior. The DAT polymorphism is of particular interest because the 9-repeat allele has been associated with a 22% reduction in dopamine transporter protein (Heinz et al., 2000). Since a reduction in dopamine transporter level would result in less clearance and greater bioavailability of dopamine, it is speculated that individuals who have the 9-repeat may have less need to use nicotine to stimulate dopamine activity. The association of the *DAT* gene with smoking behavior has been supported in one study (Sabol et al., 1999), but not replicated in two other studies (Jorm et al., 2000; Vandenbergh, 2002). Thus, the role of *DAT* in smoking behavior remains unclear.

The serotonin pathway is also under investigation in genetic studies of smoking behavior. Candidate polymorphisms (genetic variants) include those in genes that are involved in serotonin biosynthesis (e.g., tryptophan hydroxylase, *TPH*) and serotonin reuptake (serotonin transporter, *5HTTLPR*). Two recent studies have shown that individuals who are homozygous for the more rare A allele of *TPH* are more likely to initiate smoking and to start smoking at an earlier age (Lerman et al., 2001; Sullivan et al., 2001). Although *5HTTLPR* was not associated with smoking status (Lerman et al., 1998), there is evidence from two studies that this polymorphism modifies the effect of anxiety-related traits on smoking behavior (Hu et al., 2000; Lerman et al., 2000).

While genes in the dopamine and serotonin pathways may have generalized effects on risk for substance abuse, genes that regulate nicotine metabolism should be specifically relevant to smoking behavior. One hypothesis is that slower metabolizers of nicotine may be less prone to initiate smoking because they may experience more aversive effects (Pianezza, Sellers, & Tyndale, 1998). Once smoking is initiated, slower metabolizers may require fewer cigarettes to maintain nicotine titers at an optimal level (Benowitz Perez-Stable, Herrera, & Jacobs, 2002). Initial support for this premise was provided in a study of the P450 *CYP2A6* gene, which encodes the key enzyme involved in metabolism of nicotine to inactive cotinine (Pianezza et al., 1998). Unfortunately, however, later studies did not support this finding and suggested that the *CYP2A6* variant is much more rare than originally reported (London, Idle, Daly, & Coetzee, 1999; Oscarson et al., 1998; Sabol et al., 1999).

Although genes regulating nicotine receptor function would be prime candidates for smoking risk, data on functional genetic variation in humans are not yet available. In two recent studies of the B2 nicotinic receptor, several single nucleotide polymorphisms (of unknown functional significance) were identified, but none were associated with smoking behavior (Lueders et al., 2002; Silverman et al., 2001).

As mentioned above, linkage analysis can also be used to scan the genome for regions that may harbor nicotine dependence susceptibility genes. There are, however, a limited number of reports using this approach. Straub and colleagues (1999) performed a complete genomic scan to search for loci that may confer susceptibility to nicotine dependence. Using a sample of affected sibling pairs, linkage analysis provided preliminary evidence for linkage to regions on chromosomes 2, 4, 10, 16, 17, and 18. But these results were not statistically significant, and the sample size in this study (130 families) may not have been large enough to identify genes with small effects. Two other studies used families from the Collaborative Study on the Genetics of Alcoholism (COGA) and reported evidence for linkage of smoking behavior to chromosomes 5 (Duggirala et al., 1999), 6, and 9 (Bergen et al., 1999). Notably, the regions identified in the different studies do not overlap. This may be attributable to the fact that regions identified in the COGA sample may harbor loci predisposing to addiction to both alcohol and smoking.

Genetic Contributions to Alcohol Use

As with tobacco, twin studies of alcohol use provide consistent evidence for significant genetic effects. Estimates for the proportion of variance accounted for by genetic factors range from about 30% to 70%, depending on whether the studies used population-based or treatment samples (Kendler, 2001) and on the specific phenotype examined (van den Bree, Johnson, Neale, & Pickens, 1998). One study of over 1,500 twin pairs, ages 20 to 30 years old, reported that 47% of the variance in use (vs. abstinence) in males was attributable to genetic factors with 48% of the variance being due to shared environment (and the remainder due to individual environmental effects; Heath & Martin, 1988). The comparable figures for females were 35% and 32%, respectively. Heritability estimates in other studies ranged from about 50% for alcohol dependence to 73% for early age of onset for alcohol problems (McGue, Pickens, & Svikis, 1992; Pickens, & Svikis, 1991; Prescott & Kendler, 1999). Physical symptoms of alcohol dependence also appear to have a significant heritable component (e.g., binge drinking, withdrawal), although the potential behavioral consequences appear to be less heritable (e.g., job trouble, arrests; Slutske et al., 1999). Of particular relevance to the biobehavioral model of substance abuse, there is evidence for shared genetic influences for tobacco and alcohol consumption (Swan, Carmelli, & Cardon, 1996).

The search for specific genetic effects on alcohol use has led to the discovery of genes in key neurotransmitter pathways and genes that influence the metabolism of alcohol. Once again, the dopamine pathway has been a central focus of this research. An initial study relating the *DRD2* A1 allele to alcoholism attracted a great deal of attention (Blum et al., 1990); however, several studies failed to replicate this initial result (Bolos et al., 1990). Noble (1993) reviewed nine independent studies including 491 alcoholics and 495 controls. Across these studies, the more rare A1 allele of the *DRD2* gene was carried by 43% of alcoholics, compared with 25% of nonalcoholic controls. When only severe alcoholics were examined, the prevalence of the A1 allele was 56%. Hill, Zezza, Wipprecht, Locke and Neiswanger (1999) used the more conservative family-based approach to test for linkage between *DRD2* and alcoholism. Although an overall association with alcoholism was not supported, there was evidence for linkage when only severe cases were examined. Studies examining other genes within the dopamine pathway for association with alcoholism have yielded mostly negative results (Parsian, Chakraverty, Fishler, & Cloninger, 1997).

Genes in the serotonin pathway are also plausible candidates for alcohol dependence because of the effects of alcohol on brain serotonin levels (Lesch & Merschdorf, 2000). The low activity S allele of the serotonin transporter gene (*5HTTLPR*) has been linked with alcoholism in one family-based study (Lichtermann et al., 2000). Although the prevalence of this variant has not been found to differ significantly in case–control studies comparing alcoholics and nonalcoholics, there is evidence that it increases risk for particular alcoholism subtypes, including binge drinking (Matsushita et al., 2001) and early-onset alcoholism with violent features (Hallikainen et al., 1999). Similarly, the *TPH* gene has been linked with alcoholism with comorbid impulse control problems, such as antisocial behavior or suicidal tendencies (Ishiguro et al., 1999; Nielsen et al., 1998).

The most consistent evidence for genetic effects on alcoholism has been generated from studies of genes that regulate the metabolism of alcohol. Alcohol is converted to its major metabolite acetaldehyde by the enzyme alcohol dehydrogenase (ADH). Decreased metabolism results in more aversive effects of alcohol consumption, such as flushing and toxicity. A reduced-activity allele of the *ADH2* gene (*ADH2*2*) is found more commonly in Asian populations and has been shown to be protective for alcohol dependence in Chinese (Chen et al., 1999) and European (Borras et al., 2000) populations. There is some evidence that the genetic effect is stronger for males than for females (Whitfield et al., 1998). The reduced-activity allele of *ADH2* is also found more commonly in Ashkenazi Jewish populations and has been associated with reduced alcohol consumption among Jewish college students (Shea, Wall, Carr, & Li, 2001).

The opioid system has also been implicated in the reinforcing effects of alcohol as well as other drugs of abuse (see below). With respect to alcoholism, the results of initial studies have been mixed. Two studies have suggested that variants of the μ-opioid receptor gene may be associated with a general liability to substance dependence, including alcohol (Kranzler et al., 1998; Schinka et al., 2002). However, another larger study did not find significant differences in allele frequencies in dependent and nondependent individuals (Gelernter, Kranzler, & Cubells, 1999).

Genetic Contributions to Illegal Substance Use

The Harvard Twin study is one of the most extensive investigations of the role of heritable factors in drug use (Tsuang, Bar, Harley, & Lyons, 2001; Tsuang et al., 1999). Summarizing the results from 8,000 twin pairs, Tsuang and colleagues (2001) reported heritability estimates ranging from .38 for sedative drugs to .44 for stimulant drugs. Interestingly, the variance in illicit drug use attributed to shared environmental influences tended to be much smaller than that due to individual environmental effects. Somewhat higher estimates for heritability were generated from a study of twins ascertained through alcohol and drug programs and thus exhibiting more severe forms of substance abuse disorders (van den Bree et al., 1998). Among males, heritability estimates for substance dependence were 58% for sedatives, 57% for opiates, 74% for cocaine, 78% for stimulants, and 68% for marijuana. With the exception of dependence on stimulants, estimates were significantly lower for females. In general, the genetic variance appeared to be greater for heavy use or abuse than for ever using (Kendler, Gardner, & Gardner, 1998).

Of particular relevance to youth substance abuse is the finding that the transitions in survey drug use categories (never used to ever used to regular use) have a significant heritable component. For example, genetic variance for the transition from never to ever using was reported to be 44% for marijuana, 61% for amphetamine, and 54% for cocaine (Tsuang et al., 1999). For the transition to regular use, the comparable figures were 30%, 39%, and 34%. As was shown for tobacco and alcohol, family studies showed evidence for common genetic variance underlying dependence on illegal drugs (Pickens, Svikis, McGue, & LaBuda, 1995; Tsuang et al., 2001).

Because many drugs of abuse increase levels of dopamine (Dackis & O'Brien, 2001; Shimada et al., 1991), initial genetic investigations have focused on this pathway. Genetic variations affecting mesocorticolimbic function might affect drug-induced reward and thereby contribute to addiction vulnerability. Uhl, Blum, Noble, and Smith (1995) summarized data from nine studies of mixed groups of substance abusers and reported a 2-fold increase in risk in individuals who have at least one copy of the DRD2 A1 allele. The risk ratio was nearly 3-fold for more severe substance abuse. A high activity allele of the catechol-O-methyltransferase gene, which codes for a dopamine metabolizing enzyme, has also been associated with polysubstance abuse (Vandenbergh, Rodriguez, Miller, Uhl, & Lachman, 1997).

Several twin, family, and adoption studies have concluded that the vulnerability to develop heroin dependence is partially inherited. Twin studies have reported significantly higher concordance rates for identical twins than for nonidentical twins (Tsuang et al., 1996), and an estimated heritability of .34 has been published for heroin-dependent males (van den Bree et al., 1998). One study of male and female subjects who were adopted away from their natural parents found that opioid dependence correlated with genetic loading for antisocial personality and alcoholism, and with environmental factors such as divorce and turmoil in the adoptive family (Cadoret et al., 1986). Another study reported that subjects with opioid dependence had an 8-fold increase in addiction prevalence among their first-degree relatives, independent of alcoholism and antisocial personality disorder, with evidence of specificity for familial opioid dependence (Merikangas et al., 1998). Therefore, a family history of addiction appears to be a potent risk factor for the development of opioid dependence. Specific genes associated with increased vulnerability for heroin dependence have not been identified, although animal models demonstrate that genes encoding the μ-opioid receptor might influence the animal's opioid preference, as evidenced by their willingness to self-administer morphine (Berrettini, Alexander, Ferraro, & Vogel, 1994). However, human studies of the gene (OPRM1) that encodes the human μ-opioid receptor are mixed with regard to opioid dependence vulnerability (Crowley et al., 2003; Hoehe et al., 2000).

Key Findings from Research on Genetics of Substance Use

There is no "gene for addiction." Although heritable factors are clearly important in substance abuse and dependence, such effects involve a complex interaction between multiple genes in different biological pathways. Some genetic variants may result in a more generalized predisposition to substance use and dependence, while other variants may influence risk for dependence on specific substances. These genetic effects interact with environmental factors, and any individual genetic variant is likely to account for only a small proportion of the overall variance in a substance use behavior.

Findings on the effects of specific genetic variants are not consistent. The use of different study designs and methods of subject ascertainment, the focus on polymorphisms of unknown functional significance, and ethnic admixture have resulted in inconsistent findings in this field. Very large studies using both population-based and family-based designs are needed to validate specific genetic effects and to identify the set(s) of genetic variants that predispose to general addiction potential and dependence on specific substances.

Genetic effects on substance abuse are mediated by personality traits. Such traits particularly involve the drive for sensation and novelty and deficits in impulse control. Individuals exhibiting these traits may be more prone to drug use, and as such, these traits may serve as liability markers for susceptibility to substance use and dependence. Whether these trait markers provide greater predictive value than the underlying genetic markers remains to be determined.

A complete understanding of specific genetic influences on substance dependence will reveal only part of the picture. On average, genetic influences account for roughly one-half of the variance in specific substance use behaviors. Such effects occur in the context of complex socioenvironmental and psychological influences. Even the best panel of genetic tests to identify individuals predisposed to substance abuse will have low sensitivity and specificity unless nongenetic influences are incorporated into the model. Increased understanding of the role of genetic factors in addiction will never diminish the importance of behavioral and social influences.

Treatment of Substance Use Disorders

The high rate of adolescent substance abuse in the United States (Johnsten, O'Malley, & Bachman, 1998) makes the identification of effective treatment approaches a significant priority. Effective early intervention is crucial. Adolescents who initiate alcohol use by age 14 are significantly more likely to develop alcohol dependence as adults than those who initiate use by age 20, with significant reductions in the odds of developing dependence for each year of delayed initiation (Grant & Dawson, 1997). Effective early intervention is also crucial with substance-abusing adolescents because it can play a preventive role in later years (Borduin et al., 1995; Kazdin, 1991, 1993; Santisteban et al., 2003).

While alcohol remains the most commonly used substance (illegal among adolescents; Kandel, & Faust, 1975; Kandel & Yamaguchi, 1993), a marked trend in recent years is the increased use of cannabis among adolescents, which has led to an increased demand for cannabis treatment. From 1992 to 1998, the number of adolescents with primary, secondary, or tertiary problems related to cannabis who presented to the U.S. public treatment system grew from 51,081 to 109,875 (a 115% increase) (Dennis et al., 2002). In 1998, over 80% of these adolescents received treatment in an outpatient setting. The bulk of treatment evaluation studies and clinical trials report the most prevalent types of substance use in clinical populations are alcohol and marijuana, with some cocaine, heroin, methamphetamine, hallucinogen, and polysubstance use as well, based on setting and sample.

Treatment of substance-abusing adolescents is complicated by a number of factors that appear to be particularly prevalent or problematic among adolescents (although they complicate treatment for adults as well). First, as noted previously, adolescents in treatment samples usually use multiple substances, typically alcohol and marijuana with occasional cocaine use (Henggeler, Pickrel, Brondino, & Crouch, 1996; Kaminer, Burleson, & Goldberger, 2002; Winters, Stinchfield, Opland, Weller, & Latimer, 2000) and, increasingly, heroin as well.

Second, as highlighted at several points throughout this volume, substance-using adolescents have very high rates of comorbid psychiatric disorders, which can greatly complicate treatment delivery and outcome. For example, Henggeler et al. (1996) reported that 35% of participants in a clinical trial of family approaches (described in more detail below) met criteria for conduct disorder, 19% for social phobia, 12% for oppositional defiant disorder, and 9% for major depression. In Waldron, Slesnick, Brody, Turner, and Peterson's (2001) sample, 89.8% had a history of significant delinquent behavior, 29.7% met criteria for anxiety and depressive disorders, and 27.3% had attention problems. Kaminer and colleagues (2002) reported that 55% met criteria for an externalizing disorder, 39% for conduct disorder, 18% for attention-deficit hyperactivity disorder (ADHD), 22% for depression, and 26% for an anxiety disorder. As discussed in more detail below, the presence of a comorbid disorder often indicates the need for evaluation for pharmacotherapy as well and for close monitoring of treatment adherence and response. The presence of conduct disorder is particularly significant among substance-abusing adolescents as it is often associated with poor long-term treatment outcome and persistence of antisocial behavior in this population (Myers, Stewart, & Brown, 1998). Moreover, in some circumstances (e.g., deviant adolescents assigned to interactional groups), inclusion of a high proportion of adolescents with conduct disorders in some types of unstructured groups may lead to generally poor outcomes (Arnold & Hughes, 1999; Dishion, McCord, & Poulin, 1999).

Treatment of substance-abusing adolescents is also complicated by high rates of substance abuse in their immediate families. Henggeler et al. (1996) reported that a substance abuse problem was present in 18% of birth mothers and 56% of the fathers of youth in their treatment sample. Winters et al. (2000) reported that 66% of participants had at least one parent with substance use disorder. This complication is significant because parental substance use is associated with poor parenting practices and low levels of parent monitoring, which can further exacerbate adolescent substance use (Chilcoat, Dishion, & Anthony, 1995). Furthermore, exposure to drug use and drug-related cues within the household is likely to provoke craving in established, adolescent substance abusers.

Another obstacle to treatment for adolescents is that adolescents rarely seek treatment voluntarily but are usually coerced at some level after experiencing school, legal, or medical problems (Brown, 1993). Treatment is also complicated by their involvement in the multiple systems in which their legal, school, and medical problems are being addressed, as these problems may be identified prior to recognition of the presence of a substance use disorder (Henggeler, Borduin, & Melton, 1991).

Finally, high attrition from treatment is a particular problem among adolescents, with treatment completion rates for adolescents in therapeutic communities estimated at less than 20%. Completion rates for outpatient programs are generally estimated at 50% (Henggeler et al., 1996).

PSYCHOSOCIAL TREATMENTS

Treatment Evaluation Studies

There are few rigorous evaluations of the effectiveness of standard treatment approaches for adolescents. As of 2001, two major reviews identified between 32 and 53 published studies (Dennis & White, 2003; Williams et al., 2000), 21 of which were published in the last 5 years. Overall, most of these were program evaluation studies of inpatient services, and only about 15 were randomized clinical trials in outpatient settings. The older studies tend to suffer from a range of methodological problems. A number of newer studies have been recently published or are under way. These studies are more likely to have high inclusion rates (over 80%), experimental designs, manualized protocols, standardized measures, validation substudies, repeated measures, long-term follow-up (e.g., 12 or more months), and high follow-up rates (80% to 90% or more). They also include economic analysis of the cost and benefits to society (Dennis & White, 2003).

The existing program evaluation research has focused primarily on four types of programs. First, the bulk of studies have focused on the "Minnesota model," generally a 4- to 6-week inpatient program that offers a range of services (i.e., individual, group, and family counseling, and school and recreational activities). Many of these programs are guided by an Alcoholics Anonymous or Narcotics Anonymous Twelve-Step orientation. A second major class of treatment delivery is outpatient drug-free programs. These usually consist of individual and group counseling, often with some family involvement. A third, less commonly studied treatment approach for adolescents is the "therapeutic community." Based on adult therapeutic community approaches, these programs are typically highly disciplined, 6- to 12-month residential programs that tend to offer a Twelve-Step orientation. The final form of treatment that has been investigated is the Outward Bound or life skills training programs. These wilderness programs typically last 3 to 4 weeks and use the challenges of survival and group interdependency as the key therapeutic ingredients.

Until recently, the three more intensive programs (inpatient, residential, and Outward Bound) had received the most attention from investigators. Roughly 30 to 40 studies exist, which involved primarily uncontrolled evaluations of a single treatment program (Williams et al., 2000). In these studies, it is difficult to determine the relative effectiveness of the approach because few included any type of comparison or control group; however, in some studies, patients who dropped out of treatment served as a quasi-experimental control group (although this is clearly not an ideal comparison because of the possibility of selection bias). The primary outcome measures used in these studies are typically abstinence, drug use reduction, and treatment retention, although different studies tend to define these differently. Outcomes are almost always measured by self-report and often taken from clinical records, rather than assessed by an independent evaluator. The use of validated outcome measures or biologic indicators of substance use is rare. Thus, the highly positive outcomes typically reported by these studies should be tempered by an understanding of the substantial limitations of their designs. On average about 50% of patients reported significant decreases in substance use, typically measured as days of any drug use (Williams et al., 2000).

Given that most of these programs emphasized complete abstinence, on average only 38% of those followed reported complete abstinence at 6 months.

Evaluation of Outpatient Approaches

Although residential and inpatient treatment warrants more research, focus on improving the effectiveness of outpatient services seems the most promising, given that nearly 80% of adolescents with substance abuse at least initially receive outpatient treatment. In addition, outpatient services have many benefits (e.g., ability to characterize or dictate specific treatments, potential use of randomized designs, larger sample size, etc.).

Although few well-designed treatment evaluations of outpatient services exist, there are some important large-scale studies that involve primarily cannabis use, and these are summarized here. These multisite studies of existing practice generally defined minimal or no treatment as less than 90 days (13 weeks) of outpatient service, even though nearly 80% met that criteria. Changes in days of marijuana use were assessed in most of these studies, allowing some cross-study comparison. Among the 111 to 158 youths (under age 21) followed through the Drug Abuse Reporting Program (DARP; Simpson, Savage, & Sells, 1978; Sells & Simpson, 1979) in the early 1970s, cannabis use rose from 3% to 10% in the 3 years following their discharge. Among the 87 adolescents receiving outpatient treatment in the Treatment Outcome Prospective Study (TOPS; Hubbard, Cavanaugh, Craddock, & Rachel, 1985) in the early 1980s, the change in daily cannabis use from the year before to the year after treatment varied from a decrease of 42% (for those with less than 3 months of treatment) to an increase of 13% (for those with 3 or more months of treatment). Among the 156 adolescents receiving treatment (predominantly outpatient) in the Services Research Outcome Study (SROS) during the late 1980s to early 1990s (Office of Applied Studies, 2000), cannabis use rose 2% to 9% between the year before and 5 years after treatment. Among the 236 adolescents in the National Treatment Improvement

Evaluation Study (NTIES; Center for Substance Abuse Treatment [CSAT], 1999; Gerstein & Johnson, 1999) during the early 1990s, there was a 10% to 18% reduction in use between the year before and year after treatment. Among the 445 adolescents followed up after outpatient treatment in the Drug Abuse Treatment Outcome Study of Adolescents (DATOS-A; Grella, Hser, Joshi, Rounds-Bryant, 2001; Hser et al., 2001) in the mid- to late 1990s, there was a 21% to 25% reduction in cannabis use between the years before and after treatment.

The Effectiveness of Specific Approaches: Randomized Clinical Trials

Randomized clinical trials are the gold standard for establishing the efficacy of a given approach, as they are the most rigorous approach that clinical investigators have for evaluating the effectiveness of a given treatment in comparison with a well-defined control treatment and while controlling for multiple threats to internal validity. Although the number of well-designed controlled clinical trials of well-defined treatment approaches for substance-abusing adolescents is steadily increasing, the knowledge base regarding effective treatments continues to lag well behind that for adult substance use disorders. Drawing firm conclusions about treatment outcome and the relative benefits of different approaches is difficult, as there remain only a few controlled clinical trials that meet the rigorous standards required for determining that a treatment be called "empirically supported" (Chambless & Hollon, 1998). Many of the studies reviewed here are characterized by several threats to internal validity, including differential attrition, lack of validated independent outcome measures with objective evaluation of drug use, small sample sizes, lack of specification and evaluation of treatment fidelity and quality, dilution of interventions, and limited follow-up (Cottrell & Boston, 2002; Deas & Thomas, 2001; Kaminer et al., 2002; Waldron, 1997). Thus, with only a few exceptions, caution must be used in making conclusions about the effectiveness of these approaches.

Family and Multisystem Therapies

A key defining feature of family and multisystem approaches is that they treat adolescents in the context of the family and social systems in which substance use develops and may be maintained. Thus, inclusion of family members in treatment (often with the provision of home visits) is seen as a critical strategy for reducing attrition and addressing multiple issues simultaneously (Henggeler et al., 1996; Liddle et al., 2001). Because they are grounded solidly in the knowledge base on adolescents and development and thus are well suited to the specific problems of this population, family-based approaches have been among the most widely studied approaches for adolescents in controlled trials and have the highest levels of empirical support (Deas & Thomas, 2001; Liddle & Dakof, 1995; Waldron, 1997). Waldron et al. (2001) summarizes their success as follows:

> Reviews of formal clinical trials of family-based treatments have consistently found that more drug-abusing adolescents enter, engage in, and remain in family therapy than in other treatments and that family therapy produces significant reductions in substance use from pre- to post-treatment. . . . In seven of eight studies comparing family therapy with a non-family-based intervention, adolescents receiving family therapy showed greater reductions in substance use than did those receiving adolescent group therapy, family education, and individual therapy, individual tracking through schools, or juvenile justice system interventions.

Moreover, the high level of support for family and multisystemic approaches parallels findings from large meta-analyses pointing to the effectiveness of family therapies for adult substance users (Stanton & Shadish, 1997). It should be noted that family-based approaches are diverse, and many combine a variety of techniques, including family and individual therapies and skills and communication training, which may broaden the benefits of treatment by allowing greater individualization and enabling clinicians to address multiple factors in treatment (Waldron et al., 2001). Those family-based approaches with the highest level of support with this population include multisystemic therapy (MST) (Henggeler & Borduin, 1990), brief strategic family therapy (Szapocznik & Hervis, 2003), and multidimensional family therapy (Liddle et al., 2001).

Multisystemic therapy (MST) is a manualized approach that addresses the multiple determinants of drug use and antisocial behavior. It is intended to promote fuller family involvement through engaging family members as collaborators in treatment, stressing the strength of the youth and their families, and addressing a broad and comprehensive array of barriers to attaining treatment goals. Therapists must be familiar with several empirically based therapies (including structural family therapy and cognitive-behavioral therapy) and make frequent visits to the home and be available on a full-time basis to families. Henggeler and colleagues (1996) conducted a controlled trial with 118 substance-abusing or substance-dependent juvenile offenders (mean age 16) in which participants were randomly assigned to home-based MST and compared with usual community treatment services. The comparison condition involved referral by the youth's probation officer to outpatient adolescent group meetings. Ninety-eight percent of families completed a full course of treatment (an average of 130 days and 40 hr of service provision), compared with very little service access among the youth assigned to the control group (78% of youths received no substance abuse or mental health services, and only 5% received both substance use and mental health services). In other studies, MST has been shown to reduce re-arrest rates up to 64% and to be associated with significantly lower rates of substance-related arrests (Henggeler et al., 1991; Henggeler, Melton, Brondino, Scherer, & Hanley, 1997).

Brief strategic family therapy (BSFT; Szapocznik & Hervis, 2003) is a somewhat less intensive approach (as it targets fewer systems and can be delivered through a once-per-week office-based format) that has also achieved an impressive level of empirical support. In BSFT, patterns of interaction in the family system are targeted that have been shown to influence adolescent drug abuse. The therapy consists of three classes of interventions: engaging all family members in treatment, identifying family strengths as well as roles and relationships linked to adolescent problems, and developing new family interactions (e.g., improved parenting skills and conflict resolution) to protect the adolescent. Home visits and use of specific engagement strategies are encouraged. In a study of 126 drug-abusing adolescents and their families that compared BSFT to a group control condition, 75% of those assigned to BSFT showed reliable improvement and 56% could be classified as recovered. In the control condition, only 14% showed reliable improvement, whereas 43% showed reliable deterioration in marijuana use (Santisteban et al., 2003). Brief strategic family therapy has also been shown to be associated with improved retention (Santisteban et al., 1996; Szapocznik et al., 1988) as well as significant reductions in the frequency of externalizing behaviors (aggression, delinquency) (Szapocznik, Kurtines, Foote, Perez-Vidal, & Hervis, 1986).

Multidimensional family therapy (MDFT) is a multicomponent, staged, family therapy that targets the substance-abusing adolescents, their families, and their interactions. Liddle and colleagues (2001) assigned 182 substance-abusing adolescents who were referred by the criminal justice system or the schools to either MDFT, group therapy, or multifamily education. Treatment was delivered in weekly sessions over 6 months, with roughly 70% of participants completing treatment across conditions. Superior outcomes for the adolescents assigned to MDFT relative to other approaches were seen at termination and 1-year follow-up. At termination, 42% of those assigned to MDFT, 25% of those in group therapy, and 32% of those in family education had clinically significant reductions in their drug use. Positive outcomes have also been reported for other models of family therapy, including family system therapy (Joanning, Thomas, & Quinn, 1992) and functional family therapy (Friedman, 1989).

Behavioral Therapies

A wide range of individual behavioral interventions, including those which seek to provide alternate reinforcers to drugs or reduce reinforcing aspects of abused substances, are based on operant conditioning theory and recognition of the reinforcing properties of abused substances (Aigner, 1978; Bigelow, Stitzer, & Liebson, 1984; Thompson & Pickens, 1971). Among adult substance users, these approaches have among the highest of empirical support (Griffith, Rowan-Szal, Roark, & Simpson, 2000; National Institute on Drug Abuse [NIDA], 2000). Examples include the work of Stitzer and colleagues, which has demonstrated that methadone-maintained opioid addicts will reduce illicit drug use when incentives such as take-home methadone are offered for abstinence (Stitzer & Bigelow, 1978; Stitzer, Iguchi, & Felch, 1992; Stitzer, Iguchi, Kidorf, & Bigelow, 1993). Contingency management incentive systems (Budney & Higgins, 1998; Budney, Higgins, Radonovich, & Novy, 2000; Higgins, Delany, Budney, Bickel, Hughes, et al., 1991, 1999; Kirby, Marlowe, Festinger, Lamb, & Platt, 1998; Petry, Martin, Cooney, & Kranzler, 2000; Silverman et al., 1996) offer incentives for targeted treatment goals (e.g., retention, drug-free urines) on an escalating schedule of reinforcement.

Behavioral approaches have only recently begun to be evaluated among substance-abusing adolescents. Azrin, Donahue, and Besalel (1994) assigned 26 substance-using adolescents to supportive counseling or behavior therapy, which consisted of therapist modeling and rehearsal, self-monitoring, and written assignments. After 6 months, urine toxicology screens and self-reports suggested significantly less substance abuse among the group assigned to behavioral therapy relative to supportive counseling, as well as better school and family functioning.

Contingency management approaches have not yet been widely used or evaluated with adolescents. In a feasibility study that involved adolescent smokers as a model for drug use, Corby, Roll, Ledgerwood, and Schuster (2000) found that providing cash incentives for not smoking to adolescents enrolled in a smoking cessation project (as assessed by twice daily CO levels) reduced adolescent smoking and appeared to improve their mood. In a pilot study involving young adult marijuana users referred by the criminal justice system, Sinha, Easton, and Kemp (2003) studied the use of vouchers that could be used to purchase items in neighborhood stores. By providing these vouchers as rewards contingent on session attendance, treatment retention improved significantly.

Cognitive-Behavioral Therapies

Cognitive-behavioral approaches, based on social learning theory, are among the approaches with highest levels of empirical support for the treatment of adult substance use disorders. Key defining features of most cognitive-behavioral approaches for substance use disorders are *(1)* an emphasis on functional analysis of drug use, that is, understanding instances of substance use with respect to its antecedents and consequences, and *(2)* emphasis on skills training and self-regulation. Cognitive-behavioral therapy (CBT) has been shown to be effective across a wide range of substance use disorders (Carroll, 1996; Bowers, Dunn, & Wong, Irvin, 1999), including alcohol dependence (Miller & Wilbourne, 2002; Morgenstern & Longabaugh, 2000), marijuana dependence (MTP Research Group, 2001; Stephens, Roffman, & Curtin, 2000), cocaine dependence (Carroll, Rounsaville & Nich, 1994; Carroll, Nich, Ball, McCance-Katz, & Rounsaville, 1998; McKay, 1997; Rohsenow, Montl, Martin, Michalec, & Abrams, 2000), and nicotine dependence (Fiore, Smith, Jorenberg, & Baker, 1994; Hall, 1998; Patten et al., 1998). These findings are consistent with evidence supporting the effectiveness of CBT across a number of other psychiatric disorders as well, including depression, anxiety disorders, and eating disorders (DeRubeis & Crits-Christoph, 1998).

Cognitive-behavioral therapy has also been evaluated as a treatment for adolescent substance use disorders. In an extremely well-done study, Waldron and colleagues (2001) randomly assigned 120 adolescents who were abusers of illicit drugs (primarily marijuana) to one of four treatment conditions: family therapy alone (functional family therapy), individual CBT alone, a combination of individual and family therapy, and a psychoeducational group. Completion rates were high (70% to 80% across groups). In general, while there were meaningful reductions in drug use in all conditions, there were larger and more durable reductions in substance use for the combined and family conditions relative to the individual CBT and group conditions. Treatment effects were strongest immediately after treatment but persisted through a 7-month follow-up.

Kaminer and colleagues (2002) compared group CBT to psychoeducational substance abuse treatment for 88 adolescents referred for treatment of a substance abuse problem. Eighty-six percent of the sample completed treatment and 9-month follow-up data were available for 65% of the sample. The presence of a conduct disorder was associated with treatment dropout. Cognitive-behavioral therapy was significantly more effective than psychoeducation only for male subjects; females appeared to improve regardless of treatment condition. Nevertheless, there were no significant differences between the two conditions at the 9-month follow-up. The relatively high rates of relapse in this sample (52% had a urinalysis that was positive for marijuana at the 9-month follow-up evaluation) suggest that an eight-session stand-alone approach may not be adequately intensive or structured for this population.

Motivational Approaches

Motivational approaches are brief treatment approaches designed to produce rapid, internally motivated change in addictive behavior and other problem behaviors. Grounded in principles of motivational psychology and patient-centered counseling, motivational interviewing (MI; Miller & Rollnick, 1991, 2002) arose out of several recent theoretical and empirical advances (Miller, 2000). Motivational interviewing has a high level of empirical support in the adult substance abuse treatment literature (Burke, Arkowitz, & Menchola, 2003; Dunn, Deroo, & Rivara, 2001; Miller, 2002; Wilk, Jensen, & Havighurst, 1997). The core principles of MI are as follows: *(1)* express empathy; *(2)* develop discrepancy; *(3)* avoid argumentation; *(4)* roll with resistance; *(5)* support self-efficacy. Motivational interviewing makes the important assumption that ambivalence and fluctuating motivations define substance abuse recovery and need to be thoroughly explored rather than confronted harshly. Ambivalence is considered a normal event, not something that indicates the patient is unsuitable for treatment or needs vigorous confrontation in hopes of forcing a sudden change. The patient's point of view is respected, which in some cases may mean accepting that major change, or even any change, is not what the patient wants, at least at the present time (Carroll, Ball, & Martino, 2004). Thus, while the bulk of research on efficacy of MI is in the adult literature, this nonconfrontational approach appears quite well suited for application to adolescents and young adults, given its flexibility around goals and recognition of abstinence as part of the change process.

Another distinct advantage of using MI with adolescent populations is that it can be implemented in a range of settings, given that adolescents with substance abuse problems rarely seek treatment of their own volition in traditional substance abuse settings. Monti and colleagues (1999) studied 94 adolescents treated at an emergency room for a problem related to alcohol use (e.g., injuries related to drinking, drunk driving). They were randomly assigned to MI or standard care, with all interventions and assessments conducted in the emergency room. At a 6-month follow-up, there were significantly fewer incidents of drunk driving, traffic violations, and alcohol-related problems in the group assigned to receive MI. Not only does this study suggest the promise of brief motivational approaches for this population, but it also underlines the importance of intervening with adolescents in nontraditional settings.

Disease Model Approaches

While disease model treatments and other approaches associated with the Twelve Steps of Alcoholics Anonymous dominate the treatment system for both adults and adolescents, there are no randomized controlled trials evaluating the effectiveness of these approaches in adolescents. Recent reports from randomized controlled trials evaluating the efficacy of manualized Twelve-Step approaches have found evidence to suggest their effectiveness with adult substance users (Carroll et al., 1998; Crits-Christoph et al., 1999; Project MATCH Research Group, 1997). It is important to note, however, that these manual-guided approaches are highly structured, delivered as individual (rather than group) therapy, and might be quite different from the nonmanualized group approaches typically delivered in community settings with adolescents. In addition, since individual drug counseling emphasizes and encourages frequent Twelve-Step group attendance, its effectiveness might reflect increased patient involvement in rehabilitative groups. It is important to note that the absence of sufficient research on Twelve-Step treatment should not lead one to conclude that this widespread and popular approach is ineffective.

Data on the effectiveness of more traditional programs are beginning to emerge, but no data from randomized trials comparing these approaches to alternatives are available. Winters and colleagues (2000) reported on a large nonrandomized evaluation comparing a group of substance-abusing youth who completed the Twelve-Step Minnesota Model treatment to similar individuals who did not complete treatment and to a group on a waiting list for treatment. The treatment was multimodal, based on the principles of the Twelve Steps of Alcoholics Anonymous, and included group therapy and individual counseling, family therapy, lectures about the Twelve Steps, and reading assignments. Better substance use and psychosocial outcomes at 6 and 12 months were reported for those who completed treatment compared with those who did not complete or who did not receive treatment. Although a high rate of abstinence was reported among treatment completers, it is difficult to interpret these findings, given the self-selection due to lack of randomization and lack of measurement of treatment delivery or process.

Multisite Studies Comparing Several Approaches

Recently, the Center for Substance Abuse Treatment (CSAT) funded the largest multisite clinical trial comparing an array of diverse outpatient treatments targeting adolescent marijuana abuse and dependence. The study, conducted at four sites, involved 600 randomized patients and evaluated five manualized treatments. Notably, the study had a follow-up rate of 95% for up to 30 months. Treatment modalities covered the full range of treatments (individual, group, family, and comprehensive multicomponent) that took place between 5 and 12 weeks and included 6 to 21 sessions (Diamond et al., 2002). All five treatments performed equally well and were associated with marked (50%) reductions in frequency of marijuana use; these improvements were maintained through a 30-month follow-up evaluation. It is noteworthy that these very promising outcomes were seen even for the less costly 6-week, five-session treatment.

Process Research and Mechanisms of Action

As new effective therapies for adolescents are identified, it is imperative that the field move toward evaluating how these treatments exert their effects, by looking at mediators and moderators of outcome. Several recent investigations have examined these variables. In terms of retention and engagement, Szapocznik and colleagues' impressive work on engaging teens and families in treatment has been replicated and further developed (e.g., Coatsworth, Santisteban, McBride, & Szapocznik, 2001; Santisteban et al., 1996). Henggeler and colleagues (1996) demonstrated a 98% treatment completion rate for home-based MST (Szapocznik et al., 1983). They have also demonstrated that adherence to the treatment was significantly associated with better treatment outcome. Liddle and colleagues have conducted several process studies looking at mechanisms of change, including in-session patterns of change associated with the resolution of parent–adolescent conflict (Diamond & Liddle, 1996) and the link between improvement in

parenting and better substance use outcome (Schmidt, Liddle, & Dakof, 1996). These kinds of studies will help identify key treatment ingredients that might lead to increased treatment potency.

Assessment

Another area relevant to treatment research that may be influenced by developmental perspective concerns assessment. While self-report of substance use by adolescents has been confirmed as fairly reliable (Buchan, Dennis, Tims, & Diamond, 2002), recent analysis from the Cannabis Youth Treatment Study suggests the addition of parent reports adds additional information not provided by the adolescent. Although adolescents and parents reported about the same number of substance use symptoms, there was a very low concordance between the types of symptom endorsed. Parents tended to report more symptoms related to role failure, tolerance, and substance-induced psychological problems (Dennis, Babor, Roebuck, & Donaldson, 2002). Similar findings were discovered regarding mental health symptoms. Specifically, parents tended to endorse more symptoms of depression and attention problems (Diamond, Panichelli-Mindel, Shera, Tims, & Ungemack, in press). This was particularly true for African-American adolescents. Thus parent report may have a unique contribution when working with a minority population, a community that has been characterized as suspicious of the research community.

The Challenge of Comorbidity

One area that has received strikingly little research with adolescents is the integration of substance use and other mental health services that can treat adolescents with both kinds of disorders. Historically there has been a divide between treatment systems for substance abuse and mental health disorders. Substance abuse counselors often have little or no training in mental health issues, and programs either ignore co-occurring problems or refer patients to other systems during (parallel) or after (sequential) substance abuse treatment. There is emerging consensus that lack of integration leads to poor coordination of services, interagency miscommunication, and funding conflicts, all of which contribute to attrition and poor outcomes for patients (Osher & Drake, 1996; Report to Congress, 2002). This is particularly troubling since co-occurring mental health distress is associated with substance use severity, greater psychosocial impairment, treatment resistance, and poorer long-term prognosis (Diamond, Panichelli-Mindel, Shera, Tims, & Ungemack, in press; Drake, Mueser, Clark, & Wallach, 1996; Shane et al., under review). Consequently, the most severe and chronic patients often receive the poorest care, leading to repeated visits to hospital emergency rooms and inpatient and residential facilities (Richardson, Craig, & Haughland, 1995). The end result is that comorbid patients in need of care are consuming a major portion of treatment funding (Ridgely, Goldman, & Willenbring, 1990).

The gap between substance abuse and mental health dates back to the 1930s (Rosenthal & Westreich, 1999). At that time, psychodynamic therapists, who dominated the treatment world, believed that addicts' personality structure was not amenable to the analytic method, and therefore addicts were not treatable. This attitude may persist today among practitioners in the mental health community, who tend to view addiction as inhibiting treatment of other "underlying" problems. Simultaneously, the self-help movement developed independent of the mental health community, and as the self-help philosophies and programs matured, educational and professional licensure pathways emerged that legitimized and strengthened these approaches (Rosenthal & Westreich, 1999). As often happens, these ideological differences became institutionalized and perpetuated a division that does not reflect the clinical realities of the patients.

Recognition of this schism has inspired many attempts to integrate substance abuse and mental health treatment programs for adult dual-diagnosis populations (Drake, Mchugo, & Noordsy, 1993; Miller & DelBoca, 1994; Minkoff & Drake, 1991). At least 36 studies have evaluated different versions of integrated programs at all levels of care (e.g., outpatient, day treatment,

inpatient, residential, etc). Some studies added a substance abuse group to outpatient mental health services, resulting in reduced dropout, decreased hospitalization, and increased abstinence (e.g., Hellerstein, Rosenthal, & Miner, 2001; Osher & Kofoed, 1989). Studies that combined substance abuse services with inpatient, day treatment, and residential care have also shown some benefits as long as patients remained in the program. Unfortunately, attrition was often high and once patients were discharged, relapse rates were high as well (e.g., Rahav et al., 1995).

A major contribution to this area was the 1987 funding of 13 dual-diagnosis demonstration projects. These studies demonstrated that integrated programs could be implemented in a number of settings, resulting in increased engagement and services utilization and reduced drug use. Five recent studies were conducted on comprehensive integrated systems using more sophisticated treatment programs and quasiexperimental or true experimental designs (e.g., Drake, Mercer-McFadden, Muesser, McHugo, & Blond, 1998; Ridgely & Lambert, 1999; Godley, 1994; Jerrell & Ridgely, 1995). These studies showed significant reductions in substance use, program readmission, and hospitalization and improvement in other functional outcomes (Drake et al., 1998). However, there has been little or no comparable research on the effectiveness of integrated programs for adolescent substance users.

Summary of Psychosocial Treatment

Clinical research during the past 10 years has identified a number of effective treatments for adolescent substance users. Although the field is still young, this growing body of work has yielded several important findings that support the effectiveness of carefully implemented, structured behavioral approaches for adolescent substance use (Liddle & Rowe, in press; Stanton & Shaddish, 1997; Williams et al., 2000). These can be summarized as follows:

- The field has been inadequately studied.
- Most studies indicate that treatment can be effective for most adolescents. In most stud-

ies, well-defined structured approaches tend to be more effective and durable at reducing adolescent substance use and improving related problems than no treatment, treatment as usual, or other comparison approaches. Treatments that focus on broad aspects of functioning seem to be most promising (Williams et al., 2000). That is, in addition to addressing substance use, interventions should also target other domains such as family functioning, school success, delinquency, peer group associations, and other risky behaviors.

- Adolescents who complete treatment tend to have the best outcomes, although this may be related to factors such as higher motivation for treatment, better or more intact family and social supports, less severe substance use, better school competency, and less psychopathology, all of which are associated with more treatment success.

- In general, inclusion of family members improves retention and outcome among substance-using adolescents. To date, there is no evidence from controlled studies that involvement of family members in treatment has a negative effect on outcome. In the studies of family-based therapy reviewed here, retention rates were generally high (in the 70% to 80% range), and retention was often sustained over comparatively long periods. At least two studies have demonstrated that outpatient family therapy was more effective and less costly than residential placement (Liddle & Dakof, 2002; Schoenwald et al., 1996). Finally, long-term effectiveness of family-based models has also gained some empirical support (Henggler, Schoenwald, Borduin, Rowland, & Cunningham, 1998; Stanton & Shadish, 1997).

- Behavioral therapies, especially those that target multiple systems, also appear to have some promise. However, contingency management approaches, which have been shown to be highly flexible and effective with a range of adult populations, have only rarely been applied to adolescents. The success of these approaches among adult populations suggests great promise in the treatment of adolescents. Contingency management approaches might be used, for example, to target retention, encourage patients to meet specific treatment goals (e.g., reducing truancy and improving school performance), or enhance compliance with pharmacotherapies (Carroll, Ball, & Martino, 2004). The literature indicates that adults with antisocial personality disorders respond relatively well to contingency management approaches (Messina, Farabee, & Rawson, 2003). In view of the high rates of conduct and externalizing disorders among substance-abusing adolescents, further evaluation of contingency management approaches with this population is warranted.

- Cognitive-behavioral approaches appear to have some promise, but the existing evidence suggests they may be most effective when delivered in conjunction with family therapy. The delayed emergence of effects after CBT that have been noted after termination of treatment with adults (Carroll, Rounsaville, Nitch, et al., 1994; Rawson et al., 2002) has not been reported among adolescent populations. However, CBT has generally been delivered to adolescents in a group format and for a comparatively brief period. Longer or more intensive CBT approaches, or delivery of CBT as an individual treatment, may be necessary with this population.

- The data suggesting that some deviant, high-risk adolescents may escalate problem behavior in the contexts of interventions delivered in peer groups (Dishion et al., 1999) have important implications for behavioral treatments of substance-using youth. While poor outcomes for group approaches for adolescents have not uniformly been reported in the studies reviewed here, it is clearly important to be aware of this possibility when group approaches are used, to monitor behavior closely, and to involve adults and parents as well.

PHARMACOLOGICAL TREATMENTS

Pharmacotherapy for substance dependence is a relatively young field of medicine, and the proven treatments for adults have not been adequately researched in adolescents. Therefore, few conclusions regarding this modality can be stated conclusively at this time. However, the actual usage of pharmacotherapy for psychiatric syndromes has been steadily increasing among adolescents and children for the last 15 years, despite lack of data. Prescriptions for these young patients between 1987 and 1996 rose 300% overall (Magno Zito et al., 2003). By 1996 stimulants and antidepressants were ranked first and second in terms of total prescriptions. These two medications also had the greatest increase in prescribing (400% each): stimulant prescribing rose from 10/1,000 youth to 40/1,000 youth, and antidepressants rose from 3/1,000 to 13/1,000.

What does this phenomenal increase in psychopharmacology reflect in the medical and psychiatric evaluation of adolescents? Does it have any relationship to substance abuse, which has also been rising among these adolescents and children? There is probably a strong association, since adolescents who abuse drugs and have substance use disorders typically have behavioral problems, skills deficits, academic difficulties, family problems, and mental health problems (Tarter, 2002; Tims et al., 2002). While these problems usually reflect more than neurochemical defects that may be reversed with medications, adolescents with substance dependence and comorbid psychiatric disorders can benefit from pharmacotherapy. But pharmacotherapy should be justified by careful evaluations of the diagnoses in these young patients. These medical and psychiatric evaluations can be informed by structured interviews for common comorbid disorders such as depression and bipolar disorders, ADHD, and substance dependence. Medical disorders including infections, endocrine problems, and various developmental disorders also need consideration, but are beyond this review.

Adolescents who enter substance abuse treatment programs are more likely than non–drug-abusing peers to have experienced abuse or neglect, to have significant family problems, and to have developed a psychiatric disorder during childhood such as ADHD and mood disorder. These behavioral, psychosocial, and mental health problems are coupled with the neurohormonal changes of puberty and lead to poor adjustment in the school environment, thereby increasing the risk for school failure (Riggs & Whitmore, 1999; Tarter, 2002). These school experiences may also lead to the early onset of substance abuse (Crowley & Riggs, 1995; Rutter, Giller, & Hagell, 1998). Substance abuse exacerbates preexisting psychiatric disorders such as ADHD as well as mood and anxiety disorders (Kruesi et al., 1990; Markou, Kosten, & Koob, 1998; Rutter et al., 1998).

The multidimensionality of the problems that substance-abusing youth typically bring to treatment underscores their need for multimodal treatment that addresses a broad range of mental health and psychosocial problems integrated with treatment for drug abuse. The role of pharmacotherapy targeted specifically to substance abuse may therefore be relatively limited, and there is no research base to provide guidance on dosing or duration of treatment for adolescents with dependence on alcohol, nicotine, opiates, or other addictions for which we have pharmacotherapies. Furthermore, the other most commonly abused drug, cannabis, has no specific pharmacotherapy. Pharmacotherapies are also entirely lacking for club drugs such as MDMA, GHB, and various hallucinogens.

Specific Pharmacotherapy for Substance Use Disorders in Adolescents

Given the clinical importance of drug euphoria and drug craving, most pharmacological strategies for addiction target these primary reinforcers. Drug-induced reward is attenuated in animal models by a number of agents, depending on the drug in question. These medications act on dopamine, opioid, glutamate, or GABA systems. These reward-blocking medications have been tested in human substance abusers to determine whether they reduce drug euphoria under controlled settings or promote abstinence in clinical trials. Other means of reducing reward have also been tested, including vaccines that block the entry of an addictive substance into the brain, and agents like disulfiram that produce aversive symptoms when alcohol is consumed. In addition to strategies that reduce drug euphoria, strategies that reduce craving have also been tested and prescribed. Agonist treatment (prescribing a substance that replaces the addictive drug) has been used in opioid (e.g., methadone, buprenorphine) and nicotine (e.g., nicotine gum) dependence with considerable success, providing a means of bypassing dangerous routes of administration or hazards associated with drug procurement. The reversing of clinically relevant neuroadaptations associated with chronic exposure to addictive substances has the theoretical ability to reduce craving and other aversive aspects of addiction.

Unfortunately, there has been little research directed toward the pharmacological treatment of substance dependence in adolescents. For a number of reasons, there are no controlled trials evaluating the effectiveness of substitution or replacement therapies (e.g., methadone, buprenorphine), antagonists (e.g., naltrexone), aversive therapies (e.g., disulfiram), or anticraving medications (e.g., bupropion, naltrexone) in this subpopulation. Therefore, if such medications are used in adolescents, they must be used with caution, careful monitoring, and consideration of the developmental characteristics that distinguish adult patients from adolescents (e.g., greater impulsivity and polydrug use; Solhkhah & Grenyer, 1998). More research is clearly needed in this area.

Since the most commonly abused substances by adolescents are nicotine, alcohol, and cannabis, these are the most likely drugs for which pharmacotherapy questions might arise. We will review these medications briefly, starting with those used in detoxification. Advances in our understanding of the mechanisms of drug craving and drug-induced euphoria should guide future research and shed light on more effective pharmacological treatments for addiction in adolescents.

Detoxification

Medical detoxification is required for alcohol, sedatives, and opiates, but not for other abused drugs. Detoxification from alcohol dependence can be effectively attained by using benzodiazepines or barbiturates, and anticonvulsants such as valproate and carbamazepine to block or reverse withdrawal symptoms (Kosten & O'Connor, 2003). These detoxification medications should be used in adolescents if withdrawal symptoms are significant, particularly because alcohol withdrawal is potentially life threatening. Detoxification from sedative hypnotic dependence can also be accomplished by prescribing descending doses of benzodiazepines and barbiturates.

For opioid dependence, the most common means of detoxification involves prescribing descending doses of methadone for a period of 2 to 4 days while carefully monitoring the patient's response. Methadone is a long-acting opioid agonist that reverses heroin withdrawal by replacing heroin at the opioid receptor. Since methadone has the potential to cause lethal opioid overdose, and opioid withdrawal is not medically dangerous, it is imperative to avoid prescribing an excessive dose of methadone to adolescents. The appropriate dose is best selected by closely monitoring the signs of opioid withdrawal, which should be given more weight than reported symptoms that might be exaggerated or feigned by drug-seeking patients.

A new treatment for detoxification and maintenance, the partial agonist buprenorphine, was made available in the United States in 2003. It may be ideally suited to adolescents and is currently in clinical trials in this population. Detoxification with this medication is very simple because overdose is almost impossible. The patient can be transferred from the opiate of abuse to buprenorphine and then the dose is gradually reduced with minimal or absent withdrawal symptoms. Yet another option is the nonopioid clonidine, an antihypertensive medication that blocks many of the opiate withdrawal symptoms (Gold, Dackis, & Washton, 1984). Most patients prefer methadone or buprenorphine because of greater comfort.

The treatment of heroin and other opioid dependence often begins with inpatient detoxification of heroin withdrawal that should also involve specialized drug rehabilitation and aftercare referral (Dackis & O'Brien, 2003b). Unfortunately, considerable availability and access problems preclude many adolescents from receiving appropriate inpatient treatment. Still, hospitalization is the safest and most conservative treatment approach to this potentially lethal condition (Dackis & Gold, 1992). Inpatient treatment provides a controlled environment in which abstinence can be assured while a comprehensive medical and psychiatric evaluation is conducted. The high mortality rate in intravenous adolescent heroin users results not only from overdose but also from trauma, medical conditions related to the use of needles, and the concomitant use of other drugs and alcohol. Therefore, as reviewed elsewhere (Dackis & Gold, 1992), a comprehensive physical examination, medical history, and laboratory evaluation are indicated in all addicted adolescents.

Familiarity with the medical and psychiatric complications of heroin dependence enhances the clinician's ability to identify and treat these commonly occurring conditions. Infections related to intravenous heroin use include acquired immunodeficiency syndrome (AIDS), viral hepatitis, endocarditis, meningitis, tuberculosis, abscesses, infected injection sites, and pneumonia. Additionally, unprotected sex is common among addicted adolescents (Crome, Christian, & Green, 1998), leading to a preponderance of sexually transmitted diseases. Heroin often produces irregular menses in women and sexual performance problems in men, apparently by dysregulating the hypothalamic–pituitary–gonadal axis (Malik, Khan, Jabbar, & Iqbal, 1992). The most common psychiatric problem associated with heroin dependence is depression (Handelsman, Aronson, Ness, Cochrane, & Kanof, 1992), which should be expeditiously identified and appropriately treated to avoid the risk of suicide and to facilitate the recovery process.

Inpatient detoxification treatment should not be restricted merely to the medical management of heroin withdrawal. This intensive intervention provides the physician with an ideal opportunity to establish a therapeutic alliance with adolescent patients by concomitantly addressing the critical treatment issues of honesty, openness, trust, denial, and engagement. Inpatient detoxification also provides an opportunity to fully evaluate the patient, assess their readiness for change, and provide critical family therapy. Since families require education, support, and guidance throughout the process, clinicians

should be familiar with psychosocial as well as medical aspects of heroin addiction. It is essential to emphasize that detoxification, in and of itself, is not sufficient treatment for heroin dependence and must therefore be followed by ongoing outpatient drug rehabilitation. The recent fad of very rapid detoxification with general anesthesia has not been shown to produce better outcomes than standard detoxification.

Abstinence and Relapse Prevention

The nature of addiction requires that, after detoxification, complete abstinence be the treatment goal for addicted adolescents, rather than the mere reduction of drug and alcohol use. Once the cycle of addiction has become entrenched, casual use is seldom possible. Indeed, even the use of other addictive agents, such as alcohol by a cocaine-dependent adolescent, often leads to relapse to the drug of choice. Thus, total abstinence from all addicting drugs should be the goal when treating adolescents. After attaining abstinence, preventing relapse to drug dependence is the primary clinical target in adolescents, and to that end, medications for relapse prevention are likely to be useful. A few specific relapse prevention pharmacotherapies are U.S. Food and Drug Administration (FDA) approved for nicotine and alcohol, but none has been tested in adolescents. For nicotine the medications are nicotine replacement and bupropion, and for alcohol the medications are disulfiram and naltrexone. However, before medicating adolescents, it is imperative to determine that they will be cooperative, that parental consent has been obtained, and that the adolescents and parents have the same understanding of treatment goals and approaches.

Adolescent Smoking Cessation Research

Despite the prevalence of adolescent tobacco use and nicotine dependence, there have been relatively fewer studies that evaluate adolescent smoking treatment programs. The settings for and approaches to the treatment of adolescent tobacco use are similar to those described for adolescent smoking prevention, with the addition of pharmacological approaches. However, the challenges inherent in adolescent smoking treatment appear to be greater than those for prevention. Recruitment to adolescent smoking treatment programs is difficult, in part because of adolescents' desires to keep their smoking practices confidential. Moreover, among those adolescents who enroll in treatment programs, attrition rates are very high (Mermelstein, 2003).

For the most part, available data on the effectiveness of adolescent smoking treatment have been disappointing. Quit rates for adolescents receiving behavioral smoking cessation treatment are roughly 10% to 15%, compared with 5% to 10% in control conditions (Pomerleau, Pomerleau, & Namenek, 1998). The results of pharmacological trials using nicotine replacement therapy (e.g., nicotine patch) have also been disappointing, yielding 6-month quit rates of only 5% (Hurt et al., 2000; Smith et al., 1996). While not yet thoroughly investigated, interventions delivered by pediatricians and family physicians may have great promise for assisting youth to quit smoking (Pbert et al., 2003). Adolescents with comorbid psychiatric conditions are an important target group for treatment, given the greater predisposition to tobacco use (Moolchan, Ernst, & Henningfield, 2000).

Medications for Smoking Cessation

Because nicotine replacement therapy (NRT) is readily available in over-the-counter preparations, many adolescents have already used these agents before seeing practitioners. Low-dose NRT is clearly preferable to smoking cigarettes, given the risks of lung damage that are associated with inhaling carbon monoxide and carcinogens. The forms of NRT include patches, gum, inhalers (oral absorptions), nasal spray, and lozenges (McCance & Kosten, 1998). If NRT is used, it should probably be discontinued after 8 to 12 weeks to avoid continued nicotine dependence. Although some patients continue to use nicotine gum for up to a year, such an extended duration of treatment should probably be discouraged in NRT-treated adolescents. In summary, NRT may be a reasonable treatment for adolescents who want to quit smoking and are experiencing acute withdrawal symptoms that interfere with abstinence.

Bupropion has a long record of relatively safe use in depression, and several large studies have shown its efficacy for smoking cessation in adults, with higher success rates than NRT alone (McCance & Kosten, 1998). Thus, this medication is another option for treating adolescents who want to quit smoking. Recent discussion has considered vaccines for nicotine dependence (Kosten & Biegel, 2002). These immunotherapies can attenuate the rewarding effects of nicotine and have been considered as a potential prophylactic for preventing nicotine dependence. Immunotherapies might also be used as a secondary prevention for adolescents who have begun to smoke (Kosten & Biegel, 2002). However, this type of invasive and long-lasting intervention has potential ethical problems, particularly in adolescents who do not want to stop smoking.

Medications for Alcohol Abuse and Alcoholism in Adolescents

One of the actions of alcohol in the body is to release endogenous opioids. Thus a drug such as naltrexone that blocks opiate receptors will reduce the reward of alcohol and help to prevent relapse. The majority of controlled studies have shown that naltrexone increases abstinence. Although there are case reports in adolescents (Lifrak et al., 1997), no controlled studies of naltrexone have been conducted in this population. Side effects of naltrexone in adults have generally been minimal at usual doses. Naltrexone also has substantial hormonal effects that include raising cortisol and various sex hormone levels (e.g., luteinizing hormone), and these actions could interfere with growth and development in adolescents (Morgan & Kosten, 1990).

Disulfiram promotes abstinence by blocking the metabolism of alcohol, resulting in the production of acetaldehyde, a noxious compound. It can produce severe reactions, including death, when mixed with alcohol, and there is significant risk associated with prescribing this medication to impulsive adolescent alcohol abusers. Thus, disulfiram is rarely used for younger patients. Other medications such as acamprosate and topiramate have been found effective in relapse prevention in clinical trials in adult populations but have not yet received FDA approval. There have been no studies of these medications in adolescents.

Medications for Long-Term Treatment of Opioid Dependence

Opioid dependence is relatively uncommon in adolescents, particularly those seeking treatment. However, many regions of the United States have experienced a rise in opioid addiction, particularly with the availability of potent, smokable heroin. Naltrexone, by blocking opiate receptors, can absolutely prevent relapse to opioid dependence as long as it is ingested. Adolescents, however, are not likely to take this medication regularly. Several naltrexone depot preparations are currently in clinical trials. When these become available, a monthly injection will effectively prevent relapse.

Agonist maintenance with methadone or buprenorphine is the most generally effective treatment for adolescent opioid addiction currently available (Gonzalez, Oliveto, & Kosten, 2002). Buprenorphine, which became available in 2003, may be particularly promising in adolescent opioid patients because of the ease of detoxification and legal status that permits prescribing from an individual practitioner's office. A large multiclinic trial of buprenorphine in adolescents is currently in progress.

These pharmacological treatments should be integrated with psychosocial interventions including individual, family, and group therapy approaches to promote continued abstinence from the drug of abuse. Agonist treatment with methadone or buprenorphine replaces intravenous heroin with a prescribed, long-acting oral agent that is administered in a clinic. The need to procure heroin on a daily basis is eliminated and the risk of medical complications associated with intravenous use is averted. When combined with psychosocial treatment, methadone has been shown to stabilize adult patients and reduce medical complications associated with needle use (Sees et al., 2000).

Heroin-addicted patients continue to crave heroin even after they have completed detoxification, however, and are particularly vulnerable to craving that is evoked by environmental cues previously associated with heroin use. Cue-induced craving, often precipitated by viewing syringes, visiting places where heroin was previously used, or interacting with people using heroin, can actually be associated with physiological symptoms of heroin withdrawal even after months or years of abstinence (O'Brien, Childress, McLellan, & Ehrman, 1992). Consequently, an essential strategy of drug rehabilitation involves avoiding situations that might expose recovering adolescents to cue-induced craving. Treatment recommendations often involve terminating friendships with addicted friends, eliminating risky social events, and otherwise changing one's lifestyle in ways that might not be palatable to adolescents who are focused on peer interactions and achieving autonomy. Denial also contributes to the adolescent's reluctance to follow treatment recommendations that involve motivation, sacrifice, and protracted effort. Practitioners trained in addiction treatment should use age-appropriate clinical approaches to engage adolescent heroin users in this challenging process. Considerable therapeutic flexibility and skill are often required to negotiate a therapeutic alliance that can help adolescents overcome their pleasure-reinforced compulsion to use heroin.

Treatments for Stimulant Abuse and Dependence

There has been little research on the treatment of adolescent stimulant dependence and most regions of the United States do not provide adequate treatment options for the large population of afflicted adolescents. Unfortunately, no pharmacological treatments with proven efficacy have been identified for cocaine dependence in general, and few clinical trials have even included adolescents. Similarly, psychosocial treatments have been minimally researched in stimulant addicted adolescents. Group-based treatments, following the principles of Alcoholics Anonymous (AA) and Narcotics Anonymous (NA), are commonly employed in specialized adolescent treatment programs in the United States. Adolescents will naturally resist treatment approaches that ignore normal developmental issues, including their need for peer acceptance, autonomy, and individualization. In addition, they cannot be treated in a vacuum and it is important to address maladaptive family patterns with family therapy. Parents should also receive education about cocaine addiction that includes the warning signs of relapse and specific behavioral guidance.

Treatment approaches have limited effectiveness when adolescent patients do not view their use as problematic or are not sufficiently motivated to quit using cocaine. It is even more difficult to establish a therapeutic alliance when adolescents have been pressured into treatment by their parents, the legal system, or school authorities. Even internally motivated adolescents are often difficult to engage, and treatment facilities should be staffed with practitioners who are familiar with the dynamics of addiction, normal adolescent development, and the nuances of treating adolescent patients.

A large number of medications have been examined and some hold promise, such as disulfiram and several agents that enhance GABA activity, such as baclofen, topiramate, and tiagabine (Kosten, in press). Experimental agents include immunotherapies, such as a cocaine vaccine (Kosten & Biegel, 2002). Glutamatergic agents such as modafinil may promote abstinence by reducing cocaine euphoria and cocaine craving (Dackis et al., 2003). At present, however, no medication has been consistently beneficial in preventing relapse to stimulant abuse and dependence.

Treatment of Co-occurring Psychiatric Disorders in Adolescents

Current research provides fairly solid support for integrated pharmacotherapy of co-occurring psychiatric disorders and substance dependence in adolescents. The first consideration in this research is that adolescents with substance dependence and comorbid psychiatric disorders have poorer treatment outcomes than those with single disorders. If the comorbid disorders are left untreated, the likelihood of successful engagement, retention, and completion of substance treatment is reduced (Grella, Hser, Joshi, &

Rounds-Bryant, 2001; Lohman, Riggs, Hall, Mikulich, & Klein, 2002; Whitmore et al., 1997; Wise, Cuffe, & Fischer, 2001). Second, pharmacotherapy of comorbid disorders alone is not likely to reduce or "treat" substance abuse in the absence of specific substance treatment interventions in adolescents with substance dependence. This has been demonstrated in controlled trials for comorbid ADHD, bipolar disorder, and depression (Deas & Thomas, 2001; Geller et al., 1998; Lohman et al., 2002; Riggs, Mikulich, & Hall, 2001). Third, treatment of substance dependence (or achievement of abstinence) alone does not "treat" comorbid psychiatric disorders, such as ADHD, bipolar disorder, or major depression, in the absence of specific pharmacotherapy for the comorbid disorder. Even depression is much less likely to remit with abstinence in adolescents compared to findings in depressed adults with chronic alcohol or drug dependence (Bukstein, Glancy, & Kaminer, 1992; Riggs et al., 1996). Fourth, controlled trials indicate that some medications commonly used to treat psychiatric disorders in children and adolescents may be safe and effective in treating comorbid disorders in adolescents with substance dependence, even if the adolescent is nonabstinent. Specific studies have examined fluoxetine for depression (Lohman et al., 2002), lithium for bipolar disorder (Geller et al., 1998), and pemoline for ADHD (Riggs et al., 2001).

Taken together, current research supports integrated, concurrent treatment of comorbid psychiatric disorders and substance abuse in adolescents. Sequential treatment models requiring adolescents to first complete substance treatment and achieve abstinence as a prerequisite for medicating comorbidity are much less effective and probably contraindicated. Although research now supports integrated treatment models, it is understandable that sequential models evolved and have been perpetuated. Some of the reasons for this include a shortage of child and adolescent psychiatrists with training in addictions; shortages of addiction clinicians with substantial psychiatric training; separate provider networks for mental health and substance treatment services; and poor third-party payer coverage for integrated treatment services. Although coordinated treatment of co-occurring disorders in adolescents provides significant clinical advantage, it is often unavailable because of inadequacies in the health delivery system.

The dearth of research related to pharmacological treatment of addiction in adolescents results in part from the traditional exclusion of addicted adolescents from clinical trials evaluating the safety and efficacy of medications, even when prescribed for psychiatric illnesses. Until very recently, virtually nothing was known about the safety and effectiveness of these medications in adolescents with substance dependence or the potential for adverse interactions of medications with drugs of abuse. Clinicians were therefore reluctant to use medications to treat psychiatric disorders in substance-abusing adolescents, often referring such youth for substance treatment before considering treatment of comorbidity. This reluctance to use pharmacotherapy is often cited as one reason for poorer treatment outcomes in dually diagnosed adolescents, as untreated psychiatric illness significantly diminishes the likelihood of successful substance treatment. The risks of treatment must be balanced with risks associated with not treating psychiatric comorbidity. Recent controlled clinical trials have begun to extricate clinicians from this therapeutic conundrum by demonstrating the safety and efficacy of some medications used to treat the most common psychiatric comorbidities, including bipolar disorder, ADHD, and depression (Geller et al., 1998; Lohman et al., 2002; Riggs et al., 2001).

Attention-Deficit Hyperactivity Disorder

Pharmacotherapy with psychostimulants is considered the first-line treatment for ADHD in children and adolescents without substance dependence. Only one controlled medication trial has been conducted in adolescents with ADHD and substance dependence. In this study, 69 out-of-treatment adolescents with conduct disorder, substance dependence, and ADHD were recruited from the community and randomized to receive either placebo or pemoline (a low-abuse potential psychostimulant). Results showed that pemoline had similar safety and efficacy for ADHD in nonabstinent adolescents to that reported in adolescents without substance depen-

dence. Despite its efficacy for ADHD, pemoline did not reduce substance use or conduct problems when specific treatment for substance dependence was not provided. Although no patients in this trial developed serious side effects or elevations in liver enzymes, recent concerns about the rare but serious potential for liver toxicity with pemoline have led to recommendations for frequent monitoring of liver enzymes (Safer, Zito, & Gardner, 2001; Willy, Manda, Shatin, Drinkard, & Graham, 2002). This restriction has diminished the clinical feasibility of using pemoline in outpatient settings. Nonetheless, pemoline is still considered an important treatment option for ADHD in settings requiring the use of medications with low-abuse potential (e.g., substance abuse treatment programs) and once-per-day dosing regimens. The stimulants used for ADHD have good efficacy but a relatively high-abuse potential and have been placed in schedule II psychostimulants (e.g., methylphenidate, dextroamphetamine; Klein-Schwartz, & McGrath, 2003).

Fortunately, newer medications with low abuse liability, such as bupropion and atomoxetine, have been developed and shown to be effective for ADHD in adults and adolescents without substance dependence (Barrickman et al., 1995; Michelson et al., 2002; Riggs, Leon, Mikulich, & Pottle, 1998; Spencer et al., 2002; Wilens et al., 2001). Although no controlled trials have been conducted, preliminary data indicate that these medications are sufficiently safe to be considered in treating ADHD in dually diagnosed adolescents. Bupropion has also been shown to be effective in treating both ADHD and depression in adolescents and adults without substance dependence (Daviss et al., 2001). Clinicians may therefore wish to consider bupropion as a first-line treatment in adolescents who have substance dependence, ADHD, and depression, again with the caveat that there are no controlled trials in adolescents with substance dependence (Riggs et al., 1998).

Bipolar Disorder

Pharmacotherapy with mood stabilizers (e.g., lithium, valproic acid, carbamazepine) is the first-line treatment for bipolar disorder in adolescents without substance dependence. Only one controlled trial (lithium vs. placebo) has been conducted in adolescents with bipolar disorder and substance dependence (Geller et al., 1998). In this study, lithium had a relatively good safety profile and was shown to be effective in stabilizing mania or hypomania in adolescents with substance dependence, many of whom were not abstinent during the trial (Geller et al., 1998). Although there was a somewhat greater decline in substance use in the lithium-treated group than in those who received placebo, the pharmacological treatment of bipolar disorder did not effectively treat substance dependence in the absence of specific substance treatment. The available data would support treating bipolar disorder only in the context of concurrent treatment for substance dependence in dually diagnosed adolescents. No data are yet available from controlled trials about the safety or efficacy of other mood stabilizers in dually diagnosed adolescents.

Depression

In standard practice, adolescents with major (severe) depression would receive both psychotherapy and pharmacotherapy, whereas those with mild or moderate symptoms might be given a trial of psychotherapy alone before considering medications. When medications are used, selective serotonin reuptake inhibitors (SSRIs; specifically fluoxetine and paroxetine) are considered first-line medication choices for adolescent depression without comorbid substance dependence (Emslie et al., 1997). No adequately powered controlled trials of SSRIs have yet been completed in depressed adolescents with substance dependence. Preliminary data from an ongoing randomized, controlled trial of fluoxetine for depression in 120 depressed and addicted adolescents indicate that fluoxetine appears to have a very good safety profile even in nonabstinent adolescents with polydrug abuse (Lohman et al., 2002). Since this trial is not yet completed, no data are yet available on the efficacy of fluoxetine for depression, although preliminary data from open trials and a small controlled trial indicate some promise for the efficacy of SSRIs for depression in adolescents

with substance dependence (Deas & Thomas, 2001; Riggs, Mikulich, Coffman, & Crowley, 1997). Clinically, the SSRIs are currently considered by many adult and adolescent addiction psychiatrists to be the first-line medication choice for depression co-occurring with substance dependence (Deas & Thomas, 2001; Lohman et al., 2002; Riggs et al., 1997). If ADHD is also present, bupropion may be a first-line choice, as mentioned above. These recommendations must be regarded as provisional, since no antidepressant medications have yet demonstrated safety and efficacy in a conclusive controlled, clinical trial with adolescents with substance dependence. Moreover, there is currently a controversy over the possibility that all SSRIs, except fluoxetine, may increase the risk of suicide in adolescents. This issue is thoroughly discussed in Chapter 2, which deals with depression in adolescence.

Tricyclic antidepressants are relatively contraindicated for the treatment of depression or ADHD in adolescents with substance dependence. These agents have significant anticholinergic and cardiac side effects, a relatively high potential for adverse interactions with substances of abuse, and considerable danger of causing death if an overdose should occur (Wilens, Spencer, Biederman, & Schleifer, 1997).

Anxiety Disorders

Cognitive-behavioral therapies, often used in combination with SSRI medications, are considered standard treatment for a variety of anxiety disorders (including obsessive compulsive disorder, social anxiety disorder, generalized anxiety disorder, and posttraumatic stress disorder [PTSD]) in adolescents without substance dependence. While SSRI treatment for adolescent anxiety disorders that are comorbid with substance dependence has not yet been well studied, the data support their relatively good safety profile in treating depression in adolescents with substance dependence. Furthermore, the high rates of co-occurring depression with anxiety disorders suggest that clinicians may wish to consider SSRIs in dually diagnosed adolescents with anxiety disorders. Good target symptoms for SSRIs include the management of sleep problems, depressive symptoms, intrusive memories, and hy-perarousal symptoms often associated with PTSD (Davies, Gabbert, & Riggs, 2001; Lohman et al., 2002). Benzodiazepines are contraindi-cated for anxiety disorders in patients with sub-stance dependence because of their well-known abuse potential.

Pharmacotherapy in Adolescents: Special Considerations in Treating Comorbidity

If the adolescent has a comorbid disorder for which medication is being considered (e.g., ADHD, major depression), abstinence is ideal be-fore initiating medication for comorbidity. How-ever, abstinence is not a realistic goal for many adolescent patients. Clinicians must therefore weigh the risk of potential drug–medication in-teractions against the risk that the untreated psy-chiatric illness will thwart treatment engage-ment or precipitate early dropout. Once the adolescent is engaged in substance abuse treat-ment, both urine drug screening and self-report should indicate either abstinence or significant reduction in substance use, although it is often necessary to tolerate some ongoing alcohol or cannabis use. The mental health professional or psychiatrist should then develop a plan for regular drug abuse monitoring (e.g., urine toxi-cology, breath alcohol) and for information exchange regarding compliance with substance treatment, urine toxicology results, target symp-tom response, and emergence of adverse side ef-fects. When initiating medications, the patient should be compliant with at least weekly therapy sessions. Our clinical experience suggests benefit from motivational enhancement therapy cou-pled with CBT and an empathic, encouraging therapeutic style. Such an approach typically leads to successful medication stabilization for comorbidity during the first month of treatment. Early treatment of a psychiatric disorder can be critically important in facilitating treatment en-gagement and retention during the initial months of substance abuse treatment.

The following principles also may be helpful when using medications to treat comorbid dis-orders concurrently with substance dependence. First, when medication is indicated, consider medications with good safety profiles, low-abuse liability, and once-per-day dosing, if possible. Second, use a single medication if at all possible. Third, provide the patient and family with edu-cation about the potential for adverse interac-tions of medications with substances of abuse and the need for abstinence or reduced sub-stance use to ensure safety and efficacy. Fourth, establish mechanisms to closely monitor medi-cation compliance (initially weekly), adverse ef-fects, target symptom response, and ongoing substance use (using both self-report and urine drug screening). Fifth, monitor compliance with regular substance treatment (generally, individ-ual or family counseling at least weekly) and reg-ular urine drug screening (if not the primary sub-stance abuse treatment provider). Sixth, monitor patient treatment motivation and target symp-tom response as well as behavior changes and psychosocial functioning throughout treatment. If substance abuse or target symptoms of the comorbid disorder do not significantly improve within the first 2 months after initiating treat-ment, or if there is evidence of escalation in drug abuse or clinical deterioration, consider several options. First, evaluate the medication efficacy and change the medication. Second, reassess the diagnostic formulation (e.g., bipolar vs. unipolar depression). Third, increase the treatment inten-sity (frequency or level of care). Adherence to these principles should facilitate pharmacother-apy in adolescents who frequently have comor-bid Axis I psychiatric disorders with their sub-stance dependence. Medications primarily targeted at the substance dependence, such as bupropion or NRT for nicotine dependence, might also be considered, but behavior treat-ments should be tried first for most adolescents with primary substance dependence and no other Axis I psychopathology.

Prevention of Substance
Use Disorders

On the basis of findings from extensive epidemiological research, the Centers for Disease Control and Prevention (CDC) has identified a set of interrelated problem behaviors, typically originating during childhood and adolescence, that are critically important from a public health standpoint. For youths, central among these risk-related health behaviors are alcohol, tobacco, and other drug use (CDC, 2002b). Prevalence rates of alcohol, tobacco, and marijuana use among adolescents remain high. For example, recent prevalence of lifetime alcohol use among 12th graders was 80%; for cigarette use the lifetime rate was 64.7%, and for marijuana it was 49.7% (Johnston, O'Malley, & Bachman, 2000). Early initiation and use of these substances are associated with a wide range of problems, including risky sexual practices, impaired mental health functioning, and behaviors that result in unintentional and intentional injuries (CDC, 2002a; Duncan, Duncan, Strycker, Li, & Alpert, 1999; Windle & Windle, 2001). Thus, legal and moral implications aside, adolescent substance abuse must be regarded as a public health issue. The effective prevention and treatment of adolescent substance abuse, like that for any public health problem, require a clear understanding of causes and the context in which these causes operate. One cannot effectively stem a pneumonia epidemic without knowing the following:

- Which microbe or microbes produce the disease?
- Under which environmental conditions do the microbes flourish?
- Are there individual sensitivities to the infection?
- What are the most common patterns of contagion?
- To which antibiotic treatments are the microbes most sensitive?
- What are the patterns and factors associated with relapse?

Research on the origins of adolescent substance abuse is asking similar questions: How do different drugs affect the brains of different adolescents at different stages of maturation? How do environmental conditions increase or decrease the probability of substance abuse? Are there individual sensitivities to drugs of abuse that increase the risk of a substance use disorder? How do social factors produce contagion of drug abuse among adolescents? Are there specific treatments or prevention interventions for specific types of adolescent substance abuse? How do biological, psychological, and social factors account for failed prevention efforts or drug treatment relapse, and how common is it? This promising body of research carries with it the potential to create more effective approaches to the prevention of adolescent substance abuse as well as guiding treatment efforts.

THEORETICAL AND CONCEPTUAL MODELS OF PREVENTION AND CHANGE

There is no generally agreed-upon theoretical or conceptual model for prevention of substance abuse. Most prevention interventionists and researchers use both theory and empirical research to plan prevention programs. For example, Hawkins and colleagues Hawkins, Catalano, & Miller, (1992) derive a psychosocial model of drug abuse prevention based on an etiological model that incorporates laws, social norms, substance availability, the quality of the neighborhood, peer values, peer behavior, parental values, parental behavior, individual values, and individual behavior. However, there is no widespread agreement that these domains are the most salient in the cause or prevention of a drug abuse disorder. The development and implementation of a prevention intervention that efficaciously addresses all of these broad domains are daunting tasks.

RISK AND PROTECTIVE FACTORS: THE COMPLEX CAUSES OF ADOLESCENT SUBSTANCE ABUSE

It has been recognized for over 30 years that the risk for becoming a substance abuser is not equally distributed in the population. Originally this observation came from research that followed children into adulthood and used childhood demographic and psychological data to uncover pathways to an adolescent or adult substance abuse disorder. Subsequently, this view was bolstered by epidemiological surveys in the United States that revealed that only 27% of individuals who have experimentally used drugs six or more times actually progress to become daily drug users, and only about a half of young adult daily drug users go on to develop a drug abuse or dependence disorder (Robins & Regier, 1991). While it is possible that chance plays a role in the acquisition of a substance abuse problem, it is more likely that the complex interplay of risk and protective factors determine who progresses from experimentation to regular use and from regular use to problematic involvement. Furthermore, the interplay of risk and protective factors exists in a maturational context such that at some stages of human development certain biological, psychological, or social factors may be totally benign, while at other stages of development these same factors may confer considerable risk for problematic involvement with drugs of abuse. These risk factors are subject to effects of gender and ethnicity, so risk factors may operate differently in boys and girls, and in Caucasians and African Americans. To further complicate the issue, individual risk and protective factors must be viewed against a backdrop of laws, cultural and social norms, drug availability, economic circumstances, and regional and community factors. For example, a white Chicago adolescent male who has a variety of individual risk factors for alcoholism might develop alcohol problems, but if that same child were raised in Saudi Arabia (where drinking alcohol is forbidden), it is less likely that he would develop an alcohol problem. However, it is possible that these risk factors might manifest themselves in other forms of problematic behavior (e.g., aggressive behavior). Thus, substance abuse is a multifaceted problem.

Geneticists refer to multidetermined problems like substance abuse as "complex disorders" because a multiplicity of individual biological and behavioral factors interact with environmental factors (e.g., social and societal phenomena) in complicated ways across human development to produce a good or bad outcome. To the best of our knowledge, there is no single cause of adolescent substance abuse, and so it is unlikely that there will be a single preventive

measure to forestall its development. For this reason, the reader is cautioned to be skeptical of overly simplistic causal explanations for substance abuse problems and of facile and obvious solutions. The likelihood that approaches guided by conventional wisdom will achieve their promised results is diminished by the realities of our current understanding of the complex pathways to a substance abuse disorder.

INFLUENTIAL THEORIES OF THE DEVELOPMENT OF ADOLESCENT SUBSTANCE ABUSE

Theories develop as an effort to summarize and explain research data generated by observation and experimentation. Theories are used to organize future research studies that ultimately test the validity of the original theory and provide an opportunity for the initial theory to evolve and undergo revision. Thus, theories are scientific "works in progress," not facts. Several influential theories have guided our understanding of the origins of adolescent substance abuse, and provide a framework for ongoing research in this area. These theories also provide a useful structure to guide approaches to the prevention and treatment of adolescent substance abuse problems. The following are among the most influential of these theories. There are many areas of commonality and overlap; yet each has contributed and advanced our understanding of the origins of substance abuse. Other theories abound and it is noteworthy that the "general field theorem" for the vulnerability to adolescent substance abuse has yet to be fully articulated.

The "Gateway" or Stage Theory

This theory comes from epidemiological research that has examined the patterning of alcohol and other drug use progression among adolescents. However, recently this theory has become a battleground for those both for and against the decriminalization of marijuana. The theory is based on the delineation of four stages in the sequence of involvement with drugs. The original findings suggested that surveyed adolescents engage in use of either alcohol or cigarettes (as legal and culturally accepted drugs) then progress to marijuana, and then on to other illicit drugs, such as heroin and cocaine. The legal drugs are necessary intermediates between nonuse and marijuana. Thus, the use of tobacco, alcohol, and marijuana by adolescents was viewed as a crucial step, or "gateway," to the use of other illicit drugs (Kandel, 1975). However, opponents of this theory suggest that, if there were a risk factor that was common to both marijuana and other drugs, it could easily account for the relationship between both marijuana and other drug use. Examples of a theorized "third factor" include the genetic predisposition to drug use, a predisposition toward adolescent risk behavior in general, or shared opportunities to obtain both marijuana and other drugs (Morral, McCaffrey, & Paddock, 2002). Nonetheless, surveys of American high school students suggest that by 12th grade, 37% of students have tried marijuana, whereas 0.9% have tried heroin and 4.8% have tried cocaine (Johnston, O'Malley, & Bachman, 2002b). The discrepancies in these prevalence rates indicate that although hard drug users may have started with marijuana, it is clear that marijuana use does not invariably progress to adolescent use of hard drugs.

A less controversial aspect of this theory deals with age of initiation of experimentation with drugs of abuse (whether it is alcohol, tobacco, marijuana, or hard drugs), and the timing of stages of regular use and problematic involvement. The literature converges around the observation that the earlier the onset of substance use, the greater the likelihood of problematic involvement (Choi, Gilpin, Farkas, & Pierce, 2001; Choi, Pierce, Gilpin, Farkas, & Berry, 1997; Kandel & Logan, 1984; Schuckit & Russell, 1983; Yamaguchi & Kandel, 1984b). For this reason, substantial effort has been placed on prevention interventions that delay the initiation of initial substance exposure.

Problem Behavior Theory

Problem behavior theory is an influential conceptual framework for understanding not only substance abuse but a wide variety of other types

of risky adolescent behaviors (Jessor & Jessor, 1977). The theory proposes that there exists a syndrome of adolescent problem behaviors that may co-occur within the same individual (Jessor, 1991). For example, those who experiment with substance use also tend to engage in risky sexual practices and illegal behavior. These adolescent problem behaviors include

- Problematic involvement with alcohol
- Illicit drug use
- Delinquent behaviors (e.g., truancy, petty theft, vandalism, lying, running away)
- Risky and precocious sexual activity
- Other high-risk behaviors (e.g., drag racing, driving drunk)

These deviant behaviors are thought to emanate from a single underlying factor (perhaps of genetic origin) that may exist prior to adolescence, resulting in a general syndrome of deviance. The risky behaviors may also be adaptive to the extent that they serve a social or maturational goal, such as separating from parents, achieving adult status, or gaining peer acceptance, and these behaviors may help an adolescent cope with failure, boredom, social anxiety or isolation, unhappiness, rejection, and low self-esteem. One example of a risk behavior syndrome is an adolescent's reported use of substances as a means of gaining social status and acceptance from peers and, at the same time, enhancing mood and feelings of low self-worth (DuRant, 1995; DuRant, Getts, Cadenhead, Emans, & Woods, 1995). Thus, this theory posits that substance abuse for some adolescents may be a maladaptive means to cope with the stresses and social pressures that are characteristic of the adolescent stage of development. This theoretical perspective suggests that prevention interventions that offer alternative means of coping and social adaptation might reduce adolescent substance use behavior.

Patterson's Developmental Theory

Patterson's theory was originally proposed to explain the development of juvenile delinquency, and however consistent with the observation that problem behaviors frequently co-occur in adolescents, it has also been used to understand and address problematic involvement with alcohol and other drugs of abuse. Patterson and colleagues (Dishion, Patterson, Stoolmiller, & Skinner, 1991; Patterson, DeBaryshe, & Ramsey, 1989) are proponents of a developmental theory of conduct problems that posits that adolescent problem behavior is a consequence of poor parental family management practices interacting with the child's own aggressive and oppositional temperament. Here, *temperament* refers to the early and genetically determined behavioral characteristics that over time and life experiences evolve into personality. Deficits in parenting skill, such as harsh and inconsistent punishment, increased parent–child conflict, low parental involvement, and poor parental monitoring, result in school behavior and performance problems. The poorly performing and poorly behaving child may be socially rejected by average children, but he or she forms close friendships with other problematic children. This process of forming close peer relationships is augmented by the negative interactions with caregivers in the home.

As the child affiliates with more deviant children, he or she adopts deviant behavior as a norm and becomes less involved in home life. Other deviant children become powerful social role models from whom the child learns further deviant and socially unacceptable behavior, including experimentation with drugs of abuse. Early experimentation has consistently been found as a risk factor for later problematic involvement with a wide variety of drugs. These children may therefore be viewed as being on a developmental trajectory of deviancy and substance abuse that begins in infancy and is compounded by unskilled parenting and the formation of social relationships with other problem children (Vuchinich, Bank, & Patterson, 1992).

Prevention interventions based on this theoretical approach offer parenting skill training to teach parents more effective ways to discipline and monitor their children and reduce the negative environment of the home. Tutoring and other forms of education support may be provided to reduce academic failure. Social skills

training may also be offered the child to reduce normal peer rejection and provide a mechanism to gracefully resist peer pressure to use alcohol and illicit drugs.

Behavior Genetic Theory: Adolescent Substance Abuse as a Complex Familial Trait

Plutarch noted 2,000 years ago that alcohol problems run in families ("Drunkards beget drunkards"; Plutarch, *The Training of Children*, 110 CE). More recently, research continues to demonstrate that there is significant familial aggregation of substance use disorders. If substance abuse problems run in families, then there must be some familial influence on the development of these problems. The behavior genetic theory proposes that those factors that are transmitted within families tend to make family members more similar on a given characteristic such as substance abuse. These within-family factors can be genetic, since parents, children, and siblings share about 50% of their genes; or they can be nongenetic. These nongenetic family factors include the modeling of behaviors, the teaching of values and beliefs, parenting practices, the structure of the home environment, the quality of neighborhood, and the standards of the society at-large in which the family lives. Those factors experienced uniquely by each family member tend to make family members different from each other. These nonshared factors include peers, work, school, and all aspects of life experiences outside the family. In families where there is little substance abuse but there is an adolescent with substance problems, it is less likely to be due to a family factor than to an unshared factor outside the family. If there are many within the family with substance abuse problems, then these are likely to be due to something in the family—either genes, the home environment, or the complicated effects of genes and environment working together.

Substantial evidence suggests that substance abuse, for both adolescents and adults, is a complex trait. However, while research clearly reveals that genes are an important determinant for substance abuse problems, it does not tell us which genes. For other complex traits such as high blood pressure or diabetes or high cholesterol, it is clear that there are multiple genes involved and multiple genetic and biological pathways are involved in producing disease. It is unlikely that there is a single gene for alcoholism or cocaine dependence or cigarette addiction. There may be hundreds or thousands of genes in a given pattern producing risk, and that risk may only be present in a given environmental context. The nature of the genetic risk may be a common factor for abuse across a wide variety of drugs or a genetic risk for conduct difficulties or problem behaviors, or a set of genes that delay the maturation of the brain so one is less able to control the habituating effects of drugs. The effects of genes may be protective rather than associated with risk, and what we think of as genetic effects producing substance abuse may actually be the *absence* of protective genes. There is good evidence that specific genetic mutations protect against the development of alcoholism in certain ethnic groups, and some evidence that there is a mutation that protects against smoking.

Applying New Knowledge of Genetics to Reduce Adolescent Smoking

The enormous toll that tobacco use takes on youth may also lead prevention experts to consider ways in which genetic risk information might be used to identify high-risk subgroups that might benefit from more intensive or tailored prevention approaches. As reviewed in greater detail elsewhere (Lerman, Patterson, & Shields, 2003; Wilfond, Geller, Lerman, Audrain-McGovern, & Shields, 2002), there are many ethical challenges and considerations. From a scientific perspective, research on genetics and tobacco use is still in its infancy. There is no single "tobacco use gene," and as such, risk estimates will need to take into account multiple interactions between genetic, social, and psychological factors. Even considering genetic variants with widely validated effects on smoking behavior, these effects are likely to be small, and risk estimates will be highly probabilistic. Additional risks of genetic testing of adolescents include stigmatization, discrimination, and

potential adverse psychological effects (Lerman et al., 2003).

Nonetheless, it is tempting to consider whether individualized feedback about genetic susceptibility to tobacco addiction could overcome adolescents' perceptions of invulnerability and reduce the chances of initial tobacco use or the transition to tobacco dependence. Despite acknowledging that nicotine is an addictive chemical, a large proportion (62%) of adolescents who smoke cigarettes report that quitting smoking was either easy or manageable for most people if they tried hard enough (Jamieson & Romer, 2001). Likewise, data from the 2002 Legacy Tracking Survey indicate that among current smokers ages 12–18, 60% reported that they would definitely be able to quit smoking if they wanted to and 28% said they probably would be able to quit (American Legacy Foundation, 2002).

While intriguing, data from research on genetic testing for disease susceptibility do not provide strong support for an effect of genetic risk communication on health protective behaviors (Marteau & Lerman, 2001). With regard to cigarette smoking, Lerman and colleagues (1997) conducted a clinical trial to determine whether feedback on genetic susceptibility to lung cancer would motivate smoking cessation in an adult population. The results showed that such information did have beneficial effects on risk perceptions and the perceived benefits of quitting smoking; however, there was no significant effect on smoking behavior. Whether communication of genetic risk for addiction to adolescents would have a significant impact on relevant attitudes and behavior is an open empirical question.

In summary, ongoing research is elucidating the determinants of tobacco use and dependence in youth. Although scientific advances in the genetics arena offer some promise, biology offers less than half the answer for those seeking to reduce tobacco use among youth, with social and environmental factors playing an equal or larger role. Thus, the expertise of multiple disciplines and methodological approaches is needed to meet the needs of the most vulnerable adolescents.

MEDIATING FACTORS

While adolescents in the United States are widely exposed to a spectrum of drugs of abuse, research suggests that adolescent substance abuse problems are due to multiple factors (Table 19.1). Most theories suggest that genetic, psychological, familial, and nonfamilial environmental factors are thought to interact in a complex way to determine an adverse or protective outcome. Thus, genes, temperament, attitudes and beliefs, family environment, peer affiliation, and social norms all mediate the relationship between the individual and a substance use disorder outcome. The developmental timing of these factors adds an additional level of complexity. The question of "nature or nurture" has been rendered moot, primarily by research conducted over the last 10 years. It is clear that both nature and nurture are involved, set against the backdrop of child development. Thus, there is no single cause of adolescent substance abuse, and any single prevention approach is unlikely to have broad universal success.

The behavior genetic theory does help us to identify high-risk children for prevention interventions. Clearly, offspring of parents with sub-

Table 19.1 Who Is at High Risk?

Children engaged in early alcohol or drug experimentation

Offspring of substance-dependent parents

Children with substance-abusing siblings

Children with conduct disturbances

Children with psychiatric disorders

Children with deviant and substance-abusing peers

Children temperamentally seeking high sensation

Children with impulse and self-control problems

Children under poor parental supervision

Children living in heavy drug-use neighborhoods

Children with school problems

Children with social skills deficits

Children of parents with poor parenting skills

Children who are victims of trauma, abuse, and neglect

stance abuse problems are themselves at significant risk for becoming substance abusers. We can't alter the effects of genes, but we can modify the environmental experiences of high-risk children. Interventions that improve parenting practices may be important, not only for instilling appropriate disciplinary practices in the parents of high-risk children but also for enhancing parental involvement and monitoring. Social skills training may keep high-risk children from being rejected by high-functioning children forced into deviant peer groups. Thus, the revolution in genetics may allow us to learn how to best change the environments of children at risk for adolescent substance abuse.

TYPES OF PREVENTION INTERVENTIONS AND MODEL PROGRAMS

Prevention programs are categorized according to the following recently adopted definitions based on the audience they are designed to reach (Mrazek & Haggerty, 1994).

Universal Intervention Programs

Universal intervention programs are designed to reach the general population, such as all students in a given school or school district, through media campaigns, for example. Broadly speaking, universal interventions represent the most widely utilized approach to drug abuse prevention. In a review of major findings of research on adolescent risk, Jamieson and Romer (2003) have recommended special focus on universal interventions, indicating that they have "great promise." They specifically note that early and continuous universal interventions that encourage mature decision making and healthy choices among youth have considerable potential. From a universalist intervention perspective, public health problems and their solutions are inextricably a part of the community social system; solutions are essentially universal, with some types of universal interventions facilitating access to higher-risk groups within the community that may warrant more intensive intervention. Implementation of these types of interventions is typically supported by local community partnerships or coalitions.

The largest group of universal programs is the in-school intervention, typified by the well-known original Drug Abuse Resistance Education (DARE), a school-based primary drug prevention curriculum designed for introduction during the last year of elementary education. DARE is the most widely disseminated school-based prevention curriculum in the United States. Despite its popularity, independent evaluations of DARE have failed to demonstrate its effectiveness (Clayton, Cattarello, & Johnstone, 1996; Lynam et al., 1999). Recently, an enhanced version of DARE has been developed and tested (DARE Plus). Additional components added to the original DARE curriculum include a peer-led parental involvement classroom program called "On the VERGE," youth-led extracurricular activities, community adult action teams, and postcard mailings to parents. Evidence suggests that DARE Plus produced significant reductions in alcohol, tobacco, and polydrug use among boys; but had no effect on girls (Perry et al., 2003).

Other school-based universal programs provide more promising results for both boys and girls. For example, the Life Skills Training Program (Botvin, Baker, Dusenbury, Botvin, & Diaz, 1995) emphasizes teaching of drug resistance skills, self-management skills, and general social skills in the junior high school classroom setting. The program has been shown to demonstrate significant reductions in drug experimentation among student participants.

Another important group of universal interventions are family focused. An example of this type of intervention that has been rigorously evaluated and found to be effective is the Strengthening Families Program: For Parents and Youth 10–14 (SFP 10–14; Kumpfer, Molgaard, & Spoth, 1996; Molgaard & Kumpfer, 1995). Implementation of the SFP 10–14 entails seven sessions occurring once a week for 7 weeks. The SFP 10–14 has separate sessions for parents and children that run concurrently for 1 hour and focus on skills building. During the second hour parents and children participate together in a joint

hour-long family session, during which they practice the skills learned in their preceding, separate sessions. The family session affords the opportunity for higher-risk families and those with special needs to identify available services. In addition, the family session includes activities designed to encourage family cohesiveness and positive involvement of the child in family activities. For the parental sessions the essential content and key concepts of the program are also presented on videotape. Further details regarding the SFP 10–14 is provided in published reports (Spoth, Guyll, & Day, 2002; Spoth, Redmond, & Shin, 2000, 2001; Spoth, Reyes, Redmond, & Shin, 1999).

Yet another group includes interventions that combine school-based interventions with those engaging parents and sometimes other community institutions. An example of this type of expanded program is Project STAR (Pentz et al., 1989). This approach attempts to involve the entire community with a comprehensive school program, a mass media campaign, a parent program, a community organizing component, and health policy change component. Project STAR has been shown to be effective in terms of reductions in drug use behavior in high school for those youth that began the program in junior high school.

In addition to these interventions, there are universal interventions that have made use of mass media in a primary role, either in one community or, in the most interesting cases, nationwide, to address drug use. Below is a discussion in some detail of a universal intervention in the form of mass media campaigns.

Case Study: Media Drug Abuse Prevention Campaigns

Although the money committed to mass media–based campaign interventions is now substantial, evaluations of serious mass media–based interventions addressing drug use are few. One was a field experiment in Kentucky, a second was an evaluation of the Partnership for Drug-Free America (PDFA) campaign in its earlier phase, 1987–1990, along with some ancillary trend data. Another evaluation was one of the Office

of National Drug Control Policy's campaign between 1999 and the present. In addition to these
evaluations, there is a literature on mass media
campaigns that addresses adolescent smoking.

The Kentucky Intervention

The research group at the University of Kentucky
(Donohew, Lorch, & Palmgreen, 1991) has a long
history of anti-drug communication research
based in the core construct of "sensation seeking." They argue that this personality construct
accounts for a substantially increased risk of drug
use among youth, and thus would provide a
basis for the development of a mass-media intervention. This work culminated in their development of a two-city test of a televised anti-
marijuana campaign in 1997 and 1998. The
project was an interrupted time series following
youth in grades 7 through 10 in Fayette County
(Lexington), Kentucky, and Knox County (Knoxville), Tennessee, for 32 months. The televised
ads first ran for 4 months in Lexington, 8
months into the time series, and 1 year later for
4 months in both Lexington and in Knoxville.
The campaign was developed so as to appeal particularly to high sensation–seeking youth. The
ads were designed to have high sensation value;
they were pretested with these youth; and they
were shown in the context of high–sensation
value television programs preferred by these
youth. During a campaign period, enough ad
time was purchased or donated so that 70% of
the target audience should have seen ads three
times per week.

The reported results of the evaluation were
positive. Self-reported 30-day use of marijuana
among high sensation–seeking youth declined
(or climbed less than would have been expected)
during all three campaign periods, and not during other periods. Strikingly, few youth seeking
low sensation reported use of marijuana, regardless of the presence or absence of the campaign.

The Partnership for a Drug-Free America

The Partnership has been operating a mass media campaign since mid-1987. It describes itself
as "a non-profit coalition of professionals from

the communications industry." Through its national drug-education advertising campaign and
other forms of media communication, the Partnership seeks to help kids and teens reject substance abuse by influencing attitudes through
persuasive information.

One evaluation approach notes correlated secular trends: the first 5 years of the PDFA's existence, between 1987 and 1992, match a period
of substantial decline in youth reports of drug
use. That is the period when PDFA had its heav-
iest presence in the advertising marketplace. After 1992, when it became less successful in generating donated advertising time, particularly on
television, the decline in youth reports of use
was reversed, and drug use continued to climb
through 1998. In a similar analysis focused on
inhalant use, Johnston, O'Malley, and Bachman
(2002a) found that the PDFA's initiation of
strong anti-inhalants advertising in 1996 fore-
cast a period of decline in inhalant use among
youth. However, data drawn from secular trends
are inevitably open to other interpretations, recognizing that there are many exogenous influences on such trends. Indeed, the secular trends
in marijuana use, for example, establish that the
start of the decline in such use preceded the introduction of the PDFA campaign in 1987. This
is evident in the time trend data from the Monitoring the Future (MTF) surveys for 12th graders
reporting annual use of marijuana. The downward trend was fairly constant from 1983 on-
ward, 4 years prior to initiation of the PDFA campaign. Although it is possible that the decline
might have stalled absent the initiation of the
campaign, that is not the only possible interpretation of the pattern (Johnston, O'Malley, &
Bachman, 2003a).

The National Youth Anti-Drug Media Campaign

The National Youth Anti-Drug Media Campaign
is the direct inheritor of the PDFA campaign. It
came out of the PDFA's recognition that it was
no longer able to generate the donated media
time it had previously received, and reflected intensive lobbying of Congress and the administration to make up the deficit. The long decline

in marijuana use had ended in 1992, and had climbed substantially by 1997, also raising congressional concern. The PDFA envisioned the new campaign operating with the government buying media time for the ads generated by PDFA, but the eventual legislation shifted control of the Campaign to the White House Office of National Drug Control Policy (ONDCP) and added other provisions. While most money was allocated to the purchase of time for advertising largely produced under the PDFA mechanism, the overall message strategy was designed outside of PDFA, and the advertising was to be complemented by public relations efforts including community outreach and institutional partnerships. Youth were addressed directly, but the campaign spent its resources equally on parent-focused messages, particularly encouraging parenting skills and monitoring of youth behavior.

The Congress funded an independent evaluation through National Institute on Drug Abuse (NIDA) which contracted with Westat and the Annenberg School for Communication at the University of Pennsylvania. The evaluation is ongoing, with the most recent report covering the first 2.5 years of the fully implemented campaign (Hornik et al., 2002). Pertinent results thus far are as follows.

- Most parents and youth in the surveys recalled exposure to Campaign anti-drug messages. About 70 percent of both groups reported exposure to one or more messages through all media channels every week. The average (median) youth recalled seeing one television ad per week. In 2000 and the first half of 2001, less than 25 percent of parents recalled seeing a television ad every week; this increased to 40 percent in the second half of 2001 and to 50 percent in the first half of 2002.
- There is evidence consistent with a favorable Campaign effect on some parent outcomes. Overall, there are favorable changes in three out of five parent belief and behavior outcome measures, including talking about drugs with children and monitoring of children. Moreover, parents who reported more

exposure to Campaign messages scored better on four out of five outcomes after statistical controls were applied to adjust for the possible influence of other explanatory factors. In addition, parents who had more exposure the first time they were measured were more likely to talk with their children and do fun activities with their children subsequently. However, there was little evidence for Campaign effects on parents' monitoring behavior. That has been the focus of the parent Campaign and the one parent behavior most associated with youth nonuse of marijuana. In addition, there is no evidence for favorable indirect effects on youth behavior as a result of parent exposure to the Campaign.
- There is also little evidence of favorable direct Campaign effects on youth. There is no statistically significant decline in marijuana use to date in the surveys undertaken for the evaluation (although the MTF study suggested that there was a small but significant decline in marijuana use between 2001 and 2002 at the 10th-grade level; Johnston, O'Malley, & Bachman, 2003a). However, there were no improvements in surveyed beliefs and attitudes about marijuana use between 2000 and the first half of 2002. Regardless of whether the trends were stable or showing a slight decline, there is no basis for attributing any youth changes to the Campaign specifically. Also, and of most concern, there is evidence for an unfavorable delayed effect of Campaign exposure from September 1999 through June 2001 on intentions to use marijuana and on other beliefs expressed 12 to 18 months subsequently.

Several hypotheses have been suggested to explain why a campaign might produce a boomerang effect. One comes from reactance theory (Brehm, 1966; Brehm & Brehm, 1981), an argument that youth react against adult threats to their freedom by feeling pressure to re-establish that freedom, including some pressure to engage in the forbidden behavior. The Campaign might represent such a threat. Another theory argues that the heavy dose of anti-drug messages carries a meta-message, the idea that many youth must be using drugs if there is so much attention being paid to them. Indeed, for this hypothesis there is some consistent evidence: youth more exposed to the campaign advertising are more likely to progress subsequently to a belief that most other kids are using marijuana, and that belief predicts subsequent initiation of marijuana use. Other hypotheses include the idea that ads that contain relatively weak arguments serve to stimulate strong counterarguments (J., 2003), or the idea that for some youth, the ads provide novel information and thus provoke curiosity about drugs.

Selective Intervention Programs

Selective intervention programs are designed to target groups at risk as subsets of the general population, such as children of drug addicts or children with school problems.

The Strengthening Families Program (Kumpfer & Alvardo, 1995) and the Focus on Families Program (Catalano, Gainey, Fleming, Haggerty, & Johnson, 1999; Catalano, Haggerty, Gainey, & Hoppe, 1997) represent examples of selective interventions for children with drug-abusing parents, with slightly different approaches. Strengthening Families contains three elements: a parent training component, a child skills training component, and a family skills training component. The goal of the parent training component is to reduce parental substance abuse and improve parenting skills. The goal of the child skills training component is to decrease the child's negative and socially unacceptable behavior. The goal of the family skills training component is to improve the family environment. Evaluations of efficacy so far have found short-term benefits for this intervention; longer-term studies have not been done.

Focus on Families is for parents receiving methadone maintenance. Here parents are taught skills for relapse prevention and coping to help improve their treatment outcomes, as well as family management and parenting skills. Preliminary data suggest that this program improves treatment outcomes of parents and enhances their parenting skills.

Indicated Intervention Programs

Indicated intervention programs are those designed for groups already experimenting with drugs or engaging in other risky practices. To a great extent, indicated programs traverse the fine line between prevention and treatment interventions. The Reconnecting Youth Program (Eggert, Thompson, Herting, & Nicholas, 1995; Eggert, Thompson, Herting, Nicholas, & Dicker, 1994) is a prime example. This program is for adolescents in grades 9 to 12 who show signs of poor school achievement and the potential to drop out. The program teaches skills to build resiliency toward risk factors and to moderate early signs of drug abuse. It consists of several components, such as a personal growth class designed to enhance self-esteem, decision making, personal control, and interpersonal communications; a social activities and school bonding program to establish drug-free peer relationships; and a school system crisis response plan to address suicide prevention. Evaluations of this intervention have documented only short-term benefits, with long-term studies yet to be done.

Multilevel Intervention Programs

Multilevel intervention programs are typically ambitious combinations of the above intervention models. They include universal, selected, and indicated strategies gauged to the needs of the adolescent.

The Adolescent Transitions Program (Dishion & Kavanagh, 2000) is an example of a multilevel intervention designed to address the needs of families of young adolescents that present with a range of problem behaviors and diverse developmental histories. This ambitious program incorporates universal, selective, and indicated prevention components. The universal prevention intervention is in the form of a school-based family resource room to establish a venue for exchange between school professionals and families. The selective intervention is in the form of a family check-up that offers family assessment and support, and the motivation to change behaviors. The indicated intervention provides a menu of services that includes a brief family intervention, school monitoring system, parent groups, behavioral family therapy, and case management services.

SUMMARIES AND REVIEWS OF MODEL PREVENTIVE INTERVENTIONS

Over the past decade numerous efforts have been undertaken to identify and disseminate descriptive information about model preventive interventions. In the family-focused prevention area alone, for instance, at least 11 of these model intervention reviews have gained some currency (Metzler, Biglan, Rusby, & Sprague, 2001). Reviews of model preventive interventions typically include descriptions of selection criteria or rules of evidence applied and summaries of the intervention review process. Many also delineate salient characteristics of the types of programs that have proven to be effective. A major issue for the field is the variability in the rules of evidence and intervention selection criteria, with the level of scientific rigor applied ranging considerably.

Frequently, model interventions are classified by the level of supportive evidence for the intervention (e.g., exemplary or promising). Most reviews of interventions consider the level of evidence for a particular intervention; some, however, create categories of interventions and critically evaluate the evidence *only* for specified types of interventions. Table 19.2 summarizes selected reviews of particular evidence-based interventions; it does not include reviews of types of programs. Rather, these are included in the following summary of meta-analysis and reviews of outcome studies of interventions from the relevant literature. Although some of the reviews are focused exclusively on interventions designed to prevent substance use or abuse among youth, many include interventions that target other youth problem behaviors as well. All of the reviews selected for inclusion in Table 19.2 have critically evaluated at least some substance-

related preventive interventions described in published reports. Included in Table 19.2 is an especially instructive "review of reviews" of particular family-focused preventive interventions (Meltzer et al., 2002).

THE FUTURE OF YOUTH PREVENTION PROGRAMS: NEW DIRECTIONS

Recently, prevention professionals have broadened the target of their interventions, extending beyond substance abuse to globally address the quality of youth development. Advocates of positive youth development approaches emphasize that efforts to address public health concerns by preventing youth problem behaviors must be pursued in concert with youth-related health promotion goals. The need to integrate prevention and youth-related health promotion—or positive youth development—has emerged as a consequence of the observation that problem-free youth are not necessarily fully prepared youth (Pittman, Irby, & Ferber, 2000). In keeping with this concept, several scholars (Eccles & Gootman, 2002; Flay, 2002; Lerner, 2001; Roth & Brooks-Gunn, 2002; Villarruel, Perkins, Bordon, & Keith, 2003) have cogently argued for the need for strategies and interventions that prepare young people to fully participate in school and career, by reducing the level of harmful or risk behaviors *and* building "external" developmental assets (e.g., support from parents, peers, teachers) along with "internal" assets (e.g., social competencies—see Scales, Benson, Leffert, & Blyth, 2000).

Community-based intervention researchers have underscored how difficult it is to accomplish substantial behavior change in large populations (e.g., Holder, 2002), in part because of natural tensions between researchers and community-based practitioners (Greenberg & Spoth, in press; Spoth & Greenberg et al., in press; Price & Behrens, 2003; Wandersman, 2003). This conclusion is consistent with earlier admonitions about ways in which prevailing economic, political, and social forces can perpetuate unhealthy behaviors such as problem drinking (Giesbrecht, Krempulec, & West, 1993). Many researchers agree that the key to address-

Table 19.2 Reviews of Particular Evidence-Based Interventions

Reference	Level of Intervention	Summary
Alvarado, Kendall, Beesley, & Lee-Cavaness, 2000	Family	This review entails "Two page summaries of family-focused programs which have been proven to be effective. . . . The programs in this booklet are divided into categories based upon the degree, quality and outcomes of research associated with them" (p. vi). "Numerous criteria were utilized by the review committee to rate and categorize programs. The criteria included: theory, fidelity of the interventions, sampling strategy and implementation, attrition, measures, data collection, missing data, analysis, replications, dissemination capability, cultural and age appropriateness, integrity and program utility. Each program was rated independently by reviewers, discussed and a final determination made regarding the appropriate category" (p. vii).
Catalano, Berglund, Ryan, Lonczak, & Hawkins, 2002	Multiple	This review "Describes the findings from evaluations of positive youth development programs. The chapter highlights 25 well-evaluated programs and their results. Elements of the programs are described, including positive youth development constructs, social domains, and strategies." (http://www.journals.apa.org/prevention/volume5/pre0050015a.html)
Center for the Study and Prevention of Violence, 2003	Multiple	The center "Has identified 11 prevention and intervention programs that meet a strict scientific standard of program effectiveness. . . . The 11 model programs, called Blueprints, have been effective in reducing adolescent violent crime, aggression, delinquency, and substance abuse. Another 21 programs have been identified as promising programs." (http://www.colorado.edu/cspv/blueprints/)
Developmental Research and Programs, 2000	Multiple	Communities that Care (CTC) is an integrated approach to positive youth development and the prevention of problem behaviors including substance abuse, academic failure, unplanned pregnancy, school dropout, and violence. This program is based on prevention science—social development theory—which aims to identify and reduce risk factors and promote protective factors in the development of problem behaviors among young people. (http://www.channing-bete.com/positiveyouth)
Drug Strategies, 1999	School	This assessment "is based on careful review of curriculum materials and other information provided by curriculum developers and distributors as well as evaluation reports on 14 curricula. . . . Extensive research during the past two decades points to certain key elements of successful prevention curricula . . . assesses the extent to which curricula address these key areas" (p. 1).
Eccles & Gootman, 2002	Community	"We considered reviews that included both programs for youth with a primary focus on prevention and programs explicitly focused on a youth development framework. . . . Programs based on clinical theories of behavior change and sound instructional practices are effective at both reducing problem behaviors and increasing a wide range of social and emotional competencies. In addition, interventions in the field of mental health promotion use high evaluation standards. All evaluations included in both reviews used both control group comparisons, and the majority used random assignment. The high level of evaluation rigor obtained was understandably facilitated by the short-term nature of the programs, the integration of these programs into the school day, and the fact that program participation was more likely to be seen by participants as required rather than voluntary" (pp. 148, 172).

(continued)

Table 19.2 Continued

Reference	Level of Intervention	Summary
Greenberg, Domitrovich, & Bumbarger, 2000	Multiple	"The goals of this report were to . . . identify universal, selective and indicated programs that reduce symptoms of both externalizing and internalizing disorders; summarize the state-of-the art programs in the prevention of mental disorders in school-age children; identify elements that contribute to program success; and provide suggestions to improve the quality of program development and evaluation." (http://www.prevention.psu.edu/resources.html) The scope of interest for this review included prevention programs for children ages 5 to 18 that produce improvements in specific psychological symptoms or in factors directly associated with increased risk for child mental disorders. Programs were excluded if they produced outcomes solely related to substance abuse, sexuality or health promotion or positive youth development.
Hansen, 1992	School	"Substance use prevention studies published between 1980 and 1990 are reviewed for content, methodology and behavioral outcomes. . . . Studies were classified based on the inclusion of 12 content areas: Information, Decision-Making, Pledges, Values Clarification, Goal Setting, Stress Management, Self-Esteem, Resistance Skills Training, Life Skills Training, Norm Setting, Assistance and Alternatives. Comprehensive and Social Influence programs are found to be most successful in preventing the onset of substance use" (p. 403).
Olds, Robinson, Song, Little, & Hill, 1999	Family	This study is a review of research that tested universal, selected, or indicated interventions that took place between the prenatal period and a child's fifth year (0–5) and examined outcomes indicative of either child behavioral adjustment problems or major parent or family risk factors (e.g., maternal mental health and use of substance; relationship disturbance).
Promising Practices, 2001	Multiple	"PPN [Promising Practices Network] has organized information on effective programs under six broad result areas that are associated with the well-being of children, youth, and families. For each of these results areas, one or more specific benchmarks have been identified. . . . PPN provides a summary of each program that identifies key information about its effectiveness. . . . We've included programs that meet a minimum level of evidence and are labeled as follows: (1) *Proven*—at least one credible, scientifically rigorous study that shows the program improves at least one benchmark; *Promising*—at least some direct evidence that the program improves outcomes for children and families." (http://www.promisingpractices.net)
Roth, Brooks-Gunn, Murray, & Foster, 1998	Multiple	"We evaluate the usefulness of the youth development framework based on 15 program evaluations. The results of the evaluations are discussed and 3 general themes emerge" (p. 423).
SAMHSA Model Programs, 2003	Multiple	Programs are evaluated according to 18 methodological criteria, three appropriateness criteria, and program descriptors for evaluating general substance abuse and treatment programs. "Individual scores from members of each reviewer team are compiled, together with their narrative descriptions of the review program's strengths, weaknesses, and major components and outcome findings. Summary scores from two parameters, Integrity and Utility, are then used to rank programs respectively on the scientific rigor of their evaluation and the practicality of their findings." (http://modelprograms.samhsa.gov/pdfs/compmatrix.pdf)

Strengthening America's Families, 1999	Multiple	This Web site describes effective family programs for the prevention of delinquency. Programs for the prevention of delinquency and other negative outcomes are described and rated against a set of criteria as "Exemplary," "Model," or "Promising." The Web site also contains a literature review and an organizational matrix of programs, arranged by type of prevention program (universal, selected, indicated). Available on-line at: http://www.strengtheningfamilies.org/html/model_programs/mfp_pg1.html
U.S. Department of Education, 2001	School	"This publication provides descriptions of the 9 exemplary and 33 promising programs selected by the 15-member Expert Panel for Safe, Disciplined, and Drug-Free Schools in 2001. . . . The task was to develop and oversee a process for identifying and designating as promising and exemplary programs that promote safe, disciplined, and drug-free schools. The seven criteria are: (1) The program reports relevant evidence of efficacy/effectiveness based on a methodologically sound evaluation; (2) The program's goals with respect to changing behavior and/or risk and protective factors are clear and appropriate for the intended population and setting; (3) The rationale underlying the program is clearly stated, and the program's content and processes are aligned with its goals; (4) The program's content takes into consideration the characteristics of the intended population and setting (e.g., developmental stage, motivational status, language, disabilities, culture) and the needs implied by these characteristics; (5) The program implementation process effectively engages the intended population; (6) The application describes how the program is integrated into schools' educational missions; (7) The program provides necessary information and guidance for replication in other appropriate settings" (pp. 1–2).

SAMHSA, Substance Abuse and Mental Health Administration.

ing this challenge lies in universal, community-based innovations (e.g., Holder, 2001).

Holder (2001, 2002) notes that there have been two different approaches to addressing substance-related public health goals—namely, the catchment and community-system approaches. In the catchment approach to prevention of substance-related problems, a community is viewed as a collection of target groups with adverse behaviors and correlated risks. Operationally this involves locating persons at risk, identifying their risk factors, and implementing interventions to reduce risk factors, often entailing education-based programs. Notably, there is little attention to social dynamics or organizational- and systems-level factors influencing individual target group behaviors. Consistent with the emphasis on environmental influences and potential supports for youth development is the focus of the community-systems approach on the community at large, defined as a set of persons "engaged in shared, social, cultural, political, and economic processes" (Holder, 2002, p. 906). Thus a wide range of problems is collectively considered and the focus is on interventions that address a variety of aspects of the shared behavioral environment in a community. This focus is consistent with the idea of a comprehensive youth strategy recommended by Jamieson and Romer (2003) and others (e.g., Flay, 2002; Roth & Brooks-Gunn, 2002).

A recurring theme in the literature on community partnerships, particularly that concerning diffusion of evidence-based interventions, is the need for community intervention capacity-building, as a way to sustain quality implementation of preventive and developmental competency-building interventions (e.g., Altman, 1995; Lerner, 1995; Morrisey et al., 1997). In this case, capacity building can be defined as efforts designed to enhance and coordinate human, technical and scientific, financial, and other organizational resources directed toward quality implementation of evidence-based, developmentally oriented, preventive interventions for youth (see Spoth et al., 2004). A lack of capacity for sustained intervention implementation is frequently cited as a primary reason for

failures in community-based dissemination of interventions (e.g., Arthur, Ayers, Graham, & Hawkins, 2003; Feinberg, Greenberg, Osgood, Anderson, & Babinski, 2002; Goodman, 2000). This is particularly true in the case of school-based interventions (Gottfredson & Wilson, 2003; Hallfors, 2001). Especially problematic is the fact that efficacious school-based interventions are frequently unable to survive the withdrawal of grant funding (Adelman & Taylor, 2003).

FUTURE CHALLENGES

It is fitting to close this chapter on prevention by highlighting the challenge of the necessary bridge building for an improved youth development strategy. Just as there must be a construction plan for building a viable bridge across a chasm or gorge, requiring careful integration of input from a diverse group of designers, planning for a comprehensive strategy to foster positive youth development and prevent youth substance-related problems necessitates a sustained, well-organized effort, with input from a range of community interventionists, scientists, and policymakers at the state and federal levels. One potential contribution to this larger planning effort is a design for universities and communities to partner together to foster a higher prevalence of capable and problem-free youth. However, the wide range of tasks for those involved in community–university partnerships, the many barriers to task accomplishment, and the limited resources available highlight the challenges to design implementation that lie ahead. The single most salient feature of this particular challenge is the apparent gap between necessary human, technical and scientific, and funding resources on the one hand and the limited resource availability on the other. Nonetheless, the salience of the resource gap underscores the potential benefits of efficient and effective capacity building, particularly that which is based in existing community, state, and national infrastructures for coordinated activities supportive of youth.

Research Agenda for Substance Use Disorders

chapter

20

For a variety of reasons, little research has been conducted among adolescents with substance abuse problems. We operate as though data obtained from studies in adults applies to adolescents, but we know that there are critical differences. Thus assumptions about adolescents must be empirically tested. The following are a series of questions compiled by the Commission on Abuse of Alcohol and Other Drugs that we believe should be given high priority.

What We Know

- Substance abuse will often progress to addiction and become a lifelong illness, if not treated.
- Long-term treatment is usually required to arrest addiction.
- Motivation is an important ingredient for successful treatment.
    Changes in lifestyle are required.
    Drug use is a pleasure-reinforced compulsion.
    Drug craving may lead to relapse.
- Adolescents are different from adults.
    There are differences in brain development and plasticity.
    Specialized treatment approaches are necessary, including:
        Age-appropriate interventions
        More focus on family treatment
        Longitudinal continuation of treatment.
- Heredity affects the vulnerability to addiction.
- Availability of drugs is a key variable in developing drug abuse.

What We Do Not Know

- Which psychosocial treatments are most effective? All of the following show some promise:
    Individual therapy (cognitive-behavioral therapy, maturation enhancement therapy)
    Family therapy
    Group therapy
    Twelve-Step rehabilitation

- Is group therapy an effective modality for adolescents?
    If so, how should it be structured?
    Should adolescents always be segregated from adults in group treatment?
- What is the neurobiology of adolescent addiction?
    Initiation of addictive patterns
    Progression of addiction
    Vulnerability to specific agents
- Is it necessary to require complete abstinence in adolescents attempting recovery?
    Does this mean ceasing use of all addicting drugs?
    Does nicotine use impede recovery?
- How can we enhance perceived risk for experimenting with drugs?
- How can we best match patients with treatments?
    Matching problems to treatments has been found effective in small studies, but rarely used in practice.
- How can the judicial system positively influence outcome?

What We Urgently Need to Know—The Priorities

- Prevention programs: which ones are most effective or ineffective?
    Mass media campaigns?
    Drug Abuse Resistance Education (DARE)?
    Urine testing?
    Other approaches?
- Which specialized treatments for adolescent addiction provide the best outcomes?
- Which specialized programs can prevent binge drinking in college?
- Which pharmacological treatments work best for adolescents with substance use disorders?
    Pharmaceutical companies have shown little interest in developing medications for adult addictions and none for substance abuse in adolescence. How can we recruit the pharmaceutical industry into the area of prevention and treatment?
- What are the best means of identifying adolescents at risk for addiction?

- How can we recruit scientists into the area of addiction research?

How Can We Improve the Treatment System?

- How can we obtain adequate reimbursement for treatment providers?
  Adolescent treatment programs are scarce and underfunded.
- How can we provide an accessible continuum of care with age-appropriate expertise?
  Medical and psychiatric evaluation capability
  Inpatient facilities
  Partial hospitalization and intensive outpatient programs
  Outpatient treatment with long-term capability
- How can we integrate substance abuse treatment with other mental health treatment?
  Comorbidity of substance abuse with other mental disorders is very common.
  Few treatment programs are equipped to treat dual diagnosis.
- How can we disseminate scientific evidence supporting the disease concept of addiction?
- How can political initiatives secure appropriate resource allocation?

Youth Suicide

COMMISSION ON ADOLESCENT SUICIDE PREVENTION

Herbert Hendin, *Commission Chair*

David A. Brent

Jack R. Cornelius

Tamera Coyne-Beasley

Ted Greenberg

Madelyn Gould

Ann Pollinger Haas

Jill Harkavy-Friedman

Richard Harrington

Gregg Henriques

Douglas G. Jacobs

John Kalafat

Mary Margaret Kerr

Cheryl A. King

Richard Ramsay

David Shaffer

Anthony Spirito

Howard Sudak

Elaine Adams Thompson

VI
part

Defining Youth Suicide

chapter 21

SCOPE AND DEMOGRAPHICS

Fifty years ago suicide among young people aged 15–24 was a relatively infrequent event and suicides in this age group constituted less than 5% of all suicides in the United States. As can be seen in Figure 21.1, between the mid-1950s and the late 1970s, the rate of suicide rose markedly among this age group. This increase was observed most dramatically among young males, whose suicide rates more than tripled between 1955 and 1977 (from 6.3 per 100,000 to 21.3). Among females ages 15–24, the suicide rate more than doubled during this same period (from 2.0 per 100,000 to 5.2). By 1980, suicides by 15- to 24-year-olds constituted almost 17% of the approximately 30,000 suicides in the United States (National Center for Health Statistics, n.d.).

Rising suicide rates continued, albeit at a slower pace, during the 1980s and early 1990s, reaching a peak rate of 13.6 suicides per 100,000 youth aged 15–24 in 1994. At that point, rates began to steadily decline, decreasing to 9.9 per 100,000 by 2002 (the last year for which national data are currently available), a drop of over 27% (National Center for Health Statistics, n.d.).

Figures available since 1970 (also depicted in Fig. 21.1) show that among the younger subset of youth, those aged 15–19, the suicide rate rose relatively consistently up until 1990 (from 5.9 per 100,000 to 11.1), and has dropped considerably since that time to 7.4 suicides per 100,000 population in 2002. Even with these declines, the overall youth suicide rate remains more than twice what it had been before the marked rise began, and currently constitutes almost 13% of all U.S. suicides (Centers for Disease Control and Prevention [CDC] n.d.a).

Suicide before the age of 12 is rare, but increases with every year past puberty (CDC, n.d.a). In 2002, youth aged 20–24 had a suicide rate of 12.3 per 100,000, compared to the rate of 7.4 among adolescents aged 15–19. A total of 4,010 young people aged 15–24 died by suicide during that one year, 1,513 between the ages of 15–19, and 2,497 between the ages of 20–24. Currently in the United States suicide is the third leading cause of death among youth; only accidents and homicide claim more young lives. Among college students specifically, suicide is

the second leading cause of death, surpassed only by accidental injury.

How is one to explain the rise in the rate of youth suicide in the United States during the latter half of the last century? It has been suggested that the increase in the youth suicide rate paralleled an increase in the rate of depression since the 1950s. Documenting an increase in the rate of depression is not easy, however, since clinical studies undertaken prior to the 1980s did not use a standard definition of depression. In addition, such a dramatic rise in suicide in a relatively short time frame is likely to reflect some broad environmental change. Thus, medical and social scientists have sought other explanations (Berman & Jobes, 1995; Gould, Greenberg, Velting, & Shaffer, 2003; Hendin, 1978).

Increased availability of firearms as a contributing factor is suggested by increases in the rate of suicide by firearms among young people in the United States during the 1980s (Boyd & Moscicki, 1986; Brent, Perper, & Allman, 1987; Brent et al., 1991). Similar increases in youth suicide have been seen in countries such as New Zealand and in Europe, however, where firearms are not a common suicide method (World Health Organization, 2003).

The diminishing cohesion of the family observed since World War II has frequently been blamed for a wide range of youth problem behaviors, including both drug abuse and suicide. The psychosocial revolution that swept the Western world beginning in the 1960s, which embraced a greater freedom in sexual behavior, as well as changes in the expectations that young men and women had for themselves and for their relationships, is also thought to have contributed to youth suicide (Hendin, 1978, 1995). A marked and well-documented increase in drug and alcohol exposure took place during that period (Johnston, O'Malley, & Bachman, 2002), and the relationship between substance abuse and suicide has been clearly established in a number of studies of both adults (Barraclough, Bunch, Nelson, & Sainsbury, 1974; Robins, Murphy, Wilkinson, Gassner, & Kayes, 1959) and youth (Marttunen, Aro, Henriksson, & Lonnqvist, 1991; Shaffer et al., 1996).

The question of why youth suicide rates have declined in recent years is equally important. Al-

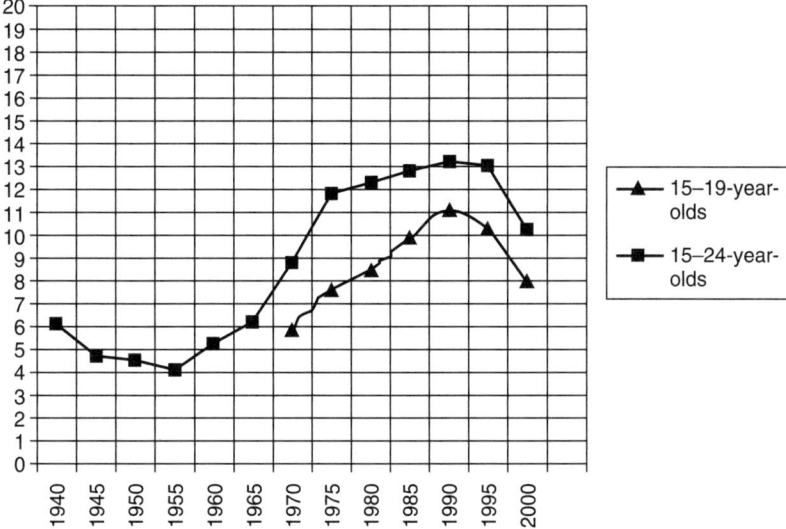

Figure 21.1 Rates of suicide for 15- to 19-year-olds and 15- to 24-year-olds, both sexes, all races [*source:* National Center for Health Statistics]. Rates for 15- to 19-year-olds are not available for pre-1970.

though we shall return to this question later in this section, it should be kept in mind that from a historical perspective, the declines we have seen recently are not unique. Twice previously in the 20th century, the rate of suicide among young men declined precipitously: once between 1908 and 1922, when the young male suicide rate went from almost 14 per 100,000 to 6, a drop of over 100%; and again between 1938 and 1944, when the rate fell from almost 9 per 100,000 to 6, a decline of 35%.

Recent decreases have been attributed to efforts to restrict firearms availability among youth (Brent, Baugher, Bridge, Chen, & Chiappetta, 1999; Miller & Heminway, 1999). In the United States the proportion of suicides that involve firearms has decreased somewhat in recent years, although firearms are still used in about 60% of all suicide deaths (CDC, n.d.a). Parallel declines in the youth suicide rate and in the rate of suicide by firearms, therefore, are not surprising. It should also be noted that among older white males, who have the highest suicide rate of any demographic group in the United States, the proportion of suicides that involve firearms has not declined. Furthermore, suicide rates have decreased in other countries where firearms are not a commonly used method.

The decline in the rate of youth suicide has also been linked to the increased use of antidepressant medication in treating young depressed people (Olfson, Shaffer, Marcus, & Greenberg, 2003). Although more precise data than are currently available may well substantiate the link between antidepressant use and suicide deaths, it should be noted that other problem behaviors among youth, notably substance abuse and violent crime, have generally risen and fallen parallel with changes in the suicide rate. And the recent drop in violent crime by young people in recent years seems less likely to be related to increased use of antidepressants.

Improved economic conditions in the 1990s have been credited for the recent decline in youth suicide, just as they were blamed for the high national rates during the depression of the 1930s. The decline in youth suicide has been noted, however, in countries that did not experience the prosperity that occurred in the United States during the last decade of the 20th century.

It is only relatively recently that tracking studies such as the CDC's Youth Risk Behavior Survey (YRBS) have been undertaken to provide accurate data about suicide attempts by young people. Thus, it is not possible to determine whether the increase in youth suicide deaths seen between the mid-1950s and 1990 was matched by an increase in suicide attempts among young people. The YRBS data reported since the early 1990s show that among high schools students (the target group for the YRBS), the recent decline in suicide deaths has not been accompanied by a comparable decline in suicide attempts (CDC, n.d.b).

The most current YRBS data (2003) indicate that 8.5 percent of U.S. high school youth surveyed (5.4% of males and 11.5% of females) made one or more suicide attempts in the prior 12-month period; 2.9 percent (2.4% of males and 3.2% of females) required medical attention as a result of a suicide attempt. Seventeen percent of the students indicated that they had seriously considered attempting suicide during the past 12 months. Since youth who are not currently attending school have been found to be at higher risk for suicide attempts and suicide deaths than those who are in school (Gould, Greenberg, et al., 2003; Gould, Fisher, Parides, Flory, & Shaffer, 1996), YRBS high school–based data likely underestimate the extent of these events among young people overall.

Patterns of suicidal behavior vary widely among youth from different demographic backgrounds. Among young people ages 15–24, males die by suicide almost six times more frequently than females. In 2002, the suicide rate among young men ages 15–24 was 16.4 per 100,000, and the rate among young women was 2.9. Although young males die by suicide more often than females, females report suicidal ideation and attempts more often than males (CDC, n.d.b.).

Youth suicide rates also vary widely among different racial and ethnic groups. In 2002, white youth had a suicide rate of 10.6 per 100,000, compared to rates of 6.5 for African Americans, 6.6 for Hispanic youth, 5.3 for Asian Americans/Pacific Islanders, and 17.9 for American Indians and Alaskan Natives (CDC, n.d.a). The elevated rate of suicide among Native Americans of all ages is substantially accounted for by the particularly high suicide rate of young Native American males (Berlin, 1987; Wallace, Calhoun, Powell, O'Neil, & James, 1996).

Suicide attempt rates appear to be particularly high among young Latinos, surpassing rates among either whites or African Americans, whose attempt rates are similar (CDC, n.d.a). Although these patterns have been relatively stable, the reasons underlying the differential distribution of suicide attempts and suicide completions among racial and ethnic groups in the United States have not yet been adequately explored.

Since the mid-1980s, significant public attention has been focused on youth suicide prevention. During that decade, a proliferation of youth suicide prevention programs were developed and implemented, particularly in schools where they targeted students, parents, teachers, and other school personnel. This coincided with increasing recognition of childhood and adolescent depression, and mental health professionals and medical practitioners likewise began looking for ways to prevent the tragic loss of young lives to suicide. Many of these early youth suicide prevention efforts have not been sustained because of a lack of demonstrable success and/or a lack of funding.

In recent years, renewed attention to the problem of youth suicide has resulted from the National Strategy for Suicide Prevention, developed by the Department of Health and Human Services Administration and the Office of the former Surgeon General, David Satcher (U.S. Department of Health and Human Services, 2001). This initiative called for the development of statewide suicide prevention programs to address youth as well as other priority target populations.

Our primary goal in this section of the book is to examine youth suicide prevention strategies and interventions with an eye toward identifying what works, what does not appear to work, and what research needs to be undertaken to move the field forward. We begin with a review of the multiple factors that have been suggested to put youth at risk for suicide.

ETIOLOGY OF YOUTH SUICIDE

It is generally agreed upon that suicidal behavior is multiply determined. In the following pages, we review the factors that have been identified in the research literature as conveying primary risk for suicide among young people, as well as factors that have been suggested to mediate or protect against suicidal behavior. These risk factors are summarized in Table 21.1. Different aspects of the problem have been addressed in a number of previous reviews (Gould, Greenberg, et al., 2003; Guo & Harstall, 2002; Wagner, 1997; Wagner, Silverman & Martin, 2003) and we have drawn on these in the discussion that follows and throughout the rest of this section.

Risk Factors

Although true causation is difficult to establish, a number of factors, or sets of factors, appear, on

Table 21.1 Factors Associated with Risk for Suicidal Behavior in Adolescents[a]

Psychopathology

Depression
Drug and alcohol abuse
Aggressive-impulsive behavior
Hopelessness
Pessimism
Conduct disorder (male)
Panic disorder (female)

Family and Genetic

Family history of suicidal behavior
Parental psychopathology

Environment

Firearm availability
Diminished family cohesion
Lack of parental support
Parent–child conflict
Negative life events
Child sex abuse
Suicide contagion

Biology

High 5-HT receptor expression in prefrontal cortex and hippocampus
Serotonergic dysfunction

Previous suicidal behavior

Suicide attempts

Sexual orientation

Same-sex sexual orientation

[a] Factors noted have been found to be associated with increased risk for suicidal behavior individually but overlap and shared underlying factors have not been assessed.

the basis of existing research, to be primary risk factors for youth suicide. Clearly, there is considerable overlap and mutual reinforcement among these factors, although most studies have considered them separately.

Psychopathology and Substance Abuse

There is overwhelming evidence that psychopathology is the most significant risk factor for both suicide deaths and suicide attempts among adolescents (Brent et al., 1999; Groholt, Ekeberg, Wichstrom, & Haldorsen, 1997; Shaffer et al., 1996). Psychological autopsy studies have determined that the vast majority of adolescents who die by suicide have significant psychiatric problems, including previous suicidal behavior, depressive disorder, substance abuse, and conduct disorder. The initial onset of such problems often precedes the suicide by several years. Suicide risk among adolescents has also been established to increase with the number of psychiatric diagnoses, with comorbidity between affective disorders and substance abuse being of particular importance (Shaffer et al., 1996). One recent analysis (Gould, 2003) has suggested that eliminating psychopathology could prevent 78%–87% of youth suicides.

The psychiatric problems and gender-specific diagnostic profiles of youth who attempt suicide have been found to be similar to those who die by suicide, with relatively more females than males presenting with affective disorder (Brent et al., 1999; Shaffer et al., 1996) and more males than females having substance abuse, particularly among older male adolescents (Gould et al., 1998; Marttunnen, Avo, Henriksson, & Lönnqvist, 1991; Shaffer et al., 1996). Conduct disorder is also prevalent in young males with suicidal behavior, often comorbid with substance use disorders and anxiety and mood disorders (Brent et al., 1993a; Gould et al., 1998; Shaffer et al., 1996).

Panic disorder has been found to be related to suicidal behavior, particularly among girls (Gould et al., 1996, 1998). Among adults, however, no association has been found when controlling for comorbid depression (Warshaw, Dolan, & Keller, 2000). Other anxiety disorders such as posttraumatic stress disorder have not been shown to be associated with suicidal behavior among young people when other comorbid psychiatric conditions are taken into consideration (Wunderlich, Bronisch, & Wittchen, 1998). Some studies have reported a relationship between bipolar disorder and both suicide deaths and suicide attempts among youth (Brent et al., 1988; Brent, Perper, & Moritz, 1993; Marttunnen et al., 1991; Shaffer & Hicks, 1994). Although suicide is relatively common among adults with bipolar disorder, given the relative rarity of the disorder, it accounts for only a small proportion of suicide deaths (Appleby, Cooper, Amos, & Faragher, 1999; Vijayakumar & Rajkumar, 1999). Suicidal ideation appears to be less directly related to psychopathology than either suicide attempts or suicide death (Andrews & Lewinsohn, 1992; Reinherz et al., 1995), perhaps because ideation, while occurring with higher frequency, is less persistent and may be fleeting. Gould et al. (1998) found suicidal ideation to be associated with depression in adolescent females and with depression and disruptive disorders in young males.

Aggressive-impulsive behavior (Apter, Plutchik, & van Praag, 1993; Gould et al., 1998; McKeown, et al., 1998; Sourander, Helstela, Haavisto, & Bergroth, 2001) has an increased association with suicidal behavior, particularly in the context of a mood disorder (Brent, Johnson, et al., 1994; Johnson, Brent, Bridge, & Connolly, 1998). Aggressive-impulsive behavior has been found to discriminate suicide attempters from psychiatric controls, and also appears to be related to familial transmission of suicidal behavior.

Hopelessness has also been implicated as an important factor associated with youth suicidal behavior, although its relationship is not independent of depression and depressed mood (Rotheram-Borus & Trautman, 1988; Rotheram-Borus, Trautman, Dopkins, & Shrout, 1990). Among a depressed subgroup that is at high risk for suicide, hopelessness may be an important marker. Pessimism, a negative cognitive style that may be related to hopelessness, has been found to characterize suicide attempters independent of depression (Lewinsohn, Rhode, & Seeley, 1996).

Previous Suicidal Behavior

Studies among adults have consistently identified previous suicidal behavior to be the most important factor associated with risk of suicide (Hawton & Sinclair, 2003), with repetition of suicide attempts significantly increasing the risk of a fatal outcome (Sakinovsky, 2000). Studies of youth have likewise found previous suicide attempts to be one of the strongest predictors of both subsequent attempts and suicide deaths (McKeown et al., 1998; Shaffer et al., 1996; Wichstrom, 2000). This relationship is particularly strong among youth with mood disorders (Brent et al., 1999; Shaffer et al., 1996). The risk for future suicidal behavior has been estimated to increase 3–17 times when a previous attempt has occurred (Groholt et al., 1997). One study of a high school sample found that half of adolescent suicide attempters had made more than one attempt (Harkavy-Friedman, Asnis, Boeck, & DiFiore, 1987), and this finding is confirmed by data reported by the YRBS (CDC, n.d.b). Overall, it is estimated that one quarter to one third of adolescents who die by suicide had made a previous attempt (Brent et al., 1993a; Groholt et al., 1997; Shaffer at al., 1996).

While prior attempts figure prominently in the histories of many young persons who die by suicide, the nature of the linkage between earlier and subsequent suicidal behavior is less clear. Existing evidence suggests, however, that previous suicide attempts convey an increased risk for suicide death even after controlling for psychiatric risk factors (Brent et al., 1999; Shaffer et al., 1996).

Sexual Orientation

An additional personal factor that has been suggested to be associated with youth suicide is homosexuality. A number of individual studies (Faulkner & Cranston, 1998; Fergusson, Horwood, & Beautrais, 1999; Garofalo et al., 1998; Remafedi, French, Story, Resnick, & Bloom, 1998; Russell & Joyner, 2001; Wichstrom & Hegna, 2003) as well as a comprehensive review article (McDaniel, Purcell, & D'Augelli, 2001) report increased rates of nonlethal suicidal behavior among youth with same-sex sexual orientation. Wichstrom and Hegna (2003) found that the suicide attempt rate was higher for those with same-sex orientation regardless of whether they had actually had same-sex sexual contact. They found that those who had had same-sex sexual contact had the highest rate. Stigmatization, victimization, isolation, and parental rejection have been identified as factors in suicidal behavior among gay, lesbian, and bisexual youth (McDaniel et al., 2001).

There is no empirical evidence that links suicide deaths among youth to sexual orientation (Shaffer, Fisher, Hicks, Parides, & Gould, 1995). Research in this area is likely to be limited by methodological challenges, notably inaccuracies in the reporting of sexual orientation or sexual behavior (McDaniel et al., 2001; Russell, 2003).

Biological and Genetic Factors

Some studies have linked youth suicidal behavior to parental psychopathology (Brent et al., 1988; Brent, Perper, et al., 1994; Gould et al., 1996), although others have found rates of family psychopathology among young suicide attempters and completers to be similar to those of other clinical samples (see Wagner, 1997; Wagner et al., 2003). Both suicide and suicide attempts have been found to be increased in families in which a parent has died by suicide or attempted suicide, even when controlling for the impact of parental psychopathology (Brent, Bridge, Johnson, & Connolly, 1996; Brent et al., 2002; Glowinski et al., 2001). This relationship may be mediated by familial transmission of impulsive aggression (Brent et al., 2003).

The mechanisms through which psychopathology and suicidality among parents may influence youth suicidal behavior are not yet clear. Although little is currently known about the genetics of youth suicide, adult studies suggest that biological factors play a significant role in suicide. Neurobiological abnormalities, in particular lower levels of central nervous system serotonin (5-HT), have been implicated in aggressive impulsivity and suicidal behavior in adults (Oquendo & Mann, 2000). Postmortem studies of the brains of adult suicide victims have also shown higher levels of 5-HT receptors than in

normal controls (Arango et al., 1990; Mann, Stanley, McBride, & McEwen, 1986).

Postmortem studies of youth who have died by suicide are rare, and therefore the implications of adult findings for understanding youth suicide are not clear. One postmortem study involving 15 teenage suicide victims and 15 normal matched control subjects found significantly higher levels of 5-HT receptor expression in the prefrontal cortex and hippocampus of those who had died by suicide, suggesting that this abnormality may be a marker of adolescent as well as adult suicide (Pandey et al., 2002). These authors noted that higher levels of serotonin receptor expression have been implicated in alterations in emotion, stress, and cognition, which suggests promising avenues of exploration for understanding the neurobiology of youth suicide. Further studies are needed to confirm these findings and to clarify genetic relationships.

Family Environment

The familial expression of suicidality is likely a function of example as well as biology. Certain factors related to the family environment such as lack of family support and parent–child conflict have been found to contribute to risk for youth suicidal behavior (see Wagner, 1997; Wagner et al., 2003 for reviews). Particularly among younger suicide victims, parent–child conflict has been identified as a common precipitant to suicidal behavior (Brent et al., 1999; (Groholt, Ekeberg, Wichstrom, & Haldorsen, 1998).

Negative Life Events

There is considerable evidence that various negative life events contribute independently to youth suicide (see Wagner, 1997; Wagner et al., 2003), over and above other risk factors (Gould et al., 1996; Johnson, Cohen, et al., 2002). Physical abuse, for example, has been demonstrated to increase risk in case–control (Brent, Johnson, et al., 1994; Brent et al., 1999) and longitudinal studies (Brown, Cohen, Johnson, & Smailes, 1999; Johnson et al., 2002; Silverman, Reinherz, & Giaconia, 1996), and has been associated with youth suicidal behavior even after controlling for other contributory factors such as parental psychopathology (see Johnson et al., 2002; Wagner, 1997; Wagner et al., 2003).

Child sexual abuse has also been found to be associated with increased risk for suicidal behavior (Johnson et al., 2002; Silverman et al., 1996), as well as with many other adverse psychological outcomes (Fergusson, Horwood, & Lynskey, 1996.). Some of the suicide risk conferred by child sexual abuse is likely related more generally to parental psychopathology, although one longitudinal study that controlled for many other risk factors (Fergusson et al., 1996) identified a unique contribution of this variable to suicidality.

Stressful life events have been found to be associated with suicide deaths (Beautrais, 2001; Brent, Perper, & Moritz, 1993; Gould et al., 1996; Marttunen, Aro, & Lönnqvist, 1993) and suicide attempts (Beautrais, Joyce, & Mulder, 1997; Fergusson, Woodward, & Horwood, 2000; Lewinsohn et al., 1996). Studies of young suicide attempters suggest that the type of stressor associated with suicidal behavior is age related, with suicidal behavior in younger adolescents most frequently precipitated by conflicts with parents, and in older adolescents by interpersonal loss, in particular the loss of a romantic relationship (Brent et al., 1999; Groholt et al., 1998). Interpersonal loss has also been identified as a significant stressor among youth with substance abuse problems (Brent et al., 1993b; Gould, Greenberg, et al., 2003; Marttunen, Aro, Henriksson, & Lönnqvist, 1994).

Bullying has also been suggested as a precipitant, with at least one study finding both victims and perpetrators to be more likely to engage in suicidal behavior than youth not involved in bullying (Kaltiala-Heino, Rimpela, Marttunen, Rimpela, & Rantanen, 1999). There appear to be commonalities between bullying and other forms of social maligning, such as those reported by gay and lesbian youth. Although media accounts of suicide among young people frequently allude to bullying as a cause, scientific evidence for this is lacking. No studies of bullying have controlled for the presence of other risk factors in suicide victims, in particular psychopathology, and to date in the United States, no systematic suicide prevention efforts have targeted this factor.

Legal or disciplinary problems have been found to precipitate suicidal behavior in youth with conduct disorder and other disruptive disorders (Brent, Perper, & Moritz, 1993; Gould et al., 1996). Academic difficulties have also been found to be associated with increased risk for suicidal behavior. Several studies have demonstrated increased suicidal ideation or behavior among students at risk for dropping out of high school (Beautrais, Joyce, & Mulder, 1996; Thompson & Eggert, 1999; Wunderlich et al., 1998). Gould et al. (1996) also reported that school problems and not being in school or in a work situation pose considerable risk for suicide death.

Contagion

There is evidence that young people are particularly vulnerable to the impact of suicide contagion, whether through media coverage or direct knowledge of a peer's suicide (Gould, 2001; Gould, Jamieson, & Romer, 2003). Research has described outbreaks or clusters of both suicide deaths (Gould, Wallenstein, & Kleinman, 1990; Gould, Wallenstein, Kleinman, O'Carroll, & Mercy, 1990) and attempted suicides (Gould, Petrie, Kleinman, & Wallenstein, 1994) among young people. Having a friend who has attempted suicide has been found to discriminate depressed adolescents who themselves make a suicide attempt from those who do not (Lewinsohn, Rohde, & Seeley, 1994). The causality of the association between a youngster's knowledge of a friend or family member who attempts suicide and the youth's subsequent suicidal behavior has been supported using two waves of data from the National Longitudinal Study of Adolescent Health (Add Health), a nationally representative study of youth in grades 7 through 12 (Cutler, Glaeser, & Norberg, 2001). Despite some research reporting no association between media reporting and subsequent suicides (Mercy et al., 2001), the evidence of the significant impact of media coverage on suicide is ample and continues to grow (see Gould, 2001; Pirkis & Blood, 2001a, 2001b; Schmidtke & Shaller, 2000; Stack, 2000).

Availability of Means

Over half of the 4,000 youths aged 15–24 years who died by suicide in 2002 used firearms (CDC, n.d.a), and there is strong evidence that firearms used for both suicides and unintentional injuries by adolescents are mainly from the home environment (Bailey et al., 1997; Beautrais et al., 1996; Brent et al., 1993d; Grossman, Reay, & Baker 1999; Shah, Hoffman, Wake, & Marine, 2000).

Family firearm ownership has been found to correlate with the youth suicide rate for 15- to 24-year-olds (Birckmayer & Hemenway, 2001). Almost three quarters of youth suicides and suicide attempts have been found to involve the use of a firearm belonging to a household member; in more than half of the cases, a parent's gun was involved (Grossman et al., 1999; Reza, Modzeleski, Feucht, Anderson, & Barrios, 2003). A disproportionate number of parents with guns in the household have been found to leave their guns loaded and not locked up (Coyne-Beasley, McGee, Johnson, & Bordley, 2002; Coyne-Beasley, Schoenback, & Johnson, 2001).

Guns have been estimated to be four to five times more prevalent in the homes of suicide victims compared to controls (Brent et al., 1993d; Kellermann et al., 1992; Shah et al., 2000). There appears to be a gradient of risk, with loaded guns and handguns posing the greatest risk. In a recent review of case–control studies, Brent and Bridge (2003) reported that the odds of a youth dying by suicide was 31.3–107.9 times higher in homes where a gun was present than in homes without guns.

Of note, youth who use firearms for suicide reportedly have fewer identifiable risk factors, such as expressing suicidal thoughts, suicidal intent, psychopathology, and substance abuse, compared to those using other means (Azrael, 2001; Brent et al., 1999; Groholt et al., 1998), and firearm suicides appear to be more impulsive and spontaneous (Azrael, 2001). Thus, to at least some extent, means availability appears to function as a contributing factor to youth suicide, independent of other factors. Among the approximately 10% of youth who died by suicide and had no clear psychiatric diagnosis, the only factor found to discriminate this group from nor-

mal controls was the presence of a loaded gun in the home (Brent et al., 1993d; Kellerman et al., 1992).

Despite strong evidence for the role of firearms in youth suicide, it should be noted that restricting access to guns may not always result in a decrease in overall suicide deaths. A study that examined suicide methods used by Australian males between 1975 and 1998 (De Leo, Dwyer, Firman, & Neulinger, 2003) reported a declining rate of firearm suicide among males overall as well as among a subset of males aged 15–24, attributed in part to increased restrictions on weapons purchases. In both samples, however, these declines coincided with an increase in the rate of suicide by hanging. Among young males, the increased rate of hanging coincided with an increase in the overall suicide rate.

Protective Factors

Several factors, identified below, have been suggested as protecting youth against suicidal behavior. In reviewing protective factors, several limitations should be noted, in particular, the likelihood that they are features of psychological health and thus nonspecific for suicidality as opposed to other forms of mental illness. Further, it has not been empirically determined whether patterns and behaviors consistent with psychological health actually protect against mental illness and suicidality, or whether they are manifestations of a lack of mental illness. In addition, conclusions are limited by the fact that studies have not generally examined protective factors in a broader context of risk factors.

Connectedness to Family, School, and Other Institutions

Researchers have found that students who describe their families as emotionally involved and supportive were much less likely to report suicidal behavior than students who described their families as less supportive and involved (McKeown et al., 1998; Resnick et al., 1997; Rubenstein, Halton, Kasten, Rubin, & Stechler, 1998, Rubenstein, Heeren, Housman, Rubin, & Stechler, 1989; Zhang & Jin, 1996). There is limited evidence that family cohesion is independent of the adolescent's levels of depression or life stress (Rubenstein et al., 1989, 1998).

The National Longitudinal Study on Adolescent Health (Resnick et al., 1997) reported that student connectedness to school was also a primary protective factor. Similarly, there is limited evidence that perceived suicide risk is inversely related to religious orthodoxy, particularly among racial and ethnic minorities (Greening & Stoppelbein, 2002).

Social Skills

Jessor (1991) suggested that a range of social skills, including decision making and problem solving, may be protective factors for suicidal behavior, and this relationship has received considerable attention among school administrators. The impact of social skills on youth suicidal behavior has not been directly tested, however, and there is no evidence that students with good decision-making or problem-solving skills are overall less suicidal. Although some studies have found that at-risk students who participated in interventions designed to improve social skills showed decreased depression and suicidal behavior (LaFramboise & Howard-Pitney, 1995; Thompson, Eggert, & Herting, 2000; Thompson, Eggert, Randell, & Pike, 2001), it is not clear that these decreases were accounted for by any increase in acquired social skills.

YOUTH SUICIDE PREVENTION

Given the multiplicity of risk and protective factors that have been related to youth suicide, it is understandable that many different approaches have been taken in the attempt to prevent this behavior. In the next three chapters, we discuss and critique the major preventive strategies and treatment approaches that have been used. Rather than undertaking an exhaustive review of every program that has been identified, we have selected those that have been most fully described in published reports and/or those we feel best illustrate a general type or approach. Reflecting the strategies that have received the widest application, our review focuses primarily on

suicide prevention programs targeting groups of youth, rather than on clinical care or evaluation of individual youth who are potentially suicidal.

Before turning to this discussion, we would like to share some observations regarding the accumulated literature on youth suicide prevention. Although many different programs have been developed and implemented, very few have been systematically evaluated for their immediate or long-term efficacy and effectiveness. In contrast to programs addressing other high-risk behaviors such as drug use, few if any youth suicide prevention programs are supported by conclusive empirical evidence of effectiveness.

In part, this is due to the unique impact of ethical considerations on suicide research in general and outcomes evaluation in particular. Such considerations have served to limit participation of suicidal individuals in clinical trials and other interventions, and to restrict the availability of appropriate control groups by discouraging selective offering of potentially helpful interventions (Fisher, Pearson, Kim, & Reynolds, 2002).

Also important to note are the difficulties inherent in attempting to determine the impact of programs implemented among relatively small samples on the statistically rare events of suicide death or attempted suicide. In addition, the application of many suicide prevention strategies and programs in settings in which contact with participants is transitory has limited the ability of such programs to employ longitudinal evaluation designs that might reveal long-term outcomes, including suicide attempts and suicide deaths. In the absence of large-scale, long-term studies, programs have tended to rely on proximal outcomes such as knowledge, attitudes, and referrals to treatment, whose relationship to suicide attempts and suicide deaths has been incompletely established, if at all.

Further, it should be noted that with respect to almost all suicide prevention efforts, reports of effectiveness have been internally produced, typically by the program developers, often using designs, outcomes, effectiveness criteria and measures unique to an individual site. This has limited the degree to which different approaches can be compared. Rather than using a careful before-and-after design in a case–control setting, evaluations have frequently been confined to determining whether a program was found to be interesting or acceptable to a particular target group.

In spite of these limitations, the programs and interventions reviewed in the subsequent chapters suggest a great deal about what appears to work, and what doesn't, in the prevention of suicide among adolescents and young adults.

Universal Approaches to Youth Suicide Prevention

In this chapter, we focus on suicide prevention programs that have taken a universal approach, targeting youth in specific settings regardless of individual risk factors. One particularly widespread approach targets youth where they are most accessible—in the schools. Although the ultimate goal of all suicide prevention programs is to reduce death by suicide, school-based programs typically focus on more proximal outcomes.

Two broad types of universal prevention programs have been especially common. The first includes educational programs that aim to increase students' knowledge and awareness about suicidal behavior, encourage troubled students to seek help, and improve recognition of at-risk students by teachers, counselors, and other "gatekeepers" within the school or community settings. In the second category are screening programs that seek to identify and refer to treatment youth who are at risk for suicidal behavior.

In each category, suicide prevention efforts have been separately designed for high school and college students. In the following pages, we summarize these universal programs, identifying for each broad type the underlying assumptions and specific program examples, and providing a summary critique of the approach.

SUICIDE AWARENESS AND EDUCATION PROGRAMS

Assumptions

A wide range of suicide education and awareness programs have been developed; these are summarized in Table 22.1 The key assumptions underlying such programs are that the conditions that contribute to suicide risk in adolescents and young adults often go unrecognized, undiagnosed, and untreated, and that educating students and gatekeepers about the warning signs for suicide and appropriate responses will result in better identification of at-risk youth, and an increase in help seeking and referrals for treatment.

Program Examples

Most suicide awareness and education programs described in the literature have been implemented at the high school level and share a core of common programmatic features, centering on a suicide education curriculum, supplemented in some cases with training directed toward teachers and other gatekeepers. Such programs are exemplified by those developed by Kalafat and colleagues (Kalafat & Elias, 1992, 1994; Kalafat & Gagliano, 1996; Kalafat & Ryerson, 1999), which incorporate education about the warning signs of suicide and appropriate help-seeking behaviors into the regular physical education or related curricula. Such education has been reported by the program developers to result in students' increased knowledge about suicidal behavior, more positive attitudes about talking to friends they believe to be suicidal, and seeking of help from adults. In its most fully developed form, the Adolescent Suicide Awareness Program (ASAP) includes education for teachers, school staff, and parents, as well as students. Although no controlled evaluations have been reported, the developers cited anecdotal reports of increased referrals of at-risk youth, following implementation of ASAP in a number of schools (Kalafat & Ryerson, 1999).

Another widely applied curriculum-based prevention effort is the Signs of Suicide (SOS) program, developed by Jacobs and colleagues. The SOS program delivers the core message that suicidal behavior is directly related to mental illness, particularly depression, and needs to be responded to as a mental health emergency. The instructional component, which occurs over one to two class periods, may be augmented with screening and parent-awareness activities. Schools in which the program has been implemented have reported substantial increases in students' help-seeking behavior and high satisfaction with the program among school officials (Aseltine, Jacobs, Kopans, & Bloom, 2003). In a recent posttest-only evaluation involving five high schools in Columbus, Georgia, and Hartford, Connecticut, 2,100 students were randomly assigned to intervention and control groups. In self-administered questionnaires 3

Table 22.1 Suicide Education Programs

Reference	Intervention	Study Design	Program Length	Sample Size	Comments
Spirito et al., 1988	Samaritan-based program	Nonrandom pre–postcontrol group design	8 hr	Experimental: 291 high school students Control: 182 high school students	Program-exposed group demonstrated increase in knowledge Females increased knowledge more than males
Overholser et al., 1989	Samaritan-based program with didactics, handouts, discussion, and role-playing	Nonrandom pre–postcontrol group design	5 health classes	Experimental: 215 ninth-grade students from two schools Control: 256 ninth-grade students from one school 53% male from suburban middle class	Gender and personal experience related to students' knowledge and attitudes at baseline and after the program More positive effect of program for females and slightly negative in some aspects for males Students who knew suicidal peer were more likely to increase knowledge All students except males with personal experience with suicidal behavior had decreased negative attitudes No comparisons with controls presented
Shaffer et al., 1990	Didactics and discussion led by trained, regular education classroom teachers	Nonequivalent control group with 2×2 (attempt yes/no × program yes/no) pre–post design	1–3 hr, depending on school	Initial sample: $N = 1,551$ ninth graders Final sample: $N = 63$ suicide attempters (35 program/28 control) $N = 910$ nonattempters (489 program/421 Control)	Majority felt others should participate in program Changes in knowledge and attitudes tended to be in intended direction Male attempters more likely than nonattempters to feel uncomfortable dealing with friends' problems, to know someone upset by program, and to discourage participation

(continued)

Table 22.1 Continued

Reference	Intervention	Study Design	Program Length	Sample Size	Comments
Shaffer et al., 1991 Vieland et al., 1991	Didactic instruction and discussion	Pretest–posttest design with comparison group Follow-ups at 1 month and of a subsample at 18 months	3 different suicide-awareness programs, each lasting 3–4 hr, focusing on symptom identification and help seeking; differences between programs in use of teachers and focus on help seeking, problem solving, or mobilizing networks	11 schools n = 758 from 6 program schools (2 for each program) n = 680 from 5 control schools 9th and 10th graders 5 urban 2 suburban 4 rural/suburban	Reaction to program was good Females and nonwhite ethnic groups rated programs more highly Base knowledge high; exposure increased controversial beliefs supported by the programs Programs increased knowledge about where to get help but did not improve help-seeking behavior
Kalafat & Elias, 1994	Adolescent Suicide Awareness Program (ASAP) Didactics and discussion program	Solomon four-group design	3 health class periods	253 suburban 10th graders	Increased knowledge about warning signs Improved attitudes about help seeking More likely to talk about a friend's suicidal behavior and refer for help
Kalafat & Gagliano, 1996	ASAP Didactics, discussion, and simulated encounters with suicidal peers	Stratified random sample Pre–post control group	5 health class periods	109 eighth graders (whole grade) White n = 52 experimental n = 57 controls	Experimental group was more likely to tell an adult about suicidal peers Less likely to report suicidal behavior to an adult when ambiguous
Zenere & Lazarus, 1997	Didactics and discussion	Epidemiological comparison No control group	One class in 5-year program	Reports from department of crisis management	Decreased rate of suicide completions and suicide attempts No change in suicidal ideation
Aseltine et al., 2003	Signs of Suicide (SOS) Video, didactics, discussion, school kit with materials for screening and parents	One group posttest only, 1- and 3-month follow-up	1–2 class periods	376 high schools postscreen 233/376 schools at 1 month 64% white 12% African American 10% Latino 27% urban 33% suburban 41% rural 21% school lunch eligible 177/376 schools at 3 months	63% completed program and evaluation Schools reported increased help-seeking behavior of students, increased help-seeking on behalf of friend, low cost 1% of teachers thought program might have had adverse effect

Source	Program/Materials	Design	Setting	Sample	Results
Thompson, 2003a	YSPP Needs assessment and school-based student-led campaign program	Single group(s) qualitative design	Ongoing program	Gatekeepers, crisis teams, community groups, and high school students willing to participate	Increased awareness, knowledge, and number of students advising peers to get help Direct involvement of students in antisuicide campaign development
National Mental Health Association	Booklets and offers of help to develop mental health programs	Not yet evaluated	Booklet	Distributed to college students, administrators, and student leaders, and on Web site	Not yet evaluated
Aseltine & DeMartine, 2004	SOS Video and discussion guide Columbia Depression Screen (CDS)	Posttest only Stratified random assignment with delayed-treatment comparison group	2 health or social studies classes	$N = 2,100$ $n = 1,435$ 3 classes from Hartford, CT High School grades 9–12, "economically disadvantaged" 47% male 59% Hispanic 20% non-Hispanic black 20% in remedial English or ESL $n = 665$ from two Columbus, GA high schools ninth graders 52% male "working class" 39% white 37% African American 15% remedial English or ESL	*SOS vs. Comparison* 3.6 vs. 5.4 suicide attempts SOS had higher posttest knowledge and more positive attitudes than comparison No difference in suicidal ideation or treatment seeking Combined schools without comparing Don't know about pretest differences

ESL, English as a second language.

months after program implementation, students who had participated in the SOS intervention reported significantly lower rates of suicide attempts and greater knowledge and more adaptive attitudes about depression and suicide (Aseltine & DeMartino, 2004).

Educational efforts in the Dade County, Florida, Public School System provide an example of universal programs applied on a community-wide level. This program, which began in 1989, included related curricula across kindergarten through 12th grade, although only 10th graders received direct discussion of suicide and suicide prevention. In addition to the instructional components, it also included intervention and postvention activities by school-based crisis teams.

A 5-year longitudinal study of the Dade County program examined rates of suicide deaths and suicide attempts by youth in the county in the years during which the program was operative (1989–1994), comparing them to comparable rates over the 8-year period preceding the program (Zenere & Lazarus, 1997). The annual suicide rate was reported to have decreased from an average of 12.9 deaths per 100,000 youth prior to the program to 4.6 per 100,000 during the 5 years of program operation. Known suicide attempts were reported to have dropped from 87 to 37 per 100,000 youth. No significant change was reported in rates of suicidal ideation.

The lack of a contemporaneous local control group in this study makes it difficult to determine the linkage between the educational program and the reported decline in suicide rates. Although this report concludes that the comprehensive educational program contributed to the declines, it should be noted that youth suicide rates were declining nationally during the 5-year period of the program's implementation, although not as sharply as were reported in this particular county. In addition, the county under study was quite small (330,000 students), so that relatively large fluctuations in suicide rates are not as meaningful as they would be for the national population.

Many states are currently implementing universal youth suicide prevention programs that, in addition to student education, frequently include parent and gatekeeper training. Like other programs of this type, controlled evaluation studies have not yet been reported. In an internally published report (Eggert, Karovsky, & Pike, 1999), positive results have been reported for one of the most fully developed such programs, the Youth Suicide Prevention Program (YSPP) in Washington State.

Some efforts to address suicide prevention on a universal level have concentrated specifically on gatekeeper training. These programs are summarized in Table 22.2. The Suicide Options, Awareness and Relief (SOAR) program, for example, trains school counselors to identify students at risk of suicide and increase the likelihood and effectiveness of their interventions. This program has been reported to result in improved knowledge and increased comfort and confidence in dealing with at-risk students. More positive results were found among the most recently trained counselors, suggesting the need for ongoing training (King & Smith, 2000).

The broadest and most frequently applied gatekeeper training program, the Applied Suicide Intervention Skills Training (ASIST), has been developed by LivingWorks Education for application in a wider community setting (Ramsay, Cooke, & Lang, 1990; Rothman, 1980). Developed over the last 20 years, ASIST is a 2-day workshop for teachers, counselors, youth leaders, and other community caregivers that seeks to increase their awareness and understanding of suicide, address the associated stigma and taboos, develop their readiness and ability to use "first-aid" actions to prevent suicidal behavior, and network with other gatekeepers to improve communication and continuity of care. An estimated 25,000 caregivers participate in the program each year, and to date more than 300,000 have been trained worldwide.

Pre- to postevaluations of participants suggest increased knowledge about suicidal behavior, greater willingness to intervene, and improved competence in dealing with suicidal individuals (Eggert et al., 1999; Tierney, 1994). In one evaluation report of training programs in Australia, more than three quarters of ASIST workshop participants reported using their knowledge and intervention skills directly during the 4 months following their participation in the program (Turley & Tanney, 1998). There is some evidence

Table 22.2 Gatekeeper Training Programs

References	Intervention	Study Design	Program Length	Sample Size	Comments
Turley & Tanney, 1998	Suicide Aware Program (SA) Interventions Workshop (IW)	Pre–post No control or comparison group	1–3 hr presentation (SA) 2-day IW	N = 3,972 participants in SA across 3 sites (4 groups per site) N = 2,870 participants in IW across 4 sites, 1996–1998 Participants were from all areas of school, mental health and administrative programs	89% of trainers plan to continue program Most trainers continue to meet 3 trainings/year requirement after 2 years Most participants reported increased comfort, competence, and confidence immediately after training and 4 months later Knowledge increased Willingness to intervene with suicidal youth increased Most attrition was from rural areas
Fendrich et al., 2000	Team Up to Save Lives: what your school should know about preventing suicide CD-ROM mailed to schools with written instructions	Posttest only No comparison or control group	CD-ROM available for viewing	CD-ROM was sent by mass mailing to every high school, K–12 school, or junior high school in the U.S. in January 1997 n = 301 Chicago-area schools were contacted in 1998 Public and private schools n = 202/301 responded to survey n = 79/202 participated in the evaluation	The majority of schools did not know that they had received the CD-ROM (only 20% knew about CD-ROM) Only 39% of schools contacted participated in review of CD-ROM Lack of time, computer equipment, and training were cited as factors preventing review of CD-ROM Those who reviewed CD-ROM had positive evaluations and negative reactions were rare Most respondents said either they had made use of the information (40%) or planned to (87%)

(continued)

Table 22.2 Continued

References	Intervention	Study Design	Program Length	Sample Size	Comments
King & Smith, 2000	Project SOAR: Suicide Opinions, Awareness and Relief Program for school counselors	Posttest only No comparison or control group	8-hr training course	All school counselors in Independent School District of Dallas, TX N = 186/247 60% counselors ≤ 10 years 48% received SOAR training 3 years ago 88% had assessed a suicidal student	More than half of school counselors had adequate knowledge in most areas Almost all knew risk signs for suicide including depression, previous attempt, low self esteem, recent break-up of relationship, child abuse There were gaps in knowledge related to drug use and gun accessibility Most had good knowledge of appropriate interventions Almost two-thirds thought they could effectively offer support for suicidal student
Turley, 2000	ASIST: Applied Suicide Intervention Skills Training	Posttest only No ASIST comparison group	2-day workshop	$n = 91$ ASIST 75% female $n = 40$ No ASIST 63% female Participants include school, mental health, and medical personal	Increased readiness to make suicide intervention Increased knowledge, especially relative to control group Comparison group did not change in readiness to intervene
Pfaff et al., 2001	Youth suicide prevention workshop for general practitioners, focused on recognizing and responding to distress and suicidal ideation in adolescents	Pre–post case reviews	1 training session	N = 23 general practitioners N = 423 patients ages 15–24 N = 203 cases preworkshop N = 220 cases postworkshop	48% increase in identifying psychological distress 40% increase in identification of depression 33% increase in inquiry about suicidal ideation 130% increase in recognition of suicidal patients No change in patient management strategy

Maine et al., 2001	Youth Suicide: Recognizing the Signs Video for parents with booklet	Pretest–posttest No comparison or control group	1 session with 1–20 people	$N = 112$ parents with no experience of suicide within the family from South Australia Parents with a child ≥ 15 years old 84% females No indigent parents	Knowledge of suicidal signs increased Improved ability to choose a more appropriate response to suicidal statements Parents became more rejecting of suicide Parents indicated higher intention to help
Toumbourou & Gregg, 2002	Parenting Adolescents: A Creative Experience (PACE) Didactic training for parents, focused on improving communication and relationships with adolescents Discussion, pamphlets, booklets, and behavioral homework for reinforcing program	Pretest–posttest Random assignment to program or control group	7 sessions for groups of 10 parents at a time	$N = 577$ eighth-grade students from 28 school campuses in Melbourne, Australia $n = 305$ parents from 14 schools in PACE $n = 272$ parents from 14 control schools Private and public schools	PACE schools had reduced elevation of substance use but this did not lead to cessation Delinquent behavior decreased in PACE schools and increased in control schools Suicidal behavior and depressive symptoms were stable in both groups Family conflict and parental care increased in PACE schools relative to control schools

of an increase in referral to treatment as a result of gatekeeper training (Turley, 2000; Walsh & Perry, 2000).

A second component of LivingWorks' efforts is the Training for Trainers (T4T) program. This 5-day course, offered worldwide, trains and certifies gatekeepers to provide the ASIST training in their local communities. A CD-ROM program has recently been developed by LivingWorks to provide posttraining retention and reinforcement of intervention skills through virtual simulation of interactions with suicidal individuals.

Less proactive training strategies for school personnel and parents have used audiovisual materials to enhance suicide awareness and encourage early identification of youth at risk. Preliminary evaluations of two such efforts (Fendrich, Mackesy-Amiti, & Kruesi, 2000; Maine, Shute, & Martin, 2001) suggest that while most of those who view CD-ROMs and films about suicide prevention react positively, lack of time and inaccessibility of computer equipment may limit the effectiveness of such efforts, particularly within schools.

Another approach to gatekeeper training has involved educating general practitioners to more effectively identify suicidal patients. One such intervention was a youth suicide prevention workshop for general practitioners in Australia, which sought to encourage screening of young patients for psychological distress, depression, and suicidal behavior. The workshop was reported to have resulted in increased identification of distressed, depressed, and suicidal adolescents; no changes were reported, however, in physicians' management of such patients (McKelvey, Davies, Pfaff, Acres, & Edwards, 1998; McKelvey, Pfaff, & Acres, 2001).

In comparison with programs addressed to high school students and the adults who have frequent contact with them, suicide awareness and education programs for college students are far less cohesive and identifiable (Haas, Hendin, & Mann, 2003). One of the few programs that involve more than a single campus is Finding Hope and Help, developed by the National Mental Health Association in 2001. This program facilitates partnerships between a local mental health association and a university to develop and implement campus educational programs on suicide and related mental health problems. These "campus coalitions" typically work with residence hall advisers, campus counseling centers, relevant academic departments, campus ministries, and other student affairs personnel to design trainings for students and staff, peer counseling programs, and other activities to increase knowledge and awareness of mental health concerns (National Mental Health Association, 2005).

Another effort that targets colleges and universities is the recently produced film developed by the American Foundation for Suicide Prevention (AFSP), "The Truth About Suicide: Real Stories of Depression in College." The film is accompanied by a Facilitator's Guide that includes recommendations for its use in classrooms, orientation sessions, and dorm meetings and at other student activities, as well as educational materials to assist faculty and other facilitators in guiding student discussions and answering specific questions about suicide. Although no formal evaluation of the film's effectiveness is currently planned, AFSP is gathering feedback data from viewers and facilitators.

Critique

Most suicide awareness and suicide education programs involve one or a limited number of relatively brief sessions focused on suicidal behavior, frequently as part of a larger curricular effort aimed at reducing multiple high-risk behaviors. Although pre- to postevidence suggests that such programs can increase students' knowledge and awareness of suicide risk and improve their help-seeking behaviors, little attention has been paid to determining the scientific accuracy of program content. Examination of curricular materials used by some of these programs reveals considerable variation in regard to their portrayal of suicide risk factors, in particular, the relationship between suicide and mental illness, as well as suicide demographics.

Generalizable conclusions about the efficacy and effectiveness of suicide education programs for both high school and college students are further limited by the lack of control or comparison groups that would make it possible to differentiate program impact from broader co-occurring trends. In the case of the comprehensive, multilevel educational programs, insufficient attention has been paid to documenting which program components are responsible for the reported outcomes.

An additional limitation of currently available data on the impact of universal education programs is their short-term focus. It is not clear if ongoing interventions might serve as "booster shots" to enhance and reinforce a program's impact. In addition, follow-up evaluations of these programs have been rare, and thus little is currently known about their impact on reducing suicidal behavior among the targeted group. Longitudinal controlled studies that look at youth several years after participating in educational programs are needed to address the question of long-term behavioral change. This will require addressing the fact that neither high schools nor colleges currently have a reliable system for reporting suicidal behaviors among students, thus hampering collection of reliable data to determine an educational program's impact. Also, students graduate and leave the school environment, making follow-up difficult.

Long-term controlled studies of gatekeeper training programs are likewise needed to determine the frequency or the effectiveness of participants' direct interventions during the years following the training. Because little is known about particular approaches that make referral efforts safe and effective, further evaluation is needed of the impact of such programs on referral processes, adequate treatment, and, in turn, the reduction of suicide risk factors and suicidal behavior among youth.

Some concerns have been voiced by high school personnel and parents that overt discussion of suicide in the school curriculum may increase suicidal thoughts and behavior, and adequate attention has generally not been given by evaluators to documenting adverse effects. One study found statistically significant increases in hopelessness and maladaptive coping resources among some male students after exposure to a suicide awareness curriculum (Overholser, Hemstreet, Spirito, & Vyse, 1989). Studies by Shaffer and colleagues (1990, 1991) and Vieland and colleagues (1991) found that students who had pre-

viously made a suicide attempt were less likely to recommend suicide awareness programs in the schools, and were more likely to feel that talking about suicide in the classroom would increase suicidal behavior among some students. While the small number of students reporting past suicidal behavior limit generalization of these findings, they point to the need for evaluations of school-based suicide education programs to include better assessment of potential harmful effects and identification of adolescents who may be vulnerable to adverse effects. Educational programs should also include a plan for clinical assessment and referral for students who are identified to be at risk for suicidal behavior. It is essential that school personnel be made aware of referral sources in the community and for the school to have in place a plan of action for identified students that includes a debriefing component for peers and faculty who are involved in making referrals.

In the case of college-based programs, concerns about effects on the institution's legal liability, reputation, and student enrollment sometimes encourages campus officials to avoid or minimize the problem of student suicide, which appears to have limited the development of educational programs directed to this population. In addition, providing suicide education to college students poses unique issues. In contrast to high school students, who follow a tightly prescribed core curriculum that typically includes at least a minimal amount of health education, college students are not generally required to take any courses in which education about depression and suicide may be appropriately incorporated. Other than a limited number of mandatory orientation sessions, few opportunities exist to reach large numbers of college students with information about mental health issues and services. Involvement of parents in educational programs on such issues is also extremely limited in most college settings.

Finally, it should be noted that most suicide prevention programs directed to young adults are designed specifically for college students, who represent less than half of all persons aged 18–24 in the United States. Although few research studies have examined suicide risk among young adults not in college, this population may have particular risk factors, including more involvement with substance use, as well as less access to mental health resources.

One effort that may have applicability to youth in noncollege settings is the U.S. Air Force suicide prevention program, which has focused on removing the stigma of seeking help for mental health and psychosocial problems, enhancing understanding of mental health, and changing policies and social norms within the service. Introduced in 1996–97, the Air Force program has been described as highly effective in reducing suicide and other adverse outcomes, including family violence and homicide, among its five million members. A recent evaluation that compared 5-year cohorts before and after program implementation reported a 33% relative risk reduction for suicide and reductions ranging between 18% and 54% for other outcomes (Knox, Litts, Talcott, Feig, & Caine, 2003). The impact of the program on young servicemen in particular has not been reported, and thus the program is not listed as a youth suicide prevention program in the current review.

SCREENING PROGRAMS

Assumptions

Screening for depression in adults has been demonstrated to increase the likelihood of depressed adults seeking mental health treatment (Greenfield et al., 1997, 2000). Universal screening programs as a youth suicide prevention strategy (listed in Table 22.3) are designed to identify young people at risk for suicidal behavior and refer them to treatment. Some programs focus specifically on identifying symptoms of psychopathology known to be related to adolescent and young adult suicidal behavior, while others assess specifically for signs of suicidality.

The primary assumption underlying screening programs is that because anxiety, depression, substance abuse, and suicidal preoccupation among youth often go unnoticed and untreated, a systematic, universally applied effort is needed to improve identification of at-risk individuals. Although not always explicitly stated, screening programs also rest on the assumptions that iden-

tification of youth with psychiatric disorders will substantially increase the number receiving treatment, the treatment will be sufficiently effective, and effective treatment will decrease suicides.

Program Examples

Reynolds (1991) described one of the first high school–based screening programs for youth at risk for suicide. The program involved a two-stage method, in which a general population of students was first screened using the Suicide Ideation Questionnaire (Reynolds, 1988). Students with scores above a defined cutoff value were subsequently evaluated clinically with the Suicide Behavior Interview, and those identified as being at risk were referred for treatment.

The program devoted particular attention to determining an appropriate cutoff score for identifying at-risk youth, comparing two different scores with regard to sensitivity (the ability to identify correctly those who have the problem, with few false negatives) and specificity (the ability to identify correctly those who do not have the problem, with few false positives). Reynolds found that increasing the cutoff score led to missing a disproportionate number of at-risk youth. The impact on suicidal behavior and the adherence to treatment recommendations were not reported.

Perhaps the most widely used high school screening program, the Columbia TeenScreen Program (CTSP), likewise employs a multistage procedure. In one variant of the CTSP, students complete a brief, self-report questionnaire, i.e., the Columbia Suicide Screen. Those who screen positive on this measure are given a computerized instrument, the Voice DISC 2.3, a version of the Diagnostic Interview Schedule for Children, which has been found to accurately identify a comprehensive range of psychiatric disorders in children and adolescents (Shaffer, Fisher, Lucas, Dulcan, & Schwab-Stone, 2000; Shaffer et al., 2004). This stage of the screen is regarded as particularly important for avoiding over-identification of students at risk. In the final stage, youth who have been identified through Voice DISC 2.3 as meeting specific diagnostic cri-

Table 22.3 Screening Programs

Reference	Intervention	Study Design	Study Length	Sample Size	Comments
Reynolds 1991	2-stage depression and suicide screening	No comparison or control group	Stage 1: Suicide Ideation Questionnaire Stage 2: Suicide Behavior Interview	N = 121 General high school	Used 90% as cutoff for adequate sensitivity and specificity Lowering cutoff improves sensitivity but decreases specificity below acceptable levels
Lewinsohn et al., 1996	Baseline assessment with 1-year follow-up, no intervention	No comparison or control group	Baseline comprehensive diagnostic assessment with K-SADS repeated at 1 year	N = 1,709 at baseline N = 1,507 at follow-up 14- to 18-year-olds in community	Poor to excellent sensitivity and specificity 80% false-positive rate
Thompson & Eggert, 1999	Suicide Risk Screen (SRS) and Measure for Adolescent Potential for Suicide (MAPS)	No comparison or control group	1. Identify potential dropouts 2. Screen with SRS 3. Comprehensive assessment with MAPS 4. Validity measures of depression and suicide	N = 581 potential high school dropouts, ages 14–20 58% male 43% minority 63% did not live with both biological parents	Excellent specificity Poor specificity No false negatives Validity supported by expected associations with measures of risk and protective factors
Aseltine et al., 2003	Signs of Suicide (SOS) anonymous depression and suicide screening	No comparison or control group	1 class period complete Columbia Depression Scale and item about suicide risk	N = 233 high schools 64% white 12% African American 10% Latino 27% urban 33% suburban 41% rural 21% eligible for free/reduced price lunch (Age and number screened varies by school)	Not evaluated

Table 22.3 Continued

Reference	Intervention	Study Design	Study Length	Sample Size	Comments
Shaffer et al., 2004	Columbia Suicide Screen	Group matched sample of youths who did not endorse risk items	5 phases with attrition at each phase: 1. Self-report questionnaire (1 class period) 2. DISC (2 hr) 3. Clinical evaluation (1 hr) 4. Case manager 5. Treatment	N = 1,729 high school students from 7 metropolitan schools 57% female 56% white 18% African American 13% Hispanic	35% scored positively on screen High sensitivity, specificity, and negative predictive value (.75–.99) Low positive predictive value (.16)
Jacobs, 2003	The Comprehensive College Initiative			451 colleges used in-person events 215 colleges used on-line screening tool N = 9,964 in-person screens N = 12,351 on-line screens for depression N = 3,858 on-line screens for bipolar disorder	35% of in-person and 65% of on-line screens scored positive for depression 19% in-person and 25% on-line screens scored positive for bipolar disorder 89% of those with on-line positive risk reported intent to seek further evaluation Based on on-line evaluation: Seniors and freshman had highest rates of suicidal ideation (2.0% and 5.6%, respectively) On-campus students had higher rates of suicidal ideation than off-campus students

Source	Program	Comparison/Control	Intervention	Sample	Follow-up/Evaluation
Jed Foundation, 2003	ULifeLine Program	No comparison or control groups	Compares student screening questionnaire with computer-generated values to identify students at risk Provides recommendations for treatment as indicated	Anonymous No information available	No follow-up information or evaluation
Haas, 2003	American Foundation for Suicide Prevention College Screening Project	No comparison or control groups	1. Anonymous on-line questionnaire, using ID and password after e-mail invitation 2. Student risk determined 3. Counselor assesses responses and provides assessment and access to treatment info via e-mail 4. Student reviews feedback and can access referral	Sample from one college based on response to anonymous on-line questionnaire No sample information available	8% of target students responded 15% of identified students sought evaluation and referral as needed

DISC, Diagnostic Interview for Children; K-SADS, Kiddie Schizophrenia and Affective Disorders Schedule; SRS teria for a psychiatric disorder are evaluated by a clinician, who determines whether the student needs to be referred for treatment or further evaluation. Ideally, the program also includes a case manager who contacts the parents of students who are referred and establishes links with a clinic to facilitate treatment adherence.

Evaluation results indicate that most of the adolescents identified as being at high risk for suicide through the program were not previously recognized as such, and very few had received prior treatment. About half of the students referred for treatment attended at least one treatment visit, however. In addition, the program's requirements of a clinician and a case manager may be a resource burden for many schools.

The screening strategy developed by Thompson and Eggert (1999) as part of their comprehensive Reconnecting Youth program (discussed in detail in Chapter 24) is based on a public health prevention model that emphasizes the identification of at-risk students on the basis of observable behaviors. The first level of screening involves a review of high school attendance registers to identify students having high absenteeism. Teachers and guidance counselors are asked to recommend students they deem to be at risk. Identified youth are then assessed by means of the Suicide Risk Screen (SRS). Those with elevated risk for suicidal behaviors are given an appropriate intervention within the school setting or are referred for further evaluation and treatment (Thompson & Eggert, 1999).

Recent screening initiatives for college students include the Comprehensive College Initiative (CCI), developed by Jacobs (2003) to identify students at risk for depression and facilitate them to get treatment. The program has been offered at a large number of colleges in conjunction with National Depression Screening Day. In addition to the in-person screenings offered at this annual event, the program includes an on-line year-round screening component.

In campuses where it has been implemented, the CCI has been described by its developers as effective in identifying at-risk students and motivating them to seek treatment (Jacobs, 2003). Almost 20% of students taking the screening measure scored "very likely" to be suffering from depression and 5% reported persistent suicidal ideation. Both student participants and college officials were reported to have positive reactions to the in-person and on-line program components. No data have yet been reported, however, on treatment follow-up or outcomes, or on changes in suicidal behavior on the participating campuses.

Another recent program is the College Screening Project developed by the American Foundation for Suicide Prevention (Haas et al., 2003). This project, which is currently being pilot tested at selected colleges, uses the campus e-mail network to target students and encourage them to complete a Depression Screening Questionnaire, which is found on a project-developed Web site. This instrument is an adaptation of the Patient Health Questionnaire, which has been established to be an effective tool for identifying depression among community samples (Spitzer, Kroenke, Williams, & The Patient Health Questionnaire Study Group, 1999; Spitzer et al., 2000). In addition to depression, the screening questionnaire includes items dealing with current suicidal ideation, past suicide attempts, anxiety and other affects, drugs, alcohol, and eating disorders. Students use a self-assigned user name and password to log into the Web site; the user name is the sole identification on the submitted questionnaire.

Assisted by a computer program, a clinically trained counselor evaluates the responses and assigns the student into one of three tiers on the basis of their suicide risk. The counselor then writes a personalized reply that the student accesses on the Web site, using their user name and password. Students with significant problems as determined by a well-defined set of criteria are urged to come in for a face-to-face evaluation. The Web site also contains a "Dialogue" feature that allows students to communicate with the counselor on-line to discuss concerns they may have prior to an evaluation.

During the face-to-face meeting, treatment options, including medication and psychotherapy, are discussed and referrals are made to appropriate services on and off campus. In an effort to evaluate treatment effects, the project collects data on an ongoing basis from treatment providers on student adherence, treatment progress, and disposition.

Initial reports indicate that about 80% of the students who respond to the screening questionnaire indicate some mental health problems, with almost half of all respondents falling into the highest-risk tier. Fewer than 15% of identified students, however, comply with recommendations for evaluation, which suggests that recommendations need to be refined to make them more acceptable, or that innovative strategies need to be developed to encourage greater numbers of at-risk students to seek help. Almost all students who receive a clinical evaluation through the College Screening Project are referred for treatment. Over 90% of students coming for evaluation have reported that the screening questionnaire and the counselor's responses were critical factors in their decision to seek help (Haas, 2003).

One other Web-based screening program for college students, the ULifeLine program, has recently been developed by the Jed Foundation (2003). This program provides computer-generated results to students who complete the screening instrument. Although identified students are provided with recommendations regarding treatment possibilities, no follow-up is offered. It is not clear whether without a personal connection, such Web-based screenings will succeed in motivating students in need to seek treatment.

Critique

In their basic assumptions, screening programs as implemented within both high school and college settings closely conform to scientifically validated premises regarding the causes of suicide—i.e., that suicide risk is not randomly distributed, but rather is conferred by certain factors that are both identifiable and, to a considerable extent, alterable. At the same time, such programs face a number of challenges.

Screening measures with acceptable test characteristics (e.g., a sensitivity of 80% and a specificity of 70%, figures similar to screens for depression) will necessarily miss some in the population who will go on to make suicide attempts, while identifying many more as at risk when they are not. The often transient or episodic nature of suicidality among young people makes screening this population even more difficult. Given that costs are involved each time a segment of the target group is screened, most school-based screening programs assess students only once a year, and in some cases, only once during a several-year period. The timing of the screening may increase the likelihood of identifying students in need of referral (e.g., close to exams, at the beginning of high school or college, or during the senior year) or at other times may reduce this likelihood.

Both high school- and college-based screening programs report relatively low adherence with treatment recommendations among those identified through the screening instrument to be at risk. Although this is likely due to a range of problems that are beyond the scope of the screening effort (e.g., lack of parental support, perceived quality of available treatment, and attitudes of treatment providers), additional strategies appear to be needed to encourage students at risk to access and make effective use of needed treatment services. In this regard, better integration of suicide education, gatekeeper training programs, and screening programs may be helpful.

All school-based suicide screening programs need to be mindful of the availability and quality of mental health services for students who are identified as at risk. On college campuses, this is sometimes a formidable problem. It is estimated that only 38% of colleges provide mental health services (Gallagher, 2001), and most of those that do limit the number of sessions or offer only group therapy that may not be appropriate for students at risk for suicide. Although many colleges require students to have health insurance, most students (as well as most people in the general population) are not adequately covered for acute or long-term mental health services.

Even when implemented under ideal conditions, there is no clear evidence that screening for suicide in general populations improves rate reduction outcomes. In addition, as yet, no data have been reported on the effectiveness of high school- or college-based screening programs in reducing suicide risk factors, including depression and suicidal ideation, or suicidal behavior at the schools where screening programs are being implemented.

Within high schools, there is evidence that administrators prefer suicide education and awareness programs over screening programs (Miller, Eckert, DuPaul, & White, 1999). Many colleges and universities have also expressed reluctance about implementing depression and suicide screening programs. This appears to reflect, in part, concerns about the liability schools may assume in the event that students identified as at risk for suicide do not follow through with treatment recommendations and actually engage in suicidal behavior. Identification of at-risk students may also put universities into a difficult legal and ethical position with respect to parents. Because students over the age of 18 are considered adults, parents of students cannot typically be contacted without written permission from the student. Although confidentiality can be waived in situations in which threat to life is concerned, universities are reluctant to become embroiled in such matters. Further, monitoring students identified as in need of mental health services is difficult because of their diverse living arrangements and lack of supervision by other adults.

Although Web-based programs show promise as a tool for suicide screening with youth, one complication is the recent Health Insurance Portability and Accountability Act (HIPAA), which limits the use of electronic technology to transmit identifiable health information, because of the potential threats to patient confidentiality. This has been interpreted as requiring that a student's actual identity not be revealed on-line, making it impossible for the counselor to intervene to help a student believed to be suicidal unless he or she presents in person for evaluation.

Finally, as was earlier noted in discussing suicide prevention education, most screening programs directed at young adults are designed specifically for college students. Although screening programs are expensive to administer and monitor, creative strategies are needed for integrating and supporting screening into existing health-care settings that reach all youth.

Targeted Youth Suicide Prevention Programs

chapter

23

In this chapter we review examples of selective suicide prevention programs that have been developed for youth identified or presumed to be at increased risk for suicidal behavior. Although the youth targeted by such programs are considered to be particularly vulnerable to suicide, in most cases they have not yet exhibited specific signs of suicidality.

Discussed here are programs for three specific groups, each of which has shown elevated rates of suicidal behavior: Native American youth, youth with recent exposure to a suicide in the school or community, and youth who have access to firearms in the home. While there has been considerable research suggesting that adolescents and young adults in these groups are at greater risk for suicide, relatively few intervention programs for these populations have been developed to date.

PROGRAMS FOR NATIVE AMERICAN YOUTH

Assumptions

Based on research indicating markedly different rates of suicide among different Native American tribes, May and Van Winkle (1994) suggested that high suicide rates among certain tribes were linked to a loosening of social integration within the tribe as members become increasingly acculturated into the broader society. The underlying assumption for a small number of programs is that instilling certain personal traits and social skills in Native American youth will counter the negative effects of the acculturation process and protect these youth against suicidality.

Program Examples

The Zuni Life Skills Curriculum for preventing suicidal behavior (LaFramboise & Howard-Pitney, 1995) is illustrative of programmatic efforts in this category. This program, developed specifically for Zuni youth, featured a 30-week,

three-times-a-week, course focused on building self-esteem, helping youth identify feelings and stresses, improving communication and problem-solving skills, decreasing self-destructive behavior, and setting goals. The curriculum also provided information about suicide and training for intervening with suicidal peers. Results of the program were mixed, with students showing a decrease in hopelessness but not depression after the intervention. Although the program was not specifically addressed to suicidal youth, some of those who participated reported decreased suicidal behaviors. Adult judges rated the impact of the skills training program as positive, but youth overall reported few effects on social functioning.

Critique

Although the Zuni curriculum demonstrated some success, more specific evaluation of program efficacy is needed that incorporates a control-group design and links outcomes to specific program components. In particular, studies that suggest differential acculturation to be pivotal in explaining suicide rates among Native American youth have not controlled for other variables such as psychopathology or family influences. It should also be emphasized that no empirical evidence has been put forth that supports a link between high suicide rates among Native American youth and deficits in personal or social skills.

The program has not been replicated in other at-risk tribes. Resources available for the development, implementation, and evaluation of suicide prevention programs for Native American youth appear to be limited (Middle-brook, LeMaster, Beals, Novins, & Manson, 2001). An additional observation is that although programs targeting Native American youth are based in part on the premise that external forces in the social and cultural environment contribute to the difficulties these young people face, the strategies focus on changing individuals rather than the external influences themselves.

PROGRAMS FOR YOUTH
EXPOSED TO SUICIDE

Assumptions

Studies show that adolescents' exposure to the suicide of a family member or peer can trigger new-onset or recurrent major depressive disorder, posttraumatic stress disorder, and suicidal ideation, especially within the month following the suicide (Brent et al., 1993c). Youth who were already at risk for depression because of family history, a prior episode of depression, or recent interpersonal conflict were found to be at increased risk for suicidal ideation following a suicide, as were those who knew about the victim's plan, felt responsible for the death, or had a conversation with the victim within 24 hours of the suicide. Although the study by Brent and colleagues cited above did not find evidence of increased risk for suicide attempts among such youth, studies of the contagion effect of suicide (Gould et al., 1994; Gould, Wallenstein, & Kleinman, 1990) also report increased suicidal ideation among exposed youth, as was discussed in Chapter 21. It may be that contagion effects are most pronounced in adolescents who are not closely linked with the suicide victim.

The assumption of programs targeting youth exposed to suicide, referred to as "postvention," is that suicide exposure carries increased risk for suicidal ideation, and possibly suicidal behavior, in a school or community where a recent suicide has occurred. Postvention within schools generally seeks to support those grieving the loss, to identify and assist those at risk for developing depression or posttraumatic stress disorder in response to the suicide, and to return the community or school to its normal routines.

Program Examples

One well-described postvention program is the Services for Teens at Risk (STAR) Center Outreach program implemented in Pennsylvania (Kerr, Brent, & McKain, 1997). This program provides a protocol that identifies specific steps to be taken by school staff, community officials, students and parents in the event of a suicide. Central to the protocol is the development of a school-based crisis team to coordinate postvention activities. The STAR-Center Outreach program provides free training to crisis teams, upon request by school districts throughout the state. Such training consists of an initial 6–12 hr that includes designation of a postvention coordinator, assignment of tasks to team members, simulations and problem-based learning activities, team-building exercises, preparation of Crisis Team Members Kits that include needed documents and supplies, and "dry runs" to test the postvention response. The crisis team then meets for a monthly refresher at the school. This postvention effort emphasizes the importance of including information about warning signs for suicidal behavior with students and staff and the need for ongoing monitoring of at-risk students and staff following implementation. The program specifically discourages school and local officials, family members, and friends from having direct contacts with media in the aftermath of a suicide.

Many other less comprehensive postvention efforts have been implemented in schools across the country (Hazell & Lewin, 1993), as well as abroad (Poijula, Wahlberg, & Dyregrov, 2001). The limited nature of the interventions that were implemented, limited articulation of the intervention models, and the small samples that were studied preclude meaningful conclusions about their impact.

Critique

Although there has been a proliferation of postvention programs in recent years, there are no published studies that systematically assess the impact of these programs or identify specific components that are particularly helpful or potentially harmful. Guidelines for postvention responses by schools have been in existence for some time (CDC, 1988), but the interventions implemented by individual school districts and communities are varied. The Substance Abuse and Mental Health Services Administration (SAMHSA) is currently funding a project to develop research-based guidelines for schools to help them to implement timely and effective postvention programs (Gould, 2000).

Staffing for postvention programs and follow-up can be costly for schools both financially and emotionally, and this may be a significant impediment to their implementation. Conducting formal evaluations of the impact of such programs within schools is fraught with difficult ethical issues such as parental consent and confidentiality of data regarding students' emotional and behavioral responses to suicide.

FIREARMS RESTRICTION PROGRAMS

Assumptions

As summarized in Table 23.1, several different programs have been developed to encourage restriction of access to firearms by children and adolescents. The key assumption underlying such programs is that accessibility is a primary risk factor for suicide. Programs of this type have been directed primarily at parents.

Program Examples

A core strategy of firearms restriction programs has involved firearm safety counseling to parents that encourages removal or safe storage of firearms from homes where children reside. One such effort, entitled Love our Kids: Lock your Guns, was developed by Coyne-Beasley, Schoenbach, and Johnson (2001), following research that documented the presence of unlocked and loaded weapons within many households in which children and adolescents live (Azrael, Miller, & Hemenway, 2000; Coyne-Beasley et al., 2002; Schuster, Franke, Bastian, Sor, & Halfon, 2000; Senturia, Christoffel, & Donovan, 1994, 1996; Stennies, Ikeda, Leadbetter, Houston, & Sacks, 1999). Prior research by Coyne-Beasley and colleagues (2002) established that firearm storage practices were frequently lax even among parents who demonstrated high safety consciousness of other potential hazards in the home.

The intervention aimed essentially to reach male gun owners who lived with children, and thus was implemented in an outdoor community setting. Program developers provided firearm safety counseling, distributed free gunlocks, and demonstrated their use on a community-wide basis. Politicians, law enforcement personnel, and the media participated in the program along with youth and their parents; T-shirts and certificates were presented to participants. A 6-month follow-up evaluation found improved safe storage habits among gun owners who had participated in the program. Participants with children, who overall were more likely than other gun owners to store weapons unlocked and loaded at baseline, were found in the post-test to be more likely to have removed guns from the home and to lock the guns that remained. Those who had participated in the counseling were also more likely to report talking with friends about safe storage practices.

A few attempts have been made to deliver firearms and other means restriction education in mental health settings. One such effort involved education for parents of children who made a visit to an emergency room mental health department of a rural, Midwestern hospital (Kruesi et al., 1999). At 6-month follow-up, these investigators found that the education led to decreased youth access to guns, prescription medications, and over-the-counter medication but not alcohol. Firm conclusions were limited, however, by the high attrition rate at follow-up.

A similar effort was made with parents of depressed adolescents who participated in a randomized clinical trial of psychotherapy (Brent, Baugher, Birmaher, Kolko, & Bridge, 2000). Parents who reported the presence of firearms in the homes of these adolescents received an intervention designed to encourage gun removal. Although compliance with recommendations was more likely in the homes of adolescents with active suicidality and in single-parent homes, overall, less than one third of the targeted parents removed their guns from the home. Urban families and families in which there was marital discord or a father with a drinking problem were less likely to remove guns. The investigators emphasized the need to talk directly with the parent who owned the gun. In addition, 17% of parents

Table 23.1 Firearms Restriction Programs

Reference	Intervention	Study Design	Program Length	Sample Size	Comments
Kruesi et al., 1999	Injury prevention program provided by staff: 1. Inform parents that child was at risk for suicide 2. Tell parents they can decrease risk by limiting access to lethal means 3. Educate parents and teach problem solving about limiting access	Prospective follow-up design No exposure to training comparison group	1 session of education in emergency department Follow-up phone interview (mean 2 months after training (range .03–5.6 months)	**Baseline** N = 103 parents whose children (ages 6–19) made a visit to ED in a Midwest rural hospital for mental health N = 62 trained N = 42 untrained Parent and child were English speaking, lived together, accessible for telephone follow-up 75% white, +50% female Child was assessed as being at high risk for "high-risk" behavior **Follow-up** N = 27 trained N = 36 untrained	30% lost to follow-up Most locked up lethal means rather than disposing of them No guns were disposed of Training group was more likely to take action limiting firearms and prescription and over-the-counter medications, but not alcohol
Brent et al., 2000	Treating clinician presented suicide risk associated with firearms in the home and the importance of removal or storage elsewhere	Prospective follow-up design No comparison or control group	Brief review by clinician of danger of firearms in the home at treatment intake and at follow-up assessments Only for those reporting firearms in the home	N = 106 Ages 13–18 years with DSM-III-R major depressive disorder who agreed to enter a randomized clinical trial using psychotherapy to treat major depression 76% female 83% white 43% lived with both biological parents	26% of those with firearms at baseline removed them from home by the end of treatment 36% of those with firearms assessed at 2-year follow-up continued to keep guns from the home 5.5% of those without firearms at intake acquired guns by the end of treatment 17% of those without firearms at intake acquired guns by the 2-year follow-up Need to train all families

(continued)

Table 23.1 Continued

Reference	Intervention	Study Design	Program Length	Sample Size	Comments
Coyne-Beasley et al., 2001	Love our Kids, Lock your Guns community intervention program 1. Gun safety information 2. Provided with gun locks and instruction for use	Pre- to postintervention assessment No comparison group	One brief baseline assessment and intervention session 6-month follow-up telephone interview	$N = 112$ adult gun owners recruited through media advertising campaign 62% white 63% male 58% had children 74% owned gun for protection No assessment of suicidal behavior	Increased number of participants who stored their guns in locked compartment (up 29%) 72% started using gun locks 9% reduction in number of people leaving guns loaded and unlocked Intervention was most effective for people with children

ED, emergency department.

who reported no gun in the home at intake and therefore were not targeted by the intervention purchased a gun during the study. This points to the advisability of weapons restriction interventions for all parents and not just those who own a gun at the outset of the intervention.

The policy statement on firearm safety of the American Academy of Pediatrics (2000) has urged parents to remove guns from the environment where children live and visit, and if guns remain in the home, to store them unloaded and locked, with ammunition stored separately. One attempt to apply this policy in an intervention program (although not specifically a suicide prevention program) is the Steps to Prevent Firearms Injury Program (STOP) of the American Academy of Pediatrics and the Center to Prevent Handgun Violence. This intervention provides counseling to parents in primary care clinics. Evaluations have not found the program to be effective in reducing firearm safety and removal (Grossman et al., 2000; Oatis, Fenn Buderer, Cummings, & Fleitz, 1999), possibly because it has reached primarily mothers, whereas fathers and other males in the household are more often responsible for the presence and storage practices of the guns in the home.

Critique

In assessing the effectiveness of firearms restriction programs on reducing youth suicide, it is important to note that the activities described here have been implemented during a period of declining use and ownership of firearms in U.S. homes, notable since 1980. Thus, care must be exercised in drawing conclusions about the role of specific interventions in removing guns from American households.

Assessment of the impact of firearms removal and firearms safety on youth suicidal behavior is likewise a difficult task. It is not surprising that young people who use guns for self-injury live in a house where there are firearms, and where the firearms are accessible. This does not mean, however, that the presence of firearms has set in motion the lengthy and complex process that leads to suicide. The methodological challenge ultimately facing firearms restriction programs is to demonstrate that suicide-prone youth survive in firearms-free homes, but not in homes where firearms are accessible. As was noted in Chapter 21, it is not clear the extent to which a decrease in youth suicide deaths from firearms may be offset by increases in the use of other lethal methods (Beautrais, 2001; De Leo et al., 2003), and this possibility needs to be considered in evaluating the impact of firearms restriction programs.

Although comprehensive evaluations of this sort have not yet been undertaken, existing programs suggest the potential of community-based programs that provide firearms restriction education to males within households in which children and youth live. It should be noted that means restriction programs have not received widespread funding, in part because of political pressures and in part because they address a more limited audience than universal interventions that can be easily incorporated into public school systems.

Preventive Interventions and Treatments for Suicidal Youth

chapter

24

The third and last category of youth suicide prevention efforts includes indicated interventions and treatments that target those who have already shown signs of suicidality. Such efforts seek essentially to reduce and prevent subsequent suicidal ideation and suicide attempts and prevent suicide completion. The interventions and treatments described in this chapter differ widely in the groups they target, the methods they use, and the settings in which they have been implemented.

SCHOOL-BASED PROGRAMS FOR SUICIDAL STUDENTS

Assumptions

The central underlying assumption of school-based programs for suicidal students is that subsequent suicidal thoughts and behavior can be reduced by enhancing protective factors, in particular, students' personal and social support resources.

Program Examples

The most comprehensive school-based programs are those developed and tested by Eggert, Thompson, and their colleagues (Eggert, Karovsky, & Pike, 1999; Eggert, Thompson, Herting, & Nichols, 1994, 1995; Thompson, Eggert, & Herting, 2000; Thompson, Eggert, Randell, & Pike, 2001), as part of the Reconnecting Youth (RY) Prevention Research Program. The interventions are directed at students who are deemed to be at risk of dropping out of high school, based primarily on school attendance data and observations of teachers, counselors, and other gatekeepers. Such students have been reported to have multiple co-occurring problems that, in addition to school performance difficulties, include depression, suicidality, drug involvement, and tendencies toward aggressive and violent behaviors (Eggert et al., 1994; Lewinsohn, Rohde, & Seeley, 1993).

The interventions are based on a theoretical model that rests essentially on improving students' personal resources, leading to an enhanced sense of personal control and self-esteem, improved decision making, increased use of social support resources, and reduced suicidal behavior. The early research involved systematic evaluation of a semester-long, school-based, small-group intervention called the Personal Growth Class (PGC). The intervention included life skills training using strategies of group process, teacher and peer support, goal setting, and weekly monitoring of mood management, school performance, and drug involvement.

Evaluation studies by Thompson, Eggert, and colleagues (Eggert et al., 1994, 1995; Thompson et al., 2000) involved approximately 100 high school students at risk for dropping out of high school, as determined by a set of defined criteria, who screened positive for suicidal behavior (as discussed in Chapter 22). The students were randomly assigned to one of three conditions: assessment protocol plus one semester of PGC, assessment protocol plus two semesters of PGC, and assessment protocol only. Participants were assessed at baseline and at 5 and 10 months post-intervention. Participants in all three groups showed significant declines in suicidal behavior. Unlike the students who received the assessment protocol only, PGC participants showed significant improvement in self-perceived ability to manage problem circumstances. Also reported was a significant positive impact of both teacher and peer support in decreasing suicide risk behaviors and depression.

Thompson, Eggert, and colleagues (2001) subsequently tested two additional school-based prevention programs based on the PGC: a brief one-on-one intervention known as Counselors Care (C-CARE), and a small-group skills-building intervention program, Coping and Support Training (CAST), derived directly from the PGC program. Both interventions, compared to a usual care control group, were found to reduce suicide risk behaviors and depression, even at the 9-month follow-up assessment; CAST was most effective in enhancing and sustaining protective factors such as problem-solving coping.

Currently, the CARE intervention, expanded to include a parent intervention component, P-CARE (Randell, 1999), is being studied to determine the added benefit of this component to further reduce depression, anger, and suicide risk behaviors. Preliminary results suggest that C-CARE, coupled with the parent intervention, is associated with more rapid rates of decline in suicidal ideation, direct suicide threats, depression, hopelessness, and anxiety when compared to usual care (Thompson, 2003b).

Critique

These programs for suicidal students at risk of dropping out of high school have demonstrated efficacy in reducing suicidal behavior and depression. There is some indication that prolonged intervention results in the most positive outcomes related to suicide, although it is not clear whether these effects are due to repeated contact with the treatment or to the nature of the treatment itself. As is often the case with programs involving multiple components, identifying which component is most responsible for the outcomes reported by these programs is difficult. Preliminary reports suggest that the inclusion of parents in the intervention is particularly effective.

The target groups addressed by the studies of Eggert and Thompson may limit the generalizability of the findings to other populations of suicidal youth. From the outset, the focus of these programs has been on students at risk of dropping out of high school as principally defined through attendance records. There is some evidence that high school dropouts may come from more deviant and neglecting families and thus may not be representative of suicidal adolescents overall. In addition, the inclusion criteria for these programs are somewhat idiosyncratic in their use of gatekeeper identification of problematic students, which may limit the exportability and testing of the model.

In addition, it should be noted that these interventions were designed and implemented by highly skilled, university-based professionals, who devoted considerable attention to ensuring program fidelity, evaluating program results, and making improvements based on empirical findings. Although results appear promising, replication of the program in schools that do not have such resources may be difficult. A

community-based dissemination of the CAST intervention is currently being implemented and evaluated in three sites (Randell, 2003), which will begin to address this concern.

EMERGENCY DEPARTMENT INTERVENTIONS FOR YOUNG SUICIDE ATTEMPTERS

Assumptions

A considerable number of youth who make suicide attempts obtain some form of medical intervention (Grunbaum et al., 2002), typically beginning in a hospital emergency department (ED). This suggests that the ED may be a prime location for initiating treatment programs aimed at suicidal youth.

Numerous studies have documented, however, that young suicide attempters' adherence to outpatient treatment recommendations made in the ED is poor, with over 15% never attending any recommended outpatient sessions, and fewer than half attending more than a few sessions (Spirito et al., 1992; Stewart, Manion, Davidson, & Cloutier, 2001; Trautman, Stewart, & Morishima, 1993). Poor adherence has been attributed to ED factors, such as long waits, repetitive evaluations, and poor communication by ED staff, and also to cultural factors including the perception that mental health treatment is shameful (Spirito, 2003).

Table 24.1 lists the key ED interventions that have been developed to date for young suicide attempters. The primary assumption underlying these interventions is that improved treatment adherence will result in decreased suicidal behavior. Thus, their goal is to develop mechanisms for engaging suicide attempters in the treatment process.

Program Examples

Rotheram-Borus and colleagues (1996, 2000) designed an intervention that targeted both the ED staff and families of Latino adolescent females who attempted suicide and followed participants over 18 months. Using videotapes and thera-

Table 24.1 Emergency Department Programs

Reference	Intervention	Study Design	Study Length	Sample Size	Comments
Rotheram-Borus et al., 1996	Specialized emergency room program including: 1. Staff training 2. Videotape for adolescent and parent addressing treatment expectations 3. On-call family therapist	Quasi-experimental design with nonrandom assignment and treatment-as-usual comparison group	Presentation during ED visit and referral to 6-month therapy program	$N = 140$ Latina adolescent suicide attempters and their mothers Ages 12–18 years $N = 65$ specialized care $N = 75$ no specialized care	Specialized care group reported less depression and mothers reported more positive attitudes towards treatment than those with no specialized care after intervention Specialized care group more likely to attend at least one follow-up treatment session (95.4% vs. 82.7%) Trend toward those in specialized care attending more treatment than those without specialized care (5.7 vs. 4.7 sessions) Mothers of adolescent attempters in specialized care were less likely to complete treatment
Rotheram-Borus et al., 2000	See above	See above	See above 18-month follow-up (92% participation follow-up rate)	See above	Rates of suicide re-attempts and re-ideation attempts were lower than expected and not different between groups Impact of specialized care was greatest for most symptomatic suicide attempters when maternal distress and family cohesion were improved

Study	Intervention	Design	Sample	Results
Spirito et al., 2002	Compliance-enhancement, problem-solving intervention in ED: 1. Review treatment expectations 2. Address treatment misconceptions 3. Review factors that impede treatment attendance 4. Verbal contract to attend at least 4 outpatient sessions	Random assignment to enhanced or standard disposition planning in ED; 1-hr ED intervention with 3-month follow-up	N = 63 suicide attempters receiving medical care in ED; Ages 12–18 years (mean 15 years); N = 29 in enhanced care (25 female); N = 34 in standard care (32 female); 73% white; SES: 47% middle class, 49% below middle class; Over 50% were hospitalized after ED visit as part of disposition	Adherence to treatment was not different between groups unless controlled for barriers to treatment
Greenfield et al., 2002	Rapid-response (RR) outpatient model: Psychiatrist and psychiatric nurse were available to assist in making outpatient appointment, prescribe medication, and discuss misconceptions, maladaptive behaviors, and communications contributing to stress	Nonrandom assignment to RR or control group; Assignment yoked to ED psychiatrist's access to RR team	N = 286 adolescents with "suicidal risk" seen in 2 pediatric EDs and assessed to not need medical hospitalization; Ages 12–17 (mean 14 years); 70% female; +70% white; N = 158 RR; N = 128 control	RR group was less likely to be hospitalized (11% vs. 41%); RR group had first outpatient contact and first outpatient appointment sooner; At 6-month follow-up: RR had 59% fewer hospitalizations; No difference between RR and control for number of ED visits or subsequent suicide attempts

ED, emergency department; SES, Socioeconomic status.

pists, this program involved ED staff and families with a focus on encouraging participation in outpatient treatment. In comparison with patients who received family therapy alone, participants who received both family therapy and the emergency room intervention were found to adhere more frequently to the recommendation to attend a first treatment session. Families receiving the combined intervention also had more favorable outcomes in terms of maternal depression and general psychopathology, patient ideation, and parent-reported family interaction.

Spirito, Boergers, Donaldson, Bishop, and Lewander (2002) also developed an adherence enhancement intervention to improve engagement in therapy. Treatment expectations, misperceptions, and reasons for treatment dropout were separately presented to adolescents and parents, along with a brief intervention to facilitate problem solving around factors that might impede treatment attendance. After this ED intervention, telephone contacts were made at 1, 2, and 6 weeks with adolescents and parents. Many service barriers were reported such as delays in getting an appointment, being placed on a waiting list, and insurance and out-of-pocket expenses. Family barriers to treatment included parental emotional problems, transportation difficulties, language difficulties, and scheduling problems. The adherence enhancement program increased the number of sessions attended, although premature termination of treatment continued to be a problem. The program developers emphasized the importance of reducing service barriers for adolescents who have attempted suicide.

Hospitalization for suicidal behavior, though often securing the safety of the suicidal individual, is quite costly and not always beneficial. In an effort to decrease hospitalization rates and suicidality and improve functioning, Greenfield, Larson, Hechtman, Rousseau, and Platt (2002) implemented the Rapid Response (RR) ED intervention for suicidal adolescents who were not considered to require immediate medical or psychiatric hospitalization. The intervention included family therapy, medication, and community intervention, as indicated. Hospitalization rates were decreased and outpatient therapy

was initiated more rapidly as a result of the RR intervention when compared with standard care. In addition, adolescents receiving the intervention were less likely to be rehospitalized during the 6 months after their visit to the ED. Neither hospitalization nor RR was found to prevent subsequent suicidal behavior or ED visits.

Critique

The results of programs implemented to date suggest that some improvement in outpatient treatment adherence by young suicide attempters, as well as reduced hospitalizations, can be achieved by concerted efforts in the ED. Such efforts, however, require education of ED staff on suicide risks and treatment needs of young suicide attempters. Barriers to outpatient treatment appear to remain significant and difficult to surmount, even for the most cohesive and well-functioning families. It seems essential that ED interventions provide some continuity of contact with the youth beyond the initial ED visit, which will require additional staffing. While this may seem costly, the cost reductions associated with decreasing immediate and future hospitalization are significant.

PSYCHOTHERAPEUTIC TREATMENTS FOR SUICIDAL YOUTH

Effectiveness of Psychotherapeutic and Psychosocial Treatments for Adults

As noted in Chapter 21, previous suicidal behavior is the most important factor associated with suicide risk among both adults and youth. Recognizing that repetition of a suicide attempt vastly increases the risk of a fatal outcome (Sakinofsky, 2000), considerable effort has been directed towards developing psychotherapeutic and other psychosocial treatment modalities to prevent subsequent suicidal behavior among identified individuals. Although suicide attempts and other forms of deliberate self-harm occur with greater frequency among young people than among adults, virtually all such treatments have been systematically studied only among adults, primarily because of restrictions against including suicidal youth in randomized trials and other research.

In a comprehensive review of psychological and pharmacological treatments for preventing repetition of suicide attempts (primarily among adults), undertaken in conjunction with the Cochrane Collaboration's Database of Systematic Reviews, Hawton and colleagues synthesized findings from 20 randomized controlled trials (RCTs), involving 2,641 patients in which repetition of deliberate self-harm was reported as an outcome variable (Hawton et al., 1998, 2000; Townsend et al., 2001). Most of these trials studied psychotherapeutic or other psychosocial treatments.

Reports on these RCTs were independently rated by two reviewers, blind to authorship, using the recommended Cochrane criteria for quality assessment. These include determination of the study's overall validity, the quality of the randomization procedures used to assign subjects into groups, the potential biases regarding sample selection and attrition, and intervention delivery (Alderson, Green, & Higgins, 2003). Overall, Hawton and colleagues concluded that there is currently insufficient evidence on which to make firm recommendations about the most effective forms of treatment for patients who have engaged in suicidal behavior, primarily because most treatment studies to date involving identified suicide attempters have included far too few subjects to have the statistical power to detect meaningful differences in rates of repetition of suicide attempts between experimental and control treatments, if such differences existed (Hawton et al., 1998). Nevertheless, promising results were found for several psychotherapeutic modalities.

In one promising approach, dialectical behavior therapy (DBT), a number of cognitive and behavioral strategies are used to target suicidal and other dysfunctional behaviors. In DBT relatively long-term individual treatment is combined with group behavioral skills training. This therapeutic technique was developed by Linehan (1993a, 1993b) for adult suicide attempters, specifically to address the problems of poor emotional regulation that are commonly found in this population. Because individuals with borderline personality disorder (BPD) are particularly prone to affective dysregulation and maladaptive problem-solving behaviors including self-harm, DBT has been described as especially effective for this subgroup of suicide attempters (Linehan 1993a, 1993b).

Dialectical behavior therapy is designed to be given in several sessions a week for approximately a year. Its components include (1) training the patient in self-acceptance through the technique of mindfulness; (2) increasing assertiveness to reduce interpersonal conflicts; (3) training the patient to avoid situations that trigger negative moods; and (4) increasing tolerance of distress. In DBT, the suicidal behavior itself is regarded as the primary focal point of treatment; although efficacious treatment for underlying problems such as depression is important, it does not necessarily reduce suicidality (Linehan, Armstrong, Suarez, Allmon, & Heard, 1991). An adaptation of DBT (DBT-A) has been developed for adolescents (Miller, Rathus, Linehan, Wetzler, & Leigh, 1997). Given for 6 months rather than for a year, DBT-A has not yet been tested in a controlled study.

During a 1-year course of treatment with DBT, Linehan and colleagues (1991) found that a sample of adult female patients with BPD had significantly fewer suicide attempts, less medically significant attempts, and fewer inpatient psychiatric days. They were also more likely to stay in individual therapy than were comparable patients who received treatment as usual. Between-group differences in depression, hopelessness, suicidal ideation, and reasons for living were not significant, although the DBT group showed decreases in all four measures throughout the treatment year. In a 1-year posttreatment follow-up, the DBT patients were found to have significantly higher global functioning, better social adjustment, less anger, less suicidal behavior, and fewer psychiatric inpatient days compared to control patients (Linehan, Heard, & Armstrong, 1993).

Although the efficacy of DBT was strongly supported in studies of female suicide attempters with BPD, Hawton and colleagues (1998) noted that the intensive nature of the treatment could limit its application within general psychiatric services, and that its efficacy among male patients had not been determined.

Short-term problem-solving therapy based on a cognitive behavioral model (Gibbons, Butler, Irwin, & Gibbons, 1978; McLeavey, Daly, Ludgate, & Murray, 1994) was also found in Hawton's review to result in reductions in subsequent suicidal behaviors by adult patients who had engaged in self-poisoning, although comparisons with patients who received treatment as usual were not statistically significant, likely because of the small numbers of patients studied in these trials. A subsequent meta-analysis of data reported by six trials in which brief problem-solving therapy was compared with control treatment showed that patients who were offered problem-solving therapy had significantly greater improvement in depression as hopelessness, as well as perceived improvement in the problems these patients faced (Townsend et al., 2001). These findings suggest that short-term therapy might be as efficacious as long-term treatment in preventing repetition of suicidal behavior, although Hawton and colleagues noted the need for confirmation of these findings in a large trial.

Also noted as promising in this review were studies in which experimental group patients were given, in addition to standard aftercare, 24-hour emergency access to a psychiatrist or hospital. Two such studies (Cotgrove, Zirinski, Black, & Weston, 1995; Morgan, Jones, & Owen, 1993) reported a tendency towards less repetition of self-harm among patients who were encouraged to make emergency contact with services if needed. In the only RCT reviewed by Hawton that involved adolescent patients, Cotgrove and colleagues (1995) gave tokens allowing readmission upon demand to a random sample of adolescents who had been hospitalized following a suicide attempt, in addition to standard management. Although only 11% of the sample used the tokens, the group overall showed a somewhat (but not significantly) lower rate of repeat attempts, compared to comparable adolescents who were given standard management but no tokens.

Because of small sample sizes, Hawton's review noted that meaningful conclusions could not be reached about the efficacy of hospital ad-

mission following a suicide attempt vs. outpatient treatment, or about the relative impact of inpatient behavior therapy compared to inpatient insight-oriented therapy.

Psychotherapeutic interventions that encourage compliance with treatment and attempt to decrease depression and other negative affects in the context of a supportive interpersonal relationship should theoretically reduce suicide risk. There is some evidence, however, that reexamination of painful problems may have adverse effects on some vulnerable individuals (Nemeroff, Compton, & Berger, 2001). Although no systematic attention has been given to documenting adverse outcomes of psychotherapy for suicidal individuals, one study has reported negative outcomes of "life history" interviews with elderly suicidal women who had abusive histories (Haight & Hendrix, 1998).

Assumptions Underlying Psychotherapeutic Treatments for Suicidal Youth

Psychotherapeutic approaches for treating suicidal youth are summarized in Table 24.2. Most such interventions have employed variations of cognitive behavioral therapy. The underlying assumption is that the primary focus of treatment should be the suicidal behavior itself, rather than the underlying psychopathology (Brent et al., 1997; Harrington et al., 1998). As was earlier noted, restrictions regarding the inclusion of suicidal youth in RCTs have limited systematic evaluation of some of these approaches.

Program Examples

Rudd and colleagues provided the first description of a cognitive behavioral skills group intervention designed to treat young adults with suicidal ideation or suicidal behavior (Rudd et al., 1996). The intervention, an intensive 2-week program that participants attended for 9 hr/day, included an experiential affective group, psychoeducational classes with homework, and a problem-solving and social competence group. A variety of strategies such as behavioral rehearsal, role-playing, and modeling were used to im-

Table 24.2 Psychotherapeutic Interventions

Reference	Intervention	Study Design	Program Length	Sample Size	Comments
Rudd et al., 1996	Outpatient, intensive, structured, time-limited group treatment using problem-solving and social competence approach to improve social functioning and adaptive coping	Pretest to posttest Follow-up (24 months) Random assignment to treatment vs. TAU comparison group	9 hr/day for 2-week period with minimum of 8 individuals	N = 264 members of military medical center in southwest U.S. Reflects 21% dropout rate N = 143 treatment N = 121 TAU (inpatient and outpatient care) Mean age = 22 years 70% completed high school 82% male 61% White 26% African American 11% Hispanic 39% married 42% never married 30% had previous hospitalization 110 suicidal ideation 107 single attempters 47 multiple attempter	Both groups improved and there were no between-group differences at posttest or follow-up Treatment was more effective at retaining poor problem solvers over 24-month period relative to TAU controls
Harrington et al., 1998	Home-based family intervention	Random assignment to home-based intervention or TAU with 6-month follow-up	5 sessions in family home	N = 162 of 435 referred cases Adolescents ages 10–16 seen in the hospital for self-poisoning n = 85 home-based Mean age, 14.4 years 89% female 63% not living with both parents 66% with DSM-III-R MDD n = 77 TAU Mean age, 14.6 years 90% female 70% not living with both parents 60% with DSM-III-R MDD	The groups did not differ with respect to suicidal behavior after treatment Parents from home-based treatment were more satisfied at 2-month follow-up than TAU parents While the MDD group did not evidence group differences, the home-based intervention was more effective than TAU for nondepressed adolescents with respect to suicidal ideation

(continued)

Table 24.2 Continued

Reference	Intervention	Study Design	Program Length	Sample Size	Comments
Wood et al., 2001	Developmental group psychotherapy (DGP)	Random assignment to DGP or TAU Follow-up at 7 months	6 "acute" group sessions followed by weekly "long-term group" until patient ready to leave	N = 63 adolescents aged 12–16 years (mean age 14 years) who were referred to mental health service of South Manchester, England, and had reported at least one other act of deliberate self-harm in the previous year (mean, 4 attempts) Primarily from disadvantaged families Approximately 50% had history of abuse Majority not living with both parents n = 32 DGP 78% female n = 31 TAU 77% female	Those in DGP attended more sessions than those in TAU Those in TAU were more likely to make repeat attempts and to make them sooner than those in DGP who made repeat attempts The groups did not differ with respect to suicidal ideation or depression at follow-up The DGP group demonstrated a reduction in behavioral disorder at 7 months relative to TAU Adolescents with more DGP were less likely to make repeat attempts
Rathus & Miller, 2002	Dialectical behavior therapy (DBT)	Pretest to posttest Nonrandom assignment to DBT or TAU	12 weeks of twice-weekly DBT including individual and multifamily skills therapy	N = 111 67% Hispanic 17% African American 8% white n = 29 adolescents receiving DBT Mean age, 16.1 years 93% female suicide attempt within the last 16 weeks and minimum of 3 borderline personality features n = 82 adolescents receiving TAU Mean age, 15 years 73% female either suicide attempt in last 16 weeks or evidenced 3 borderline personality features but not both	DBT vs. TAU Despite greater psychopathology, the DBT group had no psychiatric hospitalizations vs. 13% of the TAU group hospitalized DBT group had 3.4% attempts vs. 8.6% of TAU group 62% of DBT vs. 40% of TAU group completed 12 weeks of treatment Within DBT Group Suicidal ideation, depression, overall symptom level, and specific borderline personality features were reduced at the end of treatment

DBT, dialectical behavior therapy; DGP, developmental group therapy; MDD, major depressive disorder; TAU, treatment as usual.

prove basic social skills and effective coping. Participants (*N* = 264) were randomly assigned to either the experimental intervention or a treatment-as-usual condition involving long-term outpatient treatment. In a 2-year follow-up, Rudd et al. found that participants in both groups showed significant reductions in suicidal ideation and behavior and experienced stress, and improvements in self-appraised problem-solving ability. The intensive time-limited intervention was found to be more effective than long-term treatment in retaining the highest-risk participants. Subsequent analyses showed that patients with psychiatric symptomatology experienced the most improvement in response to this intervention (Joiner, Voelz, & Rudd, 2001). The rate of suicide attempts at follow-up was not reported for either the experimental or control group, however, and conclusions were limited by high attrition rates in both the experimental and control group.

Harrington and colleagues in Great Britain (Byford et al., 1999; Harrington et al., 1998, 2000) developed a home-based family intervention for adolescents with a history of deliberate self-poisoning. This intervention used a cognitive behavioral approach to address family dysfunction assumed to be related to the suicide attempt (Kerfoot, 1988; Keerfoot, Dyer, Harrington, Woodham, & Harrington, 1996), and to improve adherence to treatment by bringing it into the home. The intervention consisted of five highly structured sessions focusing of goal setting, reviewing the self-poisoning episode, communication, problem solving, and discussing issues related to the family. The program included a treatment manual and videotape for training.

This brief intervention was found to be effective primarily among those adolescents who were not seriously depressed and had less severe suicidal ideation, who made up about one third of the 85 participants (Harrington et al., 1998, 2000). Adherence and parental satisfaction with treatment were better for participants in this treatment relative to treatment as usual. The intervention was found to be no more costly than routine care alone (Byford et al., 1999).

Wood and colleagues have developed an additional psychotherapeutic variant, using developmental group therapy as an alternative to usual care for adolescents who have repeatedly attempted to harm themselves (Wood, Harrington, & Moore, 1996; Wood, Trainor, Rothwell, Moore, & Harrington, 2001). The group-therapy format was hypothesized to be useful in providing an arena for working on social problem-solving and relationship skills that are often considered core to suicidal behavior. Using a developmental approach to address issues unique to adolescents, the intervention combines problem-solving and cognitive behavioral interventions (Harrington, et al., 1998), DBT (Linehan et al., 1991), and psychodynamic approaches. An acute phase focusing on core themes (family and peer relationships, school problems, anger management, depression, self-harm, and hopelessness) is followed by a longer phase that concentrates on group processes. In interviews conducted about 7 months after treatment began, participants in the developmental group therapy reported engaging in less self-harm than did adolescents who received routine care, although depression did not appear to improve. Episodes of self-harm became less frequent as participants attended more sessions of the group therapy, whereas among those in usual care, self-harm behaviors were found to increase compared to baseline. Participants in the developmental group therapy, particularly youth who had made multiple suicide attempts, also showed reductions in conduct problems.

Considering suicidal behavior as the primary problem rather than the symptom, Henriques, Beck, and Brown (2003) have developed and examined a brief cognitive intervention for suicide attempters ages 18 and over. The intervention consists of 10 sessions, beginning with the identification of proximal thoughts and associated core beliefs that were activated just prior to the adolescent's suicide attempt. Cognitive and behavioral strategies are then applied to help individuals develop more adaptive ways of thinking about their situation and more functional ways of responding during periods of acute emotional distress. Specific attention is given to the role of hopelessness.

The intervention follows a structured protocol with specific therapeutic strategies developed for the early, middle, and late phases of treatment, which are designed for replication by mental health professionals working with suicidal youth. Early sessions focus on engaging the patient, setting goals, and increasing hopefulness. Middle sessions involve changing maladaptive beliefs and addressing problem-solving deficits and impulsivity while developing reasons for living, increasing adherence with health-care professionals, and increasing social support. Later sessions focus on relapse prevention, terminations, therapy extensions, and booster sessions as necessary. The efficacy and effectiveness of the intervention are currently being evaluated in a randomized controlled clinical trial. To date, the approach has not been used in the treatment of younger adolescents.

In another variation, Miller and colleagues (Miller et al., 1997; Rathus & Miller, 2002) have used a modification of DBT in their treatment of adolescent suicide attempters who demonstrated at least three features of BPD. The intervention developed by Miller et al. consists of 12 weeks of twice-weekly individual and family skills training. In one specific trial (Rathus & Miller, 2002), participants in the DBT group were found to have better adherence to treatment and fewer hospitalizations than those receiving treatment as usual, despite the fact that they had greater psychiatric comorbidity than control subjects. The DBT treatment was also found to be associated with reduced suicidal ideation, symptom severity, and distress. Although suicide attempts were less likely in the DBT group than among controls, this difference was not found to be significant.

Critique

Results reported to date suggest the effectiveness of cognitive behavioral interventions in improving social functioning and reducing suicidal ideation among suicidal adolescents, particularly those with mild to moderate depression and those with borderline features. In some cases, however, the outcomes of experimental treatments have not been substantially better than those obtained by comparison or standard care treatments. Long-term effects of psychotherapy interventions on suicidal behavior have not yet been reported. Given that maladaptive cogni-

tions and behaviors have likely developed over a long period of time, it is not clear that short-term psychotherapies will ultimately be found to be effective in reducing suicidal behavior.

PHARMACOLOGICAL TREATMENTS FOR SUICIDAL YOUTH

Effectiveness of Pharmacological Treatments for Adults

The neurobiological underpinnings of suicidal behavior are currently the subject of considerable research, and new information that broadens our understanding of this complex area continues to emerge. Recent reviews have identified serotonergic dysfunction, noradrenergic dysfunction, dopaminergic dysfunction, and hypothalamic–pituitary–adrenal (HPA) axis hyperactivity as the key neurobiological correlates of suicidality (Mann, 2003; Nemeroff et al., 2001).

The most extensively replicated studies have focused on the role of serotonergic dysfunction. Studies have reported that depressed patients who have made suicide attempts have lower levels of 5-hydroxyindoleacetic acid (5-HIAA) in the brainstem and in cerebrospinal fluid (CSF) compared to depressed nonattempters (Nemeroff et al., 2001). Decreased CSF 5-HIAA is hypothesized to be a marker of the impulsive, aggressive, and violent nature of suicide, and appears to correlate with a high degree of suicidal planning and a high level of lethality of suicide attempts. Central nervous system (CNS) serotonergic dysfunction has also been associated with suicidal behavior.

One early small RCT study of adult chronic suicide attempters (Montgomery et al., 1979) found that depot neuroleptic medications were effective in preventing repetition of suicidal behavior, although patient reluctance and negative side effects were noted as limitations. Hawton and colleagues, in their exhaustive search using Cochrane criteria (1998), were unable to identify any other RCT conducted through the mid-1990s that found antidepressant medications to be effective in preventing subsequent suicidal behavior in patients who had made prior attempts. They noted, however, that the only antidepressants that had been systematically studied for suicide-related outcomes, nomifensine and mianserin, had been discontinued for general use at the time of their review.

A number of studies have reported decreased suicidality among mood-disordered adult patients receiving long-term lithium treatment (Sharma, 2003; Tondo, Jamison, & Baldessarini, 1997). Pooling results reported by several individual studies conducted between 1974 and 1996, Tondo and colleagues estimated that lithium treatment was associated with an almost 9-fold reduction in risk of suicide and suicide attempts. They noted that it is not clear whether the protection lithium provides against suicide derives from its general mood-stabilizing effect or its effects on reducing aggression and impulsivity through improved serotonergic functioning.

Long-term treatment with clozapine, an atypical antipsychotic, has been shown to produce similar effects among patients with schizophrenia, reducing suicidal behavior among this high-risk population (Sharma, 2003; Spivak, Shabash, Sheitman, Weizman, & Mester, 2003). Randomized controlled trials involving both lithium and clozapine are needed to determine the extent to which positive outcomes are related to patient characteristics that are correlated with their ability to adhere to long-term treatment.

Among patients suffering from unipolar depression, selective serotonin reuptake inhibitors (SSRIs) are currently considered superior to other antidepressants for improving both suicidal behavior and suicidal ideation (Nemeroff et al., 2001). Although no large RCTs of SSRIs have included outcomes related to suicide (due to the exclusion of suicidal patients from most pharmaceutical-sponsored trials), there is considerable evidence pointing to the positive effects of such medications on the CNS serotonergic dysfunction noted above to be associated with suicidality in adults (Oquendo, Malone, & Mann, 1997).

In recent years, several European studies have reported inverse correlations between use of SSRIs and suicide deaths, suggesting their potential significance for reducing suicide risk (Barbui, Campomori, D'Avanzo, Negri, & Garattini, 1999; Carlsten, Waern, Ekedahl, & Ranstam, 2001; Gunnel, Middleton, Whitley, Dorling, &

Frankel, 2003; Isacsson, 2000). Although large RCTs need to be conducted to determine causative linkages, SSRIs appear to be a potent means of treating suicidality. The SSRIs have been reported to have less inherent toxicity than the previously widely used tricyclic antidepressants (TCAs), and are thus less likely to be related to death from overdoses. Although side effects such as gastrointestinal upset, insomnia, and sexual dysfunction are fairly common, most SSRIs appear to be well tolerated.

Assumptions Underlying Pharmacological Treatments for Suicidal Youth

To date there are few publicly reported studies involving the use of pharmacological interventions to treat suicidal behavior among young people. Although the effectiveness of antidepressants in treating children and adolescents has not been definitively established, use of SSRIs in treating depressed and suicidal youth has nonetheless become widespread. A recent U.S. analysis by Olfson, Shaffer, and colleagues (2003) reported an inverse relationship between regional change in use of antidepressants among youth aged 10–19 and suicide mortality. The relationship was found to be significant specifically among males, among youth aged 15–19, and in geographic regions with lower family median incomes.

Although these studies do not establish use of antidepressants to be causally linked to decreases in suicide deaths, some efforts are under way to implement and evaluate pharmacological treatments among youth with serious psychopathology, including suicidal ideation or behavior. The key assumption of these efforts is suicide risk among youth, as in adults, can be reduced through the use of antidepressant medications.

Program Examples

An intervention by Cornelius and colleagues used fluoxetine (Prozac) to treat adolescents with comorbid major depression and an alcohol use disorder, including some who demonstrated suicidal ideation at baseline (Cornelius, Bukstein, et al., 2001). The intervention was based on findings that reducing depression and problem drinking in adults resulted in a reduction of suicidal behavior (Dinh-Zarr, Diguiseppi, Heitman, & Roberts, 1999). Cornelius and colleagues also found fluoxetine to be effective in treating suicidal adults with an alcohol use disorder. Such treatment improved but did not completely eliminate both depressive symptoms (including suicidal ideations) and the level of drinking (Cornelius, Salhoum, Lynch, Clark, & Mann, 2001).

In their studies involving youth, all patients receiving fluoxetine improved with respect to depressive symptoms, and over half improved in symptoms of alcohol dependence. Among participants with suicidal ideation at baseline, ideation decreased and these decreases remained 1 year after treatment (Cornelius, 2003). Cornelius reported no serious adverse effects of fluoxetine among youth.

A definitive study supported by the National Institute of Mental Health, known as the Treatment of Adolescents with Depression Study (TADS), has provided the strongest evidence to date of the effectiveness of fluoxetine in treating adolescent depression and suicidality. This study randomly assigned 439 youths ages 12 to 17 diagnosed with moderate to severe depression to one of four treatment conditions for a period of 36 weeks: fluoxetine therapy alone, cognitive-behavioral therapy (CBT) alone, fluoxetine and CBT, and a placebo drug treatment. Based on the results obtained during the first 12 weeks of the study, the highest rate of clinical improvement (71%) was found among those receiving the combination treatment, followed by 61% of those who received fluoxetine alone, 43% of those who received CBT alone, and 35% of those who received the placebo drug treatment (March et al., 2004). It should be noted that the most seriously suicidal adolescents were excluded from the TADS sample, and thus only 29% of participants reported having clinically significant suicidal ideation at baseline. This percent decreased to 10% by week 12. Although no suicides occurred during the trial, the risk of a suicide attempt among study participants during the first weeks on fluoxetine was reported to be twice that for participants not receiving the medication. The study investigators concluded, however, that the benefits of the medication far outweighed its associated risk.

Critique

Since fluoxetine is presently the only antidepressant medication approved by the U.S. Food and Drug Administration (FDA) for the treatment of major depression in children and adolescents, the findings reported by Cornelius and colleagues and by the (NIMH) study have important implications for suicide prevention among depressed youth. It is encouraging that publicly supported large-scale RCTs are beginning to be undertaken. Much additional research is needed, however, to further illuminate the impact of fluoxetine, as well as that of other medications, for reducing suicidal ideation and behavior among both substance-abusing and nonabusing adolescents.

Since 2003, concerns have been raised about the safety of the newer antidepressant medications for use by children and adolescents, based initially on unpublished data from drug company studies linking use of SSRIs by children and adolescents to suicidal ideation and self-harm behaviors. In late 2003, these reports led the British drug regulatory agency to recommend against the use of all SSRIs except fluoxetine in treating depression among youth under age 18 (Goode, 2003).

In 2004, the U.S. Food and Drug Administration undertook a review of 23 clinical trials involving the use of nine different antidepressant medications by over 4,000 children and adolescents. The results of this analysis, presented in September 2004, found that the medications increased the risk of suicidal thinking and behavior (suicidality) in children and adolescents with major depressive disorder (MDD) or other psychiatric disorders (Hammad, 2004). Specifically, 4% of all youth taking medication reported an "adverse event," i.e., thoughts of suicide and/or potentially dangerous behavior, compared to 2% of those taking a placebo drug.

On October 15, 2004, the FDA directed pharmaceutical companies to label all antidepressant medications distributed in the U.S. with a black box warning to this effect (FDA, 2004), even though their analysis had only included nine specific drugs. The warning states that the increased risk of suicidal thinking and/or behavior occurs in a small proportion of youth and is most likely to occur during the early phases of treatment. Although the FDA did not prohibit the use of antidepressants by children and adolescents, it called upon physicians and parents to closely monitor youth who are taking the medications for a worsening in symptoms of depression or unusual changes in behavior.

On February 1, 2005, the American Psychiatric Association (APA) and a coalition of other leading health, mental health, and advocacy organizations released detailed fact sheets for physicians and parents on the use of medications in treating childhood and adolescent depression (American Psychiatric Association, 2005). The fact sheets were developed because of concern that the FDA black box warning could have the unintended effect of limiting necessary, appropriate, and effective treatment of depression and other psychiatric disorders in youth.

The APA fact sheets were particularly critical of the FDA's measurement of suicidality following antidepressant use among children and adolescents, which essentially used thoughts of suicide or potentially dangerous behaviors that had been spontaneously shared by the young participants and subsequently recorded in the researchers' "adverse events reports." Although the FDA analysis showed more such spontaneous reports among those taking an antidepressant medication as compared to placebo (4% vs. 2%), this finding was not supported by data from 17 of the 23 studies examined that had systematically asked all participants about their suicidal thoughts and behaviors, using standardized forms. The FDA's analysis of these data concluded that medication neither increased suicidality that had been present before the treatment, nor induced new suicidality in those who were not thinking about suicide at the start of the study. All studies collecting such data reported a reduction in suicidality over the course of treatment. The APA critique noted that while the FDA reported both sets of findings, it did not comment on the contradiction between them. It further questioned the reliability of the 2% and 4% spontaneous report rates, noting findings

from numerous community samples that as many as half of adolescents with major depression were thinking of suicide at the time of diagnosis and 16%–35% reported making a suicide attempt.

The fact sheets included suggestions for physicians and parents in monitoring youth receiving antidepressant medication, and called for the development of a readily-accessible registry of clinical trials that could aid in resolving the controversy and conflicting information surrounding the prescribing of antidepressants to children and adolescents.

POSTHOSPITALIZATION PROGRAMS FOR SUICIDAL YOUTH

Assumptions

Research has pointed to a lack of posthospital treatment adherence among the many youth who are hospitalized in inpatient psychiatric units following serious suicidal behavior (Cohen-Sandler, Berman, & King, 1982; Spirito, Brown, Overholser, & Fritz, 1989). One result is frequent rehospitalization for repeated suicidality (Greenfield et al., 2002; Stewart et al., 2001). The key assumption of posthospitalization programs is that providing consistent support and improving adherence to aftercare recommendations will help to prevent future suicidal behavior.

Program Examples

The only full-developed program of this sort is the Youth-Nominated Support Team (YST) intervention, developed by King and colleagues (King, 2003; King, Preuss, & Kramer, 2001). This program was an outgrowth of the developers' finding that family dysfunction and parental psychopathology significantly impact treatment adherence by suicidal youth after hospitalization (King, Hovey, Brand, Wilson, & Ghaziuddin, 1997). Concentrating on the high-risk period for suicidality immediately following psychiatric hospitalization, the program specifically targets poor treatment adherence and negative perceptions of family support and helpfulness.

Before leaving the hospital, program participants nominate specific adults from their home, school, or community to support them when they are released. The YST conducts a psycho-education session with these adults, then engages them in weekly consultations designed to improve their understanding of the suicidal youngster and how he or she can be effectively supported. A social network is encouraged among the adults, who typically come from diverse settings. The program is designed to supplement usual treatments.

Response to YST by participating youth and the nominated adults has been positive (King, 2003), with 80% of those nominated actually participating in the program. Positive effects have been reported for adolescent females, including reduced suicidal ideation and mood impairment. Similar benefits were not evidenced among male participants, although some described YST as having beneficial effects.

Critique

Since this intervention has only recently been implemented, it is too early to know whether the positive effects found among the suicidal girls will be translated into reductions of suicide attempts and rehospitalizations. It will also be important to identify the reasons underlying the lack of clear effects among male participants and to incorporate the necessary programmatic changes. The fact that the program has been manualized will likely encourage its replication, while permitting independent assessment of specific program components.

TREATMENT PROGRAMS FOR SUICIDE ATTEMPTERS ON COLLEGE CAMPUSES

Assumptions

As was noted in Chapter 22 there has been marked reluctance among college and university officials to specifically identify suicidal students or offer treatment services that specifically address this problem. One university-based treatment program has been identified, which is based on the assumption that students who engage in suicidal threats or behavior will not voluntarily submit to a clinical assessment, and thus that such assessment must be mandated as a condition of the student's continued enrollment at the university.

Program Examples

For the last 17 years, the University of Illinois has had in place a policy that requires mandatory reporting of all suicide threats and attempts by students, and mandatory clinical assessment sessions for all students identified as engaging in such behavior. Specifically, identified students are required to attend four weekly sessions with a social worker or psychologist at the University Counseling Center, during which the student receives a comprehensive clinical assessment and referral to additional treatment if needed. Students who do not attend the mandated sessions can be suspended or expelled from the university.

The program's primary developer reported high compliance among students over the past 17 years, with only one student being involuntarily dismissed from the university for refusing to attend the mandatory sessions. A significant decrease in the suicide rate at the university as a function of this policy has also been reported (Joffe, 2003).

Critique

Although the program has claimed to be uniquely successful in reducing suicidal behavior at the one campus where it has been implemented, confirmatory evidence is lacking. Comparative statistics on suicide rates over the last 17 years from universities with a similar student body to that of the University of Illinois are lacking, and it is possible the reported reductions are reflective of a general trend toward decreasing numbers of suicides among adolescents and young adults during the time period described, rather than the result of this specific program. Further, it is not clear how many suicidal students voluntarily withdrew from the university prior to identification, or how many troubled students may have decided not to enroll at all because of this particular policy.

Research Agenda for Youth
Suicide Prevention

In the preceding chapters, we have reviewed what is currently known about youth suicide, how it can be prevented, and how the problems associated with suicidal behavior can be treated. We begin this last chapter with a summary of what we currently know.

WHAT WE KNOW

About Youth Suicide

- Between the mid-1950s and the late 1970s, the suicide rate among U.S. males aged 15–24 more than tripled. Among females aged 15–24, the rate more than doubled during this period. The youth suicide rate generally leveled off during the 1980s and early 1990s, and since the mid-1990s, it has been steadily decreasing.
- About 4,000 people aged 15–24 die by suicide each year in the United States.
- In the United States suicide is currently the third leading cause of death among all youth ages 15–24.
- Among young people aged 15–24, males die by suicide almost six times more frequently than females.
- Youth suicide rates vary widely among different racial and ethnic groups. The rate for African-American, Hispanic, and Asian-American youth are currently less than that of white youth; the highest suicide rate is seen among American Indian and Alaskan Native youth.
- Over eight percent of American high school students make a suicide attempt. Seventeen percent of high school students report having seriously considered suicide during the previous 12 months.
- The vast majority of youth (70%–90%) who die by suicide had at least one psychiatric illness at the time of death. The most common diagnoses among youth are depression, substance abuse, and conduct disorders.
- Other factors associated with youth suicide include physical abuse, sexual abuse, serious conflict with parents, interpersonal loss, not being in school or not working, knowing someone who has attempted suicide or died by suicide, and access to firearms.
- Suicide and suicide attempts are increased in families in which a parent has died by suicide or attempted suicide.
- Among youth (and adults), a prior suicide attempt is a strong predictor of subsequent attempts and suicide death.

About Youth Suicide Prevention Programs

- Under adequate conditions of implementation, programs that educate high school students about suicide can increase students' knowledge of mental illness and suicide, encourage more adaptive attitudes about these problems, encourage help-seeking behaviors, and increase referrals of at-risk students to treatment.
- Programs that train teachers, counselors, and community gatekeepers about suicide intervention can increase participants' knowledge about suicide and suicide prevention, increase self-confidence and willingness to intervene, and increase referrals to treatment.
- Programs that screen high school and college students to identify those at risk for suicide and refer them for treatment can identify some high-risk individuals who were not previously recognized or treated. Most at-risk students who are identified, however, do not adhere to recommendations regarding treatment.

About Treatment of Suicidality and Underlying Disorders Among Youth

- Under adequate conditions of implementation, intensive school-based programs for students at risk of dropping out of school can reduce depression and suicidality in students who exhibit these problems.
- Programs that engage young suicide attempters and their families while they are in the emergency department can increase adherence to outpatient treatment and de-

crease immediate and subsequent hospitalizations.

- Cognitive behavior therapy can improve social functioning and reduce suicidal ideation and self-harm behaviors among suicidal youth.
- There appears to be increasing evidence that treatment with fluoxetine (Prozac) can reduce depression, alcohol dependence, and suicidal ideation in youth.
- Combination treatment involving Prozac and psychotherapy appears to result in the most positive outcomes for depressed, suicidal youth.
- There is some evidence that posthospitalization programs for suicidal youth can reduce subsequent suicidal ideation and mood impairment among female participants.

In spite of considerable research and program development focusing on youth suicide, there is much we do not yet know about the factors that cause or significantly influence suicidal behavior among youth and the interventions that must be made if this behavior is to be prevented or treated. Listed below are the key knowledge needs our review has identified that constitute a future research agenda for youth suicide. Clearly, the task that lies ahead for researchers and program developers is formidable.

WHAT WE DON'T KNOW

About Youth Suicide

- Although the problem of youth suicide is disproportionately due to its prevalence in young males, explanations for this phenomenon are currently lacking.
- Also not well understood is the impact of race and ethnicity on suicide vulnerability among youth. What particular risk or protective factors are conferred by membership in particular racial or ethnic groups?
- Studies of the relationship of sexual orientation to youth suicidality have to date produced equivocal findings. Better understanding is needed of the interrelationships among sexual orientation and other risk factors, including psychopathology, substance abuse, and family and peer conflicts, and of what appears to be an increased number of suicide attempts (but not suicide deaths) among homosexual and bisexual youth.
- What external environments increase or decrease youth vulnerability and susceptibility to suicide? How can these be improved?
- Although psychopathology has been well documented to be the most potent factor underlying suicide among all age groups, relatively little is known about the specific clinical pathways to youth suicide. In particular, much more needs to be known about the contribution of bipolar disorder, panic attacks, and posttraumatic stress disorder (PTSD) to suicide deaths among youth. The impact of race and ethnicity on diagnostic profiles and clinical pathways to suicide likewise needs greater scrutiny. Longitudinal studies of young suicide ideators and attempters are particularly needed. In addition, because most people with psychopathology do not engage in suicidal behavior and suicidal behavior crosses many different psychopathologies, the interactions among specific forms of psychopathology, other suicide risk factors less associated with mental disorders, and factors that protect against suicide need greater research attention.
- Much more needs to be known about the role of neurobiological abnormalities that contribute to youth suicidal behavior, and the degree to which these may be inherited. Family studies of adults and adolescents who have attempted suicide or died by suicide can provide important information about inherited characteristics, and it is essential that youth be included in such research.
- The extent to which parental and familial psychopathology influences suicide ideation, attempts, and completions among youth, over and above genetic influences, needs to be examined. Specifically, what is the effect of exposure to parental suicide attempts and completion, and suicide risk among youth? Does childhood physical and sexual abuse confer suicide risk independent of other effects of family psychopathology?

- Although suicide clusters have been identified among youth, the characteristics of those most vulnerable to "contagion" and the mechanisms through which contagion occurs have not been precisely identified.
- Much more needs to be understood about the role of personal and social skills in protecting youth from suicidal behavior. Do strong problem-solving skills, decision-making abilities, and support from family and schools actually protect young people from developing suicidal impulses, or is the absence of such skills a manifestation of psychopathology that is more directly related to suicidal thoughts or behavior? What is the role of culture, identity, and religious beliefs in reducing suicide risk?
- Both theoretically and in practical programmatic terms, it is essential to have better understanding of which combinations of risk and protective factors have the greatest predictive value for youth suicide. Current research points to the identification and treatment of psychopathology among adolescents as a priority suicide prevention strategy, but better understanding is needed of the wide range of interpersonal, cultural, and environmental factors that may exacerbate or mitigate the impact of psychopathology among particular groups of high-risk youth. In addition, some treatments have been found to reduce suicidality without significantly affecting psychopathology. Research to date has focused almost exclusively on looking at relationships between single risk or protective factors and adolescent suicidal behavior. Comprehensive analyses that simultaneously consider a number of individual variables are essential.

About Youth Suicide Prevention Programs

- Most suicide education programs have not identified the active ingredients responsible for the outcomes they produce.
- Most suicide education programs target outcomes whose relationship to youth suicide has not been precisely identified. Many, for example, have reported increased knowl-edge of mental illness and suicide among students, although the impact of this outcome on suicidal behavior is not known. Greater attention needs to be given identifying long-term behavioral outcomes among students who have received such education, particularly those with particular risk factors.
- Although increasing the number of referrals to treatment is a key goal of screening programs, there is no clear evidence of a direct linkage between increased referrals and decreased suicidal behavior among youth.
- Screening programs have generally not identified effective mechanisms for encouraging larger numbers of youth identified as at risk for suicide into treatment.
- Little data are currently available about the cost-effectiveness of school-based screening programs.
- Although popular in recent years, the effects of postvention programs, both positive and adverse, on youth exposed to a suicide death have not been clearly documented.
- Despite limited evidence that educational programs directed at parents, particularly fathers, can decrease youth access to firearms, the impact of means restriction programs on decreasing suicide attempts and suicide deaths among youth has not been documented.

About Treatment of Suicidality and Underlying Disorders Among Youth

- The active ingredients of comprehensive high school–based programs for treating students at risk of dropping out, including some who are depressed and suicidal, have not been clearly identified.
- It has not been demonstrated that students at risk of dropping out of school are representative of suicidal youth generally, and therefore that programs that address this population have wide applicability.
- The replication of such programs, which require considerable personnel and financial resources, has not been established.
- The impact of emergency department pro-

grams for young suicide attempters and their families on decreasing suicide deaths has not been established.

- Although some promising outcomes have been reported, long-term effects of cognitive behavior therapy with suicidal youth are not yet known.
- Although there is increasing evidence of the safety and efficacy of Prozac in treating depressed and suicidal youth, the safety and efficacy of the many other antidepressants currently being used have not been established.
- Much more needs to be known about the combinations of psychotherapeutic and pharmacological treatment that produce the most positive short- and long-term outcomes for depressed, suicidal youth.
- Long-term effects of posthospitalization programs for suicidal youth have not been documented.

RESEARCH NEEDS

In order to effectively address the knowledge needs that have been identified, youth suicide research must expand beyond its present relatively narrow focus to incorporate standards of research design and program evaluation that are routinely used in other prevention fields. Our review has made clear the extent to which scientifically valid evaluation of youth suicide prevention programs has lagged far behind their development and implementation. As a result, many efforts show considerable promise but very few have been established with reasonable certainty to be effective in preventing suicidal ideation, suicide attempts, or suicide deaths among youth.

Evaluation strategies that have been employed have relied largely on pre–post designs that do not adequately link outcomes to program components. Prospective controlled studies are needed to determine the effectiveness, safety, and active ingredients of universal and targeted suicide prevention programs, including school-based education, screening, and skills development programs; and school and community interventions for at-risk populations, in-

cluding firearms restriction programs and gatekeeper training programs.

A development that is expected to encourage and support the use of scientifically valid evaluation designs by suicide prevention programs is the recent decision of the Substance Abuse and Mental Health Administration (SAMHSA) to expand its National Registry of Effective Programs and Practices (NREPP) from its original focus on substance abuse prevention programs to include mental health promotion and treatment programs, including those associated with suicide prevention. NREPP is currently in the process of developing a unified set of evaluation criteria for all prevention programs that would define precise standards regarding research design, sampling, measurement, statistical analysis, and other methodological aspects. These criteria will then be used to systematically evaluate programs and classify then into one of five categories: *(1)* Insufficient Data to Make a Determination, *(2)* Program or Practice of Interest, *(3)* Promising Program or Practice, *(4)* Conditionally Effective, or *(5)* Effective Program or Practice. Beginning in May 2005, suicide prevention programs that are determined to be evidence-based will be included in NREPP's online registry (SAMHSA Model Programs, 2005).

To meet the NREPP criteria, suicide prevention programs will need to give particular attention to several issues that have been particularly problematic.

Theoretical Justification of Expected Outcomes

As has been noted earlier in this chapter, some suicide prevention programs, in particular universal education programs, have targeted outcome variables whose relationship to youth suicide has not been precisely identified. Evaluation of program outcomes must include careful consideration of the theoretical relevance of program goals and expected outcomes.

Theory-driven prevention strategies, programs, and treatments are most likely to inform the field in a cumulative manner. Specific variables believed to contribute to youth suicidal behavior (e.g., impaired problem-solving) need to be justified theoretically and addressed in the prevention strategy. Following the intervention, change in the variable must be specifically measured to determine if it functions, in fact, as a mediator of suicide-related outcomes. Without a theoretical base, findings from many studies are difficult to integrate, leaving the field with an absence of information as to what actually worked, and what directions (and theoretical models) are worthy of further investigation.

Sampling Strategies

Relatively few suicide prevention programs have systematically studied adequate numbers of representative at-risk youth to allow meaningful conclusions to be reached about program effectiveness, and only rarely have appropriate comparison groups been simultaneously studied. Further, most outcome studies have had access to program participants for a short period of time, which precludes attention to long-term effects of the program, including adverse effects.

Use of Third-Party vs. Internal Evaluator

Evaluation reports on the outcomes of youth suicide prevention programs have most frequently been issued by the program developers themselves. Third-party evaluation, rare in this field, may provide a more objective assessment of program accomplishments.

Funding for Evaluation Studies

Few youth suicide prevention programs have had the necessary personnel or financial resources to conduct independent program evaluations. If the field is to move forward, however, mechanisms need to be established that mandate and support comprehensive, well-designed outcome studies as a regular part of prevention programming. In regard to school-based programs in particular, effective evaluation requires follow-up of students who have participated in curricular or screening activities, to determine long-term outcomes. To date, sufficient resources

for such research programs have not been available.

We have noted that much more attention also needs to be given to evaluating the outcome of treatment programs for suicidal youth. Since universal and selective suicide prevention programs focus heavily on encouraging help seeking and on identifying vulnerable youth and referring them to treatment, their impact on reducing youth suicide depends ultimately on the effectiveness of the treatments that are available to such young people. Thus, the single highest priority must be given to determining the relative efficacy and effectiveness of all currently employed treatments and indicated interventions for suicidal youth.

As has been noted, randomized controlled trials (RCT) of treatments used for suicidal youth are seriously lacking. These are clearly needed to determine the impact of brief interventions with young suicide attempters presenting to emergency departments; psychotherapeutic strategies for suicidal youth and pharmacological treatments for young suicide ideators and attempters; as well as hospitalization, partial hospitalization, and posthospitalization support programs for youth. In addition to studies focusing on individual treatments, simultaneous evaluations of multiple treatment approaches (e.g., psychotherapy and medication) are especially needed. Adverse effects of treatment, including the potential of certain antidepressant medications to induce suicidality among vulnerable youth, also need to be more closely evaluated. It is also important to encourage psychiatric treatment studies to include a systematic assessment of suicidal behavior, even if this is not their primary focus.

In addition to the general evaluation concerns noted above, treatment evaluations need to give particular attention to building appropriate safeguards into treatment trials involving high-risk youth populations. Maintaining troubled youth in treatment trials over an adequate period of time to observe both short- and long-term outcomes is a particular challenge. Time-limited treatments, while easier to evaluate, leave unresolved questions about long-term effectiveness. Although control or comparison groups are essential, the inclusion of such groups necessitates ethical consideration of appropriate "control" treatments. Few studies involving treatments for suicidality among youth have adequately defined or measured the therapeutic effects of treatment as usual.

The ultimate criteria for effectiveness in suicide prevention remain reduction in suicide attempts and suicide deaths, events for which the population base rate is low. The primary limitation of virtually all studies of the effectiveness of treatments for suicidal patients has been their relatively small size and thus their limited power to detect significant differences between or among alternative strategies (Hawton & Sinclair, 2003). Enrolling adequate numbers of appropriate participants into treatment trials can best be achieved through a number of centrally coordinated treatment research centers that can pursue common studies of treatment effectiveness. We know, for example, that antidepressant medication is effective against depression, and there is suggestive but not conclusive evidence that it reduces suicide in both adolescents and adults. Treatment research centers would make it possible to determine if this is so, to identify which medications are most effective, and to determine what degree their effectiveness is increased by combining them with various forms of psychotherapy. The formation of such centers was a primary recommendation of a recent Institute of Medicine report on suicide (Goldsmith, Pellmar, Kleinman, & Bunney, 2002).

Youth who engage in suicidal behavior vary considerably with respect to specific forms of psychopathology, substance abuse, and other psychosocial problems, and treatment trials must address this variability (Hawton & Sinclair, 2003). Particular protections must be developed to allow inclusion in such trials of suicidal youth with serious alcohol and drug problems, which confers considerable risk for subsequent attempts and suicide death.

In assessing the outcomes of treatment studies primary measures should focus on suicide-related outcomes, specifically suicidal ideation and behavior, and should also include as secondary outcomes measures of mood and social functioning. Based on their review of RCTs that have used repeated suicidal behavior as an outcome, Hawton and Sinclair (2003) have emphasized the importance of including measures of deliberate self-harm that did not lead to medical treatment. Their analysis also points to the importance of including measures of the costs of various intervention programs, and their cost-effectiveness, in assessing the impact of treatment strategies on reducing suicidality.

Finally, longitudinal studies are needed to follow up suicidal or at-risk youth through their young-adult, middle-adult, and later life years. It is clear that psychopathology can be lethal, and sustained attention to the problems evidenced by this vulnerable population is needed across the lifespan.

Beyond Disorder

COMMISSION ON POSITIVE YOUTH DEVELOPMENT

Martin E.P. Seligman, *Commission Chair*

Marvin W. Berkowitz

Richard F. Catalano

William Damon

Jacquelynne S. Eccles

Jane E. Gillham

Kristin A. Moore

Heather Johnston Nicholson

Nansook Park

David L. Penn

Christopher Peterson

Margaret Shih

Tracy A. Steen

Robert J. Sternberg

Joseph P. Tierney

Roger P. Weissberg

Jonathan F. Zaff

part VII

The Positive Perspective on Youth Development

chapter

26

How can we promote the mental health of children and adolescents? Earlier sections in this volume have provided one answer to this question by reviewing what is known about the treatment and prevention of psychological disorders among youth: anxiety, depression and suicide, substance abuse, eating disorders, and schizophrenia. As valuable as these reviews are, the insights they provide are necessarily incomplete.

Imagine a society in which no young person meets the diagnostic criteria for mental illness, because treatment and prevention have been pervasively and perfectly implemented. No one reports any symptoms of a disorder. All risks have been purged. In such a society, individual suffering due to psychological problems is eliminated, along with staggering societal costs. *Such a society is still not a psychological utopia.* There are huge differences between a teenager who is not depressed or anxious and one who bounds out of bed in the morning with twinkling eyes; between an adolescent who says no to drugs and one who says yes to meaningful involvement in family, school, and community activities; and between one who costs society little and one who actually benefits it.

The field of mental health has long been one of mental illness negated, but young people who are problem-free are not fully prepared for the business of life, not if skill, talent, character, happiness, engagement, and social involvement are its hallmarks (Pittman, 1991, 2000). As important as it is to reduce or eliminate problems among children and adolescents, it is just as important to help them thrive and form positive connections to the larger world. If asked what they most desire for their children, few parents would say that "falling short of DSM diagnostic criteria" is their primary wish. Rather, parents want their children to be safe, healthy, happy, moral, fully engaged in life, and productive contributors to the communities in which they live (Noddings, 2003). These are the ultimate goals not only of all capable parents but of all viable societies.

So how can we promote the mental health of children and adolescents? In decades of focus on psychopathology, clinical psychology, psychiatry, and allied disciplines have begun the task of improving the lives of young people and the adults they will become. Effective treatment strategies and risk-based prevention programs such as those described earlier in this volume are among our most notable scientific achievements. But they represent a journey just begun. In recent years, these traditional approaches—all based on a disease model in which well-being is defined only by the absence of distress and disorder—have been challenged. Calls have been made for balanced attention to the positive aspects of human development as well as the negative ones.

Several contemporary approaches address people from the positive perspective—e.g., assets-based community development, competence-based primary prevention, the cultural strengths perspective, positive organizational studies, positive psychology, positive youth development, strengths-based social work, and the whole-school reform movement, among others (Maton, Schellenbach, Leadbetter, & Solarz, 2003; Peterson, 2004). These approaches overlap substantially in their basic assumptions about the authenticity of human excellence, meaning that clear distinctions among them are not always possible or even necessary. In the present contribution, we focus on positive youth development because of its explicit concern with how to encourage the well-being of children and adolescents. We also draw on positive psychology because of its interest in the underlying psychological processes leading to well-being and optimal functioning.

We should be explicit that the history of the positive perspective on youth development long predates its explicit recognition as a common viewpoint. Some of the best-known youth programs in the United States—e.g., YWCA of the USA (1851), YMCA of the USA (1855), Boys Clubs (1860) and Girls Clubs of America (1906), Girls Incorporated (1864), American Red Cross (1881), Big Brothers (1903)/Big Sisters (1908) of America, Boy Scouts of America (1910), Camp Fire USA (1910), Girl Scouts of the USA (1912), and 4-H (1914)—were founded a century or more ago to promote the health and character of young people through structured activities (Erickson, 1999). Today's positive perspective is rediscovering and reaffirming the premise of these programs.

More recently setting the stage for the positive perspective on development are humanistic psychology as popularized by Rogers (1951) and Maslow (1970); utopian visions of education such as those of Neill (1960); primary prevention programs based on notions of wellness, sometimes dubbed "promotion programs," as pioneered by Albee (1982) and Cowen (1994); developmental theories emphasizing person–envionment interactions (e.g., Bronfenbrenner, 1979; Lerner & Kauffman, 1985); work by Bandura (1989) and others on human agency; studies of giftedness, genius, and talent (e.g., Winner, 2000); conceptions of intelligence as multiple (e.g., Gardner, 1983; Sternberg, 1985); and studies of the quality of life among psychiatric patients that went beyond an exclusive focus on symptoms and diseases (e.g., Levitt, Hogan, & Bucosky, 1990).

We should also note that the positive perspective on youth development is still evolving, and there are still gaps in the work. Notably, the positive perspective has been embraced most strongly by social scientists, who by and large have *not* placed optimal development in its biological context. All acknowledge that physical health, good nutrition, and safety importantly set the stage for positive development, and there is a growing interest in, for example, the ways in which temperament influences positive affect and life satisfaction. But the positive perspective is still detailed largely in terms of environmental and/or purely psychological (cognitive, emotional, and behavioral) influences on development, which makes it challenging to meld this perspective with the increasingly biological approach on disorder taken by psychiatrists and clinical psychologists. As the positive perspective matures, it will need to take into full account the contribution of biogenetic factors.

We stress that there is no incompatibility between a positive approach and one that is informed by biology (cf. Wright, 1994). When we criticize the "disease model," we do not deny the existence of disorder or the important contribution of biology to disorder. Rather, we are criticizing this model as a global vision of human nature. The positive perspective is the necessary complement to one that focuses on disorder (and vice versa).

Another area in which the positive perspective must expand is the role of culture in defining and determining optimal development. Youth development practitioners have long taken seriously the importance of cultural (i.e., ethnic) differences within the United States, but a great deal of theorizing and research addresses youth development only as it occurs in the United States. The scope of this work must eventually include youth around the world, and we can expect to find both similarities and differences (e.g., Park, Huebner, Laughlin, Valois, & Gilman, 2004).

A third gap, or at least shortcoming, of the positive perspective is that some of its advocates may strike the skeptic as naively enthusiastic. Grim reality seems to be glossed over, and claims seem to be exaggerated beyond available evidence. We have argued elsewhere for the need to be even-handed about being positive (Peterson & Park, 2003) and for the importance of checking theories against the facts of the matter (Peterson & Seligman, 2003). As important as it is for social science to acknowledge and study human excellence, prescription should not override description and explanation. The positive perspective obviously resides in a value-laden domain, but so too does a focus on disease and distress, albeit more subtly. To be taken most seriously, the positive perspective needs to be based on good science. Enough good science already exists to justify continued interest in the positive perspective.

Our goal in the present contribution is to review the positive perspective as it exists today and use it to complement the more problem-oriented disciplines (cf. Larson, 2000; Maton et al., 2003). A balanced view of youth must acknowledge assets along with problems, addressing the good and the bad within youth in tandem, including risk factors and protective factors (Pollard, Hawkins, & Arthur, 1999). We have two working assumptions, each buttressed by some suggestive evidence:

1. The sorts of psychological characteristics of interest to positive social scientists are associated with reduced problems and increased well-being among youth.
2. Youth development programs with specifia-

ble features can encourage these positive characteristics and at the same time increase the likelihood of desired outcomes.

Not only are positive characteristics valuable in their own right, but they may buffer against the development of psychological problems among youth. Attention to positive characteristics may help us promote the full potential of all youth, including those with current or past psychological problems.

This contribution therefore addresses positive youth development with respect to mental illness *and* mental health. We discuss positive characteristics of youth and their settings and how these are related to thriving. We summarize what is known about programs and institutions that promote positive development. In conclusion, we take stock of what we know and what we do not know.

WHAT IS POSITIVE YOUTH DEVELOPMENT?

The field of *positive youth development* recognizes the good in young people, focusing on each and every child's unique talents, strengths, interests, and future potential (Damon, 2004). As much as we want to raise up children of soundest body and mind, those with straight A grades and perfect school attendance, kids who play in the marching band and star on a high school sports team, the real world is not Lake Woebegone. Real youth, no less than real adults, are a mix of those whose lives are above average and those who are not doing well at all. Some adolescents are anxious and depressed; some develop eating disorders; some use drugs and take other risks; some drop out of school; some become pregnant; and some fail to find praiseworthy pursuits in or out of school.

What are we to make of these young people? The positive perspective avoids labeling them as across-the-board failures. Calling someone a schizophrenic, a depressive, a drug user, or a high school dropout overlooks what else may be true about that individual. John Nash, Abraham Lincoln, Edgar Allan Poe, and Peter Jennings could be respectively labeled with these dismis-

sive terms, but to do so is to overlook remarkable lives and the people who have lived them.

To be sure, the problems for which these labels are shorthand are nothing to ignore and certainly nothing to glorify. We applaud those who attempt to prevent, minimize, or undo such problems, in themselves and in others. But the positive perspective urges that these problems be placed in the context of the whole person. Attention to what is good about a young person provides a foundation on which to base interventions that target what is not so good. In particular, the positive perspective urges us not to give up on children, no matter what problems they may have experienced.

These assertions seem obvious, but positive youth development nonetheless stands in contrast with approaches that have focused solely on the problems that some young people encounter while growing up, problems such as learning disabilities; affective disorders; antisocial conduct; low motivation and poor achievement; drinking, smoking, and drug use; psychosocial crises triggered by maturational episodes such as puberty; and risks of neglect, abuse, and economic deprivation that plague certain populations. Models of youth that focus on these problems have long held sway in the child-care professions, the mass media, and much of the public mind. In such models, youth is seen as a period fraught with hazards, and many young people are seen as potential problems that must be straightened out before they can do serious harm to themselves or others. This problem-centered vision of youth has dominated most of the professional fields charged with raising the young.

In education and pediatric medicine, for example, a huge share of resources has been directed to remediating the incapacities of young people with syndromes such as attention-deficit/hyperactivity disorder. In child psychology, intense attention has been directed to self-esteem deficits, especially among girls; to damage created by childhood trauma such as poverty, abuse, and early separation; and to destructive patterns such as violence. Descriptions such as the *at-risk child*, the *learning-disabled child*, the *juvenile delinquent*, the *bully*, and even the *super-predator* have filled professional journals as well as the popular press. The old suspicion that there are "bad seeds," or, switching metaphors, that there are "rotten apples" that will spoil the barrel if not removed in time has been kept alive in the guise of scientific theories that propose a genetic determinism for youth crime. The job of youth professionals has been to identify the problem early enough to defray and then patch up the damage.

This focus on problems and deficits is part of a mental health model left over from the work of child psychoanalysts such as Fritz Redl (Redl & Wineman, 1951). It is also drawn from a criminal justice model that has stressed punishment over prevention and rehabilitation. One of the legacies of this problem-focused tradition has been its influence on the way young people have been portrayed in the mass culture and, as a consequence, in the popular mind. "According to a recent examination of a month of network and local TV news coverage of American youth . . . just 2% of teenagers were shown at home, while only 1% were portrayed in a work setting. In contrast, the criminal justice system accounted for nearly one out of every five visual backdrops" (Communitarian Network, 2000). A recent survey of adults in the United States found that the majority describe youth in negative terms and believe that young people will leave the world in worse shape than they found it (Public Agenda Online, 1999).

But during the past two decades or so, the field of youth development has articulated a more affirmative vision of young people as resources rather than as problems for society. This vision focuses on the manifest potentials rather than on the supposed incapacities of young people— including young people from the most disadvantaged backgrounds and those with the most troubled histories.

The positive youth development approach recognizes the existence of adversities and developmental challenges that may affect children in various ways, but it resists conceiving of the developmental process as mainly an effort to overcome deficits and risk. Instead, it begins with a vision of a fully able child eager to explore the world, to gain competence, and to acquire the capacity to contribute importantly to the world. The positive youth development ap-

proach aims at understanding, educating, and engaging children in productive activities rather than at correcting, curing, or treating them for maladaptive tendencies or so-called disabilities.

As already noted, the change brought about by this shift to a more positive vision of youth potential has taken place on a number of fronts. Positive youth development today is an interdisciplinary field with roots in developmental psychology, developmental epidemiology, and prevention science (Larson, 2000). It embraces an explicit developmental stance: children and adolescents are not miniature adults, and they need to be understood in their own terms.

The youth development field emphasizes the multiple contexts in which development occurs. Particularly influential as an organizing framework has been Bronfenbrenner's (1977, 1979, 1986) *ecological approach,* which articulates different contexts in terms of their immediacy to the behaving individual. So, the *microsystem* refers to ecologies with which the individual directly interacts: family, peers, school, and neighborhood. The *mesosystem* is Bronfenbrenner's term for relationships between and among various microsystems. The *exosystem* is made up of larger ecologies that indirectly affect development and behavior, such as the legal system, the social welfare system, and mass media. Finally, the *macrosystem* consists of broad ideological and institutional patterns that collectively define a culture. There is the risk of losing the individual amid all of these systems, but the developmental perspective reminds us that different children are not interchangeable puppets. Each young person brings his or her own characteristics to the business of life, and these interact with the different ecologies to produce behavior.

The youth development field has always had a strong interest in application (Catalano, Berglund, Ryan, Lonczak, & Hawkins, 1999). From their very beginning, national youth groups embraced promotion goals, but throughout the 20th century other applications were increasingly directed at youth problems such as school dropout, juvenile crime, alcohol and drug use, and unwanted pregnancy. These early interventions often targeted young people in crisis—i.e., they helped youth with problems—and the more recent interventions were preventive—i.e., they supported youth before problems developed. The earliest applications were informed more by common sense and intuition than by research. This state of affairs has changed in light of information from longitudinal studies about the predictors of specific problems (e.g., Jessor & Jessor, 1977). This information provides explicit targets for interventions, and theory has begun to guide practice.

Another change that occurred as the field of youth development matured is that prevention efforts targeting but a single problem came under criticism. Many problems co-occur and have the same risk factors. Broad-based interventions can therefore have broad effects. Part of the broadening of youth development and its applications was a call for studying and eventually cultivating what has come to be known as positive youth development—desirable outcomes such as school achievement, vocational aspirations, community involvement, good interpersonal relations, and the like. Pittman (1991, 2000) has phrased this change, "problem-free is not fully prepared." Here is where youth development converges with positive psychology and its premise that the best in life is not simply the absence of disorder and dysfunction.

As an applied field, youth development marches to the drummer of societal priorities. At least as far as the nation's youth are concerned, the reduction in their problems has been the priority, for good reasons. "Positive" outcomes can be a difficult sell when juxtaposed with tax cuts, pothole repairs, and defense spending. But there is ample reason to believe that attention to positive outcomes has the additional effect of reducing negative outcomes. Researchers at the Search Institute in Minneapolis have studied what they call *developmental assets,* which include external factors such as family support and adult role models and internal factors such as commitment to learning, positive values, and sense of purpose (Benson, Leffert, Scales, & Blyth, 1998; Leffert et al., 1998; Scales, Benson, Leffert, & Blyth, 2000). Youth with more of these assets not only show fewer problems but also display more thriving (e.g., school success, leadership, helping others, and physical health).

Among the important ideas that frame this emerging positive vision of youth are the following:

1. Children can overcome adversity and thrive. Many by nature are hardy, not delicate. The term *resiliency* is used to describe the quality that enables young people to thrive even in the face of adversity (Werner, 1982). Associated with resiliency are persistence, hardiness, goal-directedness, an orientation to success, achievement motivation, educational aspirations, a belief in the future, a sense of anticipation, a sense of purpose, and a sense of coherence (Benard, 1991).

2. It is important to recognize, however, that resiliency does not operate in a vacuum. Few if any children are impervious to unrelenting adversity. Without appropriate environmental or social support, children will likely succumb to problems. What allows young people to thrive is a combination of individual hardiness *and* protective factors embedded in socializing institutions (cf. Bonnano, 2004).

3. Accordingly, the assets of youth that protect against problems and allow young people to do well include not only individual psychological characteristics such as talents, energies, strengths, and constructive interests but also characteristics of their social settings such as family support, parental involvement in schooling, adult role models outside the family, high expectations within the community, and the availability of creative activities (Benson, 1997). The agenda of positive youth development is to maximize the potential of young people by encouraging both personal and environmental assets. To do so requires a recognition of the reciprocal relation between them (Bronfenbrenner & Ceci, 1994; Riegel, 1973).

4. The emerging positive youth development tradition takes a deliberately broad perspective on the qualities of young people that should be promoted. For example, following extensive literature reviews and consensus meetings of experts in the field, Catalano, Berglund, Ryan, Lonczak, and Hawkins (2004) identified the following goals of positive youth development.

Promoting bonding. *Bonding* is the emotional attachment and commitment a child makes to social relationships in the family, peer group, school, community, or culture. Child development studies frequently describe bonding and attachment processes as internal working models for means by which a child forms social connections with others (Ainsworth, Blehar, Waters, & Wall, 1978; Bowlby, 1969, 1973, 1980; Mahler, Pine, & Bergman, 1975). The interactions between a child and his or her caregivers build the foundation for bonding that is key to the development of the child's capacity for motivated behavior (Erikson, 1968). Positive bonding with an adult is crucial to the development of a capacity for adaptive responses to change, and growth into a healthy and functional adult. Good bonding establishes the child's trust in self and others. Inadequate bonding establishes patterns of insecurity and self-doubt. Very poor bonding establishes a fundamental mistrust in self and others, creating an emotional emptiness that the child may try to fill in other ways, possibly through drugs, impulsive acts, antisocial peer relations, or other problem behaviors (Braucht, Kirby, & Berry, 1978; Brook, Brook, Gordon, Whiteman, & Cohen, 1990; Kandel, Kessler, & Margulies, 1978).

The importance of bonding reaches beyond the family. How a child establishes early bonds to caregivers will directly affect the manner in which the child later bonds to peers, school, the community, and culture(s). The quality of a child's bonds to these other domains are essential aspects of positive development into a healthy adult (Brophy, 1988; Brophy & Good, 1986; Dolan, Kellam, & Brown, 1989; Hawkins, Catalano, & Miller, 1992). Strategies to promote positive bonding combined with the development of skills have proven to be an effective intervention for adolescents at risk for antisocial behavior (Caplan et al., 1992; Dryfoos, 1990).

Fostering of resiliency. *Resilience* refers to any instance of displayed competence despite adversity, whereas *resiliency* is the individual's capacity to adapt to stressful events in healthy and flexible ways (Luthar, Cicchetti, & Becker, 2000). As already described, resiliency has been identified in research studies as a characteristic of youth who, when exposed to multiple risk factors, show successful responses to challenge and use this learning to achieve successful outcomes (Hawkins, Catalano, & Miller, 1992; Masten, Best, & Garmezy, 1990; Rutter, 1985; Werner, 1989, 1995).

Promoting competencies. The construct of *competence* covers at least five areas of youth functioning—specifically, social, emotional, cognitive, behavioral, and moral abilities. The multidimensionality of competence has been increasingly recognized in the past two decades (Gardner, 1993; Harter, 1985; Zigler & Berman, 1983). More recently, Weissberg and Greenberg (1997) urged that competence be viewed and measured in research studies as an important developmental outcome. While the enhancement of competence can help to prevent negative outcomes (Botvin, Baker, Dusenbury, Botvin, & Diaz, 1995), competence can also be specified and measured as an important outcome in its own right, indicative of positive development.

Social competence encompasses the range of interpersonal skills that help youth integrate feelings, thinking, and actions to achieve specific social and interpersonal goals (Caplan et al., 1992; Weissberg, Caplan, & Sivo, 1989). These skills include encoding relevant social cues, accurately interpreting those social cues, generating effective solutions to interpersonal problems, realistically anticipating consequences and potential obstacles to one's actions, and translating social decisions into effective behavior.

In a review of 650 articles on biopsychosocial risk factors and preventive interventions, Kornberg and Caplan (1980) concluded that competence training to promote adaptive behavior and mental health is one of the most significant developments in recent primary prevention research. In general, social competence promotion programs have been designed to enhance personal and interpersonal effectiveness and to prevent the development of maladaptive behavior through *(a)* teaching students developmentally appropriate skills and information, *(b)* fostering prosocial and health-enhancing values and beliefs, and *(c)* creating environmental supports to reinforce the real-life application of skills (Weissberg et al., 1989). To produce meaningful effects on specific target behaviors, it also appears necessary to include opportunities for students to practice and apply learned skills to specific, relevant social tasks (Hawkins & Weis, 1985).

Emotional competence is the ability to identify and respond to feelings and emotional reactions in oneself and others. Salovey and Mayer (1989) identified five elements of emotional competence, including knowing one's emotions, managing emotions, motivating oneself, recognizing emotions in others, and handling relationships. The W. T. Grant Consortium on the School-Based Promotion of Social Competence (1992, p. 136) provided a similar list of emotional skills that are ingredients of many prevention programs: "identifying and labeling feelings, expressing feelings, assessing the intensity of feelings, managing feelings, delaying gratification, controlling impulses, and reducing stress."

Cognitive competence includes two overlapping constructs. The W. T. Grant Consortium on the School-Based Promotion of Social Competence (1992, p. 136) defined the first form of cognitive competence as the "ability to develop and apply the cognitive skills of self-talk, the reading and interpretation of social cues, using steps for problem-solving and decision-making, understanding the perspective of others, understanding behavioral norms, a positive attitude toward life, and self awareness." The second aspect of cognitive competence is related to academic and intellectual achievement. The emphasis here is on the development of core capacities, including the ability to use logic, analytic thinking, and abstract reasoning.

Behavioral competence encompasses the skills required for effective action. The W. T. Grant Consortium on the School-Based Promotion of Social Competence (1992, p. 136) identified three dimensions of behavioral competence: "nonverbal communication (through facial expressions, tone of voice, style of dress, gesture or eye contact), verbal communication (making clear requests, responding effectively to criticism, expressing feelings clearly), and taking action (helping others, walking away from negative situations, participating in positive activities)."

Moral competence is a youth's ability to assess and respond to the ethical, affective, or social justice dimensions of a situation. Piaget (1952, 1965) described moral maturity as both a respect

for rules and a sense of social justice. Kohlberg (1963, 1969, 1981) defined moral development as a multistage process through which children acquire society's standards of right and wrong, focusing on choices made in facing moral dilemmas. Gilligan (1982) countered that morality is as much about relationships and interdependence as it is about societal rules, and Hoffman (1981) proposed that the roots of morality are in empathy, or empathic arousal, which has a neurological basis and can be either fostered or suppressed by environmental influences. He also asserted that empathic arousal eventually becomes an important mediator of altruism, a quality that many youth interventions try to promote in young people.

Encouraging self-determination. Self-determination is the ability to think for oneself and to take action consistent with those thoughts. Fetterman, Kaftarian, and Wandersman (1996) defined self-determination as the ability to chart one's own course. Much of the literature on self-determination has emerged from work with disabled youth (Brotherson, Cook, Lahr, & Wehmeyer, 1995; Field, 1996; Sands & Doll, 1996; Wehmeyer, 1996) and from cultural identity work with ethnic and minority populations (Snyder & Zoann, 1994; Swisher, 1996). Although some writers have expressed concern that self-determination may emphasize individual development at the expense of group-oriented values (Ewalt & Mokuau, 1995), others link self-determination to innate psychological needs for competence, autonomy, and relatedness (Deci & Ryan, 1994).

Fostering spirituality. Spirituality has been associated in some research with the development of a youth's moral reasoning, moral commitment, or a belief in the moral order (Hirschi, 1969; Stark & Bainbridge, 1997). Recent reviews of the relationship between religiosity and adolescent well-being have found that religiosity is positively associated with prosocial values and behavior, and negatively related to suicide ideation and attempts, substance abuse, premature sexual involvement, and delinquency (Johnson, Tierney, & Siegel, 2003).

Developing self-efficacy. Self-efficacy is the perception that one can achieve desired goals through one's own action. Bandura (1989,

p. 1175) proposed that "self-efficacy beliefs function as an important set of proximal determinants of human motivation, affect, and action. They operate on action through motivational, cognitive, and affective intervening processes." Strategies associated with self-efficacy beliefs include personal goal setting, which is influenced by self-appraisal of one's capabilities (Bandura, 1986, 1993). Others have documented that the stronger the perceived self-efficacy, the higher the goals people set for themselves and the firmer their commitment to them (Locke, Frederick, Lee, & Bobko, 1984).

Nurturing a clear and positive identity.   Clear and positive identity is the internal organization of a coherent sense of self. The construct is associated with the theory of identity development emerging from studies of how children establish their identities across different social contexts, cultural groups, and genders. Identity is viewed as a "self-structure," an internal, self-constructed, dynamic organization of drives, abilities, beliefs, and individual history, which is shaped by the child's navigation of normal crises or challenges at each stage of development (Erikson, 1968). Erikson described overlapping yet distinct stages of psychosocial development that influence a child's sense of identity throughout life, but which are especially critical in the first 20 years. If the adolescent or young adult does not achieve a healthy identity, role confusion can result. Developmental theorists assert that successful identity achievement during adolescence depends on the child's successful resolution of earlier stages.

Stages of identity development are linked to gender differences in childhood and adolescence, revealing a series of identity aspects for girls that are not strictly parallel to those of boys (Gilligan, 1982). Investigations of the positive identity development of gay and bisexual youth have become a focus for some researchers (Johnston & Bell, 1995). For youth of color, the development of positive identity and its role in healthy psychological functioning is closely linked with the development of ethnic identity (Mendelberg, 1986; Parham & Helms, 1985; Phinney, 1990, 1991; Phinney, Lochner, & Murphy, 1990; Plummer, 1995), issues of bicultural identification (Phinney & Devich-Navarro,

1997), and bicultural or cross-cultural competence (LaFromboise, Coleman, & Gerton, 1993; LaFromboise & Rowe, 1983). Some researchers have suggested that it is healthy for ethnic minority youth to be socialized to understand the multiple demands and expectations of both the majority and minority culture (Spencer, 1990; Spencer & Markstrom-Adams, 1990). This process may offer psychological protection through providing a sense of identity that captures the strengths of the ethnic culture and helps buffer experiences of racism and other risk factors (Hill, Piper, & Moberg, 1994). This may also enhance prosocial bonding to adults who can help youths to counter potential interpersonal violence in their peer groups (Wilson, 1990).

Fostering belief in the future.   Belief in the future is the internalization of hope and optimism about possible outcomes. This construct is linked to studies on long-range goal setting, belief in higher education, and beliefs that support employment or work values. "Having a future gives a teenager reasons for trying and reasons for valuing his life" (Prothrow-Stith, 1991, p. 57). Research demonstrates that positive future expectations predict better social and emotional adjustment in school and a stronger internal locus of control, while acting as a protective factor in reducing the negative effects of high stress on self-rated competence (Wyman, Cowen, Work, & Kerley, 1993).

Recognizing positive behavior.   Recognition for positive involvement is the positive response of those in the social environment to desired behaviors by youths. According to social learning theory, behavior is in large part a consequence of the reinforcement or lack of reinforcement that follows action (Akers, Krohn, Lanza-Kaduce, & Radosevich, 1979; Bandura, 1973). Reinforcement affects an individual's motivation to engage in similar behavior in the future. Social reinforcers have major effects on behavior. These social reinforcers can come from the peer group, family, school, or community.

Providing opportunities for prosocial involvement. Opportunity for prosocial involvement is the presentation of events and activities across different social environments that encourage youths to participate in prosocial actions. The provision of prosocial opportunities in the nonschool hours has been the focus of much discussion and study (Carnegie Council on Adolescent Development, 1992; Pittman, 1991). For a child to acquire key interpersonal skills in early development, positive opportunities for interaction and participation must be available (Hawkins, Catalano, Jones, & Fine, 1987; Patterson, Chamberlain, & Reid, 1982; Pentz et al., 1989). In adolescence, it is especially important that youth have the opportunity for interaction with positively oriented peers and for involvement in roles in which they can make a contribution to the group, whether family, school, neighborhood, peer group, or larger community (Dryfoos, 1990).

Establishing prosocial norms. Social institutions that foster prosocial norms seek to encourage youth to adopt healthy beliefs and clear standards for behavior through a range of approaches. These may include providing youth with data about the small numbers of people their age who use illegal drugs, so that they decide that they do not need to use drugs to be normal; encouraging youth to make explicit commitments in the presence of peers or mentors not to use drugs or to skip school; involving older youth in communicating healthy standards for behavior to younger children; or encouraging youth to identify personal goals and set standards for themselves that will help them achieve these goals (Hawkins, Catalano, & Miller, 1992; Hawkins, Catalano, Morrison, O'Donnell, Abbott, & Day, 1992).

WHAT IS POSITIVE PSYCHOLOGY?

The field of positive psychology was christened in 1998 as one of the initiatives of Martin Seligman in his role as President of the American Psychological Association (Seligman, 1998, 1999). The trigger for positive psychology was the premise that psychology since World War II has focused much of its efforts on human problems and how to remedy them. The yield of this focus on pathology has been considerable. Great strides have been made in understanding, treating, and preventing psychological disorders. Widely accepted classification manuals—the *Diagnostic and Statistical Manual of Mental Disorders*

(DSM) sponsored by the American Psychiatric Association (1994) and the *International Classification of Diseases* (ICD) sponsored by the World Health Organization (1990)—allow disorders to be described and have given rise to a family of reliable assessment strategies. There now exist effective treatments, psychological and pharmacological, for more than a dozen disorders that in the recent past were frighteningly intractable (Barrett & Ollendick, 2004 Hibbs & Jensen, 1996; Kazdin & Weisz, 2003; Nathan & Gorman, 1998, 2002; Seligman, 1994).

But there has been a cost to this emphasis. Much of scientific psychology has neglected the study of what can go right with people and often has little more to say about the good life than do pop psychologists, inspirational speakers, and armchair gurus. More subtly, the underlying assumptions of psychology have shifted to embrace a disease model of human nature. Human beings are seen as flawed and fragile, casualties of cruel environments or bad genetics, and if not in denial then at best in recovery. This worldview has crept into the common culture of the United States. We have become a nation of self-identified victims, and our heroes and heroines are called survivors and nothing more.

Positive psychology proposes that it is time to correct this imbalance and to challenge the pervasive assumptions of the disease model (Maddux, 2002). Proponents of positive psychology call for as much focus on strength as on weakness, as much interest in building the best things in life as in repairing the worst, and as much attention to fulfilling the lives of healthy people as to healing the wounds of the distressed (Seligman, 2002; Seligman & Csikszentmihalyi, 2000). The concern of psychology with human problems is of course understandable. It will not and should not be abandoned; people experience difficulties that demand and deserve scientifically informed solutions. Positive psychologists are merely saying that the psychology of the past 60 years is incomplete. But as simple as this proposal sounds, it demands a sea change in perspective. Psychologists interested in promoting human potential need to start with different assumptions and to pose different questions from their peers who assume only a disease model.

The most basic assumption that positive psychology urges is that human goodness and excellence are as authentic as disease, disorder, and distress. Positive psychologists are adamant that these topics not be secondary, derivative, illusory, epiphenomenal, or otherwise suspect. The good news for positive psychology is that our generalizations about business-as-usual psychology over the past 60 years are simply that—generalizations. As already noted, there are many good examples of psychological research, past and present, that can be claimed as positive psychology.

Positive psychologists do not claim to have invented notions of happiness and well-being, or even to have ushered in their scientific study. Rather, the contribution of positive psychology has been to provide an umbrella term for what have been isolated lines of theory and research and to make the self-conscious argument that what makes life worth living deserves its own field of inquiry within psychology, at least until that day when all of psychology embraces the study of what is good along with the study of what is bad.

Within the framework of positive psychology (Seligman & Csikszentmihalyi, 2000) one can find a comprehensive scheme for understanding and promoting positive youth development. Research and practice efforts should include the domains identified by positive psychology as critical in thriving. We can parse the concerns of positive psychology into three related topics: the study of *positive subjective experiences* (happiness, pleasure, gratification, fulfillment), the study of *positive individual traits* (strengths of character, talents, interests, values), and the study of *enabling institutions* (families, schools, businesses, communities, societies). A theory is implied here: Enabling institutions facilitate the development and display of positive traits, which in turn facilitate positive subjective experiences (Park & Peterson, 2003).

The term *facilitate* deliberately avoids strict causal language. It is possible for people to be happy or content even in the absence of good character, and people can have good character even when living outside the realm of enabling institutions. The example of apartheid's demise in South Africa shows that citizens can do the right thing even in the face of historical prece-

dent. The example of whistleblowers shows that employees do not always conform with workplace norms. And the example of excellent students from underfunded school districts shows that intellectual curiosity is not always stamped out by educational mediocrity.

But matters are simpler when institutions, traits, and experiences are in alignment (cf. Gardner, Csikszentmihalyi, & Damon, 2001). Indeed, doing well in life probably represents a coming together of these three domains and demonstrates why positive psychology and positive youth development programs are potentially good partners.

Psychologists have only recently devoted their full attention to the conceptualization and measurement of core positive psychology constructs such as life satisfaction and strength of character. And even more recent is the examination of these constructs among young people. Regardless, we believe that these are important. They contribute to a variety of positive outcomes and at the same time work as a buffer against a variety of negative outcomes, including psychological disorders. Life satisfaction and character strengths serve not only as key indicators of positive youth development but also as broad enabling factors in the promotion and maintenance of optimal mental health among youth. The task in applying these notions to the field of youth development is to understand how they confer benefits and, ultimately, how they can be deliberately encouraged.

YOUTH DEVELOPMENT FROM THE POSITIVE PERSPECTIVE

Despite its initially radical notions about young people, the positive youth development perspective has become so widely endorsed, at least in the abstract, that the label is sometimes used to describe any and all programs that involve young people. The result is that the self-identified positive youth development field is sprawling. In an overview of the youth development field, Benson and Saito (2000, p. 136) went so far as to conclude that "if one commissioned 10 writers to compose reviews of what we know about youth development, 10 very different papers would emerge. Perhaps a few studies and a few names would be constant. Ultimately, the overlap in references cited would be minimal." We are not as dismayed about the coherence of the youth development field as these authors, but we do agree with their conclusion that "the conceptual terrain is murky" (p. 136).

In the contemporary United States alone, the vast majority of the 30+ million adolescents participate in one or more programs or organizations with other young people: middle school, high school, church groups, mentoring programs, Little League baseball, the Boy Scouts of America, and other after-school programs. Many of these programs have adopted "positive" language to frame their goals and rationales. But we stop short of calling all of these programs positive in their actual stance toward youth. Consider, for example, juvenile boot camp programs that try to scare children "straight" (Tyler, Darville, & Stalnaker, 2001). And we certainly refrain from saying that all of these programs succeed; otherwise 99+% of our young people would be doing extremely well.

Part of the human condition, in the contemporary United States as well as elsewhere, is the embeddedness of individuals in multiple social systems—some that encourage thriving and some that do not. A close and analytic look is needed, not just at existing outcome evidence but also at the actual programs in which young people participate and the active ingredients in those programs that work (Larson, 2000). Positive psychology provides a way to think about the goals of positive youth development and how they are achieved. If we are trying to develop young people, just what is our destination, and how will we know that we have arrived— that positive development has indeed occurred?

Everyday people may equate happiness with momentary positive affect, but positive psychology proposes that "authentic" happiness is a broad concept that includes three distinct orientations to life (Seligman, 2002). First is the *pursuit of pleasure,* the venerable doctrine of hedonism and the underpinning of psychoanalysis and all but the most radical of the behaviorisms. We may not want our children to become hedonists or epicureans, but we certainly want them to be full of cheer, free of worry, and content with the choices they have made. Second is the *pursuit of engagement,* involvement and absorption in activities that produce the state of flow. We want our children to find activities at school, at play, and eventually at work in which they can lose themselves. Third is the *pursuit of meaning* in which one attempts to connect with external factors or forces larger than the self by embracing social responsibility or experiencing the immaterial and transcendent. We want our children to make a life that matters to the world and creates a difference for the better.

The vision of the thriving youth that emerges here is a young person who experiences more positive affect than negative affect, who is satisfied with his or her life as it has been lived, who has identified what he or she does well and uses these talents and strengths in a variety of fulfilling pursuits; and who is a contributing member of a social community. And, of course, safety and health are importantly in place as the context of this vision. From the perspective of positive psychology, a positive youth development program is one that effectively targets one or more of these facets. It is worth noting that business-as-usual clinical psychology and psychiatry have been concerned with but one of these features: the reduction of negative affect (i.e., depression and anxiety).

As explained already, youth development proponents have also addressed the vision of a healthy child, and their lists of desirable attributes overlap considerably with what we have just specified:

- Benson (1997) proposed a number of developmental assets (discussed earlier).
- Also popular are the alliterative five Cs: caring, competence, character, connection, and confidence (cf. Roth & Brooks-Gunn, 2003).
- The National Research Council Committee on Community-based Programs for Youth similarly proposed that positive youth possess good health habits; knowledge of life skills; emotional self-regulation; optimism; prosocial values; spirituality or a sense of purpose; trusting relationships with peers, parents, and other adults; attachment to positive institutions; and commitment to

civic engagement (Eccles & Gootman, 2002).

- Weissberg and O'Brien (2004) described positive youth in terms of core social and emotional competencies: self-awareness, social awareness, emotional self-management, relationship skills, and responsible decision making.
- Finally, as described in detail, Catalano et al. (2004) pointed to such features as attachment and commitment to social relationships in the family, peer group, school, community, or culture; resiliency; competence (social, emotional, cognitive, behavioral, and moral); self-determination; spirituality; clear and positive identity; optimism; opportunities for involvement; recognition for positive behavior; and prosocial norms.

These different visions of thriving by a young person overlap substantially. Taken together, they currently guide the development of comprehensive ways to measure their components. Both positive youth development (e.g., Arthur, Hawkins, Pollard, Catalano, & Baglioni, 2002; Moore, Lippman, & Brown, 2004) and positive psychology (e.g., Lopez & Snyder, 2003; Ong & van Dulmen, 2005; Peterson & Seligman, 2004) provide useful research tools. These measures and indices allow important matters to be addressed that are unanswerable if our only vision is a list of unsorted desiderata. For example:

- How are positive characteristics distributed in the population of young people?
- How do various positive characteristics co-vary?
- Are some positive characteristics primary and others derivative?
- Are some more crucial than others in predicting the presence of good outcomes or the absence of bad outcomes?
- Are there levels of positive characteristics that are "good enough" as judged by the individual or society in terms of what they produce, or is more always better?
- Which positive characteristics are the easiest to nurture, and which are the most difficult?
- Are there critical, or at least optimal, periods

for the cultivation of positive characteristics?
- What sorts of competencies—intellectual, behavioral, emotional, social, and moral—need to be in place for other positive characteristics to be nurtured?
- What sorts of settings lend themselves to the development of positive characteristics, and what sorts of settings hinder them?
- How do positive characteristics interact with risk factors?
- What is the relative strength of positive characteristics compared to risk factors in promoting healthy outcomes and preventing adverse ones?

In sum, the availability of reliable and valid research instruments draws our attention to mechanisms and pathways by which optimal development occurs. Interventions that do less than throw the proverbial kitchen sink at youth then become possible (Linley & Joseph, 2004).

If we are successful in merging positive youth development and positive psychology, the initial stages may be awkward. Positive psychology is a new perspective within academic psychology. Positive youth development is a more established subject matter embraced by multiple disciplines. The integration of these approaches will result from deliberation, negotiation, and trade-offs.

Positive psychologists will need to "get real" about the fuzzy world in which youth live and to do more than bracket social institutions for study by other disciplines (Nicholson, Collins, & Holmer, 2004). Positive psychologists must do more than generalize downward to adolescents from empirical studies of young adults in introductory psychology subject pools (cf. Hawkins, Catalano, Kosterman, Abbott, & Hill, 1999). Positive youth development practitioners in contrast must become more comfortable with the notion of individual agency and take their own rhetoric seriously that young people are indeed resourceful and resilient (Larson, 2000). Some youth development proponents seem to have an ambivalent relation with the notion of personality traits and especially character, perhaps because of its implication that youth would be okay if they only learned to say no.

Needless to say, a concern with character does not preclude acknowledging the role played by multiple social systems in shaping the person, for better or for worse. If youth are to be developed, one needs to ask just what it is about them that develops. One important answer is individual psychological characteristics (Peterson & Seligman, 2004). To be specific, these characteristics include the following:

- *Positive emotions*, such as joy, contentment, and love. Positive emotions have been linked by recent research to the broadening and building of psychological skills and abilities (Fredrickson, 1998, 2000, 2001).
- *Flow*, the psychological state that accompanies highly engaging activities (Csikszentmihalyi, 1990). The frequent experience of flow during adolescence foreshadows long-term desirable consequences, such as achievement in creative domains (Rathunde & Csikszentmihalyi, 1993).
- *Life satisfaction*, the overall judgment that one's life is a good one (Diener, 1984). Life satisfaction among youth is pervasively associated with the presence of desirable psychological characteristics (e.g., self-esteem, resiliency, hope, self-reliance, health-promoting habits, and prosocial behavior) and the absence of negative characteristics (anxiety, depression, loneliness, school discipline problems, drug and alcohol use, teenage pregnancy, and violence). Life satisfaction also buffers against the development of depression in the wake of stressful life events (Park, 2004b).
- *Character strengths*, which include positive traits such as curiosity, kindness, gratitude, hope, and humor (Peterson & Seligman, 2004). Among young people, such strengths are robustly linked to life satisfaction and can function as buffers against the negative effects of stress and trauma (Park, 2004a).
- *Competencies*, or skills and abilities in social, emotional, cognitive, behavioral, and moral domains (Weissberg & O'Brien, 2004)

Researchers have already identified many of the precursors of these valuable characteristics and are now turning their attention to their deliberate cultivation (Seligman et al., 2003).

Both fields must compromise—positive psychology by refraining from the cautious "further basic research is needed" mantra of the academy, and youth development by examining the enthusiastic "more is better" truism of liberal social activism. We already know enough to mount interventions with a good likelihood of short-term success (Catalano et al., 2003), but we need to examine further these interventions in terms of their long-term consequences, their cost-effectiveness, and their active ingredients. We also need to listen to youth as we try to help them.

IDENTIFYING EFFECTIVE YOUTH DEVELOPMENT PROGRAMS

In a classification similar to Bronfenbrenner's more abstract distinctions among ecological systems, Benson and Saito (2000) have proposed that the institutions that enable positive youth development be categorized from the specific to the general:

- *Programs* entail semistructured or structured group activities for youth, usually led by adults, deliberately designed to achieve specific goals and outcomes—e.g., service learning requirements in high schools, drug prevention interventions, transition-to-work programs, Big Brothers and Big Sisters.
- *Organizations* are settings that provide activities and relationships intended to improve the well-being of young people—e.g., YWCA, youth soccer leagues, church retreats.
- *Socializing systems* are "naturally occurring" social institutions that intend, among other goals, to enhance processes and outcomes consistent with positive youth development—e.g., families, schools, religious institutions, museums, libraries, neighborhoods.
- *Community* is an overarching institution that includes the geographical setting within which programs, organizations, and socializing systems interact. The social

norms, resources, and relationships that influence youth development take place here.

These categories of institutions of course overlap. For example, programs are often embedded in organizations, and a common way to categorize youth development programs is in terms of the setting (organization) in which they occur—e.g., school-based programs, after-school programs; and faith-based programs. And as Bronfenbrenner has emphasized, instances of these categories interact.

However we categorize enabling institutions, just what are they vis-à-vis positive youth development? Do critical features recur and function as the institutional equivalent of the nonspecific factors identified by psychotherapy researchers? Are these features the sorts of things that we can deliberately create or modify, or must we simply hope that they will appear in the lives of young people?

Like much of social science over the past 60 years, what we know about institutions and their impact on youth has been decidedly slanted toward problems and pathology. We know a fair amount about family chaos, underfunded schools, and unsafe neighborhoods, especially in terms of the toll that they can take on children and adolescents. We know a fair amount about the risk factors for unhealthy behaviors and for various psychological disorders. Indeed, we can almost write an exact formula for producing a drug-using, violent, alienated school dropout who satisfies one or more DSM diagnoses and is resistant to treatment. In contrast, we need to know more about the institutions that produce positive outcomes, those that move young people above the zero points of disorder, distress, and dysfunction (Peterson, 2000).

Frequently used measures for tracking youth development also tend to have a negative bias, reflecting societal concerns with youth problems and those of funding agencies that sponsor the development and use of indicators (Moore, et al., 2004). In the current U.S. indicators system, measures of child well-being focus primarily on negative outcomes and problems. We measure and track those behaviors that adults wish to prevent: homicide, school dropout, substance use, teen childbearing, low birth weight, and crime.

But for the most part, the indicators system does not monitor positive development and outcomes. With exceptions, such as the measure of volunteering included in *America's Children* (Federal Interagency Forum on Child and Family Statistics, 2001) and measures of academic success such as the percentages of students meeting grade level standards, high school graduation rates, and college entrance examination scores, the indicators system lacks a vision of what might be desired and fostered in the development of the next generation. However, as emphasized, both positive youth development and positive psychology suggest a rich array of positive indicators (and ways of measuring them) that should be formally incorporated into state and federal indicators systems (e.g., Arthur et al., 2002).

Methodological Issues

Eccles and Templeton (2003) amplified these criticisms in a recent discussion of how to identify successful youth development programs. As they reviewed the research done on programs for youth, they were struck by the heterogeneity in virtually all design features:

- The heterogeneity of the youth along dimensions of age, gender, sexual orientation, ethnicity, family social class, and place of residence
- The research designs used, which ranged from in-depth ethnographic studies of small to large local programs to carefully controlled quantitative evaluation studies and included both cross-sectional and longitudinal survey-type studies, large- and small-scale experimental evaluations, descriptive studies of programs considered to be effective by the communities in which they reside, meta-analyses of other published articles, and more traditional summative reviews of both published and nonpublished reports.
- The outcomes studied, which ranged from such youth characteristics as increases in academic achievement, school engagement, mental health, and life skills to decreases in

or avoidance of such problematic outcomes as teen pregnancy, alcohol and drug use and abuse, and involvement in delinquent and violent behaviors

- The quality of implementation of the program goals, what psychotherapy outcome researchers call *fidelity of treatment*
- The level of both the study focus and the analyses, which ranged from fairly micro-level changes at the level of the individual youth or staff person to macrolevel changes at the level of the community or even the city or state

It is worth emphasizing that the evaluation of program effectiveness can be compromised by how the program itself is run. If it encounters difficulties with the recuitment or retention of participants, if it is delivered inconsistently, if it is changed before its effects have a chance to play themselves out, or if it is unduly affected by societal fads (some of which may be legislatively mandated), one can say little about its success.

A variety of methods are used to study programs for youth. Most studies rely on either cross-sectional or longitudinal surveys that link activity participation to individual level outcomes—such as school achievement and engagement, mental health, social development, and/or involvement in various problem behaviors—with the primary research goal of describing the relation between participation and outcomes. Unfortunately, few of these studies measure characteristics of the programs themselves. Consequently, the studies tell us little about the actual features of the programs that might explain any observed change in participants.

Selection concerns are a constant threat to understanding the effects of extracurricular activities and after-school activities. When participation is a choice, those who opt for a given program may well differ in the first place from those who do not; the program itself may be irrelevant in producing long-term differences. Some recent longitudinal studies have included the most obvious third variables. And other longitudinal studies have gathered data consistent with a theory-based evaluation perspective. In these studies, the researchers measure the hy-pothesized mediators of participation on individual change and then use causal modeling techniques to test these hypotheses. Such designs tell us something about the plausible "causes" of the many longitudinal changes that might be associated with participation in the activity. Too few of the studies of extracurricular activities have used experimental designs with random assignment to pin down more definitively the consequences of activity participation.

Researchers studying after-school programs, whether in schools or in community organizations, have typically used two research strategies: nonexperimental descriptive studies and quasi-experimental or experimental program evaluation strategies. Although experimental methods using random assignment are rightly considered the gold standard of program evaluation, they can be quite expensive and difficult to implement. Accordingly, they may not always be the best method to study community-based after-school programs (cf. Agodin & Dynarski, 2001; Hollister & Hill, 1999).

Rather, the best method depends on the question(s) being asked. The method also depends on the nature of the thing being studied. Studies of these types of experiences on positive youth development have focused on at least four different levels: the individual across time, programs, organizations, and communities. Programs themselves are also composed of different types of specific activities. Similarly, organizations usually contain a wide variety of programs and activities. Finally, organizations themselves are very heterogeneous, ranging from after-school centers tied to such national youth organizations as the YMCA, YWCA, 4-H, Girls Incorporated, Beacons, and the 21st Century Learning Centers, to local parks and recreation centers, amateur sports leagues, and faith-based centers. The best method of study depends on the level one wants to study.

The most comprehensive theories about programming effects typically focus on either the program level or the activities within the program. Not surprisingly, most of the quasiexperimental or experimental program evaluations focus on this level for three major reasons: *(1)* programs and activities are simple enough to allow for explicit theories regarding the nature of the proposed impact of the program on youth development; (2) programs and activities are small enough to make random assignment to the treatment and control groups possible; and (3) programs often have sufficiently well-developed manuals and resources materials to allow dissemination.

Doing randomized trial experimental evaluations is much more difficult at the organization and community level. For example, there are a variety of challenges to using experimental designs to evaluate large nationally visible organizations such as the YMCAs or YWCAs. First, national organizations differ in their local programming. Consequently, even if one could successfully implement a truly randomized trial evaluation design for specific sites, it is not clear that the information gained would generalize to other sites. This is why multisite trials are advocated in this setting. However, this is a common feature of experimentation that highlights internal validity at the cost of external validity. Replication and extension are part of the experimental mantra. In addition, because these organizations are complex and offer a varied assortment of programs, the level of evaluation needs to be quite general. Such information is likely to tell us little about which specific aspects of the organizational context produce positive developmental results for the participating children and adolescents.

Even evaluation of programs within organizations can be quite difficult. Most after-school and in-school nonacademic programs are voluntary. Although parents may try to insist that their children attend, their ability to enforce their desires on their children declines as their children move into and through adolescence. In addition, as noted above, many community organizations for youth include a diverse array of programs from which youth select. Often their selections vary from week to week or day to day, making each individual youth's experiences at the organization quite unique. Again, there are methods to meet the messiness of the real world.

Each of these program and organizational characteristics has implications for experimental program evaluation. For example, the voluntary nature of many community-based programs cre-

ates a problem with selection bias. When such programs are offered at school during the regular school hours, random assignment may be easier and more successful because the participants are more likely to attend regularly and complete the program. In contrast, the voluntary nature of joining and attending after-school community-based youth programs, particularly if they are in nonschool settings during nonschool hours, leads to more sporadic attendance and higher rates of dropping out. Consequently, researchers are faced with uncontrolled factors that influence attendance. In this case, rigid adherence to random assignment classification in analyzing one's results is likely to underestimate the program's effectiveness for those youth who are actually exposed to it over an extended period of time (Zaff, O'Neill, & Eccles, 2002). Length of participation is not an infallible moderator of program effectiveness, however, if youth who are more likely to stay with a given program do so because of preexisting differences.

The challenge for program evaluators is to specify the features that make complex programs effective. Because individual participants may select which parts of a program to attend and how often, evaluators may know little about each individual's exposure to various aspects of the center's programming. Such variation makes it difficult to determine the aspects of the program that are responsible for certain developmental outcomes.

Finally, the evolving nature of many youth programs poses problems for evaluation. Experimental methods usually assume a static treatment. Nonexperimental research on youth programs suggests that the most highly respected and well-attended programs are dynamic—changing, for example, in response to seasonal activity structures, changing clientele, changing staff, and information derived from ongoing reflective practice and self-evaluation, as well as from the youth themselves (McLaughlin, 2000; McLaughlin, Irby, & Langman, 1994). These are often the problems associated with ineffective treatment, shifting client presenting issues, shifting responses, never knowing if anything works. Rather than make these chaotic and unorganized aspects of the environment the driving aspects of the field, the professionalization of and disciplined approach by the field needs to understand what works.

Given these concerns, it is not surprising that some of the most careful studies of extracurricular and other positive youth developmental programs use either nonexperimental methods or mixed methods in which small experiments are embedded as part of an action research agenda. Also not surprisingly, some of the strongest experimental evaluations of nonacademic programs for youth have been conducted on school-based programs offered during regular school hours.

Studying organized community efforts at increasing the provision of quality experiences for youth is even more challenging. Nonetheless, there is a growing interest in efforts at this level. Both researchers and policy advocates are coming to the conclusion that substantial and sustainable increments in the quantity and accessibility of high-quality after-school experiences for America's youth need community-wide initiatives.

In principle, the best design remains one that uses random assignment. The policy question invariably posed is whether Program X adds value to business as usual; only a true experiment can allow this question to be answered with certainty. If there are no demonstrable differences, policy makers will not see the point in supporting new programs. Accordingly, there is a practical as well as a scientific reason for true experiments in the "real" world.

These are controversial issues, and we think the wisest conclusion is cautiously even-handed: Use a variety of methods, each with its strengths and weaknesses for given purposes, and look for convergence in conclusions. For instance, in the arena of psychotherapy research for adults, randomized clinical trials established conclusively that therapy can work (Smith & Glass, 1977), and nonexperimental studies extended this conclusion by suggesting that therapy as typically practiced does work (Seligman, 1995).

Especially given the struggle for credibility over the years, the field of positive youth development should not give up on experimental designs simply because they are difficult to implement or are too expensive or too messy. To do so would invite justified skepticism. To sustain and

further the gains made by the positive youth development field, we must demand rigorous evaluation, despite demands on cost and imagination.

Youth Development Programs That Work

As noted, enough outcome studies have been done to warrant reviews of these programs to abstract what works and why. We offer the provocative conclusion that at least as much is known about effective youth development programs as is known about effective clinical interventions—psychotherapeutic and pharmacological—for adolescents that are described earlier in this volume. Indeed, recent years have seen the publication of many reviews of the effectiveness of youth development programs, some qualitative (narrative reviews) and others quantitative (meta-analytic reviews). Before we turn to an overview of these reviews and their conclusions, some framing is in order.

Each review starts by demarcating its terrain—e.g., character education programs, school-based programs, after-school programs, prevention programs (those that decrease problems or risky behaviors), promotion programs (those that encourage positive outcomes like social skills). In some cases, two reviews overlap in their terrain (and hence the research studies included), and in other cases, the terrains are distinct enough to result in completely nonoverlapping studies. Some large number of outcomes studies from either published or unpublished sources are then identified and then winnowed according to one or more design criteria (e.g., comparison groups, quantitative data, adequate statistical power, behavioral measures, replication). Among included studies, some reviews distinguish between high-quality evaluations and others, a criterion difficult to judge because relatively few programs assess fidelity or quality of implementation. And in some reviews, only programs that work in the sense of yielding significant differences between intervention groups and comparison groups are examined in detail.

This latter strategy makes sense if one is trying to discover best-practice interventions—model programs—but it is suspect if one is trying to arrive at overall conclusions about youth development programs. Before identifying "best practice," we need to know that there is "good practice," otherwise such selectivity runs the risk of capitalizing on chance findings or inadvertently highlighting unusual programs.

Of the many thousands of youth development programs in the United States, a reviewer seems able to find at most several hundred evaluation efforts, of which a few dozen typically satisfy the methodological criteria set forth. Often the reviews conclude by identifying a small number of model programs (as judged by rigorous evaluations) that are then described in detail. Table 26.1 lists some of the frequently cited model programs and their design features. (More detailed descriptions of most of these programs as well as many others are available at http:// www.casel.org/about_sel/SELintro.php by following the link to programs/curricula). These programs are not the only ones that work, but the evidence for their effectivess is especially solid because it usually involved evaluation with random assignment, multiple outcome measures, and long-term follow-up.

Table 26.2 summarizes some of the more recent reviews of empirical studies of the effectiveness of youth development programs in reducing problems and/or promoting well-being. As can be seen, the outcome measures ranged from the positive to the negative, although individual reviews tended to focus on only a few classes of outcomes. Every review offered its own conclusions about what works, but we rely here on syntheses provided by Eccles and Gootman (2002), Nation et al. (2003), and Park and Peterson (2004). The bottom line is that *youth development programs can promote the positive and reduce the negative.* Each of the reviews was able to point to empirical evidence that at least some programs achieved one or more of their stated goals, as shown by demonstrable effects on the outcomes of interest. However, caution is introduced by the following disclaimers: *(1)* lack of random assignment in many program evaluations; *(2)* inconsistent measures across studies, especially of positive outcomes; and *(3)* in most cases, lack of long-term follow-up data (i.e., years after the program is done).

A common thread of programs that work is supportive relationships (between youth participants and group leaders, teachers, parents, and so on) and, not surprisingly, fidelity of implementation. One-shot programs do not work well, although it is unclear just how long a program needs to be before it begins to work. Structured programs are more effective, a feature that can be achieved by manualizing the program, or spelling out in detail just what one does to make the program a reality. Everyone concludes, although these may be articles of faith more than evidence-based facts, that programs need to take account of the multiple links among socializing agents and that community norms supporting the goals of a program must be in place (cf. Schinke & Matthieu, 2003).

The reader will note that most of the reviews have been of programs and not of more general institutions that might promote well-being among youth. The Johnson et al. (2003) review is an exception—the socializing system of religion has been consistently associated with desired outcomes, although this is a purely correlational conclusion and leaves unanswered the hypothetical question of what coerced participation in religious activities would produce. (History tells us that this would be a disaster if done on a large scale, but we also wonder about the effects of parents forcing unwilling offspring to attend church.) The Child Trends (2003) research briefs are another exception, because they survey the effects of not only specific programs but also more general institutions and socializing systems.

And what about communities? Epidemiological research tells us that problems are more likely to occur in some communities than others, but the studies are not fine-grained and in any event we know that problems co-occur. Not enough is known about the community settings that help youth thrive in all the ways that we have described, although extensive research with subjective well-being shows that demographic variables (a proxy for certain community-level variables given ethnic, socioeconomic, and educational stratification in the United States) are but weakly associated with life satisfaction. Recent studies of character strengths in adults similarly show few consistent demographic correlates except gender and,

Table 26.1 Model Youth Development Programs

Big Brothers and Big Sisters (Tierney & Grossman, 2000)

- Ongoing community-based mentoring program (3–5 contact hours per week) that matches low-income children and adolescents, many from single-parent homes, with adult volunteers with the expectation that a caring and supportive relationship will develop
- Evaluated with random-assignment design, long-term follow-up
- Outcome measures included academic achievement, parental trust, violence, alcohol and drug use, and truancy.

Caring School Community (Solomon, Battistich, Watson, Schaps, & Lewis, 2000)

- Twenty-five-session school-based program that targets drug use and violence through community-building exercises
- Evaluated with quasiexperimental design using multiple comparison groups, long-term follow-up
- Outcome measures included social acceptance, alcohol and drug use, loneliness, social anxiety, and antisocial behavior (carrying weapons, vehicle theft).

Penn Resiliency Program (Gillham & Reivich, 2004)

- Twelve-session school-based program for preventing depression among children and adolescents by teaching cognitive-behavioral skills, especially those involved in optimistic thinking
- Evaluated with random-assignment design, long-term follow-up
- Outcome measures included depression and anxiety (symptoms and diagnoses), physical health, violence, and optimism.

Promoting Alternative Thinking Strategies (Greenberg & Kusche, 1998)

- Thirty- to 45-session school-based program that promotes emotional and social competence through structured exercises emphasizing self-control and social problem-solving
- Evaluated with random-assignment design, long-term follow-up
- Outcome measures included social problem-solving, emotional understanding, conduct problems, adaptive behavior, social planning, and impulsivity.

Quantum Opportunities Program (Hahn, Leavitt, & Aaron, 1994)

- Year-round multiyear community-based program (750 contact hours per year) for very poor adolescents that provides educational, community service, and development activities and financial incentives for participation
- Evaluated with random-assignment design, long-term follow-up
- Outcome measures included high school graduation, college attendance, positive attitudes, volunteer work, and criminal activity.

Queensland Early Intervention and Prevention of Anxiety Project (Spence, 1996)

- Ten-session school-based program for preventing anxiety disorders among children by teaching cognitive-behavior skills, especially how to cope with anxiety by graduated exposure
- Evaluated with random-assignment design, long-term follow-up
- Outcome measures included anxiety (symptoms and diagnoses).

Skills, Opportunities, and Recognition (Hawkins, Catalano, Kosterman, Abbott, & Hill, 1999)

- Multiyear school-based program infused into the entire curriculum that targets positive development and academic competence by reducing risk factors and increasing connections to school and family through cooperative classroom learning
- Evaluated with random-assignment design, long-term follow-up
- Outcome measures included academic achievement, attachment to school, violence, alcohol use, and sexual intercourse.

Teen Outreach Program (Allen, Philiber, Herrling, & Kuperminc, 1997)

- Nine-month school-based weekly discussion curriculum for adolescents that focuses on life skills, parent–child communication, future planning, and volunteer service (20 hours per week)
- Evaluated with random-assignment design, long-term follow-up
- Outcome measures included initiation of intercourse and contraceptive use.

Table 26.2 Reviews of Empirical Studies of Youth Development Programs

Hattie, Neill, & Richards (1997)

- Reviewed 96 evaluations of adventure programs (e.g., Outward Bound) and excluded 9 as being of poor scientific quality. Also excluded school-based programs as insufficiently challenging. Included only programs that had comparison groups, adequate measures, and detailed methodological descriptions
- Outcome measures included self-control, self-confidence, decision making, school achievement, leadership, assertiveness, emotional stability, time management, and flexibility.

Kirby (1997)

- Reviewed 50 pregnancy prevention programs, each of which included at least 100 teenagers, had comparison groups
- Outcome measures included sexual behavior, contraceptive behavior, and pregnancy and birth rates.

Durlak & Wells (1997)

- Reviewed 177 primary prevention programs for "normal" youth under the age of 19; included only programs with comparison groups, about 60% with random assignment, most based in school settings
- Outcome measures included psychological problems such as anxiety, conduct disorder, and depression, and personal competencies (assertiveness, communication, self-confidence).

Durlak & Wells (1998)

- Reviewed 130 secondary prevention programs for "at-risk" youth under the age of 19; included only programs with comparison groups, about 70% with random assignment, most based in school settings
- Outcome measures included psychological problems such as anxiety, conduct disorder, and depression, and personal competencies (assertiveness, communication, self-confidence).

Elliot & Tolan (1998)

- Reviewed 10 violence prevention programs (chosen from 450) with comparison groups and random assignment, "significant" results, replication, results sustained for at least 1 year.
- Outcome measures included delinquency, drug use, and violent behavior.

Roth, Brooks-Gunn, Murray, & Foster (1998)

- Reviewed 60 community-based prevention and intervention programs for youth and selected 15 for their final review; included only studies with comparison groups
- Outcome measures included positive behaviors and competencies, problem behaviors, and resistance skills.

Greenberg, Domitrovich, & Bumbarger (1999)

- Started with 130 prevention programs that were either universal (targeting all youth), selective (targeting at risk youth), or indicated (targeting youth showing early signs of disorders but not meeting diagnostic criteria) and reviewed 34 in detail that included a comparison group, pre- and post-test measures, and a written manual specifying theory and procedures
- Outcome measures included symptoms of externalizing and/or internalizing disorders.

Catalano, Berglund, Ryan, Lonczak, & Hawkins (1999)

- Reviewed 77 promotion programs for youth, and 25 in detail; included only programs with comparison groups and at least one significant result
- Outcome measures included bonding, resilience, competence, self-determination, spirituality, self-efficacy, opportunities for positive involvement, recognition for positive involvement, identity, belief in the future, and prosocial norms.

(continued)

Table 26.2 Continued

Tobler et al. (2000)

• Reviewed 207 school-based drug use prevention programs targeted at youth in general; included only programs with comparison groups; about two-thirds used random assignment of participants

• Outcome measures included self-reported drug use.

Wilson, Gottfredson, & Najaka (2001)

• Reviewed 165 school-based programs for youth attempting to reduce problem behaviors; included only studies with comparison groups

• Outcome measures included crime, substance abuse, truancy, school dropout, and other conduct problems.

Center for the Study and Prevention of Violence (2003)

• Elaborated the Elliot and Tolan (1998) review to include 33 programs

• Outcome measures included delinquency, drug use, and violent behavior.

CASEL (2003)

• Reviewed 242 school-based programs whose descriptions were rated by experts as satisfying the principles of how to impart social and emotional intelligence and in particular the 80 programs that were multiyear

• Outcome measures included social and emotional competence.

Roth & Brooks-Gunn (2003)

• Drawing on earlier reviews to identify programs, evaluated 48 studies of programs that targeted one or more of these positive youth outcomes. Notable was the attempt to categorize programs according to program goals, program atmosphere, and program activities, and relate these features to effectiveness.

• Outcome measures included competence, confidence, connections, character, and caring.

Johnson, Tierney, & Siegel (2003)

• Reviewed "hundreds" of studies of religiousness and participation (e.g., frequency of religious attendance, frequency of prayer, and/or degree of religious salience) and their correlates; none of these studies was experimental, but the results were overwhelmingly supportive of the hypothesis that religious participation is associated with reduced negative outcomes and increased positive outcomes.

• Outcome measures included problem behavior (suicide, promiscuous sexuality, drug and alcohol use, delinquency) and prosocial behavior.

Child Trends (2003)

• Reviewed 1,100 studies of youth development, summarizing them in research briefs identifying "what works"

• Outcome measures included teenage pregnancy, healthy lifestyle, social skills, educational achievement, positive mental and emotional health, and civic engagement.

Berkowitz & Bier (2004)

• Reviewed 72 different school-based character education programs; included only studies with character-relevant outcomes, comparison groups, and pre–post (change) data.

• Outcome measures included academic motivation and aspirations, academic achievement, prosocial behavior, bonding to school, democratic values, conflict resolution skills, moral reasoning maturity, responsibility, respect, self-efficacy, self-control, self-esteem, social skills, and trust in and respect for teachers.

Table 26.2 Continued

Nelson, Westhues, & Macleod (2004)
- Reviewed 34 programs for at-risk preschoolers in terms of positive and negative outcomes classified as cognitive or socioemotional. Included studies with comparison groups and long-term follow-up.
- Outcome measures included cognitive, socioemotional, and parent/family outcomes.

Stice & Shaw (2004)
- Reviewed 51 programs for preventing eating disorders among adolescents; included only studies with comparison groups
- Outcome measures included body dissatisfaction, dieting, negative affect, and bulimic symptoms.

---

among African-Americans, religiosity, a finding reported by many previous researchers (Peterson & Seligman, 2004).

CONCLUSIONS AND FUTURE DIRECTIONS

In this final section, we take stock of the youth development field from the positive perspective. We start with what we know, and we conclude with our recommendations for ways in which positive youth development research and application might counter mental disorders in youth at risk.

What Do We Know?

There is agreement at least within the contemporary United States about the positive characteristics of youth. Labels will vary, but the features proposed by different groups overlap substantially. These are best regarded as a family of characteristics, each of which exists in degrees. Children and adolescents are not simply doing well or doing poorly, and accordingly, we need to take a broad and nuanced view of the goals of positive youth development.

There is agreement that indicators and indices of positive youth development must do more than ascertain the absence of disorder and distress. Much further work needs to be done to craft generally useful measures of positive constructs and to see that these are routinely used in evaluations of youth programs (Moore et al., 2004).

There is, of course, agreement that positive characteristics are valuable in their own right but, more importantly for the purpose of this volume, that positive characteristics can buffer against the development of the most common psychological disorders among youth (Pollard et al., 1999). Furthermore, we can encourage optimal development through youth programs, either those that already exist (e.g., Big Brothers and Big Sisters) or those explicitly designed by psychologists, prevention scientists, and youth development practitioners for this purpose (e.g., the Penn Resiliency Program). There is also agreement that the personal characteristics of group leaders are critical for the success of their programs, as is parental support.

From the existing program evaluation research, investigators have agreed that programs are apt to be most successful—increasing positive outcomes and reducing negative outcomes—if they have the following features:

- *More is better.* Weekend workshops are not effective interventions; however, programs in which youth spend many hours over extended periods of time are effective in reducing negative outcomes and encouraging positive outcomes.
- *Earlier is better.* In general, the most effective programs do not wait for their participants to enter adolescence but instead start with younger children (cf. Zigler & Berman, 1983). However, among preschoolers, the optimal age remains unclear (Nelson, Westhues, & MacLeod, 2004). For eating disorders, prevention programs work better for older adolescents (Stice & Shaw, 2004).
- *Appropriate timing is better.* When do inter-

ventions have maximal impact? Programs work best when put in place before the target behavior is set in place. And, of course programs must be developmentally appropriate. Developers of programs that require metacognitive skills on the part of participants need to be sure that these skills exist (e.g., Gillham & Reivich, 2004).

- *Structured is better.* Programs that work best have a clear plan that is monitored on an ongoing basis.
- *Accurate is better.* Programs are most effective when implemented with fidelity. Our enthusiasm for youth development programs must be tempered by caution about bad (or at least slipshod) company.
- *Supportive is better.* The best programs are those in which youth have at least one supportive relationship with an adult.
- *Active is better.* The most effective programs actively teach skills related to the target outcome, through hands-on and minds-on engagement.
- *Broad is better.* The most effective programs target several systems simultaneously—e.g., home and school. Programs that work best provide ways for youth to not only think differently but also act differently.
- *Socioculturally relevant is better.* Programs work best when tailored to the cultural background of their participants.
- *Contextual is better.* Programs that work best take a sophisticated "person-in-environment" approach. They do not address just internal factors such as character strengths, and they do not address just external factors such as school safety. Instead, they address both.
- *Theoretical is better.* Along these lines, programs work best when guided by explicit theories about the causes of outcomes and the mechanisms of change.

Not enough is known about the parameters of these truisms. All program evaluations report statistical significance levels but not necessarily effect sizes, making it difficult to say which of the features just described are more or less important in producing outcomes. Also, almost nothing is known about the cost-effectiveness of

different programs (or program features) with respect to various outcomes (see Newman, Smith, & Murphy, 2000). We do not know if promotion programs help troubled youth as much as they do youth in general, or if prevention programs are as helpful for youth per se as they are for young people at risk. We have no idea whether preexisting programs work better than "designer" programs. We are not sure whether programs in general are more effective when they target at-risk adolescents or young people per se, although violence prevention programs and eating disorder prevention programs seem more successful when they target at-risk individuals (Stice & Shaw, 2004).

More generally, except for age and cultural background (ethnicity) of participants, we do not know if programs work better if matched to preexisting characteristics of youth (e.g., gender, temperament, religiosity) or whether one size indeed fits and benefits all. Although such positive characteristics as life satisfaction and strengths of character vary little across gender, ethnicity, and social class, the prevalence of psychological disorders varies considerably as a function of these contrasts, which means that they cannot be neglected in future research. For example, if the risk factors for a disorder vary by gender, do males and females require different prevention strategies?

There is agreement about the most desirable features of program evaluation studies—i.e., random assignment, manualization and checks on program fidelity, and designs that are multivariate, multimethod, and longitudinal—and the importance of using explicit theory in designing interventions and studies (cf. Coalition for Evidence-Based Policy, 2003). Theory need not be ultimately correct (and it is unlikely that it will be), but is extremely helpful in making sense of research findings, both positive and negative.

Compounding the difficulty in drawing conclusions from existing reviews is that many of those we surveyed were sponsored by private foundations or government agencies interested in bottom-line conclusions about what works and not in theories about why something works. The good news is that individual interventions are usually based on strong theories about youth development; the problem is that these underlying theories are often downplayed in commissioned reviews (see Eccles & Gootman, 2002, for an exception).

In any event, a consensual theory of change would be a boon. Within other fields, e.g., public health, explicit theories of change such as the reasoned-action model (Fishbein & Ajzen, 1975), the health belief model (Becker, 1974), the social development model (Catalano & Hawkins, 1996), and the transtheoretical model of change (Prochaska, Redding, & Evers, 1997) are used to design and evaluate interventions. The youth development field would do well to follow these examples and use the same theory across different programs. Frequently cited as a program rationale is social learning theory (Bandura, 1986), but this "theory" is often applied metaphorically rather than rigorously.

What Do We Need To Know?

As promised, we have made two arguments: *(1)* the sorts of psychological characteristics of interest to positive psychology—notably life satisfaction, strength of character, and competencies, but also positive emotions and the frequent experience of flow—are associated with reduced problems and increased well-being among youth; and *(2)* youth development programs with specifiable features can encourage these positive characteristics and at the same time increase the likelihood of the outcomes in which we are interested. We would like to treat these two statements as the components of a syllogism, but the implied conclusion, that programs reduce problems and increase desirable outcomes because they develop positive psychological features, may or may not follow. A number of the reviews we have mentioned attempted to identify mediators of effective interventions, but the included studies in almost all cases did not allow this to be done.

Given the typical absence of long-term outcome data, we do not know with certainty whether positive youth characteristics, either naturally occurring or deliberately produced, limit, contain, or preclude subsequent adult problems (see Lonczak, Abbott, Hawkins, Koster-

man & Catalano, 2002, for an exception). Said another way, we need to know whether youth intervention programs are palliative or curative. The disappointing fact about therapeutic interventions for adult disorders, whether psychosocial or pharmacological, is that they are rarely cures (Seligman, 1994). They usually need to stay in place for their benefits to remain. Are youth development programs somehow different? If so, they would represent a huge preventive investment for society.

There is a methodological disconnect between intervention programs that attempts to prevent problems and promote well-being and the therapeutic interventions, psychosocial or pharmacological, reviewed in earlier sections of this volume. Most of the latter studies use individuals who satisfy certain DSM diagnoses and not others according to structured clinical interviews. In contrast, prevention and promotion interventions often use different ways of ascertaining problems: self-report symptom checklists or single-item indicators. We have no doubt that an adolescent formally diagnosed with depression also reports symptoms of depression on a self-report questionnaire and evidences problematic indicators, although the concordance will not be perfect.

We also note that prevention programs exist for many of the common psychological problems among youth—anxiety, depression and suicide, alcohol and substance abuse—but there are fewer for the less common but often more severe disorders of schizophrenia and bipolar disorder. The relative absence of prevention programs for these problems may represent a deliberate choice on the part of prevention scientists to focus on more common disorders with less obvious genetic contributions. But heritable problems are not necessarily immutable. Perhaps prevention programs, if nothing else, might reduce the severity or chronicity of psychotic episodes, and some suggestive evidence supports this important possibility.

There is little agreement, again because much of the relevant research is skeletal, whether positive characteristics are causes of program benefits or merely correlated markers. If they are causes, there is little agreement about the mechanisms by which different benefits might take place (mastery and internalization of prosocial norms are promising mediators). There is little agreement about which of these outcomes is more or less likely and whether they are independent or entwined. There is little discussion of the possibility that these positive characteristics might destigmatize disorders and as a result increase help-seeking and facilitate community reintegration of youth following treatment (Penn, 2003).

Needed are studies of programs that look explicitly at what mediates gains. To do such studies, we would probably want to start with some of the best-practice programs (Table 26.1) and repeat their evaluations with multiple waves of data collection that explicitly measure hypothesized mediators. These studies would establish the relative salience and temporal or causal ordering of these characteristics.

For whom do youth development programs *not* work? Even successful programs with a moderate effect size help only 60% of participants (cf. Rosenthal & Rubin, 1982). Do the other 40% of participants represent error or noise, or is there something more systematic that might be said about them? Indeed, we can even raise the issue of intervention casualties, participants in youth development programs who end up worse off for the intervention. We know that traditional psychotherapy can hurt some adults (cf. Mays & Franks, 1985). As unpalatable as the possibility may be, the matter also deserves attention within the youth development field. For example, participants in eating disorders programs may learn new ways to starve themselves and participants in substance abuse programs may be turned on to new drugs (cf. Mann et al., 1997; Shin, 2001).

Finally, little is known about the benefits of positive youth development programs for adolescents already displaying a psychological disorder. We know that past problems predict future problems, which could lead to the unfortunate and gravely stigmatizing implication that young people who develop a disorder are beyond the help of youth development programs. The positive perspective challenges this implication, but there are no data showing, for example, that a youth development program can help a depressed teen achieve his or her full potential, transcending a diagnostic label to lead a satisfying life (Shih, 2004).

What Do We Urgently Need To Know?

Let us move from these general comments to propose studies that would advance our knowledge and practice of positive youth development vis-à-vis mental health and mental illness.

The Natural History of Positive Youth Development

What is a healthy child? We have concluded that the positive perspectives provides a consensual answer to this question, but it is only a snapshot. We know relatively little about who these young people are except that they can be found in all walks of life. Urgently needed is a broader characterization of youth who are doing well—where do they come from, where do they go, and what are the choices made and routes taken in between? A good first step has already been taken by studies already underway that use epidemiological samples followed over many years (e.g., Hawkins, Catalano, & Miller, 1992).

We propose further studies of this sort that use the full array of positive measures and indicators now at our disposal. These studies should be patterned on the Terman (1925) study of adolescent geniuses and the Grant Study of the best and brightest of Harvard University undergraduates (Vaillant, 1977) in the sense that they be large scale—i.e., have big samples, longitudinal designs, and multiwave assessments—but *not* start with the most fortunate or the most privileged in our society. Dissemination of information about youth who are thriving might help combat negative stereotypes about teenagers. Realistic portrayals of young people, including their flaws and problems and how they cope with them, might inspire other teenagers to focus on what they do well and to eschew a victim mentality (Shih, 2004).

We propose that these studies of the natural history of positive youth development include, obviously, measures of positive characteristics (positive emotions, flow, life satisfaction, character strengths, skills, talents, and callings), measures of risk, and measures of problems (negative emotions, risky behaviors, symptoms, and psychological disorders). It would be a shame if the positive psychology perspective leads researchers to repeat the error of business-as-usual psychology by ruling out a balanced view of youth and the adults they become.

Inclusion of both positive and negative measures over time allows the critical questions we have posed to be answered with hard data (cf. deVries, 1992). Do positive characteristics preclude recurrence of problems? Do they limit them? Do they allow youth to learn lessons from crises, episodes of disorder, and misfortunes? Which positive characteristics provide the best buffers against depression, substance abuse, or anxiety disorders?

A retrospective study we have done with several thousand adults asked respondents if they had ever experienced a severe psychological disorder and, if so, how well they had recovered from it (Park et al., 2003). We also measured their life satisfaction and various strengths of character. Individuals who had fully recovered from a disorder were just as satisfied with their lives as those who had never experienced a disorder. At least for some, there is light at the end of the psychopathology tunnel: "Tis an ill wind that blows no good." And individuals who had fully recovered from a disorder also reported higher levels of specific strengths of character—i.e., appreciation of beauty, bravery, creativity, curiosity, forgiveness, gratitude, love of learning, and spirituality—compared to those who had never experienced a psychological disorder. Whether these character strengths were in place before the disorder and helped in recovery or whether they represent lessons learned during dark days is unclear from the research design; the need for a richer prospective study is implied (Linley & Joseph, 2004).

Prospective studies of psychological problems need to be informed by varying base rates of different disorders. Depression and substance abuse are so common in the contemporary United States that their eventual onset can arguably be investigated in unselected samples of several hundred youth. In contrast, other sorts of problems—e.g., schizophrenia, bipolar disorder, anorexia, and bulimia—are less common, which means that studies would need to oversample at-risk youth, but we stress that we are not calling for studies of only at-risk adolescents. That strategy would deny the premises of the positive perspective and preclude the lessons to be learned from charting the positive development of youth per se.

We are interested in an approach to psychological disorder that we dub "dealing with it," or keeping on with life despite problems. Our interest was stimulated by conversations with those in the military about how they train personnel to perform optimally under the most extreme circumstances. How does a sniper learn to shoot accurately after crawling into a position and staying there for 48+ hours? How does a pilot learn to fly skillfully in a dizzying free fall? How does a submariner learn to live and work with others in extremely cramped quarters? Business-as-usual psychologists would probably target and then relieve the negative emotional states that accompany these circumstances—boredom, fear, anxiety, fatigue, and discomfort. But that is not how the military proceeds. They teach their personnel how to perform in spite of these circumstances. They teach personnel to deal with aversive states, to do what needs to be done regardless of how they feel at the moment.

If these examples are too militaristic to be compelling, then what of the identical lessons we learned from interviewing firefighters and paramedics who perform well—heroically, in our view—under frightening circumstances (Peterson & Seligman, 2004). In no case did anyone we interviewed say that they had eradicated their fear. Rather, they learned to do their job so well that their fear did not get in the way (cf. Rachman, 1990). One of our firefighters told us of rescuing an infant from a smoke-filled building: He lost control of his bladder, but never his grip on the baby. Extraordinary? Yes and no. Deserving of study are the more mundane among us who go to school or show up at work or raise our families even when we are depressed or anxious.

Crucial in studying youth from a positive perspective is taking into account the institutions that influence them—programs, organizations, and communities; friends and families; mental health professionals; and the media. Needed here is an elaboration of institutions and their features that can be applied throughout the lifespan, and not just to youth (cf. Cameron, Dutton, & Quinn, 2003).

The data from such studies can be productively examined with the techniques of causal modeling (e.g., Connell, Gambone, & Smith, 2000; Gambone, 1997; Halpern, Barker, & Mollard, 2000; Walker, 2001). Sample sizes must be large enough, especially to discern interactions between and among variables. But with adequately powered designs, these models allow inferences about what might prevent what and why. As already emphasized, explicit theory is imperative to specify hypothesized links prior to causal modeling.

Positive Interventions for At-Risk and Troubled Youth

Some practitioners in the youth development field have called for extremely ambitious community-level interventions, in which all of the institutions that influence youth development would be explicitly programmed and linked. Interventions would target all children and adolescents and presumably last for years. In the abstract, we understand the sentiment behind this recommendation and agree that the links among different institutions and socializing agents deserve study in terms of their effect on youth development.

But in the real world, there are many objections to this research agenda (cf. Wandersman & Florin, 2003). On scientific grounds, community interventions cannot be easily manualized (i.e., explicitly described in detail and thus generalized), and if all youth in a given community are to be included, then what sorts of comparisons are possible? It is difficult to think of a meaningful control group to isolate the active ingredients of such global and enduring interventions. These problems can be surmounted, but it is still unlikely that a society with dwindling resources would be willing or able to initiate such grand interventions on a routine basis, which makes those already under way all the more worthy of attention. Thus with respect to urgently needed intervention studies, we believe that there are two promising research avenues to pursue that

are somewhat more modest but infinitely more feasible.

Positive prevention. Positive prevention would use already-established best-practice youth development interventions to help at-risk youth. Although we know that these interventions in general make disorder less likely, we need to know more about why and how prevention works when it does, especially among those at-risk. We have proposed that prevention programs are effective because they cultivate the ingredients of the good life—i.e., positive emotions, flow, strength of character, competencies, and social engagement. An opposing hypothesis is that prevention directly undoes causes found in biological anomalies. By this view, the cultivation of the positive should be irrelevant in predicting who benefits from prevention programs, especially in the long run.

Contrast the prevention of infectious diseases by strengthening the immune system instead of eradicating germs. Positive prevention is aligned with the first strategy as opposed to the second. Immunocompetence can be increased in specific ways (through vaccination) or in general ways (through good nutrition and physical fitness). Positive youth development programs similarly benefit young people in specific ways (e.g., by teaching techniques of disputation in the Penn Resiliency program) or in general ways (e.g., by providing supportive mentors in the Big Brothers and Big Sisters programs).

Using what is known about optimal research design, investigators can randomly assign at-risk teenagers to manualized youth development programs of different sorts (and to no-intervention comparison groups). An important contrast among candidate programs is whether they are specific in their techniques and goals or are more general. There are best-practice examples of both (Table 26.1), and each has strengths and weaknesses. Specific programs are usually briefer, easier to characterize, and thus more generalizable; general programs are less so. But specific programs need to be created anew each time they are mounted, whereas general programs are already in place and sustained for repeated cohorts of youth by an infrastructure that need not be the concern of the researcher. Comparison and contrast of these two types of programs, not only with respect to psychological outcomes but also with respect to their cost, would provide unique and valuable information about ways to cultivate positive youth development most efficiently.

Along with assessment of symptoms and diagnoses, the measurement of positive characteristics should be thorough. Existing measures of positive emotions, flow, subjective well-being, character strengths, and competencies should be included, not just pre- and postintervention but also in the course of the program, to allow the hypothesized mediating roles of these positive constructs to be tested explicitly through causal modeling. We also call for long-term follow-up with the full battery of positive and negative measures. *Long-term* means years following the end of the program. In particular, it would be important to see how cultivated positive characteristics help a young person make transitions out of high school and into college, into the work force, and into lasting relationships—the important societal institutions that help young people become fulfilled adults.

The questions of immediate interest are which individuals develop a disorder and which do not, and whether some disorders are more easily prevented than others. We are also interested in determining what happens to those youth who do develop a disorder despite these interventions. Some will show recurrent problems, and some will not. What factors predict differing courses following initial episodes? The positive psychology prediction is that even if cultivated positive characteristics do not prevent a disorder, they might well limit recurrence and allow the eventual achievement of a good life.

Positive rehabilitation.   The second sort of intervention study we propose again uses existing best-practice youth development programs, not with youth in general or with at-risk youth, but instead with troubled teens mid- or postepisode. In other words, we call for positive rehabilitation and hypothesize that positive interventions like those developed by positive psychologists and positive youth development practitioners may maximize the likelihood that the individual will grow up to lead a full and productive life.

Adults in therapy can usually expect some relief (Nathan & Gorman, 1998, 2002), but most can also expect to be in and out of treatment for the rest of their lives. At its worst, this phenomenon is dubbed "revolving-door psychiatry." Even at its best, this phenomenon leads to perpetual aftercare in the form of support groups, booster psychotherapy sessions, and/or prophylactic medication (Weissman, 1994). Self-identification as being always "in recovery" may be inevitable, and ongoing stigma is likely (Penn, 2003).

Matters may be different for young people. Among adults, it seems clear that prognosis worsens with age for almost all psychological disorders (e.g., Seivewright, Tyrer, & Johnson, 1998). Although the apparent magnitude of this effect may be an artifact of studying patient samples rather than community samples, past psychological problems remain the best predictor of future psychological problems. A depressed middle-aged adult will likely become depressed again, no matter how effective treatment may be in the short term, but young people who become depressed may not become depressed again if early intervention takes place (e.g., Birmaher, Arbelaez, & Brent, 2002; Clarke et al., 2001; Lewinsohn, Pettit, Joiner, & Seeley, 2003; but cf. Weissman et al., 1999).

The same is true for many other problems, such as anxiety disorders (Dadds et al., 1999). Indeed, among adolescents showing early (prodromal) symptoms of schizophrenia, early intervention may help stave off the full-blown disorder (Cannon et al., 2002; Harrigan, McGorry, & Krstev, 2003; McGorry et al., 2002; Phillips, Yung, Yuen, Pantelis, & McGorry, 2002; Schaeffer & Ross, 2002). And it is clear that many teenagers experiment with drugs or alcohol without dooming themselves to a life in recovery (Spooner, Mattick, & Noffs, 2001). At least for some young people and for some disorders, it becomes meaningful to speak of curing mental illness, which provides a powerful rationale for the focus on youth taken by this volume.

Why are young people different? We speculate that it is not age per se that is the crucial factor but rather the number of untreated episodes someone experiences and the psychosocial consequences of these episodes that determine long-term prognosis—the doors closed by lost time, missed opportunities, and pervasive stigma. Indeed, the more episodes of a disorder, the greater the likelihood of still more episodes and the worse the prognosis for an individual. If this downward spiral can be interrupted at a sufficiently early point, perhaps the business of life can take over as a curative agent.

Consistent with this analysis, Joiner (2000) grappled with the self-propagating nature of depression and argued that interpersonal processes such as excessive reassurance seeking and conflict avoidance are largely responsible for its persistence and/or recurrence. Other interpersonal processes by implication set the person on a different course that entails true recovery. Perhaps youth development programs can preclude recurrence of depression, and other psychological problems, by imparting appropriate strengths and competencies on which the person can rely when troubled.

Along these lines, recent longitudinal studies of life satisfaction imply that job loss (especially for males) and divorce (especially for females) can leave lasting "scars" in the sense that individuals never return to their initial levels of well-being, even with new jobs and new marriages (Clark, Georgellis, Lucas, & Diener, 2004; Lucas, Clark, Georgellis, & Diener, 2003). The mechanisms responsible for these effects, which are not inevitable, have yet to be identified, but if they are interpersonal, the implication again is that youth development programs may work against them.

Supporting this possibility is the consistent finding that assets such as intelligence and an intact family predict better long-term prognosis for youth posttreatment (e.g., Otto & Otto, 1978). The constructs of concern to positive youth development and positive psychology provide a more articulate starting point for understanding how life can cure. Relationships with other people are established, positive emotions are experienced, talents and strengths are identified and used, and meaningful careers are chosen and pursued (Richter, Brown, & Mott, 1991; Shoemaker & Sherry, 1991; Todis, Bullis, Waintrup, Schultz, & D'Ambrosio, 2001). If life becomes satisfying, one can navigate it well. The overall likelihood of psychological disorder is decreased, and the likelihood of successfully dealing with disorder is increased.

It is difficult to mount such an argument with existing data. For example, among children and youth, early onset of a disorder is usually associated with worse prognosis, which seems to contradict our hypothesis (e.g., Jarbin & von Knorring, 2003). However, early onset may reflect a greater biological contribution to disorder and certainly greater severity. Early onset may reflect a more chaotic social context to which successfully treated youth return. Consider as well the ongoing challenge in reliably diagnosing disorders among the very young and the associated reluctance by professionals to label youth unless the problem is unambiguous.

We nonetheless know that some youth who enter the mental health system are successfully treated and are never seen again, just as we know that the majority of young peole who enter the juvenile justice system never return again (Snyder & Sickmund, 1999). The skeptic might argue that these cases are not really cures; maybe the initial diagnoses were simply wrong, maybe the problems recurred but further treatment was not sought, and so on. The positive perspective suggests that we take this phenomenon at face value and fill in its details with the facts. The natural history studies we have proposed would begin to yield critical information about single-episode individuals. How many are literally cured?

But the studies of positive rehabilitation that we propose would go further in trying to influence prognosis by deliberately cultivating the ingredients of a healthy life. Our proposal is supported by studies of psychosocial rehabilitation for troubled adolescents. *Psychosocial rehabilitation* embraces an educational model, in contrast to a disease model, and tries to teach psychological and social skills that facilitate productive community reintegration of youth following treatment (Byalin, Smith, Chatkin, & Wilmot, 1987; Fruedenberger & Carbone, 1984). Such programs are effective in reducing recurrence of a variety of problems and seem to be cost-effective (e.g., Barasch, 1994; Mishna, Michalski, & Cummings, 2001; Rund et al., 1994). The positive psychology perspective goes beyond typical psychosocial rehabilitation to specify the active ingredients that allow imparted skills to be deployed to best effect.

Studies of positive rehabilitation would use

the same general research design already sketched for studies of positive prevention: randomly assign research participants, in this case adolescents with disorders, to intervention and comparison groups and do thorough assessment of both positive and negative characteristics before, during, and after the intervention. Measures of perceived stigma would be an informative addition to the assessment battery. Those in comparison groups would, of course, receive conventional (business-as-usual) aftercare. Both specific and general programs should be included. It might also be of interest to see if the timing of positive rehabilitation matters: Should it begin during treatment of a disorder (mid-episode) or following symptom relief (postepisode)?

Studies of positive prevention and especially positive rehabilitation for youth would represent a strong test of the perspective put forward here. When positive psychology was first formulated, its goal was phrased as moving people not from −3 to zero but from +2 to +5 (Seligman, 2002). But if the positive perspective on youth development has legs, it should also be able to move young people from −3 to +5 and keep them there.

APPENDIX A
Glossary

Character strengths Positive traits (individual difference), such as curiosity, kindness, hope, and teamwork, that contribute to fulfillment

Competencies Social, emotional, cognitive, behavioral, and moral abilities

"Dealing with it" Keeping on with life despite problem(s)

Ecological approach Bronfenbrenner's approach to development, emphasizing the multiple contexts in which behavior occurs

Flow Psychological state that accompanies highly engaging activities

Life satisfaction Overall judgment that one's life is a good one

Positive emotions Emotions such as joy, contentment, and love that are thought to broaden and build cognitive and behavioral repertoires

Positive prevention Positive youth development programs that prevent problems by encouraging assets

Positive psychology Umbrella term for the new field within psychology that studies processes and states underlying optimal functioning

Positive rehabilitation Positive youth development programs that promote recovery by encouraging assets

Positive youth development Umbrella term for approaches that recognize and encourage what is good in young people

Prevention programs Interventions that prevent problems

Promotion programs Interventions that promote well-being

Resiliency Quality that enables young people to thrive in the face of adversity

Summary of Conclusions, Recommendations, Priorities

Joyce Garczynski
Michael Hennessy
Kimberly Hoagwood
Kathleen Hall Jamieson
Patrick Jamieson
Abigail Judge
Mary McIntosh
A. Thomas McLellan
Kathleen Meyers
David Penn
Daniel Romer

VIII
part

Stigma

David L. Penn
Abigail Judge
Patrick Jamieson
Joyce Garczynski
Michael Hennessy
Daniel Romer

chapter 27

Reducing the stigma of mental illness is among the goals of those seeking to increase the diagnosis, improve the treatment, and enhance the well-being of those with mental disorders in the United States. Both the U.S. Surgeon General's report (U.S. Department of Health and Human Services, 1999) and the first stated goal of President George W. Bush's New Freedom Commission on Mental Health advocate "a national campaign to reduce the stigma of seeking care" (President's New Freedom Commission, 2003, p. 7).

Stigma occurs when a person or group is labeled in a pejoratively categorized way that sets them apart from the majority and, as a result, is treated in ways that mark the person as socially unacceptable. Stigma has serious consequences for individuals with mental illness. Those with severe mental illness (SMI) are less likely to have apartments leased to them (Page, 1995), be given job opportunities (Farina & Felner, 1973; Link & Phelan, 2001), or be provided with adequate health care (Lawrie, 1999) relative to individuals without a mental illness. Furthermore, stigmatization is associated with a lowered quality of life (Mechanic, McAlpine, Rosenfield, & Davis, 1994), reduced self-esteem (Link, Struening, Neese-Todd, Asmussen, & Phelan, 2001; Wright, Gronfein, & Owens, 2000), and increased symptoms and stress (Markowitz, 1998). To manage stigma, individuals with mental illness may avoid others or engage in secrecy (Link, Mirotznik, & Cullen, 1991), strategies that may lead to social isolation (Perlick et al., 2001), which in turn could lower social support and increase the likelihood of relapse. Therefore, stigma poses a significant threat to the recovery of persons with SMI.

The purpose of this chapter is to propose methods for reducing stigmatization of mental illness in adolescents. It begins with a brief summary of community attitudes toward persons with mental illness, including a discussion of a recent nationwide survey of young people. We argue that addressing stigma in adolescence is important for two primary reasons. First, stigma appears to have an adverse effect on the course of mental illness once the person has been diagnosed with a disorder. Second, concerns about stigma may delay the seeking of and continuing

in treatment. This section is followed by a discussion of factors that contribute to stigma and methods for reducing it. We conclude by recommending strategies for addressing mental illness stigma in adolescents.

COMMUNITY ATTITUDES TOWARD PERSONS WITH MENTAL ILLNESS

In both Western (Crisp, Gelder, Rix, Meltzer, & Rowlands, 2000) and Eastern societies (Chou & Mak, 1998; Tsang, Tam, Chan, & Cheung, 2003), individuals with serious mental illness, such as schizophrenia and other psychotic disorders, are stigmatized by society (Farina, 1998). The extent of this phenomenon may be increasing (Phelan, Link, Stueve, & Pescosolido, 2000). Stigmatizing attitudes toward persons with SMI have a number of recurring themes: persons with SMI are viewed as dangerous, unpredictable, irresponsible, and childlike (Brockington, Hall, Levings, & Murphy, 1993; Levey & Howells, 1995), and unable to manage their own treatment needs (Pescosolido, Monahan, Link, Stueve, & Kikuzawa, 1999). These attitudes are not only held by those in the community but also may be present among mental health professionals and trainees. Specifically, there is evidence that some mental health professionals, including psychiatrists (Chaplin, 2000; Miller, Shepard, & Magen, 2001), social workers (Dudley, 2000; Minkoff, 1987), general mental health providers (Ryan, Robinson, & Hausmann, 2001; Sartorius, 2002), and medical and mental health graduate students (Hasui, Sakamoto, Sugiura, & Kitamua, 2000; Mukherjee, Fialho, Wijetunge, Checinski, & Surgenor, 2002; Werrbach & DePoy, 1993) may hold stigmatizing beliefs about those with mental disorders. The effects include "discrimination in housing, education and employment, and increased feelings of hopelessness in people with schizophrenia" (Hocking, 2003, p. S47). These findings suggest that efforts to destigmatize mental illness should not be limited to community members, but also should include mental health and medical training professionals.

The tendency to stigmatize individuals with mental illness is not a byproduct of adult experiences but has its roots in childhood. In a recent review of the literature, Wahl (2002) concluded that negative attitudes toward persons with mental illness are evident as early as in third grade. In general, those with mental illness are viewed more negatively and with more fear than are individuals with physical disabilities (Wahl, 2002). Wahl reported that there is evidence that these negative attitudes increase over time, suggesting a longitudinal process in which negative stereotypes become increasingly ingrained, culminating in potentially discriminating behaviors in adulthood.

Direct evidence for the presence of stigmatizing beliefs about peers with mental illness was obtained from a recent national survey of young people (ages 14–22) conducted by the Adolescent Risk Communication Institute of The University of Pennyslvania's Annenberg Public Policy Center (APPC). The National Annenberg Risk Survey of Youth (NARSY) was conducted by telephone in the spring of 2002 with 900 respondents who were selected by means of random digit dialing procedures. The response rate for the survey (52.7%), taking into account those who could not be reached as well as those who refused, was comparable to the rates achieved by the Centers for Disease Control and Prevention (CDC; about 49%) in its national surveys of risk behavior (CDC, 2003; see Romer, 2003, for a description of the survey methods and sample).

Respondents were asked if they were aware of four mental disorders: major depression, bipolar disorder, schizophrenia, and eating disorders. Awareness was highest for eating disorders (89%) and depression (86%), but high levels of awareness were registered for the other disorders as well (81% for schizophrenia and 73% for bipolar disorder). Respondents who were aware of at least one disorder were asked a series of questions concerning two disorders selected at random from among those with which they reported familiarity. In particular, they were asked to imagine someone their age who had the disorder and to indicate whether they thought this person was "more likely, less likely, or about as likely as other people to be" *(a)* "violent," *(b)* "prone to committing suicide," and *(c)* "good in school." The order of the traits was randomized across respondents.

Responses to the three items for each of the disorders indicate (Table 27.1) that large proportions of young people believe that persons with these disorders are different from other people. Over half thought that persons with major depression are more likely to be violent, whereas over 90% said that such persons are more prone to suicide, and about three quarters said they are less likely to be good in school than other people. Although all of the disorders displayed the same pattern, violence was most associated with schizophrenia, and doing badly in school was linked the most with major depression. Eating disorders were somewhat of an exception in that they were less associated with violence than the other disorders.

There were few differences in these stereotypes by age, gender, or education. African-American and Latino youth were more likely than others to think that the persons with the disorders were not different from others (data not shown).

Correlational analyses using gamma coefficients (to compensate for the skewed distributions) indicated that the three items were highly intercorrelated for each disorder (with "good in school" reverse scored). Coefficient alphas based on the gamma correlation coefficients were .64 for depression, .61 for bipolar disorder, .68 for schizophrenia, and .53 for eating disorders. These findings suggest that each disorder had an underlying stereotype that could guide respondents' reactions to persons with mental disorders. In addition, the stereotypes were correlated across disorders, from a low of .35 to a high of .52. It appears, therefore, that young people hold a general stereotype of mental disorder that includes a heightened risk for suicide and violence as well as the inability to function in an adaptive manner.

The survey also included questions to identify youth with potential symptoms of depression. In particular, respondents were asked if (a) "during the past 12 months have you ever felt so sad or hopeless for 2 weeks or more in a row that you stopped doing your usual activities," and if (b) "during the past 12 months have you ever seriously considered attempting suicide." Nearly a quarter of the sample (N = 221) responded affirmatively to one of these questions. However,

Table 27.1 Percentage of Respondents Who Said That Three Characteristics Are More, Less, or About as Likely in a Peer with a Mental Disorder as in Other Persons Without the Disorder

	Disorder			
Characteristic	*Major Depression (%)*	*Bipolar Disorder (%)*	*Schizophrenia (%)*	*Eating Disorder (%)*
Violent				
More	55.7	65.1	72.1	28.9
As likely	22.1	20.5	21.4	35.5
Less	22.2	14.4	6.5	35.6
Suicidal				
More	91.9	79.9	75.9	80.0
As likely	4.5	12.1	16.5	13.2
Less	3.6	8.0	7.6	6.8
Good in School				
More	6.7	8.5	4.1	12.1
As likely	16.8	29.0	26.2	31.9
Less	76.5	62.5	69.7	56.0
Respondents (*n*)	512	390	462	537

Data were weighted by age, gender, racial-ethnic background, and region of the country to match national demographic profiles.

youth who had experienced these conditions were as likely to report the stereotypes as those who had not.

CONSEQUENCES OF STIGMA

Stigmatization also plays a role in whether an individual initiates and adheres to treatment. Interestingly, failure to initiate treatment may not only be due to having a mental illness but also result from the stigma attached to seeking help. For example, Ben-Porath (2002) found that a case vignette describing someone with depression was rated most negatively when the target individual sought help for the disorder. This suggests that individuals with a mental illness have to wrestle with the fear of both being stigmatized for having a disorder and for seeking help for it.

There is growing evidence that stigma affects individuals with mental disorders in ways that minimize the likelihood that they will be successfully treated. For example, concerns that others will learn that their child is receiving

mental health treatment is a common worry for parents of children between the ages of 5 and 19 (Richardson, 2001). In addition, higher levels of stigma are associated with greater treatment delay among individuals with SMI (Okazaki, 2000), parents of rural children with emotional disorders (Starr, Campbell, & Herrick, 2002), athletes (Ferraro & Rush, 2000), individuals with HIV (or concerns of having HIV) (Chesney & Smith, 1999; Fortenberry et al., 2002), general community participants unselected for presence of mental illness (Cooper, Corrigan, & Watson, 2003), and women with alcohol or drug addictions (Copeland, 1997).

Once in treatment, perceived stigma may be a barrier to medication compliance and treatment continuation (Buck, Baker, Chadwick, & Jacoby, 1997; Pugatch, Bennett, & Patterson, 2002; Sirey et al., 2001a, 2001b). Buck et al. (1997) reported that feelings of being stigmatized were associated with lower adherence to antiepileptic drug treatment. Pugatch et al. (2002) reported similar findings; fears of being stigmatized were associated with poorer adherence to drug regimens among young adults (ages 16–24) who were HIV posi-tive. In a series of studies, Sirey and colleagues found that perceived stigmatization predicted medication adherence and treatment continua-tion (in older adults only) among individuals with depression. These findings indicate that stigma may impact the course of the illness by interfering with commitment to treatment.

Reluctance to seek psychological or psychiat-ric treatment is especially relevant to adoles-cents, because numerous disorders, such as major depression, bipolar disorder, anxiety dis-orders, anorexia and bulimia, and schizophrenia begin in late adolescence or early adulthood. Such delays in seeking treatment have important prognostic implications for individuals in this age group. Post, Leverich, Xing, and Weiss (2001) found that individuals with a greater number of affective episodes prior to receiving pharmaco-therapy had a less favorable prognosis than in-dividuals who began medications after fewer episodes. In schizophrenia, it has been hypoth-esized that the duration of untreated psychotic episodes prior to illness onset is associated with poorer long-term prognosis (Lieberman et al., 2001; Norman & Malla, 2001). Thus, the role of stigma in delaying treatment may contribute to greater severity of illness among adolescents with a newly diagnosed disorder.

SURVEY EVIDENCE FOR THE ROLE OF STIGMA ON HELP SEEKING

To determine the role of unfavorable stereotypes on help seeking behavior, we examined the ex-tent to which youth who had experienced symp-toms of depression or suicidal ideation in the past 12 months had failed to seek help from a variety of sources as a function of negative beliefs about mental health treatment. A revised version of the NARSY conducted a year after the first sur-vey (2003) included questions to examine this question. In this survey, we again identified a large number of respondents ($N = 211$; 23.4%) who had experienced symptoms of depression or suicidal ideation. Hence, we focused on the stigma associated with this disorder.

We also assessed perceptions of the effective-ness of treatment. We did so under the hypoth-

esis that the stigma associated with mental ill-ness should be reduced if the disorder has been successfully treated (see discussion of interven-tions below). If stigma continues to be attached to those who have been successfully treated, then persons with symptoms could be inhibited from seeking help. Hence, perceived treatment effectiveness could be an important moderator of stigma's effects on help seeking.

To determine the effects of potential treat-ment, we asked respondents the following ques-tion: "If you had major depression, do you think you could get the help you need from any of the following:" *(a)* "a doctor," *(b)* "your friends," *(c)* "your parents," *(d)* "a counselor," *(e)* "an Internet site," and *(f)* "a telephone helpline."

Actual help-seeking behavior on the part of re-spondents who had experienced depressed symptoms or suicidal ideation was assessed by asking, "Have you ever done any of the follow-ing to try to get help?" Responses were grouped into four categories based on a factor analysis that indicated that help seeking tended to occur in the following ways:

- Gone to a doctor or nurse; or, taken medi-cation prescribed by a doctor;
- Gone to a counselor;
- Talked to a friend; or talked to a parent, and
- Gone to an Internet site; or used a telephone helpline.

Respondents were scored as having tried any cat-egory if they had sought help from any of the sources within the category. In addition, treat-ment effectiveness scores were created for each category on the basis of ratings of each source.

Perceptions of treatment effectiveness (Table 27.2) indicated that seeing a doctor was viewed as most effective, whereas going to an Internet site or using a telephone helpline were viewed as the least effective. Although the differences are small in magnitude, seeing a doctor was viewed as significantly more effective in the entire sam-ple than seeing a counselor, $t(814) = 3.02$, $p < .01$, or talking to a parent, $t(814) = 2.53$, $p < .02$. Other differences that are larger in magnitude are even more statistically discernable.

With the exception of seeking help from par-ents, the rank order of perceived effectiveness of

Table 27.2 Perceptions of Efficacy of Sources of Help for Depression by Those With or Those Without Symptoms Associated With Depression

| Help Source | Respondents Who Reported | | |
	Symptoms of Depression or Suicidality (N = 180) (%)	No Symptoms of Depression or Suicidality (N = 635) (%)	Total (N=815) (%)
Doctor	77.7	90.6	87.8
Counselor	74.6	86.1	83.5
Friend	73.6	79.6	78.3
Parent	71.0	87.6	83.9
Telephone helpline	34.7	47.2	44.5
Internet site	25.2	28.0	27.4

Data include only those who were aware of major depression and were weighted to match national demographics; unweighted Ns were 191 for depressed group and 619 for others (total = 810).

the help sources was comparable between those with and without symptoms of depression. Nevertheless, there were differences between the groups. With the exception of one help source (the Internet), persons with symptoms were less likely to perceive any of the help sources as effective. Therefore, perceived treatment ineffectiveness is a source of concern in itself for youth with symptoms of mental disorder (Shaffer et al., 1990).

Analysis of Help Seeking

To determine the role of stigma on help seeking, we conducted regression analyses of the relation between stereotypes of depression and reported help seeking for respondents with symptoms of major depression or suicidality. Stereotypes were defined as the average of three beliefs associated with mental disorder in the first NARSY: violence, suicidality, and good performance in school (reversed scored). The scale ranged from (1) less likely than the average person to have the undesirable trait to (3) more likely than the average person to have the trait. We used probit regression because it is appropriate for dichoto-

mous outcomes and because it also provides an estimate of the percentage change in the probability of the outcome given a unit change in the predictor for an average respondent, e.g., as the change in probability of seeing a counselor vs. not seeing one for a unit change in stereotypes (Agresti, 1990; Greene, 1993).

Table 27.3 has the descriptive statistics of the variables used in the analysis. The four dichotomous outcome variables indicate that talking to parents or friends is the most common help sought (88.6%), followed by seeing a doctor or taking medication (45.4%), getting counseling (40.7%), and going to the Internet or using a telephone helpline (16.1%). The expected help results show a somewhat similar ordering; most respondents with symptoms of major depression expect help from physicians, followed by counselors, parents and friends, and lastly from the Internet and helplines.

Table 27.4 summarizes the regression results for each of the four outcomes holding constant demographic variables (not shown). Except in two cases (counseling and seeing a physician/taking medications), there were no effects of any demographic characteristic on help seeking for these young respondents. Stereotypes of depression were negatively related to help seeking in three out of the four cases (the small positive effect is for seeing a doctor or nurse or taking medication). The effect of stereotypes on counseling was about −12%, and the effect of stereotypes on talking to parents or friends was about −6%, but these effects were not reliably different from zero. The strongest observed effect was for the impact of stereotypes on using the Internet or calling a helpline, which was almost −14%. Note that in two cases (counselors and Internet/helplines), expected efficacy of the treatment modality and help seeking were positively and significantly related, indicating that young people are more likely to seek help from sources that are seen as effective.

The results of this survey suggest that young people need not attach stigma to help seeking when the source of help is seen as particularly effective, as in the case of seeing a doctor or nurse or taking medication. For the other less effective sources of help, by contrast, stereotypes tended to be negatively related to help seeking

Table 27.3 Descriptive Statistics for Help Seeking–Dependent Variables Predicted by
Stigma, Expectations of Positive Help by Source, and Demographic Data

Variable	N	Mean	Standard Deviation
Help seeking: doctor/nurse/meds (%)	191	.454	.499
Help seeking: counselor (%)	191	.407	.492
Help seeking: parents/friends (%)	191	.886	.318
Help seeking: Internet/helplines (%)	191	.161	.368
Stereotype scale	190	2.53	.471
Expected help from physician (%)	191	.785	.411
Expected help from parents/friends	185	.748	.35
Expected help from counselor (%)	191	.769	.422
Expected help from Internet/helplines	191	.291	.383
Age (years)	191	17.672	2.38
Male (%)	191	.383	.487
Education (1 to 5 years)	190	4.8	2.745
African American (%)	191	.199	.4
Asian (%)	191	.028	.166
Other ethnicity (%)	191	.113	.318

Doctor/nurse/meds: seeing a physician or nurse or taking medications. Counselor: seeing a counselor. Parents/friend: talking to parents or friends. Internet/help: going to an Internet Web site or calling a helpline. Stereotype: mean stereotype score on 1 to 3 scale. Expected Help: expected help from specified sources. When expected help sources were multiple, the average of the two scores was used.

and most reliably so for the least effective sources, the Internet and telephone helplines. The findings are also consistent with recently reported results from a large (N = 1,387) national survey conducted with adults in the United Kingdom, which found that the most common reason that individuals with "neurotic disorders" did not seek treatment was that they didn't think anyone could help them (reported by 22% of the sample; Meltzer et al., 2003).

Increasing the perceived effectiveness of appropriate treatment may be an important strategy for reducing the effects of unfavorable stereotypes associated with mental disorder and for increasing help seeking in general. It is noteworthy that our sample of youth with symptoms of depression reported poorer perceptions of treatment effectiveness for all but one of the sources of help compared to youth without those symptoms (Table 27.2). Hence increasing the perceived effectiveness of appropriate treatment among this vulnerable youth segment could be a strategy to increase their help seeking.

FACTORS THAT CONTRIBUTE TO STIGMA

Given the role of stigma on help-seeking behavior in youth, it is critical to identify the factors that contribute to stigma. In this section, we summarize the research on factors that contribute to stigma in both the general population and among youth. A comprehensive review of this literature is beyond the scope of this chapter, so a brief summary is provided. In general, factors contributing to stigma include (a) labels; (b) symptoms and/or anomalous behaviors associated with labels and mental illness; (c) attributions about mental illness; (d) misinformation about mental illness and negative images promulgated by the mass media; and (e) lack of contact with persons who have been successfully treated for mental illness.

According to the modified labeling theory, labels are one of a number of factors that contribute to stigma, perhaps via their association with specific behaviors, media accounts, or experiences (Link & Phelan, 1999; Phelan & Link,

Table 27.4 Results of Probit Regressions Predicting Four Help-Seeking Outcomes[a]

	Δ in Prob[b]	Z[c]	P|z|	95% Confidence Interval for Prob. Δ	
1. Doctor/Nurse/Medication					
(Pseudo R-squared = .042, N = 189)					
Stereotype	.055	0.69	0.49	−.101	.211
Expected help	.119	1.25	0.211	−.067	.306
2. Counselor					
(Pseudo R-squared = .115, N = 189)					
Stereotype	−.116	−1.43	0.153	−.274	.043
Expected help	.374	3.76	0	.18	.567
3. Parents/Friends					
(Pseudo R-squared = .097, N = 183)					
Stereotype	−.059	−1.28	0.201	−.149	.03
Expected help	.087	1.61	0.108	−.019	.193
4. Internet/Helplines					
(Pseudo R-squared = .212, N = 179)					
Stereotype	−.135	−2.63	0.009	−.238	−.032
Expected help	.278	4.49	0	.141	.401

[a] All coefficients are adjusted for gender, ethnicity, age, and education.

[b] Δ in Prob is the change in the probability of the outcome given a one-unit change in the predictor.

[c] Z = ratio of probit coefficient to its standard error.

Significance tests refer to probit estimates, not change in probability values (Δ) for an average respondent. For outcomes (1) and (2) there is a significant negative effect of the "other" ethnicity category. For all other outcomes and all other demographic variables, there are no discernable effects.

1999). This is especially true for pejorative labels, such as "schizo," "psycho," "wacko," and so on, which may be linked with violent and erratic behavior. Therefore, labels may be stigmatizing in their own right.

Labels clearly do not exist in a vacuum, but derive meaning from their relationship with characteristics of the disorder, both real (e.g., hearing voices) and exaggerated (e.g., being a homicidal maniac). Thus, the behaviors associated with mental illness may be stigmatizing in their own right. Evidence in support of this hypothesis is garnered from studies showing that the social behaviors of individuals with depression can elicit negative reactions from others (reviewed in Segrin, 2000), and that the social skill deficits present in schizophrenia (Mueser & Bellack, 1998) may increase stigma, even beyond the contribution of symptoms (Penn, Kohlmaier, & Corrigan, 2000).

Research on the role of attributions on stigma has its roots in the work of Weiner and colleagues (Weiner, 1993; Weiner, Perry, & Magnusson, 1988) and asserts that our explanations for mental and physical illness (i.e., in terms of controllability and responsibility) will affect our attitudes toward these disorders. Tests of this model applied to severe mental illnesses, such as schizophrenia, indicate that when such conditions are seen as under the person's control and something for which she or he is responsible, the tendency to blame and stigmatize that individual increases (Corrigan, 2000). Interestingly, ascribing causality to biological factors (e.g., genetics) leads to lower responsibility attributions, but in addition, to beliefs that the problem cannot be changed and that family members may have similar problems (i.e., a courtesy stigma; Phelan, Cruz-Rojas, & Reiff, in press).

Perhaps the most consistent predictors of

stigma are misinformation about mental illness. This is not surprising in view of the large role of the mass media in providing information about mental illness. In fact, the media are the most frequent source of information about mental illness for people in this country (Wahl, 1995). This suggests that the media have an important role in shaping public perception of mental illness.

Interestingly, there has been scant research directly linking media images of mental illness to stigma. There is evidence that greater exposure to the media, particularly television viewing, is associated with greater intolerance toward persons with mental illness (Granello & Pauley, 2000). However, there is convincing evidence that the media depict persons with SMI in a negative rather than positive light. Persons with SMI are disproportionately portrayed in films, television, and newspapers as violent, erratic, and dangerous (Angermeyer & Schulze, 2001; Diefenbach, 1997; Granello, Pauley, & Carmichael, 1999; Hyler, Gabbard, & Schneider, 1991; Monahan, 1992; Nairn, Coverdale, & Claasen, 2001; Signorielli, 2001; Wahl, 1995; Wahl & Roth, 1982; Williams & Taylor, 1995). As noted by Wahl (2002), media depictions of the violence committed by persons with a SMI are more graphic and disturbing than that depicted in persons without a SMI.

In an analysis of 31 major U.S. newspapers over a period of 2 months during the year 2000, APPC found that 64.7% of the stories about persons with schizophrenia had an association with violence. While associations with violence in stories about persons with bipolar disorder (29.1%) and depression (15.2%) were lower, these rates still exaggerate the incidence of violence in persons with SMI (Silver, 2001). These negative and inaccurate depictions of persons with SMI are not limited to adult media, but are unfortunately present in children's media as well (Wahl, 2002; 2003; Wahl, Wood, Zaveri, Drapalski, & Mann, 2003; Wilson, Nairn, Coverdale, & Panapa, 2000).

The role of the mass media is potentially increased because of the relative lack of direct contact with individuals who have been successfully treated for mental illness. Although there are exceptions, the research generally supports a re-

lationship between greater retrospective self-reported contact with persons with mental illness and less stigmatizing attitudes (Couture & Penn, 2003). Although retrospective reports have inherent flaws, such as being influenced by memory biases, the consistency of the findings is compelling.

Most of the research on stigma has been conducted with adult and community samples. However, findings from one of our own laboratories reveal that labels, previous contact, and anomalous behaviors also influence the attitudes of older adolescents (i.e., college-age samples) toward persons with mental illness. For example, labels that varied in "political correctness" (e.g., "schizophrenic" vs. "consumer of mental health services") exerted similar effects on the attitudes of undergraduates and a community adult sample (Penn & Drummond, 2001). Regarding contact effects, most of our studies (Penn & Corrigan, 2002; Penn et al., 1994; Penn, Kommana, Mansfield, & Link, 1999), as well as those in other laboratories (reviewed in Couture & Penn, 2003), replicate the findings with adults that greater self-reported contact is associated with lower stigma. Therefore, it appears that the factors that contribute to stigma development in adulthood are also important in adolescence.

Our review of the factors that influence stigma of mental illness suggests that one approach with potential for influencing the attitudes of adolescents toward mental illness is the use of mass media. Adolescents are heavy consumers of mass media. It has been estimated that approximately ⅔ of individuals between the ages of 8 and 18 have a television in their bedroom (Roberts, Henriksen, & Foehr, in press; Woodard & Gridina, 2000). Television viewing averages approximately 3½ hours daily in 11- to 14-year-olds (Roberts, Henriksen, & Foehr, in press), which decreases to 2½ hours daily by late adolescence (15–18; Brown & Witherspoon, 2001; Roberts, Henriksen, & Foehr, in press). However, these numbers may underestimate media exposure, as adolescents also devote a great deal of time (and money) to movies, video rentals, and the Internet (Brown & Witherspoon, 2001; Roberts & Foehr, in press).

The attitudes and behaviors of adolescents are influenced by exposure to the mass media. Reviews of the literature indicate a relationship between media exposure and the formation of gender stereotypes (Signorielli, 2001), aggression and desensitization to violence (Bushman & Anderson, 2001), particularly among children and young adolescents (Roberts, Henriksen, & Foehr, in press), and body image in adolescent women (Groesz, Levine, & Murnen, 2002). Furthermore, the media serve as a source of information for youth; over half of teenage women report learning about sex and birth control from TV, movies, and magazines (discussed in Brown & Witherspoon, 2001). Similar findings have been observed for knowledge about mental illness. In a qualitative study with 12- to 14-year-olds, all of the participants reported that television was their primary source of information about mental illness (Secker, Armstrong, & Hill, 1999). These findings suggest that the media can influence adolescent beliefs about mental illness, perhaps in a positive way. This notion will be discussed in more detail below.

REDUCING THE STIGMA OF MENTAL ILLNESS

Various approaches to reducing stigma of mental disorders have been attempted, mostly in the areas of education and promoting personal contact (Corrigan & Penn, 1999). Educational interventions have included various strategies, ranging from those that are brief (e.g., fact sheets, brochures; Penn et al., 1994; 1999) to more extensive interventions (e.g., semester-long courses) that provided factual information on mental illness and dispelled myths (e.g., Holmes, Corrigan, Williams, Canar, & Kubiak, 1999; reviewed in Corrigan & Penn, 1999; Hinshaw & Cicchetti, 2000; Mayville & Penn, 1999). In general, education appears to have a short-term impact on attitudes; however, the longitudinal stability of the findings has not been adequately evaluated (Corrigan & Penn, 1999). There is some evidence that education also has an effect on helping behaviors (e.g., donating money to the National Alliance for the Mentally Ill (NAMI); discussed in Corrigan, 2002), but the impact of education on specific discriminatory behaviors (e.g., treatment at work) has to this point not been assessed.

Promoting personal contact between a stigmatized group and community members is based on the "contact hypothesis," which has an extensive history in the study of racism (Jackson, 1993; Kolodziej & Johnson, 1996). According to this hypothesis, contact effects will be strongest when the individuals meet as equals, have a chance to work cooperatively, rather than competitively, on a task, and when the target person mildly disconfirms the stereotype. The last criterion refers to the finding that encountering someone who greatly disconfirms a stereotype may result in categorizing that target as an "exception" to the rule. Therefore, positive experiences with the target individual will not generalize to the broader group (Johnstone & Hewstone, 1992).

With respect to mental illness stigma, contact has been provided in the context of volunteer activities, classroom experiences, job training, and simulated laboratory encounters (reviewed by Couture & Penn, 2003; Kolodziej & Johnson, 1996). The findings suggest that contact effects are especially impressive and robust (Corrigan, 2002; Couture & Penn, 2003); a recent meta-analysis of the literature reported that the average effect size of contact on attitudes was .34 (Kolodziej & Johnson, 1996). These effects were largest when the contact was provided to students, rather than professionals, especially if the contact was not a required part of the classroom or training experience (Kolodziej & Johnson, 1996). These findings indicate that promoting personal contact can reduce stigma toward persons with mental illness.

Most of these studies were conducted with either college-age student samples or with adults in the community. In addition, there have been numerous grass roots or community efforts to reduce stigma, some focused on children and adolescents (Estroff, Penn, & Toporek, in press; WPA, 2002). However, most of these community efforts either did not collect outcome data or are in the process of collecting it. Therefore, we will report on the few studies that have been conducted with younger adolescents that evaluated outcomes related to stigma.

Petchers, Biegel, and Drescher (1988) implemented a video-based educational program in two high schools. The program included a videotape of teenagers discussing their experiences of having a person with mental illness in the family, along with a six-lesson educational supplement. The results of a posttest-only design showed that participation in the video-based program was associated with higher ratings on a measure that assessed both knowledge about and attitudes toward mental illness, relative to participants who did not participate in this program. These findings are limited by the posttest-only design and use of a nonstandard measure of stigma.

Esters, Cooker, and Ittenbach (1998) assigned two classes of rural high school students to receive either 3 days of instruction on mental health, which included an instructional video, and information pertaining to sources of help in the community, or instruction unrelated to mental health. Participants completed measures that assessed attitudes toward receiving treatment and to persons with mental illness, prior to and following the course instruction and at 12-week follow-up. The results showed that the mental health instruction was significantly associated with improved attitudes both toward persons with mental illness and with seeking professional help; findings that held at follow-up.

Schulze, Richter-Werling, Matschinger, and Angermeyer (2003) also implemented an educational intervention, but one which included a contact component. Ninety high school students signed up for a program entitled *Crazy? So What*, a 5-day program that involved the presentation of information about mental illness, meeting someone with schizophrenia (who discussed their personal experiences with the illness, treatment, and stigma), and group discussions. Participants in this program were compared to high school students who chose to sign up for non–mental health–related projects. The results showed that *Crazy? So What* produced a significant reduction in negative stereotypes and a trend toward less social distance after participation in the project. These results remained stable at 1-month follow-up. Interpretation of these findings needs to be tempered by the fact that participants self-selected into the project. Thus, the preexisting characteristics that led to partic-

ipation in the mental health project may have also been the underlying mechanism by which the program exerted its effects.

Finally, Pinfold et al. (2003) evaluated the effectiveness of two mental health awareness workshops on attitudes toward and knowledge of mental illness in 472 secondary school children in the United Kingdom. An individual who worked in the mental health field led the first workshop, which included viewing a videotape about people living with mental illness and challenging negative stereotypes of mental illness. An individual who shared her or his personal experience with having a mental illness facilitated the second workshop. The results showed that the workshops had a positive impact on attitudes and knowledge of mental illness, with attitudinal changes remaining stable across 6-month follow-up. These results were especially strong for individuals who reported previous contact with someone with a mental illness. Again, the value of these findings was circumscribed by the uncontrolled design.

Although limited in number and by methodological limitations, these findings are nevertheless promising. The findings also converge on a number of themes. In particular, consistent with previous findings obtained from adult samples (Couture & Penn, 2003), promoting contact seems to be a key element in reducing stigma. In addition, there is indirect evidence that demonstrating the effectiveness of psychiatric and psychological treatments, either through direct instruction (Esters et al., 1998) or via role models (Schulze et al., 2003), may reduce stigma, a finding consistent with the survey data reported earlier in this chapter (Table 27.4). Therefore, facilitating personal contact between members of the community and individuals with mental illness, and promoting the effectiveness of treatments for mental illness, may be crucial to reducing stigma among youth.

Because adolescents are heavy media users, greater use of mass media to reduce, rather than augment, stigmatizing attitudes should be explored. This can be done in a number of ways. First, the media can serve as a resource for adolescents with a mental illness. For example, Gould, Munfakh, Lubell, Kleinman, and Parker (2002) found that nearly one fifth of New York adolescents reported using the Internet to help with emotional disorders. Unfortunately, over 20% of the respondents were not satisfied with the information they found, which suggests that the content and links provided by some of the Web sites were inadequate. Second, the media can be educated to report on mental illness responsibly (Gould & Kramer, 2001; Salter & Byrne, 2002). This has been advocated in the context of suicide in adolescents by addressing contagion, the increase in suicides that follow from the reporting of suicide stories in the news media (Gould & Kramer, 2001; Gould, Jamieson, & Romer, 2003). Such responsible reporting can also be extended to presenting information about mental illness with the aim of educating the public about the efficacy of treatment for mental disorders, providing the information in a more balanced manner, and avoiding attention-grabbing, pejorative headlines (Gould et al., 2003; Wahl, 1995).

Stigma reduction may also be achieved by integrating mental illness messages into the entertainment value of film and television. Anecdotally, this appears to be the case with the film *A Beautiful Mind,* which seems to have served the dual purpose of both entertaining and educating audiences about mental illness. Another recent example is the collaboration between Barbara Hocking from www.sane.org with the staff of *Home and Away,* the most popular soap opera in Australia. This collaboration resulted in a storyline of a current character, Joey Rainbow, who gradually develops schizophrenia. Hocking consulted with the program's staff and provided educational materials on schizophrenia to the 18-year-old actor who played the character who developed schizophrenia. This culminated in a more accurate portrayal of schizophrenia (e.g., prodromal symptoms, acute episode, residual symptoms) than typically manifest on screen. What is especially appealing about this approach is that the character was already well established on the program, so the development of his schizophrenia was arguably comparable to observing a family member or friend develop the disorder. Thus, it would appear the producers for *Home and Away* provided an opportunity to promote a mediated form of contact between the audience and someone with mental illness.

We recently investigated the effects of a documentary film about schizophrenia on the attitudes of undergraduates toward schizophrenia (Penn, Chamberlin, & Mueser, 2003). The documentary *I'm Still Here* depicts individuals with schizophrenia in a balanced light; individuals with both remitted and acute symptoms are portrayed, with both humor and sensitivity. These depictions were supplemented by interviews with family members and mental health professionals. The results showed that this documentary resulted in more benign attributions about schizophrenia (i.e., that persons with schizophrenia are not to blame for having this disorder and that they are not responsible for causing it themselves) relative to two control documentary films. The film did not have a significant effect on participant attitudes toward individuals with schizophrenia, although the pattern of performance (i.e., task means) was in the expected direction. Participant ratings revealed that they found this film enjoyable, suggesting that documentaries can be an effective and entertaining medium for delivering information about mental illness.

CONCLUSIONS

This chapter has reviewed evidence that addressing the stigma of mental illness in adolescence is a worthy endeavor. It is likely that adolescents who are informed about mental illness, both in terms of facts and the dispelling of myths, will be less likely to stigmatize others and more likely to seek and stay in treatment for their own symptoms. In particular, there is promising evidence in both our survey findings and the results of interventions that increasing awareness of the efficacy of treatment can reduce the role of stigma in inhibiting help seeking and in discriminating against persons with mental disorders.

This chapter has also highlighted the potential role of mass media in destigmatizing mental illness, a role that will be more effective if expressed in partnerships between media and mental health professionals. Of course, the media can only do so much to address stigma; much is also dependent on educators and the mental health field. For example, bringing persons with mental illness to the classroom as guest speakers and providing opportunities for adolescents to volunteer with persons with mental illness have shown promise as stigma reduction strategies (Couture & Penn, 2003). In sum, the high school and classroom can promote activities that may challenge negative stereotypes.

In a similar manner, mental health professionals should strive to make the process of seeking and staying in treatment as destigmatizing as possible. Part of the challenge is developing liaisons between primary-care practitioners and school counselors, the gatekeepers who may be the first to encounter adolescents with emotional problems. This will facilitate appropriate mental health referrals and reduce the time from symptom onset and treatment. In addition, there have been recent efforts to provide treatment at home or in settings that are not identified as psychiatric facilities to address the stigma or shame of seeking treatment for physical disorders (e.g., AIDS; Gewirtz & Gossart-Walker, 2000) or psychiatric disorders (prodromal symptoms; McGorry, Yung, & Phillips, 2001). These approaches, coupled with early education and contact opportunities, and working with the media to provide balanced views of mental illness, are important steps in addressing stigma and ensuring that adolescents get early treatment for mental disorders.

The Research, Policy, and Practice Context for Delivery of Evidence-Based Mental Health Treatments for Adolescents: A Systems Perspective

Kimberly Hoagwood

28

chapter

Research discoveries in the past 20 years have led to major breakthroughs in identifying treatments for adolescents that are most likely to improve their mental health functioning. Problems of attention, depression, and various forms of anxiety, including those related to traumatic abuse and obsessive-compulsive disorders, can now be treated and treated effectively through cognitive-behavioral, interpersonal, and medication therapies and, in some cases, a combination of these therapies (Lonigan, Elbert, & Johnson, 1998; March, Amaya, Jackson, Murray, & Schulte, 1998; March and the TADS Consortium, MTA Cooperative Group, 1999a; Mufson, Dorta, Olfson, Weissman, & Hoagwood, 2004; Silverman, Kurtines, & Hoagwood, 2004). A range of community-based services to support youth and families in accessing or continuing with treatments have also been examined rigorously. Some of this work is demonstrating how engagement techniques, particularly forms of intensive case management, in-home therapeutic services, and functional family therapies can help parents or caregivers care for their children (Alexander & Sexton, 2002; Burns, Costello, Angold, et al., 1995; Chamberlain & Reid, 1991; Evans, Banks, Huz, McNulty, 1994; Farmer, Dorsey & Mustillo, 2004; Henggeler & Schoenwald, 1998; McKay & Lynn, in press). Research progress in these areas has been of unprecedented proportions, in part because there was a tripling of funding at the National Institute of Mental Health (NIMH) between 1989 and 2001 for studies of children's mental health in general (National Advisory Mental Health Council, 2001). Although in general research on child and adolescent mental health has lagged far behind studies of adult mental illness, research on the efficacy of specific treatment and service models for youth is now in an era of expansion.

The nexus for this progress has arisen because of the growing popularity of evidence-based practices (EBPs). At least 26 federal Web sites use this term to refer to their practices. A MEDLINE search from 1995 to 2002 found over 5,400 citations that included the terms *evidence-based medicine, evidence-based treatment,* or *evidence-based practice.* Between 1900 and 1995 there were only 70 such citations. The term *evidence-based practice* has captured the public imagination in part because it provides what appears to be a scientific imprimatur upon a body of work whose application in real-world clinical practice is presumed to lead to improvements in children's emotional or behavioral functioning. Because the state of current mental health service delivery has been widely criticized as being fragmented, ineffective, and insufficient (Bickman, 1996c; Stroul & Friedman, 1986), policymakers' hopes for improvements in service delivery and practices are now largely linked to delivery of EBPs. Logically, this is a reasonable assumption.

However, the growth in empirical knowledge and focus on community-based care has drawn attention to the "different worlds of research and practice" (Ringeisen, Henderson, & Hoagwood, 2003). A series of influential reports, including the Institute of Medicine Report (1998), the *Surgeon General's Report on Mental Health* (U.S. Department of Health and Human Services [DHHS], 1999), and the Surgeon General's National Action Plan on Children's Mental Health (U.S. Public Health Service [USPHS] 2001b), have uniformly voiced a single theme: the gap between research and practice must be closed.

Yet, despite this progress, there exist numerous challenges to providing quality care for youth and their families within the systems that serve these populations. These challenges are largely *systemic* and, unfortunately, have become *endemic* to the current structure of youth mental health care in this country. As Flynn points out in a recent special issue on EBP, "Many parents are frankly doubtful that grafting evidence based practices onto a failed and fragmented system will succeed" (Flynn, in press).

Among the challenges to embedding effective treatments within the current system of mental health care for youth are a range of both research-based knowledge gaps and systemic barriers. Gaps in research knowledge exist in five major areas: treatment development for specific disorders; the comorbidities that exist among these disorders and psychiatric classification more generally; ways of bridging the gap between research and practice; the categorizations of EBPs; and means of implementing or disseminating effective practices. Systemic barriers exist in five areas: service fragmentation; access and use of services, which are especially relevant to ethnic and cultural variations; lack of sustained family involvement; regulatory practices; and fiscal disincentives.

The purpose of this chapter is to outline these challenges to improving delivery of effective treatments for adolescents and their families and to define a set of research and policy directions that may help improve delivery. In particular, a number of major multisite studies supported by several foundations and federal agencies are currently under way to examine contextual influences on delivery of youth mental health services. These studies will very likely lead to new ways of thinking about implementation and dissemination of effective practices.

RESEARCH GAPS

Gaps in Treatment Development

A recent report from the National Alliance for Mental Illness (NAMI, 2004) indicated that research on serious mental illness has been underfunded, compared to other chronic, disabling illnesses, and consequently is insufficiently prioritized. As a result, little is known about the safety, efficacy, or effectiveness of treatments for bipolar disorders, eating disorders, depression, and trauma. The placebo effect in medication research, particularly in studies of adolescent depression, can be higher than 50% (Emslie, Walkup, Pliska & Ernst, 1999), thus calling into serious question the mechanisms whereby treatment affects outcomes. Furthermore, when families of youth with these kinds of problems are seeking treatment, they are unlikely to be able to identify any providers sufficiently well informed to be able to diagnose and treat these disorders. In addition, despite progress in identifying the efficacy of certain medication treatments for certain conditions (e.g., attention-deficit hyperactivity disorder [ADHD], obsessive-compulsive disorder [OCD], aggression), no studies have yet been completed on the long-term safety and efficacy of these medications. Thus families do not know what the long-term effects may be of treating their children with medication therapies.

Gaps in Comorbidity and Issues in Psychiatric Diagnosis

The strength of the evidence in research-based knowledge centers largely on discrete treatments for discrete disorders (Weisz et al., 1995a; Weisz, Donenberg, Han, & Weiss, 1995b). Unfortunately, many children present with multiple, chronic, and severe problems. The strength of the evidence about mental health care for these youth is weak. This is a major problem because comorbidity of disorders among youth is relatively common. The Great Smoky Mountain Study (GSMS; Costello, Farmer, Angold, Burns, & Erkanli (1997) Costello et al., (1996a,b), conducted in North Carolina, found that while the prevalence of psychiatric disorders in an epidemiological sample among youth was 20%, a full third of the youth had more than one diagnosis. In addition, studies by Weisz and colleagues conducted within public mental health clinics in Los Angeles found that the modal number of diagnoses among youth presenting to these clinics was 5, and that youth with single disorders were extremely rare (Weisz et al., 1995a, 1995b). As a consequence, the lack of a developed research base on the effectiveness of treatments for youth with more than one problem presents serious problems for delivery of services within complex service systems that routinely are responsible for multiproblem youth.

A more fundamental problem exists with respect to psychiatric classification itself, especially in the field of children's mental health. Diagnostic vicissitudes are the norm rather than the exception. This has given rise to a variety of perspectives, not to mention tensions, on what constitutes mental health, mental illness, or psychiatric impairments among children and on their etiology (Jensen & Hoagwood, 1997). The epistemological issues surrounding diagnostic classification and its nomenclature have been described elsewhere. Diagnostic criteria for children rely primarily on observational markers subject to clinical bias (Bickman, 1999), cultural inferences, and these problems are compounded by lack of reliability between research-based diagnoses and community-based diagnoses (Lewczyk, Garland, Hurlburt, Gearity, & Haugh, 2001). These issues raise questions about the nature of psychiatric knowledge itself, and under-score the importance of inclusion and collaboration of family members, teachers, and other persons knowledgeable about the behavior of children prior to assigning a diagnosis. In short, the complexities surrounding psychiatric diagnosis for children push the notion of collaboration into a place of conceptual prominence with respect to children's mental health.

Lab-to-Clinic Translatability

Meta-analyses of psychosocial treatments for youth have indicated that psychosocial treatment appears to work equally well for internalizing conditions (which include depression and anxiety disorders) and externalizing disorders (those directed more outwardly, including disruptive behavior problems such as conduct disorder). However, most of these studies have been conducted in university or laboratory settings rather than in community clinics. Thus the degree of adaptation (either cultural, practical, or organizational) needed to translate a protocol from a laboratory setting into a community clinic is unknown and is not built into the design or methods for developing treatments in the first place, even though it is a critical ingredient for the ultimate fit of a treatment to a clinical context (Hoagwood, Jensen, Roper, Arnold, Odbert et al., in press).

Studies by Weisz and colleagues have demonstrated that mental health interventions used to treat youth in everyday clinical practice are not only different from those studied in academic settings but also potentially less effective (Weisz et al., 1992; 1995b). Weisz et al. (1992) found that the vast majority of studies supporting the effectiveness of these models were conducted in either university, school, or laboratory settings. Under these conditions, the interventions improve the outcomes for the children. However, the dozen studies that investigated outcomes of these treatments in naturalistic (clinic) settings demonstrated a negative effect. The implications of these different outcomes are that the conditions of routine clinic care are vastly different from the conditions under which

most studies of treatment effectiveness have been conducted.

Weisz and colleagues (Weisz, 2000; Weisz et al., 1992, 1995a, 1995b) also identified some possible explanations for the disparity between results in laboratory and clinic settings. One is that laboratory settings may be more conducive to therapeutic gain, simply because they have more resources. Providers may be better trained and have more modern equipment and intensive supervision, making it a better setting in which to deliver services. Another explanation is that psychosocial treatment provided in laboratory settings may result in better outcomes because it is more likely to use behavioral treatment methods, which are well established. Studies are currently under way to examine how and whether research-based treatment models can be delivered in clinic settings and whether these models actually improve clinical outcomes beyond treatments usually delivered within these settings (MacArthur Foundation Network on Youth Mental Health, 2004; J. Weisz, personal communication, March 2004). This study is described in greater detail below.

Limitations and Discrepancies in the Categorization of Evidence-Based Practices

Kazdin (in press-a) suggests that an emphasis on the distinctions between evidence-based and not evidence-based is misguided and limits the potential of research studies to further the goal of improving practices. Instead, he suggests broadening the continuum of evidence to include a range of categories for differentiating studies about treatments. The categories he suggests are *(1)* not evaluated; *(2)* evaluated, but unclear, no, or possibly negative effects at this time; *(3)* promising (some evidence); *(4)* well-established (parallel to well-established in conventional schemes); and *(5)* better/best treatments (treatments shown to be more effective than other evidence-based treatments). He also points out that an exclusive focus on outcomes rather than on the reasons that treatments work—i.e., on the mechanisms or processes of change within therapies—is leading to a proliferation of treatments, many of which are likely to be similar. Attention to mechanisms of change can create better efficiencies of effort and improve treatments more generally (Kazdin, in press).

In addition to these limitations, there is currently no consensus on how to define *evidence-based*, nor on when the evidence base, however it is defined, is ready to be deployed, moved out, or used in community settings. While the term is generally used to demarcate research-based, generally structured and manualized practices that have been examined with randomized trial designs from less rigorous or well-tested practices, no currently agreed-upon definition exists, and it is becoming a popular phrase with which to capture public attention and public funds (Tannenbaum, 2003).

In this chapter I use the term *evidence-based practices* to refer to a set of research-based treatments, preventive interventions, services, or clinical practices (e.g., assessment, screening, referral). *Evidence-based policies* refer to local, state, or federal mandates or initiatives promoting the use or adoption of evidence-based practices.

In fact, numerous and discrepant criteria are being used by professional associations and by the scientific community to differentiate evidence based from non–evidence based. The varying definitions make it difficult for policymakers or practitioners to decide which among the practices to adopt in any given circumstance. Currently foundations and federal agencies are attempting to create agreed-upon criteria and an archive of research-based practices that can be updated to assist field practitioners and the scientific community in evaluating the quality, strength, and fit of evidence for specific clinical practice.

In addition, the standards for entry into the lists of EBPs vary widely. Operational criteria have been proposed by the Division of Clinical Psychology of the American Psychological Association (APA; Lonigan et al., 1998) and applied to studies of specific psychosocial treatments for childhood disorders. A similar process has been developed for evaluating the evidence for pharmacological treatments (Jensen, Bhatara, et al., 1999), preventive programs (Greenberg, Domitrovich, & Bumbarger et al., 2001), and school-based mental health services (Rones & Hoagwood, 2000). Yet, because inclusion criteria

vary, the ways in which delivery variables have been taken into account also vary. For example, the APA standards apply criteria that ignore parameters of effectiveness that would be likely to yield answers to questions about the readiness of a treatment model to be implemented. Such factors are often excluded from clinical trials of specific treatments for the very reason that they may create "noise" around the interpretation of treatment effects. Yet it is precisely these "nuisance" factors that are essential to understand if implementation of a treatment is likely to be successful. So the relevance of the applicability of most EBPs' integration into routine services is largely unknown (Mufson et al., in press). These different definitions make it difficult for policymakers, families, treatment developers, and consumer organizations to speak in a uniform voice or to learn from each other's lessons in the complex task of implementing these models.

Gaps in Knowledge About Implementation and Dissemination

Knowledge about ways in which to integrate evidence-based practices within complex, dynamic service systems is currently lacking. Challenges remain in "scaling up" interventions from local sites to states. The use of the term *evidence-based practice* is thus far associated with specific models of child or family interventions; it has not yet been applied to system- or organization-level interventions (e.g., quality assurance methods) (Chambers, Ringeisen, & Hickman, in press). Studies from outside of mental health (in AIDS or cancer trials, for example) have found that characteristics of the environment within which an intervention is placed influence the delivery of the model and the outcomes associated with it. Consequently, studies that examine how to build an infrastructure to support delivery of quality clinical care are greatly needed.

As Ringeisen and colleagues (2003) point out, both content-specific and contextual factors influence the ability to disseminate services and treatments. For example, Kendall et al. (1997) examined specific mechanisms of action within a cognitive-behavioral intervention for childhood anxiety disorders and found that exposure accounted for the response. This component of the intervention—a feature of its content—is critical to reducing reported childhood fears and anxiety responses. Other factors that reside outside of the content of specific EBPs also influence outcomes. Such factors might include degree or intensity of clinical supervision, or an organization's support for employees. These factors of context are beginning to be examined. For example, Henggeler, Schoenwald, Liao, Letourneau, and Edwards (2002) describe the positive relationship between model-consistent clinical supervision and a therapist's fidelity to multisystemic therapy (MST). Supervision consistent with the MST approach is also positively related to clinical improvement. New studies just beginning to be undertaken in the field of child and adolescent mental health services are examining how systemic features, such as organizational leadership, work attitudes, and climate, may explain variance in the quality of provided services (e.g., Glisson & James, 2002).

Another type of context factor that limits the ability to disseminate EBP models is the small number of studies on the cost-effectiveness of these models. In fact, in mental health, those empirically based interventions that currently have the widest dissemination are also those that have had cost-effectiveness data to support their impact relative to usual care prior to wide-scale promotion (e.g., functional family therapy, Alexander & Parsons, 1973; multisystemic therapy, Henggeler, Schoenwald, Rowland, & Cunningham, 2002; nurse visitation model, Kitzman, Olds, Sidora, Henderson, Hanks et al., 2000). The paucity of studies on the cost-effectiveness of service or treatment models seriously limits the adoption by policymakers of these interventions. These studies are labor-intensive and costly and require careful delineation of the service or treatment components.

Another kind of problem in the spread of empirically based practices occurs because of the rapidity with which knowledge about effective practices is being deployed, coupled with the dearth of knowledge about how best to implement them. This problem has become a kind of catch-22 for the field (Hoagwood et al., in press). The problem arises when treatment developers

or organizations not affiliated with the development and testing of a particular treatment model design strategies to take that model to scale. Considerable resources are required to design strategies for overcoming the obstacles enumerated above—for example, in strengthening the capacity of clinicians to implement a model with fidelity. Yet resources must be expended in advance in order to garner research funding for assessing the impact of those strategies (Schoenwald & Henggeler, 2002; Torrey et al., 2001). Thus, although several groups of treatment and service developers have produced similar multilevel approaches to the problem of taking an effective model to scale (Schoenwald & Henggeler, 2002), the methods used to do so have been idiosyncratic, bootstrapped, and informed as much by field experience as by theory and research on the diffusion of innovation, technology transfer, and organizational behavior.

SYSTEM BARRIERS

In the mid-1980s a series of federal and state initiatives focused on strengthening the community-based service system for children and adolescents. Called the Child and Adolescent Service System Program (CASSP), a group of state grants were awarded by the NIMH to create youth and family bureaus within state systems. This initiative was given principled footing through the development of an influential model, called the System of Care (Stroul and Friedman, 1986). This model articulated a series of values, centered around maintaining children within their communities, coordinating services, involving families integrally in delivery and planning of treatments and services, and attending to the cultural relevance of services. The most recent iteration of the model has been under an important federal initiative designed to support local community-based services for children and adolescents. Called the Comprehensive Community Mental Health Services for Children and Families (CMHSC) and supported by the Center for Mental Health Services (CMHS) of the Substance Abuse and Mental Health Services Administration (SAMHSA), this program constitutes the single largest federal program supporting mental health services for youth with serious emotional or behavioral problems. The program is currently financed at close to $100 million per year. One major focus of this program in recent years has been the inclusion of EBPs into the local community-based programs.

Despite the importance of this program, it exists only in a small percentage of communities in the United States. As a consequence, most families seeking mental health care do not have access to these federally funded programs and instead face significant system barriers in accessing effective treatment models. Some of these barriers are outlined below.

Fragmentation

Many sectors are involved in delivering services for children, adolescents, and their families, a characteristic that makes them cumbersome to study. In general, at least six separate sectors or administrative structures may be involved in serving youth with mental health problems: specialty mental health; primary health care; child welfare; education; juvenile justice; and substance abuse (Stroul & Friedman, 1986). Across most of the United States, these sectors are administratively, fiscally, and structurally distinct. As a consequence, the responsibility for providing services for a youth with mental health problems or for his or her family is divided among different agencies, each with a unique set of regulations, intake procedures, rules for inclusion and exclusion, and service options. This fragmentation creates enormous problems for families whose children often need different kinds of services for different kinds of problems (Burns, 2003; Burns et al., 1995; Friedman, 2003).

Studies of the impact of coordinated models for delivering services to youth with mental health problems have found that integrated models improve access to care, reduce restrictiveness of placements (e.g., reduce in-patient stays), and improve family satisfaction (Bickman, 1996a, 1996b). However, these same studies have found that these integrated models do nothing in the way of improving clinical outcomes, and concerted calls for improving the clinical care that can be embedded within coordinated systems models have been made repeatedly (Burns, 2003; Henggeler, Schoenwald, & Munger, 1996; Hoagwood, Hibbs, Brent, & Jensen, 1995; Hoagwood, Jensen, Petti, & Burns, 1996).

Access

Underrecognition of youth mental disorders is well documented across all ethnic and racial groups (Costello et al., 1996; DHHS, 1999; Horwitz, Leaf, & Leventhal, 1998; Horwitz, Leaf, Leventhal, Forsyth, & Speechley, 1992; Lavigne et al., 1993; National Advisory Mental Health Council, 2001; Attkisson & Rosenblatt, 1998; Fisher, Dulcan, Davies, Piacentini et al., 1996; Roberts, 1998, 1999; Shaffer, USPHS, 2001a, 2001b). Current evidence suggests that these difficulties disproportionately affect minority youth and families because they are also less likely to have access to general health-care services (DHHS, 1999; USPHS, 2001b). The recent supplement to the Surgeon General's Report on Mental Health, Culture, Race, and Ethnicity (USPHS, 2001c) notes that the disparities affecting mental health services for racial and ethnic minorities have several key characteristics, namely that minorities *(1)* have more barriers and less access to mental health services, *(2)* are less likely to receive needed mental health services, *(3)* often receive a poorer quality of services, and *(4)* are underrepresented in studies of mental health. Minority parents are at further disadvantage because they and their children are exposed to proportionately greater levels of strains and risks under normal day-to-day conditions, all of which are increased even further when they must deal with a child with emotional or behavioral disabilities (Leaf et al., 1996).

The cumulative impact of lack of access to mental health services, higher levels of risk factors, and historical and current societal discriminatory attitudes place these children on a dangerous trajectory that can lead to more serious emotional or behavioral problems later in life (Loeber & Farrington, 1998; USPHS, 2000). Furthermore, studies have documented that less than one third of children with suicide ideation, conduct disorder, and substance abuse or dependency seek or receive help for these problems, and that less than half of youth with major depression seek or receive help for depression (Stiffman, Earls, Robins, & Jung, 1988). By necessity, access to mental health services for youth usually depends on the recognition and actions of key adults (Pescosolido, 1992; Stiffman, Chen, Elze, Dore, & Cheng, 1997), some of whom themselves may suffer from mental health problems. Other barriers such as stigma, lack of availability of services, lack of specialists, long waiting lists, and lack of insurance also impede use of services.

According to numerous recent reports and studies (Kataoke et al., 2002; USPHS 2001a; NIMH, 2001; Ringel & Sturm, 2001; Stiffman et al., 1997), the majority of all children—both minority and nonminority—with mental health problems do not receive any mental health service. The recently released report of the President's New Freedom Commission on Mental Health (2003) has identified access to services among children as a top priority. In addition, a report released by the NIMH (2001) indicated that approximately three quarters of children with mental health needs do not receive any type of mental health service, and the disparity between need and use of services is highest among minority youth. These rates are identical to those reported in the mid-1980s by the U.S. Congress, Office of Technology Assessment (1991), which shows that the level of need for services remains unchanged despite decades of scientific progress in developing evidence-based assessments, treatments, and services for these children.

Underidentification is of particular concern in the gatekeeping systems such as schools and primary care settings, where almost all children are seen at some point and where early identification is especially feasible (Costello et al., 1988a, 1988b; Horwitz et al., 1992, 1998; Lavigne et al., 1993; USPHS, 2001a). In fact, in a prospective cohort study, Horwitz et al. (1998) examined the effect of families' attitudes about the appropriateness of discussing psychosocial concerns on pediatric providers' identification of psychoso-

cial problems. The authors found considerable discrepancy between what parents reported as appropriate to do and what they actually did when they recognized mental health problems in their children. Most (81.1%) believed it was appropriate to discuss four or more of the six hypothetical situations with their children's physician, whereas only 40.9% actually did discuss any of these problems with a physician when a problem occurred.

Directly connected to lack of access are significant problems in capacity: most communities in the United States have few if any child psychiatrists to treat children or adolescents (IOM, 2000). Furthermore, the training of other professionals who are most likely to come in contact with children or adolescents (e.g., family physicians or pediatricians, school counselors, psychologists, social workers) is unlikely to have included any content on empirically based practices (American Academy of Pediatrics [AAP], 2000; National Association of Social Workers). Consequently, the mental health system's ability to accommodate the needs of children and adolescents with mental health problems is acutely compromised.

Cultural Barriers to Access

Additional barriers to access deter racial and ethnic minorities, including mistrust of treatment, discrimination, and differences in communication (McKay & Lynn, in press). Mental health care disparities may also stem from minorities' historical and current struggles with racism and discrimination, which may affect their mental health or contribute to lower economic, social, and political status (USPHS, 2001b). The cumulative weight of all barriers to care, not any single one alone, is likely responsible for mental health disparities.

In addition, studies by Takeuchi, Leaf, and Kuo (1988) have demonstrated that different ethnic groups gain access to services through different routes or pathways. For example, Takeuchi found that African-American families entered community mental health care through referrals from social agencies more often than Caucasian families did, and that Mexican-American families entered more often than Caucasian families through school referrals. The patterns of service use also vary across different racial and ethnic groups (McCabe, Yeh, Hough, Landsverk, Hurlburt et al., 1999). These findings have implications for the ways service systems should be organized to serve those who need them and to increase access to care.

Lack of Attention to Family-Driven Practices

Treatments that are inaccessible to those who may benefit from them may be effective but are essentially useless if not accessed. However, a series of important studies have found that successful efforts can be made to enhance a family's service engagement and decrease rates of premature treatment termination. Using brief telephone interviews prior to service entry, a range of studies have been undertaken to troubleshoot barriers to service engagement and increase minority families' participation in services (McKay & Lynn, in press; Santisteban et al., 1996; Szapocznik et al., 1988). Unfortunately, attempts to integrate evidence-based and family-driven engagement strategies with evidence-based clinical treatments are rare. A notable exception to this is a series of studies in New York State, linking implementation of EBPs for child trauma to family-driven practices (Murray, Rodriguez, Hoagwood, & Jensen, in press).

Among the values that have become intrinsic to community-based services have been those that stipulate that parents, guardians, or consumers must be integrally involved in treatment planning and delivery if the quality of care for children is to improve. The federal government through SAMHSA has supported the development of an infrastructure within state mental health agencies to support consumer involvement in service planning, and most states have consumer or recipient offices to strengthen this involvement. Numerous family advocacy organizations now exist to support the needs of families with children who have emotional or behavioral problems more generally, and for those with specific psychiatric disorders (e.g., ADHD, bipolar disorders, depressive disorders, etc.). Simultaneously, there have been several major initiatives in primary care (through Institutes for Healthcare Improvement, for example) to reform health-care services nationally by positioning consumers centrally in treatment planning so that they are empowered to make decisions about their own health care. These initiatives within both general health care and mental health care are leading to innovations in delivery, such as providing families with vouchers to function as case managers for their child's care. The movement away from office-based practice and toward empowerment of consumers is likely to increase significantly over the next decade.

A major issue affecting the acceptability of EBPs to many families is the concern that use of EBPs may interfere with the individualization of services. For many families, the single most important criterion of acceptability is the extent to which services can be individually tailored (Flynn, in press). Evidence-based practices are often seen as prescriptive and constraining. Thus efforts are being made to meld family-based preferences for individualization of care with EBPs, such as the development of parent empowerment programs taught by parent advocate and professional teams to improve knowledge about EBPs (Hoagwood & Johnson, 2003; Jensen, Hoagwood, & Trickett, 1999). Family advocacy groups, such as the Federation of Families, are also developing family-friendly guides to describe in detail the expectations and levels of involvement that specific EBPs require for their implementation (T. Osher, personal communication, April 2004).

Regulatory Practices

Across the range of what are called EBPs (for psychosocial treatments, medications, services, or preventive programs) there are differences in the ways in which deployment occurs. For example, in pharmaceutical medicine, evidence-based approaches have been built into the regulatory standards developed by the U.S. Food and Drug Administration (FDA) to review scientific evidence and identify effective medications. The strength of the evidence for pharmacological treatments is regulated by the FDA, and an industry for their distribution has grown up around this. In contrast, psychosocial treatments, services, and preventive interventions do not have regulatory backing, and their distribution depends largely on the resourcefulness of individuals who developed the treatments or services (Hoagwood et al., 2001)

Financing Policies

A series of financing policies are shaping the reimbursement mechanisms for mental health services for children and their families and consequently the possibilities for delivering new effective clinical treatment models. The most significant of the federal policies are those targeting the financing of children's mental health services. These have included significant increases in funding from sources outside of traditional mental health block grants, including expanded funding for Medicaid, State Children's Health Insurance Program (SCHIP), certain educational programs (e.g., Head Start, Safe and Drug-Free Schools), and privately insured pharmacy benefits, among other sources. Policies focusing on the application of behavioral managed care in the public and private sectors and on expansion of health insurance coverage under SCHIP for uninsured children are reducing the role of mental health agencies to effect policy reforms single-handedly. A related set of financing issues has included expansion of the parity for mental health and general health benefits. These are outlined below.

Medicaid Expansion and State Children's Health Insurance Program

The policies involving expansions of public health insurance, including Medicaid expansions in the late 1980s and the introduction of SCHIP in the late 1990s, changed the insurance distribution for youth who use mental health services. The share of all children, and of children using services, who were uninsured fell (Glied & Cuellar, 2003) because public insurance covered children who would otherwise have been uninsured. Public insurance coverage has also displaced private insurance. In 1998 about

25% of children with a diagnosed mental health problem were publicly insured (Glied & Cuellar, 2003). Among poor minority children, those eligible for Medicaid are likely to have higher rates of mental health problems than privately insured children (Glied & Cuellar, 2003). These policy shifts in health insurance coverage mean that state Medicaid directors must now consider both seriously and less-seriously ill children in making decisions about service distribution.

Behavioral Managed Care

Medicaid programs in most states have shifted their mental health coverage into behavioral managed care. By 1999, for example, 42 states operated some form of managed behavioral health care, and this was triple the number in 1996 (Glied & Cuellar, 2003). Behavioral managed care for youth mental health care has generated substantial savings, mainly through marked reductions in the use of inpatient services and a consequent rise in outpatient services. It is not clear whether these reductions have generated negative outcomes for children, because no studies have yet examined the overall effects of behavioral managed care on mental health outcomes for youth. Cost savings have occurred. The movement toward managed care creates a risk for decreased service, cost shifting, and disenrollment. A study of Medicaid managed care in Pennsylvania found a higher rate of disenrollment for children with psychiatric admissions than for those with nonpsychiatric admissions (Scholle, Kelleher, Childs, Mendeloff, & Gardner, 1997). There is also a potential for this sudden rise of managed care to shift the burden of mental health care to public systems, such as juvenile justice, special education, or child welfare (Hutchinson & Foster, 2003).

Parity

Over the past 8 years, some legislative efforts have targeted parity of mental health and general health benefits. In 1996, the federal government passed the Mental Health Parity Act (which was implemented in 1998), requiring parity in benefits if mental health coverage was also offered. Although it applied only to lifetime and annual dollar limits (and did not require parity in copayments, deductibles, or limits on days or visits), it represented a major policy advance by offering for the first time mental health coverage. The impact of this legislation on service use and costs are being examined (Goldman & Azrin, 2003).

RECENT INITIATIVES ADDRESSING RESEARCH AND SYSTEM FAILURES

There are several significant initiatives currently under way and supported by foundations and federal agencies to reform some of the system failures referenced above.

National Registry of Effective Practices

The Substance Abuse and Mental Health Services Administration (SAMHSA) has recently launched a new expansion of its National Registry on Effective Practices (NREP) to include mental health. This registry creates a standard set of criteria with which to establish an archive of research-based practices that can be updated to provide assistance to field practitioners on the quality and strength of effective mental health practices. This registry marks a major effort to bring order to the plethora of usages of the term *evidence-based practice.*

MacArthur Foundation Youth Mental Health Network

A major new 4-year initiative from the MacArthur Foundation, entitled the Youth Mental Health Initiative, under the leadership of John Weisz, is further extending the reach of EBPs by reviewing the evidence for therapies targeted at the most common childhood disorders. A set of studies will address gaps between research-based treatments and their delivery within clinic systems by examining how best to bring effective treatment practices to youth in mental health service settings. Studies of technology transfer in medicine, nutrition, agriculture, and other fields

have shown that effective dissemination requires *(a)* adaptation of the technologies to fit their intended users, and *(b)* an understanding of organizational and system barriers to change. This initiative includes two components. A *Clinic Treatment Project* will test two alternative methods of delivering EBPs within public community-based mental health clinics, using training and supervision procedures designed for the settings and users. A *Clinic Systems Project* will investigate the organizational, system, and payment issues that influence the ability of providers and clinics to use EBPs. The findings from these two projects are likely to yield answers to significant questions about the readiness of research-based treatments for integration into community practices and the readiness of community practices for adoption of new clinical strategies.

Annie E. Casey Blue Sky

Another new initiative of the Annie E. Casey Foundation is also focusing on disseminating EBPs by melding training and supervisory models across different sets of interventions. The foundation, through its BlueSky Project, has enlisted the involvement of the developers of three evidence-based interventions for youth with disruptive behavior problems who are likely to be involved in the juvenile justice system (Multisystemic Therapy [FFT], Treatment Foster Care, and Functional Family Therapy) to create an integrated training and supervision model. An implementation demonstration program is being planned with two to three states beginning in September 2004.

State Initiatives

A group of states are undertaking major efforts to create state-level strategies for disseminating single or, in some cases, multiple EBPs. In several of the states, these efforts also include providing comprehensive training, supervision, or regulatory activities to support the implementation of these EBPs. A brief description of some of the state efforts is provided below.

New York

New York is implementing a range of EBPs and is engaged in a major effort to evaluate the impact of the implementation processes. For example, FFT, a research-based treatment for youth with antisocial behavior problems and delinquency, is being implemented in approximately 12 sites statewide, following an active process of community involvement that sought stakeholder input about needs and options. Another large-scale implementation effort is being undertaken to carry out and evaluate a set of evidence-based cognitive-behavioral trauma treatments for approximately 600 youth affected by the September 11th World Trade Center disaster. New York State has also created a research bureau specifically focused on EBPs for children and adolescents, to track the implementation of research-based services and to include assessment tools, engagement strategies (McKay, Pennington, Lynn, & McCadam, 2001), and outcomes monitoring (Bickman, Smith, Lambert, & Andrade, 2003). In addition, New York has been awarded one of the NIMH-SAMHSA State Planning Grants to develop a set of tools and methodological approaches for assessing the fit between specific EBP models and organizational and contextual factors within mental health clinics and schools statewide. The focus of this effort is to improve understanding about differences among families, clinicians, administrators, and treatment developers in their perspectives on organizational issues relevant to the adoption of new clinical practices.

Texas

A different strategy has been undertaken in Texas, where the state is formulating a benefit design package of selected EBPs, supported through training, supervision, and monitoring. In 2003, a Consensus Conference was convened to assist state policymakers in designing the new benefit package. The Consensus Conference included family advocates, policymakers, clinical practitioners, and treatment and service model developers. The recommended benefit package includes both diagnostic-specific psychotherapies and comprehensive community-based services to address the full range of mental health needs of youth and families. This benefit design was implemented in 2004.

Michigan

In Michigan, a state planning process led to the identification of specific interventions to address the most common clinical problems and a statewide initiative to embed a standardized measure of functioning (CAFAS) into clinical practice. A plan was developed to train practitioners to provide cognitive behavior therapy for internalizing disorders, with assistance from UCLA, and parent management training to address externalizing disorders, with assistance from the Oregon Social Learning Center.

Center for Mental Health Services System of Care and EBPs in Kentucky, Ohio, and California

The Center for Mental Health Services (CMHS) is funding implementation initiatives of specific EBP models in several states, including Kentucky, Ohio, and California. In conjunction with Kentucky's Children's Services Grant Program, CMHS is supporting formal implementation of parent–child interaction treatment (PCIT) in a system-of-care site in eastern Kentucky. Although many randomized clinical trials of PCIT have been conducted, this is the first one conducted outside of academia. The PCIT is being randomized to schools and will also be implemented in a large county in Oregon where mental health centers will be the locus of treatment. Through the Center on Innovative Practices, Ohio is implementing Multisystemic Therapy, intensive home-based services, and wraparound services. Through the California Institute of Mental Health, the state of California is implementing Treatment Foster Care, FFT, and Webster-Stratton's Incredible Years.

Hawaii

An ambitious dissemination approach has been undertaken in Hawaii, called the Hawaii Experiment (Chorpita, Yim, Donkervoet, Arensdorf, Amundsen et al., 2002). The combination of a 14-month review of the research literature on psychosocial treatments for youth by a group of stakeholders, including families, policymakers, researchers, and practitioners, identified a set of treatments that have been systematically deployed into Hawaii schools. A partnership between academia and the state led to the implementation effort. A process of distillation of EBPs into core practice components, has enabled more clinician flexibility in selecting treatments that fit with parent, child, and clinical needs. This statewide initiative is being carefully evaluated and a set of clinical practice guidelines and tools are being developed (Chorpita, Daleiden, & Weisz, in press).

RESEARCH ON ORGANIZATIONAL CONTEXT AND ITS IMPACT ON SERVICE DELIVERY

During the past decade, a series of studies originally conducted within business and industry has been applied to human service agencies, most recently including mental health (Glisson, 2002; Glisson & James, 2002; Schoenwald, Sheidow, Letourneu, & Liao, 2003). This application has arisen because it has become apparent that theory and constructs about organizational behavior have much to offer as interpretive frameworks within which to understand the capacity of mental health systems to change, adapt, or adopt new technologies, including EBPs. In the mental health field, *organizations* or *organizational systems* refer to the range of service delivery settings where treatments or mental health services are delivered (e.g., clinics, schools, group homes, or other work environments).

Much of the new thinking about the application of organizational theory to mental health service delivery is derived from the diffusion of innovation literature, generally ascribed to Everett Rogers (1995). Rogers delineated different stages of adoption that characterize the uptake of new technologies and identified characteristics of the diffusion process that lead to their sustainability over time (Van de Ven, Polly, Garud, & Ventkataraman, 1999). For example, Rogers (1995) noted that the characteristics and moti-

vations of adopters tend to differ among those adopting at the beginning, middle, and end periods of an innovation, and he identified attributes of innovations that can be used to design new technologies for their later successful diffusion. These characteristics include the extent to which an innovation is believed to be better than the current model of care, the degree to which an innovation is perceived to be consistent with existing values, the ease with which an innovation can be used, and the extent to which results of an innovation are visible to others.

Empirical studies from the diffusion of innovation literature indicate that organizations and systems are not equally innovative and that some are much more open than others to adopting and implementing new practices. The factors that affect the capacity of an organizational system to change, adapt, or take up new innovations have been examined in a series of studies mostly outside of the human services field. These studies have identified a core group of dimensions along which work environments or service systems vary. In recent work, most notably by Glisson (2002) and Schoenwald et al. (2003), key factors within mental health agencies have been identified that affect delivery of services.

Some of the key constructs within the organizational literature found to influence the behavior of providers are summarized below.

Organizational Culture and Climate

The constructs of organizational culture and climate have been measured in tandem and recently found to be discrete (Glisson & James 2002; Verbeke, Volgering, & Hessels, 1998). In general, organizational theorists define *climate* as the way people perceive their work environment, and *culture* as the way things are done in an organization (Verbeke et al., 1998). In other words, climate is defined as a property of the individual and culture as a property of the organization.

Climate is further subdivided into psychological climate and organizational climate (Glisson & James, 2002; James & James, 1989; Jones, James, & Bruni, 1975; James, James, & Ashe, 1990). *Psychological climate* is defined as an individual's perception of the psychological impact of their work environment on their well-being (James & James, 1989). *Organizational climate* occurs when employees in the same organizational unit have the same perceptions about their work environment (Jones & James, 1979; Joyce & Slocum, 1984). Some of the core components of the psychological climate of a work environment include emotional exhaustion, depersonalization, and role conflict. A general psychological climate factor (PCg), reflecting the workers' overall perception of the positive or negative valence within the organization, is believed to constitute the core features underlying this construct (James & James, 1989; James et al., 1990; Brown & Leigh, 1996; Glisson & Hemmelgarn, 1998; Glisson & James, 2002).

Culture is described as a "deep" construct that reflects the normative beliefs and shared behavioral expectations in an organization or work unit (Cooke & Szumal, 1993). These beliefs and expectations provide a guiding framework by which the priorities of the organization are made explicit. These priorities or values include conformity, consensus, and motivation. According to Glisson (2000), organizational culture is often described as layered, with behavioral expectations and norms representing an outer layer and values and assumptions representing an inner layer (Rousseau, 1990). Hofstede (1998) described behavior as the visible part of culture and values as the invisible part.

Organizational Structure

Structure refers to the formal organization of an agency or unit. This construct has the longest history and has been studied in greater depth and detail than the other organizational constructs. Core components of organizational structure include the centralization of power and the formalization of responsibilities and position in an organization. Structural functions such as participation in decision making, hierarchy of authority, ways in which roles are divided, and the procedural specifications that guide the division of labor all comprise elements of an organization's structure (Glisson, 2002).

Work Attitudes

Job satisfaction and organizational commitment have been studied since 1976 and appear to comprise features associated with work attitudes (Glisson & Durick, 1988). The distinction between satisfaction and commitment inheres in the difference between attachment to an organization and positive acceptance of one's duties within it (Mowday, Porter, and Steers, 1982; Williams & Hazer, 1986).

Leadership

The characteristics of effective leadership have been identified largely through studies of staff perceptions about this quality. In these studies, three types of skills have been identified (Glisson & Durick, 1988): the extent to which a leader is perceived as willing to make key decisions and comfortable with this responsibility; the extent to which a leader is perceived as using the power to make decisions without authoritarianism; and the perceptions of the leader as intelligent. These dimensions are believed to comprise a single factor reflecting overall staff perceptions of a leader's capabilities (Glisson & Durick, 1998).

Organizational Readiness to Change

The construct of readiness to change is a recent addition to the dialogue within the organizational literature. It is a construct that has arisen within the substance abuse literature and includes aspects of culture, climate, structure, leadership, and work attitudes (Simpson, 2002). It has been examined with reference to the question as to why some organizations are more apt to adopt innovations than others (Simpson, 2002). Debate currently exists as to whether readiness to change is a separate dimension from the other constructs or whether it constitutes a whole subsumed within which are the other dimensions of organizational behavior. One of the research projects being undertaken in New York state is targeted at constructing a typology for organizational readiness, which will reflect multiple stakeholder perspectives, including, importantly, families and consumers. This typology will be used to assess for policy-planning purposes the readiness for uptake of a set of specific EBPs for youth (Hoagwood et al., in press).

Studies of Organizational Effectiveness

Recent work by Glisson and colleagues suggests that considerable variation exists among organizations in their capacity to accept innovations and to implement new technologies. These studies have demonstrated that an organization's structure and leadership affect the extent to which work environments allow experimentation with innovations or the adoption of new technologies. Studies from literatures within business and industrial organizational research suggest that work environments vary considerably along the dimension of innovativeness and openness to adoption. Structure and leadership are known to be important dimensions of organizations, but other variables—notably organizational culture, climate, and work attitudes—are also factors that predict innovation. These studies suggest that flexible structures, strong leadership, constructive cultures, nonrestrictive climates, and positive work attitudes contribute to innovation in organizations and the adoption of cutting-edge technologies (Glisson & James, 2002).

In addition, Glisson has identified four organizational requirements for effective work environments (2002): use of assessments and treatment interventions that are appropriate, valid, and effective for the populations targeted by the service system; assurance that adherence to the protocols is obtained; positive alliances between the clinicians and the clients; and finally, provision of services that are available, responsive, and characterized by continuity. Glisson has found that these characteristics can be modeled and that they improve the culture and climate of child welfare and juvenile justice systems (Glisson, 2002). Whether this will hold true for mental health–care agencies remains to be determined.

Summary of Organizational Research Findings

Characteristics of organizations that promote adoption, adherence, alliance, and service responsivity have been identified in relatively global ways. Yet a specific understanding of the complex relationships that coexist among culture, climate, structure, leadership, attitudes, and the complex therapeutic process of alliance, adherence, and fidelity has yet to be delineated. According to Glisson, constructive and nondefensive organizational cultures, less centralized and formalized organizational structures, safe organizational climates, and positive work attitudes promote these attributes of service delivery. In identifying ways to improve healthcare delivery and quality, it is likely that attention to issues of the specific fit among organizational elements and therapeutic processes will need to be identified if EBPs are to be sustained.

SUMMARY AND RECOMMENDATIONS

Create a Context for Constant Empirical Inquiry in Routine Practice

Current approaches to the implementation of EBPs within state and local service systems are largely characterized as unidirectional: research-based models are taken off the academic shelf and put into place within routine practice settings. An alternative approach is to encourage routine practice settings to become the seat of empirical inquiry—to become empirically driven centers for both delivering and examining practices and their link to outcomes (Kazdin, 2004). Such normalization of research-based approaches to practice would demystify the scientific enterprise and create services that could be constantly reevaluated, refined, and improved. This kind of revolution in thinking could lead to the creation of service clinics that construct locally relevant evidence. This approach could be used to create a context for empiricism within routine service settings, leading ultimately to improvements in quality.

Ensure That all Studies of Treatment Development and Delivery Include Perspectives of Families and Providers

If the goal is to enhance the generalizability and uptake of research findings into practice, then from the outset research models should incorporate the perspectives of families, providers, and other stakeholders into the design of new treatments, preventive strategies, and services. Only by doing so can issues relating to the relevance of the intervention for stakeholders, the cost-effectiveness of the intervention, and the extent to which it reflects the values and traditions of families and community leaders be addressed. These issues are ultimately essential for the evidence base to be of any practical utility.

Put into Action Clinic and Community Intervention Development and Deployment Models

The time lag between creation of an EBP and its acceptance into routine practice is estimated to be 20 years (IOM, 2001). To accelerate the pace of development of EBPs and their deployment into routine practice, new models for their creation have been proposed. Building on the deployment focused model (DFM) of Weisz (2003, 2005), Hoagwood, Burns, and Weisz (2002) developed the clinic–community intervention model (CID) to extend the DFM by attending to those context variables such as characteristics of the practice setting (e.g., practitioner behaviors, organizational variables, community characteristics) and involvement of families and community from piloting, manualization, and dissemination that are essential to the ultimate acceptability of new services. These models are proposed as a way to ensure strong scientifically based practices and to accelerate the pace of the uptake of research findings into practice.

CONCLUSION

It does little good to know what treatments are effective if those treatments cannot reach the children and families who need them. Likewise, it does little good to have effective treatment protocols sitting idly on academic shelves.

Significant state and national policy initiatives are currently focused on more closely aligning science and practice. These initiatives present unique opportunities for linking scientific developments on effective clinical care to organizational system and policy reform. The availability of a growing research base on effective clinical treatments and practices offers an opportunity to tap into a reservoir of scientifically based strategies. Testing their applicability within locally based service systems is the key question for the next generation of services research. However, limitations in the evidence base as well as limitations in understanding *the fit* of EBPs to service contexts pose considerable challenges to treatment developers, policymakers, administrators, clinicians, and families. New models for crossing the boundaries between research and practice and accelerating delivery of quality care need to be applied. Creating family-driven and empirically based services and supporting these services through policies that provide fiscal incentives for delivery of outcome-based practices requires commitment to empirical inquiry and to the "obstinate questioning" (Wordsworth, *Intimations of Immortality: An Ode*, 1819) that alone sustains creative change.

The American Treatment System for Adolescent Substance Abuse: Formidable Challenges, Fundamental Revisions, and Mechanisms for Improvements

Kathleen Meyers
and A. Thomas McLellan

The multifaceted problems of adolescent substance abuse represent a pressing national
concern. Despite research advances in efficacious treatment models for these youth, such
as cognitive-behavioral therapy, multisystemic
therapy, and multidimensional family therapy
(Rahdert & Czechowicz, 1995; Wagner & Waldron, 2001), few substance-abusing youth receive
treatment and are therefore unable to take advantage of these developments.

In 2001 (the latest data currently available),
1.1 million U.S. youth aged 12–17 were estimated to need substance abuse treatment (Substance Abuse and Mental Health Services Administration [SAMHSA], 2001a, 2001b). Of these,
100,000 actually received treatment, leaving a
gap of approximately one million untreated adolescents nationwide (SAMHSA, 2001a, 2001b).
Female adolescents who abuse substances fare
even worse than their male counterparts: although the percentage of male and female teens
in the United States who needed substance abuse
treatment was almost identical (4.9% vs. 4.8%),
male adolescents were more likely to receive
treatment (11.4% vs. 8.8%).

There are many reasons why adolescents fail
to receive treatment. At the individual level, adolescents (perhaps even more than adults) fail to
recognize an alcohol or other drug (AOD) problem or minimize the problem (Melnick, DeLeon,
Hawke, Jainchill, & Kressel, 1997). Moreover, adolescent concerns about disclosing sensitive information to parents and competing priorities
for multiproblem families render access problematic (Cheng, Savageaue, Sattler, & DeWitt,
1993; Cornelius, Pringle, Jernigan, Kirisi, &
Clark, 2001; Ford, Milstein, Halpern-Fisher, & Irwin, 1997). While these individual problems are
significant, there are already efforts to bring
about problem recognition and motivation for
change (Rahdert & Czechowicz, 1995; Wagner &
Waldron, 2001).

The purpose of this chapter is to discuss an
additional complicating factor that impacts adolescent treatment and goes beyond the individual youth and his or her family: the service delivery system. These systems (e.g., educational
institutions, health care, juvenile justice, and
mental health systems) are complex environments that offer opportunities to identify, treat,
and monitor adolescent substance abusers. However, the architecture and operating procedures
of these systems often serve to inhibit access to
needed services and to confuse or confound coordination of complementary service delivery
across systems. The result can be formidable
challenges to the identification and subsequent
intervention and treatment of the adolescent
who uses, abuses, or is dependent upon substances. In the text that follows, we identify
problems within the current "standard" system
of care leading to failure to identify these adolescents, inadequate access to even basic substance abuse intervention for those identified,
and failure to provide adequate amounts or types
of services to those who do access the care system. We also present mechanisms for enhancements and conclude with a summary of three
innovative approaches targeted to systems improvement.

IDENTIFICATION OF ADOLESCENTS WHO USE SUBSTANCES

Adolescents with varying degrees of substance
use can be found throughout U.S. communities,
coming into contact with a variety of settings
and service systems. Identification of these
teens, regardless of their level of use, is important
so that targeted, developmentally focused interventions can be delivered (e.g., brief interventions, outpatient treatment, long-term residential treatment, all followed by the appropriate
form of reintervention, step-down, or continuing care services). Such identification has the potential to reduce the morbidity and mortality related to this condition.

The settings within a community can be categorized into two tiers: *(1)* first-gate generalist
settings, and *(2)* more specialized, problem-
focused systems of care (e.g., mental health,
child welfare). Generalist settings (e.g., health-
care settings, schools) are settings where many
adolescents can be found, and they have the opportunity to provide the "first gate" into needed
behavioral health and social services. Specialized, problem-focused systems of care, by con-

trast, center on adolescents with more serious and specific problems (e.g., the mental health system, the juvenile justice system, the child welfare system, the drug treatment system). In a well-structured system, the general settings and the problem-focused systems would have the training and ability to screen and refer adolescents with presumptive evidence of substance use (or any other specific problem) *(a)* for a more in-depth assessment; or *(b)* to problem-focused agencies for intervention (e.g., mental health clinic, substance abuse program). Moreover, an optimized system would have interagency working arrangements in place to assure multidimensional service provision and continuity of care without unnecessary overlap of services.

With respect to early identification, it is important for early screening efforts to differentiate substance *use* from substance *abuse or dependence*. This is important for both the efficiency of system operation (i.e., conservation of more intensive services for those with more severe problems) and because these different stages of substance use require qualitatively different types of interventions (Wagner & Waldron, 2001; Winters, 1999).

An appropriate clinical response to identified substance use is likely to be one of a variety of recently developed brief interventions designed to prevent escalation of use into abuse or dependence and the associated penetration into the juvenile justice and social service systems that typically is associated with more severe use (Bilchik, 1995; Greenwood, Model, Rydell, & Chiesa, 1998; RAND, 1996; Wagner & Waldron, 2001; Winters, 1999). Because the effects of brief interventions may weaken after 12 months, the delivery of a brief reintervention is critical if prevention of escalation is to be maintained (Conners, Tarbox, & Faillace, 1992; Connors & Walitzer, 2001; Stanton & Burns, 2003; U.S. Department of Health and Human Services, 1993). In contrast to the appropriate clinical response to substance use, the appropriate clinical response to an identified case of abuse or dependence is likely to be much more intensive, structured, and long-lasting (Wagner & Waldron, 2001; Winters, 1999), designed to change (or slow) the trajectory of a long-term drug-using career. Thus, for both clinical and cost-effectiveness reasons, it is critical for both systems to be able to identify use, to differentiate use from abuse or dependence, to appropriately refer for a comprehensive assessment based on identification, and to provide rapid linkage to the appropriate level of clinical intervention for each type of case. As will be described below, we have found that both service tiers are deficient in these important skills.

Primary Care Settings

There are numerous studies documenting the failure of primary care settings to identify and differentiate individuals who use, abuse, or are dependent upon substances (Hack & Adger, 2002; Miller & Swift, 1996). This is problematic in that primary care clinics can be particularly good sites for adolescent substance-use case finding (National Association of State Alcohol and Drug Abuse Directors [NASADAD], 1998, 2002). In a recent survey, however, U.S. teens reported that the topic of substance abuse was rarely initiated. Only about one third of youth (35%) reported discussing substance use, even though about twice that number (65%) wanted it to be discussed. In order of preference, adolescents would like their health-care provider to talk with them about substance use (reported by 65%), smoking (reported by 59% of youth), and sexually transmitted diseases (STDs; reported by 61% of youth) (Ackard & Neumark-Sztainer, 2001; Klein & Wilson, 2002). Instead, physicians and/or nurses discuss diet, weight, and exercise with their adolescent patients. While these issues are, of course, very important, they should not be the only health issues discussed. When primary care providers do not initiate discussions about alcohol or drugs or are not attuned to the subtle signs of early use, the opportunity for identification and early intervention or treatment is missed.

Emergency Rooms

Adolescents make fewer visits to primary care physicians than any other age group, in part because they generally are in good health, but also because they lack health insurance (Kokotailo, 1995; Newacheck, 1999). In fact, only about 38% of teens surveyed reported that they had a routine health-care source (Grove, Lazebnik, & Petrack, 2000). Hence, many adolescents use the emergency room (ER) as their primary source of medical care: studies report that approximately 16% of all ER patients are adolescents who present with numerous complaints: abdominal pain, injuries, gynecological problems, asthma, and diabetes (Grove et al., 2000; Lehmann, Barr, & Kelly, 1994; Melzer-Lange, & Lye 1996; Mader, Smithline, Nyquist, & Letourneau, 2001).

A major element in adolescent use of the ER is alcohol, such as alcohol-related injuries, motor vehicle accidents, and violence (Mader et al., 2001; Maio, Portnoy, Blow, & Hill, 1994). According to the National Pediatric Trauma Registry (Mader et al., 2001), 15.5% of all ER trauma patients were alcohol-positive adolescents (Mader et al., 2001).

Substance use other than alcohol has also been an increasing factor in ER use. For example, recent data from the American Association of Poison Control Center's Toxic Exposure Surveillance System show a growing number of teens (about 759 cases over a 5-year period) are presenting in the ER with tachycardia, hypertension, and agitation as a result of methylphenidate abuse (Klein-Schwartz & McGrath, 2003). Further, The Drug Abuse Warning Network (DAWN; i.e., the study that monitors ER utilization as a result of drug use) reports a 17% increase in ER drug-related episodes among youth ages 12–17 between 1999 and 2001 (SAMHSA, 2002b). Drug abuse deaths among teens seen in the ER accounted for approximately 20% of all DAWN cases (SAMHSA, 2003).

Thus, adolescents in general as well as those who use, abuse, and are dependent on substances frequent the ER. Despite this fact, substance use is rarely assessed or addressed by ER health-care staff. Indeed, it is remarkable that less than 50% of cases are referred to any form of drug treatment (Mader et al., 2001). Unless the substance-abusing youth is the driver of the car in an alcohol-related motor vehicle accident, referral for substance abuse assessment or intervention is rare (Mader et al., 2001).

Schools and School Health

Schools are among the most important institutions for adolescents, have the most efficient and continuous access to them, and thus constitute perhaps the most important site for initial case finding. Hence, schools are in a unique position to *(1)* identify substance-using youth needing treatment at earlier stages of impairment; *(2)* reduce the stigma of receiving treatment; and *(3)* increase access to care (Rappaport, 1999). However, while schools may have identified use among students through zero-tolerance policies, drug testing, and locker searches (Center on Addiction and Substance Abuse [CASA], 2001), they have not increased access to care, thereby making limited contributions to the subsequent well-being of these adolescents (Lear, 2002; Wagner, Kortlander, & Morris, 2001). In fact, only 11% of admissions to alcohol and drug treatment are from school referrals (SAMHSA, 2002c).

In fairness to school personnel, the identification of a student who uses substances can be problematic. First, few school districts provide the resources for appropriate identification of use among youth or for subsequent intervention. Student assistance programs (SAPs, which are similar to employee assistance programs [EAPs]) can be found in only 9.5% of school districts in the United States, and there is widespread variation in the types of SAPs and in how they are run (CASA, 2001; Wagner et al., 2001). When a SAP does exist, identification is compromised because few use standardized assessment measures. Second, only 36% of public schools and 14.4% of private schools offer alcohol and drug counseling to substance-using youth (CASA, 2001). Issues of inadequate reimbursement for assessment and intervention services and arguments over the appropriate level of responsibility of teachers and assessment specialists further hamper identification of the student who uses, abuses, or is dependent on substances (Lear, 2002). Combined, these issues seriously compromise a school's ability to play a major role in substance use intervention and call into question the true role of a school (e.g., should a school be responsible for case finding only and then partner with other organizations for intervention services?).

The situation has become even more problematic by the introduction of zero-tolerance policies, drug-testing programs, and locker searchers in the schools. These supposedly serve as deterrent and detective mechanisms and almost always have predetermined consequences. Zero-tolerance policies, introduced in 1994 to address weapons in schools, with Elementary and Secondary Education Act (ESEA) funding contingent on their enactment (Martin, 2000), quickly expanded to include a wide range of disciplinary issues such as drug use. As of 2001, 88% of schools across this country had zero tolerance policies for drugs, 87% for alcohol, and 79% for tobacco (CASA, 2001; ERIC, 2001), with most states treating minor or major incidents identically (e.g., in Maine, the policy was enforced for a high school girl who brought Tylenol to school for menstrual cramps [Rosenbaum, 2003]; in Georgia, an asthmatic child was barred by local school policy for carrying his asthma inhaler and died after a severe asthmatic attack while boarding a school bus [Reuters Health, 2002]). Rarely is an assessment and treatment referral a consequence. Instead, infractions are typically handled only by punitive measures such as suspension or expulsion, or referral to an alternative school (CASA, 2001; ERIC, 2001).

Drug Testing in Schools

Drug testing of public school students who participate in athletics or other extracurricular activities has been introduced to deter use among the larger student body. It seems paradoxical that youth who display those protective factors shown in research studies to reduce the likelihood and severity of substance use among youth (e.g., extracurricular activities, school bonding; Hawkins, Catalano, & Miller, 1992) would be targeted for drug testing. However, parents want to be sure that their children attend drug-free schools and school systems are regularly chided by parents and community groups to "get tough on drugs," not only while students are in school but also when they are participating in school-related activities after school or on the weekends.

In a large, multiyear national study, research-ers from the University of Michigan's Institute for Social Research concluded that drug testing of public school students (conducted in approximately 19% of all U.S. secondary schools) did not deter use (Yamaguchi, Johnston, & O'Malley, 2003). At each of three grade levels (i.e., 8, 10, 12), there were identical prevalence and frequency rates of drug use over the 12 months prior to the examination in the schools with and without drug-testing programs. These data are critical in that the Supreme Court's split decision upholding the constitutionality of drug testing in schools was highly influenced by the notion that drug testing among public school students is a deterrent to use. Hence, the debate over a student's right to privacy and unreasonable and suspicionless searches continues.

Not only has school-based drug testing not been found to deter use, Chaloupka and Laixuthai (2002) found that it can result in an increase in alcohol use. Aware that alcohol is almost impossible to detect after 1 day (as are cocaine and heroin), students decreased their use of marijuana but increased their use of alcohol (Chaloupka & Laixuthai, 2002; Zeese, 2002). Consequently, there is concern that school-based drug testing could pose a number of unintended effects vis-a-vis switching to more dangerous forms of drugs to avoid detection. Finally, and again paradoxically, teens in schools that had drug-testing programs tended to view drugs as less risky and believed that drug testing must have been initiated because more students were using drugs, beliefs that have been consistently shown to lead to increases in using behaviors.

The second tier of the services system (i.e., agencies that focus on a specific problem area) often fares no better with respect to identification of the adolescent who uses, abuses, or is dependent upon substances. Since adolescent substance use disorders (SUD) are clinically complex, typically compromising numerous life domains (behavioral, mood, family, legal), it is not surprising that substance-abusing adolescents are prevalent in many different service systems. In one of the first studies to date, Aarons and colleagues (2001) found that 62% of youth in the juvenile justice system, 41% of youth in the mental health system, 24% of youth in the special-education system, and 19% of youth in the child welfare system met criteria for a SUD. In each of these systems, adolescents had been assessed for some other disorder, illness, or problem behavior and were receiving some form of system-specific services (e.g., mental health services if in the mental health system, educational services if in the special education system). It is noteworthy that despite the high prevalence rates of SUD in these settings, most cases of SUD were not identified by staff in these systems. One must wonder whether and to what extent the unidentified SUD may have compromised the accuracy of the assessments for the targeted problems and the effects of the services that were provided.

Reasons for Lack of Identification

It is unfortunate that those delivering health or social services as part of larger agencies or systems (e.g., hospital systems, mental health systems) rarely screen for alcohol and drug problems (Center for Substance Abuse Treatment [CSAT], 2000). There are several reasons for this. First, there has been little effort to train key personnel from these various systems (e.g., school nurses, probation officers, case workers) in the use of some of the proven substance abuse screening instruments (CSAT, 2000; NASADAD, 1998; SAMHSA, 1993). With respect to healthcare practitioners, sizable portions of physicians feel ill equipped to discuss these topics with their adolescent patients (Karam-Hage, Nerenberg, & Brower, 2001). In a survey assessing medical residents' perception of substance abuse knowledge and assessment skills, only half felt that they were adequately prepared to identify, manage, or refer a substance-abusing adolescent (Siegal, Cole, & Eddy 2000; Steg, Mann, Schwartz, & Wise, 1992). Further, staffs from diverse service systems do not possess sufficient knowledge of disorders outside of their respective disciplines to adequately diagnose or comprehensively assess comorbid conditions (NASADAD, 1998, 1999). These problems are compounded by systems issues that dictate exclusion of each other's clients, confidentiality requirements that stifle collaboration, and the lack of bridges between systems of care that limit coordination of need-

based services (NASADAD, 1998, 1999). These issues alone and in combination cause a number of multi-problem youth to fall through the cracks.

Second, and intimately connected to the first reason, is the lack of reimbursement for screening and early intervention activities. Few states currently reimburse adolescent screening efforts outside the specialty sector substance abuse treatment system and there are a number of payment restrictions for AOD screening and diagnostic assessments within primary care settings (Buck & Umland, 1997; Rivera, Tollefson, Tesh, & Gentilello, 2000; CSAT, 2001). Even if the services are reimbursed through insurance programs, roughly 4 million adolescents in this country are without any form of health insurance, with additional youth covered by plans that do not provide for preventive care or behavioral health treatments (Center for Adolescent Health and the Law, 2000). As in all other areas of health and social services, the only sure way of increasing the probability of clinically recommended practices is through reimbursement.

Third, the complex interrelationships between the parents' right to know about assessment and the legal protection of the adolescent's privacy and confidentiality can further complicate identification. Adolescents want their health issues to be kept private and want to receive certain services without their parents' or guardians' consent (Ford & English, 2002; Ford et al., 1997). Without these guarantees, adolescents will forego services (Ford, Bearman, & Moody, 1999; Klein, Wilson, McNulty, Kapphahn, & Collins, 1999) until their problems escalate to a point when they can no longer be ignored. Fortunately, as illustrated below, most states give youth the sole authority to consent to assessment and treatment for those conditions in which parental knowledge would curtail adolescent treatment seeking (e.g., STD testing, alcohol or drug use).

- Twenty-five states and the District of Columbia accept minor consent for contraceptive services.
- Twenty-seven states and the District of Columbia accept minor consent for prenatal care.

- Fifty states and the District of Columbia accept minor consent for STD and HIV services.
- Forty-four states and the District of Columbia accept minor consent for alcohol and drug assessment and treatment.
- Twenty states and the District of Columbia accept minor consent for mental health services.

However, in some states that accept minor consent for services, *(1)* the physician has the discretion to notify the parent without the adolescent's consent (e.g., in Colorado, Oklahoma, and Louisiana [Colorado, 1995; Oklahoma, 1995; Louisiana, 1995]); and *(2)* parental involvement is required prior to the end of mental health or alcohol and drug treatment (Oregon; OAHHS, 2004). While statutes that give the adolescent the right to consent to treatment are vitally important, adolescents are not knowledgeable about what they can and cannot obtain without their parents' permission and there is movement to restore parental consent for all conditions (Boonstra & Nash, 2000; Cheng, Savageau et al., 1993; Ford et al., 1997; Marks, Malizio, Hoch, Brody, & Fisher, 1983). Mandated compliance with the Health Insurance Portability and Accountability Act (HIPPA) of 1996 may further complicate these issues. In section 164.502(g) of the Privacy Rule of December 2000, parents are generally able to access and control health information about their minor child. Consequently, they generally have access to all charts, medical records, etc., thereby affording them access to information their adolescent children may not want them to have. However, 164.502(g)(3)(ii) A&B states that if a state or other law permits a minor to obtain a particular health service without the consent of the parent, it is the minor and not the parent who has control over the information. If state or other applicable law is silent or unclear, service providers have the discretion to permit or prohibit parental access without interference from the Federal Privacy Rule.

Finally, critics of early identification argue that it unnecessarily widens the net for behavioral health services and stigmatizes at-risk youth or youth with low-level problem behaviors (Goldson, 2001; Kammer, Minor, & Wells, 1997). Although many in the substance abuse field advocate early identification so that brief interventions and/or referrals will result, the intended positive outcomes may not always occur. As indicated above, many and even most zero-tolerance programs are simply punitive, with no clear benefits for the substance-using adolescent who may wish to seek help. In contrast, if the same identification efforts were linked to programs of useful and desirable rehabilitative services, short- and long-term benefits to the substance-using adolescent could result. Thus, the philosophy of the setting and intent of identification (i.e., habilitative treatment or punitive expulsion or incarceration) can impact the outcome of the substance-using youth identified early. More research is needed to evaluate the effectiveness of various post–substance use identification strategies so that early identification and intervention programs can be based on empirical data rather than on individual or public opinion.

System Change Considerations

Improve Identification of Adolescent Substance Use, Abuse, and Dependence

When substance use is not identified and when differentiations between use and abuse or dependence are not made, the opportunity for interventions in general and for targeted interventions specifically is lost (e.g., brief interventions for use or the delivery of conjoint, complementary treatments for abuse or dependence). Obviously, it makes good clinical sense to encourage screening for substance use, abuse, and dependence within all sectors of the service delivery system (CSAT, 2000; SAMHSA, 1993). There is a need, however, to develop necessary training procedures, common definitions, reimbursement mechanisms, confidentiality safeguards, and protection from stigma and institutional backlash if this is to become standard clinical practice (Aarons, Brown, Hough, Garland, & Wood, 2001; Buck & Umland, 1997; Miller & Brown, 1997; Rivera, Tollefson, Tesh, & Gentilello, 2000; Tracy & Farkas, 1994).

Training. Expanding medical and nursing school curricula and developing addiction rotations within residency and nursing programs comprise a first step in skill enhancement. Research shows that 1-day to 6-month chemical dependency training programs improve *(1)* physician attitude toward patients with SUD; *(2)* SUD assessment skills; *(3)* comfort with discussing chemical dependency; and *(4)* knowledge of the addiction service system (Brauzer, Lefley, & Steinbook, 1996; Karam-Hage et al., 2001; Kokotailo, Fleming, & Koscik, 1995; Matthews et al., 2002; Siegal et al., 2000; Westreich & Galantar, 1997). Because not all adolescents who are identified as using AOD in these first-gate settings will require formal treatment (Rahdert & Czechowicz, 1995; Wagner & Waldron, 2001; Winters, 1999), teaching of motivational interviewing and brief interventions with appropriate follow-up contact should become a standard component in clinical training curricula. These practices have been shown to have widespread applicability and documented effectiveness even within ER settings (Barnett, Monti, & Wood, 2001; Greenwood et al., 1998; Monti et al., 1999; RAND, 1996). Further, because these interventions do not assume that the client is interested in changing, they are particularly relevant to adolescents who are generally disinterested in changing their behavior.

The training of public school and alternative-school personnel (as well as other systems' personnel such as social workers and correctional officers) to "spot" the signs of alcohol and drug use through undergraduate and graduate education, state qualification exams that include a set of identification-related questions, in-service programs, and orientation of new staff members is a step in the right direction (CASA, 2001). Bry and Attaway (2001) have trained staff to refer youth who display academic and conduct problems to school-based programs. This risk-focused approach has been found to consistently identify the student user and Bry's subsequent intervention has been effective in preventing increases in and problems associated with use. In either case, punishment-only policies will likely need to be revised so that when youth are identified, continued education and services in ad-dition to clear consequences result (CASA, 2001). Further, for those who have repeat infractions, fail to follow through on assessment and treatment referrals, or fail to complete a required treatment, a program of graduated school-based sanctions (e.g., detention, in-school suspension) should be designed and made available for dissemination to a range of schools.

Common problem definitions. As part of any training program, adoption of a common language with common definitions will be necessary. To this end, a focus on symptom multiplicity and severity rather than diagnosis has been suggested (Angold, Costello, Farmer, Burns, & Erkanli, 1999; NASADAD, 1998, 1999; Pollock & Martin, 1999; Winters, Latimer, & Stinchfield, 1999). First, research indicates that not all adolescents who have experienced serious consequences as a result of substance use will meet DSM-IV criteria for a substance use disorder (Pollock & Martin, 1999). Called "diagnostic orphans," these youth present with serious use patterns and problems that require treatment (Pollock & Martin, 1999; Winters et al., 1999), but symptom constellations do not meet a specific diagnosis. Similar findings appear in the mental health literature, where symptoms may be at a subthreshold diagnostic level but serious functional impairment exists nonetheless (Angold et al., 1999). These issues call the applicability of the DSM system into question, can impact eligibility decisions and reimbursement mechanisms, and will require policy changes. At a minimum, however, the use of common assessment tools (or common data elements obtained from one of a list of approved tools) would initially address this complex topic by providing greater comparability of terms that can be used across discrete systems of care (e.g., mental health, substance abuse, juvenile justice; Meyers et al., 1999; NASADAD, 1999; U.S. Public Health System, 2000).

Within this definitional arena, training programs must also address differentiation of behaviors indicative of true problems from behaviors that are "typically adolescent." Although adolescent assessment may seem simple at first glance, this developmental period presents unique challenges for the assessor (Meyers,

Hagan, Zanis, & Webb, 1999; Meyers, Hagan, McDermott, Webb, Frantz, & Randall, submitted; Winters, Latimer, & Stinchfield, 2001). Because of the youth's state of biological, emotional, neurocognitive, and social development, youth will sporadically display challenging behaviors as part of the normal course of development (e.g., rebelliousness, defiance, moodiness, marijuana experimentation), and these behaviors do not automatically indicate the need for intervention. In other words, the presentation of "a problem behavior" with subsequent identification of "dysfunction and need for intervention" can be confounded by the normal course of development. False-positive cases result when normative developmental behaviors are considered aberrant and false-negative cases occur when problem behaviors needing intervention are thought to be "just a function of being an adolescent." Consequently, training curricula need to address the various ways in which normative behaviors can be disentangled from problematic ones through modules teaching assessment of the typography, frequency, and age of onset of various behaviors.

Financing. Financing mechanisms will undoubtedly need to be improved if there is to be an increase in assessment services so that the adolescent who uses, abuses, or is dependent on substances is identified. This area is particularly challenging, with few proven answers. Consequently, economic research is needed so that informed decisions about resource allocation, alternative payment systems, public and private financing mechanisms, and development of responsive insurance packages can be made. Elimination of payment restrictions for screening and diagnostic assessments through changes in systems, policy, and public and private insurance will be needed to improve the identification process.

Confidentiality. Continued attention to ways in which service access policies and data-sharing technologies affect confidentiality is vital. Facilitation of appropriate ways for adolescents to initiate contact with providers independently of families may enhance identification and subsequent engagement in substance abuse services (Flisher et al., 1997; Rappaport, 2001). To this end, providing teens with a listing of services that do or do not require parental consent or notification may be helpful.

ACCESS TO ADOLESCENT-SPECIFIC SUBSTANCE ABUSE TREATMENT

We have discussed the multiple and complex system level problems associated with identifying adolescents who use, abuse, or are dependent upon substances. It might be thought that once these hurdles are overcome, it would at least be comparatively easy for substance-abusing adolescents to access treatments suited to their needs. This is not the case even for adults with substance use disorders, and it is even worse for adolescents.

In a recent survey of a national sample of 175 adult substance abuse treatment facilities in the United States, McLellan and colleagues (2003) found a disturbing degree of erosion in the infrastructure of those programs. For example, this report found closure rates of 21% over a 16-month period; of the remaining sample, an additional 18% had been reorganized or taken over by a different company (in the case of privately owned programs) or a different agency (in the case of government-run programs). In addition, these researchers found turnover rates of over 50% among *both* the directors of these programs and their counseling staffs. The result was confusion at the staff level and disorganization of service delivery.

The situation is arguably worse for the substance abuse treatment programs that are specifically designed for adolescents. First, there have always been relatively few of these adolescent programs (White, 1998). In the early 1980s when it became apparent that adolescents with substance use disorders were a unique client group requiring specific assessment and particular therapeutic approaches (see Deas, Riggs, Langenbucher, Goldman, & Brown, 2000, for a discussion; Poulin, Dishion, & Burraston, 2001), traditional substance abuse treatment facilities had to adapt their adult-oriented programs if they were to accept and appropriately treat an adolescent clientele (Winters, Stinchfield, Opland, Weller, & Latimer, 2000). To be responsive to the needs of this age group, programs needed to address the key developmental tasks of adolescence within an ecological context that included individual (e.g., self-regulation) and proximal (e.g., peer, family) influences (Bronfenbrenner, 1986, 1989; Deas et al., 2000; Liddle & Hogue, 2001; Wagner & Waldron, 2001). Hence, to be considered adolescent-specific, interventions needed to be revised so that they were sensitive to and focused on identity formation, autonomy seeking, social-role development, moral and cognitive development, self-regulation, peer group influences, and family management practices. When faced with such an undertaking, few substance abuse treatment providers responded to this challenge. Only 37% of approximately 14,000 substance abuse treatment programs in this country offer services to adolescents (SAMHSA, 2001a).

When the availability of substance abuse service within other systems is reviewed, the picture is equally discouraging. The systems in which one would most expect adequate capacity for treatment of the adolescent substance abuser are the juvenile justice system and the mental health system. Despite increases in arrests for drug offenses among juveniles (Butts, 1997) and the continued use of substances among juvenile detainees (Arrestee Drug Abuse Monitoring [ADAM], 2003), only 37% of the 3,127 juvenile correctional facilities in the United States deliver substance abuse treatment (SAMHSA, 2002a). Compounding limited access is questionable service appropriateness. Of the 13 states that operate their own substance abuse treatment programs within their state Department for Juvenile Justice and Corrections, only 6 states require that these programs meet state AOD agency licensing and accreditation standards (NASADAD, 2002). Further, of the 25 states within which the state Department for Juvenile Justice and Corrections purchases substance abuse treatment, only 7 states (28%) exclusively do so from licensed providers.

Given the high rates of comorbidity, with up to 75% of SUD youth having a coexisting mental health disorder (Crowley & Riggs, 1995; Greenbaum, Foster-Johnson, & Petrilla, 1996), and the finding that two-fifths (41%) of youth in the mental health system meet criteria for a substance use diagnosis (Aarons et al., 2001), one would logically expect that the mental health system would have adequate capacity or at least referral linkages to substance abuse treatment. In a study of the purchasers of drug treatment, conducted by NASADAD (2002), the mental health system was not even recorded as a service purchaser. Among the major purchasers of services were drug courts (by 31 states), Temporary Assistance of Needy Families (TANF) and welfare-to-work programs (by 27 states), the juvenile justice system (by 25 states), and the child welfare system (by 24 states). Similarly, when NASADAD examined units of state government that operated their own drug treatment programs, only three states described drug treatment services operated by the state's Department of Mental Health. The two most common governmental units that operate their own programs are the Department of Corrections (38 states) and the Department of Child Welfare (7 states). Hence, neither the general community nor the justice system nor the mental health system have, by themselves, adequate capacity (and questionable appropriateness) for intervening with the adolescent substance abuser.

Lack of Credentialed Staff

No state in the United States offers adolescent-specific provider certification and only five states require adolescent-specific knowledge for licensure (Northwest Fronteir Addiction Technology Transfer Center, 2000; Pollio, 2002). At the national level, the National Association of Alcoholism and Drug Abuse Counselors (NAADAC) certification program employs a competency-based tiered system of national-level credentials: national certified addictions counselor, level I, national certified addictions counselor, level II, and master addictions counselor. There are no adolescent-specific knowledge requirements for any level, including the highest level (NAADAC, 2003). Since knowledge of adolescent development and skill and interest in treating youth are of paramount importance to treatment of adolescents (Deas et al., 2000; Winters et al., 2000), questions arise as to *(1)* whether the few staff who do treat adolescents are sufficiently skilled to do so, and *(2)* why state and national credentialing processes do not require adolescent-specific knowledge. This is particularly perplexing given that the NAADAC recently added a national tobacco addiction specialist certification program. Judging from the scientific literature, a national certification program for adolescent addiction specialist appears to be equally important. At the very least, incorporation of adolescent-specific knowledge requirements into all certification programs should result in a more informed group of providers.

Restricted Funding for Services

Compounding the paucity of properly credentialed adolescent services is the failure of programs to accept an array of insurance types: less than 50% of adolescent AOD programs accept Medicaid; less than two thirds accept private insurance; and less than two thirds have a sliding fee scale (SAMHSA, 2001a). Even when insurance is accepted, adolescents are the most uninsured group in this country, rendering many of them unable to finance their treatment (Ford et al., 1999; Klein et al., 1999). As stated earlier, approximately 4 million youth in this country are without any form of health insurance, with many more having insurance that does not cover behavioral health treatment (Center for Adolescent Health and the Law, 2000). Inadequate financing mechanisms and lack of insurance coverage, coupled with the insufficient number of adolescent programs, further reduces the already limited odds of gaining access to treatment once identified.

Summary of System Change: Focus on Access

Improvement in early problem identification is only the beginning to a very large and complex problem. If the system is to meet the needs of identified youth, other service system inadequacies will need to be addressed simultaneously: *(1)* the demand for adolescent substance abuse treatment—current demand already exceeds the system's capacity to intervene; and *(2)* inade-

quate financing mechanisms—too few dollars and too few funding mechanisms render it difficult to support a treatment episode.

System Change Considerations

Improving Access: Expand Treatment Capacity

Although the creation of additional adolescent-specific treatment slots would initially increase system capacity, it would fail to get at the roots of the problems discussed, and the impact on long-term improvement would be minimal. One of the important and fundamental problems associated with substance abuse treatment for adolescents is the large and rapid rate of relapse following treatment termination. Currently, about half of adolescents with SUD relapse (Winters et al., 2000), with 60%–70% doing so within the first 3–4 months following treatment (Brown, Vik, & Creamer, 1989). Although there is no doubt that additional adolescent-specific services are needed, if there were means by which treatment effects might be enhanced or extended even slightly, it would be possible to limit the cycling in and out of existing programs and thus increase system capacity (Dembo, Walters, & Meyers, in press). The delivery of evidence-based interventions by a properly trained and credentialed staff could go a long way toward this goal. To this end, the transfer of evidence-based interventions into real-world settings and revision of the credentialing process to include adolescent-specific licensure have the potential to increase treatment effectiveness, thereby increasing treatment availability and subsequent access. Until an adolescent-specific certification program can be developed, an immediate revision of the credentialing process must be undertaken so that adolescent-specific knowledge is incorporated as a requirement for licensures. In the short term, this change would have the effect of increasing the population of personnel who would at least be sensitive to the unique needs of this group. Establishment of the Clinical Trials Networks (CTN) of the National Institute on Drug Abuse (NIDA) and Addiction Technology Transfer Centers of the Substance Abuse and Mental Health Services Administration (SAMHSA) is a beginning step in this direction.

Improving Access: Expand Financing Mechanisms

The topic of financing for early intervention and drug treatment services has received much attention with little resolution. For example, development of targeted utilization rates based on epidemiological estimates of need for care has been suggested (CSAT, 2000; Minnesota Department of Human Services, 1997). Such a public funding mechanism would provide incentives to ensure that health plans and public funding streams identify, refer, and reimburse treatment for adolescents with an SUD. Increasing benefits in the private sector through parity and comprehensive coverage packages, improving the flexibility of funding, tying reimbursement to performance measures and quality treatment standards, and reallocating interdiction and incarceration funds to treatment have also been proposed (CSAT, 2000). Research examining the effects of these suggestions has been called for (CSAT, 2000; NIDA RFA# DA-03-003; NIDA PA-01-097), but the results of these empirical studies are not yet available. Nonetheless, revisions to the way in which services are reimbursed are critical if system improvement is to be realized.

Beyond general financing of treatment services and insurance coverage are additional issues unique to adolescents. First, of the 4 million uninsured adolescents, approximately 2.3 million are eligible for Medicaid or State Children's Health Insurance Program (SCHIP) (Center for Adolescent Health and the Law, 2000; Newacheck, 1999). Increased access to SCHIP is needed and may be accomplished through staff training within presumptive eligibility sites and use of Early and Periodic Screening, Diagnostic, and Treatment (EPSDT), Maternal and Child Health (MCH), and community-based staff to enroll teens. This would result in fewer uninsured adolescents, who would then have a greater probability of accessing the care that does exist. Concomitant attention is also essential in *(1)* developing mechanisms for health plans and providers to adapt medical records, billing and laboratory procedures to protect confidentiality

(e.g., currently the insurance summary is sent to the customer [parent] listing payment or coverage of confidential services rendered to the patient [adolescent]); *(2)* disseminating accurate information to adolescent members about what services they can receive with their own consent; and *(3)* communicating clearly about confidentiality protections, particularly about what types of information are not confidential (Ford et al., 1999; Klein et al., 1999; Newacheck, 2000).

DELIVERY OF COMPREHENSIVE, NEED-BASED, AND DEVELOPMENTALLY SENSITIVE SERVICES

Once an adolescent is identified and able to access services, one might assume that the treatment provided would meet at least most of an adolescent's identified needs. Unfortunately, service delivery often falls short for several reasons. Because so few adolescents receive comprehensive assessments (Weinberg, Rahdert, Colliver, & Glantz, 1998), very few are provided with comprehensive need-based services (Delany, Broome, Flynn, & Fletcher, 2001; Dembo, 1995, 1996; Terry, VanderWaal, McBride, & Van Buren, 2000). In turn, few receive step-down or continuing care (Alford, Koehler, & Leonard, 1991; Spear & Skala, 1995; Brown, Meyers, Mott, & Vik, 1994; Winters, 1999). Finally, few adolescents are able to access services that even minimally address key developmental challenges of this period (e.g., individuation coupled with age-appropriate limit setting within the context of family-specific services).

Limited Assessment Practices

Despite research advances in adolescent assessment practices (Winters & Stinchfield, 1995), the standard clinical intake does not identify the full range of problems and strengths brought to a substance abuse treatment program by an individual youth, nor does it assess youth within a developmental context of measurement (Weinberg et al., 1998). In a typical program, an unstructured interview (generally with program-developed forms) is conducted to obtain an in-depth drug use history, a psychiatric review, and a physical examination. These components are the mainstay for treatment planning (Weinberg et al., 1998). As we and others have shown, adolescents with SUD are characterized by interconnected, complex problems (Hawkins et al., 1992; Fleming, Leventhal, Glynn, & Ershley, 1989; Helzer, 1981; Hirschi, Hindelang, & Weis, 1980; Meyers et al., 1999; Morrison, McCusker, Stoddard, & Bigelow, 1995; Prout & Chuzik, 1988; Winters & Stinchfield, 1995).

In a recent study of 205 youth in drug treatment (Meyers, Hagan, & McDermott et al., under review), many individuals had an array of problem behaviors, with typical onset occurring in early or middle childhood. Excluding tobacco, alcohol and other drugs were tried at approximately 11 years of age on average (11.3; SD = 2.5), with at least weekly use starting by the age of 13 (12.9; SD = 1.8). Alcohol, marijuana, hallucinogens, heroin, and cocaine tended to be the most predominant substances of abuse; 89% of the youth were daily cigarette smokers. With respect to mental health issues, 93% of youth had at least three symptoms of a mental health disorder at treatment admission, with 82% meeting criteria for an Axis I nondrug diagnosis by the age of 12 years. Family problems were prevalent in that 50% of the youth lived with active substance abusers, 53% had run away from home, 53% reported transient living arrangements, and 31% reported police or child welfare involvement with their family. Inconsistent discipline practices (46%), harsh discipline practices (35%), and a lack of supervision (46%) were also reported. In 21% of cases, youth assumed the adult or parental role within the household. Educational deficits were the norm, with 77% reporting a history of academic problems, 74% reporting attendance problems, and 80% reporting discipline problems. It is therefore not surprising that 57% of these teens had dropped out of school by the age of 15. Further, 75% had been or were currently involved with the justice system, 55% actively carried guns, and 43% had witnessed a murder or an attempted murder in their community. Eighty-three percent of the youth were sexually active; all (100%) reported hanging out with peers who either had AOD problems or were involved in the juvenile justice system.

In addition to these descriptive data illustrating the clinical complexities of substance-abusing youth, we empirically identified seven treatment-oriented youth prototypes (Meyers, McDermott, Webb, & Hagan, in press).

- General low-severity problems
- Moderate-severity delinquency and chemical dependency; low-severity psychosocial problems and sexual risk behavior
- Moderate-severity psychosocial problems and sexual risk behavior; low-severity delinquency and chemical dependency
- High-severity delinquency and sexual risk behavior; moderate-severity chemical dependency and psychosocial problems
- High-severity psychosocial problems and delinquency; moderate-severity chemical dependency and sexual risk behavior
- Very high-severity psychosocial problems; low-severity chemical dependency, delinquency, sexual risk behavior
- Very high-severity chemical dependency; moderate-severity psychosocial problems, delinquency, sexual risk behavior

These typologies suggest that adolescents in substance abuse treatment programs are a very diverse group of youth. While it is clear that effective treatment needs to address these multiple problems, neither the simple availability of multiple services nor even the broad, undifferentiated provision of multiple services appears to be appropriate for producing treatment gains. Instead, gains are most likely to be obtained when the facets of treatment relate directly (i.e., are matched) to the life areas of the teen that are in need of remediation (Meyers et al., 1999). Given the degradation of services available within many service programs (Delany et al., 2001; Etheridge, Smith, Rounds-Bryant, & Hubbard, 2001; SAMHSA, 2001b), service coordination between programs and systems will be necessary if treatment matching is to become a reality.

When limited assessments are conducted, there is a risk that services will focus on just a few issues or provide services that are irrelevant to a youth's profile. These scenarios are rarely associated with significant clinical benefits (Henggeler, Schoenwald, Pickrel, Rowland, & Santos, 1994; Kiestenbaum, 1985). Limited assessments can result in a cascading effect of inadequate treatment plans, incomplete treatment matching, limited service coordination, poor treatment engagement and retention, and poor utilization of scarce resources. In turn, this can lead the youth and the family to conclude that "treatment doesn't work." Hence, once youth are identified and find access to substance abuse treatment, there is a strong need for the use of standardized multidimensional assessment tools.

Limited Scope (and Appropriateness) of Services

Even if comprehensive assessments leading to prioritized but multifocused treatment planning can become standard clinical practice, another barrier will become even more apparent. Few if any programs are able to deliver even a minimal constellation of developmentally sensitive educational, social, or health services. Within the last few years, there has been a severe decline in the number and types of on-site services provided by adolescent substance abuse treatment programs in the United States (Etheridge et al., 2001). This occurs at a time when it is widely recognized that (1) treatment decisions for adolescents are better informed by pretreatment psychosocial factors than by drug use severity (Latimer, Newcomb, Winters, & Stinchfield, 2000), and (2) treatment effectiveness is contingent upon treatment for the array of comorbid dysfunctions within clinical samples (Kazdin & Weisz, 1998; Williams & Chang, 2000).

As a result of limited assessment and service decline, adolescents who are fortunate enough to obtain substance abuse treatment will probably not receive the type or amount of services required to minimally address their needs (Delany et al., 2001; Etheridge et al., 2001; SAMHSA, 2001b). Even adolescents are aware of service deficiencies: many of those who had received substance abuse treatment reported that their needs were not met by the services they received (Eth-

ridge et al., 2001), with family and psychiatric needs most often going unmet (40%–50%). Since these are perhaps the two domains most comorbid with adolescent substance abuse, it is likely that these unmet needs may particularly compromise the effects of the services (typically drug counseling) that can be provided.

The effects of provided services can also be compromised if they are not developmentally focused. Adolescents are a unique client group in that (1) they are in a continuous state of social, biological, cognitive, and emotional development; and (2) risk taking and experimentation characterize normal development (Deas et al., 2000; Eccles et al., 1993; Gottlieb, Wahisten, & Licklieter, 1998; Greene, 1993). Consequently, evidence continues to mount demonstrating the effectiveness of interventions that address the developmental processes of social-identity development, peer group influences, self-regulation, moral and cognitive development (e.g., perspective-taking), and autonomy seeking (i.e., separation from the family [classic view] or movement toward family interdependence [contemporary view]; Deas et al., 2000; Wagner & Waldron, 2001). To obtain optimal effects, ecologically framed interventions that address individual and proximal factors are necessary (Bronfenbrenner, 1986, 1989; Liddle & Hogue, 2001). Because the family or household is a principle ecological context for child and adolescent development, targeted interventions with the family as a unit that address limit setting, monitoring and supervision, consistent discipline practices, and communication patterns are required to compliment individually based services. When there is limited availability of these core components, treatment delivery falls short of meeting individual needs. This has a negative impact on retention, one of the most consistent predictors of treatment outcome (Hubbard, Craddock, Flynn, Anderson, & Etheridge, 1997; Simpson, Joe, & Brown, 1997; Simpson, Joe, Broome et al., 1997). When the treatment landscape has been compromised by service deterioration and nondevelopmentally focused care, it is not surprising that few adolescents complete treatment, thus reducing their chances of having a good outcome (Battjes, Onken, & Delany, 1999; Williams & Chang, 2000; Winters, 1999).

Restricted Access to Step-Down Services

Further complicating service delivery is the fact that step-down and continuing care services rarely follow an index treatment episode. Hence, the chronic nature of the substance use disorder is typically not addressed. Without less intensive step-down services there is a significant risk of relapse and return of substance abuse problems (Alford et al., 1991; Armstrong & Altschuler, 1998; Brown, Meyers, Mott, & Vik 1994; Latimer et al., 2000; Spear & Skala, 1995; Stewart & Brown, 1993; Winters, 1999; Winters et al., 2000). This causes readmissions to treatment, expending the already limited pool of resources.

System Change Considerations

Improve Delivery of Comprehensive Need-Based Services

As stated previously, research indicates declines in the number and type of on-site services in substance abuse treatment programs throughout the country. Since substance abuse treatment programs are part of a larger network of care (Denmead & Rouse, 1994), one would expect corresponding increases in the partnering between substance abuse treatment programs and other service providers (e.g., those within the mental health, educational, and sexual health systems) to compensate for service deficits. This is not occurring (Ethridge, Hubbard, Anderson, Craddock, & Flynn, 1997). Admittedly, obtaining out-of-program and continuing care services is not simple.

The larger network of care within which drug treatment programs operate consists of components that function as discrete entities, reporting to separate budget authorities and with minimal coordination among them—the so-called administrative "silos" (Dembo et al., in press; NASADAD, 2002; Solar, 1992). Competing priorities of these different entities, rigidly drawn boundary turfs and budgetary categories, competition for reimbursement dollars, and barriers to data sharing stifle collaboration (Gerstein & Harwood, 1990; Krisberg & Austin, 1993). In addition, with different eligibility criteria, various data collection and reporting requirements, and

different coverage policies, codes, and procedures, it becomes clear why so many service providers operate independently from one another (Gerstein & Harwood, 1990; Johnson, 1999; Moss, 1998). Without system coordination, the same youth loops in and out of all treatment systems (Solar, 1992), with each intervention failure in one system accompanied by a repeat cost to some other sector of the system. Again, capacity is diminished and the pool of financial resources is unnecessarily reduced.

If comprehensive services are to be delivered through provider partnering, the development of interorganizational networks of care is critical (Baker, 1991; CASA, 2001; Krisberg & Austin, 1993; Kutash, Duchnowski, Meyers, & King, 1997; Marsden, 1998; Meyers & Davis, 1997; US Public Health Service, 2000; Murray & Belenko, under review; Rose, Zweben, & Stoffel, 1999). Such an undertaking requires substantial systems change and ongoing commitments. First, policymakers should begin to facilitate a change in "business as usual" by developing *(1)* new representative authority, governance structures, and funding streams; *(2)* universal, consolidated, and standardized data collection and reporting requirements; and *(3)* consolidated coverage policies, codes, and procedures (Gerstein & Harwood, 1990; Johnson, 1999; Moss, 1998). Next, partnering agencies could develop information-sharing partnerships and adopt written agreements—e.g., about the level at which information will be shared (i.e., case level, department or agency level, community level), when information will be shared, or the purpose and use of information sharing. This can be an effective way to provide coordinated, nonduplicative services through streamlined assessment and service referral activities, case management support, and availability of real-time information for necessary case plan adjustments (Meyers, 1998, 2000). Interdependence among these independent systems could be achieved by developing *(1)* centralized intake, referral, and case management services; and *(2)* colocation of services. To this end, all youth who present (or call) for services would be referred to the central intake unit (CIU). At the CIU, the youth would receive a standardized assessment followed by a case plan and referral to needed services. Referral may be back to the original system of contact or perhaps not, depending upon the case plan. Through colocating diverse services at the CIU or at various service sites (e.g., mental health services located at drug treatment programs) and holding staffing meetings at these locations, collaboration between provider and system can occur. Colocated services could also improve service compliance and retention because youth would not have to go to multiple locations to have their needs met. If service providers, service systems, and policymakers could commit to systems change and participate in an interorganizational network of care, competitors could become collaborators, limited resources could be better matched and maximized, and services could move from being fragmented to coordinated. All of this could ultimately improve the delivery of clinically appropriate, nonduplicative, and cost-effective services within a continuum of care. Within such a system, substance abuse treatment providers (as well as other types of providers) could then partner with agencies to provide services they do not offer but that youth need.

EMERGING TRENDS IN SYSTEM CHANGES

Despite the many challenges discussed, there is movement toward improvement in Community Assessment Centers (CACs), Juvenile Drug Courts, and CASASTART (described below) have been designed to address systemic barriers to appropriate intervention. Each includes a comprehensive assessment followed by coordination of need-based services provided through intersystem linkages. Although outcome data are scarce at this time, the innovations they represent warrant discussion.

Community Assessment Centers

Community Assessment Centers originated within the U.S. Office of Juvenile Justice and Delinquency Prevention (OJJDP) to address multiple and decentralized points of entry, inadequate assessment practices, scarce resources, system fragmentation, and lack of early intervention

among at-risk and delinquent youth (Bilchik, 1995; Oldenettel & Wordes, 2000). There are 67 CACs distributed throughout the United States (e.g., California, Colorado, Florida, Kansas, Maryland, Nebraska) and a formal evaluation of their effectiveness is under way (National Council on Crime and Delinquency, 2003). Four interrelated components make up the CAC. First, these centers serve as a single point of entry (component # 1) into the entire system of care within a target community. All agencies regardless of the service system within which they are embedded (e.g., mental health, substance abuse) triage youth to the CAC. If the youth has been arrested, the arresting officer transports the youth to the CAC, where they are booked prior to being assessed. In other words, CACs function as a centralized intake facility for all sectors of a community's service system. Administration of a standardized screening instrument (e.g., Massachusetts Youth Screening Instrument [MAYSI-2]; Grisso & Barnum, 2000) is followed by a standardized comprehensive assessment (component #2), when indicated (e.g., Comprehensive Adolescent Severity Inventory [CASI]; Meyers, Hagan, et al., in press). Arrested youth also receive a risk assessment so that the level of needed security can be determined. Assessment data are reviewed by an interdisciplinary team comprised of CAC staff and colocated staff from multiple community agencies. The data are stored in an integrated management information system (component #3) for data sharing and performance monitoring and are synthesized into a case plan for ongoing case management (component #4). Colocated staff work with case management staff to minimize the red tape that case managers may face when accessing an array of community services. When implemented as designed, CACs *(1)* enable identification of issues that impede community youths' ability to function (whether they are in the juvenile justice system or not) so that *(2)* effective services can be delivered in a coordinated, nonduplicative fashion by systems staff working together for the purpose of *(3)* improving the functional status of youth (and possibly their families), thereby preventing penetration (or further penetration) into various systems of care (Meyers, 1998, 2000). Although evaluation data are not yet available in this area, CACs are nonetheless a promising approach to systems change for youth who use, abuse, or are dependent upon substances, regardless of their presenting problem or the system to which they present. Given the obvious potential of this approach, there is clear need for additional research and evaluation and, if effectiveness is shown, for dissemination and community training.

Juvenile Drug Courts

Although there are recent indications that violent crime has decreased among juveniles, youth crime overall is at unacceptably high levels, with younger and more impaired youth being arrested at an increasing rate (Snyder & Sickmund, 1999). As social services are reduced, the juvenile justice system has become the focal point for interventions with many youth. Hence, the justice system has responded by providing a number of innovative programs (Jenson & Howard, 1998; Office of Juvenile Justice and Delinquency Prevention, 1995).

One such program is the juvenile drug court (American University, 1997; Belanko, 2001; Office of Justice Programs Drug Court Clearinghouse and Technical Assistance Project, 1998). Modeled after adult drug court programs, juvenile drug courts (of which there are 167 as of June 2001; American University, 2001) combine identification of a youth's problems with systemic interventions monitored and enforced by the presiding judge. Although the name implies that drug treatment is the sole focus of these courts, juvenile drug courts generally take a multifaceted approach. Educational deficits, family problems, and behavioral difficulties are addressed by staff of local provider agencies who attend weekly meetings, share information, work together, and change intervention plans where indicated. Participating providers serve as a team delivering coordinated, noncompeting services to youth.

Outcome results are still preliminary, but there are a few studies that found reduced recidivism rates and increased time to rearrest among juvenile drug court participants (Belenko, 2001; Meyers, O'Brien, et al., under review). While ad-

ditional research is needed, juvenile drug courts appear to be a promising systems intervention for substance-abusing juvenile offenders. These courts enact some of the core principles described above for a more effective systems approach to identifying and treating SUDs among adolescents.

CASASTART *(Striving Together to Achieve Rewarding Tomorrows)*

CASASTART, originally called the Children at Risk program, was developed by the National Center on Addiction and Substance Abuse (CASA) at Columbia University through foundation and U.S. Department of Justice funding to address service gaps among high-risk 8- to 13-year-olds, their families, and their communities (Murray and Belanko, under review). Similar to the programs discussed above, CASASTART forges a working partnership of schools, law enforcement, and community-based health and social service organizations, and all are housed under one roof. Through intensive case management, a coordinated constellation of eight core services is provided to varying degrees according to the needs of the youth and his or her family: social support; family services; educational services; after-school and summer recreational activities; mentoring; incentives; community policing; and criminal and juvenile justice interventions. Evaluation data illustrate that CASASTART participants were less likely to use or deal drugs, engage in violent crime, or be influenced by negative peers (Harrell, Cavanagh, & Sridharan, 1998). Further, these same youth were more likely to belong to positive peer groups and to advance to the next grade. These data suggest that CASASTART is a promising systems change model that results in positive outcomes among its participants.

SUMMARY

Adolescents who use, abuse, or are dependent upon substances are served by a service delivery system that often *(1)* fails to identify them; *(2)* fails to make the important distinction between use and abuse or dependence and thus may make inappropriate referrals; *(3)* renders multiple barriers to treatment access for those who are referred; and *(4)* delivers fewer developmentally sensitive services than are indicated. As a result, a large group of adolescents who use, abuse, or are dependent upon substances are not being appropriately cared for at a time when there are more and better evidence-based treatment and intervention options than ever before (e.g., motivational interviewing, cognitive-behavioral therapy, multidimensional family therapy).

This chapter has shown that designing ways to address service system inadequacies is just as important as developing evidence-based interventions to treat the disorder itself. Hence, it is clear that the same type of focused research attention and political support that led to the recent developments in evidence-based treatments will be even more important to address service system inadequacies. Examination of ways to efficiently improve the identification of adolescent substance users through staff training, adoption of common definitions and mechanisms for assessment within a developmental context of measurement, and financing arrangements are all needed. The translation of evidence-based research into practice through technology transfer projects has the potential to improve adolescent outcomes, thereby improving access. The Clinical Trials Network within the National Institute on Drug Abuse and Addiction Technology Transfer Centers supported by the Center for Substance Abuse Treatment are a very good beginning in this endeavor. Although complex environments, service delivery systems are comprised of components primed for intervention and three integrative models have been developed. We recognize that systems reform will not be quick or easy and will undoubtedly require policy change and national leadership. But such reform is necessary if adolescents are to take advantage of improved interventions and curtail a trajectory of life-long problems.

Acknowledgments

This work was supported in part by NIDA grant # DA07705-06. The authors thank Siobhan O'Brien and Sarah Teague for literature and citation assistance.

The Role of Primary Care Physicians in Detection and Treatment of Adolescent Mental Health Problems

Daniel Romer
and Mary McIntosh

chapter

30

This chapter presents research conducted as part of the Sunnylands Adolescent Mental Health Initiative (SAMHI) to determine primary care provider practices in identifying and referring adolescents for treatment of mental health problems. It is estimated that over 70% of youth visit a primary care physician in an average year (Wells, Kataoka, & Asarnow, 2001), and with the advent of managed care, primary care physicians also serve as the gateway to obtaining specialist care, including mental health services (Glied & Neufield, 2001). However, research suggests that less than half of adolescents in the United States with a significant mental disorder are seen by an appropriate mental health service provider (Costello et al., 1998; Horwitz, Leaf, Leventhal, Borsyth, & Speechley, 1992; Sturm, Ringel, & Andreyeva, 2003).

Several explanations have been proposed for the poor treatment rate of adolescents with mental health problems. Most primary care providers are not extensively trained to identify or treat mental health problems (Wells et al., 2001), and their ability to screen patients for mental disorders is limited by time constraints per office visit (Chang, Warner, & Weissman, 1988) and restrictive reimbursement policies (Wells et al., 2001). Indeed, studies of primary care providers indicate that they recognize symptoms of mental disorder in only about 50% of adolescents reporting those symptoms prior to their visit (Horwitz et al., 1992; Kelleher et al., 1997). Even when symptoms are recognized, less than half of youth are referred for care to mental health specialists (Gardner et al., 2000; Rushton, Bruckman, & Kelleher, 2002). Although pediatric primary care providers increasingly recognize mental health problems in their patients (Kelleher, McInerny, Gardner, Childs, & Wasserman, 2000), it is clear that improving identification and referral practices represents a significant opportunity to increase appropriate treatment of adolescent mental disorders.

Despite long-standing weaknesses in the primary care system, recent changes in the delivery of mental health services may be influencing the treatment of adolescent mental disorders. Many managed care plans now contain dedicated services, or "carve-outs," for mental health care that may encourage referral to specialists (Conti,

Frank, & McGuire, 2004; Forrest et al., 1999; Glied & Neufield, 2001). Experience with these arrangements in adult managed care suggests that they may eliminate costly (and ineffective) inpatient mental health services, but very little is known about the effects of managed care on youth (Glied & Neufield, 2001; Scholle & Kelleher, 1998). Another development is the increase in public financing of children's health. More children are now covered by Medicaid and the State Children's Health Insurance Program, both of which may provide more comprehensive coverage than available through other mechanisms (Glied & Cuellar, 2003).

In addition to changes in the financing of health care, many initiatives have focused on the need for better mental health screening of children and adolescents, most notably the *Report of the Surgeon General on Child Mental Health* (U.S. Department of Health and Human Services, 2000) and the President's New Freedom Commission on Mental Health (2003). Furthermore, the American Academy of Pediatrics as part of its Bright Futures program (Jellinek, Patel, & Froehle, 2002) and the National Association of Pediatric Nurse Practitioners as part of its Keep Your Children/Yourself Safe and Secure initiative (KySS) (Melnyk, Brown, Jones, Kreipe, & Novak, 2003) now encourage primary care practitioners to screen their patients for common mental disorders and to refer those who meet diagnostic criteria to appropriate providers.

In this ever-changing policy environment, it is important to determine how well primary care physicians, especially those serving patients in managed care, are able to identify and refer adolescent patients with serious mental disorders. In particular, we were interested to determine if primary care physicians who treat adolescents view the mental health of their patients as their responsibility and, if so, whether their diagnostic skills and office practices enable them to identify a variety of mental health problems and to seek referrals for those in need of treatment. We were also interested in providers' views of stigma and beliefs about the efficacy of treatment in their decisions about mental health care.

To determine the status of current practices in adolescent primary care, the Annenberg Public Policy Center, with funding from SAMHI, commissioned Princeton Survey Research Associates to conduct a survey of over 700 primary care physicians who regularly treat adolescents ages 10 to 18 (pediatricians, family physicians, and general practitioners). The interviews were conducted by telephone between September 29, 2003, and January 23, 2004. The details of the methodology are provided in the Appendix to this chapter.

SURVEY OF PRIMARY CARE PHYSICIANS WHO TREAT ADOLESCENTS

Sample Characteristics

Table 30.1 shows the demographic composition of the sample in comparison to the universe of

Table 30.1 Sample Composition in Comparison to National Population Characteristics (*N* = 727)

Characteristic	Population (%)	Unweighted Sample (%)	Weighted Sample (%)
Age			
Under 45 years	40	33	32
45 years and older	60	63	65
Gender			
Women	49	54	58
Men	51	46	42
Type			
Pediatrician	80	92	80
Family or general practitioner	20	8	20
Urbanity			
Urban	40	42	40
Suburban	46	42	43
Rural	14	11	12
Region			
Northeast	26	32	30
Midwest	20	17	19
South	31	27	26
West	24	24	25

physicians from which it was drawn. The sample of 727 primary care providers closely mirrored the demographic characteristics of U.S. pediatricians, family practitioners, and general practitioners. The one exception was type of physician—pediatrician or family or general practitioners. Fewer family and general practitioners were willing to participate in the survey than were sampled. To compensate for their underrepresentation, the data were weighted to the proportions (80%/20%) originally sampled.

The sample of providers reported seeing an average of 27.4 adolescents in an average week (range, 1 to 200). Approximately 45% reported that the majority of their adolescent patients were enrolled in managed care, and about 50% reported that the majority of their patients were insured through public programs. Hence, this sample provides a unique look at the practices of providers who treat large numbers of adolescents in the United States within an ever-expanding universe of managed care and public reimbursement programs.

FINDINGS

Adolescent Mental Health Is a Strong Responsibility

Most primary care physicians believe that they have a responsibility to tend to both the physical and mental well-being of their adolescent patients (Table 30.2). When asked to what degree they believe it is their job to talk to adolescent patients about their mental health, more than 7 in 10 (76%) said it is their job to a great extent. Only a handful (3%) did not feel it is their job to ask about mental health issues.

In addition to mental health issues, most physicians feel strongly that it is their job to ask about other aspects of their adolescent patients' lives. A large majority of physicians felt a great deal of responsibility to bring up risky behaviors such as use of tobacco (80%), alcohol (78%), marijuana (74%), and other illegal drugs (76%). As many physicians believed it is very much their job to ask how things are going at school (79%) and about sexual activity (76%). And nearly as many physicians believed it is very

Table 30.2 Physician Responsibilities in Regard to Mental Health Topics[a]

| Topic | Physician's Response | | |
	A Great Deal (%)	A Fair Amount (%)	Not Too Much/ Not At All (%)
Mental health	76	21	3
Use of tobacco	80	18	2
School work and how things are going	79	20	1
Use of alcohol	78	19	2
Sexual activity	76	21	3
Use of other illegal drugs	76	20	3
Use of marijuana	74	22	3
Eating habits	73	25	2
Relationships with their family and friends	73	24	3

[a]According to response to the question, "In general, how much do you feel it is your job to talk to adolescent patients about their (Insert)?"

much a part of their job to ask about adolescents' eating habits (73%) and their relationships with family and friends (73%).

Physicians who felt it is their responsibility to ask adolescents about mental health issues were also more likely to strongly believe it is their job to ask about all of these other issues. This suggests that many physicians see their job as clearly encompassing much more than just the treatment of their patient's physical health.

Mental Health Is Not Always a Priority During Physical Exams

Despite the fact that most physicians are convinced that paying attention to their adolescent patients' mental health is part of their job, primary care physicians do not always ask adolescents about mental health issues during routine exams (Table 30.3). Roughly half of physicians (48%) said they always ask their patients about their mental health—most of the rest (43%) asked about it sometimes. The good news is that substantially fewer rarely or never (9%) asked their adolescent patients about their mental health during their routine physical exams.

Physicians who say they always ask adolescents about their mental health tend to think that mental health is a big part of their job. We

also found that female physicians are more likely to say they always ask about mental health than male physicians. And pediatricians make a point to always ask about mental health more often than family and general practitioners.

Perhaps because it is such a natural topic to ask an adolescent about, more than 8 in 10 physicians (84%) said they always ask how things are going in school. Physicians were also more likely to always address use of tobacco (74%), sexual activity (66%), and use of alcohol (65%) than they were to address mental health. In addition, more than half of physicians said they always ask about use of marijuana (54%) and other illegal drugs (57%). And most physicians asked about these issues at least sometimes. Roughly 1 in 10 or fewer said they rarely or never address these issues.

Knowledge Is Good But Not Excellent

Despite their strong conviction that mental health is integral to their mission, primary care providers do not feel particularly qualified to treat mental health problems. Only 1 in 10 physicians (11%) said their knowledge of mental health issues is "excellent." A slim majority said it is good (56%), while 33% said their knowledge is only somewhat good or weak.

We found no demographic differences be-

Table 30.3 Frequency of Asking Questions on Various Mental Health Topics
During Physical Exams in the Past Year

	Physician's Response		
	---	---	---
Topic	A Great Deal (%)	A Fair Amount (%)	Not Too Much/ Not At All (%)
Mental health	48	43	9
School work and how things are going	84	15	1
Use of tobacco	74	21	4
Sexual activity (for those who have reached puberty)	66	29	5
Use of alcohol	65	30	4
Use of other illegal drugs	57	34	8
Use of marijuana	54	35	12

tween primary care physicians who say they have excellent knowledge of adolescent mental health and those who describe their knowledge as good. For example, female physicians were no more likely than male physicians to believe their knowledge level is excellent. And even though younger physicians were probably exposed to more information about mental health in medical school, physicians under age 50 described their knowledge base as excellent as often as older physicians. Furthermore, regardless of whether the physician practiced medicine in a rural, urban, or suburban location, there was no difference in their reported knowledge levels. Likewise, pediatricians were as likely as family and general practitioners to say they have excellent knowledge of mental health issues. The same conclusion applies to physicians whose patients are primarily enrolled in managed care or with private insurers.

Many physicians also report a lack of confidence in how to handle information they receive from adolescent patients about their mental status. Only half of physicians (50%) said they very often "know how to handle" this type of information. But 40% reported being less confident and said they only *somewhat* often rather than *very* often knew how to handle the information they get. At the same time, relatively few physicians (9%) said they are often unsure about how to handle the information they get on a patient's mental health.

Not surprisingly, physicians who said they have excellent knowledge about adolescent mental health were much more likely to say they very often know how to handle the information they get from patients about their mental health (86%) than those who describe their knowledge base as good (55%) or only somewhat good or weak (30%).

Ability to Identify Mental Health Problems

When asked about specific mental health conditions, most physicians felt at least somewhat capable of identifying these problems in adolescents (Table 30.4). However, physicians expressed more confidence in their ability to identify some conditions than others. Regardless of the condition they were asked about, only half or fewer felt *very* capable of identifying these disorders.

Physicians are most confident in their ability to identify depression. Still, only half (50%) said they feel very capable of identifying depression in adolescents. Almost all (98%), however, said they are at least somewhat capable of identifying adolescent depression.

In identifying anxiety and eating disorders, physicians are even less confident than they are for depression. Although over 9 in 10 said they are at least somewhat capable of identifying these conditions, only about 4 in 10 reported

Table 30.4 Ability to Identify Various Mental Health Problems in Adolescents

| | Physician's Response | | | |
	Very Capable (%)	Somewhat Capable (%)	Not Too Capable (%)	Not Capable at All (%)
Mental Health Problem				
Depression	50	48	2	—
Anxiety disorders such as panic disorder, social phobias, and obsessive/compulsive disorders	43	52	5	—
Eating disorders	39	55	5	1
Alcohol abuse	31	61	7	1
Drug abuse	25	65	8	—
Sexual abuse	22	59	16	2
Schizophrenia	21	51	23	4
Bipolar disorder	18	59	20	3

that they are very capable of identifying anxiety (43%) and eating disorders (39%). Next in order are drug and alcohol abuse. Only 3 in 10 or fewer said they are very capable of identifying alcohol (31%) and drug (25%) abuse. But again, 9 in 10 physicians said they are at least somewhat capable of identifying these behaviors.

When it comes to identifying victims of sexual abuse, quite a few physicians feel unsure. Only 22% said they are very capable of identifying victims of sexual abuse. Although 81% reported feeling at least somewhat capable, 18% seriously doubted their abilities to identify sexual abuse.

Physicians are most likely to express doubts about their capabilities when it comes to patients with either of two mental conditions—schizophrenia and bipolar disorders. Perhaps because of its low incidence, only 21% said they are very capable of identifying schizophrenia in adolescents. And although a solid majority (72%) reported feeling at least somewhat capable, 27% said they are not too or not at all capable of identifying this condition.

Bipolar disorder is another condition that quite a few express doubts about. Only 18% of physicians said they are very capable of identifying bipolar disorders. Although 77% reported feeling at least somewhat capable, 23% were less sure of their ability to identify this disorder in adolescents.

Experience Matters

There is reason to believe that for at least some of these conditions, steps can be taken to increase physicians' confidence in diagnosing them. For example, by improving physicians' knowledge, they may be better able to diagnose depression, anxiety, and eating disorders. Solid majorities who described their knowledge base as excellent reported feeling very capable of identifying depression (85%), anxiety (76%), and eating disorders (71%). Knowledge may also help in identifying other conditions, although even among those with excellent knowledge, only half or fewer reported feeling very capable of identifying bipolar disorders (49%), sex abuse victims (47%), or schizophrenia (46%).

According to the physicians surveyed, they learn to diagnose mental health problems through a combination of patient care experiences and formal training. More than 4 in 10 attributed their diagnostic skills most to their patient care experience (43%), while almost as many referred to their medical training (40%).

Female physicians (50%) were more likely to attribute their skills to their patient care experience than male physicians (38%), and physicians over age 50 (21%) more often than their younger colleagues (7%) attributed their confidence to their personal experiences.

Treatment Viewed as Effective

Physician competence in diagnosing and treating adolescent mental conditions obviously matters, but it is especially important because virtually all agree that with adequate care adolescents can be successfully treated for mental health conditions. Some physicians reported feeling more strongly about this than others: 71% strongly agreed that with adequate care adolescents can be successfully treated, whereas an additional 25% agreed somewhat. Very few physicians (3%) reported feeling that mental disorders cannot be successfully treated with adequate care.

Screening for Mental Disorders

The most systematic way to learn about potential mental health problems is to screen patients for these conditions. According to physicians surveyed, not quite one in two adolescents will encounter such a test during an office visit.[1] Roughly half of providers (48%) said that their office "routinely screens adolescent patients for mental health disorders." However, slightly more physicians said their office does not routinely conduct a screening test (51%). Physicians who are more likely to screen are also more likely to be open and engaged and to be knowledgeable about mental health issues. Physicians who say they always ask about mental health issues, who strongly feel it is their responsibility to talk to adolescents about mental health issues, and who describe their knowledge as excellent are more likely to say they routinely screen their patients for mental disorders.

Physicians who reported screening patients tended to use either a screening instrument developed by the physician (36%) or a standard patient questionnaire that is administered to the adolescent (34%) (Table 30.5). Considerably fewer physicians reported using a standard questionnaire that is administered to the parent (4%) or do the screening themselves or have an associate do the screening (17%).

1. A brief fax survey of nonrespondents indicates that the number of doctors who routinely screen adolescent patients for mental health disorders could be even lower.

Table 30.5 Reported Method of Screening[a]

Method	Physician's Response (%)
Use our own screening instrument	36
Standard patient questionnaire administered to adolescents	34
I or one of my associates does screening during the visit	17
Standard patient questionnaire administered to parent, such as the Pediatric Symptom Checklist	4
Other	7

[a]Among those saying they screen, $N = 357$.

Physicians who routinely screen patients for mental disorders were more likely to do so during the office visit itself (81%) rather than while the patient is in the waiting room (13%) or at some other time (6%).

A majority of physicians who do not routinely screen patients reported being aware (64%) that there are screening instruments for common mental conditions that can be completed by adolescents while they wait to see the physician. At the same time, more than a third (36%) said they are not aware of these screening instruments.

Treatment Decisions Are Quite Consistent

To find out more about physicians' actual treatment practices, we asked how they would proceed given a set of symptoms often associated with different mental health conditions—depression, anxiety disorders, bipolar disorders, eating disorders, alcohol abuse, and schizophrenia. (To reduce respondent burden, we only asked each physician about three of the disorders.) In particular, we asked if they would talk to the adolescent's parents about the symptoms, refer the patient to a mental health professional, or treat the patient themselves. We also asked physicians to estimate how many patients with each set of symptoms they actually referred in the last year and to what type of professional.

Physicians were remarkably consistent in their chosen course of treatment across different mental health conditions. Most physicians reported that they would talk to the adolescent's parents and would refer the adolescent to another professional. In a smaller percentage of cases, physicians claimed they would treat the patient themselves.

As seen in Table 30.6, physicians said they would be very likely to talk to parents of adolescents who presented symptoms of depression (91%) or schizophrenia (90%). A large majority also said they would be very likely to consult parents if an adolescent had symptoms of bipolar disorder (83%), eating disorder (81%), or an anxiety disorder (78%) or if an adolescent was showing signs of alcohol abuse (75%).

Very few among the physicians interviewed said they would not be likely to talk to the parent of an adolescent who had symptoms of one of these conditions.

In addition to talking to a parent, a majority of physicians said they would be very likely to refer an adolescent to a mental health professional for further testing or treatment (Table 30.7). Fewer than 1 in 10 physicians said they would not be likely to make a referral if a patient was showing symptoms associated with a mental disorder.

An adolescent presenting with symptoms of schizophrenia was most likely to be referred to a mental health professional (94%). A large majority of physicians also said they would be very likely to make a referral for symptoms associated with depression (79%), anxiety disorders (76%), alcohol abuse (76%), or bipolar disorders (71%). Somewhat fewer but still a solid majority said they would be very likely to refer an adolescent with symptoms of an eating disorder (61%) to a mental health professional.

Referring a patient to a mental health professional for further diagnostic tests does not mean that the physician will refrain from treating the patient in-house. Many physicians who said

Table 30.6 Reported Likelihood of Talking to Parents About Adolescents Exhibiting Various Symptoms

Symptom	Likelihood		
	Very Likely (%)	Somewhat Likely (%)	Not Too Likely (%)
Depression: lost interest in school and work, stopped getting together with friends, often refused to get out of bed in the morning	91	7	1
Schizophrenia: had trouble focusing on school work, no interest in hanging out with friends, convinced other people were reading their mind, suffered from disorganized speech	90	6	3
Bipolar disorder: displayed mood swings; very depressed at times and overexcited at other times	83	14	2
Eating disorder: lost weight even though did not need to, exercises rigorously, expressed concern about appearance	81	15	3
Anxiety: often intensely worried to the point that it disrupts daily life	78	19	1
Alcohol abuse: drunk at least once a week, consuming 5 or more drinks and sometimes would not remember what happened the night before	75	16	6

One group of respondents was randomly selected to receive questions about depression, schizophrenia, and eating disorders ($N = 373$), whereas the other group was asked about bipolar disorder, anxiety, and alcohol abuse ($N = 355$).

Table 30.7 Reported Likelihood of Referral to a Mental Health
Professional for Further Diagnostic Tests and/or Counseling

Symptom	Likelihood		
	Very Likely (%)	Somewhat Likely (%)	Not Too Likely (%)
Schizophrenia: had trouble focusing on school work, no interest in hanging out with friends, convinced other people were reading their mind, suffered from disorganized speech	94	5	1
Depression: lost interest in school and work, stopped getting together with friends, often refused to get out of bed in the morning	79	18	3
Anxiety: often intensely worried to the point that it disrupts daily life	76	18	5
Alcohol abuse: drunk at least once a week, consuming 5 or more drinks and sometimes would not remember what happened the night before	76	15	7
Bipolar disorder: displayed mood swings; very depressed at times and overexcited at other times	71	20	8
Eating disorder: lost weight even though did not need to, exercises rigorously, expressed concern about appearance	61	31	7

One group of respondents was randomly selected to receive questions about depression, schizophrenia, and eating disorders ($N = 373$), whereas the other group was asked about bipolar disorder, anxiety, and alcohol abuse ($N = 355$).

they are very likely to refer adolescents with symptoms of a specific disorder to another professional also said they would be likely to treat the patient themselves.

When asked about treating an adolescent with a mental health condition, roughly half said they are likely to treat these patients themselves, but relatively few said they are *very* likely to do so (Table 30.8).

Physicians were particularly cautious about treating patients with symptoms of schizophrenia. Only 9% said they would be very likely to treat the patient themselves. By contrast, a solid majority (72%) said they would not be too likely (34%) or not likely at all (38%) to treat an adolescent with these symptoms.

Physicians express greater willingness to treat adolescents with symptoms associated with other conditions. Even so, only a quarter or fewer said they would be *very* likely to treat any of these conditions themselves. Slim majorities, however, said they would be very or somewhat

likely to treat adolescents with symptoms of depression (57%), eating disorders (56%), bipolar disorders (52%), or anxiety disorders (51%). Somewhat fewer said they would be somewhat or very likely to treat symptoms of alcohol abuse (46%).

Physicians who say they are very likely to treat a particular condition themselves are more likely to say they are very capable of identifying that disorder than those who say they are not likely to treat the condition themselves. This is true for all mental conditions except for schizophrenia, a condition which very few physicians, regardless of their confidence in their diagnostic skills, say they are very likely to treat themselves.

It is encouraging that physicians who feel less than total confidence in their diagnostic skills with regard to a particular disorder are less likely to treat that disorder themselves. At the same time, however, many physicians who said they are very likely to treat a condition themselves also said that they are only *somewhat* or *not too*

Table 30.8 Reported Likelihood of Personally Counseling or Treating the Adolescent

Symptom	Likelihood			
	Very likely (%)	*Somewhat Likely (%)*	*Not Too Likely (%)*	*Not Likely At All (%)*
Depression: lost interest in school and work, stopped getting together with friends, often refused to get out of bed in the morning	25	32	27	16
Alcohol abuse: drunk at least once a week, consuming 5 or more drinks and sometimes would not remember what happened the night before	23	23	25	28
Eating disorder: lost weight even though did not need to, exercises rigorously, expressed concern about appearance	21	35	26	17
Bipolar disorder: displayed mood swings; very depressed at times and overexcited at other times	21	31	24	23
Anxiety: often intensely worried to the point that it disrupts daily life	21	30	28	21

One group of respondents was randomly selected to receive questions about depression, schizophrenia, and eating disorders ($N = 373$), whereas the other group was asked about bipolar disorder, anxiety, and alcohol abuse ($N = 355$).

confident in their ability to diagnose that condition. Of those physicians who said they are very likely to treat a condition, large proportions said they are less than very capable to identify alcohol abuse (47%), eating disorders (39%), and depression (37%). A majority of physicians (56%) who said they are very likely to treat bipolar disorders themselves said they are only somewhat confident in their diagnostic ability when it comes to identifying adolescents with this disorder.

Psychiatrists Are Preferred

Providers who say they are likely to refer their adolescent patients are most likely to refer to a psychiatrist. More than half of physicians who reported being at least somewhat likely to refer, said they would refer an adolescent with symptoms of schizophrenia (63%), bipolar disorders (57%), or anxiety disorders (55%) to a psychiatrist.

Referrals to psychologists were second most likely, with nearly as many saying they would refer an adolescent showing signs of depression, eating disorders, or alcohol abuse to a psychol-ogist as a psychiatrist. Substantially fewer said they would refer adolescents to a mental health worker or social worker. Alcohol abuse is an exception, with a sizable minority of physicians (28%) saying they would send adolescents showing signs of alcohol abuse to a mental health worker, such as a substance abuse counselor.

Concerns About Stigma

Providers talk to parents and make referrals to mental health professionals despite the fact that many of them worry about stigmatizing their adolescent patients with the diagnosis of a mental disorder. About one in two physicians (54%) said they very often (16%) or somewhat often (38%) worry that diagnosing an adolescent with a mental disorder will stigmatize the patient. Only 15% of physicians said they rarely worry about stigmatizing their patients.

A sizable minority of providers who said they often worried about the stigma of a mental health problem acknowledged that this makes them reluctant to actually diagnose an adolescent with a mental health disorder. Forty-three percent said that this concern causes them to be reluctant to a great (7%) or moderate extent (36%). Only about a quarter (24%) said that this concern plays no role in their diagnostic decision.

Based on responses to the two stigma questions, we created a single stigma score that reflected the degree to which physicians were concerned about diagnosing an adolescent with a mental disorder. Those who thought about stigma infrequently were given the two lowest scores ("not too often" and "not often at all"). Those who thought about stigma more often were given the highest score if they expressed either great or moderate reluctance to diagnose a patient with a mental disorder and an intermediate score if they only expressed a small or nonexistent reluctance to diagnose.

A regression analysis of this score indicated that providers with greater diagnostic knowledge about the disorders were less likely to be concerned about stigma than those with less knowledge. In addition, those with a patient population that contained high proportions of privately insured adolescents were less likely to be concerned about stigma. Belief in treatment efficacy was not related to concerns about stigma.

Inadequate Treatment Resources

Most providers say they would refer adolescent patients with symptoms of a mental disorder to another health professional. But only 32% said that there are adequate mental health treatment resources in their community, whereas 67% reported that the treatment resources are inadequate. Indeed, 44% reported that they felt very strongly about this.

Views about treatment resources are apparently shaped in part by the type of patient being treated and the location the doctor practices in. Providers who treat predominantly low-income patients were more likely to say that treatment resources are inadequate (71%) than those who treat mostly middle- or high-income patients (57%). We also found that physicians who practice in rural communities (80%) were much more likely than those who practice in an urban (64%) or suburban setting (65%) to say that the

treatment resources in their community are inadequate. Views about the adequacy of treatment resources were unrelated to beliefs about the potential efficacy of treatment.

Collaborative Relationship with Mental Health Professionals

Despite inadequate resources, many primary care physicians often work closely with mental health care specialists. It is generally accepted that patients experience better outcomes when the referring physician works closely with the mental health specialist treating the patient. A solid majority of providers (68%) reported that they collaborate to a great (27%) or moderate (41%) extent with the mental health professionals to whom they refer their adolescent patients. An additional 27% reported collaborating to a small extent. Only a handful of doctors (5%) said they do not work with the mental health care professionals at all. Physicians who practiced in rural areas were much more likely to say they collaborate to a great extent (41%) than those who practice in suburban (26%) or urban areas (24%).

Physicians who claimed to collaborate with mental health specialists tended to view the experience in positive terms: 85% said they have a good relationship with these mental health professionals, and 42% said the relationship is very good.

PREDICTORS OF IDENTIFICATION AND REFERRAL FOR CARE

The survey results suggest that primary care physicians agree about the importance of treating mental health problems in their adolescent patients and about referring those who are identified to a mental health specialist. The weak link in the process is the poor ability of physicians to identify patients who are in need of mental health services. Nevertheless, providers who report greater diagnostic skills should identify mental health conditions in their patients at a greater rate. If screening helps providers to recognize and diagnose mental disorder, we would also expect those who employ screening to report higher rates of mental health problems. In addition, if mental health carve-outs within managed care provide a ready link with mental health specialists, we would expect those with large proportions of patients in managed care to be more likely to refer patients for mental health care. We examined the role of these and other provider characteristics in reported prevalence of disorder and rates of referral.

Prevalence of Mental Health Conditions Reported by Physicians

We asked physicians to estimate the percentage of adolescent patients they saw in the last year who had specific mental disorders. In addition to mental disorders, we asked about the percentage of adolescent patients who engaged in risky behaviors such as excessive alcohol use. The estimates given by the physicians roughly resemble the reported prevalence of these mental health conditions in the adolescent population (Table 30.9).

Depression was the most commonly seen mental disorder, followed by anxiety disorders and alcohol abuse. On average, physicians said that in the last year about 16% of their adolescent patients were depressed. Anxiety disorders and alcohol abuse were the next most commonly seen disorders, with physicians saying that, on average, about 10% of their patients had these conditions. About 9% of adolescent patients were thought to have an eating disorder. And physicians reported that about 5% of their patients, on average, were suffering from bipolar disorders and a little over 1% from schizophrenia.

These estimates are not far off from reported national prevalence of mental health conditions in adolescents. Approximately 10% to 15% of adolescents exhibit *some* signs of depression, although the percentage of adolescents who meet the criteria for a full-fledged diagnosis of depression is closer to 5% to 8%. Similarly, while only 1% of adolescents meet the full criteria for bipolar disorders, nearly 6% of adolescents present with many of the classic symptoms of the con-

dition. Additionally, 13% of the adolescent population is thought to have an anxiety disorder, whereas 1% is believed to have schizophrenia (National Institutes of Mental Health, 2000a, 2000b); U.S. Department of Health and Human Services, 1999). Estimates of alcohol *dependence* are lower than the estimated rate found here; however, alcohol abuse is quite common among adolescents.

We conducted regression analyses to determine significant predictors of prevalence estimates. Table 30.9 shows the changes in prevalence rates attributable to several differences in provider characteristics with other differences held constant. Not shown are differences in provider gender, age, rural vs. urban location, reported weekly adolescent patient load, and income level of patient population. It is clear that the self-reported diagnostic skill of the provider is a consistent predictor of estimated prevalence. This was measured by taking the mean response to the questions concerning self-assessed diagnostic ability (Table 30.4) for the five mental disorders (alpha = .79). For alcohol abuse, we used the reported diagnostic knowledge for alcohol abuse. The only condition not predicted by self-assessed skill was the prevalence of eating disorders. Screening for mental disorders was also a predictor of anxiety and schizophrenia.

It is important to note that diagnostic skill was assessed on a four-point scale. The distribution of this scale was such that the difference between those who were most confident in their diagnostic skill (the top 15%) and those who were least confident (the lowest 15%) produced a difference of about 5 percentage points in reported prevalence of depression, anxiety, and alcohol abuse.

Concern about stigma was a predictor of diagnosis for alcohol abuse but was not systematically related to any of the other disorders. Belief in treatment efficacy (not shown) was also not related to any diagnosis rates. Family physicians and general practitioners also gave higher prevalence estimates for all the conditions but bipolar disorder. Prevalence estimates did not differ according to the proportion of the patient population that had private insurance or that was served by managed care.

Table 30.9 Estimated Prevalence of Six Disorders in Annual Patient Load and Differences Attributable to Provider Characteristics ($p < .05$)

Predictor	*Diagnosis*					
	Anxiety	*Depression*	*Bipolar Disorder*	*Schizophrenia*	*Eating Disorder*	*Alcohol Abuse*
Mean prevalence (%)	10.84	16.46	4.75	1.81	9.20	10.86
Diagnostic knowledge[a]	3.89	4.32	1.49	0.65	—	3.50
Screening	1.28	—	—	0.26[b]	—	—
Stigma[a]	—	—	—	—	—	−1.32
Managed care	−0.53	—	—	—	—	—
Private insurance	—	—	—	—	—	—
Family or general practice	3.58	5.49	—	1.60	3.36[b]	4.28

[a] Scored on a 1-to-4 scale.

[b] Significant only at the $p < .10$ level.

We cannot confirm that the estimated prevalence rates are valid; however, the predictors are consistent with the hypothesis that providers with better diagnostic skills (or those who screen for disorder) are more likely to identify mental disorders. Furthermore, by holding constant other provider and practice characteristics that might affect prevalence rates, we can be more confident that the differences are a reflection of diagnostic skill and not patient populations.

Rates of Referral for Treatment

We also asked providers to estimate the percentage of patients with symptoms of each mental condition they had referred to other professionals in the past year. Although referral rates did not differ dramatically across diagnoses (Table 30.10), the rates did differ considerably within each diagnosis. Roughly 30% to 45% of providers said they referred most adolescent patients with the given symptoms to other professionals. About 4 in 10 physicians said they referred most of their adolescent patients with symptoms of schizophrenia (44%) or alcohol abuse (38%). Somewhat fewer referred most of their patients with symptoms of bipolar disorders (35%), anxiety disorders (33%), depression (32%), or eating disorders (28%).

At the same time, many physicians referred 25% or fewer of their patients with symptoms of

Table 30.10 Mean Estimated Rates of Referral for Treatment of Six Mental Health Problems in Past Year and Differences Attributable to Provider Characteristics ($p < .05$)

Predictor	*Diagnosis*					
	Anxiety	*Depression*	*Bipolar Disorder*	*Schizophrenia*	*Eating Disorder*	*Alcohol Abuse*
Mean referral rate (%)	51.20	52.70	52.49	54.59	43.84	48.37
Managed care	2.89	—	3.21	—	—	4.26
Private insurance	—	—	—	3.19	3.66	—
Screening	—	6.78	—	—	5.60	—

Respondents were randomly assigned to answer this question for one of two groups of conditions: depression, schizophrenia, and eating disorders ($N = 373$) or anxiety, bipolar disorder, and alcohol abuse ($N = 355$).

a mental health problem. Roughly 4 in 10 did not make a referral for most of their adolescent patients with signs of eating disorders (46%), alcohol abuse (46%), anxiety disorders (43%), schizophrenia (41%), bipolar disorders (40%), or depression (38%).

A regression analysis of referral rates indicated that types of practice and insurance were the major predictors (Table 30.10). Providers with most of their patients in managed care plans were more likely to refer patients with anxiety, bipolar, and alcohol problems. Providers with patients who were mostly privately insured were more likely to refer patients with schizophrenia and eating disorders. Providers who screened their patients for mental disorders were also more likely to refer them for treatment of depression and eating disorders. Diagnostic knowledge, stigma, belief in treatment efficacy, or type of provider were not significantly related to referral rates.

Although not shown in Table 30.10, our analysis also revealed that providers who were more likely to refer patients to mental health specialists were more likely to rate the treatment resources in their community as *inadequate*. This was especially true for the referral of anxiety disorders and bipolar disorder. Evaluations of treatment resources were not related to practice characteristics such as managed care or private insurance status.

SUMMARY AND CONCLUSIONS

This survey of primary care providers who treat adolescents indicates that these physicians are concerned about the mental health of their adolescent patients and regard mental health as an important responsibility. In addition, the vast majority of primary care providers believe in the efficacy of treatment for mental disorders. However, primary care providers report only weak ability to diagnose mental health problems, and at best, only half employ any screening technique at all to detect mental health problems in their adolescent patients. Indeed, a separate survey of nonresponders to the survey indicated

that the true rate of screening as well as diagnostic knowledge may well be lower.

Weak Confidence in Detecting Disorders

The low levels of confidence in recognizing depression that were observed in this study are consistent with another recent survey of primary care pediatricians (Olson et al., 2001). Although the present survey indicates that providers feel most capable of identifying depression (about 50%), their confidence in identifying other disorders is even lower. For example, only 25% reported being very capable of identifying drug abuse in their adolescent patients. In the absence of effective screening procedures, primary care providers will continue to be unable to recognize mental and substance abuse disorders in their adolescent patients.

Providers' estimated prevalence of mental disorders in their patient populations indicated that although the rates are in line with national estimates, variation across providers was strongly related to diagnostic knowledge. Providers who were more confident in their ability to diagnose mental conditions reported higher prevalence of disorders in their patients. In addition, those who regularly screened for mental disorders were also more likely to recognize some of the conditions. The importance of appropriate diagnosis is also underlined in the finding that providers who screened their patients were more likely to refer them for treatment of depression and eating disorder.

The inability to detect mental disorders in adolescents is a serious flaw in the primary care system. No matter how well intentioned providers may be, there is little that can be done to help adolescents in need of treatment if they are not first identified. Although providers recognize the importance of referring their patients to mental health specialists and of including parents in the treatment of mental disorders, these intentions do not come into play without adequate resources and abilities to detect patients at risk for mental and substance abuse disorders.

Pediatricians as a group were even less likely to report mental health problems in their patients than family doctors or general practitioners. In view of the much higher representation of pediatricians in the adolescent primary care system, there is a large opportunity to increase the ability to detect mental disorders in primary care. The Bright Futures and KySS programs already recommend screening and referral for adolescent mental disorders and have materials in place that could advance the adoption of better screening practices. Research would also be valuable to determine if computer-assisted screening mechanisms such as that developed by the Columbia Teen Screen program (McGuire & Flynn, 2003) could be adopted in primary care.

Increased knowledge and ability to diagnose mental health problems may also reduce concerns about stigma, a factor that could also impede appropriate referral and treatment. Providers with greater confidence in their understanding of mental disorders were also less likely to express concerns about the stigma of mental disorder. Although concerns about stigma were only related to the estimated prevalence of alcohol abuse, substance abuse is highly comorbid with other disorders and its association with stigma is likely to reflect a failure to identify these disorders as well (American Academy of Pediatrics, 2000).

Rates of Referral for Mental Health Problems

Recognition of mental disorder is only a first step in delivering appropriate care. Providers must also make decisions about appropriate treatment. Estimates of rates of treatment referral indicated that about half of patients with major mental disorders are referred on average. It is difficult to evaluate the optimal level of referral without greater knowledge of the diagnostic criteria used by providers. However, given these reported rates of referral, it is not surprising that less than half of adolescents with serious mental conditions are estimated to receive appropriate mental health services (Costello et al., 1998; Horwitz et al., 1992; Sturm et al., 2003).

Practice characteristics were the strongest predictors of reported referral rates. In particular, providers whose patient population was primar-

ily served by managed care were more likely to refer those patients for anxiety disorder, bipolar disorder, and alcohol abuse. This finding may reflect the influence of increased deployment of mental health carve-outs in managed care. This approach is designed to contain costs for mental health treatment, but it could also encourage referral for those who are appropriately diagnosed with mental conditions (Conti et al., 2004). Unfortunately, the present research could not assess the quality of the referrals that are being made in managed care. There is evidence to suggest that the barriers to successful referral are actually greater in pediatric managed-care systems (Walders, Childs, Comer, Kelleher, & Drotar, 2003). Hence, many have expressed concerns that mental health carve-outs will encourage referral to less than optimal care providers (Glied & Neufield, 2001; Jellinek & Little, 1998; Kelleher, Scholle, Feldman, & Nace, 1999). Research to determine the fate of adolescents with mental disorders in managed care is clearly a high priority.

Providers whose patient population was primarily served by private insurance were more likely to refer them for treatment of some disorders (schizophrenia and eating disorder). This finding suggests that patients in the public sector may be receiving even less appropriate treatment for these conditions.

Treatment Resources Are Often Inadequate

An important concern in the findings is the unfavorable evaluation that most providers report of treatment resources in their communities. Indeed, providers who were more likely to refer patients to mental health specialists were also more likely to evaluate those services as inadequate. This finding suggests that better screening will only solve a part of the mental health service delivery problem for adolescents. Better treatment resources will also be needed (cf. Walders et al., 2003). In sum, this survey indicates that appropriate screening and diagnosis of adolescents in primary care is a critical step in advancing the mental health of youth. At the same time, however, increased referral to mental health specialists may have the potential to make providers even more aware of the limitations in the mental health treatment system for adolescents.

Appendix
Design and Data Collection Procedures

As part of its Sunnylands Adolescent Mental Health Initiative, the Annenberg Public Policy Center commissioned Princeton Survey Research Associates International (PSRAI) to conduct the survey. The fieldwork was conducted by Princeton Data Source, LLC, and Braun Research, Inc., from September 29, 2003, to January 23, 2004. In total, 727 interviews were conducted with a nationally representative sample of pediatricians, family practitioners, and general practitioners who regularly treat adolescents between the ages of 10 and 18. The interviews took approximately 25 min to complete. The maximum margin of sampling error for results based on the full sample is ±4%.

SAMPLE DESIGN

A nationally representative sample of 5,000 pediatricians, family practitioners, and general practitioners was drawn from the American Medical Association's (AMA) Physician Masterfile. The AMA Physician Masterfile is the nation's largest repository of primary-source physician data and includes both members and nonmembers in the United States and all of its foreign territories. Since the population of interest was physicians who are currently practicing medicine, we drew our sample from a prescreened list provided by SK&A Information Services, Inc., that had removed fellows, residents, students, and retired doctors.

The sample was drawn among the three main types of primary care physicians who are likely to treat adolescents—pediatricians, family practitioners, and general practitioners. The composition of the sample reflects the fact that most adolescents are treated by pediatricians rather than by family and general practitioners, who

tend to have a broader patient base. On the basis of this information, the sample was drawn so that it comprised 80% pediatricians and 20% family and general practitioners.

CONTACT PROCEDURES

Interviews were conducted by telephone with as many as 35 attempts to contact each provider. Calls were staggered over different times of day and days of the week to maximize the chance of making contact with potential respondents. Prior to being called, each physician was sent a letter introducing the research and explaining that the doctor could expect a call to participate in the study in the coming weeks. In addition, doctors were told that for their participation, a $20 charitable donation[2] would be made in their name and that they would receive a complimentary copy of the Oxford University Press book that will include the detailed findings of the study and other research on treating adolescent mental health conditions. The letter also gave a 1-800 number so that doctors could call in and take the survey at their own convenience.

RESPONSE RATE

The response rate estimates the fraction of all eligible respondents in the sample that were ultimately interviewed. At PSRAI it is calculated by taking the product of three component rates as recommended by the American Association for Public Opinion Research:

- Contact rate—the proportion of working numbers through which a request for interview was accomplished (66%)
- Cooperation rate—the proportion of contacted numbers through which a consent for interview was at least initially obtained, vs. those refused (41%)
- Completion rate—the proportion of initially cooperating and eligible interviews that were completed (99%)

2. In an effort to increase the response rate, the incentive for participating was increased to $100. The higher donation amount seemed to have little effect on participation rates and was again lowered to $20 after a couple of weeks.

The response rate for this survey was 27%. Despite the high number of contact attempts and the use of incentives, a 27% response rate is not surprising, given that physicians are a notoriously difficult population to reach. Although the response rate is somewhat lower than what is normally targeted, the sample of physicians who were interviewed closely resembles that of pediatricians and family and general practitioners in various important characteristics (see Table 30.1).

In order to evaluate the representativeness of the survey data and to verify that there were no systematic differences between doctors who participated in the telephone survey and those who declined to participate, PSRAI conducted a separate fax survey of a random sample of doctors who did not participate in the survey. Three hundred nonrespondents of the telephone survey were faxed a cover letter and a one-page questionnaire that covered the core topics of the telephone survey. A total of 77 (26%) responses to this request were received.

With one exception, responses to the fax survey were very similar to those of the original telephone survey. Based on the fax survey, there is reason to believe that providers who did not participate in the telephone survey may be less likely to routinely screen their adolescent patients for mental illnesses than those who participated in the telephone survey. Whereas about 48% of the telephone sample claimed to routinely screen their patients for mental health problems, only about 31% of the nonresponders to the telephone survey claimed that they do this routinely, $\chi^2(1) = 9.25, p < .01$.

ACKNOWLEDGMENTS

We wish to thank Kelly Kelleher and Michael Murphy for their helpful comments on an earlier version of this chapter.

The Roles and Perspectives of School Mental Health Professionals in Promoting Adolescent Mental Health

Daniel Romer
and Mary McIntosh

chapter

This chapter presents research conducted as part of the Sunnylands Adolescent Mental Health Initiative to gain a greater understanding of the roles and prespectives of school mental health professionals in identifying, treating and preventing mental health problems in adolescents. The Surgeon General's report on the mental health of children (U.S. Department of Health and Human Services, 2000) estimated that 1 in 10 adolescents in the United States struggles with a mental health disorder that is severe enough to cause significant impairment. Because over 90% of adolescents under age 18 attend schools in the United States (U.S. Census, 2002), there is a unique opportunity to promote the mental health of youth in this setting, a role that has long been recognized by the public and mental health community (Allinsmith & Goethals, 1962; Starr, 1982).

The failure to treat adolescents suffering from mental conditions has severe consequences. Adolescents with mental disorders are at increased risk for poor academic achievement as well as continued mental disability (Puig-Antich, Kaufman, & Ryan, 1993; Randall, Henggeler, & Pickrel, 1999; Willcutt & Pennington, 2000). Many youth who suffer from mental disorders also end up in the juvenile justice system (Bilchik, 1998), an outcome that could be prevented if they were treated while still in school (American Psychiatric Association, 2004). Unfortunately, less than half of adolescents with significant mental health conditions are seen by a mental health professional in an average year (Costello, Angold, & Burns, 1996; Leaf et al., 1996; Sturm, Ringel, & Andreyeva, 2003). Therefore, increased efforts to identify and treat youth in need of services are a high priority.

The President's New Freedom Commission on Mental Health (2003) called for a transformation of the nation's mental health system and emphasized the importance of schools in this endeavor. In line with this agenda, this research was designed to learn what schools are doing to promote the mental health of adolescents and where future efforts should be directed to improve the delivery of services. To accomplish these goals, we interviewed professionals who are responsible for the mental health of adolescents in public schools to determine the programs they have in place, how well they think those programs are performing, and what changes they would make to improve their performance.

Previous research on the availability of mental health services in schools has found wide variation across states, regions of the country, and urban vs. rural locations (Brener, Martindale, & Weist, 2001; Slade, 2003). The largest of these surveys was conducted by the Centers for Disease Control and Prevention in 2000 (Brener et al., 2003). Another important source is the Add Health Study of school administrators conducted in 1994 (Slade, 2003). These studies indicate that only about half of all high schools have formal mental health counseling services on site. According to the President's New Freedom Commission, one of the biggest obstacles to receiving care for mental illness, especially for children, is the fragmentation of the mental health service delivery system. One way to integrate the system, according to the Commission, is to "rethink how state and Federal funding streams can be more efficiently partnered and utilized by school systems to deliver these services."

Two major programs to improve access to health services in schools have shown growth in recent years: school-based health centers (SBHCs) and student assistance programs (SAPs). According to a recent survey (Center for Health and Health Care in Schools, 2003), over 1,500 SBHCs in at least 43 states frequently treat mental health conditions (Anglin, Naylor, & Kaplan, 1996; American Academy of Pediatrics, 2001). Student assistance programs, which were inspired by the employee assistance programs for workplaces, have also grown with over 60% of schools now offering such services (Brener et al., 2001). A third approach that overlaps with SAPs is the referral of students with mental health conditions to providers at other sites in the community. About half of all schools adopt the third approach for mental health care (Brener et al., 2001).

In addition to formal programs, most schools have at least one professional on staff on at least a part-time basis who is responsible for mental health programming. The three most common professionals, guidance counselors, school psychologists, and school social workers, tend to have a masters degree in their discipline (Brener et al., 2001). Guidance counselors are present in over three-quarters of schools and have a wide range of responsibilities, including assisting students who are experiencing problems in coping with school (American School Counselors Association, 2004). Approximately two-thirds of schools have a part-time or full-time psychologist whose major responsibilities involve the assessment of cognitive, behavioral, and emotional conditions that may affect school performance (National Association of School Psychologists, 2004). About 40% of schools have a part-time or full-time social worker who serves as a liaison with parents and coordinates care with outside agencies (National Association of Social Workers, 2004).

Despite considerable information about the presence of mental health services in schools, the quality of these services is largely unknown (Rones & Hoagwood, 2000). Research trials of model school-based programs indicate that many are effective (Armbruster & Lichtman, 1999; Rones & Hoagwood, 2000), but actual school programs are more difficult to assess. In this research, we took a step toward assessing quality by asking school professionals to evaluate the overall effectiveness of their mental health programs. We then used these evaluations to assess the contribution of various components to overall success.

We also were interested to learn about the potential roles that school mental health professionals can play to promote the mental health of adolescents. One approach already noted is to create school-based mental health services in schools that can diagnose and treat adolescents on site. Although this strategy has the ability to increase access to effective services for many adolescents (American Academy of Pediatrics, 2001; Armbrister & Lichtman, 1999), it is one that will be difficult to implement on a wide scale in the near term. In another, school professionals refer students for diagnosis and treatment off site by mental health specialists, much as expert panels recommend to primary care providers (Jellinek, Patel, & Froehle, 2002; Melnyk, Brown, Jones, Kreipe, & Novak, 2003).

In a third approach, school mental health pro-

fessionals design programs for schools to prevent the onset of mental health problems and at the same time identify symptoms so that students can be referred to mental health specialists for care. This public-health approach may have the ability to use the skills of school mental health professionals to their best advantage while also benefiting all students (Adelman & Taylor, 1998; 2000; Atkins, Graczyk, Frazier, & Abdul-Adif, 2003; Hoagwood & Johnson, 2003; Strein, Hoagwood, & Cohn, 2003; Weist, 2003; Weist & Christodulu, 2000).

In evaluating different strategies for school programming, we were also interested in examining potential obstacles to quality mental health care, including limitations in access due to inadequate or no insurance coverage and to inadequate resources in low-income schools. We also asked school professionals to identify solutions to inadequacies in mental health services in schools.

To accomplish these many objectives, the Annenberg Public Policy Center, with funding from the Sunnylands Adolescent Mental Health Initiative, commissioned Princeton Survey Research Associates International to conduct a nationwide survey of over 1,400 school mental health professionals. Interviews were conducted between April and May of 2004. A complete description of the survey methodology is contained in Appendix 31.1.

SURVEY METHODOLOGY

A sample of 2,000 public schools was drawn from the *Common Core of Data Public Elementary/Secondary School Universe 2002–2003*, a database of virtually all public elementary and secondary schools in the United States that is produced annually by the National Center for Education Statistics (NCES). The sample was selected to represent all schools that have at least 100 students and have classes in at least one middle or high school grade. This sample frame represents more than 90% of all adolescent students in the United States. The database is compiled from the administrative records provided by state education agencies.

The sample was drawn by taking into account

the percentage of students enrolled nationwide defined by four parameters—region, urbanity, level, and school size. To illustrate, we determined from the NCES database that approximately 18 percent of the nation's middle and high school students attend schools in the Northeast. Hence, the sample design aimed for 18 percent of the complete interviews to occur among mental health professionals who work in schools that are located in the northeastern United States.

As seen in Table 31.1, the resulting sample of mental health professionals closely resembled the student population with the exception of school size. To correct for the slight underrepresentation of mental health professionals working in very large schools, the sample was weighted to more accurately reflect the NCES database. A small proportion of schools (11%) contained seventh-grade students or higher that

were either in primary or other types of schools. These schools were included because they also contained adolescents, even though they could not be classified as either middle or high schools.

In each of the sampled schools, we asked to speak to the school psychologist, counselor, social worker, or other school professional who was most knowledgeable about the mental health services offered in the school. The resulting distribution of professionals by title is shown in Table 31.2. In schools where more than one staff member met the criterion, one professional was randomly selected for the interview. Only one professional from each sampled school was eligible to participate. Professionals working in more than one school were asked to respond to the survey questions in reference to the school in which they were contacted. Most of the professionals interviewed were women who worked

Table 31.1 Sample Composition (*N* = 1402)

	Schools in Unweighted Sample (N)	Students Nationwide (%)	Schools in Unweighted Sample (%)	Schools in Weighted Sample (%)
Region				
Northeast	231	18	17	16
Midwest	356	24	25	25
South	490	36	35	35
West	325	22	23	24
Urbanity				
Urban	317	24	23	23
Suburban	636	46	45	45
Rural	279	18	20	19
Missing	170	12	12	12
School Level				
Primary and other	162	13	12	11
Middle school	515	36	37	36
High school	725	51	52	53
Size of School				
Less than 500	217	16	16	15
500–1000	518	35	37	35
1001–1500	395	22	28	22
More than 1500	272	27	19	27

Table 31.2 Sampled Professionals by Title and Demographic Characteristics (*N* = 1402)

	Characteristic				
Title	Sample (%)	Female (%)	Masters Degree (%)	Under Age 50 (%)	Current Position 10 Years (%)
School or guidance counselor	49.1	72.0	95.1	54.9	49.9
Psychologist	25.7	63.6	80.0	63.1	41.0
Social worker	11.2	84.7	90.4	66.2	41.6
Nurse or nurse practitioner	3.0	97.6	35.7	64.3	41.5
Special educator	2.9	80.0	75.0	60.0	52.5
Principal or assistant principal	2.8	46.2	79.5	51.3	64.1
Special services or student services director	2.3	81.3	71.9	56.3	54.6
Teacher	0.3	75.0	75.0	25.0	60.0
Other	2.8	80.0	70.0	55.0	40.0

full time, were younger than age 50, and had a master's degree in their discipline. Over 40% of the respondents had worked in their school for more than 10 years.

The response rate for the survey was 72%, and the maximum margin of error ($p < .05$) for the entire survey sample was ± 2.7%. Significant differences between subsets of the sample, such as between professionals working in middle vs. high schools, are reported whenever relevant.

MAJOR FINDINGS

Depression and Anxiety Serious Problems

We asked our respondents to rate the extent to which various behaviors and conditions were problems in their schools. These ratings, shown in Table 31.3, are organized into three clusters obtained in a factor analysis of respondents' answers. The first cluster, corresponding to mental health problems, indicates that these conditions were seen as related and among the more serious problems affecting students. Indeed, according to the professionals, adolescent depression is one of the more serious problems in their schools, with over 60% saying it is either very (12%) or moderately serious (51%). Anxiety disorders were seen as somewhat less prevalent than depression. Nevertheless, 43% of professionals be-

lieved students struggle with anxiety at least to a moderate extent. At the same time, however, a majority of professionals (57%) said that anxiety disorders are at most a small problem in their schools.

Cutting or inflicting other forms of self-harm was also generally described as occurring to a small extent. A solid majority of professionals (75%) reported that students' attempting to harm themselves is at most a small problem, but about one in four described it as a problem to a moderate (21%) or great (4%) extent. Similarly, a majority of professionals (81%) said that eating disorders occur to a small or no extent. Fewer than 20% reported that eating disorders are a problem to a moderate (17%) or great (1%) extent.

The second cluster, corresponding to various drug-related behaviors, was also seen as an important set of problems. About half of respondents felt that alcohol (50%) and illegal drug (55%) use presented at least a moderate problem. Illegal use of prescription drugs was not as prevalent as the abuse of illegal substances. A majority of professionals (58%) reported that illegal use of prescription drugs is a small problem, and one in four (21%) said that this is not a problem at all.

Actual sale of drugs on school property was generally not seen as a big problem. A majority of mental health professionals (75%) said that

Table 31.3 Problems Reported by School Professionals

Problem	Severity of Problem			
	Great Extent (%)	Moderate Extent (%)	Small Extent (%)	Not at All (%)
Mental Health				
Depression	12	51	36	1
Anxiety disorder	6	37	54	3
Cutting or other forms of self-harm	4	21	66	9
Eating disorders	1	17	71	10
Substance Abuse Related				
Use of illegal drugs, such as marijuana	12	43	40	4
Excessive use of alcohol	12	38	39	9
Drug dealing	3	19	59	16
Illegal use of prescription drugs	2	13	58	21
Violence and Truancy				
Truancy	20	40	37	2
Bullying or picking on other students	18	48	33	0
Fighting among students	10	36	51	3
Carrying or using weapons	0	5	60	33

drug dealing is at worst a small problem in their schools. This is not to say that drug dealing was never a problem. About 22% reported that drug dealing presents a moderate or great problem in their schools.

The third cluster, conflict between individual students and school truancy, also contained some of the bigger problems in schools. A solid majority of professionals (66%) said that bullying or picking on other students is at least a moderate problem. Actual fighting among students was described as somewhat less prevalent. Nonetheless, close to half of mental health professionals said physical violence directed at other students is a problem to a great (10%) or moderate (36%) extent. In addition to interpersonal conflict, a majority of professionals (60%) described truancy as at least a moderate problem.

Despite the media attention of the past few years, students carrying or using weapons was rarely considered a big problem. Very few professionals (5%) reported that weapons are even

a moderate problem, with a vast majority either characterizing it as a small problem (60%) or saying that it is not a problem at all (33%).

Although the three problem clusters tended to be distinct, they were also interrelated. Schools with high levels of mental health problems also were seen as having high rates of drug use ($r = .48, p < .01$) and interpersonal conflict ($r = .47, p < .01$). Drug use and conflict were slightly less related ($r = .31, p < .01$).

Different Schools—Different Problems

The context in which school professionals work greatly influences their perceptions of student problems. These perceptions vary greatly depending on the size and location of the school and the demographic characteristics of the student population, especially their age and socioeconomic background. We analyzed school characteristics by conducting multiple regression analyses for each problem with size of school, urban vs. rural location, poverty level (percent eligible for school lunch), middle vs. high school, and region of the country as predictors.

Professionals working in middle schools often described a different set of problems from those described by mental health professionals working with adolescents attending high school. Interpersonal conflict problems tend to take center stage during the middle school years, whereas drug and alcohol use are more prevalent in high school. Professionals working in middle schools were considerably more likely ($p < .001$) to report that bullying or picking on other students (82% vs. 54%) and fighting (57% vs. 37%) are moderate or great problems than their counterparts working with high school students. At the same time, high school professionals were more likely ($p < .001$) to describe the use of illegal drugs (72% vs. 36%), excessive use of alcohol (71% vs. 28%), drug dealing (31% vs. 12%), and illegal use of prescription drugs (23% vs. 7%) as problematic.

Mental health conditions were also described as more prevalent in high schools than in middle schools. Professionals in high schools were more likely ($p < .01$) to say that depression (68% vs. 57%) and eating disorders (22% vs. 13%) are problems to a great or moderate extent than professionals in middle schools. However, anxiety disorders (44% vs. 42%) and cutting (26% vs. 26%) were seen as equally prevalent in middle and high schools.

We also found that larger schools tend to have more problems than smaller ones. It is not clear whether this perception is the result of the sheer likelihood that more problems occur in a larger school or that the prevalence is greater. Nevertheless, mental health conditions, such as depression (69% vs. 48%), anxiety (44% vs. 32%), and cutting (29% vs. 19%), were seen as more of a problem ($p < .05$) in schools with more than 1,500 students than in schools with less than 500 students. The same is true when it comes to students engaging in risky behaviors ($p < .01$). In particular, a solid majority of professionals (65%) working in schools with more than 1,500 students reported that the use of illegal drugs is a moderate or a great problem, compared to fewer than half of professionals (45%) working in schools with less than 500 students. Fighting (50% vs. 33%) and drug dealing (28% vs. 11%) were also seen as more problematic in very large schools than in small schools. Nevertheless, perceptions of excessive use of alcohol (55% vs. 49%), eating disorders (20% vs. 16%), and bullying (51% vs. 51%) were not related to school size.

Where the school is located also makes a difference. Professionals working in urban schools (69%) were more likely ($p < .01$) to see depression as a problem than those working in rural areas (53%). The same was true for fighting among students (59% vs. 33%) and weapon carrying (12% vs. 2%). At the same time, professionals in urban schools felt that alcohol abuse was less of a problem than those working in rural areas (40% vs. 52%).

Regionally, mental health professionals working in the South tended to see fewer problems than those working in other areas of the country. For example, professionals in southern schools (54%) were less likely ($p < .01$) to consider depression problematic than their colleagues in the Northeast (71%), Midwest (66%), and West (66%). Southerners also reported fewer problems regarding eating disorders, cutting, use of illegal drugs, alcohol abuse, fighting, and weapon carrying than professionals in other regions. The one exception was for abuse of prescription drugs, for which southerners saw more problems than professionals working in other regions ($p < .01$). Professionals working in the Northeast (56%) were also more likely to describe anxiety disorders as a great or moderate problem than either southern (39%) or western (36%) mental health professionals, with their counterparts in the Midwest (46%) falling in between.

The socioeconomic composition of the student population (measured by the proportion of students eligible for a free or reduced lunch program) also leads to differences in problems. Abuse of alcohol and prescription drugs, eating disorders, and cutting tended to be more problematic in wealthier schools than they were in schools with a higher proportion of low-income students. At the same time, drug dealing, fighting, bullying, and weapon carrying tended to be more problematic in low-income schools.

Half Offer Counseling on Premises

Consistent with earlier research, we found that many schools already offer at least some mental health services on site (Table 31.4). About half of the professionals reported that their schools offer counseling for conditions such as anxiety and depression on school premises (47%), and many (44%) have a program for dealing with students who have mental health issues, such as an SAP. Most of the schools that do not offer counseling on school premises are prepared to refer students to other providers in the community (48%). Only 1 percent of professionals reported that their school neither provides counseling for depressed or anxious students nor refers these students to a service provider outside the school.

Large proportions of schools (67%) also reported the presence of programs to counsel students on the prevention of alcohol and drug abuse or the prevention of suicide (68%). However, smaller proportions of schools have programs to help students who want to quit the use of tobacco (43%) or other drugs such as alcohol (24%).

Schools are also less likely to be prepared to handle victims of abuse or the families of students with mental health conditions. Only 38% of schools offer counseling in the district for students who are victims of physical, sexual, or emotional abuse, and only 29% offer counseling or help for families of students who have a mental health condition. Nevertheless, nearly all of the schools that do not have programs on site refer students and families to outside providers.

Only Half Have a Full-Time Professional

Only a little more than half of the schools sampled (53%) have full-time access to a mental health professional—a psychologist, counselor, or social worker—whose main job is to deal with students' mental health issues. Even if one considers part-time staff, 23% do not even have access to a part-time mental health professional.

But even if mental health professionals are not always available, most schools employ other health professionals. A slim majority of schools (51%) have a school nurse on the premises full-time, while an additional 32% of schools employ a part-time nurse. If one considers all potential health professionals, including physicians and nurses, then about 74% of schools have a full-time health professional on site. If one considers both full-time and part-time staff, then nearly all schools (96%) have at least one health professional on site.

Seven percent of schools have a full-service health center on school property where students can receive primary health care, including diagnostic and treatment services by a doctor, nurse practitioner, or physician's assistant. However, not all of these centers offer mental health services (38% do not). It is clear that these centers

Table 31.4 Reported Availability of Services

Service	How Provided			
	Provided at School (%)	Provided by District but Not on Site (%)	Referred to Other Providers (%)	Neither Provided nor Referred (%)
Counseling for mental health conditions, such as anxiety or depression	47	4	48	1
Counseling for students who are victims of physical, sexual, or emotional abuse	34	4	61	1
Counseling or help for families of students who have a mental health condition	25	4	68	3

Table 31.5 Health Resources by Region of the Country

| Health Resource | Region | | | | |
	Northeast (N = 226)	Midwest (N = 349)	West (N = 492)	South (N = 333)	Total (N = 1402)
School nurse	90[a]	84[b]	76[c]	84[b]	83
Counselor	62[a]	48[b]	50[b]	49[b]	51
Psychologist	58[a]	48[c]	55[b]	47[c]	51
Social worker	58[a]	56[a]	33[b]	26[c]	41
Student assistance program	52[a]	54[a]	39[b]	37[b]	44
Physician or nurse practitioner	32[a]	16[b]	20[b]	17[b]	20
School-based health center	8[a]	6[a]	7[a]	7[a]	7

Significant differences between regions are indicated by superscripts ($p < .05$).

[a] Percentages not significantly different from the Northeast. ($p > .05$)

[b] Percentages significantly lower than the Northeast ($p < .05$)

[c] Percentages significantly lower than outcomes labeled by footnote b.

are currently only able to care for a small percentage of adolescent mental health problems.

Adolescents in some parts of the country are much more likely to have access to health professionals on school premises than others (Table 31.5). In particular, schools in the Northeast are considerably more likely to employ mental health professionals than schools elsewhere in the country. The regional gap is also reflected in the fact that 32% of the schools in the Northeast employ a physician or nurse practitioner, whereas nearly as high a percentage of schools in the West (24%) do not even have a part-time school nurse.

We also found that schools located in both the Northeast (52%) and the Midwest (54%) are more likely ($p < .01$) to have a program, such as an SAP, for dealing with students who have mental health issues than schools in the western (39%) or southern (37%) parts of the country. Such programs are also more common in schools with a wealthier student base, defined as less than 25 percent of the student body eligible for free or reduced lunches, than schools in which more than half of students are eligible (53% vs. 36%). This disparity is somewhat offset by the fact that schools that receive Medicaid funding for the purpose of providing health care services to their students are more likely to offer counseling for mental health conditions on school premises than schools that do not receive Medicaid funding (54% vs. 42%). These schools are also more likely to employ a full-time psychologist (21% vs. 13%) or social worker (24% vs. 15%). However, almost as high a percentage of schools with low proportions of poor students avail themselves of Medicaid funding as schools with high proportions of poor students (41% vs. 48%).

As might be expected, we also found that larger schools are more likely to employ full-time mental health professionals than smaller schools. Professionals working in larger schools were more likely to report that their school employs a full-time school nurse, counselor, social worker, or psychologist than mental health professionals working in smaller schools.

What Do School Mental Health Professionals Do?

What school mental health professionals do varies considerably both across and within their job titles. We asked respondents with each of the three major job titles (Table 31.2) how they viewed their responsibilities in regard to mental health issues. The clearest finding (Table 31.6) is

Table 31.6 Self-Described Job Responsibilities by Job Title (% Great to Moderate Extent)

Description	Title		
	Counselor (N = 675)	Psychologist (N = 374)	Social Worker (N = 154)
Refer students who may have a mental health condition such as an anxiety disorder or depression to other professionals for further testing and treatment	89	87	99
Identify students who may have a mental health condition such as an anxiety disorder or depression	65	82[a]	88[a]
Counsel students with mental health conditions	63	57[a]	86[a]
Develop programs to enhance the mental health of the entire student body	66	38[a]	66
Counsel or help families of students who may have a mental health condition	53	46[a]	82[a]
Administer tests to diagnose students with specific mental health conditions such as an anxiety disorder or depression	6	68[a]	24[a]

[a] Percentages were significantly different from counselors ($p < .01$).

that all three types of professionals viewed their job as referring students who might have a mental health condition such as depression or anxiety disorder to other professionals for further testing and treatment. Social workers appear the most likely of the three to see their job as performing any treatment themselves (86%). Both counselors (63%) and psychologists (57%) often viewed this as part of their job but not to the same level as social workers. The same general pattern appeared in regard to counseling parents; only the large majority of social workers viewed this as their responsibility.

When it comes to identifying students with potential mental health conditions, the vast majority of psychologists (82%) and social workers (88%) regarded this as part of their job. However, a smaller yet significant majority of school counselors agreed with this job description (65%). Differences were also apparent when the development of mental health programs for the entire school is considered. Here about two-thirds of counselors and social workers agreed with this description, but less than 40% of psychologists viewed this as a priority. School psychologists appear to have the major responsibility of administering tests to identify mental health conditions in students. Whereas about two-thirds of psychologists agreed with

this description, very few counselors (6%) and only about a quarter of social workers saw this as part of their job.

These job descriptions suggest that school mental health professionals can help to identify students with mental health conditions and provide referrals but that actual treatment is more likely to occur elsewhere or with different providers. Most school mental health professionals are likely to refer students who are displaying symptoms of mental health conditions to another professional for further testing and counseling. As seen in Table 31.7, roughly 8 in 10 school professionals would refer students who were showing signs of depression (80%), anxiety (79%), or alcohol abuse (77%). Most of the rest said they would be somewhat likely to do so.

School mental health professionals are considerably less likely to say that they would treat or counsel students with potential mental health problems themselves. In the case of depression, fewer than 40% said they would be very likely to treat or counsel the student (Table 31.7). Even fewer said they would be very likely to treat or counsel students who were displaying symptoms of an anxiety disorder (30%) or alcohol abuse (27%). Sizable minorities indicated that they would not be too likely or would not be likely at all to treat or counsel students who were de-

Table 31.7 Likely Course of Action in Treating a Student with a Common Mental Condition: Refer to Another Professional or Treat (% Very Likely)

| Condition and Action Taken | Title | | | | |
	Counselor (N = 675)	Psychologist (N = 374)	Social Worker (N = 154)	Other (N = 199)	Total (N = 1402)
Alcohol Abuse					
Refer	75	77	83	82	77
Treat	30	17[a]	33	26[a]	27
Depression					
Refer	75	81	86	88[a]	80
Treat	38	33[a]	47	25[a]	36
Anxiety					
Refer	80	73	81	85	79
Treat	31	28	42[a]	24[a]	30

All differences between rates of referral and treatment within each condition were statistically significant, $p < .01$.
[a] Significant differences ($p < .01$) compared to counselors.

pressed (27%), had an anxiety disorder (34%), or were using excessive amounts of alcohol (38%).

Limited Time for Direct Care of Students

Counseling or working with students who have mental health problems is clearly not the only thing that school mental health professionals do. Most school professionals actually spend much of their time doing other things. A majority of professionals (76%) spend less than half of their work week counseling or working with students who have mental health problems, and nearly half (47%) do this for less than 10 hours a week. A small minority (9%) spends more than 30 hours per week on this activity.

Not only do school professionals divide their time between a multitude of tasks, some also work in more than one school. Although a solid majority of professionals (69%) spend all their time in one school, 31% said they work in more than one school. Among psychologists, a solid majority (62%) reported that they work in more than one school.

Spending more time working with students who have mental health issues may sensitize one to the problem. Mental health professionals who spent at least 10 hours a week counseling or

working with students who have mental health issues were considerably more likely to consider depression (73% vs. 52%), anxiety disorders (52% vs. 33%), cutting (31% vs. 18%), and eating disorders (21% vs. 14%) to be a problem in their school to a great or moderate extent than professionals who spent less time with such students (all differences significant at $p < .01$).

Processes for Referrals, but Not Necessarily for Identification

Given the extent to which mental health professionals have to stretch their time, it is important to understand the procedures that schools employ to identify and deal with students who may have a mental health condition. We found that a solid majority of professionals claimed their schools have a clearly defined and coordinated process for providing *referrals* for students who may have a mental health condition. However, having an equally clear process for *identifying, diagnosing,* or *treating* students is less common.

In particular, 66% of professionals said their school has a "clearly defined and coordinated process for providing referrals to students who may have a mental health condition." However, before students can be referred for further testing and counseling, their condition needs to reach the attention of the professional in charge of referrals. Schools are less likely to have a clearly defined and coordinated process for identifying students who may have a mental health condition than they are to have a referral process. Only 37% of professionals said that their schools have a process to a great extent for identifying students. As many (37%) are in schools with a moderately clear process, and one in four said (25%) their process is only coordinated to a small extent or not at all.

Schools are even less likely to have a clear process for diagnosing students with a specific mental health condition. In fact, about half of professionals said (51%) their schools have a diagnostic process that is clearly defined and coordinated only to a small extent or not at all. Only half of professionals (49%) are in schools with a very (26%) or moderately (23%) clear and coordinated diagnostic process.

Similarly, the process for treating students with mental health conditions is clear to only a small extent or not at all in the about half of schools (53%). Less than half of professionals (46%) are in schools that have a very (17%) or moderately (29%) clear and defined process for treating students.

Procedures for Identification

One way to minimize the chance that students with problems are overlooked is to systematically screen the entire student population. At present, however, only 2% of schools screen all and only 7% screen most of their students for mental health problems. Although a majority of schools (63%) report screening some of the students, about 26% conduct no screening at all.

One solution to increasing the identification of students in need of assistance is to train teachers to identify symptoms of mental health conditions. Here the situation is a little more encouraging. Only about 19% of schools provide no training at all to teachers in identifying mental health problems in students. However, it is unusual for schools to train all (9%) or most (12%) of the teachers to identify such problems. A little more than half (53%) trains only some of

their teachers to identify mental health problems.

Another potential way to increase the likelihood that students will seek and find help when necessary is to teach students to identify potential symptoms of mental health conditions in themselves and in peers. A sizable minority of schools (38%) follows this practice for all or most of the students. However, in a solid majority of schools (59%), only some or none of them are taught these skills. Schools in the Northeast (49%) and Midwest (48%) are more likely ($p < .01$) to teach students to identify symptoms of mental health conditions than schools in the West (32%) or the South (30%).

It is also important that students feel comfortable asking for help themselves when they feel they need it. Most schools seem to recognize this, as a strong majority of professionals reported that all (60%) or most (21%) of the students in their school are encouraged to seek help if they think they or their peers might have a mental health condition. About 57% of respondents reported that they encouraged all of the parents in their school to seek help if they need it; 20% reported that they encouraged most of the parents in their school in the same way.

When it comes to identifying students who may have mental health issues, "clearly defined and coordinated" often means that the entire school is involved. Mental health professionals who said that their school's program for identifying students is clearly defined and coordinated to a great extent were more likely to indicate that not only mental health professionals but also other professionals working in the school are involved in the identification process. In particular, higher proportions ($p < .01$) of teachers (77% vs. 46%), supervisors of after-school programs (77% vs. 46%), health care professionals (70% vs. 54%), and administrators (66% vs. 44%) have at least moderate responsibility for identifying students than professionals who described their identification process as only coordinated to a small extent or not at all.

We asked school professionals to evaluate how well various staff members identify students with mental conditions. The results shown in Table 31.8 indicate that among those responsible for identifying students with potential mental

Table 31.8 Perceived Success of Staff in Identifying Students with a Mental Health Condition (if Responsible for This Activity)

Staff Category (% Responsible)	Success		
	Very Good (%)	Somewhat Good (%)	Somewhat or Very Bad (%)
Mental health professionals (97%)	73	25	1
Health care professionals, such as school nurse (86%)	56	37	4
Principal or assistant principal (92%)	38	50	9
Teachers (96%)	33	59	8
Coaches and other adults who supervise after-school activities (87%)	19	54	17

health problems, mental health professionals believed that both they and school nurses do a very good job. However, it is possible for teachers, administrators, and coaches to do a good job as well.

According to our respondents, mental health professionals and teachers are the ones who are seen as most often identifying a student who needs mental health services (Table 31.9). At the same time, more than half of respondents said that referrals by parents, peers, or the students themselves are also somewhat common. About 19% of school professionals reported that students who use the school's mental health services very often do so because they were referred by parents, and over half (55%) said parents are the initiating party somewhat often. At the same time, school professionals (24%) indicated that parents are not too often or not often at all involved.

Students are seen as somewhat less likely to ask for help on their own accord. About 38% of school professionals said that students do not often approach them on their own. Yet, a majority (60%) said this happens at least somewhat often. Sometimes peers identify students with mental health concerns, although school professionals were divided on how frequently this occurs. A slim majority (52%) said that peers identify students who may have a mental health condition at least somewhat often, but nearly as many (46%) said this happens not too often or not at all.

Adolescents in schools where the students are taught to identify symptoms of mental health conditions are said to be more likely ($p < .01$) to enter the system on their own accord (65% vs. 47%) or because peers identified them (60% vs. 33%) than adolescents in schools where only some or none of the students learn these skills.

Table 31.9 Perceived Source of Identification of Students Needing Attention for a Mental Health Condition

Source of Identification	Likelihood			
	Very often (%)	Somewhat Often (%)	Not Too Often (%)	Not Often at All (%)
School mental health professional	43	45	8	3
Teacher	29	54	13	3
Parent or guardian	19	55	20	4
Students on their own	16	44	28	10
Another student	10	42	32	14

Barriers to Receiving Care

We asked school professionals to evaluate two common barriers to receiving mental health care: inadequate insurance coverage and inadequate treatment resources in the community. A large proportion of professionals (85%) reported agreement with the statement that "inadequate insurance coverage prevents many students from getting the mental health services they need." In addition, 54% of professionals agreed with the statement that the "treatment resources for adolescent mental health are adequate in the community." These evaluations suggest that school professionals see the treatment barriers often cited by panels such as the President's New Freedom Commission as significant problems in the schools.

Similar to primary care physicians who see adolescents for routine check-ups (see Chapter 30), mental health professionals working in rural schools (52%) were more likely ($p < .01$) to indicate that the resources in their community are inadequate than mental health professionals working in suburban (44%) or urban (41%) schools. As a whole, mental health professionals gave a more positive picture of community resources than primary care physicians. Compared to fewer than half of school mental health professionals (46%), a solid majority of primary care physicians (67%) reported that the treatment resources for adolescent mental health disorders are inadequate in their community (Chapter 30).

Schools Serving Low-Income Students Differ from Higher-Income Schools

Adolescents going to schools in which a high proportion of their classmates come from low-income households are no more likely to have mental health services available than adolescents going to wealthier schools. In fact, as noted earlier, SAPs are actually less available in schools with high proportions of poor students. There are signs, however, that schools serving low-income students try to provide more services on site. First, schools that serve mostly low-income students (more than 75% qualify for free lunch) are more likely to have a school-based health

center than schools that serve wealthier students (fewer than 25% qualify) (13% vs. 4%, $p < .01$). Second, professionals serving in low-income schools are more likely to report that their school has a well-defined process for treating students with mental health problems (24% vs. 15%, $p < .05$). In addition, schools that avail themselves of Medicaid funding are more likely ($p < .01$) to have a very clearly defined and coordinated process for diagnosing (31% vs. 21%) and treating (20% vs. 13%) students who may have a mental health condition. Schools that have Medicaid funding are also slightly more likely ($p < .05$) to screen all or most students for mental health problems (9% vs. 7%). Nevertheless, as noted earlier, schools with high proportions of poor students are only marginally more likely to take advantage of Medicaid funding than schools with wealthier students (48% vs. 41%).

Despite the signs that schools serving low-income students deliver more care, other practices promoting mental health are more likely to take place in wealthier schools. Students who go to schools in which fewer than 25 percent of the student body qualify for the free or reduced lunch program are more likely ($p < .01$) to be taught to identify symptoms of mental health conditions in themselves and others than students who go to schools with a large low-income population (50% vs. 27%). Parents in wealthier schools are also encouraged to a greater extent to get involved in identifying students who need help (62% vs. 53%). Perhaps as a consequence, professionals working in schools with a wealthier student population are more likely ($p < .01$) to report that students who are using the mental health services offered by the school often seek them on their own accord (65% vs. 53%) or because they were identified by another student (62% vs. 39%).

Evaluation of Available Services

To assess the quality and effectiveness of the available programs and services from the perspective of school professionals, we examined three somewhat related outcomes that might serve as criteria for the success of the services currently in place in schools serving adolescents

Table 31.10 Distributions of Response to Program Effectiveness Questions

Overall Effectiveness	%	Received Services in Total	%	Received Services on Site	%
Very effective	18	All	7	All	7
Somewhat effective	67	Most	30	Most	24
Not too effective	13	About ½	29	About ½	20
Not at all effective	2	About ¼	17	About ¼	19
Don't know	1	Only a few	13	Only a few	26
		Don't know	4	Don't know	4

(Table 31.10). The first was a rating of the overall effectiveness of the school's services. Most professionals (85%), regardless of the demographic characteristics of their schools, described the mental health services offered in their schools as at least somewhat effective. However, only about 18% believed they are "very effective," with 67% characterizing the services offered as just "somewhat effective." Fifteen percent of respondents described their mental health services as "not too effective" or "not effective at all."

A second set of outcomes, school professionals' estimates of how well their programs connect students in their school with needed mental health services, depends on their perceptions of the need for such services. These perceptions varied widely, but on average, school professionals estimated that 18 percent of adolescents are in need of "counseling for mental health conditions such as anxiety disorders or depression." According to several estimates, approximately 20 percent of adolescents suffer from a diagnosable mental disorder (U.S. Department of Health and Human Services, 2000), so their estimates were clearly in line with prevailing evidence.

More than half of professionals (59%) estimated that only about half or fewer of students who are in need of counseling actually receive these services either at school or elsewhere. Only about 37% of professionals reported that all (7%) or most (30%) of the students receive the care they need. When asked about the proportion that receives the services they need on site, the level of success understandably dropped even lower. In this case, 65% of professionals estimated that half or fewer of the students received the services they needed at the school. Despite the weak performance of most of the school programs, there was considerable variation in perceived success in delivering care to students in need, with a solid core of school professionals seeing their schools' programs as reaching most of the students in need.

Predictors of School Effectiveness

Which of the things that schools do to promote the mental health of their students best predict whether a school is evaluated as effective in dealing with students who may have a mental health condition? To answer this question, we first conducted a factor analysis of the services and programs provided, including the professionals on staff and the procedures for identification and screening as well as those for diagnosis, treatment, and referral. We then grouped the results of this analysis into 10 factors that represented the dominant clusters of services, providers, and policies in place in schools. The 10 factors were then entered stepwise into a regression analysis after first holding constant demographic differences between schools, including region of the country, size of school, type of school (primary, middle, high, other), urban vs. rural location, percent of students eligible for free lunch, use of Medicaid funding for health services, and differences between respondents, including age, gender, professional title, length of service at school, and number of hours per week spent on counseling of students. We also included the two measures that assessed the adequacy of treatment resources in the community and the importance of access to health insurance as an obstacle to receiving care in the community. Because the three measures of school effectiveness were only moderately correlated with each other (*r* values ranging from .30 to .40), we analyzed each one separately.

Table 31.11 shows the results of the analysis for each outcome: overall evaluation of the school's mental health program, proportion of students in need of services who received them in total, and proportion of students in need of services who received them primarily at school. Five of the 10 school program factors consistently predicted success. Schools that had well-defined and coordinated processes for both identifying and referring students and for diagnosing and treating them were significantly more likely to perform well on all three criteria. The same was true of schools that had staff that were effective in identifying students at risk for mental health problems, as well as schools that had counseling programs on site and schools that were in communities with adequate treatment resources.

Schools that had mental health professionals on site full time and that had screening programs and staff training for identification of mental health problems were more likely to perform well on overall effectiveness and on delivery of services in total. Schools that encouraged students and parents to seek care performed well on the two service delivery outcomes. Finally, schools that had student health centers were seen as more effective in providing services on site. Prevention programs for problems such as suicide and drugs as well as SAPs did not appear to add any incremental effectiveness beyond the other programs.

In addition to the programs employed in the school, community resources outside the school also mattered. Schools were judged more effective and providing more services if the treatment resources for students in the community were viewed as adequate. In addition, it was seen as easier to deliver services to students if their families had insurance coverage for mental health treatment.

Table 31.11 Regression Analysis of Three School Program Outcomes as a Function of Program Characteristics (Significant Standardized Coefficients)

	Outcome		
Program Factor	*Overall Effectiveness*	*Receipt of Services (Total)*	*Receipt of Services in School*
Procedures for identification and Referral	.201	.125	.081
Staff effectiveness in identifying students	.134	.057	.047[a]
Mental health professionals on staff	.133	.064	—
Screening programs and staff training	.110	.061	—
Good treatment resources in community	.098	.052[a]	.062
Counseling programs on site	.104	.059	.197
Procedures for diagnosis or treatment	.053	.162	.229
Parents and students encouraged to seek care	—	.135	.048
Adequate insurance for mental health care	—	.105	—
Student health center	—	—	.050

Adjusted R^2 were 26.1% for effectiveness, 18.5% for total service, and 22.5% for service on site.

[a] $p < .10$

When we examined the many school and respondent characteristics in the analysis, a few school characteristics were consistent predictors of success. In particular, professionals working in middle schools consistently saw their schools as more effective and as delivering services to a higher proportion of students. Schools with high proportions of students eligible for free lunch and those in rural areas were more likely to have successful programs for delivering care on site. In addition, professionals working in schools in the Northeast and South felt their programs did a better job of delivering services on site than those working in the West and Midwest. However, perceptions of overall school effectiveness did not vary by region of the country, urbanity, or income.

SUMMARY AND DISCUSSION

This survey of school professionals' knowledge about mental health issues supports the need for increased resources and programming in the nations' schools for adolescent mental health promotion and care. Mental health problems are seen as extremely prevalent in schools that serve adolescents, and the schools are seen as only somewhat effective in meeting the mental health needs of students. Most schools have a well-defined and coordinated program to *refer* students for mental health problems. However, a much smaller proportion of schools have a similar system to *identify* students who may need assistance. Although about half of schools have some form of counseling on site to help students with mental health concerns, resources in these programs are stretched very thin, with most professionals not able to spend even half their time on these activities.

The findings that depression and substance use are highly prevalent and serious problems, especially in high schools, is consistent with considerable research indicating that most adolescents with mental health problems do not receive appropriate treatment for their conditions (Kataoka, Zhang, & Wells, 2002; Sturm, Ringel, & Andreyeva, 2003). In addition, adolescent substance use is often comorbid with mental health conditions (see Part V). However, adolescents who experience substance use dependency are either not appropriately treated (see Chapter 29) or, when they are treated, do not receive care for comorbid mental health conditions (Jaycox, Morral, & Juvonen, 2003). Indeed, it is disheartening to find that so few schools (24%) have treatment programs for drug dependence available on site. Hence, our findings indicate that despite the considerable resources devoted to adolescent mental health in schools, the unmet need for services remains large and is unlikely to be reduced without additional resources devoted to the prevention and identification of mental health problems.

In view of our findings, it is not surprising that many school professionals say they could use more help to identify and treat students in need of care. In a separate set of questions, roughly half of mental health professionals (47%) said that having more mental health professionals is one of the top ways that the mental health services in their school could be improved. More than half of mental health professionals (53%) said they very often feel limited by time constraints to adequately assess and deal with students who may have a mental health condition. Many mental health professionals (32%) also reported feeling hampered because of a lack of available support resources.

Despite the limitations in the school mental health system, the results suggest that some schools have the capability of identifying students with mental conditions sufficiently early so that school staff can take appropriate action. Schools that are seen as doing this effectively involve the entire professional staff as well as students to identify persons needing help. They also encourage parents and students to identify themselves if they feel that they are in need of mental health evaluation. Nevertheless, most schools do not have adequate diagnostic and treatment facilities on site, and so many students need to be referred to outside providers for care. In these schools, mental health professionals serve primarily as facilitators of early identification and referral for mental health care. They are also in the best position to train teachers and other staff in the adoption of other schoolwide practices that can create a favorable climate for promoting mental health.

One possible direction for mental health care in the schools is to increase the presence of school-based health centers. At present, very few schools have these facilities, and many of those that exist do not have the capability to provide a full range of mental health care. This approach will take considerable time and cost to implement. However, based on the perceived effectiveness of the programs that are currently in place in many schools, it is possible to have an effective program that provides some counseling on site for less serious mental health conditions if the entire school is poised to identify students in need of help. If these programs were supplemented by other schoolwide programs that can advance the positive development of students (see Romer, 2003; Chapter 26, this volume), many student mental health problems may also be prevented.

The approach that emphasizes prevention and schoolwide programming is consistent with recent calls for school mental health professionals to adopt more of a public health outlook on their role (Adelman & Taylor, 2000; Atkins et al., 2003; Hoagwood & Johnson, 2003; Weist & Christodulu, 2000). This approach emphasizes universal programming that can also be supplemented by selective programs for students in need of special care. Such an approach focuses on the strengths of school mental health professionals as the experts on mental health in school settings without taxing their time and skills to provide one-on-one counseling and treatment for students who need selective and indicated care better provided by other mental health specialists. This facilitator role is already consistent with how school mental health professionals view their job; the majority view their work as identifying students in need of further care and providing referral to other providers for treatment.

Even if schools could do a perfect job of identifying students at risk for mental health problems, two major barriers to effective care for adolescents would remain. One is the inadequacy of treatment resources in the community, a reality endorsed by school professionals as well as primary care providers (Chapter 30). This barrier is greatest in rural areas where appropriate medical providers are less available. A second barrier

is inadequate insurance coverage for mental health treatment. However, it is encouraging that schools with high proportions of poor youth are reported to be able to provide mental health services in schools. This may reflect the use of Medicaid funding to provide those services or greater ability to bill for services under State Children's Health Insurance Programs.

Despite evidence that schools serving poor children are managing to deliver mental health services, it is also clear that many of these schools do not avail themselves of Medicaid funding to provide mental health services. Use of Medicaid funding appears to be nearly as prevalent in schools serving wealthier students as in those serving poorer students. Hence, there appears to be a large opportunity to improve the delivery of services to poor youth by greater use of Medicaid funds than is currently the practice.

A major limitation in our research's conclusions regarding effective services is that we relied completely on school professionals' perceptions of their programs. However, we did hold constant many characteristics of both the respondents and their schools. Hence, the relations between school programs and perceived effectiveness were not simply the result of those characteristics. It remains for future research to evaluate the effectiveness of school programs using actual mental health outcomes as criteria. In conducting this research, our findings suggest that schoolwide programs that involve the entire teaching and administrative staff as well as parents and students should be evaluated as potential strategies to promote the mental health of students. Universal screening programs, such as the Columbia Teen Screen (McGuire & Flynn, 2003), could also be evaluated as potential mechanisms to identify and refer students in need of further diagnosis and care.

According to the President's New Freedom Commission on Mental Health (2003),

> In a transformed mental health system, the early detection of mental health problems in children and adults—through routine and comprehensive testing and screening—will be an expected and typical occurrence. At the first sign of difficulties, preventive interventions will be started to keep problems

from escalating . . . Quality screening and early intervention will occur in both readily accessible, low-stigma settings, such as primary health care facilities and schools.

Our findings indicate that this objective is attainable in the nations' schools if we are willing to make the needed investments.

APPENDIX 31.1
Survey Methodology

To assess the status of mental health services provided in American schools and to learn what types of barriers and opportunities school mental health service providers face, the Annenberg Public Policy Center commissioned Princeton Survey Research Associates International (PSRAI) to conduct a nationwide telephone survey of 1,402 school mental health professionals. The survey was funded by the Sunnylands Adolescent Mental Health Initiative and follows a fall 2003 survey that examined the attitudes and practices of 727 primary care physicians who regularly treat adolescents.

A total of 1,402 school-based mental health professionals were interviewed by Princeton Data Source, LLC, between April 5 and May 28, 2004. The margin of sampling error for results based on the full sample is ± 2.6%. Details on the design, execution, and analysis of the survey are discussed below.

Contact Procedures

Interviews were conducted by telephone from April 5 to May 28, 2004. A minimum of 20 attempts were made to contact a mental health professional at each school. Calls were staggered over different times of the day and days of the week to maximize the chance of making contact with potential respondents. Prior to being called, the principal of each school was sent a letter introducing the research and explaining that a mental health professional in the school could

expect a call to participate in the study in the coming weeks. In addition, the principals as well as the respondents were told that for their participation a $20,000 charitable donation would be made in the name of all participating schools to an organization that works to improve mental health care among adolescents. The letter also gave a toll-free telephone number so that mental health professionals could call in and take the survey at their own convenience.

The sample was released for interviewing in replicates, which are representative subsamples of the larger sample. Use of replicates to control the release of sample ensures that complete call procedures are followed for the entire sample.

Response Rate

The response rate estimates the fraction of all eligible schools in the sample where a mental health professional was interviewed. At PSRAI, the response rate is calculated by taking the product of three component rates as recommended by the American Association for Public Opinion Research:

- Contact rate: the proportion of working numbers through which a request for interview was made (84%)
- Cooperation rate: the proportion of contacted numbers through which a consent for interview was at least initially obtained, vs. those refused (87%)
- Completion rate: the proportion of initially cooperating and eligible interviews that were completed (100%)

The response rate for the survey was 72%.

Acknowledgments

We wish to thank Marc Atkins, Kimberly Hoagwood, and James G. Kelly for their helpful comments on an earlier version of this chapter.

A Call to Action on Adolescent Mental Health

Kathleen Hall Jamieson
and Daniel Romer

chapter 32

In this final chapter, we summarize important policy implications of the commission reports and highlight steps they suggest to advance the healthy development of America's youth. The reports provide a hopeful assessment of our ability to treat the most prevalent adolescent disorders. At the same time, enormous hurdles remain in our ability to deliver these treatments, and our knowledge base of effective treatments still has important gaps. These considerations suggest that we face formidable challenges if we wish to ensure the healthy development of our youth. Nevertheless, our ever-growing understanding of environments that encourage healthy development bodes well for our future ability to both treat and prevent adolescent mental disorder.

TREATMENT WORKS

The good news in the commission reports is that the most common disorders (anxiety and depression) have effective treatments that can help more than 70% of those who are afflicted. Those who do not respond to particular treatments can be given alternative therapies that can raise the success rate even higher. Although combination treatments involving both drugs and psychotherapy are often most effective, it is also the case that psychotherapy, in particular cognitive-behavior (CBT) or interpersonal (IPT) approaches, can reduce symptoms and lead to improvement without the use of medication.

There is also progress in the treatment of the less prevalent conditions. Treatments for bipolar disorder have a high success rate, and therapeutic interventions for anorexia nervosa can lead to recovery from this illness. Early intervention can also benefit those with schizophrenia, reducing the severity of the illness and leading to better adaptation to the disorder. Since many with severe mental disorders are at risk for suicide, these interventions can be not only life altering but also life saving.

As discussed below, the findings also have important implications for the reduction of stigma associated with mental illness. Public awareness of the effectiveness of treatment for mental disorders should increase the willingness of parents and youth to seek treatment before illness pro-

gresses. Stigma reduction throughout society should also increase the likelihood that those who have been successfully treated will lead productive and satisfying lives.

RECENT DEVELOPMENTS IN THE USE OF MEDICATION TO TREAT ADOLESCENT DEPRESSION

As this book goes to press, there is vigorous discussion about the safety and efficacy of antidepressants in particular, selective serotonin reuptake inhibitors (SSRIs), for treatment of adolescent depression. Many clinical trials supported by the pharmaceutical industry suggest the potential for adverse events in the use of SSRIs, including increased suicidal ideation and suicide attempts (Harris, 2004a, b). Unfortunately, these trials were often kept from public view. This has led to increased pressure to make all clinical trials involving drugs available for public inspection. In addition, an FDA panel has determined that these trials support the conclusion that SSRIs may carry an increased risk for suicidal ideation or behavior for a small proportion of users (perhaps 2 or 3%) and as a result labels warning of these effects will now be placed on all antidepressants (FDA, 2004).

A recent trial with adolescents suffering from major depression (Glass, 2004; March et al., 2004) indicated that treatment with a particular SSRI (Prozac) was *less* likely to produce adverse events when combined with CBT. Based on this evidence as well as considerable research suggesting the effectiveness of CBT as well as IPT with adolescents (reviewed by the depression-bipolar commission), it may be that combined treatment is the best approach for adolescents who present with depression and suicidal thoughts or behaviors. Since many physicians and mental health providers may not be trained to deliver CBT or IPT, there is a clear need to increase the number of practitioners who can provide these alternatives. Use of CBT or IPT may be the preferred alternative for less severe cases, since it has proven efficacy and does not run the risk of increased suicidal behavior.

It is encouraging to note the appearance of several initiatives designed to increase public access to the results of clinical trials evaluating the effects of therapeutic interventions. Eleven major medical journals have established a policy requiring the registration of such trials at inception before findings can be considered for publication (DeAngelis, Drazen, Frizelle, Haug, Hoey, Horton, et al., 2004). The American Medical Association has endorsed the concept of a federally mandated registry of clinical trials (Council of Scientific Affairs, 2004). Legislation mandating registration has been introduced in both the House and Senate (Fair Access to Clinical Trials Act, 2004). All of these efforts encourage greater use of the existing federally-sponsored but voluntary repository of clinical trails, www.clinicaltrials.gov. We look forward to the eventual open access to all results regarding the efficacy of medication and other therapies as well as reports of adverse reactions experienced following regulatory approval.

TREATMENT FOR SUBSTANCE ABUSE

Treatment for drug dependence in adolescents raises a host of issues because some drugs of dependence (e.g., marijuana) are banned by law and their use is treated as criminal behavior. This is unfortunate because dependence on most drugs can be successfully treated if the family is involved in the therapy (see Chapter 18). Furthermore, drug dependence is often comorbid with other mental conditions that would benefit from treatment as a medical problem rather than as criminal behavior. Because the treatment system for substance abuse is not integrated with treatment for mental conditions (see below), those with both suffer needlessly.

EARLY DETECTION AND TREATMENT AS A PREVENTION STRATEGY

It is now clear that most cases of adult mental disorders make their first appearance prior to or during adolescence (Kim-Cohen, et al., 2003; Roza, Hofstra, van der Ende, & Verhulst, 2003). This reality makes the early detection and treatment of mental disorders even more critical (see also The President's New Freedom Commission

on Mental Health, 2003). The earlier a condition is identified and treatment begun, the less serious the course of illness and the lower the likelihood that it will disrupt healthy adolescent development. This is particularly important for substance dependence, including smoking, because there is evidence of nervous system plasticity during adolescence. A drug habit learned early produces brain changes that may be lifelong. If early detection and treatment of mental disorders were the norm, the possibility of reducing subsequent disorder would be increased. Furthermore, given the high rates of mental disorders as precursors to suicide, their early treatment would boost our chances of preventing this fatal outcome in youth.

Because it is clear that early detection and referral for treatment should be a high national priority, it is disappointing to learn from research conducted as part of the commissions (Chapters 30 and 31) that the primary care system and schools are inadequately prepared to meet this challenge. Primary care physicians are not trained to detect mental disorders or substance abuse problems, and most do not employ screening programs to identify youth at risk for these conditions. A similar situation exists in the schools where mental health professionals do not have the resources to identify youth at risk for problems. As a result, schools do not intervene until illnesses progress and come to the attention of staff. Unfortunately, the most common disorders in adolescence (depression, anxiety, and substance abuse) are not as easily recognized as conduct disorder and attention-deficit hyperactivity disorder (ADHD), conditions that make their first appearance in the elementary years. Waiting until adolescent conditions seriously interfere with school performance forestalls treatment and reduces the odds of successful recovery.

Treatment systems also are poorly designed for delivering care to adolescents. The most glaring example of this, treatment for substance abuse, is a case study of inadequate response to a large but potentially manageable problem (Chapter 29). The long-standing dichotomy between treatment for drug dependence and other mental conditions creates a barrier that prevents comprehensive treatment. Since substance abuse and mental conditions often co-occur, they should be treated within the same service system. Furthermore, substance dependence treatment programs often employ ineffective interventions despite the existence of evidence-based therapies (involving the family) that can produce greater treatment adherence and success.

The integration of treatment services (mental health, addiction treatment, behavioral health) across different practitioners in different settings (primary care, specialty care, schools, juvenile justice) requires coordination that is difficult to achieve under the current health care system. New systems of treatment for mental health that integrate services are sorely needed. As noted in Chapter 28 by Hoagwood, several states, most notably Hawaii, Michigan, and New York, are attempting to implement new public programs that include evidence-based treatments and are coordinating structures to ensure that youth are effectively served. We await further evaluations of these programs to see if they can solve the service fragmentation problems that have plagued mental health treatment for both youth and adults.

UNIVERSAL PREVENTION

Aside from early detection of mental disorders, there is growing evidence that universal prevention programs in schools and other youth settings can help to increase resilience to stress and encourage healthy growth and decision making. The evidence in the case of drugs and alcohol as well as depression is particularly encouraging (see Chapters 3, 19, and 26). Suicide prevention programs are also showing encouraging signs (see Chapter 24). However, in our recommendations for further research (below), we observe that much remains to be learned about these programs.

INSURANCE COVERAGE

No discussion of treatment problems can ignore the weaknesses in insurance coverage for mental health. The Mental Health Parity law that went into effect in 1998 is due for renewal in 2004, and several changes have been proposed in the latest legislation to make coverage of mental health conditions more inclusive. Achievement of full parity is an important policy goal. As a report by the Congressional Research Service notes (Redhead, 2003), "Requiring parity for mental health benefits establishes a uniform 'floor' of mental health coverage across all plans." This has the desirable effect of reducing wasteful competition among health-insurers to attract the least risky policyholders. In addition, experience in the implementation of full parity in federal health insurance programs indicates that the short-term increases in costs are small (about 1.6% in fee-for-service plans and less than 1% in managed care) (Redhead, 2003). Hence, short-term cost does not appear to be a barrier to the implementation of full parity for mental health services, and the long-term cost savings and benefits to consumers should make parity cost-effective.

Despite the importance of parity legislation, this policy effort also has serious limitations. At least 15% of Americans have no health insurance coverage whatsoever (Mills & Bhandari, 2003). This means that nearly 12% of youth under the age of 18 and 30% of young people between the ages of 18 and 24 without coverage will not be helped by parity. In addition, parity legislation affects only those whose insurance already includes coverage for mental health, and it does not cover treatment for substance dependence (Redhead, 2003). Hence, even if the current parity legislation were enacted, it would not solve the problems inherent in the current system of treatment for mental health.

A potentially favorable development in the search for solutions to inadequate mental health coverage is the prospect that managed care programs, which now cover more than half of youth (Glied & Neufield, 2001), will evolve to adequately ensure treatment for mental conditions. One approach adopted by managed care involves the use of specialized services or "carve-outs" for behavioral treatment. Through this approach, costs for mental health services can be contained while patients are directed to appropriate care by specialists (Conti, Frank, & McGuire, 2004). In principle, the *short-term* costs of mental health services can be effectively managed. Nevertheless, it remains to be seen if managed care can adequately accommodate youth who require more long-term treatment to either complete a full course of psychotherapy or maintain treatment and avoid relapse (Glied & Neufield, 2001; Kelleher, Scholle, Feldman, & Nace, 1999).

Another challenge for managed care and other insurance plans is to identify those practitioners who can treat adolescent mental problems effectively. Surveys of both primary care providers and school mental health professionals indicate widespread dissatisfaction with the quality of care available in local communities for adolescents having the disorders studied by our commissions. The effectiveness of early detection and treatment of adolescent mental disorders is thus limited. There is an urgent need to increase the pool of providers able to deliver evidence-based treatments to youth so that availability of such services is no longer a barrier to referral by schools and primary care providers. School mental health professionals and nurses as well as primary care providers need links with quality treatment centers to which they can refer adolescents in need.

STIGMA OF MENTAL DISORDER

Research conducted by Penn and colleagues (Chapter 27) indicates that young people hold stigmatizing beliefs about mental disorders and that these beliefs can influence their treatment decisions. If youth feel that they will be stigmatized for seeking treatment, they will resist coming forward when experiencing symptoms. One approach to reducing this dysfunctional response is to increase public awareness of the efficacy of treatment for mental disorders. If adolescents (and their parents) recognize the potential effectiveness of early detection and treatment, they may be more inclined to seek help from providers who are seen as effective in treating their problems. Hence, through awareness of treatment efficacy, the effects of stigmatizing beliefs may be moderated and youth encouraged to seek help from providers.

Educating the public about the effectiveness of treatment and the reality that persons with mental disorders can lead productive lives is a strategy that deserves the support of the advocacy community and government agencies. The current mental health media campaign sponsored by the Substance Abuse and Mental Health Services Administration (SAMHSA) as part of its Elimination of Barriers Initiative (2004) is one example of such an effort.

RESEARCH NEEDS

Estimates of the economic costs of mental and substance abuse disorders in the United States are in excess of $200 billion per year (Redhead, 2003; U.S. Department of Health and Human Services, 1999). By increasing our ability to prevent and treat these disorders in young people, we have the potential to reduce this burden significantly while substantially increasing the nation's welfare. We see two kinds of research opportunities for improving our ability to prevent and treat mental disorders in youth. At the procedural level, there are many unanswered questions about appropriate protocols and systems for treatment. Although we have treatments that work, we still don't know enough about the best ways to combine treatments for maximum effect or the optimal ways to withdraw treatments without leading to relapse. We also need more research on the best ways to treat persons with comorbid conditions, especially addiction. Moreover, we have no direct evidence of efficacy for the treatment of some adolescent anxiety and eating disorders, and schizophrenia still remains a treatment challenge.

We also know that universal prevention of some conditions is possible (Chapters 3 and 19) and that the healthy development of youth can be enhanced considerably using positive youth development strategies (see Chapter 26). Nevertheless, much remains to be learned about integrating effective programs into schools and communities in a cost-effective way. The promise of positive psychology is still untested and requires more research.

We also lack knowledge of the best ways to conduct screening of youth in schools and primary care settings so that care is delivered to them. Many young people identified in screening programs as needing services fail to seek them. There are several promising models (discussed by the suicide commission) but not enough evidence about their efficacy or ability to be taken to scale to permit widespread adoption.

A second major opportunity for research is to increase our understanding of the multiple pathways to both healthy and unhealthy development. Because we know little about the ways in which disorders unfold, it is difficult to design appropriate interventions at the earliest signs of disorder. One shortcoming in previous research is that investigators inevitably focused on the one or two disorders in which they had expertise. Unfortunately, the many disorders that appear in adolescence do not accommodate this neat developmental pattern. Disorders that first appear in childhood may later develop into other forms and some may develop together (Kim-Cohen et al., 2003). Early emergence of some conditions may be left behind never to appear again. These complex patterns of comorbidity and development have been a frequent finding in the commission reports. The challenge for future research is to examine a broad range of potential psychopathology as well as sources of resilience in one design in which different developmental pathways can be studied at the same time.

Fortunately, research strategies to better understand the causal influences on varied developmental trajectories are available (Curtis & Cicchetti, 2003; Masten, 2004). Longitudinal studies of representative populations can help to identify the paths and influences that affect the emergence of a disorder (e.g., Caspi et al., 2002; Kim-Cohen et al., 2003). Studies of twins embedded in such studies make it possible to identify genetic and interacting environmental factors that alter trajectories toward either resilience or disability (Rutter et al., 1997; Waldman, 2003). Once potential causal influences have been isolated, their effects can be studied in more focused longitudinal designs that select high-risk youth for prospective investigation. Clinical trials that follow young people over time can test the effects of theoretically derived interventions,

thereby adding further knowledge of causally efficacious treatments (Masten, 2004).

A research project designed to follow a large representative sample of children and twins that will enable the study of different developmental pathways throughout the early years and into adulthood is prohibitively expensive, even for the National Institute of Mental Health. Funding for such an endeavor will require the collaboration of a multitude of investigators with different areas of expertise, and it will necessitate the cooperation of both federal and private funding sources. It is clear, however, that such a study would greatly advance our understanding of the emergence of mental disorder and resilience in youth and allow further tests of intervention strategies that could reduce the burden of mental disorders in adolescence and adulthood.

THE FUTURE

With recent advances in neuroscience, it is now clear that adolescence is a period of dramatic change in brain structure and function (Giedd, 2004; Spear, 2000). The brain is an eminently plastic organ that develops both in accord with genetic rules and in response to its environment (Huttenlocher, 2002). Adolescence is particularly critical because it is the period during which significant "pruning" of synaptic connections occurs. The connections that remain may allow experience to mold a more adaptive brain, but they also open the door to illness and dysfunctional behavior. We remain far from understanding the mechanisms that produce these varied outcomes, but the potential for therapeutic interventions to correct dysfunctional neurodevelopment and to enhance resilience is a clear possibility. As we learn more about these effects, possibilities for dramatic breakthroughs in our ability to prevent and alter dysfunctional trajectories will present themselves (Kandel, 1998).

Our new understanding of brain development is rendering the old debates between nature and nurture or biology vs. behavior increasingly irrelevant (Kandel, 1998). Gene expression is responsive to environments and hormonal changes. As Kandel (1998) put it, "nurture will become nature," and our ability to influence such developments in positive ways will greatly enlarge the scope of preventive interventions. Increasing evidence of brain plasticity during the adolescent years suggests that both biologically and socially based interventions can influence development and alter dysfunctional developmental paths. The battleground between opposing biological and environmental viewpoints may be merging into a synthesis that recognizes the value and promise of both sides of these debates. These new frontiers in the study of psychopathology make this a most exciting time for advancing our knowledge and ultimately for preventing the onset and development of mental disorders at the earliest signs of presentation.

References

Introduction

Benes, F. M. (1989). Myelination of cortical–hippocampal relays during late adolescence. *Schizophrenia Bulletin, 15,* 585–593.

Benson, P. L., Leffert, N., Scales, P. C., & Blyth, D. A. (1998). Beyond the "village" rhetoric: Creating health communities for children and adolescents. *Applied Developmental Science, 2,* 138–159.

Booth, A., Johnson, D. R., Granger, D. A., Crouter, A., & McHale, S. (2003). Testosterone and child and adolescent adjustment: The moderating role of parent–child relationships. *Developmental Psychology, 39,* 85–98.

Brener, N. D., Martindale, J., & Weist, M. D. (2001). Mental health and social services: Results from the School Health Policies and Programs Study 2000. *Journal of School Health, 71,* 305–312.

Burns, B. J., Costello, E. J., Angold, A., Tweed, D., Stangl, D., Farmer, E. M., et al. (1995). Children's mental health service use across service sectors. *Health Affairs, 14,* 147–159.

Casey, B. J., Giedd, J. N., & Thomas, K. M. (2000). Structural and functional brain development and its relation to cognitive development. *Biological Psychology, 54,* 241–257.

Caspi, A., Sugden, K., Moffitt, T. E., Taylor, A., Craig, I. W., Harrington, H., et al. (2003). Influence of life stress on depression: Moderation by a polymorphism in the 5-HTT gene. *Science, 301*(5631), 386–389.

Charney, D. S., & Deutch, A. (1996). A functional neuroanatomy of anxiety and fear: Implications for the pathophysiology and treatment of anxiety disorders. *Critical Reviews in Neurobiology, 10,* 419–446.

Chin, H. P., Guillermo, G., Prakken, S., & Eisendrath, S. (2000). Psychiatric training in primary care residency programs. A national survey. *Psychosomatics, 41,* 412–417.

Chugani, H. T. (1996). Neuroimaging of developmental nonlinearity and developmental pathologies. In R. W. Thatcher, G. R. Lyon, J. Rumsey, & N. Krasnegor (Eds.), *Developmental neuroimaging: Mapping the development of brain and behavior* (pp. 187–195). San Diego: Academic Press.

Commission on Chronic Illness. (1957). Chronic illness in the United States. In L. Breslow (Ed.), *Prevention of chronic illness, Vol. 1.* Cambridge, MA: Harvard University Press.

Cunningham, M. G., Bhattacharyya, S., & Benes, F. M. (2002). Amygdalo-cortical sprouting continues into early adulthood: Implications for the development of normal and abnormal function during adolescence. *Journal of Comparative Neurology, 453,* 116–130.

Dahl, R. E. (2004). Adolescent brain development: A period of vulnerabilities and opportunities. *Annals of the New York Academy of Sciences, 1021,* 1–21.

Davidson, R. J., Abercrombie, H., Nitschke, J. B., & Putnam, K. (1999). Regional brain function, emotion and disorders of emotion. *Current Opinion in Neurobiology, 9,* 228–234.

Dorn, L. D., & Chrousos, G. P. (1997). The neurobiology of stress: Understanding regulation of affect during female biological transitions. *Seminars in Reproductive Endocrinology, 15,* 19–35.

Dorn, L. D., Hitt, S. F., & Rotenstein, D. (1999). Biopsychological and cognitive differences in children with premature vs. on-time adrenarche. *Archives of Pediatrics and Adolescent Medicine, 153,* 137–146.

Falloon, I.R.H., Kydd, R. R., Coverdale, J. H., & Laidlaw, T. M. (1996). Early detection and intervention for initial episodes of schizophrenia. *Schizophrenia Bulletin, 22,* 271–282.

FDA Public Health Advisory (2004, Mar. 22). Retrieved May 21, 2004, from http://www.fda.gov/ cder/ drug/antidepressants/*Antidepressants PHA.htm.*

Fitzpatrick, K. M. (1997). Aggression and environmental risk among low income African-American youth. *Journal of Adolescent Health, 21,* 172–178.

Forman, R. F. (2003). Availability of opioids on the Internet. *Journal of the American Medical Association, 290,* 889.

Fuster, J. M. (1989). *The prefrontal cortex: anatomy, physiology, and neuropsychology of the frontal lobe.* New York: Raven Press.

Garland, A. F., Hough, R. L., McCabe, K. M., Yeh, M., Wood, P. A., Aarons, G. A. (2001). Prevalence of psychiatric disorders in youth across five sectors of care. *Journal of the American Academy of Child and Adolescent Psychiatry, 40,* 409–418.

Giedd, J. N. (2004). Structural magnetic resonance imaging of the adolescent brain. *Annals of the New York Academy of Sciences, 1021,* 77–85.

Giedd, J. N., Blumenthal, J., Jeffries, N. O., Castellanos, F. X., Liu, H., Zijdenbos, A., et al. (1999). Brain development during childhood and adolescence: A longitudinal MRI study. *Nature Neuroscience, 2,* 861–863.

Giedd, J. N., Castellanos, F. X., Rajapakse, J. C., Vaituzis, A. C., & Rapoport, J. L. (1997). Sexual dimorphism of the developing human brain. *Progress in Neuropsyphopharmacology and Biological Psychiatry, 21,* 1185–1201.

Goldman-Rakic, P. S., Isseroff, A., Schwartz, M. L., & Bugbee, N. M. (1983). The neurobiology of cognitive development. In P. H. Mussen (Ed.), *Handbook of child psychology: Vol. II. Infancy and developmental psychobiology* (pp. 281–344). New York: John Wiley & Sons.

Goode, E. (2003, December 11). British warning on antidepressant use for youth. *New York Times.* Retrieved December 11, 2003, from http://www.nytimes.com.

Gordon, R. (1983). An operational classification of disease prevention. *Public Health Reports, 98,* 107–109.

Gordon, R. (1987). An operational classification of disease prevention. In J. Steinberg & M. Silverman (Eds.), *Preventing mental disorders: A research perspective* (DHHS Publication No. (ADM) 87–1492: pp. 20–26. Rockville, MD: Alcohol, Drug Abuse, and Mental Health Administration.

Haggerty, R. J., & Mrazek, P. J. (1994). *Reducing the risk of mental disorders.* Washington, DC: National Academy Press.

Harris, G. (2004, March 23). Regulators want antidepressants to list warning. *New York Times.* Retrieved March 24, 2004, from http://www.nytimes.com.

Harris, J. R. (1995). Where is the child's environment? A group socialization theory of development. *Psychological Review, 102,* 458–459.

Hessl, D., Glaser, B., Dyer-Friedman, J., Blasey, C., Hastie, T., Gunnar, M., et al. (2002). Cortisol and behavior in fragile X syndrome. *Psychoneuroendocrinology, 27,* 855–872.

Holden, C. (2004). Psychopharmacology. FDA weighs suicide risk in children on antidepressants. *Science, 303,* 745.

Huttenlocher, P. R. (1979). Synaptic density of human frontal cortex—developmental changes and effects of aging. *Brain Research, 163,* 195–205.

Institute of Medicine. (1989). *Research on children and adolescents with mental, behavioral, and developmental disorders.* Washington, DC: National Academy Press.

Institute of Medicine. (1994). *Reducing risk for mental disorders: Frontiers for prevention intervention research.* Washington, DC: National Academy Press.

Irwin, C. E., Burg, S. J., & Cart, C. U. (2002). America's adolescents: Where have we been, where are we going? *Journal of Adolescent Health, 31,* 91–121.

Jacobson, K. C., Prescott, C. A., & Kendler, K. S. (2002). Sex differences in the genetic and environmental influences on the development of antisocial behavior. *Development and Psychopathology, 14,* 395–416.

Kellogg, C. K. (1998). Early developmental modulation of GABA(A) receptor function: Influence on adaptive responses. *Perspectives on Developmental Neurobiology, 5,* 219–234.

Killgore, W.D.S., Oki, M., & Yurgelun-Todd, D. A. (2001). Sex-specific developmental changes in amygdala responses to affective faces. *Neuroreport, 12,* 427–433.

Leavell, H. R., & Clark, E. G. (1965). *Preventive medicine for the doctor in his community* (3rd ed.) New York: McGraw-Hill.

Leffert, N., Benson, P. L., Scales, P. C., Sharma, A. R., Drake, D. R., & Blyth, D. A. (1998). Developmental assets: Measurement and prediction of risk behaviors among adolescents. *Applied Developmental Science, 2,* 209–230.

Levisohn, L., Cronin-Golomb, A., & Schmahmann, J. D. (2000). Neuropsychological consequences of cerebellar tumour resection in children: Cerebellar cognition affective syndrome in a paediatric population. *Brain, 123,* 1041–1050.

Luna, B., & Sweeney, J. A. (2004). fMRI studies of the development of response inhibition. *Annals of the New York Academy of Sciences, 1021,* 296–309.

Nathan, P. E., & Gorman, J. M. (2002). *A guide to treatments that work.* (2nd ed.) New York: Oxford University Press.

National Drug Intelligence Center. (2002, October). *Information bulletin: Drugs, youth and the Internet.* Washington, DC: U.S. Dept. of Justice.

Nelson, C. A. (2004). Brain development during puberty and adolescence. *Annals of the New York Academy of Sciences, 1021,* 105–109.

Nottelmann, E. D., Susman, E. J., Inoff-Germain, G., Cutler, G. B., Jr., Loriaux, D. L., & Chrousos, G. P. (1987). Developmental processes in early adolescence: Relationships between adolescent adjustment problems and chronologic age, pubertal stage, and puberty-related serum hormone levels. *Journal of Pediatrics, 110,* 473–480.

Nurse, S., & Lacaille, J. C. (1999). Late maturation of GABA(B) synaptic transmission in area CA1 of the rat hippocampus. *Neuropharmacology, 38,* 1733–1742.

Olfson, M., Marcus, S. C., Weissman, M. M., & Jensen, P. S. (2002). National trends in the use of psychotropic medications by children. *Journal of the American Academy of Child and Adolescent Psychiatry, 41,* 514–521.

Parent, A. S., Teilmann, G., Juul, A., Skakkebaek, N. E., Toppari, J., & Bourguignon, J. P. (2003). The timing of normal puberty and the age limits of sexual precocity: Variations around the world, secular trends, and changes after migration. *Endocrine Reviews 24,* 668–693.

Pine, D. S., Grun, J., Zarahn, E., Fyer, A., Koda, V., Li, W., et al. (2001). Cortical brain regions engaged by masked emotional faces in adolescents and adults: An fMRI study. *Emotion, 1,* 137–147.

Prather, M. D., Lavenex, P., Mauldin-Jourdain, M. L., Mason, W. A., Capitanio, J. P., Mendoza, S. P., et al. (2001). Increased social fear and decreased fear of objects in monkeys with neonatal amygdala lesions. *Neuroscience, 106,* 653–658.

Rakic, P., Bourgeois, J.-P., & Goldman-Rakic, P. S. (1994). Synaptic development of the cerebral cortex: Implications for learning, memory, and mental illness. In J. van Pelt, M. A. Corner, H.B.M. Uylings, & F. H. Lopes da Silva (Eds.), *Progress in brain research: Vol. 102. The self-organizing brain: From growth cones to functional networks* (pp. 227–243). Amsterdam: Elsevier.

Rieger, D. (1990). Adolescent pregnancy prevention: Primary, secondary, and tertiary. *Journal of the American Medical Association, 263,* 813.

Rosso, I. M., Young, A. D., Femia L. A., & Yurgelun-Todd, D. A. (2004). Cognitive and emotional components of frontal lobe functioning in childhood and adolescence. *Annals of the New York Academy of Sciences, 1021,* 355–362.

Rupprecht, R., & Holsboer, F. (1999). Neuroactive steroids: Mechanisms of action and neuropsychopharmacological perspectives. *Trends in Neurosciences, 22,* 410–416.

Rushton, J. L., & Whitmire, J. T. (2001). Pediatric stimulant and selective serotonin reuptake inhibitor prescription trends: 1992 to 1998. *Archives of Pediatric and Adolescent Medicine 155,* 560–565.

Scales, P. C., Benson, P. L., Leffert, N., & Blyth, D. A. (2000). Contributions of developmental assets to the prediction of thriving among adolescents. *Applied Developmental Science, 4,* 27–46.

Schmahmann, J. D., & Sherman, J. C. (1998). The cerebellar cognitive affective syndrome. *Brain, 121,* 561–579.

Silberg, J., Pickles, A., Rutter, M., Hewitt, J., Simonoff, E., Maes, H., et al. (1999). The influence of genetic factors and life stres on depression among adolescent girls. *Archives of General Psychiatry, 56,* 225–232.

Slade, E. P. (2003). The relationship between school characteristics and the availability of mental health and related health services in middle and high schools in the United States. *Journal of Behavorial Health Services and Research, 30,* 382–392.

Sowell, E. R., Thompson, P. M., Holmes, C. J., Batth, R., Jernigan, T. L., & Toga, A. W. (1999a). Localizing age-related changes in brain structure between childhood and adolescence using statistical parametric mapping. *Neuroimage, 9,* 587–597.

Sowell, E. R., Thompson, P. M., Holmes, C. J., Jernigan, T. L., & Toga, A. W. (1999b). In vivo evidence for post-adolescent brain maturation in frontal and striatal regions. *Nature Neuroscience, 2,* 859–861.

Spear, L. P. (2000). The adolescent brain and age-related behavioral manifestations. *Neuroscience and Biobehavioral Reviews, 24,* 417–463.

Teicher, M. H., & Andersen, S. L. (1999, October). *Limbic serotonin turnover plunges during puberty.* Poster session presented at the annual meeting of the Society for Neuroscience, Miami Beach, FL.

Terasawa, E., & Timiras, P. S. (1968). Electrophysiological study of the limbic system in the rat at onset of puberty. *American Journal of Physiology, 215,* 1462–1467.

U.S. Department of Health and Human Services. (1999). *Mental health: A report of the surgeon general.* Rockville, MD: U.S. Department of Health and Human Services, Substance Abuse and Mental Health Services Administration, Center for Mental Health Services, National Institutes of Health, National Institute of Mental Health.

van Eden, C. G., Kros, J. M., & Uylings, H.B.M. (1990). The development of the rat prefrontal cortex: Its size and development of connections with thalamus, spinal cord and other cortical areas. In H.B.M. Uylings, C. G. van Eden, J.P.C. De Bruin, M. A. Corner, & M.G.P. Feenstra (Eds.), *Progress in Brain Research: Vol. 85. The prefrontal cortex: Its structure, function and pathology* (pp. 169–183). Amsterdam: Elsevier.

Walker, E. F., Walder, D. J., & Reynolds, F. (2001). Developmental changes in cortisol secretion in normal and at-risk youth. *Development and Psychopathology, 13,* 721–732.

Wells, K. B., Kataoka, S. H., & Asarnow, J. R. (2001). Affective disorders in children and adolescents: Addressing unmet need in primary care settings. *Biological Psychiatry, 49,* 1111–1120.

White, T., & Nelson, C. A. (in press). Neurobiological development during childhood and adolescence. In R. L. Findling & S. C. Schulz (Eds.), *Juvenile-onset schizophrenia: assessment, neurobiology, and treatment.* Baltimore, MD: John Hopkins University Press.

Wolfer, D. P., & Lipp, H. P. (1995). Evidence for physiological growth of hippocampal mossy fiber collaterals in the guinea pig during puberty and adulthood. *Hippocampus, 5,* 329–340.

Wren, F. J., Scholle, S. H., Heo, J., & Comer, D. M. (2003). Pediatric mood and anxiety syndromes in primary care: who gets identified? *International Journal of Psychiatry in Medicine, 33,* 1–16.

Yurgelun-Todd, D. A., Killgore, W.D.S., & Cintron, C. B. (2003). Cognitive correlates of medial temporal lobe development across adolescence: A magnetic resonance imaging study. *Perceptual and Motor Skills, 96,* 3–17.

Zill, N., & Schoenborn, C. A. (1990). Developmental, learning, and emotional problems: Health of our nation's children, United States, 1988. In *Advance data from vital and health statistics (No. 190).* Hyattsville, MD: National Center for Health Statistics.

Zito, J. M., Safer, D. J., dos Reis, S., Gardner, J. F., Magder, L., Soeken, K., et al. (2003). Psychotropic practice patterns for youth: A 10-year perspective. *Archives of Pediatric and Adolescent Medicine, 157,* 17–25.

Part I: Depression and Bipolar Disorder

Aalto-Setälä, T. Marttunen, M., Tuulio-Hendriksson, A., Poikolainen, K., & Lonnqvist, J. (2001). One month prevalence of depression and other PSM-IV disorders among young adults. *Psychological Medicine 31,* 791–801.

Aber, J. L., Bennett, N. G., Conley, D. C., & Li, J. (1997). The effects of poverty on child health and development. *Annual Review of Public Health, 18,* 463–483.

Abramson, L. Y., Metalsky, G. I., & Alloy, L. B. (1989). Hopelessness depression: A theory-based subtype of depression. *Psychological Review, 96,* 358–372.

Abramson, L. Y., Seligman, M. E. P., & Teasdale, I. (1978). Learned helplessness in humans: Critique and reformulation. *Journal of Abnormal Psychology, 87,* 49–59.

Ackerson, J., Scogin, F., McKendree-Smith, N., & Lyman, R. D. (1998). Cognitive bibliotherapy for mild and moderate adolescent depressive symptomatology. *Journal of Consulting and Clinical Psychology, 66,* 685–690.

Agency for Health Care Policy Research. (1993). *Treatment of major depression. Clinical guidelines, Vol. 5, No. 2.* (AHCPR Publication No. 93-0551). Rockville, MD: U.S. Department of Health and Human Services.

Agency for Health Care Policy and Research. (1999). *Treatment of depression—Newer pharmacotherapies: Summary, evidence report/technology assessment, No. 7.* Rockville, MD: U.S. Department of Health and Human Services, retrieved from http://www.ahcpr.gov/clinic/deprsumm.htm

Akiskal, H. S., Downs, J., Jordan, P., Watson, S., Daugherty, D., & Pruitt, D. B. (1985). Affective disorders in referred children and younger siblings of manic-depressives: Mode of onset and prospective course. *Archives of General Psychiatry, 42,* 996–1003.

Akiskal, H. S., & McKinney, W. T. (1975). Overview of recent research in depression: Integration of ten conceptual models into a comprehensive clinical frame. *Archives of General Psychiatry, 32,* 285–305.

Allgood-Merten, B., Lewinson, P. M., & Hops, H. (1990). Sex differences and adolescent depression. *Journal of Abnormal Psychology, 99,* 55–63.

Alloy, L. B., Abramson, L. Y., Hogan, M. E., Whitehouse, W. G., Rose, D. T., Robinson, M. S., et al. (2000). The Temple-Wisconsin Cognitive Vulnerability to Depression Project: Lifetime history of Axis I psychopathology in individuals at high and low cognitive risk for depression. *Journal of Abnormal Psychology, 109,* 403–418.

Altmann, E. O., & Gotlib, I. H. (1988). The social behavior of depressed children: An observational study. *Journal of Abnormal Child Psychology, 16,* 29–44.

American Psychiatric Association. (1994). *Diagnostic and statistical manual of mental disorders* (4th ed., text revisions). Washington, DC.

American Psychiatric Association (2000). *Practice*

guidelines for the treatment of patients with major depressive disorder, 2nd Ed. Washington, DC: American Psychiatric Publishing, Inc.

American Psychiatric Association. *Practice guideline for the treatment of patients with bipolar disorder.* (1994). Washington DC: American Psychiatric Publishing, Inc.

Andrews, B. (1995). Bodily shame as a mediator between abusive experiences and depression. *Journal of Abnormal Psychology, 104,* 277–285.

Andrews, B., Valentine, E. R., & Valentine, J. D. (1995). Depression and eating disorders following abuse in childhood in two generations of women. *British Journal of Clinical Psychology, 34* (Pt 1), 37–52.

Angold, A., & Costello, E. J. (1993). Depressive comorbidity in children and adolescents: Empirical, theoretical and methodological issues. *American Journal of Psychiatry, 150,* 1779–1791.

Angold, A., Costello, E. J., & Erkanli, A. (1999). Comorbidity. *Journal of Child Psychology and Psychiatry, 40,* 57–87.

Angold, A., Costello, E. J., & Worthman, C. M. (1998). Puberty and depression: The roles of age, pubertal status and pubertal timing. *Psychological Medicine, 28,* 51–61.

Arean, P. A., Perri, M. G., Nezu, A. M., Schein, R. L., Christopher, F., & Joseph, T. X. (1993). Comparative effectiveness of social problem-solving therapy and reminiscence therapy as treatments for depression in older adults. *Journal of Consulting and Clinical Psychology, 61,* 1003–1010.

Arnarson, E. O., & Craighead, W. E. (2004, November). *Prevention of depression among adolescents in Iceland.* Paper presented at the meeting of the Association for the Advancement of Behavior Therapy, New Orleans.

Aronson, R., Offman, H. J., Joffe, R. T., & Naylor, C. D. (1996) Triiodothyronine augmentation in the treatment of refractory depression. A meta-analysis. *Archives of General Psychiatry, 53,* 842–848.

Asarnow, J. R., Carlson, G. A., & Guthrie, D. (1987). Coping strategies, self-perceptions, hopelessness, and perceived family environments in depressed and suicidal children. *Journal of Consulting and Clinical Psychology, 55,* 361–366.

Asarnow, J. R., Goldstein, M. J., Tompson, M., & Guthrie, D. (1993). One-year outcomes of depressive disorders in child psychiatric inpatients: Evaluation of the prognostic power of a brief measure of expressed emotion. *Journal of Child Psychology and Psychiatry, 34,* 129–137.

Aseltine, R. H., Jr., Gore, S., & Colten, M. E. (1994).

Depression and the social developmental context of adolescence. *Journal of Personality and Social Psychology, 67,* 252–263.

Bandura, A. (1977). *Social learning theory.* Englewood Cliff, NJ: Prentice Hall.

Barbe, R. P., Bridge, J., Birmaher, B., Kolko, D. J., & Brent, D. A. (2004a). Lifetime history of sexual abuse, clinical presentation, and outcome in a clinical trial for adolescent depression. *Journal of Clinical Psychiatry, 65,* 77–83.

Barbe, R. P., Bridge, J., Birmaher, B., Kolko, D., & Brent, D. A. (2004b). Suicidality and its relationship to treatment outcome in depressed adolescents. *Suicide and Life-Threatening Behavior, 34,* 44–55.

Barber, B. K. (1996). Parental psychological control: Revisiting a neglected construct. *Child Development, 67,* 3296–3319.

Barkham, M., Hardy, G. E., & Startup, M. (1994) The structure, validity and clinical relevance of the inventory of interpersonal problems. *British Journal of Medical Psychology, 67* (Pt 2), 171–185.

Barrera, A. Z., & Craighead, W. E. (2004). *Depression among adolescent and adult Latinos in the United States: A review.* Unpublished manuscript. Available from Alinne Z. Barrera, Department of Psychology, University of Colorado, Boulder, CO 80309–0345.

Bassuk, E. L., Buckner, J. C., Perloff, J. N., & Bassuk, S. S. (1998). Prevalence of mental health and substance use disorders among homeless and low-income housed mothers. *American Journal of Psychiatry, 155,* 1561–1564.

Bauer, M. S., McBride, L., Chase, G., Sachs, G., & Shea, N. (1998) Manual-based group psychotherapy for bipolar disorder: A feasibility study. *Journal of Clinical Psychiatry, 59,* 449–455.

Baumann, P. (1996) Pharmacokinetic–pharmacodynamic relationship of the selective serotonin reuptake inhibitors. *Clinical Pharmacokinetics, 31,* 444–469.

Beardslee, W. R., Gladstone, T. R. G., Wright, E. J., & Cooper, A. B. (2003). A family-based approach to the prevention of depressive symptoms in children at risk: Evidence of parental and child change. *Pediatrics, 112,* e119–131.

Beardslee, W. R., Keller, M. B., Seifer, R., Lavori, P. W., Staley, D., Poderefsky, D., et al. (1996). Prediction of adolescent affective disorder: Effects of prior parental affective disorders and child psychopathology. *Journal of the American Academy of Child and Adolescent Psychiatry, 35,* 279–288.

Beardslee, W. R., Versage, E. M., & Gladstone,

T. R. G. (1998). Children of affectively ill parents: A review of the past ten years. *Journal of the American Academy of Child and Adolescent Psychiatry, 37*, 1134–1141.

Beck, A. T. (1967). *Depression: Clinical experimental and theoretical aspects*. New York: Harper and Row.

Beck, A. T. (1983). Cognitive therapy of depression: new perspectives. In P. Clayton & J. E. Barrett (Eds.), *Treatment of depression: old controversies and new approaches* (pp. 265–290). New York: Raven Press.

Beck, A. T., Rush, A. J., Shaw, B. F., & Emery, G. (1979). *Cognitive therapy of depression*. New York: Guilford Press.

Bennett, D. S., Pendley, J. S., & Bates, J. E. (1995). Daughter and mother report of individual symptoms on the Children's Depression Inventory. *Journal of Adolescent Health, 20*, 51–57.

Berns, G. S., & Nemeroff, C. B. (2003). The neurobiology of bipolar disorder. *American Journal of Medical Genetics, 123C*, 76–84.

Berrettini, W. H., Ferraro, T. N., Goldin, L. R., Weeks, D. E., Detera-Wadleigh, S., Nurnberger, J. I., et al. (1994). Chromosome 18 DNA markers and manic depressive illness: evidence for a susceptibility gene. *Proceedings of the National Academy of Sciences of the United States of America, 91*, 5918–5921.

Berrettini, W. H., Ferraro T. N., Goldin, L. R., Detera-Wadleigh, S. D., Choi, H., Muniec, D., et al. (1997). Linkage studies of bipolar illness. *Archives of General Psychiatry, 54*, 32–39.

Biederman, J. (1998). Resolved: Mania is mistaken for ADHD in prepubertal children. *Journal of the American Academy of Child and Adolescent Psychiatry, 37*, 1091–1093.

Biederman, J. Faraone, S., Mick, E., Lelon, E. (1995). Psychiatric comorbidity among referred juveniles with major depression: fact or artifact? *Journal of the American Academy of Child and Adolescent Psychiatry 34*, 579–590.

Biederman, J., Faraone, S. V., Chu, M., Wozniak, J. (1999). Further evidence of a bidirectional overlap between juvenile mania and conduct disorder in children. *Journal of the American Academy of Child and Adolescent Psychiatry, 38*, 468–476.

Biederman, J., Faraone, S. V., Hatch, M., Menin, D., Taylor, A., & George, P. (1997). Conduct disorder with and without mania in a referred sample of ADHD children. *Journal of Affective Disorders, 44*, 177–188.

Biederman, J., Faraone, S. V., Marrs, A., Moore, P., Garcia, J., Ablon, S., et al. (1997). Panic disorder and agoraphobia in consecutively referred children and adolescents. *Journal of the American Academy of Child and Adolescent Psychiatry, 36*, 214–223.

Biederman, J., Faraone, S. V., Mick, E., Wozniak, J., Chen L., Ouellette, C., et al. (1996). Attention deficit hyperactivity disorder and juvenile mania: An overlooked comorbidity? *Journal of the American Academy of Child and Adolescent Psychiatry, 35*, 997–1008.

Biederman, J., Klein, R. G., Pine, D. S., & Klein, D. F. (1998). Resolved: Mania is mistaken for ADHD in prepubertal children. *Journal of the American Academy of Child and Adolescent Psychiatry, 37*, 1091–1096; discussion 1096–1099.

Biederman, J., Rosenbaum, J. F., Hirshfeld, D. R., Faraone, S. V., Bolduc, E. A., Gersten, M., et al. (1990) Psychiatric correlates of behavioral inhibition in young children of parents with and without psychiatric disorders. *Archives of General Psychiatry, 47*, 21–26.

Biederman, J., Wilens, T. E., Mick, E., Faraone, S., Weber, W., Curtis, S., et al. (1997). Is ADHD a risk factor for psychoactive substance use disorders? Findings from a four-year prospective follow-up study. *Journal of the American Academy of Child and Adolescent Psychiatry, 36*, 21–29.

Bifulco, A., Brown, G. W., & Adler, Z. (1991). Early sexual abuse and clinical depression in adult life. *British Journal of Psychiatry, 159*, 115–122.

Billings, A. G., & Moos, R. H. (1983). Comparisons of children of depressed and nondepressed parents: A social–environmental perspective. *Journal of Abnormal Child Psychology, 11*, 463–485.

Birmaher, B., Brent, D. A., Kolko, D., Baugher, M., Bridge, J., Iyengar, S., et al. (2000). Clinical outcome after short-term psychotherapy for adolescents with major depressive disorder. *Archives of General Psychiatry, 57*, 29–36.

Birmaher, B., McCafferty, J. P., Bellew, K. M., & Beebe, K. L. (2001). *Disruptive disorders as predictors of response in adolescents with depression*. Poster presented at the 48th annual meeting of the American Academy of Child and Adolescent Psychiatry, Honolulu, HI.

Birmaher, B., Ryan, N. D., Williamson, D. E., Brent, D. A., Kaufman, J., Dahl, R. E., et al. (1996a). Childhood and adolescent depression: a review of the past 10 years. Part I. *Journal of the American Academy of Child and Adolescent Psychiatry, 35*, 1427–1439.

Birmaher, B., Ryan, N. D., Williamson, D. E., Brent, D. A., & Kaufman, J. (1996b) Childhood and adolescent depression: a review of the past 10 years. Part II. *Journal of the American Academy of Child and Adolescent Psychiatry, 35,* 1575–1583.

Blackburn, I. M., Eunson, K. M., & Bishop, S. (1986). A two-year naturalistic follow-up of depressed patients treated with cognitive therapy, pharmacotherapy and a combination of both. *Journal of Affective Disorders, 10,* 67–75.

Blackburn, I. M., & Moore, R. G. (1997). Controlled acute and follow-up trial of cognitive therapy and pharmacotherapy in outpatients with recurrent depression. *British Journal of Psychiatry, 171,* 328–334.

Blackwood, D. H. R., He, L., Morris, S. W., McLean, A., Whitton, C., Thomson, M., et al. (1996). A locus for bipolar affection disorder on chromosome 4p. *Nature Genetics, 12,* 427–430.

Blatt, S. J., Quinlan, D. M., Chevron, E. S., McDonald, C., & Zuroff, D. (1982). Dependency and self-criticism: Psychological dimensions of depression. *Journal of Consulting and Clinical Psychology, 50,* 113–124.

Bolton, P., Bass, J., Neugebauer, R., Verdeli, H., Clougherty, K. F., Wickramaratne, P., et al. (2003). Group interpersonal psychotherapy for depression in rural Uganda: A randomized controlled trial. *Journal of the American Medical Association, 289,* 3117–3124.

Borchardt, C. M., & Bernstein, G. A. (1995). Comorbid disorders in hospitalized bipolar adolescents compared with unipolar depressed adolescents. *Child Psychiatry and Human Development, 26,* 11–18.

Bowden, C. L., Brugger, A. M., Swann, A. C., Calabrese, J. R., Janicak, P. G., Petty, F., et al. (1994). Efficacy of divalproes vs. lithium and placebo in the treatment of mania. The Depakote Mania Study Group. *Journal of the American Medical Association, 271,* 918–924.

Bowden, C. L., Calabrese, J. R., McElroy, S. L., Rhodes, L. J., Keck, P. E., Jr., Cookson, J., et al. (1999). The efficacy of lamotrigine in rapid cycling and non-rapid cycling patients with bipolar disorder. *Biological Psychiatry, 45,* 953–958.

Bowden, C. L., Davis, J., Morris, D., Swann, A., Calabrese, J., Lambert, M., & Goodnick, P. (1997). Effect size of efficacy measures comparing divalproex, lithium and placebo in acute mania. *Depression and Anxiety, 6,* 26–30.

Bowden, C. L., Lecrubier, Y., Bauer, M., Goodwin, G., Greil, W., & Sachs, G. (2000). Maintenance therapies for classic and other forms of bipolar disorder. *Journal of Affective Disorders, 59* (Suppl. 1), S57–S67.

Bowen, R., South, M., & Hawkes, J. (1994). Mood swings in patients with panic disorder. *Canadian Journal of Psychiatry, 39,* 91–94.

Bowlby, J. (1980). By ethology out of psychoanalysis: An experiment in interbreeding. *Animal Behavior, 28* (Pt 3), 649–656.

Brent, D. A., Holder, D., Kolko, D., Birmaher, B., Baugher, M., Roth, C., et al. (1997). A clinical psychotherapy trial for adolescent depression comparing cognitive, family, and supportive treatments. *Archives of General Psychiatry, 54,* 877–885.

Brent, D. A., Kolko, D., Birmaher, B., Baugher, M., & Bridge, J. (1999). A clinical trial for adolescent depression: Predictors of additional treatment in the acute and follow-up phases of the trial. *Journal of the American Academy of Child and Adolescent Psychiatry, 38,* 263–270.

Brent, D. A., Kolko, D., Birmaher, B., Baugher, M., Bridge, J., Roth, C., et al. (1998). Predictors of treatment efficacy in a clinical trial of three psychosocial treatments for adolescent depression. *Journal of the American Academy of Child and Adolescent Psychiatry, 37,* 906–914.

Brent, D. A., Perper, J. A., Goldstein, C. E., Kolko, D. J., Allan, M. J., Allman, C. J., et al. (1988). Risk factors for adolescent suicide: A comparison of adolescent suicide victims with suicidal inpatients. *Archives of General Psychiatry, 45,* 581–588.

Breslau, N., & Davis, G. C. (1992). Posttraumatic stress disorder in an urban population of young adults: Risk factors for chronicity. *American Journal of Psychiatry, 149,* 671–675.

Breslau, N., Davis, G. C., & Andreski, P. (1995). Risk factors for PTSD-related traumatic events: A prospective analysis. *American Journal of Psychiatry, 152,* 529–535.

Bruce, M. L., Takeuchi, D. T., & Leaf, P. J. (1991). Poverty and psychiatric status: Longitudinal evidence from the New Haven Epidemiologic Catchment Area Study. *Archives of General Psychiatry, 48,* 470–474.

Brunson, K. L., Eghbal-Ahmadi, M., Bender, R., Chen, Y., & Baram, T. Z. (2001). Long-term, progressive hippocampal cell loss and dysfunction induced by early-life administration of corticotropin-releasing hormone reproduce the effects of early-life stress. *Proceedings of the National Academy of Sciences of the United States of America, 98,* 8856–8861.

Buka, S. L., Stichick, T. L., Birdthistle, I., & Earls, F. J. (2001). Youth exposure to violence: Prevalence, risks, and consequences. *American Journal of Orthopsychiatry, 71,* 298–310.

Burge, D., Hammen, C., Davila, J., Daley, S. E., Paley, B., Lindberg, N., et al. (1997). The relationship between attachment cognitions and psychological adjustment in late adolescent women. *Development and Psychopathology, 9,* 151–167.

Burnam, M. A., Stein, J. A., Golding, J. M., Siegel, J. M., Sorenson, S. B., Forsythe, A. B., et al. (1988). Sexual assault and mental disorders in a community population. *Journal of Consulting and Clinical Psychology, 56,* 843–850.

Burnam, M. A., Wells, K. B., Leake, B., & Landsverk, J. (1988). Development of a brief screening instrument for detecting depressive disorders. *Medical Care, 26,* 775–789.

Burns, D. D. (1990). *Feeling good: The new mood therapy.* New York: Avon Books.

Burt, C. E., Cohen, L. H., & Bjorck, J. P. (1988). Perceived family environment as a moderator of young adolescents' life stress adjustment. *American Journal of Community Psychology, 16,* 101–122.

Butler, L. F., Meizitis, S., & Friedman, R. J. (1980). The effect of two school-based intervention programs on depressive symptoms in preadolescent children. *American Education Research Journal, 17,* 111–119.

Carlson, G. A. (1983). Bipolar affective disorders in childhood and adolescence. In D. P. Cantwell & G. A. Carlson (Eds.), *Affective disorders in childhood and adolescence: An update* (pp. 61–83). New York: Spectrum Publications.

Carlson, G. A. (1984). Classification issues of bipolar disorders in childhood. *Psychiatric Developments, 2,* 273–285.

Carlson, G. A., Bromet, E. J., & Sievers, S. (2000). Phenomenology and outcome of subjects with early- and adult-onset psychotic mania. *American Journal of Psychiatry, 157,* 213–219.

Carlson, G. A., & Kelly, K. L. (1998). Manic symptoms in psychiatrically hospitalized children—What do they mean? *Journal of Affective Disorders, 51,* 123–135.

Carlson, G. A., & Weintraub, S. (1993). Childhood behavior problems and bipolar disorder—Relationship or coincidence? *Journal of Affective Disorders, 28,* 143–153.

Caspi, A., Moffitt, T. E., Newman, D. L., & Silva, P. A. (1996). Behavioral observations at age 3 years predict adult psychiatric disorders. Longitudinal evidence from a birth cohort. *Archives of General Psychiatry, 53,* 1033–1039.

Caspi, A., Sugden, K., Moffitt, T. E., Taylor, A., Craig, I. W., Harrington, H., et al. (2003). Influence of life stress on depression: Moderation by a polymorphism in the 5-HTT gene. *Science, 301*(5631), 386–389.

Catalan, J., Gath, D. H., Anastasiades, P., Bond, S. A., Day, A., & Hall, L. (1991). Evaluation of a brief psychological treatment for emotional disorders in primary care. *Psychological Medicine, 21,* 1013–1018.

Chang, K., Adleman, N., Dienes, K., Barnea-Goraly, N., Reiss, A., & Ketter, T. (2003). Decreased N-acetyl-aspartate in children with familial bipolar disorder. *Biological Psychology, 53,* 1059–1065.

Chang, K., Adleman, N., Dienes, K., Simeonova, D., Menon, V., & Reiss, A. (2004). Anomalous prefrontal–subcortical activation in familial pediatric bipolar disorder. *Archives of General Psychiatry, 61,* 781–792.

Chang K. D., Ketter, T. A. (2001). Special issues in the treatment of paediatric bipolar disorder. *Expert Opinion on Pharmacotherapy 2,* 613–622.

Chang, K. D., Steiner, H., & Ketter, T. (2000). Psychiatric phenomenology of child and adolescent bipolar offspring. *Journal of the American Academy of Child and Adolescent Psychiatry, 39,* 453–460.

Cicchetti, D., Rogosch, F. A., & Toth, S. L. (1998). Maternal depressive disorder and contextual risk: Contributions to the development of attachment insecurity and behavior problems in toddlerhood. *Development and Psychopathology, 10,* 283–300.

Clark, L. A., Vittengl, J. R., Kraft, D., & Jarrett, R. B. (2003). Shared, not unique, components of personality and psychosocial functioning predict depression severity after acute-phase cognitive therapy. *Journal of Personality Disorders, 17,* 406–430.

Clark, L. A., Watson, D., & Mineka, S. (1994). Temperament, personality, and the mood and anxiety disorders. *Journal of Abnormal Psychology, 103,* 103–116.

Clarke, A. S., & Schneider, M. L. (1993). Prenatal stress has long-term effects on behavioral responses to stress in juvenile rhesus monkeys. *Developmental Psychobiology, 26,* 293–304.

Clarke, A. S., Wittwer, D. J., Abbott, D. H., & Schneider, M. L. (1994). Long-term effects of prenatal stress on HPA axis activity in juvenile rhesus monkeys. *Developmental Psychobiology, 27,* 257–269.

Clarke, G. N., Hawkins, W., Murphy, M., Sheeber, L. B., Lewinsohn, P. M., & Seeley, J. R. (1995). Targeted prevention of unipolar depressive disorder in an at-risk sample of high school adolescents: A randomized trial of a group cognitive intervention. *Journal of the American Academy of Child and Adolescent Psychiatry, 34,* 312–321.

Clarke, G., Hops, H., Lewinsohn, P. M., Andrew, J., & Williams, J. (1992). Cognitive-behavioral group treatment of adolescent depression: Prediction of outcome. *Behavior Therapy, 23,* 341–354.

Clarke, G. N., Hornbrook, M., Lynch, F., Polen, M., Gale, J., O'Connor, E., et al. (2002). Group cognitive-behavioral treatment for depressed adolescent offspring of depressed parents in a health maintenance organization. *Journal of the American Academy of Child and Adolescent Psychiatry, 41,* 305–313.

Clarke, G. N., Hornbrook, M., Lynch, F., Polen, M., Gale, J., Beardslee, W., et al. (2001). A randomized trail of a group cognitive intervention for preventing depression in adolescent offspring of depressed parents. *Archives of General Psychiatry, 58,* 1127–1134.

Clarke, G. N., Lewinsohn, P. N., & Hops, H. (1990). *Instructor's manual for the adolescent: Coping with depression course.* Portland, OR: Kaiser Permanente Center for Health Research. Available at: http//www.kpchr.org/acwd/acwd.html

Clarke, G. N., Lewinsohn, P. M., Rohde, P., Hops, H., & Seeley, J. R. (1999). Cognitive-behavioral group treatment of adolescent depression: Efficacy of acute group treatment and booster sessions. *Journal of the American Academy of Child and Adolescent Psychiatry, 38,* 272–279.

Clarkin, J. F., Glick, I. D., Haas, G. L., Spencer, J. H., Lewis, A. B., Peyser, J., et al. (1990). A randomized clinical trial of inpatient family intervention. Results for affective disorders. *Journal of Affective Disorders, 18,* 17–28.

Cloninger, C. R. (1987). A systematic method for clinical description and classification of personality variants: A proposal. *Archives of General Psychiatry, 44,* 573–588.

Cohen, I. H. (1987). Masked depression revisited. *Maryland Medical Journal, 36,* 571.

Cohen, P., Cohen, J., Kasen, S., Velez, C. N., Hartmark, C., Johnson, J., et al. (1993). An epidemiological study of disorders in late childhood and adolescence—I. Age- and gender-specific prevalence. *Journal of Child Psychology and Psychiatry, 34,* 851–867.

Cohn, J. F., & Tronick, E. (1989). Specificity of infants' response to mothers' affective behavior. *Journal of the American Academy of Child and Adolescent Psychiatry, 28,* 242–248.

Cole, D. A., & Rehm, L. P. (1986). Family interaction patterns and childhood depression. *Journal of Abnormal Child Psychology, 14,* 297–314.

Colom, F., Vieta, E., Reinares, M., Martinez-Aran, A., Torrent C., Goikolea, J. M., et al. (2003). Psychoeducation efficacy in bipolar disorders: Beyond compliance enhancement. *Journal of Clinical Psychiatry, 64,* 1101–1105.

Commission on Chronic Illness. (1957). *Chronic illness in the United States, Vol. 1.* Cambridge, MA: Harvard University Press.

Compas, B. E., Grant, K. E., & Ey, S. (1994). Psychosocial stress and child and adolescent depression: Can we be more specific? In W. M. Reynolds & H. F. Johnston (Eds.), *Handbook of depression in children and adolescents* (pp. 509–523). New York: Plenum Press.

Conte, H. R., Plutchik, R., Wild, K. V., & Karasu, T. B. (1986). Combined psychotherapy and pharmacotherapy for depression. *Archives of General Psychiatry, 43,* 471–479.

Cook, E. H., Wagner, K. D., March, J. S., March, J. S., Biederman J., Landau P., et al. (2001). Long-term sertraline treatment of children and adolescents with obsessive-compulsive disorder. *Journal of the American Academy of Child and Adolescent Psychiatry, 40,* 1175–1181.

Coplan, J. D., Andrews, M. W., Rosenblum, L. A., Owens, M. J., Friedman, S., Gorman, J. M., et al. (1996). Persistent elevations of cerebrospinal fluid concentrations of corticotropin-releasing factor in adult nonhuman primates exposed to early-life stressors: Implications for the pathophysiology of mood and anxiety disorders. *Proceedings of the National Academy of Sciences of the United States of America, 93,* 1619–1623.

Coplan, J. D., Smith, E. L., Altemus, M., Scharf, B. A., Owens, M. J., Nemeroff, C. B., et al. (2001). Variable foraging demand rearing: Sustained elevations in cisternal cerebrospinal fluid corticotropin-releasing factor concentrations in adult primates. *Biological Psychiatry, 50,* 200–204.

Costa, P. T., & McCrae, R. R. (1980). Influence of extraversion and neuroticism on subjective well-being: Happy and unhappy people. *Journal of Personality and Social Psychology, 38,* 668–678.

Costello, E. J., Angold, A., Burns, B. J., Erkanli, A., Stangl, D. K., & Tweed, D. L. (1996). The Great Smoky Mountains Study of Youth. Functional impairment and serious emotional disturbance. *Archives of General Psychiatry, 53,* 1137–1143.

Costello, E. J., Pine, D. S., Hammen, C., March, J. S., Plotsky, P. M., Weissman, M. M., et al. (2002). Development and natural history of mood disorders. *Biological Psychiatry, 52,* 529–542.

Coyle, J. T., Pine, D. S., Charney, D. S., Lewis, L., Nemeroff, C. B., Carlson, G. A., et al. (2003). Depression and Bipolar Support Alliance Consensus Development Panel. *Journal of the American Academy of Child and Adolescent Psychiatry, 42,* 1494–1503.

Craighead, W. E., Hart, A. B., Craighead, L. W., & Ilardi, S. S. (2002). Psychosocial treatments for major depressive disorder. In P. Nathan & J. Gorman (Eds.), *A guide to treatments that work* (2nd ed.) (pp. 245–261). New York: Oxford University Press.

Craighead, W. E., Miklowitz, D. J., Frank, E., & Vajk, F. C. (2002). Psychosocial treatments for bipolar disorder. In P. E. Nathan & J. M. Gorman (Eds.), *A guide to treatments that work* (2nd ed.) (pp. 263–275). New York: Oxford University Press.

Cross-National Collaborative Group. (1992). The changing rate of major depression: Cross-national comparisons. *Journal of the American Medical Association, 268,* 3098–3106.

Dahl, R. E. (2001). Affect regulation, brain development, and behavioral/emotional health in adolescence. *International Journal of Neuropsychiatric Medicine, 6,* 60–72.

Davanzo, P., Thomas, M. A., Yoe, K. Oshiro, T., Belin, T., Strober, M., et al. (2001). Decreased anterior cingulate myo-inositol creatine spectroscopy resonance with lithium treatment in children with bipolar disorder. *Neuropsychopharmacology 24,* 359–369.

De Bruyn, A., Soucry, D., Mendelbaum, K., Mendlewicz, J., & Van Broeckhoven, C. (1996). Linkage analysis of families with bipolar illness and chromosome 18 markers. *Biological Psychiatry, 39,* 679–688.

Decina, P., Kestenbaum, C. J., Farber, S., Kron, L., Gargan, M., Sackeim, H. A., et al. (1983). Clinical and psychological assessment of children of bipolar probands. *American Journal of Psychiatry, 140,* 548–553.

DelBello, M. P., Schwiers, M. L., Rosenberg, H. L., & Strakowski, S. M. (2002). A double-blind, randomized, placebo-controlled study of quetiapine as adjunctive treatment for adolescent mania. *Journal of the American Academy of Child and Adolescent Psychiatry, 41,* 1216–1223.

DeMulder, E. K., & Radke-Yarrow, M. (1991). Attachment with affectively ill and well mothers: Concurrent behavioral correlates. *Development and Psychopathology, 3,* 227–242.

Depression Guideline Panel. (1993). *Depression in primary care: Detection, diagnosis, and treatment. Quick reference guide for clinicians, No. 5.* (AHCPR publication No. 93-0552). Rockville, MD: U.S. Department of Health and Human Services, Public Health Service, Agency for Health Care Policy and Research.

Detra-Wadleigh, S. D., Badner, J. A., Goldin, L. R., Berrettini, W. H., Sanders, A. R., Rollins, D. Y., et al. (1996). Affected sib-pair analyses reveal support of prior evidence for a susceptibility locus for bipolar disorder on 21q. *American Journal of Human Genetics, 58,* 279–1285.

Detra-Wadleigh, S. D., Hsieh, W. T., Berrettini, W. H., Goldin, L. R., Rollins, D. Y., Muniec, D., et al. (1997). Genetic-linkage mapping for a susceptibility locus to bipolar illness: Chromosomes 2,3,4,7,9,10p, 11p, 22 and Xpter. *Neuropsychiatric Genetics, 74,* 206–218.

Detra-Wadleigh, S. D., Badner, J. A., Berrettini, W. H., Yoshikawa, T., Goldin, L. R., Turner, G., et al. (1999). Evidence for a bipolar susceptibility locus on 13q32 and other potential locion 1q32 and 18p11.2. *Proceedings of the National Academy of Sciences of the United States of America, 96,* 5604–5609.

DeRubeis, R. J., Gelfand, L. A., Tang, T. Z., & Simons, A. D. (1999). Medication versus cognitive behavior therapy for severely depressed outpatients: Mega-analysis of four randomized comparisons. *American Journal of Psychiatry, 156,* 1007–1013.

DeRubeis, R. J., Hollon, S. D., Amsterdam, J. D., Shelton, R. C., Young, P. R., Salomon, R. M., O'Reardon, J. P., Lovett, M. L., Gladis, M. M., Brown, L. L., & Gallop, R. (in press). Cognitive Therapy vs. medications in the treatment of moderate to severe depression. *Archives of General Psychiatry.* Paper presented at the World Congress of Behavioral and Cognitive Behavior Therapy, Vancouver, Canada.

Devine, D., Kempton, T., & Forehand, R. (1994). Adolescent depressed mood and young adult functioning: A longitudinal study. *Journal of Abnormal Child Psychology, 22,* 629–640.

Diamond, G. S., Reis, B. F., Diamond, G. M., Siqueland, L., & Isaacs, L. (2002). Attachment-based family therapy for depressed adolescents: A treatment development study. *Journal of the American Academy of Child and Adolescent Psychiatry, 41,* 1190–1196.

Digman J. M. (1989). Five robust trait dimensions: Development, stability, and utility. *Journal of Personality, 57,* 195–214.

Digman, J. M., & Inouye, J. (1986). Further specification of the five robust factors of personality. *Journal of Personality and Social Psychology, 50,* 116–123.

Digman, J. M., & Shmelyov, A. G. (1996). The structure of temperament and personality in Russian children. *Journal of Personality and Social Psychology, 71,* 341–351.

DiMascio, A., Weissman, M. M., Prusoff, B. A., Neu, C., Zwilling, M., & Klerman, G. L. (1979). Differential symptom reduction by drugs and psychotherapy in acute depression. *Archives of General Psychiatry, 36,* 1450–1456.

Dixon, J. F., & Ahrens, A. H. (1992). Stress and attributional style as predictors of self-reported depression in children. *Cognitive Therapy and Research, 16,* 623–634.

Dobson, K. S. (1989). A meta-analysis of the efficacy of cognitive therapy for depression. *Journal of Consulting and Clinical Psychology, 57,* 411–419.

Dohrenwend, B. P., Levav, I., Shrout, P. E., Schwartz, S., Naveh, G., Link, B. G., et al. (1992). Socioeconomic status and psychiatric disorders: The causation–selection issue. *Science, 255,* 946–952.

Dong, J., & Blier, P. (2001). Modification of norepinephrine and serotonin, but not dopamine, neuron firing by sustained bupropion treatment. *Psychopharmacology, 155,* 52–57.

Dube, S. R., Anda, R. F., Felitti, V. J., Chapman, D. P., Williamson, D. F., & Giles, W. H. (2001). Childhood abuse, household dysfunction, and the risk of attempted suicide throughout the lifespan: Findings from the Adverse Childhood Experiences Study. *Journal of the American Medical Association, 286,* 3089–3096.

DuBois, D. L., Felner, R. D., Brand, S., & George, G. R. (1999). Profiles of self-esteem in early adolescence: Identification and investigation of adaptive correlates. *American Journal of Community Psychology, 27,* 899–932.

Ehlers, C. L., Frank, E., & Kupfer, D. J. (1988). Social zeitgebers and biological rhythms. A unified approach to understanding the etiology of depression. *Archives of General Psychiatry, 45,* 948–952.

Elkin, I., Gibbons, R. D., Shea, T., Sotsky, S. M., Watkins, J. T., Pilkonis, P. A., et al. (1995). Initial severity and differential treatment outcome in the National Institute of Mental Health Treatment of Depression Collaborative Research Program. *Journal of Consulting and Clinical Psychology, 63,* 841–847.

Elkin, I., Shea, M. T., Watkins, J. T., Imber, S. D.,
Sotsky, S. M., Collins, J. F., et al. (1989). National Institute of Mental Health Treatment of Depression Collaborative Research Program: General effectiveness of treatments. *Archives of General Psychiatry, 46,* 971–982.

Emslie, G. J., Heiligenstein, J. H., Hoog, S. L., Wagner, K. D., Findling, R. L., McCracken, J. T., et al., (2004). Fluoxetine treatment for prevention of relapse of depression in children and adolescents: A double blind, placebo-controlled study. *Journal of the American Academy of Child and Adolescent Psychiatry, 43,* 1397–1405.

Emslie, G. J., Heiligenstein, J. H., Wagner, K. D., Hoog, S. L., Ernest, D. E., Brown, E., et al. (2002). Fluoxetine for acute treatment of depression in children and adolescents: A placebo-controlled, randomized clinical trial. *Journal of the American Academy of Child and Adolescent Psychiatry, 41,* 1205–1215.

Emslie, G. J., Rush, A. J., Weinberg, W. A., Kowatch, R. A., Hughes, C. W., Carmody, T., Rintelmann, J. (1997). A double-blind, randomized, placebo-controlled trial of fluoxetine in children and adolescents with depression. *Archives of General Psychiatry, 54,* 1031–1037.

Evans, M. D., Hollon, S. D., DeRubeis, R. J., Piasecki, J., Grove, W. M., Garvey, M. J., et al. (1992). Differential relapse following cognitive therapy and pharmacotherapy for depression. *Archives of General Psychiatry, 49,* 802–808.

Evans, D. L., & Nemeroff, C. B. (1983). The dexamethasone suppression test in mixed bipolar disorder. *American Journal of Psychiatry 140,* 615–617.

Ewald, H., Degn, B., Mors, B., & Kruse, T. A. (1998a). Significant linkage between bipolar affective disorder and chromosome 12q24. *Psychiatric Genetics, 3,* 131–140.

Ewald, H., Degn, B., Mors, B., & Kruse, T. A. (1998b). Support for the possible locus on chromosome 4p15 for bipolar affective disorder. *Molecular Psychiatry, 3,* 442–448.

Eysenck, H. J. (1947). *Dimensions of personality.* London: Kegan Paul.

Faedda, G., Baldessarini, R., Suppes, T., Tondo, L., Becker, I., & Lipschitz, D. S. (1995). Pediatric-onset bipolar disorder: A neglected clinical and public health problem. *Harvard Review of Psychiatry, 3,* 171–195.

Faraone, S. V., Biederman, J., Mennin, D., & Russel, R. I. (1998). Bipolar and antisocial disorders among relatives of ADHD children: Parsing familial subtypes of illness. *Neuropsychiatric Genetics, 81,* 108–116.

Faraone, S. V., Biederman, J., & Monuteaux, M. C. (2001). Attention deficit hyperactivity disorder with bipolar disorder in girls: Further evidence for a familial subtype? *Journal of Affective Disorders, 64,* 19–26.

Faraone, S. V., Biederman, J., Wozniak, J., Munday, E., Mennin, D., & O'Donnell, D. (1997). Is comorbidity with ADHD a marker for juvenile onset mania? *Journal of the American Academy of Child and Adolescent Psychiatry, 36,* 1046–1055.

Faraone, S. V., & Tsuang, M. T. (1995). Methods in psychiatric genetics. In M. Tohen, M. T. Tsuang, & G. E. P. Zahner (Eds.), *Textbook in psychiatric epidemiology* (pp. 81–134). New York: John Wiley & Sons.

Faraone, S. V., Tsuang, D., & Tsuang, D. (1999). *Genetics and mental disorders: A guide for students, clinicians, and researchers.* New York: Guilford Press.

Farvolden, P., Kennedy, S. H., & Lam, R. W. (2003). Recent developments in the psychobiology and pharmacotherapy of depression: Optimising existing treatments and novel approaches for the future. *Expert Opinion on Investigational Drugs, 12,* 65–86.

Fava, G. A. (1999). Subclinical symptoms in mood disorders: Pathological and therapeutic implications. *Psychological Medicine, 29,* 47–61.

Fava, G. A., Grandi, S., Zielezny, M., Rafanelli, C., & Canestrari, R. (1996). Four-year outcome for cognitive behavioral treatment of residual symptoms in major depression. *American Journal of Psychiatry, 153,* 945–947.

Fava, G. A., Rafanelli, C., Grandi, S., Conti, S., & Belluardo, P. (1998). Prevention of recurrent depression with cognitive behavioral therapy. *Archives of General Psychiatry, 55,* 816–820.

Feder, A., Coplan, J. D., Goetz, R. R., Mathew, S. J., Pine, D. S., Dahl, R. E., et al. (2004). Twenty-four-hour cortisol secretion patterns in prepubertal children with anxiety or depressive disorders. *Biological Psychiatry, 56,* 198–204.

Feinstein, S. C., & Wolpert, E. A. (1973). Juvenile manic-depressive illness: Clinical and therapeutic considerations. *Journal of the American Academy of Child and Adolescent Psychiatry, 12,* 123–136.

Felitti, V. J., Anda, R. F., Nordenberg, D., Williamson, D. F., Spitz, A. M., Edwards, V., et al. (1998). Relationship of childhood abuse and household dysfunction to many leading causes of death in adults: The Adverse Childhood Experiences (ACE) Study. *American Journal of Preventive Medicine, 14,* 245–258.

Fendrich, M., Warner, V., & Weissman, M. M. (1990). Family risk factors, parental depression and psychopathology in offspring. *Developmental Psychology, 25,* 40–50.

Fergusson, D. M., & Woodward, L. J. (2002). Mental health, educational, and social role outcomes of adolescents with depression. *Archives of General Psychiatry, 59,* 225–231.

Field, T. (1995). Massage therapy for infants and children. *Journal of Developmental and Behavioral Pediatrics, 16,* 105–111.

Findling, R. L., Gracious, B. L., McNamara, N. K., & Calabrese, J. R. (2000). The rationale, design, and progress of two novel maintenance treatment studies in pediatric bipolarity. *Acta Neuropsychiatrica, 12,* 136–138.

Findling, R. L., McNamara, N. K., Gracious, B. L., Youngstrom, E. A., Stansbrey, R. J., Reed, M. D., et al. (2003). Combination lithium and divalproex sodium in pediatric bipolarity. *Journal of the American Academy of Child and Adolescent Psychiatry, 42,* 895–901.

Fine, S., Forth, A., Gilbert, M., & Haley, G. (1991). Group therapy for adolescent depressive disorder: A comparison of social skills and therapeutic support. *Journal of the American Academy of Child and Adolescent Psychiatry, 30,* 79–85.

Flemming, J. E., Offord, D. R., & Boyle, M. H. (1989). Prevalence of childhood and adolescent depression in the community: Ontario child health study. *British Journal of Psychiatry, 155,* 647–654.

Flores, D. L., Alvarado, I., Wong, M. L., Licinio, J., & Flockhart, D. (2004). Clinical implications of genetic polymorphism of *CYP2D6* in Mexican Americans. *Annals of Internal Medicine, 140*(11), W71.

Frank, E., Hlastala, S., Ritenour, A., Houck, P., Tu, X. M., Monk, T. H., et al. (1997) Inducing lifestyle regularity in recovering bipolar disorder patients: Results from the maintenance therapies in bipolar disorder protocol. *Biological Psychiatry 41,* 1165–1173.

Frank, E., Kupfer, D. J., Perel, J. M., Cornes, C., Jarrett, D. B., Mallinger, A. G., et al. (1990). Three-year outcomes for maintenance therapies in recurrent depression. *Archives of General Psychiatry, 47,* 1093–1099.

Frazier, J. A., Biederman, J., Tohen, M., Feldman, P. D., Jacobs, T. G., Toma, V., et al. (2001). A prospective open-label trial of olanzapine monotherapy in children and adolescents with bipolar disorder. *Journal of Child and Adolescent Psychopharmacology, 11,* 239–250.

Frazier, J. A., Meyer, M. C., Biederman, J., Wozniak, J., Wilens, T. E., Spencer, T. J., et al. (1999). Risperidone treatment for juvenile bipolar disorder: A retrospective chart review. *Journal of the American Academy of Child and Adolescent Psychiatry, 38*, 960–965.

Freemantle, N., Anderson, I. M., & Young, P. (2000). Predictive value of pharmacological activity for the relative efficacy of antidepressant drugs. Meta-regression analysis. *British Journal of Psychiatry, 177*, 292–302.

French, D. C., Conrad, J., & Turner, T. M. (1995). Adjustment of antisocial and nonantisocial rejected adolescents. *Development and Psychopathology, 7*, 857–874.

Freimer, N. B., Reus, V. I. Escamilla, M. A., McInnes, L. A., Spesny, M., Leon, P., et al. (1996). Genetic mapping using haplotype, association and linkage methods suggests a locus for severe bipolar disorder (BPI) at 18q22–q23. *Nature Genetics, 12*, 436–441.

Frombonne, E., Wostear, G., Cooper, V., Harrington, R., & Rutter, M. (2001). The Maudsley long-term follow-up of child and adolescent depression. I. Psychiatric outcomes in adulthood. *British Journal of Psychiatry, 179*, 210–217.

Frost, A. K., Reinherz, H. Z., Pakiz-Camra, B., Fiaconia, R. M., & Lekowitz, E. E. (1999). Risk factors for depressive symptoms in late adolescence; a longitudinal community study. *American Journal of Orthopsychiatry, 69*, 370–381.

Gaensbauer, T. J., Harmon, R. J., Cytryn, L., & McKnew, D. H. (1984). Social and affective development in infants with a manic-depressive parent. *American Journal of Psychiatry, 141*, 223–229.

Gaffan, E. A., Tsaousis, I., & Kemp-Wheeler, S. M. (1995). Researcher allegiance and meta-analysis: The case of cognitive therapy for depression. *Journal of Consulting and Clinical Psychology, 63*, 966–980.

Gallagher, D. E., & Thompson, L. W. (1982). Treatment of major depressive disorder in older adult outpatients with brief psychotherapies. *Psychotherapy: Theory, Research and Practice, 19*, 482–490.

Gallagher-Thompson, D., & Steffen, A. M. (1994). Comparative effects of cognitive behavioral and brief psychodynamic psychotherapy for depressed family caregivers. *Journal of Consulting and Clinical Psychology, 62*, 543–549.

Garber, J., & Hilsman, R. (1992). Cognition, stress, and depression in children and adolescents. *Child and Adolescent Psychiatric Clinics of North America, 1*, 129–167.

Garber, J., & Kaminski, K. M. (2000). Laboratory and performance-based measures of depression in children and adolescents. *Journal of Clinical and Child Psychology, 29*, 509–525.

Garber, J., Keiley, M. K., & Martin, N. C. (2002). Developmental trajectories of adolescents' depressive symptoms: Predictors of change. *Journal of Consulting and Clinical Psychology, 70*, 79–95.

Garber, J., & Little, S. (1999). Predictors of competence among offspring of depressed mothers. *Journal of Adolescent Research, 14*, 44–71.

Garber, J., Little, S., Hilsman, R., & Weaver, K. R. (1998). Family predictors of suicidal symptoms in young adolescents. *Journal of Adolescence, 21*, 445–457.

Garber, J., & Martin, N. C. (2002). Negative cognitions in offspring of depressed parents: Mechanisms of risk. In S. H. Goodman & I. H. Gotlib (Eds.), *Children of depressed parents: Mechanisms of risk and implications for treatment* (pp. 121–153). Washington, DC: American Psychological Association.

Garber, J., Martin, N. C., & Keiley, M. K. (2002). *Predictors of the first onset of major depressive disorder.* Presented at the Society for Research on Psychopathology, San Francisco, CA.

Garber, J., & Robinson, N. S. (1997). Cognitive vulnerability in children at risk for depression. *Cognitions and Emotions, 11*, 619–635.

Garber, J., Wiess, B., & Shanley, N. (1993). Cognitions, depressive symptoms, and development in adolescents. *Journal of Abnormal Psychology, 102*, 248–258.

Garrison, C. Z., Jackson, K. L., Marsteller, F., McKeown, R., & Addy, C. (1990). A longitudinal study of depressive symptomatology in young adolescents. *Journal of the American Academy of Child and Adolescent Psychiatry, 29*, 581–585.

Ge, X., Conger, R. D., Lorenz, F. O., & Simons, R. L. (1994). Parents' stressful life events and adolescent depressed mood. *Journal of Health and Social Behavior, 35*(1), 28–44.

Gelenberg, A. J., Kane, J. M., Keller, M. B., Lavori, P., Rosenbaum, J. F., Cole, K., et al. (1989). Comparison of standard and low serum levels of lithium for maintenance treatment of bipolar disorder. *New England Journal of Medicine, 321*, 1489–1493.

Geller, B., Cooper, T. B., Sun, K., Zimerman, B., Frazier, J., Williams, M., et al. (1998). Double-blind and placebo-controlled study of lithium for adolescent bipolar disorders with secondary substance dependency. *Journal of the American Academy of Child and Adolescent Psychiatry, 37,* 171–178.

Geller, B., Craney, J. L. Bolhofner, K., Nichelsburg, M. J., Williams, M., & Zimerman, B. (2002). Two-year prospective follow-up of children with a prepubertal and early adolescent bipolar disorder phenotype. *American Journal of Psychiatry, 159,* 927–933.

Geller, B., Fox, L., & Clark, K. A. (1994). Rate and predictors of prepubertal bipolarity during follow-up of 6- to 12-year-old depressed children. *Journal of the American Academy of Child and Adolescent Psychiatry, 33,* 461–468.

Geller, B., & Luby, J. (1997). Child and adolescent bipolar disorder: A review of the past 10 years. *Journal of the American Academy of Child and Adolescent Psychiatry, 36,* 1168–1176.

Geller, B., Sun, K., Zinerman, B., Luby, J., Frazier, J., & Williams, M. (1995). Complex and rapid-cycling in bipolar children and adolescents: A preliminary study. *Journal of Affective Disorders, 34,* 259–268.

Gershon, E. S., McKnew, D., Cytryn, L., Hamovit, J., Schreiber, J., Hibbs, E., et al. (1985). Diagnoses in school-age children of bipolar affective disorder patients and normal controls. *Journal of Affective Disorders, 16,* 167–179.

Gershuny, B. S., & Sher, K. J. (1998). The relation between personality and anxiety: Findings from a 3-year prospective study. *Journal of Abnormal Psychology, 107,* 252–262.

Gillham, J. E., & Reivich, K. J. (1999). Prevention of depressive symptoms in school children: A research update. *Psychological Science, 10,* 461–462.

Gillham, J. E., Reivich, K. J., Jaycox, L. H., & Seligman, M. E. P. (1995). Prevention of depressive symptoms in school children: Two-year follow-up. *Psychological Science, 6,* 343–351.

Gilman, S. E., Kawachi, I., Fitzmaurice, G. M., & Buka, S. L. (2002). Socioeconomic status in childhood and the lifetime risk of major depression. *International Journal of Epidemiology, 31,* 359–367.

Ginns, E. I., St. Jean, P., & Philibert, R. A. (1998). A genome search for chromosomal loci linked to mental health wellness in relatives at high risk for bipolar affective disorder among the Old Order Amish. *Proceedings of the National Academy of Sciences of the United States of America, 95,* 15531.

Gjerde, P. F. (1995). Alternative pathways to chronic depressive symptoms in young adults:

Gender differences in developmental trajectories. *Child Development, 66,* 1277–1300.

Gladstone, T. R., & Kaslow, N. J. (1995). Depression and attributions in children and adolescents: A meta-analytic review. *Journal of Abnormal and Child Psychology, 23,* 597–606.

Goldberg, L. R. (1992). The development of markers for the Big-Five factor structure. *Psychological Assessment, 4,* 26–42.

Goleman, D. (1995). *Emotional intelligence.* New York: Bantam Books.

Goodman, S. H., & Gotlib, I. H. (1999). Risk for psychopathology in the children of depressed mothers: A developmental model for understanding mechanisms of transmission. *Psychological Review, 106,* 458–490.

Goodyer, I. M., Herbert, J., & Altham, P. M. (1998). Adrenal steroid secretion and major depression in 8- to 16-year-olds, III. Influence of cortisol/DHEA ratio at presentation on subsequent rates of disappointing life events and persistent major depression. *Psychological Medicine, 28,* 265–273.

Goodyer, I. M., Herbert, J., Tamplin, A., & Altham, P. M. (2000). Recent life events, cortisol, dehydroepiandrosterone and the onset of major depression in high-risk adolescents. *British Journal of Psychiatry, 177,* 499–504.

Goodyer, I. M., Wright, C., & Altham, P. M. (1988). Maternal adversity and recent stressful life events in anxious and depressed children. *Journal of Child Psychology and Psychiatry, 29,* 651–667.

Gordon, R. (1983). An operational classification of disease prevention. *Public Health Reports, 98,* 107–109.

Gordon, R. (1987). An operational classification of disease prevention. In J. Steinberg & M. Silverman (Eds.), *Preventing mental disorders: A research perspective* (pp. 20–26). Rockville, MD: Dept. of Health and Human Services.

Gordon, D., Burge, D., Hammen, C., Adrian, C., Jaenicke, C., & Hiroto, D. (1989). Observations of interactions of depressed women with their children. *American Journal of Psychiatry, 146,* 50–55.

Gotlib, I. H., & Hammen, C. (1992). Psychological aspects of depression: Toward a cognitive-interpersonal integration. In: *The Wiley series in clinical psychology.* Chichester, UK: John Wiley & Sons.

Gould, M., King, R., Greenwald, S., Fisher, P., Schwab-Stone, M., Kramer, R., et al. (1998). Psychopathology associated with suicidal ideation and attempts among children and adolescents.

Journal of the American Academy of Child and Adolescent Psychiatry, 37, 915–923.

Grant, K. E., Compas, B. E., Stuhlmacher, A. F., Thurm, A. E., McMahon, S. D., & Halpert, J. A. (2003). Stressors and child and adolescent psychopathology: Moving from markers to mechanisms of risk. *Psychological Bulletin, 129,* 447–466.

Gray, J. A. (1982). *The neuropsychology of anxiety: An enquiry into the functions of the septo-hippocampal system.* New York: Oxford University Press.

Graziano, W. G., & Ward, D. (1992). Probing the big five in adolescence: Personality and adjustment during a developmental transition. *Journal of Personality, 60,* 425–439.

Hammen, C. (1991). Generation of stress in the course of unipolar depression. *Journal of Abnormal Psychology, 100,* 555–561.

Hammen, C., Burge, D., Burney, E., & Adrian, C. (1990). Longitudinal study of diagnosis in children of women with unipolar and bipolar affective disorder. *Archives of General Psychiatry, 47,* 1112–1117.

Hankin, B. L., Abramson, L. Y., Moffitt, T. E., Silva, P. A., McGee, R., & Angell, K. E. (1998). Development of depression from preadolescence to young adulthood: Emerging gender differences in a 10-year longitudinal study. *Journal of Abnormal Psychology, 107,* 128–140.

Harrington, R., Fudge, H., Rutter, M., Pickles, A., & Hill J. (1990) Adult outcomes of childhood and adolescent depression. *Archives of General Psychiatry 47,* 465–473.

Harrington, R., Kerfoot, M., Dyer, E., McNiven, F., Gill, J., Harrington, V., et al. (1998). Randomized trial of a home-based family intervention for children who have deliberately poisoned themselves. *Journal of the American Academy of Child and Adolescent Psychiatry, 37,* 512–518.

Hart, A. B., Craighead, W. E., & Craighead, L. W. (2001). Predicting recurrence of major depressive disorder in young adults: A prospective study. *Journal of Abnormal Psychology, 110,* 633–643.

Hayward, C., Gotlib, I. H., & Schraedley, P. K. (1999). Ethnic differences in the association between pubertal status and symptoms of depression in adolescent girls. *Journal of Adolescent Health, 25,* 143–149.

Hayward, C., Killen, J. D., Kraemer, H. C., & Taylor, C. B. (2000). Predictors of panic attacks in adolescence. *Journal of the American Academy of Child and Adolescent Psychiatry, 39,* 207–214.

Heim, C., & Nemeroff, C. B. (2001). The role of childhood trauma in the neurobiology of mood and anxiety disorders: Preclinical and clinical studies. *Biological Psychiatry 49,* 1023–1039.

Heim, C., Newport, J. D., Bonsall, R., Miller, A. H., & Nemeroff, C. B. (2001). Altered pituitary–adrenal axis responses to provocative challenge tests in adult survivors of childhood abuse. *American Journal of Psychiatry, 158,* 575–581.

Heim, C., Newport, J. D., Heit, S., Graham, Y. P., Wilcox, M., Bonsall, R., et al. (2000). Pituitary–adrenal and autonomic responses to stress in women after sexual and physical abuse in childhood. *Journal of the American Medical Association, 284,* 592–597.

Heim, C., Plotsky, P. M., & Nemeroff, C. B. (2004). The importance of studying the contributions of early adverse experience to neurobiological findings in depression. *Neuropsychopharmacology, 29,* 641–648.

Helzer, J. E., Robins, L. N., & McEvoy, L. (1987). Post-traumatic stress disorder in the general population. Findings of the epidemiologic catchment area survey. *New England Journal of Medicine, 317,* 1630–1634.

Henry, C., Kabbaj, M., Simon, H., Le Moal, M., & Maccari, S. (1994). Prenatal stress increases the hypothalamo–pituitary–adrenal axis response in young and adult rats. *Journal of Neuroendocrinology, 6,* 341–345.

Hilsman, R., & Garber, J. (1995). A test of the cognitive diathesis–stress model of depression in children: Academic stressors, attributional style, perceived competence, and control. *Journal of Personality and Social Psychology, 69,* 370–380.

Hirshfeld, D. R., Rosenbaum, J. F., Biederman, J., Bolduc, E. A., Faraone, S. V., Snidman, N., et al. (1992). Stable behavioral inhibition and its association with anxiety disorder. *Journal of the American Academy of Child and Adolescent Psychiatry, 31,* 103–111.

Hirschfeld, R. M., Klerman, G. L., Lavori, P., Keller, M. B., Griffith, P., & Coryell, W. (1989). Premorbid personality assessments of first onset of major depression. *Archives of General Psychiatry, 46,* 345–350.

Hirschfeld, R. M., Montgomery, S. A., Aguglia, E., Amore, M., Delgado, P. L., Gastpar, M., et al. (2002). Partial response and nonresponse to antidepressant therapy: Current approaches and treatment options. *Journal of Clinical Psychiatry 63,* 826–837.

Hoffman, K. B., Cole, D. A., Martin, J. M., Tram, J., & Serocynski, A. D. (2001). Are the discrepancies between self- and others' appraisals of competence predictive or reflective of depressive symptoms in children and adolescents: A longitudinal study, Part II. *Journal of Abnormal Psychology, 109,* 651–662.

Hollon, S. D., DeRubeis, R. J., Evans, M. D., Wiemer, M. J., Garvey, M. J., Grove, W. M., et al. (1992). Cognitive therapy and pharmacotherapy for depression: Singly and in combination. *Archives of General Psychiatry, 49,* 774–781.

Ingram, R. E., Miranda, J., & Segal, Z. V. (1998). *Cognitive vulnerability to depression.* New York: Guilford Press.

Institute of Medicine (IOM). (1994). *Reducing risks for mental disorders: Frontiers for preventive intervention research.* Washington, DC: National Academy Press.

Jacobson, N. S., Dobson, K., Fruzzetti, A. E., Schmaling, K. B., & Salusky, S. (1991). Marital therapy as a treatment for depression. *Journal of Consulting and Clinical Psychology, 59(4).*

Jacobson, N. S., Dobson, K. S., Truax, P. A., Addis, M. E., Koerner, K., Gollan, J. K., et al. (1996). A component analysis of cognitive-behavior treatment for depression. *Journal of Consulting and Clinical Psychology, 64,* 295–304.

Jacobson, N. S., & Truax, P. A. (1991). Clinical significance: A statistical approach to defining meaningful change in psychotherapy research. *Journal of Consulting and Clinical Psychology, 59,* 12–19.

Jarrett, R. B., Kraft, D., Doyle, J., Foster, B. M., Eaves, G. G., & Silver, P. C. (2001). Preventing recurrent depression using cognitive therapy with and without a continuation phase: A randomized clinical trial. *Archives of General Psychiatry, 58,* 381–388.

Jaycox, L. H., Reivich, K. J., Gillham, J., & Seligman, M. E. P. (1994). Prevention of depressive symptoms in school children. *Behaviour Research and Therapy, 32,* 801–816.

Jayson, D., Wood, A., Kroll, L., Fraser, J., & Harrington, R. (1998). Which depressed patients respond to cognitive-behavioral treatment? *Journal of the American Academy of Child and Adolescent Psychiatry, 37,* 35–39.

Johnson, J. G., Cohen, P., Dohrenwend, B. P., Link, B. G., & Brook, J. S. (1999). A longitudinal investigation of social causation and social selection processes involved in the association between socioeconomic status and psychiatric disorders. *Journal of Abnormal Psychology, 108,* 490–499.

Johnson, J., Weissman, M. M., & Klerman, G. L. (1992). Service utilization and social morbidity associated with depressive symptoms in the community. *Journal of the American Medical Association, 267,* 1478–1483.

Johnston, J. A., Lineberry, C. G., Ascher, J. A., Davidson, J., Khayrallah, M. A., Feighner, J. P., et al. (1991). A 102-center prospective study of seizure in association with bupropion. *Journal of Clinical Psychiatry 52,* 450–456.

Joiner, T. E., Jr., & Wagner, K. D. (1995). Attributional style and depression in children and adolescents: A meta-analytic review. *Clinical Psychology Review, 8,* 777–798.

Jorm, A. F., Christensen, H., Henderson, A. S., & Jacomb, P. A. (2000). Predicting anxiety and depression from personality: Is there a synergistic effect of neuroticism and extraversion? *Journal of Abnormal Psychology, 109,* 145–149.

Judd, L. L., Akiskal, H. S., & Paulus, M. P. (1997). The role and clinical significance of subsyndromal depressive symptoms (SSD) in unipolar major depressive disorder. *Journal of Affective Disorders, 45,* 5–18.

Kafantaris, V., Coletti, D. J., Dicker, R., Padula, G., & Kane, J. M. (2001). Adjunctive antipsychotic treatment of adolescents with bipolar psychosis. *Journal of the American Academy of Child and Adolescent Psychiatry, 40,* 1448–1456.

Kagan, J., Reznick, J. S., & Snidman, N. (1987). The physiology and psychology of behavioral inhibition in children. *Child Development, 55,* 1459–1473.

Kagan, J., & Snidman, N. (1991). Temperamental factors in human development. *American Psychologist, 46,* 856–862.

Kahn, J. S., Kehle, T. J., Jenson, W. R., & Clark, E. (1990). Comparison of cognitive-behavioral relaxation, and self-modeling interventions for depression among middle-school students. *School Psychology Review, 19,* 196–211.

Kalin, N. H., & Carnes, M. (1984). Biological correlates of attachment bond disruption in humans and nonhuman primates. *Progress in Neuropsychopharmacology and Biological Psychiatry, 8,* 459–469.

Kaslow, N. J., Rehm, L. P., & Siegel, A. W. (1984). Social-cognitive and cognitive correlates of depression in children. *Journal of Abnormal and Child Psychology, 12,* 605–620.

Kaslow, N. J., & Thompson, M. (1998). Applying the criteria for empirically supported treatments to studies of psychosocial interventions for child and adolescent depression. *Journal of Clinical Child Psychology, 27,* 146–155.

Katainen, S., Raikkonen, K., Keskivaara, P., &

Keltikangas-Jarvinen, L. (1999). Maternal child-rearing attitudes and role satisfaction and children's temperament as antecedents of adolescent depressive tendencies: Follow-up study of 6- to 15-year-olds. *Journal of Youth and Adolescence, 2,* 139–163.

Katona, C. L., Robertson, M. M., Abou-Saleh, M. T., Nairac, B. L., Edwards, D. R., Lock, T., et al. (1993) Placebo-controlled trial of lithium augmentation of fluoxetine and lofepramine. *International Clinical Psychopharmacology, 8,* 323.

Kaufman, J., Martin, A., King, R. A., & Charney, D. (2001). Are child-, adolescent-, and adult-onset depression one and the same disorder? *Biological Psychiatry, 49,* 980–1001.

Kazdin, A. E., & Weisz, J. R. (1998). Identifying and developing empirically supported child and adolescent treatments. *Journal of Consulting and Clinical Psychology, 66,* 19–36.

Keller M. B. (2003) Past, present, and future directions for defining optimal treatment outcome in depression: Remission and beyond. *Journal of the American Medical Association, 289,* 3152–3160.

Keller, M. B., McCullough, J. P., Klein, D. N., Arnow, B., Dunner, D. L., Gelenberg, A. J., et al. (2000). A comparison of nefazodone, the cognitive behavioral-analysis system of psychotherapy, and their combination for the treatment of chronic depression. *New England Journal of Medicine, 342,* 1462–1470.

Keller, M. B., Ryan, N. D., Strober, M., Klein, R., Kutcher, S. P., Birmaher, B., et al., (2001). Efficacy of paroxetine in the treatment of adolescent major depression: A randomized, controlled trial. *Journal of the American Academy of Child and Adolescent Psychiatry, 40,* 762–772.

Kelsoe, J. R., Spence, M. A., Loetscher E., Fogurt, M., Sadovnick, A. D., Remick, R. A., et al. (2001). A genome survey indicates a susceptibility locus for bipolar disorder on chromosome 22. *Proceedings of the National Academy of Sciences of the United States of America, 98,* 585–590.

Kendler, K. S., Gardner, C. O., & Prescott, C. A. (2002). Toward a comprehensive developmental model for major depression in women. *American Journal of Psychiatry, 159,* 1133–1145.

Kendler, K. S., Kessler, R. C., Neale, M. C., Heath, A. C., & Eaves, L. J. (1993). The prediction of major depression in women: Toward an integrated etiologic model. *American Journal of Psychiatry, 150,* 1139–1148.

Kendler, K. S., Kuhn, J., & Prescott, C. A. (2004). The interrelationship of neuroticism, sex, and stressful life events in the prediction of episodes of major depression. *American Journal of Psychology, 16,* 631–636.

Kenny, M. E., Moilanen, D. M., Lomax, R., & Brabeck, M. D. (1993). Contributions of parental attachment to view of self and depressive symptoms among early adolescents. *Journal of Youth and Adolescence, 13,* 408–430.

Kessler, R. C., Avenevoli, S., & Merikangas, K. R. (2001). Mood disorders in children and adolescents: An epidemiologic perspective. *Social Biology and Psychiatry, 49,* 1002–1014.

Kessler, R. C., Berglund, P., Demler, O., Jin, R., Koretz, D., Merikangas, K. R., et al. (2003). National Comorbidity Survey Replication. The epidemiology of major depressive disorder: Results from the National Comorbidity Survey Replication (NCS-R). *Journal of the American Medical Association, 289,* 3095–3105.

Kessler, R. C., Foster, C., Webster, P. S., & House, J. S. (1992). The relationship between age and depressive symptoms in two national surveys. *Psychology and Aging, 7,* 119–126.

Kessler, R., McGonagle, K., Zhao, S., Nelson, C., Hughes, M., Eshleman, S., et al. (1994). Lifetime and 12-month prevalence of DSM-III-R psychiatric disorders in the United States: Results from the national comorbidity survey. *Archives of General Psychiatry, 51,* 8–19.

Kessler, R., & Walters, E. E. (1998). Epidemiology of DSM-III-R major depression and minor depression among adolescents and young adults in the National Comorbidity Survey. *Depression and Anxiety, 7,* 3–15.

Khantzian, E. (1997). The self-medication hypothesis of substance use disorders: A reconsideration and recent applications. *Harvard Review of Psychiatry, 4,* 231–244.

Kilpatrick, D. G., Ruggiero, K. J., Acierno, R., Saunders, B. E., Resnick, H. S., & Best, C. L. (2003). Violence and risk of PTSD, major depression, substance abuse/dependence, and comorbidity: Results from the National Survey of Adolescents. *Journal of Consulting and Clinical Psychology, 71,* 692–700.

Kistner, J., Balthazor, M., Risi, S., & Burton, C. (1999). Predicting dysphoria in adolescence from actual and perceived peer acceptance in childhood. *Journal of Clinical Child Psychology, 28,* 94–104.

Klein, D. N., Depue, R. A., & Slater, J. F. (1985). Cyclothymia in the adolescent offspring of parents with bipolar affective disorder. *Journal of Abnormal Psychology, 94,* 115–127.

Klein, D. N., Durbin, C. E., Shankman, S. A., & Santiago, N. J. (2002). Depression and personality. In I. H. Gotlib & C. L. Hammen (Eds.), *Handbook of depression and its treatment* (pp. 115–140). New York: Guilford Press.

Klein, R. G., Pine, D. S., & Klein, D. (1998). Resolved: Mania is mistaken for ADHD in prepubertal children. Negative. *Journal of the American Academy of Child and Adolescent Psychiatry, 37,* 1093–1095.

Klerman, G. L. (1989). Evaluating the efficacy of psychotherapy for depression: The USA experience. *European Archives of Psychiatry and Neurological Sciences, 238,* 240–246.

Klerman, G. L., Weissman, M. M., Rounsaville, B. J., & Chevron, E. S. (1984). *Interpersonal psychotherapy of depression.* New York: Basic Books.

Klerman, G. L., & Weissman, M. M. (1989). Increasing rates of depression. *Journal of the American Medical Association, 261,* 2229–2235.

Kobak, R. R., Cole, H. E., Ferenz-Gillies, R., Fleming, W. S., & Gamble, W. (1993). Attachment and emotion regulation during mother–teen problem solving: A control theory analysis. *Child Development, 64,* 231–245.

Kochanska, G., & Kuczynski, L. (1991). Maternal autonomy granting: Predictors of normal and depressed mothers' compliance and noncompliance with the requests of five-year-olds. *Child Development, 62,* 1449–1459.

Kochanska, G., Kuczynski, L., Radke-Yarrow, M., & Welsh, J. D. (1987). Resolutions of control episodes between well and affectively ill mothers and their young children. *Journal of Abnormal Child Psychology, 15,* 441–456.

Kolko, D. J., Brent, D. A., Baugher, M., Bridge, J., & Birmaher, B. (2000). Cognitive and family therapies for adolescent depression: Treatment specificity, mediation, and moderation. *Journal of Consulting and Clinical Psychology, 68,* 603–614.

Kovacs, M. (1990). Comorbid anxiety disorders in childhood-onset depression. In J. D. Maser & C. R. Cloninger (Eds.), *Comorbidity of mood and anxiety disorders* (pp. 271–282). Washington, DC: American Psychiatric Press.

Kovacs, M. (1996). Presentation and course of major depressive disorder during childhood and later years of the life span. *Journal of the American Academy of Child and Adolescent Psychiatry, 35,* 705–715.

Kovacs, M., Akiskal, H., Gatsonis, C., & Parrone, P. (1994). Childhood-onset dysthymic disorder: Clinical features and prospective naturalistic outcome. *Archives of General Psychiatry, 51,* 365–374.

Kovacs, M., Feinberg, T. L., Crouse-Novak, M., Paulauskas, S. L., Pollack, M., & Finkelstein, R. (1984). Depressive disorders in childhood. II. A longitudinal study of the risk source for a subsequent major depression. *Archives of General Psychiatry, 41,* 643–649.

Kovacs, M., & Gatsonis, C. (1994). Secular trends in age at onset of major depressive disorders in a clinical sample of children. *Journal of Psychiatric Research, 28,* 319–329.

Kovacs, M., Paulauskas, S., Gatsonis, C., & Richards, C. (1998). Depressive disorders in childhood. III. A longitudinal study of comorbidity with and risk for conduct disorders. *Journal of Affective Disorders, 15,* 205–217.

Kovacs, M., & Pollock, M. (1995). Bipolar disorder and comorbid conduct disorder in childhood and adolescence. *Journal of the American Academy of Child and Adolescent Psychiatry, 34,* 715–723.

Kovacs, M., Rush, A. J., Beck, A. T., & Hollon, S. D. (1981). Depressed outpatients treated with cognitive therapy or pharmacotherapy. *Archives of General Psychiatry, 38,* 33–39.

Kowatch, R. A., & DelBello, M. P. (2003). The use of mood stabilizers and atypical antipsychotics in children and adolescents with bipolar disorders. *CNS Spectrums, 8,* 273–280.

Kowatch, R. A., Suppes, T., Carmody, T. J., Bucci, J. P., Hume, J. H., Kromelis, M., et al. (2000). Effect size of lithium, divalproex sodium, and carbamazepine in children and adolescents with bipolar disorder. *Journal of the American Academy of Child and Adolescent Psychiatry, 39,* 713–720.

Kowatch, R. A., Suppes, T., Gilfillian, S. K., Fuentes, R. M., Grannemann, B. D., & Emslie, G. J. (1995). Clozapine treatment of children and adolescents with bipolar disorder and schizophrenia: A clinical case series. *Journal of Child and Adolescent Psychopharmacology, 5,* 241–253.

Kramer, R. A., Warner, V., Olfson, M., Ebanks, C. M., Chaput, F., & Weissman, M. M. (1998). General medical problems among the offspring of depressed parents: A ten-year follow-up. *Journal of the Academy of Child and Adolescent Psychiatry, 37,* 602–611.

Kroll, L., Harrington, R., Jayson, D., Fraser, J., & Gowers, S. (1996). Pilot study of continuation cognitive-behavioral therapy for major depression in adolescent psychiatric patients. *Journal of the American Academy of Child and Adolescent Psychiatry, 35,* 1156–1161.

Krueger, R. F., Caspi, A., Moffitt, T. E., Silva, P., McGee, R. (1996). Personality traits are differentially linked to mental disorders: A multitrait–

multidiagnosis study of an adolescent birth cohort. *Journal of Abnormal Psychology, 105*, 299–312.

Kutcher, S. P., Marton, P., & Korenblum, M. (1989). Relationship between psychiatric illness and conduct disorder in adolescents. *Canadian Journal of Psychiatry, 34*, 526–529.

Kwok, J. B., Adams, I. J., Salmon, J. A., Donald, J. A., Mitchell, P. B., & Schofield, P. R. (1999). Non-parametric simulation-based statistical analyses for bipolar affective disorder locus on chromosome 21q22.3. *American Journal of Medical Genetics 88*, 99–102.

Ladd, C. O., Huot, R. L., Thrivikraman, K. V., Nemeroff, C. B., Meaney, M. J., & Plotsky, P. M. (2000). Long-term behavioral and neuroendocrine adaptations to adverse early experience. *Progress in Brain Research, 122*, 81–103.

Ladd, C. O., Huot, R. L., Thrivikraman, K. V., Nemeroff, C. B., & Plotsky, P. M. (2004). Long-term adaptations in glucocorticoid receptor and mineralocorticoid receptor mRNA and negative feedback on the hypothalamo–pituitary–adrenal axis following neonatal maternal separation. *Biological Psychiatry, 55*, 367–375.

Lahey, B. B., Flagg, E. W., Bird, H. R., Schwab-Stone, M. E., Canino, G., Dulcan, M. K., et al. (1996). The NIMH Methods for the Epidemiology of Child and Adolescent Mental Disorders (MECA) Study: Background and methodology. *Journal of the American Academy of Child and Adolescent Psychiatry, 35*, 855–864.

Larson, R. J. (1992). Neuroticism and selective encoding and recall of symptoms: Evidence from a combined concurrent retrospective study. *Journal of Personality and Social Psychology, 62*, 480–488.

Lazarus, R. S., DeLongis, A., Folkman, S., & Gruen, R. (1985). Stress and adaptational outcomes. The problem of confounded measures. *American Psychologist, 40*, 770–785.

Leibenluft, E., Charney, D. S., Towbin, K. E., Bhangoo, R. K., & Pine, D. S. (2003). Defining clinical phenotypes of juvenile mania. *American Journal of Psychiatry, 160*, 430–437.

Levenson, M. R., Aldwin, C. M., Bosse, R., & Spiro, A. (1988). Emotionality and mental health: Longitudinal findings from the normative aging study. *Journal of Abnormal Psychology, 97*, 94–96.

Leventhal, T., & Brooks-Gunn, J. (2000). The neighborhoods they live in: The effects of neighborhood residence on child and adolescent outcomes. *Psychological Bulletin, 126*, 309–337.

Lewinsohn, P. M., & Clarke, G. N. (1999). Psychosocial treatments for adolescent depression. *Clinical Psychology Review, 19*, 329–342.

Lewinsohn, P. M., Clarke, G. N., Hops, H., & Andrews, J. (1990). Cognitive-behavioral treatment for depressed adolescents. *Behavior Therapy, 21*, 385–401.

Lewinsohn, P. M., Hops, H., Roberts, R. E., Seeley, J. R., & Andrews, J. A. (1993). Adolescent psychopathology. I. Prevalence and incidence of depression and other DSM-III-R disorders in high school students. *Journal of Abnormal Psychology, 102*, 133–144.

Lewinsohn, P., Joiner, T., & Rohde, P. (2001). Evaluation of cognitive diathesis–stress models in predicting major depressive disorder in adolescents. *Journal of Abnormal Psychology, 110*, 203–215.

Lewinsohn, P. M., Klein, D. N., & Seeley, M. S. (1995). Bipolar disorders in a community sample of older adolescents: Prevalence, phenomenology, comorbidity and course. *Journal of the American Academy of Child and Adolescent Psychiatry, 34*, 454–463.

Lewinsohn, P. M., & MacPhillamy, D. J. (1974). The relationship between age and engagement in pleasant activities. *Journal of Gerontology, 29*, 290–294.

Lewinsohn, P. M., Rohde, P., & Seeley, J. R. (1996). Adolescent suicidal ideation and attempts: Prevalence, risk factors, and clinical implications. *Clinical Psychology and Scientific Practice, 3*, 25–46.

Lewinsohn, P. M., Rohde, P., & Seeley, J. R. (1998). Major depressive disorder in older adolescents: Prevalence, risk factors and clinical implications. *Clinical Psychology Review, 18*, 765–794.

Lewinsohn, P. M., Rohde, P., Seeley, J. R., & Fischer, S. A. (1993). Age-cohort changes in the lifetime occurrence of depression and other mental disorders. *Journal of Abnormal Psychology, 10*, 110–120.

Lewinsohn, P. M., Rohde, P., Seeley, J. R., Klein, D. N., & Gotlib, I. H. (2000). Natural course or adolescent major depressive disorder in a community sample: Predictors of recurrence in young adults. *American Journal of Psychiatry, 157*, 1585–1591.

Lewinsohn, P. M., Solomon, A., Seeley, J. R., & Zeiss, A. (2000). Clinical implications of "subthreshold" depressive symptoms. *Journal of Abnormal Psychology, 109*, 345–351.

Liddle, B. J., & Spence, S. H. (1990). Cognitive-behavior therapy with depressed primary school children: A cautionary note. *Behavioral Psychotherapy, 18*, 85–102.

Lou, H. C., Hansen, D., Nordentoft, M., Pryds, O., Jensen, F., Nim, J., et al. (1994). Prenatal stressors of human life affect fetal brain development. *Developmental Medicine and Child Neurology, 36,* 826–832.

Lovejoy, M. C. (1991). Maternal depression: Effects on social cognition and behavior in parent–child interactions. *Journal of Abnormal Child Psychology, 19,* 693–706.

MacMillan, H. L., Fleming, J. E., Streiner, D. L., Lin, E., Boyle, M. H., Jamieson, E., et al. (2001). Childhood abuse and lifetime psychopathology in a community sample. *American Journal of Psychiatry, 158,* 1878–1883.

Mann, J. J., Aarons, S. F., Wilner, P. J., Keilp, J. G., Sweeney, J. A., Pearlstein, T., et al. (1989). A controlled study of the antidepressant efficacy and side effects of (-)-deprenyl. A selective monoamine oxidase inhibitor. *Archives of General Psychiatry, 46,* 45–50.

March, J., Silva, S., Petrycki, S., Curry, J., Wells, K., Fairbank, J., et al. (2004). Fluoxetine, cognitive behavioral therapy, and their combination for adolescents with depression: Treatment for Adolescents with Depression Study (TADS) randomized controlled trial. *JAMA, 292,* 807–820.

Marikangas, K. R., Avenevoli, D., Dierker, L. C., & Grillon, D. (1999). Vulnerability factors among children at risk for anxiety disorders. *Biological Psychiatry, 46,* 1523–1535.

Markowitz, J. C., Svartberg, M., & Swartz, H. A. (1998). Is IPT time-limited psychodynamic psychotherapy? *Journal of Psychotherapeutic Practice Research, 7,* 185–195.

Matas, L., Arend, R., & Sroufe, L. (1978). Continuity of adaptation in the second year: The relationship between quality of attachment and later competence. *Child Development, 49,* 547–556.

McCrae, R. R., & Costa, P. T. (1987). Validation of the five-factor model of personality across instruments and observers. *Journal of Personality and Social Psychology, 52,* 81–90.

McElroy, S. L., Strakowski, S. M., West, S. A., Keck, P. E., & McConville, B. J. (1997). Phenomenology of adolescent and adult mania in hospitalized patients with bipolar disorder. *American Journal of Psychiatry, 154,* 44–49.

McFarlane, A. H., Bellissimo, A., & Norman, G. R. (1995). The role of family and peers in social self-efficacy: Links to depression in adolescence. *American Journal of Orthopsychiatry, 65,* 402–410.

McGlashan, T. (1988). Adolescent versus adult onset of mania. *American Journal of Psychiatry, 145,* 221–223.

McInnes, L. A., Escamilla, M. A., Service, S. K, Reus, V. I., Leon, P., Silva, S., et al. (1996). A complete genome screen for genes predisposing to severe bipolar disorder in two Costa Rican pedigrees. *Proceedings of the National Academy of Sciences of the United States of America, 93,* 13060–13065.

McLean, P. D., & Hakstian, A. R. (1979). Clinical depression: Comparative efficacy of outpatient treatments. *Journal of Consulting and Clinical Psychology, 47,* 818–836.

McLoyd, V. C. (1998). Socioeconomic disadvantage and child development. *American Psychologist, 53,* 185–204.

McMahan, F. J., Hopkins P. J., Xu, J., McInnis, M. G., Shaw, S., Cardon, L., et al. (1997). Linkage of bipolar affective disorder to chromosome 18 markers in a new pedigree series. *American Journal of Medical Genetics, 61,* 1397–1404.

Merali, Z., Du, L., Hrdini, P., Palkovits, M., Faludi, G., Poulter, M. O., et al. (2004). Dysregulation in the suicide brain: mRNA expression of corticotrophin-releasing hormone receptors and GABA$_A$ receptor subunits in frontal cortical brain region. *Journal of Neuroscience, 24,* 1478–1485.

Mervaala, E., Foehr, J., Koenoenen, M., Valkonen-Korhonen, M., Vainio, P., Partanen, K., et al. (2000). Quantitative MRI of the hippocampus and amygdala in severe depression. *Psychological Medicine, 30,* 117–125.

Miklowitz, D. J., & Goldstein, M. J. (1990). Behavioral family treatment for patients with bipolar affective disorder. *Behavior Modification, 14,* 457–458.

Miklowitz, D. J., Goldstein, M. J., Nuechterlein, K. H., Snyder, K. S., & Mintz J. (1988). Family factors and the course of bipolar affective disorder. *Archives of General Psychiatry, 45,* 225–231.

Miklowitz, D. J., Simoneau, T. L., George, E. L., Richards, J. A., Kalbag, A., Sachs-Ericsson, N., et al. (2000). Family-focused treatment of bipolar disorder: 1 year effects of a psychoeducational program in conjunction with pharmacotherapy. *Biological Psychiatry, 48,* 582–592.

Moller, H. J., & Nasrallah, H. A. (2003). Treatment of bipolar disorder. *Journal of Clinical Psychiatry 64,* 9–17; discussion 28.

Monroe, S. M., Rohde, P., Seeley, J. R., & Lewinsohn, P. M. (1999). Life events and depression in adolescence: relationship loss as a prospective risk factor for first onset of major depressive disorder. *Journal of Abnormal Psychology, 108,* 606–614.

Moreau, D. (1996). Depression in the young. *An-*

nals of the New York Academy of Sciences, 789, 31–44.

Morissette J., Villeneuve, A., Bordeleau, I., Rochette, D., Laberge C., Gagne, B., et al. (1999). Genome-wide search for linkage of bipolar affective disorders in a very large pedigree derived from a homogeneous population in Quebec points to a locus of major effect on chromosome 12q23-q24. *American Journal of Medical Genetics, 88,* 567–587.

Mortensen, P. B., Pedersen, C. B., Melbye, M., Mors, O., & Ewald, H. (2003). Individual and familial risk factors for bipolar affective disorders in Denmark. *Archives of General Psychiatry, 60,* 1209–1215.

Mrazek, D. A., Schuman, W. B., & Klinnert, M. (1998). Early asthma onset: Risk of emotional and behavioral difficulties. *Journal of Child Psychology and Psychiatry, 39,* 247–254.

Mueller, C., & Orvaschel, H. (1997). The failure of "adult" interventions with adolescent depression: What does it mean for theory, research, and practice? *Journal of Affective Disorders, 44,* 203–215.

Mufson L., Dorta K. P., Wickramaratne P., Nomura Y., Olfson M., & Weissman, M. M. (2004). A randomized effectiveness trial of interpersonal psychotherapy for depressed adolescents. *Archives of General Psychiatry, 61,* 577–584.

Mufson, L., Moreau, D., Weissman, M. M., Wickramaratne, P., Martin, J., & Samoilov, A. (1994). A. Modification of interpersonal psychotherapy with depressed adolescents (IPT-A): Phase I and II studies. *Journal of the American Academy of Child and Adolescent Psychiatry, 33,* 695–705.

Mufson, L., Weissman, M. M., Moreau, D., & Garfinkel, R. (1999). Efficacy of interpersonal psychotherapy for depressed adolescents. *Archives of General Psychiatry, 56,* 573–579.

Murphy, G. E., Simons, A. D., Wetzel, R. D., & Lustman, P. J. (1984). Cognitive therapy and pharmacotherapy, singly and together, in the treatment of depression. *Archives of General Psychiatry, 41,* 33–41.

Murray, C. J., & Lopez, A. D. (1997). Alternative projections of mortality and disability by cause 1990–2020: Global Burden of Disease Study. *Lancet, 34,* 1498–1504.

Mynors-Wallis, L. M., Gath, D. H., Lloyd-Thomas, A. R., & Tomlinson, D. (1995). Randomised controlled trial comparing problem solving treatment with amitriptyline and placebo for major depression in primary care. *British Medical Journal, 310*(6977), 441–445.

National Institute of Mental Health (NIMH). (1998). Priorities for prevention research at NIMH: A report by the National Advisory Mental Health Council Workgroup on Mental Disorders Prevention Research, National Institutes of Health. Bethesda, MD: Author.

Nemeroff, C. B. (2004). Neurobiological consequences of childhood trauma. *Journal of Clinical Psychiatry, 65,* 18–28.

Nezu, A. M. (1986). Cognitive appraisal of problem solving effectiveness: Relation to depression and depressive symptoms. *Journal of Clinical Psychology, 42,* 42–48.

Nezu, A. M., & Perri, M. G. (1989) Social-problem solving therapy for unipolar depression: An initial dismantling. *Journal of Consulting and Clinical Psychology, 57,* 408–413.

Nolan, S., Flynn, C., & Garber, J. (2003). The relation between rejection and depression in adolescents. *Journal of Personality and Social Psychology, 85,* 745–755.

Nolen-Hoeksema S. (2000). The role of rumination in depressive disorders and mixed anxiety/depressive symptoms. *Journal of Abnormal Psychology, 109,* 504–511.

Nolen-Hoeksema, S., Girgus, J. S., & Seligman, M. E. (1986). Learned helplessness in children: A longitudinal study of depression, achievement, and explanatory style. *Journal of Personality and Social Psychology, 51,* 435–444.

Nolen-Hoeksema, S., Girgus, J. S., & Seligman, M. E. P. (1992). Predictors and consequences of childhood depressive symptoms: A 5-year longitudinal study. *Journal of Abnormal Psychology, 101,* 405–422.

Nomura, Y., Wickramaratne, P. J., Warner, V., Mufson, L., & Weissman, M. M. (2002). Family discord, parental depression and psychopathology in offspring: 10-year follow-up. *Journal of the American Academy of Child and Adolescent Psychiatry, 41,* 402–409.

North, C. S., Nixon, S. J., Shariat, S., Mallonee, S., McMillen, J. C., Spitznagel, E. L., et al. (1999). Psychiatric disorders among survivors of the Oklahoma City Bombing. *Journal of the American Medical Association, 282,* 755–762.

Nothen, M. M., Cichon, S., Rohleder, H., Hemmer, S., Franzek, E., Fritze, J., et al. (1999). Evaluation of linkage of bipolar affective disorder to chromosome 18 in a sample of 57 German families. *Molecular Psychiatry, 4,* 76.

Nothen, M. M., Cichon, S., Franzek, E., Albus, M., Bormann, M., Rietschel, M., et al. (1997). Systematic search for susceptibility genes in bipolar affective disorder—evidence for disease loci at 18p and 4p. *American Journal of Human Genetics, 61 (S)*, A288.

Nottelman, E. D., & Jensen, P. S. (1998). Current issues in childhood bipolarity. *Journal of Affective Disorders, 51*, 77–80.

Nurnberger, J. I., Hamovit, J., Hibbs, E. D., Pelligrini, D., Guroff, J. J., Maxwell, M. E., et al. (1988). A high-risk study of primary affective disorder: Selection of subjects, initial assessment, and 1- to 2-year follow-up. In D. L. Dunner, E. S. Gershon, & J. E. Barrett (Eds.), *Relatives at risk for mental disorder* (pp. 161–177). New York: Raven Press.

Offord, D. R., Boyle, M. H., Szatmari, P., Rae-Grant, J. I., Links, P. S., Cadman, D. T., et al. (1987). Ontario Child Health Study. II. Six-month prevalence of disorder and rates of service utilization. *Archives of General Psychiatry, 44*, 832–836.

O'Hara, M. W., Stuart, S., Gorman, L. L., & Wenzel, A. (2000). Efficacy of interpersonal psychotherapy for postpartum depression. *Archives of General Psychiatry, 57*, 1039–1045.

Panak, W. F., & Garber, J. (1992). Role of aggression, rejection, and attributions in the prediction of depression in children. *Development and Psychopathology, 4*, 145–165.

Papolos, D., & Papolos, J. (1999). *Bipolar child: The definitive and reassuring guide to childhood's most misunderstood disorder, Vol. 1*. New York: Broadway.

Papolos, D., & Papolos, J. (2002). *The bipolar child: The definitive and reassuring guide to childhood's most misunderstood disorder* (revised and expanded ed.). New York: Broadway.

Parker, G. (1993). Parental rearing style: Examining for links with personality vulnerability factors for depression. *Social Psychiatry and Psychiatric Epidemiology, 28*, 97–100.

Paykel, E. S., Scott, J., Teasdale, J. D., Johnson, A. L., Garland, A., Moore, R., et al. (1999). Prevention of relapse in residual depression by cognitive therapy. *Archives of General Psychiatry, 56*, 829–835.

Perlis, R. H., Nierenberg, A. A., Alpert, J. E., Pava, J., Matthews, J. D., Buchin, J., et al. (2002). Effects of adding cognitive therapy to fluoxetine dose increase on risk of relapse and residual depressive symptoms in continuation treatment of major depressive disorder. *Journal of Clinical Psychopharmacology, 22*, 474–480.

Petersen, T., Gordon, J. A., Kant, A., Fava, M., Rosenbaum, J. R., & Nierenberg, A. A. (2001). Treatment-resistant depression and Axis I comorbidity. *Psychological Medicine, 31*, 1223–1229.

Peterson, L., Mullins, L. L., & Ridley-Johnson, R. (1985). Childhood depression: Peer reactions to depression and life stress. *Journal of Abnormal Child Psychology, 13*, 597–609.

Pine, D. S., Cohen, P., & Brook, J. (1996). The association between major depression and headache: Results of a longitudinal epidemiologic study in youth. *Journal of Child and Adolescent Psychopharmacology, 6*, 153–164.

Pine, D. S., Cohen, E., Cohen, P., & Brook, J. (1999). Adolescent depressive symptoms as predictors of adult depression: Moodiness or mood disorder? *American Journal of Psychiatry, 156*, 133–135.

Pine, D. S., Cohen, E., Gurley, D., Brook, J., & Ma, Y. (1998). The risk for early-adulthood anxiety and depressive disorders in adolescents with anxiety and depressive disorders. *Archives of General Psychiatry, 55*, 56–64.

Pine, D. S., Goldstein, R. B., Wolk, S., & Weissman, M. M. (2001). The association between childhood depression and adulthood body mass index. *Pediatrics, 107*, 1049–1056.

Plotsky, P. M., & Meaney, M. J. (1993). Early, postnatal experience alters hypothalamic corticotropin-releasing factor (CRF) mRNA, median eminence CRF content and stress-induced release in adult rats. *Brain Research. Molecular Brain Research, 18*, 195–200.

Poltyrev, T., Keshet, G. I., Kay, G., & Weinstock, M. (1996). Role of experimental conditions in determining differences in exploratory behavior of prenatally stressed rats. *Developmental Psychobiology, 29*, 453–462.

Puig-Antich, J., Lukens, E., Davies, M., Goetz, D., Brennan-Quattrock, J., & Todak, G. (1985a). Psychosocial functioning in prepubertal major depressive disorders. I. Interpersonal relationships during the depressive episode. *Archives of General Psychiatry, 42*, 500–507.

Puig-Antich, J., Lukens, E., Davies, M., Goetz, D., Brennan-Quattrock, J., & Todak, G. (1985b). Psychosocial functioning in prepubertal major depressive disorders. II. Interpersonal relationships after sustained recovery from affective episode. *Archives of General Psychiatry, 42*, 511–517.

Quiggle, N. L., Garber, J., Panak, W. F., & Dodge, K. A. (1992). Social information processing in aggressive and depressed children. *Child Development, 63*, 1305–1320.

Radke-Yarrow, M., Nottleman, E., Martinez, P., Fox, M., & Belmont, B. (1992). Young children of affectively ill parents: A longitudinal study of psychological development. *Journal of the American Academy of Child and Adolescent Psychiatry, 31,* 68–76.

Rao, O., Ryan, N. D., Birmaher, B., Dahl, R. E., Williamson, D. E., Kaufman, J., et al. (1995). Unipolar depression in adolescents: Clinical outcome in adulthood. *Journal of the American Academy of Child and Adolescent Psychiatry, 34,* 566–578.

Rapee, R. M. (1997). Potential role of childrearing practices in the development of anxiety and depression. *Clinical Psychology Review, 17,* 47–67.

Rehm, L. P. (1977). A self-control model of depression. *Behavior Therapy, 8,* 787–804.

Reinecke, M. A., Ryan, N. E., & DuBois, L. (1998). Cognitive-behavioral therapy of depression and depressive symptoms during adolescence: A review and meta-analysis. *Journal of the American Academy of Child and Adolescent Psychiatry, 37,* 26–34.

Reinherz, H. A., Giaconia, R. M., Hauf, A. M., Wasserman, M. S., & Silverman, A. B. (1999). Major depression in the transition to adult hood: Risk and impairments. *Journal of Abnormal Psychology, 108,* 500–510.

Reiss, D., Neiderhiser, J. M., Hetherington, E. M., & Plomin, R. (2000). *The relationship code: Deciphering genetic and social influences on adolescent development.* Cambridge, MA: Harvard University Press.

Reynolds, C. F., Frank, E., Perel, J. M., Imber, S. D., Cornes, C., Miller, M. D., et al. (1999). Nortriptyline and interpersonal psychotherapy as maintenance therapies for recurrent depression: A randomized controlled trial in patients older than 59 years. *Journal of the American Medical Association, 281,* 39–45.

Reynolds, W. M., & Coats, K. I. (1986). A comparison of cognitive-behavioral therapy and relaxation training for the treatment of depression in adolescents. *Journal of Consulting and Clinical Psychology, 54,* 653–660.

Rice, F., Harold, G., & Thapar, A. (2002). The genetic etiology of childhood depression: A review. *Journal of Child Psychology and Psychiatry, 43,* 65–79.

Roberts, R. E., Roberts, C. R., & Chen, Y. R. (1997). Ethnocultural differences in prevalence of adolescent depression. *American Journal of Community Psychology, 25,* 95–110.

Roberts, S. B., & Kendler, K. S. (1999). Neuroticism and self-esteem as indices of the vulnerability to major depression in women. *Psychological Medicine, 29,* 1101–1109.

Robins, L. N., Locke, B. Z., & Regier, D. A. (1991). An overview of psychiatric disorders in America. In L. N. Robins & D. A. Regier (Eds.), *Psychiatric disorders in America: The Epidemiologic Catchment Area Project* (pp. 328–366). New York: The Free Press.

Robins, L. N., & Price, R. (1991). Adult disorders predicted by childhood conduct problems: Results from the NIMH Epidemiologic Catchment Area Project. *Psychiatry, 54,* 116–132.

Robinson, N. S., Garber, J., & Hilsman, R. (1995). Cognitions and stress: direct and moderating effects on depressive versus externalizing symptoms during the junior high school transition. *Journal of Abnormal Psychology 104,* 453–463.

Robinson, R. M., Powers, J. M., Cleveland, P. H., & Thyer, B. A. (1990). Inpatient treatment for depressed children and adolescents: Preliminary evaluations. *Psychiatric Hospital, 21,* 107–112.

Rohde, P., Clarke, G. N., Lewinsohn, P. M., Seeley, J. R., & Kaufman, N. K. (2001). Impact of comorbidity on a cognitive-behavioral group treatment for adolescent depression. *Journal of the American Academy of Child and Adolescent Psychiatry, 40,* 795–802.

Rohde, P., Lewinsohn, P. M., & Seeley, J. R. (1990). Are people changed by the experience of having an episode of depression? A further test of the scar hypothesis. *Journal of Abnormal Psychology, 99,* 264–271.

Rohde, P., Lewinsohn, P. M., & Seeley, J. R. (1994). Are adolescents changed by an episode of major depression? *Journal of the American Academy of Child and Adolescent Psychiatry, 33,* 1289–1298.

Rosenbaum, J. F., Biederman, J., Hirshfeld-Becker, D. R., Kagan, J., Snidman, N., & Friedman, D. (2000). A controlled study of behavioral inhibition in children of parents with panic disorder and depression. *American Journal of Psychiatry, 157,* 2002–2010.

Rossello, J., & Bernal, G. (1999). The efficacy of cognitive-behavioral and interpersonal treatments for depression in Puerto Rican adolescents. *Journal of Consulting and Clinical Psychology, 67,* 734–745.

Rotheram-Borus, M. J., Piacentini, J., Van Rossem, R., Graae, F., Cantwell, C., Castro-Blanco, D., et al. (1996). Enhancing treatment adherence with a specialized emergency room program for adolescent suicide attempters. *Journal of the American Academy of Child and Adolescent Psychiatry, 35,* 654–663.

Rubin, K., Booth, L., Zahn-Waxler, C., Cummings, E. M., & Wilkinson, M. (1991). Dyadic play behaviors of children of well and depressed mothers. *Development and Psychopathology, 3,* 243–251.

Rudolph, K. D., Hammen, C., & Burge, D. (1994). Interpersonal functioning and depressive symptoms in childhood: Addressing the issues of specificity and comorbidity. *Journal of Abnormal Child Psychology, 22,* 355–371.

Rueter, M. A., Scaramella, L., Wallace, L. E., & Conger, R. D. (1999). First onset of depressive or anxiety disorders predicted by the longitudinal course of internalizing symptoms and parent–adolescent disagreements. *Archives of General Psychiatry, 56,* 726–732.

Rutter, M. (1996). Connections between child and adult psychopathology. *European Child and Adolescent Psychiatry, 5* (Suppl. 1), 4–7.

Ryan, C. E. (2002) Clinical and research issues in the evaluation and treatment of families. *Medicine and Health, Rhode Island, 85,* 278–280.

Ryan, N. D. (2003). Medication treatment for depression in children and adolescents. *CNS Spectrums, 8,* 283–287.

Ryan, N. D., Meyer, V., Dachille, S., Mazzie, D., & Puig-Antich, J. (1988). Lithium antidepressant augmentation in TCA-refractory depression in adolescents. *Journal of the American Academy of Child and Adolescent Psychiatry, 27,* 371–376.

Ryan, N. D., Puig-Antich, J., Rabinovich, H., Fried, J., Ambrosin, P., Meyer, V., et al. (1988). MAOIs in adolescent major depression unresponsive to tricyclic antidepressants. *Journal of the American Academy of Child and Adolescent Psychiatry, 27,* 755–758.

Rynn, M. A., Findling, R., Emslie, G., Marcus, R. N., Fernandes, L. A., D'Amico, M. F., et al. (2002). *Efficacy and safety of nefazodone in adolescents with MDD.* Poster presented at the 155th annual meeting of the American Psychiatric Association, Philadelphia, PA.

Sachs, G. S., Baldassano, C. F., Truman, C., & Guille, C. (2000). Comorbidity of attention deficit hyperactivity disorder with early- and late-onset bipolar disorder. *American Journal of Psychiatry, 157,* 466–468.

Sachs, G. S., Grossman, F., Ghaemi, S. N., Okamoto, A., & Bowden, C. L. (2002). Combination of a mood stabilizer with risperidone or haloperidol for treatment of acute mania: A double-blind, placebo-controlled comparison of efficacy and safety. *American Journal of Psychiatry, 159,* 1146–1154.

Schlenger, W. E., Caddell, J. M., Ebert, L., Jordan, B. K., Rourke, K. M., Wilson, D., et al. (2002).

Psychological reactions to terrorist attacks: Findings from the National Study of Americans' Reactions to September 11. *Journal of the American Medical Association, 288,* 581–588.

Schneider, L. S., Cooper, T. B., Staples, F. R., & Sloane, R. B. (1987). Prediction of individual dosage of nortriptyline in depressed elderly outpatients. *Journal of Clinical Psychopharmacology, 7,* 311–314.

Schulberg, H. C., Block, M. R., Madonia, M. J., Scott, C. P., Rodriguez, E., Imber, S. D., et al. (1996). Treating major depression in primary care practice. Eight-month clinical outcomes. *Archives of General Psychiatry, 53,* 913–919.

Schulze, T. G., & McMahon, F. J. (2003). Genetic linkage and associate studies in bipolar affective disorder: A time for optimism. *American Journal of Medical Genetics, 123C,* 36–47.

Schwab, S. G., Hallmayer, J., Lerer B., Albus, M., Bormann, M., Honig, S., et al. (1998). Support for a chromosome 18p locus conferring susceptibility to functional psychoses in families with schizophrenia, by association and linkage analysis. *American Journal of Human Genetics, 63,* 1139.

Sedlak, A. J., & Broadhurst, D. D. (1996). *Executive summary of the Third National Incidence Study of Child Abuse and Neglect.* Washington, DC: U.S. Department of Health and Human Services, Administration for Children and Families, Administration on Children, Youth and Families, National Center on Child Abuse and Neglect.

Segal, J., Berk, M., & Brook, S. (1998). Risperidone compared with both lithium and haloperidol in mania: A double-blind randomized controlled trial. *Clinical Neuropharmacology, 21,* 176–180.

Seligman, M. E. P. (1975). *Helplessness: On depression, development and death.* New York: Freeman.

Seth, R., Jennings, A. L., Bindman, J., Phillips, J., & Bergmann, K. (1992). Combination treatment with noradrenalin and serotonin reuptake inhibitors in resistant depression. *British Journal of Psychiatry, 161,* 562–565.

Shapiro, D. A., Barkham, M., Rees, A., Hardy, G. E., Reynolds, S., & Startup, M. (1994) Effects of treatment duration and severity of depression on the effectiveness of cognitive-behavioral and psychodynamic-interpersonal psychotherapy. *Journal of Consulting and Clinical Psychology, 62,* 522–534.

Shaw, B. F. (1977). Comparison of cognitive therapy and behavior therapy in the treatment of depression. *Journal of Consulting and Clinical Psychology, 45,* 543–551.

Sheeber, L., Hops, H., & Davis, B. (2001). Family processes in adolescent depression. *Clinical Child and Family Psychology Review, 4*, 19–35.

Sheeber, L., Hops, H., Albert, A., Davis, B., & Andrews, J. (1997). Family support and conflict: prospective relations to adolescent depression. *Journal of Abnormal Child Psychology, 25*, 333–344.

Shelton, R. C., Tollefson, G. D., Tohen, M., Stahl, S., Gannon, K. S., Jacobs, T. G., et al. (2001). A novel augmentation strategy for treating resistant major depression. *American Journal of Psychiatry, 158*, 131–134.

Shochet, I. M., Dadds, M. R., Holland, D., Whitefield, K., Harnett, P. H., & Osgarby, S. (2001). The efficacy of a universal school-based program to prevent adolescent depression. *Journal of Clinical Child Psychology, 30*, 303–315.

Shulterbrant, J. G. & Ruskin, A. (ed.) 1977. *Depression in childhood: diagnosis, treatment and conceptual models*. New York: Raven Press.

Silberg, J., Pickles, A., Rutter, M., Hewitt, J., Simonoff, E., Maes, H., et al. (1999). The influence of genetic factors and life stress on depression among adolescent girls. *Archives of General Psychiatry, 56*, 225–232.

Simons, A. D., Murphy, G. E., Levine, J. E., & Wetzel, R. D. (1986). Cognitive therapy and pharmacotherapy for depression: Sustained improvement over one year. *Archives of General Psychiatry, 43*, 43–49.

Smoller, J. W., & Finn, C. T. (2003). Family, twin, and adoption studies of bipolar disorder. *American Journal of Medical Genetics, 123C*(1), 48–58.

Smyth, C., Kalsi, G., Brynjolfsson, J., O'Neil, J., Curtis, D., Rifkin, L., et al. (1996). Further tests for linkage of bipolar affective disorder to the tyrosine hydroxylase gene locus on chromosome 11p15 in a new series of multiplex British affective disorder pedigrees. *American Journal of Psychiatry, 153*, 271–274.

Solomon, D. A., Keitner, G. I., Miller, I. W., Shea, M. T., & Keller, M. B. (1995). Course of illness and maintenance treatments for patients with bipolar disorder. *Journal of Clinical Psychiatry, 56*, 5–13.

Spence, S., Najman, J. M., Bor, W., O'Callaghan, M. J., & Williams, G. M. (2002). Maternal anxiety and depression, poverty and marital relationship factors during early childhood as predictors of anxiety and depressive symptoms in adolescence. *Journal of Child Psychology and Psychiatry and Allied Disciplines, 43*, 457–469.

Spence, S. H., Sheffield, J. K., & Donovan, C. L. (2003). Preventing adolescent depression: An evaluation of the Problem Solving for Life program. *Journal of Consulting and Clinical Psychology, 71*, 3–13.

Spinelli, M. G., & Endicott, J. (2003). Controlled clinical trial or interpersonal psychotherapy versus parenting education program for depressed pregnant women. *American Journal of Psychiatry, 160*, 555–562.

Spitz, R. A., & Wolf, K. M. (1946). Anaclitic depression: An inquiry into the genesis of psychiatric conditions in childhood, 11. *The Psychoanalytic Study of the Child, 2*, 313–342.

Stanger, C., McConaughy, S. H., & Achenbach, T. M. (1992). Three-year course of behavioral/emotional problems in a national sample of 4- to 16-year-olds: II. Predictors of syndromes. *Journal of the American Academy of Child and Adolescent Psychiatry, 31*, 941–950.

Stark, K. D., Reynolds, W. M., & Kaslow, N. J. (1987). A comparison of the relative efficacy of self-control therapy and a behavioral problem-solving therapy for depression in children. *Journal of Abnormal Child Psychology, 15*, 91–113.

Stein, D., Williamson, D. E., Birmaher, B., Brent, D. A., Kaufman, J., Dahl, R. E., et al. (2000). Parent–child bonding and family functioning in depressed children and children at high risk and low risk for future depression. *Journal of the American Academy of Child and Adolescent Psychiatry, 39*, 1387–1395.

Steingard, R. J., Renshaw, A. F., Hennen, J., Lenox, M., Cintron, C., Young, A., et al. (2002). Smaller frontal lobe white matter volumes in depressed adolescents. *Biological Psychiatry, 52*, 413–417.

Steingard, R. J., Yurgelun-Todd, D. A., Hennen, J., Moore, J., Moore, C., Vakil, K., et al. (2000). Increased orbitofrontal cortex levels of choline in depressed adolescents as detected by in vivo MRS. *Biological Psychiatry, 48*, 1053–1066.

Straub, R. E., Lehrer T., Luo, Y., Loth, J. E., Wei, S., Sharpe, L., et al. (1994). A possible vulnerability locus for bipolar affective disorder on chromosome 21q22.3. *Nature Genetics, 8*, 291–296.

Stine, O. C., Xu, J., Koskela R., McMahon, F. J., Gschwend, M., Friddle, C., et al. (1995). Evidence for linkage of bipolar disorder to chromosome 18 with a parent-of-origin effect. *American Journal of Human Genetics, 57*, 1384–1394.

Strober, M., & Carlson, G. (1982). Bipolar illness in adolescents with major depression: Clinical, genetic, and psychopharmacologic predictors in a three- to four-year prospective follow-up investigation. *Archives of General Psychiatry, 39,* 549–555.

Strober, M., Freeman, R., Rigali, J., Schmidt, S., & Diamond, D. (1992). The pharmacotherapy of depressive illness in adolescence: II. Effects of lithium augmentation in nonresponders to imipramine. *Journal of the American Academy of Child and Adolescent Psychiatry, 31,* 16–20.

Strober, M., Morrell, W., Lampert, C., & Burroughs, J. (1990). Relapse following discontinuation of lithium maintenance therapy in adolescents with bipolar I illness: A naturalistic study. *American Journal of Psychiatry, 147,* 457–461.

Swann, A. C., Stokes, P. E., Casper, F., Secunda, S., Bowden, C., Berman, N., et al. (1992). Hypothalmic–pituitary–adrenocortical function in mixed and pure mania. *Acta Psychiatrica Scandinavia, 85,* 270–274.

Takahashi, L. K., Baker, E. W., & Kalin, N. H. (1990). Ontogeny of behavioral and hormonal responses to stress in prenatally stressed male rat pups. *Physiology and Behavior, 47,* 357–364.

Tanner, J. M. (1962). *Growth at adolescence: With a general consideration of effects of hereditary and environmental factors upon growth and maturation from birth to maturity.* Oxford: Blackwell Scientific Publications.

Teasdale, J. D., Segal, Z., Williams, J. M. G., Ridgeway, V. A., Soulsby, J. M., & Lau, M. A. (2000). Prevention of relapse/recurrence in major depression by mindfulness-based cognitive therapy. *Journal of Consulting and Clinical Psychology, 68,* 615–623.

Teicher, M. H. (2002). Scars that won't heal: The neurobiology of child abuse. *Scientific American, 286*(3), 68–75.

Teti, D. M., Gelfand, D. M., Messinger, D., & Isabella, R. (1995). Maternal depression and the quality of early attachment: An examination of infants, preschoolers and their mothers. *Developmental Psychology, 31,* 364–376.

Thase, M. E., Bhargave, M., & Sachs, G. S. (2003). Treatment of bipolar depression: Current status, continued challenges, and the STEP-BD approach. *Psychiatric Clinics of North America, 26,* 495–518.

Thase, M. E., Entsuah, A. R., & Rudolph, R. L. (2001). Remission rates during treatment with venlafaxine or selective serotonin reuptake inhibitors. *British Journal of Psychiatry, 178,* 234–241.

Thase, M. E., Greenhouse, J. B., Frank, E., Reynolds, C. F., Pilkonis, P. A., Hurley, K., et al. (1997). Treatment of major depression with psychotherapy–pharmacotherapy combinations. *Archives of General Psychiatry, 54,* 1009–1015.

Thase, M. E., Trivedi, M. H., & Rush, A. J. (1995). MAOIs in the contemporary treatment of depression. *Neuropsychopharmacology, 12,* 185–219.

Thompson, L. W., Gallagher, D., & Breckenridge, J. S. (1987). Comparative effectiveness of psychotherapies for depressed elders. *Journal of Consulting and Clinical Psychology, 55,* 385–390.

Todd, R. D., Reich, W., Petti, T. A., Joshi, P., DePaulo, J. R., Nurneberger, J., et al. (1996). Psychiatric diagnoses in the child and adolescent members extended families identified through adult bipolar affective disorder probands. *Journal of the American Academy of Child and Adolescent Psychiatry, 35,* 664–671.

Tohen, M., Sanger, T. M., McElroy, S. L., Tollefson, G. D., Chengappa, K. N., Daniel, D. G., et al. (1999). Olanzapine versus placebo in the treatment of acute mania. Olanzapine HGEH Study Group. *American Journal of Psychiatry, 156,* 702–709.

Trad, P. V. (1987). *Infant and childhood depression: developmental factors.* New York: John Wiley & Sons.

Trad, P. V. (1994). Save our children. *American Journal of Psychotherapy, 48,* 175–178.

Treatment for Adolescents With Depression Study Team. (2003). Treatment for Adolescents With Depression Study Team (TADS): Rationale, design, and methods. *Journal of the American Academy of Child and Adolescent Psychiatry, 42,* 531–542.

Tsuang, M. T., Taylor, L., & Faraone, S. V. (2004). An overview of the genetics of psychotic mood disorders. *Journal of Psychiatric Research, 38,* 3–15.

Turecki, G., Grof, P., Cavazzoni, P., Duffy, A., Grof, E., Martin, R., et al. (1999). Lithium responsive bipolar disorder, unilineality and chromosome 18: a linkage study. *American Journal of Medical Genetics, 88,* 411–415.

Turner, J. E., Jr., & Cole, D. A. (1994). Developmental differences in cognitive diatheses for child depression. *Journal of Abnormal Child Psychology, 22,* 15–32.

Turner, R. J., & Lloyd, D. A. (1999). The stress process and the social distribution of depression. *Journal of Health and Social Behavior, 40,* 374–404.

U. S. Department of Health and Human Services (US-DHHS). (1999). *Mental health: A report of the Surgeon General.* Washington, DC: Author.

van Os, J., Jones, P., Lewis, G., Wadsworth, M., &

Murray, R. (1997). Developmental precursors of affective illness in a general population birth cohort. *Archives of General Psychiatry, 54,* 625–631.

Vitaro, F., Pelletier, D., Gagnon, C., & Baron, P. (1995). Correlates of depressive symptoms in early adolescence. *Journal of Emotional and Behavioral Disorders, 3,* 241–251.

Voekler, R. (2003). Mounting student depression taxing campus mental health services. *Journal of the American Medical Association, 289,* 2055–2056.

Vostanis, P., Feehan, C., Grattan, E., & Bickerton, W. (1996). A randomised controlled out-patient trial of cognitive-behavioural treatment for children and adolescents with depression: 9-month follow-up. *Journal of Affective Disorders, 40,* 105–116.

Vythilingam, M., Heim, C., Newport, J., Miller, A. H., Anderson, E., Bronen, R., et al. (2002). Childhood trauma associated with smaller hippocampal volume in women with major depression. *Amrican Journal of Psychiatry, 159,* 2072–2080.

Wagner, K. D. (2002). Management of bipolar disorder in children and adolescents. *Psychopharmacology Bulletin, 36,* 151–159.

Wagner, K. D., & Ambrosini, P. J. (2001). Childhood depression: Pharmacological therapy/treatment (pharmacotherapy of childhood depression). *Journal of Clinical Child Psychology, 30,* 88–97.

Wagner, K. D., Ambrosini, P., Rynn, M., Wohlberg, C., Yang, R., Greenbaum, M. S., et al. (2003). Efficacy of sertraline in the treatment of children and adolescents with major depressive disorder: Two randomized controlled trials. *Journal of the American Medical Association, 290,* 1033–1041.

Wagner, K. D., Robb, A. S., Findling, R., Jin, J., Gutierroz, M. M., & Heydorn, W. E. (2001). *Citalopram is effective in the treatment of major depressive disorder in children and adolescents: Results of a placebo-controlled trial.* Poster presented at the 40th annual meeting of the American College of Neuropsychopharmacology, Waikoloa, HI.

Wagner, K. D., Weller, E. B., Carlson, G. A., Sachs, G., Biederman, J., Frazier, J. A., et al. (2002). An open-label trial of divalproex in children and adolescents with bipolar disorder. *Journal of the American Academy of Child and Adolescent Psychiatry, 41,* 1224–1230.

Walker, L. S., Garber, J., & Greene, J. W. (1993). Psychosocial correlates of recurrent childhood pain: A comparison of pediatric patients with recurrent abdominal pain, organic illness, and psychiatric disorders. *Journal of Abnormal Psychology, 102,* 248–258.

Walker, L. S., Garber, J., & Greene, J. W. (1994). Somatic complaints in pediatric patients: A prospective study of the role of negative life events, child social and academic competence, and parental somatic symptoms. *Journal of Consulting and Clinical Psychology, 62,* 1213–1221.

Wang, X., & Nemeroff, C. B. (2003). Biological distinction between unipolar and bipolar disorder. In J. C. Soares & S. Gershon (Eds.), *Handbook of medical psychiatry* (pp. 407–422). New York: Marcel Dekker.

Warner, V., Weissman, M. M., Mufson, L., & Wickramaratne, P. J. (1999). Grandparents, parents, and grandchildren at high risk for depression: A three-generation study. *Journal of the American Academy of Child and Adolescent Psychiatry, 38,* 289–296.

Watson, D., & Tellegen, A. (1985). Toward a consensual structure of mood. *Psychological Bulletin, 98,* 219–235.

Webster-Stratton, C., & Hammond, M. (1988). Maternal depression and its relationship to life stress, perceptions of child behavior problems, parenting behaviors, and child conduct problems. *Journal of Abnormal Child Psychology, 16,* 299–315.

Weersing, V. R., Iyengar, S., Birmaher, B., Kolko, D. J., & Brent, D. A. (in press). Effectiveness of cognitive-behavioral therapy for adolescent depression under clinically representative conditions. *Behavior Therapy.*

Weinfield, N. S., Stroufe, L. A., & Egeland, B. (2000). Attachment from infancy to early adulthood in a high risk sample: Continuity, discontinuity, and their correlates. *Child Development, 71,* 695–702.

Weiss, E. L., Longhurst, J. G., & Mazure, C. M. (1999). Childhood sexual abuse as a risk factor for depression in women: Psychosocial and neurobiological correlates. *American Journal of Psychiatry, 156,* 816–828.

Weissman, M. M., Bland, R., Canino, G., Faravelli, C., Greenwald, S., Hwu, H. G., et al. (1996). Cross-national epidemiology of major depression and bipolar disorder. *Journal of the American Medical Association, 276,* 293–299.

Weissman, M. M., Paykel, E. S., Siegel, R., & Klerman, G. L. (1971). The social role performance of depressed women: Comparisons with a normal group. *American Journal of Orthopsychiatry, 41*, 390–405.

Weissman, M. M., Warner, V., Wickramaratne, P., Moreau, D., & Olfson, M. (1997). Offspring of depressed parents. 10 years later. *Archives of General Psychiatry, 54*, 932–940.

Weissman, M. M., Warner, V., Wickramaratne, P. J., Nomura, Y., Merikangas, K., Bruder, G., et al. (2004). Offspring at high risk for anxiety and depression: Preliminary findings from a three-generation study. In J. Gorman (Ed.), *Fear and anxiety: Benefits of translational research* (pp. 65–85). Washington, DC: American Psychiatric Association Press.

Weissman, M. M., Wolk, S., Goldstein, R. B., Moreau, D., Adams, P., Greenwald, S., et al. (1999) Depressed adolescents grown up. *Journal of the American Medical Association, 281*, 1707–1713.

Weissman, M. M., Wolk, S., Wickramaratne, P., Goldstein, R. B., Adams, P., Greenwald, S., et al. (1999). Children with prepubertal-onset major depressive disorder and anxiety grown up. *Archives of General Psychiatry, 56*, 794–801.

Weisz, J. R., Southam-Gerow, M. A., & McCarty, C. A. (2001). Control-related beliefs and self-reported depressive symptoms in clinic-referred children and adolescents. *Journal of Abnormal Psychology, 110*, 97–109.

Weisz, J. R., Thurber, C. A., Sweeney, L., Proffitt, V. D., & LeGagnoux, G. L. (1997). Brief treatment of mild-to-moderate child depression using primary and secondary control enhancement training. *Journal of Consulting and Clinical Psychology, 65*, 703–707.

Weisz, J. R., & Weersing, V. R. (1999). Psychotherapy with children and adolescents: Efficacy, effectiveness, and developmental concerns in Rochester symposium on developmental psychopathology. In D. Cicchetti and S. L. Toth (Ed.), *Developmental approaches to prevention and intervention*. Rochester, NY: Univ. of Rochester Press.

Weisz, J. R., & Weersing, V. R. (2002). Community clinic treatment of depressed youth: Benchmarking usual care against CBT clinical trials. *Journal of Consulting and Clinical Psychology, 70*, 299–310.

Weller, E., Weller, R., & Fristad, M. (1995). Bipolar disorder in children: Misdiagnosis, underdiagnosis, and future directions. *Journal of the American Academy of Child and Adolescent Psychiatry, 34*, 709–714.

Weller, R. A., Weller, E. B., Tucker, S., & Fristad, M.

(1986). Mania in prepubertal children: Has it been underdiagnosed? *Journal of Affective Disorders, 11*, 151–154.

West, S., McElroy, S., Strakowski, S., Keck, P., & McConville, B. (1995). Attention deficit hyperactivity disorder in adolescent mania. *American Journal of Psychiatry, 152*, 271–274.

West, S. A., Strakowski, S. M., Sax, K., McElroy, S., Keck, P., & McConville, B. (1996). Phenomenology and comorbidity of adolescents hospitalized for the treatment of acute mania. *Biological Psychiatry, 39*, 458–460.

Whittaker, A., Johnson, J., Shaffer, D., Rappaport, J. L., Kalikow, K., Walsh, B. T., et al. (1990). Uncommon troubles in young people: Prevalence estimates of selected psychiatric disorders in a nonreferred population. *Archives of General Psychiatry, 47*, 487–496.

Wicki, W., & Angst, J. (1991). The Zurich study. X. Hypomania in a 28- to 30-year-old cohort. *European Archives of Psychiatry and Clinical Neuroscience, 240*, 339–348.

Wilens, T. E., Biederman, J., Abrantes, M., Spencer, B., & Thomas, J. (1997a). Attention deficit hyperactivity disorder (ADHD) is associated with early onset substance use disorders. *Journal of Nervous and Mental Diseases, 185*, 475–482.

Wilens, T., Biederman, J., Abrantes, M., Spencer, B., & Thomas, J. (1997b). Clinical characteristics of psychiatrically referred adolescent outpatients with substance use disorder. *Journal of the American Academy of Child and Adolescent Psychiatry, 36*, 941–947.

Wilens, T., Biederman, J., Millstein, R., Wozniak, J., Hahesy, A., & Spencer B. (1999). Risk for substance use disorders in youths with child- and adolescent-onset bipolar disorder. *Journal of the American Academy of Child and Adolescent Psychiatry, 36*, 680–685.

Wittchen, H. U., Nelson, C. B., & Lachner, G. (1998). Prevalence of mental disorders and psychosocial impairments in adolescents and young adults. *Psychological Medicine, 28*, 109–126.

Wong, K. C., Kenndy, P. J., & Lee, S. (1999). Clinical manifestations and outcomes in 17 cases of Stevens-Johnson syndrome and toxic epidermal necrolysis. *Australasian Journal of Dermatology, 40*, 131–134.

Wood, A., Harrington, R., & Moore, A. (1996). Controlled trial of a brief cognitive-behavioural intervention in adolescent patients with depressive disorders. *Journal of Child Psychology and Psychiatry, 37*, 737–746.

Wood, A., Trainor, G., Rothwell, J., Moore, A., & Harrington, R. (2001). Randomized trial of a group therapy for repeated deliberate self-harm in adolescents. *Journal of the American Academy of Child and Adolescent Psychiatry, 40,* 1246–1253.

Wozniak, J., Biederman, J., Kiely, K., Ablon, J., Faraone, S. Mundy, E., et al. (1995). Mania-like symptoms suggestive of childhood-onset bipolar disorder in clinically referred children. *Journal of the American Academy of Child and Adolescent Psychiatry, 34,* 867–876.

Wozniak, J., Biederman, J., Mundy, E., Mennin, D., & Faraone, S. V. (1995). A pilot family study of childhood-onset mania. *Journal of the American Academy of Child and Adolescent Psychiatry, 34,* 1577–1583.

Wozniak, J., Crawford, M. H., Biederman, J., Faraone, S. V., Spencer, T. J., Taylor, A., et al. (1999). Antecedents and complications of trauma in boys with ADHD: Findings from a longitudinal study. *Journal of the American Academy of Child and Adolescent Psychiatry, 38,* 48–55.

Part II: Schizophrenia

Addington, D., Addington, J., & Patten, S. (1998). Depression in people with first-episode schizophrenia. *British Journal of Psychiatry Supplement, 172,* 90–92.

Addington, J. (2002). Draft consensus statement-principles and practice in early psychosis. In J. Edwards & P. McGorry (Eds.), *Implementing early intervention in psychosis: A guide to establishing early psychosis services* (1st ed., pp. 145–155). London: Martin Dunitz.

Addington, J., & Addington, D. (1998). Effect of substance misuse in early psychosis. *British Journal of Psychiatry Supplement, 172,* 134–136.

Adler, L. E., & Waldo, M. C. (1991). Counterpoint: Sensory gating-hippocampal model of schizophrenia, *Schizophrenia Bulletin, 17,* 19–24.

Adler, L. E., Waldo, M. C., & Freeman, R. (1985). Neurophysiological studies of sensory gating in schizophrenia: Comparison of auditory and visual responses. *Biological Psychiatry, 20,* 1284–1296.

Akil, M., Kolachana, B. S., Rothmond, D. A., Hyde, T. M., Weinberger, D. R., & Kleinman, J. E. (2003). Catechol-*O*-methyltransferase genotype and dopamine regulation in the human brain. *Journal of Neuroscience, 23,* 2008–2013.

Alaghband-Rad, J., McKenna, K., Gordon, C. T., Albus, K. E., Hamburger, S. D., Rumsey, J. M., et al. (1995). Childhood-onset schizophrenia: The severity of premorbid course. *Journal of the American Academy of Child and Adolescent Psychiatry, 34,* 1273–1283.

Alexander, G. E., & Crutcher, M. D. (1990). Functional architecture of basal ganglia circuits: Neural substrates of parallel processing [review]. *Trends in Neuroscience, 13,* 266–271.

Ambelas, A. (1992). Preschizophrenics: Adding to the evidence, sharpening the focus. *British Journal of Psychiatry, 160,* 401–404.

American Psychiatric Association. (1994). *Diagnostic and statistical manual of mental disorders* (4th ed.). Washington, DC: Author.

Amin, S., Singh, S. P., Brewin, J., Jones, P. B., Medley, I., & Harrison, G. (1999). Diagnostic stability of first-episode psychosis. Comparison of ICD-10 and DSM-III-R systems. *British Journal of Psychiatry, 175,* 537–543.

Andreasen, N. C. (1986). *Can schizophrenia be localized in the brain?* Washington, DC: American Psychiatric Press.

Andreasen, N. C. (1999). A unitary model of schizophrenia: Bleuler's "fragmented phrene" as schizencephaly. *Archives of General Psychiatry, 56,* 781–787.

Andreasen, N. C., Arndt, S., Alliger, R., Miller, D., & Flaum, M. (1995). Symptoms of schizophrenia. Methods, meanings, and mechanisms. *Archives of General Psychiatry, 52,* 341–351.

Andreasen, N. C., O'Leary, D. S., Arndt, S., Cizadlo, T., Rezai, K., Watkins, G. L., et al. (1995). I. PET studies of memory: Novel and practiced free recall of complex narratives. *Neuroimage, 2,* 284–295.

Andreasen, N. C., O'Leary, D. S., Flaum, M., Nopoulos, P., Watkins, G. L., Boles Ponto, L. L., et al. (1997). Hypofrontality in schizophrenia: Distributed dysfunctional circuits in neuroleptic-naive patients. *Lancet, 349,* 1730–1734.

Andreasen, N. C., Olsen, S. A., & Dennert, J. W. (1982). Ventricular enlargement in schizophrenia: Relationship to positive and negative symptoms. *American Journal of Psychiatry, 139,* 297–302.

Andreasen, N. C., Rajarethinam, R., Cizadlo, T., Arndt, S., Swayze, V. W., Flashman, L. A., et al. (1996). Automatic atlas-based volume estimation of human brain regions from MR images. *Journal of Computer Assisted Tomography, 20,* 98–106.

Arndt, S., Alliger, R. J., & Andreasen, N. C. (1991).

The distinction of positive and negative symptoms. The failure of a two-dimensional model. *British Journal of Psychiatry, 158,* 317–322.

Arndt, S., Andreasen, N. C., Flaum, M., Miller, D., & Nopoulos, P. (1995). A longitudinal study of symptom dimensions in schizophrenia. Prediction and patterns of change. *Archives of General Psychiatry, 52,* 352–360.

Arseneault, L., Cannon, M., Poulton, R., Murray, R., Caspi, A., & Moffitt, T. E. (2002). Cannabis use in adolescence and risk for adult psychosis: longitudinal prospective study. *British Medical Journal, 325,* 1212–1213.

Arsenault, L., Cannon, M., Witton, J., & Murray, R. (2003). The causal association between cannabis and psychosis: An examination of the evidence. *British Journal of Psychiatry.*

Asarnow, J. R. (1994). Annotation: childhood—onset schizophrenia. *Journal of Child Psychology and Psychiatry, and Allied Disciplines, 35,* 1345–1371.

Asarnow, J. (1988). Children at risk for schizophrenia: Converging lines of evidence. *Schizophrenia Bulletin, 14,* 613–631.

Asarnow, J. R., Tompson, M. C., & Goldstein, M. J. (2001). Psychosocial factors: The social context of child and adolescent-onset schizophrenia. In H. Remschmidt (Ed.), *Schizophrenia in children and adolescents* (pp. 168–181). Cambridge, UK: Cambridge University Press.

Asarnow, J. R., Tompson, M., Hamilton, E. B., Goldstein, M. J., & Guthrie, D. (1994). Family-expressed emotion, childhood-onset depression, and childhood-onset schizophrenia spectrum disorders: Is expressed emotion a non-specific correlate of child psychopathology or a specific risk factor for depression? *Journal of Abnormal Child Psychology, 22,* 129–146.

Asarnow, J. R., & Goldstein, M. J. (1986). Schizophrenia during adolescence and early adulthood: A developmental perspective on risk research. *Clinical Psychology Review, 6,* 211–235.

Asarnow, R. (1983). Schizophrenia. In R. Tartar (Ed.), *The child at psychiatric risk* (pp. 150–194). New York: Oxford University Press.

Asarnow, R., Brown W., & Strandburg, R. (1995). Children with a schizophrenic disorder: Neurobehavioral studies. *European Archives of Psychiatry and Clinical Neuroscience, 245,* 70–79.

Asarnow, R. F., Nuechterlein, K. H., Fogelson, D., Subotnik, K. L., Payne, D. A., Russell, A. T., et al. (2001). Schizophrenia and schizophrenia-spectrum personality disorders in the first-degree relatives of children with schizophrenia: The UCLA family study. *Archives of General Psychiatry, 58,* 581–588.

Asarnow, R., Steffy, R., MacCrimmon, D., & Cleghorn, J. (1978). An attentional assessment of foster children at risk for schizophrenia. In L. Wynne, R. Cromwell, & S. Matthysse (Eds.), *The nature of schizophrenia: New approaches to research and treatment* (p. 356). New York: John Wiley & Sons.

Asarnow, R., Tanguay, P., Bott, L., & Freeman, B. (1987). Patterns of intellectual functioning in non-retarded autistic and schizophrenic children. *Journal of Child Psychology and Psychiatry, and Allied Disciplines, 28,* 273–280.

Axelsson, R., & Lagerkvist-Briggs, M. (1992). Factors predicting suicide in psychotic patients. *European Archives of Psychiatry and Clinical Neuroscience, 241,* 259–266.

Aylward, E., Walker, E., & Bettes, B. (1984). Intelligence in schizophrenia: Meta-analysis of the research. *Schizophrenia Bulletin, 10,* 430–459.

Barbee, J. G., Mancuso, D. M., Freed, C. R., & Todorov, A. A. (1992). Alprazolam as a neuroleptic adjunct in the emergency treatment of schizophrenia. *American Journal of Psychiatry, 149,* 506–510.

Baribeau-Braun J., Picton T., & Gosselin J. (1983). Schizophrenia: A neurophysiological evaluation of abnormal information processing. *Science, 219,* 874–876.

Battaglia, J., Moss, S., Rush, J., Kang, J., Mendoza, R., Leedom, L., et al. (1997). Haloperidol, lorazepam, or both for psychotic agitation? A multicenter, prospective, double-blind, emergency department study. *American Journal of Emergency Medicine, 15,* 335–340.

Beck, A. T., Sokol, L., Clark, D. A., Berchick, R., & Wright, F. (1992). A crossover study of focused cognitive therapy for panic disorder. *American Journal of Psychiatry, 149,* 778–83.

Bellack, A. S., & Brown, S. A. (2001). Psychosocial treatments for schizophrenia. *Current Psychiatry Reports, 3,* 407–412.

Bellack, A. S., & Mueser, K. T. (1993). Psychosocial treatment for schizophrenia. *Schizophrenia Bulletin, 19,* 317–336.

Bentsen, H. (2003). Correspondence. *Psychological Medicine, 33,* 755.

Berk, M., Ichim, C., & Brook, S. (2001). Efficacy of mirtazapine add on therapy to haloperidol in the treatment of the negative symptoms of schizophrenia: A double-blind randomized placebo-controlled study. *International Clinical Psychopharmacology, 16,* 87–92.

Berman, K. F., Torrey, E. F., Daniel, D. G., & Weinberger, D. R. (1992). Regional cerebral blood flow in monozygotic twins discordant and concordant for schizophrenia. *Archives of General Psychiatry, 49*, 927–934.

Bertolino, A., Breier, A., Callicott, J. H., Adler, C., Mattay, V. S., Shapiro, M., et al. (2000). The relationship between dorsolateral prefrontal neuronal *N*- acetylaspartate and evoked release of striatal dopamine in schizophrenia. *Neuropsychopharmacology, 22*, 125–132.

Bhana, N., Foster, R. H., Olney, R., & Plosker, G. L. (2001). Olanzapine: an updated review of its use in the management of schizophrenia. *Drugs, 61*, 111–161.

Bilder, R. M., Goldman, R. S., Robinson, D., Reiter, G., Bell, L., Bates, J. A., et al. (2000). Neuropsychology of first-episode schizophrenia: Initial characterization and clinical correlates. *American Journal of Psychiatry, 157*, 549–559.

Bilder, R. M., Mukherjee, S., Rieder, R. O., & Pandurangi, A. K. (1985). Symptomatic and neuropsychological components of defect states. *Schizophrenia Bulletin, 11*, 409–491.

Blatter, D. D., Bigler, E. D., Gale, S. D., Johnson, S. C., Anderson, C. V., Burnett, B. M., et al. (1995). Quantitative volumetric analysis of brain MR: Normative database spanning 5 decades of life. *American Journal of Neuroradiology, 16*, 241–251.

Bleuler, E. (1950). *Dementia praecox or the group of schizophrenias*, Trans. New York: International University Press. (Original work published 1911)

Bleuler, M. (1978). *The schizophrenic disorders: Long-term patient and family studies*. New Haven: Yale University Press.

Bleuler, M. (1980). Schizophrenia-neurosis. *Deutsche Medizinische Wochenschrift, 105*, 209–212.

Bleuler, E. (1987). The prognosis of dementia praecox—Group of schizophrenias. In J. Cutting & M. Shepherd (Eds.), *The clinical roots of the schizophrenia concept* (pp. 59–74). Cambridge, UK: Cambridge University Press. (Original work published 1908)

Booth, A., Johnson, D. R., Granger, D. A., Crouter, A., & McHale, S. (2003). Testosterone and child and adolescent adjustment: The moderating role of parent-child relationships. *Developmental Psychology, 39*, 85–98.

Bourdon, K. H., Rae, D. S., Locke, B. Z., Narrow, W. E., & Regier, D. A. (1992). Estimating the prevalence of mental disorders in U.S. adults from the Epidemiologic Catchment Area Survey. *Public Health Report, 107*, 663–668.

Bracha, H. S., Torrey, E. F., Gottesman, I. I., Bigelow, L. B., & Cunniff, C. (1992). Second-trimester markers of fetal size in schizophrenia: A study of monozygotic twins. *American Journal of Psychiatry, 149*, 1355–1361.

Braff, D., Stone, C., Callaway, E., Geyer, M., Glick, I., & Bali, L. (1978). Prestimulus effects on human startle reflex in normals and schizophrenics. *Psychophysiology, 15*, 339–343.

Brown, G. W., Monck, E. M., Carstairs, G. M., & Wing, J. K. (1962). Influence of family life on the course of schizophrenic illness. *British Journal of Preventative and Social Medicine, 16*, 55–68.

Browne, S., Clarke, M., Gervin, M., Waddington, J. L., Larkin, C., & O'Callaghan E. (2000). Determinants of quality of life at first presentation with schizophrenia. *British Journal of Psychiatry, 176*, 173–176.

Bustillo, J. R., Lauriello, J., Horan, W. P., & Keith, S. J. (2001). The psychosocial treatment of schizophrenia: An update. *American Journal of Psychiatry, 158*, 163–175.

Bustillo, J. R., Lauriello, J., & Keith, S. J. (1999). Schizophrenia: Improving outcome. *Harvard Review of Psychiatry, 6*, 229–240.

Butzlaff, R. L., & Hooley, J. M. (1998). Expressed emotion and psychiatric relapse. A meta-analysis. *Archives of General Psychiatry, 55*, 547–552.

Callicott, J. H., Bertolino, A., Mattay, V. S., Langheim, F. J., Duyn, J., Coppola, R., et al. (2000). Physiological dysfunction of the dorsolateral prefrontal cortex in schizophrenia revisited. *Cerebral Cortex, 10*, 1078–1092.

Cannon, M., Caspi, A., Moffitt, T. E., Harrington, H., Taylor A., & Murray, R. M. (2002). Evidence for early-childhood, pan-developmental impairment specific to schizophreniform disorder: Results from a longitudinal birth cohort. *Archives of General Psychiatry, 59*, 449–456.

Cannon, M., Jones, P., Gilvarry, C., Rifkin, L., McKenzie, K., Foerster, A., et al. (1997). Premorbid social functioning in schizophrenia and bipolar disorder. Similarities and differences. *American Journal of Psychiatry, 154*, 1544–1550.

Cannon, M., Jones, P., Huttunen, M., Tanskanen, A., & Murray, R. M. (1999a). Motor coordination deficits as predictors of schizophrenia among Finnish school children. *Human Psychopharmacology, 14*, 491–497.

Cannon, T. D., Mednick, S. A., Parnas, J., Schulsinger, F., Praestholm, J., & Vestergaard, A. (1993). Developmental brain abnormalities in the offspring of schizophrenic mothers. I. Contributions of genetic and perinatal factors. *Archives of General Psychiatry, 50,* 551–564.

Cannon-Spoor, H. E., Potkin, S. G., & Wyatt, R. J. (1982). Measurement of premorbid adjustment in chronic schizophrenia. *Schizophrenia Bulletin, 8,* 470–484.

Carpenter, W. T., Jr., Buchanan, R. W., Kirkpatrick, B., & Breier, A. F. (1999). Diazepam treatment of early signs of exacerbation in schizophrenia. *American Journal of Psychiatry, 156,* 299–303.

Caviness, V. S., Jr., Kennedy, D. N., Richelme, C., Rademacher, J., & Filipek, P. A. (1996). The human brain age 7–11 years: A volumetric analysis based on magnetic resonance images. *Cerebral Cortex, 6,* 726–736.

Censits, D. M., Ragland, J. D., Gur, R. C., & Gur, R. E. (1997). Neuropsychological evidence supporting a neurodevelopmental model of schizophrenia: A longitudinal study. *Schizophrenia Research, 24,* 289–298.

Chakos, M. H., Mayerhoff, D. I., Loebel, A. D., Alvir, J. M., & Lieberman, J. A. (1992). Incidence and correlates of acute extrapyramidal symptoms in first episode of schizophrenia. *Psychopharmacological Bulletin, 28,* 81–86.

Chouljian, T. L., Shumway, M., Balancio, E., Dwyer, E. V., Surber, R., & Jacobs, M. (1995). Substance use among schizophrenic outpatients: Prevalence, course, and relation to functional status. *Annals of Clinical Psychiatry, 7,* 19–24.

Chowdari, K. V., Mirnics, K., Semwal, P., Wood, J., Lawrence, E., Bhatia, T., et al. (2002). Association and linkage analyses of RGS4 polymorphisms in schizophrenia. *Human Molecular Genetics, 11,* 1373–1380.

Christison, G. W., Kirch, D. G., & Wyatt, R. J. (1991). When symptoms persist: Choosing among alternative somatic treatments for schizophrenia. *Schizophrenia Bulletin, 17,* 217–245.

Chumakov, I., Blumenfeld, M., Guerassimenko, O., Cavarec, L. Palicio, M., Abderrahim, H., et al. (2002). Genetic and physiological data implicating the new human gene *G72* and the gene for D-amino acid oxidase in schizophrenia. *Proceeding of the National Academy of Science of the United States of America, 99,* 13675–13680.

Citrome, L., Levine, J., & Allingham, B. (2000). Changes in use of valproate and other mood stabilizers for patients with schizophrenia from 1994 to 1998. *Psychiatric Service, 51,* 634–638.

Clouston, T. S. (1892). *Clinical lectures on mental diseases* (3rd ed.) London: Churchill.

Cohen, R. (1990). Event-related potentials and cognitive dysfunction in schizophrenia. In H. Hafner, & W. Gattaz (Eds.), *Search for the causes of schizophrenia* (Vol. II, pp. 342–360). New York: Springer-Verlag.

Cohen, S., Lavelle, J., Rich, C. L., & Bromet, E. (1994). Rates and correlates of suicide attempts in first-admission psychotic patients. *Acta Psychiatrica Scandinavica, 90,* 167–171.

Cormac, I., Jones, C., & Campbell, C. (2002). Cognitive behaviour therapy for schizophrenia. *Cochrane Database of Systematic Reviews.*

Cornblatt, B. A. (2002). The New York high-risk project to the Hillside recognition and prevention (RAP) program. *American Journal of Medical Genetics, 114,* 956–966.

Cornblatt, B., Lenzenweger, M., Dworkin R., & Erlenmeyer-Kimling, L. (1992). Childhood attentional dysfunctions predict social deficits in unaffected adults at risk for schizophrenia. *British Journal of Psychiatry, 161,* 59–64.

Cornblatt, B., & Obuchowski, M. (1997). Update of high-risk research: 1987–1997. *International Review of Psychiatry, 9,* 437–447.

Cosway, R., Byrne, M., Clafferty, R., Hodges, A., Grant, E., Abukmeil, S. S., et al. (2000). Neuropsychological change in young people at high risk for schizophrenia: Results from the first two neuropsychological assessments of the Edinburgh High-Risk Study. *Psychological Medicine, 30,* 1111–1121.

Crow, T. J., Done, D. J., & Sacker, A. (1995). Childhood precursors of psychosis as clues to its evolutionary origins. *European Archives of Psychiatry & Clinical Neuroscience, 245,* 61–69.

Crow, T. J., MacMillan, J. F., Johnson, A. L., & Johnstone, E. C. (1986). A randomized controlled trial of prophylactic neuroleptic treatment. *British Journal of Psychiatry, 148,* 120–127.

Cullberg, J. (1999). Integrating intensive psychosocial therapy and low-dose medical treatment in a total material of first-episode psychotic patients compared to "treatment as usual"—a 3-year follow-up. *Medicinski Arhiv, 53,* 167–170.

David, A. S., & Cutting, J. (1994). *The neuropsychology of schizophrenia.* Hove: Lawrence Erlbaum.

David, A. S., Malmberg, A., Brandt, L., Allebeck, P., & Lewis, G. (1997). IQ and risk for schizophrenia: A population-based cohort study. *Psychological Medicine, 27,* 1311–1323.

Davidson, M., Reichenberg, A., Rabinowitz, J., Weiser, M., Kaplan, Z., & Mark, M. (1999). Behavioral and intellectual markers for schizophrenia in apparently healthy male adolescents. *American Journal of Psychiatry, 156,* 1328–1335.

Degreef, G., Ashtari, M., Bogerts, B., Bilder, R. M., Jody, D. N., Alvir, J. M., et al. (1992). Volumes of ventricular system subdivisions measured from magnetic resonance images in first-episode schizophrenic patients. *Archives of General Psychiatry, 49,* 531–537.

de Haan, L., Linszen, D. H., Lenior, M. E., de Win, E. D., & Gorsira, R. (2003). Duration of untreated psychosis and outcome of schizophrenia: Delay in intensive psychosocial treatment versus delay in treatment with antipsychotic medication. *Schizophrenia Bulletin, 29,* 341–348.

DeLisi, L. E. (1997). Is schizophrenia a lifetime disorder of brain plasticity, growth and aging? *Schizophrenia Research, 23,* 119–129.

DeLisi, L. E., Hoff, A. L., Schwartz, J. E., Shields, G. W., Halthore, S. N., Gupta, S. M., et al. (1991). Brain morphology in first-episode schizophrenic-like psychotic patients: a quantitative magnetic resonance imaging study. *Biological Psychiatry, 29,* 159–175.

DeLisi, L. E., Stritzke, P., Riordan, H., Holan, V., Boccio, A., Kushner, M., et al. (1992). The timing of brain morphological changes in schizophrenia and their relationship to clinical outcome. *Biological Psychiatry, 31,* 241–254.

DeLisi, L. E., Tew, W., Xie, S., Hoff, A. L., Sakuma, M., Kushner, M., et al. (1995). A prospective follow-up study of brain morphology and cognition in first-episode schizophrenic patients: preliminary findings. *Biological Psychiatry, 38,* 349–360.

DeQuardo, J. R., Carpenter, C. F., & Tandon, R. (1994). Patterns of substance abuse in schizophrenia: Nature and significance. *Journal of Psychiatric Research, 28,* 267–275.

Dickerson, F. B. (2000). Cognitive behavioural psychotherapy for schizophrenia: A review of recent empirical studies. *Schizophrenia Research, 43,* 71–90.

Done, D., Crow, T., Johnson, E., & Sacker, A. (1994). Childhood antecedents of schizophrenia and affective illness: Social adjustment at ages 7 and 11. *British Medical Journal, 309,* 699–703.

Dorn, L. D., & Chrousos, G. P. (1997). The neurobiology of stress: Understanding regulation of affect during female biological transitions. *Seminars in Reproductive Endocrinology, 15,* 19–35.

Dorn, L. D., Hitt, S. F., & Rotenstein, D. (1999). Biopsychological and cognitive differences in children with premature vs. on-time adrenarche. *Archives of Pediatrics and Adolescent Medicine, 153,* 137–146.

Dubertret, C., Gorwood, P., Ades, J., Feingold, J., Schwartz, J. C., & Sokoloff, P. (1998). Meta-analysis of DRD3 gene and schizophrenia: Ethnic heterogeneity and significant association in Caucasians. *American Journal of Medical Genetics, 81,* 318–322.

Dworkin, R. H., Cornblatt, B. A., Friedmann, R., Kaplansky, L. M., Lewis, J. A., Rinaldi, A., et al. (1993). Childhood precursors of affective vs. social deficits in adolescents at risk for schizophrenia. *Schizophrenia Bulletin, 19,* 563–577.

Eaton, W. W. (1985). Epidemiology of schizophrenia. *Epidemiologic Reviews, 7,* 105–126.

Eaton, W. W., Badawi, M., & Melton, B. (1995). Prodromes and precursors: Epidemiologic data for primary prevention of disorders with slow onset. *American Journal of Psychiatry, 152,* 967–972.

Eckman, T. A., Wirshing, W. C., Marder, S. R., Liberman, R. P., Johnston-Cronk, K., Zimmermann, K., et al. (1992). Technique for training schizophrenic patients in illness self-management: A controlled trial. *American Journal of Psychiatry, 149,* 1549–1555.

Edwards, J., & McGorry, P. (2002). *Implementing early intervention in psychosis: A guide to establishing early psychosis services.* London: Martin Dunitz.

Egan, M. F., Goldberg, T. E., Kolachana, B. S., Callicott, J. H., Mazzanti, C. M., Straub, R. E., et al. (2001). Effect of COMT Val108/158 Met genotype on frontal lobe function and risk for schizophrenia. *Proceedings of the National Academy of Sciences of the United States of America, 98,* 6917–6922.

Elvevag, B., & Goldberg, T. E. (2000). Cognitive impairment in schizophrenia is the core of the disorder. *Critical Reviews in Neurobiology, 14,* 1–21.

Emsley, R. A. (1999). Risperidone in the treatment of first-episode psychotic patients: A double-blind multicenter study. Risperidone Working Group. *Schizophrenia Bulletin, 25,* 721–729.

Erickson, D. H., Beiser, M., Iacono, W. G., Fleming, J. A., & Lin, T. Y. (1989). The role of social relationships in the course of first-episode schizophrenia and affective psychosis. *American Journal of Psychiatry, 146,* 1456–1461.

Erlenmeyer-Kimling, L. (2001). Early neurobehavioral deficits as phenotypic indicators of the schizophrenia genotype and predictors of later psychosis. *American Journal of Medical Genetics, 105,* 23–24.

Erlenmeyer-Kimling, L., & Cornblatt, B. A. (1992). Summary of attentional findings in the New York high-risk project. *Journal of Psychiatric Research, 26,* 405–426.

Erlenmeyer-Kimling, L., Cornblatt, B., Friedman, D., Marcuse, Y., Rutschmann, J., Simmens, S., et al. (1982). Neurological, electrophysiological and attentional deviations in children at risk of schizophrenia. In F. A. Henn & H. Nasrallah (Eds.), *Schizophrenia as a brain disease* (pp. 61–98). New York: Oxford University Press.

Erlenmeyer-Kimling, L., Rock, D., Roberts, S., Jamal, M., Kestenbaum, C., Cornblatt, B., et al. (2000). Attention, memory, and motor skills as childhood predictors of schizophrenia-related psychoses: The New York high-risk project. *American Journal of Psychiatry, 157,* 1416–1422.

Falloon, I.R.H., Boyd, J. L., & McGill, C. W. (1984). *Family care of schizophrenia*. New York: Guilford Press.

Falloon, I.R.H., Kydd, R. R., Coverdale, J. H., & Laidlaw, T. M. (1996). Early detection and intervention for initial episodes of schizophrenia. *Schizophrenia Bulletin, 22,* 271–282.

Faraone, S. V., Kremen, W. S., Lyons, M. J., Pepple, J. R., Seidman, L. J., & Tsuang, M. T. (1995). Diagnostic accuracy and linkage analysis: How useful are schizophrenia spectrum phenotypes? *American Journal of Psychiatry, 152,* 1286–1290.

Feinberg, I. (1982a). Schizophrenia and late maturational brain changes in man. *Psychopharmacology Bulletin, 18,* 29–31.

Feinberg I. (1982b). Schizophrenia: Caused by a fault in programmed synaptic elimination during adolescence? *Journal of Psychiatric Research, 17,* 319–334.

Filipek, P. A., Richelme, C., Kennedy, D. N., & Caviness, V. S., Jr. (1994). The young adult human brain: An MRI-based morphometric analysis. *Cerebral Cortex, 4,* 334–360.

Fish, B. (1977). Neurobiological antecedents of schizophrenia in children. *Archives of General Psychiatry, 34,* 1297–1313.

Fish, B. (1984). Characteristics and sequelae of the neurointegrative disorder in infants at risk for schizophrenia: 1952–1982. In N. Watt, E. Anthony, L. Wynne, & J. Rolf (Eds.), *Children at risk for schizophrenia: A longitudinal perspective* (pp. 423–439). New York: Cambridge University Press.

Fish, B. (1987). Infant predictors of the longitudinal course of schizophrenic development. *Schizophrenia Bulletin, 13,* 395–409.

Fish, B., Marcus, J., Hans, S. L., & Auerbach, J. G. (1993). Infants at risk for schizophrenia: Sequelae of a genetic neurointegrative defect: A review and replication analysis of pandysmaturation in the Jerusalem Infant Development Study. *Annual Progress in Child Psychiatry and Child Development,* 153–190.

Fish, B., Marcus, J., Hans, S. L., Auerbach, J. G., & Perdue, S. (1992). Infants at risk for schizophrenia: Sequelae of a genetic neurointergrative defect. *Archives of General Psychiatry, 49,* 221–235.

Flaum, M., O'Leary, D. S., Johnson, D., Arndt, S., Cizadlo, T., Hichwa, R., et al. (1997). Relationship between symptom dimensions and cerebral blood flow in schizophrenia as assessed by 15H$_2$O PET. *Schizophrenia Research, 24,* 165.

Flaum, M., O'Leary, D. S., Swayze, V. W., II, Miller, D. D., Arndt, S., & Andreasen, N. C. (1995). Symptom dimensions and brain morphology in schizophrenia and related psychotic disorders. *Journal of Psychiatric Research, 29,* 261–276.

Foerster, A., Lewis, S. W., Owen, M. J., & Murray, R. M. (1991). Pre-morbid adjustment and personality in psychosis. Effects of sex and diagnosis. *British Journal of Psychiatry, 158,* 171–176.

Ford, J. M., White, P. M., Csernansky, J. G., Faustman, W. O., Roth, W. T., & Pfefferbaum, A. (1994). ERPs in schizophrenia: Effects of antipsychotic medication. *Biological Psychiatry, 36,* 153–170.

Freedman, L., Rock, D., Roberts, S., Cornblatt, B., & Erlenmeyer-Kimling, L. (1998). The New York high-risk project: Attention, anhedonia, and social outcome. *Schizophrenia Research, 30,* 1–9.

Freedman, R. F., Adler, L. E., Bickford, P., Byerley, W., Coon, H., Cullum, C. M., et al. (1994). Schizophrenia and nicotinic receptors. *Harvard Review of Psychiatry, 2,* 179–192.

Freedman, R., Adler, L., Waldo, M., Oachtman, E., & Franks, R. (1983). Neurophysiological evidence for a defect in inhibitory pathways in schizophrenia: Comparison of medicated and drug-free patients. *Biological Psychiatry, 18,* 537–551.

Gervin, M., Browne, S., Lane, A., Clarke, M., Waddington, J. L., Larkin, C., et al. (1998). Spontaneous abnormal involuntary movements in first episode schizophrenia and schizophreniform disorder: Baseline rate in a group of patients from an Irish catchment area. *American Journal of Psychiatry, 155,* 1202–1206.

Giedd, J. N., Blumenthal, J., Jeffries, N. O., Castellanos, F. X., Liu, H., Zijdenbos, A., et al. (1999). Brain development during childhood and adolescence: A longitudinal MRI study. *Nature Neuroscience, 2,* 861–863.

Giedd, J. N., Snell, J. W., Lange, N., Rajapakse, J. C., Casey, B. J., Kozuch, P. L., et al. (1996). Quantitative magnetic resonance imaging of human brain development: Ages 4–18. *Cerebral Cortex, 6,* 551–560.

Gitlin, M., Nuechterlein, K., Subotnik, K. L., Ventura, J., Mintz, J., Fogelson, D. L., et al. (2001). Clinical outcome following neuroleptic discontinuation in patients with remitted recent-onset schizophrenia. *American Journal of Psychiatry, 158,* 1835–1842.

Gittleman-Klein, R., & Klein, D. F. (1969). Premorbid social adjustment and prognosis in schizophrenia. *Journal of Psychiatric Research, 7,* 35–53.

Glatt, S. J., Faraone, S. V., & Tsuang, M. T. (2003). Meta-analysis identifies an association between the dopamine D2 receptor gene and schizophrenia. *Molecular Psychiatry, 8,* 911–915.

Gogate, N., Giedd, J., Janson, K., Rapoport, J. L. (2001). Brain imaging in normal and abnormal brain development: New perspectives for child psychiatry. *Clinical Neuroscience Research, 1,* 283–290.

Gottesman, I. I. (1991). *Schizophrenia genesis: The origin of madness.* New York: W. H. Freeman.

Gottesman, I. I., & Erlenmeyer-Kimling, L. (2001). Family and twin strategies as a head start in defining prodromes and endophenotypes for hypothetical early-interventions in schizophrenia. *Schizophrenia Research, 51,* 93–102.

Gottesman, I. I., & Gould, T. D. (2003). The endophenotype concept in psychiatry: Etymology and strategic intentions. *American Journal of Psychiatry, 160,* 636–645.

Gottesman, I. I., & Shields, J. (1973). Genetic theorizing and schizophrenia. *British Journal of Psychiatry, 122,* 15–30.

Gottesman, I. I., & Shields, J. (1982). *Schizophrenia: The epigenetic puzzle.* Cambridge, UK: Cambridge University Press.

Green, A. I., & Schildkraut, J. J. (1995). Should clozapine be a first-line treatment for schizophrenia? The rationale for a double-blind clinical trial in first-episode patients. *Harvard Review of Psychiatry, 3,* 1–9.

Green, M. F. (1996). What are the functional consequences of neurocognitive deficits in schizophrenia? *American Journal of Psychiatry, 153,* 321–330.

Green, M. F. (1998). *Schizophrenia from a neurocognitive perspective. Probing the impenetrable darkness.* Needham Heights, MA: Allyn & Bacon.

Green, M. F., Satz, P., Gaier, D. J., Ganzell, S., & Kharabi, F. (1989). Minor physical anomalies in schizophrenia. *Schizophrenia Bulletin, 15,* 91–99.

Gualtieri, C. T., Adams, A., Shen, C. D., & Loiselle, D. (1982). Minor physical anomalies in alcoholic and schizophrenic adults and hyperactive and autistic children. *American Journal of Psychiatry, 139,* 640–643.

Gupta, S., Hendricks, S., Kenkel, A. M., Bhatia, S. C., & Haffke, E. A. (1996). Relapse in schizophrenia: Is there a relationship to substance abuse? *Schizophrenia Research, 20,* 153–156.

Gur, R. E., Cowell, P., Turetsky, B. I., Gallacher, F., Cannon, T., Bilker, W., et al. (1998). A follow-up MRI study of schizophrenia: Relationship of neuroanatomic changes with clinical and neurobehavioral measures. *Archives of General Psychiatry, 55,* 145–152.

Gur, R. E., Maany, V., Mozley, P. D., Swanson, C., Bilker, W., & Gur, R. C. (1998). Subcortical MRI volumes in neuroleptic-naive and treated patients with schizophrenia. *American Journal of Psychiatry, 155,* 1711–1717.

Gur, R. E., Mozley, P. D., Resnick, S. M., Levick, S., Erwin, R., Saykin, A. J., et al. (1991). Relations among clinical scales in schizophrenia. *American Journal of Psychiatry, 148,* 472–478.

Gur, R. C., Ragland, J. D., Moberg, P. J., Bilker, W. B., Kohler, C., Siegel, S. J., et al. (2001). Computerized neurocognitive scanning II: The profile of schizophrenia. *Neuropsychopharmacology, 25,* 777–788.

Gur, R. C., Ragland, J. D., Mozley, L. H., Mozley, P. D., Smith, R., Alavi, A., et al. (1997). Lateralized changes in regional cerebral blood flow during performance of verbal and facial recognition tasks: Correlations with performance and "effort." *Brain and Cognition, 33,* 388–414.

Gur, R. E., Turetsky, B. I., Bilker, W. B., & Gur, R. C. (1999). Reduced gray matter volume in schizophrenia. *Archives of General Psychiatry, 56,* 905–911.

Gur, R. E., Turetsky, B. I., Cowell, P. E., Finkelman, C., Maany, V., Grossman, R. I., et al. (2000a). Temporolimbic volume reductions in schizophrenia. *Archives of General Psychiatry, 57,* 769–775.

Gur, R. E., Cowell, P. E., Latshaw, A., Turetsky, B. I., Grossman, R. I., Arnold, S. E., et al. (2000b). Reduced dorsal and orbital prefrontal gray matter volumes in schizophrenia. *Archives of General Psychiatry, 57,* 761–768.

Guy, J. D., Majorski, L. V., Wallace, C. J., & Guy, M. P. (1983). The incidence of minor physical anomalies in adult male schizophrenics. *Schizophrenia Bulletin, 9,* 571–582.

Häfner, H., Löffler, W., Maurer, K., Hambrecht, M.,

& an der Heiden, W. (1999). Depression, negative symptoms, social stagnation and social decline in the early course of schizophrenia. *Acta Psychiatrica Scandinavica, 100,* 105–118.

Häfner, H., Maurer, K., Löffler, W., & Riecher-Rossler, A. (1993). The influence of age and sex on the onset and early course of schizophrenia. *British Journal of Psychiatry, 162,* 80–86.

Hambrecht, M., & Hafner, H. (2000). Cannabis, vulnerability, and the onset of schizophrenia: an epidemiological perspective. *The Australian and New Zealand Journal of Psychiatry, 34,* 468–475.

Hans, S., Marcus, J., Nuechterlein K., Asarnow, R., Styr, B., & Auerbach, J. (1999). Neurobehavioral deficits at adolescence in children at risk for schizophrenia: The Jerusalem Infant Development Study. *Archives of General Psychiatry, 56,* 741–748.

Hare, E. H. (1987). Epidemiology of schizophrenia and affective psychoses. *British Medical Bulletin, 43,* 514–530.

Harrison, G., Hopper, K., Craig, T., Laska, E., Siegel, C., Wanderling, J., et al. (2001). Recovery from psychotic illness: A 15- and 25-year international follow-up study. *British Journal of Psychiatry, 178,* 506–517.

Heckers, S., Rausch, S. L., Goff, D., Savage, C. R., Schacter, D. L., Fischman, A. J., et al. (1998). Impaired recruitment of the hippocampus during conscious recollection in schizophrenia. *Nature Neuroscience, 1,* 318–323.

Helgason, T. (1964). Epidemiology of mental disorders in Iceland. A psychiatric and demographic investigation of 5395 Icelanders. *Acta Psychiatrica Scandinavica, Supplement 40,* 173.

Hessl, D., Glaser, B., Dyer-Friedman, J., Blasey, C., Hastie, T., Gunnar, M., et al. (2002). Cortisol and behavior in fragile X syndrome. *Psychoneuroendocrinology, 27,* 855–872.

Hillyard, S., & Hansen, J. (1986). Attention: Electrophysiological approaches. In: M. Coles, E. Donchin, & S. Porges (Eds.), *Psychophysiology: Systems, processes, and applications* (pp. 227–243). New York: Guilford.

Hillyard, S., & Kutas, M. (1983). Electrophysiology of cognitive processing. *Annual Review of Psychology, 34,* 33–61.

Ho, B. C., Alicata, D., Ward, J., Moser, D. J., O'Leary, D. S., Arndt, S., et al. (2003). Untreated initial psychosis: Relation to cognitive deficits and brain morphology in first-episode schizophrenia. *American Journal of Psychiatry, 160,* 142–148.

Hogarty, G., Anderson, C., Reiss, D., Kornblith, S., Greenwald, D., Ulrich, R., et al. (1997). Family psychoeducation, social skills training and maintenance chemotherapy in the aftercare treatment of schizophrenia, II: Two-year effects of a controlled study on relapse and adjustment. *Archives of General Psychiatry, 48,* 340–347.

Hogarty, G. E., McEvoy, J. P., Ulrich, R. F., DiBarry, A. L., Bartone, P., Cooley, S., et al. (1995). Pharmacotherapy of impaired affect in recovering schizophrenic patients. *Archives of General Psychiatry, 52,* 29.

Holcomb, H. H., Cascella, N. G., Thaker, G. K., Medoff, D. R., Dannals, R. F., & Tamminga, C. A. (1996). Functional sites of neuroleptic drug action in the human brain: PET/FDG studies with and without haloperidol. *American Journal of Psychiatry, 153,* 41–49.

Holcomb, H. H., Lahti, A. C., Medoff, D. R., Weiler, M., Dannals, R. F., & Tamminga, C. A. (2000). Brain activation patterns in schizophrenic and comparison volunteers during a matched-performance auditory recognition task. *American Journal of Psychiatry, 157,* 1634–1645.

Huber, T. J., Rollnik, J., Wilhelms, J., von zur Muhlen, A., Emrich, H. M., & Schneider, U. (2001). Estradiol levels in psychotic disorders. *Psychoneuroendocrinology, 26,* 27–35.

Huston, P. E., & Shakow, D. (1946). Studies of motor function in schizophrenia: III. Steadiness. *Journal of General Psychology, 34,* 119–126.

Huttenlocher, P. R. (1984). Synaptic elimination and plasticity in developing human cerebral cortex. *American Journal of Mental Deficiency, 88,* 488–496.

Huttenlocher, P. R., de Courten, C., Garey, L. J., & Van der Loos, H. (1982). Synaptogenesis in human visual cortex—evidence for synapse elimination during normal development. *Neuroscience Letters, 33,* 247–252.

Ingraham, L., Kugelmass, S., Frankel, E., Nathan, M., & Mirsky, A. (1995). Twenty-five-year follow-up of the Israeli high-risk study: Current and lifetime psychopathology. *Schizophrenia Bulletin, 21,* 183–192.

Isohanni, M., Jones, P. B., Moilanen, K., Rantakallio, P., Veijola, J., Oja, H., et al. (2001). Early developmental milestones in adult schizophrenia and other psychoses. A 31-year follow-up of the north Finland 1966 birth cohort. *Schizophrenia Research, 52,* 1–19.

Isohanni, M., Isohanni, I., Koponen, H., Koskinen, J., Laine, P., Lauronen, E., et al. (2004). Developmental precursors of psychosis. *Current Psychiatry Reports, 6,* 168–175.

Jablensky, A. (1986). Epidemiology of schizophrenia: A European perspective. *Schizophrenia Bulletin, 12,* 52–73.

Jackson, H., McGorry, P., Henry, L., Edwards, J., Hulbert, C., Harrigan, S., et al. (2001). Cognitively oriented psychotherapy for early psychosis (COPE): A 1-year follow-up. *British Journal of Clinical Psychology, 40,* 57–70.

Jacobsen, L. K., Giedd, J. N., Castellanos, F. X., Vaituzis, A. C., Hamburger, S. D., Kumra, S., et al. (1998). Progressive reduction of temporal lobe structures in childhood-onset schizophrenia. *American Journal of Psychiatry, 155,* 678–685.

Jacobson, K. C., Prescott, C. A., & Kendler, K. S. (2002). Sex differences in the genetic and environmental influences on the development of antisocial behavior. *Development and Psychopathology, 14,* 395–416.

Jarbin, H., Yngve, O., & Von Knorring, A. (2003). Adult outcome of social function in adolescent-onset schizophrenia and affective psychosis. *Journal of the American Academy of Child and Adolescent Psychiatry, 42,* 176–183.

Jernigan, T. L., & Tallal, P. (1990). Late childhood changes in brain morphology observable with MRI. *Developmental Medicine and Child Neurology, 32,* 379–385.

Johannessen, J. L., McGlashan, T. H., Larsen, T. K., Horneland, M., Joa, I., Mardal, S., et al. (2001). Early detection strategies for untreated first-episode psychosis. *Schizophrenia Research, 51,* 39–46.

Johns, A. (2001). Psychiatric effects of cannabis. *British Journal of Psychiatry, 178,* 116–122.

Jones, P. B. (1999). Longitudinal approaches to the search for the causes of schizophrenia: Past, present and future. In: W. F. Gattaz & H. Hafner (Eds.), *Search for the causes of schizophrenia* (Vol. 4, pp. 91–120). Berlin: Springer-Verlag.

Jones, P., & Done, D. (1997). From birth to onset: A developmental perspective of schizophrenia in two national birth cohorts. In M. Keshavan & R. Murray (Eds.), *Neurodevelopment and adult psychopathology* (pp. 119–136). Cambridge, UK: Cambridge University Press.

Jones, P. B., & Murray, R. M. (1991). The genetics of schizophrenia is the genetics of neurodevelopment. *British Journal of Psychiatry, 158,* 615–623.

Jones, P. B., Rodgers, B., Murray, R. M., & Marmot, M. G. (1994). Child developmental risk factors for adult schizophrenia in the British 1946 birth cohort. *Lancet, 344,* 1398–1402.

Jones, P., & Tarrant, J. (1999). Specificity of developmental precursors to schizophrenia and affective disorders. *Schizophrenia Research, 39,* 121–125.

Jones, P. B., & van Os, J. J. (2000). Commentary on Davidson, M., Reichenberg, A., Rabinowitz, J., Weiser, M., Kaplan, Z., & Mark, M. (1999). Behavioural and intellectual markers for schizophrenia in apparently healthy male adolescents. *American Journal of Psychiatry, 156,* 1328–1335; *Evidence-Based Mental Health, 3,* 89.

Kane, J. M. (1996). Treatment-resistant schizophrenic patients. *Journal of Clinical Psychiatry, 57,* 35–40.

Kane, J. M., Rifkin, A., Quitkin, F., Nayak, D., & Ramos-Lorenzi, J. (1982). Fluphenazine vs. placebo in patients with remitted, acute first-episode schizophrenia. *Archives of General Psychiatry, 39,* 70–73.

Kasai, K., Shenton, M. E., Salisbury, D. F., Hirayasu, Y., Lee, C. U., Ciszewski, A. A., et al. (2003a). Progressive decrease of left superior temporal gyrus gray matter volume in patients with first-episode schizophrenia. *American Journal of Psychiatry, 160,* 156–164.

Kasai, K., Shenton, M. E., Salisbury, D. F., Hirayasu, Y., Onitsuka, T., Spencer, M., et al. (2003b). Progressive decrease of left Heschl's gyrus and planum temporale gray matter volume in schizophrenia: A longitudinal MRI study of first-episode patients. *Archives of General Psychiatry, 60,* 766–775.

Kellner, R., Wilson, R. M., Muldawer, M. D., & Pathak, D. (1975). Anxiety in schizophrenia. The responses to chlordiazepoxide in an intensive design study. *Archives of General Psychiatry, 32,* 1246–1254.

Kemp, R., Hayward, P., Applewhaite, G., Everitt, B., & David, A. (1996). Compliance therapy in psychotic patients: Randomised controlled trial. *British Medical Journal, 312,* 345–349.

Kemp, R., Kirov, G., Everitt, B., Hayward, P., & David, A. (1998). Randomised controlled trial of compliance therapy: 18-month follow-up. *British Journal of Psychiatry, 172,* 413–419.

Kendler, K. S. (2000). Schizophrenia: Genetics. In B. J. Sadock & V. A. Sadock (Eds.), *Comprehensive textbook of psychiatry* (7th ed., pp. 1147–1159). New York: Lippincott, Williams, & Wilkins.

Keshavan, M. S., Anderson, S., & Pettegrew, J. W. (1994). Is schizophrenia due to excessive synaptic pruning in the prefrontal cortex? The Feinberg hypothesis revisited. *Journal of Psychiatric Research, 29,* 239–265.

Keshavan, M. S., & Hogarty, G. E. (1999). Brain maturational processes and delayed onset in schizophrenia. *Development and Psychopathology, 11,* 525–543.

Keshavan, M. S., & Schooler, N. (1992). First episode studies of schizophrenia: Criteria and characterization. *Schizophrenia Bulletin, 18,* 491–513.

Kety, S. S., Wender, P., Jacobsen, B., Ingraham, L. J., Jansson, L., Faber, B., et al. (1994). Mental illness in the biological and adoptive relatives of schizophrenic adoptees: Replication of the Copenhagen study in the rest of Denmark. *Archives of General Psychiatry, 51,* 442–455.

Kim, J., Caspi, A., Moffitt, T., Harrington, H., Milene, B., & Poulton, R. (in press). How may adults with mental disorder have prior juvenile diagnoses? Developmental follow-back of a prospective longitudinal cohort. *Archives of General Psychiatry.*

Klorman, R. (1991). Cognitive event-related potentials in attention deficit disorder. *Journal of Learning Disabilities, 24,* 130–140.

Knight, R. T., Hillyard, S. A., Woods, D. L., Neville, H. J. (1981). The effects of frontal cortex lesions on event-related potentials during auditory selective attention. *Electroencephalography and Clinical Neurophysiology, 52,* 571–582.

Ko, G. N., Korpi, E. R., Freed, W. J., Zalcman, S. J., & Bigelow, L. B. (1985). Effect of valproic acid on behavior and plasma amino acid concentrations in chronic schizophrenic patients. *Biological Psychiatry, 20,* 209–215.

Kohler, C. G., Turner, T. H., Bilker, W. B., Brensinger, C. M., Siegel, S. J., Kanes, S. J., et al. (2003). Facial emotion recognition in schizophrenia: Intensity effects and error pattern. *American Journal of Psychiatry, 160,* 1768–1774.

Kohn, M. I., Tanna, N. K., Herman, G. T., Resnick, S. M., Mozley, P. D., Gur, R. E., et al. (1991). Analysis of brain and CSF volumes from magnetic resonance imaging: Methodology, reliability and validation. *Radiology, 178,* 115–122.

Kopala, L. C., Fredrikson, D., Good, K. P., & Honer, W. G. (1996). Symptoms in neuroleptic-naive, first-episode schizophrenia: Response to risperidone. *Biological Psychiatry, 39,* 296–298.

Koreen, A. R., Siris, S. G., Chakos, M., Alvir, J., Mayerhoff, D., & Lieberman, J. (1993). Depression in first-episode schizophrenia. *American Journal of Psychiatry, 150,* 1643–1648.

Kovacs, M., Rush, A. J., Beck, A. T., & Hollon, S. D. (1981). Depressed outpatients treated with cognitive therapy or pharmacotherapy. A one-year follow-up. *Archives of General Psychiatry, 38,* 33–39.

Kraepelin, E. (1987). Dementia praecox. In J. Cutting & M. Shepherd (Eds. and Trans.), *The clinical roots of the schizophrenia concept* (pp. 13–24). Cambridge, UK: Cambridge University Press. (Original work published 1896)

Kraepelin, E. (1919). *Dementia praecox and paraphrenia.* Edinburgh: Livingstone.

Kramer, M. (1969). Cross-national study of diagnosis of the mental disorders: Origin of the problem. *American Journal of Psychiatry, 10,* 1–11.

Kravariti, E., Dazzan, P., Fearon, P., & Murray, R. (2003). Can one identify preschizophrenic children? In M. Keshavan, J. L. Kennedy, & R. Murray (Eds.), *Neurodevelopment and schizophrenia.* New York: Oxford University Press.

Kring, A. M., Barrett, L. F., & Gard, D. E. (2003). On the broad applicability of the affective circumplex: Representations of affective knowledge among schizophrenia patients. *Psychological Science, 14,* 207–214.

Kubicki, M., McCarley, R. W., Nestor, P. G., Huh, T., Kikinis, R., Shenton, M. E., et al. (2003). An fMRI study of semantic processing in men with schizophrenia. *Neuroimage, 20,* 1923–1933.

Kubicki, M., Westin, C. F., Maier, S., Frumin, M., Nestor, P. G., Salisbury, D., et al. (2002). Uncinate fasciculus findings in schizophrenia: A magnetic resonance diffusion tensor imaging study. *American Journal of Psychiatry, 159,* 813–820.

Kulhara, P., Kota, S. K., & Joseph, S. (1986). Positive and negative subtypes of schizophrenia: A study from India. *Acta Psychiatrica Scandinavica, 74,* 353–359.

Kumra, S., Frazier, J. A., Jacobsen, L. K., McKenna, K., Gordon, C. T., Lenane, M. C., et al. (1996). Childhood-onset schizophrenia. A double-blind clozapine-haloperidol comparison. *Archives of General Psychiatry, 53,* 1090–1097.

Kumra, S., Giedd, J. N., Vaituzis, A. C., Jacobsen, L. K., McKenna, K., Bedwell, J., et al. (2000). Childhood-onset psychotic disorders: Magnetic resonance imaging of volumetric differences in brain structure. *American Journal of Psychiatry, 157,* 1467–1474.

Kumra, S., Jacobsen, L. K., Lenane, M., Smith, A., Lee, P., Malanga, C. J., et al. (1998). Case series: Spectrum of neuroleptic-induced movement disorders and extrapyramidal side effects in childhood-onset schizophrenia. *Journal of Amer-*

ican Academy Child and Adolescent Psychiatry, 37, 221–227.

Kwon, J. S., O'Donnell, B. F., Wallenstein, G. V., Greene, R. W., Hirayasu, Y., Nestor, P. G., et al. (1999). Gamma frequency-range abnormalities to auditory stimulation in schizophrenia. *Archives of General Psychiatry, 56,* 1001–1005.

Lambe, E. K., Krimer, L. S., & Goldman-Rakic, P. S. (2000). Differential postnatal development of catecholamine and serotonin inputs to identified neurons in prefrontal cortex of rhesus monkey. *Journal of Neuroscience, 20,* 8780–8787.

Lammers, C. H., Garcia-Borreguero, D., Schmider, J., Gotthardt, U., Dettling, M., Holsboer, F., et al. (1995). Combined dexamethasone/corticotropin-releasing hormone test in patients with schizophrenia and in normal controls. *Biological Psychiatry, 38,* 803–807.

Lane, A., Kinsella, A., Murphy, P., Byrne, M., Keenan, J., Colgan, K., et al. (1997). The anthropometric assessment of dysmorphic features in schizophrenia as an index of its developmental origins. *Psychological Medicine, 27,* 1155–1164.

Laruelle, M. (2000). The role of endogenous sensitization in the pathophysiology of schizophrenia: Implications from recent brain imaging studies. *Brain Research. Brain Research Reviews, 31,* 371–384.

Lay, B., Blanz, B., Hartmann, M., & Schmidt, M. H. (2000). The psychosocial outcome of adolescent-onset schizophrenia: A 12-year follow-up. *Schizophrenia Bulletin, 26,* 801–816.

Lee, J. H., Woo, J. I., & Meltzer, H. Y. (2001). Effects of clozapine on sleep measures and sleep-associated changes in growth hormone and cortisol in patients with schizophrenia. *Psychiatry Research, 103,* 157–166.

Leff, J., Kuipers, L., Berkowitz, R., Eberlein-Vries, R., & Sturgeon, D. (1982). A controlled trial of social intervention in the families of schizophrenic patients. *British Journal of Psychiatry, 141,* 121–134.

Lehman, A. F., & Steinwachs, D. M. (1998). Translating research into practice: the Schiozphrenia Patient Outcomes Research Team (PORT) treatment recommendations. *Schizophrenia Bulletin, 24,* 1–10.

Lenior, M. E., Dingemans, P. M., Schene, A. H., Hart, A. A., & Linszen, D. H. (2002). The course of parental expressed emotion and psychotic episodes after family intervention in recent-onset schizophrenia. A longitudinal study. *Schizophrenia Research, 57,* 183–190.

Lenzenweger, M., Dworkin, R., & Wethington, E. (1989). Models of positive and negative symp-toms in schizophrenia: An empirical evaluation of latent structures. *Journal of Abnormal Psychology, 98,* 62–70.

Leonard, S., Adams, C., Breese, C. R., Adler, L. E., Bickford, P., Byerley, W., et al. (1996). Nicotinic receptor function in schizophrenia. *Schizophrenia Bulletin 22,* 431–445.

Leonard, S. C., Gault, J., Hopkins, J., Logel, J., Vianzon, R., Short, M., et al (2002). Association of promoter variants in the alpha 7 nicotinic acetylcholine receptor subunit gene with an inhibitory deficit found in schizophrenia. *Archives of General Psychiatry, 59,* 1085–1096.

Leucht, S., McGrath, J., White, P., & Kissling, W. (2002). Carbamazepine augmentation for schizophrenia: How good is the evidence? *Journal of Clinical Psychiatry, 63,* 218–224.

Lewis, C. M., Levinson, D. F., Wise, L. H., Delisi, L., Straub, R. E., Hovatta, I., et al. (2003). Genome scan meta-analysis of schizophrenia and bipolar disorder, Part II: Schizophrenia. *American Journal of Human Genetics.*

Lewis, R. (1998). Typical and atypical antipsychotics in adolescent schizophrenia: Efficacy, tolerability, and differential sensitivity to extrapyramidal symptoms. *Canadian Journal of Psychiatry, 43,* 596–604.

Lewis, S., Tarrier, N., Haddock, G., Bentall, R., Kinderman, P., Kingdon, D., et al. (2002). Randomised controlled trial of cognitive-behavioural therapy in early schizophrenia: acute-phase outcomes. *British Journal of Psychiatry, 43,* s91–97.

Liddle, P. (1987). The symptoms of chronic schizophrenia. A re-examination of the positive-negative dichotomy. *British Journal of Psychiatry, 151,* 145–151.

Liddle, P. F., Spence, S. A., & Sharma, T. (1995). A PET study of obligate carriers of the predisposition to schizophrenia. *Schizophrenia Research, 15,* 90.

Lieberman, J. A. (1996). Atypical antipsychotic drugs as a first-line treatment of schizophrenia: A rationale and hypothesis. *Journal of Clinical Psychiatry, 57,* 68–71.

Lieberman, J. A. (1999). Is schizophrenia a neurodegenerative disorder? A clinical and neurobiological perspective. *Biological Psychiatry, 46,* 729–739.

Lieberman, J. A., Alvir, J. M., Koreen, A., Geisler, S., Chakos, M., Sheitman, B., et al. (1996). Psychobiologic correlates of treatment response in schizophrenia. *Neuropsychopharmacology, 14,* 13S–21S.

Lieberman, J., Chakos, M., Wu, H., Alvir, J., Hoffman, E., Robinson, D., et al. (2001). Longitudinal study of brain morphology in first episode schizophrenia. *Biological Psychiatry, 49,* 487–499.

Lieberman, J. A., Gu, H., Stroup, S., Zhang, P., Kong, L., Ji, Z., et al. (2003). Atypical and conventional antipsychotic drugs in first episode schizophrenia: Comparison of clozapine versus chlorpromazine in a 52-week randomized double-blind trial. *Neuropsychopharmacology, 28,* 995–1003.

Lieberman, J., Jody, D., Geisler, S., Alvir, J., Loebel, A., Szymanski, S., et al. (1993). Time course and biologic correlates of treatment response in first-episode schizophrenia. *Archives of General Psychiatry, 50,* 369–376.

Lieberman, J. A., Perkins, D., Belger, A., Chakos, M., Jarskog, F., Boteva, K., et al. (2001). The early stages of schizophrenia: Speculations on pathogenesis, pathophysiology, and therapeutic approaches. *Biological Psychiatry, 50,* 884–897.

Lieberman, J. A., Tollefson, G., Tohen, M., Green, A. I., Gur, R. E., et al. (HGDH Study Group). (2003). Comparative efficacy and safety of atypical and conventional antipsychotic drugs in first-episode psychosis: A randomized double-blind trial of olanzapine vs. haloperidol. *American Journal of Psychiatry, 160,* 1396–1404.

Linnoila, M., & Viukari, M. (1979). Sodium valproate and tardive dyskinesia. *British Journal of Psychiatry, 134,* 223–224.

Linszen, D. H., Dingemans, P. M., & Lenior, M. E. (1994). Cannabis abuse and the course of recent-onset schizophrenic disorders. *Archives of General Psychiatry, 51,* 273–279.

Linszen, D., Dingemans, P., Van der Does, J. W., Nugter, A., Scholte, P., Lenoir, R., et al. (1996). Treatment, expressed emotion and relapse in recent onset schizophrenic disorders. *Psychological Medicine, 26,* 333–342.

Lohr, J. B., & Flynn, K. (1993). Minor physical anomalies in schizophrenia and mood disorders. *Schizophrenia Bulletin, 19,* 551–556.

Loiselle, D., Stamm, J., Maitinsky, S., & Whipple, S. (1980). Evoked potential and behavioral signs of attention dysfunction in hyperactive boys. *Psychophysiology, 17,* 193–201.

Malmberg, A., Lewis, G., David, A., & Allebeck, P. (1998). Premorbid adjustment and personality in people with schizophrenia. *British Journal of Psychiatry, 172,* 308–313.

Manschreck, T. C., Maher, B. A., Rucklos, M. E., & Vereen, D. R. (1982). Disturbed voluntary motor activity in schizophrenic disorder. *Psychological Medicine, 12,* 73–84.

Marcus, J., Hans, S., Auerbach, J., & Auerbach, A. (1993). Children at risk for schizophrenia: The Jerusalem Infant Development Study: II. Neurobehavioral deficits at school age. *Archives of General Psychiatry, 50,* 797–809.

Marcus, J., Hans, S., Nagler, S., Auerbach, J., Mirsky, A., & Aubrey, A. (1987). Review of the NIMH Israeli Kibbutz-city study and the Jerusalem Infant Development Study. *Schizophrenia Bulletin, 13,* 425–438.

Marenco, S., & Weinberger, D. R. (2000). The neurodevelopmental hypothesis of schizophrenia: Following a rail of evidence from cradle to grave. *Development and Psychopathology, 12,* 501–527.

Matsuzawa, J., Matsui, M., Konishi, T., Noguchi, K., Gur, R. C., Bilker, W., et al. (2001). Age-related volumetric changes of brain gray and white matter in healthy infants and children. *Cerebral Cortex, 11,* 335–342.

May, P. R., Tuma, A. H., Yale, C., Potepan, P., & Dixon, W. J. (1976). Schizophrenia—a follow-up study of results of treatment. *Archives of General Psychiatry, 33,* 481–486.

McCarley, R. W., Hsiao, J. K., Freedman, R., Pfefferbaum, A., & Donchin, E. (1996). Neuroimaging and the cognitive neuroscience of schizophrenia. *Schizophrenia Bulletin, 22,* 703–725.

McCarley, R. W., Salisbury, D. F., Hirayasu, Y., Yurgelun-Todd, D. A., Tohen, M., Zarate, C., et al. (2002). Association between smaller left posterior superior temporal gyrus MRI volume and smaller left temporal P300 amplitude in first episode schizophrenia. *Archives of General Psychiatry, 59,* 321–331.

McCarley, R. W., Shenton, M. E., O'Donnell, B. F., Faux, S. F., Kikinis, R., Nestor, P. G., et al. (1993). Auditory P300 abnormalities and left posterior superior temporal gyrus volume reduction in schizophrenia. *Archives of General Psychiatry, 50,* 190–197.

McCreadie, R. G., Wiles, D., Grant, S., Crockett, G. T., Mahmood, Z., Livingston, M. G., et al. (1989). The Scottish first episode schizophrenia study. VII. Two-year follow-up. Scottish Schizophrenia Research Group. *Acta Psychiatrica Scandinavica, 80,* 597–602.

McEvoy, J. P., Hogarty, G. E., & Steingard, S. (1991). Optimal dose of neuroleptic in acute schizophrenia. A controlled study of the neuroleptic threshold and higher haloperidol dose. *Archives of General Psychiatry, 48,* 739–745.

McFarlane, W. R., Lukens, E., Link, B., Dushay, R., Deakins, S. A., Newmark, M., et al. (1995). Multiple family groups and psychoeducation in the treatment of schizophrenia. *Archives of General Psychiatry, 52,* 679–687.

McGlashan, T. H. (1988). A selective review of recent North American long-term follow-up studies of schizophrenia. *Schizophrenia Bulletin, 14,* 515–542.

McGlashan, T. H. (1996). Early detection and intervention in schizophrenia: Research. *Schizophrenia Bulletin, 22,* 327–345.

McGorry, P. D., & Killackey, E. J. (2002). Early intervention in psychosis: A new evidence-based paradigm. *Epidemiologia e Psichiatria Sociale, 11,* 237–247.

McGorry, P. D., Yung, A. F., Phillips, L. J., Yuen, H. P., Francey, S., Cosgrave, E. M., et al. (2002). Randomized controlled trial of interventions designed to reduce the risk of progression to first-episode psychosis in a clinical sample with subthreshold symptoms. *Archives of General Psychiatry, 59,* 921–928.

McGrath, J. J., van Os, J., Hoyos, C., Jones, P. B., Harvey, I., & Murray, R. M. (1996). Minor physical abnormalities in psychoses: Associations with clinical and putative aetiological variables. *Schizophrenia Research, 18,* 9–20.

McNeil, T., Harty, B., Blennow, G., & Cantor-Graae, E. (1993). Neuromotor deviation in offspring of psychotic mothers: A selective developmental deficiency in two groups of children at heightened psychiatric risk? *Journal of Psychiatric Research, 27,* 39–54.

Mednick, S. A., Parnas, J., & Schulsinger, R. (1987). The Copenhagen High-Risk Project. *Schizophrenia Bulletin, 13,* 485–495.

Mednick, S., & Schulsinger, F. (1968). Some premorbid characteristics related to breakdown in children with schizophrenic mothers. In D. Rosenthal & S. Kety (Eds.), *The transmission of schizophrenia* (pp. 267–291). Oxford: Pergamon Press.

Medoff, D. R., Holcomb, H. H., Lahti, A. C., & Tamminga, C. A. (2001). Probing the human hippocampus using rCBF: Contrasts in schizophrenia. *Hippocampus, 11,* 543–550.

Meltzer, H. Y., Alphs, L., Green, A. I., Altamura, A. C., Anand, R., Bertoldi, A., et al. (2003). Clozapine treatment for suicidality in schizophrenia: International Suicide Prevention Trial (InterSePT). *Archives of General Psychiatry, 60,* 82–91.

Meltzer, H. Y., & Okayli, G. (1995). Reduction of suicidality during clozapine treatment of neuroleptic-resistant schizophrenia: Impact on risk-benefit assessment. *American Journal of Psychiatry, 152,* 183–190.

Merlo, M. C., Hofer, H., Gekle, W., Berger, G., Ventura, J., Panhuber, I., et al. (2002). Risperidone, 2 mg/day vs. 4 mg/day, in first-episode, acutely psychotic patients: Treatment efficacy and effects on fine motor functioning. *Journal of Clinical Psychiatry, 63,* 885–891.

Meyer-Lindenberg, A., Miletich, R. S., Kohn, P. D., Esposito, G., Carson, R. E., Quarantelli, M., et al. (2002). Reduced prefrontal activity predicts exaggerated striatal dopaminergic function in schizophrenia. *Nature Neuroscience, 5,* 267–271.

Meyer-Lindenberg, A., Poline, J-P., Kohn, P. D., Holt, J. L., Egan, M., Weinberger, D. R., et al. (2001). Evidence for abnormal cortical functional connectivity during working memory in schizophrenia. *American Journal of Psychiatry, 158,* 1809–1817.

Michie, P., Fox, A., Ward, P., Catts, S., & McConaghy, N. (1990). Event-related potential indices of selective attention and cortical lateralization in schizophrenia. *Psychophysiology, 27,* 207–227.

Miklowitz, D. J., Goldstein, M. J., Doane, J. A., Nuechterlein, K. H., Strachan, A. M., Snyder, K. S., et al. (1989). Is expressed emotion an index of a transactional process? Relative's affective style. *Family Process, 28,* 153–167.

Millar, J. K., Wilson-Annan, J. C., Anderson, S., Christie, S., Taylor, M. S., Semple, C. A., et al. (2000). Disruption of two novel genes by a translocation co-segregating with schizophrenia. *Human Molecular Genetics, 9,* 1415–1423.

Miller, D. D., Arndt, S., & Andreasen, N. C. (1993). Alogia, attentional impairment, and inappropriate affect: Their status in the dimensions of schizophrenia. *Comprehensive Psychiatry, 34,* 221–226.

Miller, P., Byrne, M., Hodges, A., Lawrie, S. M., Owens, D. G., & Johnstone, E. C. (2002). Schizotypal components in people at high risk of developing schizophrenia: Early findings from the Edinburgh High-Risk Study. *British Journal of Psychiatry, 180,* 179–184.

Moises, H. W., Yang, L., Kristbjarnarson, H., Wiese, C., Byerley, W., Macciardi, F., et al. (1995). An international two-stage genome-wide search for schizophrenia susceptibility genes. *Nature Genetics, 11,* 321–324.

Muck-Seler, D., Pivac, N., Jakovljevic, M., & Brzovic, Z. (1999). Platelet serotonin, plasma cortisol, and dexamethasone suppression test in schizophrenic patients. *Biological Psychiatry, 45,* 1433–1439.

Murray, G., Isohanni, M., Isohanni, I., & Jones, P. (in press). School and schizophrenia. In A. Grispini (Ed.), *Preventative strategies for schizophrenic disorders.* Rome: Giovanni Fioriti Editore.

Murray, R. M. (1994). Neurodevelopmental schizophrenia: The rediscovery of dementia praecox. *British Journal of Psychiatry, 165,* 6–12.

Murray, R. M., & Jones, P. B. (1995). Schizophrenia: Disease or syndrome? In H. Hafner & W. F. Gattaz (Eds.), *Search for the causes of schizophrenia* (Vol. III, pp. 186–192). Heidelberg: Springer-Verlag.

Murray, R., & Lewis, S. (1987). Is schizophrenia a neurodevelopmental disorder? [editorial]. *British Medical Journal Clinical Research Edition, 295,* 681–682.

Naatanen. R. (1982). Processing negativity: An evoked potential reflection of selective attention. *Psychological Bulletin, 92,* 605–640.

Nagy, J., & Szatmari, P. (1986). A chart review of schizotypal personality disorders in children. *Journal of Autism and Developmental Disorders, 16,* 351–367.

National Institute for Clinical Excellence [NICE] (2002). *Clinical guideline I: Schizophrenia. Core interventions in the treatment and management of schizophrenia in primary and secondary care.* London: Author.

Nicolson, R., Lenane, M., Singaracharlu, S., Malaspina, D., Giedd, J. N., Hamburger, S. D., et al. (2000). Premorbid speech and language impairments in childhood-onset schizophrenia: Association with risk factors. *American Journal of Psychiatry, 157,* 794–800.

Nicolson, R., & Rapoport, J. L. (1999). Childhood-onset schizophrenia: Rare but worth studying. *Biological Psychiatry, 46,* 1418–1428.

Niemi, L. T., Suvisaari, J. M., Tuulio-Henriksson, A., & Loennqvist, J. K. (2003). Childhood developmental abnormalities in schizophrenia: Evidence from high-risk studies. *Schizophrenia Research, 60,* 239–258.

Norman, R. M., & Malla, A. K. (2001). Duration of untreated psychosis: A critical examination of the concept and its importance. *Psychological Medicine, 31,* 381–400.

Nottelmann, E. D., Susman, E. J., Inoff-Germain, G., Cutler, G. B., Jr., Loriaux, D. L., & Chrousos, G. P. (1987). Developmental processes in early adolescence: Relationships between adolescent adjustment problems and chronologic age, pubertal stage, and puberty-related serum hormone levels. *Journal of Pediatrics, 110,* 473–480.

Nuechterlein, K. H., Dawson, M. E., Ventura, J., Gitlin, M., Subotnik, K. L., Snyder, K. S., et al. (1994). The vulnerability/stress model of schizophrenic relapse: A longitudinal study. *Acta Psychiatrica Scandinavica Supplement, 382,* 58–64.

Nugter, A., Dingemans, P., Van der Does, J. W., Linszen, D., & Gersons, B. (1997). Family treatment, expressed emotion and relapse in recent onset schizophrenia. *Psychiatry Research, 72,* 23–31.

O'Donnell, C., Donohoe, G., Sharkey, L., Owens, N., Migone, M., Harries, R., et al. (2003). Compliance therapy: A randomised controlled trial in schizophrenia. *British Medical Journal, 327,* 834.

O'Leary, D. S., Flaum, M., Kesler, M. L., Flashman, L. A., Arndt, S., & Andreasen, N. C. (2000). Cognitive correlates of the negative, disorganized, and psychotic symptom dimensions of schizophrenia. *Journal of Neuropsychiatry and Clinical Neurosciences, 12,* 4–15.

Pantelis, C., Velakoulis, D., McGorry, P. D., Wood, S. J., Suckling, J., Phillips, L. J., et al. (2003). Neuroanatomical abnormalities before and after onset of psychosis: a cross-sectional and longitudinal MRI comparison. *Lancet, 361,* 281–288.

Parnas, J. (1982). Behavioral precursors of schizophrenia spectrum: A prospective study. *Archives of General Psychiatry, 39,* 658–664.

Paus, T., Zijdenbos, A., Worsley, K., Collins, D. L., Blumenthal, J., Giedd, J. N., et al. (1999). Structural maturation of neural pathway in children and adolescents: In vivo study. *Science, 283,* 1908–1911.

Pfefferbaum, A., Mathalon, D. H., Sullivan, E. V., Rawles, J. M., Zipursky, R. B., & Lim, K. O. (1994). A quantitative magnetic resonance imaging study of changes in brain morphology from infancy to late adulthood. *Archives of Neurology, 51,* 874–887.

Philippe, A., Martinez, M., Guilloud-Bataille, M., Gillberg, C., Rastam, M., Sponheim, E., et al. (1999). Genome-wide scan for autism susceptibility genes. Paris Autism Research International Sibpair Study. *Human Molecular Genetics, 8,* 805–812.

Phillips, L. J., Yung, A. R., Yuen, H. P., Pantelis, C., & McGorry, P. D. (2002). Prediction and prevention of transition to psychosis in young people at incipient risk for schizophrenia. *American*

Journal of Medical Genetics (Neuropsychiatric Genetics), 114, 929–937.

Pidgeon, D. A. (1964). Tests used in the 1954 and 1957 surveys. In J.W.B. Douglas. (Ed.), *The home and the school* (pp. 129–132). London: MacGibbon & Kee.

Pidgeon, D. A. (1968). Appendix: Details of the fifteen-year tests. In J.W.B. Douglas, J. M. Ross, & H. R. Simpson (Eds.), *All our futures* (pp. 194–197). London: Peter Davies.

Pilling, S., Bebbington, P., Kuipers, E., Garety, P., Geddes, J., Orbach, G., et al. (2002). Psychological treatments in schizophrenia: I. Meta-analysis of family intervention and cognitive behaviour therapy. *Psychological Medicine, 32,* 763–782.

Plocka-Lewandowska, M., Araszkiewicz, A., & Rybakowski, J. K. (2001). Dexamethasone suppression test and suicide attempts in schizophrenic patients. *European Psychiatry: The Journal of the Association of European Psychiatrists, 16,* 428–431.

Plomin, R., Reiss, D., Hetherington, E. M., & Howe, G. W. (1994). Nature and nurture: Genetic contributions to measures of the family environment. *Developmental Psychology, 30,* 32–43.

Pogue-Geile, M. F. (1997). Developmental aspects of schizophrenia. In M. S. Keshavan & R. M. Murray (Eds.), *Neurodevelopment and adult psychopathology* (pp. 137–154). Cambridge, UK: Cambridge University Press.

Poulton, R., Caspi, A., Moffitt, T. E., Cannon, M., Murray, R., & Harrington, H. (2000). Children's self-reported psychotic symptoms and adult schizophreniform disorder: A 15-year longitudinal study. *Archives of General Psychiatry, 57,* 1053–1058.

Pritchard, W. (1986). Cognitive event-related potential correlates of schizophrenia. *Psychological Bulletin, 100,* 43–66.

Rabinowitz, J., Bromet, E. J., Lavelle, J., Carlson, G., Kovasznay, B., & Schwartz, J. E. (1998). Prevalence and severity of substance use disorders and onset of psychosis in first-admission psychotic patients. *Psychological Medicine, 28,* 1411–1419.

Rantakallio, P. (1969). Groups at risk in low birth weight infants and perinatal mortality. *Acta Paediatrica Scandinavica, 193,* 1–71.

Rapoport, J. L., Giedd, J., Kumra, S., Jacobsen, L., Smith, A., Lee, P., et al. (1997). Childhood-onset schizophrenia. Progressive ventricular change during adolescence. *Archives of General Psychiatry, 54,* 897–903.

Raux, G., Bonnet-Brilhault, F., Louchart, S., Houy, E., Gantier, R., Levillain, D., et al. (2002). The −2 bp deletion in exon 6 of the 'alpha 7-like' nicotinic receptor subunit gene is a risk factor for the P50 sensory gating deficit. *Molecular Psychiatry, 7,* 1006–1011.

Rector, N. A., & Beck, A. T. (2002). Cognitive therapy for schizophrenia: From conceptualization to intervention. *Canadian Journal of Psychiatry, 47,* 41–50.

Reid, W. H., Mason, M., & Hogan, T. (1998). Suicide prevention effects associated with clozapine therapy in schizophrenia and schizoaffective disorder. *Psychiatric Service, 49,* 1029–1033.

Reiss, A. L., Abrams, M. T., Singer, H. S., Ross, J. L., & Denckla, M. B. (1996). Brain development, gender and IQ in children: A volumetric imaging study. *Brain, 119,* 1763–1774.

Reite, M., Teale, P., & Rojas, D. C. (1999). Magnetoencephalography: Applications in psychiatry. *Biological Psychiatry, 45,* 1553–1563.

Reveley, A. M., Reveley, M. A., & Clifford, R. M. (1982). Cerebral ventricular size in twins discordant for schizophrenia. *Lancet, 1,* 540–541.

Robins, L. N. (1966). *Deviant children grown up. A sociological and psychiatric study of sociopathic personality.* Baltimore: Williams and Wilkins.

Robins, L. N., Helzer, J. E., Weissman, M. M., Orvaschel, H., Gruenberg, E., Burke, J. D., Jr., et al. (1984). Lifetime prevalence of specific psychiatric disorders in three sites. *Archives of General Psychiatry, 41,* 949–958.

Robinson, D., Woerner, M. G., Alvir, J. M., Bilder, R., Goldman, R., Geisler, S., et al. (1999a). Predictors of relapse following response from a first episode of schizophrenia or schizoaffective disorder. *Archives of General Psychiatry, 56,* 241–247.

Robinson, D. G., Woerner, M. G., Alvir, J. M., Geisler, S., Koreen, A., Sheitman, B., et al. (1999b). Predictors of treatment response from a first episode of schizophrenia or schizoaffective disorder. *American Journal of Psychiatry, 156,* 544–549.

Rodriguez, E., George, N., Lachaux, J-P., Martinerie, J., Renault, B., & Varela, F. J. (1999). Perception's shadow: Long-distance synchronization of human brain activity. *Nature, 397,* 430–433.

Rohrbaugh, J., McCallum, W., Galliard, A., Simons, R., Birbaumer, N., & Papakostopoulos, D. (1986). ERPs associated with preparatory and movement-related processes: A review. In M. McCallum, R. Zappoli, & F. Denoth (Eds.), *Cerebral psychophysiology: Studies in event-related potentials* (pp. 189–229). *EEG Supplement 38,* Amsterdam: Elsevier.

Rose, V. L. (1997). APA practice guideline for the

treatment of patients with schizophrenia. *American Family Physician, 56,* 1217–1220.

Rupprecht, R., & Holsboer, F. (1999). Neuroactive steroids: Mechanisms of action and neuropsychopharmacological perspectives. *Trends in Neurosciences, 22,* 410–416.

Saint-Cyr, J. (2003). Frontal-striatal circuit functions: Context, sequence, and consequence. *Journal of the International Neuropsychological Society, 9,* 103–128.

Salisbury, D. F., Bonner-Jackson, A., Griggs, C. B., Shenton, M. E., & McCarley, R. W. (2001). Mismatch negativity in schizophrenia: Does MMN amplitude decline with disease duration? *Biological Psychiatry, 49* (Suppl.), 85S.

Salzman, C., Solomon, D., Miyawaki, E., Glassman, R., Rood, L., Flowers, E., et al. (1991). Parenteral lorazepam versus parenteral haloperidol for the control of psychotic disruptive behavior. *Journal of Clinical Psychiatry, 52,* 177–180.

Sanger, T. M., Lieberman, J. A., Tohen, M., Grundy, S., Beasley, C., Jr., & Tollefson, G. D. (1999). Olanzapine versus haloperidol treatment in first-episode psychosis. *American Journal of Psychiatry, 156,* 79–87.

Sartorius, N., Fleischhacker, W., Gjerris, A., Kern, U., Knapp, M., Leonard, B. E., et al. (2002). The usefulness and use of second-generation antipsychotic medications. *Current Opinion in Psychiatry, 15,* S1–S51.

Satterfield, J., Schell, A., Nicholar, T., Satterfield, B., & Freese, T. (1990). Ontogeny of selective attention effects on event-related potentials in attention-deficit hyperactivity disorder and normal boys. *Biological Psychiatry, 28,* 879–903.

Saykin, A. J., Shtasel, D. L., Gur, R. E., Kester, D. B., Mozley, L. H., Stafiniak, P., et al. (1994). Neuropsychological deficits in neuroleptic naive, first episode schizophrenic patients. *Archives of General Psychiatry, 51,* 124–131.

Schaffner, K. F., & McGorry, P. D. (2001). Preventing severe mental illnesses—New prospects and ethical challenges. *Schizophrenia Research, 51,* 3–15.

Schooler, N., Keith, S., Severe, J., Matthews, S., Bellack, A., Glick, I., et al. (1997). Relapse and rehospitalization during maintenance treatment of schizophrenia. *Archives of General Psychiatry, 54,* 453–463.

Schreiber, H., Stolz-Born, G., Heinrich, H., & Kornhuber, H. H. (1992). Attention, cognition, and motor perseveration in adolescents at genetic risk for schizophrenia and control subjects. *Psychiatry Research, 44,* 125–140.

Schwab, S. G., Knapp, M., Mondabon, S., Hallmayer, J., Borrmann-Hassenbach, M., Albus, M., et al. (2003). Support for association of schizophrenia with genetic variation in the 6p22.3 gene, dysbindin, in sib-pair families with linkage and in an additional sample of triad families. *American Journal of Human Genetics, 72,* 185–190.

Scottish Schizophrenia Research Group. (1987). The Scottish First Episode Schizophrenia Study. II. Treatment: Pimozide versus flupenthixol. The Scottish Schizophrenia Research Group. *British Journal of Psychiatry, 150,* 334–338.

Seeman, M. V. (1997). Psychopathology in women and men: Focus on female hormones. *American Journal of Psychiatry, 154,* 1641–1647.

Seidman, L. J., Faraone, S. V., Goldstein, J. M., Goodman, J. M., Kremen, W. S., Matsuda, G., et al. (1997). Reduced subcortical brain volumes in nonpsychotic siblings of schizophrenic patients: A pilot MRI Study. *American Journal of Medical Genetics, 74,* 507–514.

Selemon, L., & Goldman-Rakic, P. (1999). The reduced neuropil hypothesis: A circuit based model of schizophrenia. *Biological Psychiatry, 45,* 17–25.

Sernyak, M. J., Desai, R., Stolar, M., & Rosenheck, R. (2001). Impact of clozapine on completed suicide. *American Journal of Psychiatry, 158,* 931–937.

Sharma, S., & Lal, R. (1986). Minor physical anomalies in schizophrenia. *International Journal of Neuroscience, 31,* 138.

Shenton, M., Kikinis, R., Jolesz, F., Pollak, S., LeMay, M., Wible, C., et al. (1992). Abnormalities of the left temporal lobe and thought disorder in schizophrenia: A quantitative magnetic resonance imaging study. *New England Journal of Medicine, 327,* 604–612.

Shifman, S., Bronstein, M., Sternfeld, M., Pisante-Shalom, A., Lev-Lehman, E., Weizman, A., et al. (2002). A highly significant association between a COMT haplotype and schizophrenia. *American Journal of Human Genetics, 71,* 1296–1302.

Shinkai, T., Ohmori, O., Hori, H., & Nakamura, J. (2002). Allelic association of the neuronal nitric oxide synthase (NOS1) gene with schizophrenia. *Molecular Psychiatry, 7,* 560–563.

Silberg, J., Pickles, A., Rutter, M., Hewitt, J., Simonoff, E., Maes, H., et al. (1999). The influence of genetic factors and life stress on depression among adolescent girls. *Archives of General Psychiatry, 56,* 225–232.

Silbersweig, D. A., Stern, E., Frith, C., Cahill, C.,

Holmes, A., Grootoonk, S., et al. (1995). A functional neuroanatomy of hallucinations in schizophrenia. *Nature, 378,* 176–179.

Silver, H., Barash, I., Aharon, N., Kaplan, A., & Poyurovsky, M. (2000). Fluvoxamine augmentation of antipsychotics improves negative symptoms in psychotic chronic schizophrenic patients: A placebo-controlled study. *International Clinical Psychopharmacology, 15,* 257–261.

Silver, H., & Nassar, A. (1992). Fluvoxamine improves negative symptoms in treated chronic schizophrenia: An add-on double-blind, placebo-controlled study. *Biological Psychiatry, 31,* 698–704.

Sowell, E. R., Thompson, P. M., Holmes, C. J., Jernigen, T. L., & Toga, A. W. (1999). In vivo evidence for post-adolescent brain maturation in frontal and striatal regions. *Nature Neuroscience, 2,* 859–861.

Spencer, K. M., Nestor, P. G., Niznikiewicz, M. A., Salisbury, D. F., Shenton, M. E., & McCarley, R. W. (2003). Abnormal neural synchrony in schizophrenia. *Journal of Neuroscience, 23,* 7407–7411.

Stefansson, H., Sarginson, J., Kong, A., Yates, P., Steinthorsdottir, V., Gudfinnsson, E., et al. (2003). Association of neuregulin 1 with schizophrenia confirmed in a Scottish population. *American Journal of Human Genetics, 72,* 83–87.

Stefansson, H., Sigurdsson, E., Steinthorsdottir, V., Bjornsdottir, S., Sigmundsson, T., Ghosh, S., et al. (2002). Neuregulin 1 and susceptibility to schizophrenia. *American Journal of Human Genetics, 71,* 877–892.

Steinert, T., Wiebe, C., & Gebhardt, R. P. (1999). Aggressive behavior against self and others among first-admission patients with schizophrenia. *Psychiatric Services, 50,* 85–90.

Stevens, J. R. (2002). Schizophrenia: Reproductive hormones and the brain. *American Journal of Psychiatry, 159,* 713–719.

Strandburg, R., Marsh, J., Brown, W., Asarnow, R., & Guthrie, D. (1984). Event-related potentials concomitants of information processing dysfunction in schizophrenic children. *Electroencephalography and Clinical Neurophysiology, 57,* 236–253.

Strandburg, R., Marsh, J., Brown, W., Asarnow, R., Guthrie, D., & Higa, J. (1990). Event-related potential correlates of impaired attention in schizophrenic children. *Biological Psychiatry, 27,* 1103–1115.

Strandburg, R., Marsh, J., Brown, W., Asarnow, R.,

Guthrie, D., & Higa, J. (1994a). Continuity of information processing deficits across childhood- and adult-onset schizophrenia: ERP correlates. *Schizophrenia Bulletin, 20,* 685–696.

Strandburg, R., Marsh, J., Brown, W., Asarnow, R., Guthrie, D., & Higa, J. (1994b). Reduced attention-related negative potentials in schizophrenic adults. *Psychophysiology, 31,* 272–281.

Strandburg, R., Marsh, J., Brown, W., Asarnow, R., Higa, J., & Guthrie, D. (1994c). Continuous processing-related ERPs in schizophrenic and normal children. *Biological Psychiatry, 35,* 525–538.

Straub, R. E., Jiang, Y., MacLean, C. J., Ma, Y., Webb, B. T., Myakishev, M. V., et al. (2002). Genetic variation in the 6p22.3 gene DTNBP1, the human ortholog of the mouse dysbindin gene, is associated with schizophrenia. *American Journal of Human Genetics, 71,* 337–348.

Straub, R. E., MacLean, C. J., Ma, Y., Webb, B. T., Myakishev, M. V., Harris-Kerr, C., et al. (2002). Genome-wide scans of three independent sets of 90 Irish multiplex schizophrenia families and follow-up of selected regions in all families provides evidence for multiple susceptibility genes. *Molecular Psychiatry, 7,* 542–559.

Szymanski, S., Masiar, S., Mayerhoff, D., Loebel, A., Geisler, S., Pollack, S., et al. (1994). Clozapine response in treatment-refractory first-episode schizophrenia. *Biological Psychiatry, 35,* 278–280.

Tallon-Baudry, C., & Bertrand, O. (1999). Oscillatory gamma activity in humans and its role in object representation. *Trends in Cognitive Science, 3,* 151–162.

Tamminga, C. A., Thaker, G. K., & Medoff, D. R. (2002). Neuropsychiatric aspects of schizophrenia. In S. C. Yudofsky & R. E. Hales (Eds.), *The American Psychiatric Publishing textbook of neuropsychiatry and clinical neurosciences* (4th ed., pp. 989–1020). Washington, DC: American Psychiatric Publishing.

Tarrant, C., & Jones, P. (1999). Precursors to schizophrenia: Do biological markers have specificity? *Canadian Journal of Psychiatry, 44,* 335–349.

Thompson, K. N., McGorry, P. D., & Harrigan, S. M. (2001). Reduced awareness of illness in first-episode psychosis. *Comprehensive Psychiatry, 42,* 498–503.

Thompson, P. M., Vidal, C., Giedd, J. N., Gochman, P., Blumenthal, J., Nicolson, R., et al. (2001). Mapping adolescent brain change reveals dynamic wave of accelerated gray matter loss in very early-onset schizophrenia. *Proceedings of the*

National Academy of Sciences of the United States of America, 98, 11650–11655.

Tkachev, D., Mimmack, M. L., Ryan, M. M., Wayland, M., Freeman, T., Jones, P. B., et al. (2003). Oligodendrocyte dysfunction in schizophrenia and bipolar disorder. *Lancet, 362,* 798–805.

Tompson, M. C., Asarnow, J. R., Hamilton, E. B., Newell, L. E., & Goldstein, M. J. (1997). Children with schizophrenia-spectrum disorders: Thought disorder and communication problems in a family interactional context. *Journal of Child Psychology and Psychiatry, 38,* 421–429.

Tsuang, M. T., Stone, W. S., Tarbox, S. I., & Faraone, S. V. (2002). An integration of schizophrenia with schizotypy: Identification of schizotaxia and implications for research on treatment and prevention. *Schizophrenia Research, 54,* 169–175.

Tucker, D., & Williamson, P. (1984). Asymmetric neural control systems in human self-regulation. *Psychological Review, 91,* 185–215.

Ueland, T., & Rund, B. R. (2004). A controlled randomised treatment study: The effects of a cognitive training program on adolescents with early onset psychosis. *Acta Psychiatrica Scandinavica, 109,* 70–74.

Ueland, T., Rund, B., Borg, N., Newton, E., Purvis, R., & Wykes, T. (2004). Modification of performance on the Span of Apprehension Task in a group of young people with early onset psychosis. *Scandinavian Journal of Psychology, 45,* 55–60.

Umbricht, D., Javitt, D. C., Bates, J., Kane, J., & Lieberman, J. A. (2002). Auditory event-related potentials (ERP): Indices of both premorbid and illness-related progressive neuropathology in schizophrenia? *Schizophrenia Research, 53,* 18.

Umbricht, D., Javitt, D. C., Novak, G., Pollack, S., Liberman, J., & Kane, J. (1998). Effects of clozapine on auditory event-related potentials in schizophrenia. *Biological Psychiatry, 44,* 716–725.

van Oel, C. J., Sitskoorn, M. M., Cremer, M.P.M., & Kahn, R. S. (2002). School performance as a premorbid marker for schizophrenia: A twin study. *Schizophrenia Bulletin, 28,* 401–414.

Van Os, J., Jones, P., Lewis, G., Wadsworth, M., & Murray, R. (1997). Developmental precursors of affective illness in a general population birth cohort. *Archives of General Psychiatry, 54,* 625–631.

Walder, D. J., Walker, E. F., & Lewine, R. J. (2000). Cognitive functioning, cortisol release, and symptom severity in patients with schizophrenia. *Biological Psychiatry, 48,* 1121–1132.

Waldo, M. C., Carey, G., Myles-Worsley, M., Cawthra, E., Adler, L. E., Nagamoto, H. T., et al. (1991). Codistribution of a sensory gating deficit and schizophrenia in multi-affected families. *Psychiatry Research, 39,* 257–268.

Walker, E. (1991). Research on life-span development in schizophrenia. In E. Walker (Ed.), *Schizophrenia: A life-course developmental perspective* (pp. 1–6). San Diego: Academic Press.

Walker, E. F. (1994). Developmentally moderated expressions of the neuropathology underlying schizophrenia. *Schizophrenia Bulletin, 20,* 453–480.

Walker, E. F. (2002). Adolescent neurodevelopment and psychopathology. *Current Directions in Psychological Science, 11,* 24–28.

Walker, E., & Bollini, A.-M. (2002). Pubertal neurodevelopment and the emergence of psychotic symptoms. *Schizophrenia Research, 54,* 17–23.

Walker, E. F., & Diforio, D. (1997). Schizophrenia: A neural diathesis-stress model. *Psychological Review, 104,* 667–685.

Walker, E., & Emory, E. (1985). Infants at risk for psychopathology: Offspring of schizophrenic parents. *Child Development, 54,* 1269–1285.

Walker, E. F., Grimes, K. E., Davis, D. M., & Smith, A. J. (1993). Childhood precursors of schizophrenia: Facial expressions of emotion. *American Journal of Psychiatry, 150,* 1654–1660.

Walker, E., & Lewine, R. J. (1990). Prediction of adult-onset schizophrenia from childhood home movies of the patients. *American Journal of Psychiatry, 147,* 1052–1056.

Walker, E. F., Lewine, R.R.J., & Neumann, C. (1996). Childhood behavioral characteristics and adult brain morphology in schizophrenia. *Schizophrenia Research, 22,* 93–101.

Walker, E., Lewis, N., Loewy, R., & Palyo, S. (1999). Motor dysfunction and risk for schizophrenia. *Development and Psychopathology, 11,* 509–523.

Walker, E. F., Savoie, T., & Davis, D. (1994). Neuromotor precursors of schizophrenia. *Schizophrenia Bulletin, 20,* 441–451.

Walker, E. F., Walder, D. J., & Reynolds, F. (2001). Developmental changes in cortisol secretion in normal and at-risk youth. *Development and Psychopathology, 13,* 721–732.

Wassef, A. A., Dott, S. G., Harris, A., Brown, A., O'Boyle, M., Meyer, W. J., 3rd, et al. (2000). Randomized, placebo-controlled pilot study of divalproex sodium in the treatment of acute exacerbations of chronic schizophrenia. *Journal of Clinical Psychopharmacology, 20,* 357–361.

Watkins, J., Asarnow, R., & Tanguay, P. (1988). Symptom development in childhood-onset schizophrenia. *Journal of Child Psychology and Psychiatry, 29,* 865–878.

Watt, N. F. (1978). Patterns of childhood social development in adult schizophrenics. *Archives of General Psychiatry, 35,* 160–165.

Watt, N., Grubb, T., & Erlenmeyer-Kimling, L. (1982). Social, emotional, and intellectual behavior at school among children at high risk for schizophrenia. *Journal of Consulting and Clinical Psychology, 50,* 171–181.

Watt, N., & Lubensky, A. (1976). Childhood roots of schizophrenia. *Journal of Consulting and Clinical Psychology, 44,* 363–375.

Watt, N., & Saiz, C. (1991). Longitudinal studies of premorbid development of adult schizophrenics. In E. Walker (Ed.), *Schizophrenia: A life-course developmental perspective* (pp. 158–185). San Diego: Academic Press.

Weinberger, D. (1986). The pathogenesis of schizophrenia: A neurodevelopmental theory. In H. Nasrallah & D. Weinberger (Eds.), *The neurobiology of schizophrenia* (pp. 397–406). Amsterdam: Elsevier Science Publishers.

Weinberger, D. R. (1987). Implications of normal brain development for the pathogenesis of schizophrenia. *Archives of General Psychiatry, 44,* 660–669.

Weinberger, D. R. (1995). From neuropathology to neurodevelopment. *Lancet, 346,* 552–557.

Weinberger, D. R., Berman, K. F., Suddath, R., & Torrey, E. F. (1992). Evidence of dysfunction of a prefrontal-limbic network in schizophrenia: A magnetic resonance imaging and regional cerebral blood flow study of discordant monozygotic twins. *American Journal of Psychiatry, 149,* 890–897.

Weinberger, D. R., DeLisi, L. E., Neophytides, A. N., & Wyatt, R. J. (1981). Familial aspects of CT scan abnormalities in chronic schizophrenic patients. *Psychiatry Research, 4,* 65–71.

Weinberger, D. R., Egan, M. F., Bertolino, A., Calicott, J. H., Mattay, V. S., Lipska, B. K., et al. (2001). Prefrontal neurons and the genetics of schizophrenia. *Biological Psychiatry, 50,* 825–844.

Weinstein, D. D., Diforio, D., Schiffman, J., Walker, E., & Bonsall, R. (1999). Minor physical anomalies, dermatoglyphic asymmetries, and cortisol levels in adolescents with schizotypal personality disorder. *American Journal of Psychiatry, 156,* 617–623.

Werry, J. S. (1981). Drugs and learning. *Journal of Child Psychology and Psychiatry, 22,* 283–290.

Werry, J. S., McClellan, J. M., & Chard, L. (1991). Childhood and adolescent schizophrenic, bipolar, and schizoaffective disorders: A clinical and outcome study. *Journal of the American Academy of Child and Adolescent Psychiatry, 30,* 457–465.

Wible, C. F., Kubicki, M., Yoo, S-S, Kacher, D. F., Salisbury, D. F., Anderson, M. C., et al. (2001). A functional magnetic resonance imaging study of auditory mismatch in schizophrenia. *American Journal of Psychiatry, 158,* 938–943.

Wiersma, D., Wanderling, J., Dragomirecka, E., Ganev, K., Harrison, G., an der Heiden, W., et al. (2000). Social disability in schizophrenia: Its development and prediction over 15 years in incidence cohorts in six European centres. *Psychological Medicine, 30,* 1155–1167.

Wiersma, D., Nienhuis, F. J., Slooff, C. J., & Giel, R. (1998). Natural course of schizophrenic disorders: A 15-year follow-up of a Dutch incidence cohort. *Schizophrenia Bulletin, 24,* 75–85.

Williams, J., McGuffin, P., Nothen, M., & Owen, M. J. (1997). Meta-analysis of association between the 5-HT2a receptor T102C polymorphism and schizophrenia. EMASS Collaborative Group. European Multicentre Association Study of Schizophrenia. *Lancet, 349,* 1221.

Wolff, A. L., & O'Driscoll, G. A. (1999). Motor deficits and schizophrenia: The evidence from neuroleptic-naive patients and populations at risk. *Journal of Psychiatry and Neuroscience, 24,* 304–314.

Wood, S. J., Pantelis, C., Proffitt, T., Phillips, L. J., Stuart, G. W., Buchanan, J.-A., et al. (2003). Spatial working memory ability is a marker of risk-for-psychosis. *Psychological Medicine, 33,* 1239–1247.

Woods, S. W., Miller, T. J., Davidson, L., Hawkins, K. A., Sernyak, M. J., & McGlashan, T. H. (2001). Estimated yield of early detection of prodromal or first episode patients by screening first-degree relatives of schizophrenic patients. *Schizophrenia Research, 52,* 21–27.

Woods, S., Zipursky, R., Perkins, D., Addington, J., Marquez, E., Breier, A., et al. (2002). Olanzapine vs. placebo for prodromal symptoms. *Acta Psychiatrica Scandinavica, 106,* 43.

World Health Organization. (1992). International classification of diseases (10th revision). Geneva: Author.

Wykes, T., Reeder, C., Williams, C., Corner, J., Rice, C., & Everitt, B. (2001). Are the effects of cognitive remediation therapy (CRT) durable? Results from an exploratory trial in schizophrenia. *Schizophrenia Research, 61,* 163–174.

Wykes, T., & van der Gaag, M. (2001). Is it time to

develop a new cognitive therapy for psychosis-Cognitive remediation therapy (CRT)? *Clinical Psychology Review, 21,* 1227–1256.

Yakovlev, P. L., & Lecours, A. R. (1967). The myelogenetic cycles of regional maturation of the brain. In A. Minkowski (Ed.), *Regional development of the brain in early life* (pp. 3–70). Oxford: Blackwell.

Yap, H. L., Mahendran, R., Lim, D., Liow, P. H., Lee, A., Phang, S., et al. (2001). Risperidone in the treatment of first episode psychosis. *Singapore Medical Journal, 42,* 170–173.

Yarden, P. E., & Discipio, W. J. (1971). Abnormal movements and prognosis in schizophrenia. *American Journal of Psychiatry, 128,* 317–323.

Yung, A. R., & McGorry, P. D. (1996). The prodromal phase of first-episode psychosis: Past and current conceptualizations. *Schizophrenia Bulletin, 22,* 353–370.

Yung, A. R., Phillips, L. J., Yuen, H. P., Francey, S. M., McFarlane, C. A., Hallgren, M., et al. (2003). Psychosis prediction: 12-month follow up of a high-risk ("prodromal") group. *Schizophrenia Research, 60,* 21–32.

Zammit, S., Allebeck, P., Andreasson, S., Lunberg, I., & Lewis, G. (2002). Self reported cannabis use as a risk factor for schizophrenia in Swedish conscripts of 1969: Historical cohort study. *British Medical Journal, 325,* 1199–1201.

Zhang-Wong, J., Zipursky, R. B., Beiser, M., & Bean, G. (1999). Optimal haloperidol dosage in first-episode psychosis. *Canadian Journal of Psychiatry, 44,* 164–167.

Zornberg, G. L., Buka, S. L., & Tsuang, M. T. (2000). Hypoxic-ischemia-related fetal/neonatal complications and risk of schizophrenia and other nonaffective psychoses: A 19-year longitudinal study. *American Journal of Psychiatry, 157,* 196–202.

Part III: Anxiety Disorders

Achenbach, T. M. (1991). *Manual for the Child Behaviour Checklist/4-18 and 1991 profile.* Burlington, VT: University of Vermont Department of Psychiatry.

Ainsworth, M.D.S., Blehar, M. C., Waters, E., & Wall, E. (1978). *Patterns of attachment: A psychological study of the strange situation.* Hillsdale, NJ: Lawrence Erlbaum Associates.

Albano, A. M. (2003). Treatment of social anxiety disorder. In M. A. Reinecke, F. M. Dattilio, & A. Freeman (Eds.), *Cognitive therapy with children and adolescents: A casebook for clinical practice* (2nd ed.). New York: Guilford Press.

Albano, A. M., Chorpita, B. F., & Barlow, D. (2003). Childhood anxiety disorders. In E. J. Mash & R. A. Barkley (Eds.), *Child psychopathology* (2nd ed., pp. 279–329). New York: Guilford Press.

Albano, A. M., Detweiler, M. F., Logsden-Conrdsen, S., Russ, S. W., & Ollendick, T. (1999). Cognitive-behavioral interventions with socially phobic children. In *Handbook of psychotherapies with children and families. Issues in clinical child psychology* (pp. 255–280). Dordrecht, Netherlands: Kluwer Academic Publishers.

Albucher, R. C., & Liberzon, I. (2002). Psychopharmacological treatment in PTSD: A critical review. *Journal of Psychiatric Research, 36,* 355–367.

Alderman, J., Wolkow, R., Chung, M., & Johnston, H. F. (1998). Sertraline treatment of children and adolescents with obsessive compulsive disorder or depression: Pharmacokinetics, tolerability, and efficacy. *Journal of the American Academy of Child and Adolescent Psychiatry, 37,* 386–394.

Allen, A., Leonard H., & Swedo, S. E. (1995). Current knowledge of medications for the treatment of childhood anxiety disorders. *Journal of the American Academy of Child and Adolescent Psychiatry, 34,* 976–986.

Alloy, L. B., Kelly, K. A., Mineka, S., & Clements, C. M. (1990). Comorbidity in anxiety and depressive disorders: A helplessness-hopelessness perspective. In J. D. Maser and C. R. Cloninger (Eds.), *Comorbidity of mood and anxiety disorders* (pp. 449–544). Washington, DC: American Psychiatric Press.

Alpert-Gillis, L. J., Pedro-Carroll, J. L., & Cowen, E. L. (1989). The children of divorce intervention program: Development, implementation, and evaluation of a program for young urban children. *Journal of Consulting and Clinical Psychology, 57,* 583–589.

American Psychiatric Association. (1994). *Diagnostic and statistical manual of mental disorders* (4th ed.). Washington, DC: Author.

Andrykowski, M. A., & Cordova, M. J. (1998). Factors associated with PTSD symptoms following treatment for breast cancer: Test of the Andersen model. *Journal of Traumatic Stress, 11,* 189–203.

Anisman, H., & Zacharko, R. M. (1992). Depression as a consequence of inadequate neurochemical adaptation in response to stress. *British Journal of Psychiatry, 160,* 36–43.

Anstendig, K. D. (1998). Selective mutism: A review of the treatment literature by modality from

1980–1996. *Psychotherapy: Theory, Research, Practice, Training, 35,* 381–391.

Anstendig, K. D. (1999). Is selective mutism an anxiety disorder? Rethinking its DSM-IV classification. *Journal of Anxiety Disorders, 13,* 417–434.

Apter, A., Ratzoni, G., King, R., Weizman, A., Doncy, I., Ginder, M. et al. (1994). Fluvoxamine open-label treatment of adolescent inpatients with obsessive-compulsive disorder or depression. *Journal of the American Academy of Child and Adolescent Psychiatry, 33,* 342–348.

Arbelle, S., Benjamin, J., Galin, M., Kremer, I., Belmaker, R. H., & Ebstein, R. P. (2003). Relation of shyness in grade school children in the genotype for the long form of the serotonin transporter promoter region polymorphism. *American Journal of Psychiatry, 160,* 671–676.

Astin, M. C., Lawrence, K. F., & Foy, D. W. (1993). Posttraumatic stress disorder among battered women: Risk and resiliency factors. *Violence and Victims, 8,* 17–28.

Bakker, A., Spinhoven, P., van der Does, A.J.W., van Balkom, A.J.L.M., & van Dyck, R. (2002). Locus of control orientation in panic disorder and the differential effects of treatment. *Psychotherapy and Psychosomatics, 71,* 85–89.

Ballenger, J. C., Davidson, J.R.T., Lecrubier, Y., Nutt, D. J., Bobes, J., Beidel, D. C., et al. (1998). Consensus statement on social anxiety disorder from the International Consensus Group on Depression and Anxiety. *Journal of Clinical Psychiatry, 59,* 54–60.

Ballenger, J. C., Davidson, J.R.T., Wheadon, D. E., Steiner, M., Bushnell, W. & Gergel, I. P. (1998). Double-blind, fixed-dose, placebo-controlled study of paroxetine in the treatment of panic disorder. *American Journal of Psychiatry, 155,* 36–42.

Barbee, J. G., Black, F. W., & Todorov, A. A. (1992). Differential effects of alprazolam and buspirone upon acquisition, retention, and retrieval processes in memory. *Journal of Neuropsychiatry, 4,* 308–314.

Barlow, D. H. (1988). *Anxiety and its disorders: The nature and treatment of anxiety and panic.* New York: Guilford Press.

Barlow, D. H. (2001). *Anxiety and its disorders: The nature and treatment of anxiety and panic* (2nd ed.). New York: Guilford Press.

Barlow, D. H., Gorman, J. M., Shear, M. K., & Woods, S. W. (2000). Cognitive-behavioral therapy, imipramine, or their combination for panic disorder: A randomized controlled trial. *Journal of the American Medical Association, 283,* 2529–2536.

Barlow, D. H., & Seidner, A. L. (1983). Treatment of adolescent agoraphobics: Effects on parent–adolescent relations. *Behaviour Research and Therapy, 21,* 519–526.

Barnas, M. V., Pollina, L., & Cummings, E. M. (1991). Life-span attachment: Relations between attachment and socioemotional functioning in adult women. *Genetic, Social, and General Psychology Monographs, 117,* 175–202.

Barrett, P. M. (1998). Evaluation of cognitive-behavioral group treatments for childhood anxiety disorders. *Journal of Clinical Child Psychology, 27,* 459–468.

Barrett, P. M., Dadds, M. R., & Rapee, R. M. (1996). Family treatment of childhood anxiety: A controlled trial. *Journal of Consulting and Clinical Psychology, 64,* 333–342.

Barrett, P. M., Rapee, R. M., Dadds, M. M., & Ryan, S. M. (1996). Family enhancement of cognitive style in anxious and aggressive children. *Journal of Abnormal Child Psychology, 24,* 187–203.

Barrett, P. M., Sonderegger, R., & Sonderegger, N. L. (2001). Evaluation of an anxiety-prevention and positive-coping program (FRIENDS) for children and adolescents of non-English-speaking background. *Behaviour Change, 18,* 78–91.

Barrett, P. M., & Turner, C. (2001). Prevention of anxiety symptoms in primary school children: Preliminary results from a universal school-based trial. *British Journal of Clinical Psychology, 40,* 399–410.

Barrett, T. W., & Mizes, J. S. (1988). Combat level and social support in the development of posttraumatic stress disorder in Vietnam veterans. *Behavior Modification, 12,* 100–115.

Basile, V. S., Masellis, M., Potkin, S. G., & Kennedy, J. L. (2002). Pharmacogenomics in schizophrenia: The quest for individualized therapy. *Human Molecular Genetics, 11,* 2517–2530.

Beck, A. T., Emery, G., & Greenberg, R. L. (1985). *Anxiety disorders and phobias: A cognitive perspective.* New York: Basic Books.

Beidel, D. C., & Turner, S. M. (1988). Comorbidity of test anxiety and other anxiety disorders in children. *Journal of Abnormal Child Psychology, 16,* 275–287.

Beidel, D. C., Turner, S. M., & Morris, T. L. (1995). A new inventory to assess childhood social anxiety and phobia: The Social Phobia and Anxiety Inventory for Children. *Psychological Assessment, 7,* 73–79.

Beidel, D. C., Turner, S. M., & Morris, T. L. (1999).

Psychopathology of childhood social phobia. *Journal of the American Academy of Child and Adolescent Psychiatry, 38,* 643–650.

Beidel, D. C., Turner, S. M., & Morris, T. L. (2000). Behavioral treatment of childhood social phobia. *Journal of Consulting and Clinical Psychology, 68,* 1072–1080.

Beidel, D. C., Turner, S. M., & Trager, K. N. (1994). Test anxiety and childhood anxiety disorders in African American and white school children. *Journal of Anxiety Disorders, 8,* 169–174.

Bell-Dolan, D. J. (1995). Social cue interpretation of anxious children. *Journal of Clinical Child Psychology, 24,* 1–10.

Belsky, J., & Rovine, M. (1987). Temperament and attachment security in the strange situation: An empirical rapprochement. *Child Development, 58,* 787–795.

Bendor, S. J. (1990). Anxiety and isolation in siblings of pediatric cancer patients: The need for prevention. *Social Work in Health Care, 14,* 17–35.

Benes, F. M. (1989). Myelination of cortical–hippocampal relays during late adolescence. *Schizophrenia Bulletin, 15,* 585–593.

Berman, S. L., Kurtines, W. M., Silverman, W. K., & Serafini, L. T. (1996). The impact of exposure to crime and violence on urban youth. *American Journal of Orthopsychiatry, 66,* 329–336.

Berney, T. P., Bhate, S. R., Kolvin, I., Famuyiwa, O. O., Barrett, M. L., Fundudis, T., et al. (1991). The context childhood depression: The Newcastle Childhood Depression Project. *British Journal of Psychiatry, 159,* 28–35.

Berney, T., Kolvin, I., Bhate, S. R., Garside, R. F., Jeans, J., Kay, B., et al. (1981). School phobia: A therapeutic trial with clomipramine and short-term outcome. *British Journal of Psychiatry, 138,* 110–118.

Bernstein, G. A., Borchardt, C. M., & Perwien, A. R. (1996). Anxiety disorders in children and adolescents: A review of the past 10 years. *Journal of the American Academy of Child and Adolescent Psychiatry, 35,* 1110–1119.

Bernstein, G. A., Borchardt, C. M., Perwien, A. R., Crosby, R. D., Kushner, M. G., Thuras, P. D., et al. (2000). Imipramine plus cognitive-behavioral therapy in the treatment of school refusal. *Journal of the American Academy of Child and Adolescent Psychiatry, 39,* 276–283.

Bernstein, G. A., Garfinkel, B. D., & Borchardt, C. M. (1990). Comparative studies of pharmacotherapy for school refusal. *Journal of the American Academy of Child and Adolescent Psychiatry, 29,* 773–781.

Biederman, J. (1987). Clonazepam in the treatment of prepubertal children with panic-like symptoms. *Journal of Clinical Psychiatry, 48,* 38–41.

Biederman, J., Faraone, S. V., Hirshfeld-Becker, D. R., Friedman, D., Robin, J. A., & Rosenbaum, J. F. (2001). Patterns of psychopathology and dysfunction in high-risk children of parents with panic disorder and major depression. *American Journal of Psychiatry, 158,* 49–57.

Biederman, J., Hirshfeld-Becker, D. R., Rosenbaum, J. F., Herot, C., Freidman, D. Snidman, N., et al. (2001). Further evidence of association between behavioral inhibition and social anxiety in children. *American Journal of Psychiatry, 158,* 1673–1679.

Biederman, J., Rosenbaum, J. R., Chaloff, J., & Kagan, J. (1995). Behavioral inhibition as a risk factor for anxiety disorders. In J. S. March (Ed.), *Anxiety disorders in children and adolescents.* New York: Guilford Press.

Birmaher, B., Khetarpal, S., Brent, D., Cully, M., Balach, L., Kaufman, J., et al. (1997). The Screen for Child Anxiety Related Emotional Disorders (SCARED): Scale construction and psychometric characteristics. *Journal of the American Academy of Child and Adolescent Psychiatry, 36,* 545–553.

Birmaher, B., & Ollendick, T. H. (2004). Childhood onset panic disorder. In T. H. Ollendick & J. S. March (Eds.), *Phobic and anxiety disorders in children and adolescents: A clinician's guide to effective psychosocial and pharmacological interventions.* New York: Oxford University Press.

Birmaher, B., Waterman, G. S., Ryan, N., Cully, M., Balach, L., Ingram, J., et al. (1994). Fluoxetine for childhood anxiety disorders. *Journal of the American Academy of Child and Adolescent Psychiatry, 33,* 993–999.

Bisson, J. I. (2003). Single-session early psychological interventions following traumatic events. *Clinical Psychology Review, 23,* 481–499.

Bisson, J. I., & Shepherd, J. P. (1995). Psychological reactions of victims of violent crime. *British Journal of Psychiatry, 167,* 718–720.

Black, B. (1994). Separation anxiety disorder and panic disorder. In J. March (Ed.), *Anxiety disorders in children and adolescents.* New York: Guilford Press.

Black, B., & Uhde, T. W. (1992). Elective mutism as a variant of social phobia. *Journal of the American Academy of Child and Adolescent Psychiatry, 31,* 1090–1094.

Black, B., & Uhde, T. W. (1994). Treatment of elective mutism with fluoxetine: A double-blind, placebo-controlled study. *Journal of the American Academy of Child and Adolescent Psychiatry, 33,* 1000–1006.

Black, B., & Uhde, T. W. (1995). Psychiatric characteristics of children with selective mutism: A pilot study. *Journal of the American Academy of Child and Adolescent Psychiatry, 34,* 847–856.

Blagg, N. R., & Yule, W. (1984). The behavioural treatment of school refusal: A comparative study. *Behaviour Research and Therapy, 22,* 119–127.

Boer, F. (1998). Anxiety disorders in the family: The contributions of heredity and family interactions. In D. A. Treffers (Ed.), *Emotionele Stoornissen en Somatoforme Stoornissen bij Kenderen en Adolescenten: de Stand van Zaken* (pp. 109–114). Leiden: Boerhaave Commissie.

Borkovec, T. D., Newman, M. G., & Castonguay, L. G. (2003). Cognitive-behavioral therapy for generalized anxiety disorder with integrations from interpersonal and experiential therapies. *CNS Spectrums, 8,* 382–389.

Borkovec, T. D., & Ruscio, A. M. (2001). Psychotherapy for generalized anxiety disorder. *Journal of Clinical Psychiatry, 62,* 37–42.

Boscarino, J. A. (1995). Post-traumatic stress and associated disorders among Vietnam veterans: The significance of combat exposure and social support. *Journal of Traumatic Stress, 8,* 317–336.

Bouton, M. E. (1994). Context, ambiguity, and classical conditioning. *Current Directions in Psychological Science, 3*(2), 49–53.

Bouton, M. E. (2000). A learning theory perspective on lapse, relapse, and the maintenance of behavior change. *Health Psychology,* 19(Suppl 1), 57–63.

Bouwer, C., & Stein, D. J. (1997). Association of panic disorder with a history of traumatic suffocation. *American Journal of Psychiatry, 154,* 1566–1570.

Brady, E. U., & Kendall, P. C. (1992). Comorbidity of anxiety and depression in children and adolescents. *Psychological Bulletin, 11,* 244–255.

Bremner, J. D. (1999). Does stress damage the brain? *Biological Psychiatry, 45,* 797–805.

Bremner, J. D., Krystal, J. H., Charney, D. S., & Southwick, S. M. (1996). Neural mechanisms in dissociative amnesia for childhood abuse: Relevance to the current controversy surrounding the "false memory syndrome." *American Journal of Psychiatry, 153,* 71–82.

Bremner, J. D., Staib, L. H., Kaloupek, D., Southwick, S. M., Soufer, R., & Charney, D. S. (1999). Neural correlates of exposure to traumatic pictures and sound in Vietnam combat veterans with and without posttraumatic stress disorder: A positron emission tomography study. *Biological Psychiatry, 45,* 806–816.

Brent, D. A., Holder, D., Kolko, D., Birmaher, B., Baugher, M., Roth, C., et al. (1997). A clinical psychotherapy trial for adolescent depression comparing cognitive, family, and supportive therapy. *Archives of General Psychiatry, 54,* 877–885.

Breslau, N., Schultz, L., & Peterson, E. (1995). Sex differences in depression: A role for preexisting anxiety. *Journal of Psychiatric Research, 58,* 1–12.

Brooks-Gunn, J., Graber, J. A., & Paikoff, R. L. (1994). Studying links between hormones and negative affect: Models and measures. *Journal of Research on Adolescence, 4,* 469–486.

Brown, J. M., O'Keeffe, J., Sanders, S. H., & Baker, B. (1986). Developmental changes in children's cognition to stressful and painful situations. *Journal of Pediatric Psychology, 11,* 343–357.

Brownell, K. D., Marlatt, G. A., Lichtenstein, E., & Wilson, G. T. (1986). Understanding and preventing relapse. *American Psychologist, 41,* 765–782.

Bryant, R. A., Harvey, A. G., Sackville, T., Dangh, S. T., & Basten, C. (1998). Treatment of acute stress disorder: A comparison between cognitive-behavioral therapy and supportive counseling. *Journal of Consulting and Clinical Psychology, 66,* 862–866.

Bryant, R. A., Sackville, T., Dangh, S. T., Moulds, M., & Guthrie, R. (1999). Treating acute stress disorder: An evaluation of cognitive behavior therapy and supportive counseling techniques. *American Journal of Psychiatry, 156,* 1780–1786.

Buckley, T. C., Blanchard, E. B., & Hickling, E. J. (1996). A prospective examination of delayed onset PTSD secondary to motor vehicle accidents. *Journal of Abnormal Psychology, 105,* 617–625.

Bush, J. P., Melamed, B. G., Cockrell, C. S. (1989). Parenting children in a stressful medical situation. In T. W. Miller (Ed.), *Stressful life events. International Universities Press stress and health series, Monograph 4* (pp. 643–657).

Cahill, L., & McGaugh, J. L. (1990). Amygdaloid complex lesions differentially affect retention of tasks using appetitive and aversive reinforcement. *Behavioral Neuroscience, 104,* 532–543.

Cahill, S. P., & Foa, E. B. (2003). A glass half empty or half full? Where we are and directions for future research in the treatment of PTSD. In S. Taylor (Ed.), *Advances in the treatment of posttraumatic stress disorder: Cognitive-behavioral perspectives*. New York: Springer.

Cahill, S. P., Foa, E. B., Rothbaum, B. O., Davidson, R. T., Connor, K., & Compton, J. (2004, March). Augmentation of setraline with cognitive behavior therapy in the treatment of posttraumatic stress disorder: Effects on acute treatment outcome and maintenance of treatment gains. In N. C. Feeny (Chair), *Psychosocial and pharmacological interventions for PTSD: Recent advances*. Convention Proceedings of the 24th annual meeting of the Anxiety Disorders Association of America. Silver Springs, MD: ADAA.

Capps, L., Sigman, M., Sena, R., & Henker, B. (1996). Fear, anxiety and perceived control in children of agoraphobic parents. *Journal of Child Psychology and Psychiatry and Allied Disciplines, 37*, 445–452.

Casey, B. J., Giedd, J. N., & Thomas, K. M. (2000). Structural and functional brain development and its relation to cognitive development. *Biological Psychology, 54*, 241–257.

Caspi, A., & Moffitt, T. E. (1991). Individual differences as accentuated during periods of social changes: The sample case of girls at puberty. *Journal of Personality and Social Psychology, 61*, 157–168.

Cassidy, J. (1995). Attachment and generalized anxiety disorder. In D. Cicchetti & S. Toth (Eds.), *Emotion, cognition, and representation: Rochester Symposium on Developmental Psychopathology VI*, (pp. 343–370). Rochester, NY: University of Rochester Press.

Cassidy, J., & Berlin, L. J. (1994). The insecure/ambivalent pattern of attachment: Theory and research. *Child Development, 65*, 971–991.

Cavaiola, A. A., & Schiff, M. (1988). Behavioral sequelae of physical and/or sexual abuse in adolescents. *Child Abuse and Neglect, 12*, 181–188.

Chambless, D. L., & Hollon, S. D. (1998). Defining empirically supported therapies. *Journal of Consulting and Clinical Psychology, 66*, 7–18.

Chambless, D. L., & Ollendick, T. H. (2000). Empirically supported psychological interventions: Controversies and evidence. *Annual Review of Psychology, 52*, 685–716.

Charney, D. S., & Deutch, A. (1996). A functional neuroanatomy of anxiety and fear: Implications for the pathophysiology and treatment of anxiety disorders. *Critical Reviews in Neurobiology, 10*, 419–446.

Chemtob, C. M., Nakashima, J., & Carlson, J. G. (2002). Brief treatment for elementary school children with disaster-related posttraumatic stress disorder: A field study. *Journal of Clinical Psychology, 58*, 99–112.

Chorpita, B. F., Albano, A. M., & Barlow, D. H. (1996). Cognitive processing in children: Relation to anxiety and family influences. *Journal of Clinical Child Psychology, 25*, 170–176.

Chorpita, B. F., Brown, T. A., & Barlow, D. H. (1998). Perceived control as a mediator of family environment in etiological models of childhood anxiety. *Behavior Therapy, 29*, 457–476.

Chugani, H. T. (1996). Neuroimaging of developmental nonlinearity and developmental pathologies. In R. W. Thatcher, G. R. Lyon, J. Rumsey, & N. Krasnegor (Eds.), *Developmental neuroimaging: Mapping the development of brain and behavior* (pp. 187–195). San Diego: Academic Press.

Clark, D. M. (1986). A cognitive approach to panic. *Behaviour Research and Therapy, 24*, 461–470.

Clark, D. M. (1996). Panic disorder: From theory to therapy. In P. M. Salkovskis (Ed.), *Frontiers of cognitive therapy* (pp. 318–344). New York: Guilford Press.

Clark, D. M., Salkovskis, P. M., Hackmann, A., Wells, A., Ludgate, J., & Gelder, M. (1999). Brief cognitive therapy for panic disorder: A randomized controlled trial. *Journal of Consulting and Clinical Psychology, 67*, 583–589.

Cobham, V. E., Dadds, M. R., & Spence, S. H. (1998). The role of parental anxiety in the treatment of childhood anxiety. *Journal of Consulting and Clinical Psychology, 66*, 893–905.

Cohen, J. A. (2001). Pharmacologic treatment of traumatized children. *Trauma, Violence, and Abuse, 2*, 155–171.

Cohen, J. A., & Mannarino, A. P. (1996a). A treatment outcome study for sexually abused preschool children: Initial findings. *Journal of the American Academy of Child and Adolescent Psychiatry, 35*, 42–50.

Cohen, J. A., & Mannarino, A. P. (1996b). "A treatment outcome study for sexually abused preschool children: Initial findings": Errata. *Journal of the American Academy of Child and Adolescent Psychiatry, 35*, 835.

Cohen, J. A., & Mannarino, A. P. (1998). Factors that mediate treatment outcome of sexually abused preschool children: Six- and twelve-month follow-up. *Journal of the American Academy of Child and Adolescent Psychiatry, 37*, 44–51.

Cohen, J. A., Mannarino, A. P., Greenberg, T., Padlo, S., & Shipley, C. (2002). Childhood traumatic grief: Concepts and controversies. *Trauma Violence and Abuse, 3*, 307–327.

Collins, J. J., & Bailey, S. L. (1990). Traumatic stress disorder and violent behavior. *Journal of Traumatic Stress, 3*, 203–220.

Comeau, N., Stuart, S. H., & Loba, P. (2001). The relations of trait anxiety, anxiety sensitivity and sensation seeking to adolescents' motivations for alcohol, cigarette and marijuana use. *Addictive Behaviors, 26*, 803–825.

Conners, C. K. (1997). *Conners Rating Scales-revised technical manual.* Toronto: Multi-Health Systems.

Cooper, N. A., & Clum, G. A. (1989). Imaginal flooding as a supplementary treatment for PTSD in combat veterans: A controlled study. *Behavior Therapy, 20*, 381–391.

Coplan, J. D., Moreau, D., Chaput, F., Martinez, J. M., Hoven, C. W., Mandell, D. J., et al. (2002). Salivary cortisol concentrations before and after carbon dioxide inhalations in children. *Biological Psychiatry, 51*, 326–333.

Coplan, J. D., Papp, L. A., Pine, D., Martinez, J., Cooper, T., Rosenblum, L. A., et al. (1997). Clinical improvement with fluoxetine therapy and noradrenergic function in patients with panic disorder. *Archives of General Psychiatry, 54*, 643–648.

Coryell, W., Fyer, A., Pine, D., Martinez, J., & Arndt, S. (2001). Aberrant respiratory sensitivity to CO(2) as a trait of familial panic disorder. *Biological Psychiatry, 49*, 582–587.

Costello, E. J., & Angold, A. (1988). Scales to assess child and adolescent depression: Checklists, screens, and nets. *Journal of the American Academy of Child and Adolescent Psychiatry, 27*, 726–737.

Costello, E. J., & Angold, A. (1995). Epidemiology. In J. S. March (Ed.), *Anxiety disorders in children and adolescents* (pp. 109–124). New York: Guilford Press.

Costello, E. J., Burns, B. J., Angold, A., & Leaf, P. J. (1993). How can epidemiology improve mental health services for children and adolescents? *Journal of the American Academy of Child and Adolescent Psychiatry, 32*, 1106–1113.

Costello, E. J., Egger, H. L., & Angold, A. (2004). The developmental epidemiology of anxiety disorders. In T. Ollendick & J. March (Eds.). *Phobic and anxiety disorders in children and adolescents* (pp. 61–91). New York: Oxford University Press.

Costello, E. J., Erkanli, A., Federman, E., & Angold, A. (1999). Development of psychiatric comorbidity with substance abuse in adolescents: Effects of timing and sex. *Journal of Clinical Child Psychology, 28*, 298–311.

Costello, E. J., Mustillo, S., Erkanli, A., Keeler, G., & Angold, A. (2003). Prevalence and development of psychiatric disorders in childhood and adolescence. *Archives of General Psychiatry, 60*, 837–844.

Cottraux, J., Mollard, E., Bouvard, M., Marks, I., Sluys, M., Nury, A. M., et al. (1990). A controlled study of fluvoxamine and exposure in obsessive-compulsive disorder. *International Clinical Psychopharmacology, 5*, 17–30.

Cowen, E. L., Wyman, P. A., Work, W. C., & Parker, G. R. (1990). The Rochester Child Resilience Project: Overview and summary of first year findings. *Development and Psychopathology, 2*, 193–212.

Craske, M. G., & Zucker, B. G. (2001). Prevention of anxiety disorders: A model for intervention. *Applied and Preventive Psychology, 10*, 155–175.

Crowe, R. (1985). The genetics of panic disorder and agoraphobia. *Psychiatric Developments, 3*, 171–185.

Crowell, J. A., O' Connor, E., Wollmers, G., & Sprafkin, J. (1991). Mothers' conceptualizations of parent–child relationships: Relation to mother–child interaction and child behavior problems. *Development and Psychopathology, 3*, 431–444.

Cunningham, C. E., Cataldo, M. F., Mallion, C., Keyes, J. B. (1984). A review and controlled single case evaluation of behavioral approaches to the management of elective mutism. *Child and Family Behavior Therapy, 5*, 25–49.

Cunningham, M. G., Bhattacharyya, S., & Benes, F. M. (2002). Amygdalo-cortical sprouting continues into early adulthood: Implications for the development of normal and abnormal function during adolescence. *Journal of Comparative Neurology, 453*, 116–130.

Dadds, M. R., Barrett, P. M., Rapee, R. M., & Ryan, S. (1996). Family process and child anxiety and aggression: An observational analysis. *Journal of Abnormal Child Psychology, 24*, 715–734.

Dadds, M. R., Holland, D. E., Laurens, K. R., Mullins, M., Barrett, P. M., & Spence, S. H. (1999). Early intervention and prevention of anxiety disorders in children: Results at 2-year follow-up. *Journal of Consulting and Clinical Psychology, 67*, 145–150.

Dadds, M. R., Spence, S. H., Holland, D. E., Barrett, P. M., & Laurens, K. R. (1997). Prevention and early intervention for anxiety disorders: A controlled trial. *Journal of Consulting and Clinical Psychology, 65,* 627–635.

Dalgleish, T., Moradi, A. R., Taghavi, M. R., Neshat-Doost, H. T., & Yule, W. (2001). An experimental investigation of hypervigilance for threat in children and adolescents with post-traumatic stress disorder. *Psychological Medicine, 31,* 541–547.

Dalgleish, T., Taghavi, R., Neshat-Doost, H., Moradi, A., Canterbury, R., & Yule, W. (2003). Patterns of processing bias for emotional information across clinical disorders: A comparison of attention, memory, and prospective cognition in children and adolescents with depression, generalized anxiety, and posttraumatic stress disorder. *Journal of Clinical Child and Adolescent Psychology, 32,* 10–21.

Daniels, D., & Plomin, R. (1985). Origins of individual differences in infant shyness. *Developmental Psychology, 21,* 118–121.

Davidson, J. R., Rothbaum, B. O., van der Kolk, B. A., Sikes, C. R., & Farfel, G. M. (2001). Multicenter, double-blind comparison of sertraline and placebo in the treatment of posttraumatic stress disorder. *Archives of General Psychiatry, 58,* 485–492.

Davidson, R. J., Abercrombie, H., Nitschke, J. B., & Putnam, K. (1999). Regional brain function, emotion and disorders of emotion. *Current Opinion in Neurobiology, 9,* 228–234.

Davis, M. (1992). The role of the amygdala in fear and anxiety. *Annual Review of Neuroscience, 15,* 353–375.

Davis, M. (1998). Are different parts of the external amygdala involved in fear versus anxiety? *Biological Psychiatry, 44,* 1239–1247.

De Bellis, M. D. (2001). Developmental traumatology: The psychobiological development of maltreated children and its implication for research, treatment, and policy. *Development and Psychopathology, 13,* 539–564.

De Bellis, M. D., Keshavan, M. S., Clark, D. B., Casey, B. J., Giedd, J. N., Boring, A. M., et al. (1999). A. E. Bennett Research Award. Developmental traumatology. Part II: Brain development. *Biological Psychiatry, 45,* 1271–1284.

De Bellis, M. D., Keshavan, M. S., Shifflett, H., Iyengar, S., Dahl, R. E., Axelson, D. A., et al. (2002). Superior temporal gyrus volumes in pediatric generalized anxiety disorder. *Biological Psychiatry, 51,* 553–562.

De Bellis, M. D., Keshavan, M. S., Spencer, S., & Hall, J. (2000). N-acetylaspartate concentration in the anterior cingulate of maltreated children

and adolescents with PTSD. *American Journal of Psychiatry, 157,* 1175–1177.

Deblinger, E., & Heflin, A. H. (1996). Treating sexually abused children and their nonoffending parents: A cognitive behavioral approach. *Interpersonal violence: The practice series, 16,* 256.

Deblinger, E., Lippmann, J., & Steer, R. A. (1996). Sexually abused children suffering posttraumatic stress symptoms: Initial treatment outcome findings. *Child Maltreatment, 1,* 310–321.

Deblinger, E., Steer, R. A., & Lippmann, J. (1999). Two-year follow-up study of cognitive behavioral therapy for sexually abused children suffering post-traumatic stress symptoms. *Child Abuse and Neglect, 23,* 1371–1378.

De Haan, E., Hoogduin, K. A., Buitelaar, J. K., & Keijsers, G. P. (1998). Behavior therapy versus clomipramine for the treatment of obsessive-compulsive disorder. *Journal of the American Academy of Child and Adolescent Psychiatry, 37,* 1022–1029.

Derivan, A. T., Entsuah, R., Haskins, T., Rudolph, R., & Aguiar, L. (1997, December). Double-blind, placebo-controlled study of once-daily venlafaxine XR and buspirone in outpatients with generalized anxiety disorder (GAD). Paper presented at the annual meeting of the American College of Neuropsychopharmacology, Honolulu, Hawaii.

DeVeaugh-Geiss, J., Moroz, G., Biederman, J., Cantwell, D. P., Fontaine, R., Greist, J. H., et al. (1992). Clomipramine hydrochloride in childhood and adolescent obsessive-compulsive disorder—A multicenter trial. *Journal of the American Academy of Child and Adolescent Psychiatry, 31,* 45–49.

Devilly, G. J., & Spence, S. H. (1999). The relative efficacy and treatment distress of EMDR and a cognitive-behavior trauma treatment protocol in the amelioration of posttraumatic stress disorder. *Journal of Anxiety Disorders, 13,* 131–157.

Deykin, E. Y., & Buka, S. L. (1997). Prevalence and risk factors for posttraumatic stress disorder among chemically dependent adolescents. *American Journal of Psychiatry, 154,* 752–757.

Dick-Niederhauser, A., & Silverman, W. K. (2003). *Courage and fearlessness: A positive approach to the etiology and treatment of anxiety disorders.* Paper submitted for publication.

Dierker, L. C., Albano, A. M., Clarke, G. N., Heimberg, R. G., et al. (2001). Screening for anxiety and depression in early adolescence. *Journal of the American Academy of Child and Adolescent Psychiatry, 40,* 929–936.

DiLalla, L. F., Kagan, J., & Reznick, J. S. (1994). Genetic etiology of behavioral inhibition among 2-year-old children. *Infant Behavior and Development, 17*, 405–412.

Donovan, C. L., & Spence, S. H. (2000). Prevention of childhood anxiety disorders. *Clinical Psychology Review, 20*, 509–531.

Dougherty, D. D., Rauch, S. L., & Jenike, M. A. (2002). Pharmacological treatments for obsessive compulsive disorder. In P. E. Nathan & J. M. Gorman (Eds.), *A guide to treatments that work* (2nd ed.) London: Oxford University Press.

Dubner, A. E., & Motta, R. W. (1999). Sexually and physically abused foster care children and posttraumatic stress disorder. *Journal of Consulting and Clinical Psychology, 67*, 367–373.

Dummit, E. S., Klein, R. G., Tancer, N. K., Asche, B., Martin, J., & Fairbanks, J. A. (1997). Systematic assessment of 50 children with selective mutism. *Journal of the American Academy of Child and Adolescent Psychiatry, 36*, 653–660.

D'Zurilla, T. J., & Goldfried, M. R. (1971). Problem solving and behavior modification. *Journal of Abnormal Psychology, 78*, 107–126.

Eaves, L. J., Eysenck, H. J., & Martin M. (1989). *Genes, culture and personality; An empirical approach.* New York: Academic Press.

Eaves, L. J., Silberg, J. L., Maes, H. H., Simonoff, E., Pickles, A., Rutter, M., et al. (1997). Genetics and developmental psychopathology: The main effects of genes and environment on behavioral problems in the Virginia Twin Study of adolescent behavior development. *Journal of Child Psychology and Psychiatry and Allied Disciplines, 38*, 965–980.

Ebata, A. T., & Moos, R. H. (1991). Coping and adjustment in distressed and healthy adolescents. *Journal of Applied Developmental Psychology, 12*, 33–54.

Echeburua, E., de Corral, P., Zubizarreta, I., & Sarsua, B. (1997). Psychological treatment of chronic posttraumatic stress disorder in victims of sexual aggression. *Behavior Modification, 21*, 433–456.

Eisen, A. R., & Silverman, W. K. (1998). Prescriptive treatment for generalized anxiety disorder in children. *Behavior Therapy, 29*, 105–121.

Ellis, H. (1899). The evolution of modesty. *Psychological Review, 6*, 134–145.

Emslie, G. J., Rush, A. J., Weinberg, W. A., Kowatch, R. A., Hughes, C. W., Carmody, T., et al. (1997). A double-blind, randomized, placebo-controlled trial of fluoxetine in children and adolescents with depression. *Archives of General Psychiatry, 54*, 1031–1037.

Epkins, C. C. (2002). A comparison of two self-report measures of children's social anxiety in clinical and community samples. *Journal of Clinical Child and Adolescent Psychology, 31*, 69–79.

Eriksson, P. S., Perfilieva, E., Björk-Eriksson, T., Alborn, A.-M., Nordborg, C., Peterson, D. A., et al. (1998). Neurogenesis in the adult human hippocampus. *Nature Medicine, 4*, 1313–1317.

Essau, C. A., Conradt, J., & Petermann, F. (1999). Frequency of panic attacks and panic disorder in adolescents. *Depression and Anxiety, 9*, 19–26.

Essex, M. J., Klein, M. H., Cho, E., & Kalin, N. H. (2002). Maternal stress beginning in infancy may sensitize children to later stress exposure: Effects on cortisol and behavior. *Biological Psychiatry, 52*, 776–784.

Fairbanks, J. M., Pine, D. S., Tancer, N. K., Dummit E. S., III, Kentgen, L. M., Asche, B. K., et al. (1997). Open fluoxetine treatment of mixed anxiety disorders in children and adolescents. *Journal of the American Academy of Child and Adolescent Psychiatry, 7*, 17–29.

Famularo, R., Spivak, G., Bunshaft, D., & Berkson, J. (1988). Advisability of substance abuse testing in parents who severely maltreat their children: The issue of drug testing before the juvenile/family courts. *Bulletin of the American Academy of Psychiatry and the Law, 16*, 217–223.

Farrell, A. D., & Bruce, S. E. (1997). Impact of exposure to community violence on violent behavior and emotional distress among urban adolescents. *Journal of Clinical Child Psychology, 26*, 2–14.

Feigon, S., Waldman, I., Irwin, D., Levy, F., & Hay, D. A. (2001). Genetic and environmental influences on separation anxiety disorder symptoms and their moderation by age and sex. *Behavior Genetics, 31*, 403–411.

Felner, R. D., & Adan, A. M. (1988). The School Transitional Environment Project: An ecological intervention and evaluation. In R. H. Price, E. L. Cowen, L. Emory, et al. (Eds.), *Fourteen ounces of prevention: A casebook for practitioners* (pp. 111–122). Washington, DC: American Psychological Association.

Findling, R. L., Reed, M. D., Myers, C., O'Riordan, M. A., Fiala, S., Branicky, L., et al. (1999). Paroxetine pharmacokinetics in depressed children and adolescents. *Journal of the American Academy of Child and Adolescent Psychiatry, 38*, 952–959.

Fitzgerald, K. D., Stewart, C. M., Tawile, V., & Rosenberg, D. R. (1999). Risperidone augmentation of serotonin reuptake inhibitor treatment of pediatric obsessive compulsive disorder. *Journal of Child and Adolescent Psychopharmacology, 9,* 115–123.

Flament, M. F., Rapoport, J. L., Berg, C. J., Sceery, W., Kilts, C., Mellstrom, B., et al. (1985). Clomipramine treatment of childhood obsessive-compulsive disorder. *Archives of General Psychiatry, 42,* 977–983.

Flannery-Schroeder, E. C., & Kendall, P. C. (2000). Group and individual cognitive-behavioral treatments for youth with anxiety disorders: A randomized clinical trial. *Cognitive Therapy and Research, 24,* 251–278.

Foa, E. B., Cashman, L., Jaycox, L., & Perry, K. (1997). The validation of a self-report measure of posttraumatic stress disorder: The Posttraumatic Diagnostic Scale. *Psychological Assessment, 9,* 445–451.

Foa, E. B., Dancu, C. V., Hembree, E. A., Jaycox, L. H., Meadows, E. A., & Street, G. P. (1999). A comparison of exposure therapy, stress inoculation training, and their combination for reducing posttraumatic stress disorder in female assault victims. *Journal of Consulting and Clinical Psychology, 67,* 194–200.

Foa, E. B., Feske, U., Murdock, T. B., Kozak, M. J., McCarthy, P. R. (1991). Processing of threat-related information in rape victims. *Journal of Abnormal Psychology, 100,* 156–162.

Foa, E. B., Franklin, M. E., & Moser, J. (2002). Context in the clinic: How well do cognitive-behavioral therapies and medications work in combination? *Biological Psychiatry, 52,* 989–997.

Foa, E. B., Hearst-Ikeda, D., & Perry, K. J. (1995). Evaluation of a brief cognitive-behavioral program for the prevention of chronic PTSD in recent assault victims. *Journal of Consulting and Clinical Psychology, 63,* 948–955.

Foa, E. B., Johnson, K. M., Feeny, N. C., & Treadwell, K.R.H. (2001). The Child PTSD Symptom Scale (CPSS): A preliminary examination of its psychometric properties. *Journal of Clinical Child Psychology, 30,* 376–384.

Foa, E. B., & Kozak, M. J. (1985). Treatment of anxiety disorders: Implications for psychopathology. In A. H. Tuma & J. D. Maser (Eds.), *Anxiety and the anxiety disorders.* Hillsdale, NJ: Lawrence Erlbaum Associates.

Foa, E. B., & Kozak, M. J. (1986). Emotional processing of fear: Exposure to corrective information. *Psychological Bulletin, 90,* 20–35.

Foa, E. B., Liebowitz, M. R., Kozak, M. J., Davies, S. O., Campeas, R., Franklin, M. E., et al. (2005).

Treatment of obsessive compulsive disorder by exposure and ritual prevention, clomipramine, and their combination: A randomized, placebo-controlled trial. *American Journal of Psychiatry, 162,* 151–161.

Foa, E. B., & Riggs, D. S. (1993). Post traumatic stress disorder in rape victims. In J. M. Oldham, M. B. Riba, & A. Tasman (Eds.), *American Psychiatric Press review of psychiatry, Vol. 12.* Washington, DC: American Psychiatric Press.

Foa, E. B., & Rothbaum, B. O. (1998). *Treating the trauma of rape: Cognitive-behavioral therapy for PTSD.* New York: The Guilford Press.

Foa, E. B., Rothbaum, B. O., & Furr, J. M. (2003). Augmenting exposure therapy with other CBT procedures. *Psychiatric Annals, 33,* 47–53.

Foa, E. B., Zoellner, L., & Feeny, N. (2004). *An evaluation of three brief programs for facilitating recovery after trauma.* Manuscript submitted for publication.

Fontana, A., & Rosenheck, R. (1998). Duty-related and sexual stress in the etiology of PTSD among women veterans who seek treatment. *Psychiatric Services, 49,* 658–662.

Fontana, A., Schwartz, L. S., & Rosenheck, R. (1997). Posttraumatic stress disorder among female Vietnam veterans: A causal model of etiology. *American Journal of Public Health, 87,* 169–175.

Fox, N. A., & Bell, M. A. (1990). Electrophysiological indexes of frontal lobe development. *Annals of the New York Academy of Sciences, 608,* 677–698.

Fox, N. A., Henderson, H. A., Rabin, K. H., Caikins, S. D., & Schmidt, L. A. (2001). Continuity and discontinuity of behavioral inhibition and exuberance. *Child Development, 72,* 1–21.

Foy, D. W., Resnick, H. S., Sipprelle, R. C., & Carroll, E. M. (1987). Premilitary, military, and post-military factors in the development of combat-related posttraumatic stress disorder. *Behavior Therapist, 10,* 3–9.

Francis, G., Last, C. G., & Strauss, C. C. (1987). Expression of separation anxiety disorder: The roles of age and gender. *Child Psychiatry and Human Development, 18,* 82–89.

Franklin, M. E., & Foa, E. B. (2002). Cognitive behavioral treatments for obsessive compulsive disorder. In P. E. Nathan & J. M. Gormon (Eds.), *A guide to treatments that work* (2nd ed.). New York: Oxford University Press.

Franklin, M. E., Foa, E. B., & March, J. S. (2003). The Pediatric OCD Treatment Study (POTS): Rationale, design and methods. *Journal of Child and*

Adolescent Psychopharmacology, 13 (Suppl. 1), 39–52.

Franklin, M. E., Kozak, M. J., Cashman, L. A., Coles, M. E., Rheingold, A. A., Foa, E. B. (1998). Cognitive-behavioral treatment of pediatric obsessive-compulsive disorder: An open clinical trial. *Journal of the American Academy of Child and Adolescent Psychiatry 37*, 412–419.

Franklin, M. E., Tolin, D. F., March, J. S., & Foa, E. B. (2001). Treatment of pediatric obsessive-compulsive disorder: A case example of intensive cognitive-behavioral therapy involving exposure and ritual prevention. *Cognitive and Behavioral Practice, 8*, 297–304.

Frederick, C. J., Pynoos, R. S., & Nader, K. (1992). *Reaction Index to Psychic Trauma Form C (Child).* Unpublished manuscript, University of California at Los Angeles.

Freeman, C. P., Trimble, M. R., Deakin, J. F. W., Stokes, T. M., & Ashford, J. J. (1994). Fluvoxamine versus clomipramine in the treatment of obsessive compulsive disorder: A multicenter, randomized, double-blind, parallel group comparison. *Journal of Clinical Psychiatry, 55*, 301–305.

Freeman, J. E., Garcia, A. M., Fucci, C., Karitani, M., Miller, L., & Leonard, H. L. (2003). Family-based treatment of early-onset obsessive-compulsive disorder. *Journal of Child and Adolescent Psychopharmacology, 13*, (Suppl. 1), 571–580.

Gardenswartz, C. A., & Craske, M. G. (2001). Prevention of panic disorder. *Behavior Therapy, 32*, 725–737.

Garvey, M. A., Perlmutter, S. J., Allen, A. J., Hamburger, S., Lougee, L., Leonard, H. I., et al. (1999). A pilot study of penicillin prophylaxis for neuropsychiatric exacerbations triggered by streptococcal infections. *Biological Psychiatry, 45*, 1564–1571.

Geller, D. A., Hoog, S. L., Heiligenstein, J. H., Ricardi, R. K., Tamura, R., Kluszynski, S., et al. (2001). Fluoxetine treatment for obsessive-compulsive disorder in children and adolescents: A placebo-controlled clinical trial. *Journal of the American Academy of Child and Adolescent Psychiatry, 40*, 773–779.

Gerlsma, C., Emmelkamp, P.M.G., & Arrindell, W. A. (1990). Anxiety, depression, and perception of early parenting: A meta-analysis. *Clinical Psychology Review, 10*, 251–277.

Giedd, J. N., Blumenthal, J., Jeffries, N. O., Castellanos, F. X., Liu, H., Zijdenbos, A., et al. (1999). Brain development during childhood and adolescence: A longitudinal MRI study. *Nature Neuroscience, 2*, 861–863.

Giedd, J. N., Castellanos, F. X., Rajapakse, J. C., Vaituzis, A. C., & Rapoport, J. L. (1997). Sexual dimorphism of the developing human brain. *Progress in Neuro-psyphopharmacology and Biological Psychiatry, 21*, 1185–1201.

Ginsburg, G. S., & Schlossberg, M. C. (2002). Family-based treatment of childhood anxiety disorders. *International Review of Psychiatry, 14*, 143–154.

Ginsburg, G. S., Silverman, W. K., & Kurtines, W. M. (1995). Family involvement in treating children with phobic and anxiety disorders: A look ahead. *Clinical Psychology Review, 15*, 457–473.

Ginsburg, G. S., & Walkup, J. T. (2004). Treatment of specific phobias. In T. H. Ollendick & J. S. March (Eds.), *Phobic and anxiety disorders in children and adolescents: A clinician's guide to effective psychosocial and pharmacological interventions.* New York: Oxford University Press.

Gittelman-Klein, R. (1975). Pharmacotherapy and management of pathological separation anxiety. *International Journal of Mental Health 4*, 255–272.

Gittelman-Klein, R., & Klein, D. F. (1971). Controlled imipramine treatment of school phobia. *Archives of General Psychiatry, 2*, 204–207.

Gittelman-Klein, R., & Klein, D. F. (1973). School phobia: Diagnostic considerations in the light of imipramine effects. *Journal of Nervous and Mental Disease, 156*, 199–215.

Glynn, S. M., Eth, S., Randolph, E. T., Foy, D. W., Urbaitis, M., Boxer, L., et al. (1999). A test of behavioral family therapy to augment exposure for combat-related posttraumatic stress disorder. *Journal of Consulting and Clinical Psychology, 67*, 243–251.

Goddard, A. W., Brouette, T., Almai, A., Jetty, P., Woods, S. W., Charney, D. (2001). Early coadministration of clonazepam with sertraline for panic disorder. *Archives of General Psychiatry, 58*, 681–686.

Goenjian, A. K., Karayan, I., Pynoos, R. S., Minassian, D., Najarian, L. M., Steinberg, A. M., et al. (1997). Outcome of psychotherapy among early adolescents after trauma. *American Journal of Psychiatry, 154*, 536–542.

Goenjian, A., Stilwell, B. M., Steinberg, A. M., Fairbanks, L. A., Galvin, M. R., Karayan, I., et al. (1999). Moral development and psychopathological interference in conscience functioning among adolescents after trauma. *Journal of the American Academy of Child and Adolescent Psychiatry, 38*, 376–384.

Goldman-Rakic, P. S., Isseroff, A., Schwartz, M. L.,

& Bugbee, N. M. (1983). The neurobiology of cognitive development. In P. H. Mussen (Ed.), *Handbook of child psychology. Vol. II. Infancy and developmental psychobiology* (pp. 281–344). New York: John Wiley & Sons.

Gorman, J. M., & Sloan, R. P. (2000). Heart rate variability in depressive and anxiety disorders. *American Heart Journal, 140,* 77–83.

Gorwood, P., Feingold, J., & Ades, J. (1999). Genetic epidemiology and psychiatry. D: Scope and limitations of familial studies. Case of panic disorder. *Encephale, 25,* 21–29.

Gottesman, I. I., & Gould, T. D. (2003). The endophenotype concept in psychiatry: Etymology and strategic intentions. *American Journal of Psychiatry, 160,* 636–645.

Gould, R. A., Buckminster, S., Pollack, M. H., Otto, M. W. & Yap, L. (1997). Cognitive-behavioral and pharmacological treatment for social phobia: A meta-analysis. *Clinical Psychology: Science and Practice, 4,* 291–306.

Graae, F., Milner, J., Rizzotto, L., & Klein, R. G. (1994). Clonazepam in childhood anxiety disorders. *Journal of the American Academy of Child and Adolescent Psychiatry, 33,* 372–376.

Graber, J. A., Brooks-Gunn, J., Paikoff, R. L., & Warren, M. P. (1994). Prediction of eating problems: an 8-year study of adolescent girls. *Developmental Psychology, 30,* 823–834.

Gray, J. A. (1987). Interactions between drugs and behavior therapy. In H. J. Eysenck & I. Martin (Eds.), *Theoretical foundations of behavior therapy* (pp. 433–447). New York: Plenum Press.

Graybiel, A. M., & Rauch, S. L. (2000). Toward a neurobiology of obsessive-compulsive disorder. *Neuron, 28,* 343–347.

Green, B. L., Grace, M. C., & Gleser, G. C. (1985). Identifying survivors at risk: Long-term impairment following the Beverly Hills Supper Club fire. *Journal of Consulting and Clinical Psychology, 53,* 672–678.

Greenberg, P. E., Sisitsky, T., Kessler, R. C., Finkelstein, S. N., Berndt, E. R., Davidson, R. R. T., et al. (1999). The economic burden of anxiety disorders in the 1990s. *Journal of Clinical Psychiatry, 60,* 427–435.

Greist, J. H., Jefferson, J. W., Kobak, K. A., & Katzelnick, D. J. (1995). Efficacy and tolerability of serotonin transport inhibitors in obsessive-compulsive disorder: A meta-analysis. *Archives of General Psychiatry, 52,* 53–60.

Griffith, J. (1985). Social support providers: Who are they? Where are they met?—and the relationship of network characteristics to psychological distress. *Basic and Applied Social Psychology, 6,* 41–60.

Gullone, E. (2000). The development of normal fear: A century of research. *Clinical Psychology Review, 20,* 429–451.

Hadwin, J., Frost, S., French, C. C., & Richards, A. (1997). Cognitive processing and trait anxiety in typically developing children: Evidence for an interpretation bias. *Journal of Abnormal Psychology, 106,* 486–490.

Hageman, I., Andersen, H. S., & Jorgensen, M. B. (2001). Post-traumatic stress disorder: A review of psychobiology and pharmacotherapy. *Acta Psychiatrica Scandinavia, 104,* 411–422.

Hagemann, D., Naumann, E., Thayer, J. F., & Bartussek, D. (2002). Does resting EEG asymmetry reflect a trait? *Journal of Personality and Social Psychology 82,* 619–641.

Hallowell, A. I. (1955). *Culture and experience.* Philadelphia: University of Pennsylvania Press.

Hambick, J. P., Turk, C. L., Heimberg, R. G., Schneier, F. R., & Liebowitz, M. R. (2003). The experience of disability and quality of life in social anxiety disorder. *Depression and Anxiety, 18,* 46–50.

Harmon, M. G., Morse, D. T., & Morse, L. W. (1996). Confirmatory factor analysis of the Gibb Experimental Test of Testwiseness. *Educational and Psychological Measurement, 56,* 276–286.

Harvey, A. G., & Bryant, R. A. (1998). The relationship between acute stress disorder and post-traumatic stress disorder: A prospective evaluation of motor vehicle accident survivors. *Journal of Consulting and Clinical Psychology, 66,* 507–512.

Hayward, C., Killen, J. D., Kraemer, H. C., Blair-Greiner, A., Strachowski, D., Cunning, D., et al. (1997). Assessment and phenomenology of nonclinical panic attacks in adolescent girls. *Journal of Anxiety Disorders, 11,* 17–32.

Hayward, C., Killen, J. D., Wilson, D. M., & Hammer, L. D. (1997). Psychiatric risk associated with early puberty in adolescent girls. *Journal of the American Academy of Child and Adolescent Psychiatry, 36,* 255–262.

Hayward, C., Varady, S., Albano, A. M., Thienemann, M., Henderson, L., Schatzberg, A. F. (2000). Cognitive-behavioral group therapy for social phobia in female adolescents: Results of a pilot study. *Journal of the American Academy of Child and Adolescent Psychiatry, 39,* 721–726.

Heim, C., & Nemeroff, C. B. (2002). Neurobiology of early life stress: Clinical studies. *Seminars in Clinical Neuropsychiatry, 7,* 147–159.

Heim, C., Owens, M. J., Plotsky, P. M., & Nemeroff, C. B. (1997). Persistent changes in corticotropin-releasing factor systems due to early life stress: Relationship to the pathophysiology of major depression and post-traumatic stress disorder. *Psychopharmacology Bulletin, 33,* 185–192.

Hembree, E. A., & Foa, E. B. (2003). Interventions for trauma-related emotional disturbances in adult victims of crime. *Journal of Traumatic Stress, 16,* 187–199.

Herman, J. L. (1992). Complex PTSD: A syndrome in survivors of prolonged and repeated trauma. *Journal of Traumatic Stress, 5,* 377–391.

Hettema, J., Neale, M. C., & Kendler, K. S. (2001). A review and meta-analysis of the genetic epidemiology of anxiety disorders. *American Journal of Psychiatry, 158,* 1568–1578.

Hettema, J., Prescott, C., & Kendler, K. S. (2001). A population-based twin study of generalized anxiety disorder in men and women. *Journal of Nervous and Mental Disease,189,* 413–420.

Heyne, D., King, N. J., Tonge, B. J., Rollings, S., Young, D., Pritchard, M., et al. (2002). Evaluation of child therapy and caregiver training in the treatment of school refusal. *Journal of the American Academy of Child and Adolescent Psychiatry, 41,* 687–695.

Hightower, A. D., & Braden, J. (1991). Prevention. In T. R. Kratochwill & R. J. Morris (Eds.), *The practice of child therapy* (pp. 410–440). New York: Pergamon Press.

Hill, H. M., Levermore, M., Twaite, J., & Jones, L. P. (1996). Exposure to community violence and social support as predictors of anxiety and social and emotional behavior among African American children. *Journal of Child and Family Studies, 5,* 399–414.

Hirschmann, S., Dannon, P. N., Iancu, J., Dolberg, O. T., Zohar, J., & Grunhaus, L. (2000). Pindolol augmentation in patients with treatment-resistant panic disorder: A double-blind, placebo-controlled trial. *Journal of Clinical Psychopharmacology, 20, 5,* 556–559.

Hodges, K., Doucette–Gates, A., & Liao, Q. (1999). The relationship between the Child and Adolescent Functional Assessment Scale (CAFAS) and indicators of functioning. *Journal of Child and Family Studies, 8,* 109–122.

Hodges, W. F. (1991). *Interventions for children of divorce.* New York: John Wiley & Sons.

Hohagen, F., Winklemann, G., Rasche-Raeuchle, H., Hand, I., Koenig, A., Muenchau, N., et al. (1998). Combination of behaviour therapy with fluvoxamine in comparison with behaviour therapy and placebo: Results of a multicentre study. *British Journal of Psychiatry, 173,* 71–78.

Holmbeck, G. N., Colder, C., Shapera, W., Westhoven, V., Kenealy, L., & Updegrove, A. (2000). Working with adolescents: Guides from developmental psychology. In P. C. Kendall (Ed.), *Child and adolescent therapy: Cognitive-behavioral procedures* (2nd ed., pp. 334–385). New York: Guilford Press.

Holmbeck, G. N., & Lavigne, J. V. (1992). Combining self-modeling and stimulus fading in the treatment of an electively mute child. *Psychotherapy: Theory, Research, Practice, Training, 29,* 661–667.

Howard, B. L., & Kendall, P. C. (1996). Cognitive-behavioral family therapy for anxiety-disordered children: A multiple-baseline evaluation. *Cognitive Therapy and Research, 20,* 423–443.

Hudson, J. L., Flannery-Shroeder, E., & Kendall, P. C. (2004). Primary prevention of anxiety disorders. In D. J. A. Dozois & K. S. Dobson (Eds.), *The prevention of anxiety and depression: Theory, research, and practice,* Washington, DC: American Psychological Association.

Hudson, J. L., & Rapee, R. M. (2002). Parent–child interactions in clinically anxious children and their siblings. *Journal of Clinical Child and Adolescent Psychology, 31,* 548–555.

Hughes, H. E., & Sparber, S. B. (1978). D-Amphetamine unmasks postnatal consequences of exposure to methylmercury in utero: Methods for studying behavioral teratogenesis. *Pharmacology, Biochemistry and Behavior, 8,* 365–375.

Huttenlocher, P. R. (1979). Synaptic density of human frontal cortex—Developmental changes and effects of aging. *Brain Research, 163,* 195–205.

Ialongo, N., Edelsohn, G., Werthamer-Larsson, L., Crockett, L., & Kellam, S. (1993). Are self-reported depressive symptoms in first-grade children developmentally transient phenomena? A further look. *Development and Psychopathology, 5,* 433–452.

Jerremalm, A., Jansson, L., & Öst, L. (1986). Individual response patterns and the effects of different behavioral methods in the treatment of dental phobia. *Behaviour Research and Therapy, 24,* 587–596.

Johnson, J. G., Cohen, P., Pine, D. S., Kline, D. F., Kasen, S., & Book, J. S. (2000). Association between cigarette smoking and anxiety disorders during adolescence and early adulthood. *Journal of the American Medical Association, 284,* 2348–2351.

Joiner, T. E., Jr., Schmidt, N. B., Schmidt, K. L., Laurent, J., Catanzaro, S. J., Perez, M., et al. (2002). Anxiety sensitivity as a specific and unique marker of anxious symptoms in youth psychiatric inpatients. *Journal of Abnormal Child Psychology, 30,* 167–175.

Kagan, J. (1994). Inhibited and uninhibited temperaments. In W. B. Carey & S. C. McDevitt (Eds.), *Prevention and early intervention: Individual differences as risk factors for the mental health of children: A festschrift for Stella Chess and Alexander Thomas* (pp. 35–41). Philadelphia: Brunner/Mazel.

Kagan, J. (2002). Childhood predictors of states of anxiety. *Dialogues in Clinical Neuroscience, 4,* 287–292.

Kagan, J., Snidman, N., McManis, M., & Woodward, S. (2001). Temperamental contributions to the affect family of anxiety. *Psychiatric Clinics of North America, 24,* 677–688.

Kampman, M., Keijsers, G. P., Hoogduin, C. A., & Hendriks, G. J. (2002). A randomized, double-blind, placebo-controlled study of the effects of adjunctive paroxetine in panic disorder patients unsuccessfully treated with cognitive-behavioral therapy alone. *Journal of Clinical Psychiatry, 63,* 772–777.

Kaplan, S. J., Pelcoviz, D., Salzinger, S., Weiner, M., Mandel, F. S., Lesser, M., et al. (1998). Adolescent physical abuse: Risk for adolescent psychiatric disorders. *American Journal of Psychiatry, 155,* 954–959.

Kaplow, J. B., Curran, P. J., Angold, A., & Costello, E. J. (2001). The prospective relation between dimensions of anxiety and the initiation of adolescent alcohol use. *Journal of Clinical Child Psychology, 30,* 316–326.

Kaufman, J., Plotsky, P. M., Nemeroff, C. B., & Charney, D. S. (2000). Effects of early adverse experiences on brain structure and function: clinical implications. *Biological Psychiatry, 48,* 778–790.

Kazak, A. E., Barakat, L. P., Meeske, K., Christakis, D., Meadows, A. T., Casey, R., et al. (1997). Posttraumatic stress, family functioning, and social support in survivors of childhood leukemia and their mothers and fathers. *Journal of Consulting and Clinical Psychology, 65,* 120–129.

Kazdin, A. E. (1997). Parent management training: Evidence, outcomes, and issues. *Journal of the American Academy of Child and Adolescent Psychiatry, 36,* 1349–1356.

Kazdin, A. E., & Weisz, J. R. (1998). Identifying and developing empirically supported child and adolescent treatments. *Journal of Consulting and Clinical Psychology, 66,* 19–36.

Keane, T. M., Fairbank, J. A., Caddell, J. M., & Zimmering, R. T. (1989b). Implosive (flooding) therapy reduces symptoms of PTSD in Vietnam combat veterans. *Behavior Therapy, 20,* 245–260.

Keane, T. M., Fairbank, J. A., Caddell, J. M., Zimmering, R. T., et al. (1989a). Clinical evaluation of a measure to assess combat exposure. *Psychological Assessment, 1,* 53–55.

Keane, T. M., Zimmering, R. T., & Caddell, J. M. (1985). A behavioral formulation of posttraumatic stress disorder in Vietnam veterans. *Behavior Therapist, 8,* 9–12.

Kearney, C. A., & Drake, K. L. (2002). Social phobia. In M. Hersen (Ed.), *Clinical behavior therapy: Adults and children.* New York: John Wiley & Sons.

Kearney, C. A., & Silverman, W. K. (1997). The evolution and reconciliation of taxonomic strategies for school refusal behavior. *Clinical Psychology: Science and Practice, 3,* 339–354.

Kehle, T. J., Owen, S. V., & Cressy, E. T. (1990). The use of self-modeling as an intervention in school psychology: A case study of an elective mute. *School Psychology Review, 19,* 115–121.

Kellogg, C. K. (1998). Early developmental modulation of GABA(A) receptor function: Influence on adaptive responses. *Perspectives on Developmental Neurobiology, 5,* 219–234.

Kemp, A., Green, B. L., Hovanitz, C., & Rawlings, E. I. (1995). Incidence and correlates of posttraumatic stress disorder in battered women: Shelter and community samples. *Journal of Interpersonal Violence, 10,* 43–55.

Kendall, P. C. (1984). Cognitive-behavioural self-control therapy for children. *Journal of Child Psychology and Psychiatry and Allied Disciplines, 25,* 173–179.

Kendall, P. C. (1989). The generalization and maintenance of behavior change: Comments, considerations and the "no-cure" criticism. *Behavior Therapy, 20,* 357–364.

Kendall, P. C. (1994). Treating anxiety disorders in youth: Results of a randomized clinical trial. *Journal of Consulting and Clinical Psychology, 62,* 100–110.

Kendall, P. C. (2000a). *Coping cat workbook.* Ardmore, PA: Workbook Publishing.

Kendall, P. C. (2000b). *Cognitive-behavioral therapy for anxious children: Treatment manual* (2nd ed.). Ardmore, PA: Workbook Publishing.

Kendall, P. C., Cantwell, D. P., & Kazdin, A. E. (1989). Depression in children and adolescents: Assessment issues and recommendations. *Cognitive Therapy and Research, 13,* 109–146.

Kendall, P. C., Chu, B., Gifford, A., Hayes, C., & Nauta, M. (1998). Breathing life into a manual: Flexibility and creativity with manual-based treatments. *Cognitive and Behavioral Practice, 5,* 177–198.

Kendall, P. C., Chu, B. C., Pimentel, S. S., & Choudhury, M. (2000). In P. C. Kendall (Ed.), *Child and adolescent therapy: Cognitive-behavioral procedures* (2nd ed., pp. 235–287). New York: Guilford Press.

Kendall, P. C., & Clarkin, J. F. (1992). Introduction to special section: Comorbidity and treatment implications. *Journal of Clinical and Consulting Psychology, 60,* 833–834.

Kendall, P. C., Flannery-Schroeder, E., Panichelli-Mindel, S., Southam-Gerow, M., Henin, A., & Warman, M. (1997). Therapy for youth with anxiety disorders: A second randomized clinical trial. *Journal of Consulting and Clinical Psychology, 65,* 366–380.

Kendall, P. C., Kortlander, E., Chantsky, T. E., & Brady, E. U. (1992). Comorbidity of anxiety and depression in youth: Treatment implications. *Journal of Consulting and Clinical Psychology, 60,* 869–880.

Kendall, P. C., Krain, A. L., & Treadwell, K. R. H. (1999). Generalized anxiety disorder. In R. Ammerman, C. Last, & M. Hersen (Eds.), *Handbook of prescriptive treatments for children and adolescents* (2nd ed.). Needham, MA: Allyn and Bacon.

Kendall, P. C., & Pimentel, S. S. (2003). On the physiological symptom constellation in youth with generalized anxiety disorder (GAD). *Journal of Anxiety Disorders, 17,* 211–221.

Kendall, P. C., Safford, S., Flannery-Schroeder, E., & Webb, A. (2004). Child anxiety treatment: Outcomes in adolescence and impact on substance use and depression at 7.4-year follow-up. *Journal of Consulting and Clinical Psychology, 72,* 276–287.

Kendall, P. C., & Southam-Gerow, M. A. (1995). Issues in the transportability of treatment: the case of anxiety disorders in youths. *Journal of Consulting and Clinical Psychology, 63,* 702–708.

Kendall, P. C., & Southam-Gerow, M. A. (1996). Long-term follow-up of a cognitive-behavioral therapy for anxiety-disordered youth. *Journal of Consulting and Clinical Psychology, 64,* 724–730.

Kendall, P. C., & Williams, C. L. (1986). Therapy with adolescents: Treating the "marginal man." *Behavior Therapy, 17,* 522–537.

Kendler, K. S., Heath, A. C., Martin, N. G., & Eaves, L. J. (1987). Symptoms of anxiety and symptoms of depression. Same genes, different environments? *Archives of General Psychiatry, 44,* 451–457.

Kendler, K. S., Neale, M. C., Kessler, R. C., Heath, A. C., & Eaves, L. J. (1992). Major depression and generalized anxiety disorder: Same genes, (partly) different environments? *Archives of General Psychiatry, 51,* 716–722.

Kessler, R. C. 1994. The National Comorbidity Survey of the United States. *International Review of Psychiatry, 6,* 365–376.

Kessler, R. C., Sonnega, A., Bromet, E., Hughes, M., Nelson, C. B. (1995). Posttraumatic stress disorder in the National Comorbidity Survey. *Archives of General Psychiatry, 52,* 1048–1060.

Killgore, W. D. S., Oki, M., & Yurgelun-Todd, D. A. (2001). Sex-specific developmental changes in amygdala responses to affective faces. *Neuroreport, 12,* 427–433.

Kilpatrick, D. G., Acierno, R., Resnick, H. S., Saunders, B. E., & Best, C. L. (1997). A 2-year longitudinal analysis of the relationships between violent assault and substance use in women. *Journal of Consulting and Clinical Psychology, 65,* 834–847.

Kilpatrick, D. G., Acierno, R., Saunders, B., Resnick, H. S., Best, C. L., & Schnurr, P. P. (2000). Risk factors for adolescent substance abuse and dependence: Data from a national sample. *Journal of Consulting and Clinical Psychology, 68, 1,* 19–30.

Kilpatrick, D. G., Ruggerio, K. J., Acierno, R., Saunders, B. E., Resnick, H. S., & Best, C. L. (2003). Violence and risk of PTSD, major depression, substance abuse/dependence, and comorbidity: Results from the National Survey of Adolescents. *Journal of Consulting and Clinical Psychology, 71,* 692–700.

Kilpatrick, D. G., Saunders, B. E., Resnick, H. S., & Smith, D. W. (1995). The National Survey of Adolescents: Preliminary findings on lifetime prevalence of traumatic events and mental health correlates. Charleston: Medical University of South Carolina, National Crime Victims Research and Treatment Center.

Kindt, M., Bierman, D., & Brosschot, J. F. (1997). Cognitive bias in spider fear and control children: Assessment of emotional interference by a card format and a single-trial format of the Stroop task. *Journal of Experimental Child Psychology, 66,* 163–179.

Kindt, M., Brosschot, J. F., & Everaerd, W. (1997). Cognitive processing bias of children in a real life stress situation and a neutral situation. *Journal of Experimental Child Psychology, 64,* 79–97.

Kindt, M., van den Hout, M., de Jong, P., & Hoekzema, B. (2000). Cognitive bias for pictorial and linguistic threat cues in children. *Journal of Psychopathology and Behavioral Assessment, 22,* 201–219.

King, N. J., Hamilton, D. I., & Ollendick, T. H. (1994). *Children's phobias: A behavioural perspective.* Oxford, UK: John Wiley & Sons.

King, R., Gaines, L. S., Lambert, E. W., Summerfelt, W. T., & Bickman, L. (2000). The co-occurrence of psychiatric substance use diagnoses in adolescents in different service systems: Frequency, recognition, cost, and outcomes. *Journal of Behavioral Health Services and Research, 27,* 417–430.

King, R. A., Leonard, H., & March, J. (1998). Practice parameters for the assessment and treatment of children and adolescents with obsessive-compulsive disorder. *Journal of the American Academy of Child and Adolescent Psychiatry, 37,* 27S–45S.

Klein, D. F. (1964). Delineation of two drug-responsive anxiety syndromes. *Psychopharmacologia (Berlin), 5,* 397.

Klein, D. F. (1993). Panic may be a misfiring suffocation alarm. *Archives of General Psychiatry, 50,* 306–317.

Klein, D. F., & Fink, M. (1962). Behavioral reaction patterns with phenothiazines. *Archives of General Psychiatry, 7,* 449–459.

Klein, D. F., Mannuzza, S., Chapman, T., & Fyer, A. J. (1992). Child panic revisited. *Journal of the American Academy of Child and Adolescent Psychiatry, 31,* 112–114.

Klein, R. G. (1995). Is panic disorder associated with childhood separation anxiety disorder? *Clinical Neuropharmacology, 18,* (Suppl. 2), S7–S14.

Klein, R. G., Koplewicz, H. S., & Kanner, A. (1992). Imipramine treatment of children with separation anxiety disorder. *Journal of the American Academy of Child and Adolescent Psychiatry, 31,* 21–28.

Klein, R. G., & Pine, D. S. (2001). Anxiety disorders. In M. Rutter, E. Taylor, & M. Hersov (Eds.), *Child and adolescent psychiatry* (3rd ed.). New York: Blackwell Scientific.

Koran, L. M., Hackett, E., Rubin, A., Wolkow, R., & Robinson, D. (2002). Efficacy of sertraline in the long-term treatment of obsessive-compulsive disorder. *American Journal of Psychiatry, 159,* 88–95.

Kutcher, S. P., & MacKenzie, S. (1988). Successful clonazepam treatment of adolescents with panic disorder. *Journal of Clinical Psychopharmacology, 8,* 299–301.

La Bar, K. S., Gatenby, C., Gore, J. C., Le Doux, J. E., & Phelphs, E. A. (1998). Human amygdala activation during conditioned fear acquisition and extinction. *Neuron, 29,* 937–945.

Labellarte, M. J., Ginsburg, G. S., Walkup, J. T., & Riddle, M. A. (1999). The treatment of anxiety disorders in children and adolescents. *Biological Psychiatry, 46,* 1567–1578.

Labellarte, M. J., Walkup, J. T., & Riddle, M. A. (1998). The new antidepressants. Selective serotonin reuptake inhibitors. *Pediatric Clinics of North America, 45,* 1137–1155.

LaFreniere, P. J., & Capuano, F. (1997). Preventive intervention as means of clarifying direction of effects in socialization: Anxious-withdrawn preschoolers case. *Development and Psychopathology, 9,* 551–564.

La Greca, A. M., & Lopez, N. (1998). Social anxiety among adolescents: Linkages with peer relations and friendships. *Journal of Abnormal Child Psychology, 26,* 83–94.

La Greca, A. M., Silverman, W. K., Vernberg, E. M., & Prinstein, M. J. (1996). Symptoms of posttraumatic stress in children following Hurricane Andrew: A prospective study. *Journal of Consulting and Clinical Psychology, 105,* 712–723.

La Greca, A. M., & Stone, W. L. (1993). Social Anxiety Scale for Children–Revised: Factor structure and concurrent validity. *Journal of Clinical Child Psychology, 22,* 17–27.

Lang, P. J. (1977). Imagery in therapy: An information processing analysis of fear. *Behavior Therapy, 8,* 862–886.

Last, C. G., Hansen, C., & Franco, N. (1998). Cognitive-behavioral treatment of school phobia. *Journal of the American Academy of Child and Adolescent Psychiatry, 37,* 404–411.

Lavigne, J. V., Arend, R., Rosenbaum, D., Binns, H. J., Christoffel, K. K., & Gibbons, R. D. (1998). Psychiatric disorders with onset in the preschool years: I. Stability of diagnoses. *Journal of the American Academy of Child and Adolescent Psychiatry, 37,* 1246–1254.

Lavigne, J. V., Cicchetti, C., Gibbons, R. D., Binns, H. J., Larsen, L., & DeVito, C. (2001). Oppositional defiant disorder with onset in preschool years: Longitudinal stability and pathways to other disorders. *Journal of the American Academy of Child and Adolescent Psychiatry, 40,* 1393–1400.

Lavigne, J. V., Gibbons, R. D., Christoffel, K. K., Arend, R., Rosenbaum, D., Binns, H., et al. (1996). Prevalence rates and correlates of psychiatric disorders among preschool children. *Journal of the American Academy of Child and Adolescent Psychiatry, 35,* 204–214.

Layne, C. M., Pynoos, R. S., & Cardenas, J. (2001). Wounded adolescence: School-based group psychotherapy for adolescents who sustained or witnessed violent injury. In M. Shafi & S. L. Shafi (Eds.), *School violence: Assessment, management, prevention.* Washington, DC: American Psychiatric Association.

Layne, C. M., Pynoos, R. S., Saltzman, W. R., Arslanagic, B., Black, M., Savjak, N., et al. (2001). Trauma/grief-focused group psychotherapy: School-based postwar intervention with traumatized Bosnian adolescents. *Group Dynamics, 5,* 277–290.

Leckman, J. F., & Mayes, L. C. (1998). Understanding developmental psychopathology: How useful are evolutionary accounts? *Journal of the American Academy of Child and Adolescent Psychiatry, 37,* 1011–1021.

Lecrubier, Y., Bakker, A., Dunbar, G., & Judge, R. (1997). A comparison of paroxetine, clomipramine and placebo in the treatment of panic disorder. *Acta Psychiatrica Scandinavica, 95,* 145–152.

LeDoux, J. E. (1996). *The emotional brain.* New York: Simon & Schuster.

LeDoux, J. (1998). Fear and the brain: Where have we been, and where are we going? *Biological Psychiatry, 44,* 1229–1238.

LeDoux, J. E. (2000). Emotion circuits in the brain. *Annual Review of Neuroscience, 23,* 155–184.

Leonard, H. L., & Swedo, S. E. (2001). Paediatric autoimmune neuropsychiatric disorders associated with streptococcal infection (PANDAS). *International Journal of Neuropsychopharmacology, 4,* 191–198.

Leonard, H. L., Swedo, S. E., Lenane, M. C., Rettew, D. C., Cheslow, D. L., Hamburger, S. D., et al. (1991). A double-blind desipramine substitution during long-term clomipramine treatment in children and adolescents with obsessive compulsive disorder. *Archives of General Psychiatry, 48,* 922–926.

Leonard, H. L., Swedo, S. E., Lenane, M. C., Rettew, D. C., Hamburger, S. D., Bartko, J. J., et al. (1993). A 2- to 7-year follow-up study of 54 obsessive compulsive children and adolescents. *Archives of General Psychiatry, 50,* 429–439.

Leonard, H. L., Swedo, S., Rapoport, J. L., Koby, E. V., Lenane, M. C., Cheslow, D. L., et al. (1989). Treatment of obsessive compulsive disorder with clomipramine and desipramine in children and adolescents: A double-blind crossover comparison. *Archives of General Psychiatry, 46,* 1088–1092.

Leonard, H. L., Topol, D., Bukstein, O., Hindmarsh, D., Allen, A. J., & Swedo, S. E. (1994). Clonazepam as an augmenting agent in the treatment of childhood onset obsessive compulsive disorder. *Journal of the American Academy of Child and Adolescent Psychiatry, 33,* 792–794.

Levisohn, L., Cronin-Golomb, A., & Schmahmann, J. D. (2000). Neuropsychological consequences of cerebellar tumour resection in children: Cerebellar cognition affective syndrome in a paediatric population. *Brain, 123,* 1041–1050.

Lewinsohn, P. M., Gotlib, I. H., Lewinsohn, M., Seeley, J. R., & Allen, N. B. (1998). Gender differences in anxiety disorders and anxiety symptoms in adolescents. *Journal of Abnormal Psychology, 107,* 109–117.

Lewinsohn, P., Zinbarg, J., Seeley, J. R., Lewinsohn, S., & Sack, W. H. (1997). Lifetime comorbidity among anxiety disorders and between anxiety disorders and other mental disorders in adolescents. *Journal of Anxiety Disorders, 14,* 377–394.

Lichtenstein, P., & Annas, P. (2000). Heritability and prevalence of specific fears and phobias in childhood. *Journal of Child Psychology and Psychiatry, 41,* 927–937.

Liebowitz, M. R., Schneier, R., Campeas, R., Hollander, E., Hatterer, J., Fyer, A., et al. (1992). Phenelzine vs. atenolol in social phobia. *Archives of General Psychiatry, 49,* 290–300.

Liebowitz, M. R., Turner, S. M., Piacentini, J., Beidel, D. C., Clarvit, S. O., Graue, F., et al. (2002). Fluoxetine in children and adolescents with OCD: A placebo-controlled trial. *Journal of the American Academy of Child and Adolescent Psychiatry 41,* 1431–1438.

Lin, K. M. (2001). Biological differences in depression and anxiety across races and ethnic groups. *Journal of Clinical Psychiatry 62* (Suppl. 13), 13–19; discussion 20–21.

Loeber, R., Green, S. M., & Lahey, B. B. (1990). Mental health professionals' perception of the utility of children, mothers, and teachers as informants on childhood psychopathology. *Journal of Clinical Child Psychology, 19,* 136–143.

Lowry-Webster, H. M., Barrett, P. M., & Dadds, M. R. (2001). A universal prevention trial of anxiety and depressive symptomatology in childhood: Preliminary data from an Australian study. *Behaviour Change, 18,* 36–50.

Lumpkin, P. W., Silverman, W. K., Weems, C. F., Markham, M. R., & Kurtines, W. M. (2002). Treating a heterogeneous set of anxiety disorders in youths with group cognitive behavioral therapy: A partially nonconcurrent multiple-baseline evaluation. *Behavior Therapy, 33,* 163–177.

Lutz, W. J., & Hock, E. (1995). Maternal separation anxiety: Relations to adult attachment representations in mothers of infants. *Journal of Genetic Psychology, 156,* 57–72.

MacLeod, C., Mathews, A., & Tata, P. (1986). Attentional bias in emotional disorders. *Journal of Abnormal Psychology, 95,* 15–20.

Madakasira, S., & O'Brien, K. F. (1987). Acute posttraumatic stress disorder in victims of a natural disaster. *Journal of Nervous and Mental Disease, 175,* 286–290.

Main, M., & Goldwyn, R. (1991). Adult attachment classification system. In M. Main (Ed.), *Behavior and the development of representational models of attachment: Five methods of assessment.* Cambridge, UK: Cambridge University Press.

Main, M., & Solomon, J. (1990). Procedures for identifying infants as disorganized/disoriented during the Ainsworth Strange Situation. In M. T. Greenberg & D. Cicchetti (Eds.), *Attachment in the preschool years: Theory, research, and intervention.* The John D. and Catherine T. MacArthur Foundation series on mental health and development (pp. 121–160). Chicago: The University of Chicago Press.

Malinosky-Rummell, R., & Hansen, D. J. (1993). Long-term consequences of childhood physical abuse. *Psychological Bulletin, 114,* 68–79.

Manassis, K., & Bradley, S. J. (1994). The development of childhood anxiety disorders: Toward an integrated model. *Journal of Applied Developmental Psychology, 15,* 345–366.

Manassis, K., Bradley, S., Goldberg, S., Hood, J., & Swinson, R. P. (1994). Attachment in mothers with anxiety disorders and their children. *Journal of the American Academy of Child and Adolescent Psychiatry, 33,* 1106–1113.

Manassis, K., Mendlowitz, S. L., Scapillato, D., Avery, D., Fiksenbaum, L., Freire, M., et al. (2002). Group and individual cognitive-behavioral therapy for childhood anxiety disorders. A randomized trial. *Journal of the American Academy of Child and Adolescent Psychiatry, 41,* 1423–1430.

Manicavasagar, V., Silove, D., Rapee, R., Waters, F., & Momartin, S. (2001). Parent–child concordance for separation anxiety: A clinical study. *Journal of Affective Disorders, 65,* 81–84.

March, D., & Yonkers, K. A. (2001). Panic disorder. In K. Yonkers & B. Little (Eds.), *Management of psychiatric disorders in pregnancy* (pp. 134–148). New York: Oxford University Press.

March, J. S. (1995). Cognitive-behavioral psychotherapy for children and adolescents with OCD: A review and recommendations for treatment. *Journal of the American Academy of Child and Adolescent Psychiatry, 34,* 7–18.

March, J. (1999). Current status of pharmacotherapy for pediatric anxiety disorders. In D. Beidel (Ed.), *Treating anxiety disorders in youth: Current problems and future solutions (ADAA/NIMH)* (pp. 42–62). Washington, DC: Anxiety Disorders Association of America.

March, J. S., Amaya-Jackson, L., Murry, M. C., & Schulte, A. (1998). Cognitive-behavioral psychotherapy for children and adolescents with posttraumatic stress disorder after a single-incident stressor. *Journal of the American Academy of Child and Adolescent Psychiatry, 37,* 585–593.

March, J. S., Amaya-Jackson, L., Terry, R., & Costanzo, P. (1997). Posttraumatic symptomatology in children and adolescents after an industrial fire. *Journal of the American Academy of Child and Adolescent Psychiatry, 36,* 1080–1088.

March, J. S., Biederman, J., Wolkow, R., Safferman, A., Mardekian, J., Cook, E. H., et al. (1998). Sertraline in children and adolescents with obsessive-compulsive disorder: A multicenter randomized controlled trial. *Journal of the American Medical Association, 280,* 1752–1756.

March, J. S., Conners, C., Arnold, G., Epstein, J., Parker, J., Hinshaw, S., et al. (1999). The Multidimensional Anxiety Scale for Children (MASC): Confirmatory factor analysis in a pediatric ADHD sample. *Journal of Attention Disorders, 3,* 85–89.

March, J., Frances, A., Kahn, D., & Carpenter, D. (1997). Expert Consensus Guidelines: Treatment of obsessive-compulsive disorder. *Journal of Clinical Psychiatry, 58,* 1–72.

March, J. S., & Leonard, H. L. (1998). Obsessive-compulsive disorder in children and adolescents. In R. P. Swinson & M. M. Antony (Eds.), *Obsessive-compulsive disorder: Theory, research, and treatment.* New York: Guilford Press.

March, J. S., & Mulle, K. (1998). *OCD in children and*

adolescents: A cognitive-behavioral treatment manual. New York: Guilford Press.

March, J., Mulle, K., & Herbel, B. (1994). Behavioral psychotherapy for children and adolescents with obsessive-compulsive disorder: an open trial of a new protocol driven treatment package. *Journal of the American Academy of Child and Adolescent Psychiatry, 33,* 333–341.

March, J. S., Parker, J. D. A., Sullivan, K., & Stallings, P. (1997). The Multidimensional Anxiety Scale for Children (MASC): Factor structure, reliability, and validity. *Journal of the American Academy of Child and Adolescent Psychiatry, 36,* 554–564.

Marks, I. (1986). Genetics of fear and anxiety disorders [review]. *British Journal of Psychiatry, 149,* 408–418.

Marks, I. M. (1987). *Fears, phobias, and rituals.* New York: Oxford University Press.

Marks, I. M., Lelliott, P. T., Basoglu, M., Noshirvani, H., Monteiro, W., Cohen, D., et al. (1988). Clomipramine, self-exposure and therapist-aided exposure for obsessive-compulsive rituals. *British Journal of Psychiatry, 152,* 522–534.

Marks, I., Lovell, K., Noshirvani, H., Livanou, M., & Thrasher, S. (1998). Treatment of posttraumatic stress disorder by exposure and/or cognitive restructuring: A controlled study. *Archives of General Psychiatry, 55,* 317–325.

Marks, I. M., Swinson, R. P., Basoglu, M., Kuch K., Noshirvani, H., O'Sullivan, G., et al. (1993). Alprazolam and exposure alone and combined in panic disorder with agoraphobia: A controlled study in London and Toronto. *British Journal of Psychiatry, 162,* 776–787.

Marlatt, G. A., & Gordon, J. J. (1985). *Relapse prevention.* New York: Guilford Press.

Marshall, R. D., Beebe, K. L., Oldhan, M., & Zaninelli, R. (2001). Efficacy and safety of paroxetine treatment for chronic PTSD: A fixed-dose, placebo-controlled study. *American Journal of Psychiatry, 158,* 1982–1988.

Martenyi, F., Brown, E. B., Zhang, H., Koke, S. C., & Prakash, A. (2002a). Fluoxetine v. placebo in prevention of relapse in post-traumatic stress disorder. *British Journal of Psychiatry, 181,* 315–320.

Martenyi, F., Brown, E. B., Zhang, H., Prakash, A., & Koke, S. C. (2002b). Fluoxetine versus placebo in posttraumatic stress disorder. *Journal of Clinical Psychiatry, 63,* 199–206.

Martin, M., Horder, P., & Jones, G. V. (1992). Integral bias in naming of phobia-related words. *Cognition and Emotion, 6,* 479–486.

Martin, M., & Jones, G. V. (1995). Integral bias in

the cognitive processing of emotionally linked pictures. *British Journal of Psychology, 86,* 419–435.

Masia, C. L., Klein, R. G., Storch, E. A., & Corda, B. (2001). School-based behavioral treatment for social anxiety disorder in adolescents: Results of a pilot study. *Journal of the American Academy of Child and Adolescent Psychiatry, 40,* 780–786.

Mathew, S. J., Coplan, J. D., & Gorman, J. M. (2001). Management of treatment-refractory panic disorder. *Psychopharmacology Bulletin, 35,* 97–110.

Mattis, S. G., Hoffman, E. C., Cohen, E. M., Pincus, D. B., Choate, M. L., & Micco, J. A. (2001). Cognitive-behavioral treatment of panic disorder in adolescence. In C. L. Masia & E. A. Storch (Chairs), Treatment of childhood anxiety: Innovative interventions and future directions. Symposium presented at the meeting of the Anxiety Disorders Association of America, Atlanta, Georgia.

Mattis, S. G., & Ollendick, T. H. (2002). School refusal and separation anxiety. In M. Hersen (Ed.), *Clinical behavior therapy: Adults and children* (pp. 304–325). New York: John Wiley & Sons.

Mavissakalian, M. R., & Perel, J. M. (1992). Clinical experiments in maintenance and discontinuation of imipramine therapy in panic disorder with agoraphobia. *Archives of General Psychiatry, 49,* 318–323.

Mavissakalian, M. R., & Perel, J. M. (2001). 2nd year maintenance and discontinuation of imipramine in panic disorder with agoraphobia. *Annals of Clinical Psychiatry, 13,* 63–67.

Mayou, R., Bryant, B., & Ehlers, A. (2001). Prediction of psychological outcomes one year after a motor vehicle accident. *American Journal of Psychiatry, 158,* 1231–1238.

Mayou, R. A., Gill, D., Thompson, D. R., Day, A., Hicks, N., Volmink, J., et al. (2000). Depression and anxiety as predictors of outcome after myocardial infarction. *Psychosomatic Medicine, 62,* 212–219.

McCracken, J. T., Walkup, J. T., & Koplewicz, H. S. (2002). Childhood and early-onset anxiety: Treatment and biomarker studies. *Journal of Clinical Psychiatry, 63,* 8–11.

McDougle, C. J., Epperson, C. N., Pelton, G. H., Wasylink, S., & Price, L. H. (2000). A double-blind, placebo-controlled study of risperidone addition in serotonin reuptake inhibitor-refractory obsessive-compulsive disorder. *Archives General Psychiatry, 57,* 794–801.

McDougle, C. J., Fleischmann, R. L., Epperson,

C. N., Wasylink, S., Leckman, J. F., & Price, L. H. (1995). Risperidone addition in fluvoxamine-refractory obsessive-compulsive disorder: Three cases [see comments]. *Journal of Clinical Psychiatry, 56,* 526–528.

McManis, M. H., Kagan, J., Snidman, N. C., & Woodward, S. A. (2002). EEG asymmetry, power, and temperament in children. *Developmental Psychobiology, 41,* 169–177.

McNally, R. J. (1996). Cognitive bias in the anxiety disorders. *Nebraska Symposium on Motivation, 43,* 211–250.

McNally, R. J. (2001a). On Wakefield's harmful dysfunction analysis of mental disorder. *Behaviour Research and Therapy, 39,* 309–314.

McNally, R. J. (2001b). On the scientific status of cognitive appraisal models of anxiety disorder. *Behaviour Research and Therapy, 39,* 513–521.

McNally, R. J. (2003). *Remembering trauma.* Cambridge, MA: Belknap Press/Harvard University Press.

McNally, R. J., & Steketee, G. S. (1985). The etiology and maintenance of severe animal phobias. *Behaviour Research and Therapy, 23,* 431–435.

Meaney, M. J. (2001). Nature, nurture, and the disunity of knowledge. *Annals of the New York Academy of Sciences, 935,* 50–61.

Meeske, K. A., Ruccione, K., Globe, D. R., & Stuber, M. L. (2001). Posttraumatic stress, quality of life, and psychological distress in young adult survivors of childhood cancer. *Oncology Nursing Forum, 28,* 481–489.

Mendlowitz, S., Manassis, K., Bradley, S., Scapillato, D., Miezitis, S., & Shaw, B. (1999). Cognitive-behavioral group treatments in childhood anxiety disorders: The role of parental involvement. *Journal of the American Academy of Child and Adolescent Psychiatry, 38,* 1223–1229.

Merikangas, K. R., & Avenevoli, S. (2002). Epidemiology of mood and anxiety disorders in children and adolescents. In M. T. Tsuang & M. Tohen (Eds), *Textbook in psychiatric epidemiology* (2nd ed., pp. 657–704). New York: Wiley-Liss.

Merikangas, K. R., Avenevoli, S., Dierker, L., & Grillon, C. (1999). Vulnerability factors among children at risk for anxiety disorders. *Biological Psychiatry, 46,* 1523–1535.

Merikangas, K. R., and Risch, N. (2003). Will the genomic revolution revolutionize psychiatry? *American Journal of Psychiatry, 160,* 625–635.

Modigh, K., Westberg P., & Eriksson, E. (1992). Superiority of clomipramine over imipramine in the treatment of panic disorder: A placebo-controlled trial. *Journal of Clinical Psychopharmacology, 12,* 251–261.

Moffitt, T. E., Caspi, A., Belsky, J., & Silva, P. A. (1992). Childhood experience and the onset of menarche: a test of a sociobiological model. *Child Development, 63,* 47–58.

Monk, C. S., Pine, D. S., & Charney, D. S. (2002). A developmental and neurobiological approach to early trauma research. *Seminars in Clinical Neuropsychiatry, 7,* 137–146.

Montoya, A. G., Sorrentino, R., Lukas, S. E., & Price, B. H. (2002). Long-term neuropsychiatric consequences of "ecstasy" (MDMA): A review. *Harvard Review of Psychiatry, 10,* 212–220.

Moradi, A. R., Taghavi, M. R., Neshat Doost, H. T., Yule, W., & Dalgleish, T. (1999). Performance of children and adolescents with PTSD on the Stroop colour-naming task. *Psychological Medicine, 29,* 415–419.

Moreau, D. L., & Follet, C. (1993). Panic disorder in children and adolescents. *Child and Adolescent Psychiatric Clinics of North America, 2,* 581–602.

Moreau, D. L., & Weissman, M. M. (1992). Panic disorder in children and adolescents: A review. *American Journal of Psychiatry, 149,* 1306–1314.

Morris, T. L., & Masia, C. L. (1998). Psychometric evaluation of the Social Phobia and Anxiety Inventory for Children: Concurrent validity and normative data. *Journal of Clinical Child Psychology, 27,* 452–458.

Moss, H., & Damasio, A. R. (2001). Emotion, cognition, and the human brain. *Annals of the New York Academy of Sciences, 935,* 98–100.

Mrazek, P. J., & Haggerty, R. J. (1994). *Reducing risks for mental disorders: Frontiers for preventive intervention research.* National Academy of Sciences, Institute of Medicine, Division of Biobehavioral Sciences and Mental Disorders, Committee on Prevention of Mental Disorders. Washington, DC: National Academy Press.

Mundo, E., Bareggi, S. R., Pirola, R., & Bellodi, L. (1997). Long-term pharmacotherapy of obsessive-compulsive disorder: A double-blind controlled study. *Journal of Clinical Psychopharmacology, 17,* 4–10.

Munoz, R. F., Mrazek, P. J., & Haggerty, R. J. (1996). Institute of Medicine report on prevention of mental disorders: Summary and commentary. *American Psychologist, 51,* 1116–1122.

Muris, P., Merckelbach, H., Holdrinet, I., & Sijeenaar, M. (1998). Treating phobic children: Effects of EMDR versus exposure. *Journal of Consulting and Clinical Psychology, 66,* 193–198.

Muris, P., Merckelbach, H., Ollendick, T. H., King,

N., & Bogie, N. (2002). Three traditional and three new childhood anxiety questionnaires: Their reliability and validity in a normal adolescent sample. *Behaviour Research and Therapy, 40,* 753–772.

Murphy, G. M., Jr., Kremer, C., Rodrigues, H. E., & Schatzberg, A. F. (2003). Pharmacogenetics of antidepressant medication intolerance. *American Journal of Psychiatry, 160,* 1830–1835.

Murphy, M. L., & Pichichero, M. E. (2002). Prospective identification and treatment of children with pediatric autoimmune neuropsychiatric disorder associated with group A streptococcal infection (PANDAS). *Archives of Pediatric and Adolescent Medicine 156,* 356–361.

Myers, H. F., & Durvasula, R. S. (1999). Psychiatric disorders in African American men and women living with HIV/AIDS. *Cultural Diversity and Ethnic Minority Psychology, 5,* 249–262.

Nader, P. R., Wexler, D. B., Patterson, T. L, McKusick, L., et al. (1989). Comparison of beliefs about AIDS among urban, suburban, incarcerated, and gay adolescents. *Journal of Adolescent Health Care, 10,* 413–418.

Nelson, C. B., & Wittchen, H. U. (1998). DSM IV alcohol disorders in a general population sample of adolescents and young adults. *Addiction, 93,* 1065–1077.

Nelson, E. E., Shelton, S. E., & Kalin, N. H. (2003). Individual differences in the responses of naïve Rhesus monkeys to snakes. *Emotion, 3,* 3–11.

Nurse, S., & Lacaille, J.-C. (1999). Late maturation of GABA(B) synaptic transmission in area CA1 of the rat hippocampus. *Neuropharmacology, 38,* 1733–1742.

Ohman, A., & Mineka, S., 2001. Fears, phobias, and preparedness. *Psychological Review, 108,* 483–522.

Ollendick, T. H. (1995). Cognitive behavioral treatment of panic disorder with agoraphobia in adolescents: A multiple baseline design analysis. *Behavior Therapy, 26,* 517–531.

Ollendick, T. H., & Cerny, J. A. (1981). *Clinical behavior therapy with children.* New York: Plenum Press.

Ollendick, T. H., & King, N. J. (1998). Empirically supported treatments for children with phobic and anxiety disorders: Current status. *Journal of Clinical Child Psychology, 27,* 156–167.

Ollendick, T. H., & King, N. J. (2000). Empirically supported treatments for children and adolescents. In P. C. Kendall (Ed.), *Child and adolescent therapy* (pp. 386–425). New York: Guilford Press.

Ollendick, T. H., King, N. J., & Muris, P. (2002). Fears and phobias in children: Phenomenology, epidemiology, and aetiology. *Child and Adolescent Mental Health, 7,* 98–106.

Ollendick, T. H., & March, J. S. (Eds.) (2004). *Phobic and anxiety disorders in children and adolescents: A clinician's guide to effective psychosocial and pharmacological interventions.* New York: Oxford University Press.

Ollendick, T. H., Mattis, S. G., & King, N. J. (1994). Panic in children and adolescents: A review. *Journal of Child Psychology and Psychiatry and Allied Disciplines, 35,* 113–134.

Orsillo, S. M., Roemer, L., & Barlow, D. H. (2003). Integrating acceptance and mindfulness into existing cognitive-behavioral treatment for GAD: A case study. *Cognitive and Behavioral Practice, 10,* 222–230.

Orvaschel, H., Lewinsohn, P. M., & Seeley, J. R. (1995). Continuity of psychopathology in a community sample of adolescents. *Journal of the American Academy of Child and Adolescent Psychiatry, 34,* 1525–1535.

Öst, L. (1989). One-session treatment for specific phobias. *Behaviour Research and Therapy, 27,* 1–7.

Öst, L., Ferbee, I., & Furmark, T. (1997). One-session group therapy of spider phobia: Direct versus indirect treatments. *Behaviour Research and Therapy, 35,* 721–732.

Öst, L., Salkovskis, P. M., & Hellstroem, K. (1991). One-session therapist-directed exposure vs. self-exposure in the treatment of spider phobia. *Behavior Therapy, 22,* 407–422.

Öst, L., Svensson, L., Hellstrom, K., & Lindwall, R. (2001). One-session treatment of specific phobias in youths: A randomized clinical trial. *Journal of Consulting and Clinical Psychology, 69,* 814–824.

Owley, T., Owley, S., Leventhal, B., & Cook, E. (2002). Case series: Adderall augmentation of serotonin reuptake inhibitors in childhood-onset obsessive compulsive disorder. *Journal of Child and Adolescent Psychopharmacology 12,* 165–171.

Papp, L. A., Klein, D. F., Martinez, J., Schneier, F., Cole, R., Liebowitz, M. R., et al. (1993). The diagnostic and substance specificity of carbon-dioxide-induced panic. *American Journal of Psychiatry, 150,* 250–257.

Papp, L. A., Martinez, J. M., Klein, D. F., Coplan, J., & Gorman, J. M. (1995). Rebreathing tests in panic disorder. *Biological Psychiatry, 38,* 240–245.

Pato, M. T., Zohar-Kadouch, R., Zohar, J., & Murphy, D. L. (1988). Return of symptoms after discontinuation of clomipramine in patients with obsessive-compulsive disorder. *American Journal of Psychiatry, 145,* 1521–1525.

Pediatric OCD Treatment Study Team (2004). Cognitive-behavioral therapy, sertraline, and their combination for children and adolescents with obsessive-compulsive disorder: The Pediatric OCD Treatment Study (POTS) randomized controlled trial. *Journal of the American Medical Association, 292,* 1969–1976.

Pedro-Carroll, J. L., & Cowen, E. L. (1985). The Children of Divorce Intervention Program: An investigation of the efficacy of a school-based prevention program. *Journal of Consulting and Clinical Psychology, 53,* 603–611.

Pela, O. A., & Reynolds, C. R. (1982). Cross-cultural application of the Revised-Children's Manifest Anxiety Scale: Normative and reliability data for Nigerian primary school children. *Psychological Reports, 51,* 1135–1138.

Pelcovitz, D., Kaplan, S. J., DeRosa, R. R., Mandel, F. S., & Salzinger, S. (2000). Psychiatric disorders in adolescents exposed to violence and physical abuse. *American Journal of Orthopsychiatry, 70,* 360–369.

Pelcovitz, D., Kaplan, S. J., Ellenberg, A., Labruna, V., Salzinger, S., Mandel, F., et al. (2000). Adolescent physical abuse: Age at time of abuse and adolescent perception of family functioning. *Journal of Family Violence, 15,* 375–389.

Pennebaker, J. W., & Seagal, J. D. (1999). Forming a story: The health benefits of narrative. *Journal of Clinical Psychology, 55,* 1243–1254.

Perlmutter, S. J., Leitman, S. F., Garvey, M. A., et al. (1999). Therapeutic plasma exchange and intravenous immunoglobulin for OCD and tic disorders in children. *Lancet, 354,* 1153–1158.

Peterson, L., & Shigetomi, C. (1981). The use of coping techniques to minimize anxiety in hospitalized children. *Behavioral Therapy, 12,* 1–14.

Petty, F., Brannan, S., Casada, J., Davis, L. L., Gajewski, V., Kramer, G. L., et al. (2001). Olanzapine treatment for post-traumatic stress disorder: An open-label study. *International Clinical Psychopharmacology, 16,* 331–337.

Piacentini, J. (1999). Cognitive behavioral therapy of childhood OCD. *Child and Adolescent Psychiatric Clinics of North America, 8,* 599–616.

Piacentini, J., Bergman, R. L., Jacobs, C., McCracken, J. T., & Kretchman, J. (2002). Open trial of cognitive behavior therapy for childhood obsessive-compulsive disorder. *Journal of Anxiety Disorders, 16,* 207–219.

Piacentini, J., Gitow, A., Jaffer, M., Graae, F., et al. (1994). Outpatient behavioral treatment of child and adolescent obsessive compulsive disorder. *Journal of Anxiety Disorders, 8,* 277–289.

Pickar, D. (2003). Pharmacogenomics of psychiatric drug treatment. *Psychiatric Clinics of North America, 26,* 303–21.

Pina, A. A., Silverman, W. K., Alfano, C. A., & Saavedra, L. M. (2002). Diagnostic efficiency of symptoms in the diagnosis of DSM-IV: Generalized anxiety disorder in youth. *Journal of Child Psychology and Psychiatry and Allied Disciplines, 43,* 959–967.

Pincus, H. A., Tunielian, T. L., Marcus, S. C., Olfson, M., Zarin, D. A., Thompson, J., et al. (1998). Prescribing trends in psychotropic medications: Primary care, psychiatry, and other medical specialties. *Journal of the American Medical Association, 279,* 526–531.

Pine, D. S. (1999). Pathophysiology of childhood anxiety disorders. *Biological Psychiatry, 46,* 1555–1566.

Pine, D. S. (2001). Affective neuroscience and the development of social anxiety disorder. *Psychiatric Clinics of North America, 24,* 689–705.

Pine, D. S. (2002). Brain development and the onset of mood disorders. *Seminars in Clinical Neuropsychiatry, 7,* 223–233.

Pine, D. S., Cohen, P., & Brook, J. (2001). Adolescent fears as predictors of depression. *Biological Psychiatry, 50,* 721–724.

Pine, D. S., Cohen, P., Gurley, D., Brook, J., & Ma, Y. (1998). The risk for early-adulthood anxiety and depressive disorders in adolescents with anxiety and depressive disorders. *Archives of General Psychiatry, 55,* 56–64.

Pine, D. S., Fyer, A., Grun, J., Phelps, E. A., Szeszko, P. R., Koda, V., et al. (2001). Methods for developmental studies of fear conditioning circuitry. *Biological Psychiatry, 50,* 225–228.

Pine, D. S., & Grun, J. S. (1999). Childhood anxiety: Integrating developmental psychopathology and affective neuroscience. *Journal of Child and Adolescent Psychopharmacology, 9,* 1–12.

Pine, D. S., Grun, J., Zarahn, E., Fyer, A., Koda, V., Li, W., et al. (2001). Cortical brain regions engaged by masked emotional faces in adolescents and adults: An fMRI study. *Emotion, 1,* 137–147.

Pine, D. S., Klein, R. G., Coplan, J. D., Papp, L. A., Hoven, C. W., Martinez, J., et al. (2000). Differential carbon dioxide sensitivity in childhood anxiety disorders and nonill comparison group. *Archives of General Psychiatry, 57,* 960–967.

Pine, D. S., Wasserman, G. A., & Workman, S. B. (1999). Memory and anxiety in prepubertal boys at risk for delinquency. *Journal of the American*

Academy of Child and Adolescent Psychiatry, 38, 1024–1031.

Pohl, R., Balon, R., Yergani, V. K., & Gershon, S. (1989). Serotonergic anxiolytics in the treatment of panic disorder: A controlled study with buspirone. *Psychopathology, 22,* 60–67.

Pohl, R. B., Wolkow, R. M., & Clary, C. M. (1998). Sertraline in the treatment of panic disorder: A double-blind multicenter trial. *American Journal of Psychiatry, 155,* 1189–1195.

Popper, C. W., & Ziminitzky, B. (1995). Sudden death putatively related to desipramine treatment in youth: A fifth case and a review of speculative mechanisms. *Journal of Child and Adolescent Psychopharmacology, 5,* 283–300.

Power, K. G., Simpson, R. J., Swanson, V., Wallace L. A., et al. (1990). A controlled comparison of cognitive-behaviour therapy, diazepam, and placebo, alone and in combination, for the treatment of generalised anxiety disorder. *Journal of Anxiety Disorders, 4,* 267–292.

Prather, M. D., Lavenex, P., Mauldin-Jourdain, M. L., Mason, W. A., Capitanio, J. P., Mendoza, S. P., et al. (2001). Increased social fear and decreased fear of objects in monkeys with neonatal amygdala lesions. *Neuroscience, 106,* 653–658.

Prins, P. J. M., & Ollendick, T. H. (2003). Cognitive change and enhanced coping: Missing mediational links in cognitive behavior therapy with anxiety-disordered children. *Clinical Child and Family Psychology Review, 6,* 87–105.

Pynoos, R. S. (1992). Grief and trauma in children and adolescents. *Bereavement Care, 11,* 2–10.

Pynoos, R. S., Frederick, C., Nader, K., & Arroyo, W. (1987). Life threat and posttraumatic stress in school-age children. *Archives of General Psychiatry, 44,* 1057–1063.

Pynoos, R. S., Kinzie, J. D., & Gordon, M. (2001). Children, adolescents and families exposed to extreme trauma and torture. In: E. Gerrity, T. M. Keane, F. Fuma, & F. Tuma (Eds.), *Mental health consequences of torture and related violence and trauma* (pp. 211–225). New York: Plenum Press.

Pynoos, R. S., Steinberg, A. M., & Piacentini, J. C. (1999). A developmental psychopathology model of childhood traumatic stress and intersection with anxiety disorders. *Biological Psychiatry, 46,* 1542–1554.

Radke-Yarrow, M., DeMulder, E., & Belmont, B. (1995). Attachment in the context of high risk conditions. *Development and Psychopathology, 7,* 247–265.

Rakic, P., Bourgeois, J.-P., & Goldman-Rakic, P. S. (1994). Synaptic development of the cerebral cortex: Implications for learning, memory, and mental illness. In J. van Pelt, M. A. Corner, H.B.M. Uylings, & F. H. Lopes da Silva (Eds.), *Progress in brain research: Vol. 102. The self-organizing brain: From growth cones to functional networks* (pp. 227–243). Amsterdam: Elsevier.

Rapee, R. M. (1997). Potential role of childrearing practices in the development of anxiety and depression. *Clinical Psychology Review, 17,* 47–67.

Rapee, R. M. (2002). The development and modification of temperamental risk for anxiety disorders: Prevention of a lifetime of anxiety. *Biological Psychiatry, 52,* 947–957.

Rapee, R. M., Brown, T. A., Antony, M. M., & Barlow, D. H. (1992). Response to hyperventilation and inhalation of 5.5% carbon dioxide–enriched air across the DSM-III-R anxiety disorders. *Journal of Abnormal Psychology, 101,* 538–552.

Rapee, R. M., & Heimberg, R. G. (1997). A cognitive-behavioral model of anxiety in social phobia. *Behaviour Research and Therapy, 35,* 741–756.

Rauch, S. L., Savage, C. R., Alpert, N. M., Fischman, A. J., & Jenike, M. A. (1997). The functional neuroanatomy of anxiety: A study of three disorders using positron emission tomography and symptom provocation. *Biological Psychiatry, 42,* 446–452.

Rauch, S. L., Whalen, P. J., Shin, L. M., McInerney, S. C., Macklin, M. L., Lasko, N. B., et al. (2000). Exaggerated amygdala response to masked facial stimuli in posttraumatic stress disorder: A functional MRI study. *Biological Psychiatry, 47,* 769–776.

Reiss, S., & McNally, R. J. (1985). Expectancy model of fear. In S. Reiss & R. R. Bootzin (Eds.), *Theoretical issues in behavior therapy* (pp. 107–121). New York: Academic Press.

Renaud, J., Birmaher, B., Wassick, S. C., & Bridge, J. (1999). Use of selective serotonin reuptake inhibitors for the treatment of childhood panic disorder: A pilot study. *Journal of Child and Adolescent Psychopharmacology, 9,* 73–83.

Rescorla, R. A. (1988). Pavlovian conditioning: It's not what you think it is. *American Psychologist 43,* 151–160.

Research Units of Pediatric Psychopharmacology (RUPP) Anxiety Group. (2001). Fluvoxamine for the treatment of anxiety disorders in children and adolescents. *New England Journal of Medicine, 344,* 1279–1285.

Research Units on Pediatric Psychopharmacology Anxiety Study Group (RUPP). (2003). Searching for moderators and mediators of pharmacological treatment effects in children and adolescents with anxiety disorders. *Journal of the American Academy of Child and Adolescent Psychiatry, 42,* 13–21.

Resick, P. A. (1993). The psychological impact of rape. *Journal of Interpersonal Violence, 8,* 223–255.

Resick, P. A., Nishith, P., & Griffin, M. G. (2003). How well does cognitive-behavioral therapy treat symptoms of complex PTSD? An examination of child sexual abuse survivors within a clinical trial. *CNS Spectrum, 8,* 340–355.

Reynolds, C. R., & Richmond, B. O. (1978). What I think and feel: A revised measure of children's manifest anxiety. *Journal of Abnormal Child Psychology, 6,* 271–280.

Richards, D. A., Lovell, K. & Marks, I. M. (1994). Post-traumatic stress disorder: Evaluation of a behavioral treatment program. *Journal of Traumatic Stress, 7,* 669–680.

Rickels, K., Amsterdam, J. D., Clary, C., Puzzuoli, G., Schweizer, E. (1991). Buspirone in major depression: A controlled study. *Journal of Clinical Psychiatry, 52,* 34–38.

Rickels, K., Case, W. G., & Diamond, L. R. (1980). Relapse after short-term drug therapy in neurotic outpatients. *International Pharmacopsychiatry, 15,* 186–192.

Rickels, K., Case, W. G., Downing, R. W., & Fridman, R. (1986). One-year follow-up of anxious patients treated with diazepam. *Journal of Clinical Psychopharmacology, 6,* 32–36.

Rickels, K., Csanalosi, I., Greisman, P., Cohen, D., Werblowsky, J., Ross, H. A., et al. (1983). A controlled clinical trial of alprazolam for the treatment of anxiety. *American Journal of Psychiatry, 140,* 82–85.

Rickels, K., Downing, R., Schweizer, E., & Hassman, H. (1993). Antidepressants for the treatment of generalized anxiety disorder: A placebo-controlled comparison of imipramine, trazodone and diazepam. *Archives of General Psychiatry, 50,* 884–895.

Rickels, K., Pollack, M. H., Sheehan, D. V., & Haskins, J. T. (2000). Efficacy of extended-release venlafaxine in nondepressed patients with generalized anxiety disorder. *American Journal of Psychiatry, 157,* 968–974.

Rickels, K., Schweizer, E., Case, W. G., & Greenblatt, D. J. (1990). Long-term therapeutic use of benzodiazepines I. Effects of abrupt discontinuation. *Archives of General Psychiatry, 47,* 899–907.

Riddle, M. A., Geller, B., & Ryan, N. (1993). Case study: Another sudden death with a child treated with desipramine. *Journal of the American Academy of Child and Adolescent Psychiatry, 32,* 792–797.

Riddle, M. A., Hardin, M. T., & King, R. A. (1990). Fluoxetine treatment of children and adolescents with Tourette's and obsessive compulsive disorders: Preliminary clinical experience. *Journal of the American Academy of Child and Adolescent Psychiatry, 29,* 45–48.

Riddle, M. A., King, R. A., Hardin, M. T., et al. (1991). Behavioral side effects of fluoxetine in children and adolescents. *Journal of Child and Adolescent Psychopharmacology, 1,* 193.

Riddle, M. A., Nelson, J. C., Kleinman, C. S., Rasmusson, A., Leckman, J. F., King, R. A., et al. (1991). Case study: Sudden death in children receiving Norpramine: A review of three reported cases and commentary. *Journal of the American Academy of Child and Adolescent Psychiatry, 30,* 104–108.

Riddle, M., Reeve, E., Yaryura-Tobias, J., Yang, H. M., Claghorn, J. L., Gaffney, G., et al. (2001). Fluvoxamine for children and adolescents with obsessive compulsive disorder: A randomized controlled multicenter trial. *Journal of the American Academy of Child and Adolescent Psychiatry, 40,* 222–229.

Riggs, D. S., Rothbaum, B. O., & Foa, E. B. (1995). A prospective examination of symptoms of post-traumatic stress disorder in victims of nonsexual assault. *Journal of Interpersonal Violence, 10,* 201–214.

Roberts, R. E., Lewinsohn, P. M., & Seeley, J. R. (1991). Screening for adolescent depression: A comparison of depression scales. *Journal of the American Academy of Child and Adolescent Psychiatry, 30,* 58–66.

Rohde, L. A., Roman, T., & Hutz, M. H. (2003). Attention-deficit/hyperactivity disorder: Current aspects on pharmacogenetics. *Pharmacogenomics, 3,* 11–13.

Romano, S., Goodman, W., Tamura, R., Gonzales, J., and the Collaborative Research Group (2001). Long-term treatment of obsessive-compulsive disorder after an acute response: A comparison of fluoxetine versus placebo. *Journal of Clinical Psychopharmacology, 21,* 46–52.

Rose, S., Brewin, C. R., Andrews, B., & Kirk, M. (1999). A randomized controlled trial of individual psychological debriefing for victims of violent crime. *Psychological Medicine, 29,* 793–799.

Rosenbaum, J. F., Moroz, G., & Bowden, C. L. (1997). Clonazepam in the treatment of panic disorder with or without agoraphobia: A dose–response study of efficacy, safety, and discontinuance. *Journal of Clinical Psychopharmacology, 17,* 390–400.

Rosenberg, D. R., & Hanna, G. L. (2000). Genetic and imaging strategies in obsessive-compulsive disorder: Potential implications for treatment development. *Biological Psychiatry, 48,* 1210–1222.

Rosenberg, D. R., MacMillan, S. N., & Moore, G. J. (2001). Brain anatomy and chemistry may predict treatment response in paediatric obsessive-compulsive disorder. *International Journal of Neuropsychopharmacology, 4,* 179–190.

Rosenberg, D. R., Stewart, C. M., Fitzgerald, K. D., Tawile, V., & Carroll, E. (1999). Paroxetine open-label treatment of pediatric outpatients with obsessive-compulsive disorder. *Journal of the American Academy of Child and Adolescent Psychiatry, 38,* 1180–1185.

Rothbaum, B. O., Foa, E. B., Riggs, D. S., Murdock, T., et al. (1992). A prospective examination of post-traumatic stress disorder in rape victims. *Journal of Traumatic Stress, 5,* 455–475.

Roy-Byrne, P. P., & Cowley, D. S. (2002). Pharmacological treatments for panic disorder, generalized anxiety disorder, specific phobia, and social anxiety disorder. In P. E. Nathan & J. M. Gorman (Eds.), *A guide to treatments that work* (2nd ed., pp. 337–365). New York: Oxford University Press.

Rutter, M., Bolton, P., Harrington, R., Le Couteur, A. Macdonald, H., & Siminoff, E. (1990). Genetic factors in child psychiatric disorders: I. A review of research strategies. *Journal of Child Psychology and Psychiatry and Allied Disciplines, 31,* 3–37.

Rutter, M., Silberg, J., O'Connor, T., & Siminoff, E. (1999a). Genetics and child psychiatry: I Advances in quantitative and molecular genetics. *Journal of Child Psychology and Psychiatry, 40,* 3–18.

Rutter, M., Silberg, J., O'Connor, T., & Siminoff, E. (1999b). Genetics and child psychiatry: II Empirical research findings. *Journal of Child Psychology and Psychiatry, 40,* 19–56.

Rynn, M. A., Siqueland, L., & Rickels, K. (2001). Placebo-controlled trial of sertraline in the treatment of children with generalized anxiety disorder. *American Journal of Psychiatry, 158,* 2008–2014.

Saigh, P. A., Mroueh, M., & Bremner, J. D. (1997). Scholastic impairments among traumatized adolescents. *Behaviour Research and Therapy, 35,* 429–436.

Salkovskis, P. M. (1985). Obsessional-compulsive problems: A cognitive-behavioural analysis. *Behaviour Research and Therapy, 23,* 571–583.

Sallee, F. R., & March, J. S. (2001). Neuropsychiatry of paediatric anxiety disorders. In W. K. Silverman & P. A. D. Treffers (Eds.), *Anxiety disorders in children and adolescents: Research, assessment and intervention* (pp. 90–125). New York: Cambridge University Press.

Sallee, F. R., Richman, H., Sethuraman, G., Dougherty, D., Sine, L., & Altman-Hamamdzic, S. (1998). Clonidine challenge in childhood anxiety disorder. *Journal of the American Academy of Child and Adolescent Psychiatry, 37,* 655–662.

Sallee, F. R., Sethuraman, G., Sine, L., & Liu, H. (2000). Yohimbine challenge in children with anxiety disorders. *American Journal of Psychiatry, 157,* 1236–1242.

Salzman, C. (1993). Benzodiazepine treatment of panic and agoraphobic symptoms: Use, dependence, toxicity, abuse. *Journal of Psychiatric Research, 27,* 97–110.

Saltzman, W. R., Pynoos, R. S., Layne, C. M., Steinberg, A. M., & Aisenberg, E. (2001). Trauma- and grief-focused intervention for adolescents exposed to community violence: Results of a school-based screening and group treatment protocol. *Group Dynamics, 5,* 291–303.

Sanders, M. R. (1996). New directions in behavioral family intervention with children. In T. H. Ollendick & R. J. Prinz (Eds.), *Advances in clinical child psychology* (pp. 283–330). New York: Plenum Press.

Sanderson, W. C., & Wetzler, S. (1993). Observations on the cognitive behavioral treatment of panic disorder: Impact of benzodiazepines. *Psychotherapy, 30,* 125–132.

Sanson, A., Pedlow, R., Cann, W., Prior, M., & Oberklaid, F. (1996). Shyness ratings: Stability and correlates in early childhood. *Journal of the American Academy of Child and Adolescent Psychiatry, 38,* 1008–1015.

Saranson, S., Davidson, K., Lighthall, F., & Waite, R. (1958). A test anxiety scale for children. *Child Development, 29,* 105–113.

Scahill, L., Riddle, M. A., McSwiggin-Hardin, M., Ort, S. I., King, R. A., Goodman, W. K., et al. (1997). Children's Yale-Brown Obsessive Compulsive Scale: Reliability and validity. *Journal of the American Academy of Child and Adolescent Psychiatry, 36,* 844–852.

Schlegel, A., & Barry, H., III. (1991). *Adolescence: An anthropological inquiry.* New York: The Free Press, Maxwell MacMillan International.

Schmahmann, J. D., & Sherman, J. C. (1998). The

cerebellar cognitive affective syndrome. *Brain, 121*, 561–579.

Schmidt, N. B., Koselka, M., & Woolaway-Bickel, K. (2001). Combined treatments for phobic anxiety disorders. In M. T. Sammons & N. B. Schmidt (Eds.), *Combined treatment for mental disorders: A guide to psychological and pharmacological interventions* (pp. 81–110). Washington, DC: American Psychological Association.

Schmidt, N. B., Woolaway-Bickel, K., Trakowski, J., Santiago, H., Storey, J., Koselka, M., et al. (2000). Dismantling cognitive-behavioral treatment for panic disorder: Questioning the utility of breathing retraining. *Journal of Consulting and Clinical Psychology, 68*, 417–424.

Schuster, M. A., Stein, B. D., Jaycox, L. H., Collins, R. L., Marshall, G. N., Elliot, M. N., et al. (2001). A national survey of stress reactions after the September 11, 2001, terrorist attacks. *New England Journal of Medicine, 345*, 1507–1512.

Schwartz, C. E., Wright, C. I., Shin, L. M., Kagan, J., Whalen, P. J., McMullin, K. G., et al. (2003). Differential amygdalar response to novel versus familiar neutral faces. *Biological Psychiatry, 53*, 854–862.

Seligman, M. E. P. (2002). Positive psychology, positive prevention, and positive therapy. In C. R. Snyder & S. J. Lopez (Eds.), *Handbook of positive psychology* (pp. 3–9). New York: Oxford University Press.

Shaffer, D., Fisher, P., Dulcan, M. K., & Davies, M. (1996). The NIMH Diagnostic Interview Schedule for Children Version 2.3 (DISC 2.3): Description, acceptability, prevalence rates, and performance in the MECA study. *Journal of the American Academy of Child and Adolescent Psychiatry, 35*, 865–877.

Shaffer, D., Gould, M. S., Brasic, J., Ambrosini, P., Fisher, P., Bird, H., et al. (1983). A Children's Global Assessment Scale (CGAS). *Archives of General Psychiatry, 40*, 1228–1231.

Shear, M. K., & Oommen, M. (1995). Anxiety disorders in pregnant and postpartum women. *Psychopharmacology Bulletin, 31*, 693–703.

Sheehan, D. V., Raj, A. B., Sheehan, K. H., & Soto, S. (1990). Is buspirone effective for panic disorder? *Journal of Clinical Psychopharmacology, 10*, 3–11.

Shemesh, E., Rudnick, A., Kaluski, E., Milovanov, O., Salah, A., Alon, D., et al. (2001). A prospective study of posttraumatic stress symptoms and nonadherence in survivors of a myocardial infarction (MI). *General Hospital Psychiatry, 23*, 215–222.

Short, J. L. (1998). Evaluation of a substance abuse prevention and mental health promotion program for children of divorce. *Journal of Divorce and Remarriage, 28*, 139–155.

Silberg, J., Rutter, M., & Eaves, L. (2001a). Genetic and environmental influences on the temporal association between earlier anxiety and later depression in girls. *Biological Psychiatry, 49*, 1040–1049.

Silberg, J. L., Rutter, M., & Eaves, L. (2001b). Genetic and environmental influences on the temporal association between earlier anxiety and later depression in girls: Erratum. *Biological Psychiatry, 50*, 393.

Silberg, J., Rutter, M., Neale, M., & Eaves, L. (2001). Genetic moderation of environmental risk for depression and anxiety in adolescent girls. *British Journal of Psychiatry, 179*, 116–121.

Silove, D., Manicavasagar, V., Curtis, J., & Blaszczynski, A. (1996). Is early separation anxiety a risk factor for adult panic disorder? A critical review. *Comprehensive Psychiatry, 37*, 167–179.

Silverman, J. J., Singh, N. N., Carmanico, S. J., Lindstrom, K. A., Best, A. M., & Clearfield, S. (1999). Psychological distress and symptoms of posttraumatic stress disorder in Jewish adolescents following a brief exposure to concentration camps. *Journal of Child and Family Studies, 8*, 71–89.

Silverman, W. K., & Albano, A. M. (1996). *The Anxiety Disorders Interview Schedule for Children-IV (Child and parent versions)*. San Antonio, TX: Psychological Corporation.

Silverman, W. K., & Carter, R. (in press). Anxiety disturbance in girls and women. In J. Worell and C. Goodheart (Eds.), *Handbook of girls' and women's psychological health*. New York: Oxford University Press.

Silverman, W. K., Cerny, J. A., Nelles, W. B., & Burke, A. E. (1988). Behavior problems in children of parents with anxiety disorders. *Journal of the American Academy of Child and Adolescent Psychiatry, 27*, 779–784.

Silverman, W. K., Fleisig, W., Rabian, B., & Peterson, R. A. (1991). Childhood anxiety sensitivity index. *Journal of Clinical Child Psychology, 20*, 162–168.

Silverman, W. K., Goedhart, A. W., Barrett, P., & Turner, C. (2003). The facets of anxiety sensitivity represented in the Childhood Anxiety Sensitivity Index: Confirmatory analyses of factor models from past studies. *Journal of Abnormal Psychology, 112*, 364–374.

Silverman, W. K., Kurtines, W. M., Ginsburg, G. S.,

Weems, C. F., Lumpkin, P. W., & Carmichael, D. H. (1999a). Treating anxiety disorders in children with group cognitive behavior therapy: A randomized clinical trial. *Journal of Consulting and Clinical Psychology, 67,* 995–1003.

Silverman, W. K., Kurtines, W. M., Ginsburg, G. S., Weems, C. F., Rabian, B., & Serafini, L. T. (1999b). Contingency management, self-control, and education support in the treatment of childhood phobic disorders: A randomized clinical trial. *Journal of Consulting and Clinical Psychology, 67,* 675–687.

Silverman, W. K., La Greca, A. M., & Wasserstein, S. (1995). What do children worry about? Worries and their relation to anxiety. *Child Development, 66,* 671–686.

Silverman, W. K., Saavedra, L. M., & Pina, A. A. (2001). Test–retest reliability of anxiety symptoms and diagnoses with anxiety disorders interview schedule for DSM-IV: Child and parent versions. *Journal of the American Academy of Child and Adolescent Psychiatry, 40,* 937–944.

Silverman, W. K., & Weems, C. F. (1999). Anxiety sensitivity in children. In S. Taylor (Ed.), *Anxiety sensitivity: Theory, research, and treatment of the fear of anxiety* (pp. 239–268). Mahwah, NJ: Lawrence Erlbaum Associates.

Simeon, J. G., Ferguson, H. B., Knott, V., Roberts, N., Gauthier, B., Dubois, C., et al. (1992). Clinical, cognitive, and neurophysiological effects of alprazolam in children and adolescents with overanxious and avoidant disorders. *Journal of the American Academy of Child and Adolescent Psychiatry, 31,* 29–33.

Simon, N. M., Safren, S. A., Otto, M. W., Sharma, S. G., Lanka, G. D., & Pollack, M. H. (2002). Longitudinal outcome with pharmacotherapy in a naturalistic study of panic disorder. *Journal of Affective Disorders, 69,* 201–208.

Simpson, H. B., Liebowitz, M. R., Foa, E. B., Kozak, M. J., Schmidt, A. B., Rowan, V., et al. (2004). Post-treatment effects of exposure therapy and clomipramine in obsessive-compulsive disorder. *Depression and Anxiety, 19,* 225–233.

Siqueland, L., & Diamond, G. S. (1998). Engaging parents in cognitive behavioral treatment for children with anxiety disorders. *Cognitive and Behavioral Practice, 5,* 81–102.

Siqueland, L., Kendall, P. C., & Steinberg, L. (1996). Anxiety in children: Perceived family environments and observed family interaction. *Journal of Clinical Child Psychology, 25,* 225–237.

Skre, I., Onstad, S., Torgersen, S., Lygren, S., & Kringlen, E. (1993). A twin study of DSM-111-R anx-iety disorders. *Acta Psychiatrica Scandinavica, 88,* 85–92.

Slattery, M. J., Klein, D. F., Mannuzza, S., Moulton, J. L., III, Pine, D. S., & Klein, R. G. (2002). Relationship between separation anxiety disorder, parental panic disorder, and atopic disorders in children: A controlled high-risk study. *Journal of the American Academy of Child and Adolescent Psychiatry, 41,* 947–954.

Smajkic, A., Weine, S., Djuric-Bijedic, Z., Boskailo, E., Lewis, J., & Pavkovic, I. (2001). Sertraline, paroxetine, and venlafaxine in refugee posttraumatic stress disorder with depression symptoms. *Journal of Traumatic Stress, 14,* 445–452.

Smoller, J. W., Rosenbaum, J. F., Biederman, J., Kennedy, J., Dai, D., Racette, S. R., et al. (2003). Association of a genetic marker at the corticotropin-releasing hormone locus with behavioral inhibition. *Biological Psychiatry, 54,* 1376–1381.

Solomon, Z., Mikulincer, M., & Avitzur, E. (1988). Coping, locus of control, social support, and combat-related posttraumatic stress disorder: A prospective study. *Journal of Personality and Social Psychology, 55,* 279–285.

Sowell, E. R., Thompson, P. M., Holmes, C. J., Batth, R., Jernigan, T. L., & Toga, A. W. (1999a). Localizing age-related changes in brain structure between childhood and adolescence using statistical parametric mapping. *Neuroimage, 9,* 587–597.

Sowell, E. R., Thompson, P. M., Holmes, C. J., Jernigan, T. L., & Toga, A. W. (1999b). In vivo evidence for post-adolescent brain maturation in frontal and striatal regions. *Nature Neuroscience, 2,* 859–861.

Spear, L. P. (2000). The adolescent brain and age-related behavioral manifestations. *Neuroscience and Biobehavioral Reviews, 24,* 417–463.

Spence, S. H., Donovan, C., & Brechman-Toussaint, M. (2000). The treatment of childhood social phobia: The effectiveness of a social skills training-based, cognitive-behavioural intervention, with and without parental involvement. *Journal of Child Psychology and Psychiatry and Allied Disciplines, 41,* 713–726.

Spiegel, D. A., & Bruce, T. J. (1997). Benzodiazepines and exposure-based cognitive behavior therapies for panic disorder: Conclusions from combined treatment trials. *American Journal of Psychiatry, 154,* 773–781.

Stein, D. J., Westenberg, H. G. M., & Liebowitz, M. R. (2002). Social anxiety disorder and generalized anxiety disorder: Serotonergic and dopaminergic neurocircuitry. *Journal of Clinical Psychiatry, 63,* 12–19.

Stein, M. B., Chartier, M. J., Hazen, A. L., Kroft, C. D. L., Chale, R. A., Cote, D., et al. (1996). Paroxetine in the treatment of generalized social phobia: Open label and double-blind placebo-controlled discontinuation. *Journal of Clinical Psychopharmacology, 16,* 218–222.

Stein, M. B., Chavira, D. A., & Jang, K. L. (2001). Bringing up bashful baby. Developmental pathways to social phobia. *Psychiatric Clinics of North America, 24,* 661–675.

Steinhausen, H., & Juzi, C. (1996). Elective mutism: An analysis of 100 cases. *Journal of the American Academy of Child and Adolescent Psychiatry, 35,* 606–614.

Steketee, G., & Foa, E. B. (1987). Rape victims: Posttraumatic stress responses and their treatment: A review of the literature. *Journal of Anxiety Disorders, 1,* 69–86.

Stevens, S. J., Murphy, B. S., & McKnight, K. (2003). Traumatic stress and gender differences in relationship to substance abuse, mental health, physical health and HIV risk behavior in a sample of adolescents enrolled in drug treatment. *Child Maltreatment, 8,* 46–57.

Stevenson-Hinde, J., & Shouldice, A. (1990). Fear and attachment in 2.5-year-olds. *British Journal of Developmental Psychology, 8,* 319–333.

Strauss, C. C., Lease, C., Last, C. G., & Francis, G. (1988). Overanxious disorder: An examination of developmental differences. *Journal of Abnormal Child Psychology, 16,* 433–443.

Stretch, R. H. (1985). Posttraumatic stress disorder among U.S. Army Reserve Vietnam and Vietnam-era veterans. *Journal of Consulting and Clinical Psychology, 53,* 935–936.

Stretch, R. H. (1989). Incidence and etiology of posttraumatic stress disorder among active duty Army personnel. *Journal of Applied Social Psychology, 16,* 464–481.

Sullivan, G. M., Coplan, J. D., & Gorman, J. M. (1998). Psychoneuroendocrinology of anxiety disorders. *Psychiatric Clinics of North America, 21,* 397–412.

Sullivan, G. M., Coplan, J. D., Kent, J. M., & Gorman, J. M. (1999). The noradenergic system in pathological anxiety: A focus on panic with relevance to generalized anxiety and phobias. *Biological Psychiatry, 46,* 1205–1218.

Sutker, P. B., Davis, J. M., Uddo, M., & Ditta, S. R. (1995). War zone stress, personal resources, and PTSD in Persian Gulf War returnees. *Journal of Abnormal Psychology, 104,* 444–452.

Swadi, H. (1999). Individual risk factors for adolescent substance abuse. *Drug and Alcohol Dependence, 55,* 209–224.

Swedo, S. E. (1994). Sydenham's chorea: A model for childhood autoimmune neuropsychiatric disorders. *Journal of the American Medical Association, 272,* 1788–1791.

Swedo, S. E. (2002). Pediatric autoimmune neuropsychiatric disorders associated with streptococcal infections (PANDAS). *Molecular Psychiatry, 7,* S24–S25.

Swedo, S. E., Leonard, H. L., Garvey, M., Mittleman, B., Allen, A. J., Perlmutter, S., et al. (1998). Pediatric autoimmune neuropsychiatric disorders associated with streptococcal infections: Clinical description of the first 50 cases. *American Journal of Psychiatry, 155,* 264–271.

Sweeny, M., & Pine, D. (2004). Etiology of fear and anxiety. In T. H. Ollendick & J. S. March (Eds.), *Phobic and anxiety disorders in children and adolescents: A clinician's guide to effective psychosocial and pharmacological interventions* (pp. 34–60). New York: Oxford University Press.

Swinson, R. P., Soulios, C., Cox, B. J., & Kuch, K. (1992). Brief treatment of emergency room patients with panic attacks. *American Journal of Psychiatry, 14,* 944–946.

Taghavi, M. R., Moradi, A. R., Neshat-Doost, H. T., Yule, W., & Dalgleish, T. (2000). Interpretation of ambiguous emotional information in clinically anxious children and adolescents. *Cognition and Emotion, 14,* 809–822.

Taghavi, M. R., Neshat-Doost, H. T., Moradi, A. R., Yule, W., & Dalgleish, T. (1999). Biases in visual attention in children and adolescents with clinical anxiety and mixed anxiety—Depression. *Journal of Abnormal Child Psychology, 27,* 215–223.

Teicher, M. H., & Andersen, S. L. (1999, October). *Limbic serotonin turnover plunges during puberty.* Poster session presented at the Annual Meeting of the Society for Neuroscience, Miami Beach, FL.

Teplin, L. A., Abram, K. M., McClelland, G. M., Dulcan, M. K., & Mericle, A. A. (2002). Psychiatric disorders in youth in juvenile detention. *Archives of General Psychiatry, 59,* 1133–1143.

Terasawa, E., & Timiras, P. S. (1968). Electrophysiological study of the limbic system in the rat at onset of puberty. *American Journal of Physiology, 215,* 1462–1467.

Thomas, K. M., Drevets, W. C., Dahl, R. E., Ryan, N. D., Birmaher, B., Eccard, C. H., et al. (2001a). Amygdala response to fearful faces in anxious and depressed children. *Archives of General Psychiatry, 58,* 1057–1063.

Thomas, K. M., Drevets, W. C., Whalen, P. J., Eccard, C. H., Dahl, R. E., Ryan, N. D., et al. (2001b). Amygdala response to facial expressions in children and adults. *Biological Psychiatry, 49,* 309–316.

Thomsen, P. H. (1997). Child and adolescent obsessive-compulsive disorder treated with citalopram: Findings from an open trial of 23 cases. *Journal of Child and Adolescent Psychopharmacology, 7,* 157–166.

Thrasher, S. M., Dalgleish, T., & Yule, W. (1994). Information processing in post-traumatic stress disorder. *Behaviour Research and Therapy, 32,* 247–254.

Topolski, T. D., Hewitt, J. K., Eaves, L. J., Silberg, J. L., Meyer, J. M., Rutter, M., et al. (1997). Genetic and environmental influences on child reports of manifest anxiety and symptoms of separation anxiety and overanxious disorders: A community-based twin study. *Behavior Genetics, 27,* 15–28.

Treadwell, K. H., & Kendall, P. C. (1996). Self-talk in anxiety-disordered youth: States-of-mind, content specificity, and treatment outcome. *Journal of Consulting and Clinical Psychology, 64,* 941–950.

Tucker, P., Zaninelli, R., Yehuda, R., Ruggiero, L., Dillingham, K., & Pitts, C. D. (2001). Paroxetine in the treatment of chronic posttraumatic stress disorder: Results of a placebo-controlled, flexible-dosage trial. *Journal of Clinical Psychiatry, 62,* 860–868.

U.S. Department of Health and Human Services, Administration on Children, Youth and Families. (2003). *Child maltreatment 2001.* Washington, DC: Government Printing Office.

U.S. Department of Justice. (2002). *Juvenile residential facility census, 2000: Selected findings.* Washington, DC: Office of Juvenile Justice and Delinquency Prevention.

Upadhyaya, H., Deas, D., Brady, K., & Kruesi, M. (2002). Cigarette smoking and psychiatric comorbidity in children and adolescents. *Journal of the American Academy of Child and Adolescent Psychiatry, 41,* 1295–1303.

van Balkom, A. J. L. M., de Haan, E., van Oppen, P., Spinhoven, P., Hoogduin, K. A. L., Vermeulen, A. W. A., & van Dyck, R. (1998). Cognitive and behavioral therapies alone and in combination with fluvoxamine in the treatment of obsessive compulsive disorder. *Journal of Nervous and Mental Disease, 186,* 492–499.

van Eden, C. G., Kros, J. M., & Uylings, H. B. M. (1990). The development of the rat prefrontal cortex: Its size and development of connections with thalamus, spinal cord and other cortical areas. In H. B. M. Uylings, C. G. van Eden, J. P. C. De Bruin, M. A. Corner, & M. G. P. Feenstra (Eds.), *Progress in brain research: Vol. 85. The prefrontal cortex: Its structure, function and pathology* (pp. 169–183). Amsterdam: Elsevier.

Varley, C. K., & McClellan, J. (1997). Case study: Two additional sudden deaths with tricyclic antidepressants. *American Journal of Child and Adolescent Psychiatry, 36,* 390–394.

Vasey, M. W., Daleiden, E. L., Williams, L. L., & Brown., L. M. (1995). Biased attention in childhood anxiety disorders: A preliminary study. *Journal of Abnormal Child Psychology, 23,* 267–279.

Vasey, M. W., Dalgleish, T., & Silverman, W. K. (2003). Research on information-processing factors in child and adolescent psychopathology: A critical commentary. *Journal of Clinical Child and Adolescent Psychology, 32,* 81–93.

Vasey, M. W., El-Hag, N., & Daleiden, E. L. (1996). Anxiety and the processing of emotionally threatening stimuli: Distinctive patterns of selective attention among high- and low-test-anxious children. *Child Development, 67,* 1173–1185.

Vasey, M. W., & MacLeod, C. (2001). Information-processing factors in childhood anxiety: A developmental perspective. In M. W. Vasey & M. R. Dadds (Eds.), *The developmental psychopathology of anxiety* (pp. 253–277). New York: Oxford University Press.

Vecchio, T. (1996). Predictive value of a single diagnostic test in unselected populations. *New England Journal of Medicine, 275,* 1171–1173.

Vernberg, E. M., La Greca, A. M., Silverman, W. K., Silverman, W. K., & Prinstein, M. J. (1996). Predictors of children's post-disaster functioning following hurricane Andrew. *Journal of Abnormal Psychology, 105,* 237–248.

Wakefield, J. C. (1992). The concept of mental disorder: On the boundary between biological facts and social values. *American Psychologist, 47,* 373–388.

Walker, J. R., Van Amerigen, M. A., Swinson, R., Bowen, R. C., Cokka, P. R., Goldner, E., et al. (2000). Prevention of relapse in generalized social phobia: Results of a 24-week study in responders to 20 weeks of sertraline treatment. *Journal of Clinical Psychopharmacology, 20,* 636–643.

Walkup, J. T., Labellarte, M. J., Riddle, M. A., Pine, D. S., Greenhill, L., Klein, R., et al. (2001). Fluvoxamine for the treatment of anxiety disorders in children and adolescents. *New England Journal of Medicine, 344,* 1279–1285.

Warner, B. S., & Weist, M. D. (1996). Urban youth as witnesses to violence: Beginning assessment and treatment efforts. *Journal of Youth and Adolescence, 25,* 361–377.

Warren, S. L., Huston, L., Egeland, B., & Sroufe, L. A. (1997). Child and adolescent anxiety disorders and early attachment. *Journal of the American Academy of Child and Adolescent Psychiatry, 36,* 637–644.

Wasserman, G. A., McReynolds, L. S., Lucal, C. P., Fisher, P., & Santos, L. (2002). The Voice DISC-IV with incarcerated male youths: Prevalence of disorder. *Journal of the American Academy of Child and Adolescent Psychiatry, 41,* 314–321.

Weems, C. F., Hayward, C., Killen, J., & Taylor, C. B. (2002). A longitudinal investigation of anxiety sensitivity in adolescence. *Journal of Abnormal Psychology, 111,* 471–477.

Weems, C. F., Silverman, W. K., and La Greca, A. M. (2000). What do youth referred for anxiety problems worry about? Worry and its relation to anxiety and anxiety disorders in children and adolescents. *Journal of Abnormal Child Psychology, 28,* 63–72.

Wegner, D. M. (1989). *White bears and other unwanted thoughts: Suppression, obsession, and the psychology of mental control.* New York: Penguin Books.

Weissberg, R. P., Kumpfer, K. L., & Seligman, M. E. P. (2003). Prevention that works for children and youth: An introduction. *American Psychologist, 58,* 425–432.

Weissman, M. M. (1988). The epidemiology of anxiety disorders: Rates, risks and familial patterns. *Journal of Psychiatric Research, 22* (Suppl. 1), 99–114.

Weissman, M. M., Bland, R. C., Canino, G. J., Faravelli, C., Greenwald, S., Hwu, H., et al. (1997). The Cross-National Epidemiology of Panic Disorder Study. *Archives of General Psychiatry, 54,* 305–309.

Weissman, M. M., Wolk, S., Wickramaratne, P., Goldstein, R. B., Adams, P., Greenwald, S., et al. (1999). Children with prepubertal–onset major depressive disorder and anxiety grown up. *Archives of General Psychiatry, 56,* 794–801.

Weisz, J. R., & Hawley, K. M. (2002). Developmental factors in the treatment on adolescents. *Journal of Consulting and Clinical Psychology, 70,* 21–43.

Weizman, A., & Weizman, R. (2000). Serotonin transporter polymorphism and response to SSRIs in major depression and relevance to anxiety disorders and substance abuse. *Pharmacogenomics 1,* 335–341.

Westra, H. A., & Stewart, S. H. (1998). Cognitive behavioral therapy and pharmacotherapy: Complimentary or contradictory approaches to the treatment of anxiety? *Clinical Psychology Review, 18,* 307–340.

Wever, C., & Rey, J. M. (1997). Juvenile OCD. *Australian and New Zealand Journal of Psychiatry 31,* 105–113.

White, K. S., Bruce, S. E., Farrell, A. D., & Kliewer, W. (1998). Impact of exposure to community violence on anxiety: A longitudinal study of family social support as a protective factor for urban children. *Journal of Child and Family Studies, 7,* 187–203.

Wilhelm, F. H., & Roth, W. T. (1997). Acute and delayed effects of alprazolam on flight phobics during exposure. *Behavior Research and Therapy, 35,* 831–841.

Williams, J. M. G., Mathews, A., & MacLeod, C. (1996). The Emotional Stroop Task and psychopathology. *Psychological Bulletin, 120,* 3–24.

Williams, J. M. G., Watts, F. N., MacLeod, C., & Mathews, A. (1997). *Cognitive psychology and emotional disorders* (2nd ed.). Chichester, UK: John Wiley & Sons.

Wills, T. A., Vaccaro, D., & McNammar, G. (1992). The role of life events, family support and competence in adolescent substance abuse: A test of vulnerability and protective factors. *American Journal of Community Psychology, 20,* 349–374.

Wilson, F. A., & Rolls, E. T. (1993). The effect of stimulus novelty and familiarity on neuronal activity in the amygdala of monkeys performing recognition memory tasks. *Experimental Brain Research, 93,* 367–382.

Winett, R. A. (1998a). Prevention: A proactive-developmental-ecological perspective. In T. H. Ollendick & M. Hersen (Eds.), *Handbook of child psychopathology* (3rd ed., pp. 637–671). New York: Plenum Press.

Winett, R. A. (1998b). Developing more effective health-behavior programs: Analyzing the epidemiological and biological bases for activity and exercise programs. *Applied and Preventive Psychology, 7,* 209–224.

Wolfe, D. A., Scott, K., Reitzel-Jaffe, D., Wekerle, C.,

Grasley, C., & Straatman, A. (2001). Development and validation of the Conflict in Adolescent Dating Relationships Inventory. *Psychological Assessment, 13,* 277–293.

Wolfe, D. A., Scott, K., Wekerle, C., & Pittman, A. (2001). Child maltreatment: Risk of adjustment problems and dating violence in adolescence. *Journal of the American Academy of Child and Adolescent Psychiatry, 40,* 282–289.

Wolfer, D. P., & Lipp, H.-P. (1995). Evidence for physiological growth of hippocampal mossy fiber collaterals in the guinea pig during puberty and adulthood. *Hippocampus, 5,* 329–340.

Wood, J., Foy, D., Layne, D., Pynoos, R., & James, C. B. (2002). An examination of the relationships among violence, posttraumatic stress symptomotology, and delinquent activity: An 'ecological' model of delinquent behavior among incarcerated adolescents. *Journal of Aggression, Maltreatment and Trauma, 6,* 127–147.

Woods, S. W., & Charney, D. S. (1998). Applications of the pharmacologic challenge strategy in panic disorders research. *Journal of Anxiety Disorders, 2,* 31–49.

Yehuda, R. (2002). Post-traumatic stress disorder. *New England Journal of Medicine, 346,* 108–114.

Young, S. E., Smolen, A., Stallings, M. C., Corley, R. P., & Hewitt, J. K. (2003). Sibling-based association analyses of the serotonin transporter polymorphism and internalizing behavior problems in children. *Journal of Child Psychology and Psychiatry, 44,* 961–967.

Yurgelun-Todd, D. A., Killgore, W. D. S., & Cintron, C. B. (2003). Cognitive correlates of medial temporal lobe development across adolescence: A magnetic resonance imaging study. *Perceptual and Motor Skills, 96,* 3–17.

Zabin, & Melamed, (1980).

Zarate, R., Craske, M. G., & Barlow, D. H. (1990). Situational exposure treatment versus panic control treatment for agoraphobia. A case study. *Journal of Behavior Therapy and Experimental Psychiatry, 21,* 311–324.

Zito, M. J. M., Safer, D. J., dosReis, S., Gardner, J. F., Boles, M., & Lynch, F. (2000). Trends in the prescribing of psychotropic medications to preschoolers. *Journal of the American Medical Association, 283,* 1025–1030.

Zoellner, L. A., Foa, E. B., & Brigidi, B. D. (1999). Interpersonal friction and PTSD in female victims of sexual and nonsexual assault. *Journal of Traumatic Stress, 12,* 689–700.

Zubernis, L. S., Cassidy, K. W., Gillham, J. E., Reivich, K. J., & Jaycox, L. H. (1999). Prevention of depressive symptoms in preadolescent children of divorce. *Journal of Divorce and Remarriage, 30,* 11–36.

Zucker, B. G., Craske, M. G., Barrios, B., & Holguin, M. (2002). Thought action fusion: Can it be corrected? *Behaviour Research and Therapy, 40,* 652–664.

Part IV: Eating Disorders

Abbassi, V. (1998). Growth and normal puberty. *Pediatrics, 102,* 507–511.

Achenbach, T. M. (1991). *Manual for the child behavior checklist.* Burlington, VT: University of Vermont, Department of Psychiatry.

Ackard, D. M., Neumark-Sztainer, D., Story, M., & Perry, C. (2003). Overeating among adolescents: Prevalence and associations with weight-related characteristics and psychological health. *Pediatrics, 111,* 67–74.

Agras, W. S. (1997). Pharmacotherapy of bulimia nervosa and binge eating disorder: Longer-term outcomes. *Psychopharmacology Bulletin, 33,* 433–436.

Agras, W. S., Walsh, B. T., Fairburn, C. G., Wilson, G. T., & Kraemer, H. C. (2000). A multicenter comparison of cognitive-behavioral therapy and interpersonal psychotherapy for bulimia nervosa. *Archives of General Psychiatry, 57,* 459–466.

Alexander, P. (1992). Application of attachment theory to the study of sexual abuse. *Journal of Consulting and Clinical Psychology, 60,* 185–195.

American Academy of Child and Adolescent Psychiatry (1998). Practice parameters. *Journal of the American Academy of Child and Adolescent Psychiatry, 37* (Suppl.), 1–55.

American Academy of Pediatrics Committee on Nutrition (1999). Calcium requirements of infants, children, and adolescents. *Pediatrics, 104,* 1152–1157.

American Psychiatric Association (1980). *Diagnostic and statistical manual of mental disorders* (3rd ed.). Washington, DC: Author.

American Psychiatric Association. (1987). *Diagnostic and statistical manual of mental disorders* (3rd ed., rev.). Washington, DC: Author.

American Psychiatric Association. (1994). *Diagnostic and statistical manual of mental disorders* (4th ed.). Washington, DC: Author.

American Psychiatric Association. (2000). *Diagnos-*

tic and statistical manual of mental disorders (4th ed., text revision). Washington, DC: Author.

American Psychiatric Association Work Group on Eating Disorders (2000). American Psychiatric Association practice guideline for the treatment of patients with eating disorders. *American Journal of Psychiatry, 157* (Suppl.), 1–39.

Anderluh, M., Tchanturia, K., Rabe-Hesketh, S., & Treasure, J. (2003). Childhood obsessive-compulsive personality traits in adult women with eating disorders: Defining a broader eating disorder phenotype. *American Journal of Psychiatry, 160*, 242–247.

Andersen, I., Parry-Billings, M., Newsholme, E., Fairburn, C., & Cowen, P. (1990). Dieting reduces plasma tryptophan and alters brain serotonin function in women. *Journal of Psychological Medicine, 20*, 785–791.

Anderson, A. E., Bowers, W., & Evans, K. (1997). Inpatient treatment of anorexia nervosa. In D. M. Garner & P. E. Garfinkel (Eds.), *Handbook of treatment for eating disorders* (pp. 327–353). New York: Guilford Press.

Anderson, J. C., Williams, S. M., McGee, R., & Silva, P. A. (1987). DSM-III disorders in preadolescent children: Prevalence in a large sample from the general population. *Archives of General Psychiatry, 44*, 69–76.

Appolinario, J. C., Godoy-Matos, A., Fontenelle, L. F., Cararro, L., Cabral, M., Vieira, A., & Countinho, W. (2002). An open-label trial of sibutramine in obese patients with binge-eating disorder. *Journal of Clinical Psychiatry, 63*, 28–30.

Arden, M. R., Weiselberg, E. C., Nussbaum, M. P., Shenker, I. R., & Jacobson, M. S. (1990). Effect of weight restoration on the dyslipoproteinemia of anorexia nervosa. *Journal of Adolescent Health Care, 11*, 199–202.

Armstrong, J., & Roth, D. (1989). Attachment and separation difficulties in eating disorders: A preliminary investigation. *International Journal of Eating Disorders, 8*, 141–155.

Attia, E., Haiman, C., Walsh, B. T., & Flater, S. (1998). Does fluoxetine augment the inpatient treatment of anorexia nervosa? *American Journal of Psychiatry, 155*, 548–551.

Austin, S. B., Field, A. E., & Gortmaker, S. L. (2002, April). The impact of a school-based nutrition and physical activity intervention on onset of disordered eating behaviors in early adolescent girls over two years. Paper presented at the Academy for Eating Disorders International Conference, Boston, MA.

Bachrach, L. K., Guido, D., Katzman, D., Litt, I. F.,

& Marcus, R. (1990). Decreased bone density in adolescent girls with anorexia nervosa. *Pediatrics, 86*, 440–447.

Bachrach, L. K., Katzman, D. K., Litt, I. F., Guido, D., & Marcus, R. (1991). Recovery from osteopenia in adolescent girls with anorexia nervosa. *Journal of Clinical Endocrinology and Metabolism, 72*, 602–606.

Baran, S., Weltzin, T., & Kaye, W. (1995). Low discharge weight and outcome in anorexia nervosa. *American Journal of Psychiatry, 152*, 1070–1072.

Barlow, D. H. (2002). *Anxiety and its disorders* (2nd ed.). New York: Guilford Press.

Bates, G. W., Bates, S. R., Whitworth, N. S. (1982). Reproductive failure in women who practice weight control. *Fertility and Sterility, 37*, 373–378.

Bearman, S. K., Stice, E., & Chase, A. (2003). Evaluation of an intervention targeting both depressive and bulimic pathology: A randomized prevention trial. *Behavior Therapy, 34*, 277–293.

Bearman, S. K., Stice, E., & Chase, Allison. (2003). Evaluation of an intervention targeting both depressive and bulimic pathology: A randomized prevention trial. *Behavior Therapy, 34*, 277–293.

Beck, D., Casper, R., & Andersen, A. (1996). Truly late onset of eating disorders: A study of 11 cases averaging 60 years of age at presentation. *International Journal of Eating Disorders, 20*, 389–395.

Becker, A., Burwell, R., Gilman, S., Herzog, D., & Hamburg, P. (2002). Eating behaviours and attitudes following prolonged exposure to television among ethnic Fijian adolescent girls. *British Journal of Psychiatry, 180*, 509–514.

Becker, B., Bell, M., & Billington, R. (1987). Objects relations ego deficits in bulimic college women. *Journal of Clinical Psychology, 43*, 92–95.

Berkowitz, B. E., Stunkard, A. J., & Stallings, V. A. (1993). Binge-eating disorder in obese adolescent girls. *Annals of the New York Academy of Sciences, 699*, 200–206.

Bhugra, D., & Kamaldeep, B. (2003). Eating disorders in teenagers in East London: A survey. *European Eating Disorders Review, 11*, 46–57.

Biederman, J., Herzog, D. B., Rivinus, T. M., Harper, G. P., Ferber, R. A., Rosenbaurm, J. F., et al. (1985). Amitriptyline in the treatment of anorexia nervosa: A double-blind placebo-controlled study. *Journal of Clinical Psychopharmacology, 5*, 10–16.

Birmingham, C. L., Goldmer, E. M., & Bakan, R. (1994). Controlled trial of zinc supplementation in anorexia nervosa. *International Journal of Eating Disorders, 15*, 251–255.

Bloomfield, F., Oliver, M., Hawkins, P., Campbell, M., Phillips, D., Gluckman, P., et al. (2003). A periconceptional nutritional origin for noninfectious preterm birth. *Science, 300,* 606.

Boachie, A., Goldfield, G. S., & Spettigue, W. (2003). Olanzapine use as an adjunctive treatment for hospitalized children with anorexia nervosa: Case reports. *International Journal of Eating Disorders, 33,* 98–103.

Boland, B., Beguin, C., Zech, F., Desager, J. P., & Lambert, M. (2001). Serum beta-carotene in anorexia nervosa patients: a case-control study. *International Journal of Eating Disorders, 30,* 299–305.

Bonjour, J. P., Theintz, G., Buchs, B., Slosman, D., & Rizzoli, R. (1991). Critical years and stages of puberty for spinal and femoral bone mass accumulation during adolescence. *Journal of Clinical Endocrinology and Metabolism, 73,* 555–563.

Braet, C., & Van Winckel, M. (2000). Long-term follow-up of a cognitive behavioral treatment program for obese children. *Behavior Therapy, 31,* 55–74.

Braun, D. L., Sunday, S. R., & Halmi, K. A. (1994). Psychiatric comorbidity in patients with eating disorders. *Psychological Medicine, 24,* 859–867.

Brent, D. A., Holder, D., Kolko, K. J., Birmaher, B., Baugher, M., Roth, C., et al. (1997). A clinical psychotherapy trial for adolescent depression comparing cognitive, family, and supportive treatments. *Archives of General Psychiatry, 54,* 877–885.

Brewerton, T. D. (2002). Bulimia in children and adolescents. *Child and Adolescent Psychiatric Clinics of North America, 11,* 237–256.

Brewerton, T. D., Dorn, L. J., & Bishop, E. R. (1992). The tridimensional personality quesionnaire in eating disorders. *Biological Psychiatry, 31,* 91A.

Brewerton, T. D., Lydiard, R. B., Herzog, D. B., Brotman, A. W., O'Neil, P. M., & Ballenger, J. C. (1995). Comorbidity of axis I psychiatric disorders in bulimia nervosa. *Journal of Clinical Psychiatry, 56,* 77–80.

Brownell, K. (1991). Dieting and the search for the perfect body: Where physiology and culture collide. *Behavior Therapy, 22,* 1–12.

Brownell, K. D., Marlatt, G. A., Lichtenstein, E., & Wilson, G. T. (1986). Understanding and preventing relapse. *American Psychologist, 41,* 765–782.

Bruch, H. (1973). *Eating disorders.* New York: Basic Books.

Bryant-Waugh, R. J., Cooper, P. J., Taylor, C. L., & Lask, B. D. (1996). The use of the eating disorder examination with children: A pilot study. *International Journal of Eating Disorders, 19,* 391–397.

Buddeberg-Fischer, B., Klaghofer, R., Reed, V., & Buddeberg, C. (2000). Psychosomatic health promotion in adolescents: An intervention study in 2 high schools. *Gesundheitswesen, 62,* 499–504.

Bulik, C. (1987). Eating disorders in immigrants: Two case studies. *International Journal of Eating Disorders, 6,* 133–141.

Bulik, C. M. (2001). Anxiety and depression in eating disorders. In K. Brownell (Ed.), *Eating disorders and obesity: A comprehensive handbook* (Vol. 2, pp. 193–198). New York: Guilford Press.

Bulik, C. (2002). Anxiety, depression, and eating disorders. In C. G. Fairburn & K. D. Brownell (Eds.), *Eating disorders and obesity* (2nd ed., pp. 193–198). New York: Guilford Press.

Bulik, C. (2003). Genetic and biological risk factors. In J. K. Thompson (Ed.), *Handbook of eating disorders and obesity* (pp. 3–16). New York: Wiley.

Bulik, C. M., Devlin, B., Bacanu, S. A., Thornton, L., Klump, K. L., Fichter, M. M., et al. (2003). Significant linkage on chromosome 10p in families with bulimia nervosa. *American Journal of Human Genetics, 72,* 200–207.

Bulik, C., Sullivan, P., Fear, J., & Joyce, P. (1997). Eating disorders and antecedent anxiety disorders: A controlled study. *Acta Psychiatrica Scandinavica, 96,* 101–107.

Bulik, C., Sullivan, P., Fear, J., & Pickering, A. (2000). Outcome of anorexia nervosa: Eating attitudes, personality, and parental bonding. *International Journal of Eating Disorders, 28,* 139–147.

Bulik, C., Sullivan, P., Fear, J., Pickering, A., & Dawn, A. (1999). Fertility and reproduction in women with anorexia nervosa: a controlled study. *Journal of Clinical Psychiatry, 2,* 130–135.

Bulik, C. M., Sullivan, P. F., Joyce, P. R., Carter, F. A., & McIntosh, V. V. (1998). Predictors of one-year treatment outcome in bulimia nervosa. *Comprehensive Psychiatry, 39,* 206–214.

Bulik, C. M., Sullivan, P. F., & Kendler, K. S. (1998). Heritability of binge-eating and broadly defined bulimia nervosa. *Biological Psychiatry, 44,* 1210–1218.

Bulik, C. M., Sullivan, P. F., McKee, M., Weltzin, T. E., & Kaye, W. H. (1994). Characteristics of bulimic women with and without alcohol abuse. *American Journal of Drug & Alcohol Abuse, 20,* 273–283.

Bulik, C., Sullivan, P., Weltzin, T., & Kaye, W. (1995). Temperament in eating disorders. *International Journal of Eating Disorders, 17,* 251–262.

Bulik, C., Tozzi, F., Anderson, C., Mazzeo, S., Aggen, S., & Sullivan, P. (2003). The relation between eating disorders and components of perfectionism. *American Journal of Psychiatry, 160,* 366–368.

Burton, E. M., Stice, E., Bearman, S. K., & Rohde, P. (under review). Evaluation of a brief depression prevention program: Results from a randomized efficacy trial.

Bushnell, J. A., Wells, J. E., Hornblow, A. R., Oakley-Browne, M. A., & Joyce, P. (1990). Prevalence of three bulimia syndromes in the general population. *Psychological Medicine, 20,* 671–680.

Cachelin, F. M., & Maher, B. A. (1998). Is amenorrhea a critical criterion for anorexia nervosa? *Journal of Psychosomatic Research, 44,* 435–440.

Cadogan, J., Eastell, R., Jones, N., & Barker, M. E. (1997). Milk intake and bone mineral acquisition in adolescent girls: Randomised, controlled intervention trial. *British Medical Journal, 315,* 1255–1260.

Casey, V. A., Dwyer, J. T., Coleman, K. A., & Valadian, I. (1992). Body mass index from childhood to middle age: A 50-year-follow-up. *American Journal of Clinical Nutrition, 56,* 14–18.

Cash, T., & Henry, P. (1995). Women's body images: The results of a national survey in the U.S.A. *Sex Roles, 33,* 19–28.

Casper, R. (1990). Personality features of women with good outcome from restricting anorexia nervosa. *Psychosomatic Medicine, 52,* 156–170.

Casper, R. C., Eckert, E. D., Halmi, K. A., Goldberg, S. C., & Davis, J. M. (1980). Bulimia: Its incidence and clinical importance in patients with anorexia nervosa. *Archives of General Psychiatry, 37,* 1030–1035.

Cattarin, J. A., & Thompson, J. K. (1994). A 3-year longitudinal study of body image, eating disturbance, and general psychological functioning in adolescent females. *Eating Disorders: Journal of Treatment and Prevention, 2,* 114–125.

Cattarin, J. A., Thompson, J. K., Thomas, C., & Williams, R. (2000). Body image, mood, and televised images of attractiveness: The role of social comparison. *Journal of Social and Clinical Psychology, 19,* 220–239.

Childress, A. C., Jarrell, M. P., & Brewerton, T. D. (1993). The Kids' Eating Disorders Survey (KEDS): Internal consistency, component analysis, and reliability. *Eating Disorders: Journal of Treatment and Prevention, 1,* 123–133.

Chumlea, W. C., Schubert, C. M., Roche, A. F., Kulin, H. E., Lee, P. A., Himes, J. H., et al. (2003). Age at menarche and racial comparisons in US girls. *Pediatrics, 111,* 110–113.

Clarke, G. N., Hornbrook, M. C., Lynch, F., Polen, M., Gale, J., Beardslee, W. R., et al. (2001). Offspring of depressed parents in a HMO: A randomized trial of a group cognitive intervention for preventing adolescent depressive disorder. *Archives of General Psychiatry, 58,* 1127–1134.

Cnattingius, S., Hultman, C., Dahl, M., & Sparen, P. (1999). Very preterm birth, birth trauma, and the risk of anorexia nervosa among girls. *Archives of General Psychiatry, 56,* 634–638.

Committee on Dietary Reference Intakes (2002). *Dietary reference intakes for energy, carbohydrate, fiber, fat, fatty acids, cholesterol, protein, and amino acids.* Washington, DC: National Academies Press.

Cooley, E., & Toray, T. (2001a). Body image and personality predictors of eating disorder symptoms during the college years. *International Journal of Eating Disorders, 30,* 28–36.

Cooley, E., & Toray, T. (2001b). Disordered eating in college freshman women: A prospective study. *Journal of American College Health, 49,* 229–235.

Cooper, P. J., Watkins, B., Bryant-Waugh, R., & Lask, B. (2002). The nosological status of early onset anorexia nervosa. *Psychological Medicine, 32,* 873–880.

Curry, J. F. (2001). Specific psychotherapies for childhood and adolescent depression. *Biological Psychiatry, 49,* 1091–1100.

Dalrymple, T. (August 13, 2003). A new pill for every ill. *Medical Letter on the FDA and CDC.*

Dancyger, I. F., & Garfinkel, P. E. (1995). The relationship of partial syndrome eating disorders to anorexia nervosa and bulimia nervosa. *Psychological Medicine, 25,* 1019–1025.

Dare, C., & Eisler, I. (2000). A multi-family group day treatment programme for adolescent eating disorder. *European Eating Disorders Review, 8,* 4–18.

Dare, C., & Eisler, I. (2002). Family therapy and eating disorders. In C. G. Fairburn & K. D. Brownell (Eds.), *Eating disorders and obesity: A comprehensive handbook.* (2nd ed., pp. 314–319). New York: Guilford Press.

Dare, C., Eisler, I., Russell, G., Treasure, J., & Dodge, L. (2001). Psychological therapies for adults with anorexia nervosa: Randomised controlled trial of out-patient treatments. *The British Journal of Psychiatry, 178,* 216–221.

Deep, A., Nagy, L., Weltzin, T., Rao, R., & Kaye, W. (1995). Premorbid onset of psychopathology in long-term recovered anorexia nervosa. *International Journal of Eating Disorders, 17,* 291–298.

Delgado, P. A., Charnedy, D. S., Price, L. H., Agha-janian, G. K., Landis, H., & Neninger, G. R. (1990). Serotonin function and the mechanism of antidepressant action: Reversal of antidepressant-induced remission by rapid depletion of plasma tryptophan. *Archives of General Psychiatry, 47,* 411–418.

Devlin, B., Bacanu, S., Klump, K., Bulik, C., Fichter, M., Halmi, K., et al. (2002). Linkage analysis of anorexia nervosa incorporating behavioral co-variates. *Human Molecular Genetics, 11,* 689–696.

DiPietro, L., Mossberg, H. O., & Stunkard, A. J. (1994). A 40-year history of overweight children in Stockholm: Life-time overweight, morbidity, and mortality. *International Journal of Obesity, 18,* 585–590.

Donovan, C. L., & Spence, S. H. (2001). Anxiety disorders in children. In N. Smelser & P. Baltes (Eds.), *International encyclopedia of the social and behavioral sciences* (pp. 570–576). Oxford: Elsevier Science Ltd.

Durlak, J. L., & Wells, A. M. (1997). Primary prevention mental health programs for children and adolescents: A meta-analytic review. *American Journal of Community Psychology, 25,* 115–152.

Eckert, E. D., Halmi, K. A., Marchi, P., Grove, W., & Crosby, R. (1995). Ten-year follow-up of anorexia nervosa: Clinical course and outcome. *Psychological Medicine, 25,* 143–156.

Eddy, K. T., Keel, P. K., Dorer, D. J., Delinsky, S. S., Franko, D. L., & Herzog, D. B. (2002). Longitudinal comparison of anorexia nervosa subtypes. *International Journal of Eating Disorders, 31,* 191–201.

Eisler I., Dare C., Hodes M., Russell, G., Dodge, E., & LeGrange, D. (2000). Family therapy for adolescent anorexia nervosa: The results of a controlled comparison of two family interventions. *Journal of Child Psychology and Psychiatry, 41,* 727–736.

Eisler, I., Dare, C., Russell, G.F.M., Szmukler, G. I., LeGrange, D., & Dodge, E. (1997). Family and individual therapy in anorexia nervosa: A 5-year follow-up. *Archives of General Psychiatry, 54,* 1025–1030.

Eliot, A. O., & Baker, C. W. (2001). Eating disordered adolescent males. *Adolescence, 36,* 535–543.

Emerson, E. (2003). Prevalence of psychiatric disorders in children and adolescents with and without intellectual disability. *Journal of Intellectual Disability Research, 47,* 51–58.

Engelsen, B. K. (1999). Multidimensionality in adolescent eating problems: A two-phase measurement study. *Eating and Weight Disorders, 4,* 63–75.

Enzmann, D. R., & Lane, B. (1977). Cranial computed tomography findings in anorexia nervosa. *Journal of Computer Assisted Tomography, 1,* 410–414.

Epstein, L. H., Myers, M. D., Raynor, H. A., & Saelens, B. E. (1998). Treatment of pediatric obesity. *Pediatrics, 101,* 554–547.

Epstein, L. H., Paluch, R. A., Saelens, B. E., Ernst, M. M., & Wilfley, D. E. (2001). Changes in eating disorder symptoms with pediatric obesity treatment. *Journal of Pediatrics, 139,* 58–65.

Epstein, L. H., & Squires, S. (1988). *The stop-light diet for children.* Boston: Little, Brown.

Epstein, L. H., Valoski, A. M., Vara, L. S., McCurley, J., Wisniewski, L., Kalarchian, M. A., et al. (1995). Effects of decreasing sedentary behavior and increasing activity on weight change in obese children. *Health Psychology, 14,* 109–115.

Epstein, L. H., Valoski, A., Wing, R. R., & McCurley, J. (1994). Ten–year outcomes of behavioral family-based treatment for childhood obesity. *Health Psychology, 13,* 373–383.

Fairburn, C. G. (1997a). Eating disorders. In D. M. Clark & C. G. Fairburn (Eds.), *The science and practice of cognitive behaviour therapy* (pp. 209–242). Oxford: Oxford University Press.

Fairburn, C. G. (1997b). Interpersonal psychotherapy for bulimia nervosa. In D. M. Garner & P. E. Garfinkel (Eds.), *Handbook of treatment for eating disorders,* (pp. 278–294). New York: Guilford Press.

Fairburn, C. G., & Beglin, S. A. (1990). Studies of the epidemiology of bulimia nervosa. *American Journal of Psychiatry, 147,* 401–408.

Fairburn, C. G., & Cooper, Z. (1993). The eating disorder examination (12th ed.). In C. G. Fairburn & G. T. Wilson (Eds.), *Binge eating: Nature, assessment, and treatment* (pp. 317–360). New York: Guilford Press.

Fairburn, C. G., Cooper, Z., Doll, H. A., Norman, P., & O'Connor, M. (2000). The natural course of bulimia nervosa and binge eating disorder in young women. *Archives of General Psychiatry, 57,* 659–665.

Fairburn, C. G., Cooper, Z., Doll, H. A., & Welch, S. L. (1999). Risk factors for anorexia nervosa: Three integrated case-control comparisons. *Archives of General Psychiatry, 56,* 468–476.

Fairburn, C. G., Cooper, Z., & Shafran, R. (2003). Cognitive behaviour therapy for eating disorders: A "transdiagnostic" theory and treatment. *Behaviour Research and Therapy, 41,* 509–528.

Fairburn, C. G., & Harrison, P. J. (2003). Eating disorders. *Lancet, 361,* 407–416.

Fairburn, C. G., Marcus, M. D., & Wilson, G. T. (1993). Cognitive-behavioral therapy for binge eating and bulimia nervosa: A comprehensive treatment manual. In C. G. Fairburn & G. T. Wilson (Eds.), *Binge eating: Nature, assessment, and treatment* (pp. 361–404). New York: Guilford Press.

Fairburn, C. G., Norman, P. A., Welch, S. L., O'Connor, M. E., Doll, H. A., & Peveler, R. C. (1995). A prospective study of outcome in bulimia nervosa and the long-term effects of three psychological treatments. *Archives of General Psychiatry, 52,* 304–312.

Fairburn, C. G., Shafran, R., & Cooper, Z. (1999). A cognitive behavioural theory of anorexia nervosa. *Behaviour Research and Therapy, 37,* 1–13.

Fairburn, C. G., Stice, E., Cooper, Z., Doll, H. A., Norman, P. A., & O'Connor, M. E. (2003). Understanding persistence in bulimia nervosa: a 5-year naturalistic study. *Journal of Consulting and Clinical Psychology, 71,* 103–109.

Fairburn, C. G., Welch, S. L., Doll, H. A., Davies, B. A., & O'Connor, M. E. (1997). Risk factors for bulimia nervosa: A community-based case-control study. *Archives of General Psychiatry, 54,* 509–517.

Faris, P. L., Kim, S. W., Meller, W. H., Goodale, R. L., Oakman, S. A., Hofbauer, R. D., et al. (2000). Effect of decreasing afferent vagal activity with ondansetron on symptoms of bulimia nervosa: A randomised, double-blind trial. *Lancet, 355,* 792–797.

Faulkner, R. A., Bailey, D. A., Drinkwater, D. T., McKay, H. A., Arnold, C., & Wilkinson, A. A. (1996). Bone densitometry in Canadian children 8–17 years of age. *Calcified Tissue International, 59,* 344–351.

Fava, M., Herzog, D. B., Hamburg, P., Reiss, H., Anfang, S., & Rosenbaum, J. F. (1990). Long-term use of fluoxetine in bulimia nervosa: A retrospective study. *Annals of Clinical Psychiatry, 2,* 53–56.

Feehan, M., McGee, R., Raja, S. N., & Williams, S. M. (1994). DSM-III-R disorders in New Zealand 18-year-olds. *Australian & New Zealand Journal of Psychiatry, 28,* 87–99.

Feehan, M., McGee, R., & Williams, S. M. (1993). Mental health disorders from age 15 to age 18 years. *Journal of the American Academy of Child and Adolescent Psychiatry, 32,* 1118–1126.

Fichter, M. M., Kruger, R., Rief, W., Holland, R., & Dohne, J. (1996). Fluvoxamine in prevention of relapse in bulimia nervosa: Effects on eating-specific psychopathology. *Journal of Clinical Psychopharmacology, 16,* 9–18.

Fichter, M., & Quadflieg, N. (1997). Six-year course of bulimia nervosa. *International Journal of Eating Disorders, 22,* 361–384.

Fichter, M. M., Weyerer, S., Sourdi, L., & Sourdi, Z. (1983). The epidemiology of anorexia nervosa: A comparison of Greek adolescents living in Germany and Greek adolescents living in Greece. In P. L. Darby, P. E. Garfinkel, D. M. Garner, & D. V. Coscina (Eds.), *Anorexia nervosa: Recent developments in research* (pp. 95–101). New York: Alan R. Liss.

Field, A. E., Camargo, C. A., Taylor, C. B., Berkey, C. S., & Colditz, G. A. (1999). Relation of peer and media influences to the development of purging behaviors among preadolescent and adolescent girls. *Archives of Pediatric Adolescent Medicine, 153,* 1184–1189.

Field, A. E., Camargo, C. A., Taylor, C. B., Berkey, C. S., Roberts, S. B., & Colditz, G. A. (2001). Peer, parent, and media influences on the development of weight concerns and frequent dieting among preadolescent and adolescent girls and boys. *Pediatrics, 107,* 54–60.

Fisher, M., Golden, N. H., Katzman, D. K., Kreipe, R. E., Rees, J., Schebendach, J., et al. (1995). Eating disorders in adolescents: A background paper. *Journal of Adolescent Health, 16,* 420–437.

Fisher, M., Schneider, M., Burns, J., Symons, H., & Mandel, F. S. (2001). Differences between adolescents and young adults at presentation to an eating disorders program. *Journal of Adolescent Health, 28,* 222–227.

Foster, G. D., Wadden, T. A., Kendall, P. C., Stunkard, A. J., & Vogt, R. A. (1996). Psychological effects of weight loss and regain: A prospective evaluation. *Journal of Consulting and Clinical Psychology, 64,* 752–757.

Franko, D. L. (1998). Secondary prevention of eating disorders in college women at risk. *Eating Disorders: The Journal of Treatment & Prevention, 6,* 29–40.

Franko, D., Blais, M., Becker, A., Delinsky, S., Greenwood, D., Flores, A., et al. (2001). Pregnancy complications and neonatal outcomes in women with eating disorders. *American Journal of Psychiatry, 158,* 1461–1466.

Franko, D. L., & Walton, B. E. (1993). Pregnancy and eating disorders: A review and clinical implications. *International Journal of Eating Disorders, 13,* 41–48.

French, S. A., Perry, C. L., Leon, G. R., & Fulkerson, J. A. (1994). Food preferences, eating patterns, and physical activity among adolescents: Correlates of eating disorders symptoms. *Journal of Adolescent Health, 15,* 286–294.

French, S., Story, M., Downes, B., Resnick, M., & Blum, R. (1995). Frequent dieting among adolescents: Psychosocial and health behavior correlates. *American Journal of Public Health, 85,* 695–701.

Frost, L. A., Moffitt, T. E., & McGee, R. (1989). Neuropsychological correlates of psychopathology in an unselected cohort of young adolescents. *Journal of Abnormal Psychology, 98,* 307–313.

Furman, K., & Thompson, J. K. (2002). Body image, teasing, and mood alterations: An experimental study of exposure to negative verbal commentary. *International Journal of Eating Disorders, 32,* 449–457.

Galetta, F., Franzoni, F., Cupisti, A., Belliti, D., Prattichizzo, F., & Rolla, M. (2002). QT interval dispersion in young women with anorexia nervosa. *Journal of Pediatrics, 140,* 456–460.

Garfinkel, P. E., Lin, E., Goering, P., Spegg, C., Goldbloom, D. S., Kennedy, S., et al. (1995). Bulimia nervosa in a Canadian community sample: Prevalence and comparison of subgroups. *American Journal of Psychiatry, 152,* 1052–1058.

Garfinkel, P. E., Lin, E., Goering, P., Spegg, C., Goldbloom, D., Kennedy, S., et al. (1996). Should amenorrhea be necessary for the diagnosis of anorexia nervosa? *British Journal of Psychiatry, 168,* 500–506.

Garfinkel, P. E., Moldofsky, H., & Garner, D. (1980). The heterogeneity of anorexia nervosa: Bulimia as a distinct group. *Archives of General Psychiatry, 37,* 1036–1040.

Garn, S. M., Sullivan, T. V., & Hawthorne, V. M. (1989). Fatness and obesity of the parents of obese individuals. *American Journal of Clinical Nutrition, 50,* 1308–1313.

Garner, D. M., & Garfinkel, P. E. (1979). The Eating Attitudes Test: An index of the symptoms of anorexia nervosa. *Psychological Medicine, 9,* 273–279.

Garner, D., & Garfinkel, P. (1980). Socio-cultural factors in the development of anorexia nervosa. *Psychological Medicine, 10,* 647–656.

Garner, D. M., & Garfinkel, P. E. (Eds.). (1997). *Handbook of treatment for eating disorders.* New York: Guilford Press.

Garner, D. M., & Needleman, L. D. (1997). Sequencing and integration of treatments. In D. M. Garner & P. E. Garfinkel (Eds.), *Handbook of treatment for eating disorders* (2nd ed., pp. 50–66). New York: Guilford Press.

Garner, D. M., Vitousek, K., & Pike, K. M. (1997). Cognitive behavioral therapy for anorexia nervosa. In D. M. Garner & P. E. Garfinkel (Eds.), *Handbook of treatment for eating disorders* (2nd ed., pp. 94–144). New York: Guilford Press.

Garner, D. M., & Wooley, S. C. (1991). Confronting the failure of behavioral and dietary treatments for obesity. *Clinical Psychology Review, 11,* 729–780.

Gaskill, J. A., Treat, T. A., McCabe, E. B., & Marcus, M. D. (2001, May). *Does olanzapine affect the rate of weight gain among inpatients with eating disorders?* Paper presented at the International Conference on Eating Disorders, Vancouver, BC.

Geist, R., Heinmaa, M., Stephens, D., Davis, R., & Katzman, D. K. (2000). Comparison of family therapy and family group psychoeducation in adolescents with anorexia nervosa. *Canadian Journal of Psychiatry, 45,* 173–178.

Geller, B., Reising, D., Leonard, H. L., Riddle, M. A., & Walsh, B. T. (1999). Critical review of tricyclic antidepressant use in children and adolescents. *Journal of the American Academy of Child and Adolescent Psychiatry, 38,* 513–516.

Gershon, E., Schreiber, J., Hamovit, J., Dibble, E., Kaye, W., Nurnberger, J., et al. (1983). Anorexia nervosa and major affective disorders associated in families: A preliminary report. In S. B. Guze, F. J. Earls, & J. E. Barrett (Eds.), *Childhood psychopathology and development* (pp. 279–284). New York: Raven Press.

Gershon, E., Schreiber, J., Hamovit, J., Dibble, E., Kaye, W., Nurnberger, J., et al. (1984). Clinical findings in patients with anorexia nervosa and affective illness in their relatives. *American Journal of Psychiatry, 141,* 1419–1422.

Glaser, N. S. (1997). Non–insulin-dependent diabetes mellitus in childhood and adolescence. *Pediatric Clinics of North America, 44,* 307–337.

Glastre, C., Braillon, P., David, L., Cochat, P., Meunier, P. J., & Delmas, P. D. (1990). Measurement of bone mineral content of the lumbar spine by dual energy x-ray absorptiometry in normal children: correlations with growth parameters. *Journal of Clinical Endocrinology and Metabolism, 70,* 1330–1333.

Godart, N. T., Flament, M. F., Perdereau, F., & Jeammet, P. (2002). Comorbidity between eating disorders and anxiety disorders: A review. *International Journal of Eating Disorders, 32,* 253–270.

Goebel, G., Schweiger, U., Kruger, R., & Fichter, M. M. (1999). Predictors of bone mineral density in patients with eating disorders. *International Journal of Eating Disorders, 25,* 143–150.

Golan, M., Weizman, A., Apterm, A., & Fainaru, M. (1998). Parents as exclusive agents of change in the treatment of childhood obesity. *American Journal of Clinical Nutrition, 67,* 1130–1135.

Golden, N. H. (2003). Osteopenia and osteoporosis in anorexia nervosa. *Adolescent Medicine, 14,* 97–108.

Golden, N. H., Ashtari, M., Kohn, M. R., Patel, M., Jacobson, M. S., Fletcher, A., et al. (1996). Reversibility of cerebral ventricular enlargement in anorexia nervosa, demonstrated by quantitative magnetic resonance imaging. *Journal of Pediatrics, 128,* 296–301.

Golden, N. H., Jacobson, M. S., Schebendach, J., Solanto, M. V., Hertz, S. M., & Shenker, I. R. (1997). Resumption of menses in anorexia nervosa. *Archives of Pediatrics and Adolescent Medicine, 151,* 16–21.

Golden, N. H., Katzman, D. K., Kreipe, R. E., Stevens, S. L., Sawyer, S. M., Rees, J., et al. (2003). Eating disorders in adolescents: A position paper of the Society for Adolescent Medicine. *Journal of Adolescent Health, 33,* 496–503.

Golden, N. H., Lanzkowsky, L., Schebendach, J., Palestro, C. J., Jacobson, M. S., & Shenker, I. R. (2002). The effect of estrogen-progestin treatment on bone mineral density in anorexia nervosa. *Journal of Pediatric and Adolescent Gynecology, 15,* 135–143.

Golden, N. H., & Shenker, I. R. (1992). Amenorrhea in anorexia nervosa: Etiology and implications. In M. P. Nussbaum & J. T. Dwer (Eds.), *Adolescent nutrition and eating disorders* (3rd ed., pp. 503–518). Philadelphia: Hanley & Belfus Inc.

Goldfield, G. S., & Epstein, L. H. (2002). Management of obesity in children. In C. G. Fairburn & K. D. Brownell (Eds.), *Eating disorders and obesity: A comprehensive handbook* (2nd ed., pp. 573–577). New York: Guilford Press.

Goldfield, G. S., Raynor, H. A., & Eptein, L. H. (2002). Treatment of pediatric obesity. In T. A. Wadden & A. J. Stunkard (Eds.), *Handbook of obesity treatment* (pp. 532–555). New York: Guilford Press.

Goldsmith, S. J., Anger-Friedfeld, K., Beren, S., Rudolph, D., Boeck, M., & Aronne, L. (1992). Psychiatric illness in patients presenting for obesity treatment. *International Journal of Eating Disorders, 12,* 63–71.

Goodrick, G. K., Poston, W. S., Kimball, K. T., Reeves, R. S., & Foreyt, J. P. (1998). Nondieting versus dieting treatments for overweight binge-eating women. *Journal of Consulting and Clinical Psychology, 66,* 363–368.

Gordon, C. M., Goodman, E., Emans, S. J., Grace, E., Becker, K. A., Rosen, C. J., et al. (2002). Physiologic regulators of bone turnover in young women with anorexia nervosa. *Journal of Pediatrics, 141,* 64–70.

Gordon, C. M., Grace, E., Emans, S. J., Feldman, H. A., Goodman, E., Becker, K. A., et al. (2002). Effects of oral dehydroepiandrosterone on bone density in young women with anorexia nervosa: A randomized trial. *Journal of Clinical Endocrinology and Metabolism, 87,* 4935–4941.

Gordon, C. M., Grace, E., Emans, S. J., Goodman, E., Crawford, M. H., & LeBoff, M. S. (1999). Changes in bone turnover markers and menstrual function after short-term oral DHEA in young women with anorexia nervosa. *Journal of Bone and Mineral Research, 14,* 136–145.

Gordon, I., Lask, B., Bryant-Waugh, R., Christie, D., & Timimi, S. (1997). Childhood-onset anorexia nervosa: Towards identifying a biological substrate. *International Journal of Eating Disorders, 22,* 159–165.

Götestam, K., & Agras, W. (1995). General population-based epidemiology study of eating disorders in Norway. *International Journal of Eating Disorders, 18,* 119–126.

Gowers, S., & Shore, A. (2001). Development of weight and shape concerns in the etiology of eating disorders. *British Journal of Psychiatry, 179,* 236–242.

Graber, J., Brooks-Gunn, J., Paikoff, R., & Warren, M. (1994). Prediction of eating problems: An 8-year study of adolescent girls. *Developmental Psychology, 30,* 823–834.

Graber, J. A., Tyrka, A. R., & Brooks-Gunn, J. (2003). How similar are correlates of different subclinical eating problems and bulimia nervosa? *Journal of Child Psychology and Psychiatry, 44,* 262–273.

Grace, P. S., Jacobson, R. S., & Fullager, C. J. (1985). A pilot comparison of purging and non-purging bulimics. *Journal of Clinical Psychology, 41,* 173–180.

Grice, D. E., Halmi, K. A., Fichter, M. M., Strober, M., Woodside, D. B., Treasure, J. T., et al. (2002). Evidence for a susceptibility gene for anorexia nervosa on chromosome 1. *American Journal of Human Genetics, 70,* 787–792.

Grinspoon, S., Baum, H., Lee, K., Anderson, E., Herzog, D., & Klibanski, A. (1996). Effects of short-term recombinant human insulin-like growth factor I administration on bone turnover in osteopenic women with anorexia nervosa. *Journal of Clinical Endocrinology and Metabolism, 81,* 3864–3870.

Grinspoon, S., Miller, K., Coyle, C., Krempin, J., Armstrong, C., Pitts, S., et al. (1999). Severity of osteopenia in estrogen-deficient women with anorexia nervosa and hypothalamic amenorrhea. *Journal of Clinical Endocrinology and Metabolism, 84,* 2049–2055.

Grinspoon, S., Thomas, L., Miller, K., Herzog, D., & Klibanski, A. (2002). Effects of recombinant human IGF-I and oral contraceptive administration on bone density in anorexia nervosa. *Journal of Clinical Endocrinology and Metabolism, 87,* 2883–2891.

Grinspoon, S., Thomas, E., Pitts, S., Gross, E., Mickley, D., Miller, D., et al. (2000). Prevalence and predictive factors for regional osteopenia in women with anorexia nervosa. *Annals of Internal Medicine 133,* 790–794.

Groesz, L. M., Levine, M. P., & Murnen, S. K. (2002). The effects of experimental presentation of thin media images on body satisfaction: A meta-analytic review. *International Journal of Eating Disorders, 31,* 1–16.

Gross, H. A., Ebert, M. H., Faden, C. B., Goldberg, S. C., Nee, L. E., & Kaye, W. H. (1981). A double-blind controlled trial of lithium carbonate in primary anorexia nervosa. *Journal of Clinical Psychopharmacology, 1,* 376–381.

Grunbaum, J. A., Kann, L., Kinchen, S. A., Williams, B., Ross, J. G., Lowry, R., et al. (2002). Youth risk behavior surveillance: United States, 2001. *Journal of School Health, 72,* 313–328.

Gual, P., Pérez-Gaspar, M., Martínez-González, M. A., Lahortiga, F., de Irala-Estévez, J., Cervera-Enguix, S. (2002). Self-esteem, personality and eating disorders: Baseline assessment of a prospective population-based cohort. *International Journal of Eating Disorders, 31,* 261–273.

Halmi, K. A. (2002). Eating disorders. In A. Martin, L. Scahill, D. S. Charney, & J. F. Leckman (Eds.), *Pediatric psychopharmacology* (pp. 592–602). Oxford: Oxford University Press.

Halmi, K. A., Agras, W. S., Mitchell, J., Wilson, G. T., Crow, S., Bryson, S. W., et al. (2002). Relapse predictors of patients with bulimia nervosa who achieved abstinence through cognitive behavioral therapy. *Archives of General Psychiatry, 59,* 1105–1109.

Halmi, K. A., Casper, R. C., Eckert, E. D., Goldberg, S. C., & Davis, J. M. (1979). Unique features associated with age of onset of anorexia nervosa. *Psychiatry Research, 1,* 209–215.

Halmi, K. A., Eckert, E., LaDu, T. J., & Cohen, J. (1986). Anorexia nervosa: Treatment efficacy of cyproheptadine and amitriptyline. *Archives of General Psychiatry, 43,* 177–181.

Halmi, K. A., Eckert, E., Marchi, P., Sampugnaro, V., Apple, R., & Cohen, J. (1991). Comorbidity of psychiatric diagnoses in anorexia nervosa. *Archives of General Psychiatry, 48,* 712–718.

Halmi, K. A., Struss, A., & Goldberg, S. C. (1978). An investigation of weights in the parents of anorexia nervosa patients. *Journal of Nervous and Mental Disease, 166,* 358–361.

Hansen, L. (1999). Olanzapine in the treatment of anorexia nervosa. *British Journal of Psychiatry, 175,* 592.

Harris, G. (2003, August 7). Debate resumes on the safety of depression's wonder drugs. *The New York Times,* p. A1.

Hartman, D., Crisp, A., Rooney, B., Rackow, C., Atkinson, R., & Patel, S. (2000). Bone density of women who have recovered from anorexia nervosa. *International Journal of Eating Disorders, 28,* 107–112.

Hawkins, R., & Clement, P. (1984). Binge-eating: Measurement problems and a conceptual model. In R. Hawkins, W. Fremouw, & P. Clement (Eds.), *The binge–purge syndrome: Diagnosis, treatment and research* (pp. 229–251). New York: Springer-Verlag.

Hay, P. J., & Bacaltchuk, J. (2000). Psychotherapy for bulimia nervosa and binging (Cochrane Review). In *The Cochrane Library,* Issue 4, 2000. Oxford: Update Software.

Hayward, C., Killen, J. D., Wilson, D., Hammer, L. D., Litt, I., Kraemer, H. C., et al., (1997). Psychiatric risk associated with early puberty in adolescent girls. *Journal of the American Academy of Child and Adolescent Psychiatry, 36,* 255–262.

Hazell, P., O'Connell, D., Heathcote, D., Robertson, J., & Henry, D. (1995). Efficacy of tricyclic drugs in treatment of child and adolescent depression: A meta-analysis. *British Medical Journal, 310,* 897–901.

Heebink, D., Sunday, S., & Halmi, K. A. (1995). Anorexia nervosa and bulimia nervosa in adolescence: Effects of age and menstrual status on psychological variables. *Journal of the American Academy of Child and Adolescent Psychiatry, 34,* 378–382.

Heesacker, R., & Neimeyer, G. (1990). Assessing object relations and social cognitive correlates of eating disorders. *Journal of Counseling Psychology, 37*, 419–426.

Henderson, N. K., Price, R. I., Cole, J. H., Gutteridge, D. H., & Bhagat, C. I. (1995). Bone density in young women is associated with body weight and muscle strength but not dietary intakes. *Journal of Bone and Mineral Research, 10*, 384–393.

Herpertz-Dahlmann, B., Muller, B., Herpertz, S., Heussen, N., Hebebrand, J., & Remschmidt, H. (2001). Prospective 10-year follow-up in adolescent anorexia nervosa: Course, outcome, psychiatric comorbidity, and psychosocial adaptation. *Journal of Child Psychology and Psychiatry and Allied Disciplines, 42*, 603–162.

Herzog, D. B., Dorer, D. J., Keel, P. K., Selwyn, S. E., Ekeblad, E. R., Flores, A. T., et al. (1999). Recovery and relapse in anorexia and bulimia nervosa: A 7.5-year follow-up study. *Journal of the American Academy of Child and Adolescent Psychiatry, 38*, 829–837.

Herzog, D. B., Keller, M. B., Lavori, P. W., Kenny, G. M., & Sacks, N. R. (1992). The prevalence of personality disorders in 210 women with eating disorders. *Journal of Clinical Psychiatry, 53*, 147–152.

Herzog, D. B., Keller, M. B., Sacks, N. R., Yeh, C. J., & Lavori, P. W. (1992). Psychiatric comorbidity in treatment-seeking anorexics and bulimics. *Journal of the American Academy of Child and Adolescent Psychiatry, 31*, 810–818.

Herzog, D. B., Nussbaum, K. M., & Marmor, A. K. (1996). Comorbidity and outcome in eating disorders. *Psychiatric Clinics of North America, 19*, 843–859.

Herzog, D. B., Staley, J. E., Carmody, S., Robbins, W. M., & van der Kolk, B. A. (1993). Childhood sexual abuse in anorexia nervosa and bulimia nervosa. *Journal of the American Academy of Child and Adolescent Psychiatry, 32*, 962–966.

Hirschmann, J. R., & Munter, C. H. (1988). *Overcoming overeating: Living free in the world of food.* Reading, MA: Addison-Wesley.

Hoek, H. W. (1991). The incidence and prevalence of anorexia nervosa and bulimia nervosa in primary care. *Psychological Medicine, 21*, 455–460.

Hoek, H. W. (2002). Distribution of eating disorders. In C. G. Fairburn & K. D. Brownell (Eds.), *Eating disorders and obesity: A comprehensive handbook* (pp. 233–237). New York: Guilford Press.

Hoek, H., Bartelds, A., Bosveld, J., van der Graaf, Y., Limpens, V., Maiwald, M., et al. (1995). Impact of urbanization on detection rates of eating disorders. *American Journal of Psychiatry, 152*, 1272–1278.

Hoek, H., van Harten, P., van Hoeken, D., & Susser, E. (1998). Lack of relation between culture and anorexia nervosa—results of an incidence study on Curacao. *New England Journal of Medicine, 23*, 1231–1232.

Hoek, H. W., & van Hoeken, D. (2003). Review of the prevalence and incidence of eating disorders. *International Journal of Eating Disorders, 34*, 383–396.

Hoek, H. W., van Hoeken, D., & Katzman, M. A. (2003). Epidemiology and cultural aspects of eating disorders: A review. In M. Maj, K. Halmi, J. J. Lopez-Ibor, & N. Sartorius (Eds.), *Eating disorders* (pp. 75–104). Chichester, England: Wiley.

Hollon, S. D., Thase, M. E., & Markowitz, J. (2002). Treatment and prevention of depression. *Psychological Science in the Public Interest, 3*, 39–77.

Holmbeck, G. N., Colder, C., Shapera, W., Westhoven, V., Kenealy, L., & Updegrove, A. (2000). Working with adolescents: Guides from developmental psychology. In P. C. Kendall (Ed.), *Child and adolescent therapy. Cognitive-behavioral procedures* (2nd ed., pp. 334–385). New York: Guilford Press.

Horesh, N., Apter, A., Lepkifker, E., Ratzoni, G., Weizman, R., & Tyano, S. (1995). Life events and severe anorexia nervosa in adolescence. *Acta Psychiatrica Scandinavica, 91*, 5–9.

Hudson, J., Pope, H., Jonas, J., & Yurgelun-Todd, D. (1983). Phenomenologic relationship of eating disorders to major affective disorder. *Psychiatry Research, 9*, 345–354.

Hudson, J. I., Pope, H. G., Jonas, J. M., Yurgelun-Todd, D., & Frankenburg, F. R. (1987). A controlled family history study of bulimia. *Psychological Medicine, 17*, 883–890.

Hughes, P. L., Wells, L. A., & Cunningham, C. J. (1986). The dexamethasone suppression test in bulimia before and after successful treatment with desipramine. *Journal of Clinical Psychiatry, 47*, 515–517.

Huon, G. F., Mingyi, Q., Oliver, K., & Xiao, G. (2002). A large-scale survey of eating disorder symptomatology among female adolescents in the People's Republic of China. *International Journal of Eating Disorders, 32*, 192–205.

Inagaki, T., Horiguchi, J., Tsubouchi, K., Miyaoka, T., Uegaki, J., & Seno, H. (2002). Late onset anorexia nervosa: Two case reports. *International Journal of Psychiatry Medicine, 32*, 91–95.

Irving, L. M. (1990). Mirror images: Effects of the standard of beauty on the self- and body-esteem of women exhibiting varying levels of bulimic symptoms. *Journal of Social and Clinical Psychology, 9,* 230–242.

Isner, J. M., Roberts, W. C., Heymsfield, S. B., & Yager, J. (1985). Anorexia nervosa and sudden death. *Annals of Internal Medicine, 102,* 49–52.

Jackson, T. D., Grilo, C. M., & Masheb, R. M. (2000). Teasing history, onset of obesity, current eating disorder psychopathology, body dissatisfaction, and psychological functioning in binge eating disorder. *Obesity Research, 8,* 451–458.

Jensen, V. S., & Mejlhede, A. (2000). Anorexia nervosa: Treatment with olanzapine. *British Journal of Psychiatry, 177,* 87.

Johnson, G. L., Humphries, L. L., Shirley, P. B., Mazzoleni, A., & Noonan, J. A. (1986). Mitral valve prolapse in patients with anorexia nervosa and bulimia. *Archives of Internal Medicine, 146,* 1525–1529.

Johnson, J. G., Cohen, P., Kasen, S., & Brook, J. S. (2002). Eating disorders during adolescence and the risk for physical and mental disorders during early adulthood. *Archives of General Psychiatry, 59,* 545–552.

Johnson, J. G., Cohen, P., Kotler, L., Kasen, S., & Brook, J. S. (2002). Psychiatric disorders associated with risk for the development of eating disorders during adolescence and early adulthood. *Journal of Consulting and Clinical Psychology, 70,* 1119–1128.

Johnson, J. G., Harris, E. S., Spitzer, R., & Williams, J.B.W. (2002). The patient health questionnaire for adolescents. *Journal of Adolescent Health, 30,* 196–204.

Johnson-Sabine, E., Wood, K., Patton, G., Mann, A., & Wakeling, A. (1988). Abnormal eating attitudes in London schoolgirls: A prospective epidemiological study: Factors associated with abnormal response on screening questionnaires. *Psychological Medicine, 18,* 615–622.

Johnston, C. C., Jr., Miller, J. Z., Slemenda, C. W., Reister, T. K., Hui, S., Christian, J. C., et al. (1992). Calcium supplementation and increases in bone mineral density in children. *New England Journal of Medicine, 327,* 82–87.

Jones, D., Fox, M., Babigan, H., & Hutton, H. (1980). Epidemiology of anorexia nervosa in Monroe County, New York: 1960–76. *Psychosomatic Medicine, 42,* 551–558.

Kaminski, P. L., & McNamara, K. (1996). A treatment for college women at risk for bulimia: A controlled evaluation. *Journal of Counseling & Development, 74,* 288–294.

Karwautz, A., Rabe-Hesketh, S., Hu, X., Zhao, J., Sham, P., Collier, D. A., et al. (2001). Individual-specific risk factors for anorexia nervosa: A pilot study using a discordant sister-pair design. *Psychological Medicine, 31,* 317–329.

Kassett, J., Gershon, E., Maxwell, M., Guroff, J., Kazuba, D., Smith, A., et al. (1989). Psychiatric disorders in the first-degree relatives of probands with bulimia nervosa. *American Journal of Psychiatry, 146,* 1468–1471.

Kassett, J. A., Gwirtsman, H. E., Kaye, W. H., Brandt, H. A., & Jimerson, D. C. (1988). Pattern of onset of bulimic symptoms in anorexia nervosa. *American Journal of Psychiatry, 145,* 1287–1288.

Kater, K. J., Rohwer, J., & Levine, M. P. (2000). An elementary school project for developing healthy body image and reducing risk factors for unhealthy and disordered eating. *Eating Disorders: The Journal of Treatment and Prevention, 8,* 3–16.

Katz, J. L., Boyar, R., Roffwarg, H., Hellman, L., & Weiner, H. (1978). Weight and circadian lutenizing hormone secretory pattern in anorexia nervosa. *Psychosomatic Medicine, 40,* 549–567.

Katz, R. L., Keen, C. L., Litt, I. F., Hurley, L. S., Kellams-Harrison, K. M., & Glader, L. J. (1987). Zinc deficiency in anorexia nervosa. *Journal of Adolescent Health Care, 8,* 400–406.

Katzman, D. K., Bachrach, L. K., Carter, D. R., & Marcus, R. (1991). Clinical and anthropometric correlates of bone mineral acquisition in healthy adolescent girls. *Journal of Clinical Endocrinology and Metabolism, 73,* 1332–1339.

Katzman, D. K., Lambe, E. K., Mikulis, D. J., Ridgley, J. N., Goldbloom, D. S., & Zipursky, R. B. (1996). Cerebral gray matter and white matter volume deficits in adolescent girls with anorexia nervosa. *Journal of Pediatrics, 129,* 794–803.

Katzman, D. K., Zipursky, R. B., Lambe, E. K., & Mikulis, D. J. (1997). A longitudinal magnetic resonance imaging study of brain changes in adolescents with anorexia nervosa. *Archives of Pediatrics and Adolescent Medicine, 151,* 793–797.

Katzman, M., Nasser, M., & Gordon, R. (2001). *Eating disorders and cultures in transition.* London: Routledge Press.

Kaye, W., Frank, G., Meltzer, C., Price, J., Drevets, W., & Mathis, C. (submitted). Enhanced pre- and postsynaptic 5HT1A receptor binding after recovery from anorexia nervosa: Relationship to anxiety and harm avoidance.

Kaye, W. H., Gwirtsman, H. E., George, D. T., &

Ebert, M. H. (1991). Altered serotonin activity in anorexia nervosa after long-term weight restoration: Does elevated cerebrospinal fluid 5-hydroxyindoleacetic acid level correlate with rigid and obsessive behavior? *Archives of General Psychiatry, 48,* 556–562.

Kaye, W. H., Gwirtsman, H. E., George, D. T., Jimerson, D. C., & Ebert, M. H. (1988). CSF 5-HIAA concentrations in anorexia nervosa: Reduced values in underweight subjects normalize after weight gain. *Biological Psychiatry, 23,* 102–105.

Kaye, W. H., Nagata, T., Weltzin, T. E., Hsu, L.K.G., Sokol, M. S., McConaha, C., et al. (2001). Double-blind placebo-controlled administration of fluoxetine in restricting- and restricting-purging type anorexia nervosa. *Biological Psychiatry, 49,* 644–652.

Kaye, W., Weltzin, T., & Hsu, L. (1993). Relationship between anorexia nervosa and obsessive and compulsive behaviors. *Psychiatric Annals, 23,* 365–373.

Kazdin, A. E. (2003). Psychotherapy for children and adolescents. *Annual Review of Psychology, 54,* 253–276.

Kazdin, A. E., Bass, D., Ayers, W. A., & Rodgers, A. (1990). Empirical and clinical focus of child and adolescent psychotherapy research. *Journal of Consulting and Clinical Psychology, 58,* 729–740.

Keel, P. K., Dorer, D. J., Eddy, K. T., Franko, D., Charatan, D. L., & Herzog, D. B. (2003). Predictors of mortality in eating disorders. *Archives of General Psychiatry, 60,* 179–183.

Keel, P. K., & Mitchell, J. E. (1997). Outcome in bulimia nervosa. *American Journal of Psychiatry, 154,* 313–321.

Keel, P. K., Mitchell, J. E., Miller, K. B., Davis, T. L., & Crow, S. J. (1999). Long-term outcome of bulimia nervosa. *Archives of General Psychiatry, 56,* 63–69.

Kelton-Locke, S. (2001). Revisiting the question: Can helping hurt? *The California Therapist, 56–*58.

Kendall, P. C. (2000). *Child and adolescent therapy. Cognitive-behavioral procedures* (2nd ed.). New York: Guilford Press.

Kendall, P. C., Flannery-Schroeder, E., Panichelli-Mindel, S. M., Southam-Gerow, M., Henin, A., & Warman, M. (1997). Therapy for youths with anxiety disorders: A second randomized clinical trial. *Journal of Consulting and Clinical Psychology, 65,* 366–380.

Kendler, K. S., MacLean, C., Neale, M. C., Kessler, R. C., Heath, A. C., & Eaves, L. J. (1991). The genetic epidemiology of bulimia nervosa. *American Journal of Psychiatry, 148,* 1627–1637.

Kenny, M. E., & Hart, K. (1992). Relationship between parental attachment and eating disorders in an inpatient and a college sample. *Journal of Counseling Psychology, 39,* 521–526.

Keys, A., Brozek, K., Henschel, A., Mickelson, O., & Taylor, H. L. (1950). *The biology of human starvation.* Minneapolis: University of Minnesota Press.

Khan, K., Green, R., Saul, A., Bennell, K., Crichton, K., Hopper, J., et al. (1996). Retired elite female ballet dancers and nonathletic controls have similar bone mineral density at weightbearing sites. *Journal of Bone and Mineral Research, 11,* 1566–1574.

Killen, J. D., Taylor, C. B., Hammer, L. D., Litt, I, Wilson, D. M., Rich, T., et al. (1993). An attempt to modify unhealthful eating attitudes and weight regulation practices of young adolescent girls. *International Journal of Eating Disorders, 13,* 369–384.

Killen, J. D., Taylor, C. B., Hayward, C., Haydel, K. F., Wilson, D. M., Hammer, L., et al. (1996). Weight concerns influence the development of eating disorders: A 4-year prospective study. *Journal of Consulting and Clinical Psychology, 64,* 936–940.

Killen, J. D., Taylor, C. B., Hayward, C., Wilson, D., Haydel, K., Hammer, L., et al. (1994). Pursuit of thinness and onset of eating disorder symptoms in a community sample of adolescent girls: A three-year prospective analysis. *International Journal of Eating Disorders, 16,* 227–238.

Kingston, K., Szmukler, G., Andrewes, D., Tress, B., & Desmond, P. (1996). Neuropsychological and structural brain changes in anorexia nervosa before and after refeeding. *Psychological Medicine, 26,* 15–28.

Kinzl, J., Traweger, C., Guenther, V., & Biebl, W. (1994). Family background and sexual abuse associated with eating disorders. *American Journal of Psychiatry, 151,* 1127–1131.

Kleifield, E., Sunday, S., Hurt, S., & Halmi, K. (1994). The tridimensional personality questionnaire: An exploration of personality traits in eating disorders. *Journal of Psychiatric Research, 28,* 413–423.

Klem, M. L., Wing, R. R., Simkin-Silverman, L., & Kuller, L. H. (1997). The psychological consequences of weight gain prevention in healthy, premenopausal women. *International Journal of Eating Disorders, 21,* 167–174.

Klerman, G. L., Weissman, M. M., Rounsaville,

B. J., & Chevron, E. S. (1984). *Interpersonal psychotherapy of depression*. New York: Basic Books.

Klibanski, A., Biller, B.M.K., Schoenfeld, D. A., Herzog, D. B., & Saxe, V. C. (1995). The effects of estrogen administration on trabecular bone loss in young women with anorexia nervosa. *Journal of Clinical Endocrinology and Metabolism, 80,* 898–903.

Klump, K. L., Miller, K. B., Keel, P. K., McGue, M., & Iacono, W. G. (2001). Genetic and environmental influences on anorexia nervosa syndromes in a population-based twin sample. *Psychological Medicine, 31,* 737–740.

Klump, K., Ringham, R., Marcus, M., & Kaye, W. (2001). *A family history/family study approach to examining the nature of eating disorder risk in ballet dancers: Evidence for gene–environment combinations?* Paper presented at the Eating Disorder Research Society Annual Meeting, Albuquerque, NM.

Kohn, M. R., Golden, N. H., & Shenker, I. R. (1998). Cardiac arrest and delirium: presentations of the refeeding syndrome in severely malnourished adolescents with anorexia nervosa. *Journal of Adolescent Health, 22,* 239–243.

Kortegaard, L. S., Hoerder, K., Joergensen, J., Gillberg, C., & Kyvik, K. O. (2001). A preliminary population-based twin study of self-reported eating disorder. *Psychological Medicine, 31,* 361–365.

Kotler, L., Cohen, P., Davies, M., Pine, D., & Walsh, B. T. (2001). Longitudinal relationships between childhood, adolescent, and adult eating disorders. *Journal of the American Academy of Child and Adolescent Psychiatry, 40,* 1434–1440.

Kotler, L. A., Devlin, M. J., Davies, M., & Walsh, B. T. (2003). An open trial of fluoxetine for adolescents with bulimia nervosa. *Journal of Child and Adolescent Psychopharmacology, 13,* 329–335.

Kotler, L. A., & Walsh, B. T. (2000). Eating disorders in children and adolescents: Pharmacological therapies. *European Child and Adolescent Psychiatry, 9,* 108–116.

Kreipe, R. E., Golden, N. H., Katzman, D. K., Fisher, M., Rees, J., & Tonkin, R. S., et al. (1995). Eating disorders in adolescents: A position paper of the Society for Adolescent Medicine. *Journal of Adolescent Health, 16,* 476–480.

Lacey, J. H., & Crisp, A. H. (1980). Hunger, food intake and weight: The impact of clomipramine on a refeeding anorexia nervosa population. *Postgraduate Medical Journal, 56,* 79–85.

Lantzouni, E., Frank, G. R., Golden, N. H., & Shenker, R. I. (2002). Reversibility of growth stunting in early onset anorexia nervosa: A prospective study. *Journal of Adolescent Health, 31,* 162–165.

Lask, B., & Bryant-Waugh, R. (Eds.). (2000). *Anorexia nervosa and related eating disorders in childhood and adolescence* (2nd ed.). East Sussex, UK: Psychology Press.

Lask, B., Fosson, A., Rolfe, U., & Thomas, S. (1993). Zinc deficiency and childhood-onset anorexia nervosa. *Journal of Clinical Psychiatry, 54,* 63–66.

La Via, M. C., Gray, N., & Kaye, W. H. (2000). Case reports of olanzapine treatment of anorexia nervosa. *International Journal of Eating Disorders, 27,* 363–366.

Lay, B., Jennen-Steinmetz, C., Reinhard, I., & Schmidt, M. (2002). Characteristics of inpatient weight gain in adolescent anorexia nervosa: Relation to speed of relapse and re-admission. *European Eating Disorders Review, 10,* 22–40.

Le Grange, D., Eisler, I., Dare, C., & Russell, G.F.M. (1992). Evaluation of family treatments in adolescent anorexia nervosa—A pilot study. *International Journal of Eating Disorders, 12,* 347–357.

Le Grange, D., Lock, J., & Dymek, M. (2003). Family-based therapy for adolescents with bulimia nervosa. *American Journal of Psychotherapy, 57,* 237–251.

Leon, G., Fulkerson, J., Perry, C., & Cudeck, R. (1993). Personality and behavioral vulnerabilities associated with risk status for eating disorders in adolescent girls. *Journal of Abnormal Psychology, 102,* 438–444.

Levine, M. D., Ringham, R. M., Kalarchian, M. A., Wisniewski, L., & Marcus, M. D. (2001). Is family-based behavioral weight control appropriate for severe pediatric obesity? *International Journal of Eating Disorders, 30,* 318–328.

Levine, M. P., & Piran, N. (2001). The prevention of eating disorders: Towards a participatory ecology of knowledge, action, and advocacy. In R. Striegel-Moore & L. Smolak (Eds.), *Eating disorders: New directions for research and practice* (pp. 233–253). Washington, DC: American Psychological Association.

Lewinsohn, P. M., Hops, H., Roberts, R. E., Seeley, J. R., & Andrews, J. A. (1993). Adolescent psychopathology: I. Prevalence and incidence of depression and other DSM-III-R disorders in high school students. *Journal of Abnormal Psychology, 102,* 133–144.

Lewinsohn, P. M., Roberts, R. E., Seeley, J. R., Rohde, P., Gotlib, I. H., & Hops, H. (1994). Adolescent psychopathology: II. Psychosocial risk factors for depression. *Journal of Abnormal Psychology, 103,* 302–315.

Lewinsohn, P. M., Striegel-Moore, R. H., & Seeley, J. P. (2000). Epidemiology and natural course of eating disorders in young women from adolescence to young adulthood. *Journal of the American Academy of Child and Adolescent Psychiatry, 39,* 1284–1292.

Lilenfeld, L., Kaye, W., Greeno, C., Merikangas, K., Plotnikov, K., Pollice, C., et al. (1998). A controlled family study of restricting anorexia and bulimia nervosa: Comorbidity in probands and disorders in first-degree relatives. *Archives of General Psychiatry, 55,* 603–610.

Lilenfeld, L., Kaye, W., & Strober, M. (1997). Genetics and family studies of anorexia nervosa and bulimia nervosa. *Balliere's Clinical Psychiatry, 3,* 177–197.

Lloyd, T., Andon, M. B., Rollings, N., Martel, J. K., Landis, J. R., Demers, L. M., et al. (1993). Calcium supplementation and bone mineral density in adolescent girls. *Journal of the American Medical Association, 270,* 841–844.

Lock, J., Le Grange, D., Agras, W. S., & Dare, C. (2001). *Treatment manual for anorexia nervosa: A family-based approach.* New York: Guilford Press.

Logue, C. M., Crowe, R. R., & Bean, J. A. (1989). A family study of anorexia nervosa and bulimia. *Comprehensive Psychiatry, 30,* 179–188.

Löwe, B., Zipfel, S., Buchholz, C., Dupont, Y., Reas, D. L., & Herzog, W. (2001). Long-term outcome of anorexia nervosa in a prospective 21-year follow-up study. *Psychological Medicine, 31,* 881–890.

Lowe, M. R. (1993). The effects of dieting on eating behavior: A three factor model. *Psychological Bulletin, 114,* 100–121.

Lowry, R., Galuska, D. A., Galuska, D. A., Fulton, J. E., Wechsler, H., & Kann, L. (2002). Weight management goals and practices among U.S. high school students: Associations with physical activity, diet, and smoking. *Journal of Adolescent Health, 31,* 133–144.

Lucas, A. R., Beard, C. M., O'Fallon, W. M., & Kurland, L. T. (1988). Anorexia nervosa in Rochester, Minnesota: A 45-year study. *Mayo Clinic Proceedings, 63,* 433–442.

Lucas, A. R., Beard, C. M., O'Fallon, W. M., & Kurland, L. T. (1991). 50-year trends in the incidence of anorexia nervosa in Rochester, Minn.: A population-based study. *American Journal of Psychiatry, 148,* 917–922.

Luce, K. H., Osborne, M. I., Winzelberg, A. J., Abascal, L. B., Celio, A., Wilfley, D., et al. (submitted). Acceptance of internet weight and body image intervention recommendations: Application of algorithm-driven internet-delivered programs.

Mann, T., Nolen-Hoeksema, S., Huang, K., Burgard, D., Wright, A., & Hanson, K. (1997). Are two interventions worse than none? Joint primary and secondary prevention of eating disorders in college females. *Health Psychology, 16,* 1–11.

Marchi, M., & Cohen, P. (1990). Early childhood eating behaviors and adolescent eating disorders. *Journal of the American Academy of Child and Adolescent Psychiatry, 29,* 112–117.

Marino, D. D., & King, J. C. (1980). Nutritional concerns during adolescence. *Pediatric Clinics of North America, 27,* 125–139.

Marlatt, G. A., & Gordon, J. R. (1985). *Relapse prevention: Maintenance strategies in the treatment of addictive behaviors.* New York: Guilford Press.

McElroy, S. L., Arnold, L. M., Shapira, N. A., Keck, P. E. Jr., Rosenthal, N. R., Karim, M. R., et al. (2003). Topiramate in the treatment of binge eating disorder associated with obesity: A randomized, placebo-controlled trial. *American Journal of Psychiatry, 160,* 255–261.

McGee, R., Feehan, M., Williams, S., Partridge, F., Silva, P. A., & Kelly, J. (1990). DSM-III disorders in a large sample of adolescents. *Journal of the American Academy of Child and Adolescent Psychiatry, 29,* 611–619.

McIntosh, V. V., Jordan, J., Carter, F. A., Luty, S. E., McKenzie, J. M., Bulik, C. M., et al. (2002, April). *Three psychotherapies for anorexia nervosa: A controlled trial.* Paper presented at the International Conference on Eating Disorders, Boston, MA.

McKay, H. A., Petit, M. A., Schutz, R. W., Prior, J. C., Barr, S. I., & Khan, K. M. (2000). Augmented trochanteric bone mineral density after modified physical education classes: A randomized school-based exercise intervention study in prepubescent and early pubescent children. *Journal of Pediatrics, 136,* 156–162.

McKnight Investigators. (2003). Risk factors for the onset of eating disorders in adolescent girls: Results of the McKnight longitudinal risk factor study. *American Journal of Psychiatry, 160,* 248–254.

McVey, G., & Davis, R. (2002). A program to promote positive body image: A 1-year follow-up evaluation. *Journal of Early Adolescence, 22,* 96–108.

Mecklenberg, R. S., Loriaux, D. L., Thompson, R. L., Andersen, A. E., & Lipsett, M. B. (1976). Hypothalamic dysfunction in patients with anorexia nervosa. *Medicine, 53,* 147–157.

Mehler, P. S., Lezotte, D., & Eckel, R. (1998). Lipid levels in anorexia nervosa. *International Journal of Eating Disorders, 24,* 217–221.

Mehler, C., Wewetzer, C., Schulze, U., Warnke, A., Theisen, F., Dittman, R. W. (2001). Olanzapine in children and adolescents with chronic anorexia nervosa: A study of five cases. *European Child and Adolescent Psychiatry, 10,* 151–157.

Meyers, D. G., Starke, H., Pearson, P. H., & Wilken, M. K. (1986). Mitral valve prolapse in anorexia nervosa. *Annals of Internal Medicine, 105,* 384–386.

Mickley, D., Greenfeld, D., Quinlan, D. M., Roloff, P., & Zwas, F. (1996). Abnormal liver enzymes in outpatients with eating disorders. *International Journal of Eating Disorders, 20,* 325–329.

Middleman, A. B., Vasquez, I., & Durant, R. H. (1998). Eating patterns, physical activity, and attempts to change weight among adolescents. *Journal of Adolescent Health, 42,* 22–37.

Minuchin, S, Rosman, B. L., & Baker, L. (1978). *Psychosomatic families: Anorexia nervosa in context.* Cambridge, MA: Harvard University Press.

Mitchell, J. E., Hatsukami, D., Eckert, E. D., & Pyle, R. L. (1985). Characteristics of 275 patients with bulimia. *American Journal of Psychiatry, 142,* 482–485.

Mitchell, J. E., Specker, S. M., & de Zwaan, M. (1991). Comorbidity and medical complications of bulimia nervosa. *Journal of Clinical Psychiatry, 52,* 13–20.

Modan-Moses, D., Yaroslavsky, A., Novikov, I., Segev, S., Toledano, A., Miterany, E., et al. (2003). Stunting of growth as a major feature of anorexia nervosa in male adolescents. *Pediatrics, 111,* 270–276.

Morgan, H. G., Purgold, J., & Welbourne, J. (1983). Management and outcome in anorexia nervosa: A standardized prognostic study. *British Journal of Psychiatry, 143,* 282–287.

Morgan, H. G., & Russell, G.F.M. (1975). Value of family background and clinical features as predictors of long-term outcome in anorexia nervosa: Four-year follow-up study of 41 patients. *Psychological Medicine, 5,* 355–371.

Moriarty, D., Shore, R., & Maxim, N. (1990). Evaluation of an eating disorders curriculum. *Evaluation and Program Planning, 13,* 407–413.

Mufson, L., Weissman, M. M., Moreau, D., & Garfinkel, R. (1999). Efficacy of interpersonal psychotherapy for depressed adolescents. *Archives of General Psychiatry, 56,* 573–579.

Muñoz, M., & Argente, J. (2002). Anorexia nervosa in female adolescents: Endocrine and bone mineral density disturbances. *European Journal of Endocrinology, 147,* 275–286.

Murphy, F., Troop, N., & Treasure, J. (2000). Differential environmental factors in anorexia nervosa: A sibling pair study. *British Journal of Clinical Psychology, 39,* 193–203.

Muscari, M. (2002). Effective management of adolescents with anorexia and bulimia. *Journal of Psychosocial Nursing and Mental Health Services, 40,* 22–31.

Must, A. Jacques, P. F., Dallal, G. E., Bajema, C. J., & Dietz, W. H. (1992). Long-term morbidity and mortality of overweight adolescents: A follow-up of the Harvard Growth Study of 1922 to 1935. *New England Journal of Medicine, 327,* 1350–1355.

Myers, M. D., Raynor, H. A., & Epstein, L. H. (1998). Predictors of child psychological changes during family-based treatment for obesity. *Archives of Pediatric and Adolescent Medicine, 152,* 855–861.

Nakash-Eisikovits, O., Dierberger, A., & Westen, D. (2002). A multidimensional meta-analysis of pharmacotherapy for bulimia nervosa: Summarizing the range of outcomes in controlled clinical trials. *Harvard Review of Psychiatry, 10,* 193–211.

Nathan, P. E., & Gorman, J. M. (Eds.). (2002). *A guide to treatments that work* (2nd ed.). New York: Oxford University Press.

Nation, M., Crusto, C., Wandersman, A., Kumpfer, K. L., Syebolt, D., Morrissey-Kane, E., et al. (2003). What works in prevention: Principles of effective prevention programs. *American Psychologist, 58,* 449–456.

National Center for Health Statistics. (1973). *Height and weight of youths 12–17 years, United States, vital and health statistics.* Series 11, No. 124. Health Services and Mental Health Administration. Washington, DC: United States Government Printing Office.

National Center for Health Statistics (2003). *Overweight children and adolescents: United States, 1999–2000.* Washington, DC: United States Government Printing Office.

National Institute for Clinical Excellence. (2004). *Eating disorders. Core interventions in the treatment and management of eating disorders in primary and secondary care.* London: Author.

National Task Force on the Prevention and Treatment of Obesity. (2000). Dieting and the development of eating disorders in overweight and obese adults. *Archives of Internal Medicine, 160,* 2581–2589.

Neumark-Sztainer, D. (1996). School-based programs for preventing eating disturbances. *Journal of School Health, 66,* 64–71.

Neumark-Sztainer, D., Butler, R., & Palti, H. (1995). Eating disturbances among adolescent girls: Evaluation of a school-based primary prevention program. *Journal of Nutrition Education, 27,* 24–30.

Neumark-Sztainer D., Sherwood N., Coller T., & Hannan, P. J. (2000). Primary prevention of disordered eating among pre-adolescent girls: Feasibility and short-term impact of a community-based intervention. *Journal of the American Dietetic Association, 100,* 1466–1473.

Newman, D. L., Moffitt, T. E., Caspi, A., Magdol, L., Silva, P. A., & Stanton, W. R. (1996). Psychiatric disorder in a birth cohort of young adults: Prevalence, comorbidity, clinical significance, and new case incidence from ages 11 to 21. *Journal of Consulting and Clinical Psychology, 64,* 552–562.

Nicholls, D., Chater, R., & Lask, B. (2000). Children into DSM don't go: A comparison of classification systems for eating disorders in childhood and early adolescence. *International Journal of Eating Disorders, 28,* 317–324.

Nobakht, M., & Dezhkam, M. (2000). An epidemiological study of eating disorders in Iran. *International Journal of Eating Disorders, 28,* 265–271

Norman, D., & Herzog, D. (1984). Persistent social maladjustment in bulimia: A 1-year follow-up. *American Journal of Psychiatry, 141,* 444–446.

Nussbaum, M., Baird, D., Sonnenblick, M., Cowan, K., & Shenker, I. R. (1985). Short stature in anorexia nervosa patients. *Journal of Adolescent Health Care, 6,* 453–455.

Nussbaum, M., Shenker, I. R., Marc, J., & Klein, M. (1980). Cerebral atrophy in anorexia nervosa. *Journal of Pediatrics, 96,* 867–869.

O'Connor, P., Lewis, R., Kirchner, E., & Cook, D. (1996). Eating disorder symptoms in former female college gymnasts: Relations with body composition. *American Journal of Clinical Nutrition, 64,* 840–843.

Ogren, F. P., Huerter, J. V., Pearson, P. H., Antonson, C. W., & Moore, G. F. (1987). Transient salivary gland hypertrophy in bulimics. *Laryngoscope, 97,* 951–953.

Olmsted, M. P., Daneman, D., Rydall, A. C., Lawson, M. L., & Rodin, G. M. (2002). The effects of psychoeducation on disturbed eating attitudes and behavior in young women with type 1 diabetes mellitus. *International Journal of Eating Disorders, 32,* 230–239.

Olmsted, M. P., Kaplan, A. S., & Rockert, W. (1994). Rate and prediction of relapse in bulimia nervosa. *American Journal of Psychiatry, 151,* 738–743.

Orimoto, L., & Vitousek, K. (1992). Anorexia nervosa and bulimia nervosa. In P. W. Wilson (Ed.), *Principles and practices of relapse prevention* (pp. 85–127). New York: Guilford Press.

Ornstein, R. M., Golden, N. H., Jacobson, M. S., & Shenker, I. R. (2003). Hypophosphatemia during nutritional rehabilitation in anorexia nervosa: Implications for refeeding and monitoring. *Journal of Adolescent Health, 32,* 83–88.

Palla, B., & Litt, I. F. (1988). Medical complications of eating disorders in adolescents. *Pediatrics, 81,* 613–623.

Patton, G. C. (1988). Mortality in eating disorders. *Psychological Medicine, 18,* 947–951.

Patton, G. C., Coffey, C., & Sawyer, S. M. (2003). The outcome of adolescent eating disorders: Findings from the Victorian Adolescent Health Cohort Study. *European Child and Adolescent Psychiatry, 12* (Suppl.), 25–29.

Patton, G. C., Johnson-Sabine, E., Wood, K., Mann, A. H., & Wakeling, A. (1990). Abnormal eating attitudes in London schoolgirls: A prospective epidemiological study: Outcome at twelve-month follow-up. *Psychological Medicine, 20,* 383–394.

Paxton, S. J. (1993). A prevention program for disturbed eating and body dissatisfaction in adolescent girls: A 1 year follow-up. *Health Education Research: Theory & Practice, 8,* 43–51.

Phelps, L., Sapia, J., Nathanson, D., & Nelson, L. (2000). An empirically supported eating disorder prevention program. *Psychology in the Schools, 37,* 443–452.

Phillips, D. I., & Young, J. B. (2000). Birth weight, climate at birth and the risk of obesity in adult life. *International Journal of Obesity, 24,* 281–287.

Pike K. M. (1998). Long-term course of anorexia nervosa. *Clinical Psychology Review, 18,* 447–475.

Pike, K. M., Devlin, M. J., & Loeb, K. L. (2003). Cognitive behavior therapy in the treatment of anorexia nervosa, bulimia nervosa, and binge eating disorder. In J. K. Thompson (Ed.), Handbook of eating disorders and obesity (pp. 130–162). New York: Wiley.

Pike, K. M., & Rodin, J. (1991). Mothers, daughters, and disordered eating. *Journal of Abnormal Psychology, 100,* 198–204.

Pike, K. M., Walsh, B. T., Vitousek, K. B., Wilson,

G. T., & Bauer, J. (2003). Cognitive behavioral therapy in the post-hospital treatment of anorexia nervosa. *American Journal of Psychiatry, 160,* 2046–2049.

Pinhas-Hamiel, O., Dolan, L. M., Daniels, S. R., Standiford, D., Khoury, R. P., & Zeitler, P. (1996). Increased incidence of non-insulin dependent diabetes mellitus among adolescents. *Journal of Pediatrics, 12,* 608–615.

Piran, N. (1999). Eating disorders: A trial of prevention in a high risk school setting. *Journal of Primary Prevention, 20,* 75–90.

Pirke, K. M., Fichter, M. M., Lund, R., & Doerr, P. (1979). Twenty-four hours sleep: Wake pattern of plasma LH in patients with anorexia nervosa. *Acta Endocrinology, 92,* 193–204.

Polivy, J., & Herman, C. P. (1985). Dieting and bingeing: A causal analysis. *American Psychologist, 40,* 193–201.

Powers, P. S. (1982). Heart failure during treatment of anorexia nervosa. *American Journal of Psychiatry, 139,* 1167–1170.

Powers, P. S., Santana, C. A., & Bannon, Y. S. (2002). Olanzapine in the treatment of anorexia nervosa: An open label trial. *International Journal of Eating Disorders, 32,* 146–154.

Powers, P., Schocken, D., & Boyd, F. (1998). Comparison of habitual runners and anorexia nervosa patients. *International Journal of Eating Disorders, 23,* 133–143.

Pratt, B. M., & Woolfenden, S. R. (2002). Interventions for preventing eating disorders in children and adolescents (Cochrane Review). *The Cochrane Library, Issue 2.* Oxford: Update Software (http://www.update-software.com/abstracts/main index.html).

Presnell, K., & Stice, E. (2003). An experimental test of the effect of weight-loss dieting on bulimic pathology: Tipping the scales in a different direction. *Journal of Abnormal Psychology, 112,* 166–170.

Pyle, R. L., Mitchell, J. E., Ecker, E. D., Hatsukami, D., Pomeroy, C., & Zimmerman, R. (1990). Maintenance treatment and 6-month outcome for bulimic patients who respond to initial treatment. *American Journal of Psychiatry, 147,* 871–875.

Rand, C.S.W., & Kuldau, J. M. (1992). Epidemiology of bulimia and symptoms in a general population: Sex, age, race, and socioeconomic status. *International Journal of Eating Disorders, 11,* 37–44.

Rastam, M., Gillberg, C., & Garton, M. (1989). Anorexia nervosa in a Swedish urban region: A population-based study. *British Journal of Psychiatry, 155,* 642–646.

Rathner, G., & Messner, K. (1993). Detection of eating disorders in a small rural town: An epidemiological study. *Psychological Medicine, 23,* 175–184.

Reeves, R. S., McPherson, R. S., Nichaman, M. Z., Harrist, R. B., Foreyt, J. P., & Goodrick, G. K. (2001). Nutrient intake of obese female binge eaters. *Journal of the American Dietetic Association, 101,* 209–215.

Reichborn-Kjennerud, T., Bulik, C. M., Tambs, K., Harris, J. R., & Sullivan, P. F. (submitted). Psychiatric and medical symptoms in binge eating in the absence of compensatory behaviors.

Reid, I. R., Ames, R. W., Evans, M. C., Gamble, G. D., & Sharpe, S. J. (1995). Long-term effects of calcium supplementation on bone loss and fractures in postmenopausal women: A randomized controlled trial. *American Journal of Medicine, 98,* 331–335.

Rierdan, J., Koff, E., & Stubbs, M. L. (1989). A longitudinal analysis of body image as a predictor of the onset and persistence of adolescent girls' depression. *Journal of Early Adolescence, 9,* 454–466.

Rigotti, N. A., Neer, R. M., Skates, S. J., Herzog, D. B., & Nussbaum, S. R. (1991). The clinical course of osteoporosis in anorexia nervosa: A longitudinal study of cortical bone mass. *Journal of the American Medical Association, 265,* 1133–1138.

Rivinus, T., Biederman, J., Herzog, D., Kemper, K., Harper, G., Harmatz, J., et al. (1984). Anorexia nervosa and affective disorders: A controlled family history study. *American Journal of Psychiatry, 141,* 1414–1418.

Robin, A. L., Siegel, P. T., Koepke, T., Moye, A. W., & Tice, S. (1994). Family therapy versus individual therapy for adolescent females with anorexia nervosa. *Journal of Developmental and Behavioral Pediatrics, 15,* 111–116.

Robin, A. L., Siegel, P. T., Moye, A. W., Gilroy, M., Baker-Dennis, A., & Sikand, A. (1999). A controlled comparison of family versus individual therapy for adolescents with anorexia nervosa. *Journal of the American Academy of Child and Adolescent Psychiatry, 38,* 1482–1489.

Robins, L. N., & Regier, D. A. (1991). *Psychiatric disorders in America: The epidemiologic catchment area study.* New York: The Free Press.

Robinson, E., Bachrach, L. K., & Katzman, D. K. (2000). Use of hormone replacement therapy to reduce the risk of osteopenia in adolescent girls with anorexia nervosa. *Journal of Adolescent Health, 26,* 343–348.

Rodin, J., Silberstein, L., & Striegel-Moore, R. (1985). Women and weight: A normative discontent. In T. Sonderegger (Ed.), *Psychology and gender: Nebraska Symposium on Motivation.* Lincoln: University of Nebraska Press.

Romano, S. J., Halmi, K. A., Sarkar, N. P., Koke, S. C., & Lee, J. S. (2002). A placebo-controlled study of fluoxetine in continued treatment of bulimia nervosa after successful acute fluoxetine treatment. *American Journal of Psychiatry, 159,* 96–102.

Romans, S., Martin, J., & Mullen, P. (1994). Child sexual abuse (CSA) and later eating disorders: A New Zealand epidemiological study. *Neuropsychopharmacology, 10(3S),* 92S.

Rome, E. S., Ammerman, S., Rosen, D. S., Keller, R. J., Lock, J., Mammel, K. A., et al. (2003). Children and adolescents with eating disorders: The state of the art. *Pediatrics, 111,* 98–108.

Root, A. W., & Powers, P. S. (1983). Anorexia nervosa presenting as growth retardation in adolescents. *Journal of Adolescent Health Care, 4,* 25–30.

Rosenvinge, J. H., Borgen, J. S., & Boerresen, R. (1999). The prevalence and psychological correlates of anorexia nervosa, bulimia nervosa and binge eating among 15-year-old students: A controlled epidemiological study. *European Eating Disorders Review, 7,* 382–391.

Rossello, J., & Bernal, G. (1999). The efficacy of cognitive-behavioral and interpersonal treatments for depression in Puerto Rican adolescents. *Journal of Consulting and Clinical Psychology, 67,* 734–745.

Russell, G. F. (1969). Metabolic, endocrine and psychiatric aspects of anorexia nervosa. *Scientific Basis Medical Annual Reviews, 15,* 236–255.

Russell, G. F. (1985). Premenarchal anorexia nervosa and its sequelae. *Journal of Psychiatric Research, 19,* 363–369.

Russell, G.F.M., Szmukler, G. I., Dare, C., & Eisler, I. (1987). An evaluation of family therapy in anorexia nervosa and bulimia nervosa. *Archives of General Psychiatry, 44,* 1047–1056.

Sands, R., Tricker, J., Sherman, C., Armatas, C., & Maschette, W. (1997). Disordered eating patterns, body image, self-esteem, and physical activity in preadolescent school children. *International Journal of Eating Disorders, 21,* 159–166.

Santonastaso, P., Zanetti, T., Ferrara, S., Olivetto, M. C., Magnavita, N., & Favaro, A. (1999). A preventive intervention program in adolescent schoolgirls: A longitudinal study. *Psychotherapy and Psychosomatics, 68,* 46–50.

Santonastaso, P., Zanetti, T., Sala, A., & Favaretto, G. (1996). Prevalence of eating disorders in Italy: A survey on a sample of 16-year-old female students. *Psychotherapy & Psychosomatics, 65,* 158–162.

Schebendach, J., Golden, N. H., Jacobson, M. S., Arden, M., Pettei, M., Hardoff, D., et al. (1995). Indirect calorimetry in the nutritional management of eating disorders. *International Journal of Eating Disorders, 17,* 59–66.

Schebendach, J. E., Golden, N. H., Jacobson, M. S., Hertz, S., & Shenker, I. R. (1997). The metabolic responses to starvation and refeeding in adolescents with anorexia nervosa. *Annals of the New York Academy of Sciences, 817,* 110–119.

Schiff, R. J., Wurzel, C. L., Brunson, S. C., Kasloff, I., Nussbaum, M. P., & Frank, S. D. (1986). Death due to chronic syrup of ipecac use in a patient with bulimia. *Pediatrics, 78,* 412–416.

Schmidt, U. (2002). Risk factors for eating disorders. In C. G. Fairburn & K. D. Brownell (Eds.), *Eating disorders and obesity: A comprehensive handbook* (2nd ed., pp. 247–251). New York: Guilford Press.

Schmidt, U., Hodes, M., & Treasure, J. (1992). Early onset bulimia nervosa: Who is at risk? A retrospective case-control study. *Psychological Medicine, 22,* 623–628.

Schmidt, U., Tiller, J., Blanchard, M., Andrews, B., & Treasure, J. (1997). Is there a specific trauma precipitating anorexia nervosa? *Psychological Medicine, 27,* 523–530.

Schmidt, U., Tiller, J., & Treasure, J. (1993). Setting the scene for eating disorders: Childhood care, classification and course of illness. *Psychological Medicine, 23,* 663–672.

Schocken, D. D., Holloway, J. D., & Powers, P. S. (1989). Weight loss and the heart: Effects of anorexia nervosa and starvation. *Archives of Internal Medicine, 149,* 877–881.

Schweiger, V., Warnhoff, M., Pahl, J., & Pirke, K. (1986). Effects of carbohydrate and protein meals on plasma large neutral amino acids, glucose, and insulin plasma levels of anorectic patients. *Metabolism, 35,* 938–943.

Serfaty, M. A., Turkington, D., Heap, M., Ledsham, L., & Jolley, E. (1999). Cognitive therapy versus dietary counseling in the outpatient treatment of anorexia nervosa: Effects of the treatment phase. *European Eating Disorders Review, 7,* 334–350.

Shamim, T., Golden, N. H., Arden, M., Filiberto, L., & Shenker, I. R. (2003). Resolution of vital sign instability: An objective measure of medical stability in anorexia nervosa. *Journal of Adolescent Health, 32,* 73–77.

Sharp, C. W., & Freeman, C. P. (1993). The medical complications of anorexia nervosa. *British Journal of Psychiatry, 162,* 452–462.

Sherman, P., Leslie, K., Goldberg, E., Rybczynski, J., & St. Louis, P. (1994). Hypercarotenemia and transaminitis in female adolescents with eating disorders: A prospective, controlled study. *Journal of Adolescent Health, 15,* 205–209.

Shoebridge, P., & Gowers, S. (2000). Parental high concern and adolescent-onset anorexia nervosa. *British Journal of Psychiatry, 176,* 132–137.

Silberg, J., & Bulik, C. (submitted). Developmental association between eating disorders symptoms and symptoms of anxiety and depression in juvenile twin girls.

Silverman, J. A., & Krongrad, E. (1983). Anorexia nervosa: A cause of pericardial effusion? *Pediatric Cardiology, 4,* 125–127.

Smolak, L., & Levine, M. P. (2001). A two-year follow-up of a primary prevention program for negative body image and unhealthy weight regulation. *Eating Disorders: The Journal of Treatment & Prevention, 9,* 313–325.

Snow-Harter, C., Bouxsein, M. L., Lewis, B. T., Carter, D. R., & Marcus, R. (1992). Effects of resistance and endurance exercise on bone mineral status of young women: A randomized exercise intervention trial. *Journal of Bone and Mineral Research, 7,* 761–769.

Soundy, T., Lucas, A., Suman, V., & Melton, L. (1995). Bulimia nervosa in Rochester, Minnesota from 1980 to 1990. *Psychological Medicine, 25,* 1065–1071.

Southard, R. N., Morris, J. D., Mahan, J. D., Hayes, J. R., Torch, M. A., Sommer, A., et al. (1991). Bone mass in healthy children: Measurement with quantitative DXA. *Radiology, 179,* 735–738.

Soyka, L. A., Misra, M., Frenchman, A., Miller, K. K., Grinspoon, S., Schoenfeld, D. A., et al. (2002). Abnormal bone mineral accrual in adolescent girls with anorexia nervosa. *Journal of Clinical Endocrinology and Metabolism, 87,* 4177–4185.

Spitzer, R. L., Williams, J. B., Kroenke, K., Hornyak, R., & McMurray, J. (2000). Validity and utility of the PRIME-MD patient health questionnaire in assessment of 3000 obstetric-gynecologic patients: The PRIME-MD patient health questionnaire obstetric-gynecology study. *American Journal of Obstetrics and Gynecology, 183,* 759–769.

Spitzer, R. L., Yanovski, S. Z., Wadden, T., Wing, R., Marcus, M. D., Stunkard, A., et al. (1993). Binge eating disorder: Its further validation in a multisite study. *International Journal of Eating Disorders, 13,* 137–153.

Springer, E. A., Winzelberg, A. J., Perkins, R., & Taylor, C. B. (1999). Effects of a body image curriculum for college students. *International Journal of Eating Disorders, 26,* 13–20.

Srinivasagam, N. M., Kaye, W. H., Plotnicov, K. H., Greeno, C., Weltzin, T. E., & Rao, R. (1995). Persistent perfectionism, symmetry, and exactness after long-term recovery from anorexia nervosa. *American Journal of Psychiatry, 152,* 1630–1634.

Standing Committee on the Scientific Evaluation of Dietary Reference Intakes, Food and Nutrition Board. (1997). *Dietary Reference Intakes for Calcium, Phosphorus, Magnesium, Vitamin D, and Fluoride.* Washington, D.C.: National Academy Press.

Stein, S., Chalhoub, N., & Hodes, M. (1998). Very early-onset bulimia nervosa: Report of two cases. *International Journal of Eating Disorders, 24,* 323–327.

Steiner-Adair, C. (1994). The politics of prevention. In P. Fallon, M. A. Katzman, & S. C. Wooley (Eds.), *Feminist perspectives on eating disorders* (pp. 381–394). New York: Guilford Press.

Steiner-Adair, C., Sjostrom, L., Franko, D. L., Pai, S., Tucker, R., Becker, A. E., et al. (2002). Primary prevention of eating disorders in adolescent girls: Learning from practice. *International Journal of Eating Disorders, 32,* 401–411.

Steinhausen, H. C. (1997). Outcome of anorexia nervosa in the younger patient. *Journal of Child Psychology and Psychiatry and Allied Disciplines, 38,* 271–276.

Steinhausen, H. C. (2002). The outcome of anorexia nervosa in the 20th century. *American Journal of Psychiatry, 159,* 1284–1293.

Steinhausen, H. C., Winkler, C., & Meier, M. (1997). Eating disorders in adolescence in a Swiss epidemiological study. *International Journal of Eating Disorders, 22,* 147–151.

Stewart, D. A., Carter, J. C., Drinkwater, J., Hainsworth, J., & Fairburn, C. G. (2001). Modification of eating attitudes and behaviour in adolescent girls: A controlled study. *International Journal of Eating Disorders, 29,* 107–118.

Stice, E. (1994). Review of the evidence for a sociocultural model of bulimia nervosa and exploration of mechanisms of action. *Clinical Psychology Review, 14,* 633–661.

Stice, E. (2001). A prospective test of the dual pathway model of bulimic pathology: Mediating effects of dieting and negative affect. *Journal of Abnormal Psychology, 110,* 124–135.

Stice, E. (2002). Risk and maintenance factors for eating pathology: A meta-analytic review. *Psychological Bulletin, 128,* 825–848.

Stice, E., & Agras, W. S. (1998). Predicting onset and cessation of bulimic behaviors during adolescence: A longitudinal grouping analyses. *Behavior Therapy, 29,* 257–276.

Stice, E., Agras, W., & Hammer, L. (1999). Risk factors for the emergence of childhood eating disturbances; A five-year prospective study. *International Journal of Eating Disorders, 25,* 375–387.

Stice, E., & Bearman, S. K. (2001). Body-image and eating disturbances prospectively predict increases in depressive symptoms in adolescent girls: A growth curve analysis. *Developmental Psychology, 37,* 1–11.

Stice, E., Fisher, M., & Lowe, M. R. (2004). Are dietary restraint scales valid measures of dietary restriction? Unobtrusive observational data suggest not. *Psychological Assessment, 16,* 51–59.

Stice, E., Hayward, C., Cameron, R., Killen, J. D., & Taylor, C. B. (2000). Body image and eating related factors predict onset of depression in female adolescents: A longitudinal study. *Journal of Abnormal Psychology, 109,* 438–444.

Stice, E., Maxfield, J., & Wells, T. (2003). Adverse effects of social pressure to be thin on young women: An experimental investigation of the effects of "fat talk." *International Journal of Eating Disorders, 34,* 108–117.

Stice, E., Presnell, K., & Bearman, S. (2001). Relation of early menarche to depression, eating disorders, substance abuse, and comorbid psychopathology among adolescent girls. *Developmental Psychology, 37,* 608–619.

Stice, E., Presnell, K., Groesz, L., & Shaw, H. (submitted). Effects of a weight maintenance diet on bulimic pathology: An experimental test of the dietary restraint theory.

Stice, E., Presnell, K., & Spangler, D. (2002). Risk factors for binge eating onset: A prospective investigation. *Health Psychology, 21,* 131–138.

Stice, E., & Ragan, J. (2002). A preliminary controlled evaluation of an eating disturbance psychoeducational intervention for college students. *International Journal of Eating Disorders, 31,* 159–171.

Stice, E., & Shaw, H. (2004). Eating disorder prevention programs: A meta-analytic review. *Psychological Bulletin, 130,* 206–227.

Stice, E., Spangler, D., & Agras, W. S. (2001). Exposure to media-portrayed thin-ideal images adversely affects vulnerable girls: A longitudinal experiment. *Journal of Social and Clinical Psychology, 20,* 270–288.

Stice, E., Trost, A., & Chase, A. (2003). Healthy weight control and dissonance-based eating disorder prevention programs: Results from a controlled trial. *International Journal of Eating Disorders, 33,* 10–21.

Stice, E., & Whitenton, K. (2002). Risk factors for body dissatisfaction in adolescent girls: A longitudinal investigation. *Developmental Psychology, 38,* 669–678.

Stock, S. L., Goldberg, E., Corbett, S., & Katzman, D. K. (2002). Substance use in female adolescents with eating disorders. *Journal of Adolescent Health, 31,* 176–182.

Strauss, R. S. (1999). Self-reported weight status and dieting in a cross-sectional sample of young adolescents: National Health and Nutrition Examination Survey III. *Archives of Pediatrics and Adolescent Medicine, 153,* 741–747.

Striegel-Moore, R. H. (1993). Etiology of binge eating: A developmental perspective. In C. G. Fairburn & G. T. Wilson (Eds.), *Binge eating: Nature, assessment, and treatment* (pp. 144–172). New York: Guilford Press.

Striegel-Moore, R. H., & Cachelin, F. M. (2001). Etiology of eating disorders in women. *Journal of Counseling Psychology, 29,* 635–661.

Striegel-Moore, R. H., Dohm, F. A., Kraemer, H. C., Taylor, C. B., Daniels, S., Crawford, P. B., et al. (2003). Eating disorders in white and black women. *American Journal of Psychiatry, 160,* 1326–1331.

Striegel-Moore, R. H., Leslie, D., Petrill, S. A., Garvin, V., & Rosenheck, R. A. (2000). One-year use and cost of inpatient and outpatient services among female and male patients with an eating disorder: Evidence from a national database of health insurance claims. *International Journal of Eating Disorders, 27,* 381–389.

Striegel-Moore, R. H., Seeley, J. P., & Lewinsohn, P. M. (2003). Psychosocial adjustment in young women who had experienced an eating disorder during adolescence. *Journal of the American Academy of Child and Adolescent Psychiatry, 42,* 587–593.

Striegel-Moore, R., Silberstein, L., & Rodin, J. (1986). Toward an understanding of risk factors for bulimia. *American Psychologist, 41,* 246–263.

Striegel-Moore, R., Silberstein, L., & Rodin, J. (1993). The social self in bulimia nervosa: Public self-consciousness, social anxiety, and perceived fraudulence. *Journal of Abnormal Psychology, 102,* 297–303.

Strober, M. (1990). Personality and symptomatological features in young, nonchronic anorexia nervosa patients. *Journal of Psychosomatic Research, 24,* 353–359.

Strober, M., Freeman, R., Lampert, C., Diamond, J., & Kaye, W. (2000). Controlled family study of anorexia nervosa and bulimia nervosa: Evidence of shared liability and transmission of partial syndromes. *American Journal of Psychiatry, 157,* 393–401.

Strober, M., Freeman, R., & Morrell, W. (1997). The long-term course of severe anorexia nervosa in adolescents: Survival analysis of recovery, relapse, and outcome predictors over 10–15 years in a prospective study. *International Journal of Eating Disorders, 22,* 339–360.

Strober, M., Lampert, C., Morrell, W., Burroughs, J., & Jacobs, C. (1990). A controlled family study of anorexia nervosa: Evidence of familial aggregation and lack of shared transmission with affective disorders. *International Journal of Eating Disorders, 9,* 239–253.

Stunkard, A. J. (1957). The dieting depression: Untoward responses to weight reduction. *American Journal of Medicine, 23,* 77–86.

Stunkard, A. J., & Rush, J. (1974). Dieting and depression reexamined: A critical review of reports of untoward responses during weight reduction for obesity. *Annals of Internal Medicine, 81,* 526–33.

Styne, D. M. (2001). Childhood and adolescent obesity. *Pediatric Clinics of North America, 48,* 1041–1053.

Sullivan, P. F. (1995). Mortality in anorexia nervosa. *American Journal of Psychiatry, 152,* 1073–1074.

Sullivan, P. F., Bulik, C. M., Fear, J. L., & Pickering, A. (1998). Outcome of anorexia nervosa. *American Journal of Psychiatry, 155,* 939–946.

Szabo, P., & Tury, F. (1991). The prevalence of bulimia nervosa in a Hungarian college and secondary school population. *Psychotherapy and Psychosomatics, 56,* 43–47.

Szmukler, G., Eisler, I., Gillies, C., & Hayward, M. (1985). The implications of anorexia nervosa in a ballet school. *Journal of Psychiatric Research, 19,* 177–181.

Taylor, C. B., Sharpe, T., Shisslak, C., Bryson, S., Estes, L. S., Gray, N., et al. (1998). Factors associated with weight concerns in adolescent girls. *International Journal of Eating Disorders, 24,* 31–42.

Taylor, C. B., Winzelberg, A. J., & Celio, A. A. (2001). The use of interactive media to prevent eating disorders. In R. Striegel-Moore & L. Smolak (Eds.), *Eating disorders: New directions for research and practice* (pp. 255–269). Washington, DC: American Psychological Association.

Taylor, M. J., & Cooper, P. J. (1992). An experimental study of the effect of mood on body size perception. *Behavior Research and Therapy, 30,* 53–58.

Telch, C. F., & Agras, W. S. (1993). The effects of a very-low-calorie diet on binge eating. *Behavior Therapy, 24,* 177–193.

Thaw, J. M., Williamson, D. A., & Martin, C. K. (2001). Impact of altering DSM-IV criteria for anorexia and bulimia nervosa on the base rates of eating disorder diagnoses. *Eating and Weight Disorders, 6,* 121–129.

Theander, S. S. (2002). Literature on eating disorders during 40 years: Increasing number of papers, emergence of bulimia nervosa. *European Eating Disorders Review, 10,* 386–398.

Theintz, G., Buchs, B., Rizzoli, R., Slosman, D., Clavien, H., Sizonenko, P. C., et al. (1992). Longitudinal monitoring of bone mass accumulation in healthy adolescents: Evidence for a marked reduction after 16 years of age at the levels of lumbar spine and femoral neck in female subjects. *Journal of Clinical Endocrinology and Metabolism, 75,* 1060–1065.

Thiels, C., Schmidt, U., Treasure, J., Garthe, R., & Troop, N. (1998). Guided self-change for bulimia nervosa incorporating use of a self-care manual. *American Journal of Psychiatry, 155,* 947–953.

Tiggemann, M. (1994). Gender differences in the interrelationships between weight dissatisfaction, restraint, and self-esteem. *Sex Roles, 30,* 319–330.

Tobler, N. S., Roona, M. R., Ochshorn, P., Marshall, D. G., Streke, A. V., & Stackpole, K. M. (2000). School-based adolescent drug prevention programs: 1998 meta-analysis. *The Journal of Primary Prevention, 20,* 275–336.

Tozzi, F., Bergen, A. W., & Bulik, C. M. (2002). Candidate gene studies in eating disorders. *Psychopharmacology Bulletin, 36,* 60–90.

Troiano, R. P., Flegal, K. M., Kuczmarski, R. K., Campbell, S. M., & Johnson, C. L. (1995). Overweight prevalence and trends for children and adolescents. *Archives of Pediatric and Adolescent Medicine, 149,* 1085–1091.

Tyrka, A., Waldron, I., Graber, J., & Brooks-Gunn, J. (2002). Prospective predictors of the onset of anorexic and bulimic syndromes. *International Journal of Eating Disorders, 32,* 282–290.

United Kingdom Department of Health. (2003, September 19). New advice on antidepressant for treatment of children with depressive illness. Retrieved September 25, 2003, from http://www.info.doh.gov.uk/doh/intpress.nsf.

United States Food and Drug Administration. (2004, March 22). Worsening depression and suicidality in patients being treated with antidepressant medication. Retrieved April 4, 2004, from http://www.fda.gov/cder/drug/antidepressants/AntidepressanstPHA.htm.

Vaisman, N., Voet, H., Akivis, A., & Sive-Ner, I. (1996). Weight perception of adolescent dancing school students. *Archives of Pediatrics and Adolescent Medicine, 150,* 187–190.

Van den Berg, P., Wertheim, E. H., Thompson, J. K., & Paxton, S. J. (2002). Development of body image, eating disturbance, and general psychological functioning in adolescent females: A replication using covariance structure modeling in an Australian sample. *International Journal of Eating Disorders, 32,* 46–51.

Vandereycken, W. (1984). Neuroleptics in the short-term treatment of anorexia nervosa: A double-blind placebo-controlled study with sulpiride. *British Journal of Psychiatry, 144,* 288–292.

Vandereycken, W., & Pierloot, R. (1982). Pimozide combined with behavior therapy in the short-term treatment of anorexia nervosa. *Acta Psychiatrica Scandinavica, 66,* 445–450.

Van Strien, T. (1989). Dieting, dissatisfaction with figure, and sex role orientation in women. *International Journal of Eating Disorders, 8,* 455–463.

Van Strien, T., Frijters, J.E.R., Bergers, G.P.A., & Defares, P. B. (1986). The Dutch Eating Behavior Questionnaire for assessment of restrained, emotional, and external eating behavior. *International Journal of Eating Disorders, 5,* 295–315.

Varley, C. K. (2003). Psychopharmacological treatment of major depressive disorder in children and adolescents. *Journal of the American Medical Association, 290,* 1091–1093.

Verhulst, F. C., van der Ende, J., Ferdinand, R. F., & Kasius, M. C. (1997). The prevalence of DSM-III-R diagnoses in a national sample of Dutch adolescents. *Archives of General Psychiatry, 54,* 329–336.

Vieselman, J., & Roig, M. (1985). Depression and suicidality in eating disorders. *Journal of Clinical Psychiatry, 46,* 118–124.

Vitousek, K., & Manke, F. (1994). Personality variables and disorders in anorexia nervosa and bulimia nervosa. *Journal of Abnormal Psychology, 103,* 137–147.

Vogeltanz-Holm, N. D., Wonderlich, S. A., Lewis, B. A., Wilsnack, S. C., Harris, T. R., Wilsnack, R. W., et al. (2000). Longitudinal predictors of binge eating, intense dieting, and weight concerns in a national sample of women. *Behavior Therapy, 31,* 221–235.

Vohs, K. D., Bardone, A. M., Joiner, T. E., Abramson, L. Y., & Heatherton, T. F. (1999). Perfectionism, perceived weight status, and self-esteem interact to predict bulimic symptoms: A model of bulimic symptom development. *Journal of Abnormal Psychology, 108,* 695–700.

Vohs, K. D., Voelz, Z. R., Pettit, J. W., Bardone, A. M., Katz, J., Abramson, L. Y., et al. (2001). Perfectionism, body dissatisfaction, and self-esteem: An interactive model of bulimic symptom development. *Journal of Social and Clinical Psychology, 20,* 476–497.

von Ranson, K. M., Kaye, W. H., Weltzin, T. E., Rao, R., & Matsunaga, H. (1999). Obsessive-compulsive disorder symptoms before and after recovery from bulimia nervosa. *American Journal of Psychiatry, 156,* 1703–1708.

Wadden, T. A., Stunkard, A. J., & Liebschutz, J. (1988). Three-year follow-up of the treatment of obesity by very low-calorie diet, behavior therapy, and their combination. *Journal of Consulting and Clinical Psychology, 56,* 925–928.

Wadden, T. A., Stunkard, A. J., & Smoller, J. W. (1986). Dieting and depression: A methodological study. *Journal of Consulting and Clinical Psychology, 54,* 869–871.

Wade, T. D., Bulik, C. M., Neale, M., & Kendler, K. S. (2000). Anorexia nervosa and major depression: shared genetic and environmental risk factors. *American Journal of Psychiatry, 157,* 469–471.

Wade, T. D., Martin, N., Neale, M., Tiggemann, M., Trealor, S., Heath, A., et al. (1999). The structure of genetic and environmental risk factors for three measures of disordered eating characteristic of bulimia nervosa. *Psychological Medicine, 29,* 925–934.

Waller, D., Guillon, C., Petty, F., Hardy, B., Murdock, M., & Ruch, A. (1993). Temperament and

Personality Questionnaire and serotonin in bulimia nervosa. *Psychiatry Research, 48,* 9–15.

Waller, G., Halek, C., & Crisp, A. (1993). Sexual abuse as a factor in anorexia nervosa: Evidence from two separate case series. *Journal of Psychosomatic Research, 37,* 873–879.

Walsh, B. T., Hadigan, C. M., Devlin, M. J., Gladis, M., & Roose, S. P. (1991). Long-term outcome of antidepressant treatment for bulimia nervosa. *American Journal of Psychiatry, 148,* 1206–1212.

Walsh, B. T., Wilson, G. T., Loeb, K. L., Devlin, M. J., Pike, K. M., Roose, S. P., et al. (1997). Medication and psychotherapy in the treatment of bulimia nervosa. *American Journal of Psychiatry, 154,* 523–531.

Walters, E. E., & Kendler, K. S. (1995). Anorexia nervosa and anorexic-like syndromes in a population-based female twin sample. *American Journal of Psychiatry, 152,* 64–71.

Weeda-Mannak, W., & Drop, M. (1985). The discriminative value of psychological characteristics in anorexia nervosa: Clinical and psychometric comparison between anorexia nervosa patients, ballet dancers and controls. *Journal of Psychiatric Research, 19,* 285–290.

Weisz, J. R., & Hawley, K. M. (2002). Developmental factors in the treatment of adolescents. *Journal of Consulting and Clinical Psychology, 70,* 21–43.

Wells, J. E., Bushnell, J. A., Hornblow, A. R., Joyce, P. R., & Oakley-Browne, M. A. (1989). Christchurch psychiatric epidemiology study, Part I: methodology and lifetime prevalence for specific psychiatric disorders. *Australian and New Zealand Journal of Psychiatry, 23,* 315–326.

Wentz, E., Gillberg, C., Gillberg, I. C., & Rastam, M. (2001). Ten-year follow-up of adolescent-onset anorexia nervosa: Psychiatric disorders and overall functioning scales. *Journal of Child Psychology and Psychiatry and Allied Disciplines, 42,* 613–622.

Wertheim, E. H., Koerner, J., & Paxton, S. (2001). Longitudinal predictors of restrictive eating and bulimic tendencies in three different age groups of adolescent girls. *Journal of Youth and Adolescence, 30,* 69–81.

Whitaker, A., Johnson, J., Shaffer, D., Rapoport, J. L., Kalikow, K., Walsh, B. T., et al. (1990). Uncommon troubles in young people: Prevalence estimates of selected psychiatric disorders in a nonreferred adolescent population. *Archives of General Psychiatry, 47,* 487–496.

Whittal, M. L., Agras, W. S., & Gould, R. A. (1999). Bulimia nervosa: A meta-analysis of psychosocial and pharmacological treatments. *Behavior Therapy, 30,* 117–135.

Wilfley, D. E., Schwartz, M. B., Spurrell, E. B., & Fairburn, C. G. (2000). Using the Eating Disorder Examination to identify the specific psychopathology of binge eating disorder. *International Journal of Eating Disorders, 27,* 259–269.

Wilson, G. T. (1999). Cognitive behavior therapy for eating disorders: Progress and problems. *Behaviour Research and Therapy, 37,* 579–596.

Wilson, G. T. (2002). The controversy over dieting. In C. G. Fairburn & K. D. Brownell (Eds.), *Eating disorders and obesity: A comprehensive handbook* (pp. 93–97). New York: Guilford Press.

Wilson, G. T., & Fairburn, C. G. (2002). Treatments for eating disorders. In P. E. Nathan & J. M. Gorman (Eds.), *A guide to treatments that work* (2nd ed., pp. 559–592). New York: Oxford University Press.

Wilson, G. T., Vitousek, K. M., & Loeb, K. L. (2000). Stepped care treatment for eating disorders. *Journal of Consulting and Clinical Psychology, 68,* 564–572.

Wiseman, C. V., Sunday, S. R., Bortolotti, F., & Halmi, K. (2002). Primary prevention of eating disorders through attitude change: A two-country comparison.

Wittchen, H. U., Nelson, C. B., & Lanchner, G. (1998). Prevalence of mental disorders and psychosocial impairments in adolescents and young adults. *Psychological Medicine, 28,* 109–126.

Wlodarczyk-Bisaga, K., & Dolan, B. (1996). A two-stage epidemiological study of abnormal eating attitudes and their prospective risk factors in Polish schoolgirls. *Psychological Medicine, 26,* 1021–1032.

Wolraich, M. L. Felice, M. E., & Drotar, D. (Eds.) (1996). *The classification of child and adolescent mental diagnoses in primary care: Diagnostic and Statistical Manual for Primary Care (DSM-PC) Child and Adolescent Version.* Elk Grove, IL: American Academy of Pediatrics.

Wonderlich, S. A., Connolly, K. M., & Stice, E. (in press). Impulsivity as a risk factor for eating disordered behavior: Assessment implications with adolescents. *International Journal of Eating Disorders.*

Wonderlich, S. A., & Mitchell, J. E. (1997). Eating disorders and comorbidity: Empirical, conceptual, and clinical implications. *Psychopharmacological Bulletin, 33,* 381–390.

Woodside, D. B., Garfinkel, P. E., Lin, E., Goering, P., Kaplan, A. S., Goldbloom, D. S., & Kennedy, S. H. (2001). Comparisons of men with full or partial eating disorders, men without eating disorders, and women with eating disorders in the community. *American Journal of Psychiatry, 158*, 570–574.

World Health Organization. (1990). *International classification of diseases and related health problems* (10th revision). Geneva: Author.

Yager, J., Landsverk, J., & Edelstein, C. K. (1987). A 20-month follow-up study of 628 women with eating disorders, I: course and severity. *American Journal of Psychiatry, 144*, 1172–1177.

Yager, J., Landsverk, J., Edelstein, C. K., & Jarvik, M. (1988). A 20-month follow-up study of 628 women with eating disorders: II. Course of associated symptoms and related clinical features. *International Journal of Eating Disorders, 7*, 503–513.

Yannakoulia, M., Sitara, M., & Matalas, A. L. (2002). Reported eating behavior and attitudes improvement after a nutrition intervention program in a group of young female dancers. *International Journal of Sports Nutrition Exercise and Metabolism, 12*, 24–32.

Yanovski, S. Z. (2002). Binge eating in obese persons. In C. G. Fairburn & K. D. Brownell (Eds.), *Eating disorders and obesity: A comprehensive handbook* (pp. 403–407). New York: Guilford Press.

Youth Risk Behavior Surveillance System. (2003). Youth Risk Behavior Survey [Web site]. Retrieved May 19, 2003, from http://www.cdc.gov/nccdphp/dash/yrbs/about_yrbss.htm

Zhu, A. J., & Walsh, B. T. (2002). Pharmacologic treatment of eating disorders. *Canadian Journal of Psychiatry, 47*, 227–234.

Part V: Substance Use Disorders

Abraham, H. D., Aldridge, A. M., & Gogia, P. (1996). The psychopharmacology of hallucinogens. *Neuropsychopharmacology, 14*, 285–298.

Abraham, H., McCann, U., & Ricaurte, G. (2002). Psychedelic drugs. In K. Davis, D. Charney, J. Coyle, & C. Nemeroff (Eds.), *Neuropsychopharmacology, the fifth generation of progress*, (pp. 1545–1556) New York: Lippincott Williams & Wilkins.

Abreu-Villaca, Y., Seidler, F. J., Qiao, D., Tate, C. A., Cousins, M. M., Thillai, I., et al. (2003). Short-term adolescent nicotine exposure has immediate and persistent effects on cholinergic systems: Critical periods, patterns of exposure, dose thresholds. *Neuropsychopharmacology,* 28(11): 1935–1949.

Addolorato, G., Caputo, F., Capristo, E., Colombo, G., Gessa, G. L., & Gasbarrini, G. (2000). Ability of baclofen in reducing alcohol craving and intake: II—Preliminary clinical evidence. *Alcoholism, Clinical and Experimental Research, 24*, 67–71.

Adelman, H. S., & Taylor, L. (2003). On sustainability of project innovations as systemic change. *Journal of Educational and Psychological Consultation,* 14(1): 1–25.

Aghajanian, G. K., & Marek, G. J. (1999). Serotonin and hallucinogens. *Neuropsychopharmacology, 21*(2 Suppl), 16S–23S.

Ahmed, S. H., & Koob, G. F. (1998). Transition from moderate to excessive drug intake: Change in hedonic set point. *Science, 282*, 298–300.

Aigner, T. G., & Balster, R. L. (1978). Choice behavior in rhesus monkeys: Cocaine versus food. *Science, 201*, 534–535.

Akhondzadeh, S., Ahmadi-Abhari, S. A., Assadi, S. M., Shabestari, O. L., Kashani, A. R., & Farzanehgan, Z. M. (2000). Double-blind randomized controlled trial of baclofen vs. clonidine in the treatment of opiates withdrawal. *Journal of Clinical Pharmacy and Therapeutics, 25*, 347–353.

Alper, K. R. (2001). Ibogaine: A review. *The Alkaloids, Chemistry & Biology, 56*, 1–38.

Altman, D. G. (1995). Sustaining interventions in community systems: On the relationship between researchers and communities. *Health Psychology, 14*, 526–536.

Alvarado, A., Kendell, K., Beesley, S., & Lee-Cavaness, C. (2000). *Strengthening American families: Model family programs for substance abuse and delinquency prevention*. Salt Lake City, UT: University of Utah, Department of Health Promotion and Education.

American Legacy Foundation. (2002). Media tracking survey (unpublished data).

American Psychiatric Association (APA). (1994). *Diagnostic and statistical manual of mental disorders* (4th ed.) (DSM IV). Washington, DC: Author.

Anderson, C. E., & Loomis, G. A. (2003). Recognition and prevention of inhalant abuse. *American Family Physician, 68*, 869–874.

Anonymous. (2003). Inhalant abuse treatment and prevention. *Public Health Reports, 118*, 276.

Anthony, J. C., Warner, L. A., & Kessler, R. C. (1994). Comparative epidemiology of dependence on tobacco, alcohol, controlled substances, and inhalants: Basic findings from the

National Comorbidity Survey. *Experimental and Clinical Psychopharmacology, 2,* 244–268.

Arnold, M. E., & Hughes, J. N. (1999). First do no harm: Adverse effects of grouping deviant youth for skills training. *Journal of School Psychology, 37,* 99–115.

Arthur, M. W., Ayers, C. D., Graham, K. A., & Hawkins, J. D. (2003). Mobilizing communities to reduce risks for drug abuse: A comparison of two strategies. In W. J. Bukoski & Z. Sloboda (Eds.), *Handbook of drug abuse theory, science and practice* (pp. 129–144). New York: Plenum Press.

Aydin, K., Sencer, S., Demir, T., Ogel, K., Tunaci, A., & Minareci, O. (2002). Cranial MR findings in chronic toluene abuse by inhalation. *American Journal of Neuroradiology, 23,* 1173–1179.

Azrin, N. H., Donohue, B., & Besalel, V. A. (1994). Youth drug abuse treatment: A controlled outcome study. *Journal of Child and Adolescent Substance Abuse, 3,* 1–16.

Bachman, J. G., Johnston, L. D., & O'Malley, P. M. (1990). Explaining the recent decline in cocaine use among young adults: Further evidence that perceived risks and disapproval lead to reduced drug use. *Journal of Health and Social Behavior, 31,* 173–184.

Bachman, J. G., Johnston, L. D., & O'Malley, P. M. (1998). Explaining the recent increases in students' marijuana use: The impacts of perceived risks and disapproval from 1976 through 1996. *American Journal of Public Health, 88,* 887–892.

Bachman, R., & Peralta, R. (2002). Relationship between drinking and violence in an adolescent population: Does gender matter? *Deviant Behavior, 23,* 1–19.

Baer, J. S. (1993). Etiology and secondary prevention of alcohol problems with young adults. In J. S. Baer, G. A. Marlatt, & R. J. McMahon (Eds.), *Addictive behaviors across the life span: Prevention, treatment, and policy issues* (pp. 111–137). Newbury Park, CA: Sage Publications.

Balster, R. L. (1987). Abuse potential evaluation of inhalants. *Drug and Alcohol Dependence, 19,* 7–15.

Balster, R. L. (1998). Neural basis of inhalant abuse. *Drug and Alcohol Dependence, 51,* 207–214.

Barrickman, L. L., Perry, P. J., Allen, A. J., Kuperman, S., Arndt, S. V., Herrmann, K. J., et al. (1995). Bupropion versus methylphenidate in the treatment of attention-deficit hyperactivity disorder. *Journal of the American Academy of Child and Adolescent Psychiatry, 34,* 649–657.

Beauvais, F., Wayman, J. C., Jumper-Thurman, P., Plested, B., & Helm, H. (2002). Inhalant abuse among American Indian, Mexican American, and non-Latino white adolescents. *American Journal of Drug and Alcohol Abuse, 28,* 171–187.

Benowitz, N. L. (1990). Pharmacokinetic considerations in understanding nicotine dependence. In G. Block & J. Marsh (Eds.), *The biology of nicotine dependence* (Vol. Ciba Foundation Symposium 152, pp. 186–209). Chichester: John Wiley & Sons.

Benowitz, N. L., & Jacob, P., III. (1999). Pharmacokinetics and metabolism of nicotine and related alkaloids. In S. P. Arneric & J. D. Brioni (Eds.), *Neuronal nicotinic receptors* (pp. 213–234). New York: Wiley-Liss.

Benowitz, N. L., Perez-Stable, E. J., Herrera, B., & Jacob, P., 3rd. (2002). Slower metabolism and reduced intake of nicotine from cigarette smoking in Chinese-Americans. *Journal of the National Cancer Institute, 94,* 108–115.

Benson, P. L., Leffert, W., Scates, P. C., & Blyth, D. A. (1998). Beyond the "village" rhetoric: Creating healthy communities for children and adolescents. *Applied Developmental Science, 2,* 138–159.

Bergen, A. W., Korczak, J. F., Weissbecker K. A., Goldstein, A. M., et al. (1999). A genome-wide search for loci contribution to smoking and alcoholism. *Genetic Epidemiology, 17,* S55–60.

Berrettini, W. H., Alexander, R., Ferraro, T. N., & Vogel, W. H. (1994). A study of oral morphine preference in inbred mouse strains. *Psychiatric Genetics, 4,* 81–86.

Biederman, J., Wilens, T., Mick, E., Faraone, S. V., Weber, W., Curtis, S., et al. (1997). Is ADHD a risk factor for psychoactive substance use disorders? Findings from a four-year prospective follow-up study. *Journal of the American Academy of Child and Adolescent Psychiatry, 36,* 21–29.

Biederman, J., Wilens, T., Mick, E., Spencer, T., & Faraone, S. V. (1999). Pharmacotherapy of attention-deficit/hyperactivity disorder reduces risk for substance use disorder. *Pediatrics, 104,* e20.

Bieurt, L., Rice, J., Edenberg, H., Goate, A., Foroud, T., & Cloninger, C. (2000). Family-based study of the association of the dopamine D2 receptor gene (DRD2) with habitual smoking. *American Journal of Medical Genetics, 90,* 299–302.

Bierut, L. J., Saccone, N. L., Rice, J. P., Goate, A., Foroud, T., Edenberg, H., et al. (2002). Defining alcohol-related phenotypes in humans. The Collaborative Study on the Genetics of Alcoholism. *Alcohol Research and Health, 26,* 208–213.

Bigelow, G. E., Stitzer, M. L., & Liebson, I. A. (1984). The role of behavioral contingency management in drug abuse treatment. In J. Grabowski, M. L. Stitzer, & J. E. Henningfield (Eds.) *Behavioral intervention techniques in drug abuse treatment* (pp. 36–52). Rockville, MD: National Institute on Drug Abuse.

Blaho, K., Merigian, K., Winbery, S., Geraci, S. A., & Smartt, C. (1997). Clinical pharmacology of lysergic acid diethylamide: Case reports and review of the treatment of intoxication. *American Journal of Therapeutics, 4,* 211–221.

Blum, K., Noble, E. P., Sheridan, P. J., Mongomery, A., Ritchie, T., Jagadeeswaran, P., et al. (1990). Allelic association of human dopamine D2 receptor gene in alcoholism. *Journal of the American Medical Association, 263,* 2055–2060.

Bolos, A. M., Dean, M., Lucas-Derse, S., Ramsburg, M., Brown, G. L., & Goldman, D. (1990). Population and pedigree studies reveal a lack of association between the dopamine D2 receptor gene and alcoholism. *Journal of the American Medical Association, 264,* 3156–3160.

Bonson, K. R., Grant, S. J., Contoreggi, C. S., Links, J. M., Metcalfe, J., Weyl, H. L., et al. (2002). Neural systems and cue-induced cocaine craving. *Neuropsychopharmacology, 26,* 376–386.

Borduin, C. M., Mann, B. J., Cone, L. T., Henggeler, S. W., Fucci, B. R., Blaske, D. M., et al. (1995). Multisystemic treatment of serious juvenile offenders: Long-term prevention of criminality and violence. *Journal of Consulting and Clinical Psychology, 63,* 569–578.

Borras, E., Coutelle, C., Rosell, A., Fernandez-Muixi, F., Broch., M., Crosas, B., et al. (2000). Genetic polymorphism of alcohol dehydrogenase in Europeans: the ADH2*2 allele decreases the risk for alcoholism and is associated with ADH3*1. *Hepatology, 31,* 984–989.

Botvin, G. J., Baker, E., Dusenbury, L., Botvin, E. M., & Diaz, T. (1995). Long-term follow-up results of a randomized drug abuse prevention trial in a white middle-class population. *Journal of the American Medical Association, 273,* 1106–1112.

Brebner, K., Childress, A. R., & Roberts, D. C. (2002). A potential role for GABA(B) agonists in the treatment of psychostimulant addiction. *Alcohol and Alcoholism, 37,* 478–484.

Brehm, J. W. (1966). *A theory of psychological reactance.* New York: Academy Press.

Brehm, S. S., & Brehm, J. W. (1981). *Psychological reactance.* New York: John Wiley & Sons.

Bresleau, N. (1995). Psychiatric comorbidity of smoking and nicotine dependence. *Behavioral Genetics, 25,* 95–101.

Brody, A. L., Mandelkern, M. A., London, E. D., Childress, A. R., Lee, G. S., Bota, R. G., et al. (2002). Brain metabolic changes during cigarette craving. *Archives of General Psychiatry, 59,* 1162–1172.

Brouette, T., & Anton, R. (2001). Clinical review of inhalants. *American Journal on Addictions, 10,* 79–94.

Brown, S. (1993). Recovery patterns in adolescent substance abuse. In J. S. Baer, G. A. Marlott, & M.R.J. (Eds.), *Addictive behaviors across the life span: Prevention, treatment, and policy issues* (pp. 161–183). Newbury Park, CA: Sage Publications.

Brown, S. A., & D'Amico, E. J. (2003). Outcomes of alcohol treatment for adolescents. *Recent Developments in Alcoholism, 16,* 289–312.

Buchan, B. J., Dennis, M. L., Tims, F. M., & Diamond, G. S. (2002). Cannabis use: Consistency and validity of self-report, on-site urine testing, and laboratory testing. *Addiction, 97* (Suppl. 1), 98–108.

Buchert, R., Obrocki, J., Thomasius, R., Vaterlein, O., Petersen, K., Jenicke, L., et al. (2001). Long-term effects of "ecstasy" abuse on the human brain studied by FDG PET. *Nuclear Medicine Communications, 22,* 889–897.

Budney, A. J., Higgins, S. T., Radonovich, K. J., & Novy, P. L. (2000). Adding voucher-based incentives to coping skills and motivational enhancement improves outcomes during treatment for marijuana dependence. *Journal of Consulting and Clinical Psychology, 68,* 1051–1061.

Budney, A. J., & Higgins, S. T. (1998). *A Community Reinforcement Plus Vouchers Approach: Treating Cocaine Addiction.* Rockville, MD: NIDA.

Budney, A. J., & Moore, B. A. (2002). Development and consequences of cannabis dependence. *Journal of Clinical Pharmacology, 42* (11 Suppl), 28S–33S.

Bukstein, O. G., Glancy, L. J., & Kaminer, Y. (1992). Patterns of affective comorbidity in a clinical population of dually diagnosed adolescent substance abusers. *Journal of the American Academy of Child and Adolescent Psychiatry, 31,* 1041–1045.

Burke, B. L., Arkowitz, H., & Menchola, M. (2003). The efficacy of motivational interviewing: A meta-analysis of controlled clinical trials. *Journal of Consulting and Clinical Psychology, 71,* 843–861.

Cadoret, R. J., Troughton, E., O'Gorman, T. W., & Heywood, E. (1986). An adoption study of genetic and environmental factors in drug abuse. *Archives of General Psychiatry, 43,* 1131–1136.

Cahill, L., & McGaugh, J. L. (1998). Mechanisms of

emotional arousal and lasting declarative memory. *Trends in Neurosciences, 21*, 294–299.

Carroll, K. M. (1996). Relapse prevention as a psychosocial treatment approach: A review of controlled clinical trials. *Experimental and Clinical Psychopharmacology, 4*, 46–54.

Carroll, K. M., Ball, S. A., & Martino, S. (2004). Cognitive, behavioral and motivational therapies. In M. Galanter & H. D. Kleber (Eds.), *The American psychiatric publishing textbook of substance abuse treatment* (3rd ed. pp. 365–376). Washington, DC: American Psychiatric Association Press.

Carroll, K. M., Nich, C., Ball, S. A., McCance-Katz, E., & Rounsaville, B. J. (1998). Treatment of cocaine and alcohol dependence with psychotherapy and disulfiram. *Addiction, 93*, 713–728.

Carroll, K. M., Rounsaville, B. J., Gordon, L. T., Nich, C., Jatlow, P. M., Bisighini, R. M., et al. (1994). Psychotherapy and pharmacotherapy for ambulatory cocaine abusers. *Archives of General Psychiatry, 51*, 177–197.

Carroll, K. M., Rounsaville, B. J., Nich, C., Gordon, L. T., Wirtz, P. W., & Gawin, F. H. (1994). One-year follow-up of psychotherapy and pharmacotherapy for cocaine dependence: Delayed emergence of psychotherapy effects. *Archives of General Psychiatry, 51*, 989–997.

Catalano, R., Gainey, R., Fleming, C., Haggerty, K., & Johnson, N. (1999). An experimental intervention with families of substance abusers: One-year follow-up of the focus on families project. *Addiction, 94*, 241–254.

Catalano, R. F., Berglund, M. L., Ryan, J.A.M., Lonczak, H. S., & Hawkins, J. D. (2004). Positive youth development in the United States: Research findings on evaluations of positive youth development programs. *Annals of the American Academy of Political and Social Science, 591*, 98–124.

Catalano, R. F., Haggerty, K., Gainey, R., & Hoppe, M. (1997). Reducing parental risk factors for children's substance misuse: Preliminary outcomes with opiate-addicted parents. *Substance Use and Misuse, 32*, 699–721.

Center for the Study and Prevention of Violence. (2003). Blueprints Model Programs. Boulder: Center for the Study and Prevention of Violence, Institute of Behavioral Science, University of Colorado at Boulder. http://colorado.edu.cspv/blueprints/

Centers for Disease Control and Prevention (CDC). (1998). Youth risk behavior surveillance—United States, 1997. Morbidity and Mortality Weekly Report, 47(SS-3), 1–89.

Center for Substance Abuse Treatment (CSAT). (1999). Adolescents and young adults in treatment. In www.health.org/nties/young/yung text.htm.

Centers for Disease Control and Prevention (CDC). (2002a). Adolescent and school health. Atlanta: National Center for Chronic Disease Prevention and Health Promotion.

Centers for Disease Control and Prevention (CDC). (2002b). Trends and cigarette smoking among high school students—United States, 1991–2001. *Morbidity and Mortality Weekly Report, 51*, 409–412.

Chambers, R. A., Taylor, J. R., & Potenza, M. N. (2003). Developmental neurocircuitry of motivation in adolescence: A critical period of addiction vulnerability. *American Journal of Psychiatry, 160*, 1041–1052.

Chambless, D. L., & Hollon, S. D. (1998). Defining empirically supported therapies. *Journal of Consulting and Clinical Psychology, 66*, 7–18.

Chen, C. C., Lu, R. B., Chen, Y. C., Wang, M. F., Chang, Y. C., Li, T. K., et al. (1999). Interaction between the functional polymorphisms of the alcohol-metabolism genes in protection against alcoholism. *American Journal of Human Genetics, 65*, 795–807.

Chen, C. Y., & Anthony, J. C. (2004). Epidemiological estimates of risk to become dependent upon cocaine: Cocaine hydrochloride powder vs. crack coccaine. *Psychopharmacology, 172*, 78–86.

Chen, X., Stacy, A., Zheng, H., Shan, J., Spruijt-Metz, D., Unger, J., et al. (2003). Sensations from initial exposure to nicotine predicting adolescent smoking in China: A potential measure of vulnerability to nicotine. *Nicotine and Tobacco Research, 5*, 455–463.

Chilcoat, H. D., Dishion, T. J., & Anthony, J. C. (1995). Parent monitoring and the incidence of drug sampling in urban elementary school children. *American Journal of Epidemiology, 14*, 25–31.

Childress, A. R., Franklin, T., Listerud, J., Acton, P., & O'Brien, C. P. (2002). Neuroimaging of cocaine craving states: Cessation, stimulant administration, and drug cue paradigms. In K. L. Davis, D. Charney, J. Coyle, & C. Nemeroff (Eds.), *Neuropsychopharmacology: The fifth generation of progress* (pp. 1575–1590). New York: Lippincott Williams & Wilkins.

Childress, A. R., McElgin, W., Franklin, T., Acton, P., & O'Brien, C. P. (1999). Impact of GABAergics on brain activity during cue-induced cocaine craving. *Society for Neuroscience* Abstracts Annual meeting. Abstract Book Vol. 328.14, 25(1), 815.

Childress, A. R., McLellan, A. T., Ehrman, R., & O'Brien, C. P. (1988). Classifically conditioned responses in opioid and cocaine dependence: a role in relapse? In B. A. Ray (Ed.), *Learning factors in substance abuse* (NIDA Research Monograph, pp. 25–43). Rockville, MD: National Institute on Drug Abuse.

Childress, A. R., Mozley, P. D., McElgin, W., Fitzgerald, J., Reivich, M., & O'Brien, C. P. (1999). Limbic activation during cue-induced cocaine craving. *American Journal of Psychiatry, 156,* 11–18.

Choi, W. S., Gilpin, E. A., Farkas, A. J., & Pierce, J. P. (2001). Determining the probability of future smoking among adolescents. *Addiction, 96,* 313–323.

Choi, W. S., Pierce, J. P., Gilpin, E. A., Farkas, A. J., & Berry, C. C. (1997). Which adolescent experimenters progress to established smoking in the United States? *American Journal of Preventive Medicine, 13,* 385–391.

Chung, T., Martin, C. S., Armstrong, T. D., & Labouvie, E. W. (2002). Prevalence of DSM-IV alcohol diagnoses and symptoms in adolescent community and clinical samples. *Journal of the American Academy of Child and Adolescent Psychiatry, 41,* 546–554.

Clark, D. B., Bukstein, O., & Cornelius, J. (2002). Alcohol use disorders in adolescents: Epidemiology, diagnosis, psychosocial interventions, and pharmacological treatment. *Paediatric Drugs, 4,* 493–502.

Clark, D. B., Pollock, N., Bukstein, O. G., Mezzich, A. C., Bromberger, J. T., & Donovan, J. E. (1997). Gender and comorbid psychopathology in adolescents with alcohol dependence. *Journal of the American Academy of Child and Adolescent Psychiatry, 36,* 1195–1203.

Clark, D. B., Vanyukov, M., & Cornelius, J. (2002). Childhood antisocial behavior and adolescent alcohol use disorders. *Alcohol Research and Health, 26,* 109–115.

Clayton, R. R., Cattarello, A. M., & Johnstone, B. M. (1996). The effectiveness of Drug Abuse Resistance Education (project DARE): 5-year follow-up results. *Preventive Medicine, 25,* 307–318.

Coatsworth, J. D., Santisteban, P. A., McBride, C. K., Szapocznik, J. (2001). Brief strategic family therapy versus community control: Engagement, retention, and an exploration of the moderating role of adolescent symptom severity. *Family Process 40,* 313–332.

Colby, S. M., Tiffany, S. T., Shiffman, S., & Niaura, R. S. (2000a). Are adolescent smokers dependent on nicotine? A review of the evidence. *Drug and Alcohol Dependence, 59* (Suppl 1), S83–95.

Colby, S. M., Tiffany, S. T., Shiffman, S., & Niaura, R. S. (2000b). Measuring nicotine dependence among youth: A review of available approaches and instruments. *Drug and Alcohol Dependence, 59* (Suppl 1), S23–39.

Cole, J. C., Bailey, M., Sumnall, H. R., Wagstaff, G. F., & King, L. A. (2002). The content of ecstasy tablets: implications for the study of their long-term effects. *Addiction, 97,* 1531–1536.

Cole, J. C., & Sumnall, H. R. (2003). Altered states: The clinical effects of Ecstasy. *Pharmacology Therapeutics, 98,* 35–58.

Comings, D., Ferry, L., Bradshaw-Robinson, S., Burchette, R., Chiu, C., & Muhleman, D. (1996). The dopamine D2 receptor (DRD2) gene: A genetic risk factor in smoking. *Pharmacogenetics, 6,* 73–79.

Comings, D. E., Wu, S., Gonzalez, M., Iacono, W. G., McGue, M., Peters, W. W., et al. (2001). Cholecystokinin(CCK) gene as a possible risk factor for smoking: A replication in two independent samples. *Molecular Genetics and Metabolism, 73,* 349–353.

Conrad, K. M., Flay, B. R., & Hill, D. (1992). Why children start smoking cigarettes: Predictors of onset. *British Journal of Addiction, 87,* 1711–1724.

Corby, E. A., Roll, J. M., Ledgerwood, D. M., & Schuster, C. R. (2000). Contingency management interventions for treating the substance abuse of adolescents: A feasibility study. *Experimental and Clinical Psychopharmacology, 8,* 371–376.

Corrigall, W. A., Zack, M., Eissenberg, T., Belsito, L., & Scher, R. (2001). Acute subjective and physiological responses to smoking in adolescents. *Addiction, 96,* 1409–1417.

Cottler, L. B., Schuckit, M. A., Helzer, J. E., Crowley, T., Woody, G., Nathan, P., et al. (1995). The DSM-IV field trial for substance use disorders: Major results. *Drug and Alcohol Dependence, 38,* 59–69; discussion 71–83.

Cottrell, D., & Boston, P. (2000). Practitioner review: The effectiveness of systemic family therapy for children and adolescents. *Journal of Child Psychology and Psychiatry, 43,* 573–586.

Crits-Christoph, P., Siqueland, L., Blaine, J. D., Frank, A., Luborsky, L., Onken, L. S., et al. (1999). Psychosocial treatments for cocaine dependence: Results of the National Institute on

Drug Abuse Collaborative Cocaine Study. *Archives of General Psychiatry, 56,* 495–502.

Crome, I. B., Christian, J., & Green, C. (1998). Tip of the national iceberg? Profile of adolescent subjects prescribed methadone in an innovative community drug service. *Drugs: Education, Prevention and Policy, 5,* 195–197.

Crowley, J. J., Oslin, D. W., Patkar, A. A., Gottheil, E., DeMaria, P. A., Jr., O'Brien, C. P., et al. (2003). A genetic association study of the mu opioid receptor and severe opioid dependence. *Psychiatric Genetics, 13,* 169–173.

Crowley, T. J., & Riggs, P. D. (1995). Adolescent substance use disorder with conduct disorder and comorbid conditions. In D. Czechowicz (Ed.), *NIDA research monograph 156: Adolescent drug abuse: Clinical assessment and therapeutic interventions* (Vol. 156, pp. 49–111). Rockville, MD: National Institute on Drug Abuse.

Dackis, C. A., & Gold, M. S. (1992). Psychiatric hospitals for treatment of dual diagnosis. In J. H. Lowinson (Ed.), *Substance abuse, a comprehensive textbook* (2nd ed., pp. 467–485). Baltimore: Williams & Wilkins.

Dackis, C. A., Lynch, K. G., Yu, E., Samaha, F. F., Kampman, K. M., Cornish, J. W., et al. (2003). Modafinil and cocaine: A double-blind, placebo-controlled drug interaction study. *Drug and Alcohol Dependence, 70,* 29–37.

Dackis, C. A., & O'Brien, C. P. (2001). Cocaine dependence: A disease of the brain's reward centers. *Journal of Substance Abuse Treatment, 21,* 111–117.

Dackis, C. A., & O'Brien, C. P. (2002). Cocaine dependence: The challenge for pharmacotherapy. *Current Opinion in Psychiatry, 15,* 261–267.

Dackis, C. A., & O'Brien, C. P. (2003b). The neurobiology of addiction. In A. Asbury, G. McKhann, W. McDonald, P. Goadsby, & J. McArthur (Eds.), *Diseases of the nervous system* (3rd ed., pp. 431–444). Cambridge, UK: Cambridge University Press.

Dackis, C. A., & O'Brien, C. P. (2003a). Glutamatergic agents for cocaine dependence. *Annals of the New York Academy of Science, 103,* 1–18.

Dackis, C., Yu, E., Samaha, F., Kampman, K., Cornish, J., Rowan, A., et al. (2001). Modafinil—Cocaine safety study; a double-blind, placebo-controlled drug interaction study. College on Problems of Drug Dependence, Presented at the Annual Meeting at San Juan, Puerto Rico.

Daglish, M. R., Weinstein, A., Malizia, A. L., Wilson, S., Melichar, J. K., Britten, S., et al. (2001). Changes in regional cerebral blood flow elicited by craving memories in abstinent opiate-dependent subjects. *American Journal of Psychiatry, 158,* 1680–1686.

Daumann, J., Schnitker, R., Weidemann, J., Schnell, K., Thron, A., & Gouzoulis-Mayfrank, E. (2003). Neural correlates of working memory in pure and polyvalent ecstasy (MDMA) users. *Neuroreport, 14,* 1983–1987.

Davies, R., Gabbert, S., & Riggs, P. D. (2001). Anxiety disorders in neurologic illness. *Current Treatment Options in Neurology, 3,* 333–346.

Daviss, W. B., Bentivoglio, P., Racusin, R., Brown, K. M., Bostic, J. Q., & Wiley, L. (2001). Bupropion sustained release in adolescents with comorbid attention-deficit/hyperactivity disorder and depression. *Journal of the American Academy of Child and Adolescent Psychiatry, 40,* 307–314.

Deas, D., Riggs, P., Langenbucher, J., Goldman, M., & Brown, S. (2000). Adolescents are not adults: Developmental considerations in alcohol users. *Alcoholism, Clinical and Experimental Research, 24,* 232–237.

Deas, D., & Thomas, S. E. (2001). An overview of controlled studies of adolescent substance abuse treatment. *American Journal on Addictions, 10,* 178–189.

Deas, D., & Thomas, S. (2002). Comorbid psychiatric factors contributing to adolescent alcohol and other drug use. *Alcohol Research and Health, 26,* 116–121.

Deas-Nesmith, D., Brady, K., & Campbell, S. (1998). Comorbid substance use and anxiety disorders in adolescents. *Journal of Psychopathology and Behavioral Assessment, 20,* 139–148.

Deas-Nesmith, D., Campbell, S., & Brady, K. T. (1998). Substance use disorders in an adolescent inpatient psychiatric population. *Journal of the National Medical Association, 90,* 233–238.

Dennis, M., Babor, T. F., Roebuck, M. C., & Donaldson, J. (2002). Changing the focus: The case for recognizing and treating cannabis use disorders. *Addiction, 97* (Suppl 1), 4–15.

Dennis, M., Titus, J. C., Diamond, G., Donaldson, J., Godley, S. H., Tims, F. M., et al. (2002). The Cannabis Youth Treatment (CYT) experiment: Rationale, study design and analysis plans. *Addiction 97,* 16–34.

Dennis, M. L., & White, M. K. (2003). *The effectiveness of adolescent substance abuse treatment: A brief summary of studies through 2001.* Bloomington, IL: Chestnut Health Systems.

DeRubeis, R. J., & Crits-Christoph, P. (1998). Empirically supported individual and group psychological treatments for adult mental disorders. *Journal of Consulting and Clinical Psychology, 66,* 37–52.

Developmental Research and Programs. (2000). In *Communities That Care: A Comprehensive Prevention Program.* Seattle, WA.

De Win, M. M., Reneman, L., Reitsma, J. B., Den Heeten, G. J., Booij, J., & Van Den Brink, W. (2004). Mood disorders and serotonin transporter density in ecstasy users—the influence of long-term abstention, dose, and gender. *Psychopharmacology (Berlin), 173,* 376–382.

DeWit, D. J., Adlaf, E. M., Offord, D. R., & Ogborne, A. C. (2000). Age at first alcohol use: A risk factor for the development of alcohol disorders. [Comment]. *American Journal of Psychiatry, 157,* 745–750.

Diamond, G. S., Godley, S. H., Liddle, H. A., Sampl, S., Webb, C., Tims, F. M., et al. (2002). Five outpatient treatment models for adolescent marijuana use: A description of the cannabis youth treatment interventions. *Addiction, 97,* 70–84.

Diamond, G. S., & Liddle, H. A. (1996). Resolving a therapeutic impasse between parents and adolescents in multidimensional family therapy. *Journal of Consulting and Clinical Psychology, 64,* 481–488.

Diamond, G., Panichelli-Mindel, S. M., Shera, D., Tims, F., Ungemack, J. (in press). Psychiatric distress in adolescents presenting for outpatient treatment for marijuana abuse and dependency: Prevalence and diagnostic algorithms. *Journal of Child and Adolescent Substance Abuse Treatment.*

Di Chiara, G. (1999). Drug addiction as dopamine-dependent associative learning disorder. *European Journal of Pharmacology, 375,* 13–30.

Di Chiara, G., Acquas, E., Tanda, G., & Cadoni, C. (1993). Drugs of abuse: Biochemical surrogates of specific aspects of natural reward? *Biochemical Society Symposium, 59,* 65–81.

Di Ciano, P., & Everitt, B. J. (2003). The GABA(B) receptor agonist baclofen attenuates cocaine- and heroin-seeking behavior by rats. *Neuropsychopharmacology, 28,* 510–518.

DiFranza, J. R., Rigotti, N. A., McNeill, A. D., Ockene, J. K., Savageau, J. A., St Cyr, D., et al. (2000). Initial symptoms of nicotine dependence in adolescents. *Tobacco Control, 9,* 313–319.

DiFranza, J. R., Savageau, J. A., Rigotti, N. A., Fletcher, K., Ockene, J. K., McNeill, A. D., et al. (2002). Development of symptoms of tobacco dependence in youths: 30-month follow-up data

from the DANDY study. *Tobacco Control, 11,* 228–235.

Dillon, P., Copeland, J., & Jansen, K. (2003). Patterns of use and harms associated with non-medical ketamine use. *Drug and Alcohol Dependence, 69,* 23–28.

Dishion, T. J., McCord, J., & Poulin, F. (1999). When interventions harm: Peer groups and problem behavior. *American Psychologist, 54,* 755–764.

Dishion, T., Patterson, G., Stoolmiller, M., & Skinner, M. (1991). Family, school and behavioral antecedents to early adolescent involvement with antisocial peers. *Developmental Psychology, 27,* 172–180.

Donohew, L., Lorch, E., & Palmgreen, P. (1991). Sensation seeking and targeting of televised anti-drug PSAs. In L. Donohew, H. E. Sypher, & W. J. Bukoski (Eds.), *Persuasive communication and drug abuse prevention* (pp. 209–226). Hillsdale, NJ: Lawrence Erlbaum.

Drake, R. E., Mchugo, G. J., & Noordsy, D. L. (1993). Treatment of alcoholism among schizophrenic outpatients: 4-year outcomes. *American Journal of Psychiatry, 150,* 328–329.

Drake, R. E., Mercer-McFadden, C., Muesser, K. T., McHugo, G. J., & Bond, G. R. (1998). A review of integrated mental health and substance abuse treatment for patients with dual disorders. *Schizophrenia Bulletin, 24,* 589–608.

Drake, R. E., Mueser, K. T., Clark, R. E., & Wallach, M. A. (1996). The course, treatment and outcome of substance disorder in persons with severe mental illness. *American Journal of Orthopsychiatry, 66,* 41–51.

Drug Strategies. (2003). In *Making the grade: A guide to school drug prevention programs.* Washington, D.C.

Duggirala, R., Almasy, L., & Blangero, J. (1999). Smoking behavior is under the influence of a major quantitative trait locus on human chromosome 5q. *Genetic Epidemiology, 17,* S139–144.

Duncan, T. E., Duncan, S. C., Strycker, L. A., Li, F., & Alpert, A. (1999). *An introduction to latent variable growth curve modeling: Concepts, issues and applications.* Mahwah, NJ: Lawrence Erlbaum.

Dunn, C., Deroo, I., & Rivara, F. P. (2001). The use of brief interventions adapted from motivational interviewing across behavioral domains: A systematic review. *Addiction, 96,* 1725–1742.

DuRant, R. H. (1995). Adolescent health research as we proceed into the twenty-first century. *Journal of Adolescent Health, 17,* 199–203.

DuRant, R. H., Getts, A., Cadenhead, C., Emans,

S. J., & Woods, E. R. (1995). Exposure to violence and victimization and depression, hopelessness, and purpose in life among adolescents living in and around public housing. *Journal of Developmental and Behavioral Pediatrics, 16,* 233–237.

Eccles, J., & Gootman, J. A. (2002). *Community programs to promote youth development* (National Research Council and Institute of Medicine). Washington, DC: National Academy Press.

Eddy, N. B., Halbach, H., Isbell, H., & Seevers, M. H. (1965). Drug dependence: Its significance and characteristics. *Bulletin of the World Health Organization, 32,* 721–733.

Eggert, L. L., Thompson, E. A., Herting, J. R., & Nicholas, L. J. (1995). Reducing suicide potential among high-risk youth: Tests of school-based prevention program. *Suicide and Life-Threatening Behavior, 25,* 276–296.

Eggert, L. L., Thompson, E. A., Herting, J. R., Nicholas, L. J., & Dicker, B. G. (1994). Preventing adolescent drug abuse and high school dropout through an intensive school-based social network development program. *American Journal of Health Promotion, 8,* 202–215.

Eissenberg, T., & Balster, R. (2000). Initial tobacco use episodes in children and adolescent: Current knowledge, future direction (review). *Drug and Alcohol Depndence, 59,* (Suppl. 51), S41–60.

Ellickson, P. L., Tucker, J. S., & Klein, D. J. (2003). Ten-year prospective study of public health problems associated with early drinking. *Pediatrics, 111*(5 Pt 1), 949–955.

Elliott, R., Newman, J. L., Longe, O. A., & Deakin, J. F. (2003). Differential response patterns in the striatum and orbitofrontal cortex to financial reward in humans: A parametric functional magnetic resonance imaging study. *Journal of Neuroscience, 23,* 303–307.

Emslie, G. J., Rush, A. J., Weinberg, W. A., Kowatch, R. A., Hughes, C. W., Carmody, T., et al. (1997). A double-blind, randomized, placebo-controlled trial of fluoxetine in children and adolescents with depression. *Archives of General Psychiatry, 54,* 1031–1037.

Escobedo, L. G., Kirch, D. G., & Anda, R. F. (1996). Depression and smoking initiation among US Latinos. *Addiction, 91,* 113–119.

Escobedo, L. G., Marcus, S. E., Holtzman, D., & Giovino, G. A. (1993). Sports participation, age at smoking initiation, and the risk of smoking among US high school students. *Journal of the American Medical Association, 269,* 1391–1395.

Farkas, A. J., Gilpin, E. A., White, M. M., & Pierce, J. P. (2000). Association between household and workplace smoking restrictions and adolescent smoking. *Journal of the American Medical Association, 284,* 717–722.

Farre, M., De La Torre, R., O Marthuna, B., Roset, P. N., Peiro, A. M., Torrens, M., Ortuno, J., Pugados, M., & Cami, J. (2004). Repeated doses administration of MDMA in humans: Pharmacological effects and pharmacokinetics. *Psychopharmacology (Berlin), 173,* 364–375.

Feinberg, M. E., Greenberg, M. T., Osgood, D. W., Anderson, A., & Babinski, L. (2002). The effects of training community leaders in prevention science: Communities that Care in Pennsylvania. *Evaluation and Program Planning, 25,* 245–259.

Fiore, M. C., Smith, S. S., Jorenberg, D. E., & Baker, T. B. (1994). The effectiveness of the nicotine patch for smoking cessation: A meta-analysis. *JAMA, 271,* 1940–1947.

Flay, B. R. (2002). Positive youth development requires comprehensive health promotion programs. *American Journal of Health Behavior, 26,* 407–424.

Flay, B. R., d'Avernas, J., Best, J., Kersell, M., & Ryan, K. (1983). Cigarette smoking: Why young people do it and ways of preventing it. In P. J. McGrath & P. Firestone (Eds.), *Pediatric and adolescent behavioral medicine* (pp. 132–183). New York: Springer-Verlag.

Fone, K. C., Beckett, S. R., Topham, I. A., Swettenham, J., Ball, M., & Maddocks, L. (2002). Long-term changes in social interaction and reward following repeated MDMA administration to adolescent rats without accompanying serotonergic neurotoxicity. *Psychopharmacology (Berlin), 159,* 437–444.

Franklin, T. R., Acton, P. D., Maldjian, J. A., Gray, J. D., Croft, J. R., OBrien, C. P., et al. (2002). Decreased gray matter density in the insular, orbitofrontal, cingulate and temporal cortices of cocaine patients. *Biological Psychiatry, 51,* 134–142.

Freese, T. E., Miotto, K., & Reback, C. J. (2002). The effects and consequences of selected club drugs. *Journal of Substance Abuse Treatment, 23,* 151–156.

French, S. A., Perry, C. L., Leon, G. R., & Fulkerson, J. A. (1994). Weight concerns, dieting behavior and smoking initiation among adolescents: A prospective study. *American Journal of Public Health, 84,* 1818–1820.

Friedman, A. (1989). Family therapy vs. parent groups: Effects on adolescent drug abusers. *American Journal of Family Therapy, 17,* 335–347.

Friedman, L., Lichtenstein, E., & Biglan, A. (1985). Smoking onset among teens: an empirical analysis of initial situation. *Addictive Behaviors, 10,* 1–13.

Galloway, G. P., Frederick-Osborne, S. L., Seymour, R., Contini, S. E., & Smith, D. E. (2000). Abuse and therapeutic potential of gamma-hydroxybutyric acid. *Alcohol, 20,* 263–269.

Garavan, H., Pankiewicz, H. J., Bloom, A., Cho, J.-K., Sperry, L., Ross, T. J., et al. (2000). Cue-induced cocaine craving: Neuroanatomical specificity for drug-users and drug stimuli. *American Journal of Psychiatry, 157,* 1789–1798.

Gelernter, J., Kranzler, H., & Cubells, J. (1999). Genetics of two mu opioid receptor gene (OPRM1) exon 1 polymorphisms: Population studies, and allele frequencies in alcohol- and drug-dependent subjects. *Molecular Psychiatry, 4,* 476–483.

Geller, B., Cooper, T. B., Sun, K., Zimerman, B., Frazier, J., Williams, M., et al. (1998). Double-blind and placebo-controlled study of lithium for adolescent bipolar disorders with secondary substance dependency. [see comment]. *Journal of the American Academy of Child and Adolescent Psychiatry, 37,* 171–178.

Gerra, G., Zaimovic, A., Ferri, M., Zambelli, U., Timpano, M., Neri, E., et al. (2000). Long-lasting effects of (+/−)3,4-methylenedioxymethamphetamine (ecstasy) on serotonin system function in humans. *Biological Psychiatry, 47,* 127–136.

Gerstein, D. R., & Johnson, R. A. (1999). Adolescents and young adults in the National Treatment Improvement Evaluation Study. Retrieved from http://www.ilpsr.umich.edu/SAMHDA/NTIES/ebm-summaries.html

Giesbrecht, H., Krempulec, L., & West, P. (1993). Community-based prevention research to reduce alcohol-related problems. *Alcohol Health and Research World, 28,* 309–321.

Gilbert, D., & Gilbert, B. (1995). Personality, psychopathology and nicotine responses as mediators of the genetics of smoking. *Behavior Genetics, 25,* 133–147.

Gilvarry, E. (2000). Substance abuse in young people. *Journal of Child Psychology and Psychiatry and Allied Disciplines, 41,* 55–80.

Godley, S. H. (1994). A treatment system for persons with mental illness and substance abuse. The Illinois ME/SA Project. Springfield, IL: Illinois Department of Mental Health and Developmental Disabilities.

Gold, M. S., Dackis, C. A., & Washton, A. M. (1984). The sequential use of clonidine and naltrexone in the treatment of opiate addicts. *Advances in Alcohol and Substance Abuse, 3,* 19–39.

Goldberg, S. R., & Schuster, C. R. (1967). Conditioned suppression by a stimulus associated with nalorphine in morphine-dependent monkeys. *Journal of the Experimental Analysis of Behavior, 10,* 235–242.

Gonzalez, G., Oliveto, A., & Kosten, T. R. (2002). Treatment of heroin (Diamorphine) addiction: Current approaches and future prospects. *Drugs, 62,* 1331–1343.

Gonzalez, R., Carey, C., & Grant, I. (2002). Nonacute (residual) neuropsychological effects of cannabis use: A qualitative analysis and systematic review. *Journal of Clinical Pharmacology, 42* (11 Suppl.), 48S–57S.

Goodman, R. M. (2000). Bridging the gap in effective program implementation: From concept to application. *Journal of Community Psychology, 28,* 309–321.

Gottfredson, D. C., & Wilson, D. B. (2003). Characteristics of effective school-based substance abuse prevention. *Prevention Science, 4,* 27–38.

Gowing, L. R., Henry-Edwards, S. M., Irvine, R. J., & Ali, R. L. (2002). The health effects of ecstasy: A literature review. *Drug and Alcohol Review, 21,* 53–63.

Grant, B. F., & Dawson, D. A. (1997). Age at onset of alcohol use and its association with DSM-IV alcohol abuse and dependence: Results from the National Longitudinal Alcohol Epidemiologic Survey. *Journal of Substance Abuse, 9,* 103–110.

Grant, S., London, E. D., Newlin, D. B., Villemagne, V. L., Liu, X., Contoreggi, C., et al. (1996). Activation of memory circuits during cue-elicited craving. *Proceedings of the National Academy of Sciences of the United States of America, 93,* 12040–12045.

Green, A. R., Mechan, A. O., Elliott, J. M., O'Shea, E., & Colado, M. I. (2003). The pharmacology and clinical pharmacology of 3,4-methylenedioxymethamphetamine (MDMA, "ecstasy"). *Pharmacological Reviews , 55,* 463–508.

Green, B., Kavanagh, D., & Young, R. (2003). Being stoned: A review of self-reported cannabis effects. *Drug and Alcohol Review, 22,* 453–460.

Greenberg, M. T., Domitrovich, C., & Bumbarger, B. (2000). Preventing mental disorders in school-aged children: A review of the effectiveness of prevention programs. *Prevention & Treatment.* Washington, DC: American Psychological Association.

Grella, C. E., Hser, Y. I., Joshi, V., & Rounds-Bryant,

J. (2001). Drug treatment outcomes for adolescents with comorbid mental and substance use disorders. Findings from the DATOS-A. *Journal of Nervous and Mental Disease, 189*, 384–392.

Griffith, J. D., Rowan-Szal, G. A., Roark, R. R., & Simpson, D. D. (2000). Contingency management in outpatient methadone treatment: A meta-analysis. *Drug and Alcohol Dependence, 58*, 55–66.

Gross, S. R., Barrett, S. P., Shestowsky, J. S., & Pihl, R. O. (2002). Ecstasy and drug consumption patterns: A Canadian rave population study. *Canadian Journal of Psychiatry, 47*, 546–551.

Grunbaum, J. A., Kann, L., Kinchen, S. A., Williams, B., Ross, J. G., Lowery, R., et al. (2002). Youth risk behavior surveillance—United States 2001. *Morbidity and Mortality Weekly Report Surveillance Summaries, 51*(SS04), 1–64.

Hall, W., & Solowij, N. (1998). Adverse effects of cannabis. *Lancet, 352*(9140), 1611–1616.

Hallfors, D. (2001, April). *Diffusion of federal policy to promote effective school-based prevention: State and local perspectives.* Paper presented at the Drug Abuse Prevention Summit, Snowbird, UT.

Hallikainen, T., Saito, T., Lachman, H. M., Volavka, J., Pohjalainen, T., Ryynanen, O. P., et al. (1999). Association between low activity serotonin transporter promoter genotype and early onset alcoholism with habitual impulsive violent behavior. *Molecular Psychiatry, 4*, 385–388.

Halpern, J. H., & Pope, H. G., Jr. (1999). Do hallucinogens cause residual neuropsychological toxicity? *Drug and Alcohol Dependence, 53*, 247–256.

Halpern, J. H., & Pope, H. G., Jr. (2001). Hallucinogens on the Internet: A vast new source of underground drug information. *American Journal of Psychiatry, 158*, 481–483.

Halpern, J. H., & Pope, H. G. (2003). Hallucinogen persisting perception disorder: What do we know after 50 years? *Drug and Alcohol Dependence, 69*, 109–119.

Handelsman, L., Aronson, M. J., Ness, R., Cochrane, K. J., & Kanof, P. D. (1992). The dysphoria of heroin addiction. *American Journal of Drug and Alcohol Abuse, 18*, 275–287.

Hansen, W. B. (1992). School-based substance abuse prevention: A review of the state of the art in curriculum, 1980–1990. *Health Education Research: Theory and Practice, 7*, 403–430.

Harrison, L. (2001). Understanding the differences in youth drug prevalence rates produced by the MTF, NHSDA, and YRBS studies. *Journal of Drug Issues, 31*, 665–694.

Hatsukami, D. K., & Fischman, M. W. (1996). Crack cocaine and cocaine hydrochloride. Are the differences myth or reality? *Journal of the American Medical Association, 276*, 1580–1588.

Hawkins, J. D., Catalano, R. F., & Miller, J. Y. (1992). Risk and protective factors for alcohol and other drug problems in adolescence and early adulthood: Implications for substance abuse prevention. *Psychological Bulletin 112*, 64–105.

Heath, A. C., Madden, P. A., Grant, J. D., McLaughlin, T. L., Todorov, A. A., & Bucholz, K. K. (1999). Resiliency factors protecting against teenage alcohol use and smoking, influences of religion, religious involvement and values and ethnicity in the Missouri Adolescent Female Twin Study. *Twin Research, 2*, 145–155.

Heath, A. C., & Martin, N. (1988). Teenage alcohol use in the Australian twin register; genetic and social determinants of starting to drink. *Alcoholism, Clinical and Experimental Research, 12*, 735–741.

Heath, A. C., & Martin, N. G. (1993). Genetic models for the natural history of smoking: Evidence for a genetic influence on smoking persistence. *Addictive Behaviors, 18*, 19–34.

Heimer, L., & Alheid, G. (1991). Piecing together the puzzle of basal forebrain anatomy. In T. C. Napier, P. W. Kalivas, & I. Hanin (Eds.), The basal forebrain: Anatomy to function (series title: *Advances in Experimental Medicine and Biology*, Vol. 295, pp. 1–42). New York: Plenum Press.

Heinz, A., Goldman, D., Jones, D. W., Palmour, R., Hommer, D., Gorey, J, G., et al. (2000). Genotype influences in vivo dopamine transporter availability in human striatum. *Neuropsychopharmacology, 22*, 133–139.

Hellerstein, D. J., Rosenthal, R. N., & Miner, C. R. (2001). Integrating services for schizophrenia and substance abuse. *Psychiatric Quarterly 72*, 291–306.

Henggeler, S. W., & Borduin, C. M. (1990). *Family therapy and beyond: A multisystemic approach to treating the behavior problems of children and adolescents.* Pacific Grove, CA: Brooks/Cole.

Henggeler, S. W., Borduin, C., & Melton, G. B. (1991). Effects of multisystemic therapy on drug use and abuse in serious juvenile offenders: A progress report from two outcome studies. *Family Dynamics and Addiction Quarterly, 1*, 40–51.

Henggeler, S. W., Melton, G. B., Brondino, M. J., Scherer, D. G., & Hanley, J. H. (1997). Multisystemic therapy with violent and chronic juvenile offenders and their families: The role of treatment fidelity. *Journal of Consulting and Clinical Psychology, 65,* 821–833.

Henggeler, S. W., Schoenwald, S. K., Borduin, C. M., Rowland, M. D., & Cunningham, P. B. (1998). *Multisystemic treatment of antisocial behavior in children and adolescents.* New York: Guilford Press.

Henggeler, S. W., Pickrel, S. G., Brondino, M. J., & Crouch, J. L. (1996). Eliminating (almost) treatment dropout of substance abusing or dependent delinquents through home-based multisystemic therapy. *American Journal of Psychiatry, 153,* 427–428.

Hibell, B., Andersson, B., Ahlstrom, S., Balakireva, O., Bjarnason, T., Kokkevi, A., et al. (2000). *The 1999 ESPAD report on alcohol and other drug use among students in 30 European countries.* Paper presented at the Information on Alcohol and Other Drugs, Stockholm, Sweden.

Higgins, S. T. (1999). We've come a long way: Comments on cocaine treatment outcome research. *Archives of General Psychiatry, 56,* 516–518.

Higgins, S. T., Delany, D. D., Budney, A. J., Bickel, W. K., Hughes, J. R., Foerg, F., et. al. (1991). A behavioral approach to achieving initial cocaine abstinence. *American Journal of Psychiatry, 148,* 1218–1224.

Hill, S. Y., Locke, J., Zezza, N., Kaplan, B., Neiswanger, K., Steinhauer, S. R., et al. (1998). Genetic association between reduced P300 amplitude and the DRD2 dopamine receptor A1 allele in children at high risk for alcoholism. *Biological Psychiatry, 43,* 40–51.

Hill, S. Y., Zezza, N., Wipprecht, G., Locke, J., & Neiswanger, K. (1999). Personality traits and dopamine receptors (D2 and D4): Linkage studies in families of alcoholics. *American Journal of Medical Genetics 88,* 634–641.

Himmelsbach, C. K. (1943). Can the euphoric, analgetic, and physical dependence effects of drugs be separated? IV With reference to physical dependence. *Federation Proceedings, 2,* 201–203.

Hingson, R. W., Heeren, T., Zakocs, R. C., Kopstein, A., & Wechsler, H. (2002). Magnitude of alcohol-related mortality and morbidity among U.S. college students ages 18–24. *Journal of Studies on Alcohol, 63,* 136–144.

Hoehe, M. R., Kopke, K., Wendel, B., Rohde, K., Flachmeier, C., Kidd, K. K., et al. (2000). Sequence variability and candidate gene analysis in complex disease: Association of mu opioid receptor gene variation with substance dependence. *Human Molecular Genetics, 9,* 2895–2908.

Hofmann, A. (1994). History of the discovery of LSD. In A. Pletscher & D. Ladewig (Eds.), *Fifty years of LSD: Current status and prospectives of hallucinogens.* Parthenon, NY: Parthenon Publishing Group.

Holder, H. D. (2001). Prevention of alcohol problems in the 21st century. *American Journal of the Addictions, 10,* 1–15.

Holder, H. D. (2002). Prevention of alcohol and drug "abuse" problems at the community level: What research tells us. *Substance Use and Misuse, 37,* 901–921.

Hollister, L. E. (1968). *Chemical psychoses: LSD and related drugs.* Springfield, IL: C. C. Thomas.

Hornik, R. (2003). Alcohol, tobacco, and marijuana use among youth: Same-time and lagged and simultaneous-change associations in a nationally representative sample of 9- to 18-year-olds. In D. Romer (Ed.), *Reducing adolescent risk: Toward an integrated approach* (pp. 335–344). Thousand Oaks, CA: Sage Publications.

Hornik, R., Maklan, D., Cadell, D., Barmada, C., Jacobsohn, L., Prado, A., et al. (2002). *Evaluation of the National Youth Anti-Drug Media Campaign: Fifth semi-annual report of findings.* Washington, DC: Campaign Publications.

Hser, Y., Hoffman, V., Grella, C. E., & Anglin, M. D. (2001). A 33-year follow-up of narcotics addicts. *Archives of General Psychiatry, 58,* 503–508.

Hu, S., Brody, C., Fisher, C., Gunzerath, L., Nelson, M., Sabol, S., et al. (2000). Interaction between the serotonin transporter gene and neuroticism in cigarette smoking behavior. *Molecular Psychiatry, 5,* 181–188.

Hurt, R. D., Croghan, G. A., Beede, S. D., Wolter, T. D., Croghan, I. T., & Patten, C. A. (2000). Nicotine patch therapy in 101 adolescent smokers: Efficacy, withdrawal symptom relief and carbon monoxide and plasma cotinine levels. *Archives of Pediatric and Adolescent Medicine, 154,* 31–37.

Hyman, S. E., & Malenka, R. C. (2001). Addiction and the brain: The neurobiology of compulsion and its persistence. *Nature Reviews Neuroscience, 2,* 695–703.

Iversen, L. (2003). Cannabis and the brain. *Brain, 126* (Pt 6), 1252–1270.

Irvin, J. E., Bowers, C. A., Dunn, M. E., & Wong, M. C. (1999). Efficacy of relapse prevention: A meta-analytic review. *Journal of Consulting and Clinical Psychology, 67,* 563–570.

Ishiguro, H., Saito, T., Akazawa, S., Mitushio, H., Tada. K., Enomoto, M., et al. (1999). Association between drinking-related antisocial behavior and a polymorphism in the serotonin transporter gene in a Japanese population. *Alcoholism, Clinical and Experimental Research, 23,* 1281–1284.

Jaffe, J. H., Cascella, N. G., Kumor, K. M., & Sherer, M. A. (1989). Cocaine-induced cocaine craving. *Psychopharmacology, 97,* 59–64.

Jaffe, S. L., & Simkin, D. R. (2002). Alcohol and drug abuse in children and adolescents. In M. Lewis (Ed.), *Child and adolescent psychiatry: A comprehensive textbook* (3rd ed., pp. 895–911). New Haven, CT: Lippincott Williams and Wilkins.

Jamieson, P., & Romer, D. (2001). What do young people think they know about the risks of smoking. In P. Slovic (Ed.), *Smoking risks, perception and policy,* (pp. 51–63). Philadelphia: Sage Publications.

Jansen, K. L., & Darracot-Cankovic, R. (2001). The nonmedical use of ketamine, part two: A review of problem use and dependence. *Journal of Psychoactive Drugs, 33,* 151–158.

Jentsch, J. D., Olausson, P., De La Garza, 2nd, R., & Taylor, J. R. (2002). Impairments of reversal learning and response perseveration after repeated, intermittent cocaine administrations to monkeys. *Neuropsychopharmacology, 26,* 183–190.

Jerrell, J. M., & Ridgely, M. S. (1995). Comparative effectiveness of three approaches to serving people with severe mental illness and substance abuse disorders. *Journal of Nervous and Mental Disease, 183,* 566–576.

Jessor, R. (1991). Risk behavior in adolescence: A psychosocial framework for understanding and action. *Journal of Adolescent Health, 12,* 597–605.

Jessor, R., & Jessor, S. L. (1977). *Problem behavior and psychological development: A longitudinal study of youth.* New York: Academic Press.

Joanning, H., Thomas, F., & Quinn, W. (1992). Treating adolescent drug abuse: A comparison of family systems therapy, group therapy, and family drug education. *Journal of Marital and Family Therapy, 18,* 345–356.

Johnston, L. D. (1973). *Drugs and American youth.* Paper presented at the Institute for Social Research, Ann Arbor, MI.

Johnston, L. D. (1991). Toward a theory of drug epidemics. In L. Donohew, H. Syper & W. Bukoski (Eds.), *Persuasive communication and drug abuse prevention* (pp. 93–131). Hillsdale, NJ: Lawrence Erlbaum.

Johnston, L. D. (2003). Alcohol and illicit drugs: The role of risk perceptions. In D. Romer (Ed.), *Reducing adolescent risk: Toward an integrated approach* (pp. 56–74). Thousand Oaks, CA: Sage Publications.

Johnston, L. D., O'Malley, P. M., & Bachman, J. G. (1998). *National survey results on drug use from the Monitoring the Future Study 1995–1997. Volume 1: Secondary school students.* Rockville, MD: National Institute on Drug Abuse.

Johnston, L. D., O'Malley, P. M., & Bachman, J. G. (2000). *National survey results on drug use from the Monitoring the Future Study, 1975–1999. Volume I: Secondary school students* (NIH publication no. 00-4802). Bethesda, MD: National Institute on Drug Abuse. 480 pp.

Johnston, L. D., O'Malley, P. M., & Bachman, J. G. (2002a). *National survey results on drug use from the Monitoring the Future Study, 1975–2001. Volume I: Secondary school students* (NIH Publication No. 02-5106). Bethesda, MD: National Institute on Drug Abuse.

Johnston, L., O'Malley, P., & Bachman, J. (2002b). *Overview of key findings of the Monitoring the Future study on drug use, national survey results 2001.* Bethesda, MD: National Institute on Drug Abuse.

Johnston, L. D., O'Malley, P. M., & Bachman, J. G. (2003a). Demographic subgroup trends for various licit and illicit drugs, 1975–2002. (Monitoring the Future Occasional Paper #58) Ann Arbor, MI: Institute for Social Research 25pp.

Johnston, L. D., O'Malley, P. M., & Bachman, J. G. (2003b). *National survey results on drug use from the Monitoring the Future Study, 1975–2002: Volume I: Secondary school students* (NIH publication no. 03-5375). Bethesda, MD: National Institute on Drug Abuse.

Johnston, L. D., O'Malley, P. M., & Bachman, J. G. (2003c). *National survey results on drug use from the Monitoring the Future study, 1975–2002. Volume II: College students and adults ages 19–40* (NIH Publication No. 03-5376). Bethesda, MD: National Institute on Drug Abuse 253pp.

Jorm, A., Henderson, A., Jacomb, P., Christensen, H., Korten, A., Rodgers, B., et al. (2000). Association of smoking and personality with a polymorphism of the dopamine transporter gene: Results from a community survey. *American Journal of Medical Genetics, 96,* 331–334.

Kaminer, Y., Burleson, J. A., & Goldberger, R. (2002). Cognitive-behavioral coping skills and psychoeducation therapies for adolescent substance abuse. *Journal of Nervous and Mental Disease, 190,* 737–745.

Kandel, D. B. (1975). Stages in adolescent involvement in drug use. *Science, 190,* 912–914.

Kandel, D. B. (Eds.). (2002). *Stages and pathways of drug involvement: Examining the gateway hypothesis.* Cambridge, UK: Cambridge University Press.

Kandel, D., & Faust, R. (1975). Sequence and stages in patterns of adolescent drug use. *Archives of General Psychiatry, 32,* 923–932.

Kandel, D. B., & Jessor, R. (2002). *The gateway hypothesis revisited.* In D. B. Kandel (Ed.), *Stages and pathways of drug involvement: Examining the gateway hypothesis.* (pp. 365–372). Cambridge, UK: Cambridge University Press.

Kandel, D. B., & Logan, J. A. (1984). Patterns of drug use from adolescence to young adulthood: I. Periods of risk for initiation, continued use, and discontinuation. *American Journal of Public Health, 74,* 660–666.

Kandel, D., & Yamaguchi, K. (1993). From beer to crack: Developmental patterns of drug involvement. *American Journal of public Health, 83,* 851–855.

Kann, L. (2002). The Youth Risk Behavior Surveillance System: Measuring health-risk behaviors. *American Journal of Health Behavior 2001, 25,* 272–277.

Karama, S., Lecours, A. R., Leroux, J. M., Bourgouin, P., Beaudoin, G., Joubert, S., & Beauregard, M. (2002). Areas of brain activation in males and females during viewing of erotic film excerpts. *Human Brain Mapping, 16,* 1–13.

Kazdin, A. E. (1991). Effectiveness of psychotherapy with children and adolescents. *Journal of Consulting and Clinical Psychology, 59,* 785–798.

Kazdin, A. E. (1993). Treatment of conduct disorder: Progress and directions in psychotherapy research. *Development and Psychopathology, 5,* 277–310.

Kendler, K. S. (2001). Twin studies of psychiatric illness an update. *Archives of General Psychiatry, 58,* 1005–1014.

Kendler, K. S., Gardner, C. O., & Gardner, C.O.J. (1998). Twin studies of adult psychiatric and substance dependence disorders: Are they biased by differences in the environmental experiences of monozygotic and dizygotic twins in childhood and adolescence? *Psychological Medicine, 28,* 625–633.

Kendler, K. S., Neale, M. C., Sullivan, P., Corey, L. A., Gardner, C. O., & Prescott, C. A. (1999). A population-based twin study in women of smoking initiation and nicotine dependence. *Psychological Medicine, 29,* 299–308.

Kessler, R. C. (1994). The National Comorbidy Survey of the United States. *International Review of Psychiatry, 6,* 365–376.

Kessler, R. C., Aguilar-Gaxiola, S., Andrade, L., Bijl, R., Borges, G., Caraveo-Anduaga, J. J., et al. (2001). Mental–substance comorbidities in the ICPE surveys. *Psychiatria Fennica, 32* (Suppl. 2), 62–80.

Kessler, R. C., McGonagle, K. A., Zhao, S., Nelson, C. B., Hughes, M., Eshleman, S., et al. (1994). Lifetime and 12-month prevalence of DSM-III-R psychiatric disorders in the United States: Results from the National Comorbidity Survey. *Archives of General Psychiatry, 51,* 8–19.

Kilpatrick, D. G., Acierno, R., Saunders, B., Resnick, H. S., Best, C. L., & Schnurr, P. P. (2000). Risk factors for adolescent substance abuse and dependence: Data from a national sample. *Journal of Consulting and Clinical Psychology, 68,* 19–30.

Kilts, C. D., Schweitzer, J. B., Quinn, C. K., Gross, R. E., Faber, T. L., Muhammad, F., et al. (2001). Neural activity related to drug craving in cocaine addiction. *Archives of General Psychiatry, 58,* 334–341.

Kirby, K. C., Marlowe, D. B., Festinger, D. S., Lamb, R. J., & Platt, J. J. (1998). Schedule of voucher delivery influences initiation of cocaine abstinence. *Journal of Consulting and Clinical Psychology, 66,* 761–767.

Klein-Schwartz, W., & McGrath, J. (2003). Poison centers' experience with methylphenidate abuse in pre-teens and adolescents. *Journal of the American Academy of Child and Adolescent Psychiatry, 42,* 288–294.

Koesters, S. C., Rogers, P. D., & Rajasingham, C. R. (2002). MDMA ('ecstasy') and other 'club drugs'. The new epidemic. *Pediatric Clinics of North America, 49,* 415–433.

Koob, G. F. (1992). Drugs of abuse: Anatomy, pharmacology, and function of reward pathways. *Trends in Pharmacological Sciences, 13,* 177–184.

Koob, G. F., & Heinricks, S. C. (1999). A role for corticotropin-releasing factors and urocortin in behavioral responses to stressors. *Brain Research, 848,* 141–152.

Koob, G. F., & Le Moal, M. (1997). Drug abuse: Hedonic homeostatic dysregulation. *Science, 278,* 52–58.

Koob, G. F., & Le Moal, M. (2001). Drug addiction, dysregulation of reward and allostasis. *Neuropsychopharmacology, 24,* 97–129.

Koob, G. F., & Nestler, E. J. (1997). The neurobiology of drug addiction. *Journal of Neuropsychiatry and Clinical Neuroscience, 9,* 482–497.

Koob, G. F., Sanna, P. P., & Bloom, F. E. (1998). Neuroscience of addiction. *Neuron, 21,* 467–476.

Kosten, T. R. (in press). Cocaine and psychostimulants. In H. R. Kranzler & D. A. Ciraulo (Eds.), *Clinical manual of addiction psychopharmacology.* Washington, DC: APPI Press.

Kosten, T. R., & Biegel, D. (2002). Therapeutic vaccines for substance dependence. *Expert Review of Vaccines, 1,* 363–371.

Kosten, T. R., & O'Connor, P. G. (2003). Current concepts—Management of drug withdrawal. *New England Journal of Medicine, 348,* 1786–1795.

Kranzler, H. R., Gelernter, J., O'Malley, S., Hernandez-Avila, C. A., & Kaufman, D. (1998). Association of alcohol or other drug dependence with alleles of the mu opioid receptor gene (OPRM1). *Alcoholism, Clinical and Experimental Research, 22,* 1359–1362.

Kruesi, M. J., Rapoport, J. L., Hamburger, S., Hibbs, E., Potter, W. Z., Lenane, M., et al. (1990). Cerebrospinal fluid monoamine metabolites, aggression, and impulsivity in disruptive behavior disorders of children and adolescents. *Archives of General Psychiatry, 47,* 419–426.

Kumpfer, K., & Alvarado, R. (1995). Strengthening families to prevent drug use in multi-ethnic youth. In G. Botvin, S. Schinke, & M. Orlandi (Eds.), *Drug abuse prevention with multi-ethnic youth* (pp. 253–292). Newbury Park, CA: Sage Publications.

Kumpfer, K., Molgaard, V., & Spoth, R. (1996). The Strengthening Families Program for the prevention of delinquency and drug use. In R. D. Peters & R. J. McMahon (Eds.), *Preventing childhood disorders, substance abuse, and delinquency* (pp. 241–267). Thousand Oaks, CA: Sage Publications.

Kurtzman, T. L., Otsuka, K. N., & Wahl, R. A. (2001). Inhalant abuse by adolescents. *Journal of Adolescent Health, 28,* 170–180.

Laviola, G., Adriani, W., Terranova, M. L., & Gerra, G. (1999). Psychobiological risk factors for vulnerability to psychostimulants in human adolescents and animal models. *Neuroscience and Biobehavorial Reviews, 23,* 993–1010.

Le Moal, M., & Simon, H. (1991). Mesocorticolimbic dopaminergic network: functional and regulatory roles. *Physiological Reviews, 71,* 155–234.

Lerman, C., Audrain, J., Main, D., Boyd, N., Caporaso, N., Bowman, E., et al. (1999). Evidence suggesting the role of specific genetic factors in cigarette smoking. *Health Psychology, 18,* 14–20.

Lerman, C., Caporaso, N. E., Audrain, J., Main, D., Boyd, N. R., & Shields, P. G. (2000). Interacting effects of the serotonin transporter gene and neuroticism in smoking practices and nicotine dependence. *Molecular Psychiatry, 5,* 189–192.

Lerman, C., Caporaso, N., Bush, A., Zheng, Y., Audrian, J., Main, D., et al. (2001). Tryptophan hydroxylase gene variant and smoking behavior. *American Journal of Medical Genetics, 105,* 518–520.

Lerman, C., Gold, K., Audrain, J., Lin, T. H., Boyd, N. R., Orleans, C. T., et al. (1997). Incorporating biomarkers of exposure and genetic susceptibility into smoking cessation treatment: Effects on smoking-related cognitions, emotions and behavior change. *Health Psychology, 16,* 87–99.

Lerman, C., Patterson, F., & Shields, P. (2003). *Genetics basis of substance use and dependence: Implication for prevention in high-risk youth.* Philadelphia: Sage Publications.

Lerman, C., Shields, P., Audrain, J., Main, D., Cobb, B., Boyd, N., et al. (1998). The role of the serotonin transporter gene in cigarette smoking. *Cancer Epidemiology, Biomarkers, and Prevention, 7,* 253–255.

Lerner, R. (1995). *America's youth in crisis: Challenges and options for programs and policies.* Thousand Oaks, CA: Sage Publications.

Lerner, R. (2001). Promoting promotion in the development of prevention science. *Applied Developmental Science, 5,* 254–257.

Lesch, K. P., & Merschdorf, U. (2000). Impulsivity, aggression, and serotonin: A molecular psychobiological perspective. *Behavioral Science Law, 18,* 581–604.

Levin, E. D., Rezvani, A. H., Montoya, D., Rose, J. E., & Swartzwelder, H. S. (2003). Adolescent-onset nicotine self-administration modeled in female rats. *Psychopharmacology, 169,* 141–149.

Lichtermann, D., Hranoiovic, D., Trixler, M., Franke, P., Jernej, B., Delmo, C. D., et al. (2000). Support for allelic association of a polymorphic site in the promoter region of the serotonin transporter gene with risk for alcohol dependence. *American Journal of Psychiatry, 159,* 2045–2047.

Liddle, H. A., & Dakof, G. (1995). Efficacy of family therapy for drug abuse: Promising but not definitive. *Journal of Marital and Family Therapy, 21,* 511–543.

Liddle, H. A., & Dakof, G. A. (2002). *A family-based, intensive outpatient alternative to residential drug treatment for co-morbid adolescent substance abusers: Preliminary finding of a controlled trial.* Santa Fe, NM: Society for Psychotherapy Research.

Liddle, H. A., Dakof, G. A., Parker, K., Diamond, G. S., Barrett, K., & Tejeda, M. (2001). Multidimensional family therapy for adolescent drug abuse: Results of a randomized clinical trial. *American Journal of Drug and Alcohol Abuse, 27,* 651–688.

Liddle, H. A., & Rowe, C. L. Sixth Edition (in press). Advances in family therapy research: Bridging gaps and expanding frontiers. In M. Nichols & R. Schwartz (Eds.), *Family therapy: Concepts and methods* (pp.). Boston: Allyn & Bacon.

Liepman, M. R., Calles, J. L., Kizilbash, L., Nazeer, A., & Sheikh, S. (2002). Genetic and nongenetic factors influencing substance use by adolescents. *Adolescent Medicine State of the Art Reviews, 13,* 375–401.

Lifrak, P. D., Alterman, A. E., O'Brien, C. P., & Volpicelli, J. R. (1997). Naltrexone for alcoholic adolescents [Letter]. *American Journal of Psychiatry, 153,* 439–441.

Ling, W., Shoptaw, S., & Majewska, M. D. (1998). Baclofen as a cocaine-anti-craving medication: A preliminary clinical study. *Neuropsychopharmacology, 18,* 403–404.

Lingford-Hughes, A. R., Acton, P. D., Gacinovic, S., Suckling, J., Busatto, G. F., Boddington, S. J., et al. (1998). Reduced levels of GABA-benzodiazepine receptor in alcohol dependency in the absence of grey matter atrophy. *British Journal of Psychiatry, 173,* 116–22.

Lohman, M., Riggs, P. D., Hall, S. K., Mikulich, S. K., & Klein, C. A. (2002). *Perceived motivations for treatment in depressed, substance-dependent adolescents with conduct disorder.* Paper presented at the College on Problems of Drug Dependence: 64th Annual Scientific Meeting, Quebec, Canada, June 2004.

London, S. J., Idle, J. R., Daly, A. K., & Coetzee, G. A. (1999). Genetic variation of CYP2A6, smoking, and risk of cancer. *Lancet, 353,* 898–899.

Lorenc, J. D. (2003). Inhalant abuse in the pediatric population: A persistent challenge. *Current Opinion in Pediatrics, 15,* 204–209.

Lueders, K. K., Hu, S., McHugh, L., Myakishev, M. V., Sirota, L. A., & Hamer, D. H. (2002). Genetic and functional analysis of single nucleotide polymorphisms in the beta2-neuronal nicotinic acetylcholine receptor gene (CHRNB2). *Nicotine and Tobacco Research, 4,* 115–125.

Luo, X., Kranzler, H. R., Zhao, H., & Gelernter, J. (2003). Haplotypes at the OPRM1 locus are associated with susceptibility to substance dependence in European-Americans. *American Journal of Medical Genetics, 120B(1),* 97–108.

Lynam, D. R., Milich, R., Zimmerman, R., Novak,

S. P., Logan, T. K., Martin, C., et al. (1999). Project DARE: No effects at 10-year follow-up. *Journal of Consulting and Clinical Psychology, 67,* 292–296.

Maas, L. C., Lukas, S. E., Kaufman, M. J., Weiss, R. C., Daniels, S. L., Rogers, V. W., et al. (1996). *Functional MRI of human brain activation during cue-induced cocaine craving.* Paper presented at the Proceedings on College on Problems of Drug Dependence 1996, Nashville, TN.

Madden, P. A., Heath, A., Pederson, N., Kaprio, J., Koskenvuo, M., & Martin, N. (1999). The genetics of smoking persistence in men and women: a multicultural study. *Behavior Genetics, 29,* 423–431.

Magno Zito, J., Safer, D. J., dosReis, S., Gardner, J. F., Magder, L., Soeken, K., et al. (2003). Psychotropic practice patterns of youth. A 10-year perspective. *Archives of Pediatrics and Adolescent Medicine, 157,* 17–25.

Malik, S. A., Khan, C., Jabbar, A., & Iqbal, A. (1992). Heroin addiction and sex hormones in males. *Journal of the Pakistan Medical Association, 42,* 210–212.

Markou, A., Kosten, T. R., & Koob, G. F. (1998). Neurobiological similarities in depression and drug dependence: A self-medication hypothesis. *Neuropsychopharmacology, 18,* 135–174.

Marteau, J., & Lerman, C. (2001). Genetic risk and behavioral change. *British Medical Journal, 322,* 1056–1059.

Martin, C. S., Kaczynski, N. A., Maisto, S. A., Bukstein, O. M., & Moss, H. B. (1995). Patterns of DSM-IV alcohol abuse and dependence symptoms in adolescent drinkers. *Journal of Studies on Alcohol, 56,* 672–680.

Martin, C. S., & Winters, K. C. (1998). Diagnosis and assessment of alcohol use disorders among adolescents. *Alcohol Health and Research World, 22,* 95–105.

Mason, P. E., & Kerns, W. P., 2nd. (2002). Gamma hydroxybutyric acid (GHB) intoxication. *Academic Emergency Medicine, 9,* 730–739.

Masse, L., & Tremblay, R. (1997). Behavior of boys in kindergarten and the onset of substance use during adolescence. *Archives of General Psychiatry, 54,* 62–68.

Matsushita, S., Yoshino, A., Murayama, M., Kimura, M., Muramatsu, T., & Higuchi, S. (2001). Association study of serotonin transporter gene regulatory region polymorphism and alcoholism. *Behavior Genetics, 31,* 231–239.

McCance, E. F., & Kosten, T. R. (1998). Psychopharmacological treatments. In R. Frances & S.

Miller (Eds.), *Clinical textbook of addictive disorders* (2nd ed., Section V, pp. 596–624). New York: Guilford Publications.

McGue, M., Pickens, R. W., & Svikis, D. S. (1992). Sex and age effects on the inheritance of alcohol problems: a twin study. *Journal of Abnormal Psychology, 101,* 3–17.

McKance-Katz, E. F., Kosten, T. R., & Jatlow, P. (1998). Concurrent use of cocaine and alcohol is more potent and potentially more toxic than use of either alone—A multiple-dose study. *Biological Psychiatry, 44,* 250–259.

McKay, J. R., Alterman, A. I., Cacciola, J. S., Rutherford, M. J., O'Brien, C. P., & Koppenhaver, J. (1997). Group counseling versus individualized relapse prevention aftercare following intensive outpatient treatment for cocaine dependence. *Journal of Consulting and Clinical Psychology, 65,* 778–788.

McLellan, A. T., Lewis, D. C., O'Brien, C. P., & Kleber, H. D. (2000). Drug dependence, a chronic medical illness: Implications for treatment, insurance, and outcomes evaluation. *Journal of the American Medical Association, 284,* 1689–1695.

Merikangas, K. R., Stolar, M., Stevens, D. E., Goulet, J., Preisig, M. A., Fenton, B., et al. (1998). Familial transmission of substance use disorders. *Archives of General Psychiatry, 55,* 973–979.

Mermelstein, R. (2003). Teen smoking cessation. *Tobacco Control,* 12(Suppl. 1), 125–134.

Messina, N., Farabee, D., & Rawson, R. A. (2003). Treatment responsivity of cocaine-dependent patients with antisocial personality disorder to cognitive-behavioral and contingency management interventions. *Journal of Consulting and Clinical Psychology, 71,* 320–329.

Metzler, C. W., Biglan, A., Rusby, J. C., & Sprague, J. R. (2001). Evaluation of a comprehensive behavior management program to improve school-wide positive behavior support. *Education and Treatment of Children, 24,* 448–479.

Michelson, D., Allen, A. J., Busner, J., Casat, C., Dunn, D., Kratochvil, C., et al. (2002). Once-daily atomoxetine treatment for children and adolescents with attention deficit hyperactivity disorder: A randomized, placebo-controlled study. *American Journal of Psychiatry, 159,* 1896–1901.

Milberger, S., Biederman, J., Faraone, S. V., Chen, L., & Jones, J. (1997). ADHD is associated with early initiation of cigarette smoking in children and adolescents. *Journal of the American Academy of Child and Adolescent Psychiatry, 36,* 37–44.

Miller, W. R., & DelBoca, F. K. (1994). Measurement of drinking behavior using the Form 90 family of instruments. *Journal of Studies on Alcohol, 12* (Suppl.), 112–117.

Miller, W. R., & Rollnick, S. (1991). *Motivational interviewing: Preparing people to change addictive behavior.* New York: Guilford Press.

Miller, W. R., & Rollnick, S. (2002). *Motivational interviewing: Preparing people for change* (2nd ed). New York: Guilford Press.

Miller, W. R., & Wilbourne, P. L. (2002). Mesa Grande: A methodological analysis of clinical trials of treatments for alcohol use disorders. *Addiction, 97,* 265–277.

Minkoff, K., & Drake, R. E. (1991). *Dual diagnosis of serious mental illness and substance disorder.* San Francisco: Jossey-Bass.

Miotto, K., Darakjian, J., Basch, J., Murray, S., Zogg, J., & Rawson, R. (2001). Gamma-hydroxybutyric acid: Patterns of use, effects and withdrawal. *American Journal of Addiction, 10,* 232–241.

Molgaard, V., & Kumpfer, K. (1995). *The Strengthening Families program for families with pre- and early teens: Leader guide.* Ames, IA: Iowa State University Extension.

Monterosso, J., Ehrman, J., Franklin, T., Napier, K., O'Brien, C. P., & Childress, A. R. (2001). *Decision-making task performance in cocaine-dependent patients.* Paper presented at the Drug and Alcohol Dependence: Abstracts for the 63rd Annual Meeting of the College on Problems of Drug Dependence, Phoenix, AZ, June 2001.

Monti, P. M., Colby, S. M., Barnett, N. P., Spirito, A., Rohsenow, D. J., Myers, M. G., et al. (1999). Brief intervention for harm reduction with alcohol-positive older adolescents in a hospital emergency department. *Journal of Consulting and Clinical Psychology, 67,* 989–994.

Moolchan, E. T., Ernst, M., & Henningfield, J. E. (2000). A review of tobacco smoking in adolescents: Treatment implications. *Journal of the American Academy of Child and Adolescent Psychiatry, 39,* 682–693.

Morgan, C., & Kosten, T. R. (1990). Potential toxicity of high dose naltrexone in patients with appetitive disorders. In L. Ried (Ed.), *Opioids, bulimia, and alcohol abuse and alcoholism* (pp. 261–274). New York: Springer-Verlag.

Morgan, D., Grant, K. A., Gage, H. D., Mach, R. H., Kaplan, J. R., Prioleau, O., et al. (2002). Social dominance in monkeys: dopamine D2 receptors and cocaine self-administration [Comment]. *Nature Neuroscience, 5,* 169–174.

Morgenstern, J., & Longabaugh, R. (2000). Cognitive-behavioral treatment for alcohol dependence: A review of the evidence for its hypothesized mechanisms of action. *Addiction, 95,* 1475–1490.

Morley-Fletcher, S., Bianchi, M., Gerra, G., & Laviola, G. (2002). Acute and carryover effects in mice of MDMA ("ecstasy") administration during periadolescence. *European Journal of Pharmacology, 448,* 31–38.

Morral, A. R., McCaffrey, D. F., & Paddock, S. M. (2002). Reassessing the marijuana gateway effect. *Addiction, 97,* 1493–1504.

Morrisey, E., Wandersmand, A., Seybolt, D., Nation, M., Crusto, C., & Davino, K. (1997). Toward a framework for bridging the gap between science and practice in prevention: A focus on evaluator and practitioner perspectives. *Evaluation and Program Planning, 20,* 367–377.

Moss, H. B., & Lynch, K. G. (2001). Comorbid disruptive behavior disorder symptoms and their relationship to adolescent alcohol use disorders. *Drug and Alcohol Dependence, 64,* 75–83.

Mrazek, P. J., & Haggerty, K. (1994). *Reducing Risks for Mental Disorders: Frontiers for Preventive Intervention Research.* Washington, DC.: National Academy Press.

MTP Research Group (Babor, T. F., Carroll, K. M., Christiansen, K., Kadden, R., Litt, M., & McRee, B. (2004). Brief treatments for cannabis dependence. Findings from a randomized multisite trial. *Journal of Consulting and Clinical Psychology, 72,* 455–466.

Myers, M. G., Stewart, D. G., & Brown, S. A. (1998). Progression from conduct disorder to antisocial personality disorder following treatment for adolescent substance abuse. *American Journal of Psychiatry, 155,* 479–485.

National Center on Alcohol and Substance Abuse (CASA). (2003). *Teen tipplers: America's underage drinking epidemic.* The National Center on Addiction and Substance Abuse at Columbia University. New York: Columbia University.

National Commission on Marihuana (1972). Marihuana: *A signal of misunderstanding.* Washington, DC: Government Printing Office.

National Institute on Alcohol Abuse and Alcoholism (NIAAA). (2003). *Alcohol alert, underage drinking: A major public health challenge* (Vol. 59). From http://www.niaaa.gov/publications/a/alerts.htm

National Institute on Drug Abuse. (2000). *Principles of drug abuse treatment: A research-based guide.* Bethesda, Maryland: NIDA.

National Research Council and Institute of Medi-

cine (NRCIM). (2003). *Reducing underage drinking: A collective responsibility.* Washington, DC: The National Academies Press.

Nestler, E. J., Kelz, M. B., Chen, J. (1999). Delta Fos B: A molecular mediator of long-term neural and behavioral plasticity. *Brain Research, 835,* 10–17.

Newcomb, M. D. (1997). Psychosocial predictors and consequences of drug use: A developmental perspective within a prospective study. *Journal of Addictive Diseases, 16,* 51–89.

Nicholson, K. L., & Balster, R. L. (2001). GHB: A new and novel drug of abuse. *Drug and Alcohol Dependence, 63,* 1–22.

Nielsen, D. A., Virkkunen, M., Lappalainen, J., Eggert, M., Brown, G. L., Long, J. C., et al. (1998). A tryptophan hydroxylase gene marker for suicidality and alcoholism. *Archives of General Psychiatry, 55,* 593–602.

Noble E. P. (1993). The D2 dopamine receptor gene: A review of association studies in alcoholism. *Behavior Genetics, 23,* 119–129.

Noble, E., Ozkaragoz, T., Ritchie, T., Zhang, X., Belin, T., & Sparkes, R. (1998). D2 and D4 dopamine receptor polymorphisms and personality. *American Journal of Medical Genetics, 81,* 257–267.

Noble, E., St Jeor, S. T., Ritchie, T., Syndulko, K., St Jeor, S. C., Fitch, R., & Brunner, R. L. (1994). D2 dopamine receptor gene and cigarette smoking: a reward gene? *Medical Hypotheses, 42,* 257–260.

O'Brien, C. (2001). Drug addiction and drug abuse. In J. G. Hardman & C. L. Lee (Eds.), *Goodman & Gilman's the pharmacological basis of therapeutics* (10th ed., pp. 621–642). New York: McGraw-Hill.

O'Brien, C. P., Childress, A. R., Ehrman, R., & Robbins, S. J. (1998). Conditioning factors in drug abuse: Can they explain compulsion? *Journal of Psychopharmacology, 12,* 15–22.

O'Brien, C. P., Childress, A. R., McLellan, A. T., & Ehrman, R. (1992). Classical conditioning in drug-dependent humans. *Annals of the New York Academy of Science, 654,* 400–415.

O'Brien, C. P., Testa, T., O'Brien, T. J., Brady, J. P., & Wells, B. (1977). Conditioning narcotic withdrawal in humans. *Science, 195,* 1000–1002.

Obrocki, J., Schmoldt, A., Buchert, R., Andresen, B., Petersen, K., & Thomasius, R. (2002). Specific neurotoxicity of chronic use of ecstasy. *Toxicology Letters, 127,* 285–297.

Olds, D., Robinson, J., Song, N., Little, C., & Hill, P. (1999). Reducing risks for mental disorders during the first five years of life: A review of preventive interventions. Rockville, MD: Center for Mental Health Services, Substance Abuse and Mental Health Services Administration. Online at: www.sshsac.org/index.asp

O'Loughlin, J., Tarasuk, J., DiFranza, J., & Paradis, G. (2002). Reliability of selected measures of nicotine dependence among adolescents. *Annals of Epidemiology, 12,* 353–362.

Oscarson, M., Gullsten, H., Rautio, A., Bernal, M. L., Sinues, B., Dahl, M. L., et al. (1998). Genotyping of human cytochrome P450 2A6 (CYP2A6), a nicotine C-oxidase. *FEBS Letters, 438,* 201–205.

Osgood, D. W., Johnston, L. D., O'Malley, P. M., & Bachman, J. G. (1988). The generality of deviance in late adolescence and early adulthood. *American Sociological Review, 53,* 81–93.

Osher, F. C., & Drake, R. E. (1996). Reversing a history of unmet needs: Approaches to care for persons with co-occurring addictive and mental disorders. *American Journal of Orthopsychiatry, 66,* 4–11.

Pal, H. R., Berry, N., Kumar, R., & Ray, R. (2002). Ketamine dependence. *Anaesthesia and Intensive Care, 30,* 382–384.

Pandey, S. C., Zhang, H., & Roy, A. (2003). Effect of PKA activator infusion into the central amygdala on anxiety and on NPY expression during ethanol withdrawal. *Alcoholism: Clinical and Experimental Research, 27* (5 Suppl.), 188A.

Parrott, A. C. (2001). Human psychopharmacology of Ecstasy (MDMA): A review of 15 years of empirical research. *Human Psychopharmacology, 16,* 557–577.

Parrott, A. C. (2002). Recreational ecstasy/MDMA, the serotonin syndrome, and serotonergic neurotoxicity. *Pharmacology, Biochemistry, and Behavior, 71,* 837–844.

Parrott, A. C., Buchanan, T., Scholey, A. B., Heffernan, T., Ling, J., & Rodgers, J. (2002). Ecstasy/MDMA-attributed problems reported by novice, moderate and heavy recreational users. *Human Psychopharmacology, 17,* 309–312.

Parsian, A., Chakraverty, S., Fishler, L., & Cloninger, C. R. (1997). No association between polymorphisms in the human dopamine D3 and D4 receptor genes and alcoholism. *American Journal of Medical Genetics, 74,* 281–285.

Patterson, G., DeBaryshe, B., & Ramsey, E. (1989). A developmental perspective on antisocial behavior. *American Psychologist, 44,* 329–335.

Patton, G. C., Carlin, J. B., Coffey, C., Wolfe, R., Hibbert, M., & Bowers, G. (1998). The course of early smoking: A population-based cohort study over three years. *Addiction, 93,* 1251–1260.

Pbert, L., Moolchan, E. T., Muramoto, M., Winickoff, J. P., Curry, S., Lando, H., et al. (2003). The state of office-based interventions for youth tobacco use. *Pediatrics, 111*(6 Pt. 1), e650–660.

Pentz, M. A., Dwyer, J. H., MacKinnon, D. P., Flay, B. R., Hansen, W. B., Wang, E. Y., et al. (1989). A multicommunity trial for primary prevention of adolescent drug abuse. Effects on drug use prevalence. *Journal of the American Medical Association, 261,* 3259–3266.

Perry, C. L., Komro, K. A., Veblen-Mortenson, S., Bosma, L. M., Farbakhsh, K., Munson, K. A., et al. (2003). A randomized controlled trial of the middle and junior high school D.A.R.E. and D.A.R.E. Plus programs. *Archives of Pediatrics and Adolescent Medicine, 157,* 178–184.

Petrakis, I. L., Gonzalez, G., Rosenheck, R., & Krystal, J. H. (2002). Comorbidity of alcoholism and psychiatric disorders: An overview. *Alcohol Research and Health, 26,* 81–90.

Petry, N. M. (2001). Substance abuse pathological gambling, and impulsiveness. *Drug and Alcohol Dependence 63,* 29–38.

Petry, N. M., Martin, B., Cooney, J. L., & Kranzler, H. R. (2000). Give them prizes and they will come: Contingency management treatment of alcohol dependence. *Journal of Consulting and Clinical Psychology, 68,* 250–257.

Pianezza, M., Sellers, E., & Tyndale, R. (1998). Nicotine metabolism defect reduces smoking. *Nature, 393,* 750.

Pickens, R. W., & Svikis, D. S. (1991). Genetic influences in human substance abuse. *Journal of Addictive Diseases, 10,* 205–213.

Pickens, R. W., Svikis, D. S., McGue, M., & LaBuda, M. C. (1995). Common genetic mechanisms in alcohol, drug, and mental disorder comorbidity. *Drug and Alcohol Dependence, 39,* 129–138.

Pierce, J. P., Choi, W. S., Gilpin, E. A., Farkas, A. J., & Berry, C. C. (1998). Tobacco industry promotion of cigarettes and adolescent smoking. *Journal of the American Medical Association, 279,* 511–515.

Pittman, K., Irby, M., & Ferber, T. (2000). Unfinished business: Further reflections on a decade of promoting youth development. In P. P. Ventures (Ed.), *Youth development: Issues, challenges, and directions* (pp. 17–64). Philadelphia, PA: Public/Private Ventures.

Pollock, N. K., & Martin, C. S. (1999). Diagnostic orphans: Adolescents with alcohol symptoms who do not qualify for DSM-IV abuse or dependence diagnoses. *American Journal of Psychiatry, 156,* 897–901.

Pomerleau, O. F., Pomerleau, C. S. (1984). Neuroregulators and the reinforcement of smoking: Towards a biobehavioral explanation. *Neuroscience and Biobehavioral Reviews, 8,* 503–513.

Pomerleau, O. F., Pomerleau, C. S., & Namenek, R. J. (1998). Early experiences with tobacco among women smokers, ex-smokers and never-smokers. *Addiction, 93,* 595–599.

Ponomarev, I., & Crabbe, J. C. (2002). A novel method to assess initial sensitivity and acute functional tolerance to hypnotic effects of ethanol. *Journal of Pharmacology and Experimental Therapeutics, 302,* 257–263.

Price, R. H., & Behrens, T. (2003). Working Pasteur's quadrant: Harnessing science and action for community change. *American Journal of Community Psychology, 31,* 219–223.

Prescott, C. A., & Kendler, K. S. (1999). Genetic and environmental contributions to alcohol abuse and dependence in a population-based sample of male twins. *American Journal of Psychiatry, 156,* 34–40.

Project MATCH Research Group. (1997). Matching alcohol treatments to client heterogeneity: Project MATCH posttreatment drinking outcomes. *Journal of Studies on Alcohol, 58,* 7–29.

Pulvirenti, L., Balducci, C., Piercy, M., & Koob, G. F. (1998). Characterization of the effects of the partial dopamine agonist terguride on cocaine self-administration in the rat. *Journal of Pharmacology and Therapeutics, 286,* 1231–1238.

Rahav, M., Rivera, J. J., Nuttbrock, L., Ng-Mak, D., Sturz, E. L., Link, B. G., et al. (1995). Characteristics and treatment of homeless, mentally ill, chemical-abusing men. *Journal of Psychoactive Drugs, 27,* 93–103.

Rawson, R. A., Huber, A., McCann, M. J., Shoptaw, S., Farabee, D., Reiber, C., et al. (2002). A comparison of contingency management and cognitive-behavioral approaches during methadone maintenance for cocaine dependence. *Archives of General Psychiatry, 59,* 817–824.

Reich, D. L., & Silvay, G. (1989). Ketamine: An update on the first twenty-five years of clinical experience. *Canadian Journal of Anaesthesiology, 36,* 186–197.

Richardson, M. A., Craig, T. J., and Haughland, G. (1985). Treatment patterns of young chronic schizophrenic patients in the era of deinstitutionalization. *Psychiatric Quarterly, 57,* 243–249.

Ridgely, M. S., Goldman, H. H., & Willenbring, M. (1990). Barriers to the care of persons with dual diagnoses: Organizational and financing issues. *Schizophrenia Bulletin, 16,* 123–132.

Ridgely, M. S., & Lambert D., et al., (1999). Interagency collaboration in services for people with co-occurring mental illness and substance use disorders. *Psychiatric Services, 49,* 236–238.

Riggs, P. D., Leon, S. L., Mikulich, S. K., & Pottle, L. C. (1998). An open trial of bupropion for ADHD in adolescents with substance use disorders and conduct disorder. *Journal of the American Academy of Child and Adolescent Psychiatry, 37,* 1271–1278.

Riggs, P. D., Mikulich, S. K., Coffman, L. M., & Crowley, T. J. (1997). Fluoxetine in drug-dependent delinquents with major depression: an open trial. *Journal of Child and Adolescent Psychopharmacology, 7,* 87–95.

Promising Practices Network. (2001). In *Proven and promising programs.* From http://www.promisingpractices.net

Riggs, P. D., Mikulich, S. K., & Hall, S. (2001). *Effects of pemoline on ADHD, antisocial behaviors, and substance use in adolescents with conduct disorder and substance use disorder.* Paper presented at the College on Problems of Drug Dependence, 63rd Annual Scientific Meeting, Scottsdale, AZ, June 2001.

Riggs, P. D., Thompson, L. L., Mikulich, S. K., Whitmore, E. A., & Crowley, T. J. (1996). An open trial of pemoline in drug-dependent delinquents with attention-deficit hyperactivity disorder. *Journal of the American Academy of Child and Adolescent Psychiatry, 35,* 1018–1024.

Riggs, P. D., & Whitmore, E. A. (1999). Substance use disorders and disruptive behavior disorders. In R. L. Hendren (Ed.), *Disruptive behavior disorders in children and adolescents* (pp. 133–173). Washington, DC: American Psychiatric Association Press.

Roberts, D.C.S., Andrews, M. M., & Vickers, G. J. (1996). Baclofen attenuates the reinforcing effects of cocaine in rats. *Neuropsychopharmacology, 15,* 417–423.

Roberts, D.C.S., & Ranaldi, R. (1995). Effect of dopaminergic drugs on cocaine reinforcement. *Clinical Neuropharmacology, 18,* S84–S95.

Robins, L., & Regier, D. (1991). *Psychiatric disorders in America: The Epidemiological Catchment Area Study.* New York: The Free Press.

Rohsenow, D. J., Monti, P. M., Martin, R. A., Michalec, E., & Abrams, D. B. (2000). Brief coping skills treatment for cocaine abuse: 12-month substance use outcomes. *Journal of Consulting and Clinical Psychology, 68,* 515–520.

Roiser, J. P., & Sahakian, B. J. (2004). Relationship between ecstasy use and depression: A study controlling for poly-drug use. *Psychopharmacology (Berlin). 173,* 411–417.

Rosenthal, R. N., & Westreich, L. (1999). Treatment of persons with dual diagnoses of substance use disorder and other psychological problems. In B. S. McCrady & E. E. Epstein (Eds.), *Addictions: A comprehensive textbook* (pp. 439–476). New York: Oxford University Press.

Roth, J. L., & Brooks-Gunn, J. (2002). Youth development programs and healthy development: Next steps. In D. Romer (Ed.), *Reducing adolescent risk: Toward an integrated approach* (pp. 355–365). Thousand Oaks, CA: Sage Publications.

Roth, J., Brooks-Gunn, J., Murray, L., & Foster, W. (1998). Promoting healthy adolescents: Synthesis of youth development program evaluations. *Journal of Research on Adolescence, 8,* 423–459.

Roy, A., & Pandey, S. C. (2002). The decreased cellular expression of neuropeptide Y protein in rat brain structures during ethanol withdrawal after chronic ethanol exposure. *Alcoholism; Clinical and Experimental Research, 26,* 796–803.

Rutter, M., Giller, H., & Hagell, A. (1998). *Antisocial behavior by young people.* Cambridge, UK: Cambridge University Press.

Sabol, S., Nelson, M., Fisher, C., Gunzerath, L., Brody, C., Hu, S., et al. (1999). A genetic association for cigarette smoking behavior. *Health Psychology, 18,* 7–13.

Safer, D. J., Zito, J. M., & Gardner, J. E. (2001). Pemoline hepatotoxicity and postmarketing surveillance. *Journal of the American Academy of Child and Adolescent Psychiatry, 40,* 622–629.

SAMHSA Model Programs. (2003). In *National registry of effective programs (NREP).* From http://modelprograms.samhsa.gov/pdfs/compmatrix.pdf.

Santisteban, D. A., Coatsworth, J. D., Perez-Vidal, A., Kurtines, W. M., Schwartz, S. J., LaPerriere, A., et al. (2003). Efficacy of brief strategic family therapy in modifying Hispanic adolescent behavior problems and substance use. *Journal of Family Psychology, 17,* 121–133.

Santisteban, D. A., Coatsworth, J. D., Perez-Vidal, A., Mitrani, V., Jean-Gilles, M., & Szapocznik, J. (1996). Engaging behavior problem/drug abusing youth and their families in treatment: A replication and further exploration of the factors that contribute to differential effectiveness. *Journal of Family Psychology, 10,* 35–44.

Scales, P., Benson, P. L., Leffert, N., & Blyth, D. A. (2000). Contribution of developmental assets to the prediction of thriving among adolescents. *Applied Developmental Science, 4,* 27–46.

Schifano, F. (2003). A bitter pill. Overview of ecstasy (MDMA, MDA) related fatalities. *Psychopharmacology (Berlin), 173,* 242–248.

Schinka, J. A., Town, T., Abdullah, L., Crawford, F. C., Ordorica, P. I., Francis, E., et al. (2002). A functional polymorphism within the mu-opioid receptor gene and risk for abuse of alcohol and other substances. *Molecular Psychiatry, 7,* 224–228.

Schmidt, S. E., Liddle, H. A., & Dakof, G. A. (1996). Changes in parental practices and adolescent drug abuse during Multidimensional Family Therapy. *Journal of Family Psychology, 10,* 12–27.

Schneider, F., Habel, U., Wagner, M., Franke, P., Salloum, J. B., Shah, N. J., et al. (2001). Subcortical correlates of craving in recently abstinent alcoholic patients. *American Journal of Psychiatry, 158,* 1075–1083.

Schoenwald, S. K., Ward, D. M., Henggeler, S. W., Pickerl, S. G., & Patel, H. (1996). Multisystemic therapy treatment of substance abusing or dependent adolescent offenders: Cost of reducing incarceration, inpatient and residential placement. *Journal of Child and Family Studies, 5,* 431–444.

Schuckit, M. A. (2000). Genetics of the risk for alcoholism. *American Journal on Addictions, 9,* 103–112.

Schuckit, M. A., & Russell, J. W. (1983). Clinical importance of age at first drink in a group of young men. *American Journal of Psychiatry, 140,* 1221–1223.

Schuckit, M. A., Smith, T. L., Danko, G. P., Bucholz, K. K., Reich, T., & Bierut, L. (2001). Five-year clinical course associated with DSM-IV alcohol abuse or dependence in a large group of men and women. *American Journal of Psychiatry, 158,* 1084–1090.

Schulenberg, J. E., & Maggs, J. L. (2002). A developmental perspective on alcohol use and heavy drinking during adolescence and the transition to young adulthood. *Journal of Studies on Alcohol Supplement, 14,* 54–70.

Schulenberg, J., O'Malley, P. M., Bachman, J. G., Wadsworth, K. N., & Johnston, L. D. (1996). Getting drunk and growing up: Trajectories of frequent binge drinking during the transition to young adulthood. *Journal of Studies on Alcohol, 57,* 289–304.

Schulteis, G., Ahmed, S. H., Morse, A. C., Koob, G. F., & Everitt, B. J. (2000). Conditioning and opiate withdrawal: The amygdala links neutral stimuli with the agony of overcoming drug addiction. *Nature, 405,* 1013–1014.

Schulteis, G., & Koob, G. F. (1996). Reinforcement processes in opiate addiction: A homeostatic model. *Neurochemical Research, 21,* 1437–1454.

Schultz, W. (2002). Getting formal with dopamine and reward. *Neuron, 36,* 241–263.

Schwartz, R. H., Milteer, R., & LeBeau, M. A. (2000). Drug-facilitated sexual assault ('date rape'). *Southern Medical Journal, 93,* 558–561.

Sees, K. L., Delucchi, K. L., Masson, C., Rosen, A., Clark, H. W., Robillard, H., et al. (2000). Methadone maintenance vs 180-day psychosocially enriched detoxification for treatment of opioid dependence: A randomized controlled trial [see comments]. *Journal of the American Medical Association, 283,* 1303–1310.

Self, D. W., & Nestler, E. J. (1995). Molecular mechanisms of drug reinforcement and addiction. *Annual Review of Neuroscience, 18,* 463–495.

Sell, L. A., Morris, J., Bearn, J., Frackowiak, R. S., Friston, K. J., & Dolan, R. J. (1999). Activation of reward circuitry in human opiate addicts. *European Journal of Neuroscience, 11,* 1042–1048.

Sellers, E. M., Tyndale, R. F., & Fernandes, L. C. (2003). Decreasing smoking behavior and risk through CYP2A6 inhibition. *Drug Discovery Today, 8,* 487–493.

Sells, S. B., & Simpson, D. D. (1979). Evaluation of treatment outcome for youths in the Drug Abuse Report Program (DARP): A follow-up study. In G. M. Beschner & A. S. Friedman (Eds.), *Youth drug abuse: Problems, issues, and treatment* (pp. 571–628). Lexington, MA: D.C. Health.

Shea, S. H. Wall, T. L., Carr, L. G., & Li, T. K. (2001). ADH2 and alcohol-treated phenotypes in Ashkenazic Jewish American college students. *Behavior Genetics, 31,* 231–239.

Sheffler, D. J., & Roth, B. L. (2003). Salvinorin A: The "magic mint" hallucinogen finds a molecular target in the kappa opioid receptor. *Trends in Pharmacological Science, 24,* 107–109.

Shimada, S., Kitayama, S., Lin, C. L., Patel, A., Nanthakumar, E., Gregor, P., et al. (1991). Cloning and expression of a cocaine-sensitive dopamine transporter complementary DNA [published erratum appears in *Science* 1992 Mar 6;255(5049); 1195]. *Science, 254* (5031), 576–578.

Siegel, S. (1975). Evidence from rats that morphine tolerance is a learned response. *Journal of Comparative and Physiological Psychology, 89,* 498–506.

Silverman, K., Higgins, S. T., Brooner, R. K., Montoya, I. D., Cone, E. J., Schuster, C. R., et al. (1996). Sustained cocaine abstinence in methadone maintenance patients through voucher-based reinforcement therapy. *Archives of General Psychiatry, 53,* 409–415.

Silverman, M., Neale, M., Sullivan, P., Harris-Kerr, C., Wormley, B., & Sadek, H. (2001). Haplotypes of four novel single nucleotide polymorphisms in the nicotine acetylcholine receptor β-subunit (CHRNB2) gene show no association smoking initiation or nicotine dependence. *American Journal of Medical Genetics, 96,* 646–653.

Simmons, M. M., & Cupp, M. J. (1998). Use and abuse of flunitrazepam. *Annals of Pharmacotherapy, 32,* 117–119.

Simpson, D. D., Savage, L. J., & Sells, S. B. (1978). *Data book on drug treatment outcomes. Follow-up study of the 1969–71 admission to the Drug Abuse Report Program.* Fort Worth, TX: Texas Christian University.

Sinha, R., Easton, C., & Kemp, K. (2003). Substance abuse treatment characteristics of probation-referred young adults in a community-based outpatient program. *American Journal of Drug and Alcohol Abuse, 29(3),* 585–597.

Slaughter, L. (2000). Involvement of drugs in sexual assault. *Journal of Reproductive Medicine, 45,* 425–430.

Slotkin, T. A. (2002). Nicotine and the adolescent brain: Insights from an animal model. *Neurotoxicology and Teratology, 24,* 369–384.

Slutske, W. S., True, W. R., Scherrer, J. F., Heath, A. C., Bucholz, K. K., Eisen, S. A., et al. (1999). The heritability of alcoholism symptoms: Indicators of genetic and environmental influence in alcohol-dependent individuals: Revisited. *Alcoholism, Clinical and Experimental Research, 23,* 757–758.

Small, D. M., Zatorre, R. J., Dagher, A., Evans, A. C., & Jones-Gotman, M. (2001). Changes in brain activity related to eating chocolate: From pleasure to aversion. *Brain, 124,* 1720–1733.

Smith, K. M., Larive, L. L., & Romanelli, F. (2002). Club drugs: Methylenedioxymethamphetamine, flunitrazepam, ketamine hydrochloride, and gamma-hydroxybutyrate. *American Journal of Health-System Pharmacy, 59,* 1067–1076.

Smith, T. A., House, R. F., Jr., Croghan, I. T., Gauvin, T. R., Colligan, R. C., Offord, K. P., et al. (1996). Nicotine patch therapy in adolescent smokers. *Pediatrics, 98* (4 Pt. 1), 659–667.

Solhkhah, R., & Wilens, T. E. (1998). Pharmacotherapy of adolescent AOD use disorders. *Alcohol Health and Research World, 22,* 122–126.

Solomon, R. L., & Corbit, J. D. (1974). An opponent-process theory of motivation: 1. Temporal dynamics of affect. *Psychological Reviews, 81,* 119–145.

Spear, L. P. (2002). The adolescent brain and the college drinker: Biological basis of propensity to use and misuse alcohol. *Journal of Studies on Alcohol Supplement, 14,* 71–81.

Spencer, T., Heiligenstein, J. H., Biederman, J., Faries, D. E., Kratochvil, C. J., Conners, C. K., et al. (2002). Results from 2 proof-of-concept, placebo-controlled studies of atomoxetine in children with attention-deficit/hyperactivity disorder. *Journal of Clinical Psychiatry, 63,* 1140–1147.

Spielman, A. I., Najai, H., Sunavala, G., Dasso., M., Breer, H., Boekhoff, I., et al. (1996). Rapid kinetics of second messenger production in bitter taste. *American Journal of Physiology, 270*(3 pt 1), C926–931.

Spitz, M., Shi, H., Yang, F., Hudmon, K., Jiang, H., & Chanberlain, R. (1998). Case–control study of the D2 dopamine receptor gene and smoking status in lung cancer patients. *Journal of the National Cancer Institute, 90,* 358–363.

Spoth, R., Greenberg, M., Bierman, K., & Redmond, C. (2004). PROSPER partnership model for state public education systems: Capacity-building for evidence-based, competence-building prevention. *Prevention Science, 5,* 31–39.

Spoth, R., Guyll, M., Chao, W., & Molgaard, V. (2003). Exploratory study of a preventive intervention with general population African American families. *Journal of Early Adolescence, 23,* 435–468.

Spoth, R., Guyll, M., & Day, S. X. (2002). Universal family-focused interventions in alcohol-use disorder prevention: Cost-effectiveness and cost-benefit analyses of two interventions. *Journal of Studies on Alcohol, 63,* 219–228.

Spoth, R., Redmond, C., & Shin, C. (2000). Reducing adolescents' aggressive and hostile behaviors: Randomized trail effects of a brief family intervention four years past baseline. *Archives of Pediatrics and Adolescent Medicine, 154,* 1248–1257.

Spoth, R., Redmond, C., & Shin, C. (2001). Randomized trail of brief family interventions for general populations: Adolescent substance use outcomes four years following baseline. *Journal of Consulting and Clinical Psychology, 69,* 627–642.

Spoth, R., Reyes, M. L., Redmond, C., & Shin, C. (1999). Assessing the public health approach to delay onset and progression of adolescent substance use: Latent transition and loglinear analyses of longitudinal family preventive intervention outcomes. *Journal of Consulting and Clinical Psychology, 67,* 619–630.

Spoth, R. L., & Greenberg, M. T. (in press). Toward a comprehensive strategy for effective practitioner-scientist partnerships and larger-scale community benefits. *American Journal of Community Psychology.*

Stanton, M. D., & Shadish, W. R. (1997). Outcome, attrition, and family-couples treatment for drug abuse: A meta-analysis and review of the controlled, comparative studies. *Psychological Bulletin, 122,* 170–191.

Stanton, W. R. (1995). DSM-III-R tobacco dependence and quitting during late adolescence. *Addictive Behaviors, 29,* 595–603.

Stephens, R., Roffman, R. A., & Curtin, L. (2000). Comparison of extended versus brief treatments for marijuana use. *Journal of Consulting and Clinical Psychology, 68,* 898–908.

Stitzer, M. L., & Bigelow, G. E. (1978). Contingency management in a methadone maintenance program: Availability of reinforcers. *International Journal of the Addictions, 13,* 737–746.

Stitzer, M. L., Iguchi, M. Y., & Felch, L. J. (1992). Contingent take-home incentive: Effects on drug use of methadone maintenance patients. *Journal of Consulting and Clinical Psychology, 60,* 927–934.

Stitzer, M. L., Iguchi, M. Y., Kidorf, M., & Bigelow, G. E. (1993). Contingency management in methadone treatment: The case for positive incentives. In L. S. Onken, J. D. Blaine, & J. J. Boren (Eds.), *Behavioral treatments for drug abuse and dependence* (pp. 19–36). Rockville, MD: National Institute on Drug Abuse.

Strassman, R. J. (1984). Adverse reactions to psychedelic drugs. A review of the literature. *Journal of Nervous and Mental Disease, 172,* 577–595.

Straub, R. E., Sullivan, P. F., Ma, Y., Myakishev, M. V., Harris-Kerr, C., Wormley, B., et al. (1999). Susceptibility genes for nicotine dependence: A genome scan and follow-up in an independent sample suggest that regions on chronosomes 2,

4 10, 16, 17 and 18 merit further study. *Molecular Psychiatry, 4,* 129–144.

Strengthening America's Families. (1999). In *Effective family programs for the prevention of delinquency:* Maintained by the University of Utah, with funding by the Office of Juvenile Justice and Delinquency Prevention. From http://www.strengtheningfamilies.org/html/model _programs/mfp_pgl.html

Substance Abuse and Mental Health Administration (SAMHSA). (1997). *Preliminary results from the 1996 National Household Survey on Drug Abuse.* Rockville, MD: U.S. Department of Health and Human Services.

Substance Abuse and Mental Health Administration (SAMHSA). (2000). *National Household Survey on Drug Use and Health.* Rockville, MD: U.S. Department of Health and Human Services.

Substance Abuse and Mental Health Services Administration (SAMHSA). (2002a). *Results from the 2001 National Household Survey on Drug Abuse: Volume 1. Summary of national findings* (Office of Applied Studies, NHSDA Series H-17, DHHS Publication No. SMA 02-3758). Rockville, MD: U.S. Department of Health and Human Services.

Substance Abuse and Mental Health Services Administration (SAMHSA). (2002b). *Emergency department trends from the Drug Abuse Warning Network, Final estimates 1994–2000* (Office of Applied Statistics, DAWN Series D-21, DHHS Publication No. SMA 02-3635. Rockville, MD: U.S. Department of Health and Human Services.

Sullivan, P., Jiang, Y., Neale, M., Kendler, K., & Straub, R. (2001). Association of the tryptophan hydroxylase gene with smoking initiation but no progression to nicotine dependence. *American Journal of Medical Genetics, 105,* 479–484.

Sullivan, P., & Kendler, K. (1999). The genetic epidemiology of smoking. *Nicotine and Tobacco Research, 1*(S), 51–57.

Swan, G. E., Carmelli, D., & Cardon, L. R. (1996). The consumption of tobacco, alcohol and coffee in Caucasian male twins: A multivariate genetic analysis. *Journal of Substance Abuse, 8,* 19–31.

Szapocznik, J., & Hervis, O. (2003). *Brief strategic family therapy.* Rockville, MD: National Institute on Drug Abuse. (NIH Pub. No. 03-4751).

Szapocznik, J., Kurtines, W. M., Foote, F. H., Perez-Vidal, A., & Hervis, O. (1986). Conjoint versus one person family therapy: Some evidence for the effectiveness of conducting family therapy through one person. *Journal of Consulting and Clinical Psychology, 54,* 395–397.

Szapocznik, J., Perez-Vidal, A., Brickman, A. L., Foote, F. H., Santisteban, D. A., Hervis, O., et al. (1988). Engaging adolescent drug abusers and their families in treatment: A strategic structural systems approach. *Journal of Consulting and Clinical Psychology, 56,* 552–557.

Tapert, S. F., Cheung, E. H., Brown, G. G., Frank, L. R., Paulus, M. P., Schweinsburg, A. D., et al. (2003). Neural response to alcohol stimuli in adolescents with alcohol use disorder. *Archives of General Psychiatry, 60,* 727–735.

Tarter, R. E. (2002). Etiology of adolescent substance abuse: A developmental perspective. *American Journal on Addictions, 11,* 171–191.

Tellier, P. P. (2002). Club drugs: Is it all ecstasy? *Pediatric Annals, 31,* 550–556.

Teter, C. J., & Guthrie, S. K. (2001). A comprehensive review of MDMA and GHB: Two common club drugs. *Pharmacotherapy, 21,* 1486–1513.

Thompson, T., & Pickens, R. W. (1971). *Stimulus properties of drugs.* New York: Appleton-Century-Crofts.

Thorlindsson, T., & Vihjalmsson, R. (1991). Factors related to cigarette smoking and alcohol use among adolescents. *Adolescence, 26,* 399–418.

Tims, F. M., Dennis, M. L., Hamilton, N., Buchanan, J. B., Diamond, G., Funk, R., & Brantley, L. B. (2002). Characteristics and problems of 600 adolescent cannabis abusers in outpatient treatment. *Addiction, 97*(Suppl 1), 46–57.

Tobacco Advisory Group Royal College of Physicians. (2000). *Nicotine addiction in Britain: A report of the Tobacco Advisory Group of the Royal College of Physicians.* London: Royal College of Physicians.

True, W. R., Xian, H., Scherrer, J. F., Madden, P., Bucholz, K. K., Heath, A. C., et al. (1999). Common genetic vulnerability for nicotine and alcohol dependence in men. *Archives of General Psychiatry, 56,* 655–661.

Tsuang, M. T., Bar, J. L., Harley, R. M., & Lyons, M. J. (2001). The Harvard Twin Study of Substance Abuse: What we have learned. *Harvard Review of Psychiatry, 9,* 267–279.

Tsuang, M. T., Lyons, M. J., Eisen, S. A., Goldberg, J., True, W., Lin, N., et al. (1996). Genetic influences on DSM-III-R drug abuse and dependence: A study of 3,372 twin pairs. *American Journal of Medical Genetics, 67,* 473–477.

Tsuang, M. T., Lyons, M. J., Harley, R. M., Xian, H., Eisen, S., Goldberg, J., et al. (1999). Genetic and environmental influences on transitions in drug use. *Behavior Genetics, 29,* 473–479.

Uhl, G., Blum, K., Noble, E., & Smith, S. (1993).

Substance abuse vulnerability and D2 receptor genes. *Trends in Neuroscience, 16*, 83–86.

U.S. Department of Education. (2001). Safe disciplined, and drug-free school programs. From http://www.ed.gov/admins/lead/safety/exemplary01/exemplary01.pdf

U.S. Department of Health and Human Services (DHHS). (2002). *High-risk drinking in college: What we know and what we need to learn* (final report of the panel on Contexts and Consequences): Task Force of the National Advisory Council on Alcohol Abuse and Alcoholism National Institutes of Health. Bethesda, MD: Author.

Vandenbergh, D., Bennett, C., Grant, M., Strasser, A., O'Connor, R., Stauffer, R., Vogler, G. P., & Kozlowski, L. T. (2002). Smoking status and the human dopamine transporting variable number of tandem repeats (VNTR) polymorphism: Failure to replicate and finding that never-smokers may be different. *Nicotine and Tobacco Research* 4, 333–340.

Vandenbergh, D. J., Rodriguez, L. A., Miller, I. T., Uhl, G. R., & Lachman, H. M. (1997). High-activity catechol-O-methyltransferase allele is more prevalent in polysubstance abusers. *American Journal of Medical Genetics, 74*, 439–442.

van den Bree, M. B., Johnson, E. O., Neale, M. C., & Pickens, R. W. (1998). Genetic and environmental influences on drug use and abuse/dependence in male and female twins. *Drug and Alcohol Dependence, 52*, 231–241.

Van Etten, M. L., & Anthony, J. C. (2001). Male-female differences in transitions from first drug opportunity to first use: Searching for subgroup variation by age, region, and urban status. *Journal of Womens Health and Gender-Based Medicine, 10*, 797–804.

Van Etten, M. L., Neumark, Y. D., & Anthony, J. C. (1999). Male-female differences in the earliest stages of drug involvement. *Addiction, 94*, 1413–1419.

Vanyukov, M. M., & Tarter, R. E. (2000). Genetic studies of substance abuse. *Drug and Alcohol Dependence, 59*, 101–123.

Varlinskava, E. L., Spear, L. P., & Spear, N. E. (2001). Acute effects of ethanol on behavior of adolescent rats: role of social context. *Alcoholism, Clinical and Experimental Research, 25*, 377–385.

Verheyden, S. L., Henry, J. A., & Curran, H. V. (2003). Acute, sub-acute and long-term subjective consequences of 'ecstasy' (MDMA) consumption in 430 regular users. *Human Psychopharmacology, 18*, 507–517.

Villarruel, F. A., Perkins, D. F., Borden, L. M., & Keith, J. G. (2003). *Community youth development: Programs, policies and practices.* Thousand Oaks, CA: Sage Publications.

Volkow, N. D., Fowler, J. S., & Wang, G. J. (1999). Imaging studies on the role of dopamine in cocaine reinforcement and addiction in humans. *Journal of Psychopharmacology, 13*, 337–345.

Volkow, N. D., Fowler, J. S., Wang, G., Hitzemann, R., Logan, J., Schlyer, D. J., et al. (1993). Decreased dopamine D2 receptor availability is associated with reduced frontal metabolism in cocaine abusers. *Synapse, 14*, 169–177.

Volkow, N. D., Fowler, J. S., Wolf, A. P., Schlyer, D., Shiue, C., Alpert, R., et al. (1990). Effects of chronic abuse on postsynaptic dopamine receptors. *American Journal of Psychiatry, 147*, 719–724.

Volkow, N. D., Hitzemann, R., Wang, G., Fowler, J. S., Wolf, A. P., Dewey, S. L., et al. (1992). Long-term frontal brain metabolic changes in cocaine abusers. *Synapse, 11*, 184–190.

Volkow, N. D., Wang, G.-J., Fischman, M. W., Foltin, R. W., Fowler, J. S., Abumrad, N. N., et al. (1997). Relationship between subjective effects of cocaine and dopamine transporter occupancy. *Nature, 386*(6627), 827–830.

Volkow, N. D., Wang, G.-J., Fowler, J. S., Logan, J., Gatley, S. J., & Gifford, A. (1999). Prediction of reinforcing responses to psychostimulants in humans by brain dopamine D2 receptor levels. *American Journal of Psychiatry, 156*, 1440–1443.

Volkow, N. D., Wang, G. J., Fowler, J. S., Logan, J., Gatley, S. J., Hitzemann, R., et al. (1997). Decreased striatal dopaminergic responsiveness in detoxified cocaine abusers. *Nature, 386*, 830–833.

Vollenweider, F. X., Liechti, M. E., Gamma, A., Greer, G., & Geyer, M. (2002). Acute psychological and neurophysiological effects of MDMA in humans. *Journal of Psychoactive Drugs, 34*, 171–184.

Vuchinich, S., Bank, L., & Patterson, G. (1992). Parents, peers, and the stability of antisocial behavior in preadolescent boys. *Developmental Psychology, 28*, 510–521.

Wagner, F. A., & Anthony, J. C. (2002a). From first drug use to drug dependence; Developmental periods of risk for dependence upon marijuana, cocaine, and alcohol. *Neuropsychopharmacology, 26*, 479–488.

Wagner, F. A., & Anthony, J. C. (2002b). Into the world of illegal drug use: Exposure opportunity and other mechanisms linking the use of alcohol, tobacco, marijuana, and cocaine. *American Journal of Epidemiology, 155*, 918–925.

Wakefield, M. A., Chaloupka, F. J., Kaufman, N. J., Orleans, C. T., Barker, D. C., & Ruel, E. E. (2000). Effect of restrictions on smoking at home, at school, and in public places on teenage smoking: Cross-sectional study. *British Medical Journal, 321*(7257), 333–337.

Waldron, H. B. (1997). Adolescent substance abuse and family therapy outcome: A review of randomized trials. *Advances in Clinical Child Psychology, 19*, 199–234.

Waldron, H. B., Slesnick, N., Brody, J. L., Turner, C. W., & Peterson, T. R. (2001). Treatment outcomes for adolescent substance abuse at 4- and 7-month assessments. *Journal of Consulting and Clinical Psychology, 69*, 802–813.

Wallace, J. M., Jr., Bachman, J. G., O'Malley, P. M., Schulenberg, J., Cooper, S. M., & Johnston, L. D. (2003). Gender and ethnic differences in smoking, drinking, and illicit drug use among American 8th, 10th and 12th grade students, 1976–2000. *Addiction, 98*, 225–234.

Wandersman, A. (2003). American Journal of Community Psychology: Introduction to special section. *American Journal of Community Psychology, 31*, 207.

Wang, M. Q., Fitzhugh, E. C., Green, B. L., Turner, L. W., Eddy, J. M., & Westerfield, R. C. (1999). Prospective social–psychological factors of adolescent smoking progression. *Journal of Adolescent Health, 24*, 2–9.

Webb, J. A., & Baer, P. E. (1995). Influence of family disharmony and parental alcohol use on adolescent social skills, self-efficacy, and alcohol use. *Addictive Behaviors, 20*, 127–135.

Weddington, W. W., Brown, B. S., Haertzen, C. A., Cone, E. J., Dax, E. M., Herning, R. I., et al. (1990). Changes in mood, craving, and sleep during short-term abstinence reported by male cocaine addicts. A controlled, residential study. *Archives of General Psychiatry, 47*, 861–868.

Weir, E. (2000). Raves: A review of the culture, the drugs and the prevention of harm. *Canadian Medical Association Journal, 162*, 1843–1848.

Weiss, F., Martin-Fardon, R., Ciccocioppo, R., Kerr, T. M., Smith, D. L., & Ben-Shahar, O. (2001). Enduring resistance to extinction of cocaine-seeking behavior induced by drug-related cues. *Neuropsychopharmacology, 25*, 361–372.

Weschler, H., Davenport, A., Dowdall, G., Moeykens, B., & Castillo, S. (1994). Health and behavioral consequences of binge drinking in college:

A national survey of students at 140 campuses. *Journal of the American Medical Association, 272*, 1672–1677.

Whitfield, J. B., Nightingale, B. N., Bucholz, K. K., Madden, P. A., Heath, A. C., & Martin, N. G. (1998). ADH genotypes and alcohol use and dependence in Europeans. *Alcoholism, Clinical and Experimental Research, 22*, 1463–1469.

Whitmore, E. A., Mikulich, S. K., Thompson, L. L., Riggs, P. D., Aarons, G. A., & Crowley, T. J. (1997). Influences on adolescent substance dependence: Conduct disorder, depression, attention deficit hyperactivity disorder, and gender. *Drug and Alcohol Dependence, 47*, 87–97.

Wilens, T. E., Faraone, S. V., Biederman, J., & Gunawardene, S. (2003). Does stimulant therapy of attention-deficit/hyperactivity disorder beget later substance abuse? A meta-analytic review of the literature. *Pediatrics, 111*, 179–185.

Wilens, T. E., Spencer, T. J., Biederman, J., Girard, K., Doyle, R., Prince, J., et al. (2001). A controlled clinical trial of bupropion for attention deficit hyperactivity disorder in adults. *American Journal of Psychiatry, 158*, 282–288.

Wilens, T. E., Spencer, T. J., Biederman, J., & Schleifer, D. (1997). Case study: Nefazodone for juvenile mood disorders. *Journal of the American Academy of Child and Adolescent Psychiatry, 36*, 481–485.

Wilfond, B., Geller, G., Lerman, C., Audrain-McGovern, J., & Shields, A. (2002). Ethical issues in conducting behavioral genetics research: The case of smoking prevention trials among adolescents. *Journal of Health Care Law and Policy, 6*, 73–87.

Wilk, A. I., Jensen, N. M., & Havighurst, T. C. (1997). Meta-analysis of randomized controlled trials addressing brief interventions in heavy alcohol drinkers. *Journal of General Internal Medicine, 12*, 274–283.

Williams, M. T., Morford, L. L., Wood, S. L., Rock, S. L., McCrea, A. E., Fukumura, M., et al. (2003). Developmental 3,4-methylenedioxymethamphetamine (MDMA) impairs sequential and spatial but not cued learning independent of growth, litter effects or injection stress. *Brain Research, 968*, 89–101.

Williams, R. J., Chang, S. Y., & Group, A.C.A.R. (2000). A comprehensive and comparative review of adolescent substance abuse treatment outcome. *Clinical Psychology in Science Practice, 7*, 138–166.

Wills, T., Vaccaro, D., & McNamara, G. (1994). Novelty seeking, risk taking and related constructs as predictors of adolescent substance use Cloninger's theory. *Journal of Substance Abuse, 6,* 1–20.

Wills, T. A., Windle, M., & Cleary, S. D. (1998). Temperament and novelty seeking in adolescent substance abuse: Convergence of dimensions of temperament with constructs from Cloninger's theory. *Journal of Personal Social Psychology, 74,* 387–406.

Willy, M. E., Manda, B., Shatin, D., Drinkard, C. R., & Graham, D. J. (2002). A study of compliance with FDA recommendations for pemoline (Cylert). *Journal of the American Academy of Child and Adolescent Psychiatry, 41,* 785–790.

Windle, M. T. (1999). *Alcohol use among adolescents* (Vol. 42). Thousand Oaks, CA: Sage Publications.

Windle, M., Miller-Tutzauer, C., & Domenico, D. (1992). Alcohol use, suicidal behavior, and risky activities among adolescents. *Journal of Research on Adolescence, 2,* 317–330.

Windle, M., & Windle, R. C. (2001). Depressive symptoms and cigarette smoking among middle adolescents: Prospective associations and intrapersonal and interpersonal influences. *Journal of Consulting and Clinical Psychology, 69,* 215–226.

Windle, M., & Windler, R. C. (1999). Adolescent tobacco, alcohol and drug use: Current findings. *Adolescent Medicine, 19,* 153–163.

Winters, K. C. (2001). Assessing adolescent substance use problems and other areas of functioning: State of the art. In P. M. Monti, S. M. Colby, & T. A. O'Leary (Eds.), *Adolescents, alcohol and substance abuse: Reaching teens through brief interventions* (pp. 80–108). New York: Guilford Publications.

Winters, K. C., Stinchfield, R. D., Opland, E., Weller, C., & Latimer, W. W. (2000). The effectiveness of the Minnesota Model approach in the treatment of adolescent drug abusers. *Addiction, 95,* 601–612.

Wise, B. K., Cuffe, S. P., & Fischer, T. (2001). Dual diagnosis and successful participation of adolescents in substance abuse treatment. *Journal of Substance Abuse Treatment, 21,* 161–165.

Wise, R. A. (1996). Neurobiology of addiction. *Current Opinions in Neurobiology, 6,* 243–251.

Yamaguchi, K., & Kandel, D. B. (1984b). Patterns of drug use from adolescence to young adulthood: III. Predictors of progression. *American Journal of Public Health, 74,* 673–681.

Zinburg, N. E., & Robertson, J. A. (1972). *Drugs and the public.* New York: Simon & Schuster.

Zuckerman, M. (1986). Sensation seeking and the endogenous deficit theory of drug abuse. *National Institute of Drug Abuse Research Monograph, 74,* 59–70.

Part VI: Youth Suicide

Alderson, P., Green, S., & Higgins, J. P. (Eds.). (2003). *Cochrane reviewers' handbook, 4.2.1.* Retrieved January 29, 2004, from http:www .cochrane.org/resources/handbook/hbook.htm

American Academy of Pediatrics, Committee on Injury and Poison Prevention. (2000). Firearm-related injuries affecting the pediatric population. *Pediatrics, 105,* 888–895.

American Psychiatric Association (2005). *APA, coalition launches parentsmedguide.org.* Retrieved February 1, 2005, from http://www.psych.org/news_room/press_releases/0509APAonNewResourcesforParentsonAntidepressants.pdf

Andrews, J. A., & Lewinsohn, P. M. (1992). Suicidal attempts among older adolescents: Prevalence and co-occurrence with psychiatric disorders. *Journal of the American Academy of Child and Adolescent Psychiatry, 31,* 655–662.

Appleby, L., Cooper, J., Amos, T., & and Faragher, B. (1999). Psychological autopsy study of suicides by people aged under 35. *British Journal of Psychiatry, 175,* 168–174.

Apter, A., Plutchik, R., & van Praag, H. M. (1993). Anxiety, impulsivity and depressed mood in relation to suicidal and violent behavior. *Acta Psychiatrica Scandinavica, 87,* 1–5.

Arango, V., Ernsberger, P., Marzuk, P. M., Chen, J. S., Tierney, H., Stanley, M., et al. (1990). Autoradiographic demonstration of increased serotonin 5HT2 and β-adrenergic receptor binding sites in the brain of suicide victims. *Archives of General Psychiatry, 47,* 1038–1046.

Aseltine, R., & DeMartino, R. (2004). An outcome evaluation of the SOS Suicide Prevention Program. *American Journal of Public Health, 94,* 446–451.

Aseltine, R., Jacobs, D., Kopans, B., & Bloom, A. (2003, June). *Evaluation of the SOS suicide prevention program.* Presented at the Annenberg Center for Communications and the American Foundation for Suicide Prevention's Youth Suicide Prevention Workshop, New York, NY.

Azrael, D. (2001). *Risk factors for suicide by children: What can we learn from Child Fatality Review Team data?* Unpublished doctoral dissertation, Harvard University, 2001.

Azrael, D., Miller, M., & Hemenway, D. (2000). Are

household firearms stored safely? It depends on whom you ask. *Pediatrics, 10, E31.*

Bailey, J. E., Kellermann, A. L., Somes, G. W., Banton, J. G., Rivara, F. P., & Rushforth, N. P. (1997). Risk factors for violent death of women in the home. *Archives of Internal Medicine, 157,* 777–782.

Barbui, C., Campomori, A., D'Avanzo, B., Negri, E., & Garattini, S. (1999). Antidepressant drug use in Italy since the introduction of SSRIs: National trends, regional differences, and impact on suicide rates. *Social Psychiatry and Psychiatric Epidemiology, 34,* 152–156.

Barraclough, B., Bunch, J., Nelson, B., & Sainsbury, P. (1974). A hundred cases of suicide: Clinical aspects. *British Journal of Psychiatry, 125,* 355–373.

Beautrais, A. L. (2001). Child and young adolescent suicide in New Zealand. *Australian New Zealand Journal of Psychiatry, 35,* 647–653.

Beautrais, A. L., Joyce, P. R., & Mulder, R. T. (1996). Risk factors for serious suicide attempts among youths aged 13–24 years. *Journal of the American Academy of Child and Adolescent Psychiatry, 35,* 1174–1182.

Beautrais, A. L., Joyce, P. R., & Mulder, R. T. (1997). Precipitating factors and life events in serious suicide attempts among youths aged 13 through 24 years. *Journal of the American Academy of Child and Adolescent Psychiatry, 25,* 1543–1551.

Berlin, I. N. (1987). Suicide among Native American adolescents: An overview. *Suicide and Life-Threatening Behavior, 17,* 218–232.

Berman, A. L., & Jobes, D. A. (1995). Suicide prevention in adolescents (age 12–18). *Suicide and Life-Threatening Behavior, 25,* 143–154.

Birckmayer, J., & Hemenway, D. (2001). Suicide and firearm prevalence: Are youth disproportionately affected? *Suicide and Life-Threatening Behavior, 31,* 303–310.

Boyd, J. H., & Moscicki, E. K. (1986). Firearms and youth suicide. *American Journal of Public Health, 76,* 1240–1242.

Brent, D. A., Baugher, M., Birmaher, B., Kolko, D. J., & Bridge, J. (2000). Compliance with recommendations to remove firearms in families participating in a clinical trial for adolescent depression. *Journal of the American Academy of Child and Adolescent Psychiatry, 39,* 1220–1226.

Brent, D. A., Baugher, M., Bridge, J., Chen, T., & Chiappetta, L. (1999). Age- and sex-related risk factors for adolescent suicide. *Journal of the American Academy of Child and Adolescent Psychiatry, 38,* 1497–1505.

Brent, D. A., & Bridge, J. (2003). Firearms availability and suicide. *American Behavioral Scientist, 46,* 1192–1210.

Brent, D. A., Bridge, J., Johnson, B. A., & Connolly, J. (1996). Suicidal behavior runs in families: A controlled family study of adolescent suicide victims. *Archives of General Psychiatry, 53,* 1145–1152.

Brent, D. A., Holder, D., Kolko, D., Birmaher, B., Baugher, M., Roth, C., et al. (1997). A clinical psychotherapy trial for adolescent depression comparing cognitive, family, and supportive therapy. *Archives of General Psychiatry, 54,* 877–885.

Brent, D. A., Johnson, B. A., Perper, J., Connolly, J., Bridge, J., Bartle, S., et al. (1994). Personality disorder, personality traits, impulsive violence, and completed suicide in adolescents. *Journal of the American Academy of Child and Adolescent Psychiatry, 33,* 1080–1086.

Brent, D. A., Oquendo, M., Birmaher, B., Greenhill, L., Kolko, D., Stanley, B., et al. (2002). Familial pathways to early-onset suicide attempt: Risk for suicidal behavior in offspring of mood-disordered suicide attempters. *Archives of General Psychiatry, 59,* 801–807.

Brent, D. A., Oquendo, M., Birmaher, B., Greenhill, L., Kolko, D., Stanley, B., et al. (2003). Peripubertal suicide attempts in offspring of suicide attempters with siblings concordant for suicidal behavior. *American Journal of Psychiatry, 160,* 1486–1493.

Brent, D. A., Perper, J. A., & Allman, C. J. (1987). Alcohol, firearms, and suicide among youth: Temporal trends in Allegheny County, Pennsylvania, 1960 to 1983. *Journal of the American Medical Association, 257,* 3369–3372.

Brent, D. A., Perper, J. A., Allman, C. J., Moritz, G. M., Wartella, M., & Zelenak, J. P. (1991). The presence and accessibility of firearms in the homes of adolescent suicides: A case–control study. *Journal of the American Medical Association, 266,* 2989–2995.

Brent, D. A., Perper, J. A., Goldstein, C. E., Kolko, D. J., Allan, M. J., Allman, C. J., et al. (1988). Risk factors for adolescent suicide: A comparison of adolescent suicide victims with suicidal inpatients. *Archives of General Psychiatry, 45,* 581–588.

Brent, D. A., Perper, J. A., & Moritz, G. M. (1993). Stressful life events, psychopathology and adolescent suicide: A case–control study. *Suicide and Life-Threatening Behavior, 23,* 179–187.

Brent, D. A., Perper, J. A., Moritz, G. M., Allman, C., Friend, A., Roth, C., et al. (1993a). Psychiatric risk factors for adolescent suicide: A case–control study. *Journal of the American Academy of Child and Adolescent Psychiatry, 32,* 521–529.

Brent, D. A., Perper, J. A., Moritz, G. M., Allman, C., Liotus, L., Schweers, J., et al. (1993b). Bereavement or depression? The impact of the loss of a friend to suicide. *Journal of the American Academy of Child and Adolescent Psychiatry, 32,* 1189–1197.

Brent, D. A., Perper, J. A., Moritz, G. M., Allman, C., Schweers, C., Roth, C., et al. (1993c). Psychiatric sequelae to the loss of an adolescent peer to suicide. *Journal of the American Academy of Child and Adolescent Psychiatry, 32,* 509–517.

Brent, D. A., Perper, J. A., Moritz, G. M., Baugher, M., Schweers, J., & Ross, C. (1993d). Firearms and adolescent suicide: A community case–control study. *American Journal of Disorders of Childhood, 147,* 1066–1071.

Brent, D. A., Perper, J. A., Moritz, G. M., Liotus, L., Schweers, J., Balach, L., et al. (1994). Familial risk factors for adolescent suicide: A case–control study. *Acta Psychiatrica Scandinavica, 89,* 52–58.

Brown, J., Cohen, P., Johnson, J. G., & Smailes, E. M. (1999). Childhood abuse and neglect: Specificity of effects on adolescent and young adult depression and suicidality. *Journal of the American Academy of Child and Adolescent Psychiatry, 38,* 1490–1496.

Byford, S., Harrington, R., Torgerson, D., Kerfoot, M., Dyer, E., Harrington, V., et al. (1999). Cost-effectiveness analysis of a home-based social work intervention for children and adolescents who have deliberately poisoned themselves: Results of a randomized control trial. *British Journal of Psychiatry, 174,* 56–62.

Carlsten, A., Waern, M., Ekedahl, A., & Ranstam, J. (2001). Antidepressant medication and suicide in Sweden. *Pharmacoepidemiology and Drug Safety, 10,* 525–530.

Centers for Disease Control and Prevention (1988). CDC recommendations for a postvention and containment of suicide clusters. *Morbidity and Mortality Weekly Report, 37,* 1–12.

Centers for Disease Control and Prevention (n.d.a). *WISQARS fatal injury mortality reports.* Retrieved February 1, 2005, from http://webappa.cdc.gov/sasweb/ncipc/mortrate.html

Centers for Disease Control and Prevention (n.d.b). *Youth risk behavior surveillance system: Online analysis of youth risk behavior survey results.* Retrieved February 1, 2005, from http://www.cdc.gov/nccdphp/dash/yrbs/2003/youth01online.htm

Cohen-Sandler, R., Berman, A. L., & King, R. A.

(1982). A follow-up study of hospitalized suicidal children. *Journal of the American Academy of Child and Adolescent Psychiatry, 20,* 398–403.

Cornelius, J. R. (2003, June). *Medication trials with depressed suicidal adolescent substance abusers.* Presented at the Annenberg Center for Communications and the American Foundation for Suicide Prevention's Youth Suicide Prevention Workshop, New York, NY.

Cornelius, J. R., Bukstein, O. G., Birmaher, B., Salloum, I. M., Lynch, K., Pollack, N. K., et al. (2001). Fluoxetine in adolescents with major depression and an alcohol use disorder: An open-label trial. *Addictive Behaviors, 26,* 735–739.

Cornelius, J. R., Salloum, I. M., Lynch, K., Clark, D. B., & Mann, J. J. (2001). Treating the substance abusing suicidal patient. In H. Hendin & J. J. Mann (Eds.), *The clinical science of suicide prevention* (pp. 78–93). New York: New York Academy of Sciences.

Cotgrove, A., Zirinsky, L., Black, D., & Weston, D. (1995). Secondary prevention of attempted suicide in adolescence. *Journal of Adolescence, 18,* 569–577.

Coyne-Beasley, T., McGee, K. S., Johnson, M. R., & Bordley, W. C. (2002). The association of handgun ownership and storage practices with safety consciousness. *Archives of Pediatric and Adolescent Medicine, 156,* 763–768.

Coyne-Beasley, T., Schoenback, V. J., & Johnson, R. M. (2001). Love our kids lock your guns: A community firearm safety counseling and gun lock distribution program. *Archives of Pediatric and Adolescent Medicine, 155,* 659–664.

Cutler, D. M., Glaeser, E. L., & Norberg, K. E. (2001). Explaining the rise in youth suicide. In J. Gruber (Ed.), *Risky behavior among youths: An economic analysis* (pp. 219–269). Chicago: University of Chicago Press.

De Leo, D., Dwyer, J., Firman, D., & Neulinger, K. (2003). Trends in hanging and firearm suicide rates in Australia: Substitution of method? *Suicide and Life-Threatening Behavior, 33,* 151–164.

Dinh-Zarr, T., Diguiseppi, C., Heitman, E., & Roberts, I. (1999). Preventing injuries through interventions for problem drinking: A systematic review of randomized controlled trials. *Alcohol and Alcoholism, 34,* 609–621.

Eggert, L. L., Karovsky, P. P., & Pike, K. C. (1999). *Washington state youth suicide prevention program: Pathways to enhancing community capacity in preventing youth suicidal behaviors, final report.* Seattle: University of Washington School of Nursing.

Eggert, L. L., Thompson, E. A., Herting, J. R., &

Nicholas, L. J. (1994). A prevention research program: Reconnecting at-risk youth. *Issues in Mental Health Nursing, 15,* 107–135.

Eggert, L. L., Thompson, E. A., Herting, J. R., & Nicholas, L. J. (1995). Reducing suicide potential among high-risk youth: Tests of a school-based prevention program. *Suicide and Life-Threatening Behavior, 25,* 276–296.

Faulkner, A. H., & Cranston, K. (1998). Correlates of same-sex behavior in a random sample of Massachusetts high school students. *American Journal of Public Health, 88,* 262–266.

Food and Drug Administration (2004, Oct. 15). *FDA public health advisory: suicidality in children and adolescents being treated with antidepressant medications* [online]. Retrieved January 5, 2005, from http://www.fda.gov/cder/drug/antidepressants/SSRIPHA200410.htm.

Fendrich, M., Mackesy-Amiti, M. E., Kruesi, M. (2000). A mass-distributed CD-ROM for school-based suicide prevention. *Crisis, 21,* 135–140.

Fergusson, D. M., Horwood, L. J., & Beautrais, A. L. (1999). Is sexual orientation related to mental health problems and suicidality in young people? *Archives of General Psychiatry, 56,* 876–880.

Fergusson, D. M., Horwood, L. J., & Lynskey, M. T. (1996). Childhood sexual abuse and psychiatric disorder in young adulthood, II: Psychiatric outcomes of childhood sexual abuse. *Journal of the American Academy of Child and Adolescent Psychiatry, 35,* 1365–1374.

Fergusson, D. M., Woodward, L. J., & Horwood, L. J. (2000). Risk factors and life processes associated with the onset of suicidal behavior during adolescence and early adulthood. *Psychological Medicine, 30,* 23–39.

Fisher, C. B., Pearson, J. L., Kim, S., & Reynolds, C. F. (2002). Ethical issues in including suicidal individuals in clinical research. *IRB: Ethics & Human Research, 24,* 9–14.

Gallagher, R. P. (2001). *National survey of counseling center directors, international campus.* Alexandria, VA: International Association of Counseling Services, Inc.

Garofalo, R., Wolf, R., Cameron, M. S., Kessel, S., Palfrey, J., & DuRant, R. H. (1998). The association between health risk behaviors and sexual orientation among a school-based sample of adolescents. *Pediatrics, 101,* 895–202.

Gibbons, J. S., Butler, J., Urwin, P., & Gibbons, J. L. (1978). Evaluation of a social work service for self-poisoning patients. *British Journal of Psychiatry, 133,* 111–118.

Glowinski, A. L., Bucholz, K. K., Nelson, E. C., Qiang, M. D., Madden, P. A., Reich, W., et al. (2001). Suicide attempts in an adolescent female twin sample. *Journal of the American Academy of Child and Adolescent Psychiatry, 40,* 1300–1307.

Goldsmith, S. K., Pellmar, T. C., Kleinman, A. M., & Bunney, W. E. (Eds.). (2002). *Reducing suicide: A national imperative.* Washington, DC: National Academies Press.

Goode, E. (2003, December 11). British warning on antidepressant use for youth. *New York Times.* Retrieved December 11, 2003, from http://www.nytimes.com

Gould, M. S. (2000). *Epidemiologic sequelae of suicide in schools.* National Institute of Mental Health, Grant R01 MH52827-04.

Gould, M. S. (2001). Suicide and the media. In H. Hendin & J. J. Mann (Eds.), *The clinical science of suicide prevention* (pp. 200–224). New York: New York Academy of Sciences.

Gould, M. S. (2003, June). *Youth suicide epidemiology and risk factors.* Presented at the Annenberg Center for Communications and the American Foundation for Suicide Prevention's Youth Suicide Prevention Workshop, New York, NY.

Gould, M. S., Fisher, P., Parides, M., Flory, M., & Shaffer, D. (1996). Psychosocial risk factors of child and adolescent completed suicide. *Archives of General Psychiatry, 53,* 1155–1162.

Gould, M. S., Greenberg, T., Velting, D. M., & Shaffer, D. (2003). Youth suicide risk and preventive interventions: A review of the past 10 years. *Journal of the American Academy of Child and Adolescent Psychiatry 42,* 386–405.

Gould, M. S., Jamieson, P., & Romer, D. (2003). Media contagion and suicide among the young. *American Behavioral Scientist, 46,* 1269–1284.

Gould, M. S., King, R., Greenwald, S., Fisher, P., Schwab-Stone, M. D., Kramer, R., et al. (1998). Psychopathology associated with suicidal ideation and attempts among children and adolescents. *Journal of the American Academy of Child and Adolescent Psychiatry, 37,* 915–923.

Gould, M. S., Petrie, K., Kleinman, M., & Wallenstein, S. (1994). Clustering of attempted suicide: New Zealand national data. *International Journal of Epidemiology, 23,* 1185–1189.

Gould, M. S., Wallenstein, S., & Kleinman, M. (1990). Time-space clustering of teenage suicide. *American Journal of Epidemiology, 131,* 71–78.

Gould, M. S., Wallenstein, S., Kleinman, M., O'Carroll, P., & Mercy, J. (1990). Suicide clusters: An examination of age-specific effects. *American Journal of Public Health, 80,* 211–212.

Greenfield, B., Larson, C., Hechtman, L., Rousseau, C., & Platt, R. (2002). A rapid-response outpatient model for reducing hospitalization rates among suicidal adolescents. *Psychiatric Services, 53*, 1574–1579.

Greenfield, S. F., Reizes, J. M., Magruder, K. M., Muenz, L. R., Kopans, B., & Jacobs, D. G. (1997). Effectiveness of community-based screening for depression. *American Journal of Psychiatry, 154,* 1391–1397.

Greenfield, S. F., Reizes, J. M., Muenz, L. R., Kopans, B., Kozloff, R. C., & Jacobs, D. G. (2000). Treatment for depression following the 1996 National Depression Screening Day. *American Journal of Psychiatry, 157,* 1867–1869.

Greening, L., & Stoppelbein, L. (2002). Religiosity, attributional style, and social support as psychosocial buffers for African American and white adolescents' perceived risk for suicide. *Suicide and Life-Threatening Behavior, 32,* 404–417.

Groholt, B., Ekeberg, O., Wichstrom, L., & Haldorsen, T. (1997). Youth suicide in Norway, 1990–1992: A comparison between children and adolescents completing suicide and age- and gender-matched controls. *Suicide and Life-Threatening Behavior, 27,* 250–263.

Groholt, B., Ekeberg, O., Wichstrom, L., & Haldorsen, T. (1998). Suicide among children and younger and older adolescents in Norway: A comparative study. *Journal of the American Academy of Child and Adolescent Psychiatry, 37,* 473–481.

Grossman, D. C., Cummings, P., Koepsell, T. D., Marshall, J., D'Ambrosio, L., Thompson, R. S., et al. (2000). Firearm safety counseling in primary care pediatrics: A randomized controlled trial. *Pediatrics, 106,* 22–26.

Grossman, D. C., Reay, D. T., & Baker, S. A. (1999). Self-inflicted and unintentional firearm injuries among children and adolescents: The source of the firearm. *Archives of Pediatric and Adolescent Medicine, 153,* 875–878.

Grunbaum, J. A., Kann, I., Kinchen, S. A., Williams, B., Ross, J. G., Lowry, R., et al. (2002). Youth suicide risk behavior surveillance—United States, 2001. *Morbidity and Mortality Weekly Report Surveillance Summary, 51*(SS4), 1–64.

Gunnel, D., Middleton, N., Whitley, E., Dorling, D., & Frankel, S. (2003). Why are suicide rates rising in young men but falling in the elderly? A time series analysis of trends in England and Wales, 1959–1998. *Social Science and Medicine, 57,* 595–611.

Guo, B., & Harstall, C. (2002, January). *Efficacy of suicide prevention programs for children and youth.* Alberta, Canada: Alberta Heritage Foundation for Medical Research.

Haas, A. P. (2003, June). *The College Screening Project: A program to identify and treat depressed college students at risk for suicide.* Presented at the Annenberg Center for Communications and the American Foundation for Suicide Prevention's Youth Suicide Prevention Workshop, New York, NY.

Haas, A. P., Hendin, H., & Mann, J. J. (2003). Suicide in college students. *American Behavioral Scientist 46,* 1224–1240.

Haight, B. K., & Hendrix, S. A. (1998). Suicidal intent/life satisfaction: Comparing the life stories of older women. *Suicide and Life-Threatening Behavior, 28,* 272–284.

Hammand, T. A. (2004, Sept. 13). *Results of the analysis of suicidality in pediatric trials of newer antidepressants.* Presentation at the FDA Center for Drug Evaluation and Research (CDER), Bethesda, MD. Retrieved January 5, 2005, from: http://www.fda.gov/ohrms/dockets/ac/cder04.html#PsychopharmacologidDrugs

Harkavy-Friedman, J. M., Asnis, G., Boeck, M., & DiFiore, J. (1987). Prevalence of specific suicidal behaviors in a high school sample. *American Journal of Psychiatry, 144,* 1203–1206.

Harrington, R., Kerfoot, M., Dyer, E., McNiven, F., Gill, J., Harrington, V., et al. (1998). Randomized trial of a home-based family intervention for children who have deliberately poisoned themselves. *Journal of the American Academy of Child and Adolescent Psychiatry 37,* 512–518.

Harrington, R., Kerfoot, M., Dyer, E., McNiven, F., Gill, J., Harrington, V., et al. (2000). Deliberate self-poisoning in adolescence: Why does a brief family intervention work in some cases and not others? *Journal of Adolescence, 23,* 13–20.

Harris, G. (2004, March 23). Regulators want antidepressants to list warning. *New York Times.* Retrieved March 24, 2004, from http://www.nytimes.com

Hawton, K., Arensmsan, E., Townsend, E., Bremner, S., Feldman, E., Goldney, R., et al. (1998). Deliberate self harm: Systematic review of efficacy of psychosocial and pharmacological treatments in preventing repetition. *British Medical Journal, 317,* 441–447.

Hawton, K., & Sinclair, J. (2003). The challenge of evaluating the effectiveness of treatments for deliberate self-harm. *Psychological Medicine, 33,* 955–958.

Hawton, K., Townsend, E., Arensmsan, E., Gunnell,

D., Hazell, P., House, A., et al. (2000). Psychosocial versus pharmacological treatments for deliberate self-harm. *Cochrane Database of Systematic Reviews, 2,* CD001764.

Hazell, P., & Lewin, T. (1993). An evaluation of postvention following adolescent suicide. *Suicide and Life-Threatening Behavior, 23,* 101–109.

Hendin, H. (1978). Suicide: The psychosocial dimension. *Suicide and Life-Threatening Behavior, 8,* 99–117.

Hendin, H. (1995). *Suicide in America* (rev. ed.). New York: W. W. Norton.

Henriques, G., Beck, A. T., & Brown, G. K. (2003). Cognitive therapy for adolescent and young adult suicide attempters. *American Behavioral Scientist, 46,* 1258–1268.

Isacsson, G. (2000). Suicide prevention—a medical breakthrough? *Acta Psychiatrica Scandinavica, 102,* 113–117.

Jacobs, D. (2003, June). *Depression screening on campus.* Present at the Annenberg Center for Communications and the American Foundation for Suicide Prevention's Youth Suicide Prevention Workshop, New York, NY.

Jed Foundation (2003). *ULifeLine: The online behavioral support system for young adults.* Retrieved November 10, 2003 from http://www.ulifeline .org/index.php

Jessor, R. (1991). Risk behavior in adolescence: A psychosocial framework for understanding and action. *Journal of Adolescent Health, 12,* 597–605.

Joffe, P. (2003, February). *An empirically supported program to prevent suicide among a college population.* Paper presented at Stetson College of Law, Clearwater Beach, FL.

Johnson, B. A., Brent, D. A., Bridge, J., & Connolly, J. (1998). The familial aggregation of adolescent suicide attempts. *Acta Psychiatrica Scandinavica, 97,* 18–24.

Johnson, J. G., Cohen, P., Gould, M. S., Kasen, S., Brown, J., & Brook, J. S. (2002). Childhood adversities, interpersonal difficulties, and risk for suicide attempts during late adolescence and early adulthood. *Archives of General Psychiatry, 59,* 741–749.

Johnston, L. D., O'Malley, P. M., & Bachman, J. G. (2002). *National survey results of the monitoring the future study 1975–2001, Volume I* (NIH Publication No. 02-5106). Bethesda, MD: National Institute on Drug Abuse, National Institutes of Health.

Joiner, T. E., Voelz, Z. R., & Rudd, M. D. (2001). For suicidal young adults with comorbid depressive

and anxiety disorders, problem-solving treatment may be better than treatment as usual. *Professional Psychology: Research and Practice, 32,* 2001.

Kalafat, J., & Elias, M. (1992). Adolescents' experience with and response to suicidal peers. *Suicide and Life-Threatening Behavior, 22,* 315–321.

Kalafat, J., & Elias, M. (1994). An evaluation of a school-based suicide awareness intervention. *Suicide and Life-Threatening Behavior, 24,* 224–233.

Kalafat, J., & Gagliano, C. (1996). The use of simulations to assess the impact of adolescent suicide response curriculum. *Suicide and Life-Threatening Behavior, 26,* 359–364.

Kalafat, J., & Ryerson, D. M. (1999). The implementation and institutionalization of a school-based youth suicide prevention program. *Journal of Primary Prevention, 19,* 157–175.

Kaltiala-Heino, R., Rimpela, M., Marttunen, M., Rimpela, A., & Rantanen, P. (1999). Bullying, depression, and suicidal ideation in Finnish adolescents: School survey. *British Medical Journal, 319,* 348–351.

Kellermann, A. L., Rivara, F. P., Somes, G., Reay, D. T., Francisco, J., Banton, J. G., et al. (1992). Suicide in the home in relation to gun ownership [comment]. *New England Journal of Medicine, 327,* 490–491.

Kerfoot, M. (1988). Deliberate self-poisoning in childhood and early adolescence. *Journal of Child Psychology and Psychiatry, 29,* 335–345.

Kerfoot, M., Dyer, E., Harrington, V., Woodham, A., & Harrington, R. C. (1996). Correlates and short-term course of self-poisoning in adolescents. *British Journal of Psychiatry, 168,* 38–42.

Kerr, M. M., Brent, D. A., & McKain, B. W. (1997). *Postvention standards guidelines: A guide for a school's response in the aftermath of a sudden death* (3rd ed.). Pittsburgh, PA: STAR-Center Outreach.

King, C. A. (2003, June). *Post-hospitalization support program for suicide survivors.* Presented at the Annenberg Center for Communications and the American Foundation for Suicide Prevention's Youth Suicide Prevention Workshop, New York, NY.

King, C. A., Hovey, J. D., Brand, E., Wilson, R., & Ghaziuddin, N. (1997). Suicidal adolescents after hospitalization: Parent and family impacts on treatment follow-through. *Journal of the American Academy of Child and Adolescent Psychiatry, 36,* 85–93.

King, C. A., Preuss, L., & Kramer, A. (2001, October). *Youth-Nominated Support Team (YST) for sui-*

cidal adolescents. Poster session presented at the 48th Annual Meeting of the American Academy of Child and Adolescent Psychiatry, Honolulu, HI.

King, K. A., & Smith, J. (2000). Project SOAR: A training program to increase school counselor's knowledge and confidence regarding suicide prevention intervention. *Journal of School Health, 70*, 402–407.

Knox, K. L., Litts, D. A., Talcott, G. W., Feig, J. C., & Caine, E. D. (2003). Risk of suicide and related adverse outcomes after exposure to a suicide prevention programme in the U.S. Air Force: Cohort study. *British Medical Journal, 327*, 1376–1380.

Kruesi, J. M., Grossman, J., Pennington, J. M., Woodward, P. J., Duda, D., & Hirsch, J. G. (1999). Suicide and violence prevention: Parent education in the emergency department. *Journal of the American Academy of Child and Adolescent Psychiatry, 38*, 250–255.

LaFramboise, T., & Howard-Pitney, B. (1995). The Zuni Life Skills curriculum: Description and evaluation of suicide prevention program. *Journal of Counseling Psychology, 42*, 479–486.

Lewinsohn, P. M., Rohde, P., & Seeley, J. R. (1993). Psychosocial characteristics of adolescents with a history of suicide attempt. *Journal of the American Academy of Child and Adolescent Psychiatry, 32*, 60–68.

Lewinsohn, P. M., Rohde, P., & Seeley, J. R. (1994). Psychosocial risk factors for future adolescent suicide attempts. *Journal of Consulting and Clinical Psychology, 62*, 297–305.

Lewinsohn, P. M., Rohde, P., & Seeley, J. R. (1996). Adolescent suicidal ideation and attempts: Prevalence, risk factors, and clinical implications. *Clinical Psychology: Science and Practice, 3*, 25–46.

Linehan, M. M. (1993a). *Cognitive behavioral therapy of borderline personality disorder.* New York: Guilford.

Linehan, M. M. (1993b). *Skills training manual for treating borderline personality disorder.* New York: Guilford.

Linehan, M. M., Armstrong, H. E., Suarez, A., Allmon, D., & Heard, H. L. (1991). Cognitive-behavioral treatment of chronically parasuicidal borderline patients. *Archives of General Psychiatry, 48*, 1060–1064.

Linehan, M. M., Heard, H. L., & Armstrong, H. E. (1993). Naturalistic follow-up of a behavioral treatment for chronically parasuicidal borderline patients. *Archives of General Psychiatry, 50*, 971–974.

Maine, S., Shute, R., & Martin, G. (2001). Educating parents about youth suicide: Knowledge, response to suicidal statements, attitudes and intention to help. *Suicide and Life-Threatening Behavior, 31*, 320–332.

Mann, J. J. (2003). Neurobiology of suicidal behaviour. *Nature Reviews Neuroscience, 4*, 819–828.

Mann, J. J., Stanley, M., McBride, P. A., & McEwen, B. S. (1986). Increased serotonin2 and β-adrenergic receptor binding in the frontal cortices of suicide victims. *Archives of General Psychiatry, 43*, 934–959.

March, J., Silva, S., Petrycki, S., Curry, J., Wells, K., Fairbank, J., et al. (2004). Fluoxetine, cognitive-behavioral therapy, and their combination for adolescents with depression: Treatment for Adolescents with Depression Study (TADS) randomized controlled trial. *JAMA, 292*, 807–820.

Marttunen, M. J., Aro, H. M., Henriksson, M. M., & Lönnqvist, J. K. (1991). Mental disorders in adolescent suicide: DSM-III-R axes I and II diagnoses in suicides among 13- to 19-year-olds in Finland. *Archives of General Psychiatry, 48*, 834–839.

Marttunen, M. J., Aro, H. M., Henriksson, M. M., & Lönnqvist, J. K. (1994). Psychosocial stressors more common in adolescent suicides with alcohol abuse compared with depressive adolescent suicides. *Journal of the American Academy of Child and Adolescent Psychiatry, 33*, 490–497.

Marttunen, M. J., Aro, H. M., & Lönnqvist, J. K. (1993). Precipitant stressors in adolescent suicide. *Journal of the American Academy of Child and Adolescent Psychiatry, 32*, 1178–1183.

May, P. A., & Van Winkle, N. (1994). Indian adolescent suicide: The epidemiologic picture in New Mexico. In C. W. Duclos & M. Manson (Eds.), *Calling from the rim: Suicide behavior among American Indian and Alaska Native adolescents* (pp. 2–23). Boulder, CO: University of Colorado Press.

McDaniel, J. S., Purcell, D., & D'Augelli, A. R. (2001). The relationship between sexual orientation and risk for suicide: Research findings and future directions for research and preventions. *Suicide and Life-Threatening Behavior, 31*, 84–105.

McKelvey, R. S., Davies, L. C., Pfaff, J. J., Acres, J., & Edwards, S. (1998). Psychological distress and suicidal ideation among 1–24 year-olds presenting to general practice: A pilot study. *Australian and New Zealand Journal of Psychiatry, 32*, 344–348.

McKelvey, R. S., Pfaff, J. J., & Acres, J. G. (2001). The relationship between chief complaints, psychological distress, and suicidal ideation in 15–24-year-old patients presenting to general practitioners. *Medical Journal of Australia, 175,* 550–552.

McKeown, R. E., Garrison, C. Z., Cuffe, S. P., Waller, J. L., Jackson, K. L., & Addy, C. L. (1998). Incidence and predictors of suicidal behaviors in a longitudinal sample of young adolescents. *Journal of the American Academy of Child and Adolescent Psychiatry, 37,* 612–619.

McLeavey, B. C., Daly, R. J., Ludgate, J. W., & Murray, C. M. (1994). Interpersonal problem-solving skills training in the treatment of self-poisoning patients. *Suicide and Life-Threatening Behavior, 24,* 382–394.

Mercy, J. A., Kresnow, M. J., O'Carroll, P. W., Lee, R. K., Powell, K. E., Potter, L. B., et al. (2001). Is suicide contagious? A study of the relationship between exposure to the suicidal behavior of others and nearly lethal suicide attempts. *American Journal of Epidemiology, 154,* 120–127.

Middlebrook, D. L., LeMaster, P. L., Beals, J., Novins, D. K., & Manson, S. M. (2001). Suicide prevention in American Indian and Alaska Native communities: A critical review of programs. *Suicide and Life Threatening Behavior, 31* (Suppl.), 132–149.

Miller, A. L., Rathus, J. H., Linehan, M. M., Wetzler, S., & Leigh, E. (1997). Dialectical behavior therapy adapted for suicidal adolescents. *Journal of Practical Psychiatry and Behavioral Health, 3,* 78–86.

Miller, D. N., Eckert, T. L., DuPaul, G. J., & White, G. P. (1999). Adolescent suicide prevention: Acceptability of school-based programs among secondary school principals. *Suicide and Life-Threatening Behavior, 29,* 72–85.

Miller, M., & Hemenway, D. (1999). The relationship between firearms and suicide: A review of the literature. *Aggression and Violent Behavior, 4,* 59–75.

Montgomery, F. A., Montgomery, D. B., Jayanthi-Rani, S., Roy, D. H., Shaw, P. J., & McAuley, R. (1979). Maintenance therapy in repeat suicidal behavior: A placebo-controlled trial. *Proceedings of the 10th International Congress for Suicide Prevention and Crisis Intervention.* Ottowa: International Congress for Suicide Prevention and Crisis Intervention.

Morgan, H. G., Jones, E. M., & Owen, J. H. (1993). Secondary prevention of non-fatal deliberate self-harm. The Green Card study. *British Journal of Psychiatry, 163,* 111–112.

National Center for Health Statistics (n.d.). *Vital Statistics of the United States, 1900–84.* Retrieved November 10, 2003, from http://www.cdc.gov/nchs/products/pubs/pubd/vsus/1963/1963.htm

National Mental Health Association. (2005). *Finding hope and help: College student and depression pilot initiative.* Retrieved February 1, 2005, from http://www.nmha.org/camh/college/index.cfm

Nemeroff, C. B., Compton, M. T., & Berger, J. (2001). The depressed suicidal patient: Assessment and treatment. In H. Hendin & J. J. Mann (Eds.), *The clinical science of suicide prevention* (pp. 1–23). New York: New York Academy of Sciences.

Oatis, P. J., Fenn Buderer, N. M., Cummings, P., & Fleitz, R. (1999). Pediatric practice based evaluation of the Steps to Prevent Firearm Injury program. *Injury Prevention, 5,* 48–52.

Olfson, M., Shaffer, D., Marcus, S. C., & Greenberg, T. (2003). Relationship between antidepressant medication treatment and suicide in adolescents. *Archives of General Psychiatry, 60,* 978–982.

Oquendo, M. A., Malone, K. M., & Mann, J. J. (1997). Suicide: Risk factors and prevention in refractory major depression. *Depression and Anxiety, 5,* 202–211.

Oquendo, M. A., & Mann, J. J. (2000). The biology of impulsivity and suicidality. *Psychiatric Clinics of North America, 23,* 11–25.

Overholser, J. C., Hemstreet, A., Spirito, A., & Vyse, S. (1989). Suicide awareness programs in the schools: Effects of gender and personal experience. *Journal of the American Academy of Child and Adolescent Psychiatry, 28,* 925–930.

Pandey, G. N., Dwivedi, Y., Rizavi, H. S., Ren, X., Pandey, S. C., Pesold, C., Roberts, R. C., Conley, R. R., & Tamminga, C. A. (2002). Higher expression of serotonin 5-HT (2A) receptors in the postmortem brains of teenage suicide victims. *American Journal of Psychiatry, 159,* 419–429.

Pfaff, J. J. Acres, J. G., & McKelvey, R. S. (2001). Training GP's to recognise and respond to psychological distress and suicidal ideation in young people. *Medical Journal of Australia, 174,* 222–226.

Pirkis, J., & Blood, R. W. (2001a). Suicide and the media: Part I. Reportage in nonfictional media. *Crisis, 22,* 146–154.

Pirkis, J., & Blood, R. W. (2001b). Suicide and the media: Part II. Reportage in fictional media. *Crisis, 22,* 155–162.

Poijula, S., Wahlberg, K. E., & Dyregrov, A. (2001). Adolescent suicide and suicide contagion in three secondary schools. *International Journal of Emergency Mental Health, 3,* 164–168.

Ramsay, R., Cooke, M., & Lang, W. (1990). Alberta's suicide prevention training programs: A retrospective comparison with Rothman's developmental research model. *Suicide and Life-Threatening Behavior, 20,* 335–351.

Randell, B. P. (1999). *Promoting CARE: Counselors & Parents Prevent Youth Suicide Risk.* Bethesda, MD: National Institutes of Health (NIH), National Institute for Nursing Research (NINR).

Randell, B. P. (2003). *CAST-Plus: A suicide prevention community partnership.* Atlanta: Centers for Disease Control and Prevention, Extramural Prevention Research Programs (EPRP).

Rathus, J. H., & Miller, A. L. (2002). Dialectical behavior therapy adapted for suicidal adolescents. *Suicide and Life-Threatening Behavior, 32,* 146–157.

Reinherz, H. A., Giaconia, R. M., Silverman, A. B., Friedman, A., Pakiz, B., Frost, A. K., et al. (1995). Early psychosocial risks for adolescent suicidal ideation and attempts. *Journal of the American Academy of Child and Adolescent Psychiatry, 34,* 599–611.

Remafedi, G., French, S., Story, M., Resnick, M., & Blum, B. (1998). The relationship between suicide risk and sexual orientation: Results of a population-based study. *American Journal of Public Health, 88,* 57–60.

Resnick, M. D., Bearman, P. S., Blum, W. R., Bauman, K. E., Harris, K. M., Jones, J., et al. (1997). Protecting adolescents from harm: Findings from the National Longitudinal Study on adolescent health. *Journal of the American Medical Association, 278,* 823–832.

Reynolds, W. M. (1988). *Suicidal ideation questionnaire: professional manual.* Odessa, FL: Psychological Assessment Resources.

Reynolds, W. M. (1991). A school-based procedure for the identification of adolescents at risk for suicidal behaviors. *Family and Community Health, 14,* 64–75.

Reza, A., Modzeleski, W., Feucht, T., Anderson, M., & Barrios, L. (2003). Source of firearms used by students in school-associated violent deaths— United States 1992–1999. *Journal of the American Medical Association, 289,* 1626–1627.

Robins, E., Murphy, G. E., Wilkinson, R. H., Gassner, S., & Kayes, J. (1959). Some clinical considerations in the prevention of suicide based on a study of 134 successful suicides. *American Journal of Public Health, 49,* 888–899.

Rotheram-Borus, M. J., Piacentini, J., Cantwell, C., Belin, T. R., & Song, J. (2000). The 18-month impact of an emergency room intervention for adolescent female suicide attempters. *Journal of Consulting and Clinical Psychology, 68,* 1081–1093.

Rotheram-Borus, M. J., Piacentini, J., Van Rossem, R., Graae, F., Cantwell, C., Castro-Blanco, D., et al. (1996). Enhancing treatment adherence with a specialized emergency room program for adolescent suicide attempters. *Journal of the American Academy of Child and Adolescent Psychiatry, 35,* 654–663.

Rotheram-Borus, M. J., & Trautman, P. D. (1988). Hopelessness, depression and suicidal intent among adolescent suicide attempters. *Journal of the American Academy of Child and Adolescent Psychiatry, 27,* 700–704.

Rotheram-Borus, M. J., Trautman, P. D., Dopkins, S. C., & Shrout, P. E. (1990). Cognitive style and pleasant activities among female adolescent suicide attempters. *Journal of Consulting and Clinical Psychology, 58,* 554–561.

Rothman, J. (1980). *Social R & D: Research Development in the Human Services.* Englewood Cliffs, New Jersey: Prentice-Hall.

Rubenstein, J. L., Halton, A., Kasten, L., Rubin, C., & Stechler, G. (1998). Suicidal behavior in adolescents: stress and protection in different family contexts. *American Journal of Orthopsychiatry, 68,* 274–284.

Rubenstein, J. L., Heeren, T., Housman, D., Rubin, C., & Stechler, G. (1989). Suicidal behavior in "normal" adolescents: Risk and protective factors. *American Journal of Orthopsychiatry, 59,* 59–71.

Rudd, M. D., Rajab, M. H., Orman, D. T., Stulman, D. A., Joiner, T., & Dixon, W. (1996). Effectiveness of an outpatient intervention targeting suicidal young adults: Preliminary results. *Journal of Consulting and Clinical Psychology, 64,* 179–190.

Russell, S. T. (2003). Sexual minority youth and suicide risk. *American Behavioral Scientist, 46,* 1241–1257.

Russell, S. T., & Joyner, K. (2001). Adolescent sexual orientation and suicide risk: Evidence from a national study. *American Journal of Public Health, 91,* 1276–1281.

Sakinofsky, I. (2000). Repetition of suicidal behaviour. In K. Hawton & K. Van Heeringen (Eds.), *The international handbook of suicide and attempted suicide* (pp. 385–404). New York: John Wiley & Sons.

SAMHSA Model Programs (2005). Retrieved February 1, 2005, from http://www.modelprograms.samhsa.gov

Schmidtke, A., & Schaller, S. (2000). The role of

mass media in suicide prevention. In K. Hawton & K. van Heeringen (Eds.), *The international handbook of suicide and attempted suicide* (pp. 675–698). New York: John Wiley & Sons.

Schuster, M. A., Franke, T. M., Bastian, A. M., Sor, S., & Halfon, N. (2000). Firearm storage patterns in US homes with children. *American Journal of Public Health, 90,* 588–594.

Senturia, Y. D., Christoffeln, K. K., & Donovan, M. (1994). Children's household exposure to guns: A pediatric practice-based survey. *Pediatrics, 93,* 469–475.

Senturia, Y. D., Christoffeln, K. K., & Donovan, M. (1996). Gun storage patterns in US homes with children: A pediatric practice-based survey, Pediatric Research Group. *Archives of Pediatric Adolescent Medicine, 150,* 265–269.

Shaffer, D., Fisher, P., Hicks, R., Pardes, H., & Gould, M. (1995). Sexual orientation in adolescents who commit suicide. *Suicide and Life-Threatening Behavior, 25* (Suppl.), 64–70.

Shaffer, D., Fisher, P., Lucas, C. P., Dulcan, M. K., & Schwab-Stone, M. E. (2000). NIMH Diagnostic Interview Schedule for Children Version IV (NIMH DISC-IV): Description, differences from previous versions, and reliability of some common diagnoses. *Journal of the American Academy of Child and Adolescent Psychiatry, 39,* 28–38.

Shaffer, D., Garland, A., Vieland, V., Underwood, M. M., & Busner, C. (1991). The impact of curriculum-based suicide prevention programs for teenagers. *Journal of the American Academy of Child and Adolescent Psychiatry, 30,* 588–596.

Shaffer, D., Gould, M. S., Fisher, P., Trautman, P., Moreau, D., Kleinman, M., et al. (1996). Psychiatric diagnosis in child and adolescent suicide. *Archives of General Psychiatry, 53,* 339–348.

Shaffer, D., & Hicks, R. (1994). Suicide. In I. B. Pless (Ed.), *The epidemiology of childhood disorders* (pp. 339–365). New York: Oxford University Press.

Shaffer, D., Scott, M., Wilcox, H., Maslow, C., Hicks, R., Lucas, C. P., et al. (2004). The Columbia Suicide Screen: Validity and reliability of a screen for youth suicide and depression. *Journal of the American Academy of Child and Adolescent Psychiatry, 43,* 71–79.

Shaffer, D., Vieland, V., Garland, A., Rojas, M., Underwood, M. M., & Busner, C. (1990). Adolescent suicide attempters: Response to suicide-prevention programs. *Journal of the American Medical Association, 264,* 3151–3155.

Shah, S., Hoffman, R. E., Wake, L., & Marine, W. M. (2000). Adolescent suicide and household access to firearms in Colorado: Results of a case–control study. *Journal of Adolescent Health, 26,* 157–163.

Sharma, V. (2003). Atypical antipsychotics and suicide in mood and anxiety disorders. *Bipolar Disorders, 5*(Suppl. 2), 48–52.

Silverman, A. B., Reinherz, H. Z., & Giaconia, R. M. (1996). The long-term sequelae of child and adolescent abuse: A longitudinal community study. *Child Abuse and Neglect, 20,* 709–723.

Sourander, A., Helstela, L., Haavisto, A., & Bergroth, L. (2001). Suicidal thoughts and attempts among adolescents: A longitudinal 8-year follow-up study. *Journal of Affective Disorders, 63,* 59–66.

Spirito, A. (2003, June). *Suicide attempters identified in emergency rooms.* Presented at the Annenberg Center for Communications and the American Foundation for Suicide Prevention's Youth Suicide Prevention Workshop, New York, NY.

Spirito, A., Boergers, J., Donaldson, D., Bishop, B., & Lewander, W. (2002). An intervention trial to improve adherence to community treatment by adolescents after a suicide attempt. *Journal of the American Academy of Child and Adolescent Psychiatry, 41,* 435–442.

Spirito, A., Brown, L., Overholser, J., & Fritz, G. (1989). Attempted suicide in adolescence: A review and critique of the literature. *Clinical Psychology Review, 9,* 335–363.

Spirito, A., Overholser, J., Ashworth, S., Morgan, J., & Benedict-Drew, C. (1988). Evaluation of a suicide awareness curriculum for high school students. *Journal of the American Academy of Child and Adolescent Psychiatry, 27,* 705–711.

Spirito, A., Plummer, B., Gispert, M., Levy, S., Kurkjian, J., Lewander, W., et al. (1992). Adolescent suicide attempts: Outcomes at follow-up. *American Journal of Orthopsychiatry, 62,* 464–468.

Spitzer, R. L., Kroenke, K., Williams, J. B. L., & the Patient Health Questionnaire Study Group. (1999). Validity and utility of a self-report version of PRIME-MD: The PHQ Primary Care Study. *Journal of the American Medical Association, 282,* 1737–1744.

Spitzer, R. L., Williams, J. B., Kroenke, K., Hornyak, R., McMurray, J., Heartwell, S. F., et al. (2000). Validity and utility of the Patient Health Questionnaire in assessment of 3000 obstetric-gynecology patients: The PRIME-MD Patient Health Questionnaire Obstetric-Gynecology Study. *American Journal of Obstetrics and Gynecology, 183,* 759–769.

Spivak, B., Shabash, E., Sheitman, B., Weizman, A., & Mester, R. (2003). The effects of clozapine versus haloperidol on measures of impulsive aggression and suicidality in chronic schizophrenic patients: An open, nonrandomized, 6-month study. *Journal of Clinical Psychiatry, 64,* 755–760.

Stack, S. (2000). Media impacts on suicide: A quantitative review of 293 findings. *Social Science Quarterly, 81,* 957–971.

Stennies, G. R., Ikeda, R., Leadbetter, S., Houston, B., & Sacks, J. (1994). Firearm storage practices and children in the home, United States, 1994. *Archives of Pediatric and Adolescent Medicine, 153,* 586–590.

Stewart, S. E., Manion, I. G., Davidson, S., & Cloutier, P. (2001). Suicidal children and adolescents with first emergency room presentations: Predictors of six-month outcome. *Journal of the American Academy of Child and Adolescent Psychiatry, 40,* 580–587.

Thompson, E. A. (2003a, June). *Washington state program.* Presented at the Annenberg Center for Communications and the American Foundation for Suicide Prevention's Youth Suicide Prevention Workshop, New York, NY.

Thompson, E. A. (2003b, June). *Potential school dropouts.* Presented at the Annenberg Center for Communications and the American Foundation for Suicide Prevention's Youth Suicide Prevention Workshop, New York, NY.

Thompson, E. A., & Eggert, L. L. (1999). Using the Suicide Risk Screen to identify suicidal adolescents among potential high school dropouts. *Journal of the American Academy of Child and Adolescent Psychiatry, 38,* 1506–1514.

Thompson, E. A., Eggert, L. L., & Herting, J. R. (2000). Mediating effects of an indicated prevention program for reducing youth depression and suicide-risk behaviors. *Suicide and Life Threatening Behavior, 30,* 252–271.

Thompson, E. A., Eggert, L. L., Randell, B. P., & Pike, K. C. (2001). Evaluation of indicated suicide-risk prevention approaches for potential high school dropouts. *American Journal of Public Health, 91,* 742–752.

Tierney, R. J. (1994). Suicide intervention training evaluation: A preliminary report. *Crisis, 15,* 70–76.

Tondo, L., Jamison, K. R., & Baldessarini, R. J. (1997). Effect of lithium maintenance on suicidal behavior in major mood disorders. In D. M. Stoff & J. J. Mann (Eds.), *The neurobiology of suicide: From the bench to the clinic* (pp. 339–351). New York: New York Academy of Sciences.

Toumbourou, J. W., & Gregg, E. (2002). Impact of an empowerment-based parent education pro-

gram on the reduction of youth suicide factors. *Journal of Adolescent Health, 31,* 277–285.

Townsend, E., Hawton, K., Altman, D. G., Arensman, E., Gunnell, D., Hazell, P., et al. (2001). The efficacy of problem-solving treatments after deliberate self-harm: Meta-analysis of randomized controlled trials with respect to depression, hopelessness and improvement of problems. *Psychological Medicine, 31,* 979–988.

Trautman, P., Stewart, M., & Morishima, A. (1993). Are adolescent suicide attempters noncompliant with outcome care? *Journal of the American Academy of Child and Adolescent Psychiatry, 32,* 89–94.

Turley, B. (2000). *Lifeline Australia youth suicide prevention project: Final evaluation report.* Deakin, Australia: Lifeline Australia, Inc.

Turley, B., & Tanney, B. (1998). *Evaluation report on suicide intervention field trial Australia.* Deakin, Australia: Lifeline Australia, Inc. and Living-Works Education., Inc.

U.S. Department of Health and Human Services (2001). *National Strategy for Suicide Prevention: Goals and objectives for action* (SMA Publication SMA01-3517). Rockville, MD: Author.

Vieland, V., Whittle, B., Garland, A., Hicks, R., & Shaffer, D. (1991). The impact of curriculum-based suicide prevention programs for teenagers: An 18-month follow-up. *Journal of the American Academy of Child and Adolescent Psychiatry, 30,* 811–815.

Vijayakumar, L., & Rajkumar, S. (1999). Are risk factors for suicide universal? A case–control study in India. *Acta Psychiatrica Scandinavica, 99,* 407–411.

Wagner, B. M. (1997). Family risk factors for child and adolescent suicidal behavior. *Psychological Bulletin, 121,* 246–298.

Wagner, B. M., Silverman, M. A., & Martin, C. E. (2003). Family factors in youth suicidal behaviors. *American Behavioral Scientist, 46,* 1171–1191.

Walsh, M., & Perry, C. M. (2000, October). *Youth-based prevention strategies in a rural community, Quesnel, BC: A community suicide prevention study.* Presented at the Canadian Association of Suicide Prevention 11th Annual Conference, Vancouver, BC, Canada.

Wallace, J. D., Calhoun, A. D., Powell, K. E., O'Neil, J., & James, S. P. (1996). Homicide and suicide among Native Americans, 1979–1992. *Violence Surveillance Summary, Series 2.* Atlanta: Centers for Disease Control and Prevention, National Center for Injury Prevention and Control.

Warshaw, M. G., Dolan, R. T., & Keller, M. B.

(2000). Suicidal behavior in patients with current or past panic disorder: Five years of prospective data from the Harvard/Brown anxiety research program. *American Journal of Psychiatry, 157,* 1876–1878.

Wichstrom, L. (2000). Predictors of adolescent suicide attempts: A nationally representative longitudinal study of Norwegian adolescents. *Journal of the American Academy of Child and Adolescent Psychiatry, 39,* 603–610.

Wichstrom, L., & Hegna, K. (2003). Sexual orientation and suicide attempt: A longitudinal study of the general Norwegian adolescent population. *Journal of Abnormal Psychology, 112,* 144–151.

Wood, A., Harrington, R., & Moore, A. (1996). Controlled trial of a brief cognitive-behavioural intervention in adolescent patients with depressive disorders. *Journal of Child Psychology and Psychiatry, 37,* 737–746.

Wood, A., Trainor, G., Rothwell, J., Moore, A., & Harrington, R. (2001). Randomized trial of group therapy for repeated deliberate self-harm adolescents. *Journal of the American Academy of Child and Adolescent Psychiatry 40,* 1246–1253.

World Health Organization (2003). *WHO suicide rates: Country reports and charts.* Retrieved November 11, 2003, from http://www.who.int/mental_health/prevention/suicide/country_reports/en/

Wunderlich, U., Bronisch, T., & Wittchen, H. U. (1998). Comorbidity patterns in adolescents and young adults with suicide attempts. *European Archives of Psychiatry and Clinical Neuroscience, 248,* 87–95.

Zenere, F. J., III, & Lazarus, P. J. (1997). The decline of youth suicidal behavior in an urban, multicultural public school system following the introduction of a suicide prevention and intervention program. *Suicide and Life Threatening Behavior, 27,* 387–403.

Zhang, J., & Jin, S. (1996). Determinants of suicide ideation: A comparison of Chinese and American college students. *Adolescence, 31,* 451–467.

Part VII: Beyond Disorder

Agodin, R., & Dynarski, M. (2001). *Are experiments the only option? A look at dropout prevention programs.* Washington, DC: Mathematical Policy Research, Inc.

Ainsworth, M. S., Blehar, M. C., Waters, E., & Wall, S. (1978). *Patterns of attachment: A psychological study of the strange situation.* Potomac, MD: Lawrence Erlbaum.

Akers, R. L., Krohn, M., Lanza-Kaduce, L., & Radosevich, M. (1979). Social learning and deviant behavior: A specific test of a general theory. *American Sociological Review, 44,* 636–655.

Albee, G. W. (1982). Preventing psychopathology and promoting human potential. *American Psychologist, 37,* 1043–1050.

Allen, J. P., Philiber, S., Herrling, S., & Kuperminc, G. P. (1997). Preventing teen pregnancy and academic failure: Experimental evaluation of a developmentally based approach. *Child Development, 68,* 729–742.

American Psychiatric Association (1994). *Diagnostic and statistical manual of mental disorders* (4th ed.). Washington, DC: Author.

Arthur, M. W., Hawkins, J. D., Pollard, J. A., Catalano, R. F., & Baglioni, A. J. (2002). Measuring risk and protective factors for substance use, delinquency, and other adolescent problem behaviors: The Communities That Care Youth Survey. *Evaluation Review, 26,* 575–601.

Bandura, A. (1973). *Aggression: A social learning analysis.* Englewood Cliffs, NJ: Prentice Hall.

Bandura, A. (1986). *Social foundations of thought and action.* Englewood Cliffs, NJ: Prentice Hall.

Bandura, A. (1989). Human agency in social cognitive theory. *American Psychologist, 14,* 175–184.

Bandura, A. (1993). Perceived self-efficacy in cognitive development and functioning. *Educational Psychologist, 28,* 117–148.

Barasch, M. (1994). Innovative approaches in a community based educational/treatment unit for mentally ill adolescents. *International Journal of Adolescent Medicine and Health, 7,* 11–26.

Barrett, P. M., & Ollendick, T. H. (Eds.) (2004). *Handbook of interventions that work with children and adolescents: Prevention and treatment.* West Sussex, England: Wiley.

Becker, M. H. (Ed.) (1974). *The health belief model and personal health behavior.* Thorofare, NJ: Charles R. Slack.

Benard, B. (1991). *Fostering resiliency in kids: Protective factors in the family, school and community.* San Francisco: Western Regional Center for Drug Free Schools and Communities, Far West Laboratory.

Benson, P. (1997). *All kids are our kids.* San Francisco: Jossey-Bass.

Benson, P. L., Leffert, N., Scales, P. C., & Blyth, D. A. (1998). Beyond the "village" rhetoric: Creating health communities for children and adolescents. *Applied Developmental Science, 2,* 138–159.

Benson, P. L., & Saito, R. N. (2000). The scientific foundations of youth development. In N. Jaffe (Ed.), *Youth development: Issues, challenges, and directions* (pp. 125–147). Philadelphia: Public/Private Ventures.

Berkowitz, M. W., & Bier, M. C. (2004). Research-based character education. *The Annals of the American Academy of Political and Social Science, 591,* 72–85.

Birmaher, B., Arbelaez, C., & Brent, D. (2002). Course and outcome of child and adolescent major depressive disorder. *Child and Adolescent Psychiatric Clinics of North America, 111,* 619–638.

Bonnano, G. A. (2004). Loss, trauma, and human resilience: Have we underestimated the human capacity to thrive after extremely aversive events? *American Psychologist, 59,* 20–28.

Botvin, G. J., Baker, E., Dusenbury, L., Botvin, E. M., & Diaz, T. (1995). Long-term follow-up results of a randomized drug abuse prevention trial in a white middle-class population. *Journal of the American Medical Association, 273,* 1106–1112.

Bowlby, J. (1969). *Attachment and loss, Vol. I. Attachment.* New York: Basic Books.

Bowlby, J. (1973). *Attachment and loss, Vol. II. Separation: Anxiety and anger.* New York: Basic Books.

Bowlby, J. (1980). *Attachment and loss, Vol. III. Loss, sadness, and depression.* New York: Basic Books.

Braucht, G. N., Kirby, M. W., & Berry, G. J. (1978). Psychosocial correlates of empirical types of multiple drug abusers. *Journal of Consulting and Clinical Psychology, 46,* 1463–1475.

Bronfenbrenner, U. (1977). Toward an experimental ecology of human development. *American Psychologist, 32,* 513–531.

Bronfenbrenner, U. (1979). *The ecology of human development: Experiments by nature and design.* Cambridge, MA: Harvard University Press.

Bronfenbrenner, U. (1986). Ecology of the family as a context for human development: Research perspectives. *Developmental Psychology, 22,* 723–742.

Bronfenbrenner, U., & Ceci, S. J. (1994). Nature-nurture reconceptualized: A bio-ecological model. *Psychological Review, 101,* 568–586.

Brook, J. S., Brook, D. W., Gordon, A. S., Whiteman, M., & Cohen, P. (1990). The psychosocial etiology of adolescent drug use: A family interactional approach. *Genetic, Social, and General Psychology Monographs, 116,* 111–267.

Brophy, J. (1988). Research linking teacher behavior to student achievement: Potential implications for instruction of Chapter 1 students. *Educational Psychologist, 23,* 235–286.

Brophy, J., & Good, T. L. (1986). Teacher behavior and student achievement. In M. C. Wittrock (Ed.), *Handbook of research on teaching* (pp. 328–375). New York: MacMillan.

Brotherson, M. J., Cook, C. C., Lahr, R. C., & Wehmeyer, M. L. (1995). Policy supporting self-determination in the environments of children with disabilities. *Education and Training in Mental Retardation and Developmental Disabilities, 30,* 3–14.

Byalin, K., Smith, A., Chatkin, M., & Wilmot, J. (1987). A bridge over troubled waters: An innovative day-treatment program for older adolescents. *International Journal of Partial Hospitalization, 4,* 217–226.

Cameron, K. S., Dutton, J. E., & Quinn, R. E. (Eds.) (2003). *Positive organizational scholarship: Foundations of a new discipline.* San Francisco: Berrett-Koehler.

Cannon, T. D., Huttunen, M. O., Dahlstrom, M., Larmo, I., Rasanen, P., & Juriloo, A. (2002). Antipsychotic drug treatment in the prodromal phase of schizophrenia. *American Journal of Psychiatry, 159,* 1230–1232.

Caplan, M., Weissberg, R. P., Grober, J. S., Sivo, P. J., Grady, K., & Jacoby, C. (1992). Social competence promotion with inner-city and suburban young adolescents: Effects on social adjustment and alcohol use. *Journal of Consulting and Clinical Psychology, 60,* 56–63.

Carnegie Council on Adolescent Development (1992). *A matter of time: Risk and opportunity in the nonschool hours. Report of the Task Force on Youth Development and Community Programs.* New York: Carnegie Corporation of New York.

CASEL (2003). *Safe and sound: An educational leader's guide to evidence-based social and emotional learning programs.* Chicago: University of Illinois at Chicago: Author.

Catalano, R. F., Berglund, M. L., Ryan, J.A.M., Lonczak, H. S., & Hawkins, J. D. (1999). *Positive youth development in the United States. Research findings on evaluations of the positive youth development programs.* New York: Carnegie Corporation of New York.

Catalano, R. F., Berglund, M. L., Ryan, J.A.M., Lonczak, H. S., & Hawkins, J. D. (2004). Positive youth development in the United States: Research findings on evaluations of positive youth development programs. *The Annals of the American Academy of Political and Social Science, 591,* 98–124.

Catalano, R. F., & Hawkins, D. F. (1996). The social development model: A theory of antisocial behavior. In J. D. Hawkins (Ed.), *Delinquency and crime; Current theories* (pp. 149–197). New York: Cambridge University Press.

Catalano, R. F., Mazza, J. J., Harachi, T. W., Abbott, R. D., Haggerty, K. P., & Fleming, C. B. (2003). Raising healthy children through enhancing social development in elementary school: Results after 1.5 years. *Journal of School Psychology, 41,* 143–164.

Center for the Study and Prevention of Violence. (2003). Blueprints for violence prevention. Retrieved October 17, 2003, from http://colorado.edu/cspv/blueprints/

Child Trends (2003). *American teens: A special look at "what works" in adolescent development.* Washington, DC: Author.

Clark, A. E., Georgellis, Y., Lucas, R. E., & Diener, E. (2004). Unemployment alters the set-point for life satisfaction. *Psychological Science, 15,* 8–13.

Clarke, G. N., Hornbrook, M., Lynch, F., Polen, M., Gale, J., Beardslee, W. R., et al. (2001). A randomized trial of a group cognitive intervention for preventing depression in adolescent offspring of depressed parents. *Archives of General Psychiatry, 58,* 1127–1134.

Coalition for Evidence-Based Policy (2003). *Identifying and implementing educational practices supported by rigorous evidence: A user-friendly guide.* Washington, DC: Author.

Communitarian Network. (2000). Media watches kids. *The Communitarian Update, 32.* Retrieved October 17, 2003, from http://www.gwu.edu/~ccps/communitarian_update_n32.html

Connell, J. P., Gambone, M. A., & Smith, T. J. (2000). Youth development in community settings: Challenges to our field and our approach. In N. Jaffe (Ed.), *Youth development: Issues, challenges, and directions* (pp. 281–300). Philadelphia: Public/Private Ventures.

Cowen, E. L. (1994). The enhancement of psychological wellness: Challenges and opportunities. *American Journal of Community Psychology, 22,* 149–179.

Csikszentmihalyi, M. (1990). *Flow: The psychology of optimal experience.* New York: HarperCollins.

Dadds, M. R., Holland, D. E., Laurens, K. R., Mullins, M., Barrett, P. M., & Spence, S. H. (1999). Early intervention and prevention of anxiety disorders in children: Results at 2-year follow-up. *Journal of Consulting and Clinical Psychology, 67,* 145–150.

Damon, W. (2004). What is positive youth development? *The Annals of the American Academy of Political and Social Science, 591,* 13–24.

Deci, E. L., & Ryan, R. M. (1994). Promoting self-determined education. *Scandinavian Journal of Educational Research, 38,* 3–14.

deVries, M. W. (Ed.) (1992). *The experience of psychopathology: Investigating mental disorders in their natural settings.* New York: Cambridge University Press.

Diener, E. (1984). Subjective well-being. *Psychological Bulletin, 95,* 542–575.

Dolan, L., Kellam, S., & Brown, C. H. (1989). *Short-term impact of a mastery learning preventive intervention on early risk behaviors.* Baltimore: Johns Hopkins University Press.

Dryfoos, J. G. (1990). *Adolescents at risk: Prevalence and prevention.* New York: Oxford University Press.

Durlak, J. A., & Wells, A. M. (1997). Primary prevention mental health programs for children and adolescents: A meta-analytic review. *American Journal of Community Psychology, 25,* 115–152.

Durlak, J. A., & Wells, A. M. (1998). Evaluation of indicated preventive intervention (secondary intervention) mental health programs for children and adolescents. *American Journal of Community Psychology, 26,* 775–802.

Eccles, J. S., & Gootman, J. A. (Eds.). (2002). *Community programs to promote youth development.* Washington, DC: National Academy Press.

Eccles, J. S., & Templeton, J. (2003). *Identifying programs that work.* Position paper prepared for Annenberg/Sunnylands Conference on Positive Youth Development (May 28–29), Philadelphia.

Elliott, D. S., & Tolan, P. H. (1998). Youth violence: Prevention, intervention, and social policy: An overview. In D. J. Flannery & C. R. Huff (Eds.), *Youth violence: Prevention, intervention, and social policy* (pp. 3–46). Washington, DC: American Psychiatric Press.

Erikson, E. H. (1968). *Identity: Youth and crisis.* New York: W. W. Norton.

Erickson, J. B. (1999). *Directory of American youth organizations: A guide to 500 clubs, groups, troops, teams, societies, lodges, and more for young people, 1998–1999* (7th ed.). Minneapolis, MN: Free Spirit.

Ewalt, P. L., & Mokuau, N. (1995). Self-determination from a Pacific perspective. *Social Work, 40,* 168–175.

Federal Interagency Forum on Child and Family Statistics. (2001). *America's children: Key national indicators of well-being.* Washington, DC: U.S. Government Printing Office.

Fetterman, D. M., Kaftarian, S. J., & Wandersman, A. (Eds.) (1996). *Empowerment evaluation. Knowledge and tools for self-assessment and accountability.* Newbury Park, CA: Sage.

Field, S. (1996). Self-determination instructional strategies for youth with learning disabilities. *Journal of Learning Disabilities, 29,* 40–52.

Fishbein, M., & Ajzen, I. (1975). *Belief, attitude, intention, and behavior.* Reading, MA: Addison-Wesley.

Fredrickson, B. L. (1998). What good are positive emotions? *Review of General Psychology, 2,* 300–319.

Fredrickson, B. L. (2000). Cultivating positive emotions to optimize health and well-being. *Prevention and Treatment, 3(0001a).* Retrieved February 15, 2004, from http://journals.apa.org/prevention/volume3/pre0030001a.html

Fredrickson, B. L. (2001). The role of positive emotions in positive psychology: The broaden-and-build theory of positive emotions. *American Psychologist, 56,* 218–226.

Fruedenberger, H. J., & Carbone, J. (1984). The re-entry process of adolescents. *Journal of Psychoactive Drugs, 16,* 95–99.

Gambone, M. A. (1997). *Launching a resident-driven initiative. Community Change for Youth Development (CCYD) from site-selection to early implementation.* Philadelphia: Public/Private Ventures.

Gardner, H. (1983). *Frames of mind: The theory of multiple intelligences.* New York: Basic Books.

Gardner, H. (1993). *Multiple intelligences: The theory in practice.* New York: Basic Books.

Gardner, H., Csikszentmihalyi, M., & Damon, W. (2001). *Good work: When excellence and ethics meets.* New York: Basic Books.

Gillham, J. E., & Reivich, K. J. (2004). Cultivating optimism in childhood and adolescence. *The Annals of the American Academy of Political and Social Science, 591,* 146–163.

Gilligan, C. (1982). *In a different voice: Psychological theory and women's development.* Cambridge, MA: Harvard University Press.

Greenberg, M., Domitrovich, C., & Bumbarger, B. (1999). *Preventing mental disorders in school-age children.* Washington, DC: Center for Mental Health Services, U.S. Department of Health and Human Services.

Greenberg, M. T., & Kusche, C. A. (1998). *Promoting alternative thinking strategies. Blueprint for violence prevention* (Book 10). Boulder: Institute of Behavioral Sciences, University of Colorado.

Hahn, A., Leavitt, T., & Aaron, P. (1994). *Evaluation of the Quantum Opportunity Program (QOP): Did the program work?* Waltham, MA: Brandeis University, Heller Graduate School.

Halpern, R., Barker, G., & Mollard, W. (2000). Youth programs as alternative spaces to be: A study of neighborhood youth programs in Chicago's West Town. *Youth and Society, 31,* 469–506.

Harrigan, S. M., McGorry, P. D., & Krstev, H. (2003). Does treatment delay in first-episode psychosis really matter? *Psychological Medicine, 33,* 97–110.

Harter, S. (1985). Competence as a dimension of self-evaluation: Toward a comprehensive model of self-worth. In R. L. Leahy (Ed.), *The development of the self* (pp. 55–122). Orlando, FL: Academic Press.

Hattie, J. M., Neill, J. T., & Richards, G. E. (1997). Adventure education and Outward Bound: Out-of-class experiences that make a lasting difference. *Review of Educational Research, 67,* 43–87.

Hawkins, J. D., Catalano, R. F., Jones, G., & Fine, D. N. (1987). Delinquency prevention through parent training: Results and issues from work in progress. In J. Q. Wilson & G. C. Loury (Eds.), *From children to citizens: Vol. III. Families, schools, and delinquency prevention* (pp. 186–204). New York: Springer-Verlag.

Hawkins, J. D., Catalano, R. F., Kosterman, R., Abbott, R., & Hill, K. G. (1999). Preventing adolescent health-risk behaviors by strengthening protection during childhood. *Archives of Pediatric Adolescent Medicine, 153,* 226–234.

Hawkins, J. D., Catalano, R. F., & Miller, J. Y. (1992). Risk and protective factors for alcohol and other drug problems in adolescence and early adulthood: Implications for substance-abuse prevention. *Psychological Bulletin, 112,* 64–105.

Hawkins, J. D., Catalano, R. F., Morrison, D. M., O'Donnell, J., Abbott, R. D., & Day, L. E. (1992). The Seattle Social Development Project: Effects of the first four years on protective factors and problem behaviors. In J. McCord & R. E. Tremblay (Eds.), *Preventing antisocial behavior: Interventions from birth through adolescence* (pp. 139–161). New York: Guilford Press.

Hawkins, J. D., & Weis, J. G. (1985). The social development model: An integrated approach to delinquency prevention. *Journal of Primary Prevention 6,* 73–97.

Hibbs, E. D., & Jensen, P. S. (Eds.) (1996). *Psychosocial treatments for child and adolescent disorders: Empirically based strategies for clinical practice.*

Washington, DC: American Psychological Association.

Hill, H., Piper, D., & Moberg, D. M. (1994). "Us planning prevention for them": The social construction of community prevention for youth. *International Quarterly of Community Health Education, 15,* 65–89.

Hirschi, T. (1969). *Causes of delinquency.* Berkeley, CA: University of California Press.

Hoffman, M. L. (1981). Is altruism part of human nature? *Journal of Personality and Social Psychology, 40,* 121–137.

Hollister, R. G., & Hill, J. (1999). Problems in the evaluation of community-wide initiatives. In J. P. Connell, A. C. Kubisch, L. B. Schorr, and C. H. Weiss (Eds.), *New approaches to evaluating community initiatives* (Vol. 1, pp. 127–172). Washington, DC: The Aspen Institute.

Jarbin, H., & von Knorring, A. L. (2003). Diagnostic stability in adolescent onset psychotic disorders. *European Child and Adolescent Psychiatry, 12,* 15–22.

Jessor, R., & Jessor, S. L. (1977). *Problem behavior and psychosocial development: A longitudinal study of youth.* New York: Academic Press.

Johnson, B., Tierney, J., & Siegel, M. (2003). *Religion and behavioral outcomes among youth: A review of the literature.* Position paper prepared for Annenberg/Sunnylands Conference on Positive Youth Development (May 28–29), Philadelphia.

Johnston, M. W., & Bell, A. P. (1995). Romantic emotional attachment: Additional factors in the development of the sexual orientation of men. *Journal of Counseling and Development, 73,* 621–625.

Joiner, T. J. (2000). Depression's vicious scree: Self-propagating and erosive processes in depression chronicity. *Clinical Psychology: Science and Practice, 72,* 203–218.

Kandel, D. B., Kessler, R. C., & Margulies, R. Z. (1978). Antecedents of adolescent initiation into stages of drug use: A developmental analysis. *Journal of Youth and Adolescence, 7,* 13–40.

Kazdin, A. E., & Weisz, J. R. (Eds.) (2003). *Evidence-based psychotherapies for children and adolescents.* New York: Guilford.

Kirby, D. (1997). *No easy answers: Research findings on programs to reduce teen pregnancy—A research review commissioned by the National Campaign to Prevent Teen Pregnancy,* Washington, DC: Task Force on Effective Programs and Research.

Kohlberg, L. (1963). The development of children's orientations toward a moral order: I. Sequence in the development of moral thought. *Vita Humana, 6,* 11–33.

Kohlberg, L. (1969). Stage and sequence: The cognitive-developmental approach. In D. A. Goslin (Ed.), *Handbook of socialization theory and research* (pp. 347–480). Chicago: Rand McNally.

Kohlberg, L. (1981). *Essays on moral development* (Vol. 1). New York: Harper and Row.

Kornberg, M. S., & Caplan, G. (1980). Risk factors and preventive intervention in child psychotherapy: A review. *Journal of Primary Prevention, 1,* 71–133.

LaFromboise, T., Coleman, H. L., & Gerton, J. (1993). Psychological impact of biculturalism: Evidence and theory. *Psychological Bulletin, 114,* 395–412.

LaFromboise, T., & Rowe, W. (1983). Skills training for bicultural competence: Rationale and application. *Journal of Counseling Psychology, 30,* 589–595.

Larson, R. W. (2000). Toward a psychology of positive youth development. *American Psychologist, 55,* 170–183.

Leffert, N., Benson, P. L., Scales, P. C., Sharma, A. R., Drake, D. R., & Blyth, D. A. (1998). Developmental assets: Measurement and prediction of risk behaviors among adolescents. *Applied Developmental Science, 2,* 209–230.

Lerner, R. M., & Kauffman, M. B. (1985). The concept of development in contextualism. *Developmental Review, 5,* 309–333.

Levitt, A. J., Hogan, T. P., & Bucosky, C. M. (1990). Quality of life in chronically mentally ill patients in day treatment. *Psychological Medicine, 20,* 703–710.

Lewinsohn, P. M., Pettit, J. W., Joiner, T. E., & Seeley, J. R. (2003). The symptomatic expression of major depressive disorder in adolescents and young adults. *Journal of Abnormal Psychology, 112,* 244–252.

Linley, P. A., & Joseph, S. (2004). Positive change following trauma and adversity: A review. *Journal of Traumatic Stress, 17,* 11–21.

Linley, P. A., & Joseph, S. (Eds.) (2004). *Positive psychology in practice.* Hoboken, NJ: John Wiley & Sons.

Locke, E. A., Frederick, E., Lee, C., & Bobko, P. (1984). Effect of self-efficacy, goals, and task strategies on task performance. *Journal of Applied Psychology, 69,* 241–251.

Lonczak, H. S., Abbott, R. D., Hawkins, D. F., Kosterman, R., & Catalano, R. F. (2002). Effects of the Seattle Social Development Project on sexual behavior, pregnancy, birth, and sexually transmitted disease outcomes by age 21 years. *Archives of Pediatrics and Adolescent Medicine, 156,* 438–447.

Lopez, S. J., & Snyder, C. R. (2003). *Positive psychological assessment: A handbook of models and measures.* Washington, DC: American Psychological Association.

Lucas, R. E., Clark, A. E., Georgellis, Y., & Diener, E. (2003). Reexaming adaptation and the set point model of happiness: Reactions to changes in marital status. *Journal of Personality and Social Psychology, 84,* 527–539.

Luthar, S. S., Cicchetti, D., & Becker, B. (2000). The construct of resilience: A critical evaluation and guidelines for future work. *Child Development, 71,* 543–562.

Maddux, J. E. (2002). Stopping the "madness." In C. R. Snyder & S. J. Lopez (Eds.), *Handbook of positive psychology* (pp. 13–25). New York: Oxford University Press.

Mahler, M. S., Pine, F., & Bergman, A. (1975). *The psychological birth of the human infant.* New York: Basic Books.

Mann, T., Nolen-Hoeksema, S., Huang, K., Burgard, D., Wright, A., & Hanson, K. (1997). Are two interventions worse than none? Joint primary and secondary prevention of eating disorders in college females. *Health Psychology, 16,* 215–225.

Maslow, A. H. (1970). *Motivation and personality* (2nd ed.). New York: Harper & Row.

Masten, A. S., Best, K. M., & Garmezy, N. (1990). Resilience and development: Contributions from the study of children who overcome adversity. *Development and Psychopathology, 2,* 425–444.

Maton, K. I., Schellenbach, C. J., Leadbetter, B. J., & Solarz, A. L. (Eds.) (2003). *Investing in children, youth, families, and communities: Strengths-based research and policy.* Washington, DC: American Psychological Association.

Mays, D. T., & Franks, C. (Eds.) (1985). *Negative outcome in psychotherapy and what to do about it.* New York: Springer-Verlag.

McGorry, P. D., Yung, A. R., Phillips, L. J., Yuen, H. P., Francey, S., Cosgrave, E. M., et al. (2002). Randomized controlled trial of interventions designed to reduce the risk of progression to first-episode psychosis in a clinical sample with subthreshold symptoms. *Archives of General Psychiatry, 59,* 921–928.

McLaughlin, M. (2000). *Community counts: How youth organizations matter for youth development.* Washington, DC: Public Education Network.

McLaughlin, M., Irby, M. A., & Langman, J. (1994). *Urban sanctuaries: Neighborhood organizations in the lives and futures of inner-city youth.* San Francisco: Jossey-Bass.

Mendelberg, H. E. (1986). Identity conflict in Mexican-American adolescents. *Adolescence, 21,* 215–224.

Mishna, F., Michalski, J., & Cummings, R. (2001). Camps as social work interventions: Returning to our roots. *Social Work with Groups, 24,* 153–171.

Moore, K. A., Lippman, L., & Brown, B. (2004). Indicators of child well-being: The promise for positive youth development. *The Annals of the American Academy of Political and Social Science, 591,* 125–145.

Nathan, P. E., & Gorman, J. M. (1998). *A guide to treatments that work.* New York: Oxford University Press.

Nathan, P. E., & Gorman, J. M. (2002). *A guide to treatments that work* (2nd ed.). New York: Oxford University Press.

Nation, M., Crusto, C., Wandersman, A., Kumpfer, K. L., Seybolt, D., Morrisey-Kane, E., et al. (2003). What works in prevention: Principles of effective prevention programs. *American Psychologist, 58,* 449–456.

Neill, A. S. (1960). *Summerhill: A radical approach to child rearing.* New York: Hart.

Nelson, G., Westhues, A., & Macleod, J. (2004). A meta-analysis of longitudinal research on preschool intervention programs for children. *Prevention and Treatment, 6(31).* Retrieved February 15, 2004, from http://journals.apa.org/prevention/volume6/pre0060031a.html

Newman, R. P., Smith, S. M., & Murphy, R. (2000). A matter of money: The cost and financing of youth development. In N. Jaffe (Ed.), *Youth development: Issues, challenges, and directions* (pp. 81–142). Philadelphia: Public/Private Ventures.

Nicholson, H. J., Collins, C., & Holmer, H. (2004). Youth as people: The protective aspects of youth development in after-school settings. *The Annals of the American Academy of Political and Social Science, 591,* 55–71.

Noddings, N. (2003). *Happiness and education.* New York: Cambridge University Press.

Ong, A. D., & van Dulmen, M. (Eds.) (2005). *Handbook of methods in positive psychology.* New York: Oxford University Press.

Otto, G., & Otto, U. (1978). Prognosis in child psychiatry: A follow-up study of a youth clientele. *Acta Psychiatrica Scandinavica Supplement 273,* 1–61.

Parham, T. A., & Helms, J. E. (1985). Relation of racial identity attitudes to self-actualization and affective states of Black students. *Journal of Counseling Psychology, 32,* 431–440.

Park, N. (2004a). Character strengths and positive youth development. *The Annals of the American Academy of Political and Social Science, 591,* 40–54.

Park, N. (2004b). The role of subjective well-being in positive youth development. *The Annals of the American Academy of Political and Social Science, 591,* 25–39.

Park, N., Huebner, E. S., Laughlin, J. E., Valois, R. F., & Gilman, R. (2004). A cross-cultural comparison of the dimensions of child and adolescent life satisfaction reports. *Social Indicators Research, 66,* 61–79.

Park, N., & Peterson, C. (2003). Virtues and organizations. In K. S. Cameron, J. E. Dutton, & R. E. Quinn (Eds.), *Positive organizational scholarship: Foundations of a new discipline* (pp. 33–47). San Francisco: Berrett-Koehler.

Park, N., & Peterson, C. (2004). Early intervention from the perspective of positive psychology. *Prevention and Treatment, 6(35).* Retrieved February 15, 2004, from http://journals.apa.org/prevention/volume6/pre0060035c.html

Park, N., Peterson, C., & Seligman, M.E.P. (2003). *Character strengths and recovery.* Unpublished data, University of Michigan.

Patterson, G. R., Chamberlain, P., & Reid, J. B. (1982). A comparative evaluation of a parent-training program. *Behavior Therapy, 13,* 638–650.

Penn, D. L. (2003). *Stigma.* Position paper prepared for Annenberg/Sunnylands Conference on Positive Youth Development (May 28–29), Philadelphia.

Pentz, M. A., MacKinnon, D. P., Dwyer, J. H., Wang, E.Y.I, Hansen, W. B., Flay, B. R., et al. (1989). Longitudinal effects of the Midwestern Prevention Project on regular and experimental smoking in adolescents. *Preventive Medicine, 18,* 304–21.

Peterson, C. (2000). The future of optimism. *American Psychologist, 55,* 44–55.

Peterson, C. (2004). Positive social science. *The Annals of the American Academy of Political and Social Science, 591,* 186–201.

Peterson, C., & Park, N. (2003). Positive psychology as the evenhanded positive psychologist views it. *Psychological Inquiry, 14,* 141–146.

Peterson, C., & Seligman, M.E.P. (2003). Positive organizational studies: Thirteen lessons from positive psychology. In K. S. Cameron, J. E. Dutton, & R. E. Quinn (Eds.), *Positive organizational scholarship: Foundations of a new discipline* (pp. 14–27). San Francisco: Berrett-Koehler.

Peterson, C., & Seligman, M.E.P. (2004). *Character strengths and virtues: A handbook and classification.* New York: Oxford University Press/Washington, DC: American Psychological Association.

Phillips, L. J., Yung, A. R., Yuen, H. P., Pantelis, C., & McGorry, P. D. (2002). Prediction and prevention of transition to psychosis in young people at incipient risk for schizophrenia. *American Journal of Medical Genetics, 114,* 929–937.

Phinney, J. S. (1990). Ethnic identity in adolescents and adults: Review of research. *Psychological Bulletin, 108,* 499–514.

Phinney, J. S. (1991). Ethnic identity and self-esteem: A review and integration. *Hispanic Journal of Behavioral Sciences, 13,* 193–208.

Phinney, J. S., Lochner, B. T., & Murphy, R. (1990). Ethnic identity development and psychological adjustment in adolescence. In A. R. Stiffman & L. E. Davis (Eds.), *Ethnic issues in adolescent mental health* (pp. 53–72). Thousand Oaks, CA: Sage.

Phinney, J. S., & Devich-Navarro, M. D. (1997). Variations in bicultural identification among African American and Mexican American adolescents. *Journal of Research on Adolescence, 7,* 3–32.

Piaget, J. (1952). *The origins of intelligence in children.* New York: International Universities Press.

Piaget, J. (1965). *The moral judgment of the child.* New York: Free Press.

Pittman, K. J. (1991). *Promoting youth development: Strengthening the role of youth-serving and community organizations.* Washington, DC: U.S. Department of Agriculture Extension Services.

Pittman, K. J. (2000, May). *What youth need: Services, supports, and opportunities, the ingredients for youth.* Paper prepared for presentation at the White House Conference on Teenagers, Washington, DC.

Plummer, D. L. (1995). Patterns of racial identity development of African American adolescent males and females. *Journal of Black Psychology, 21,* 168–180.

Pollard, J. A., Hawkins, J. D., & Arthur, M. W. (1999). Risk and protection: Are both necessary to understand diverse behavioral outcomes in adolescence? *Social Work Research, 23,* 145–158.

Prochaska, J., Redding, C., & Evers, K. (1997). The transtheoretical model and stages of change. In K. Glanz, F. Lewis, & B. Rimer (Eds.), *Health behavior and health education* (2nd ed., pp. 60–84). San Francisco: Jossey-Bass.

Prothrow-Stith, D. (1991). *Deadly consequences: How violence is destroying our teenage population and a plan to begin solving the problem.* New York: Harper Collins.

Public Agenda Online. (1999). *Kids these days: Negative reactions.* Retrieved October 17, 2003, from http://www.publicagenda.org/specials/kids/kids1.htm

Rachman, S. J. (1990). *Fear and courage* (2nd ed.). New York: W. H. Freeman and Company.

Rathunde, K. R., & Csikszentmihalyi, M. (1993). Undivided interest and the growth of talent: A longitudinal study of adolescents. *Journal of Youth and Adolescence, 22,* 385–405.

Redl, F., & Wineman, D. (1951). *Children who hate.* New York: The Free Press.

Richter, S. S., Brown, S. A., & Mott, M. A. (1991). The impact of social support and self-esteem on adolescent substance abuse treatment outcome. *Journal of Substance Abuse, 3,* 371–385.

Riegel, K. R. (1973). Dialectical operations: the final period of cognitive development. *Human Development, 16,* 346–370.

Rogers, C. R. (1951). *Client-centered therapy: Its current practice, implications, and theory.* Boston: Houghton Mifflin.

Rosenthal, R., & Rubin, D. B. (1982). A simple, general purpose display of magnitude of experimental effect. *Journal of Educational Psychology, 74,* 166–169.

Roth, J., & Brooks-Gunn, J. (2003). Youth development programs: Risk, prevention, and policy. *Journal of Adolescent Health, 32,* 170–182.

Roth, J., Brooks-Gunn, J., Murray, L., & Foster, W. (1998). Promoting healthy adolescents: Synthesis of youth development program evaluations. *Journal of Research on Adolescence, 8,* 423–459.

Rund, B. R., Moe, L., Sollien, T., Fjell, A., Borchgrevink, T., Hallert, M., et al. (1994). The Psychosis Project: Outcome and cost-effectiveness of a psychoeducational treatment program for schizophrenic adolescents. *Acta Psychiatrica Scandinavica, 89,* 211–218.

Rutter, M. (1985). Resilience in the face of adversity: Protective factors and resistance to psychiatric disorder. *British Journal of Psychiatry, 147,* 598–611.

Salovey, P., & Mayer, J. D. (1989). Emotional intelligence. *Imagination, Cognition and Personality, 9,* 185–211.

Sands, D. J., & Doll, B. (1996). Fostering self-determination is a developmental task. *Journal of Special Education, 30,* 58–76.

Scales, P. C., Benson, P. L., Leffert, N., & Blyth, D. A. (2000). Contributions of developmental assets to the prediction of thriving among adolescents. *Applied Developmental Science, 4,* 27–46.

Schaeffer, J. L., & Ross, R. G. (2002). Childhood-onset schizophrenia: premorbid and prodromal diagnostic and treatment histories. *Journal of the American Academy of Child and Adolescent Psychiatry, 41,* 538–545.

Schinke, S. P., & Matthieu, M. (2003). Primary prevention with diverse populations. In T. P. Gullotta & M. Bloom (Eds.), *Primary prevention and health promotion* (pp. 92–97). New York: Kluwer Academic/Plenum Publishers.

Seivewright, H., Tyrer, P., & Johnson, T. (1998). Prediction of outcome in neurotic disorder: A 5-year prospective study. *Psychological Medicine, 28,* 1149–1157.

Seligman, M.E.P. (1994). *What you can change and what you can't.* New York: Knopf.

Seligman, M.E.P. (1995). The effectiveness of psychotherapy: The Consumer Reports study. *American Psychologist, 50,* 965–974.

Seligman, M.E.P. (1998). Positive social science. *The APA Monitor Online, 29(4).* Retrieved October 17, 2003, from http://www.apa.org/monitor/apr98/pres.html

Seligman, M.E.P. (1999). The president's address. *American Psychologist, 54,* 559–562.

Seligman, M.E.P. (2002). *Authentic happiness.* New York: Free Press.

Seligman, M.E.P., & Csikszentmihalyi, M. (2000). Positive psychology: An introduction. *American Psychologist, 55,* 5–14.

Seligman, M.E.P., Reivich, K. J., Gillham, J. E., Peterson, C., Duckworth, A. L., Steen, T. A., et al. (2003). *Lessons for the pleasant life, the good life, and the meaningful life.* Unpublished manuscript, University of Pennsylvania.

Shih, M. (2004). Positive stigma: Examining resilience and empowerment in overcoming stigma. *The Annals of the American Academy of Political and Social Science, 591,* 175–185.

Shin, H. S. (2001). A review of school-based drug prevention program evaluations in the 1990s. *American Journal of Health Education, 32,* 139–147.

Shoemaker, R. H., & Sherry, P. (1991). Posttreatment factors influencing outcome of adolescent chemical dependency treatment. *Journal of Adolescent Chemical Dependency, 2,* 89–106.

Smith, M. L., & Glass, G. V. (1977). The meta-analysis of psychotherapy outcome studies. *American Psychologist, 32,* 752–760.

Snyder, H., & Sickmund, M. (1999). *Juvenile offend-*

ers and victims: 1999 national report. Washington, DC: Office Juvenile Justice and Delinquency Prevention.

Snyder, J., & Zoann, K. (1994). Self-determination in American Indian education: Educators' perspectives on grant, contract, and BIA-administered schools. *Journal of American Indian Education, 34,* 20–34.

Solomon, D., Battistich, V., Watson, M., Schaps, E., & Lewis, C. (2000). A six-district study of educational change: Direct and mediated effects of the Child Development Project. *Social Psychology of Education, 4,* 3–51.

Spence, S. H. (1996). The prevention of anxiety disorders in childhood. In P. Cotton (Ed.), *Early intervention and prevention in mental health* (pp. 87–107). Carlton South VIC, Australia: Australian Psychological Society.

Spencer, M. B. (1990). Development of minority children: An introduction. *Child Development, 61,* 267–269.

Spencer, M. B., & Markstrom-Adams, C. (1990). Identity processes among racial and ethnic minority children in America. *Child Development, 61,* 290–310.

Spooner, C., Mattick, R. P., & Noffs, W. (2001). Outcomes of a comprehensive treatment program for adolescents with a substance-use disorder. *Journal of Substance Abuse Treatment, 20,* 205–213.

Stark, R., & Bainbridge, W. S. (1997). *Religion, deviance, and social control.* New York: Routledge.

Sternberg, R. J. (1985). *Beyond IQ: A triarchic theory of human intelligence.* Cambridge: Cambridge University Press.

Stice, E., & Shaw, H. (2004). Eating disorder prevention programs: A meta-analytic review. *Psychological Bulletin, 130,* 179–205.

Swisher, K. G. (1996). Why Indian people should be the ones to write about Indian education. *American Indian Quarterly, 20,* 83–90.

Terman, L. M. (1925). *Genetic studies of genius* (Vol. 1) *Mental and physical traits of a thousand gifted children.* Stanford, CA: Stanford University Press.

Tierney, J. P., & Grossman, J. B. (2000). *Making a difference: An impact study of Big Brothers/Big Sisters.* Philadelphia: Public Private/Ventures.

Tobler, N. S., Roona, M. R., Ochshorn, P., Marshall, D. G., Streke, A. V., & Stackpole, K. M. (2000). School-based adolescent drug prevention programs: 1998 meta-analysis. *Journal of Primary Prevention, 20,* 275–337.

Todis, B., Bullis, M., Waintrup, M., Schultz, R., & D'Ambrosio, R. (2001). Overcoming the odds:

Qualitative examination of resilience among formerly incarcerated adolescents. *Exceptional Children, 68,* 119–139.

Tyler, J., Darville, R., & Stalnaker, K. (2001). Juvenile boot camps: A descriptive analysis of program diversity and effectiveness. *Social Science Journal, 38,* 445–460.

Vaillant, G. E. (1977). *Adaptation to life.* Boston: Little, Brown.

W. T. Grant Consortium on the School-Based Promotion of Social Competence. 1992. Drug and alcohol prevention curricula. In J. D. Hawkins, R. F. Catalano, & Associates. (Eds.), *Communities that care: Action for drug abuse prevention* (pp. 129–148). San Francisco: Jossey-Bass.

Walker, G. (2001). *The policy climate for early adolescent initiatives. P/PV Briefs.* Philadelphia, PA: Public/Private Ventures.

Wandersman, A., & Florin, P. (2003). Community interventions and effective prevention. *American Psychologist, 58,* 441–448.

Wehmeyer, M. L. (1996). Student self-report measure of self-determination for students with cognitive disabilities. *Education and Training in Mental Retardation and Developmental Disabilities, 31,* 282–293.

Weissberg, R. P., Caplan, M. Z., & Sivo, P. J. (1989). A new conceptual framework for establishing school-based social competence promotion programs. In L. A. Bond & B. E. Compas (Eds.), *Primary prevention and promotion in the schools* (pp. 255–296). Newbury Park, CA: Sage.

Weissberg, R. P., & Greenberg, M. T. (1997). School and community competence-enhancement and prevention programs. In W. Damon (Ed.), *Handbook of child psychology* (pp. 877–954). New York: John Wiley & Sons.

Weissberg, R. P., & O'Brien, M. U. (2004). What works in school-based social and emotional learning programs for positive youth development. *The Annals of the American Academy of Political and Social Science, 591,* 86–97.

Weissman, M. M. (1994). Psychotherapy in the maintenance treatment of depression. *British Journal of Psychiatry, 51,* 42–50.

Weissman, M. M., Wolk, S., Goldstein, R. B., Moreau, D., Adams, P., Greenwald, S. Klier, C. M., Ryan, N. D., Dahl, R. E., & Wickramaratne, P. (1999). Depressed adolescents grown up. *Journal of the American Medical Association, 281,* 1707–1713.

Werner, E. E. (1982). *Vulnerable but invincible: A longitudinal study of resilient children and youth.* New York: McGraw-Hill.

Werner, E. E. (1989). High-risk children in young adulthood: A longitudinal study from birth to 32 years. *American Journal of Orthopsychiatry, 59,* 72–81.

Werner, E. E. (1995). Resilience in development. *Current Directions in Psychological Science, 4,* 81–85.

Wilson, D. B., Gottfredson, D. C., & Najaka, S. S. (2001). School-based prevention of problem behaviors: A meta-analysis. *Journal of Quantitative Criminology, 17,* 247–272.

Wilson, J. Q. (1990). Drugs and crime. In M. Tonry & J. Q. Wilson (Eds.), *Crime and justice: A review of research* (Vol. 13, pp. 521–545). Chicago: University of Chicago Press.

Winner, E. (2000). The origins and ends of giftedness. *American Psychologist, 55,* 159–169.

World Health Organization (1990). *International classification of diseases and related health problems* (10th Rev.). Geneva: Author.

Wright, R. (1994). *The moral animal: The new science of evolutionary psychology.* New York: Random House.

Wyman, P. A., Cowen, E. L., Work, W. C., & Kerley, J. H. (1993). The role of children's future expectations in self-esteem functioning and adjustment to life stress: A prospective study of urban at-risk children. *Development and Psychopathology, 5,* 649–661.

Zaff, J. F., O'Neill, S. A., & Eccles, J. S. (2002). *What does arts participation in adolescence predict in early adulthood?* Washington, DC: Child Trends.

Zigler, E., & Berman, W. (1983). Discerning the future of early childhood intervention. *American Psychologist, 38,* 894–906.

Part VIII: Summary of Conclusions, Recommendations, Priorities

Chapter 27: Stigma

Agresti, A. (1990). *Categorical data analysis.* New York: John Wiley & Sons.

Angermeyer, M. C., & Schulze, B. (2001). Reinforcing stereotypes: How the focus on forensic cases in news reporting may influence public attitudes towards the mentally ill. *International Journal of Law and Psychiatry, 24,* 469–486.

Ben-Porath, D. D. (2002). Stigmatization of individuals who receive psychotherapy: An interaction between help-seeking behavior and the presence of depression. *Journal of Social and Clinical Psychology, 21,* 400–413.

Brockington, I., Hall, P., Levings, J., & Murphy, C. (1993). The community's tolerance of the mentally ill. *British Journal of Psychiatry, 162,* 93–99.

Brown, J. D., & Witherspoon, E. M. (2001). The mass media and the health of adolescents in the United States. In Y. R. Kamalipour & K. R. Rampal. (Eds.). *Media, sex, violence, and drugs in the global village* (pp. 77–96). New York: Rowman & Littlefield.

Buck, D., Baker, G. A., Chadwick, D. W., & Jacoby, A. (1997). Factors influencing compliance with antiepileptic drug regimes. *Seizure, 6,* 87–93.

Bushman, B. J., & Anderson, C. A. (2001). Media violence and the American public: Scientific fact versus media misinformation. *American Psychologist, 56,* 477–489.

Centers for Disease Control and Prevention (CDC). (2003). Public health surveillance for behavioral risk factors in a changing environment. *Morbidity and Mortality Weekly Report, 52*(RR-9), 1–12.

Chaplin, R. (2000). Psychiatrists can cause stigma too. *British Journal of Psychiatry, 177,* 467.

Chesney, M. A., & Smith, A. W. (1999). Critical delays in HIV testing and care: The potential role of stigma. *American Behavioral Scientist, 42,* 1162–1174.

Chou, K. L., & Mak, K. Y. (1998). Attitudes to mental patients among Hong Kong Chinese: A trend study over two years. *International Journal of Social Psychiatry, 44,* 215–224.

Cooper, A. E., Corrigan, P. W., & Watson, A. C. (2003). Mental illness stigma and care seeking. *Journal of Nervous and Mental Disease, 191,* 339–341.

Copeland, J. (1997). A qualitative study of barriers to formal treatment among women who self-managed change in addictive behaviors. *Journal of Substance Abuse Treatment, 14,* 183–190.

Corrigan, P. W. (2000). Mental health stigma as social attribution: Implications for research methods and attitude change. *Clinical Psychology: Science and Practice, 7,* 48–67.

Corrigan, P. W. (2002). Testing social cognitive models of mental illness stigma: The Prairie State stigma studies. *Psychiatric Rehabilitation Skills, 6,* 232–254.

Corrigan, P. W., & Penn, D. L. (1999). Lessons from social psychology on discrediting psychiatric stigma. *American Psychologist, 54,* 765–776.

Couture, S., & Penn, D. L. (2003). Contact and the stigma of mental illness: A review of the literature. *Journal of Mental Health, 12,* 291–305.

Crisp, A. H., Gelder, M. G., Rix, S., Meltzer, H. I., & Rowlands, O. J. (2000). Stigmatisation of people with mental illnesses. *British Journal of Psychiatry, 177,* 4–7.

Diefenbach, D. (1997). The portrayal of mental illness on prime-time television. *Journal of Community Psychology, 25,* 289–302.

Dudley, J. R. (2000). Confronting stigma within the services system. *Social Work, 45,* 449–455.

Esters, I. G., Cooker, P. G., & Ittenbach, R. F. (1998). Effects of a unit of instruction in mental health on rural adolescents' conceptions of mental illness and attitudes about seeking help. *Adolescence, 33,* 469–476.

Estroff, S. E., Penn, D. L., & Toporek, J. R. (in press). From stigma to discrimination: An analysis of community efforts to reduce the negative consequences of having a psychiatric disorder and label. *Schizophrenia Bulletin.*

Farina, A. (1998). Stigma. In: K. T. Mueser and N. Tarrier (Eds.), *Handbook of social functioning in schizophrenia* (pp. 247–279). Needham Heights: Allyn & Bacon.

Farina, A., & Felner, R. D. (1973). Employment interviewer reactions to former mental patients. *Journal of Abnormal Psychology, 82,* 268–272.

Ferraro, T., & Rush, S. (2000). Why athletes resist sport psychology. *Athletic Insight: Online Journal of Sport Psychology* [On-line] 2. Available: http://www.athleticinsight.com

Fortenberry, J., McFarlane, M., Bleakley, A., Bull, S., Fishbein, M., Frimley, D. M., et al. (2002). Relationships of stigma and shame to gonorrhea and HIV screening. *American Journal of Public Health, 92,* 378–381.

Gewirtz, A., & Gossart-Walker, S. (2000). Home-based treatment for children and families affected by HIV and AIDS: Dealing with stigma, secrecy, disclosure and loss. *Child and Adolescent Psychiatric Clinics of North America, 9,* 313–330.

Gould, M. S., Jamieson, P., & Romer, D. (2003). Media contagion and suicide among the young. *American Behavioral Scientist, 46,* 1269–1284.

Gould, M. S., & Kramer, R. A. (2001). Youth suicide prevention. *Suicide and Life-Threatening Behavior, 31*(Suppl.), 6–31.

Gould, M. S., Munfakh, J. L. H., Lubell, K., Kleinman, M., & Parker, S. (2002). Seeking help from the internet during adolescence. *Journal of the American Academy of Child and Adolescent Psychiatry, 41,* 1182–1189.

Granello, D., & Pauley, P. S. (2000). Television viewing habits and their relationship to tolerance toward people with mental illness. *Journal of Mental Health Counseling, 22,* 162–175.

Granello, D., Pauley, P. S., & Carmichael, A. (1999).

Relationship of the media to attitudes toward people with mental illness. *Journal of Humanistic Counseling, Education, and Development, 38,* 98–110.

Greene, W. (1993). *Econometric analysis.* Englewood Cliffs, NJ: Prentice-Hall.

Groesz, L. M., Levine, M. P., & Murnen, S. K. (2002). The effect of experimental presentation of thin media images on body satisfaction: A meta-analytic review. *International Journal of Eating Disorders, 31,* 1–16.

Hasui, C., Sakamoto, S., Sugiura, T., & Kitamua, T. (2000). Stigmatization of mental illness in Japan: Images and frequency of encounters with diagnostic categories of mental illness among medical and non-medical university students. *Journal of Psychiatry and Law, 28,* 253–266.

Hinshaw, S. P., & Cicchetti, D. (2000). Stigma and mental disorder: Conceptions of illness, public attitudes, personal disclosure, and social policy. *Development and Psychopathology, 12,* 555–598.

Hocking, B. (2003). Reducing mental illness stigma and discrimination—Everybody's business. *Medical Journal of Australia, 178* (Suppl.), S47–S48.

Holmes, P. E., Corrigan, P. W., Williams, P., Canar, J., & Kubiak, M. A. (1999). Changing attitudes about schizophrenia. *Schizophrenia Bulletin, 25,* 447–456.

Hyler, S. E., Gabbard, G. O., & Schneider, I. (1991). Homicidal maniacs and narcissistic parasites: Stigmatization of mentally ill persons in the movies. *Hospital and Community Psychiatry, 42,* 1044–1048.

Jackson, J. W. (1993). Contact theory of intergroup hostility: A review and evaluation of the theoretical and empirical literature. *International Journal of Group Tensions, 23,* 43–65.

Johnstone, L., & Hewstone, M. (1992). Cognitive models of stereotype change: 3. Subtyping and the perceived typicality of disconfirming group members. *Journal of Experimental Social Psychology, 28,* 360–386.

Kolodziej, M. E., & Johnson, B. T. (1996). Interpersonal contact and acceptance of persons with psychiatric disorders: A research synthesis. *Journal of Consulting and Clinical Psychology, 64,* 1387–1396.

Lawrie, S. M. (1999). Stigmatisation of psychiatric disorder. *Psychiatric Bulletin, 23,* 129–131.

Levey, S., & Howells, K. (1995). Dangerousness, unpredictability, and the fear of people with schizophrenia. *Journal of Forensic Psychiatry, 6,* 19–39.

Lieberman, J. A., Perkins, D. O., Belger, A., Chakos,

M., Jarskog, F., Boteva, K., et al. (2001). The early stages of schizophrenia: Speculations on pathogenesis, pathophysiology, and therapeutic approaches. *Biological Psychiatry, 50,* 884–897.

Link, B. G., Mirotznik, J., & Cullen, F. T. (1991). The effectiveness of stigma coping orientations: Can negative consequences of mental illness be avoided? *Journal of Health and Social Behavior, 32,* 302–320.

Link, B. G., & Phelan, J. C. (1999). The labeling theory of mental disorder (II): The consequences of labeling. In A. V. Horwitz & T. L. Scheid (Eds.), *A handbook for the study of mental health: Social contexts, theories, and systems* (pp. 361–376). New York: Cambridge University Press.

Link, B. G., & Phelan, J. C. (2001). Conceptualizing stigma. *Annual Review of Sociology, 27,* 363–385.

Link, B. G., Struening, E. L., Neese-Todd, S., Asmussen, S., & Phelan, J. (2001). Stigma as a barrier to recovery: The consequences of stigma for the self-esteem of people with mental illness. *Psychiatric Services, 52,* 1621–1626.

Markowitz, F. E. (1998). The effects of stigma on the psychological well-being and life satisfaction of persons with mental illness. *Journal of Health and Social Behavior, 39,* 335–347.

Mayville, E., & Penn, D. L. (1998). Changing societal attitudes toward persons with severe mental illness. *Cognitive and Behavioral Practice, 5,* 241–253.

McGorry, P. D., Yung, A., & Phillips, L. (2001). Ethics and early intervention in psychosis: Keeping the pace and staying in step. *Schizophrenia Research, 51,* 17–29.

Mechanic, D., McAlpine, D., Rosenfield, S., & Davis, D. (1994). Effects of illness attribution and depression on the quality of life among persons with serious mental illness. *Social Science and Medicine, 39,* 155–164.

Meltzer, H., Bebbington, P., Brugha, T., Farrell, M., Jenkins, R., & Lewis, G. (2003). The reluctance to seek treatment for neurotic disorders. *International Review of Psychiatry, 15,* 123–128.

Miller, N., Shepard, L. M., & Magen, J. (2001). Barriers to improving education and training in addiction medicine. *Psychiatric Annals, 31,* 649–656.

Minkoff, K. (1987). Resistance of mental health professionals to working with the chronically mentally ill. In A. T. Meyerson (Ed.), *Barriers to treating the chronic mentally ill* (pp. 3–20), *New Directions in Mental Health Services, 33.* San Francisco, CA: Jossey-Bass.

Monahan, J. (1992). Mental disorder and violent behavior: perceptions and evidence. *American Psychologist, 47,* 511–521.

Mueser, K. T., & Bellack, A. S. (1998). Social skills and social functioning. In: K. T. Mueser & N. Tarrier (Eds). *Handbook of social functioning in schizophrenia* (pp. 79–96). Needham Heights: Allyn & Bacon.

Mukherjee, R., Fialho, A., Wijetunge, A., Checinski, K., & Surgenor, T. (2002). The stigmatization of psychiatric illness: The attitudes of medical students and doctors in a London teaching hospital. *Psychiatric Bulletin, 26,* 178–181.

Nairn, R., Coverdale, J., & Claasen, D. (2001). From source material to news story in New Zealand print media: A prospective study of the stigmatizing processes depicting mental illness. *Australian and New Zealand Journal of Pyschiatry, 35,* 654–659.

Norman, R.M.G., & Malla, A. (2001). Duration of untreated psychosis: A critical examination of the concept and its importance. *Psychological Medicine, 31,* 381–400.

Okazaki, S. (2000). Treatment delay among Asian-American patients with severe mental illness. *American Journal of Orthopsychiatry, 70,* 58–64.

Page, S. (1995). Effects of the mental illness label in 1993: Acceptance and rejection in the community. *Journal of Health and Social Policy, 7,* 61–68.

Penn, D. L., Chamberlin, C., & Mueser, K. T. (2003). The effect of documentary films on psychiatric stigma. *Schizophrenia Bulletin, 29,* 383–391.

Penn, D. L., & Corrigan, P. W. (2002). The effects of stereotype suppression on psychiatric stigma. *Schizophrenia Research, 55,* 269–276.

Penn, D. L., & Drummond, A. (2001). Politically correct labels and severe mental illness: A rose by any other name? *Schizophrenia Bulletin, 27,* 197–203.

Penn, D. L., Guynan, K., Daily, T., Spaulding, W. D., Garbin, C. P., & Sullivan, M. (1994). Dispelling the stigma of schizophrenia: What sort of information is best? *Schizophrenia Bulletin, 20,* 567–577.

Penn, D. L., Kohlmaier, J., & Corrigan, P. W. (2000). Interpersonal factors contributing to the stigma of schizophrenia: Social skills, perceived attractiveness, and symptoms. *Schizophrenia Research, 45,* 37–45.

Penn, D. L., Kommana, S., Mansfield, M., & Link, B. (1999). Dispelling the stigma of schizophrenia, II: The impact of information on dangerousness. *Schizophrenia Bulletin, 25,* 437–446.

Perlick, D. A., Rosenheck, R. A., Clarkin, J. F., Sirey,

J., Salahi, J., Struening, E., et al. (2001). Stigma as a barrier to recovery: Adverse effects of perceived stigma on social adaptation of persons diagnosed with bipolar disorder. *Psychiatric Services, 52,* 1627–1632.

Pescosolido, B. A., Monahan, J., Link, B. G., Stueve, A., & Kikuzawa, S. (1999). The public's view of the competence, dangerousness, and need for legal coercion of persons with mental health problems. *American Journal of Public Health, 89,* 1339–1345.

Petchers, M. K., Biegel, D., & Drescher, R. (1988). A video-based program to educate high school students about serious mental illness. *Hospital and Community Psychiatry, 39,* 1102–1103.

Phelan, J. C., Cruz-Rojas, R., & Reiff, M. (in press). Genes and stigma. *Psychiatric Rehabilitation Skills.*

Phelan, J. C., & Link, B. G. (1999). The labeling theory of mental disorder (I): The role of social contingencies in the application of psychiatric labels. In A. V. Horwitz & T. L. Scheid (Eds.), *A handbook for the study of mental health: Social contexts, theories, and systems* (pp. 139–149). New York: Cambridge University Press.

Phelan, J. C., Link, B. G., Stueve, A., & Pescosolido, B. A. (2000). Public conceptions of mental illness in 1950 and 1996: What is mental illness and is it to be feared? *Journal of Health and Social Behavior, 41,* 188–207.

Pinfold, V., Toulmin, H., Thornicroft, G., Huxley, P., Farmer, P., & Graham, T. (2003). Reducing psychiatric stigma and discrimination: evaluation of educational interventions in UK secondary schools. *British Journal of Psychiatry, 182,* 342–346.

Post, R. M., Leverich, G., Xing, G., & Weiss, S.R.B. (2001). Developmental vulnerabilities to the onset and course of bipolar disorder. *Development and Psychopathology, 13,* 581–598.

Presidents New Freedom Commission Report on Mental Health (PNFC). (2003). Retrieved November 19, 2003, from http://www.mental healthcommission.gov/reports/reports.htm/

Pugatch, D., Bennett, L., & Patterson, D. (2002). HIV medication adherence in adolescents: A qualitative study. *Journal of HIV/AIDS Prevention and Education for Adolescents and Children, 5,* 9–29.

Richardson, L. A. (2001). Seeking and obtaining mental health services: What do parents expect? *Archives of Psychiatric Nursing, 15,* 223–231.

Roberts, D. F., & Foehr, U. G. (in press). *Kids and the media in America: Patterns of use at the millennium.* New York: Cambridge University Press.

Roberts, D. F., Henriksen, & Foehr, U. G. (in press). Adolescents and health. In R. M. Lerner, & L. Steinberg, (Eds.), *Handbook of adolescent psychology.* New York: John Wiley & Sons.

Romer, D. (2003). Prospects for an integrated approach to adolescent risk reduction. In D. Romer (Ed.), *Reducing adolescent risk: Toward an integrated approach* (pp. 1–8). Thousand Oaks, CA: Sage Publishers.

Ryan, C. S., Robinson, D. R., & Hausmann, L. R. (2001). Stereotyping among providers and consumers of public mental health services: The role of perceived group variability. *Behavior Modification, 25,* 406–442.

Salter, M., & Byrne, P. (2002). The stigma of mental illness: How you can use the media to reduce it. *Psychiatric Bulletin, 24,* 281–283.

Sartorius, N. (2002). Iatrogenic stigma of mental illness. *British Medical Journal, 324,* 1470–1471.

Schulze, B., Richter-Werling, M., Matschinger, H., & Angermeyer, M. C. (2003). Crazy? So what! Effects of a school project on students' attitudes towards people with schizophrenia. *Acta Psychiatrica Scandinavica, 107,* 142–150.

Secker, J., Armstrong, C., & Hill, M. (1999). Young people's understanding of mental illness. *Health and Education Research, 14,* 729–739.

Segrin, C. (2000). Social skill deficits associated with depression. *Clinical Psychology Review, 20* 379–403.

Shaffer, D., Vieland, V., Garland, A., Rojas, M., Underwood, M., & Busner, C. (1990). Adolescent suicide attempters: Response to suicide-prevention programs. *Journal of the American Medical Association, 26,* 3151–3155.

Signorielli, N. (2001). Television's gender role images and contribution to stereotyping: Past, present, future. In D. Singer & J. L. Singer (Eds.), *Handbook of children and the media* (pp. 341–358). Thousand Oaks, CA: Sage Publishers.

Silver, E. (2001). *Mental illness and violence: The importance of neighborhood context.* New York: LFB Scholarly Publishing LLC.

Sirey, J., Bruce, M. L., Alexopoulos, G. S., Perlick, D. A., Freidman, S. J., & Meyers, B. S. (2001a). Stigma as a barrier to recovery: Perceived stigma and patient rated severity of illness as predictors of antidepressant drug adherence. *Psychiatric Services, 52,* 1615–1620.

Sirey, J., Bruce, M. L., Alexopoulos, G. S., Perlick, D. A., Raue, P., Friedman, S. J., et al. (2001b). Perceived stigma as a predictor of treatment discontinuation in young and older outpatients with depression. *American Journal of Psychiatry, 158,* 479–481.

Starr, S., Campbell, L. R., & Herrick, C. A. (2002). Factors affecting use of the mental health system by rural children. *Issues in Mental Health Nursing, 23,* 291–304.

Tsang, H.W.H., Tam, P.K.C., Chan, F., & Cheung, W. M. (2003). Stigmatizing attitudes towards individuals with mental illness in Hong Kong: Implications for their recovery. *Journal of Community Psychology 31,* 383–396.

U.S. Department of Health and Human Services. (1999). *Mental health: A report of the Surgeon General.* Rockville, MD: U.S. Department of Health and Human Services, Substance Abuse and Mental Health Services Administration, Center for Mental Health Services, National Institutes of Health, National Institute of Mental Health.

Wahl, O. F. (1995). *Media madness: Public images of mental illness.* New Brunswick, NJ: Rutgers University Press.

Wahl, O. F. (2002). Children's view of mental illness: A review of the literature. *Psychiatric Rehabilitation Skills, 6,* 134–158.

Wahl, O. F. (2003). Depiction of mental illnesses in children's media. *Journal of Mental Health, 12,* 249–258.

Wahl, O. F., & Roth R. (1982). Television images of mental illness: Results of a metropolitan Washington Media Watch. *Journal of Broadcasting, 26,* 599–605.

Wahl, O. F., Wood, A., Zaveri, P., Drapalski, A., & Mann, B. (2003). Mental illness depiction in children's films. *Journal of Community Psychology, 31,* 553–560.

Weiner, B. (1993). On sin and sickness: A theory of perceived responsibility and social motivation. *American Psychologist, 48,* 957–965.

Weiner, B., Perry, R. P., & Magnusson, J. (1988). An attributional analysis of reactions to stigmas. *Journal of Personality and Social Psychology, 55,* 738–748.

Werrbach, G., & DePoy, E. (1993). Social work students' interest in working with persons with serious mental illness. *Journal of Social Work Education, 29,* 200–211.

Williams, M., & Taylor, J. (1995). Mental illness: Media perpetuation of stigma. *Contemporary Nurse, 4,* 41–45.

Wilson, C., Nairn, R., Coverdale, J., & Panapa, A. (2000). How mental illness is portrayed in children's television: A prospective study. *British Journal of Psychiatry, 176,* 440–443.

Woodard, E. H., & Gridina, N. (2000). *Media in the home: The fifth annual survey of parents and children.* Philadelphia: Annenberg Public Policy Center, University of Pennsylvania.

(WPA). (2002). *The WPA global programme to reduce the stigma and discrimination because of schizophrenia, Volume IV.*

Wright, E. R., Gronfein, W. P., & Owens, T. J. (2000). Deinstitutionalization, social rejection, and the self-esteem of former mental patients. *Journal of Health and Social Behavior, 41,* 68–90.

Part VIII Summary of Conclusions, Recommendations, Priorities

Chapter 28 The Research, Policy, and Practice Context for Delivery of Evidence-Based Mental Treatments for Adolescents

Alexander, J. F., & Parsons, B.V.C. (1973) Short-term behavioral intervention with delinquent families: Impact on family process and recidivism. *Journal of Abnormal Psychology, 81*(3), 219–25.

Alexander, J. F., & Sexton, T. L. (2002). Functional family therapy: A model for treating high-risk acting-out youth. Kaslow, F. W. (Ed). *Comprehensive handbook of psychotherapy: Interactive/eclectic,* Vol. 4. New York, NY: John Wiley & Sons, pp. 111–132.

American Academy of Pediatrics: Committee on Quality Improvement and Subcommittee on Attention-Deficit/Hyperactivity Disorder (2000). Clinical practice guideline: Diagnosis and evaluation of the child with attention-deficit/hyperactivity disorder. *Pediatrics, 105,* 1158–1170.

Angold, A., Messer, S. C., Stangl, D., Farmer, E.M.Z., Costello, E. J., & Burns, B. J. (1998). Perceived parental burden and service use for child and adolescent psychiatric disorders. *American Journal of Public Health, 88,* 75–80.

Bickman, L. (Ed.). (1996a). The Fort Bragg experiment [Special issue]. *Journal of Mental Health Administration, 23*(1).

Bickman, L. (1996b). A continuum of care: More is not always better. *American Psychologist, 51,* 689–701.

Bickman, L. (1996c). The evaluation of a children's mental health managed care demonstration. *Journal of Mental Health Administration, 23,* 7–15.

Bickman, L. (1999). Practice makes perfect and

other myths about mental health services. *American Psychologist, 23,* 1.

Bickman L., Smith, C. M., Lambert, E. W., & Andrade, A. R. (2003). Evaluation of a Congressionally Mandated Wraparound Demonstration. *Journal of Child & Family Studies, 12,* 135–156.

Brown, S. P., & Leigh, T. W. (1996). A new look at psychological climate and its relationship to job involvement, effort, and performance. *Journal of Applied Psychology, 81,* 358–368.

Burns, B. J. (2003). Children and evidence-based practices. *Psychiatric Clinics of North America, 36,* 955–970.

Burns, B. J., Costello, E. J., Angold, A., Tweed, D., Stangle, D., & Farmer, E.H.Z (1995). Children's mental health service use across service sectors. *Health Affairs, 124,* 147–159.

Burns, B. J., & Hoagwood, K. (in press, b). Evidence-based practices: Effecting change. *Psychiatric Clinics of North America.*

Chamberlain, P., & Reid, J. B. (1991). Using a specialized foster care treatment model for children and adolescents leaving the state mental hospital. *Journal of Community Psychology, 19,* 266–276.

Chambers, D., Ringeisen, H., & Hickman, E. (in press). A summary of federal, state, and foundation initiatives around evidence-based practices for child and adolescent mental health. *Psychiatric Clinics of North America.*

Chorpita, B. F., Yim, L. M., Donkervoet, J. C., Arensdorf, A., Amundsen, M. J., et al. (2002). Toward large-scale implementation of empirically supported treatments for children: A review and observations by the Hawaii Empirical Basis to Services Task Force. *Clinical Psychology: Science & Practice, 9,* 165–190.

Chorpita, B., Daleiden, E., & Weisz, J. R. (in press). Identifying and selecting the common elements of evidence based interventions: A distillation and matching model. *Mental Health Services Research.*

Cooke, R. A., & Szumal, J. L. (1993). Measuring normative beliefs and shared behavioral expectations in organizations: The reliability and validity of the Organizational Culture Inventory. *Psychological Reports, 72,* 1299–1330.

Costello, E. J., Angold, A., Burns, B. J., Stangl, D. K., Tweed, D. L., Erkanli, A., et al. (1996). The Great Smoky Mountains Study of Youth: Goals, design, methods and the prevalence of DSM-III-R disorders. *Archives of General Psychiatry, 53,* 1129–1136.

Costello, E. J., Farmer, E. M., Angold, A., Burns, B. J., & Erkanli, A. (1997). Psychiatric disorders among American Indian and white youth in Appalachia: the Great Smoky Mountains Study. *American Journal of Public Health, 87,* 827–832.

Emslie, G. J., Walkup, J. T., Pliszka, S. R., & Ernst, M. (1999). Nontricyclic antidepressants: current trends in children and adolescents. *Journal of the American Academy of Child and Adolescent Psychiatry, 38,* 517–528.

Evans, M. E., Banks, S. M., Huz, S., & McNulty, T. L. (1994). Initial hospitalization and community tenure outcomes of intensive case management for children and youth with serious emotional and behavioral disabilities. *Journal of Child and Family Studies, 3,* 225–234.

Farmer, E. M., Dorsey, S., & Mustillo, S. A. (2004). Intensive home and community interventions. *Child and Adolescent Psychiatric Clinic of North America, 13,* 857–884.

Flynn, L. (in press). Family perspectives on evidence-based practices. *Psychiatric Clinics of North America.*

Friedman, R. M. (2003). A conceptual framework for developing and implementing effective policy in children's mental health. *Journal of Emotional and Behavioral Disorders, 11,* 9–16.

Glied, S., & Cuellar, A. E. (2003). Trends and issues in child and adolescent mental health. *Health Affairs, 22,* 39–50.

Glisson, C. (2000). Organizational culture and climate. In R. Patti (Ed.), *The handbook of social welfare management* (pp. 195–217). Thousand Oaks, CA: Sage Publications.

Glisson, C. (2002). The organizational context of children's mental health services. *Clinical Child and Family Psychology Review, 5,* 233–253.

Glisson, C., & Durick, (1988). Predictors of job satisfaction and organizational commitment in human service organizations. *Administrative Science Quarterly, 33*(1), 61–81.

Glisson, C., & Hemmelgarn, A. (1998). The effects of organizational climate and interorganizational coordination on the quality and outcomes of children's service systems. *Child Abuse and Neglect 22,* 401–421.

Glisson, C., & James, L. R. (2002). The cross-level effects of culture and climate in human service teams. *Journal of Organizational Behavior, 23,* 767–794.

Goldman, H. H., & Azrin, S. T. (2003). Public policy and evidence-based practice. *Psychiatric Clinics of North America, 26,* 899–917.

Greenberg, M. T., Domitrovich, C., & Bumbarger, B. (2001). The prevention of mental disorders in school-aged children: Current state of the field. *Prevention and Treatment, 4*, Article 1. Available: http://journals.apa.org/prevention/volume4/pre 0040001a.html

Henggeler, S. W., & Schoenwald, S. K. (1998). *The MST supervisory manual: Promoting quality assurance at the clinical level.* Charleston, SC: MST Services, Inc.

Henggeler, S. W., Schoenwald, S. K., Liao, J. G., Letourneau, E. J., & Edwards, D. L. (2002). Transporting efficacious treatments to field settings: The link between supervisory practices and therapist fidelity in MST programs. *Journal of Clinical Child Psychology, 31*, 155–167.

Henggeler, S. W., Schoenwald, S. K., & Munger, R. L. (1996). Families and therapists achieve clinical outcomes, systems of care mediate the process. *Journal of Child and Family Studies, 5*, 177–183.

Henggeler, S. W., Schoenwald, S. K., Rowland, M. D., & Cunningham, P. B. (2002). *Serious emotional disturbance in children and adolescents: Multisystemic therapy.* New York: Guilford Press.

Hoagwood, K., Burns, B. J., & Weisz, J. R. (2002). A profitable conjunction: From science to service in children's mental health. In B. J. Burns & K. Hoagwood (Eds.), *Community treatment for youth: Evidence-based interventions for severe emotional and behavioral disorders* (pp. 327–338). Oxford: Oxford University Press.

Hoagwood, K., Hibbs, E., Brent, D., & Jensen, P. (1995). Introduction to the special section: Efficacy and effectiveness in studies of child and adolescent psychotherapy. *Journal of Consulting and Clinical Psychology, 63*, 683–687.

Hoagwood K., Horwitz, S. M., Stiffman, A. R., Weisz, J., Bean, D., Rae, D., et al. (2001). Concordance between parent reports of children's mental health services and service records: The Services Assessment for Children and Adolescents (SACA). *Journal of Child and Family Studies, 9*, 315–331.

Hoagwood, K., Jensen, P., Petti, T., & Burns, B. (1996). Outcomes of care for children and adolescents: A conceptual model. *Journal of the American Academy of Child and Adolescent Psychiatry, 35*, 1055–1063.

Hoagwood, K., Jensen, P., Roper, M., Arnold, L., Odbert, C., Severe, J. (in press). The reliability of a clinical measure of children's services: The Services for Children and Adolescents—Parent Interview (SCAPI).: II Test-retest Reliability. *Journal of the American Academy of Child & Adolescent Psychiatry.*

Hoagwood, K., & Johnson, J. (2003). School psychology: A public health framework I. From evidence-based practices to evidence-based policies. *Journal of School Psychology, 41*, 3–21.

Hoagwood, K., & Johnson, J. (2004). The Dimensions of Organizational Readiness (Door) Report from the Office of Mental Health, New York State.

Hofstede, G. (1998). Attitudes, values and organizational culture: Disentangling the concepts. *Organization Studies, 19*, 477–492.

Horwitz, S. M., Leaf, P. J., & Leventhal, J. M. (1998). Identification of psychosocial problems in primary care pediatric practice: Do family attitudes make a difference? *Archives of Pediatric and Adolescent Medicine, 152*, 367–371.

Horwitz, S. M., Leaf, P. J., Leventhal, J. M., Forsyth, B., & Speechley, K. N. (1992). Identification and management of psychosocial and developmental problems in community-based, primary care pediatric practices. *Pediatrics, 89*, 480–485.

Hutchinson, A. B., & Foster, E. M. (2003). The effect of Medicaid managed care on mental health care for children: A review of the literature. *Mental Health Services Research, 5*, 39–54.

Institute of Medicine (IOM). (2000) From neurons to neighborhoods: The science of early childhood development. Washington, DC: National Academy Press.

Institute of Medicine (IOM) (1998). Bridging the gap between practice and research: Forging partnerships with community-based drug and alcohol treatment. Washington, DC: National Academy Press.

IOM Committee on Quality of Health Care in America (2001): *Crossing the Quality Chasm: A New Health System for the 21st Century,* Washington, DC: National Academy Press.

James, L. R., & James, L. A. (1989). Causal modeling in organizational research. In C. L. Cooper, & I. T. Robertson (Eds.), *International review of industrial and organizational psychology* (pp. 371–404). Chichester, West Sussex, UK: John Wiley & Sons.

James, L. R., James, L. A., & Ashe, D. K. (1990). The meaning of organizations: The role of cognition and values. *Organizational Climate and Culture,* 40–84.

Jensen, P. S., Bhatara, V. S., Vitiello, B., Hoagwood, K., Feil, M., & Burke. L. B. (1999). Psychoactive medication prescribing practices for US children: Gaps between research and clinical practice. *Journal of the American Academy of Child and Adolescent Psychiatry, 38*(5): 557–565.

Jensen, P. S., & Hoagwood, K. (1997). The book of names: DSM-IV in context. *Development and Psychopathology, 9,* 231–249.

Jensen, P. S., Hoagwood, K., Trickett, E. (1999). Ivory tower or earthen trenches? Community collaborations to foster real-world research. *Journal of Applied Developmental Science, 3,* 206–212.

Jensen, P. S., Vitiello, B., Bhatara, V., Hoagwood, K., & Feil, M. (1999). Current trends in psychotropic prescribing practices. Clinical and policy implications. *Journal of the American Academy of Child and Adolescent Psychiatry 38,* 557–565.

Jones, A. P., & James, L. R. (1979). Psychological climate: Dimensions and relationships of individual and aggregated work environment perceptions. *Organizational Behavior and Human Performance, 23,* 201–250.

Jones, A. P., James, L. R., & Bruni, J. R. (1975). Perceived leadership behavior and employee confidence in the leader as moderated by job involvement. *Journal of Applied Psychology, 60*(1), 146–149.

Joyce, W. F., & Slocum, J. W. (1984). Collective climate: Agreement as a basis for defining aggregate climates in organizations. *Academy of Management Journal, 24,* 721–742.

Kataoka, S. H., Zhang, L., & Wells, K. B. (2002). Unmet need for mental health care among U.S. children: Variation by ethnicity and insurance status. *American Journal of Psychiatry, 159,* 1548–1555.

Kazdin, A. E. (2004). Evidence-based treatments: Challenges and priorities for practice and research. *Child and Adolescent Psychiatric Clinics of North America, 13,* 923–940.

Kazdin, A. E. (in press). Developing a research agenda for child and adolescent psychotherapy research. *Archives of General Psychiatry.*

Kelleher, J. K., Long, N. (1994). Barriers and new directions in mental health services research in the primary care setting. *Journal of Clinical Child Psychology, 23,* 133–142.

Kendall, P. C., Flannery-Schroeder, E., Panichelli-Mindel, S. M., Southam-Gerow, M., Henin, A., & Warman, M. (1997). Therapy for youths with anxiety disorders: A second randomized clinical trial. *Journal of Consulting and Clinical Psychology, 65,* 366–380.

Kitzman, H., Olds, D. L., Sidora, K., Henderson, C. R. Jr., Hanks, C., Cole, R., Luckey, D. W., Bondy, J., Cole, K., & Glazner, J. (2000). Enduring effects of nurse home visitation on maternal life course: a 3-year follow-up of a randomized trial. *Journal of the American Medical Association, 283,* 1983–1989.

Knitzer, J. (1982). *Unclaimed children: The failure of public responsibility to children and adolescents in need of mental health services.* Washington, DC: Children's Defense Fund.

Lavigne, J. V., Binns, H. J., Christoffel, K. K., Rosenbaum, D., Arend, R., Smith, K., et al. (1993). Behavioral and emotional problems among preschool children in pediatric primary care: Prevalence and pediatricians' recognition. *Pediatrics, 91,* 649–655.

Lewczyk, C. M., Garland, A. F., Hurburt, M., Gearity, J., & Hough, R. L. (2001). DISC-V vs. clinician diagnoses among youths receiving mental health services. Paper presented at the 48th Annual Meeting of the American Academy of Child and Adolescent Psychiatry, Honolulu, HI, October 27th, 2001.

Loeber, R., & Farrington, D. P. (Eds.). (1998). *Serious and violent juvenile offenders: Risk factors and successful interventions.* Thousand Oaks, CA: Sage Publications.

Lonigan, C. J., Elbert, J. C., & Johnson, S. B. (1998). Empirically supported psychosocial interventions for children: An overview. *Journal of Child Clinical Psychology, 27,* 138–145.

March, J. S., Amaya-Jackson, L., Murray, M. C., & Schulte, A. (1998). Cognitive-behavioral psychotherapy for children and adolescents with post-traumatic stress disorder after a single-incident stressor. *Journal of the American Academy of Child and Adolescent Psychiatry, 37,* 585–593.

March, J. S. and the TADS Consortium. (in press). Evidence-based medicine: Training issues. *Psychiatric Clinics of North America.*

McCabe, K., Yeh, M., Hough R., Landsverk, J., Hurlburt, M., Culver, S., et al. (1999). Racial/ethnic representation across five public sectors of care for youth. *Journal of Emotional and Behavioral Disorders, 7,* 72–82.

McKay, M., & Lynn, C. (in press). Urban families' perceptions of the process and the providers of child mental health services. *Community Mental Health Journal.*

McKay, M. M., McCadam, K., Gonzales, J. J. (1996). Addressing the barriers to mental health services for inner city children and their caretakers. *Community Mental Health Journal, 32,* 353–361.

McKay, M. M., Pennington, J., Lynn, C. J. & McCadam, K. (2001). Understanding urban child mental health service use: two studies of child, family, and environmental correlates. *Journal of Behavioral Health Services & Research, 28,* 475–483.

Mowday, R., Porter, L., & Steers, R. (1982). *Organizational linkages: The psychology of commitment, absenteeism, and turnover.* New York: Academic Press.

MTA Cooperative Group. (1999a). A 14-month randomized clinical trial of treatment strategies for attention-deficit/hyperactivity disorder: The Multimodal Treatment Study of Children with Attention-Deficit Hyperactivity Disorder (MTA Study). *Archives of General Psychiatry, 56,* 1073–1086.

MTA Cooperative Group. (1999b). Moderators and mediators of treatment response for children with attention-deficit hyperactivity disorder: The Multimodal Treatment Study of Children with Attention-Deficit Hyperactivity Disorder (MTA Study). *Archives of General Psychiatry, 56,* 1088–1096.

Mufson, L. H., Dorta, K.E.P., Olfson, M., Weissman, M. M., & Hoagwood, K. (2004). Effectiveness research: Transporting interpersonal psychotherapy for depressed adolescents (IPT-A) from the lab to school-based health clinics. *Clinical Child and Family Psychology Review, 7,* 251–261.

Murray, L., Rodriguez, J., Hoagwood, K., & Jensen, P. S. (in press). Responding to children and adolescents in the aftermath of September 11th. In Y. Neria, R. Gross, R. Marshall, E. Susser (Eds). *Health Impacts of 9/11: Treatment, Research and Public Health.* Cambridge University Press.

National Advisory Mental Health Council Workgroup on Child and Adolescent Mental Health Intervention Development and Deployment. (2001). *Blueprint for change: Research on child and adolescent mental health.* NIH Publication No. 01-4985. Rockville, MD: National Institute of Mental Health.

National Alliance for Mental Illness (NAMI). (2004). Roadmap to recovery and cure. Report of the NAMI Policy Research Institute Task Force on Serious Mental Illness Research. Arlington, VA: NAMI.

National Institute of Mental Health (NIMH). (2001). *Proceedings of a conference on research ethics in mental health science involving minority populations of children.* New York: Fordham University.

Pescosolido, B. A. (1992). Beyond rational choice: The social dynamics of how people seek help. *American Journal of Sociology, 4,* 1096–1138.

President's New Freedom Commission Report on Mental Health (2003). Retrieved from http://www.mentalhealthcommission.gov/reports/reports/htm

Ringeisen, H., Henderson, K., & Hoagwood, K. (2003). Context matters: Schools and the "research to practice gap" in children's mental health. *School Psychology Review, 32,* 153–168.

Ringel, J., & Sturm, R. (2001). National estimates of mental health utilization and expenditures for children in 1998. *Journal of Behavioral Health Services and Research, 28,* 319–333.

Roberts, R. E., Attkisson, C. C., & Rosenblatt, A. (1998). Prevalence of psychopathology among children and adolescents. *American Journal of Psychiatry, 155,* 715–725.

Rogers, E. M. (1995). *Diffusion of innovations.* New York: Free Press.

Rones, M., Hoagwood, K. (2000). School-based mental health services: A research review. *Clinical Child and Family Psychology Review, 3,* 223–241.

Rousseau, D. M. (1990). Assessing organizational culture: The case for multiple methods. In B. Schneider (Ed.), *Organizational climate and culture* (pp. 153–192). San Francisco: Jossey-Bass.

Santisteban, D. A., Szapocznik, J., Perez-Vidal, A., Kuartines, W. M., Murray, E. J., & LaPerriere, A. (1996). Efficacy of intervention for engaging youth and families into treatment and some variables that may contribute to differential effectiveness. *Journal of Family Psychology, 10,* 35–44.

Schoenwald, S. K., & Henggeler, S. W. (2002). Services research and family-based treatment. In H. A. Liddle, D. A. Santisteban, R. F. Levant, & J. H. Bray (Eds.), *Family psychology: Science-based interventions* (pp. 259–282). Washington, DC: American Psychological Association.

Schoenwald, S. K., Sheidow, A. J., Leteourneau, E. J., Liao, J. G. (2003). Transportability of Multisystemic Therapy: Evidence for Multilevel Influences. *Mental Health Services Research, 5,* 223–239.

Scholle, S. H., Kelleher, K. J., Childs, G., Mendeloff, J., & Gardner, W. P. (1997). Changes in Medicaid managed care enrollment among children. *Health Affairs, 16,* 164–170.

Shaffer, D., Fisher, P., Dulcan, M. K., Davies, M., Piacentini, J., et al. (1996). The NIMH Diagnostic Interview Schedule for Children Version 2.3 (DISC-2.3): Description, acceptability, prevalence rates, and performance in the MECA

Study. Methods for the Epidemiology of Child and Adolescent Mental Disorders Study. *Journal of the American Academy of Child and Adolescent Psychiatry, 35,* 865–877.

Simpson, D. D. (2002). A conceptual framework for transferring research to practice. *Journal of Substance Abuse Treatment, 4,* 171–182.

Silverman, W. K., Kurtines, W. M., & Hoagwood, K. (2004). Research progress on effectiveness, transportability and dissemination of empirically supported treatments: Integrating theory and research. *Clinical Psychology: Science & Practice* 11(3), 295–299.

Stiffman, A. R., Chen, Y. W., Elze, D., Dore, P., & Cheng, L. C. (1997). Adolescents' and providers' perspectives on the need for and use of mental health services. *Journal of Adolescent Health, 21* 335–342.

Stiffman, A. R., Earls, F., Robins, L. N., & Jung, K. G. (1988). Problems and help seeking in high-risk adolescent patients of health clinics. *Journal of Adolescent Health Care, 9,* 305–309.

Stroul, B., & Friedman, R. M. (1986). *A system of care for children and youth with severe emotional disturbances* (revised edition). Washington, DC: Georgetown University Child Development Center, CASSP Technical Assistance Center.

Szapocznik, J., Perez-Vidal, A., Brickman, A. L., Foote, F. H., Santisteban, D., & Hervis, O. (1988). Engaging adolescent drug abusers and their families in treatment. A strategic structural systems approach. *Journal of Consulting and Clinical Psychology, 56,* 552–557.

Takeuchi, D. T., Chung, R. C., Lin, K. M., Shen, H., Kurasaki, K., Chun, C. A., et al. (1998). Lifetime and twelve-month prevalence rates of major depressive episodes and dysthymia among Chinese Americans in Los Angeles. *American Journal of Psychiatry 155,* 1407–1414.

Takeuchi, D. T., Leaf, P. J., & Kuo, H. S. (1988). Ethnic differences in the perception of barriers to help-seeking. *Social Psychiatry and Psychiatric Epidemiology 23,* 273–280.

Tanenbaum, S. (2003). Evidence-based practice in mental health: Practical weaknesses meet political strength. *Journal of Evaluation in Clinical Practice, 9,* 287–301.

Torrey, W. C., Drake, R. E., Dixon, L., Burns, B. J., Flynn, L., Rush, A. J., et al. (2001). Implementing evidence-based practices for persons with severe mental illnesses. *Psychiatric Services 52,* 45–50.

U.S. Congress, Office of Technology Assessment. (1991). *Adolescent health—Vol. III: Cross-cutting issues in the delivery of health and related services.* OTA-H-467, Washington, DC: U.S. Government Printing Office.

U.S. Department of Health and Human Services (DHHS). (1999). *Mental health: A report of the surgeon general.* Washington, DC: Author.

U.S. Public Health Service (USPHS). (2001a). *Youth violence: A report of the surgeon general.* Washington, DC: Department of Health and Human Services.

U.S. Public Health Service (USPHS). (2001). *Mental health: Culture, Race, Ethnicity—Supplement to mental health: Report of the surgeon general.* Washington, DC: Department of Health and Human Services.

Van de Ven, A. H., Polley, D. E., Garud, R., & Ventkataraman, S. (1999). *The innovation journey.* New York: Oxford University Press.

Verbeke, W., Volgering, M., & Hessels, M. (1998). Exploring the conceptual expansion within the field of organizational behaviour: Organizational climate and organizational culture. *Journal of Management Studies, 35,* 303–329.

Weisz, J. R. (2000). Agenda for child and adolescent psychotherapy research: On the need to put science into practice. *Archives of General Psychiatry, 57,* 837–838.

Weisz, J. R. (2003). Psychotherapy for children and adolescents: Evidence-based treatments and case examples. Cambridge, UK: Cambridge University Press.

Weisz, J. R., Donenberg, G. R., Han, S. S., Kauneckis, D. (1995a). Child and adolescent psychotherapy outcomes in experiments versus clinics: Why the disparity? *Journal of Abnormal Child Psychology, 23,* 83–106.

Weisz, J. R., Donenberg, G. R., Han, S. S., & Weiss, B. (1995b). Bridging the gap between laboratory and clinic in child and adolescent psychotherapy. *Journal of Consulting and Clinical Psychology, 63,* 688–701.

Weisz, J. R., Weiss, B., & Donenberg, G. R. (1992). The lab versus the clinic: Effects of child and adolescent psychotherapy. *American Psychologist, 47,* 1578–1585.

Weisz, J. R., Weiss, B., Han, S. S., Granger, D. A., & Morton, T. (1995). Effects of psychotherapy with children and adolescents revisited: A meta-analysis of treatment outcome studies. *Psychological Bulletin, 117,* 450–468.

Weisz, J. R. (2004). *Psychotherapy for Children and Adolescents: Evidence-based treatments and case samples.* Cambridge: Cambridge University Press.

Williams, L. J., & Hazer, J. T. (1986). Antecedents

and consequences of satisfaction and commitment in turnover models: A reanalysis using latent variable structural equation methods. *Journal of Applied Psychology, 71,* 219–231.

Part VIII: Summary of Conclusions, Recommendations, Priorities

Chapter 29: The American Treatment System for Adolescent Substance Abuse

Aarons, G. A., Brown, S. A., Hough, R. L., Garland, A. F., & Wood, P. A. (2001). Prevalence of adolescent substance use disorders across five sectors of care. *Journal of the American Academy of Child and Adolescent Psychiatry, 40,* 419–426.

Ackard, D. M., & Nuemark-Sztainer, D. (2001). Health care information sources for adolescents: Age and gender differences on use, concerns, and needs. *Journal of Adolescent Health, 29,* 170–176.

Alford, G., Koehler, R. A., & Leonard, J. (1991). Alcoholics anonymous/Narcotics anonymous model inpatient treatment of chemically dependent adolescents: A 2-year outcome study. *Journal of Studies on Alcohol, 52,* 118–126.

American University. (1997). *Juvenile drug courts: Preliminary report.* Drug Court Clearinghouse and Technical Assistance Project. Washington, DC: U.S. Department of Justice, Office of Justice Programs, Drug Court Clearinghouse.

American University. (2001). *Drug court activity update: Summary.* Washington, DC: U.S. Department of Justice, Office of Justice Programs, Drug Court Clearinghouse.

Angold, A., Costello, E. J., Farmer, E., Burns, B. J., & Erkanli, A. (1999). Impaired but undiagnosed. *Journal of the American Academy of Child and Adolescent Psychiatry, 38,* 129–137.

Arrestee Drug Abuse Monitoring (ADAM). (2003). *Annual report.* Washington, DC: Office of Justice Programs.

Armstrong, T. L., & Altschuler, D. M. (1998). Recent developments in juvenile aftercare: Assessment, findings, and promising programs. In A. R. Roberts (Ed.), *Juvenile justice* (2nd ed.), Chicago: Nelson-Hall.

Baker, F. (1991). *Coordination of alcohol, drug, and mental health services.* Rockville, MD: Alcohol, Drug Abuse and Health Services Administration, Office of Treatment Improvement.

Barnett, N. P., Monti, P. M., & Wood, M. D. (2001). Motivational interviewing for alcohol-involved adolescents in the emergency room. In E. F. Wagner & H. B. Waldron (Eds.), *Innovations in adolescent substance abuse interventions* (pp. 143–168). New York: Pergamon Press, Elsevier Science.

Battjes, R. J., Onken, L. S., & Delany, P. J. (1999). Drug abuse treatment entry and engagement: Report of a meeting on treatment readiness. *Journal of Clinical Psychology, 55,* 643–657.

Belanko, S. (2001). *Research on drug courts: A critical review.* New York: National Center on Addiction and Substance Abuse at Columbia University.

Bilchik, S. (1995). *Community assessment centers: A discussion of the concepts efficacy.* Washington, DC: U.S. Department of Justice, Office of Justice Programs, Office of Juvenile Justice and Delinquency Prevention.

Boonstra, H., & Nash, E. (2003). Minors and the right to consent to health care. *The Guttmacher Report on Public Policy, 3,* (4).

Brauzer, B., Lefley, H. P., & Steinbook, R. (1996). A module for training residents in public mental health systems and community resources. *Psychiatric Services, 47,* 192–194.

Bronfenbrenner, U. (1986). Ecology of the family as a context for human development. *American Psychologist, 32,* 513–531.

Bronfenbrenner, U. (1989). Ecological systems theory. In P. Vasta (Ed.), *Annals of Child Development, Vol. 6. Six theories of child development: Revised formulations and current issues* (pp. 187–249). London: JAI Press.

Brown, S. A., Myers, M. G., Mott, M. A., & Vik, P. W. (1994). Correlates of success following treatment for adolescent substance abuse. *Journal of Substance Abuse Treatment, 5,* 365–378.

Brown, S. A., Vik, P. W., & Creamer, V. A. (1989). Characteristics of relapse following adolescent substance abuse treatment. *Addictive Behaviors, 14,* 291–300.

Bry, B. H., & Attaway, N. M. (2001). Community-based intervention. In E. F. Wagner, & H. B. Waldron. (Eds.), *Innovations in adolescent substance abuse interventions* (pp. 109–126). New York: Pergamon Press, Elsevier Science.

Buck, J. A., & Umland, B. (1997). Covering mental health and substance abuse services. *Health Affairs, 16,* 120–126.

Butts, J. (1997). More juvenile drug offenses seen by police, courts. *The Urban Institute Bulletin* (December) Washington, DC: The Urban Institute, Program on Law and Behavior.

Center for Adolescent Health and the Law. (2000). *Improving the implementation of SCHIP for adolescents: Proposed federal legislation regarding medicaid and SCHIP.* Washington, DC: Author.

Center for Substance Abuse Treatment (CSAT). (2000). *Changing the conversation: Improving substance abuse treatment: The national treatment plan initiative* (DHHS Publication # (SMA) 00-3479). Rockville, MD: Author.

Center on Addiction and Substance Abuse (CASA). (2001). *National Survey of American Attitudes on Substance Abuse VI: Teens,* National Center on Addiction and Substance Abuse at Columbia University, Author.

Chaloupka, F. J., & Laixuthal, A. (2002). Controversial drug testing yields mixed results. *Drug Policy News* [On-line]. Available: 1/2004 www .dpj.org/news/12_30_02testing.cfm

Cheng, T. L., Savageaue, J. A., Sattler, A. L., & DeWitt, T. G. (1993). Confidentiality in health care: A survey of knowledge, perceptions and attitudes among high school students. *Journal of the American Medical Association, 269,* 1404–1407.

Colorado Rev Stat 25-1-801 (d) (1995).

Conners, G. J., Tarbox, A. R., & Faillace, L. A. (1992). Achieving and maintaining gains among problem drinkers: Process and outcome results. *Behavior Therapy, 23,* 449–474.

Conners, G. J., & Walitzer, K. S. (2001). Reducing alcohol consumption among heavily drinking women: Evaluating the contributions of life skills training and booster sessions. *Journal of Consulting and Clinical Psychology, 69,* 447–456.

Cornelius, J. R., Pringle, J., Jernigan, J., Kirisci, L., & Clark, D. B. (2001). Correlates of mental health utilization and unmet need among a sample of adolescents. *Addictive Behaviors, 26,* 11–19.

Crowley, T. J., & Riggs, P. D. (1995). Adolescent substance use disorder with conduct disorder and co-morbid conditions. In E. Rahdert, & D. Czechowicz (Eds.), *Adolescent drug abuse: Clinical assessment and therapeutic interventions* (National Institute on Drug Abuse Research Monograph 156 (pp. 49–111). Government Printing Office, Washington, DC: U.S.

Deas, D., Riggs, P., Langenbucher, M., Goldman, M., & Brown, S. (2000). Adolescents are not adults: Developmental considerations in alcohol users. *Alcoholism: Clinical and Experimental Research, 24,* 232–237.

Delany, P. J., Broome, K. M., Flynn, P. M., & Fletcher, B. W. (2001). Treatment service patterns and organizational structures: An analysis of programs in DATOS-A. *Journal of Adolescent Research, 16,* 590–607.

Dembo, R. (1995). On the poignant need for substance misuse services among youth entering the juvenile justice system. *International Journal of the Addictions, 30,* 747–751.

Dembo, R., Walters, W., & Meyers, K. (in press). A practice/research collaborative: An innovative approach to identifying and responding to psychosocial functioning problems and recidivism risk among juvenile arrestees. *Journal of Offender Rehabilitation.*

Denmeade, G., & Rouse, B. A. (Eds.). (1994). *Financing drug treatment through state programs* (Services Research Monograph #1; publication #94-3543). Rockville, MD: National Institute on Drug Abuse.

Eccles, J. S., Midgely, C., Wigfield, A., Buchanan, M., Reuman, D., Flanagan, C., et al. (1993). Development during adolescence: The impact of stage-environment fit on young adolescents' experiences in schools and in families. *American Psychologist, 48,* 90–101.

ERIC (2001). Zero tolerance policies. *ERIC digest, 146.* University of Oregon, Eugene: ERIC Clearinghouse.

Etheridge, R. M., Hubbard, R. L., Anderson, J., Craddock, S. G., & Flynn, P. (1997). Treatment structure and program services in DATOS. *Psychology of Addictive Behaviors, 11,* 244–260.

Etheridge, R. M., Smith, J. C., Rounds-Bryant, J. L., & Hubbard, R. L. (2001). Drug abuse treatment and comprehensive services for adolescents. *Journal of Adolescent Research, 16,* 563–589.

Flisher, A., Kramer, R. A., Grosser, R. C., Alegria, M., Bird, H. R., Bourdon, K. H., et al. (1997). Correlates of unmet need for mental health services by children and adolescents. *Psychological Medicine, 27,* 1145–1154.

Fleming, R., Leventhal, H., Glynn, K., & Ershley, J. (1989). The role of cigarettes in the initiation and progression of early substance use. *Addictive Behavior* 14, 261–272.

Ford, C. A., Bearman, P. S., & Moody, J. (1999). Foregone health care among adolescents. *Journal of the American Medical Association, 282,* 2227–2234.

Ford, C. A. & English, A. (2002). Limiting confidentiality of adolescent health services: What are the risks? *Journal of the American Medical Association, 288,* 752–753.

Ford, C. A., Milstein, S. G., Halpern-Fisher, B. L., & Irwin, C. E. (1997). Influence of physician confidentiality assurances on adolescent's willingness to disclose information and seek future health care. *Journal of the American Medical Association, 278,* 1029–1034.

Gerstein, D., & Harwood, R. (Eds.). (1990). *Treating drug problems, Vol. I.* Washington, DC: National Academy Press.

Goldson, B. (2001). A rational youth justice: Some critical reflections on the research, policy and practice relation. *Probation-Journal, 48,* 76–85.

Gottlieb, G., Wahlsten, D., & Licklieter, R. (1998). The significance of biology for human development: A developmental psychobiological systems view. In W. Damon & R. Lerner (Eds.), *Handbook of child psychology: Theoretical models of human development* (pp. 233–273). New York: John Wiley & Sons.

Greenbaum, P. E., Foster-Johnson, L., & Petrila, A. (1996). Co-occurring addictive and mental health disorders: Prevalence research and future directions. *American Journal of Orthopsychiatry, 66,* 52–60.

Greene, M. B. (1993). Chronic exposure to violence and poverty: Interventions that work for youth. *Crime and Delinquency, 39,* 106–124.

Greenwood, P. W., Model, K. E., Rydell, C. P., & Chiesa, J. (1998). *Diverting children from a life of crime: Measuring costs and benefits* (MR-699-1-UCB/RC/IF). Santa Monica, CA: RAND Corporation.

Grisso, T., & Barnum, R. (2000). The *Massachusetts Youth Screening Instrument (MAYSI-2).* Worcester, MA: University of Massachusetts Medical School.

Grove, D. D., Lazebnik, R., & Petrack, E. M. (2000). Urban emergency department utilization by adolescents. *Clinical Pediatrics, 39,* 479–483.

Hack, M. R., & Adger, H. (2002). Medicaid reimbursement of primary care providers for treatment of substance use disorders. In: *Strategic plan for interdisciplinary faculty development: Arming the nation's health professional workforce for a new approach to substance use disorders.* Providence, RI: Association for Medical Education and Research.

Harrell, A. V., Cavanagh, S., & Sridharan, S. (1998). *Impact of the children at risk program: Comprehensive final report.* Washington, DC: The Urban Institute.

Hawkins, J. D., Catalano, R. F., & Miller, J. Y. (1992). Risk and protective factors for alcohol and other drug problems in adolescence and early adulthood: Implications for substance abuse prevention. *Psychological Bulletin 112,* 64–105.

Helzer, J. (1981). Renard Diagnostic Interview: Its reliability and procedural validity with physicians and lay interviewers. *Archives of General Psychiatry 38,* 393–398.

Henggeler, S. W., Schoenwald, S. K., Pickrel, S. G., Rowland, M. D., & Santos, A. B. (1994). The contribution of treatment outcome research to the reform of children's mental health services: Multisystemic therapy as an example. *Journal of Mental Health Administration, 21,* 229–239.

Hirschi, T., Hindelang, M. J., & Weis, J. G. (1980). The status of self-report measures. In M. W. Klein & K. S. Teilman (Eds.), *Handbook of Criminal Justice Evaluation* (pp. 473–488). Beverly Hills: Sage Publications.

Hubbard, R. L., Craddock, S. G., Flynn, P. M., Anderson, J., & Ethridge, R. M. (1997). Overview of 1-year follow-up outcomes in the Drug Abuse Treatment Outcomes Studies (DATOS). *Psychology of Addictive Behaviors, 11,* 261–278.

Jenson, J. M., & Howard, M. O. (1998). Youth crime, public policy, and practice in the juvenile justice system: Recent trends and needed reforms, *Social Work, 43,* 325–334.

Johnson, P. (1999). *Substance abuse treatment coverage in state Medicaid programs.* Washington, DC: National Conference of State Legislatures.

Kammer, J., Minor, K., & Wells, J. (1997). An outcome study of Diversion Plus program for juvenile offenders. *Federal Probation, 61,* 51–56.

Karam-Hage, M., Nerenberg, L., & Brower, K. J. (2001). Modifying residents' professional attitudes about substance abuse treatment and training. *American Journal on Addictions, 10,* 40–47.

Kazdin, A. E., & Weisz, J. R. (1998). Identifying and developing empirically supported child and adolescent treatments. *Journal of Consulting & Clinical Psychology, 66*(1): 19–36.

Kiestenbaum, C. J. (1985). Putting it all together: A multidimensional assessment of psychiatric potential in adolescence. In S. C. Feinstein, M. Sugar, A. H. Esman, J. G. Looney, A. Z. Schwartzberg, & A. D. Sorosky (Eds.), *Adolescent psychiatry 12* (pp. 5–16). Chicago: University of Chicago Press.

Klein, J. D., & Wilson, K. M. (2002). Delivering quality care: Adolescents' discussion of health risks with their providers. *Journal of Adolescent Health, 30,* 190–195.

Klein, J. D., Wilson, K. M., McNulty, M., Kapphahn, C., & Collins, K. S. (1999). Access to medical care for adolescents: Results from the 1997 Commonwealth Fund Survey of Health in

Adolescent Girls. *Journal of Adolescent Health, 25,* 120–130.

Klein-Schwartz, W., & McGrath, J. (2003). Poison centers' experience with methylphenidate abuse in pre-teens and adolescents. *Journal of the American Academy of Child and Adolescent Psychiatry, 42,* 288–294.

Kokotailo, P. K. (1995). Physical health problems associated with adolescent substance abuse. In E. Rahdert & D. Czechowicz (Eds.), *Adolescent substance abuse: Clinical assessment and therapeutic interventions.* Bethesda, MD: National Institute on Drug Abuse.

Kokotailo, P. K., Fleming, M. F., & Koscik, R. L. (1995). A model alcohol and other drug use curriculum for pediatric residents. *Academic Medicine, 70,* 495–498.

Krisberg, B., & Austin, J. F. (1993). *Reinventing Juvenile Justice.* National Council on Crime and Delinquency. Newbury Park, CA: Sage Publications.

Kutash, K., Duchnowski, A. J., Meyers, J., & King, B. (1997). Community and neighborhood services for youth. In S. W. Henggeler & A. B. Santos (Eds.), *Innovative approaches for difficult-to-treat populations.* Washington, DC: American Psychiatric Press.

Latimer, W. M., Newcomb, M., Winters, K. C., & Stinchfield, R. D. (2000). Adolescent substance abuse treatment outcome: The role of substance abuse problem severity, psychosocial, and treatment factors. *Journal of Consulting and Clinical Psychology, 68,* 684–696.

Lear, J. G. (2002). Schools and adolescent health: Strengthening services and improving outcomes. *Journal of Adolescent Health, 31,* 310–320.

Lehman, C. U., Barr, J., & Kelly, P. J. (1994). Emergency department utilization by adolescents. *Journal of Adolescent Health, 15,* 485–490.

Liddle, H. A., & Hogue, A. (2001). Multidimensional family therapy for adolescent substance abuse. In E. F. Wagner & H. B. Waldron (Eds.), *Innovations in adolescent substance abuse interventions.* (pp. 229–261). New York: Pergamon Press, Elsevier Science.

Louisiana Rev Stat Ann 40: 1095 (1995).

Mader, T. J., Smithline, H. A., Nyquist, S., & Letourneau, P. (2001). Social services referral of adolescent trauma patients admitted following alcohol-related injury. *Journal of Substance Abuse Treatment, 21,* 167–172.

Maio, R. F., Portnoy, J., Blow, F. C., & Hill, E. M. (1994). Injury type, injury severity, and repeat occurrence of alcohol-related trauma in adolescents. *Alcoholism: Clinical and Experimental Research, 18,* 261–264. abstract.

Marks, A., Malizio, J., Hoch, J., Brody, R., & Fisher, M. (1983). Assessment of health needs and willingness to utilize health care resources of adolescents in a suburban population. *Journal of Pediatrics, 102,* 456–460.

Marsden, M. E. (1998). *Organizational structures and the environmental context of drug abuse treatment:* Issue paper. Washington, DC: National Institute of Drug Abuse.

Martin, M. (2000). Does zero mean zero? *American School Board Journal, 187,* 3, 39–41.

Mathews, J., Kadish, W., Barrett, S. V., Mazor, K., Field, D., & Jonassen, J. (2002). The impact of a brief interclerkship about substance abuse on medical students' skills. *Academic Medicine, 77,* 419–426.

McLellan, A. T., Carise, D., & Kleber, H. D. (2003). The national addiction treatment infrastructure: Can it support the public's demand for quality care? *Journal of Substance Abuse Treatment, 78,* 125–129.

Melnick, G., DeLeon, G., Hawke, J., Jainchill, N., & Kressel, D. (1997). Motivation and readiness for therapeutic community treatment among adolescent and adult substance abusers. *American Journal of Drug and Alcohol Abuse, 23,* 485–506.

Melzer-Lange, M., & Lye, P. S. (1996). Adolescent health care in a pediatric emergency department. *Annals of Emergency Medicine, 27,* 633–637.

Meyers, J. C., & Davis, K. E. (1997). State and foundation partnerships to promote mental health systems reform for children and families. In C. T. Nixon, & D. A. Northrup (Eds.), *Evaluating mental health services: how do programs for children "work" in the real world? Children's mental health services, 3* (pp. 95–116). Sage Publications, Inc.

Meyers, K. (1998). *Community assessment centers: An integrated assessment and treatment approach.* Invited paper at the Office of Juvenile Justice and Delinquency Prevention Annual Conference, Washington, DC.

Meyers, K. (2000). *Community assessment centers* [Workshop]. Office of Juvenile Justice and Delinquency Prevention Juvenile Accountability Incentive Block Grant regional trainings.

Meyers, K., Hagan, T. A., McDermott, P., Webb, A., Frantz, J., & Randall, M. (in press). Design and validation of the Comprehensive Severity Inventory (CASI). *American Journal of Drug and Alcohol Abuse.*

Meyers, K., Hagan, T. A., Zanis, D., Webb, A., Frantz, J., Ring-Kurtz, S., et al. (1999). Critical issues in adolescent substance abuse assessment. *Drug and Alcohol Dependence, 55,* 40–46.

Meyers, K., McDermott, P., Webb, A., & Hagan, T. (in press). Mapping the clinical complexities of adolescents with substance use disorders: A typological study. *Journal of Child and Adolescent Substance Abuse.*

Meyers, K., O'Brien, S., Talbot, E., DiCamillo, A., & Merrill, J. (under review). Initial retention and outcome findings of an adolescent juvenile drug court.

Miller, N. S., & Swift, R. M. (1996). Primary care medicine and psychiatry: Addictions treatment. *Psychiatric Annals, 26,* 408–416.

Miller, W. R., & Brown, S. A. (1997). Why psychologists should treat alcohol and drug problems. *American Psychologist, 52,* 1269–1279.

Minnesota Department of Human Services. (1997). *Estimate of need for alcohol/drug-related services for adolescents in Minnesota: Implications for managed care organizations and health care providers.* Report to the Minnesota State Legislature. St. Paul: Minnesota Department of Human Services, Performance Measurement & Quality Improvement Division.

Monti, P. M., Colby, S. M., Barnett, N. P., Spirito, A., Rohsenow, D. J., Myers, M., et al., (1999). Brief intervention for harm reduction with alcohol-positive older adolescents in a hospital emergency department. *Journal of Consulting and Clinical Psychology, 67,* 989–994.

Morrison, C. S., McCusker, J., Stoddard, A. M., & Bigelow, C. (1995). The validity of behavioral data reported by injection drug users on a clinical risk assessment. *International Journal of Addiction, 30,* 889–899.

Moss, S. (1998). *Contracting for managed substance abuse and mental health services: A guide for public purchasers.* CSAT Technical Assistance Publication Series, #22. Rockville, MD: Center for Substance Abuse Treatment.

Murray, L. F. & Belenko, S. (under review). CASASTART: A community-based school-centered intervention for high-risk youth.

National Association of Alcoholism and Drug Abuse Counselors (NAADAC), (2003). NAADAC Certification Commission. Available: 2004 www .naadac.org/documents/certification

National Association of State Alcohol and Drug Abuse Directors (NASADAD). (1998). *Improving the dialogue in co-occurring mental health and substance abuse disorders.* Washington, DC: Author.

National Association of State Alcohol and Drug Abuse Directors (NASADAD) (1999). *Financing and marketing the new conceptual framework for co-occurring mental health and substance abuse disorders.* Washington, DC: Author.

National Association of State Alcohol and Drug Abuse Directors (NASADAD) (2002). *Identification and description of multiple alcohol and other drug treatment systems.* Final report for SAMHSA/CSAT Health Care Reform Technical Assistance and Knowledge Development, Synthesis and Dissemination Project. Washington, DC: Author.

National Council on Crime and Delinquency (2003, July). *Update on community assessment center evaluation.* Presented at the annual meeting of the Office of Justice Programs, National Institute of Justice Society of Research and Evaluation, Washington, DC.

Newacheck, P. (1999). Adolescent health insurance coverage: Recent changes and access to care. *Pediatrics, 104,* 195–202.

Northwest Frontier Addiction Technology Transfer Center. (2000). *Substance abuse treatment workforce survey: A regional needs assessment.* Portland, Oregon. RMC Research Corporation.

OAHHS: Oregon: ORS109.675(2). OAHHS HIPAA Task Force: Special Uses and Disclosures: Guidelines to Compliance. Available 2004. http://www.aracnet.com/~oahhs/issues/hipaa/parents_and_minors.htm

Office of Justice Programs Drug Court Clearinghouse and Technical Assistance Project. (1998). *Juvenile and family drug courts: An overview.* Washington, DC: U.S. Department of Justice and American University.

Office of Juvenile Justice and Delinquency Prevention. (1995). *Comprehensive strategy for serious, violent, and chronic juvenile offenders.* Washington, DC: U.S. Department of Justice.

Oldenettel, D., & Wordes, M. (2000). *The community assessment center concept. U.S. Department of Justice, Office of Justice Programs, Office of Juvenile Justice and Delinquency Prevention. Washington, DC: OJJDP.*

Oklahoma Stat Ann tit 63, 2602 (1995).

Physician Leadership on National Drug Policy. (2002). *Adolescent substance abuse: A public health priority.* Providence, RI: Center for Alcohol and Addiction Studies.

Pollio, D. E. (2002). *States need to ensure expertise of*

adolescent providers through training and certification. Connection, Washington, DC: Academy Health.

Pollock, N. K., & Martin, C. S. (1999). Diagnostic orphans: Adolescents with alcohol symptoms who do not qualify for DSM-IV abuse or dependence diagnoses. *American Journal of Psychiatry, 156,* 897–901.

Poulin, F., Dishion, T. J., & Burraston, B. (2001). Three-year iatrogenic effects associated with aggregating high-risk adolescents in cognitive-behavioral preventive interventions. *Applied Developmental Science, 5,* 214–224.

Prout, H. T., & Chizik, R. (1988). Readability of child and adolescent self-report measures. *Journal of Consulting and Clinical Psychology, 56,* 152–154.

Rahdert, E., & Czechowicz, D. (Eds.). (1995). *Adolescent drug abuse: Clinical assessment and therapeutic interventions* (National Institute on Drug Abuse Research Monograph 156). Washington, DC: U.S. Government Printing Office.

RAND. (1996). *Diverting children from a life of crime.* RAND Research Brief. Santa Monica, CA: Author.

Rappaport, N. (1999). Emerging models. *Child and Adolescent Clinics of North America, 10,* 13–24.

Rappaport, N. (2001). Psychiatric consultation to school-based health centers: Lessons learned from an emerging field. *Journal of the American Academy of Child and Adolescent Psychiatry, 40,* 1473–1475.

Reuters Health. (2002). Many US schools ban allergy, asthma meds. In *Health News,* 2002. Reuters Health: Author.

Rivera, F. P., Tollefson, S., Tesh, E., & Gentilello, L. M. (2000). Screening trauma patients for alcohol problems: Are insurance companies barriers? *Journal of Trauma: Injury, Infection, and Critical Care, 48,* 115–118.

Rose, S. J., Zweben, A., & Stoffel, V. (1999). Interfaces between substance abuse treatment and other health and social service systems. In B. S. McCrady & E. E. Epstein (Eds.), *Addictions: A comprehensive guidebook.* (pp. 421–436). New York: Oxford University Press.

Rosenbaum, M. (2003). Keeping kids off drugs: Pragmatism vs. zero tolerance—Let science be the guide. *San Francisco Chronicle,* June 2, 2003, pp. B-7.

Siegal, H. A., Cole, P. A., Li, L., & Eddy, M. F. (2000). Can a brief practicum influence physicians' communications with patients about alcohol and drug problems? Results of a long-term

follow-up. *Teaching and Learning in Medicine, 12,* 72–77.

Simpson, D. D., Joe, G. W., & Brown, B. S. (1997). Treatment retention and follow-up outcomes in the Drug Abuse Treatment Outcome Study (DATOS). *Psychology of Addictive Behaviors, 11,* 294–307.

Simpson, D. D., Joe, G. W., Broome, K. M., Hiller, M. L., Knight, K., & Rowan-Szal, G. A. (1997). Program diversity and treatment retention rates in the Drug Abuse Treatment Outcome Study (DATOS) *Psychology of Addictive Behaviors, 11,* 279–293.

Snyder, H. N., & Sickmund, M. (1999). *Juvenile offenders and victims: A national report.* Washington, DC: U.S. Department of Justice, Office of Juvenile Justice and Delinquency Prevention.

Soler, M. (1992). Interagency services in juvenile justice. In I. Schwartz (Ed.), *Juvenile justice and public policy: Toward a national agenda* (pp. 134–150). New York: Lexington Books.

Spear, S. F., & Skala, S. Y. (1995). Post-treatment services for chemically dependent adolescents. In E. Rahdert & D. Czechowicz (Eds.), *Adolescent drug abuse: Clinical assessment and therapeutic interventions,* National Institute on Drug Abuse Research Monograph 156, (pp. 341–364). Washington, DC: U.S. Government Printing Office.

Stanton, B. F., & Burnes, J. (2003). Sustaining and broadening interventions: Social norms, core values, and parents. In D. Romer (Ed.), *Reducing adolescent risk* (pp. 193–299). Thousand Oaks, CA: Sage Publications.

Steg, J. A., Mann, L. S., Schwartz, R. H., & Wise, T. N. (1992). Comparison of child psychiatry residents' and training directors' perceptions of training for alcohol and substance abuse treatment. *Academic Psychiatry, 16,* 103–108.

Stewart, M., & Brown, S. (1993). Family functioning following adolescent substance abuse treatment. *Journal of Substance Abuse, 5,* 327–339.

Substance Abuse and Mental Health Services Administration (SAMHSA). (1993). *Screening and assessment of alcohol- and other drug-abusing adolescents.* Treatment Improvement Protocol (TIP) series (DHHS Publication No. SMA 93-2009). Rockville, MD: U.S. Department of Health and Human Services, SAMHSA.

Substance Abuse and Mental Health Services Administration (SAMHSA). (2001a). *SAMHSA fact sheet: National household survey on drug abuse, 2001.* Rockville, MD: U.S. Department of Health and Human Services, SAMHSA.

Substance Abuse and Mental Health Services Administration (SAMHSA). (2001b). *National Survey of Substance Abuse Treatment Services* (N-SSATS). Rockville, MD: U.S. Department of Health and Human Services, SAMHSA.

Substance Abuse and Mental Health Services Administration (SAMHSA). (2002a). *Drug and alcohol treatment in juvenile correctional facilities*. The DASIS Report. Rockville, MD: U.S. Department of Health and Human Services, SAMHSA. Office of Applied Studies, SAMHSA.

Substance Abuse and Mental Health Services Administration (SAMHSA). (2002b). *Emergency department trends from the Drug Abuse Warning Network* (DAWN), *2002*. Rockville, MD: U.S. Department of Health and Human Services, SAMHSA.

Substance Abuse and Mental Health Services Administration (SAMHSA). (2002c). *Treatment Episode Data Set (TEDS), 1992–2000: National admissions to substance abuse treatment services*. Rockville, MD: U.S. Department of Health and Human Services, SAMHSA.

Substance Abuse and Mental Health Services Administration (SAMHSA). (2003). *Mortality from the Drug Abuse Warning Network* (DAWN), 2001. Rockville, MD: U.S. Department of Health and Human Services, SAMHSA.

Terry, Y. M., VanderWall, C. J., McBride, D. C., & Van Buren, H. (2000). Provision of drug treatment services in the juvenile justice system: A systems reform. *Journal of Behavioral Health Services Research, 27,* 194–214.

Tracy, E., & Farkas, K. J. (1994). Preparing practitioners for child welfare practice with substance-abusing families. *Child Welfare, 73,* 57–68.

U.S. Department of Health and Human Services (DHHS). (1993). *Guidelines for treatment of alcohol and other drug-abusing adolescents*. Center for Substance Abuse Treatment. Treatment Improvement Protocol series (DHHS Publication No. SMA 93-2010). Washington, DC: Author.

U.S. Public Health Service. (2000). *Report of the surgeon general's Conference on Children's Mental Health: A national action agenda*. Washington, DC: U.S. Department of Health and Human Services.

Wagner, E. F., Kortlander, E., & Morris, S. L. (2001). The teen intervention project: A school-based intervention for adolescents with substance abuse problems. In E. F. Wagner & H. B. Waldron (Eds.), *Innovations in adolescent substance abuse*

interventions (pp. 189–203). New York: Pergamon Press, Elsevier Science.

Wagner, E. F., & Waldron, H. B. (2001). *Innovations in adolescent substance abuse interventions* (pp. 189–203). New York: Pergamon Press, Elsevier Science.

Weinberg, N. Z., Rahdert, E., Colliver, J. D., & Glantz, M. D. (1998). Adolescent substance abuse: A review of the past ten years. *Journal of the American Academy of Child and Adolescent Psychiatry, 37,* 252–261.

Westreich, L., & Galanter, M. (1997). Training psychiatric residents in addiction. *Substance Abuse, 18,* 13–25.

White, W. L. (1998). *Chasing the dragon: A history of addiction and recovery in America*. Bloomington, IL: Lighthouse Institute Publications.

Williams, R. J., & Chang, S. Y. (2000). A comprehensive and comparative review of adolescent substance abuse treatment outcome. *Clinical Psychology: Science and Practice, 7,* 138–166.

Winters, K. C. (1999). Treating adolescents with substance use disorders: An overview of practice issues and treatment outcomes. *Substance Abuse, 20,* 203–225.

Winters, K. C., Latimer, W., & Stinchfield, R. D. (1999). The DSM-IV criteria for adolescent alcohol and cannabis use disorders. *Journal of Studies on Alcohol, 60,* 337–344.

Winters, K. C., Latimer, W. W., & Stinchfield, R. D. (2001). Assessing adolescent substance use. In E. F. Wagner & H. B. Waldron (Eds.), *Innovations in adolescent substance abuse interventions* (pp. 1–29). New York: Pergamon Press, Elsevier Science.

Winters, K. C., & Stinchfield, R. D. (1995). Current issues and future needs in the assessment of adolescent drug abuse. In E. Rahdert & D. Czechowicz (Eds.), *Adolescent drug abuse: Clinical assessment and therapeutic interventions* (National Institute on Drug Abuse Research Monograph 156, pp. 146–171). Washington, DC: U.S. Government Printing Office.

Winters, K. C., Stinchfield, R. D., Opland, E., Weller, C., & Latimer, W. W. (2000). The effectiveness of the Minnesota Model approach in the treatment of adolescent drug abusers. *Addiction, 95,* 601–612.

Yamaguchi, R., Johnston, L. D., & O'Malley, P. M. (2003). Relationship between student illicit drug use and school drug-testing policies. *Journal of School Health, 73,* 159–167.

Zeese, K. B. (2002). Drug testing fails at school and

work. Common Sense for Drug Policy, at http://www.csdp.org

Part VIII: Summary of Conclusions, Recommendations, Priorities

Chapter 30: The Role of Primary Care Physicians in Detection and Treatment of Adolescent Mental Health Problems

American Academy of Pediatrics, Committee on Substance Abuse. (2000). Indications for management and referral of patients involved in substance abuse. *Pediatrics, 106,* 143–148.

Chang, G., Warner, V., & Weissman, M. M. (1988). Physicians' recognition of psychiatric disorders in children and adolescents. *American Journal of Disabilities in Children, 142,* 736–739.

Conti, R., Frank, R. G., & McGuire, T. G. (2004). Insuring mental health care in the age of managed care. In B. L. Levin, J. Petrila, & K. D. Hennessy (Eds.), *Mental health services: A public health perspective* (2nd ed., pp. 15–41). New York: Oxford University Press.

Costello, E. J., Burns, B. J., Costello, A. J., Edelbrock, G., Dulcan, M., & Brent, D. (1998). Service utilization and psychiatric diagnosis in pediatric primary care: The role of the gatekeeper. *Pediatrics, 82,* 435–441.

Forrest, C. B., Glade, G. B., Starfield, B., Baker, A. E., Kang, M., & Reid, R. J. (1999). Gatekeeping and referral of children and adolescents to specialty care. *Pediatrics, 104,* 28–34.

Gardner, W., Kelleher, K. J., Wasserman, R., Childs, G., Nutting, P., Lillienfeld, H., et al. (2002). Primary Care Treatment of Pediatric Psychosocial Problems: A Study From Pediatric Research in Office Settings and Ambulatory Sentinel Practice Network. *Pediatrics,* 106(4): E44.

Glied, S., & Cuellar, A. E. (2003). Trends and issues in child and adolescent mental health. *Health Affairs, 22*(5), 39–50.

Glied, S., & Neufield, A. (2001). Service system finance: Implications for children with depression and manic depression. *Biological Psychiatry, 49,* 1128–1135.

Horwitz, S. M., Leaf, P. J., Leventhal, J. M., Borsyth, B., & Speechley, K. N. (1992). Identification and management of psychosocial and developmental problems in community-based, primary care pediatric practices. *Pediatrics, 89,* 480–485.

Jellinek, M., & Little, M. (1998). Supporting child psychiatric services using current managed care approaches: You can't get there from here. *Ar-

chives of Pediatric and Adolescent Medicine, 152,* 321–326.

Jellinek, M., Patel, B. P., & Froehle, M. C. (Eds.). (2002). *Bright futures in practice: Mental health.* Arlington, VA: National Center for Education in Maternal and Child Health.

Kelleher, K. J., Childs, G. E., Wasserman, R. C., McInerny, T. K., Nutting, P. A., & Gardner, W. P. (1997). Insurance status and recognition of psychosocial problems. *Archives of Pediatric and Adolescent Medicine, 151,* 1109–1115.

Kelleher, K. J., McInerny, T. K., Gardner, W. P., Childs, G. F., & Wasserman, R. C. (2000). Increasing identification of psychosocial problems: 1979–1996. *Pediatrics, 105,* 1313–1321.

Kelleher, K. J., Scholle, S. H., Feldman, H. M., & Nace, D. (1999). A fork in the road: Decision time for behavioral pediatrics. *Developmental and Behavioral Pediatrics, 20,* 181–186.

McGuire, L., & Flynn, L. (2003). The Columbia TeenScreen Program: Screening youth for mental illness and suicide. *Trends in Evidence-Based Neuropsychiatry, 5*(2), 56–62.

Melnyk, B. M., Brown, H. E., Jones, D. C., Kreipe, R., & Novak, J. (2003). Improving the Mental/Psychosocial Health of U.S. Children and Adolescents: Outcomes and Implementation Strategies from the National KYSS Summit. *Journal of Pediatric Health Care* 17(6): S1–S16.

National Institutes of Mental Health. (2000a). *Depression in children and adolescents: A fact sheet for physician.* Rockville, MD: U.S. Department of Health and Human Services.

National Institutes of Mental Health. (2000b). *Child and adolescent bipolar disorder: An update from the National Institute of Mental Health.* Rockville, MD: U.S. Department of Health and Human Services.

Olson, A. L., Kelleher, K. J., Kemper, K. J., Zuckerman, B. S., Hammond, C. S., & Dietrich, A. J. (2001). Primary care pediatricians' roles and perceived responsibilities in the identification and management of depression in children and adolescents. *Ambulatory Pediatrics, 1,* 91–98.

President's New Freedom Commission on Mental Health. (2003). Retrieved August 2, 2004 from http://www.mentalhealthcommission.gov/reports/reports.htm

Rushton, J., Bruckman, D., & Kelleher, K. (2002). Primary Care Referral of Children with Psychosocial Problems. *Archives of Pediatric & Adolescent Medicine, 156,* 592–598.

Scholle, S. H., & Kelleher, K. J. (1998). Managed care: Opportunities and threats for children with serious emotional disturbance and their families. In M. H. Epstein, K. Kutash, & A. Duchnowski (Eds.), *Outcomes for children and youth with emotional and behavioral disorders and their families: Programs and evaluation best practices* (pp. 659–684) Austin, TX: Pro-Ed.

Sturm, R., Ringel, J. S., & Andreyeva, T. (2003). Geographic disparities in children's mental health care, *Pediatrics, 112*(4), 308–315.

U.S. Department of Health and Human Services. (1999). *Mental health: A report of the surgeon general—executive summary.* Rockville, MD: Author.

U.S. Department of Health and Human Services. (2000). *Report of the Surgeon General's Conference on Children's Mental Health: A national action agenda.* Washington, DC: Author.

Walders, N., Childs, G. E., Comer, D., Kelleher, K. J., & Drotar, D. (2003). Barriers to mental health referral from pediatric primary care settings. *American Journal of Managed Care, 9,* 677–683.

Wells, K. B., Kataoka, S. H., & Asarnow, J. R. (2001). Affective disorders in children and adolescents: Addressing unmet need in primary care settings. *Biological Psychiatry, 49,* 1111–1120.

Chapter 31   The Roles and Perspectives of School Mental Health Professionals in Promoting Adolescent Mental Health

Adelman, H. S., & Taylor, L. (1998). Mental health in schools: Moving forward. *School Psychology Review, 27,* 175–190.

Adelman, H. S., & Taylor, L. (2000). Promoting mental health in schools in the midst of school reform. *Journal of School Health, 70,* 171–178.

Allinsmith, W., & Goethals, G. W. (1962). *The role of schools in mental health.* New York: Basic Books.

American Academy of Pediatrics Committee on School Health. (2001). School health centers and other integrated school health services. *Pediatrics, 107,* 198–201.

American Psychiatric Association. (2004). Mental illness and the criminal justice system: Redirecting resources toward treatment, not containment. Retrieved August 10, 2004, from http://www.psych.org/edu/other_res/lib_archives/archives/200401.pdf

American School Counselors Association. (2004). *National standards.* Retrieved July 14, 2004, from http://www.schoolcounselor.org/content.cfm?L1=1&L2=9

Anglin, T. M., Naylor, K. E., & Kaplan, D. W. (1996). Comprehensive, school-based healthcare: High school student's use of medical, mental health, and substance abuse services. *Pediatrics, 97,* 318–330.

Atkins, M. S., Graczyk, P. A., Frazier, S. L., & Abdul-Adil, J. (2003). Toward a new model for promoting urban children's mental health: Accessible, effective, and sustainable school-based mental health services. *School Psychology Review, 32,* 503–514.

Armbruster, P., & Lichtman, J. (1999). Are school based mental health services effective? Evidence from 36 inner city schools. *Community Mental Health Journal, 35,* 493–504.

Bilchik, S. (1998). *Mental health disorders and substance abuse problems among juveniles. Fact Sheet #82.* Washington, DC: Department of Justice, Office of Justice Programs, Office of Juvenile Justice and Delinquency Prevention.

Brener, N. D., Martindale, J., & Weist, M. D. (2001). Mental health and social services: Results from the School Health Policies and Programs Study 2000. *Journal of School Health, 71,* 305–312.

Center for Health and Health Care in Schools. (2003). *Number of school-based health centers continue to rise across the United States, national survey finds.* Washington, DC: Center for Health and Health Care in Schools at the George Washington University School of Public Health.

Costello, E. J., Angold, A., & Burns, B. J. (1996). The Great Smoky Mountains Study of youth: Goals, designs, methods, and the prevalence of DSM-III-R disorders. *Archives of General Psychiatry, 53,* 1129–1136.

Hoagwood, K., & Johnson, J. (2003). School psychology: A public health framework I. From evidence-based practices to evidence-based policies. *Journal of School Psychology, 41,* 3–21.

Hunter, L. (2003). School psychology: A public health framework III. Managing disruptive behavior in schools: The value of a public health and evidence based perspective. *Journal of School Psychology, 41,* 39–59.

Jaycox, L. H., Morral, A. R., & Juvonen, J. (2003). Mental health and medical problems and service use among adolescent substance users. *Journal of the American Academy of Child and Adolescent Psychiatry, 42,* 701–709.

Jellinek, M., Patel, B. P., & Froehle, M. C. (Eds.) (2002). *Bright futures in practice: Mental health.* Arlington, VA: National Center for Education in Maternal and Child Health.

Kataoka, S. H., Zhang, L., & Wells, K. B. (2002). Unmet need for mental health care among U.S. children: Variation by ethnicity and insurance status. *American Journal of Psychiatry, 159,* 1548–1555.

Leaf, P. J., Alegria, M., Cohen, P., Goodman, S. H., Horwitz, S., Hoven, C. W., et al. (1996). Mental health service use in the community and schools: Results from the four-community MECA study. *Journal of the American Academy of Child and Adolescent Psychiatry, 35,* 889–897.

McGuire, L., & Flynn, L. (2003). The Columbia TeenScreen Program: Screening youth for mental illness and suicide. *Trends in Evidence-Based Neuropsychiatry, 5,* 56–62.

Melnyk, B. M., Brown, H. E., Jones, D. C., Kreipe, R., & Novak, J. (2003). Improving the mental/psychological health of U.S. children and adolescents: Outcomes and implementation strategies for the national KySS summit. *Journal of Pediatric Health Care, 17*(6) (Suppl.), S1–S24.

Nabors, L. A., Weist, M. D., Tashman, N. A., & Myers, C. P. (1999). Quality assurance and school-based mental health services. *Psychology in the Schools, 36,* 485–493.

Nastasi, B. K. (1998). A model for mental health programming in schools and communities: Introduction to the mini-series. *School Psychology Review, 27,* 165–174.

National Association of School Psychologists. (2004). *Professional conduct manual: Principles for professional ethics guidelines for the provision of school psychological services.* Retrieved July 14, 2004, from http://www.nasponline.org/pdf/ProfessionalCond.pdf

National Association of Social Workers. (2002). *NASW standards for school social work services.* Retrieved July 14, 2004, from http://www.socialworkers.org/sections/credentials/school_social.asp

Puig-Antich, J., Kaufman, J., & Ryan, N. D. (1993). The psychological functioning and family environment of depressed adolescents. *Journal of the American Academy of Child and Adolescent Psychiatry, 32,* 244–253.

President's New Freedom Commission. (2003). Retrieved August 10, 2004, from www.mentalhealthcommission.gov/reports/reports.htm

Quinn, K. P., & Mcdougal, J. L. (1998). A mile wide and a mile deep: Comprehensive interventions for children and youth with emotional and behavioral disorders and their families. *School Psychology Review, 27,* 191–203.

Randall, J., Henggeler, S. W., & Pickrel, S. G. (1999). Psychiatric comorbidity and the 16-month trajectory of substance using and substance-dependent juvenile offenders. *Journal of the American Academy of Child and Adolescent Psychiatry, 38,* 1118–1124.

Romer, D. (Ed). (2003). *Reducing adolescent risk: Toward an integrated approach.* Thousand Oaks, CA: Sage Press.

Rones, M., & Hoagwood, K. (2000). School-based mental health services: A research review. *Clinical Child and Family Psychology Review, 3,* 223–241.

Slade, E. P. (2003). The relationship between school characteristics and the availability of mental health and related health services in middle and high schools in the United States. *Journal of Behavioral Health Services and Research, 30,* 382–392.

Starr, P. (1982). *The social transformation of American medicine.* New York: Basic Books.

Strein, W., Hoagwood, K., & Cohn, A. (2003). School psychology: A public health perspective I. Prevention, populations, and system change. *Journal of School Psychology, 41,* 23–38.

Sturm, R., Ringel, J. S., & Andreyeva, T. (2003). Geographic disparities in children's mental health care. *Pediatrics, 112,* 308–315.

U. S. Census Bureau. (2002). Single grade of enrollment and high school graduation status for people 3 years old and over by age, sex, race, and Hispanic origin; October 2002. Retrieved August 10, 2004, from http://www.census.gov/population/www/socdemo/school/cps2002.html

U.S. Department of Health and Human Services. (2000). *Report of the Surgeon General's Conference on Children's Mental Health: A national action agenda.* Washington, DC: U.S. Public Health Service.

Weist, M. D. (2003). Challenges and opportunities in moving toward a public health approach in school mental health. *Journal of School Psychology, 41,* 77–82.

Weist, M. D., & Christodulu, K. V. (2000). Expanded school mental health programs: Advancing reform and closing the gap between research and practice. *Journal of School Health, 70,* 195–200.

Willcutt, E. G., & Pennington, B. F. (2000). Psychiatric comorbidity in children and adolescents with reading disability. *Journal of Child Psychology and Psychiatry and Allied Disciplines, 41,* 1039–1048.

Chapter 32 A Call to Action on Adolescent Mental Health

Caspi, A., McClay, J., Moffitt, T. E., Mill, J. Martin, J., Craig, I. W., et al. (2002). Role of genotype in the cycle of violence in maltreated children. *Science, 297,* 851–854.

Conti, R., Frank, R. G., & McGuire, T. G. (2004). Insuring mental health care in the age of managed care. In B. L. Levin, J. Petrila, & K. D. Hennessy (Eds.), *Mental health services: A public health perspective* (2nd edition, pp. 15–41). New York: Oxford University Press.

Council of Scientific Affairs. (2004, June). *Featured CSA report: Influence of funding source on outcome, validity, and reliability of pharmaceutical research (A-04).* Chicago: American Medical Association.

Curtis, W. J., & Cicchetti, D. (2003). Moving research on resilience into the 21st century: Theoretical and methodological considerations in examining the biological contributors to resilience. *Development and Psychopathology, 15,* 773–810.

DeAngelis, C. D., Drazen, J. M., Firzelle, F. A., Haug, C., Hoey, J., Horton, R., et al. (2004). Clinical trial registration: A statement from the International Committee of Medical Journal Editors. *JAMA, 292,* 1363–1364.

Fair Access to Clinical Trials Act of 2004, H. R. 5252, S. 2933. 108th Congress, 2nd Session.

Giedd, J. N. (2004). Structural magnetic resonance imaging of the adolescent brain. *Annals of the New York Academy of Sciences, 1021,* 77–85.

Glass, R. M. (2004). Treatments of adolescents with major depression: Contributions of a major trial. *Journal of the American Medical Association, 292,* 861–863.

Glied, S., & Neufield, A. (2001). Service system finance: Implications for children with depression and manic depression. *Biological Psychiatry, 49,* 1128–1135.

Harris, G. (2004a, September 14). F.D.A. links drugs to being suicidal: View shifts on teenagers and antidepressants. *New York Times,* pp. A1, A19.

Harris, G. (2004b, September 15). F.D.A. panel urges stronger warning on antidepressants. *New York Times,* pp. A1, A19.

Huttenlocher, P. R. (2002). *Neural plasticity: The effects of experience on the development of the cerebral cortex.* Cambridge, MA: Harvard University Press.

Kandel, E. R. (1998). A new intellectual framework for psychiatry. *American Journal of Psychiatry, 155,* 457–469.

Kelleher, K. J., Scholle, S. H., Feldman, H. M., & Nace, D. (1999). A fork in the road: Decision time for behavioral pediatrics. *Developmental and Behavioral Pediatrics, 20,* 181–186.

Kim-Cohen, J., Caspi, A., Moffitt, T. E., Harrington, H., Milne, B. J., & Poulton, R. (2003). Prior juvenile diagnoses in adults with mental disorder. *Archives of General Psychiatry, 60,* 709–717.

March, J. S., Silva, S., Petrycki, S., Curry, J., Wells, K., Fairbank, J., et al. (2004). Fluoxetine, cognitive-behavioral therapy, and their combination for adolescents with depression: Treatment for adolescents with depression study (TADS), randomized controlled trial. *Journal of the American Medical Association, 292,* 807–820.

Masten, A. (2004). Regulatory processes, risk, and resilience in adolescent development. *Annals of the New York Academy of Sciences, 1021,* 310–319.

Mills, R. J., & Bhandari, S. (2003). *Health insurance coverage in the United States: 2002.* Washington, DC: U.S. Census Bureau.

President's New Freedom Commission. (2003). Accessed online at: www.mentalhealthcommission.gov/reports/reports.htm

Redhead, C. S. (2003). *Mental health parity.* Washington, DC: Congressional Research Service.

Roza, S. J., Hofstra, M. B., van der Ende, J., & Verhulst, F. C. (2003). Stable prediction of mood and anxiety disorders based on behavioral and emotional problems in childhood: A 14-year follow-up during childhood, adolescence, and young adulthood. *American Journal of Psychiatry, 160,* 2116–2121.

Rutter, M., Dunn, J., Plomin, R., Simonoff, E., Pickles, A., Maughan, B., et al. (1997). Integrating nature and nurture: Implications of person–environment correlations and interactions for developmental psychopathology. *Development and Psychopathology, 9,* 335–364.

Spear, L. P. (2000). The adolescent brain and age-related behavioral manifestations. *Neuroscience and Biobehavioral Reviews, 24,* 417–463.

Substance Abuse and Mental Health Administration (SAMHSA). (2004). *Mental health: It's all a part of our lives.* Accessed online at: http://allmentalhealth.samhsa.gov/english/index.html

U.S. Department of Health and Human Services. (1999). The costs of mental illness. In *Mental health: A report of the Surgeon General.* Retrieved online at: http://www.surgeongeneral.gov/library/mentalhealth/chapter6/sec2.html

U.S. Food and Drug Administration. (2004). Antidepressant use in children, adolescents, and adults. Retrieved from http://www.fda.gov/cder/drug/antidepressants/default.htm.

Waldman, I. D. (2003). Prospects and problems in the search for genetic influences on neurodevelopment and psychopathology: Application to childhood disruptive disorders. In D. Cicchetti & E. Walker (Eds.), *Neurodevelopmental mechanisms in psychopathology* (pp. 257–292). New York: Cambridge University Press.

Index

Page numbers followed by f and t indicate figures and tables, respectively.